Election Law and Litigation

ASPEN CASEBOOK SERIES

ELECTION LAW AND LITIGATION

THE JUDICIAL REGULATION OF POLITICS

SECOND EDITION

EDWARD B. FOLEY
CHARLES W. EBERSOLD AND FLORENCE WHITCOMB EBERSOLD
CHAIR IN CONSTITUTIONAL LAW AND DIRECTOR, ELECTION LAW
THE OHIO STATE UNIVERSITY, MORITZ COLLEGE OF LAW

MICHAEL J. PITTS
VICE DEAN AND PROFESSOR OF LAW
INDIANA UNIVERSITY ROBERT H. MCKINNEY SCHOOL OF LAW

JOSHUA A. DOUGLAS
ASHLAND, INC.-SPEARS DISTINGUISHED RESEARCH PROFESSOR OF LAW
UNIVERSITY OF KENTUCKY J. DAVID ROSENBERG COLLEGE OF LAW

Published by Wolters Kluwer in New York.

Wolters Kluwer Legal & Regulatory U.S. serves customers worldwide with CCH, Aspen Publishers, and Kluwer Law International products. (www.WKLegaledu.com)

To contact Customer Service, e-mail customer.service@wolterskluwer.com, call 1-800-234-1660, fax 1-800-901-9075, or mail correspondence to:

Wolters Kluwer
Attn: Order Department
PO Box 990
Frederick, MD 21705

Printed in the United States of America.

1 2 3 4 5 6 7 8 9 0

ISBN 978-1-4548-9270-0

Library of Congress Cataloging-in-Publication Data

Names: Foley, Edward B., author. | Pitts, Michael J., author. | Douglas, Joshua A., author.
Title: Election law and litigation: the judicial regulation of politics / Edward B. Foley, Charles W. Ebersold and Florence Whitcomb Ebersold Chair in Constitutional Law and Director, Election Law, The Ohio State University, Moritz College of Law; Michael J. Pitts, Vice Dean and Professor of Law, Indiana University Robert H. McKinney School of Law; Joshua A. Douglas, Ashland, Inc.-Spears Distinguished Research Professor of Law, University of Kentucky J. David Rosenberg College of Law.
Description: Second edition. | New York City: Wolters Kluwer, 2021. | Series: Aspen casebook series | Includes bibliographical references and index.
Identifiers: LCCN 2021034202 (print) | LCCN 2021034203 (ebook) | ISBN 9781454892700 (hardcover) | ISBN 9781543823424 (ebook)
Subjects: LCSH: Election law—United States. | LCGFT: Casebooks (Law)
Classification: LCC KF4886.F65 2021 (print) | LCC KF4886 (ebook) | DDC 342.73/07—dc23
LC record available at https://lccn.loc.gov/2021034202
LC ebook record available at https://lccn.loc.gov/2021034203

About Wolters Kluwer Legal & Regulatory U.S.

Wolters Kluwer Legal & Regulatory U.S. delivers expert content and solutions in the areas of law, corporate compliance, health compliance, reimbursement, and legal education. Its practical solutions help customers successfully navigate the demands of a changing environment to drive their daily activities, enhance decision quality and inspire confident outcomes.

Serving customers worldwide, its legal and regulatory portfolio includes products under the Aspen Publishers, CCH Incorporated, Kluwer Law International, ftwilliam.com and MediRegs names. They are regarded as exceptional and trusted resources for general legal and practice-specific knowledge, compliance and risk management, dynamic workflow solutions, and expert commentary.

To Miranda, Max, and Robbie, who have been enthusiastic supporters of this project ever since its origins.

—Ned

To Jenny, William, and Jonathan, who are the best family one could ever hope for.

—Mike

To Bari, who wins the campaign for my heart every day. And to Caitlyn and Harrison: May our democracy be even stronger when you are voters.

—Josh

To our wonderful students, whose feedback has helped make this book more student-friendly.

—Ned, Mike, and Josh

Summary of Contents

CONTENTS

Introduction

This book covers the law that governs the operation of elections as well as the campaigns leading up to those elections. Implicit in this very first sentence is the fact that this field can be subdivided between "election" law on the one hand and "campaign" law on the other. Further subdivisions of election law are useful. There is the law that governs the nomination of candidates, sometimes called "ballot access" law and which includes the distinctive rules concerning primary elections, to be distinguished from the law that governs the casting and counting of votes for the nominated candidates. This latter area, regulating the voting process itself, is sometimes called "election administration," although that term is confusing since the distinctive rules for nominating candidates could be considered an aspect of election administration. Consequently, we prefer to call this latter area simply "voting" law.

Another distinctive component of election law is the law that governs the drawing of boundary lines for legislative districts, to define the specific constituency that will elect each member of the legislature. Obviously, this "districting" law is inapplicable to the election of candidates for statewide offices, such as Governor or U.S. Senator. Thus, districting law might be considered as belonging to a subfield of election law that concerns the special rules for different types of election offices. The distinctive rules for the operation of the Electoral College, which uniquely govern the election of the U.S. President, would be considered another component of this office-specific set of election laws. (The same holds true for the distinctive rules concerning referenda, initiatives, and other ballot propositions, even though they involve voting on issues rather than candidates.)

Nonetheless, the U.S. Supreme Court cases in the particular area of districting law loom sufficiently large over the entire field of election law that not only do they deserve separate consideration, but they also provide a good place to start one's study of this field. In the 1960s, as the Warren Court was reaching the apex of its activism, the Court ushered in what has been called the "reapportionment revolution," whereby the Court interpreted the Equal Protection Clause of the U.S. Constitution to require both houses of every state legislature to comply with a requirement of equally populated districts (or at least approximately so—more on that later). Not only did this revolution newly subject the districting of state legislatures to federal judicial oversight, but the interpretive principle upon which this revolution relied—that the Equal Protection Clause guarantees each citizen equal voting rights and, even more broadly, equal rights with respect to participating in the electoral process in various ways—has had profound ramifications in other areas of election law besides districting.

As we shall see, soon after the reapportionment revolution, the Warren Court extended this Equal Protection principle to the nomination of candidates, to assure that each citizen had an equal opportunity to run for office. In the twenty-first century, the Supreme Court invoked this same Equal Protection principle in *Bush v. Gore*, 513 U.S. 98 (2000), to rule that a state's procedures for recounting ballots must contain standards of sufficient specificity to avoid disparate treatment of similar ballots depending upon the particular recounting panel that happens to review them.

If one had studied election law in 1950, before the reapportionment revolution occurred, the subject would have seemed entirely different than it does today. Consisting mostly of state-court cases interpreting state statutes and some state constitutional provisions, a book like this one would have contained hardly any federal law—and almost none of it federal constitutional law. Now, we have major federal statutes regulating various aspects of the subject: the Voting Rights Act of 1965, the Federal Election Campaign Act of 1974 (when its most important provisions were adopted), and the Help America Vote Act of 2002, among the most significant. Although many students today are surprised when they first learn how much state law, rather than federal law, still controls even elections to federal office (Congress and the President), the degree of federal-law control over U.S. elections, including those for state and local offices, is vastly greater than it was a half-century ago. And a considerable portion of this new federal-law control results from judicial interpretation of the U.S. Constitution, starting with the reapportionment revolution of the 1960s.

The first edition of this book was published in 2014. At the time, the field of election law was dominated primarily by the so-called "voting wars" that occurred in the aftermath of the disputed presidential election of 2000. The closeness of that race—a mere 537 votes in the pivotal state of Florida separated the two main candidates in the officially certified result—highlighted the degree to which election laws, and especially litigation over them, potentially could make a difference in the outcome of even statewide elections. That fact, combined with the increasing polarization of American politics, caused a sharp increase in litigiousness over all aspects of the voting process, both before and after the casting of ballots. Newly adopted voter identification rules became one prominent focal point of this disputation, although by no means the only one.

This second edition is going to press in the summer of 2021, in the aftermath of the 2020 election, which dwarfed all of the "voting wars" that preceded it. Before any ballots were cast in the November 2020 general election, there already had been an unprecedented spike in lawsuits over voting rules, prompted in large part due to changes in election procedures brought on by the coronavirus pandemic. President Donald Trump, running for reelection, railed against these changes, especially those involving expanded vote-by-mail. After the voting occurred, and the tally of ballot showed him to have been defeated by Joe Biden in enough states to determine the Electoral College result, Trump refused to accept defeat and claimed—falsely—that the election had been stolen from him. Recounts and litigation in the battleground states confirmed Biden's victory. In Georgia, for example, all the ballots in the state were counted multiple times, including by hand. But still Trump claimed he was cheated, spinning fantastical conspiracy theories about voting machines having been hacked by Venezuela (or Italy), a preposterous claim that even if true would be irrelevant once the ballots had all been counted by hand.

Nonetheless, Trump's "big lie" about being cheated of a second term took hold in the body politic, with the consequence that public opinion polls throughout 2021 consistently showed substantial majorities of Republican voters believing that President Biden did not take office legitimately but instead was installed by fraudulent means. For both the first and second editions, we have strived to be as nonpartisan as possible, our core credo being that a well-functioning electoral system must work properly for all voters regardless of their party affiliations, enabling them to make the choice of which party they wish to govern for the next period of time. As professors of election law, we maintain our duty to all students is to teach this subject impartially, so that all students regardless of their own political beliefs and any party affiliation have an equal opportunity to learn the material. But as professors we also have a duty to objective truth, and this duty requires us to be candid that Trump's "big lie" is indeed objectively false and has no basis in reality. In our judgment, it is the functional equivalent of claiming that the earth is flat, which is objectively false on the basis of all available empirical evidence. We cannot give any credence to the claim that Trump was robbed of a victory, when a reality-based evaluation of the vote-counting process in Georgia and the other battleground states necessitates the conclusion that Biden, not Trump, received the most valid votes in those states.

As this book goes to press, we cannot know what long-term damage to American democracy Trump's "big lie" will do. It caused the insurrection at the Capitol on January 6, when Congress met to count the Electoral College votes. That insurrection was a uniquely ugly moment in U.S. history, with its horrific violence and loss of life. But it did not negate Biden's inauguration, which was the authentic result of the votes actually cast and counted. The long-term consequences will be determined by the public's response to the insurrection and the "big lie" that instigated it. So far, the signs are troubling: after an initial moment in which leaders of both parties essentially expressed the same "never again" sentiment, there has developed a persistent effort by Trump and his allies to rehabilitate the insurrection as an understandable response of "patriots" as part of the "Stop the Steal" effort to save the country from a fraudulent Biden presidency. Only after the 2022 and 2024 elections will we be in a position to assess whether democracy survived intact, in the critical sense of the declared winners being the candidates the voters truly wanted to win.

The aftermath of the 2020 election has also produced a frenzy of election-related legislation in the states. Given the hyperpolarized nature of American politics, much (although not all) of this legislation has been one party's rules enacted over the opposition of the opposing party. Public discourse over these new laws has also, for the most part, been highly polarized. The ultimate fate of this new legislation is also unknown as we write: President Biden's Attorney General, Merrick Garland, has sued Georgia over its new law, alleging that it is motivated by an aim to suppress Black turnout and thus violates the Voting Rights Act. Private plaintiffs have also sued, and similar lawsuits can be expected in other states.

Congress is also considering potential sweeping reforms of election law. Although the prospects of adoption seem dim at this moment, because of an inability of Senate Democrats to overcome (or eliminate) a filibuster, if Congress were to enact even a portion of the changes being contemplated, it would be a dramatic transformation of the entire field. Congress has pending provisions on redistricting and campaign finance, as well as the process of casting and counting ballots. All of these provisions taken together, were they to take effect, would shift the balance between federal and state regulation of elections more significantly than any previous Act of Congress.

The four-part division of this book is designed to reflect what might be considered the natural lifecycle of the process that governs any particular election. First, it is necessary to define the office to which the election applies. Thus, we start with the law of districting, which defines each seat in the legislative body. Then, it is necessary for candidates to appear on the ballot, and so we turn in Part II to the law of candidate nominations. Once the candidates are on the ballot, the campaigning to win the election officially can begin. Consequently, we next consider, in Part III, the various regulations of campaign practices, including campaign finance. Finally, the election itself consists of casting and counting votes, and thus the Law of Voting in Part IV addresses not only the basic question of who is eligible to vote, but also the subsidiary questions of how to implement the voting process—including registration laws, voter identification rules, the times and places for casting ballots, and the procedures for resolving any disputes that may arise over the counting of ballots. This order roughly tracks the chronological cycle of an election, although there are certainly overlaps. The goal of presenting the material in this manner is to help you place the doctrine within the setting of how an election actually proceeds.

Before we move on, a note about how we edited the judicial opinions that appear in this casebook. We view a casebook as a tool for teaching students fundamental principles and as a launching off point for discussing the intricacies of election law rather than as a reference resource. For this reason, we have tried to edit the opinions in a streamlined manner so that instructors can construct assignments of reasonable length for students while still having the capability of covering the entire casebook within the confines of a three-credit law school course. We have also tried to edit the opinions to make them relatively easy to read. Many of the opinions in the area of election law are quite lengthy and in some instances we have substantially trimmed the opinions. The omissions in the opinions are not indicated with ellipses; however, we have endeavored to indicate when we have edited out an entire part (e.g., Part I) of an opinion. We also adopted the editing philosophy of limiting citations to precedent and quotations from precedent, and limiting the citations themselves to the case names, years (where necessary), and court (when it is not the U.S. Supreme Court). We did this to make the opinions easier for students to read, and on the theory that when an opinion quotes directly from a prior opinion, it is adopting that language verbatim. While we recognize there is no perfect way to edit an opinion, we hope that our editing assists students in understanding the basics of this admittedly complex area of the law. Finally, we strongly encourage you to read the notes after the cases. We believe that they are unlike the notes you may typically have encountered in other case books, which often present many "case notes" describing detailed permutations of the law or citations to law review articles. We have chosen a different path that we hope is more helpful to students: the notes are designed to present the exact kinds of questions your professor might ask in class. In this way, the notes are intended to focus your reading and help you prepare for each day's class. We hope that this book, with its focus on being as accessible to students as possible, will serve as a valued introduction to the exciting field of election law.

Edward B. Foley
Michael J. Pitts
Joshua A. Douglas

August 2021

Election Law and Litigation

PART I

THE LAW OF LEGISLATIVE DISTRICTING

Districting law, generally speaking, involves four distinct concepts, each with its own line of cases.

- The first is the constitutional principle of one person, one vote.
- The second is the prohibition against racial vote dilution under the U.S. Constitution and Section 2 of the federal Voting Rights Act.
- The third is the constitutional constraint against race-based districting (i.e., "racial gerrymandering").
- The fourth is the constitutional treatment of "political gerrymanders" — that is, the distortion of district boundaries to secure partisan advantage.

Although each of these areas has developed its own separate set of rules, it is also true that these areas are interrelated, and cases in each of these areas often refer to cases, principles, and doctrines developed in the others. This book presents the four lines of cases in the order listed, from first to fourth, because that way they become least entangled with one another. Even so, it will be necessary — especially as one reviews all four — to consider how they have affected each other's development.

In addition to the four lines of cases, there is a fifth area that merits discussion — Section 5 of the Voting Rights Act. As you will learn, Section 5 was essentially neutralized by the Supreme Court's 2013 decision in *Shelby County v. Holder*. Yet even though Section 5, in essence, has been stripped of much, if not all, of its vitality, it is still worth studying because of its importance to the development of voting rights for racial and ethnic minorities, the recency of the Supreme Court's decision in *Shelby County*, and because discussion of Section 5 and some of its basic principles will likely remain salient for the foreseeable future. Moreover, some jurisdictions have justified their consideration of race in redistricting by saying that the goal was to comply with either Sections 2 or 5 of the Voting Rights Act (or both), and that litigation has continued post-*Shelby County*. For these reasons, this book discusses Section 5 between the discussion of racial vote dilution and the constitutional constraints on race-based districting.

Before considering any of these various topics in districting law, however, it is first necessary to address whether the judiciary should review the legality of legislative districting at all, a question that implicates the so-called "political question" doctrine.

A. THE POLITICAL QUESTION DOCTRINE

The most fundamental question to be addressed in the law of legislative redistricting (at least as it relates to constitutional, rather than statutory, law) is whether there should be a "law" of legislative redistricting at all. By "law" in this context, what is connoted is whether the judiciary should pass judgment upon the merits of claims that legislative redistricting plans violate some provision of the U.S. Constitution. The case you are about to read, *Baker v. Carr*, lays the groundwork for judicial intervention in the realm of legislative redistricting, and in many respects the *Baker* decision forms the foundation for many of the federal constitutional cases that appear in this casebook.

Before reading *Baker*, it is useful to have some background on a case that was decided about 16 years earlier—*Colegrove v. Green*, 328 U.S. 549 (1946). *Colegrove* was a case that presented a similar federal constitutional question as the one you are about to encounter in *Baker v. Carr*: whether legislative malapportionment (i.e., legislative districts with unequal numbers of persons) violates the federal Constitution. In *Colegrove*, the Illinois legislature had failed to change the congressional district lines since 1901, with the result that population disparities developed between the districts. In *Colegrove*, the most populated congressional district had 914,000 persons while the least populated congressional district had 112,116. Residents of the most populated districts sued, alleging a violation of the federal Constitution.

Only seven justices participated in *Colegrove*, and they split 4-3 on the result without a majority opinion for the Court. An opinion for three justices written by Justice Frankfurter invoked the political question doctrine and refused to consider the merits of any federal constitutional challenge to the alleged malapportionment of Illinois's congressional districts. Justice Frankfurter wrote these words, which have become oft-quoted in the realm of election law:

> Courts ought not enter this political thicket. . . . The Constitution has many commands that are not enforceable by courts because they clearly fall outside the conditions and purposes that circumscribe judicial action.

Justice Rutledge, who provided the necessary fourth vote for the Court's ruling, wrote a cryptic concurrence saying that even if the federal judiciary had the power to order a redrawing of the state's congressional districts, it should decline to do so in the context of the particular case. In *Colegrove*, the plaintiffs sought injunctive relief. Because the issuance of an injunction is always a matter of equitable discretion, Justice Rutledge thought that the public interest weighed in favor of withholding injunctive relief, in part because of the timing of the litigation in relation to the next upcoming election.

Justices Black, Douglas, and Murphy dissented and would have found a violation of the Equal Protection Clause. Justice Jackson did not participate in *Colegrove*, and Chief Justice Stone had recently died without his successor yet in place.

As you are reading *Baker v. Carr*, consider the best arguments for why the judiciary should or should not become involved in reviewing the process of drawing district lines. Is line drawing a purely legislative judgment? Do judges have the necessary tools to determine when redistricting has become unfair? Note that the Court creates six categories of cases that are nonjusticiable under the political question doctrine. Ultimately, did the Supreme Court adequately justify its decision to make redistricting questions "justiciable"? What are the consequences of saying that those unhappy with legislative districts may challenge them in court? Will the Court's entanglement in "political cases" erode the public's confidence in the Court, as the dissent suggests?

Baker v. Carr

369 U.S. 186 (1962)

Mr. Justice BRENNAN delivered the opinion of the Court.

[Plaintiffs claim that they have been denied "equal protection of the Laws" within the meaning of the Fourteenth Amendment to the U.S. Constitution as a result of an apportionment of the Tennessee General Assembly pursuant to a 1901 state statute. The district court dismissed the complaint, holding] that it lacked jurisdiction of the subject matter and also that no claim was stated upon which relief could be granted. We noted probable jurisdiction of the appeal. We hold that the dismissal was error, and remand the cause to the District Court for trial and further proceedings consistent with this opinion.

The General Assembly of Tennessee consists of the Senate with 33 members and the House of Representatives with 99 members. [The facts indicate that 33 percent of the voters of Tennessee can elect 20 of the 33 Senators while 40 percent of the voters can elect 63 of the 99 members of the House. The facts also indicate that there is a wide disparity of voting strength between the large and small counties. Some examples are: Moore County has a total representation of two with a population (2,340) of only one-eleventh of Rutherford County (25,316) with the same representation; Decatur County (5,563) has the same representation as Carter (23,303) though the latter has four times the population; Loudon County (13,264), Houston County (3,084), and Anderson County (33,990) have the same representation.]

Tennessee's constitutional standard for allocating legislative representation among her counties is the total number of qualified voters resident in the respective counties, subject only to minor qualifications. Decennial reapportionment in compliance with the constitutional scheme was effected by the General Assembly each decade from 1871 to 1901. In the more than 60 years since [enactment of the 1901 statute], all proposals in both Houses of the General Assembly for reapportionment have failed to pass.

Between 1901 and 1961, Tennessee has experienced substantial growth and redistribution of her population. In 1901 the population was 2,020,616, of whom 487,380 were eligible to vote. The 1960 Federal Census reports the State's population at 3,567,089, of whom 2,092,891 are eligible to vote. The relative standings of the counties in terms of qualified voters have changed significantly. It is primarily the continued application of the 1901 Apportionment Act to this shifted and enlarged voting population which gives rise to the present controversy.

Indeed, the complaint alleges that the 1901 statute, even as of the time of its passage, "made no apportionment of Representatives and Senators in accordance with the constitutional formula . . ., but instead arbitrarily and capriciously apportioned representatives in the Senate and House without reference . . . to any logical or reasonable formula whatever." It is further alleged that "because of the population changes since 1900, and the failure of the Legislature to reapportion itself since 1901, the 1901 statute became unconstitutional and obsolete." Appellants also argue that, because of the composition of the legislature effected by the 1901 Apportionment Act, redress in the form of a state constitutional amendment to change the entire mechanism for reapportioning, or any other change short of that, is difficult or impossible.[14] The complaint concludes that "these plaintiffs and others similarly situated are denied the equal protection of the laws accorded them by the Fourteenth Amendment to the Constitution of the United States by virtue of the debasement of their votes." They seek a declaration that the 1901 statute is unconstitutional and an injunction restraining the appellees from acting to conduct any further elections under it. They also pray that unless and until the General Assembly enacts a valid reapportionment, the District Court should either decree a reapportionment by mathematical application of the Tennessee constitutional formulae to the most recent Federal Census figures, or direct the appellees to conduct legislative elections, primary and general, at large. They also pray for such other and further relief as may be appropriate.

JUSTICIABILITY

In holding that the subject matter of this suit was not justiciable, the District Court relied on *Colegrove v. Green* (1946). We understand the District Court to have read [*Colegrove*] as compelling the conclusion that since the appellants sought to have a legislative apportionment held unconstitutional, their suit presented a "political question" and was therefore nonjusticiable. We hold that this challenge to an apportionment presents no nonjusticiable "political question."

[T]he mere fact that the suit seeks protection of a political right does not mean it presents a political question. Such an objection "is little more than a play upon words." *Nixon v. Herndon.* Rather, it is argued that apportionment cases, whatever the actual wording of the complaint, can involve no federal constitutional right except one resting on the guaranty of a republican form of government[30] and that complaints based on that clause have been held to present political questions which are nonjusticiable.

14. The appellants claim that no General Assembly constituted according to the 1901 Act will submit reapportionment proposals either to the people or to a Constitutional Convention. There is no provision for popular initiative in Tennessee.

30. "The United States shall guarantee to every State in this Union a Republican Form of Government, and shall protect each of them against Invasion; and on Application of the Legislature, or of the Executive (when the Legislature cannot be convened) against domestic Violence." U.S. Const. Art IV, §4.

We hold that the claim pleaded here neither rests upon nor implicates the Guaranty Clause and that its justiciability is therefore not foreclosed by our decisions of cases involving that clause. The District Court misinterpreted *Colegrove v. Green.* Appellants' claim that they are being denied equal protection is justiciable.

[I]t is the relationship between the judiciary and the coordinate branches of the Federal Government, and not the federal judiciary's relationship to the States, which gives rise to the "political question."

The nonjusticiability of a political question is primarily a function of the separation of powers. Much confusion results from the capacity of the "political question" label to obscure the need for case-by-case inquiry. Deciding whether a matter has in any measure been committed by the Constitution to another branch of government, or whether the action of that branch exceeds whatever authority has been committed, is itself a delicate exercise in constitutional interpretation, and is a responsibility of this Court as ultimate interpreter of the Constitution.

Prominent on the surface of any case held to involve a political question is found a textually demonstrable constitutional commitment of the issue to a coordinate political department; or a lack of judicially discoverable and manageable standards for resolving it; or the impossibility of deciding without an initial policy determination of a kind clearly for nonjudicial discretion; or the impossibility of a court's undertaking independent resolution without expressing lack of the respect due coordinate branches of government; or an unusual need for unquestioning adherence to a political decision already made; or the potentiality of embarrassment from multifarious pronouncements by various departments on one question.

Unless one of these formulations is inextricable from the case at bar, there should be no dismissal for nonjusticiability on the ground of a political question's presence. The doctrine of which we treat is one of "political questions," not one of "political cases." The courts cannot reject as "no law suit" a bona fide controversy as to whether some action denominated "political" exceeds constitutional authority.

We come to the ultimate inquiry whether our precedents as to what constitutes a nonjusticiable "political question" bring the case before us under the umbrella of that doctrine. A natural beginning is to note whether any of the common characteristics which we have been able to identify and label descriptively are present. We find none: The question here is the consistency of state action with the Federal Constitution. We have no question decided, or to be decided, by a political branch of government coequal with this Court. Nor do we risk embarrassment of our government abroad, or grave disturbance at home if we take issue with Tennessee as to the constitutionality of her action here challenged. Nor need the appellants, in order to succeed in this action, ask the Court to enter upon policy determinations for which judicially manageable standards are lacking. Judicial standards under the Equal Protection Clause are well developed and familiar, and it has been open to courts since the enactment of the Fourteenth Amendment to determine, if on the particular facts they must, that a discrimination reflects no policy, but simply arbitrary and capricious action.

This case does, in one sense, involve the allocation of political power within a State, and the appellants might conceivably have added a claim under the Guaranty Clause. Of course any reliance on that clause would be futile. But because any reliance on the Guaranty Clause could not have succeeded it does not follow that appellants may not be heard on the equal protection claim which in fact they tender. True, it must be clear that the Fourteenth Amendment claim is not so enmeshed with those political question elements which render Guaranty Clause claims nonjusticiable as actually to present a political question itself. But we have found that not to be the case here.

We conclude then that the nonjusticiability of claims resting on the Guaranty Clause which arises from their embodiment of questions that were thought "political," can have no bearing upon the justiciability of the equal protection claim presented in this case. Finally, we emphasize that it is the involvement in Guaranty Clause claims of the elements thought to define "political questions," and no other feature, which could render them nonjusticiable. Specifically, we have said that such claims are not held nonjusticiable because they touch matters of state governmental organization.

We have already noted that the District Court's holding that the subject matter of this complaint was nonjusticiable relied upon *Colegrove v. Green.* In *Colegrove,* Mr. Justice Rutledge joined in the conclusion that the case was justiciable, although he held that the dismissal of the complaint should be affirmed.

No constitutional questions, including the question whether voters have a judicially enforceable constitutional right to vote at elections of congressmen from districts of equal population, were decided in *Colegrove.* Six of the participating Justices reached the questions but divided three to three on their merits. Mr. Justice Rutledge believed that it was not necessary to decide them.

Indeed, the refusal to award relief in *Colegrove* resulted only from the controlling view of a want of equity.

We conclude that the complaint's allegations of a denial of equal protection present a justiciable constitutional cause of action upon which appellants are entitled to a trial and a decision. The right asserted is within the reach of judicial protection under the Fourteenth Amendment.

The judgment of the District Court is reversed and the cause is remanded for further proceedings consistent with this opinion.

Reversed and remanded.

Mr. Justice WHITTAKER did not participate in the decision of this case.

Mr. Justice DOUGLAS, concurring.
[Omitted.]

Mr. Justice CLARK, concurring.
[Omitted.]

Mr. Justice STEWART, concurring.

The separate writings of my dissenting and concurring Brothers stray so far from the subject of today's decision as to convey, I think, a distressingly inaccurate impression of what the Court decides. For that reason, I think it appropriate, in joining the opinion of the Court, to emphasize in a few words what the opinion does and does not say.

The Court today decides three things and no more: "(a) that the court possessed jurisdiction of the subject matter; (b) that a justiciable cause of action is stated upon which appellants would be entitled to appropriate relief; and (c) . . . that the appellants have standing to challenge the Tennessee apportionment statutes."

The complaint in this case asserts that Tennessee's system of apportionment is utterly arbitrary—without any possible justification in rationality. The District Court did not reach the merits of that claim, and this Court quite properly expresses no view on the subject. Contrary to the suggestion of my Brother Harlan, the Court does not say or imply that "state legislatures must be so structured as to reflect with approximate equality the voice of every voter." The Court does not say or imply that there is anything in the Federal Constitution "to prevent a State, acting not irrationally, from choosing any electoral legislative structure it thinks best suited to the interests, temper, and customs of its people." And contrary to the suggestion of my Brother Douglas, the Court most assuredly does not decide the question, "may a State weight the vote of one county or one district more heavily than it weights the vote in another?"

My Brother Clark has made a convincing prima facie showing that Tennessee's system of apportionment is in fact utterly arbitrary—without any possible justification in rationality. My Brother Harlan has, with imagination and ingenuity, hypothesized possibly rational bases for Tennessee's system. But the merits of this case are not before us now. The defendants have not yet had an opportunity to be heard in defense of the State's system of apportionment; indeed, they have not yet even filed an answer to the complaint. As in other cases, the proper place for the trial is in the trial court, not here.

Mr. Justice FRANKFURTER, whom Mr. Justice HARLAN joins, dissenting.

The Court today reverses a uniform course of decision established by a dozen cases, including one by which the very claim now sustained was unanimously rejected only five years ago. The impressive body of rulings thus cast aside reflected the equally uniform course of our political history regarding the relationship between population and legislative representation—a wholly different matter from denial of the franchise to individuals because of race, color, religion or sex. Such a massive repudiation of the experience of our whole past in asserting destructively novel judicial power demands a detailed analysis of the role of this Court in our constitutional scheme. Disregard of inherent limits in the effective exercise of the Court's "judicial Power" not only presages the futility of judicial intervention in the essentially political conflict of forces by which the relation between population and representation has time out of mind been and now is determined. It may well impair the Court's position as the ultimate organ of "the supreme Law of the Land" in that vast range of legal problems, often strongly entangled in popular feeling, on which this Court must pronounce. The Court's authority—possessed of neither the purse nor the sword—ultimately rests on sustained public confidence in its moral sanction. Such feeling must be nourished by the Court's complete detachment, in fact and in appearance, from political entanglements and by abstention from injecting itself into the clash of political forces in political settlements.

Even assuming the indispensable intellectual disinterestedness on the part of judges in such matters, they do not have accepted legal standards or criteria or even reliable analogies to draw upon for making judicial judgments. To charge courts with the task of accommodating the incommensurable factors of policy that underlie these mathematical puzzles is to attribute, however flatteringly, omnicompetence to judges. The Framers of the Constitution persistently rejected a proposal that embodied this assumption.

Recent legislation, creating a district appropriately described as "an atrocity of ingenuity," is not unique. Considering the gross inequality among legislative electoral units within almost every State, the Court naturally shrinks from asserting that in districting at least substantial equality is a constitutional requirement enforceable by courts. Room continues to be allowed for weighting. This of course implies that geography, economics, urban-rural conflict, and all the other non-legal factors which have throughout our history entered into political districting are to some extent not to be ruled out in the undefined vista now opened up by review in the federal courts of state reapportionments. To some extent—aye, there's the rub. In effect, today's decision empowers the courts of the country to devise what should constitute the proper composition of the legislatures of the fifty States. If state courts should for one reason or another find themselves unable to discharge this task, the duty of doing so is put on the federal courts or on this Court, if State views do not satisfy this Court's notion of what is proper districting.

We were soothingly told at the bar of this Court that we need not worry about the kind of remedy a court could effectively fashion once the abstract constitutional right to have courts pass on a state-wide system of electoral districting is recognized as a matter of judicial rhetoric, because legislatures would heed the Court's admonition. This is not only a euphoric hope. It implies a sorry confession of judicial impotence in place of a frank acknowledgment that there is not under our Constitution a judicial remedy for every political mischief, for every undesirable exercise of legislative power. The Framers carefully and with deliberate forethought refused so to enthrone the judiciary. In this situation, as in others of like nature, appeal for relief does not belong here. Appeal must be to an informed, civically militant electorate. In a democratic society like ours, relief must come through an aroused popular conscience that sears the conscience of the people's representatives. In any event there is nothing judicially more unseemly nor more self-defeating than for this Court to make *interrorem* pronouncements, to indulge in merely empty rhetoric, sounding a word of promise to the ear, sure to be disappointing to the hope.

Colegrove held that a federal court should not entertain an action for declaratory and injunctive relief to adjudicate the constitutionality, under the Equal Protection Clause and other federal constitutional and statutory provisions, of a state statute establishing the respective districts for the State's election of Representatives to the Congress. Two opinions were written by the four Justices who composed the majority of the seven sitting members of the Court. Both opinions joining in the result in *Colegrove v. Green* agreed that considerations were controlling which dictated denial of jurisdiction though not in the strict sense of want of power. While the two opinions show a divergence of view regarding some of these considerations, there are important points of concurrence. Both opinions demonstrate a predominant concern, first, with avoiding federal judicial involvement in matters traditionally left to legislative policy making; second, with respect to the difficulty—in view of the nature of the problems of apportionment and its history in this country—of drawing on or devising judicial standards for judgment, as opposed to legislative determinations, of the part which mere numerical equality among voters should play as a criterion for the allocation of political power; and, third, with problems of finding appropriate modes of relief—particularly, the problem of resolving the essentially political issue of the relative merits of at large elections and elections held in districts of unequal population.

The *Colegrove* doctrine, in the form in which repeated decisions have settled it, was not an innovation. It represents long judicial thought and experience. From its earliest opinions this Court has consistently recognized a class of controversies which do not lend themselves to judicial standards and judicial remedies. To classify the various instances as "political questions" is rather a form of stating this conclusion than revealing of analysis. Some of the cases so labeled have no relevance here. But from others emerge unifying considerations that are compelling.

The cases involving Negro disfranchisement are no exception to the principle of avoiding federal judicial intervention into matters of state government in the absence of an explicit and clear constitutional imperative. For here the controlling command of Supreme Law is plain and unequivocal. An end of discrimination against the Negro was the compelling motive of the Civil War Amendments. The Fifteenth expresses this in terms, and it is no less true of the Equal Protection Clause of the Fourteenth. Thus the Court, in cases involving discrimination against the Negro's right to vote, has recognized not only the action at law for damages, but, in appropriate circumstances, the extraordinary remedy of declaratory or injunctive relief. Injunctions in these cases, it should be noted, would not have restrained statewide general elections.

The influence of these converging considerations—the caution not to undertake decision where standards meet for judicial judgment are lacking, the reluctance to interfere with matters of state government in the absence of an unquestionable and effectively enforceable mandate, the unwillingness to make courts arbiters of the broad issues of political organization historically committed to other institutions and for whose adjustment the judicial process is ill adapted—has been decisive of the settled line of cases, reaching back more than a century, which holds that Art. IV, §4, of the Constitution, guaranteeing to the States "a Republican Form of Government," is not enforceable through the courts.

The present case involves all of the elements that have made the Guarantee Clause cases nonjusticiable. It is, in effect, a Guarantee Clause claim masquerading under a different label. But it cannot make the case more fit for judicial action that appellants invoke the Fourteenth Amendment rather than Art. IV, §4, where, in fact, the gist of their complaint is the same—unless it can be found that the Fourteenth Amendment speaks with greater particularity to their situation. Art. IV, §4, is not committed by express constitutional terms to Congress. It is the nature of the controversies arising under it, nothing else, which has made it judicially unenforceable. But where judicial competence is wanting, it cannot be created by invoking one clause of the Constitution rather than another.

Here appellants assert that "a minority now rules in Tennessee," that the apportionment statute results in a "distortion of the constitutional system," that the General Assembly is no longer "a body representative of the people of the State of Tennessee," all "contrary to the basic principle of representative government. . . ." Such a claim would be nonjusticiable not merely under Art. IV, §4, but under any clause of the Constitution, by virtue of the very fact that a federal court is not a forum for political debate.

But appellants, of course, do not rest on this claim *simpliciter*. In invoking the Equal Protection Clause, they assert that the distortion of representative government complained of is produced by systematic discrimination against them, by way of "a debasement of their votes. . . ." Does this characterization, with due regard for the facts from which it is derived, add anything to appellants' case?

At first blush, this charge of discrimination based on legislative underrepresentation is given the appearance of a more private, less impersonal claim, than the assertion that the frame of government is askew. Appellants appear as representatives of a class that is prejudiced as a class, in contradistinction to the polity in its entirety. However, the discrimination relied on is the deprivation of what appellants conceive to be their proportionate share of political influence. This, of course, is the practical effect of any allocation of power within the institutions of government. Hardly any distribution of political authority that could be assailed as rendering government non-republican would fail similarly to operate to the prejudice of some groups, and to the advantage of others, within the body politic. It would be ingenuous not to see, or consciously blind to deny, that the real battle over the initiative and referendum, or over a delegation of power to local rather than state-wide authority, is the battle between forces whose influence is disparate among the various organs of government to whom power may be given. No shift of power but works a corresponding shift in political influence among the groups composing a society.

What, then, is this question of legislative apportionment? Appellants invoke the right to vote and to have their votes counted. But they are permitted to vote and their votes are counted. They go to the polls, they cast their ballots, they send their representatives to the state councils. Their complaint is simply that the representatives are not sufficiently numerous or powerful—in short, that Tennessee has adopted a basis of representation with which they are dissatisfied. Talk of "debasement" or "dilution" is circular talk. One cannot speak of "debasement" or "dilution" of the value of a vote until there is first defined a standard of reference as to what a vote should be worth. What is actually asked of the Court in this case is to choose among competing bases of representation—ultimately, really, among competing theories of political philosophy—in order to establish an appropriate frame of government for the State of Tennessee and thereby for all the States of the Union.

In such a matter, abstract analogies which ignore the facts of history deal in unrealities; they betray reason. This is not a case in which a State has, through a device however oblique and sophisticated, denied Negroes or Jews or redheaded persons a vote, or given them only a third or a sixth of a vote. What Tennessee illustrates is an old and still widespread method of representation—representation by local geographical division, only in part respective of population—in preference to others, others, forsooth, more appealing. Appellants contest this choice and seek to make this Court the arbiter of the disagreement. They would make the Equal Protection Clause the charter of adjudication, asserting that the equality which it guarantees comports, if not the assurance of equal weight to every voter's vote, at least the basic conception that representation ought to be proportionate to population, a standard by reference to which the reasonableness of apportionment plans may be judged.

To find such a political conception legally enforceable in the broad and unspecific guarantee of equal protection is to rewrite the Constitution. Certainly, "equal protection" is no more secure a foundation for judicial judgment of the permissibility of varying forms of representative government than is "Republican Form." Indeed since "equal protection of the laws" can only mean an equality of persons standing in the same relation to whatever governmental action is challenged, the determination whether treatment is equal presupposes a determination concerning the nature of the relationship. This, with respect to apportionment, means an inquiry into the theoretic base of representation in an acceptably republican state. For a court could not determine the equal-protection issue without in fact first determining the Republican-Form issue, simply because what is reasonable for equal-protection purposes will depend upon what frame of government, basically, is allowed. To divorce "equal protection" from "Republican Form" is to talk about half a question.

The notion that representation proportioned to the geographic spread of population is so universally accepted as a necessary element of equality between man and man that it must be taken to be the standard of a political equality preserved by the Fourteenth Amendment—that it is, in appellants' words "the basic principle of representative government"—is, to put it bluntly, not true. However desirable and however desired by some among the great political thinkers and framers of our government, it has never been generally practiced, today or in the past. It was not the English system, it was not the colonial system, it was not the system chosen for the national government by the Constitution, it was not the system exclusively or even predominantly practiced by the States at the time of adoption of the Fourteenth Amendment, it is not predominantly practiced by the States today. Unless judges, the judges of this Court, are to make their private views of political wisdom the measure of the Constitution—views which in all honesty cannot but give the appearance, if not reflect the reality, of involvement with the business of partisan politics so inescapably a part of apportionment controversies—the Fourteenth Amendment, "itself a historical product," provides no guide for judicial oversight of the representation problem.

The stark fact is that if among the numerous widely varying principles and practices that control state legislative apportionment today there is any generally prevailing feature, that feature is geographic inequality in relation to the population standard. Examples could be endlessly multiplied. In New Jersey, counties of thirty-five thousand and of more than nine hundred and five thousand inhabitants respectively each have a single senator. Representative districts in Minnesota range from 7,290 inhabitants to 107,246 inhabitants. Ratios of senatorial representation in California vary as much as two hundred and ninety-seven to one. In Oklahoma, the range is ten to one for House constituencies and roughly sixteen to one for Senate constituencies. Colebrook, Connecticut—population 592—elects two House representatives; Hartford—population 177,397—also elects two. The first, third and fifth of these examples are the products of constitutional provisions which subordinate population to regional considerations in apportionment; the second is the result of legislative inaction; the fourth derives from both constitutional and legislative sources. A survey made in 1955, in sum, reveals that less than thirty percent of the population inhabit districts sufficient to elect a House majority in thirteen States and a Senate majority in nineteen States. These figures show more than individual variations from a generally accepted standard of electoral equality. They show that there is not—as there has never been—a standard by which the place of equality as a factor in apportionment can be measured.

Manifestly, the Equal Protection Clause supplies no clearer guide for judicial examination of apportionment methods than would the Guarantee Clause itself. Apportionment, by its character, is a subject of extraordinary complexity, involving—even after the fundamental theoretical issues concerning what is to be represented in a representative legislature have been fought out or compromised—considerations of geography, demography, electoral convenience, economic and social cohesions or divergencies among particular local groups, communications, the practical effects of political institutions like the lobby and the city machine, ancient traditions and ties of settled usage, respect for proven incumbents of long experience and senior status, mathematical mechanics, censuses compiling relevant data, and a host of others. Legislative responses throughout the country to the reapportionment demands of the 1960 Census have glaringly confirmed that these are not factors that lend themselves to evaluations of a nature that are the staple of judicial determinations or for which judges are equipped to adjudicate by legal training or experience or native wit. And this is the more so true because in every strand of this complicated, intricate web of values meet the contending forces of partisan politics. The practical significance of apportionment is that the next election results may differ because of it. Apportionment battles are overwhelmingly party or intra-party contests. It will add a virulent source of friction and tension in federal-state relations to embroil the federal judiciary in them.

Dissenting opinion of Mr. Justice HARLAN, whom Mr. Justice FRANKFURTER joins.

[Justice Harlan noted that Tennessee might have retained the current legislative districts to "protect the State's agricultural interests from the sheer weight of numbers of those residing in its cities."]

NOTES ON *BAKER v. CARR* AND THE POLITICAL QUESTION DOCTRINE

1. As mentioned in the introduction to this case, *Colegrove v. Green* raised the exact same basic question as *Baker* yet, as you have now learned, the Court's approach in *Baker* was much different than the Court's approach in *Colegrove.* One factual difference was that *Colegrove* concerned a state's *congressional* delegation, whereas *Baker* concerned a state's own legislature. Should that factual distinction make a difference under the Equal Protection Clause?

2. Even if *Baker* did not technically overrule *Colegrove,* the two cases are very much inconsistent, as Justice Frankfurter observes in his *Baker* dissent. Why did the Court adopt a very different approach only 16 years after *Colegrove* itself? Was the Court justified in departing from the *Colegrove* approach? If so, why? Does the majority opinion in *Baker* even attempt to justify taking a different approach from *Colegrove* (as opposed to trying to cast aside *Colegrove* as irrelevant)?

3. In both *Baker* and *Colegrove,* there was a discussion of the so-called Guaranty Clause of the U.S. Constitution, which says that the federal government will

guarantee the states a "Republican Form of Government." Early in the Court's history, in a fascinating case called *Luther v. Borden*, 48 U.S. 1 (1849), the Court refused to entertain any judicial claim based on this clause. Rather, the Court held, it is up to Congress to enforce this constitutional guarantee. The context was attempted political revolution in Rhode Island, where the existing state constitution limited the suffrage to property owners, and opponents of this restriction held a constitutional convention for the state, submitted a new constitution to the citizenry for ratification, and attempted to elect a new government under the new constitution. Defenders of the old state constitution, however, refused to acquiesce, and they declared martial law and arrested supporters of the new state constitution. After their arrest, these supporters of the new state constitution filed suit in state court, claiming protection under the Guaranty Clause. The U.S. Supreme Court ruled that the federal courts were not entitled to intervene in this political dispute, thus invoking what has come to be known as the political question doctrine.

4. The significance of *Baker* is that it reinterprets the political question doctrine so that the "nonjusticiability" of Guaranty Clause claims is clause-specific, meaning that the obstacle to judicial involvement is reliance on that particular clause, not the nature of the controversy itself. *Colegrove*, by contrast, had taken the approach that the problem was the subject matter of the litigation: It would not matter which particular clause of the U.S. Constitution was invoked to challenge disparities of population among legislative districts; according to *Colegrove*, courts cannot become involved in that subject matter. *Baker* says the opposite: The federal judiciary is entitled to entertain an Equal Protection claim with respect to districting because that involves a different clause than the Guaranty Clause.

B. ONE PERSON, ONE VOTE

Baker v. Carr declared that federal courts would entertain Equal Protection challenges to state legislative districts that were malapportioned. However, as Justice Stewart notes in his concurrence in *Baker*, the *Baker* Court did not delineate the full scope of the constitutional right or remedy in this area. The next two cases illustrate both the nature of the remedy and the breadth of the right. As you are reading, remember from *Baker* that the source of the right is the Equal Protection Clause. Does the remedy crafted for the violation of the Equal Protection Clause resemble traditional equal protection doctrine?

Reynolds v. Sims

377 U.S. 533 (1964)

[This case was one of six decided the same day concerning the make-up of state legislatures. Alabama's legislature had not been redistricted for over 60 years. As a result, neither house of Alabama's legislature had representation based even remotely on population. In the Senate, the ratio between the most populated and least populated district was 41:1; in the House, the ratio between the most populated and least populated district was 16:1. Accordingly, a group of Alabama citizens sued various state officials in federal court, claiming that the make-up of Alabama's legislature violated the Equal Protection Clause. The District Court ruled in plaintiffs' favor, and the case was appealed directly to the Supreme Court.]

Mr. Chief Justice WARREN delivered the opinion of the Court.

The right to vote freely for the candidate of one's choice is of the essence of a democratic society, and any restrictions on that right strike at the heart of representative government. And the right of suffrage can be denied by a debasement or dilution of the weight of a citizen's vote just as effectively as by wholly prohibiting the free exercise of the franchise.

A predominant consideration in determining whether a State's legislative apportionment scheme constitutes an invidious discrimination violative of rights asserted under the Equal Protection Clause is that the rights allegedly impaired are individual and personal in nature. Undoubtedly, the right of suffrage is a fundamental matter in a free and democratic society. Especially since the right to exercise the franchise in a free and unimpaired manner is preservative of other basic civil and political rights, any alleged infringement of the right of citizens to vote must be carefully and meticulously scrutinized.

Legislators represent people, not trees or acres. Legislators are elected by voters, not farms or cities or economic interests. As long as ours is a representative form of government, and our legislatures are those instruments of government elected directly by and directly representative of the people, the right to elect legislators in a free and unimpaired fashion is a bedrock of our political system. It could hardly be gainsaid that a constitutional claim had been asserted by an allegation that certain otherwise qualified voters had been entirely prohibited from voting for members of their state legislature. And, if a State should provide that the votes of citizens in one part of the State should be given two times, or five times, or 10 times the weight of votes of citizens in another part of the State, it could hardly be contended that the right to vote of those residing in the disfavored areas had not been effectively diluted. It would appear extraordinary to suggest that a State could be constitutionally permitted to enact a law providing that certain of the State's voters could vote two, five, or 10 times for their legislative representatives, while voters living elsewhere could vote only once. And it is inconceivable that a state law to the effect that, in counting votes for legislators, the votes of citizens in one part of the State would be multiplied by two, five, or 10, while the votes of persons in another area would be counted only at face value, could be constitutionally sustainable. Of course, the effect of state legislative districting schemes which give the same number of representatives to unequal numbers of constituents is identical. Overweighting and overvaluation of the votes of those living here has the certain effect of dilution and undervaluation of the votes of those living there. The resulting discrimination against those individual voters living in disfavored areas is easily demonstrable mathematically. Their right to vote is simply not the same right to vote as that of those living in a favored part of the State. Two, five, or 10 of them must vote before the effect of their voting is equivalent to that of their favored neighbor. Weighting the votes of citizens differently, by any method or means, merely because of where they happen to reside, hardly seems justifiable.

State legislatures are, historically, the fountainhead of representative government in this country. A number of them have their roots in colonial times, and substantially antedate the creation of our Nation and our Federal Government. In fact, the first formal stirrings of American political independence are to be found, in large part, in the views and actions of several of the colonial legislative bodies. With the birth of our National Government, and the adoption and ratification of the Federal Constitution, state legislatures retained a most important place in our Nation's governmental structure. But representative government is in essence self-government through the medium of elected representatives of the people, and each and every citizen has an inalienable right to full and effective participation in the political processes of his State's legislative bodies. Most citizens can achieve this participation only as qualified voters through the election of legislators to represent them. Full and effective participation by all citizens in state government requires, therefore, that each citizen have an equally effective voice in the election of members of his state legislature. Modern and viable state government needs, and the Constitution demands, no less.

Logically, in a society ostensibly grounded on representative government, it would seem reasonable that a majority of the people of a State could elect a majority of that State's legislators. To conclude differently, and to sanction minority control of state legislative bodies, would appear to deny majority rights in a way that far surpasses any possible denial of minority rights that might otherwise be thought to result. Since legislatures are responsible for enacting laws by which all citizens are to be governed, they should be bodies which are collectively responsive to the popular will. And the concept of equal protection has been traditionally viewed as requiring the uniform treatment of persons standing in the same relation to the governmental action questioned or challenged. With respect to the allocation of legislative representation, all voters, as citizens of a State, stand in the same relation regardless of where they live. Any suggested criteria for the differentiation of citizens are insufficient to justify any discrimination, as to the weight of their votes, unless relevant to the permissible purposes of legislative apportionment. Since the achieving of fair and effective representation for all citizens is concededly the basic aim of legislative apportionment, we conclude that the Equal Protection Clause guarantees the opportunity for equal participation by all voters in the election of state legislators. Our constitutional system amply provides for the protection of minorities by means other than giving them majority control of state legislatures. And the democratic ideals of equality and majority rule, which have served this Nation so well in the past, are hardly of any less significance for the present and the future.

We are told that the matter of apportioning representation in a state legislature is a complex and many-faceted one. We are advised that States can rationally consider factors other than population in apportioning legislative representation. We are admonished not to restrict the power of the States to impose differing views as to political philosophy on their citizens. We are cautioned about the dangers of entering into political thickets and mathematical quagmires. Our answer is this: a denial of constitutionally protected rights demands judicial protection; our oath and our office require no less of us.

To the extent that a citizen's right to vote is debased, he is that much less a citizen. The fact that an individual lives here or there is not a legitimate reason for overweighting or diluting the efficacy of his vote. The complexions of societies and civilizations change, often with amazing rapidity. A nation once primarily rural in character becomes predominantly urban. Representation schemes once fair and equitable become archaic and outdated. But the basic principle of representative government remains, and must remain, unchanged—the weight of a citizen's vote cannot be made to depend on where he lives. Population is, of necessity, the starting point for consideration and the controlling criterion for judgment in legislative apportionment controversies. A citizen, a qualified voter, is no more nor no less so because he lives in the city or on the farm. This is the clear and strong command of our Constitution's Equal Protection Clause. This is an essential part of the concept of a government of laws and not men. This is at the heart of Lincoln's vision of "government of the people, by the people, (and) for the people." The Equal Protection Clause demands no less than substantially equal state legislative representation for all citizens, of all places as well as of all races.

We hold that, as a basic constitutional standard, the Equal Protection Clause requires that the seats in both houses of a bicameral state legislature must be apportioned on a population basis. Simply stated, an individual's right to vote for state legislators is unconstitutionally impaired when its weight is in a substantial fashion diluted when compared with votes of citizens living on other parts of the State.

Much has been written since our decision in *Baker v. Carr* about the applicability of the so-called federal analogy to state legislative apportionment arrangements. We find the federal analogy inapposite and irrelevant to state legislative districting schemes. Attempted reliance on the federal analogy appears often to be little more than an after-the-fact rationalization offered in defense of maladjusted state apportionment arrangements. The original constitutions of 36 of our States provided that representation in both houses of the state legislatures would be based completely, or predominantly, on population. And the Founding Fathers clearly had no intention of establishing a pattern or model for the apportionment of seats in state legislatures when the system of representation in the Federal Congress was adopted.

The system of representation in the two Houses of the Federal Congress is one ingrained in our Constitution, as part of the law of the land. It is one conceived out of compromise and concession indispensable to the establishment of our federal republic. Arising from unique historical circumstances, it is based on the consideration that in establishing our type of federalism a group of formerly independent States bound themselves together under one national government. Admittedly, the original 13 States surrendered some of their sovereignty in agreeing to join together "to form a more perfect Union." But at the heart of our constitutional system remains the concept of separate and distinct governmental entities which have delegated some, but not all, of their formerly held powers to the single national government. The fact that almost three-fourths of our present States were never in fact independently sovereign does not detract from our view that the so-called federal analogy is inapplicable as a sustaining precedent for state legislative apportionments. The developing history and growth of our republic cannot cloud the fact that, at the time of the inception of the system of representation in the Federal Congress, a compromise between the larger and smaller States on this matter averted a deadlock in the Constitutional Convention which had threatened to abort the birth of our Nation.

Political subdivisions of States—counties, cities, or whatever—never were and never have been considered as sovereign entities. Rather, they have been traditionally regarded as subordinate governmental instrumentalities created by the State to assist in the carrying out of state governmental functions. These governmental units are "created as convenient agencies for exercising such of the governmental powers of the state as may be entrusted to them," and the "number, nature, and duration of the powers conferred upon (them) . . . and the territory over which they shall be exercised rests in the absolute discretion of the state." The relationship of the States to the Federal Government could hardly be less analogous.

Since we find the so-called federal analogy inapposite to a consideration of the constitutional validity of state legislative apportionment schemes, we necessarily hold that the Equal Protection Clause requires both houses of a state legislature to be apportioned on a population basis. The right of a citizen to equal representation and to have his vote weighted equally with those of all other citizens in the election of members of one house of a bicameral state legislature would amount to little if States could effectively submerge the equal-population principle in the apportionment of seats in the other house. If such a scheme were permissible, an individual citizen's ability to exercise an effective voice in the only instrument of state government directly representative of the people might be almost as effectively thwarted as if neither house were apportioned on a population basis. Deadlock between the two bodies might result in compromise and concession on some issues. But in all too many cases the more probable result would be frustration of the majority will through minority veto in the house not apportioned on a population basis, stemming directly from the failure to accord adequate overall legislative representation to all of the State's citizens on a nondiscriminatory basis. In summary, we can perceive no constitutional difference, with respect to the geographical distribution of state legislative representation, between the two houses of a bicameral state legislature.

By holding that as a federal constitutional requisite both houses of a state legislature must be apportioned on a population basis, we mean that the Equal Protection Clause requires that a State make an honest and good faith effort to construct districts, in both houses of its legislature, as nearly of equal population as is practicable.* We realize that it is a practical impossibility to arrange legislative districts so that each one has an identical number of residents, or citizens, or voters. Mathematical exactness or precision is hardly a workable constitutional requirement.

For the present, we deem it expedient not to attempt to spell out any precise constitutional tests. What is marginally permissible in one State may be unsatisfactory in another, depending on the particular circumstances of the case. Developing a body of doctrine on a case-by-case basis appears to us to provide the most satisfactory means of arriving at detailed constitutional requirements in the area of state legislative apportionment. Thus, we proceed to state here only a few rather general considerations which appear to us to be relevant.

A State may legitimately desire to maintain the integrity of various political subdivisions, insofar as possible, and provide for compact districts of contiguous territory in designing a legislative apportionment scheme. Valid considerations may underlie such aims. Indiscriminate districting, without any regard for political subdivision or natural or historical boundary lines, may be little more than an open

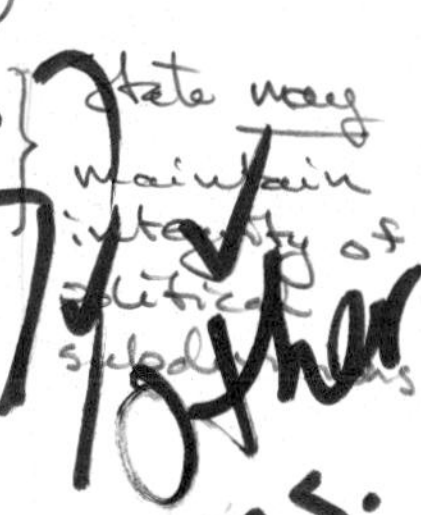

* [Re-read this sentence as it contains both the nature and the breadth of the right.—Eds.]

invitation to partisan gerrymandering. Single-member districts may be the rule in one State, while another State might desire to achieve some flexibility by creating multimember or floterial districts.* Whatever the means of accomplishment, the overriding objective must be substantial equality of population among the various districts, so that the vote of any citizen is approximately equal in weight to that of any other citizen in the State.

History indicates, however, that many States have deviated, to a greater or lesser degree, from the equal-population principle in the apportionment of seats in at least one house of their legislatures. So long as the divergences from a strict population standard are based on legitimate considerations incident to the effectuation of a rational state policy, some deviations from the equal-population principle are constitutionally permissible with respect to the apportionment of seats in either or both of the two houses of a bicameral state legislature. But neither history alone, nor economic or other sorts of group interests, are permissible factors in attempting to justify disparities from population-based representation. Citizens, not history or economic interests, cast votes. Considerations of area alone provide an insufficient justification for deviations from the equal-population principle. Again, people, not land or trees or pastures, vote. Modern developments and improvements in transportation and communications make rather hollow, in the mid-1960's, most claims that deviations from population-based representation can validly be based solely on geographical considerations. Arguments for allowing such deviations in order to insure effective representation for sparsely settled areas and to prevent legislative districts from becoming so large that the availability of access of citizens to their representatives is impaired are today, for the most part, unconvincing.

A consideration that appears to be of more substance in justifying some deviations from population-based representation in state legislatures is that of insuring some voice to political subdivisions, as political subdivisions. Several factors make more than insubstantial claims that a State can rationally consider according political subdivisions some independent representation in at least one body of the state legislature, as long as the basic standard of equality of population among districts is maintained. Local governmental entities are frequently charged with various responsibilities incident to the operation of state government. In many States much of the legislature's activity involves the enactment of so-called local legislation, directed only to the concerns of particular political subdivisions. And a State may legitimately desire to construct districts along political subdivision lines to deter the possibilities of gerrymandering. However, permitting deviations from population-based representation does not mean that each local governmental unit or political subdivision can be given separate representation, regardless of population. Carried too far, a scheme of giving at least one seat in one house to each political subdivision (for example, to each county) could easily result, in many States, in a total subversion of the equal-population principle in that legislative body. This would be especially true in a State where the number of counties is large and many of

* [A multi-member district is a district that elects more than one candidate. A floterial district is a district that elects one candidate from a combination of districts. For instance, District 1, District 2, and District 3 each elect a single candidate and then another candidate is elected from a floterial district that combines District 1, District 2, and District 3.—Eds.]

them are sparsely populated, and the number of seats in the legislative body being apportioned does not significantly exceed the number of counties. Such a result, we conclude, would be constitutionally impermissible. And careful judicial scrutiny must of course be given, in evaluating state apportionment schemes, to the character as well as the degree of deviations from a strict population basis. But if, even as a result of a clearly rational state policy of according some legislative representation to political subdivisions, population is submerged as the controlling consideration in the apportionment of seats in the particular legislative body, then the right of all of the State's citizens to cast an effective and adequately weighted vote would be unconstitutionally impaired.

That the Equal Protection Clause requires that both houses of a state legislature be apportioned on a population basis does not mean that States cannot adopt some reasonable plan for periodic revision of their apportionment schemes. Decennial reapportionment appears to be a rational approach to readjustment of legislative representation in order to take into account population shifts and growth. Reallocation of legislative seats every 10 years coincides with the prescribed practice in 41 of the States, often honored more in the breach than the observance, however. Illustratively, the Alabama Constitution requires decennial reapportionment, yet the last reapportionment of the Alabama Legislature, when this suit was brought, was in 1901. Limitations on the frequency of reapportionment are justified by the need for stability and continuity in the organization of the legislative system, although undoubtedly reapportioning no more frequently than every 10 years leads to some imbalance in the population of districts toward the end of the decennial period and also to the development of resistance to change on the part of some incumbent legislators. In substance, we do not regard the Equal Protection Clause as requiring daily, monthly, annual or biennial reapportionment, so long as a State has a reasonably conceived plan for periodic readjustment of legislative representation. While we do not intend to indicate that decennial reapportionment is a constitutional requisite, compliance with such an approach would clearly meet the minimal requirements for maintaining a reasonably current scheme of legislative representation. And we do not mean to intimate that more frequent reapportionment would not be constitutionally permissible or practicably desirable. But if reapportionment were accomplished with less frequency, it would assuredly be constitutionally suspect.

We do not consider here the difficult question of the proper remedial devices which federal courts should utilize in state legislative apportionment cases. Remedial techniques in this new and developing area of the law will probably often differ with the circumstances of the challenged apportionment and a variety of local conditions. It is enough to say now that, once a State's legislative apportionment scheme has been found to be unconstitutional, it would be the unusual case in which a court would be justified in not taking appropriate action to insure that no further elections are conducted under the invalid plan. However, under certain circumstances, such as where an impending election is imminent and a State's election machinery is already in progress, equitable considerations might justify a court in withholding the granting of immediately effective relief in a legislative apportionment case, even though the existing apportionment scheme was found invalid. In awarding or withholding immediate relief, a court is entitled to and should consider the proximity of a forthcoming election and the mechanics and complexities of state election laws, and should act and rely upon general equitable principles. With respect to the timing of relief, a court can reasonably endeavor to avoid a disruption of the election process which might result from requiring precipitate changes that could make unreasonable or embarrassing demands on a State in adjusting to the requirements of the court's decree.

Affirmed and remanded.

Mr. Justice CLARK, concurring in the affirmance.
[Omitted.]

Mr. Justice STEWART.
[Omitted.]

Mr. Justice HARLAN, dissenting.
[Omitted.]

Lucas v. 44th General Assembly of Colorado

377 U.S. 713 (1964)

[This case was a companion to *Reynolds v. Sims.* It concerned the structure of Colorado's General Assembly. As the Court noted, however, the facts of *Lucas* differed significantly from the facts of *Reynolds.* In Colorado, unlike in Alabama, the issue of the state legislature's makeup had been put directly to the electorate in a referendum held in 1962. In this referendum, which complied with the principle of one person, one vote, the Colorado voters had been asked to choose between two alternative plans.

One plan, which we shall call "Plan A," would have apportioned Colorado's House of Representatives strictly according to population, but would have apportioned the Senate based partly on population and also partly on the desire to protect the interests of those citizens who lived in sparsely populated, geographically distinctive regions within the state. The result of Plan A would be that the ratio of persons in the most populated Senate district to the least populated Senate district would have been 3:1. The other plan on the ballot, which we shall call "Plan B," would have apportioned both the House and the Senate strictly according to population.

The voters adopted Plan A and rejected Plan B by more than a three-to-two margin. Moreover, a majority of voters in every county in Colorado, *including those counties within the highly populous urban region of the state,* approved of Plan A in preference to Plan B.

Shortly thereafter, a group of Colorado voters sued the state legislature in federal district court, claiming that Plan A violated the Equal Protection Clause of the Fourteenth Amendment. The district court rejected the plaintiffs' claim, and this appeal followed.]

Chief Justice WARREN delivered the opinion of the Court.

In *Reynolds v. Sims*, we held that the Equal Protection Clause requires that both houses of a bicameral state legislature must be apportioned substantially on a population basis.

An individual's constitutionally protected right to cast an equally weighted vote cannot be denied even by a vote of a majority of a State's electorate, if the apportionment scheme adopted by the voters fails to measure up to the requirements of the Equal Protection Clause. Manifestly, the fact that an apportionment plan is adopted in a popular referendum is insufficient to sustain its constitutionality or to induce a court of equity to refuse to act. As stated by this Court in *West Virginia State Bd. of Educ. v. Barnette* "One's right to life, liberty, and property . . . and other fundamental rights may not be submitted to vote; they depend on the outcome of no elections." A citizen's constitutional rights can hardly be infringed simply because a majority of the people choose that it be. We hold that the fact that a challenged legislative apportionment plan was approved by the electorate is without federal constitutional significance, if the scheme adopted fails to satisfy the basic requirements of the Equal Protection Clause, as delineated in our opinion in *Reynolds v. Sims*.

Appellees' argument, accepted by the court below, that the apportionment of the Colorado Senate [under Plan A] is rational because it takes into account a variety of geographical, historical, topographic and economic considerations fails to provide an adequate justification for the substantial disparities from population-based representation in the allocation of Senate seats to the disfavored populous areas.

Reversed and remanded.

Mr. Justice CLARK, dissenting.

While I join my Brother Stewart's opinion, I have some additional observations with reference to this case.

I would refuse to interfere with this apportionment for several reasons. First, Colorado enjoys the initiative and referendum system which it often utilizes and which, indeed, produced the present apportionment. As a result of the action of the Legislature and the use of initiative and referendum, the State Assembly has been reapportioned eight times since 1881. This indicates the complete awareness of the people of Colorado to apportionment problems and their continuing efforts to solve them. The courts should not interfere in such a situation. Next, as my Brother Stewart has pointed out, there are rational and most persuasive reasons for some deviations in the representation in the Colorado Assembly. The State has mountainous areas which divide it into four regions, some parts of which are almost impenetrable. There are also some depressed areas, diversified industry and varied climate, as well as enormous recreational regions and difficulties in transportation. These factors give rise to problems indigenous to Colorado, which only its people can intelligently solve. This they have done in the present apportionment.

Finally, I cannot agree to the arbitrary application of the "one man, one vote" principle for both houses of a State Legislature. In my view, if one house is fairly apportioned by population (as is admitted here) then the people should have some latitude in providing, on a rational basis, for representation in the other house. The Court seems to approve the federal arrangement of two Senators from each State, on the ground that it was a compromise reached by the framers of our Constitution and is a part of the fabric of our national charter. But what the Court overlooks is that Colorado, by an overwhelming vote, has likewise written the organization of its legislative body into its Constitution, and our dual federalism requires that we give it recognition. After all, the Equal Protection Clause is not an algebraic formula. Equal protection does not rest on whether the practice assailed "results in some inequality" but rather on whether "any state of facts reasonably can be conceived that would sustain it"; and one who attacks it must show "that it does not rest upon any reasonable basis, but is essentially arbitrary." Certainly Colorado's arrangement is not arbitrary. On the contrary, it rests on reasonable grounds which, as I have pointed out, are peculiar to that State. It is argued that the Colorado apportionment would lead only to a legislative stalemate between the two houses, but the experience of the Congress completely refutes this argument. Now in its 176th year, the federal plan has worked well. It is further said that in any event Colorado's apportionment would substitute compromise for the legislative process. But most legislation is the product of compromise between the various forces acting for and against its enactment.

In striking down Colorado's plan of apportionment, the Court, I believe, is exceeding its powers under the Equal Protection Clause; it is invading the valid functioning of the procedures of the States, and thereby is committing a grievous error which will do irreparable damage to our federal-state relationship. I dissent.

Mr. Justice STEWART, whom Mr. Justice CLARK joins, dissenting.

I find it impossible to understand how or why a voter in California, for instance, either feels or is less a citizen than a voter in Nevada, simply because, despite their population disparities, each of these States is represented by two United States Senators.

The Court's draconian pronouncement, which makes unconstitutional the legislatures of most of the 50 States, finds no support in the words of the Constitution, in any prior decision of this Court, or in the 175-year political history of our Federal Union. With all respect, I am convinced these decisions mark a long step backward into that unhappy era when a majority of the members of this Court were thought by many to have convinced themselves and each other that the demands of the Constitution were to be measured not by what it says, but by their own notions of wise political theory. The rule announced today is at odds with long-established principles of constitutional adjudication under the Equal Protection Clause, and it stifles values of local individuality and initiative vital to the character of the Federal Union which it was the genius of our Constitution to create.

I

What the Court has done is to convert a particular political philosophy into a constitutional rule, binding upon each of the 50 States, from Maine to Hawaii, from Alaska to Texas, without regard and without respect for the many individualized and differentiated characteristics of each State, characteristics stemming from each State's distinct history, distinct geography, distinct distribution of population, and distinct political heritage. My own understanding of the various theories of representative government is that no one theory has ever commanded unanimous assent among political scientists, historians, or others who have considered the problem. But even if it were thought that the rule announced today by the Court is, as a matter of political theory, the most desirable general rule which can be devised as a basis for the make-up of the representative assembly of a typical State, I could not join in the fabrication of a constitutional mandate which imports and forever freezes one theory of political thought into our Constitution, and forever denies to every State any opportunity for enlightened and progressive innovation in the design of its democratic institutions, so as to accommodate within a system of representative government the interests and aspirations of diverse groups of people, without subjecting any group or class to absolute domination by a geographically concentrated or highly organized majority.

Representative government is a process of accommodating group interests through democratic institutional arrangements. Its function is to channel the numerous opinions, interests, and abilities of the people of a State into the making of the State's public policy. Appropriate legislative apportionment, therefore, should ideally be designed to insure effective representation in the State's legislature, in cooperation with other organs of political power, of the various groups and interests making up the electorate. In practice, of course, this ideal is approximated in the particular apportionment system of any State by a realistic accommodation of the diverse and often conflicting political forces operating within the State.

I do not pretend to any specialized knowledge of the myriad of individual characteristics of the several States, beyond the records in the cases before us today. But I do know enough to be aware that a system of legislative apportionment which might be best for South Dakota might be unwise for Hawaii with its many islands, or Michigan with its Northern Peninsula. I do know enough to realize that Montana with its vast distances is not Rhode Island with its heavy concentrations of people. I do know enough to be aware of the great variations among the several States in their historic manner of distributing legislative power—of the Governors' Councils in New England, of the broad powers of initiative and referendum retained in some States by the people, of the legislative power which some States give to their Governors, by the right of veto or otherwise of the widely autonomous home rule which many States give to their cities. The Court today declines to give any recognition to these considerations and countless others, tangible and intangible, in holding unconstitutional the particular systems of legislative apportionment which these States have chosen. Instead, the Court says that the requirements of the Equal Protection Clause can be met in any State only by the uncritical, simplistic, and heavy-handed application of sixth-grade arithmetic.

But legislators do not represent faceless numbers. They represent people, or, more accurately, a majority of the voters in their districts—people with identifiable needs and interests which require legislative representation, and which can often be related to the geographical areas in which these people live. The very fact of geographic districting, the constitutional validity of which the Court does not question, carries with it an acceptance of the idea of legislative representation of regional needs and interests. Yet if geographical residence is irrelevant, as the Court suggests, and the goal is solely that of equally "weighted" votes, I do not understand why the Court's constitutional rule does not require the abolition of districts and the holding of all elections at large.[12]

The fact is, of course, that population factors must often to some degree be subordinated in devising a legislative apportionment plan which is to achieve the important goal of ensuring a fair, effective, and balanced representation of the regional, social, and economic interests within a State. And the further fact is that throughout our history the apportionments of State Legislatures have reflected the strongly felt American tradition that the public interest is composed of many diverse interests, and that in the long run it can better be expressed by a medley of component voices than by the majority's monolithic command. What constitutes a rational plan reasonably designed to achieve this objective will vary from State to State, since each State is unique, in terms of topography, geography, demography, history, heterogeneity and concentration of population, variety of social and economic interests, and in the operation and interrelation of its political institutions. But so long as a State's apportionment plan reasonably achieves, in the light of the State's own characteristics, effective and balanced representation of all substantial interests, without sacrificing the principle of effective majority rule, that plan cannot be considered irrational.

II

This brings me to what I consider to be the proper constitutional standards to be applied in these cases. Quite simply, I think the cases should be decided by application of accepted principles of constitutional adjudication under the Equal Protection Clause. A recent expression by the Court of these principles will serve as a generalized compendium:

> [T]he Fourteenth Amendment permits the States a wide scope of discretion in enacting laws which affect some groups of citizens differently than others. The constitutional safeguard is offended only if the classification rests on grounds wholly irrelevant to the achievement of the State's objective. State legislatures are presumed to have acted within their constitutional power despite the fact that, in practice, their laws result in some inequality. A statutory discrimination will not be set aside if any state of facts reasonably may be conceived to justify it. *McGowan v. Maryland.*

These principles reflect an understanding respect for the unique values inherent in the Federal Union of States established by our Constitution. They reflect,

12. Even with legislative districts of exactly equal voter population, 26% of the electorate (a bare majority of the voters in a bare majority of the districts) can, as a matter of the kind of theoretical mathematics embraced by the Court, elect a majority of the legislature under our simple majority electoral system. Thus, the Court's constitutional rule permits minority rule. Students of the mechanics of voting systems tell us that if all that matters is that votes count equally, the best vote-counting electoral system is proportional representation in statewide elections. It is just because electoral systems are intended to serve functions other than satisfying mathematical theories, however, that the system of proportional representation has not been widely adopted.

too, a wise perception of this Court's role in that constitutional system. The point was never better made than by Mr. Justice Brandeis, dissenting in *New State Ice Co. v. Liebmann.* The final paragraph of that classic dissent is worth repeating here:

> To stay experimentation in things social and economic is a grave responsibility. Denial of the right to experiment may be fraught with serious consequences to the nation. It is one of the happy incidents of the federal system that a single courageous state may, if its citizens choose, serve as a laboratory; and try novel social and economic experiments without risk to the rest of the country. This Court has the power to prevent an experiment. We may strike down the statute which embodies it on the ground that, in our opinion, the measure is arbitrary, capricious or unreasonable. . . . But, in the exercise of this high power, we must be ever on our guard, lest we erect our prejudices into legal principles. If we would guide by the light of reason we must let our minds be bold.

Moving from the general to the specific, I think that the Equal Protection Clause demands but two basic attributes of any plan of state legislative apportionment. First, it demands that, in the light of the State's own characteristics and needs, the plan must be a rational one. Secondly, it demands that the plan must be such as not to permit the systematic frustration of the will of a majority of the electorate of the State. I think it is apparent that any plan of legislative apportionment which could be shown to reflect no policy, but simply arbitrary and capricious action or inaction, and that any plan which could be shown systematically to prevent ultimate effective majority rule, would be invalid under accepted Equal Protection Clause standards. But, beyond this, I think there is nothing in the Federal Constitution to prevent a State from choosing any electoral legislative structure it thinks best suited to the interests, temper, and customs of its people.

III

The Colorado plan creates a General Assembly composed of a Senate of 39 members and a House of 65 members. The State is divided into 65 equal population representative districts, with one representative to be elected from each district, and 39 senatorial districts, 14 of which include more than one county. In the Colorado House, the majority unquestionably rules supreme, with the population factor untempered by other considerations. In the Senate rural minorities do not have effective control, and therefore do not have even a veto power over the will of the urban majorities. It is true that, as a matter of theoretical arithmetic, a minority of 36% of the voters could elect a majority of the Senate, but this percentage has no real meaning in terms of the legislative process. Under the Colorado plan, no possible combination of Colorado senators from rural districts, even assuming arguendo that they would vote as a bloc, could control the Senate. To arrive at the 36% figure, one must include with the rural districts a substantial number of urban districts, districts with substantially dissimilar interests. There is absolutely no reason to assume that this theoretical majority would ever vote together on any issue so as to thwart the wishes of the majority of the voters of Colorado. Indeed, when we eschew the world of numbers, and look to the real world of effective representation, the simple fact of the matter is that Colorado's three metropolitan areas, Denver, Pueblo, and Colorado Springs, elect a majority of the Senate.[14]

[Justice Stewart then explains why Plan A is reasonable given Colorado's unique geography and issues.]

Plan is rational

The present apportionment, adopted overwhelmingly by the people in a 1962 popular referendum as a state constitutional amendment, is entirely rational, and the amendment by its terms provides for keeping the apportionment current. Thus the majority has consciously chosen to protect the minority's interests, and under the liberal initiative provisions of the Colorado Constitution, it retains the power to reverse its decision to do so. Therefore, there can be no question of frustration of the basic principle of majority rule.

NOTES ON *REYNOLDS* AND *LUCAS*

1. *Reynolds* is the famous case, but *Lucas* is the more important one because it shows the full reach of the one person, one vote principle adopted in those cases.

2. Where does the one person, one vote principle, and the corresponding constitutional "right to vote," come from? The text of the Fourteenth Amendment? Political philosophy? (Is political philosophy able to identify objectively "true" or "correct" principles of democracy?) The personal political beliefs of Chief Justice Warren and other members of the Court majority? (If so, is *Reynolds* a valid decision?)

3. Were you persuaded by the majority's rejection of the so-called "federal analogy"? In other words, if it is okay for each state to have equal representation in the U.S. Senate (should it be okay?), then why isn't it okay for each county to have equal representation in a state senate?

4. Instead of using the one person, one vote principle from *Reynolds,* Justice Stewart's opinion in *Lucas* proposes an alternative approach to adjudicating claims of malapportioned districts. He would uphold plans that were rational and that would not permit the "systematic frustration of the will of a majority of the electorate of the State." Which approach is better, Chief Justice Warren in *Reynolds* or Justice Stewart in *Lucas*?

5. Based on *Reynolds* itself, do you understand how much deviation from strict compliance with one person, one vote is permissible? In other words, would it be okay for one district to have 110,000 persons, while another district has 90,000?

14. The theoretical figure is arrived at by placing the legislative districts for each house in rank order of population, and by counting down the smallest population end of the list a sufficient distance to accumulate the minimum population which could elect a majority of the house in question. It is a meaningless abstraction as applied to a multimembered body because the factors of political party alignment and interest representation make such theoretical bloc voting a practical impossibility. For example, 31,000,000 people in the 26 least populous States representing only 17% of United States population have 52% of the Senators in the United States Senate. But no one contends that this bloc controls the Senate's legislative process.

Does the permissibility of such deviation from strict equality depend upon the state's reason for the deviation as well as its (mathematical) extent?

* * *

Reynolds and *Lucas* leave the requirement for equal population among districts relatively open-ended. The Court's more recent pronouncements in the one person, one vote area demonstrate how the Court has put a bit more definition into the standards and how the Court's doctrine seems to differentiate between state legislative and congressional districts. As the next three cases will demonstrate, the Court has generally allowed for higher deviations in population in state legislative districts than in congressional districts. The next three cases (and the notes that follow) also demonstrate that in both the legislative and congressional districting context, the Court—despite the opportunity to do so—has avoided adopting clear mathematical rules to separate those districting plans that violate one person, one vote from those districting plans that do not.

The following case, *Harris v. Arizona Independent Redistricting Commission*, involves a one person, one vote challenge to a *state* legislative redistricting plan. Before delving into that opinion, it will be helpful for you to know about a prior opinion involving state legislative redistricting in Wyoming during the 1980s.

In *Brown v. Thompson*, 462 U.S. 835 (1983), plaintiffs challenged Wyoming's plan for the State House of Representatives. The 1980 Census placed Wyoming's total population at 469,557. The plan adopted following the 1980 Census provided for 64 representatives, meaning the ideal population (i.e., the number of persons that would create totally equal population in each district)* would be 7,377 persons per representative. The overall range of relative deviation (which the courts often call "maximum deviation") for the plan was 89 percent. [Overall range of relative deviation provides the difference between the most populated district and the least populated district expressed as a percentage.]**

The *Brown* plaintiffs chose to challenge the allocation of one representative to Niobrara County, the State's least populous county. Niobrara County had a population of 2,924. The issue was whether the State of Wyoming violated the Equal Protection Clause by allocating one of the 64 seats in its House of Representatives to a county with a population considerably lower than the ideal population for a district.

* With single-member districts, the ideal population is calculated by dividing the total population by the number of districts. For example, in a city with a population of 10,000 persons and five single-member districts, the ideal population of a district is 2,000 persons (10,000 divided by 5).

** Overall range of relative deviation is calculated by looking at the largest and the smallest districts and their relation to the ideal district population. For instance, if the ideal district population is 100,000 persons and if the largest district has a population of 105,000 persons and the smallest district has a population of 97,000 persons then the overall range of relative deviation is 8%.

The Court rejected the challenge. In doing so, the Court laid out the following framework involving the basic doctrine of one person, one vote as it relates to *state legislative* redistricting plans:

> [W]e have held that minor deviations from mathematical equality among state legislative districts are insufficient to make out a prima facie case of invidious discrimination under the Fourteenth Amendment so as to require justification by the State. Our decisions have established, as a general matter, that an apportionment plan with a maximum population deviation under 10% falls within this category of minor deviations. A plan with larger disparities in population, however, creates a prima facie case of discrimination and therefore must be justified by the State. . . . The ultimate inquiry [] is whether the legislature's plan "may reasonably be said to advance [a] rational state policy" and, if so, "whether the population disparities among districts that have resulted from the pursuit of this plan exceed constitutional limits." *Mahan v. Howell.*

After laying out this framework, the Court upheld Wyoming's decision to award Niobrara County a Representative although on very limited grounds. Even though the result was a plan with an overall range of relative deviation well above 10 percent, the Court noted the plaintiffs did not challenge the entire plan but only the choice to award Niobrara a seat. Thus, the decision for the Court was between a plan that had an 89 percent overall range of relative deviation and a 66 percent overall range of relative deviation. The Court also noted that Wyoming had a policy since it had become a State of ensuring each county had one representative, that the policy had "particular force given the peculiar size and population of the State," and that there was "no evidence of a built-in bias tending to favor particular political interests or geographic areas."

The limited nature of the Court's specific holding was emphasized by the concurring opinion of Justice Sandra Day O'Connor (joined by Justice John Paul Stevens) whose votes were critical to the outcome. Justice O'Connor emphasized that the "relevant percentage in this case is not the 89 percent maximum deviation when the State of Wyoming is viewed as a whole, but the additional deviation from equality produced by the allocation of one representative to Niobrara County." She continued:

> In the past, this Court has recognized that a state legislative apportionment scheme with a maximum population deviation exceeding 10% creates a prima facie case of discrimination. Moreover, in *Mahan v. Howell,* we suggested that a 16.4% maximum deviation "may well approach tolerable limits." I have the gravest doubt that a statewide legislative plan with an 89% maximum deviation could survive constitutional scrutiny despite the presence of the State's strong interest in preserving county boundaries.

Brown involved a state justifying an overall range of relative deviation above the 10 percent threshold. The next case—*Harris*—involves a state legislative plan with an overall range of relative deviation under 10 percent and develops how the Court will treat such plans.

Harris v. Arizona Independent Redistricting Commission

136 S. Ct. 1301, 578 U.S. __ (2016)

Justice BREYER delivered the opinion of the Court.

Appellants, a group of Arizona voters, challenge a redistricting plan for the State's legislature on the ground that the plan's districts are insufficiently equal in population. Because the maximum population deviation between the largest and the smallest district is less than 10%, the appellants cannot simply rely upon the numbers to show that the plan violates the Constitution. Nor have appellants adequately supported their contentions with other evidence. We consequently affirm a 3-judge Federal District Court decision upholding the plan.

I

In 2000, Arizona voters, using the initiative process, amended the Arizona Constitution to provide for an independent redistricting commission. Each decade the Arizona Commission on Appellate Court Appointments creates three slates of individuals: one slate of 10 Republicans, one slate of 10 Democrats, and one slate of 5 individuals not affiliated with any political party. The majority and minority leader of the Arizona Legislature each select one Redistricting Commission member from the first two lists. These four selected individuals in turn choose one member from the third, nonpartisan list. Thus, the membership of the Commission consists of two Republicans, two Democrats, and one independent.

After each decennial census, the Commission redraws Arizona's 30 legislative districts. The first step in the process is to create districts of equal population in a grid-like pattern across the state. It then adjusts the grid to the extent practicable in order to take into account the need for population equality; to maintain geographic compactness and continuity; to show respect for communities of interest; to follow locality boundaries; and to use visible geographic features and undivided tracts. The Commission will favor political competitiveness as long as its efforts to do so create no significant detriment to the other goals. Finally, it must adjust boundaries as necessary to comply with the Federal Constitution and with the federal Voting Rights Act.

After the 2010 census, the legislative leadership selected the Commission's two Republican and two Democratic members, who in turn selected an independent member, Colleen Mathis. Mathis was then elected chairwoman. The Commission hired two counsel, one of whom they thought of as leaning Democrat and one as leaning Republican. It also hired consultants, including mapping specialists, a statistician, and a Voting Rights Act specialist. With the help of its staff, it drew an initial plan, based upon the gridlike map, with district boundaries that produced a maximum population deviation (calculated as the difference between the most populated and least populated district) of 4.07%. After changing several boundaries, including those of Districts 8, 24, and 26, the Commission adopted a revised plan by a vote of 3 to 2, with the two Republican members voting against it. In late April 2012, the Department of Justice approved the plan [under Section 5 of the Voting Rights Act] as consistent with the Voting Rights Act.

The next day, appellants filed this lawsuit, primarily claiming that the plan's population variations were inconsistent with the Fourteenth Amendment. A 3-judge Federal District Court heard the case. After a 5-day bench trial, the court, by a vote of 2 to 1, entered judgment for the Commission. The majority found that "the population deviations were primarily a result of good-faith efforts to comply with the Voting Rights Act . . . even though partisanship played some role." We affirm.

II

A

The Fourteenth Amendment's Equal Protection Clause requires States to "make an honest and good faith effort to construct [legislative] districts . . . as nearly of equal population as is practicable." *Reynolds.* The Constitution, however, does not demand mathematical perfection. In determining what is "practicable," we have recognized that the Constitution permits deviation when it is justified by "legitimate considerations incident to the effectuation of a rational state policy." *Id.* In related contexts, we have made clear that in addition to the traditional districting principles such as compactness and contiguity, those legitimate considerations can include a state interest in maintaining the integrity of political subdivisions, *Mahan v. Howell* (1973), or the competitive balance among political parties, *Gaffney v. Cummings.* In cases decided before *Shelby County v. Holder,** Members of the Court expressed the view that compliance with § 5 of the Voting Rights Act is also a legitimate state consideration that can justify some deviation from perfect equality of population. It was proper for the Commission to proceed on that basis here.

We have further made clear that "minor deviations from mathematical equality" do not, by themselves, "make out a prima facie case of invidious discrimination under the Fourteenth Amendment so as to require justification by the State." *Gaffney.* We have defined as "minor deviations" those in "an apportionment plan with a maximum population deviation under 10%." *Brown.* And we have refused to require States to justify deviations of 9.9% and 8%.

In sum, in a case like this one, those attacking a state-approved plan must show that it is more probable than not that a deviation of less than 10% reflects the predominance of illegitimate reapportionment factors rather than the "legitimate considerations" to which we have referred in *Reynolds* and later cases. Given the inherent difficulty of measuring and comparing factors that may legitimately account for small deviations from strict mathematical equality, we believe that attacks on deviations under 10% will succeed only rarely, in unusual cases. And we are not surprised that the appellants have failed to meet their burden here.

B

Appellants' basic claim is that deviations in their apportionment plan from absolute equality of population reflect the Commission's political efforts to help the Democratic Party. We believe that appellants failed to prove this claim because,

* [*Shelby County v. Holder,* which essentially eliminated Section 5 of the Voting Rights Act, appears *infra* at pages 116 to 139.—EDS.]

as the district court concluded, the deviations predominantly reflected Commission efforts to achieve compliance with the federal Voting Rights Act, not to secure political advantage for one party. Appellants failed to show to the contrary. And the record bears out this conclusion.

[Section 5 of] the Voting Rights Act, among other things, forbids the use of new reapportionment plans that would lead to a retrogression in the position of racial minorities with respect to their effective exercise of the electoral franchise. A plan leads to impermissible retrogression when, compared to the plan currently in effect (typically called a "benchmark plan"), the new plan diminishes the number of districts in which minority groups can "elect their preferred candidates of choice" (often called "ability-to-elect" districts). A State can obtain legal assurance that it has satisfied the non-retrogression requirement if it submits its proposed plan to the Federal Department of Justice, and the Department does not object to the plan within 60 days. While *Shelby County* struck down the § 4(b) coverage formula [and, by extension, made Section 5 largely inoperable], that decision came after the maps in this case were drawn.

The record in this case shows that the gridlike map that emerged after the first step of the redistricting process had a maximum population deviation from absolute equality of districts of 4.07%. After consulting with their Voting Rights Act expert, their mapping consultant, and their statisticians, all five Commissioners agreed that they must try to obtain Justice Department Voting Rights Act "preclearance" and that the former benchmark plan contained 10 ability-to-elect districts. They consequently set a goal of 10 such districts for the new plan. They then went through an iterative process, involving further consultation, to adjust the plan's initial boundaries in order to enhance minority voting strength. In October 2011 (by a vote of 4 to 1), they tentatively approved a draft plan with adjusted boundaries. They believed it met their goal of 10 ability-to-elect districts. And they published the plan for public comment.

In the meantime, however, the Commission received a report from one of its statisticians suggesting that the Department of Justice might not agree that the new proposed plan contained 10 ability-to-elect districts. It was difficult to know for certain because the Justice Department did not tell States how many ability-to-elect districts it believed were present in a benchmark plan, and neither did it typically explain precisely and specifically how it would calculate the number that exist in a newly submitted plan. At the same time, the ability-to-elect analysis was complex, involving more than simply adding up census figures. The Department of Justice instead conducted a functional analysis of the electoral behavior within the particular election district, and so might, for example, count as ability-to-elect districts "crossover" districts in which white voters combine their votes with minorities, see *Bartlett v. Strickland* (2009). Its calculations might take into account group voting patterns, electoral participation, election history, and voter turnout. The upshot was not random decision-making but the process did create an inevitable degree of uncertainty. And that uncertainty could lead a redistricting commission, as it led Arizona's, to make serious efforts to make certain that the districts it believed were ability-to-elect districts did in fact meet the criteria that the Department might reasonably apply.

As a result of the statistician's report, the Commission became concerned about certain of its proposed boundaries. One of the Commission's counsel advised that it would be "prudent to stay the course in terms of the ten districts that are in the draft map and look to . . . strengthen them if there is a way to strengthen them." Subsequently, the Commission adopted several changes to the boundaries of Districts 24 and 26. It reduced the populations of those districts, thereby increasing the percentage of Hispanic voters in each. The Commission approved these changes unanimously.

Changes in the boundaries of District 8, however, proved more controversial. District 8 leaned Republican. A Democrat-appointed Commissioner asked the mapping specialist to look into modifications that might make District 8 politically more competitive. The specialist returned with a draft that shifted the boundary line between District 8 and District 11 so as to keep several communities with high minority populations together in District 8. The two Republican-appointed Commissioners objected that doing so would favor Democrats by "hyperpacking" Republicans into other districts; they added that the Commission should either favor political competitiveness throughout the State or not at all.

The Democrat-appointed proponent of the change replied that District 8 had historically provided minority groups a good opportunity to elect their candidate of choice—an opportunity that the changes would preserve. The Voting Rights Act specialist then said that by slightly increasing District 8's minority population, the Commission might be able to claim an 11th ability-to-elect district; and that fact would "unquestionably enhance the submission and enhance chances for preclearance." The Commission's counsel then added that having another possible ability-to-elect district could be helpful because District 26 was not as strong an ability-to-elect district as the others.

Only then, after the counsel and consultants argued for District 8 changes for the sake of Voting Rights Act preclearance, did Chairwoman Mathis support those changes. On that basis, the Commission ultimately approved the changes to District 8 by a vote of 3 to 2 (with the two Republican-appointed commissioners dissenting). The total population deviation among districts in this final map was 8.8%. While the Commission ultimately concluded that District 8 was not a true ability-to-elect district, the State's submission to the Department of Justice cited the changes to District 8 in support of the argument for preclearance. On April 26, 2012, the Department of Justice precleared the submitted plan.

On the basis of the facts that we have summarized, the District Court majority found that "the population deviations were primarily a result of good-faith efforts to comply with the Voting Rights Act . . . even though partisanship played some role." This conclusion was well supported in the record. And, as a result, appellants have not shown that it is more probable than not that illegitimate considerations were the predominant motivation behind the plan's deviations from mathematically equal district populations—deviations that were under 10%. Consequently, they have failed to show that the Commission's plan violates the Equal Protection Clause as interpreted in *Reynolds* and subsequent cases.

C

The appellants make three additional arguments. First, they support their claim that the plan reflects unreasonable use of partisan considerations by pointing to the fact that almost all the Democratic-leaning districts are somewhat underpopulated and almost all the Republican-leaning districts are somewhat overpopulated. That is likely true. But that fact may well reflect the tendency of minority populations in Arizona in 2010 to vote disproportionately for Democrats. If so, the variations are explained by the Commission's efforts to maintain at least 10 ability-to-elect districts. The Commission may have relied on data from its statisticians and Voting Rights Act expert to create districts tailored to achieve preclearance in which minority voters were a larger percentage of the district population. That might have necessitated moving other voters out of those districts, thereby leaving them slightly underpopulated. The appellants point to nothing in the record to suggest the contrary.

Second, the appellants point to *Cox v. Larios* (2004), in which we summarily affirmed a district court's judgment that Georgia's reapportionment of representatives to state legislative districts violated the Equal Protection Clause, even though the total population deviation was less than 10%. In *Cox*, however, unlike the present case, the district court found that those attacking the plan had shown that it was more probable than not that the use of illegitimate factors significantly explained deviations from numerical equality among districts. The district court produced many examples showing that population deviation as well as the shape of many districts "did not result from any attempt to create districts that were compact or contiguous, or to keep counties whole, or to preserve the cores of prior districts." *Id.* No legitimate purposes could explain them. It is appellants' inability to show that the present plan's deviations and boundary shapes result from the predominance of similarly illegitimate factors that makes *Cox* inapposite here. Even assuming, without deciding, that partisanship is an illegitimate redistricting factor, appellants have not carried their burden.

Third, appellants point to *Shelby County v. Holder*, in which this Court held unconstitutional sections of the Voting Rights Act that are relevant to this case. Appellants contend that, as a result of that holding, Arizona's attempt to comply with the Act could not have been a legitimate state interest. The Court decided *Shelby County*, however, in 2013. Arizona created the plan at issue here in 2010. At the time, Arizona was subject to the Voting Rights Act, and we have never suggested the contrary.

* * *

For these reasons the judgment of the District Court is affirmed.

It is so ordered.

Karcher v. Daggett

462 U.S. 725 (1983)

Justice BRENNAN delivered the opinion of the Court.

The question presented by this appeal is whether an apportionment plan for congressional districts satisfies Art. I, §2* without need for further justification if

* [Art. I §2 provides, in relevant part, "Representatives . . . shall be apportioned among the several States which may be included within this Union, according to their respective Numbers. . . . The actual Enumeration shall be made within three Years after the first Meeting of the Congress of the United States, and within every subsequent Term of ten Years, in such Manner as they shall by Law direct."—EDS.]

the population of the largest district is less than one percent greater than the population of the smallest district. A three-judge District Court declared New Jersey's 1982 reapportionment plan unconstitutional because the population deviations among districts, although small, were not the result of a good-faith effort to achieve population equality. We affirm.

I

[Following the 1980 Census, the New Jersey legislature passed what was known as the Feldman Plan.] The Feldman Plan contained 14 districts with an average population per district (as determined by the 1980 census) of 526,059. Each district did not have the same population. On the average, each district differed from the "ideal" figure by 0.1384%, or about 726 people. The largest district, the Fourth District, which includes Trenton, had a population of 527,472, and the smallest, the Sixth District, embracing most of Middlesex County, a population of 523,798. The difference between them was 3,674 people, or 0.6984% of the average district.

The Legislature had before it other plans with appreciably smaller population deviations between the largest and smallest districts. . . . [One of those plans] had a maximum population difference of 2,375, or 0.4514% of the average figure.

II

Article I, §2 establishes a "high standard of justice and common sense" for the apportionment of congressional districts: "equal representation for equal numbers of people." *Wesberry v. Sanders* (1964). Precise mathematical equality, however, may be impossible to achieve in an imperfect world; therefore the "equal representation" standard is enforced only to the extent of requiring that districts be apportioned to achieve population equality "as nearly as is practicable." As we explained further in *Kirkpatrick v. Preisler*:

> "[T]he 'as nearly as practicable' standard requires that the State make a good-faith effort to achieve precise mathematical equality. Unless population variances among congressional districts are shown to have resulted despite such effort, the State must justify each variance, no matter how small."

Article I, §2, therefore, "permits only the limited population variances which are unavoidable despite a good-faith effort to achieve absolute equality, or for which justification is shown." *Id.*

Thus two basic questions shape litigation over population deviations in state legislation apportioning congressional districts. First, the court must consider whether the population differences among districts could have been reduced or eliminated altogether by a good-faith effort to draw districts of equal population. Parties challenging apportionment legislation must bear the burden of proof on this issue, and if they fail to show that the differences could have been avoided the apportionment scheme must be upheld. If, however, the plaintiffs can establish that the population differences were not the result of a good-faith effort to achieve equality, the State must bear the burden of proving that each significant variance between districts was necessary to achieve some legitimate goal.

III

Appellants' principal argument in this case is addressed to the first question described above. They contend that the Feldman Plan should be regarded *per se* as the product of a good-faith effort to achieve population equality because the maximum population deviation among districts is smaller than the predictable undercount in available census data.

A

Kirkpatrick squarely rejected a nearly identical argument. "The whole thrust of the 'as nearly as practicable' approach is inconsistent with adoption of fixed numerical standards which excuse population variances without regard to the circumstances of each particular case." Adopting any standard other than population equality, using the best census data available, would subtly erode the Constitution's ideal of equal representation. If state legislators knew that a certain *de minimis* level of population differences were acceptable, they would doubtless strive to achieve that level rather than equality. Furthermore, choosing a different standard would import a high degree of arbitrariness into the process of reviewing apportionment plans. In this case, appellants argue that a maximum deviation of approximately 0.7% should be considered *de minimis*. If we accept that argument, how are we to regard deviations of 0.8%, 0.95%, 1%, or 1.1%?

Any standard, including absolute equality, involves a certain artificiality. As appellants point out, even the census data are not perfect, and the well-known restlessness of the American people means that population counts for particular localities are outdated long before they are completed. Yet problems with the data at hand apply equally to any population-based standard we could choose. As between two standards—equality or something-less-than equality—only the former reflects the aspirations of Art. I, §2.

To accept the legitimacy of unjustified, though small population deviations in this case would mean to reject the basic premise of *Kirkpatrick* and *Wesberry*. We decline appellants' invitation to go that far. The unusual rigor of their standard has been noted several times. Because of that rigor, we have required that absolute population equality be the paramount objective of apportionment only in the case of congressional districts, for which the command of Art. I, §2 as regards the national legislature outweighs the local interests that a State may deem relevant in apportioning districts for representatives to state and local legislatures, but we have not questioned the population equality standard for congressional districts. The principle of population equality for congressional districts has not proved unjust or socially or economically harmful in experience. If anything, this standard should cause less difficulty now for state legislatures than it did when we adopted it in *Wesberry*. The rapid advances in computer technology and education during the last two decades make it relatively simple to draw contiguous districts of equal population and at the same time to further whatever secondary goals the State has. Finally, to abandon unnecessarily a clear and oft-confirmed constitutional interpretation would impair our authority in other cases, would implicitly open the door to a plethora of requests that we reexamine other rules that some may consider burdensome, and would prejudice those who have relied upon the rule of law in seeking an equipopulous congressional apportionment in New Jersey. We thus reaffirm that there are no *de minimis* population variations, which could practicably be avoided, but which nonetheless meet the standard of Art. I, §2 without justification.[6]

C

Given that the census-based population deviations in the Feldman Plan reflect real differences among the districts, it is clear that they could have been avoided or significantly reduced with a good-faith effort to achieve population equality.

The District Court found that several other plans introduced in the 200th Legislature had smaller maximum deviations than the Feldman Plan. Appellants object that the alternative plans considered by the District Court were not comparable to the Feldman Plan because their political characters differed profoundly. We have never denied that apportionment is a political process, or that state legislatures could pursue legitimate secondary objectives as long as those objectives were consistent with a good-faith effort to achieve population equality at the same time. Nevertheless, the claim that political considerations require population differences among congressional districts belongs more properly to the second level of judicial inquiry in these cases, in which the State bears the burden of justifying the differences with particularity.

In any event, it was unnecessary for the District Court to rest its finding on the existence of alternative plans with radically different political effects. As in *Kirkpatrick,* "resort to the simple device of transferring entire political subdivisions of known population between contiguous districts would have produced districts much closer to numerical equality." Starting with the Feldman Plan itself and the census data available to the Legislature at the time it was enacted, one can reduce the maximum population deviation of the plan merely by shifting a handful of municipalities from one district to another. Thus the District Court did not err in finding that appellees had met their burden of showing that the Feldman Plan did not come as nearly as practicable to population equality.

IV

By itself, the foregoing discussion does not establish that the Feldman Plan is unconstitutional. Rather, appellees' success in proving that the Feldman Plan was not the product of a good-faith effort to achieve population equality means only that the burden shifted to the State to prove that the population deviations in its plan were necessary to achieve some legitimate state objective. [W]e are willing to defer to state legislative policies, so long as they are consistent with constitutional norms, even if they require small differences in the population of congressional districts. Any number of consistently applied legislative policies might justify some

6. Justice White objects that "the rule of absolute equality is perfectly compatible with [gerrymandering] of the worst sort." That may certainly be true to some extent: beyond requiring States to justify population deviations with explicit, precise reasons, which might be expected to have some inhibitory effect, *Kirkpatrick* does little to prevent what is known as gerrymandering.

variance, including, for instance, making districts compact, respecting municipal boundaries, preserving the cores of prior districts, and avoiding contests between incumbent Representatives. As long as the criteria are nondiscriminatory, these are all legitimate objectives that on a proper showing could justify minor population deviations. The State must, however, show with some specificity that a particular objective required the specific deviations in its plan, rather than simply relying on general assertions. The showing required to justify population deviations is flexible, depending on the size of the deviations, the importance of the State's interests, the consistency with which the plan as a whole reflects those interests, and the availability of alternatives that might substantially vindicate those interests yet approximate population equality more closely. By necessity, whether deviations are justified requires case-by-case attention to these factors.

The District Court properly found that appellants did not justify the population deviations in this case. At argument before the District Court and on appeal in this Court, appellants emphasized only one justification for the Feldman Plan's population deviations—preserving the voting strength of racial minority groups. They submitted affidavits from mayors Kenneth Gibson of Newark and Thomas Cooke of East Orange, discussing the importance of having a large majority of black voters in Newark's Tenth District, as well as an affidavit from S. Howard Woodson, Jr., a candidate for mayor of Trenton, [discussing] the Feldman Plan's treatment of black voters in the Trenton and Camden areas. The District Court found, however:

> "[Appellants] have not attempted to demonstrate, nor can they demonstrate, any causal relationship between the goal of preserving minority voting strength in the Tenth District and the population variances in the other districts. . . . We find that the goal of preserving minority voting strength in the Tenth District is not related in any way to the population deviations in the Fourth and Sixth Districts."

Under the Feldman Plan, the largest districts are the Fourth and Ninth Districts, and the smallest are the Third and Sixth. None of these districts borders on the Tenth, and only one—the Fourth—is even mentioned in appellants' discussions of preserving minority voting strength. Nowhere do appellants suggest that the large population of the Fourth District was necessary to preserve minority voting strength; in fact, the deviation between the Fourth District and other districts has the effect of diluting the votes of all residents of that district, including members of racial minorities, as compared with other districts with fewer minority voters. The record is completely silent on the relationship between preserving minority voting strength and the small populations of the Third and Sixth Districts. Therefore, the District Court's findings easily pass the "clearly erroneous" test.

Affirmed.

Justice STEVENS concurring.
[Omitted.]

Justice WHITE, with whom THE CHIEF JUSTICE, Justice POWELL, and Justice REHNQUIST join, dissenting.

I respectfully dissent from the Court's unreasonable insistence on an unattainable perfection in the equalizing of congressional districts.

I

One must suspend credulity to believe that the Court's draconian response to a trifling 0.6984% maximum deviation promotes "fair and effective representation" for the people of New Jersey. The requirement that "as nearly as is practicable one man's vote in a congressional election is to be worth as much as another's," *Wesberry v. Sanders* (1964), must be understood in light of the malapportionment in the states at the time *Wesberry* was decided. The plaintiffs in *Wesberry* were voters in a congressional district (pop. 823,680) encompassing Atlanta that was three times larger than Georgia's smallest district (272,154) and more than double the size of an average district. Because the state had not reapportioned for 30 years, the Atlanta District possessing one-fifth of Georgia's population had only one-tenth of the Congressmen. Georgia was not atypical; congressional districts throughout the country had not been redrawn for decades and deviations of over 50% were the rule. These substantial differences in district size diminished, in a real sense, the representativeness of congressional elections. The Court's invalidation of these profoundly unequal districts should not be read as a demand for precise mathematical equality between the districts.

The states responded to *Wesberry* by eliminating gross disparities between congressional districts. Nevertheless, redistricting plans with far smaller variations were struck by the Court five years later in *Kirkpatrick v. Preisler*, and its companion, *Wells v. Rockefeller*. The redistricting statutes before the Court contained total percentage deviations of 5.97% and 13.1%, respectively. But *Wesberry*'s "as nearly as practicable" standard was read to require "a good faith effort to achieve precise numerical equality." [*Kirkpatrick*]. Over the objections of four Justices, *Kirkpatrick* rejected the argument that there is a fixed numerical or percentage population variance small enough to be considered *de minimis* and to satisfy the "as nearly as practicable" standard. *Kirkpatrick*'s rule was applied by the Court in *White v. Weiser* (1973) to invalidate Texas' redistricting scheme which had a maximum population variance of 4.13%.

Just as *Wesberry* did not require *Kirkpatrick*, *Kirkpatrick* does not ineluctably lead to the Court's decision today. Although the Court stated that it could see "no nonarbitrary way" to pick a *de minimis* point, the maximum deviation in *Kirkpatrick*, while small, was more than eight times as large as that posed here. Moreover, the deviation in *Kirkpatrick* was not argued to fall within the officially accepted range of statistical imprecision of the census. Accordingly, I do not view the Court's decision today as foreordained by *Kirkpatrick* and *Weiser*.

There can be little question but that the variances in the New Jersey plan are "statistically insignificant." Although the government strives to make the decennial census as accurate as humanly possible, the Census Bureau has never intimated that the results are a perfect count of the American population. The Bureau itself estimates the inexactitude in the taking of the 1970 census at 2.3%, a figure which is considerably larger than the 0.6984% maximum variance in the New Jersey plan, and which dwarfs the 0.2470% difference between the maximum deviations of the selected plan and the leading alternative plan. Because the amount of undercounting differs from district to district, there is no point for a court of law to act under an unproven assumption that such tiny differences between redistricting plans reflect actual differences in population.

Even if the 0.6984% deviation here is not encompassed within the scope of the statistical imprecision of the census, it is miniscule when compared with other variations among the districts inherent in translating census numbers into citizens' votes. First, [d]istrict populations are constantly changing, often at different rates in either direction, up or down. As the Court admits, "the well-known restlessness of the American people means that population counts for particular localities are outdated long before they are completed." Second, far larger differences among districts are introduced because a substantial percentage of the total population is too young to register or is disqualified by alienage. Third, census figures cannot account for the proportion of all those otherwise eligible individuals who fail to register. The differences in the number of eligible voters per district for these reasons overwhelm the minimal variations attributable to the districting plan itself.

Accepting that the census, and the districting plans which are based upon it, cannot be perfect represents no backsliding in our commitment to assuring fair and equal representation in the election of Congress.

If today's decision simply produced an unjustified standard with little practical import, it would be bad enough. Unfortunately, I fear that the Court's insistence that "there are no *de minimis* population variations, which could practicably be avoided, but which nonetheless meet the standard of Art. I, §2 without justification," invites further litigation of virtually every congressional redistricting plan in the nation. At least twelve states which have completed redistricting on the basis of the 1980 census have adopted plans with a higher deviation than that presented here, and four others have deviations quite similar to New Jersey's. Of course, under the Court's rationale, even Rhode Island's plan—whose two districts have a deviation of 0.02% or about 95 people—would be subject to constitutional attack.

In all such cases, state legislatures will be hard pressed to justify their preference for the selected plan. A good-faith effort to achieve population equality is not enough if the population variances are not "unavoidable." The court must consider whether the population differences could have been further "reduced or eliminated altogether." With the assistance of computers, there will generally be a plan with an even more minimal deviation from the mathematical ideal. Then, "the State must bear the burden of proving that each significant variance between districts was necessary to achieve some legitimate goal." As this case illustrates, literally any variance between districts will be considered "significant." The state's burden will not be easily met: "the State bears the burden of justifying the differences with particularity." When the state fails to sustain its burden, the result will generally be that a court must select an alternative plan. The choice will often be disputed until the very eve of an election, leaving candidates and voters in a state of confusion.

The only way a legislature or bipartisan commission can hope to avoid litigation will be to dismiss all other legitimate concerns and opt automatically for the districting plan with the smallest deviation. Yet no one can seriously contend that such an inflexible insistence upon mathematical exactness will serve to promote "fair and effective representation." The more likely result of today's extension of *Kirkpatrick* is to move closer to fulfilling Justice Fortas' prophecy that "a legislature might have to ignore the boundaries of common sense, running the congressional district line down the middle of the corridor of an apartment house or even dividing the residents of a single-family house between two districts." Such sterile and mechanistic application only brings the principle of "one man, one vote" into disrepute.

II

One might expect the Court had strong reasons to force this Sisyphean task upon the states. Yet the Court offers no positive virtues that will follow from its decision. No pretense is made that this case follows in the path of *Reynolds* and *Wesberry* in insuring the "fair and effective representation" of citizens. No effort is expended to show that Art. I, §2's requirement that Congressmen be elected "by the people," *Wesberry v. Sanders*, demands the invalidation of population deviations at this level. Any such absolute requirement, if it did exist, would be irreconcilable with the Court's recognition of certain justifications for population variances. Given no express constitutional basis for the Court's holding, and no showing that the objectives of fair representation are compromised by these minimal disparities, the normal course would be to uphold the actions of the legislature in fulfilling its constitutionally-delegated responsibility to prescribe the manner of holding elections for Senators and Representatives. Doing so would be in keeping with the Court's oft-expressed recognition that apportionment is primarily a matter for legislative judgment.

Instead the Court is purely defensive in support of its decision. The Court refuses to adopt any fixed numerical standard, below which the federal courts would not intervene, asserting that "the principle of population equality for congressional districts has not proved unjust or socially or economically harmful in experience." Of course, the *principle* of population equality is not unjust; the unreasonable *application* of this principle is the rub. Leaving aside that the principle has never been applied with the vengeance witnessed today, there are many, including myself, who take issue with the Court's self-congratulatory assumption that *Kirkpatrick* has been a success. First, a decade of experience with *Kirkpatrick* has shown that the rule of absolute equality is perfectly compatible with "gerrymandering" of the worst sort. With ever more sophisticated computers, legislators can draw countless plans for absolute population equality, but each having its own political ramifications. Although neither a rule of absolute equality nor one of substantial equality can alone prevent deliberate partisan gerrymandering, the former offers legislators a ready justification for disregarding geographical and political boundaries. In addition to providing a patina of respectability for the equipopulous gerrymander, *Kirkpatrick*'s regime assured extensive intrusion of the judiciary into legislative business.

More than a decade's experience with *Kirkpatrick* demonstrates that insistence on precise numerical equality only invites those who lost in the political arena to refight their battles in federal court. Consequently, "[m]ost estimates are that between 25 percent and 35 percent of current house district lines were drawn by the Courts." American Bar Association, Congressional Districting 20 (1981). As I have already noted, by extending *Kirkpatrick* to deviations below even the 1% level, the redistricting plan in every state with more than a single Representative is rendered vulnerable to after-the-fact attack by anyone with a complaint and a calculator.

III

Our cases dealing with state legislative apportionment have taken a more sensible approach. We have recognized that certain small deviations do not, in themselves, ordinarily constitute a *prima facie* constitutional violation. Moreover, we have upheld plans with reasonable variances that were necessary to account for political subdivisions, to preserve the voting strength of minority groups, and to insure political fairness.

Bringing together our legislative and congressional cases does not imply overlooking relevant differences between the two. States normally draw a larger number of legislative districts, which accordingly require a greater margin to account for geographical and political boundaries. "[C]ongressional districts are not so intertwined and freighted with strictly local interests as are state legislative districts." *White v. Weiser.* Furthermore, because Congressional districts are generally much larger than state legislative districts, each percentage point of variation represents a commensurately greater number of people. But these are differences of degree. They suggest that the level at which courts should entertain challenges to districting plans, absent unusual circumstances, should be lower in the congressional cases, but not altogether nonexistent.[14] Although I am not wedded to a precise figure, in light of the current range of population deviations, a 5% cutoff appears reasonable. I would not entertain judicial challenges, absent extraordinary circumstances, where the maximum deviation is less than 5%. Somewhat greater deviations, if rationally related to an important state interest, may also be permissible. Certainly, the maintaining of compact, contiguous districts, the respecting of political subdivisions, and efforts to assure political fairness, constitute such interests.

I would not hold up New Jersey's plan as a model reflection of such interests. Nevertheless, the deviation involved here is *de minimis*, and, regardless of what other infirmities the plan may have, constitutional or otherwise, there is no violation of Art. I, §2—the sole issue before us.

Justice Powell dissenting.
[Omitted.]

14. As the law has developed, our congressional cases are rooted in Art. I, §2 of the Constitution while our legislative cases rely upon the Equal Protection Clause of the Fourteenth Amendment. I am not aware, however, of anything in the respective provisions which justifies, let alone requires, the difference in treatment that has emerged between the two lines of decisions. Our early cases were frequently cross-cited, and the formulation "as nearly of equal population as is practicable" appears in *Reynolds v. Sims*, as well as *Wesberry v. Sanders.*

Figure 1-1

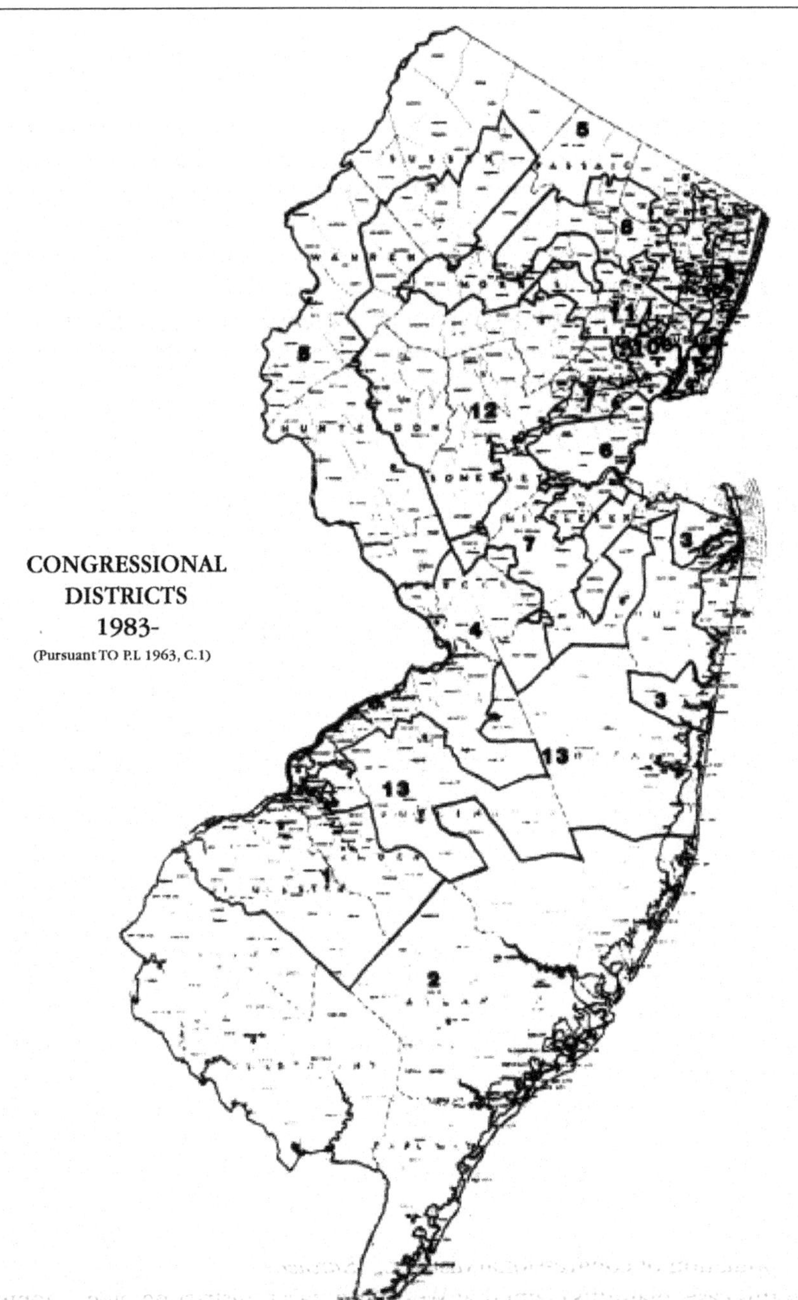

Source: *Daggett v. Kimmelman*, 535 F. Supp. 978, D.C.N.J., 1982.

Tennant v. Jefferson County Commission

567 U.S. 758 (2012)

PER CURIAM.

Plaintiffs in this case claim that West Virginia's 2011 congressional redistricting plan violates the "one person, one vote" principle that we have held to be embodied in Article I, §2, of the United States Constitution. A three-judge District Court for the Southern District of West Virginia agreed, declaring the plan "null and void" and enjoining West Virginia's Secretary of State from implementing it. The state defendants appealed directly to this Court. Because the District Court misapplied the standard for evaluating such challenges set out in *Karcher v. Daggett*, and failed to afford appropriate deference to West Virginia's reasonable exercise of its political judgment, we reverse.

* * *

Article I, §2, of the United States Constitution requires that Members of the House of Representatives "be apportioned among the several States . . . according to their respective Numbers" and "chosen every second Year by the People of the several States." In *Wesberry v. Sanders* (1964), we held that these commands require that "as nearly as is practicable one man's vote in a congressional election is to be worth as much as another's." We have since explained that the "as nearly as is practicable" standard does not require that congressional districts be drawn with "precise mathematical equality," but instead that the State justify population differences between districts that could have been avoided by "a good-faith effort to achieve absolute equality." *Karcher.*

Karcher set out a two-prong test to determine whether a State's congressional redistricting plan meets this standard. First, the parties challenging the plan bear the burden of proving the existence of population differences that "could practicably be avoided." If they do so, the burden shifts to the State to "show with some specificity" that the population differences "were necessary to achieve some legitimate state objective." This burden is a "flexible" one, which "depend[s] on the size of the deviations, the importance of the State's interests, the consistency with which the plan as a whole reflects those interests, and the availability of alternatives that might substantially vindicate those interests yet approximate population equality more closely." As we recently reaffirmed, redistricting "ordinarily involves criteria and standards that have been weighed and evaluated by the elected branches in the exercise of their political judgment." *Perry v. Perez*, 565 U.S. _______ (2012) (per curiam). "[W]e are willing to defer to [such] state legislative policies, so long as they are consistent with constitutional norms, even if they require small differences in the population of congressional districts." *Karcher.*

In this case, plaintiffs claim that West Virginia's redistricting plan, adopted following the 2010 decennial United States census, violates Article I, §2, of the United States Constitution and, separately, the West Virginia Constitution. The 2010 census did not alter West Virginia's allocation of three congressional seats. But due to population shifts within the State, West Virginia nonetheless began redistricting to comply with the requirements in our precedents.

In August 2011, the West Virginia Legislature convened an extraordinary session, and the State Senate formed a 17-member Select Committee on Redistricting. The committee first considered a redistricting plan championed by its chair, Majority Leader John Unger, and dubbed "the Perfect Plan" because it achieved a population difference of a single person between the largest and smallest districts. That appears, however, to have been the only perfect aspect of the Perfect Plan. State legislators expressed concern that the plan contravened the State's longstanding rule against splitting counties, placed two incumbents' residences in the same district, and moved one-third of the State's population from one district to another.

The following day, members of the Redistricting Committee introduced seven additional plans. The committee eventually reported to the full Senate the eighth proposal, referred to as S.B. 1008. The full Senate rejected a ninth proposal offered as an amendment on the floor and adopted S.B. 1008 by a vote of 27 to 4. The House of Delegates approved the bill without debate by a vote of 90 to 5. Governor Bill Tomblin signed the bill into law.

S.B. 1008 does not split county lines, redistrict incumbents into the same district, or require dramatic shifts in the population of the current districts. Indeed, S.B. 1008's chief selling point was that it required very little change to the existing districts: It moved just one county, representing 1.5% of the State's population, from one district to another. This was the smallest shift of any plan considered by the legislature. S.B. 1008, however, has a population variance of 0.79%, the second highest variance of the plans the legislature considered. That is, the population difference between the largest and smallest districts in S.B. 1008 equals 0.79% of the population of the average district.

The Jefferson County Commission and two of its county commissioners sued to enjoin the State from implementing S.B. 1008. At trial, the State conceded that it could have adopted a plan with lower population variations. The State argued, however, that legitimate state policies justified the slightly higher variances in S.B. 1008, citing this Court's statement from *Karcher* that "[a]ny number of consistently applied legislative policies might justify some variance, including, for instance, making districts compact, respecting municipal boundaries, preserving the cores of prior districts, and avoiding contests between incumbent Representatives." The State noted *Karcher*'s approving reference to a District Court opinion upholding a previous West Virginia redistricting plan with a population variance of 0.78%—virtually identical to the variance in S.B. 1008.

The District Court nonetheless granted the injunction, holding that the State's asserted objectives did not justify the population variance. With respect to the objective of not splitting counties, the District Court acknowledged that West Virginia had never in its history divided a county between two or more congressional districts. The court speculated, however, that the practice of other States dividing counties between districts "may portend the eventual deletion" of respecting such boundaries as a potentially legitimate justification for population variances. The court also faulted the West Virginia Legislature for failing "to create a contemporaneous record sufficient to show that S.B. 1008's entire 4,871-person variance—or even a discrete, numerically precise portion thereof—was attributable" to the State's interest in respecting county boundaries and noted that several other plans under consideration also did not split counties.

The court further questioned the State's assertion that S.B. 1008 best preserved the core of existing districts. Preserving the core of a district, the court reasoned, involved respecting the "[s]ocial, cultural, racial, ethnic, and economic interests common to the population of the area," not a "dogged insistence that change be minimized for the benefit of the delicate citizenry." The District Court concluded that although acclimating to a new congressional district and Congressperson "may give rise to a modicum of anxiety and inconvenience, avoiding constituent discomfort at the margins is not among those policies recognized in *Karcher* as capable of legitimizing a variance."

With respect to preventing contests between incumbents, the District Court again faulted the legislature for failing to build a record "linking all or a specific part of the variance" to that asserted interest. And the District Court found that although 0.79% was a minor variation when *Karcher* was decided, the feasibility of achieving smaller variances due to improved technology meant that the same variance must now be considered major.

We stayed the District Court's order pending appeal to this Court, and now reverse.

Given the State's concession that it could achieve smaller population variations, the remaining question under *Karcher* is whether the State can demonstrate that "the population deviations in its plan were necessary to achieve some legitimate state objective." Considering, as *Karcher* instructs, "the size of the deviations, the importance of the State's interests, the consistency with which the plan as a whole reflects those interests, and the availability of alternatives that might substantially vindicate those interests," it is clear that West Virginia has carried its burden.

As an initial matter, the District Court erred in concluding that improved technology has converted a "minor" variation in *Karcher* into a "major" variation today. Nothing about technological advances in redistricting and mapping software has, for example, decreased population variations between a State's counties. Thus, if a State wishes to maintain whole counties, it will inevitably have population variations between districts reflecting the fact that its districts are composed of unevenly populated counties. Despite technological advances, a variance of 0.79% results in no more (or less) vote dilution today than in 1983, when this Court said that such a minor harm could be justified by legitimate state objectives.

Moreover, our cases leave little doubt that avoiding contests between incumbents and not splitting political subdivisions are valid, neutral state districting policies. The [district court] majority cited no precedent for requiring legislative findings on the "discrete, numerically precise portion" of the variance attributable to each factor, and we are aware of none.

The District Court dismissed the State's interest in limiting the shift of population between old and new districts as "ham-handed," because the State considered only "discrete bounds of geography," rather than "[s]ocial, cultural, racial, ethnic, and economic interests common to the population of the area." According to the District Court, that did not qualify as "preserving the cores of prior districts" under *Karcher.*

Regardless of how to read that language from *Karcher*, however, our opinion made clear that its list of possible justifications for population variations was not exclusive. The desire to minimize population shifts between districts is clearly a valid, neutral state policy. S.B. 1008 achieves significantly lower population shifts than the alternative plans—more than four times lower than the closest alternative, and more than 25 times lower than others.

None of the alternative plans came close to vindicating all three of the State's legitimate objectives while achieving a lower variance. All other plans failed to serve at least one objective as well as S.B. 1008 does; several were worse with respect to two objectives; and the Perfect Plan failed as to all three of the State's objectives. This is not to say that anytime a State must choose between serving an additional legitimate objective and achieving a lower variance, it may choose the former. But here, given the small "size of the deviations," as balanced against "the importance of the State's interests, the consistency with which the plan as a whole reflects those interests," and the lack of available "alternatives that might substantially vindicate those interests yet approximate population equality more closely," *Karcher*, S.B. 1008 is justified by the State's legitimate objectives.

The judgment of the United States District Court for the Southern District of West Virginia is reversed, and the case is remanded for further proceedings consistent with this opinion.

Figure 1-2

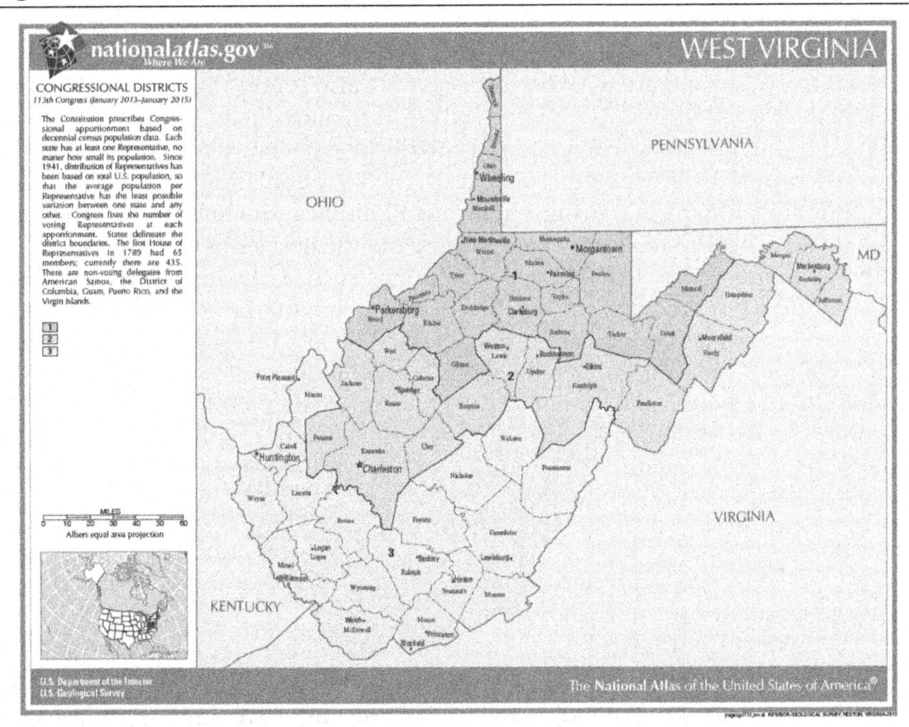

Source: http://nationalatlas.gov/printable/images/pdf/congdist/pagecgd113wv.pdf.

NOTES ON *HARRIS, KARCHER,* AND *TENNANT*

1. At one level, the cases do illustrate a difference in treatment between congressional districts (involved in *Karcher* and *Tennant*) and state legislative districts (involved in *Harris*).

2. When it comes to state legislative (and local) districts, the trend in the cases has been to give state governments a "safe harbor" against a one person, one vote challenge unless the maximum deviation (i.e., the overall range of relative deviation) exceeds 10 percent. Justice Breyer's opinion in *Harris* reflects that trend when he notes that "attacks on deviations under 10 percent will succeed only rarely, in unusual cases."

3. Consider, though, the case of *Larios v. Cox*, 300 F. Supp. 2d. 1320 (N.D. Ga. 2004) (three-judge court) that Justice Breyer mentioned in *Harris*. In *Larios*, the plaintiffs challenged the redistricting plans for the Georgia state house and senate, alleging partisan and racial gerrymandering (topics we will take up later) and a violation of one person, one vote. *Id.* at 1321. State legislators had believed there was a "safe harbor" and that any overall relative range of deviation below 10 percent could not violate one person, one vote and they developed plans that had an overall range of relative deviation of 9.98 percent. *Id.* at 1325-27. The plans were drawn by Democrats and most of the underpopulated districts favored Democrats while most of the overpopulated districts favored Republicans. *Id.* at 1326-27. The district court found that the mapmakers had a "deliberate and systematic policy of favoring rural and inner-city interests at the expense of suburban areas north, east, and west of Atlanta." *Id.* at 1327. (At the time of the drawing of the districts, Democratic incumbents represented rural and the inner-city areas and Republican incumbents represented suburban areas.) The district court also found that the other major cause of the deviations was "an intentional effort to allow incumbent Democrats to maintain or increase their delegation, primarily by systematically underpopulating the districts held by incumbent Democrats, by overpopulating those of Republicans, and by deliberately pairing numerous Republican incumbents against one another." *Id.* at 1329. The district court found that the deviations were not the result of any legitimate, consistently applied state policy, such as making districts compact and contiguous, respecting political subdivisions, maintaining the cores of prior districts, or avoiding incumbent pairings. *Id.* at 1349-50. Instead, the district court found that the deviations were "systematically and intentionally created (1) to allow rural southern Georgia and inner-city Atlanta to maintain their legislative influence even as their rate of population growth lags behind the rest of the state; and (2) to protect Democratic incumbents" and that neither of these explanations withstood Equal Protection scrutiny. *Id.* at 1338.

4. Note that cases like *Larios* that involve constitutional claims involving apportionment against state legislative districts are initially heard by three-judge district courts with a direct right to appeal to the U.S. Supreme Court. *See* 28 U.S.C. 1253; 28 U.S.C. 2284(a). In deciding that appeal, the Supreme Court generally does one of the following: (1) notes "probable jurisdiction" and hears the case with a full argument (a process akin to what typically happens when the Supreme Court grants *certiori*); or (2) summarily affirms the district court decision, with some (but perhaps not full) precedential effect. As Justice Breyer notes in *Harris, Larios* was summarily affirmed by the Supreme Court. *Cox v. Larios*, 542 U.S. 947 (2004).

5. When it comes to congressional districts, the trend in the cases—as reflected by *Karcher*—had been to push the deviations toward the minimum. For this reason, during the post-2000 redistricting cycle nearly a third of the states achieved the absolute minimum of population deviation between districts.

6. *Tennant*, however, seems to back off from requiring states to achieve the absolute minimum of population deviation between congressional districts. How much difference is there between *Tennant* and *Karcher*? If there is a difference, is it meaningful? Does *Tennant* give additional flexibility to states in their development of congressional redistricting plans? If so, is providing such flexibility a good idea?

* * *

Aside from how much deviation from strict equality of population between districts is allowed is a separate question of which *population* statistic should be used in making that assessment. Total population? Voting-age (over 18 years old) population? Citizen voting-age population? Voting-eligible population (i.e., excluding noncitizens, those under 18-years old, and disfranchised felons)? Registered voters?

The next case tackles these questions.

Evenwel v. Abbott

136 S. Ct. 1120, 578 U.S. ___ (2016)

Justice GINSBURG delivered the opinion of the Court.

Texas, like all other States, draws its legislative districts on the basis of total population. Plaintiffs-appellants are Texas voters; they challenge this uniform method of districting on the ground that it produces unequal districts when measured by voter-eligible population. Voter-eligible population, not total population, they urge, must be used to ensure that their votes will not be devalued in relation to citizens' votes in other districts. We hold, based on constitutional history, this Court's decisions, and longstanding practice, that a State may draw its legislative districts based on total population.

I

A

This Court long resisted any role in overseeing the process by which States draw legislative districts. "The remedy for unfairness in districting," the Court once held, "is to secure State legislatures that will apportion properly, or to invoke the ample powers of Congress." *Colegrove v. Green*. "Courts ought not to enter this political thicket," as Justice Frankfurter put it. *Ibid.*

Judicial abstention left pervasive malapportionment unchecked. In the opening half of the 20th century, there was a massive population shift away from rural areas and toward suburban and urban communities. Nevertheless, many States ran elections into the early 1960's based on maps drawn to equalize each district's population as it was composed around 1900. Other States used maps allocating a certain number of legislators to each county regardless of its population. These schemes left many rural districts significantly underpopulated in comparison with urban and suburban districts. But rural legislators who benefited from malapportionment had scant incentive to adopt new maps that might put them out of office.

The Court confronted this ingrained structural inequality in *Baker v. Carr,* 369 U.S. 186, 191-192, 82 S.Ct. 691, 7 L.Ed.2d 663(1962). Rather than steering clear of the political thicket yet again, the Court held for the first time that malapportionment claims are justiciable.

Although the Court in *Baker* did not reach the merits of the equal protection claim, *Baker's* justiciability ruling set the stage for what came to be known as the one-person, one-vote principle. Just two years after *Baker,* in *Wesberry v. Sanders* (1964), the Court invalidated Georgia's malapportioned congressional map, under which the population of one congressional district was "two to three times" larger than the population of the others. Relying on Article I, § 2, of the Constitution, the Court required that congressional districts be drawn with equal populations. Later that same Term, in *Reynolds v. Sims,* the Court upheld an equal protection challenge to Alabama's malapportioned state-legislative maps. "[T]he Equal Protection Clause," the Court concluded, "requires that the seats in both houses of a bicameral state legislature must be apportioned on a population basis." *Wesberry* and *Reynolds* together instructed that jurisdictions must design both congressional and state-legislative districts with equal populations, and must regularly reapportion districts to prevent malapportionment.

Over the ensuing decades, the Court has several times elaborated on the scope of the one-person, one-vote rule. States must draw congressional districts with populations as close to perfect equality as possible. See *Kirkpatrick v. Preisler* (1969). But, when drawing state and local legislative districts, jurisdictions are permitted to deviate somewhat from perfect population equality to accommodate traditional districting objectives, among them, preserving the integrity of political subdivisions, maintaining communities of interest, and creating geographic compactness. See *Brown v. Thomson* (1983). Where the maximum population deviation between the largest and smallest district is less than 10%, the Court has held, a state or local legislative map presumptively complies with the one-person, one-vote rule. Maximum deviations above 10% are presumptively impermissible. See also *Mahan v. Howell* (1973) (approving a state-legislative map with maximum population deviation of 16% to accommodate the State's interest in "maintaining the integrity of political subdivision lines," but cautioning that this deviation "may well approach tolerable limits").

In contrast to repeated disputes over the permissibility of deviating from perfect population equality, little controversy has centered on the population base jurisdictions must equalize. On rare occasions, jurisdictions have relied on the registered-voter or voter-eligible populations of districts. See *Burns v. Richardson* (1966) (holding Hawaii could use a registered-voter population base because of "Hawaii's special population problems"—in particular, its substantial temporary military population). But, in the overwhelming majority of cases, jurisdictions have equalized total population, as measured by the decennial census. Today, all States use total-population numbers from the census when designing congressional and state-legislative districts.

B

Appellants challenge that consensus. After the 2010 census, Texas redrew its State Senate districts using a total-population baseline. The map's maximum total-population deviation is 8.04%, safely within the presumptively permissible 10%

range. But measured by a voter-population baseline—eligible voters or registered voters—the map's maximum population deviation exceeds 40%.

Appellants live in Texas Senate districts with particularly large eligible- and registered-voter populations. Contending that basing apportionment on total population dilutes their votes in relation to voters in other Senate districts, in violation of the one-person, one-vote principle of the Equal Protection Clause, appellants filed suit in the U.S. District Court for the Western District of Texas. They sought a permanent injunction barring use of the existing Senate map in favor of a map that would equalize the voter population in each district.

Th[e three-judge district] court dismissed the complaint for failure to state a claim on which relief could be granted. We now affirm.

II

The parties and the United States advance different positions in this case. [A]ppellants insist that the Equal Protection Clause requires jurisdictions to draw state and local legislative districts with equal voter-eligible populations, thus protecting "voter equality," *i.e.*, "the right of eligible voters to an equal vote." To comply with their proposed rule, appellants suggest, jurisdictions should design districts based on citizen-voting-age-population (CVAP) data from the Census Bureau's American Community Survey (ACS), an annual statistical sample of the U.S. population. Texas responds that jurisdictions may, consistent with the Equal Protection Clause, design districts using any population baseline—including total population and voter-eligible population—so long as the choice is rational and not invidiously discriminatory. Although its use of total-population data from the census was permissible, Texas therefore argues, it could have used ACS CVAP data instead. Sharing Texas' position that the Equal Protection Clause does not mandate use of voter-eligible population, the United States urges us not to address Texas' separate assertion that the Constitution allows States to use alternative population baselines, including voter-eligible population. Equalizing total population, the United States maintains, vindicates the principle of representational equality by "ensur[ing] that the voters in each district have the power to elect a representative who represents the same number of constituents as all other representatives."

In agreement with Texas and the United States, we reject appellants' attempt to locate a voter-equality mandate in the Equal Protection Clause. As history, precedent, and practice demonstrate, it is plainly permissible for jurisdictions to measure equalization by the total population of state and local legislative districts.

A

We begin with constitutional history. At the time of the founding, the Framers confronted a question analogous to the one at issue here: On what basis should congressional districts be allocated to States? The Framers' solution, now known as the Great Compromise, was to provide each State the same number of seats in the Senate, and to allocate House seats based on States' total populations. "Representatives and direct Taxes," they wrote, "shall be apportioned among the several States which may be included within this Union, *according to their respective Numbers.*" U.S. Const., Art. I, § 2, cl. 3 (emphasis added). "It is a fundamental principle of the proposed constitution," James Madison explained in the Federalist Papers, "that as the aggregate number of representatives allotted to the several states, is to be . . . founded on the aggregate number of inhabitants; so, the right of choosing this allotted number in each state, is to be exercised by such part of the inhabitants, as the state itself may designate." The Federalist No. 54, p. 284 (G. Carey & J. McClellan eds. 2001). In other words, the basis of *representation* in the House was to include all inhabitants—although slaves were counted as only three-fifths of a person—even though States remained free to deny many of those inhabitants the right to participate in the selection of their representatives. Endorsing apportionment based on total population, Alexander Hamilton declared: "There can be no truer principle than this—that every individual of the community at large has an equal right to the protection of government." 1 Records of the Federal Convention of 1787, p. 473 (M. Farrand ed. 1911).[9]

When debating what is now the Fourteenth Amendment, Congress reconsidered the proper basis for apportioning House seats. Concerned that Southern States would not willingly enfranchise freed slaves, and aware that "a slave's freedom could swell his state's population for purposes of representation in the House by one person, rather than only three-fifths," the Framers of the Fourteenth Amendment considered at length the possibility of allocating House seats to States on the basis of voter population.

In December 1865, Thaddeus Stevens, a leader of the Radical Republicans, introduced a constitutional amendment that would have allocated House seats to States "according to their respective legal voters"; in addition, the proposed amendment mandated that "[a] true census of the legal voters shall be taken at the same time with the regular census." Cong. Globe, 39th Cong., 1st Sess., 10 (1866). Supporters of apportionment based on voter population employed the same voter-equality reasoning that appellants now echo. See, *e.g.*, *id.*, at 380 (remarks of Rep. Orth) ("[T]he true principle of representation in Congress is that voters alone should form the basis, and that each voter should have equal political weight in our Government. . . ."); *id.*, at 404 (remarks of Rep. Lawrence) (use of total population "disregards the fundamental idea of all just representation, that every voter should be equal in political power all over the Union").

Voter-based apportionment proponents encountered fierce resistance from proponents of total-population apportionment. Much of the opposition was

9. Justice Alito observes that Hamilton stated this principle while opposing allocation of an equal number of Senate seats to each State. That context, however, does not diminish Hamilton's principled argument for allocating seats to protect the representational rights of "every individual of the community at large." 1 Records of the Federal Convention of 1787, p. 473 (M. Farrand ed. 1911). Justice ALITO goes on to quote James Madison for the proposition that Hamilton was concerned, simply and only, with "the outcome of a contest over raw political power." Notably, in the statement Justice ALITO quotes, Madison was not attributing that motive to Hamilton; instead, according to Madison, Hamilton was attributing that motive to the advocates of equal representation for States. Farrand, *supra*, at 466. One need not gainsay that Hamilton's backdrop was the political controversies of his day. That reality, however, has not deterred this Court's past reliance on his statements of principle. See, *e.g.*, *Printz v. United States* (1997).

grounded in the principle of representational equality. "As an abstract proposition," argued Representative James G. Blaine, a leading critic of allocating House seats based on voter population, "no one will deny that population is the true basis of representation; for women, children, and other non-voting classes may have as vital an interest in the legislation of the country as those who actually deposit the ballot." *Id.*, at 141. See also *id.*, at 358 (remarks of Rep. Conkling) (arguing that use of a voter-population basis "would shut out four fifths of the citizens of the country—women and children, who are citizens, who are taxed, and who are, and always have been, represented"); *id.*, at 434 (remarks of Rep. Ward) ("[W]hat becomes of that large class of non-voting tax-payers that are found in every section? Are they in no matter to be represented? They certainly should be enumerated in making up the whole number of those entitled to a representative.").

The product of these debates was § 2 of the Fourteenth Amendment, which retained total population as the congressional apportionment base. Introducing the final version of the Amendment on the Senate floor, Senator Jacob Howard explained:

> "[The] basis of representation is numbers . . .; that is, the whole population except untaxed Indians and persons excluded by the State laws for rebellion or other crime. . . . The committee adopted numbers as the most just and satisfactory basis, and this is the principle upon which the Constitution itself was originally framed, that the basis of representation should depend upon numbers; and such, I think, after all, is the safest and most secure principle upon which the Government can rest. Numbers, not voters; numbers, not property; this is the theory of the Constitution." Cong. Globe, 39th Cong., 1st Sess., 2766-2767 (1866).

Appellants ask us to find in the Fourteenth Amendment's Equal Protection Clause a rule inconsistent with this "theory of the Constitution." But, as the Court recognized in *Wesberry*, this theory underlies not just the method of allocating House seats to States; it applies as well to the method of apportioning legislative seats within States. "The debates at the [Constitutional] Convention," the Court explained, "make at least one fact abundantly clear: that when the delegates agreed that the House should represent 'people,' they intended that in allocating Congressmen the number assigned to each state should be determined solely by the number of inhabitants." "While it may not be possible to draw congressional districts with mathematical precision," the Court acknowledged, "that is no excuse for ignoring our Constitution's plain objective of making equal representation for *equal numbers of people* the fundamental goal for the House of Representatives." (emphasis added). It cannot be that the Fourteenth Amendment calls for the apportionment of congressional districts based on total population, but simultaneously prohibits States from apportioning their own legislative districts on the same basis.

Cordoning off the constitutional history of congressional districting, appellants stress two points. First, they draw a distinction between allocating seats *to* States, and apportioning seats *within* States. The Framers selected total population for the former, appellants and their *amici* argue, because of federalism concerns inapposite to intrastate districting. These concerns included the perceived risk that a voter-population base might encourage States to expand the franchise unwisely, and the hope that a total-population base might counter States' incentive to undercount their populations, thereby reducing their share of direct taxes. *Wesberry*, however, rejected the distinction appellants now press. Even without the weight of *Wesberry*, we would find appellants' distinction unconvincing. One can accept that federalism — or, as Justice Alito emphasizes, partisan and regional political advantage — figured in the Framers' selection of total population as the basis for allocating congressional seats. Even so, it remains beyond doubt that the principle of representational equality figured prominently in the decision to count people, whether or not they qualify as voters.[11]

Second, appellants and Justice Alito urge, the Court has typically refused to analogize to features of the federal electoral system — here, the constitutional scheme governing congressional apportionment — when considering challenges to state and local election laws. True, in *Reynolds*, the Court rejected Alabama's argument that it had permissibly modeled its State Senate apportionment scheme — one Senator for each county — on the United States Senate. "[T]he federal analogy," the Court explained, "[is] inapposite and irrelevant to state legislative districting schemes" because "[t]he system of representation in the two Houses of the Federal Congress" arose "from unique historical circumstances." Likewise, in *Gray v. Sanders* (1963), Georgia unsuccessfully attempted to defend, by analogy to the electoral college, its scheme of assigning a certain number of "units" to the winner of each county in statewide elections.

Reynolds and *Gray*, however, involved features of the federal electoral system that contravene the principles of both voter *and* representational equality to favor interests that have no relevance outside the federal context. Senate seats were allocated to States on an equal basis to respect state sovereignty and increase the odds that the smaller States would ratify the Constitution. See *Wesberry* (describing the history of the Great Compromise). See also *Reynolds* ("Political subdivisions of States — counties, cities, or whatever — never were and never have been considered as sovereign entities. . . . The relationship of the States to the Federal Government could hardly be less analogous."). The [Electoral] College was created to permit the most knowledgeable members of the community to choose the executive of a nation whose continental dimensions were thought to preclude an informed choice by the citizenry at large. By contrast, as earlier developed, the constitutional scheme for congressional apportionment rests in part on the same representational concerns that exist regarding state and local legislative districting. The Framers' answer to the apportionment question in the congressional context

11. Justice Alito asserts that we have taken the statements of the Fourteenth Amendment's Framers "out of context." *Post*, at 1148. ("[C]laims about representational equality were invoked, if at all, only in service of the *real* goal: preventing southern States from acquiring too much power in the national government."). Like Alexander Hamilton, the Fourteenth Amendment's Framers doubtless made arguments rooted in practical political realities as well as in principle. That politics played a part, however, does not warrant rejecting principled argument. In any event, motivations aside, the Framers' ultimate choice of total population rather than voter population is surely relevant to whether, as appellants now argue, the Equal Protection Clause *mandates* use of voter population rather than total population.

therefore undermines appellants' contention that districts must be based on voter population.

B

Consistent with constitutional history, this Court's past decisions reinforce the conclusion that States and localities may comply with the one-person, one-vote principle by designing districts with equal total populations. Quoting language from those decisions that, in appellants' view, supports the principle of equal voting power—and emphasizing the phrase "one-person, one-vote"—appellants contend that the Court had in mind, and constantly meant, that States should equalize the voter-eligible population of districts. See *Reynolds* ("[A]n individual's right to vote for State legislators is unconstitutionally impaired when its weight is in a substantial fashion diluted when compared with votes of citizens living on other parts of the State."); *Gray,* 372 U.S., at 379-380, 83 S. Ct. 801 ("The concept of 'we the people' under the Constitution visualizes no preferred class of voters but equality among those who meet the basic qualifications."). Appellants, however, extract far too much from selectively chosen language and the "one-person, one-vote" slogan.

For every sentence appellants quote from the Court's opinions, one could respond with a line casting the one-person, one-vote guarantee in terms of equality of representation, not voter equality. In *Reynolds,* for instance, the Court described "the fundamental principle of representative government in this country" as "one of equal representation for equal numbers of people." And the Court has suggested, repeatedly, that districting based on total population serves *both* the State's interest in preventing vote dilution *and* its interest in ensuring equality of representation. See *Board of Estimate of City of New York v. Morris* (1989) ("If districts of widely unequal population elect an equal number of representatives, the voting power of each citizen in the larger constituencies is debased and the citizens in those districts have a smaller share of representation than do those in the smaller districts."). See also *Kirkpatrick* (recognizing in a congressional-districting case that "[e]qual representation for equal numbers of people is a principle designed to prevent debasement of voting power and diminution of access to elected representatives").

Moreover, from *Reynolds* on, the Court has consistently looked to total-population figures when evaluating whether districting maps violate the Equal Protection Clause by deviating impermissibly from perfect population equality. Appellants point to no instance in which the Court has determined the permissibility of deviation based on eligible- or registered-voter data. It would hardly make sense for the Court to have mandated voter equality *sub silentio* and then used a total-population baseline to evaluate compliance with that rule. More likely, we think, the Court has always assumed the permissibility of drawing districts to equalize total population.

"In the 1960s," appellants counter, "the distribution of the voting population generally did not deviate from the distribution of total population to the degree necessary to raise this issue." To support this assertion, appellants cite only a District Court decision, which found no significant deviation in the distribution of voter and total population in densely populated areas of New York State. Had this Court assumed such equivalence on a national scale, it likely would have said as much. Instead, in *Gaffney v. Cummings* (1973), the Court acknowledged that voters may be distributed unevenly within jurisdictions. "[I]f it is the weight of a person's vote that matters," the Court observed, then "total population—even if stable and accurately taken—may not actually reflect that body of voters whose votes must be counted and weighed for the purposes of reapportionment, because 'census persons' are not voters." *Id.* Nonetheless, the Court in *Gaffney* recognized that the one-person, one-vote rule is designed to facilitate "[f]air and effective representation," *id.*, and evaluated compliance with the rule based on total population alone.

C

What constitutional history and our prior decisions strongly suggest, settled practice confirms. Adopting voter-eligible apportionment as constitutional command would upset a well-functioning approach to districting that all 50 States and countless local jurisdictions have followed for decades, even centuries. Appellants have shown no reason for the Court to disturb this longstanding use of total population. As the Framers of the Constitution and the Fourteenth Amendment comprehended, representatives serve all residents, not just those eligible or registered to vote. Nonvoters have an important stake in many policy debates—children, their parents, even their grandparents, for example, have a stake in a strong public-education system—and in receiving constituent services, such as help navigating public-benefits bureaucracies. By ensuring that each representative is subject to requests and suggestions from the same number of constituents, total-population apportionment promotes equitable and effective representation.

In sum, the rule appellants urge has no mooring in the Equal Protection Clause. The Texas Senate map, we therefore conclude, complies with the requirements of the one-person, one-vote principle.[15] Because history, precedent, and practice suffice to reveal the infirmity of appellants' claims, we need not and do not resolve whether, as Texas now argues, States may draw districts to equalize voter-eligible population rather than total population.

For the reasons stated, the judgment of the United States District Court for the Western District of Texas is

Affirmed.

Justice ALITO, with whom Justice THOMAS joins except as to Part III-B, concurring in the judgment.

[Omitted.]

15. Insofar as appellants suggest that Texas could have roughly equalized both total population and eligible-voter population, this Court has never required jurisdictions to use multiple population baselines. In any event, appellants have never presented a map that manages to equalize both measures, perhaps because such a map does not exist, or because such a map would necessarily ignore other traditional redistricting principles, including maintaining communities of interest and respecting municipal boundaries.

Justice THOMAS, concurring in the judgment.

This case concerns whether Texas violated the Equal Protection Clause—as interpreted by the Court's one-person, one-vote cases—by creating legislative districts that contain approximately equal total population but vary widely in the number of eligible voters in each district. I agree with the majority that our precedents do not require a State to equalize the total number of voters in each district. States may opt to equalize total population. I therefore concur in the majority's judgment that appellants' challenge fails.

I write separately because this Court has never provided a sound basis for the one-person, one-vote principle. For 50 years, the Court has struggled to define what right that principle protects. Many of our precedents suggest that it protects the right of eligible voters to cast votes that receive equal weight. Despite that frequent explanation, our precedents often conclude that the Equal Protection Clause is satisfied when all individuals within a district—voters or not—have an equal share of representation. The majority today concedes that our cases have not produced a clear answer on this point.

In my view, the majority has failed to provide a sound basis for the one-person, one-vote principle because no such basis exists. The Constitution does not prescribe any one basis for apportionment within States. It instead leaves States significant leeway in apportioning their own districts to equalize total population, to equalize eligible voters, or to promote any other principle consistent with a republican form of government. The majority should recognize the futility of choosing only one of these options. The Constitution leaves the choice to the people alone—not to this Court.

I

The Equal Protection Clause prohibits a State from "deny[ing] to any person within its jurisdiction the equal protection of the laws." For nearly a century after its ratification, this Court interpreted the Clause as having no application to the politically charged issue of how States should apportion their populations in political districts. See, *e.g.*, *Colegrove v. Green* (1946) (plurality opinion). Instead, the Court left the drawing of States' political boundaries to the States, so long as a State did not deprive people of the right to vote for reasons prohibited by the Constitution. This meant that a State's refusal to allocate voters within districts based on population changes was a matter for States—not federal courts—to decide. And these cases were part of a larger jurisprudence holding that the question whether a state government had a "proper" republican form rested with Congress.

Since *Baker* empowered the federal courts to resolve redistricting disputes, this Court has struggled to explain whether the one-person, one-vote principle ensures equality among eligible voters or instead protects some broader right of every citizen to equal representation.

In a number of cases, this Court has said that States must protect the right of *eligible voters* to have their votes receive equal weight. On this view, there is only one way for States to comply with the one-person, one-vote principle: they must draw districts that contain a substantially equal number of eligible voters per district.

In contrast to this oft-stated aspiration of giving equal treatment to eligible voters, the Court has also expressed a different understanding of the one-person, one-vote principle. In several cases, the Court has suggested that one-person, one-vote protects the interests of *all* individuals in a district, whether they are eligible voters or not. Under this view, States cannot comply with the Equal Protection Clause by equalizing the number of eligible voters in each district. They must instead equalize the total population per district.

This lack of clarity in our redistricting cases has left States with little guidance about how their political institutions must be structured. Because the Court has not provided a firm account of what States must do when districting, States are left to guess how much flexibility (if any) they have to use different methods of apportionment.

II

This inconsistency (if not opacity) is not merely a consequence of the Court's equivocal statements on one person, one vote. The problem is more fundamental. There is simply no way to make a principled choice between interpreting one person, one vote as protecting eligible voters or as protecting total inhabitants within a State. That is because, though those theories are noble, the Constitution does not make either of them the exclusive means of apportionment for state and local representatives. In guaranteeing to the States a "Republican Form of Government," Art. IV, § 4, the Constitution did not resolve whether the ultimate basis of representation is the right of citizens to cast an equal ballot or the right of all inhabitants to have equal representation. The Constitution instead reserves these matters to the people. The majority's attempt today to divine a single " 'theory of the Constitution' "—apportionment based on representation—rests on a flawed reading of history and wrongly picks one side of a debate that the Framers did not resolve in the Constitution.

A

The Constitution lacks a single, comprehensive theory of representation. The Framers understood the tension between majority rule and protecting fundamental rights from majorities. This understanding led to a "mixed" constitutional structure that did not embrace any single theory of representation but instead struck a compromise between those who sought an equitable system of representation and those who were concerned that the majority would abuse plenary control over public policy. As Madison wrote, "A dependence on the people is no doubt the primary controul on the government; but experience has taught mankind the necessity of auxiliary precautions." The Federalist No. 51, p. 349 (J. Cooke ed. 1961). *This* was the theory of the Constitution. The Framers therefore made difficult compromises on the apportionment of federal representation, and they did not prescribe any one theory of how States had to divide their legislatures.

1

Because, in the view of the Framers, ultimate political power derives from citizens who were "created equal," The Declaration of Independence ¶ 2, beliefs in equality of representation—and by extension, majority rule—influenced the constitutional structure. In the years between the Revolution and the framing, the

Framers experimented with different ways of securing the political system against improper influence. Of all the "electoral safeguards for the representational system," the most critical was "equality of representation." G. Wood, The Creation of the American Republic 1776–1787, p. 170 (1998) (Wood).

The Framers' preference for apportionment by representation (and majority rule) was driven partially by the belief that all citizens were inherently equal. In a system where citizens were equal, a legislature should have "equal representation" so that "equal interests among the people should have equal interests in [the assembly]." Thoughts on Government, in 4 Works of John Adams 195 (C. Adams ed. 1851). The British Parliament fell short of this goal. In addition to having hereditary nobility, more than half of the members of the democratic House of Commons were elected from sparsely populated districts—so-called "rotten boroughs."

The Framers' preference for majority rule also was a reaction to the shortcomings of the Articles of Confederation. Under the Articles, each State could cast one vote regardless of population and Congress could act only with the assent of nine States. This system proved undesirable because a few small States had the ability to paralyze the National Legislature. See The Federalist No. 22, at 140-141 (Hamilton).

Consequently, when the topic of dividing representation came up at the Constitutional Convention, some Framers advocated proportional representation throughout the National Legislature. Alexander Hamilton voiced concerns about the unfairness of allowing a minority to rule over a majority. James Madison, too, opined that the general Government needed a direct mandate from the people. If federal "power [were] not immediately derived from the people, in proportion to their numbers," according to Madison, the Federal Government would be as weak as Congress under the Articles of Confederation.

In many ways, the Constitution reflects this preference for majority rule. To pass Congress, ordinary legislation requires a simple majority of present members to vote in favor. And some features of the apportionment for the House of Representatives reflected the idea that States should wield political power in approximate proportion to their number of inhabitants. Thus, "equal representation for equal numbers of people" features prominently in how representatives are apportioned among the States. These features of the Constitution reflect the preference of some members of the founding generation for equality of representation. But, as explained below, this is not the single "theory of the Constitution."

2

The Framers also understood that unchecked majorities could lead to tyranny of the majority. As a result, many viewed antidemocratic checks as indispensable to republican government. And included among the antidemocratic checks were legislatures that deviated from perfect equality of representation.

The Framers believed that a proper government promoted the common good. They conceived this good as objective and not inherently coextensive with majoritarian preferences. See, *e.g.*, The Federalist No. 1, at 4 (Hamilton) (defining the common good or "public good" as the "true interests" of the community); *id.*, No. 10, at 57 (Madison) ("the permanent and aggregate interests of the community"). For government to promote the common good, it had to do more than simply obey the will of the majority. See, *e.g.*, *ibid.* (discussing majoritarian factions). Government must also protect fundamental rights. See The Declaration of Independence ¶ 2; 1 W. Blackstone, Commentaries *124 ("[T]he principal aim of society is to protect individuals in the enjoyment of those absolute rights, which are vested in them by the immutable laws of nature").

Of particular concern for the Framers was the majority of people violating the property rights of the minority. Madison observed that "the most common and durable source of factions, has been the various and unequal distribution of property." The Federalist No. 10, at 59. A poignant example occurred in Massachusetts. In what became known as Shays' Rebellion, armed debtors attempted to block legal actions by creditors to recover debts. Although that rebellion was ultimately put down, debtors sought relief from state legislatures "under the auspices of Constitutional forms." Letter from James Madison to Thomas Jefferson (Apr. 23, 1787), in 11 The Papers of Thomas Jefferson 307 (J. Boyd ed. 1955); see Wood 412-413. With no structural political checks on democratic lawmaking, creditors found their rights jeopardized by state laws relieving debtors of their obligation to pay and authorizing forms of payment that devalued the contracts.

Because of the Framers' concerns about placing unchecked power in political majorities, the Constitution's majoritarian provisions were only part of a complex republican structure. The Framers also placed several antidemocratic provisions in the Constitution. The original Constitution permitted only the direct election of representatives. Senators and the President were selected indirectly. And the "Great Compromise" guaranteed large and small States voting equality in the Senate. By malapportioning the Senate, the Framers prevented large States from outvoting small States to adopt policies that would advance the large States' interests at the expense of the small States. See The Federalist No. 62, at 417 (Madison).

These countermajoritarian measures reflect the Framers' aspirations of promoting competing goals. Rejecting a hereditary class system, they thought political power resided with the people. At the same time, they sought to check majority rule to promote the common good and mitigate threats to fundamental rights.

B

As the Framers understood, designing a government to fulfill the conflicting tasks of respecting the fundamental equality of persons while promoting the common good requires making incommensurable tradeoffs. For this reason, they did not attempt to restrict the States to one form of government.

Instead, the Constitution broadly required that the States maintain a "Republican Form of Government." Art. IV, § 4. But the Framers otherwise left it to States to make tradeoffs and reconcile the competing goals.

Republican governments promote the common good by placing power in the hands of the people, while curtailing the majority's ability to invade the minority's fundamental rights. The Framers recognized that there is no universal formula for accomplishing these goals. At the framing, many state legislatures were bicameral, often reflecting multiple theories of representation. Only [s]ix of the original thirteen states based representation in both houses of their state legislatures on population. In most States, it was common to base representation, at least in part, on the State's political subdivisions, even if those subdivisions varied heavily in their populations.

Reflecting this history, the Constitution continued to afford States significant leeway in structuring their "Republican" governments. At the framing, "republican" referred to "[p]lacing the government in the people," and a "republick" was a "state in which the power is lodged in more than one." S. Johnson, A Dictionary of the English Language (7th ed. 1785); By requiring the States to have republican governments, the Constitution prohibited them from having monarchies and aristocracies. See *id.*, No. 43, at 291. Some would argue that the Constitution also prohibited States from adopting direct democracies.

Beyond that, however, the Constitution left matters open for the people of the States to decide. The Constitution says nothing about what type of republican government the States must follow. When the Framers wanted to deny powers to state governments, they did so explicitly. See, *e.g.*, Art. I, § 10, cl. 1 ("No State shall . . . pass any Bill of Attainder, ex post facto Law, or Law impairing the Obligation of Contracts").

None of the Reconstruction Amendments changed the original understanding of republican government. Those Amendments brought blacks within the existing American political community. The Fourteenth Amendment pressured States to adopt universal male suffrage by reducing a noncomplying State's representation in Congress. And the Fifteenth Amendment prohibited restricting the right of suffrage based on race. That is as far as those Amendments went. As Justice Harlan explained in *Reynolds,* neither Amendment provides a theory of how much "weight" a vote must receive, nor do they require a State to apportion both Houses of their legislature solely on a population basis.

C

The Court's attempt to impose its political theory upon the States has produced a morass of problems. These problems are antithetical to the values that the Framers embraced in the Constitution. These problems confirm that the Court has been wrong to entangle itself with the political process.

First, in embracing one person, one vote, the Court has arrogated to the Judiciary important value judgments that the Constitution reserves to the people. In *Reynolds,* for example, the Court proclaimed that "[l]egislators represent people, not trees or acres"; that "[l]egislators are elected by voters, not farms or cities or economic interests"; and that, accordingly, electoral districts must have roughly equal population. As I have explained, the Constitution permits, but does not impose, this view. Beyond that, *Reynolds*' assertions are driven by the belief that there is a single, correct answer to the question of how much voting strength an individual citizen should have. These assertions overlook that, to control factions that would legislate against the common good, individual voting strength must sometimes yield to countermajoritarian checks. And this principle has no less force within States than it has for the federal system. Instead of large States versus small States, those interests may pit urban areas versus rural, manufacturing versus agriculture, or those with property versus those without. There is no single method of reconciling these competing interests. And it is not the role of this Court to calibrate democracy in the vain search for an optimum solution.

The Government argues that apportioning legislators by any metric other than total population "risks rendering residents of this country who are ineligible, unwilling, or unable to vote as invisible or irrelevant to our system of representative democracy." But that argument rests on the faulty premise that "our system of representative democracy" requires specific groups to have representation in a specific manner. As I have explained, the Constitution does not impose that requirement. And as the Court recently reminded us, States are free to serve as " 'laboratories' " of democracy. *Arizona State Legislature v. Arizona Independent Redistricting Comm'n* (2015). That "laboratory" extends to experimenting about the nature of democracy itself.

Second, the Court's efforts to monitor the political process have failed to provide any consistent guidance for the States. Even if it were justifiable for this Court to enforce some principle of majority rule, it has been unable to do so in a principled manner. Our precedents do not address the myriad other ways that minorities (or fleeting majorities) entrench themselves in the political system. States can place policy choices in their constitutions or have supermajoritarian voting rules in a legislative assembly. See, *e.g.,* N.Y. Const., Art. V, § 7 (constitutionalizing public employee pensions); Ill. Const., Art. VII, § 6(g) (requiring a three-fifths vote of the General Assembly to preempt certain local ordinances). In theory, of course, it does not seem to make a difference if a state legislature is unresponsive to the majority of residents because the state assembly requires a 60% vote to pass a bill or because 40% of the population elects 51% of the representatives.

So far as the Constitution is concerned, there is no single "correct" way to design a republican government. Any republic will have to reconcile giving power to the people with diminishing the influence of special interests. The wisdom of the Framers was that they recognized this dilemma and left it to the people to resolve. In trying to impose its own theory of democracy, the Court is hopelessly adrift amid political theory and interest-group politics with no guiding legal principles.

III

This case illustrates the confusion that our cases have wrought. The parties and the Government offer three positions on what this Court's one-person, one-vote cases require States to equalize. Under appellants' view, the Fourteenth Amendment protects the right to an equal vote. Appellees, in contrast, argue that the Fourteenth Amendment protects against invidious discrimination; in their view, no such discrimination occurs when States have a rational basis for the population base that they select, even if that base leaves eligible voters malapportioned. And, the Solicitor General suggests that reapportionment by total population is the only permissible standard because *Reynolds* recognized a right of "equal representation for equal numbers of people."

Although the majority does not choose among these theories, it necessarily denies that the Equal Protection Clause protects the right to cast an equally weighted ballot. To prevail, appellants do not have to deny the importance of equal representation. Because States can equalize both total population and total voting power within the districts, they have to show only that the right to cast an equally weighted vote is part of the one-person, one-vote right that we have recognized. But the majority declines to find such a right in the Equal Protection Clause. Rather, the majority acknowledges that "[f]or every sentence appellants quote from the Court's opinions [establishing a right to an equal vote], one could respond with a line casting the one-person, one-vote guarantee in terms of equality of representation, not voter equality." Because our precedents are not consistent with appellants' position—that the only constitutionally available choice for States is to allocate districts to equalize eligible voters—the majority concludes that appellants' challenge fails.

I agree with the majority's ultimate disposition of this case. As far as the original understanding of the Constitution is concerned, a State has wide latitude in selecting its population base for apportionment. It can use total population, eligible voters, or any other nondiscriminatory voter base. And States with a bicameral legislature can have some mixture of these theories, such as one population base for its lower house and another for its upper chamber.

Our precedents do not compel a contrary conclusion. Appellants are correct that this Court's precedents have primarily based its one-person, one-vote jurisprudence on the theory that eligible voters have a right against vote dilution. But this Court's jurisprudence has vacillated too much for me to conclude that the Court's precedents preclude States from allocating districts based on total population instead. Under these circumstances, the choice is best left for the people of the States to decide for themselves how they should apportion their legislature.

* * *

There is no single "correct" method of apportioning state legislatures. And the Constitution did not make this Court "a centralized politburo appointed for life to dictate to the provinces the 'correct' theories of democratic representation, [or] the 'best' electoral systems for securing truly 'representative' government." *Holder v. Hall* (1994) (Thomas, J., concurring in judgment). Because the majority continues that misguided search, I concur only in the judgment.

NOTE ON *EVENWEL* AND THE FUTURE OF ONE-PERSON-ONE-VOTE

1. As Justice Ginsburg notes, the vast majority of plans drawn to comply with one person, one vote use total population as the baseline for comparison.

2. In *Evenwel v. Abbott*, the plaintiffs challenged Texas' use of total population on the ground that using total population produced unequal districts when measured by voter-eligible population. (Using voter-eligible population would, for example, exclude from the one person, one vote calculation those who are under 18 years of age and those who are not citizens.) The Court held Texas could use total population to draw its districts, but it is not clear from the opinion whether a state *must* use total population or could use another measure if it wanted.

3. On the other hand, at least in the context of state (as opposed to congressional) legislative districts, it would appear that states have the flexibility to use something other than total population. In *Burns v. Richardson*, 384 U.S. 73, 90-97 (1966) (mentioned in the opinions in *Evenwel*), the Supreme Court declined to invalidate Hawaii's legislative plan that used registered voters as a basis for

measuring equality amongst legislative districts. It seems likely that a future case might feature a state using voter-eligible population as the basis for drawing districts and plaintiffs challenging that decision as a violation of one person, one vote because of the decision not to use total population.

4. More broadly, how far do you think the Court might be willing to go to permit states and local governments to deviate from strict compliance with equally populated districts in order to respect special historical or geographical circumstances? For example, if Hawaii went to the Court with an argument about the need to give each of its islands distinct representation, despite their population differences, would that argument be summarily rejected based on *Reynolds*, or would the Court consider it? Would the answer depend on how far from strict equality of population Hawaii wished to deviate? In other words, is the Court more willing to *balance* the value of population equality against other historical and geographical considerations—and if *Reynolds* is now a *balancing test*, is the current doctrine vastly different than the Warren Court's own understanding of *Reynolds* as a constitutional *rule* rather than a *balancing test*?

C. MINORITY VOTE DILUTION: THE CONSTITUTION AND SECTION 2 OF THE VOTING RIGHTS ACT

The judicial doctrine of one person, one vote is one piece of the puzzle in relation to the design of electoral structures. Since deciding to enter the "political thicket" of redistricting, the Court has also made pronouncements in the area of voting rights for racial and ethnic minorities. These pronouncements have come in several forms. Initially, the Court's decisions involved an Equal Protection prohibition on minority vote dilution. Later, Congress amended Section 2 of the Voting Rights Act to address vote dilution, and so the Court moved from an interpreter of the Constitution to an interpreter of a statute. We begin with two cases involving the Constitution and then shift to cases involving the statute.

As background prior to reading the next two cases, you should know that the contours of the constitutional right prohibiting vote dilution have progressed in a nonlinear fashion. Initially, in *Whitcomb v. Chavis*, 403 U.S. 124 (1971), the Court recognized an equal protection right to an undiluted vote for minority voters. However, in that case, which involved a challenge by African-American plaintiffs to at-large elections used to elect state legislators in Marion County, Indiana, the Court declined to find a constitutional violation. The primary rationale for the Court's decision in *Whitcomb* was that the minority plaintiffs were losing not for racial reasons but rather for political reasons. In other words, plaintiffs were losing elections not because they were African Americans but because they were Democrats and Republicans were winning.

A couple of years later, though, in *White v. Regester*, 412 U.S. 755 (1973), the Court found vote dilution in the context of a challenge to the election of state legislators in two regions of Texas—Dallas and Bexar Counties (Bexar County encompasses San Antonio). In that case, the Court looked at a panoply of factors to conclude that minority vote dilution had occurred. Both *Whitcomb* and *White* are discussed extensively in the *City of Mobile v. Bolden* opinions you will read next. You should pay close attention to them, particularly the factors used in *White*, as many of those factors form the basis for both the constitutional and statutory claims in this realm.

In the next two cases, the Court considered whether an "at-large" voting system, in which all voters throughout a jurisdiction elect representatives for that jurisdiction, violated the Fourteenth or Fifteenth Amendment. As you will see, the main question becomes whether the at-large system was created or maintained with a "discriminatory purpose." Why does the Court settle on a discriminatory "purpose" standard as opposed to a discriminatory "effect" standard? In addition, what factors does the Court use to determine whether the at-large system is the product of a discriminatory purpose?

City of Mobile v. Bolden

446 U.S. 55 (1980)

Mr. Justice STEWART announced the judgment of the Court and delivered an opinion, in which THE CHIEF JUSTICE, Mr. Justice POWELL, and Mr. Justice REHNQUIST joined.

The city of Mobile, Ala., has since 1911 been governed by a City Commission consisting of three members elected by the voters of the city at large. The question in this case is whether this at-large system of municipal elections violates the rights of Mobile's Negro voters in contravention of federal statutory or constitutional law.

The appellees brought this suit in the Federal District Court for the Southern District of Alabama as a class action on behalf of all Negro citizens of Mobile.[1] The complaint alleged that the practice of electing the City Commissioners at large unfairly diluted the voting strength of Negroes in violation of §2 of the Voting Rights Act of 1965, of the Fourteenth Amendment, and of the Fifteenth Amendment. [The district court found for the plaintiffs on both the Fourteenth and Fifteenth Amendment claims and the court of appeals affirmed.]

I

The three Commissioners jointly exercise all legislative, executive and administrative power in the municipality. They are required after election to designate one of their number as Mayor, a largely ceremonial office, but no formal provision is made for allocating specific executive or administrative duties among the three. As required by the state law enacted in 1911, each candidate for the Mobile City Commission runs for election in the city at large for a term of four years in one of three numbered posts, and may be elected only by a majority of the total vote. This is the same basic electoral system that is followed by literally thousands of municipalities and other local governmental units throughout the Nation.

1. Approximately 35.4 percent of the residents of Mobile are Negro.

II

Section 2 of the Voting Rights Act provides:

"No voting qualification or prerequisite to voting, or standard, practice, or procedure shall be imposed or applied by any State or political subdivision to deny or abridge the right of any citizen of the United States to vote on account of race or color." 42 U.S.C. §1973.

Assuming, for present purposes, that there exists a private right of action to enforce this statutory provision, it is apparent that the language of §2 no more than elaborates upon that of the Fifteenth Amendment, and the sparse legislative history of §2 makes clear that it was intended to have an effect no different from that of the Fifteenth Amendment itself.

III

The Court's early decisions under the Fifteenth Amendment established that it imposes but one limitation on the powers of the States. It forbids them to discriminate against Negroes in matters having to do with voting.

Our decisions, moreover, have made clear that action by a State that is racially neutral on its face violates the Fifteenth Amendment only if motivated by a discriminatory purpose.

The Fifteenth Amendment does not entail the right to have Negro candidates elected, and [precedents of this Court do not] contain[] any implication to the contrary. That Amendment prohibits only purposefully discriminatory denial or abridgment by government of the freedom to vote "on account of race, color, or previous condition of servitude." Having found that Negroes in Mobile "register and vote without hindrance," the District Court and Court of Appeals were in error in believing that the appellants invaded the protection of that Amendment in the present case.

IV

The Court of Appeals also agreed with the District Court that Mobile's at-large electoral system violates the Equal Protection Clause of the Fourteenth Amendment. There remains for consideration, therefore, the validity of its judgment on that score.

A

Despite repeated constitutional attacks upon multimember legislative districts, the Court has consistently held that they are not unconstitutional per se. We have recognized, however, that such legislative apportionments could violate the Fourteenth Amendment if their purpose were invidiously to minimize or cancel out the voting potential of racial or ethnic minorities. *See White v. Regester, Whitcomb v. Chavis.* To prove such a purpose it is not enough to show that the group allegedly discriminated against has not elected representatives in proportion to its numbers. A plaintiff must prove that the disputed plan was "conceived or operated as [a] purposeful devic[e] to further racial . . . discrimination." [*Whitcomb.*]

This burden of proof is simply one aspect of the basic principle that only if there is purposeful discrimination can there be a violation of the Equal Protection Clause of the Fourteenth Amendment. *See Washington v. Davis.* The Court explicitly indicated in *Washington v. Davis* that this principle applies to claims of racial discrimination affecting voting just as it does to other claims of racial discrimination.

Although dicta may be drawn from a few of the Court's earlier opinions suggesting that disproportionate effects alone may establish a claim of unconstitutional racial voter dilution, the fact is that such a view is not supported by any decision of this Court.

In only one case has the Court sustained a claim that multimember legislative districts unconstitutionally diluted the voting strength of a discrete group. That case was *White v. Regester*. There the Court upheld a constitutional challenge by Negroes and Mexican-Americans to parts of a legislative reapportionment plan adopted by the State of Texas. The plaintiffs alleged that the multimember districts for the two counties in which they resided minimized the effect of their votes in violation of the Fourteenth Amendment, and the Court held that the plaintiffs had been able to "produce evidence to support findings that the political processes leading to nomination and election were not equally open to participation by the group[s] in question." In so holding, the Court relied upon evidence in the record that included a long history of official discrimination against minorities as well as indifference to their needs and interests on the part of white elected officials. The Court also found in each county additional factors that restricted the access of minority groups to the political process. In one county, Negroes effectively were excluded from the process of slating candidates for the Democratic Party, while the plaintiffs in the other county were Mexican-Americans who "suffer[ed] a cultural and language barrier" that made "participation in community processes extremely difficult, particularly with respect to the political life" of the county.

White v. Regester is thus consistent with "the basic equal protection principle that the invidious equality of a law claimed to be racially discriminatory must ultimately be traced to a racially discriminatory purpose." *Washington v. Davis*.

[I]t is clear that the evidence in the present case fell far short of showing that the appellants "conceived or operated [a] purposeful devic[e] to further racial . . . discrimination."

[T]he District Court based its conclusion of unconstitutionality primarily on the fact that no Negro had ever been elected to the City Commission, apparently because of the pervasiveness of racially polarized voting in Mobile. The trial court also found that city officials had not been as responsive to the interests of Negroes as to those of white persons. On the basis of these findings, the court concluded that the political processes in Mobile were not equally open to Negroes, despite its seemingly inconsistent findings that there were no inhibitions against Negroes becoming candidates, and that in fact Negroes had registered and voted without hindrance. Finally, with little additional discussion, the District Court held that Mobile's at-large electoral system was invidiously discriminating against Negroes in violation of the Equal Protection Clause.

[The evidentiary factors] upon which the District Court and the Court of Appeals relied were most assuredly insufficient to prove an unconstitutionally discriminatory purpose in the present case.

First, the two courts found it highly significant that no Negro had been elected to the Mobile City Commission. From this fact they concluded that the processes leading to nomination and election were not open equally to Negroes.

But the District Court's findings of fact, unquestioned on appeal, make clear that Negroes register and vote in Mobile "without hindrance," and that there are no official obstacles in the way of Negroes who wish to become candidates for election to the Commission. It may be that Negro candidates have been defeated but that fact alone does not work a constitutional deprivation.

Second, the District Court relied in part on its finding that the persons who were elected to the Commission discriminated against Negroes in municipal employment and in dispensing public services. If that is the case, those discriminated against may be entitled to relief under the Constitution, albeit of a sort quite different from that sought in the present case. The Equal Protection Clause proscribes purposeful discrimination because of race by any unit of state government, whatever the method of its election. But evidence of discrimination by white officials in Mobile is relevant only as the most tenuous and circumstantial evidence of the constitutional invalidity of the electoral system under which they attained their offices.[20]

Third, the District Court and the Court of Appeals supported their conclusion by drawing upon the substantial history of official racial discrimination in Alabama. But past discrimination cannot, in the manner of original sin, condemn governmental action that is not itself unlawful. The ultimate question remains whether a discriminatory intent has been proved in a given case. More distant instances of official discrimination in other cases are of limited help in resolving that question.

Finally, the District Court and the Court of Appeals pointed to the mechanics of the at-large electoral system itself as proof that the votes of Negroes were being invidiously canceled out. But those features of that electoral system, such as the majority vote requirement, tend naturally to disadvantage any voting minority. They are far from proof that the at-large electoral scheme represents purposeful discrimination against Negro voters.[21]

We turn finally to the arguments advanced in Part I of Mr. Justice Marshall's dissenting opinion. The theory of this dissenting opinion—a theory much more extreme than that espoused by the District Court or the Court of Appeals—appears to be that every "political group," or at least every such group that is in the minority, has a federal constitutional right to elect candidates in proportion to its numbers. Moreover, a political group's "right" to have its candidates elected is said to be a

20. Among the difficulties with the District Court's view of the evidence was its failure to identify the state officials whose intent it considered relevant in assessing the invidiousness of Mobile's system of government.

21. According to the District Court, voters in the city of Mobile are represented in the state legislature by three state senators, any one of whom can veto proposed local legislation under the existing courtesy rule. Likewise, a majority of Mobile's 11-member House delegation can prevent a local bill from reaching the floor for debate. Unanimous approval of a local measure by the city delegation, on the other hand, virtually assures passage.

There was evidence in this case that several proposals that would have altered the form of Mobile's municipal government have been defeated in the state legislature, including at least one that would have permitted Mobile to govern itself through a Mayor and City Council with members elected from individual districts within the city. Whether it may be possible ultimately to prove that Mobile's present governmental and electoral system has been retained for a racially discriminatory purpose, we are in no position now to say.

"fundamental interest," the infringement of which may be established without proof that a State has acted with the purpose of impairing anybody's access to the political process. This dissenting opinion finds the "right" infringed in the present case because no Negro has been elected to the Mobile City Commission.

Whatever appeal the dissenting opinion's view may have as a matter of political theory, it is not the law. The Equal Protection Clause of the Fourteenth Amendment does not require proportional representation as an imperative of political organization. The entitlement that the dissenting opinion assumes to exist simply is not to be found in the Constitution of the United States.

The dissenting opinion erroneously discovers the asserted entitlement to group representation within the "one person, one vote" principle of *Reynolds v. Sims*, and its progeny. Those cases established that the Equal Protection Clause guarantees the right of each voter to "have his vote weighted equally with those of all other citizens." The Court recognized that a voter's right to "have an equally effective voice" in the election of representatives is impaired where representation is not apportioned substantially on a population basis. In such cases, the votes of persons in more populous districts carry less weight than do those of persons in smaller districts. There can be, of course, no claim that the "one person, one vote" principle has been violated in this case, because the city of Mobile is a unitary electoral district and the Commission elections are conducted at large. It is therefore obvious that nobody's vote has been "diluted" in the sense in which that word was used in the *Reynolds* case.

The dissenting opinion places an extraordinary interpretation on these decisions, an interpretation not justified by *Reynolds v. Sims* itself or by any other decision of this Court. It is, of course, true that the right of a person to vote on an equal basis with other voters draws much of its significance from the political associations that its exercise reflects, but it is an altogether different matter to conclude that political groups themselves have an independent constitutional claim to representation. And the Court's decisions hold squarely that they do not.

The fact is that the Court has sternly set its face against the claim, however phrased, that the Constitution somehow guarantees proportional representation. In *Whitcomb v. Chavis*, the trial court had found that a multimember state legislative district had invidiously deprived Negroes and poor persons of rights guaranteed them by the Constitution, notwithstanding the absence of any evidence whatever of discrimination against them. Reversing the trial court, this Court said:

> "The District Court's holding, although on the facts of this case limited to guaranteeing one racial group representation, is not easily contained. It is expressive of the more general proposition that any group with distinctive interests must be represented in legislative halls if it is numerous enough to command at least one seat and represents a majority living in an area sufficiently compact to constitute a single-member district. This approach would make it difficult to reject claims of Democrats, Republicans, or members of any political organization in Marion County who live in what would be safe districts in a single-member district system but who in one year or another, or year after year, are submerged in a one-sided multi-member district vote. There are also union oriented workers, the university community, religious or ethnic groups occupying identifiable areas of our heterogeneous cities and urban areas. Indeed, it would be

difficult for a great many, if not most, multi-member districts to survive analysis under the District Court's view unless combined with some voting arrangement such as proportional representation or cumulative voting* aimed at providing representation for minority parties or interests. At the very least, affirmance of the District Court would spawn endless litigation concerning the multi-member district systems now widely employed in this country."

V

The judgment is reversed, and the case is remanded to the Court of Appeals for further proceedings.

It is so ordered.

Mr. Justice BLACKMUN, concurring in the result.

[Justice Blackmun assumed proof of intent was necessary to prevail on a vote dilution claim and was "inclined to agree with" Justice White that purposeful discrimination had been proved in this instance. However, Justice Blackmun concurred in the result because the lower courts had ordered an incorrect remedy.]

Mr. Justice STEVENS, concurring in the judgment.

[Justice Stevens would have found no constitutional violation but would have analyzed the case under a different framework than Justice Stewart.]

Mr. Justice WHITE, dissenting.

In *White v. Regester* (1973), this Court unanimously held the use of multimember districts for the election of state legislators in two counties in Texas violated the Equal Protection Clause of the Fourteenth Amendment because, based on a careful assessment of the totality of the circumstances, they were found to exclude Negroes and Mexican-Americans from effective participation in the political processes in the counties. Without questioning the vitality of *White v. Regester* and our other decisions dealing with challenges to multimember districts by racial or ethnic groups, the Court today inexplicably rejects a similar holding based on meticulous factual findings and scrupulous application of the principles of these cases by both the District Court and the Court of Appeals. The Court's decision is flatly inconsistent with *White v. Regester* and it cannot be understood to flow from our recognition in *Washington v. Davis* that the Equal Protection Clause forbids only purposeful discrimination. Both the District Court and the Court of Appeals properly found that an invidious discriminatory purpose could be inferred from the totality of facts in this case. The Court's cryptic rejection of their conclusions ignores the principles

* [Cumulative voting involves using an at-large election but allowing voters to cast more than one vote for a particular candidate. For example, assume an at-large election with three seats up for election and five candidates and where voters can cast three votes. A traditional at-large system would allow the voter to cast a single vote for three candidates. Cumulative voting would allow the voter to cast all three votes for just one candidate if the voter desired to do so. —EDS.]

that an invidious discriminatory purpose can be inferred from objective factors of the kind relied on in *White v. Regester* and that the trial courts are in a special position to make such intensely local appraisals.

I

Prior to our decision in *White v. Regester*, we upheld a number of multimember districting schemes against constitutional challenges, but we consistently recognized that such apportionment schemes could constitute invidious discrimination "where the circumstances of a particular case may operate to minimize or cancel out the voting strength of racial or political elements of the voting population." [*Whitcomb.*]

Relying on this principle, in *White v. Regester* we unanimously upheld a District Court's conclusion that the use of multimember districts in Dallas and Bexar Counties in Texas violated the Equal Protection Clause in the face of findings that they excluded Negroes and Mexican-Americans from effective participation in the political processes.

II

In the instant case the District Court and the Court of Appeals faithfully applied the principles of *White v. Regester* in assessing whether the maintenance of a system of at-large elections for the selection of Mobile City Commissioners denied Mobile Negroes their Fourteenth and Fifteenth Amendment rights. Scrupulously adhering to our admonition that "[t]he plaintiffs' burden is to produce evidence to support findings that the political processes leading to nomination and election were not equally open to participation by the group in question," the District Court conducted a detailed factual inquiry into the openness of the candidate selection process to blacks. The court noted that "Mobile blacks were subjected to massive official and private racial discrimination until the Voting Rights Act of 1965" and that "[t]he pervasive effects of past discrimination still substantially affec[t] black political participation." Although the District Court noted that "[s]ince the Voting Rights Act of 1965, blacks register and vote without hindrance," the court found that "local political processes are not equally open" to blacks. Despite the fact that Negroes constitute more than 35% of the population of Mobile, no Negro has ever been elected to the Mobile City Commission. The plaintiffs introduced extensive evidence of severe racial polarization in voting patterns during the 1960's and 1970's with "white voting for white and black for black if a white is opposed to a black," resulting in the defeat of the black candidate or, if two whites are running, the defeat of the white candidate most identified with blacks. Regression analyses covering every City Commission race in 1965, 1969, and 1973, both the primary and general election of the county commission in 1968 and 1972, selected school board races in 1962, 1966, 1970, 1972, and 1974, city referendums in 1963 and 1973, and a countywide legislative race in 1969 confirmed the existence of severe bloc voting. Nearly every active candidate for public office testified that because of racial polarization "it is highly unlikely that anytime in the foreseeable future, under the at-large system, . . . a black can be elected against a white." After single-member districts were created in Mobile County for state legislative elections, "three blacks of the present fourteen member Mobile County delegation have been elected." Based on the foregoing evidence, the District Court found "that the structure of the at-large election of city commissioners combined with strong racial polarization of Mobile's electorate continues to effectively discourage qualified black citizens from seeking office or being elected thereby denying blacks equal access to the slating or candidate selection process."

The District Court also reviewed extensive evidence that the City Commissioners elected under the at-large system have not been responsive to the needs of the Negro community. The court found that city officials have been unresponsive to the interests of Mobile Negroes in municipal employment, appointments to boards and committees, and the provision of municipal services in part because of "the political fear of a white backlash vote when black citizens' needs are at stake." The court also found that there is no clear-cut state policy preference for at-large elections and that past discrimination affecting the ability of Negroes to register and to vote "has helped preclude the effective participation of blacks in the election system today." The adverse impact of the at-large election system on minorities was found to be enhanced by the large size of the citywide election district, the majority vote requirement, the provision that candidates run for positions by place or number, and the lack of any provision for at-large candidates to run from particular geographical subdistricts.

III

Because I believe that the findings of the District Court amply support an inference of purposeful discrimination in violation of the Fourteenth and Fifteenth Amendments, I respectfully dissent.

Mr. Justice BRENNAN, dissenting.

[Justice Brennan would have held that proof of discriminatory impact was sufficient to prove a constitutional violation. In the alternative, Justice Brennan would have found that plaintiffs had proved discriminatory purpose.]

Mr. Justice MARSHALL, dissenting.

[Justice Marshall would have held that discriminatory impact was enough to prove a constitutional violation. Justice Marshall also agreed that even if Justice Stewart's standard for discriminatory purpose were correct, the plaintiffs had proven a discriminatory purpose.]

Rogers v. Lodge

458 U.S. 613 (1982)

Justice WHITE delivered the opinion of the Court.

The issue in this case is whether the at-large system of elections in Burke County, Ga., violates the Fourteenth Amendment rights of Burke County's black citizens.

I

Burke County is a large, predominately rural county located in eastern Georgia. Eight hundred and thirty-one square miles in area, it is approximately two-thirds the size of the State of Rhode Island. According to the 1980 census, Burke County had a total population of 19,349, of whom 10,385, or 53.6%, were black. The average age of blacks living there is lower than the average age of whites and therefore whites constitute a slight majority of the voting age population. As of 1978, 6,373 persons were registered to vote in Burke County, of whom 38% were black.

The Burke County Board of Commissioners governs the county. It was created in 1911, and consists of five members elected at large to concurrent 4-year terms by all qualified voters in the county. The county has never been divided into districts, either for the purpose of imposing a residency requirement on candidates or for the purpose of requiring candidates to be elected by voters residing in a district. In order to be nominated or elected, a candidate must receive a majority of the votes cast in the primary or general election, and a runoff must be held if no candidate receives a majority in the first primary or general election. Each candidate must run for a specific seat on the Board, and a voter may vote only once for any candidate. No Negro has ever been elected to the Burke County Board of Commissioners.

[The lower courts found that the at-large system was maintained for a discriminatory purpose, and we now affirm.]

II

At-large voting schemes and multimember districts tend to minimize the voting strength of minority groups by permitting the political majority to elect all representatives of the district. A distinct minority, whether it be a racial, ethnic, economic, or political group, may be unable to elect any representatives in an at-large election, yet may be able to elect several representatives if the political unit is divided into single-member districts. The minority's voting power in a multimember district is particularly diluted when bloc voting occurs and ballots are cast along strict majority-minority lines.

Arlington Heights and *Washington v. Davis* both rejected the notion that a law is invalid under the Equal Protection Clause simply because it may affect a greater proportion of one race than another. However, both cases recognized that discriminatory intent need not be proved by direct evidence. "Necessarily, an invidious discriminatory purpose may often be inferred from the totality of the relevant facts, including the fact, if it is true, that the law bears more heavily on one race than another." Thus determining the existence of a discriminatory purpose "demands a sensitive inquiry into such circumstantial and direct evidence of intent as may be available."

[Here, we reject the argument that the lower courts failed to apply the proper legal standard and conclude that the lower courts did apply the discriminatory purpose standard.]

III

A

We are also unconvinced that we should disturb the District Court's finding that the at-large system in Burke County was being maintained for the invidious purpose of diluting the voting strength of the black population.

B

The District Court found that blacks have always made up a substantial majority of the population in Burke County, but that they are a distinct minority of the registered voters. There was also overwhelming evidence of bloc voting along racial lines. Hence, although there had been black candidates, no black had ever been elected to the Burke County Commission. These facts bear heavily on the issue of purposeful discrimination. Voting along racial lines allows those elected to ignore black interests without fear of political consequences, and without bloc voting the minority candidates would not lose elections solely because of their race. Because it is sensible to expect that at least some blacks would have been elected in Burke County, the fact that none have ever been elected is important evidence of purposeful exclusion.

Under our cases, however, such facts are insufficient in themselves to prove purposeful discrimination absent other evidence such as proof that blacks have less opportunity to participate in the political processes and to elect candidates of their choice. Both the District Court and the Court of Appeals thought the supporting proof in this case was sufficient to support an inference of intentional discrimination.

The District Court began by determining the impact of past discrimination on the ability of blacks to participate effectively in the political process. Past discrimination was found to contribute to low black voter registration, because prior to the Voting Rights Act of 1965, blacks had been denied access to the political process by means such as literacy tests, poll taxes, and white primaries. The result was that "Black suffrage in Burke County was virtually non-existent." Black voter registration in Burke County has increased following the Voting Rights Act to the point that some 38% of blacks eligible to vote are registered to do so. On that basis the District Court inferred that "past discrimination has had an adverse effect on black voter registration which lingers to this date." Past discrimination against blacks in education also had the same effect. Not only did Burke County schools discriminate against blacks as recently as 1969, but also some schools still remain essentially segregated and blacks as a group have completed less formal education than whites.

The District Court found further evidence of exclusion from the political process. Past discrimination had prevented blacks from effectively participating in Democratic Party affairs and in primary elections. Until this lawsuit was filed, there had never been a black member of the County Executive Committee of the Democratic Party. There were also property ownership requirements that made it difficult for blacks to serve as chief registrar in the county. There had been discrimination in the selection of grand jurors, the hiring of county employees, and in the appointments to boards and committees which oversee the county government. The District Court thus concluded that historical discrimination had restricted the present opportunity of blacks effectively to participate in the political process. Evidence of historical discrimination is relevant to drawing an inference of purposeful discrimination, particularly in cases such as this one where the evidence shows that discriminatory practices were commonly utilized, that they were abandoned when enjoined by courts or made illegal by civil rights legislation, and that they were replaced by laws and practices which, though neutral on their face, serve to maintain the status quo.

Extensive evidence was cited by the District Court to support its finding that elected officials of Burke County have been unresponsive and insensitive to the needs of the black community, which increases the likelihood that the political process was not equally open to blacks. This evidence ranged from the effects of past discrimination which still haunt the county courthouse to the infrequent appointment of blacks to county boards and committees; the overtly discriminatory pattern of paving county roads; the reluctance of the county to remedy black complaints, which forced blacks to take legal action to obtain school and grand jury desegregation; and the role played by the County Commissioners in the incorporation of an all-white private school to which they donated public funds for the purchase of band uniforms.

The District Court also considered the depressed socio-economic status of Burke County blacks. It found that proportionately more blacks than whites have incomes below the poverty level. Nearly 53% of all black families living in Burke County had incomes equal to or less than three-fourths of a poverty-level income. Not only have blacks completed less formal education than whites, but also the education they have received "was qualitatively inferior to a marked degree." Blacks tend to receive less pay than whites, even for similar work, and they tend to be employed in menial jobs more often than whites. Seventy-three percent of houses occupied by blacks lacked all or some plumbing facilities; only 16% of white-occupied houses suffered the same deficiency. The District Court concluded that the depressed socio-economic status of blacks results in part from "the lingering effects of past discrimination."

Although finding that the state policy behind the at-large electoral system in Burke County was "neutral in origin," the District Court concluded that the policy "has been subverted to invidious purposes." As a practical matter, maintenance of the state statute providing for at-large elections in Burke County is determined by Burke County's state representatives, for the legislature defers to their wishes on matters of purely local application. The court found that Burke County's state representatives "have retained a system which has minimized the ability of Burke County Blacks to participate in the political system."

The trial court considered, in addition, several factors which this Court has indicated enhance the tendency of multimember districts to minimize the voting strength of racial minorities. It found that the sheer geographic size of the county, which is nearly two-thirds the size of Rhode Island, "has made it more difficult for Blacks to get to polling places or to campaign for office." The court concluded, as a matter of law, that the size of the county tends to impair the access of blacks to the political process. The majority vote requirement, was found "to submerge the will of the minority" and thus "deny the minority's access to the system." The court also found the requirement that candidates run for specific seats enhances appellee's lack of access because it prevents a cohesive political group from concentrating on a single candidate. Because Burke County has no residency requirement, "[a]ll candidates could reside in Waynesboro, or in 'lilly-white' [sic] neighborhoods. To that extent, the denial of access becomes enhanced."

None of the District Court's findings underlying its ultimate finding of intentional discrimination appears to us to be clearly erroneous; and as we have said, we decline to overturn the essential finding of the District Court, agreed to by the Court of Appeals, that the at-large system in Burke County has been maintained for the purpose of denying blacks equal access to the political processes in the county.

IV

We also find no reason to overturn the relief ordered by the District Court. Neither the District Court nor the Court of Appeals discerned any special circumstances that would militate against utilizing single-member districts.

The judgment of the Court of Appeals is

Affirmed.

Justice POWELL, with whom Justice REHNQUIST joins, dissenting.

Mobile v. Bolden establishes that an at-large voting system must be upheld against constitutional attack unless maintained for a discriminatory purpose. In *Mobile* we reversed a finding of unconstitutional vote dilution because the lower courts had relied on factors insufficient as a matter of law to establish discriminatory intent. The District Court and Court of Appeals in this case based their findings of unconstitutional discrimination on the same factors held insufficient in *Mobile.* Yet the Court now finds their conclusion unexceptionable. The *Mobile* plurality also affirmed that the concept of "intent" was no mere fiction, and held that the District Court had erred in "its failure to identify the state officials whose intent it considered relevant." Although the courts below did not answer that question in this case, the Court today affirms their decision.

Whatever the wisdom of *Mobile,* the Court's opinion cannot be reconciled persuasively with that case. Because I believe that *Mobile* controls this case, I dissent.

Justice STEVENS, dissenting.

In my opinion, this case raises questions that encompass more than the immediate plight of disadvantaged black citizens. I believe the Court errs by holding the structure of the local governmental unit unconstitutional without identifying an acceptable, judicially manageable standard for adjudicating cases of this kind.

I

The Court's entry into the business of electoral reapportionment in 1962 was preceded by a lengthy and scholarly debate over the role the judiciary legitimately could play in what Justice Frankfurter described as a "political thicket." In [*Colegrove v. Green*], decided in 1946, the Court declined to entertain a challenge to single-member congressional districts in Illinois that had been created in 1901 and had become grossly unequal by reason of the great growth in urban population.

In 1962, the Court changed course. In another challenge to the constitutionality of a 1901 districting statute, it held that the political question doctrine did not foreclose judicial review. That decision represents one of the great landmarks in the history of this Court's jurisprudence.

Two aspects of the Court's opinion in *Baker v. Carr* are of special relevance to the case the Court decides today. First, the Court's scholarly review of the political question doctrine focused on the dominant importance of satisfactory standards for judicial determination. Second, the Court's articulation of the relevant constitutional standard made no reference to subjective intent. The host of cases that have arisen in the wake of *Baker v. Carr* have shared these two characteristics. They have formulated, refined, and applied a judicially manageable standard that has become known as the one-person, one-vote rule; they have attached no significance to the subjective intent of the decisionmakers who adopted or maintained the official rule under attack.

In reviewing the constitutionality of the structure of a local government, two quite different methods of analysis could be employed. The Court might identify the specific features of the government that raise constitutional concerns and decide whether, singly or in combination, they are valid. This is the approach the Court has used in testing the constitutionality of rules conditioning the right to vote on payment of a poll tax, imposing burdens on independent candidates, denying new residents or members of the Armed Forces the right to vote, prohibiting crossovers in party primaries, requiring political candidates to pay filing fees, and disadvantaging minority parties in Presidential elections. In none of these cases did the validity of the electoral procedure turn on whether the legislators who enacted the rule subjectively intended to discriminate against minority voters. Under the approach employed by the Court in those cases, the objective circumstances that led to a declaration that an election procedure was unconstitutional would invalidate a similar law wherever it might be found.

Alternatively, the Court could employ a subjective approach under which the constitutionality of a challenged procedure depends entirely on federal judges' appraisals of the reasons why particular localities have chosen to govern themselves in a particular way. The Constitution would simply protect a right to have an electoral machinery established and maintained without the influence of impermissible factors. Constitutional challenges to identical procedures in neighboring communities could produce totally different results, for the subjective motivations of the legislators who enacted the procedures — or at least the admissible evidence that might be discovered concerning such motivation — could be quite different.

In deciding the question presented in this case, the Court abruptly rejects the former approach and considers only the latter. It starts from the premise that Burke County's at-large method of electing its five county commissioners is, on its face, unobjectionable. The otherwise valid system is unconstitutional, however, because it makes it more difficult for the minority to elect commissioners and because the majority that is now in power has maintained the system for that very reason. Two factors are apparently of critical importance: (1) the intent of the majority to maintain control; and (2) the racial character of the minority.

I am troubled by each aspect of the Court's analysis. In my opinion, the question whether Burke County's at-large system may survive scrutiny under a purely objective analysis is not nearly as easy to answer as the Court implies. Assuming, however, that the system is otherwise valid, I do not believe that the subjective intent of the persons who adopted the system in 1911, or the intent of those who have since declined to change it, can determine its constitutionality. Even if the intent of the political majority were the controlling constitutional consideration, I could not agree that the only political groups that are entitled to protection under the Court's rule are those defined by racial characteristics.

II

At-large voting systems generally tend to maximize the political power of the majority. There are, however, many types of at-large electoral schemes. Three features of Burke County's electoral system are noteworthy, not in my opinion because they shed special light on the subjective intent of certain unidentified people, but rather because they make it especially difficult for a minority candidate to win an election. First, although the qualifications and the duties of the office are identical for all five commissioners, each runs for a separately designated position. Second, in order to be elected, each commissioner must receive a majority of all votes cast in the primary and in the general election; if the leading candidate receives only a plurality, a runoff election must be held. Third, there are no residency requirements; thus, all candidates could reside in a single, all-white neighborhood.

Even if one assumes that a system of local government in which power is concentrated in the hands of a small group of persons elected from the community at large is an acceptable—or perhaps even a preferred—form of municipal government, it is not immediately apparent that these additional features that help to perpetuate the power of an entrenched majority are either desirable or legitimate. If the only purpose these features serve—particularly when viewed in combination—is to assist a dominant party to maintain its political power, they are no more legitimate than the Tennessee districts described in *Baker v. Carr* as "no policy, but simply arbitrary and capricious action." Unless these features are independently justified, they may be invalid simply because there is no legitimate justification for their impact on minority participation in elections.

In this case, appellees have not argued—presumably because they assumed that this Court's many references to the requirement of proving an improper motive in equal protection cases are controlling in this new context—that the special features of Burke County's at-large system have such an adverse impact on the minority's opportunity to participate in the political process that this type of government deprives the minority of equal protection of the law. Nor have the appellants sought to identify legitimate local policies that might justify the use of such rules. As a result, this record does not provide an adequate basis for determining the validity of Burke County's governmental structure on the basis of traditional objective standards.

If the governmental structure were itself found to lack a legitimate justification, inquiry into subjective intent would clearly be unnecessary. Under the Court's analysis, however, the characteristics of the particular form of government under attack are virtually irrelevant. Not only would the Court's approach uphold an arbitrary—but not invidious—system that lacked independent justification, it would invalidate—if a discriminatory intent were proved—a local rule that would be perfectly acceptable absent a showing of invidious intent. The Court's standard applies not only to Burke County and to multimember districts, but to any other form of government as well.

III

Ever since I joined the Court, I have been concerned about the Court's emphasis on subjective intent as a criterion for constitutional adjudication. Although that criterion is often regarded as a restraint on the exercise of judicial power, it may in fact provide judges with a tool for exercising power that otherwise would be confined to the legislature. My principal concern with the subjective-intent standard, however, is unrelated to the quantum of power it confers upon the judiciary. It is based on the quality of that power. For in the long run constitutional adjudication that is premised on a case-by-case appraisal of the subjective intent of local decisionmakers cannot possibly satisfy the requirement of impartial administration of the law that is embodied in the Equal Protection Clause of the Fourteenth Amendment.

The costs and the doubts associated with litigating questions of motive, which are often significant in routine trials, will be especially so in cases involving the "motives" of legislative bodies. Often there will be no evidence that the governmental system was adopted for a discriminatory reason. The reform movement in municipal government or an attempt to comply with the strictures of *Reynolds v. Sims*, may account for the enactment of countless at-large systems. In such a case the question becomes whether the system was maintained for a discriminatory purpose. Whose intentions control? Obviously not the voters, although they may be most responsible for the attitudes and actions of local government. Assuming that it is the intentions of the "state actors" that is critical, how will their mental processes be discovered? Must a specific proposal for change be defeated? What if different motives are held by different legislators or, indeed, by a single official? Is a selfish desire to stay in office sufficient to justify a failure to change a governmental system?

The Court avoids these problems by failing to answer the very question that its standard asks. Presumably, according to the Court's analysis, the Burke County governmental structure is unconstitutional because it was maintained at some point for an invidious purpose. Yet the Court scarcely identifies the manner in which changes to a county governmental structure are made. There is no reference to any unsuccessful attempt to replace the at-large system with single-member districts. It is incongruous that subjective intent is identified as the constitutional standard and yet the persons who allegedly harbored an improper intent are never identified or mentioned. Undoubtedly, the evidence relied on by the Court proves that racial prejudice has played an important role in the history of Burke County and has motivated many wrongful acts by various community leaders. But unless that evidence is sufficient to prove that every governmental action was motivated by a racial animus—and may be remedied by a federal court—the Court has failed under its own test to demonstrate that the governmental structure of Burke County was maintained for a discriminatory purpose.

Moreover, in my opinion the Court is incorrect in assuming that the intent of elected officials is invidious when they are motivated by a desire to retain control of the local political machinery. For such an intent is surely characteristic of politicians throughout the country. But if a political majority's intent to maintain control of a legitimate local government is sufficient to invalidate any electoral device that makes it more difficult for a minority group to elect candidates—regardless of the nature of the interest that gives the minority group cohesion—the Court is not just entering a "political thicket"; it is entering a vast wonderland of judicial review of political activity.

IV

I respectfully dissent.

NOTES ON *BOLDEN* AND *ROGERS*

1. As previously noted, in *White v. Regester*, 412 U.S. 755 (1973), the Court found vote dilution in the context of a challenge to the election of state legislators in two regions of Texas—Dallas and Bexar Counties (Bexar County encompasses San Antonio). In that case, the Court looked at a panoply of factors to conclude that minority vote dilution had occurred.

Justice White's dissent in *Bolden* criticizes Justice Stewart's plurality opinion for abandoning the approach the Court had previously taken in *White v. Regester*. In *Bolden*, both Justice Stewart and Justice White are applying the same legal standard—a standard of discriminatory purpose. What is the difference in the application of those standards in their opinions?

2. The approach by Justice Stewart in *Bolden* was highly criticized. In 1982, Congress amended Section 2 of the Voting Rights Act. Under amended Section 2, a court should find vote dilution whenever there are discriminatory "results."

3. Since passage of amended Section 2, most of the action in redistricting litigation related to vote dilution has been resolved under the statutory framework of the Voting Rights Act rather than the Equal Protection Clause. (The next two cases in this book involve vote dilution claims under Section 2 of the Voting Rights Act.) The fact that most litigation has been resolved under Section 2 does not, however, mean that vote dilution under the Equal Protection Clause has no modern relevance. Plaintiffs still routinely assert constitutional claims of vote dilution in their complaints and, as you will see when you read about Sections 5 and 3(c) of the Voting Rights Act in the next section of this casebook, discriminatory purpose under the Constitution still has a role to play in vote dilution cases. Indeed, in *Abbott v. Perez*, 585 U.S. ___ (2018), the Supreme Court reversed a district court finding that redistricting plans developed by Texas following the 2010 Census had been adopted with an unconstitutional discriminatory purpose.

4. *Rogers* is interesting because as Justice Powell notes, *Rogers* seems to be directly contrary to the plurality opinion in *Bolden* even though it does not overrule

Bolden. Which approach is best—Justice Stewart's in *Bolden*, Justice White's in both cases, or Justice Stevens's opinion in *Rogers* that searches for a standard not tethered to discriminatory purpose? Does the Court's ping-pong fluctuation from *White v. Regester* to *City of Mobile v. Bolden* to *Rogers v. Lodge*—where similar facts lead to dissimilar results—do a good job of bolstering Justice Stevens's contention that discriminatory purpose is not a judicially manageable standard?

* * *

As you just read, in *City of Mobile v. Bolden*, a plurality of the Supreme Court held that Section 2 of the Voting Rights Act as originally passed in 1965 could be used only to strike down laws involving individual electoral participation (i.e., laws aimed directly at voter registration and casting ballots at polling places) that were adopted with a purpose to discriminate. Congress reacted to *Bolden* by amending Section 2 to allow challenges to electoral structures that have discriminatory "results." As you will see in *Holder v. Hall*, though, Justice Clarence Thomas disputes that the amendment of Section 2 allows plaintiffs to successfully attack electoral structures such as at-large elections and redistricting plans.

Even if one disagrees with Justice Thomas's assessment as to whether the amendment of Section 2 was intended to allow for attacks on electoral structures, it is safe to say that Congress did not provide much clarity on what it intended the "results" test to mean. Instead, what essentially happened was that Congress passed an amendment and then left it to the federal courts to make sense of the "results" test.

The Supreme Court's first engagement in a substantial interpretation of what the "results" test meant came in *Thornburg v. Gingles*, 478 U.S. 30 (1986). In *Gingles*, minority plaintiffs attacked the North Carolina state legislature's use of multimember districts. While no one full opinion could garner five votes, Justice William Brennan's opinion did receive a majority for the basic sketch of how the courts should implement the "results" test. In essence, courts are to ensure that plaintiffs challenging an electoral structure prove what have come to be known as the three *Gingles* preconditions and then prove that under the "totality of the circumstances" the electoral structure is discriminatory in "results." As you read the next cases, make sure to note what the three *Gingles* preconditions are and what factors the courts use when assessing the totality of the circumstances.

In the years that immediately followed the *Gingles* decision, many of the challenges brought by plaintiffs resembled the challenges the Supreme Court had heard under the Equal Protection Clause in *White v. Regester* (1973), *City of Mobile v. Bolden* (1980), and *Rogers v. Lodge* (1983). Plaintiffs were often attacking at-large or multimember electoral structures in areas that had, among other things, racially polarized voting, a long history of discrimination, and where African-American or Latino candidates had rarely, if ever, been elected. Under these circumstances, courts often found violations of Section 2 or the jurisdictions (such as counties, cities, and school districts) settled cases with consent decrees that switched from at-large or multimember districts to single-member districts, some of which were designed to allow minority voters to control the outcomes of elections.

In the early 1990s, however, the focus began to turn away from Section 2 lawsuits involving at-large and multimember election systems; instead, plaintiffs used

Section 2 to challenge single-member districting plans. The next two cases involve redistricting claims arising under Section 2—one about statewide maps, the other about local districts. Be sure to note the test the Court employs and the most important factors in applying that test.

As you read, it will be helpful to your understanding of these decisions to have knowledge of two different redistricting techniques that can be used to diminish the political influence of a cohesive group of voters: "packing" and "cracking" (which is also known as "fragmenting"). Basically, a cohesive group is "packed" when its members are overwhelmingly placed in one district, thereby diminishing the ability of that group to have electoral power in additional districts. In contrast, a group is "cracked" (or "fragmented") when its members are divided among multiple districts so that the group cannot elect a candidate in any one single district.

It will also be helpful to your understanding of Section 2 doctrine to be familiar with four different types of districts that are discussed in redistricting cases involving minority voters:

- "Majority-minority" or "safe" districts are districts in which "a minority group composes a numerical, working majority of the voting-age population."
- "Crossover" districts are districts in which "minority voters make up less than a majority of the voting-age population . . . [but where the minority population], at least potentially, is large enough to elect the candidate of its choice with help from voters who are members of the majority and who cross over to support the minority's preferred candidate."
- "Coalition" districts are districts in which "two minority groups [e.g., African Americans and Latinos] form a coalition to elect the candidate of the coalition's choice."
- "Influence" districts are districts in which "a minority group can influence the outcome of an election even if its preferred candidate cannot be elected."

Bartlett v. Strickland, 556 U.S. 1, 13 (2009).

Johnson v. De Grandy

512 U.S. 998 (1994)

Justice Souter delivered the opinion of the Court.

[This case is] about the meaning of vote dilution and the facts required to show it, when § 2 of the Voting Rights Act of 1965 is applied to challenges to single-member legislative districts. We hold that no violation of § 2 can be found here, where, in spite of continuing discrimination and racial bloc voting, minority voters form effective voting majorities in a number of districts roughly proportional to the minority voters' respective shares in the voting-age population. While such proportionality is not dispositive in a challenge to single-member districting, it is a relevant fact in the totality of circumstances to be analyzed when determining whether members of a minority group have less opportunity than other members of the electorate to participate in the political process and to elect representatives of their choice.

I

On the first day of Florida's 1992 legislative session, a group of Hispanic voters including Miguel De Grandy (De Grandy plaintiffs) [filed a complaint alleging] that the districts from which Florida voters had chosen their state representatives since 1982 were malapportioned, failing to reflect changes in the State's population during the ensuing decade.

Several months after the first complaint was filed, on April 10, 1992, the state legislature adopted Senate Joint Resolution 2-G (SJR 2-G), providing the reapportionment plan currently at issue. The plan called for dividing Florida into 120 single-member House districts based on population data from the 1990 census.

The De Grandy plaintiffs responded to SJR 2-G by amending their federal complaints to charge the new reapportionment plan with violating § 2. They claimed that SJR 2-G "unlawfully fragments cohesive minority communities and otherwise impermissibly submerges their right to vote and to participate in the electoral process," and they pointed to areas around the State where Hispanic populations could have formed a voting majority in a politically cohesive, reasonably compact district (or in more than one), if SJR 2-G had not fragmented [Hispanic populations] among several districts or packed it into just a few.

At the end of the hearing, on July 1, 1992, the District Court ruled from the bench. It held the plan's provisions for state House districts to be in violation of § 2 because "more than [SJR 2-G's] nine Hispanic districts may be drawn without having or creating a regressive effect upon black voters," and it imposed a remedial plan offered by the De Grandy plaintiffs calling for 11 majority-Hispanic House districts.

In a later, expanded opinion the court reviewed the totality of circumstances as required by § 2 and *Thornburg v. Gingles*. In explaining Dade County's "tripartite politics," in which "ethnic factors . . . predominate over all other[s]," the court found political cohesion within each of the Hispanic and black populations but none between the two, and a tendency of non-Hispanic whites to vote as a bloc to bar minority groups from electing their chosen candidates except in a district where a given minority makes up a voting majority.[6] The court further found that the nearly one million Hispanics in the Dade County area could be combined into 11 House districts, each one relatively compact and with a functional majority of Hispanic voters, whereas SJR 2-G created fewer majority-Hispanic districts. Noting that Florida's [Hispanic population] bore the social, economic, and political effects of past discrimination, the court concluded that SJR 2-G impermissibly diluted the voting strength of Hispanics in its House districts.

II

[Omitted.]

6. The Court recognizes that the terms "black," "Hispanic," and "white" are neither mutually exclusive nor collectively exhaustive. We follow the practice of the District Court in using them as rough indicators of south Florida's three largest racial and linguistic minority groups.

III

On the merits of the vote dilution claims covering the House districts, the crux of the State's argument is the power of Hispanics under SJR 2-G to elect candidates of their choice in a number of districts that mirrors their share of the Dade County area's voting-age population (*i.e.*, 9 out of 20 House districts); this power, according to the State, bars any finding that the plan dilutes Hispanic voting strength. The District Court is said to have missed that conclusion by mistaking our precedents to require the plan to maximize the number of Hispanic-controlled districts.

The State's argument takes us back to ground covered last Term in two cases challenging single-member districts. *See Voinovich v. Quilter*; *Growe v. Emison*. In *Growe*, we held that a claim of vote dilution in a single-member district requires proof meeting the same three threshold conditions for a dilution challenge to a multimember district: that a minority group be "sufficiently large and geographically compact to constitute a majority in a single-member district"; that it be "politically cohesive"; and that "the white majority vot[e] sufficiently as a bloc to enable it . . . usually to defeat the minority's preferred candidate." (quoting *Thornburg v. Gingles*). Of course, as we reflected in *Voinovich* and amplify later in this opinion, "the *Gingles* factors cannot be applied mechanically and without regard to the nature of the claim."

In *Voinovich* we explained how manipulation of district lines can dilute the voting strength of politically cohesive minority group members, whether by fragmenting the minority voters among several districts where a bloc-voting majority can routinely outvote them, or by packing them into one or a small number of districts to minimize their influence in the districts next door. Section 2 prohibits either sort of line-drawing where its result, "interact[ing] with social and historical conditions, impairs the ability of a protected class to elect its candidate of choice on an equal basis with other voters."

A

[Omitted.]

B

The District Court found that the three *Gingles* preconditions were satisfied, and that Hispanics had suffered historically from official discrimination, the social, economic, and political effects of which they generally continued to feel. Without more, and on the apparent assumption that what could have been done to create additional Hispanic supermajority districts should have been done, the District Court found a violation of § 2. But the assumption was erroneous, and more is required, as a review of *Gingles* will show.

1

Thornburg v. Gingles prompted this Court's first reading of § 2 of the Voting Rights Act of 1965 after its 1982 amendment.[8] Section 2(a) of the amended Act

8. Congress amended the statute to reach cases in which discriminatory intent is not identified, adding new language designed to codify *White v. Regester* 412 U.S. 755 (1973).

prohibits any "standard, practice, or procedure . . . which results in a denial or abridgement of the right of any citizen of the United States to vote on account of race or color [or membership in a language minority group]. . . ." Section 2(b) provides that a denial or abridgment occurs where,

> "based on the totality of circumstances, it is shown that the political processes leading to nomination or election in the State or political subdivision are not equally open to participation by members of a class of citizens protected by subsection (a) of this section in that its members have less opportunity than other members of the electorate to participate in the political process and to elect representatives of their choice. The extent to which members of a protected class have been elected to office in the State or political subdivision is one circumstance which may be considered: *Provided,* That nothing in this section establishes a right to have members of a protected class elected in numbers equal to their proportion in the population." 42 U.S.C. §1973(b).

Gingles provided some structure to the statute's "totality of circumstances" test in a case challenging multimember legislative districts. The Court listed the factors put forward as relevant in the Senate Report treating the 1982 amendments,[9] and held that

> "[w]hile many or all of [them] may be relevant to a claim of vote dilution through submergence in multimember districts, unless there is a conjunction of the following circumstances, the use of multimember districts generally will not impede the ability of minority voters to elect representatives of their choice. Stated succinctly, a bloc voting majority must *usually* be able to defeat candidates supported by a politically cohesive, geographically insular minority group."

The Court thus summarized the three now-familiar *Gingles* factors (compactness/numerousness, minority cohesion or bloc voting, and majority bloc voting) as "necessary preconditions" for establishing vote dilution by use of a multimember district.

9. As summarized in *Gingles*: [T]he Senate Report specifies factors which typically may be relevant to a §2 claim: the history of voting-related discrimination in the State or political subdivision; the extent to which voting in the elections of the State or political subdivision is racially polarized; the extent to which the State or political subdivision has used voting practices or procedures that tend to enhance the opportunity for discrimination against the minority group, such as unusually large election districts, majority vote requirements, and prohibitions against bullet voting; the exclusion of members of the minority group from candidate slating processes; the extent to which minority group members bear the effects of past discrimination in areas such as education, employment, and health which hinder their ability to participate effectively in the political process; the use of overt or subtle racial appeals in political campaigns; and the extent to which members of the minority group have been elected to public office in the jurisdiction. The Report also notes that evidence demonstrating that elected officials are unresponsive to the particularized needs of the minority group and that the policy underlying the State's or the political subdivision's use of the contested practice or structure is tenuous may have probative value.

But if *Gingles* so clearly identified the three as generally necessary to prove a § 2 claim, it just as clearly declined to hold them sufficient in combination, either in the sense that a court's examination of relevant circumstances was complete once the three factors were found to exist, or in the sense that the three in combination necessarily and in all circumstances demonstrated dilution. This was true not only because bloc voting was a matter of degree, with a variable legal significance depending on other facts, but also because the ultimate conclusions about equality or inequality of opportunity were intended by Congress to be judgments resting on comprehensive, not limited, canvassing of relevant facts. Lack of electoral success is evidence of vote dilution, but courts must also examine other evidence in the totality of circumstances, including the extent of the opportunities minority voters enjoy to participate in the political processes.

2

If the three *Gingles* factors may not be isolated as sufficient, standing alone, to prove dilution in every multimember district challenge, *a fortiori* they must not be when the challenge goes to a series of single-member districts, where dilution may be more difficult to grasp. Plaintiffs challenging single-member districts may claim, not total submergence, but partial submergence; not the chance for some electoral success in place of none, but the chance for more success in place of some. When the question thus comes down to the reasonableness of drawing a series of district lines in one combination of places rather than another, judgments about inequality may become closer calls. As facts beyond the ambit of the three *Gingles* factors loom correspondingly larger, fact finders cannot rest uncritically on assumptions about the force of the *Gingles* factors in pointing to dilution.

The cases now before us, of course, fall on this more complex side of the divide, requiring a court to determine whether provision for somewhat fewer majority-minority districts than the number sought by the plaintiffs was dilution of the minority votes. The District Court was accordingly required to assess the probative significance of the *Gingles* factors critically after considering the further circumstances with arguable bearing on the issue of equal political opportunity. We think that in finding dilution here the District Court misjudged the relative importance of the *Gingles* factors and of historical discrimination, measured against evidence tending to show that in spite of these facts, SJR 2-G would provide minority voters with an equal measure of political and electoral opportunity.

The District Court did not, to be sure, commit the error of treating the three *Gingles* conditions as exhausting the enquiry required by § 2. Consistently with *Gingles,* the court received evidence of racial relations outside the immediate confines of voting behavior and found a history of discrimination against Hispanic voters continuing in society generally to the present day. But the District Court was not critical enough in asking whether a history of persistent discrimination reflected in the larger society and its bloc-voting behavior portended any dilutive effect from a newly proposed districting scheme, whose pertinent features were majority-minority districts in substantial proportion to the minority's share of voting-age population. The court failed to ask whether the totality of facts, including those pointing to proportionality,[11] showed that the new scheme would deny minority voters equal political opportunity.

Treating equal political opportunity as the focus of the enquiry, we do not see how these district lines, apparently providing political effectiveness in proportion to voting-age numbers, deny equal political opportunity. The record establishes that Hispanics constitute 50 percent of the voting-age population in Dade County and under SJR 2-G would make up supermajorities in 9 of the 18 House districts located primarily within the county. Likewise, if one considers the 20 House districts located at least in part within Dade County, the record indicates that Hispanics would be an effective voting majority in 45 percent of them (*i.e.*, nine), and would constitute 47 percent of the voting-age population in the area. In other words, under SJR 2-G Hispanics in the Dade County area would enjoy substantial proportionality. On this evidence, we think the State's scheme would thwart the historical tendency to exclude Hispanics, not encourage or perpetuate it. Thus in spite of that history and its legacy, including the racial cleavages that characterize Dade County politics today, we see no grounds for holding in these cases that SJR 2-G's district lines diluted the votes cast by Hispanic voters.

The De Grandy plaintiffs urge us to put more weight on the District Court's findings of packing and fragmentation, allegedly accomplished by the way the State drew certain specific lines: "[T]he line of District 116 separates heavily Hispanic neighborhoods in District 112 from the rest of the heavily Hispanic Kendall Lakes area and the Kendall area," so that the line divides "neighbors making up the same housing development in Kendall Lakes," and District 114 "packs" Hispanic voters, while Districts 102 and 109 "fragmen[t]" them. We would agree that where a State has split (or lumped) minority neighborhoods that would have been grouped into a single district (or spread among several) if the State had employed the same line-drawing standards in minority neighborhoods as it used elsewhere in the jurisdiction, the inconsistent treatment might be significant evidence of a § 2 violation, even in the face of proportionality. The district court, however, made no such finding. Indeed, the propositions the Court recites on this point are not even phrased as factual findings, but merely as recitations of testimony offered by plaintiffs' expert witness. While the District Court may well have credited the testimony, the court was apparently wary of adopting the witness's conclusions as findings. But even if one imputed a greater significance to the accounts of testimony, they would boil down to findings that several of SJR 2-G's district lines separate portions of Hispanic neighborhoods, while another district line draws several Hispanic neighborhoods into a single district. This, however, would be to say only that lines could have been drawn elsewhere, nothing more. But some dividing by district lines and

11. "Proportionality" as the term is used here links the number of majority-minority voting districts to minority members' share of the relevant population. The concept is distinct from the subject of the proportional representation clause of § 2, which provides that "nothing in this section establishes a right to have members of a protected class elected in numbers equal to their proportion in the population." 42 U.S.C. § 1973(b). This proviso speaks to the success of minority candidates, as distinct from the political or electoral power of minority voters. And the proviso also confirms what is otherwise clear from the text of the statute, namely, that the ultimate right of § 2 is equality of opportunity, not a guarantee of electoral success for minority-preferred candidates of whatever race.

combining within them is virtually inevitable and befalls any population group of substantial size. Attaching the labels "packing" and "fragmenting" to these phenomena, without more, does not make the result vote dilution when the minority group enjoys substantial proportionality.

3

It may be that the significance of the facts under § 2 was obscured by the rule of thumb apparently adopted by the District Court, that anything short of the maximum number of majority-minority districts consistent with the *Gingles* conditions would violate § 2, at least where societal discrimination against the minority had occurred and continued to occur. But reading the first *Gingles* condition in effect to define dilution as a failure to maximize in the face of bloc voting (plus some other incidents of societal bias to be expected where bloc voting occurs) causes its own dangers, and they are not to be courted.

Assume a hypothetical jurisdiction of 1,000 voters divided into 10 districts of 100 each, where members of a minority group make up 40 percent of the voting population and voting is totally polarized along racial lines. With the right geographic dispersion to satisfy the compactness requirement, and with careful manipulation of district lines, the minority voters might be placed in control of as many as 7 of the 10 districts. Each such district could be drawn with at least 51 members of the minority group, and whether the remaining minority voters were added to the groupings of 51 for safety or scattered in the other three districts, minority voters would be able to elect candidates of their choice in all seven districts.[12] The point of the hypothetical is not, of course, that any given district is likely to be open to such extreme manipulation, or that bare majorities are likely to vote in full force and strictly along racial lines, but that reading § 2 to define dilution as any failure to maximize tends to obscure the very object of the statute and to run counter to its textually stated purpose. One may suspect vote dilution from political famine, but one is not entitled to suspect (much less infer) dilution from mere failure to guarantee a political feast. However prejudiced a society might be, it would be absurd to suggest that the failure of a districting scheme to provide a minority group with effective political power 75 percent above its numerical strength[13] indicates a denial of equal participation in the political process. Failure to maximize cannot be the measure of § 2.

4

While, for obvious reasons, the State agrees that a failure to leverage minority political strength to the maximum possible point of power is not definitive of dilution in bloc-voting societies, it seeks to impart a measure of determinacy by applying a definitive rule of its own: that as a matter of law no dilution occurs whenever the percentage of single-member districts in which minority voters form an effective

12. Minority voters might instead be denied control over a single seat, of course. Each district would need to include merely 51 members of the majority group; minority voters fragmented among the 10 districts could be denied power to affect the result in any district.

13. When 40 percent of the population determines electoral outcomes in 7 out of 10 districts, the minority group can be said to enjoy effective political power 75 percent above its numerical strength.

majority mirrors the minority voters' percentage of the relevant population.[14] Proportionality so defined would thus be a safe harbor for any districting scheme.

The safety would be in derogation of the statutory text and its considered purpose, however, and of the ideal that the Voting Rights Act of 1965 attempts to foster. An inflexible rule would run counter to the textual command of § 2, that the presence or absence of a violation be assessed "based on the totality of circumstances." The need for such "totality" review springs from the demonstrated ingenuity of state and local governments in hobbling minority voting power. In a substantial number of voting jurisdictions, that past reality has included such reprehensible practices as ballot box stuffing, outright violence, discretionary registration, property requirements, the poll tax, and the white primary; and other practices censurable when the object of their use is discriminatory, such as at-large elections, runoff requirements, anti-single-shot devices, gerrymandering, the impeachment of office-holders, the annexation or deannexation of territory, and the creation or elimination of elective offices. Some of those expedients could occur even in a jurisdiction with numerically demonstrable proportionality; the harbor safe for States would thus not be safe for voters. It is, in short, for good reason that we have been, and remain, chary of entertaining a simplification of the sort the State now urges upon us.

Even if the State's safe harbor were open only in cases of alleged dilution by the manipulation of district lines, however, it would rest on an unexplored premise of highly suspect validity: that in any given voting jurisdiction (or portion of that jurisdiction under consideration), the rights of some minority voters under § 2 may be traded off against the rights of other members of the same minority class. Under the State's view, the most blatant racial gerrymandering in half of a county's single-member districts would be irrelevant under § 2 if offset by political gerrymandering in the other half, so long as proportionality was the bottom line.

Finally, we reject the safe harbor rule because of a tendency the State would itself certainly condemn, a tendency to promote and perpetuate efforts to devise majority-minority districts even in circumstances where they may not be necessary to achieve equal political and electoral opportunity. Because in its simplest form the State's rule would shield from § 2 challenge a districting scheme in which the number of majority-minority districts reflected the minority's share of the relevant population, the conclusiveness of the rule might be an irresistible inducement to create such districts. It bears recalling, however, that for all the virtues of majority-minority districts as remedial devices, they rely on a quintessentially race-conscious calculus aptly described [by some commentators] as the "politics of second best". . . . If the lesson of *Gingles* is that society's racial and ethnic cleavages sometimes necessitate majority-minority districts to ensure equal political and electoral opportunity, that

14. The parties dispute whether the relevant figure is the minority group's share of the population, or of some subset of the population, such as those who are eligible to vote, in that they are United States citizens, over 18 years of age, and not registered at another address (as students and members of the military often are). Because we do not elevate this proportion to the status of a magic parameter, and because it is not dispositive here, we do not resolve that dispute.

should not obscure the fact that there are communities in which minority citizens are able to form coalitions with voters from other racial and ethnic groups, having no need to be a majority within a single district in order to elect candidates of their choice. Those candidates may not represent perfection to every minority voter, but minority voters are not immune from the obligation to pull, haul, and trade to find common political ground, the virtue of which is not to be slighted in applying a statute meant to hasten the waning of racism in American politics.

It is enough to say that, while proportionality in the sense used here is obviously an indication that minority voters have an equal opportunity, in spite of racial polarization, "to participate in the political process and to elect representatives of their choice," 42 U.S.C. § 1973(b), the degree of probative value assigned to proportionality may vary with other facts. No single statistic provides courts with a shortcut to determine whether a set of single-member districts unlawfully dilutes minority voting strength.

5

While the United States concedes the relevance of proportionality to a § 2 claim, it would confine proportionality to an affirmative defense, and one to be made only on a statewide basis in cases that challenge districts for electing a body with statewide jurisdiction. In this litigation, the United States would have us treat any claim that evidence of proportionality supports the State's plan as having been waived because the State made no argument in the District Court that the proportion of districts statewide in which Hispanics constitute an effective voting majority mirrors the proportion of statewide Hispanic population.

The argument has two flaws. . . . There is, first, no textual reason to segregate some circumstances from the statutory totality, to be rendered insignificant unless the defendant pleads them by way of affirmative defense. Second, and just as importantly, the argument would recast these cases as they come to us, in order to bar consideration of proportionality except on statewide scope, whereas up until now the dilution claims have been litigated on a smaller geographical scale. It is, indeed, the plaintiffs themselves, including the United States, who passed up the opportunity to frame their dilution claim in statewide terms. While the United States points to language in its complaint alleging that the redistricting plans dilute the votes of "Hispanic citizens in the State of Florida," the complaint identifies "several areas of the State" where such violations of § 2 are said to occur, and then speaks in terms of Hispanics in the Dade County area. Nowhere do the allegations indicate that claims of dilution "in the State of Florida" are not to be considered in terms of the areas specifically mentioned. The complaint alleges no facts at all about the contours, demographics, or voting patterns of any districts outside the Dade County area[], and neither the evidence at trial nor the opinion of the District Court addressed white bloc voting and political cohesion of minorities statewide. The De Grandy plaintiffs even voluntarily dismissed their claims of Hispanic vote dilution outside the Dade County area. Thus we have no occasion to decide which frame of reference should have been used if the parties had not apparently agreed in the District Court on the appropriate geographical scope for analyzing the alleged § 2 violation and devising its remedy.

6

In sum, the District Court's finding of dilution did not address the statutory standard of unequal political and electoral opportunity, and reflected instead a misconstruction of § 2 that equated dilution with failure to maximize the number of reasonably compact majority-minority districts. Because the ultimate finding of dilution in districting for the Florida House was based on a misreading of the governing law, we hold it to be clearly erroneous.

Justice O'CONNOR, concurring.
[Omitted.]

Justice KENNEDY, concurring in part and concurring in the judgment.
[Omitted.]

Justice THOMAS, with whom Justice SCALIA joins, dissenting.
[Omitted.]

NOTES ON *DE GRANDY* AND SECTION 2 OF THE VOTING RIGHTS ACT

1. Section 2 of the Voting Rights Act creates a "results" test for vote dilution. However, the Court has struggled to define the contours of the results test.

2. In *Thornburg v. Gingles* (1986), Justice Brennan's plurality opinion created the basic framework that courts still use today. Courts first decide whether the three *Gingles* preconditions are met. Those preconditions are: (1) a minority group must be sufficiently large and geographically compact to comprise a majority of the district; (2) the minority group must be politically cohesive (it must demonstrate a pattern of voting for the same candidates); and (3) white voters must vote sufficiently as a bloc to usually defeat the minority group's preferred candidate. If the plaintiff can establish these three pre-conditions when challenging a redistricting plan, then the courts move to a "totality of the circumstances" test. *Gingles* said courts could use the so-called "Senate Factors" (mentioned in footnote 9 of *De Grandy*) as a guide in the totality of circumstances analysis.

3. Does the first *Gingles* analysis require that a minority group be at least 50 percent in a hypothetical single-member district, or can it have less than a numerical majority but still elect a candidate of its choice with "crossover" votes from white voters? In *Bartlett v. Strickland* (2009), the Court held that "crossover" districts do not satisfy the first *Gingles* precondition. Therefore, to establish a § 2 violation, a plaintiff must show that the minority group would actually be a majority in a single-member district without support from white voters. Does this result make sense? Why not allow minority voters to rely on crossover white voters to establish that they could comprise a majority of the district and thereby elect candidates of their choice?

4. What does *De Grandy* add to the "results" test analysis? Note the use of "proportionality." How does the Court define "proportionality," and how does that differ from proportional representation? Is proportionality even the right factor to consider?

5. The *Gingles* preconditions and use of the "Senate Factors" were designed at a time when multi-member and at-large districts were perceived as the main

barrier to minority electoral success. Should the Court have created a new test for the single-member district context? Does *De Grandy* implicitly create a three-step test (*Gingles* preconditions, Senate factors, proportionality)? If so, is such a test judicially manageable?

A NOTE ON *LEAGUE OF UNITED AMERICAN CITIZENS v. PERRY*, 548 U.S. 399 (2006)

League of United Latin American Citizens v. Perry (commonly known as *LULAC*) concerned the 2003 redistricting of Texas's congressional delegation. The case had an extremely complicated set of multiple appeals and involved multiple different claims, such as partisan gerrymandering and racial gerrymandering (topics that we will take up in a little bit). For current purposes in our consideration of Section 2 of the Voting Rights Act, we will focus on the aspect of the case involving the results standard with regard to Latino voters in south and west Texas.

The most significant changes in the 2003 redistricting occurred to District 23 and District 25. In essence, the 2003 redistricting plan was designed to protect a Latino, Republican incumbent who represented District 23 and who appeared to be on the verge of being ousted. *Id.* at 423-25. Before the redistricting, District 23 had a Latino citizen voting-age population of 57.5 percent, but the Republican incumbent had only captured 8 percent of the Latino vote and 51.5 percent of the overall vote at the most recent election in 2002. *Id.* at 423-34. In the existing plan, Webb County and the City of Laredo—an overwhelmingly Latino area—were entirely situated within District 23. *Id.* at 424. The 2003 redistricting plan divided this area, shifting 100,000 people into a neighboring district, and replaced that population with voters from counties in a largely Anglo, Republican area in central Texas. *Id.* at 424. The newly drawn District 23 had a Latino *citizen* voting-age population of 46% although the Latino share of the voting age population was just over 50 percent. *Id.* at 424.

Because the changes to District 23 may have led to a violation of another provision of the Voting Rights Act known as Section 5 (which we will discuss as our next topic), the map drawers decided to create District 25. *Id.* at 424-25. District 25 was a long, narrow strip that winded its way for about 300 miles from the Mexican border to Austin with three-quarters of the district's population residing either at the northern end or the southern end of the district. *Id.* at 424. (You could think of the population distribution of the district as looking like something of a dumbbell.) District 25 was 55 percent Latino in terms of citizen voting-age population but the Latino population was mostly divided between the north and south ends of the district, and the Court noted that the Latino communities at the opposite ends of District 25 had divergent needs and interests, owing to differences in socio-economic status, education, employment, health, and other characteristics. *Id.* at 424.

As Justice Kennedy wrote in his opinion:

> The District Court summed up the purposes underlying the redistricting in south and west Texas: "The change to Congressional District 23 served the dual goal of increasing Republican seats in general and protecting

> Bonilla's incumbency in particular, with the additional political nuance that Bonilla would be reelected in a district that had a majority of Latino voting age population—although clearly not a majority of citizen voting age population and certainly not an effective voting majority." The goal in creating District 25 was just as clear: "[t]o avoid retrogression under §5" of the Voting Rights Act given the reduced Latino voting strength in District 23.

Id. at 424-25.

Justice Kennedy's opinion finding a violation of Section 2 carried the day for a majority of the Court. In deciding a Section 2 violation had occurred, Justice Kennedy first found the existence of the *Gingles* preconditions in the area surrounding District 23. He noted that even though the previous District 23 had not yet been a district where Latino voters could elect a candidate of choice, District 23 was a Latino opportunity district because of "the increase in Latino voter registration and overall population, the concomitant rise of Latino voting power in each successive election, the near-victory of the Latino candidate of choice in 2002, and the resulting threat to the [Republican] incumbency." *Id.* at 428 (citations omitted).

Justice Kennedy rejected the State's argument that by creating District 25 as a Latino opportunity district, it had met its obligations under Section 2. In doing so, he made several points:

- That the State could use one majority-minority district to "compensate for the absence of another only when the racial group in each area had a § 2 right and both could not be accommodated." *Id.* at 429.
- That "since there is no § 2 right to a district that is not reasonably compact, the creation of a noncompact district does not compensate for the dismantling of a compact opportunity district." *Id.* at 430-31 (citations omitted).
- That "the enormous geographical distance separating Austin and Mexican-border communities, coupled with the disparate needs and interests of these populations . . . render[ed] District 25 noncompact for § 2 purposes." *Id.* at 435.

After deciding that the *Gingles* preconditions existed, Justice Kennedy then considered the totality of the circumstances and found that they demonstrated a Section 2 violation. First, he considered proportionality and decided that proportionality should be considered on a statewide basis. *Id.* at 437. In Texas, there were 32 congressional districts, and the five reasonably compact Latino opportunity districts in the 2003 plan amounted to about 16 percent of the total districts. *Id.* at 438. He then noted that Latinos made up 22 percent of the state's CVAP (citizen voting age population), meaning that Latinos were two districts short of proportionality. *Id.* at 438. In addition to considering proportionality, he noted that the changes to District 23 "undermined the progress of a racial group that has been subject to significant voting-related discrimination and that was becoming increasingly politically active and cohesive," that the state "took away Latinos' opportunity because Latinos were about to exercise it," and that the state's actions "[bore] the mark of intentional discrimination that could give rise to an equal protection violation." *Id.* at 439-40. Finally, Justice Kennedy noted that a state could cite to incumbency protection to defend its district lines if "the justification for incumbency protection is to keep the constituency intact so the officeholder is accountable for promises made or broken." *Id.* at 441. In this instance, the incumbency protection meant "excluding some voters from the district simply because they are likely to vote against the officeholder" and that such incumbency protection could not justify the impact on Latino voters. *Id.* at 441.

Several aspects of the description above are worth highlighting:

- First, *LULAC* decided a question that had been left lingering in *De Grandy*—how does one assess proportionality, by region or statewide? *LULAC's* answer is to consider proportionality on a statewide basis.
- Second, *LULAC* holds that Section 2 rights of one area cannot be traded off against another area—at least when the other area is non-compact. Does that analysis make sense when one is assessing proportionality on a statewide basis? In other words, if Latino citizens in Texas have the opportunity to elect six candidates of choice in the entire plan, should a federal court micro-manage where those districts are drawn?
- Third, *LULAC* says that a district's compactness is relevant to a Section 2 analysis and that Section 2 compactness is about both geography and the needs and interests of the populations in the district.
- Fourth, *LULAC* is interesting in that it implies that what Texas did in District 23 was not just a violation of the results standard but also something akin to intentional discrimination.

The next case, *Gonzalez v. City of Aurora,* involves a decision about a redistricting on the local level. While statewide redistricting plans grab the headlines, it is important to note that most Section 2 litigation has involved local governments. The case is also interesting because, unlike the other cases you have read in our review of vote dilution, it does not involve a jurisdiction in the South.

Gonzalez v. City of Aurora

535 F.3d 594 (7th Cir. 2008)

EASTERBROOK, Chief Judge.

In the 2000 Census, 32.6% of the population in the City of Aurora, Illinois, identified itself as Hispanic, but of the City's residents who are citizens and old enough to vote only 16.3% are Hispanic. Aurora has 10 single-seat wards, only one of which reliably elects Latino candidates to the City Council. Another ward, although about 66% Latino, has twice elected a black alderman since the redistricting that followed the 2000 Census. When the record was compiled, 2 of the 12 aldermen (there are 2 at-large seats in addition to the 10 wards) were Hispanic. One was elected and the second appointed. Plaintiffs contend in this suit under § 2 of the Voting Rights Act that these numbers are insufficient. They want an injunction compelling the City to redraw the ward boundaries so that Aurora's Latino population is concentrated in three wards, each of which then would be likely to elect a Latino candidate (would be, as plaintiffs say, "Latino effective").

Plaintiffs start with the proposition that it takes 70% or more Latino population to ensure the election of a Latino candidate. Whatever rule of thumb courts may have used in the 1960s and 1970s for black voters does not apply to Latinos, plaintiffs contend, because Latinos are younger and less likely to be citizens than are blacks and other minorities. Although the City used the rule of thumb that 65% population is enough to make a district "effective" for a minority group, plaintiffs are sure that this won't work. This table shows why 65% may not be enough:

	Latino Population	Latino Voting-Age Population	Latino Voting-Age Citizen Population
Ward 2	74.54%	71%	47.5%
Ward 7	66.27%	62.9%	43%
Ward 3	52.61%	48%	28%

These figures, all from 2000, are the right ones to use. Plaintiffs' estimates about population in 2005 don't matter, because apportionment is based on Census returns. The district court concluded that a ward with 65% or more Latino residents should be deemed sufficient no matter who it elects. If Latinos vote for candidates of other ethnic backgrounds, this means that Aurora is not afflicted by racial bloc voting, rather than that the map deprives Latinos' votes of full effect. The judge added that, with 16% of the eligible population, Latinos would receive 2 seats in a 12-seat legislature under proportional representation. As 2 of the existing 12 members were Latino, the district judge saw no problem under § 2 and granted summary judgment for the City.

The most striking thing about plaintiffs' brief on appeal is that it neither quotes from nor analyzes the text of § 2. Instead it leaps straight to the "*Gingles* factors" (from *Thornburg v. Gingles*) and language in a Senate committee report. The statute is not self-defining, so it is understandable that lawyers would turn to secondary sources such as judicial decisions and legislative history. But neither is it irrelevant. It is worth quoting. Section 2(a) says that governments cannot adopt standards, practices, or procedures that "result[] in a denial or abridgement of the right of any citizen of the United States to vote on account of race or color." This sounds like a rule that race and color cannot be used to prevent anyone from voting, or to disregard a vote once cast. Section 2(b), 42 U.S.C. § 1973(b), then adds this famously elliptical language:

> A violation of subsection (a) of this section is established if, based on the totality of circumstances, it is shown that the political processes leading to nomination or election in the State or political subdivision are not equally open to participation by members of a class of citizens protected by subsection (a) of this section in that its members have less opportunity than other members of the electorate to participate in the political process and to elect representatives of their choice. The extent to which members of a protected class have been elected to office in the State or political subdivision is one circumstance which may be considered: *Provided,* That nothing in this section establishes a right to have members of a protected class elected in numbers equal to their proportion in the population.

What does it mean to "have less opportunity than other members of the electorate to participate in the political process and to elect representatives of their choice"? *Gingles* held that gerrymandering district borders can have this effect even though everyone is entitled to vote, and all votes are counted equally. The Court set out circumstances (the "*Gingles* factors") under which clever map-drawing could have this effect and then turned to the Senate committee report for factors to consider if the conditions are met. The district judge found, and we shall assume, that these conditions are satisfied in Aurora: Latinos are sufficiently concentrated geographically that they can form a majority in some districts; Latinos are politically cohesive; and, without a large bloc of voters, Latino candidates rarely prevail. This just sets the stage.

Plaintiffs leap from satisfaction of the *Gingles* factors to the proposition that the City must do what is possible to maximize Latino voters' ability to elect Latino candidates (euphemistically "candidates of their choice"). But neither § 2 nor *Gingles* nor any later decision of the Supreme Court speaks of maximizing the influence of any racial or ethnic group. Section 2 requires an electoral process "equally open" to all, not a process that favors one group over another. One cannot maximize Latino influence without minimizing some other group's influence. A map drawn to advantage Latino candidates at the expense of black (or white ethnic) candidates violates § 2 as surely as a map drawn to maximize the influence of those groups at the expense of Latinos.

The Supreme Court emphasized in *League of United Latin American Citizens v. Perry* (2006) (*LULAC*), its most recent § 2 redistricting case, that the Voting Rights Act protects the rights of individual voters, not the rights of groups. There is a serious problem with any proposal to employ black or Asian or white citizens of some other ethnic background as "fill" in districts carefully drawn to ensure three 70%-Latino wards—wards in which the remaining 30% are (by design) never going to be able to elect a candidate of their choice. How could one explain to this 30% that the political process was "equally open" to them, as § 2 commands? A problem under § 2 arises whenever any person is moved from one district to another to minimize the value of his vote and give an advantage to someone else.

Section 2's requirement of an "equally open" process usually is described as including a prohibition of vote dilution by redistricting. Plaintiffs want the court to reduce the influence of others to produce an advantage for Latino voters. That may be necessary as a remedy for some earlier vote-dilution exercise, but the first question we need to ask is whether Latino votes have been diluted by Aurora's map. Diluted relative to what benchmark? Not the maximum influence Latinos could have, surely; as we've explained, no group is entitled to that (and all groups cannot enjoy maximum influence simultaneously). Nor is proportional representation the benchmark. *Gingles* holds that this is not the statute's objective—that it is not necessary and, *LULAC* adds, is not sufficient either, if a minority group in one part of a jurisdiction has been thrown to the wolves.

So what benchmarks are possible? One would be the outcome of a race-neutral process in which all districts are compact. Cases in which the Supreme Court has found a problem under § 2 all involve transparent gerrymandering that boosts one group's chances at the expense of another's. Nothing remotely similar happened in Aurora. A glance at the 2002 ward map reveals that the districts are compact and regular, with the few rough edges needed to ensure that they have equal population.

Still, although many opinions, of which *LULAC* is the most recent, emphasize compact districts as the benchmark for a map that does not dilute any group's influence, it is possible to locate even compact districts for political advantage.

Given the very large number of ways that reasonably compact districts of equal population can be drawn, how can a court tell whether a jurisdiction has chosen a particular arrangement in order to advantage one ethnic group over another, diluting the influence of the disfavored group? When the Voting Rights Act was enacted, the answer would have depended on the intent of those who drew the map. *See City of Mobile v. Bolden*. The 1982 amendments replaced intent with effect as the rule of decision, see *Gingles*, but did not supply a means to test whether a given map was ordinary or abnormal. Today, however, computers can use census data to generate many variations on compact districts with equal population. One could do this exercise a hundred or a thousand times, each time placing the center of the first (or "seed") district in a different location. That would generate a hundred or a thousand different maps, and the software could easily check these to determine the ethnic makeup of the districts.

Suppose that after 1,000 different maps of Aurora's wards have been generated, 10% have two or three "safe" districts for Latinos and the other 90% look something like the actual map drawn in 2002: one safe district and two "influence districts" where no candidate is likely to win without substantial Latino support. Then we could confidently conclude that Aurora's map did not dilute the effectiveness of the Latino vote. But suppose, instead, that Latinos are sufficiently concentrated that the random, race-blind exercise we have proposed yields three "Latino effective" districts at least 50% of the time. Then a court might sensibly conclude that Aurora had diluted the Latino vote by undermining the normal effects of the choices that Aurora's citizens had made about where to live. Redistricting software can not answer all hard questions, but it provides a means to implement a pure effects test without demanding proportional representation.

Plaintiffs did not conduct such an exercise, however (or, if they did, they didn't put the results in the record). What we can see from the record suggests that Latinos are not concentrated enough to support three "Latino effective" districts without serious gerrymandering. Ward 2 has 2,453 voting-age citizens who identified themselves as Hispanic in the 2000 Census. Wards 7 and 3 have fewer. Wards 1, 4, and 6 all have more than 1,000 citizen, voting-age Latinos. Ward 5 has another 668. In other words, the Latino population is not concentrated in a way that neutrally drawn compact districts would produce three "Latino effective" wards. That may be why plaintiffs have staked their all on a proposal that Latinos are entitled at least to proportional representation via two Latino-effective districts no matter what the consequences of race-blind districting would be. The Voting Rights Act does not require either outcome.

Because plaintiffs lack any evidence of dilution, there is no point in traipsing through the multiple factors mentioned in the 1982 committee reports. Although plaintiffs briefly mention the City's two at-large districts—at-large districts are a traditional means of reducing the influence of minority groups—they did not make much of them in the district court or here, devoting less than two pages of their brief to the subject. The at-large districts predate the 2002 reapportionment and, for all we know, long predate the presence of a substantial Latino population in

Aurora. After the 2000 Census, the City increased the number of single-member districts from 8 to 10, reducing the effect of the 2 at-large districts. Any contention that the at-large districts violate § 2 of the Voting Rights Act has been forfeited.

And plaintiffs have no other arguments. They ignore the fact that several wards—at least Wards 3 and 7, and likely wards 1, 4, and 6 as well—contain enough Latino citizens to produce substantial influence. (Many cases, of which *LULAC* is again the most recent example, hold that "influence districts" count in any assessment of vote dilution. *See also, e.g., Johnson v. De Grandy.*) Plaintiffs tried for the big prize (three safe districts) but did not build the sort of factual record that creates a genuine issue for trial, even under the balancing approach of *Gingles.* They thought, wrongly, that all they had to do to prevail is to show that Ward 7 is not "Latino effective." That's not enough to condemn the current map. The district court's judgment therefore is affirmed.

NOTES ON *GONZALEZ* AND THE PLAINTIFF'S BURDEN UNDER SECTION 2 OF THE VOTING RIGHTS ACT

1. Notice how Judge Easterbrook's *Gonzalez* opinion seems to criticize the plaintiffs for "neither quot[ing] nor analyz[ing]" the statutory text of Section 2. Judge Easterbrook quotes the text, but does he engage in any textual analysis?

2. Judge Easterbrook's opinion concedes the existence of the *Gingles* preconditions in Aurora. Thus, the decision to not find a violation of Section 2 would appear to be predicated on the totality of the circumstances. Consider how vague and amorphous the "totality of circumstances" test is. Does it give the Court the freedom to decide whatever it wants with respect to the issue of minority vote dilution? If this amount of judicial discretion is a problem, is it a problem of the Court's own making—or instead a consequence of the statute enacted by Congress?

3. How should courts go about analyzing challenges under the Section 2 results test in the context of single-member districts? What do you think of Judge Easterbook's idea of using randomly generated maps?

4. Why does Judge Easterbrook find no dilution? Do you agree with that analysis?

***

For many years, a majority of the Court has held that the Equal Protection Clause and amended Section 2 of the Voting Rights Act allow plaintiffs to challenge electoral structures for their failure to provide adequate representation (i.e., because the structures cause "vote dilution"). These holdings, though, are not without their critics. Perhaps the most comprehensive critique in a judicial opinion of both the constitutional and statutory decisions of the Court was written by Justice Clarence Thomas in *Holder v. Hall.*

Here is some background to assist you a bit with the specific context of the case. *Holder v. Hall* was a Section 2 challenge to the system of electing the county government in Bleckley County, Georgia. Bleckley County was 20 percent African American and had a single-commissioner form of government—which meant that a single individual elected at-large constituted the "governing body" for the county.

Plaintiffs challenged the use of the single-commissioner form of government, alleging that the one-person size was a violation of Section 2 and seeking the establishment of a larger-sized governing body that would be elected by single-member districts.

Justice Anthony Kennedy wrote the lead opinion joined in substantial part by Chief Justice William Rehnquist. Justice Sandra Day O'Connor wrote a concurrence. These three Justices all rejected the plaintiffs' challenge, although for different reasons. The details of the reasoning of the opinions by Justices Kennedy and O'Connor are not important to our purposes here, except to note that both Justices decided the case on far narrower grounds than Justice Thomas would have.

Holder v. Hall

512 U.S. 874 (1994)

Justice THOMAS, with whom Justice SCALIA joins, concurring in the judgment.

We are asked in this case to determine whether the size of a local governing body is subject to challenge under § 2 of the Voting Rights Act of 1965 as a "dilutive" practice. While I agree with Justices Kennedy and O'Connor that the size of a governing body cannot be attacked under § 2, I do not share their reasons for reaching that conclusion.

I would explicitly anchor analysis in this case in the statutory text. Only a "voting qualification or prerequisite to voting, or standard, practice, or procedure" can be challenged under § 2. I would hold that the size of a governing body is not a "standard, practice, or procedure" within the terms of the Act. In my view, however, the only principle limiting the scope of the terms "standard, practice, or procedure" that can be derived from the text of the Act would exclude, not only the challenge to size advanced today, but also challenges to allegedly dilutive election methods that we have considered within the scope of the Act in the past.

I believe that a systematic reassessment of our interpretation of § 2 is required in this case. The broad reach we have given the section might suggest that the size of a governing body, like an election method that has the potential for diluting the vote of a minority group, should come within the terms of the Act. But the gloss we have placed on the words "standard, practice, or procedure" in cases alleging dilution is at odds with the terms of the statute and has proved utterly unworkable in practice. A review of the current state of our cases shows that by construing the Act to cover potentially dilutive electoral mechanisms, we have immersed the federal courts in a hopeless project of weighing questions of political theory—questions judges must confront to establish a benchmark concept of an "undiluted" vote. Worse, in pursuing the ideal measure of voting strength, we have devised a remedial mechanism that encourages federal courts to segregate voters into racially designated districts to ensure minority electoral success. In doing so, we have collaborated in what may aptly be termed the racial "balkaniz[ation]" of the Nation.

I can no longer adhere to a reading of the Act that does not comport with the terms of the statute and that has produced such a disastrous misadventure in judicial policymaking. I would hold that the size of a government body is not a "standard, practice, or procedure" because, properly understood, those terms reach only state enactments that limit citizens' access to the ballot.

I

If one surveys the history of the Voting Rights Act, one can only be struck by the sea change that has occurred in the application and enforcement of the Act since it was passed in 1965. The statute was originally perceived as a remedial provision directed specifically at eradicating discriminatory practices that restricted blacks' ability to register and vote in the segregated South. Now, the Act has grown into something entirely different. In construing the Act to cover claims of vote dilution, we have converted the Act into a device for regulating, rationing, and apportioning political power among racial and ethnic groups. In the process, we have read the Act essentially as a grant of authority to the federal judiciary to develop theories on basic principles of representative government, for it is only a resort to political theory that can enable a court to determine which electoral systems provide the "fairest" levels of representation or the most "effective" or "undiluted" votes to minorities.

Before I turn to an analysis of the text of § 2 to explain why, in my view, the terms of the statute do not authorize the project that we have undertaken in the name of the Act, I intend first simply to describe the development of the basic contours of vote dilution actions under the Voting Rights Act.[2] An examination of the current state of our decisions should make obvious a simple fact that for far too long has gone unmentioned: Vote dilution cases have required the federal courts to make decisions based on highly political judgments—judgments that courts are inherently ill-equipped to make. A clear understanding of the destructive assumptions that have developed to guide vote dilution decisions and the role we have given the federal courts in redrawing the political landscape of the Nation should make clear the pressing need for us to reassess our interpretation of the Act.

As it was enforced in the years immediately following its enactment, the Voting Rights Act of 1965 was perceived primarily as legislation directed at eliminating literacy tests and similar devices that had been used to prevent black voter registration in the segregated South.

The Act was immediately and notably successful in removing barriers to registration and ensuring access to the ballot. For example, in Mississippi, black registration levels skyrocketed from 6.7% to 59.8% in a mere two years; in Alabama the increase was from 19.3% to 51.6% in the same time period.

The Court's decision in *Allen v. State Bd. of Elections* (1969), however, marked a fundamental shift in the focal point of the Act. In an opinion dealing with four companion cases, the *Allen* Court determined that the Act should be given "the broadest possible scope." The decision in *Allen* thus ensured that the terms "standard, practice, or procedure" would extend to encompass a wide array of electoral

2. Of course, many of the basic principles I will discuss are equally applicable to constitutional vote dilution cases. Indeed, prior to the amendment of the Voting Rights Act in 1982, dilution claims typically were brought under the Equal Protection Clause. *See, e.g., White v. Regester* (1973); *Whitcomb v. Chavis* (1971).

practices or voting systems that might be challenged for reducing the potential impact of minority votes.

As a consequence, *Allen* also ensured that courts would be required to confront a number of complex and essentially political questions in assessing claims of vote dilution under the Voting Rights Act. The central difficulty in any vote dilution case, of course, is determining a point of comparison against which dilution can be measured. As Justice Frankfurter observed several years before *Allen*, "[t]alk of 'debasement' or 'dilution' is circular talk. One cannot speak of 'debasement' or 'dilution' of the value of a vote until there is first defined a standard of reference as to what a vote should be worth." *Baker v. Carr.* But in setting the benchmark of what "undiluted" or fully "effective" voting strength should be, a court must necessarily make some judgments based purely on an assessment of principles of political theory. As Justice Harlan pointed out in his dissent in *Allen*, the Voting Rights Act supplies no rule for a court to rely upon in deciding, for example, whether a multimember at-large system of election is to be preferred to a single-member district system; that is, whether one provides a more "effective" vote than another. "Under one system, Negroes have some influence in the election of all officers; under the other, minority groups have *more* influence in the selection of *fewer* officers." *Allen.* The choice is inherently a political one, and depends upon the selection of a theory for defining the fully "effective" vote—at bottom, a theory for defining effective participation in representative government. In short, what a court is actually asked to do in a vote dilution case is to choose among competing bases of representation—ultimately, really, among competing theories of political philosophy.

Perhaps the most prominent feature of the philosophy that has emerged in vote dilution decisions since *Allen* has been the Court's preference for single-member districting schemes, both as a benchmark for measuring undiluted minority voting strength and as a remedial mechanism for guaranteeing minorities undiluted voting power. Indeed, commentators surveying the history of voting rights litigation have concluded that it has been the objective of voting rights plaintiffs to use the Act to attack multimember districting schemes and to replace them with single-member districting systems drawn with majority-minority districts to ensure minority control of seats.

It should be apparent, however, that there is no principle inherent in our constitutional system, or even in the history of the Nation's electoral practices, that makes single-member districts the "proper" mechanism for electing representatives to governmental bodies or for giving "undiluted" effect to the votes of a numerical minority. On the contrary, from the earliest days of the Republic, multimember districts were a common feature of our political systems. The Framers left unanswered in the Constitution the question whether congressional delegations from the several States should be elected on a general ticket from each State as a whole or under a districting scheme and left that matter to be resolved by the States or by Congress. It was not until 1842 that Congress determined that Representatives should be elected from single-member districts in the States. Single-member districting was no more the rule in the States themselves, for the Constitutions of most of the 13 original States provided that representatives in the state legislatures were to be elected from multimember districts. Today, although they have come under increasing attack under the Voting Rights Act, multimember district systems continue to be a feature on the American political landscape, especially in municipal governments.

The obvious advantage the Court has perceived in single-member districts, of course, is their tendency to enhance the ability of any numerical minority in the electorate to gain control of seats in a representative body. But in choosing single-member districting as a benchmark electoral plan on that basis the Court has made a political decision and, indeed, a decision that itself depends on a prior political choice made in answer to Justice Harlan's question in *Allen.* Justice Harlan asked whether a group's votes should be considered to be more "effective" when they provide influence over a greater number of seats, or control over a lesser number of seats. In answering that query, the Court has determined that the purpose of the vote—or of the fully "effective" vote—is controlling seats. In other words, in an effort to develop standards for assessing claims of dilution, the Court has adopted the view that members of any numerically significant minority are denied a fully effective use of the franchise unless they are able to control seats in an elected body. Under this theory, votes that do not control a representative are essentially wasted; those who cast them go unrepresented and are just as surely disenfranchised as if they had been barred from registering. Such conclusions, of course, depend upon a certain theory of the "effective" vote, a theory that is not inherent in the concept of representative democracy itself.[6]

In fact, it should be clear that the assumptions that have guided the Court reflect only one possible understanding of effective exercise of the franchise, an understanding based on the view that voters are "represented" only when they choose a delegate who will mirror their views in the legislative halls. But it is certainly possible to construct a theory of effective political participation that would accord greater importance to voters' ability to influence, rather than control, elections. And especially in a two-party system such as ours, the influence of a potential "swing" group of voters composing 10% to 20% of the electorate in a given district can be considerable. Even such a focus on practical influence, however, is not a necessary component of the definition of the "effective" vote. Some conceptions of representative government may primarily emphasize the formal value of the vote as a mechanism for participation in the electoral process, whether it results in control of a seat or not. Under such a theory, minorities unable to control elected posts would not be considered essentially without a vote; rather, a vote duly cast and counted would be deemed just as "effective" as any other. If a minority group is unable to control seats, that result may plausibly be attributed to the inescapable fact that, in a majoritarian system, numerical minorities lose elections.

In short, there are undoubtedly an infinite number of theories of effective suffrage, representation, and the proper apportionment of political power in a

6. Undoubtedly, one factor that has prompted our focus on control of seats has been a desire, when confronted with an abstract question of political theory concerning the measure of effective participation in government, to seize upon an objective standard for deciding cases, however much it may oversimplify the issues before us. If using control of seats as our standard does not reflect a very nuanced theory of political participation, it at least has the superficial advantage of appealing to the most easily measured indicia of political power.

representative democracy that could be drawn upon to answer the questions posed in *Allen.* I do not pretend to have provided the most sophisticated account of the various possibilities; but such matters of political theory are beyond the ordinary sphere of federal judges. And that is precisely the point. The matters the Court has set out to resolve in vote dilution cases are questions of political philosophy, not questions of law. As such, they are not readily subjected to any judicially manageable standards that can guide courts in attempting to select between competing theories.

But the political choices the Court has had to make do not end with the determination that the primary purpose of the "effective" vote is controlling seats or with the selection of single-member districting as the mechanism for providing that control. In one sense, these were not even the most critical decisions to be made in devising standards for assessing claims of dilution, for, in itself, the selection of single-member districting as a benchmark election plan will tell a judge little about the number of minority districts to create. Single-member districting tells a court "how" members of a minority are to control seats, but not "how many" seats they should be allowed to control.

But "how many" is the critical issue. Once one accepts the proposition that the effectiveness of votes is measured in terms of the control of seats, the core of any vote dilution claim is an assertion that the group in question is unable to control the "proper" number of seats—that is, the number of seats that the minority's percentage of the population would enable it to control in the benchmark "fair" system. The claim is inherently based on ratios between the numbers of the minority in the population and the numbers of seats controlled. As a result, only a mathematical calculation can answer the fundamental question posed by a claim of vote dilution. And once again, in selecting the proportion that will be used to define the undiluted strength of a minority—the ratio that will provide the principle for decision in a vote dilution case—a court must make a political choice.

The ratio for which this Court has opted, and thus the mathematical principle driving the results in our cases, is undoubtedly direct proportionality. Indeed, four Members of the Court candidly recognized in *Gingles* that the Court had adopted a rule of roughly proportional representation, at least to the extent proportionality was possible given the geographic dispersion of minority populations. While in itself that choice may strike us intuitively as the fairest or most just rule to apply, opting for proportionality is still a political choice, not a result required by any principle of law.

B

The dabbling in political theory that dilution cases have prompted, however, is hardly the worst aspect of our vote dilution jurisprudence. Far more pernicious has been the Court's willingness to accept the one underlying premise that must inform every minority vote dilution claim: the assumption that the group asserting dilution is not merely a racial or ethnic group, but a group having distinct political interests as well. Of necessity, in resolving vote dilution actions we have given credence to the view that race defines political interest. We have acted on the implicit assumption that members of racial and ethnic groups must all think alike on important matters of public policy and must have their own "minority preferred" representatives holding seats in elected bodies if they are to be considered represented at all.

[O]perating under that assumption, we have assigned federal courts the task of ensuring that minorities are assured their "just" share of seats in elected bodies throughout the Nation.

To achieve that result through the currently fashionable mechanism of drawing majority-minority single-member districts, we have embarked upon what has been aptly characterized as a process of "creating racially 'safe boroughs.'" We have involved the federal courts, and indeed the Nation, in the enterprise of systematically dividing the country into electoral districts along racial lines—an enterprise of segregating the races into political homelands that amounts, in truth, to nothing short of a system of "political apartheid." Blacks are drawn into "black districts" and given "black representatives"; Hispanics are drawn into Hispanic districts and given "Hispanic representatives"; and so on. Worse still, it is not only the courts that have taken up this project. In response to judicial decisions and the promptings of the Justice Department, the States themselves, in an attempt to avoid costly and disruptive Voting Rights Act litigation, have begun to gerrymander electoral districts according to race.

The assumptions upon which our vote dilution decisions have been based should be repugnant to any nation that strives for the ideal of a color-blind Constitution.

As a practical political matter, our drive to segregate political districts by race can only serve to deepen racial divisions by destroying any need for voters or candidates to build bridges between racial groups or to form voting coalitions. "Black-preferred" candidates are assured election in "safe black districts"; white-preferred candidates are assured election in "safe white districts." Neither group needs to draw on support from the other's constituency to win on election day.

C

While the results we have already achieved under the Voting Rights Act might seem bad enough, we should recognize that our approach to splintering the electorate into racially designated single-member districts does not by any means mark a limit on the authority federal judges may wield to rework electoral systems under our Voting Rights Act jurisprudence. On the contrary, in relying on single-member districting schemes as a touchstone, our cases so far have been somewhat arbitrarily limited to addressing the interests of minority voters who are sufficiently geographically compact to form a majority in a single-member district. There is no reason *a priori*, however, that our focus should be so constrained. The decision to rely on single-member geographic districts as a mechanism for conducting elections is merely a political choice—and one that we might reconsider in the future. Indeed, it is a choice that has undoubtedly been influenced by the adversary process: In the cases that have come before us, plaintiffs have focused largely upon attacking multimember districts and have offered single-member schemes as the benchmark of an "undiluted" alternative.

But as the destructive effects of our current penchant for majority-minority districts become more apparent, courts will undoubtedly be called upon to reconsider adherence to geographic districting as a method for ensuring minority voting power. Already, some advocates have criticized the current strategy of creating majority-minority districts and have urged the adoption of other voting mechanisms—for example, cumulative voting[15] or a system using transferable votes[16] that can produce proportional results without requiring division of the electorate into racially segregated districts.

Such changes may seem radical departures from the electoral systems with which we are most familiar. Indeed, they may be unwanted by the people in the several States who purposely have adopted districting systems in their electoral laws. But nothing in our present understanding of the Voting Rights Act places a principled limit on the authority of federal courts that would prevent them from instituting a system of cumulative voting as a remedy under § 2, or even from establishing a more elaborate mechanism for securing proportional representation based on transferable votes.

D

A full understanding of the authority that our current interpretation of the Voting Rights Act assigns to the federal courts, and of the destructive effects that our exercise of that authority is presently having upon our body politic, compels a single conclusion: A systematic reexamination of our interpretation of the Act is required.

II

Section 2(a) of the Voting Rights Act provides that "[n]o voting qualification or prerequisite to voting or standard, practice, or procedure shall be imposed or applied by any State or political subdivision in a manner which results in a denial or abridgement of the right of any citizen of the United States to vote" on account of race, color, or membership in one of the language minority groups defined in the Act. Respondents contend that the terms "standard, practice, or procedure" should extend to cover the size of a governmental body. An examination of the text of § 2 makes it clear, however, that the terms of the Act do not reach that far; indeed, the terms of the Act do not allow many of the challenges to electoral mechanisms

15. Under a cumulative voting scheme, a system commonly used in corporations to protect the interests of minority shareholders, each voter has as many votes as there are posts to be filled, and the voter may cast as many of his votes as he wishes for a single candidate. The system thus allows a numerical minority to concentrate its voting power behind a given candidate without requiring that the minority voters themselves be concentrated into a single district.

16. A system utilizing transferable votes is designed to ensure proportional representation with "mathematical exactness." Under such a system, each voter rank orders his choices of candidates. To win, a candidate must receive a fixed quota of votes, which may be set by any of several methods. Ballots listing a given candidate as the voter's first choice are counted for that candidate until the candidate has secured the quota of votes necessary for election. Remaining first-choice ballots for that candidate are then transferred to another candidate, usually the one listed as the second choice on the ballot. Like cumulative voting, the system allows a minority group to concentrate its voting power without requiring districting, and it has the additional advantage of ensuring that "surplus" votes are transferred to support the election of the minority voters' next preference.

that we have permitted in the past. Properly understood, the terms "standard, practice, or procedure" in § 2(a) refer only to practices that affect minority citizens' access to the ballot. Districting systems and electoral mechanisms that may affect the "weight" given to a ballot duly cast and counted are simply beyond the purview of the Act.

A

In determining the scope of § 2(a), as when interpreting any statute, we should begin with the statutory language. Under the plain terms of the Act, § 2(a) covers only a defined category of state actions. Only "voting qualification[s]," "prerequisite[s] to voting," or "standard[s], practice[s], or procedure[s]" are subject to challenge under the Act. The first two items in this list clearly refer to conditions or tests applied to regulate citizens' access to the ballot. They would cover, for example, any form of test or requirement imposed as a condition on registration or on the process of voting on election day.

Taken in isolation, the last grouping of terms—"standard, practice, or procedure"—may seem somewhat less precise. If we give the words their ordinary meanings, however—for they have no technical significance and are not defined in the Act—they would not normally be understood to include the size of a local governing body. Common sense indicates that the size of a governing body and other aspects of government structure do not comfortably fit within the terms "standard, practice, or procedure." Moreover, we need not simply treat the terms in isolation; indeed, it would be a mistake to do so. Reading the words in context strongly suggests that § 2(a) must be understood as referring to any standard, practice, or procedure with respect to voting.

But under our precedents, we have already stretched the terms "standard, practice, or procedure" beyond the limits of ordinary meaning. We have concluded, for example, that the choice of a certain set of district lines is a "procedure," or perhaps a "practice," concerning voting subject to challenge under the Act, even though the drawing of a given set of district lines has nothing to do with the basic process of allowing a citizen to vote—that is, the process of registering, casting a ballot, and having it counted. Similarly, we have determined that the use of multimember districts, rather than single-member districts, can be challenged under the Act.

If we return to the Act to reexamine the terms setting out the actions regulated by § 2, a careful reading of the statutory text will reveal a good deal more about the limitations on the scope of the section than suggested above. The terms "standard, practice, or procedure" appear to have been included in § 2 as a sort of catchall provision. They seem phrased with an eye to eliminating the possibility of evasion. Nevertheless, they are catchall terms that round out a list, and a sensible and long-established maxim of construction limits the way we should understand such general words appended to an enumeration of more specific items. The principle of *ejusdem generis* suggests that such general terms should be understood to refer to items belonging to the same class that is defined by the more specific terms in the list.

Here, the specific items described in § 2(a) ("voting qualification[s]" and "prerequisite[s] to voting") indicate that Congress was concerned in this section with any procedure, however it might be denominated, that regulates citizens' access to the ballot—that is, any procedure that might erect a barrier to prevent the potential voter from casting his vote. In describing the laws that would be subject to § 2, Congress focused attention upon provisions regulating the interaction between the individual voter and the voting process—on hurdles the citizen might have to cross in the form of "prerequisites" or "qualifications." The general terms in the section are most naturally understood, therefore, to refer to any methods for conducting a part of the voting process that might similarly be used to interfere with a citizen's ability to cast his vote, and they are undoubtedly intended to ensure that the entire voting process—a process that begins with registration and includes the casting of a ballot and having the ballot counted—is covered by the Act. Simply by including general terms in § 2(a) to ensure the efficacy of the restriction imposed, Congress should not be understood to have expanded the scope of the restriction beyond the logical limits implied in the specific terms of the statute.

Moreover, it is not only in the terms describing the practices regulated under the Act that § 2(a) focuses on the individual voter. The section also speaks only in the singular of the right of "any citizen" to vote. Giving the terms "standard, practice, or procedure" an expansive interpretation to reach potentially dilutive practices, however, would distort that focus on the individual, for a vote dilution claim necessarily depends on the assertion of a group right. At the heart of the claim is the contention that the members of a group collectively have been unable to exert the influence that their numbers suggest they might under an alternative system. Such a group right, however, finds no grounding in the terms of § 2(a).

Finally, as our cases have shown, reading § 2(a) to reach beyond laws that regulate in some way citizens' access to the ballot turns the section into a command for courts to evaluate abstract principles of political theory in order to develop rules for deciding which votes are "diluted" and which are not. Common sense would suggest that we should not lightly interpret the Act to require courts to address such matters so far outside the normal bounds of judicial competence, and the mere use of three more general terms at the end of the list of regulated practices in § 2(a) cannot properly be understood to incorporate such an expansive command into the Act.

Properly understood, therefore, § 2(a) is a provision designed to protect access to the ballot, and in regulating "standard[s], practice[s], and procedure[s]," it reaches only those state laws that [relate to] either voter qualifications or the manner in which elections are conducted. The section thus covers all manner of registration requirements, the practices surrounding registration (including the selection of times and places where registration takes place and the selection of registrars), the locations of polling places, the times polls are open, the use of paper ballots as opposed to voting machines, and other similar aspects of the voting process that might be manipulated to deny any citizen the right to cast a ballot and have it properly counted. The section does not cover, however, the choice of a multimember over a single-member districting system or the selection of one set of districting lines over another, or any other such electoral mechanism or method of election that might reduce the weight or influence a ballot may have in controlling the outcome of an election.

Of course, this interpretation of the terms "standard, practice, or procedure" effectively means that § 2(a) does not provide for any claims of what we have called vote "dilution." But that is precisely the result suggested by the text of the statute. Section 2(a) nowhere uses the term "vote dilution" or suggests that its goal is to ensure that votes are given their proper "weight." And an examination of § 2(b) does not suggest any different result. It is true that in construing § 2 to reach vote dilution claims in *Thornburg v. Gingles,* the Court relied largely on the gloss on § 2(b) supplied in the legislative history of the 1982 amendments to the Act. But the text of § 2(b) supplies a weak foundation indeed for reading the Act to reach such claims.

As the Court concluded in *Gingles,* the 1982 amendments incorporated into the Act, and specifically into § 2(b), a "results" test for measuring violations of § 2(a). That test was intended to replace, for § 2 purposes, the "intent" test the Court had announced in *Bolden* for voting rights claims under § 2 of the Voting Rights Act and under the Fourteenth and Fifteenth Amendments. Section 2(a) thus prohibits certain state actions that may "resul[t] in a denial or abridgement" of the right to vote, and §2(b) incorporates virtually the exact language of the "results test" employed by the Court in *White v. Regester,* and applied in constitutional voting rights cases before our decision in *Bolden.* The section directs courts to consider whether "based on the totality of circumstances," a state practice results in members of a minority group "hav[ing] less opportunity than other members of the electorate to participate in the political process and to elect representatives of their choice."

But the mere adoption of a "results" test, rather than an "intent" test, says nothing about the type of state laws that may be challenged using that test. On the contrary, the type of state law that may be challenged under § 2 is addressed explicitly in § 2(a). While § 2(a) defines and explicitly limits the type of voting practice that may be challenged under the Act, § 2(b) provides only "the test for determining the legality of such a practice." Thus, as an initial matter, there is no reason to think that § 2(b) could serve to expand the scope of the prohibition in § 2(a), which, as I described above, does not extend by its terms to electoral mechanisms that might have a dilutive effect on group voting power.

Even putting that concern aside for the moment, it should be apparent that the incorporation of a results test into the amended section does not necessarily suggest that Congress intended to allow claims of vote dilution under § 2. A results test is useful to plaintiffs whether they are challenging laws that restrict access to the ballot or laws that accomplish some diminution in the "proper weight" of a group's vote. Nothing about the test itself suggests that it is inherently tied to vote dilution claims. A law, for example, limiting the times and places at which registration can occur might be adopted with the purpose of limiting black voter registration, but it could be extremely difficult to prove the discriminatory intent behind such a facially neutral law. The results test would allow plaintiffs to mount a successful challenge to the law under § 2 without such proof.

Moreover, nothing in the language § 2(b) uses to describe the results test particularly indicates that the test was intended to be used under the Act for assessing claims of dilution. Section 2(b) directs courts to consider whether, under the "totality of circumstances," members of a minority group "have less opportunity than other members of the electorate to participate in the political process and to elect representatives of their choice." The most natural reading of that language would suggest that citizens have an equal "opportunity" to participate in the electoral process and an equal "opportunity" to elect representatives when they have been given the same free and open access to the ballot as other citizens and their votes have been properly counted. The section speaks in terms of an opportunity—a chance—to participate and to elect, not an assured ability to attain any particular result. And since the ballot provides the formal mechanism for obtaining access to the political process and for electing representatives, it would seem that one who has had the same chance as others to register and to cast his ballot has had an equal opportunity to participate and to elect, whether or not any of the candidates he chooses is ultimately successful.

To be sure, the test in § 2(b) could be read to apply to claims of vote dilution as well. But to conclude, for example, that a multimember districting system had denied a group of voters an equal opportunity to participate in the political process and to elect representatives, a court would have to embark on the extended project in political theory that I described above in Part I of this opinion. In other words, a court would have to develop some theory of the benchmark undiluted voting system that provides minorities with the "fairest" or most "equitable" share of political influence. Undoubtedly, a dizzying array of concepts of political equality might be described to aid in that task, and each could be used to attribute different values to different systems of election. But the statutory command to determine whether members of a minority have had an equal "opportunity . . . to participate in the political process and to elect representatives" provides no guidance concerning which one of the possible standards setting undiluted voting strength should be chosen over the others. And it would be contrary to common sense to read § 2(b)'s reference to equal opportunity as a charter for federal courts to embark on the ambitious project of developing a theory of political equality to be imposed on the Nation.

It is true that one factor courts may consider under the results test might fit more comfortably with an interpretation of the Act that reaches vote dilution claims. Section 2(b) provides that "one circumstance" that may be considered in assessing the results test is the "extent to which members of a protected class have been elected to office." Obviously, electoral outcomes would be relevant to claims of vote dilution (assuming, of course, that control of seats has been selected as the measure of effective voting). But in some circumstances, results in recent elections might also be relevant for demonstrating that a particular practice concerning registration or polling has served to suppress minority voting. Better factors to consider would be figures for voter registration or turnout at the last election, broken down according to race. But where such data are not readily available, election results may certainly be "one circumstance" to consider in determining whether a challenged practice has resulted in denying a minority group access to the political process. The Act merely directs courts not to ignore such evidence of electoral outcomes altogether.

Moreover, the language providing that electoral outcomes may be considered as "one circumstance" in the results test is explicitly qualified by the provision in § 2(b) that most directly speaks to the question whether § 2 was meant to reach claims of vote dilution—and which suggests that dilution claims are not covered by the section. The last clause in the subsection states in unmistakable terms that "nothing in this section establishes a right to have members of a protected class elected in numbers equal to their proportion in the population." As four Members of the Court observed in *Gingles*, there is "an inherent tension" between this disclaimer of proportional representation and an interpretation of §2 that encompasses vote dilution claims. As I explained above, dilution claims, by their very nature, depend upon a mathematical principle. The heart of the claim is an assertion that the plaintiff group does not hold the "proper" number of seats. As a result, the principle for deciding the case must be supplied by an arithmetic ratio. Either the group has attained the "proper" number of seats under the current election system, or it has not.

By declaring that the section provides no right to proportional representation, § 2(b) necessarily commands that the existence or absence of proportional electoral results should not become the deciding factor in assessing § 2 claims. But in doing so, § 2(b) removes from consideration the most logical ratio for assessing a claim of vote dilution. To resolve a dilution claim under § 2, therefore, a court either must arbitrarily select a different ratio to represent the "undiluted" norm, a ratio that would have less intuitive appeal than direct proportionality, or it must effectively apply a proportionality test in direct contravention of the text of the Act—hence the "inherent tension" between the text of the Act and vote dilution claims. Given that § 2 nowhere speaks in terms of "dilution," an explicit disclaimer removing from the field of play the most natural deciding principle in dilution cases is surely a strong signal that such claims do not fall within the ambit of the Act.

It is true that the terms "standard, practice, or procedure" in § 5 of the Act have been construed to reach districting systems and other potentially dilutive electoral mechanisms, and Congress has reenacted § 5 subsequent to our decisions adopting that expansive interpretation. Nevertheless, the text of the section suggests precisely the same focus on measures that relate to access to the ballot that appears in § 2.

B

From the foregoing, it should be clear that, as far as the text of the Voting Rights Act is concerned, "§ 2 does not speak in terms of vote dilution." *Gingles* (O'Connor, J., concurring in judgment). One might wonder, then, why we have consistently concluded that "[w]e know that Congress intended to allow vote dilution claims to be brought under § 2." *Id.* The juxtaposition of the two statements surely makes the result in our cases appear extraordinary, since it suggests a sort of statutory construction through divination that has allowed us to determine that Congress "really meant" to enact a statute about vote dilution even though Congress did not do so explicitly. In truth, our method of construing § 2 has been only little better than that, for the only source we have relied upon for the expansive meaning we have given § 2 has been the legislative history of the Act.

We first considered the amended § 2 in *Thornburg v. Gingles.* Although the precise scope of the terms "standard, practice, or procedure" was not specifically addressed in that case, *Gingles* nevertheless established our current interpretation of the amended section as a provision that addresses vote dilution, and in particular it fixed our understanding that the results test in § 2(b) is intended to measure vote dilution in terms of electoral outcomes.

In approaching § 2, the *Gingles* Court, based on little more than a bald assertion that "the authoritative source for legislative intent lies in the Committee

Reports on the bill," bypassed a consideration of the text of the Act and proceeded to interpret the section based almost exclusively on its legislative history. It was from the legislative history that the Court culled its understanding that § 2 is a provision encompassing claims that an electoral system has diluted a minority group's vote and its understanding that claims of dilution are to be evaluated based upon how closely electoral outcomes under a given system approximate the outcomes that would obtain under an alternative, undiluted norm.

Contrary to the remarkable "legislative history first" method of statutory construction pursued in *Gingles*, however, I had thought it firmly established that the "authoritative source" for legislative intent was the text of the statute passed by both Houses of Congress and presented to the President, not a series of partisan statements about purposes and objectives collected by congressional staffers and packaged into a committee report. As outlined above, had the Court addressed the text, it would have concluded that the terms of the Act do not address matters of vote "dilution."

Of course, as mentioned above, *Gingles* did not directly address the meaning of the terms "standard, practice, or procedure" in § 2(a). The understanding that those terms extend to a State's laws establishing various electoral mechanisms dates to our decision in *Allen*, in which we construed the identical terms in § 5 of the Act. But the Court's method of statutory construction in *Allen* was little different from that pursued in *Gingles*, and as the analysis of the text of § 5 above demonstrates, it similarly yielded an interpretation in tension with the terms of the Act.

Thus, to the extent that *Allen* implicitly has served as the basis for our subsequent interpretation of the terms of § 2, it hardly can be thought to provide any surer rooting in the language of the Act than the method of statutory construction pursued in *Gingles*.

C

"*Stare decisis* is not an inexorable command," *Payne v. Tennessee* (1991). Indeed, when governing decisions are unworkable or are badly reasoned, this Court has never felt constrained to follow precedent. The discussion above should make clear that our decision in *Gingles* interpreting the scope of § 2 was badly reasoned; it wholly substituted reliance on legislative history for analysis of statutory text. In doing so, it produced a far more expansive interpretation of § 2 than a careful reading of the language of the statute would allow.

Our interpretation of § 2 has also proved unworkable. As I outlined above, it has mired the federal courts in an inherently political task—one that requires answers to questions that are ill-suited to principled judicial resolution. Under § 2, we have assigned the federal judiciary a project that involves, not the application of legal standards to the facts of various cases or even the elaboration of legal principles on a case-by-case basis, but rather the creation of standards from an abstract evaluation of political philosophy.

In my view, our current practice should not continue. Not for another Term, not until the next case, not for another day. The disastrous implications of the policies we have adopted under the Act are too grave; the dissembling in our approach to the Act too damaging to the credibility of the Federal Judiciary. The "inherent tension"—indeed, I would call it an irreconcilable conflict—between the standards we have adopted for evaluating vote dilution claims and the text of the Voting Rights Act would itself be sufficient in my view to warrant overruling the interpretation of § 2 set out in *Gingles*. When that obvious conflict is combined with the destructive effects our expansive reading of the Act has had in involving the Federal Judiciary in the project of dividing the Nation into racially segregated electoral districts, I can see no reasonable alternative to abandoning our current unfortunate understanding of the Act.

I cannot adhere to the construction of § 2 embodied in our decision in *Thornburg v. Gingles*. I reject the assumption implicit in that case that the terms "standard, practice, or procedure" in § 2(a) of the Voting Rights Act can be construed to cover potentially dilutive electoral mechanisms. Understood in context, those terms extend the Act's prohibitions only to state enactments that regulate citizens' access to the ballot or the processes for counting a ballot. The terms do not include a State's or political subdivision's choice of one districting scheme over another.

III

[Omitted.]

NOTES ON JUSTICE THOMAS'S OPINION IN *HOLDER v. HALL*

1. Justice Thomas passionately attacks the Court's decisions to allow vote dilution challenges under both the Constitution (footnote 2) and the Voting Rights Act. Do you agree or disagree with his criticisms? Do you agree or disagree with his approach to interpreting the statutory language of amended Section 2?

2. Justice Thomas raises the prospect of the Court opting to order into effect a system of proportional representation (e.g., cumulative voting) rather than single-member districts as a remedy for vote dilution under Section 2. Even though Justice Thomas would not support the federal judiciary using Section 2 to install a system of proportional representation as a remedy for vote dilution, would you?

3. What does Justice Thomas's opinion (which reads like a dissent but is actually an opinion concurring in the judgment) add to the debate regarding the Court's role in resolving election disputes? Is there any way for the Court to decide redistricting cases without becoming too enmeshed in the "political thicket"? More specifically, Justice Thomas criticizes prior precedent for taking sides in what he ultimately concludes is a debate about political philosophy. Why does he think it is improper for the Court to determine, as a matter of law, what kinds of governmental structures pass muster either under the Constitution or the Voting Rights Act?

D. SECTION 5 OF THE VOTING RIGHTS ACT

The Voting Rights Act of 1965 contains another important provision related to redistricting: Section 5. As you will learn, Section 5 is quite distinct from Section 2. Section 5, however, was essentially rendered dormant by the U.S. Supreme Court's 2013 decision in *Shelby County v. Holder*. With the decision in *Shelby County*, you may wonder why it is necessary to learn about Section 5 at all. There are several reasons: (1) it is possible that Congress will address some of the constitutional concerns expressed by the Court in *Shelby County* and revive Section 5; (2) the Section 5 process—which will be described in detail below—may be revived through the use of Section 3(c) of the Voting Rights Act (which will also be described below); (3) it is possible that some of the substantive principles from Section 5—most notably Section 5's non-retrogression principle—will be imported into Section 2 litigation; (4) the decision in *Shelby County* may have implications for the constitutionality of Section 2 of the Voting Rights Act; and (5) Section 5 appeared to play an important role in the development of racial gerrymandering doctrine—which is the next topic we will tackle in relation to redistricting.

With that as an introduction, we will proceed with a somewhat lengthy description of Section 5 so as to provide adequate context for the two opinions from *Shelby County* that you will read—Chief Justice Roberts's opinion for a five-member majority and Justice Ginsburg's dissent.*

The Reason Section 5 was Created. Section 5 was part of the original Voting Rights Act of 1965. The history of Section 5 will be described in the *Shelby County* opinions, but for now it suffices to know that it was a response to what might be termed "massive resistance" on the part of Southern jurisdictions to the enfranchisement of African Americans. Prior to passage of the Voting Rights Act, many Southern jurisdictions refused to allow African-American citizens to register to vote—often through the discriminatory application of literacy tests by county boards of registrars. And even when successful lawsuits would be brought to enjoin existing discriminatory registration practices, the jurisdictions would then switch to a new discriminatory tactic not covered by the injunction. For instance, after receiving a court order to stop engaging in disparate treatment of white and African-American voters during the voter registration process, local registrars would just permanently close the voter registration office.

In reaction to these events, Congress developed Section 5. Section 5 had several features—each of which will be described in more detail below. First, Section 5 did not apply nationwide; instead, it applied only to certain jurisdictions. Second, a jurisdiction subject to Section 5 could "bail-out" and a jurisdiction not subject to Section 5 could be "bailed in." Third, Section 5 froze into place the existing voting laws, including redistricting plans, in these covered jurisdictions. Fourth, to change their existing voting laws, the covered jurisdictions would have to obtain "preclearance" from the federal government. Fifth, the federal government would review any voting changes to prevent racial discrimination. Sixth, Section 5 had a built-in sunset provision, but every time it was scheduled to lapse, Congress extended it.

* The description of Section 5 that follows is based largely on two law review articles: Michael J. Pitts, *Section 5 of the Voting Rights Act: A Once and Future Remedy?*, 81 Denv. U. L. Rev. 225 (2003) and Michael J. Pitts, *Redistricting and Discriminatory Purpose*, 59 Am. U. L. Rev. 1575 (2010).

Section 5 Coverage/Section 4 of the Voting Rights Act. Unlike amended Section 2 of the Voting Rights Act—which applies nationwide—Section 5 applied only to certain portions of the country (primarily states and counties), commonly referred to as the "covered jurisdictions." Jurisdictions were covered by Section 5 through a formula found in Section 4 of the Voting Rights Act that was designed to target places where voting discrimination had occurred. That formula, developed in 1965, focused on the combination of the use of a literacy test (or similar device) plus reduced participation in the election process as evidenced by low voter registration or low voter turnout rates. Originally (in 1965), the coverage formula captured the entire states of Alabama, Alaska, Georgia, Louisiana, Mississippi, South Carolina, and Virginia, along with 40 counties in North Carolina and a few other counties in Arizona, Hawaii, and Idaho.

Importantly, when a covered jurisdiction became subject to Section 5, all of the political subdivisions within the covered jurisdiction also fell within Section 5's ambit. For example, when the State of Alabama was covered by Section 5, the state was covered but so was every county, city, school district, and so forth within Alabama. Similarly, when Onslow County, North Carolina, was covered, the county was covered but so was every city, town, school district, and the like within Onslow County.

The coverage formula was updated in 1970 and 1975. The update in 1970 was not very significant. The update in 1975, though, expanded the notion of what a "literacy test" was to include the holding of elections solely in English where a critical mass of voters was from a single language-minority group (e.g., Spanish speakers). Notably, this change in the coverage formula resulted in, among other things, the States of Arizona and Texas becoming subject to Section 5.

The coverage formula did not undergo any changes after 1975, and this fact will become important for the majority in *Shelby County*. As of 2008 (one of the last dates on which the U.S. Department of Justice publicly published a map), the covered jurisdictions were as shown in Figure 1-3.

"Bail out." Once covered by Section 5, a jurisdiction could later escape coverage through a process known as "bail out." While the bail-out provision changed over the years, after 1982, to bail out of Section 5, a covered jurisdiction had to file for a declaratory judgment from a three-judge panel of the U.S. District Court for the District of Columbia and, essentially, prove that it had not engaged in voting-related discrimination for the previous ten years. Historically, relatively few covered jurisdictions bailed out, but, as you can see from the note at the bottom of the map in Figure 1-3, the number of jurisdictions bailing out increased quite a bit after 2000.

"Bail in" (Section 3(c) of the Voting Rights Act). A jurisdiction not originally covered by Section 5 can essentially be bailed into coverage using Section 3(c) of the Voting Rights Act. A court can order Section 3(c) coverage after "the court finds that violations of the fourteenth and fifteenth amendment justifying equitable relief have occurred" within the jurisdiction. 42 U.S.C. § 1973a. Historically, only a very few jurisdictions were "bailed in" under Section 3(c). However, with the decision in *Shelby County*, Section 3(c) may well take on greater prominence in future voting rights litigation.

Figure 1-3

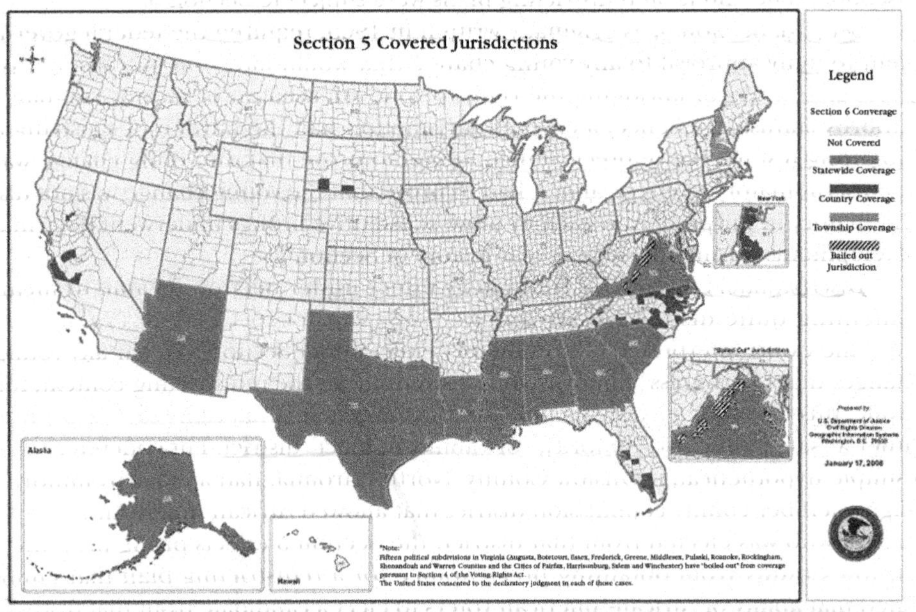

Source: U.S. Department of Justice.

Freezing of Voting Laws Until "Preclearance" Obtained. Having learned how jurisdictions were subjected to or escaped Section 5, it is time to turn to what Section 5 actually did. Section 5 froze into place the voting laws of the covered jurisdictions as of the date of coverage and required a jurisdiction to obtain "preclearance" from the federal government to implement a voting change. A covered jurisdiction could receive preclearance by litigation or through an administrative process. The litigation route involved obtaining a declaratory judgment from a three-judge panel of the U.S. District Court for the District of Columbia. The administrative process involved the covered jurisdiction submitting the voting change to the U.S. Department of Justice for review. (During Section 5's existence, the vast majority of preclearance activity took place through the administrative process.)

Here's a more concrete scenario about how Section 5 operates. After the State of Georgia passed its legislative redistricting plans following the 1970 Census, it could not immediately implement those plans. Instead, the state had to send its redistricting plans to Washington, D.C. for federal approval. Once federal approval ("preclearance") was obtained, only then could the State of Georgia hold elections under its redistricting plans.

Scope of Section 5 Review. There are two aspects important to understanding the scope of Section 5 review. The first is what types of laws were subject to Section 5. The second is the substantive standard for Section 5 preclearance.

First, Section 5 required covered jurisdictions to submit all their voting changes for Section 5 review. A voting change could be a switch in the location of a polling place, a change to voter identification laws, a shift in voting machinery from paper ballots to touch-screen machines, or any other aspect of laws that had a direct nexus to the voting process. Importantly for purposes of this section of the casebook, state and local redistricting plans were subject to Section 5.

Second, Section 5, as originally written in 1965, required the federal government to deny approval to any voting change that would have "the purpose . . . or effect of denying or abridging the right to vote" on account of race or language-minority status. In essence, a covered jurisdiction had the burden of satisfying a two-prong test to receive preclearance: It had to prove that the voting change was not discriminatory in effect; and, it had to prove that the voting change was not discriminatory in purpose. And each of these substantive prongs underwent doctrinal developments during the 40-plus year history of Section 5.

Discriminatory Effect. Discriminatory effect under Section 5 came to mean something quite distinctive. In *Beer v. United States*, 425 U.S. 130 (1976), the Supreme Court interpreted discriminatory effect under Section 5 to bar any voting changes that "retrogress" minority voting strength. In the redistricting context, for a time, this meant that a jurisdiction could not eliminate what came to be known as either a "safe," "majority-minority," or "ability to elect" district. Put concretely into a simple hypothetical, if Onslow County, North Carolina, had a majority-minority single-member county commission district that allowed African-American voters to control who was elected from that district, the Section 5 effects prong prevented Onslow County from obtaining preclearance for a redistricting plan that eliminated that ability of African-American voters to elect a candidate from that district.

In 2003, however, the Supreme Court came up with a more nuanced standard for retrogression in *Georgia v. Ashcroft*, 539 U.S. 461 (2003). A simplified description of *Ashcroft* is that the Court made the somewhat groundbreaking pronouncement that "ability to elect" districts could be traded off against so-called "influence" districts—districts where a minority group can influence an electoral outcome even if its preferred candidate cannot be elected. Put more concretely into a simplified hypothetical, a district with, say, 60 percent African-American population that provided African-American voters the ability to elect a candidate of their choice could potentially be replaced with districts that had, say, 30 percent African-American population that would not give African-American voters the ability to elect candidates of their choice, so long as African-American voters could "influence" who was elected from those districts.

However, the "tweak" to retrogression doctrine brought about by *Ashcroft* was short-lived. In 2006, when it extended Section 5, Congress also reversed the Supreme Court's decision in *Ashcroft* (which was a decision of statutory interpretation rather than a constitutional holding). Congress did so by restoring "ability to elect" as the touchstone against which retrogression should be judged in the redistricting context.

Discriminatory Purpose. The broad strokes of the discriminatory purpose prong are much like the discriminatory effect prong: Initially, the discriminatory purpose prong was interpreted one way; then, in the early 2000s, the Supreme Court reinterpreted the purpose prong; and, subsequently, Congress reversed the Supreme Court's reinterpretation.

The initial interpretation of the discriminatory purpose prong was that preclearance could be denied to a redistricting plan if it was adopted for *any* discriminatory purpose. What this meant was that preclearance could be denied if a redistricting plan resulted in unconstitutional vote dilution of the type prohibited by a case you have already encountered—*Rogers v. Lodge*. Basically, the result of this interpretation was that Section 5 could be used to compel covered jurisdictions to create additional districts that provided minority voters with the ability to elect candidates of their choice.

The Supreme Court, however, curbed the reach of Section 5's discriminatory purpose prong in *Reno v. Bossier Parish School Board*, 528 U.S. 320 (2000) (*Bossier Parish II*). In that case, the Court engaged in an interpretation of the statutory language to confine denial of preclearance under the purpose prong to redistricting plans that were adopted with a *purpose to retrogress.* Confining the purpose clause in this way ended the ability to use Section 5 to compel the creation of more single-member districts that would allow minority voters to elect candidates of their choice.

Again, though, this shift in the interpretation of the purpose prong was short-lived. In 2006, when deciding whether to extend Section 5, Congress reversed the Supreme Court's decision in *Bossier Parish II.* Congress did so by restoring the ability of the federal government to deny preclearance when a redistricting plan was adopted with *any* discriminatory purpose.

Sunset Provision and Extensions. When it was first enacted in 1965, Section 5 contained a sunset provision that would lead to its lapsing in 1970. In 1970, Congress extended Section 5 for another five years. In 1975, Congress extended Section 5 for another seven years. In 1982, Congress extended Section 5 for another 25 years. And in 2006, Congress extended Section 5 for another 25 years (until 2031). It is this most recent 2006 extension that was at issue in *Shelby County.*

Prior Challenges to Constitutionality. As you may have noticed from the above description, Section 5 was a unique and somewhat extraordinary statute. There is not really an analogous statute anywhere in the U.S. Code. For this reason, the constitutionality of Section 5 itself and all its various facets has been questioned since its initial passage in 1965. A majority of the Supreme Court upheld Section 5 in the seminal decision of *South Carolina v. Katzenbach*, 383 U.S. 301 (1966). The constitutionality of each of the subsequent extensions of Section 5 were also litigated over the years, but—prior to *Shelby County*—each time the Court declined to declare Section 5—or any of its integral component pieces—invalid. *See Georgia v. United States*, 411 U.S. 526 (1973); *City of Rome v. United States*, 446 U.S. 156 (1980); *Lopez v. Monterey County*, 526 U.S. 266 (1999).

Almost immediately after the 2006 extension, a small utility district in Texas brought a lawsuit seeking to bail out of Section 5 and also seeking to have the statute struck down as unconstitutional. *Northwest Austin Municipal Utility District No. One v. Holder*, 557 U.S. 193 (2009) ("*NAMUDNO*"). In that case, a majority of the Court declined to rule on Section 5's constitutionality and instead engaged in an interpretation of the statute that allowed the utility district to bail out. However, in several paragraphs of *dicta*, the Court made plain that Section 5 raised serious constitutional concerns. *Shelby County* then picks up where that *dicta* left off.

Shelby County v. Holder

133 S. Ct. 2612 (2013)

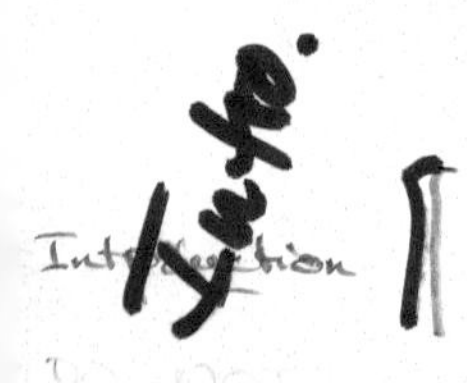

Chief Justice ROBERTS delivered the opinion of the Court.

The Voting Rights Act of 1965 employed extraordinary measures to address an extraordinary problem. Section 5 of the Act required States to obtain federal permission before enacting any law related to voting—a drastic departure from basic principles of federalism. And § 4 of the Act applied that requirement only to some States—an equally dramatic departure from the principle that all States enjoy equal sovereignty. This was strong medicine, but Congress determined it was needed to address entrenched racial discrimination in voting, "an insidious and pervasive evil which had been perpetuated in certain parts of our country through unremitting and ingenious defiance of the Constitution." *South Carolina v. Katzenbach* (1966). As we explained in upholding the law, "exceptional conditions can justify legislative measures not otherwise appropriate." Reflecting the unprecedented nature of these measures, they were scheduled to expire after five years.

Nearly 50 years later, they are still in effect; indeed, they have been made more stringent, and are now scheduled to last until 2031. There is no denying, however, that the conditions that originally justified these measures no longer characterize voting in the covered jurisdictions. By 2009, the racial gap in voter registration and turnout [was] lower in the States originally covered by § 5 than it [was] nationwide. Since that time, Census Bureau data indicate that African-American voter turnout has come to exceed white voter turnout in five of the six States originally covered by § 5, with a gap in the sixth State of less than one half of one percent.

At the same time, voting discrimination still exists; no one doubts that. The question is whether the Act's extraordinary measures, including its disparate treatment of the States, continue to satisfy constitutional requirements. As we put it a short time ago, "the Act imposes current burdens and must be justified by current needs." *Northwest Austin* [*Municipal Utility District No. One v. Holder*] (2009).

I

A

The Fifteenth Amendment was ratified in 1870, in the wake of the Civil War. It provides that "[t]he right of citizens of the United States to vote shall not be denied or abridged by the United States or by any State on account of race, color, or previous condition of servitude," and it gives Congress the "power to enforce this article by appropriate legislation."

The first century of congressional enforcement of the Amendment, however, can only be regarded as a failure. In the 1890s, Alabama, Georgia, Louisiana, Mississippi, North Carolina, South Carolina, and Virginia began to enact literacy tests for voter registration and to employ other methods designed to prevent African-Americans from voting. Congress passed statutes outlawing some of these practices and facilitating litigation against them, but litigation remained slow and expensive, and the States came up with new ways to discriminate as soon as existing ones were struck down. Voter registration of African-Americans barely improved.

Inspired to action by the civil rights movement, Congress responded in 1965 with the Voting Rights Act. Section 2 was enacted to forbid, in all 50 States, any "standard, practice, or procedure . . . imposed or applied . . . to deny or abridge the right of any citizen of the United States to vote on account of race or color." The current version forbids any "standard, practice, or procedure" that "results in a denial or abridgement of the right of any citizen of the United States to vote on account of race or color." Both the Federal Government and individuals have sued to enforce § 2, and injunctive relief is available in appropriate cases to block voting laws from going into effect. Section 2 is permanent, applies nationwide, and is not at issue in this case.

Other sections [of the Voting Rights Act] targeted only some parts of the country. At the time of the Act's passage, these "covered" jurisdictions were those States or political subdivisions that had maintained a test or device as a prerequisite to voting as of November 1, 1964, and had less than 50 percent voter registration or turnout in the 1964 Presidential election. Such tests or devices included literacy and knowledge tests, good moral character requirements, the need for vouchers from registered voters, and the like. A covered jurisdiction could "bail out" of coverage if it had not used a test or device in the preceding five years "for the purpose or with the effect of denying or abridging the right to vote on account of race or color." In 1965, the covered States included Alabama, Georgia, Louisiana, Mississippi, South Carolina, and Virginia. The additional covered subdivisions included 39 counties in North Carolina and one in Arizona.

In those jurisdictions, § 4 of the Act banned all such tests or devices. Section 5 [of the Act] provided that no change in voting procedures could take effect until it was approved by federal authorities in Washington, D.C.—either the Attorney General or a court of three judges. A jurisdiction could obtain such "preclearance" only by proving that the change had neither "the purpose [nor] the effect of denying or abridging the right to vote on account of race or color."

Sections 4 and 5 were intended to be temporary; they were set to expire after five years. In *South Carolina v. Katzenbach*, we upheld the 1965 Act against constitutional challenge, explaining that it was justified to address "voting discrimination where it persists on a pervasive scale."

In 1970, Congress reauthorized the Act for another five years, and extended the coverage formula in § 4(b) to jurisdictions that had a voting test and less than 50 percent voter registration or turnout as of 1968. That swept in several counties in California, New Hampshire, and New York. Congress also extended the ban in § 4(a) on tests and devices nationwide.

In 1975, Congress reauthorized the Act for seven more years, and extended its coverage to jurisdictions that had a voting test and less than 50 percent voter registration or turnout as of 1972. Congress also amended the definition of "test or device" to include the practice of providing English-only voting materials in places where over five percent of voting-age citizens spoke a single language other than English. As a result of these amendments, the States of Alaska, Arizona, and Texas, as well as several counties in California, Florida, Michigan, New York, North Carolina, and South Dakota, became covered jurisdictions. Congress correspondingly amended sections 2 and 5 to forbid voting discrimination on the basis of membership in a language minority group, in addition to discrimination on the basis of race or color. Finally, Congress made the nationwide ban on tests and devices permanent.

In 1982, Congress reauthorized the Act for 25 years, but did not alter its coverage formula. Congress did, however, amend the bailout provisions, allowing political subdivisions of covered jurisdictions to bail out. Among other prerequisites for bailout, jurisdictions and their subdivisions must not have used a forbidden test or device, failed to receive preclearance, or lost a § 2 suit, in the ten years prior to seeking bailout.

We upheld each of these reauthorizations against constitutional challenge. *See Georgia v. United States* (1973); *City of Rome v. United States* (1980); *Lopez v. Monterey County* (1999).

In 2006, Congress again reauthorized the Voting Rights Act for 25 years, again without change to its coverage formula. Congress also amended § 5 to prohibit more conduct than before. Section 5 now forbids voting changes with "any discriminatory purpose" as well as voting changes that diminish the ability of citizens, on account of race, color, or language minority status, "to elect their preferred candidates of choice."

Shortly after this reauthorization, a Texas utility district brought suit, seeking to bail out from the Act's coverage and, in the alternative, challenging the Act's constitutionality. *Northwest Austin.* A three-judge District Court explained that only a State or political subdivision was eligible to seek bailout under the statute, and concluded that the utility district was not a political subdivision, a term that encompassed only "counties, parishes, and voter-registering subunits." The District Court also rejected the constitutional challenge.

We reversed. We explained that "normally the Court will not decide a constitutional question if there is some other ground upon which to dispose of the case." Concluding that "underlying constitutional concerns," among other things, "compel[led] a broader reading of the bailout provision," we construed the statute to allow the utility district to seek bailout. In doing so we expressed serious doubts about the Act's continued constitutionality.

We explained that § 5 "imposes substantial federalism costs" and "differentiates between the States, despite our historic tradition that all the States enjoy equal sovereignty." We also noted that "[t]hings have changed in the South. Voter turnout and registration rates now approach parity. Blatantly discriminatory evasions of federal decrees are rare. And minority candidates hold office at unprecedented levels." Finally, we questioned whether the problems that § 5 meant to address were still "concentrated in the jurisdictions singled out for preclearance."

Eight Members of the Court subscribed to these views, and the remaining Member would have held the Act unconstitutional. Ultimately, however, the Court's construction of the bailout provision left the constitutional issues for another day.

B

Shelby County is located in Alabama, a covered jurisdiction. It has not sought bailout, as the Attorney General has recently objected to voting changes proposed from within the county. Instead, in 2010, the county sued the Attorney General in Federal District Court in Washington, D.C., seeking a declaratory judgment that sections 4(b) and 5 of the Voting Rights Act are facially unconstitutional. The District Court ruled against the county and upheld the Act. [The Court of Appeals for the D.C. Circuit affirmed, and the Court granted certiorari.]

II

In *Northwest Austin,* we stated that "the Act imposes current burdens and must be justified by current needs." And we concluded that "a departure from the fundamental principle of equal sovereignty requires a showing that a statute's disparate

geographic coverage is sufficiently related to the problem that it targets." These basic principles guide our review of the question before us.[3]

A

The Constitution and laws of the United States are "the supreme Law of the Land." U.S. Const., Art. VI, cl. 2. State legislation may not contravene federal law. The Federal Government does not, however, have a general right to review and veto state enactments before they go into effect. A proposal to grant such authority to "negative" state laws was considered at the Constitutional Convention, but rejected in favor of allowing state laws to take effect, subject to later challenge under the Supremacy Clause.

Outside the strictures of the Supremacy Clause, States retain broad autonomy in structuring their governments and pursuing legislative objectives. Indeed, the Constitution provides that all powers not specifically granted to the Federal Government are reserved to the States or citizens. Amdt. 10. This allocation of powers in our federal system preserves the integrity, dignity, and residual sovereignty of the States. But the federal balance is not just an end in itself: Rather, federalism secures to citizens the liberties that derive from the diffusion of sovereign power.

More specifically, the Framers of the Constitution intended the States to keep for themselves, as provided in the Tenth Amendment, the power to regulate elections. Of course, the Federal Government retains significant control over federal elections. For instance, the Constitution authorizes Congress to establish the time and manner for electing Senators and Representatives. Art. I, § 4, cl. 1. But States have broad powers to determine the conditions under which the right of suffrage may be exercised. And [e]ach State has the power to prescribe the qualifications of its officers and the manner in which they shall be chosen. Drawing lines for congressional districts is likewise primarily the duty and responsibility of the State.

Not only do States retain sovereignty under the Constitution, there is also a "fundamental principle of equal sovereignty" among the States. *Northwest Austin.* Over a hundred years ago, this Court explained that our Nation "was and is a union of States, equal in power, dignity and authority." *Coyle v. Smith* (1911). Indeed, the constitutional equality of the States is essential to the harmonious operation of the scheme upon which the Republic was organized. *Coyle* concerned the admission of new States, and *Katzenbach* rejected the notion that the principle operated as a bar on differential treatment outside that context. At the same time, as we made clear in *Northwest Austin,* the fundamental principle of equal sovereignty remains highly pertinent in assessing subsequent disparate treatment of States.

The Voting Rights Act sharply departs from these basic principles. It suspends all changes to state election law—however innocuous—until they have been precleared by federal authorities in Washington, D.C. States must beseech the Federal Government for permission to implement laws that they would otherwise have the right to enact and execute on their own, subject of course to any injunction in a § 2 action.

3. Both the Fourteenth and Fifteenth Amendments were at issue in *Northwest Austin,* and accordingly *Northwest Austin* guides our review under both Amendments in this case.

And despite the tradition of equal sovereignty, the Act applies to only nine States (and several additional counties). While one State waits [for preclearance], its neighbor can typically put the same law into effect immediately, through the normal legislative process. Even if a noncovered jurisdiction is sued, there are important differences between those proceedings and preclearance proceedings; the preclearance proceeding not only switches the burden of proof to the supplicant jurisdiction, but also applies substantive standards quite different from those governing the rest of the nation.

All this explains why, when we first upheld the Act in 1966, we described it as "stringent" and "potent." *Katzenbach.* We recognized that it "may have been an uncommon exercise of congressional power," but concluded that "legislative measures not otherwise appropriate" could be justified by "exceptional conditions." We have since noted that the Act authorizes federal intrusion into sensitive areas of state and local policymaking, and represents an extraordinary departure from the traditional course of relations between the States and the Federal Government. As we reiterated in *Northwest Austin,* the Act constitutes "extraordinary legislation otherwise unfamiliar to our federal system."

B

In 1966, we found these departures from the basic features of our system of government justified. The "blight of racial discrimination in voting" had "infected the electoral process in parts of our country for nearly a century." *Katzenbach.* Several States had enacted a variety of requirements and tests specifically designed to prevent African-Americans from voting. Case-by-case litigation had proved inadequate to prevent such racial discrimination in voting, in part because States "merely switched to discriminatory devices not covered by the federal decrees," "enacted difficult new tests," or simply "defied and evaded court orders." *Id.* Shortly before enactment of the Voting Rights Act, only 19.4 percent of African-Americans of voting age were registered to vote in Alabama, only 31.8 percent in Louisiana, and only 6.4 percent in Mississippi. Those figures were roughly 50 percentage points or more below the figures for whites.

In short, we concluded that "[u]nder the compulsion of these unique circumstances, Congress responded in a permissibly decisive manner." *Id.* We also noted then and have emphasized since that this extraordinary legislation was intended to be temporary, set to expire after five years.

At the time, the coverage formula—the means of linking the exercise of the unprecedented authority with the problem that warranted it—made sense. We found that "Congress chose to limit its attention to the geographic areas where immediate action seemed necessary." *Katzenbach.* The areas where Congress found "evidence of actual voting discrimination" shared two characteristics: the use of tests and devices for voter registration, and a voting rate in the 1964 presidential election at least 12 points below the national average. We explained that "[t]ests and devices are relevant to voting discrimination because of their long history as a tool for perpetrating the evil; a low voting rate is pertinent for the obvious reason that widespread disenfranchisement must inevitably affect the number of actual voters." We therefore concluded that "the coverage formula [was] rational in both practice and theory." It accurately reflected those jurisdictions uniquely characterized by voting discrimination "on a pervasive scale," linking coverage to the devices used to effectuate discrimination and to the resulting disenfranchisement. The formula ensured that the "stringent remedies [were] aimed at areas where voting discrimination ha[d] been most flagrant."

C

Nearly 50 years later, things have changed dramatically. Shelby County contends that the preclearance requirement, even without regard to its disparate coverage, is now unconstitutional. Its arguments have a good deal of force. In the covered jurisdictions, "[v]oter turnout and registration rates now approach parity. Blatantly discriminatory evasions of federal decrees are rare. And minority candidates hold office at unprecedented levels." *Northwest Austin*. The tests and devices that blocked access to the ballot have been forbidden nationwide for over 40 years.

Those conclusions are not ours alone. Congress said the same when it reauthorized the Act in 2006, writing that "[s]ignificant progress has been made in eliminating first generation barriers experienced by minority voters, including increased numbers of registered minority voters, minority voter turnout, and minority representation in Congress, State legislatures, and local elected offices." The House Report elaborated that "the number of African-Americans who are registered and who turn out to cast ballots has increased significantly over the last 40 years, particularly since 1982," and noted that "[i]n some circumstances, minorities register to vote and cast ballots at levels that surpass those of white voters." That Report also explained that there have been "significant increases in the number of African-Americans serving in elected offices"; more specifically, there has been approximately a 1,000 percent increase since 1965 in the number of African-American elected officials in the six States originally covered by the Voting Rights Act.

Census Bureau data from the most recent election indicate that African-American voter turnout exceeded white voter turnout in five of the six States originally covered by § 5, with a gap in the sixth State of less than one half of one percent. The preclearance statistics are also illuminating. In the first decade after enactment of § 5, the Attorney General objected to 14.2 percent of proposed voting changes. In the last decade before reenactment, the Attorney General objected to a mere 0.16 percent.

There is no doubt that these improvements are in large part because of the Voting Rights Act. The Act has proved immensely successful at redressing racial discrimination and integrating the voting process. During the "Freedom Summer" of 1964, in Philadelphia, Mississippi, three men were murdered while working in the area to register African-American voters. On "Bloody Sunday" in 1965, in Selma, Alabama, police beat and used tear gas against hundreds marching in support of African-American enfranchisement. Today both of those towns are governed by African-American mayors. Problems remain in these States and others, but there is no denying that, due to the Voting Rights Act, our Nation has made great strides.

Yet the Act has not eased the restrictions in § 5 or narrowed the scope of the coverage formula in § 4(b) along the way. Those extraordinary and unprecedented features were reauthorized—as if nothing had changed. In fact, the Act's unusual remedies have grown even stronger. When Congress reauthorized the Act in 2006, it did so for another 25 years on top of the previous 40—a far cry from the initial five-year period. Congress also expanded the prohibitions in § 5. We had previously interpreted § 5 to prohibit only those redistricting plans that would have the purpose or effect of worsening the position of minority groups. *Bossier II.* In 2006, Congress amended § 5 to prohibit laws that could have favored such groups but did not do so because of a discriminatory purpose. In addition, Congress expanded § 5 to prohibit any voting law "that has the purpose of or will have the effect of diminishing the ability of any citizens of the United States," on account of race, color, or language minority status, "to elect their preferred candidates of choice." § 1973c(b). In light of those two amendments, the bar that covered jurisdictions must clear has been raised even as the conditions justifying that requirement have dramatically improved.

Respondents do not deny that there have been improvements on the ground, but argue that much of this can be attributed to the deterrent effect of § 5, which dissuades covered jurisdictions from engaging in discrimination that they would resume should § 5 be struck down. Under this theory, however, § 5 would be effectively immune from scrutiny; no matter how "clean" the record of covered jurisdictions, the argument could always be made that it was deterrence that accounted for the good behavior.

The provisions of § 5 apply only to those jurisdictions singled out by § 4. We now consider whether that coverage formula is constitutional in light of current conditions.

III

A

When upholding the constitutionality of the coverage formula in 1966, we concluded that it was "rational in both practice and theory." *Katzenbach.* The formula looked to cause (discriminatory tests) and effect (low voter registration and turnout), and tailored the remedy (preclearance) to those jurisdictions exhibiting both.

By 2009, however, we concluded that the "coverage formula raise[d] serious constitutional questions." *Northwest Austin.* As we explained, a statute's "current burdens" must be justified by "current needs," and any "disparate geographic coverage" must be "sufficiently related to the problem that it targets." The coverage formula met that test in 1965, but no longer does so.

Coverage today is based on decades-old data and eradicated practices. The formula captures States by reference to literacy tests and low voter registration and turnout in the 1960s and early 1970s. But such tests have been banned nationwide for over 40 years. And voter registration and turnout numbers in the covered States have risen dramatically in the years since. Racial disparity in those numbers was compelling evidence justifying the preclearance remedy and the coverage formula. There is no longer such a disparity.

In 1965, the States could be divided into two groups: those with a recent history of voting tests and low voter registration and turnout, and those without those characteristics. Congress based its coverage formula on that distinction. Today the Nation is no longer divided along those lines, yet the Voting Rights Act continues to treat it as if it were.

B

The Government's defense of the formula is limited. First, the Government contends that the formula is "reverse-engineered": Congress identified the jurisdictions to be covered and then came up with criteria to describe them. Under that reasoning, there need not be any logical relationship between the criteria in the formula and the reason for coverage; all that is necessary is that the formula happen to capture the jurisdictions Congress wanted to single out.

The Government suggests that *Katzenbach* sanctioned such an approach, but the analysis in *Katzenbach* was quite different. *Katzenbach* reasoned that the coverage formula was rational because the "formula . . . was relevant to the problem": "Tests and devices are relevant to voting discrimination because of their long history as a tool for perpetrating the evil; a low voting rate is pertinent for the obvious reason that widespread disenfranchisement must inevitably affect the number of actual voters."

Here, by contrast, the Government's reverse-engineering argument does not even attempt to demonstrate the continued relevance of the formula to the problem it targets. And in the context of a decision as significant as this one—subjecting a disfavored subset of States to "extraordinary legislation otherwise unfamiliar to our federal system," *Northwest Austin*—that failure to establish even relevance is fatal.

The Government falls back to the argument that because the formula was relevant in 1965, its continued use is permissible so long as any discrimination remains in the States Congress identified back then—regardless of how that discrimination compares to discrimination in States unburdened by coverage. This argument does not look to "current political conditions," *Northwest Austin*, but instead relies on a comparison between the States in 1965. That comparison reflected the different histories of the North and South. It was in the South that slavery was upheld by law until uprooted by the Civil War, that the reign of Jim Crow denied African-Americans the most basic freedoms, and that state and local governments worked tirelessly to disenfranchise citizens on the basis of race. The Court invoked that history—rightly so—in sustaining the disparate coverage of the Voting Rights Act in 1966.

But history did not end in 1965. By the time the Act was reauthorized in 2006, there had been 40 more years of it. In assessing the "current need[]" for a preclearance system that treats States differently from one another today, that history cannot be ignored. During that time, largely because of the Voting Rights Act, voting tests were abolished, disparities in voter registration and turnout due to race were erased, and African-Americans attained political office in record numbers. And yet the coverage formula that Congress reauthorized in 2006 ignores these developments, keeping the focus on decades-old data relevant to decades-old problems, rather than current data reflecting current needs.

The Fifteenth Amendment commands that the right to vote shall not be denied or abridged on account of race or color, and it gives Congress the power to enforce that command. The Amendment is not designed to punish for the past; its purpose is to ensure a better future. To serve that purpose, Congress—if it is to divide the States—must identify those jurisdictions to be singled out on a basis that makes sense in light of current conditions. It cannot rely simply on the past. We made that clear in *Northwest Austin*, and we make it clear again today.

C

In defending the coverage formula, the Government, the intervenors, and the dissent also rely heavily on data from the record that they claim justify disparate coverage. Congress compiled thousands of pages of evidence before reauthorizing the Voting Rights Act. The court below and the parties have debated what that record shows. Regardless of how to look at the record, however, no one can fairly say that it shows anything approaching the "pervasive," "flagrant," "widespread," and "rampant" discrimination that faced Congress in 1965, and that clearly distinguished the covered jurisdictions from the rest of the Nation at that time.

But a more fundamental problem remains: Congress did not use the record it compiled to shape a coverage formula grounded in current conditions. It instead reenacted a formula based on 40-year-old facts having no logical relation to the present day. The dissent relies on "second-generation barriers," which are not impediments to the casting of ballots, but rather electoral arrangements that affect the weight of minority votes. That does not cure the problem. Viewing the preclearance requirements as targeting such efforts simply highlights the irrationality of continued reliance on the § 4 coverage formula, which is based on voting tests and access to the ballot, not vote dilution. We cannot pretend that we are reviewing an updated statute, or try our hand at updating the statute ourselves, based on the new record compiled by Congress. Contrary to the dissent's contention, we are not ignoring the record; we are simply recognizing that it played no role in shaping the statutory formula before us today.

The dissent also turns to the record to argue that, in light of voting discrimination in Shelby County, the county cannot complain about the provisions that subject it to preclearance. But that is like saying that a driver pulled over pursuant to a policy of stopping all redheads cannot complain about that policy, if it turns out his license has expired. Shelby County's claim is that the coverage formula here is unconstitutional in all its applications, because of how it selects the jurisdictions subjected to preclearance. The county was selected based on that formula, and may challenge it in court.

D

The dissent proceeds from a flawed premise. It quotes the famous sentence from *McCulloch v. Maryland,* with the following emphasis: "Let the end be legitimate, let it be within the scope of the constitution, and *all means which are appropriate, which are plainly adapted to that end,* which are not prohibited, but consist with the letter and spirit of the constitution, are constitutional." (Emphasis in dissent.) But this case is about a part of the sentence that the dissent does not emphasize—the part that asks whether a legislative means is "consist[ent] with the letter and spirit of the constitution." The dissent states that "[i]t cannot tenably be maintained" that this is an issue with regard to the Voting Rights Act, but four years ago, in an opinion joined by two of today's dissenters, the Court expressly stated that "[t]he Act's preclearance requirement and its coverage formula raise serious constitutional questions." *Northwest Austin.* The dissent does not explain how those "serious constitutional questions" became untenable in four short years.

The dissent treats the Act as if it were just like any other piece of legislation, but this Court has made clear from the beginning that the Voting Rights Act is far from ordinary.

In other ways as well, the dissent analyzes the question presented as if our decision in *Northwest Austin* never happened. For example, the dissent refuses to consider the principle of equal sovereignty, despite *Northwest Austin*'s emphasis on its significance. *Northwest Austin* also emphasized the "dramatic" progress since 1965, but the dissent describes current levels of discrimination as "flagrant," "widespread," and "pervasive." Despite the fact that *Northwest Austin* requires an Act's "disparate geographic coverage" to be "sufficiently related" to its targeted problems, the dissent maintains that an Act's limited coverage actually eases Congress's burdens, and suggests that a fortuitous relationship should suffice. Although *Northwest Austin* stated definitively that "current burdens" must be justified by "current needs," the dissent argues that the coverage formula can be justified by history, and that the required showing can be weaker on reenactment than when the law was first passed.

There is no valid reason to insulate the coverage formula from review merely because it was previously enacted 40 years ago. If Congress had started from scratch in 2006, it plainly could not have enacted the present coverage formula. It would have been irrational for Congress to distinguish between States in such a fundamental way based on 40-year-old data, when today's statistics tell an entirely different story. And it would have been irrational to base coverage on the use of voting tests 40 years ago, when such tests have been illegal since that time. But that is exactly what Congress has done.

3

Striking down an Act of Congress is the gravest and most delicate duty that this Court is called on to perform. We do not do so lightly. That is why, in 2009, we took care to avoid ruling on the constitutionality of the Voting Rights Act when asked to do so, and instead resolved the case then before us on statutory grounds. But in issuing that decision, we expressed our broader concerns about the constitutionality of the Act. Congress could have updated the coverage formula at that time, but did not do so. Its failure to act leaves us today with no choice but to declare § 4(b) unconstitutional. The formula in that section can no longer be used as a basis for subjecting jurisdictions to preclearance.

Our decision in no way affects the permanent, nationwide ban on racial discrimination in voting found in § 2. We issue no holding on § 5 itself, only on the coverage formula. Congress may draft another formula based on current conditions. Such a formula is an initial prerequisite to a determination that exceptional conditions still exist justifying such an extraordinary departure from the traditional course of relations between the States and the Federal Government. Our country has changed, and while any racial discrimination in voting is too much, Congress must ensure that the legislation it passes to remedy that problem speaks to current conditions.

The judgment of the Court of Appeals is reversed.

Justice THOMAS, concurring.
[Omitted.]

Justice GINSBURG, with whom Justice BREYER, Justice SOTOMAYOR, and Justice KAGAN join, dissenting.

In the Court's view, the very success of § 5 of the Voting Rights Act demands its dormancy. Congress was of another mind. Recognizing that large progress has been made, Congress determined, based on a voluminous record, that the scourge of discrimination was not yet extirpated. The question this case presents is who decides whether, as currently operative, § 5 remains justifiable[1], this Court, or a Congress charged with the obligation to enforce the post-Civil War Amendments "by appropriate legislation." With overwhelming support in both Houses, Congress concluded that, for two prime reasons, § 5 should continue in force, unabated. First, continuance would facilitate completion of the impressive gains thus far made; and second, continuance would guard against backsliding. Those assessments were well within Congress' province to make and should elicit this Court's unstinting approbation.

I

[V]oting discrimination still exists; no one doubts that. But the Court today terminates the remedy that proved to be best suited to block that discrimination. The Voting Rights Act of 1965 (VRA) has worked to combat voting discrimination where other remedies had been tried and failed. Particularly effective is the VRA's requirement of federal preclearance for all changes to voting laws in the regions of the country with the most aggravated records of rank discrimination against minority voting rights.

A century after the Fourteenth and Fifteenth Amendments guaranteed citizens the right to vote free of discrimination on the basis of race, the "blight of racial discrimination in voting" continued to "infec[t] the electoral process in parts of our country." *South Carolina v. Katzenbach.* Early attempts to cope with this vile infection resembled battling the Hydra. Whenever one form of voting discrimination was identified and prohibited, others sprang up in its place.

Congress learned from experience that laws targeting particular electoral practices or enabling case-by-case litigation were inadequate to the task [of attacking racial discrimination in voting]. In the Civil Rights Acts of 1957, 1960, and 1964, Congress authorized and then expanded the power of the Attorney General to seek injunctions against public and private interference with the right to vote on racial grounds. But circumstances reduced the ameliorative potential of these legislative Acts:

> "Voting suits are unusually onerous to prepare, sometimes requiring as many as 6,000 man-hours spent combing through registration records in preparation for trial. Litigation has been exceedingly slow, in part because of the ample opportunities for delay afforded voting officials and others involved in the proceedings. Even when favorable decisions have finally been obtained, some of the States affected have merely switched to discriminatory devices not covered by the federal decrees or have enacted difficult new tests designed to prolong the existing disparity between white and Negro registration. Alternatively, certain local officials have

1. The Court purports to declare unconstitutional only the coverage formula set out in § 4(b). But without that formula, § 5 is immobilized.

defied and evaded court orders or have simply closed their registration offices to freeze the voting rolls." [*Katzenbach.*]

Patently, a new approach was needed.

Answering that need, the Voting Rights Act became one of the most consequential, efficacious, and amply justified exercises of federal legislative power in our Nation's history. Requiring federal preclearance of changes in voting laws in the covered jurisdictions—those States and localities where opposition to the Constitution's commands were most virulent—the VRA provided a fit solution for minority voters as well as for States. Under the preclearance regime established by § 5 of the VRA, covered jurisdictions must submit proposed changes in voting laws or procedures to the Department of Justice (DOJ). In the alternative, the covered jurisdiction may seek approval by a three-judge District Court in the District of Columbia.

After a century's failure to fulfill the promise of the Fourteenth and Fifteenth Amendments, passage of the VRA finally led to signal improvement on this front. [I]n assessing the overall effects of the VRA in 2006, Congress found that "[s]ignificant progress has been made in eliminating first generation barriers experienced by minority voters, including increased numbers of registered minority voters, minority voter turnout, and minority representation in Congress, State legislatures, and local elected offices. This progress is the direct result of the Voting Rights Act of 1965." On that matter of cause and effects there can be no genuine doubt.

Although the VRA wrought dramatic changes in the realization of minority voting rights, the Act, to date, surely has not eliminated all vestiges of discrimination against the exercise of the franchise by minority citizens. Jurisdictions covered by the preclearance requirement continued to submit, in large numbers, proposed changes to voting laws that the Attorney General declined to approve, auguring that barriers to minority voting would quickly resurface were the preclearance remedy eliminated. Congress also found that as "registration and voting of minority citizens increas[ed], other measures may be resorted to which would dilute increasing minority voting strength." Efforts to reduce the impact of minority votes, in contrast to direct attempts to block access to the ballot, are aptly described as "second-generation barriers" to minority voting.

Second-generation barriers come in various forms. One of the blockages is racial gerrymandering, the redrawing of legislative districts in an "effort to segregate the races for purposes of voting." Another is adoption of a system of at-large voting in lieu of district-by-district voting in a city with a sizable black minority. By switching to at-large voting, the overall majority could control the election of each city council member, effectively eliminating the potency of the minority's votes. Whatever the device employed, this Court has long recognized that vote dilution, when adopted with a discriminatory purpose, cuts down the right to vote as certainly as denial of access to the ballot.

In response to evidence of these substituted barriers, Congress reauthorized the VRA for five years in 1970, for seven years in 1975, and for 25 years in 1982. Each time, this Court upheld the reauthorization as a valid exercise of congressional power. As the 1982 reauthorization approached its 2007 expiration date, Congress again considered whether the VRA's preclearance mechanism remained an appropriate response to the problem of voting discrimination in covered jurisdictions.

Congress did not take this task lightly. Quite the opposite. The 109th Congress that took responsibility for the renewal started early and conscientiously. In October 2005, the House began extensive hearings. In April 2006, the Senate followed suit. [Eventually, the reauthorization of the Voting Rights Act passed the House by a vote of 390 yeas to 33 nays and passed the Senate by a vote of 98 to 0. President Bush signed it on July 27, 2006.]

In the long course of the legislative process, Congress "amassed a sizable record." *Northwest Austin.* The [record] presents countless examples of flagrant racial discrimination since the last reauthorization; Congress also brought to light systematic evidence that intentional racial discrimination in voting remains so serious and widespread in covered jurisdictions that section 5 preclearance is still needed.

After considering the full legislative record, Congress made the following findings: The VRA has directly caused significant progress in eliminating first-generation barriers to ballot access, leading to a marked increase in minority voter registration and turnout and the number of minority elected officials. But despite this progress, "second generation barriers constructed to prevent minority voters from fully participating in the electoral process" continued to exist, as well as racially polarized voting in the covered jurisdictions, which increased the political vulnerability of racial and language minorities in those jurisdictions. Extensive "[e]vidence of continued discrimination," Congress concluded, "clearly show[ed] the continued need for Federal oversight" in covered jurisdictions. The overall record demonstrated to the federal lawmakers that, "without the continuation of the Voting Rights Act of 1965 protections, racial and language minority citizens will be deprived of the opportunity to exercise their right to vote, or will have their votes diluted, undermining the significant gains made by minorities in the last 40 years."

Based on these findings, Congress reauthorized preclearance for another 25 years. The question before the Court is whether Congress had the authority under the Constitution to act as it did.

II

In answering this question, the Court does not write on a clean slate. It is well established that Congress' judgment regarding exercise of its power to enforce the Fourteenth and Fifteenth Amendments warrants substantial deference. The VRA addresses the combination of race discrimination and the right to vote, which is "preservative of all rights." *Yick Wo v. Hopkins* (1886). When confronting the most constitutionally invidious form of discrimination, and the most fundamental right in our democratic system, Congress' power to act is at its height.

The basis for this deference is firmly rooted in both constitutional text and precedent. The Fifteenth Amendment, which targets precisely and only racial discrimination in voting rights, states that, in this domain, "Congress shall have power to enforce this article by appropriate legislation." [2] In choosing this language, the

2. The Constitution uses the words "right to vote" in five separate places: the Fourteenth, Fifteenth, Nineteenth, Twenty-Fourth, and Twenty-Sixth Amendments. Each of these Amendments contains the same broad empowerment of Congress to enact "appropriate

Amendment's framers invoked Chief Justice Marshall's formulation of the scope of Congress' powers under the Necessary and Proper Clause:

> "Let the end be legitimate, let it be within the scope of the constitution, and *all means which are appropriate, which are plainly adapted to that end*, which are not prohibited, but consist with the letter and spirit of the constitution, are constitutional." *McCulloch v. Maryland* (1819) (emphasis added).

It cannot tenably be maintained that the VRA, an Act of Congress adopted to shield the right to vote from racial discrimination, is inconsistent with the letter or spirit of the Fifteenth Amendment, or any provision of the Constitution read in light of the Civil War Amendments. Nowhere in today's opinion, or in *Northwest Austin*,[3] is there clear recognition of the transformative effect the Fifteenth Amendment aimed to achieve. Notably, the Founders' first successful amendment told Congress that it could make no law over a certain domain; in contrast, the Civil War Amendments used language [that] authorized transformative new federal statutes to uproot all vestiges of unfreedom and inequality and provided sweeping enforcement powers to enact appropriate legislation targeting state abuses.

Until today, in considering the constitutionality of the VRA, the Court has accorded Congress the full measure of respect its judgments in this domain should garner. *South Carolina v. Katzenbach* supplies the standard of review: "As against the reserved powers of the States, Congress may use any rational means to effectuate the constitutional prohibition of racial discrimination in voting." Faced with subsequent reauthorizations of the VRA, the Court has reaffirmed this standard. *City of Rome*. Today's Court does not purport to alter settled precedent establishing that the dispositive question is whether Congress has employed "rational means."

For three reasons, legislation reauthorizing an existing statute is especially likely to satisfy the minimal requirements of the rational-basis test. First, when reauthorization is at issue, Congress has already assembled a legislative record justifying the initial legislation. Congress is entitled to consider that preexisting record as well as the record before it at the time of the vote on reauthorization. This is especially true where, as here, the Court has repeatedly affirmed the statute's constitutionality and Congress has adhered to the very model the Court has upheld.

Second, the very fact that reauthorization is necessary arises because Congress has built a temporal limitation into the Act. It has pledged to review, after a span of years and in light of contemporary evidence, the continued need for the VRA.

Third, a reviewing court should expect the record supporting reauthorization to be less stark than the record originally made. Demand for a record of violations equivalent to the one earlier made would expose Congress to a catch-22. If the

legislation" to enforce the protected right. The implication is unmistakable: Under our constitutional structure, Congress holds the lead rein in making the right to vote equally real for all U.S. citizens. These Amendments are in line with the special role assigned to Congress in protecting the integrity of the democratic process in federal elections. U.S. Const., Art. I, §4 ("[T]he Congress may at any time by Law make or alter" regulations concerning the "Times, Places and Manner of holding Elections for Senators and Representatives.").

3. Acknowledging the existence of "serious constitutional questions," does not suggest how those questions should be answered.

statute was working, there would be less evidence of discrimination, so opponents might argue that Congress should not be allowed to renew the statute. In contrast, if the statute was not working, there would be plenty of evidence of discrimination, but scant reason to renew a failed regulatory regime.

This is not to suggest that congressional power in this area is limitless. It is this Court's responsibility to ensure that Congress has used appropriate means. The question meet for judicial review is whether the chosen means are adapted to carry out the objects the amendments have in view. The Court's role, then, is not to substitute its judgment for that of Congress, but to determine whether the legislative record sufficed to show that Congress could rationally have determined that [its chosen] provisions were appropriate methods.

In summary, the Constitution vests broad power in Congress to protect the right to vote, and in particular to combat racial discrimination in voting. This Court has repeatedly reaffirmed Congress' prerogative to use any rational means in exercise of its power in this area. And both precedent and logic dictate that the rational-means test should be easier to satisfy, and the burden on the statute's challenger should be higher, when what is at issue is the reauthorization of a remedy that the Court has previously affirmed, and that Congress found, from contemporary evidence, to be working to advance the legislature's legitimate objective.

III

The 2006 reauthorization of the Voting Rights Act fully satisfies the standard stated in *McCulloch*.

A

I begin with the evidence on which Congress based its decision to continue the preclearance remedy. The surest way to evaluate whether that remedy remains in order is to see if preclearance is still effectively preventing discriminatory changes to voting laws. On that score, the record before Congress was huge. In fact, Congress found there were more DOJ objections between 1982 and 2004 (626) than there were between 1965 and the 1982 reauthorization (490).

All told, between 1982 and 2006, DOJ objections blocked over 700 voting changes based on a determination that the changes were discriminatory. Congress found that the majority of DOJ objections included findings of discriminatory intent.

In addition to blocking proposed voting changes through preclearance, DOJ may request more information from a jurisdiction proposing a change. In turn, the jurisdiction may modify or withdraw the proposed change. The number of such modifications or withdrawals provides an indication of how many discriminatory proposals are deterred without need for formal objection. Congress received evidence that more than 800 proposed changes were altered or withdrawn since the last reauthorization in 1982.[4]

4. This number includes only changes actually proposed. Congress also received evidence that many covered jurisdictions engaged in an "informal consultation process" with DOJ before formally submitting a proposal, so that the deterrent effect of preclearance was far broader than the formal submissions alone suggest.

Congress also received evidence that litigation under § 2 of the VRA was an inadequate substitute for preclearance in the covered jurisdictions. Litigation occurs only after the fact, when the illegal voting scheme has already been put in place and individuals have been elected pursuant to it, thereby gaining the advantages of incumbency. And litigation places a heavy financial burden on minority voters. Congress also received evidence that preclearance lessened the litigation burden on covered jurisdictions themselves, because the preclearance process is far less costly than defending against a § 2 claim, and clearance by DOJ substantially reduces the likelihood that a § 2 claim will be mounted.

The number of discriminatory changes blocked or deterred by the preclearance requirement suggests that the state of voting rights in the covered jurisdictions would have been significantly different absent this remedy. Set out below are characteristic examples of changes blocked in the years leading up to the 2006 reauthorization:

- Following the 2000 census, the City of Albany, Georgia, proposed a redistricting plan that DOJ found to be "designed with the purpose to limit and retrogress the increased black voting strength . . . in the city as a whole."
- In 2006, this Court found that Texas' attempt to redraw a congressional district to reduce the strength of Latino voters bore "the mark of intentional discrimination that could give rise to an equal protection violation," and ordered the district redrawn in compliance with the VRA. *League of United Latin American Citizens v. Perry*. In response, Texas sought to undermine this Court's order by curtailing early voting in the district, but was blocked by an action to enforce the § 5 preclearance requirement.
- In 2003, after African-Americans won a majority of the seats on the school board for the first time in history, Charleston County, South Carolina, proposed an at-large voting mechanism for the board. The proposal, made without consulting any of the African-American members of the school board, was found to be an exact replica of an earlier voting scheme that, a federal court had determined, violated the VRA. DOJ invoked § 5 to block the proposal.
- In 1993, the City of Millen, Georgia, proposed to delay the election in a majority-black district by two years, leaving that district without representation on the city council while the neighboring majority-white district would have three representatives. DOJ blocked the proposal. The county then sought to move a polling place from a predominantly black neighborhood in the city to an inaccessible location in a predominantly white neighborhood outside city limits.
- In 1990, Dallas County, Alabama, whose county seat is the City of Selma, sought to purge its voter rolls of many black voters. DOJ rejected the purge as discriminatory, noting that it would have disqualified many citizens from voting "simply because they failed to pick up or return a voter update form, when there was no valid requirement that they do so."

These examples, and scores more like them, fill the pages of the legislative record. The evidence was indeed sufficient to support Congress' conclusion that "racial discrimination in voting in covered jurisdictions [remained] serious and pervasive."

True, conditions in the South have impressively improved since passage of the Voting Rights Act. Congress noted this improvement and found that the VRA was the driving force behind it. But Congress also found that voting discrimination had evolved into subtler second-generation barriers, and that eliminating preclearance would risk loss of the gains that had been made.

B

I turn next to the evidence on which Congress based its decision to reauthorize the coverage formula in § 4(b). Because Congress did not alter the coverage formula, the same jurisdictions previously subject to preclearance continue to be covered by this remedy. The evidence just described, of preclearance's continuing efficacy in blocking constitutional violations in the covered jurisdictions, itself grounded Congress' conclusion that the remedy should be retained for those jurisdictions.

There is no question, moreover, that the covered jurisdictions have a unique history of problems with racial discrimination in voting. Consideration of this long history, still in living memory, was altogether appropriate. The Court criticizes Congress for failing to recognize that "history did not end in 1965." But the Court ignores that "what's past is prologue." And "[t]hose who cannot remember the past are condemned to repeat it." Congress was especially mindful of the need to reinforce the gains already made and to prevent backsliding.

Of particular importance, even after 40 years and thousands of discriminatory changes blocked by preclearance, conditions in the covered jurisdictions demonstrated that the formula was still justified by "current needs." *Northwest Austin.*

Congress learned of these conditions through a report, known as the Katz study, that looked at § 2 suits between 1982 and 2004. Because the private right of action authorized by § 2 of the VRA applies nationwide, a comparison of § 2 lawsuits in covered and noncovered jurisdictions provides an appropriate yardstick for measuring differences between covered and noncovered jurisdictions. If differences in the risk of voting discrimination between covered and noncovered jurisdictions had disappeared, one would expect that the rate of successful § 2 lawsuits would be roughly the same in both areas.[6] The study's findings, however, indicated that racial discrimination in voting remains concentrated in the jurisdictions singled out for preclearance.

Although covered jurisdictions account for less than 25 percent of the country's population, the Katz study revealed that they accounted for 56 percent of successful § 2 litigation since 1982. The Katz study further found that § 2 lawsuits are more likely to succeed when they are filed in covered jurisdictions than in noncovered jurisdictions. From these findings—ignored by the Court—Congress reasonably concluded that the coverage formula continues to identify the jurisdictions of greatest concern.

6. Because preclearance occurs only in covered jurisdictions and can be expected to stop the most obviously objectionable measures, one would expect a lower rate of successful § 2 lawsuits in those jurisdictions if the risk of voting discrimination there were the same as elsewhere in the country.

The evidence before Congress, furthermore, indicated that voting in the covered jurisdictions was more racially polarized than elsewhere in the country. While racially polarized voting alone does not signal a constitutional violation, it is a factor that increases the vulnerability of racial minorities to discriminatory changes in voting law. The reason is twofold. First, racial polarization means that racial minorities are at risk of being systematically outvoted and having their interests underrepresented in legislatures. Second, when political preferences fall along racial lines, the natural inclinations of incumbents and ruling parties to entrench themselves have predictable racial effects. Under circumstances of severe racial polarization, efforts to gain political advantage translate into race-specific disadvantages.

In other words, a governing political coalition has an incentive to prevent changes in the existing balance of voting power. When voting is racially polarized, efforts by the ruling party to pursue that incentive will inevitably discriminate against a racial group. Just as buildings in California have a greater need to be earthquake-proofed, places where there is greater racial polarization in voting have a greater need for prophylactic measures to prevent purposeful race discrimination. This point was understood by Congress and is well recognized in the academic literature.

The case for retaining a coverage formula that met needs on the ground was therefore solid. Congress might have been charged with rigidity had it afforded covered jurisdictions no way out or ignored jurisdictions that needed superintendence. Congress, however, responded to this concern. Critical components of the congressional design are the statutory provisions allowing jurisdictions to "bail out" of preclearance, and for court-ordered "bail ins." The VRA permits a jurisdiction to bail out. It also authorizes a court to subject a noncovered jurisdiction to federal preclearance upon finding that violations of the Fourteenth and Fifteenth Amendments have occurred there.

Congress was satisfied that the VRA's bailout mechanism provided an effective means of adjusting the VRA's coverage over time. The bail-in mechanism has also worked.

This experience exposes the inaccuracy of the Court's portrayal of the Act as static, unchanged since 1965. Congress designed the VRA to be a dynamic statute, capable of adjusting to changing conditions. True, many covered jurisdictions have not been able to bail out due to recent acts of noncompliance with the VRA, but that truth reinforces the congressional judgment that these jurisdictions were rightfully subject to preclearance, and ought to remain under that regime.

IV

Congress approached the 2006 reauthorization of the VRA with great care and seriousness. The same cannot be said of the Court's opinion today. The Court makes no genuine attempt to engage with the massive legislative record that Congress assembled. Instead, it relies on increases in voter registration and turnout as if that were the whole story. Without even identifying a standard of review, the Court dismissively brushes off arguments based on "data from the record," and declines to enter the "debat[e about] what [the] record shows." One would expect more from an opinion striking at the heart of the Nation's signal piece of civil-rights legislation.

I note the most disturbing lapses. First, by what right, given its usual restraint, does the Court even address Shelby County's facial challenge to the VRA? Second, the Court veers away from controlling precedent regarding the "equal sovereignty" doctrine without even acknowledging that it is doing so. Third, hardly showing the respect ordinarily paid when Congress acts to implement the Civil War Amendments, and as just stressed, the Court does not even deign to grapple with the legislative record.

A

Shelby County launched a purely facial challenge to the VRA's 2006 reauthorization. "A facial challenge to a legislative Act," the Court has other times said, "is, of course, the most difficult challenge to mount successfully, since the challenger must establish that no set of circumstances exists under which the Act would be valid." *United States v. Salerno* (1987).

Embedded in the traditional rules governing constitutional adjudication is the principle that a person to whom a statute may constitutionally be applied will not be heard to challenge that statute on the ground that it may conceivably be applied unconstitutionally to others, in other situations not before the Court. Yet the Court's opinion in this case contains not a word explaining why Congress lacks the power to subject to preclearance the particular plaintiff that initiated this lawsuit—Shelby County, Alabama. The reason for the Court's silence is apparent, for as applied to Shelby County, the VRA's preclearance requirement is hardly contestable.

Alabama is home to Selma, site of the "Bloody Sunday" beatings of civil-rights demonstrators that served as the catalyst for the VRA's enactment. Following those events, Martin Luther King, Jr., led a march from Selma to Montgomery, Alabama's capital, where he called for passage of the VRA. If the Act passed, he foresaw, progress could be made even in Alabama, but there had to be a steadfast national commitment to see the task through to completion. In King's words, "the arc of the moral universe is long, but it bends toward justice."

History has proved King right. Although circumstances in Alabama have changed, serious concerns remain. Between 1982 and 2005, Alabama had one of the highest rates of successful § 2 suits, second only to its VRA-covered neighbor Mississippi. In other words, even while subject to the restraining effect of § 5, Alabama was found to have "deni[ed] or abridge[d]" voting rights "on account of race or color" more frequently than nearly all other States in the Union. Alabama's sorry history of § 2 violations alone provides sufficient justification for Congress' determination in 2006 that the State should remain subject to § 5's preclearance requirement.[7]

7. This lawsuit was filed by Shelby County, a political subdivision of Alabama, rather than by the State itself. Nevertheless, it is appropriate to judge Shelby County's constitutional challenge in light of instances of discrimination statewide because Shelby County is subject to § 5's preclearance requirement by virtue of Alabama's designation as a covered jurisdiction under § 4(b) of the VRA. In any event, Shelby County's recent record of employing an at-large electoral system tainted by intentional racial discrimination is by itself sufficient to justify subjecting the county to § 5's preclearance mandate.

A few examples suffice to demonstrate that, at least in Alabama, the "current burdens" imposed by § 5's preclearance requirement are "justified by current needs." *Northwest Austin.* In the interim between the VRA's 1982 and 2006 reauthorizations, this Court twice confronted purposeful racial discrimination in Alabama. In *Pleasant Grove v. United States* (1987), the Court held that Pleasant Grove—a city in Jefferson County, Shelby County's neighbor—engaged in purposeful discrimination by annexing all-white areas while rejecting the annexation request of an adjacent black neighborhood.

Two years before *Pleasant Grove,* the Court in *Hunter v. Underwood* (1985) struck down a provision of the Alabama Constitution that prohibited individuals convicted of misdemeanor offenses "involving moral turpitude" from voting. The provision violated the Fourteenth Amendment's Equal Protection Clause, the Court unanimously concluded, because "its original enactment was motivated by a desire to discriminate against blacks on account of race[,] and the [provision] continues to this day to have that effect." *Id.*

Pleasant Grove and *Hunter* were not anomalies. In 1986, a Federal District Judge concluded that the at-large election systems in several Alabama counties violated § 2. *Dillard v. Baldwin Cty. Bd. of Ed.* (M.D. Ala. 1988). Summarizing its findings, the court stated that "[f]rom the late 1800's through the present, [Alabama] has consistently erected barriers to keep black persons from full and equal participation in the social, economic, and political life of the state."

The *Dillard* litigation ultimately expanded to include 183 cities, counties, and school boards employing discriminatory at-large election systems. One of those defendants was Shelby County, which eventually signed a consent decree to resolve the claims against it.

Although the *Dillard* litigation resulted in overhauls of numerous electoral systems tainted by racial discrimination, concerns about backsliding persist. In 2008, for example, the city of Calera, located in Shelby County, requested preclearance of a redistricting plan that would have eliminated the city's sole majority-black district, which had been created pursuant to the consent decree in *Dillard.* Although DOJ objected to the plan, Calera forged ahead with elections based on the unprecleared voting changes, resulting in the defeat of the incumbent African-American councilman who represented the former majority-black district. The city's defiance required DOJ to bring a § 5 enforcement action that ultimately yielded appropriate redress, including restoration of the majority-black district.

A recent FBI investigation provides a further window into the persistence of racial discrimination in state politics. Recording devices worn by state legislators cooperating with the FBI's investigation captured conversations between members of the state legislature and their political allies. The recorded conversations are shocking. Members of the state Senate derisively refer to African-Americans as "Aborigines" and talk openly of their aim to quash a particular gambling-related referendum because the referendum, if placed on the ballot, might increase African-American voter turnout (legislators and their allies expressed concern that if the referendum were placed on the ballot, "[e]very black, every illiterate would be bused [to the polls] on HUD financed buses"). These conversations occurred not in the 1870's, or even in the 1960's, they took place in 2010. The District Judge presiding over the criminal trial at which the recorded conversations were introduced commented that the "recordings represent compelling evidence that political exclusion through racism remains a real and enduring problem" in Alabama. Racist sentiments, the judge observed, "remain regrettably entrenched in the high echelons of state government."

These recent episodes forcefully demonstrate that § 5's preclearance requirement is constitutional as applied to Alabama and its political subdivisions.[8] And under our case law, that conclusion should suffice to resolve this case.

This Court has consistently rejected constitutional challenges to legislation enacted pursuant to Congress' enforcement powers under the Civil War Amendments upon finding that the legislation was constitutional as applied to the particular set of circumstances before the Court. A similar approach is warranted here.

Leaping to resolve Shelby County's facial challenge without considering whether application of the VRA to Shelby County is constitutional can hardly be described as an exemplar of restrained and moderate decisionmaking. Quite the opposite. Hubris is a fit word for today's demolition of the VRA.

B

The Court stops any application of § 5 by holding that § 4(b)'s coverage formula is unconstitutional. It pins this result, in large measure, to "the fundamental principle of equal sovereignty." In *Katzenbach*, however, the Court held, in no uncertain terms, that the principle "*applies only to the terms upon which States are admitted to the Union*, and not to the remedies for local evils which have subsequently appeared" (emphasis added).

Katzenbach, the Court acknowledges, "rejected the notion that the [equal sovereignty] principle operate[s] as a bar on differential treatment outside [the] context [of the admission of new States]." But the Court clouds that once clear understanding by citing dictum from *Northwest Austin* to convey that the principle of equal sovereignty "remains highly pertinent in assessing subsequent disparate treatment of States." If the Court is suggesting that dictum in *Northwest Austin* silently overruled *Katzenbach*'s limitation of the equal sovereignty doctrine to "the admission of new States," the suggestion is untenable. *Northwest Austin* cited *Katzenbach's* holding in the course of declining to decide whether the VRA was constitutional or even what standard of review applied to the question. In today's decision, the Court ratchets up what was pure dictum in *Northwest Austin*, attributing breadth to the equal sovereignty principle in flat contradiction of *Katzenbach*. The Court does so with nary an explanation of why it finds *Katzenbach* wrong, let alone any discussion of whether *stare decisis* nonetheless counsels adherence to *Katzenbach*'s ruling on the limited "significance" of the equal sovereignty principle.

Today's unprecedented extension of the equal sovereignty principle outside its proper domain—the admission of new States—is capable of much mischief. Federal statutes that treat States disparately are hardly novelties. *See, e.g.*, 28 U.S.C. § 3704 (no State may operate or permit a sports-related gambling scheme, unless that State conducted such a scheme "at any time during the period beginning January 1, 1976, and ending August 31, 1990"); 26 U.S.C. § 142(l) (EPA required to

8. Congress continued preclearance over Alabama, including Shelby County, after considering evidence of current barriers there to minority voting clout. Shelby County, thus, is no "redhead" caught up in an arbitrary scheme.

locate green building project in a State meeting specified population criteria); 42 U.S.C. § 3796bb (at least 50 percent of rural drug enforcement assistance funding must be allocated to States with "a population density of fifty-two or fewer persons per square mile or a State in which the largest county has fewer than one hundred and fifty thousand people, based on the decennial census of 1990 through fiscal year 1997"). Do such provisions remain safe given the Court's expansion of equal sovereignty's sway?

Of gravest concern, Congress relied on our pathmarking *Katzenbach* decision in each reauthorization of the VRA. It had every reason to believe that the Act's limited geographical scope would weigh in favor of, not against, the Act's constitutionality. Congress could hardly have foreseen that the VRA's limited geographic reach would render the Act constitutionally suspect.

In the Court's conception, it appears, defenders of the VRA could not prevail upon showing what the record overwhelmingly bears out, i.e., that there is a need for continuing the preclearance regime in covered States. In addition, the defenders would have to disprove the existence of a comparable need elsewhere. I am aware of no precedent for imposing such a double burden on defenders of legislation.

C

[T]he Court strikes § 4(b)'s coverage provision because, in its view, the provision is not based on "current conditions." It discounts, however, that one such condition was the preclearance remedy in place in the covered jurisdictions, a remedy Congress designed both to catch discrimination before it causes harm, and to guard against return to old ways. Volumes of evidence supported Congress' determination that the prospect of retrogression was real. Throwing out preclearance when it has worked and is continuing to work to stop discriminatory changes is like throwing away your umbrella in a rainstorm because you are not getting wet.

Consider once again the components of the record before Congress in 2006. The coverage provision identified a known list of places with an undisputed history of serious problems with racial discrimination in voting. Recent evidence relating to Alabama and its counties was there for all to see. Multiple Supreme Court decisions had upheld the coverage provision, most recently in 1999. There was extensive evidence that, due to the preclearance mechanism, conditions in the covered jurisdictions had notably improved. And there was evidence that preclearance was still having a substantial real-world effect, having stopped hundreds of discriminatory voting changes in the covered jurisdictions since the last reauthorization. In addition, there was evidence that racial polarization in voting was higher in covered jurisdictions than elsewhere, increasing the vulnerability of minority citizens in those jurisdictions. And countless witnesses, reports, and case studies documented continuing problems with voting discrimination in those jurisdictions. In light of this record, Congress had more than a reasonable basis to conclude that the existing coverage formula was not out of sync with conditions on the ground in covered areas. And certainly Shelby County was no candidate for release through the mechanism Congress provided.

The Court holds § 4(b) invalid on the ground that it is "irrational to base coverage on the use of voting tests 40 years ago, when such tests have been illegal since that time." But the Court disregards what Congress set about to do in enacting the VRA. That extraordinary legislation scarcely stopped at the particular tests and devices that happened to exist in 1965. The grand aim of the Act is to secure to all in our polity equal citizenship stature, a voice in our democracy undiluted by race. As the record for the 2006 reauthorization makes abundantly clear, second-generation barriers to minority voting rights have emerged in the covered jurisdictions as attempted substitutes for the first-generation barriers that originally triggered preclearance in those jurisdictions.

The sad irony of today's decision lies in its utter failure to grasp why the VRA has proven effective. The Court appears to believe that the VRA's success in eliminating the specific devices extant in 1965 means that preclearance is no longer needed. With that belief, and the argument derived from it, history repeats itself. The same assumption—that the problem could be solved when particular methods of voting discrimination are identified and eliminated—was indulged and proved wrong repeatedly prior to the VRA's enactment. Unlike prior statutes, which singled out particular tests or devices, the VRA is grounded in Congress' recognition of the "variety and persistence" of measures designed to impair minority voting rights. *Katzenbach.* In truth, the evolution of voting discrimination into more subtle second-generation barriers is powerful evidence that a remedy as effective as preclearance remains vital to protect minority voting rights and prevent backsliding.

Beyond question, the VRA is no ordinary legislation. It is extraordinary because Congress embarked on a mission long delayed and of extraordinary importance: to realize the purpose and promise of the Fifteenth Amendment. For a half century, a concerted effort has been made to end racial discrimination in voting. Thanks to the Voting Rights Act, progress once the subject of a dream has been achieved and continues to be made.

The record supporting the 2006 reauthorization of the VRA is also extraordinary. After exhaustive evidence-gathering and deliberative process, Congress reauthorized the VRA, including the coverage provision, with overwhelming bipartisan support. It was the judgment of Congress that "40 years has not been a sufficient amount of time to eliminate the vestiges of discrimination following nearly 100 years of disregard for the dictates of the 15th amendment and to ensure that the right of all citizens to vote is protected as guaranteed by the Constitution." That determination of the body empowered to enforce the Civil War Amendments "by appropriate legislation" merits this Court's utmost respect. In my judgment, the Court errs egregiously by overriding Congress' decision.

For the reasons stated, I would affirm the judgment of the Court of Appeals.

NOTES ON *SHELBY COUNTY*

1. As a matter of policy, should Congress have extended Section 5 in 2006? Why or why not? Should Congress have amended Section 5—or just updated Section 4 (the coverage formula)? If so, how?

2. At one level, the debate between Chief Justice Roberts and Justice Ginsburg is about how much the Court should defer to Congress's legislative judgment in the context of racial discrimination in voting. Both sides appear to agree that the test is a rational basis test. The two disagree, though, as to whether the coverage

formula meets that rationality standard. Who has the better of the rational basis argument? Is Chief Justice Roberts applying a rational basis test or is he implicitly applying a tougher test?

3. Should Congress pass legislation amending the coverage formula found in Section 4? Why or why not? If so, what should that coverage formula look like? Note that even if Congress enacts a new coverage formula that passes muster with the Court's majority, *Shelby County* leaves open the question of whether Section 5 itself is constitutional. In other words, even with an updated coverage formula, a majority of the Court could still strike down Section 5. In your best judgment, how likely is it that the Court in its current composition would invalidate Section 5, even with an updated coverage formula?

4. The civil rights community vociferously called upon Congress to fix the Voting Rights Act in the wake of *Shelby County*. Yet the politics of voting rights are not what they have been for much of the last century. The passage of the Voting Rights Act in 1965, as well as its repeated extensions—including the most recent one in 2006—have been bipartisan endeavors, with both Democrats and Republicans overwhelmingly supporting the Act. (In 2006 the vote was 390–33 in the House and 98–0 in the Senate, and Republican President George W. Bush signed the reauthorization of the Voting Rights Act to much fanfare.) Yet that bipartisanship appears to have broken down. What has caused this breakdown of bipartisanship on the issue of voting rights, and is it possible to bring it back? How much, if any, of this breakdown is attributable to the fact that the United States elected President Barack Obama as its first African-American president? Or is the lack of bipartisanship on voting rights just a subset of the extreme polarization of politics that has been witnessed in recent years?

5. At oral argument in *Shelby County*, Justice Scalia controversially spoke of Section 5 as a kind of racial entitlement that, once granted, is difficult to dislodge; even if "politically incorrect," is there something valid to the point that the civil rights community, as an interest group, has become unduly enamored of the preclearance regime, which inevitably bred resentment among covered jurisdictions, and is a kind of remedy that one hopes that the nation can outgrow?

6. As a result of the decision in *Shelby County*, the Department of Justice and plaintiffs have turned to Section 3(c) of the Voting Rights Act as a mechanism to "recapture" some of the covered jurisdictions into preclearance. As of July 2019, at least two federal courts had bailed in cities that were previously subject to preclearance. *Perez v. Abbott*, No. SA-11-CV-360 (W.D. Tex. July 24, 2019), Slip. Op. at 2-3 (citing *Allen v. City of Evergreen*, No. 13-0107-CG-M, 2014 WL 12607819 (S.D. Ala. Jan. 13, 2014) and *Patino v. City of Pasadena*, 230 F. Supp. 3d 667, 729 (S.D. Tex. 2017)). In one prominent litigation, plaintiffs sought to bail-in the State of Texas. *Perez v. Abbott*, No. SA-11-CV-360 (W.D. Tex. July 24, 2019). However, the request for bail-in was denied. *Id.* Is litigation under Section 3(c) superior to the coverage formula held to be unconstitutional in *Shelby County*?

7. Following the amendment to Section 2 in 1982 that created the "results" standard, most litigation in the realm of racial and ethnic vote dilution has been resolved on statutory rather than constitutional grounds. However, with the

decision in Shelby County and bail-in under Section 3(c) requiring a finding of a constitutional violation, vote dilution plaintiffs have an renewed incentive to allege constitutional claims and press for substantive rulings on the merits of those claims.

E. *RACE-BASED GERRYMANDERS*

In relation to the intersection of race and redistricting, we have seen that the United States Constitution and Section 2 of the Voting Rights Act prohibit the implementation of districting plans that are discriminatory in purpose or result. We have also seen that, up until the summer of 2013, Section 5 of the Voting Rights Act prohibited certain state and local governments from implementing redistricting plans that were discriminatory in purpose or effect (i.e., retrogressive). These requirements were in force in one form or another since the passage of the Voting Rights Act in 1965, the initial constitutional vote dilution cases in the 1970s (*Whitcomb v. Chavis* and *White v. Regester*), and the amendment to Section 2 of the Act in 1982.

In the early 1990s, the Supreme Court added another important piece to the race and redistricting puzzle: the creation of a new constitutional doctrine of racial gerrymandering. As you will see, under certain circumstances, the doctrine of racial gerrymandering bars the use of race in the redistricting process. In this way, the doctrine of racial gerrymandering may operate as a potential counterforce to the requirements of the Voting Rights Act.

The Supreme Court's initial statement on the doctrine of racial gerrymandering came in *Shaw v. Reno* (1992). In *Shaw*, a group of North Carolina voters challenged the state's creation of two congressional districts: District 1 and District 12. These two congressional districts were drawn to comply with the Voting Rights Act by providing African-American voters the ability to elect candidates of African-American voters' choice. However, the two districts ended up being bizarrely shaped, in the eyes of some. District 1, for example, was vividly described as looking like a "bug splattered on a windshield." District 12 stretched for about 160 miles, much of it along an interstate highway, such that one legislator remarked "[i]f you drove down the interstate with both car doors open, you'd kill most of the people in the district." (Figure 1-4 shows both District 1 and District 12 as challenged in *Shaw.*)

The *Shaw* plaintiffs claimed that North Carolina's consideration of race in the creation of those districts was an unconstitutional racial gerrymander in violation of the Equal Protection Clause. A federal district court dismissed the racial gerrymandering claim for failure to state a claim upon which relief could be granted, but the Supreme Court reversed. The Supreme Court held that plaintiffs could state a cognizable claim by alleging that the redistricting was "so irrational on its face that it could be understood only as an effort to segregate voters into separate voting districts because of their race, and that the separation lack[ed] sufficient justification."

The Supreme Court set forth a number of reasons for recognizing claims of racial gerrymandering under the Equal Protection Clause. The key rationale appeared in the following two paragraphs:

> A reapportionment plan that includes in one district individuals who belong to the same race, but who are otherwise widely separated by geographical and political boundaries, and who may have little in common with one another but the color of their skin, bears an uncomfortable resemblance to political apartheid. It reinforces the perception that members of the same racial group—regardless of their age, education, economic status, or the community in which they live—think alike, share the same political interests, and will prefer the same candidates at the polls. We have rejected such perceptions elsewhere as impermissible racial stereotypes. By perpetuating such notions, a racial gerrymander may exacerbate the very patterns of racial bloc voting that majority-minority districting is sometimes said to counteract.
>
> The message that such districting sends to elected representatives is equally pernicious. When a district obviously is created solely to effectuate the perceived common interests of one racial group, elected officials are more likely to believe that their primary obligation is to represent only the members of that group, rather than their constituency as a whole. This is altogether antithetical to our system of representative democracy. *Shaw v. Reno,* 509 U.S. 630, 647-648 (1992).

In *Shaw,* the Supreme Court recognized that claims of racial gerrymandering were constitutionally cognizable but did not decide the merits of the claim. Instead, the Court remanded the case for a determination of whether North Carolina had, indeed, engaged in unconstitutional racial gerrymandering. In essence, while the Supreme Court recognized a constitutional claim, it left the standard for evaluating the claim up in the air. The next case, *Miller v. Johnson,* provides a ruling on the merits of a racial gerrymandering claim.

Figure 1-4 NORTH CAROLINA CONGRESSIONAL PLAN Chapter 7 of the 1991 Session Laws (1991 Extra Session)

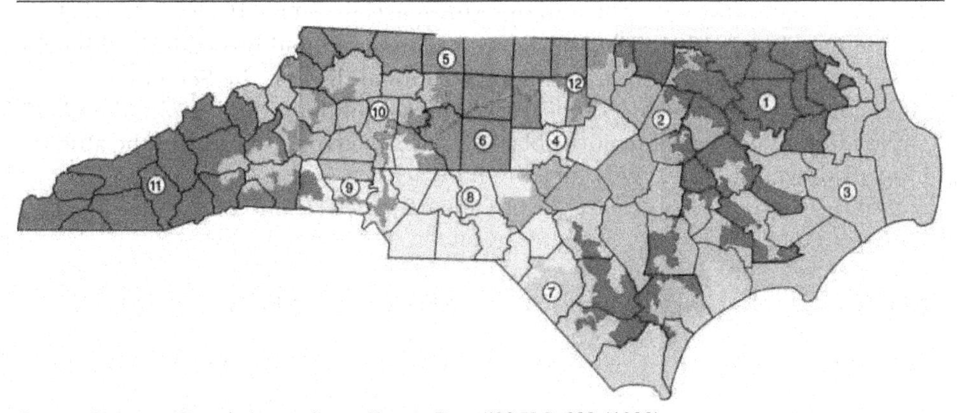

Source: Supreme Court's Appendix to *Shaw v. Reno,* 509 U.S. 630 (1993)

Miller v. Johnson

515 U.S. 900 (1995)

Justice KENNEDY delivered the opinion of the Court.

The constitutionality of Georgia's congressional redistricting plan is at issue here. In *Shaw v. Reno*, we held that a plaintiff states a claim under the Equal Protection Clause by alleging that a state redistricting plan, on its face, has no rational explanation save as an effort to separate voters on the basis of race. The question we now decide is whether Georgia's new Eleventh District gives rise to a valid equal protection claim under the principles announced in *Shaw*, and, if so, whether it can be sustained nonetheless as narrowly tailored to serve a compelling governmental interest.

I

[Section] 5 of the [Voting Rights] Act requires Georgia to obtain either administrative preclearance by the Attorney General or approval by the United States District Court for the District of Columbia of any change in a "standard, practice, or procedure with respect to voting" made after November 1, 1964. 42 U.S.C. § 1973c. The preclearance mechanism applies to congressional redistricting plans, and requires that the proposed change "not have the purpose and will not have the effect of denying or abridging the right to vote on account of race or color."

Between 1980 and 1990, one of Georgia's 10 congressional districts was a majority-black district, that is, a majority of the district's voters were black. The 1990 Decennial Census indicated that Georgia's population of 6,478,216 persons, 27% of whom are black, entitled it to an additional eleventh congressional seat, prompting Georgia's General Assembly to redraw the State's congressional districts. Both the House and the Senate adopted redistricting guidelines which, among other things, required single-member districts of equal population, contiguous geography, nondilution of minority voting strength, fidelity to precinct lines where possible, and compliance with §§ 2 and 5 of the [Voting Rights] Act. Only after these requirements were met did the guidelines permit drafters to consider other ends, such as maintaining the integrity of political subdivisions, preserving the core of existing districts, and avoiding contests between incumbents.

A special session opened in August 1991, and the General Assembly submitted a congressional redistricting plan to the Attorney General for [Section 5] preclearance on October 1, 1991. The legislature's plan contained two majority-minority districts, the Fifth and Eleventh, and an additional district, the Second, in which blacks comprised just over 35% of the voting age population. Despite the plan's increase in the number of majority-black districts from one to two and the absence of any evidence of an intent to discriminate against minority voters, the Department of Justice refused preclearance on January 21, 1992. The Department's objection letter [that refused preclearance] noted a concern that Georgia had created only two majority-minority districts, and that the proposed plan did not "recognize" certain minority populations by placing them in a majority-black district.

The General Assembly returned to the drawing board. A new plan was enacted and submitted for preclearance. This second attempt assigned the black population in Central Georgia's Baldwin County to the Eleventh District and increased the black populations in the Eleventh, Fifth, and Second Districts. The

Justice Department refused preclearance again, relying on alternative plans proposing three majority-minority districts. One of the alternative schemes relied on by the Department was the so-called "max-black" plan, drafted by the American Civil Liberties Union (ACLU) for the General Assembly's black caucus. The key to the ACLU's plan was the "Macon/Savannah trade." The dense black population in the Macon region would be transferred from the Eleventh District to the Second, converting the Second into a majority-black district, and the Eleventh District's loss in black population would be offset by extending the Eleventh to include the black populations in Savannah. Pointing to the General Assembly's refusal to enact the Macon/Savannah swap into law, the Justice Department concluded that Georgia had "failed to explain adequately" its failure to create a third majority-minority district. The State did not seek a declaratory judgment from the District Court for the District of Columbia.

Twice spurned, the General Assembly set out to create three majority-minority districts to gain preclearance. Using the ACLU's "max-black" plan as its benchmark, the General Assembly enacted a plan that

> "bore all the signs of [the Justice Department's] involvement: The black population of Meriwether County was gouged out of the Third District and attached to the Second District by the narrowest of land bridges; Effingham and Chatham Counties were split to make way for the Savannah extension, which itself split the City of Savannah; and the plan as a whole split 26 counties, 23 more than the existing congressional districts." See [the district court's opinion].

The new plan also enacted the Macon/Savannah swap necessary to create a third majority-black district. The Eleventh District lost the black population of Macon, but picked up Savannah, thereby connecting the black neighborhoods of metropolitan Atlanta and the poor black populace of coastal Chatham County, though 260 miles apart in distance and worlds apart in culture. In short, the social, political, and economic makeup of the Eleventh District tells a tale of disparity, not community. As the appendices to this opinion attest,

> "[t]he populations of the Eleventh are centered around four discrete, widely spaced urban centers that have absolutely nothing to do with each other, and stretch the district hundreds of miles across rural counties and narrow swamp corridors.
>
> "The dense population centers of the approved Eleventh District were all majority-black, all at the periphery of the district, and in the case of Atlanta, Augusta and Savannah, all tied to a sparsely populated rural core by even less populated land bridges. Extending from Atlanta to the Atlantic, the Eleventh covered 6,784.2 square miles, splitting eight counties and five municipalities along the way."

The Almanac of American Politics has this to say about the Eleventh District: "Geographically, it is a monstrosity, stretching from Atlanta to Savannah. Its core is the plantation country in the center of the state, lightly populated, but heavily black. It links by narrow corridors the black neighborhoods in Augusta, Savannah and southern DeKalb County." Georgia's plan included three majority-black districts, though, and received Justice Department preclearance on April 2, 1992.

Elections were held under the new congressional redistricting plan on November 4, 1992, and black candidates were elected to Congress from all three majority-black districts. On January 13, 1994, appellees, five white voters from the Eleventh District, filed this action against various state officials in the United States District Court for the Southern District of Georgia. As residents of the challenged Eleventh District, all appellees had standing. Their suit alleged that Georgia's Eleventh District was a racial gerrymander and so a violation of the Equal Protection Clause.

II

A

Finding that the "evidence of the General Assembly's intent to racially gerrymander the Eleventh District is overwhelming, and practically stipulated by the parties involved," the District Court held that race was the predominant, overriding factor in drawing the Eleventh District. Appellants do not take issue with the court's factual finding of this racial motivation. Rather, they contend that evidence of a legislature's deliberate classification of voters on the basis of race cannot alone suffice to state a claim under *Shaw*. They argue that, regardless of the legislature's purposes, a plaintiff must demonstrate that a district's shape is so bizarre that it is unexplainable other than on the basis of race, and that appellees failed to make that showing here. Appellants' conception of the constitutional violation misapprehends our holding in *Shaw* and the equal protection precedent upon which *Shaw* relied.

Shaw recognized a claim "analytically distinct" from a vote dilution claim. Whereas a vote dilution claim alleges that the State has enacted a particular voting scheme as a purposeful device "to minimize or cancel out the voting potential of racial or ethnic minorities," *Mobile v. Bolden*, the essence of the equal protection claim recognized in *Shaw* is that the State has used race as a basis for separating voters into districts. Just as the State may not, absent extraordinary justification, segregate citizens on the basis of race in its public parks, buses, golf courses, beaches, and schools, so did we recognize in *Shaw* that it may not separate its citizens into different voting districts on the basis of race. When the State assigns voters on the basis of race, it engages in the offensive and demeaning assumption that voters of a particular race, because of their race, "think alike, share the same political interests, and will prefer the same candidates at the polls." *Shaw*. Race-based assignments embody stereotypes that treat individuals as the product of their race, evaluating their thoughts and efforts—their very worth as citizens—according to a criterion barred to the Government by history and the Constitution.

Our observation in *Shaw* of the consequences of racial stereotyping was not meant to suggest that a district must be bizarre on its face before there is a constitutional violation. Nor was our conclusion in *Shaw* that in certain instances a district's appearance (or, to be more precise, its appearance in combination with certain demographic evidence) can give rise to an equal protection claim, a holding that bizarreness was a threshold showing. Our circumspect approach and narrow holding in *Shaw* did not erect an artificial rule barring accepted equal protection analysis in other redistricting cases. Shape is relevant not because bizarreness is a necessary element of the constitutional wrong or a threshold requirement of proof, but because it may be persuasive circumstantial evidence that race for its own sake, and not other districting principles, was the legislature's dominant and controlling rationale in drawing its district lines. The logical implication, as courts applying *Shaw* have recognized, is that parties may rely on evidence other than bizarreness to establish race-based districting.

"In some exceptional cases, a reapportionment plan may be so highly irregular that, on its face, it rationally cannot be understood as anything other than an effort to 'segregat[e] . . . voters' on the basis of race." *Shaw.* In other cases, where the district is not so bizarre on its face that it discloses a racial design, the proof will be more "difficul[t]." Although it was not necessary in *Shaw* to consider further the proof required in these more difficult cases, the logical import of our reasoning is that evidence other than a district's bizarre shape can be used to support the claim.

In sum, we make clear that parties alleging that a State has assigned voters on the basis of race are neither confined in their proof to evidence regarding the district's geometry and makeup nor required to make a threshold showing of bizarreness. Today's litigation requires us further to consider the requirements of the proof necessary to sustain this equal protection challenge.

B

Federal-court review of districting legislation represents a serious intrusion on the most vital of local functions. It is well settled that reapportionment is primarily the duty and responsibility of the State. Electoral districting is a most difficult subject for legislatures, and so the States must have discretion to exercise the political judgment necessary to balance competing interests. Although race-based decisionmaking is inherently suspect, until a claimant makes a showing sufficient to support that allegation the good faith of a state legislature must be presumed. The courts, in assessing the sufficiency of a challenge to a districting plan, must be sensitive to the complex interplay of forces that enter a legislature's redistricting calculus. Redistricting legislatures will, for example, almost always be aware of racial demographics; but it does not follow that race predominates in the redistricting process. The distinction between being aware of racial considerations and being motivated by them may be difficult to make. This evidentiary difficulty, together with the sensitive nature of redistricting and the presumption of good faith that must be accorded legislative enactments, requires courts to exercise extraordinary caution in adjudicating claims that a State has drawn district lines on the basis of race. The plaintiff's burden is to show, either through circumstantial evidence of a district's shape and demographics or more direct evidence going to legislative purpose, that race was the predominant factor motivating the legislature's decision to place a significant number of voters within or without a particular district. To make this showing, a plaintiff must prove that the legislature subordinated traditional race-neutral districting principles, including but not limited to compactness, contiguity, and respect for political subdivisions or communities defined by actual shared interests, to racial considerations. Where these or other race-neutral considerations are the basis for redistricting legislation, and are not subordinated to race, a State can "defeat a claim that a district has been gerrymandered on racial lines." *Shaw.* These principles inform the plaintiff's burden of proof at trial. Of course, courts must also recognize these principles, and the intrusive potential of judicial intervention into the legislative realm, when assessing under the Federal Rules of Civil Procedure the adequacy of a plaintiff's showing at the various stages of litigation and determining whether to permit discovery or trial to proceed.

In our view, the District Court applied the correct analysis, and its finding that race was the predominant factor motivating the drawing of the Eleventh District was not clearly erroneous. The court found it was "exceedingly obvious" from the shape of the Eleventh District, together with the relevant racial demographics, that the drawing of narrow land bridges to incorporate within the district outlying appendages containing nearly 80% of the district's total black population was a deliberate attempt to bring black populations into the district. Although by comparison with other districts the geometric shape of the Eleventh District may not seem bizarre on its face, when its shape is considered in conjunction with its racial and population densities, the story of racial gerrymandering seen by the District Court becomes much clearer. Although this evidence is quite compelling, we need not determine whether it was, standing alone, sufficient to establish a *Shaw* claim that the Eleventh District is unexplainable other than by race. The District Court had before it considerable additional evidence showing that the General Assembly was motivated by a predominant, overriding desire to assign black populations to the Eleventh District and thereby permit the creation of a third majority-black district in the Second.

The [district] court found that "it became obvious," both from the Justice Department's objection letters and the three preclearance rounds in general, "that [the Justice Department] would accept nothing less than abject surrender to its maximization agenda." It further found that the General Assembly acquiesced and as a consequence was driven by its overriding desire to comply with the Department's maximization demands. The court supported its conclusion not just with the testimony of Linda Meggers, the operator of "Herschel," Georgia's reapportionment computer, and "probably the most knowledgeable person available on the subject of Georgian redistricting," but also with the State's own concessions. The State admitted that it "would not have added those portions of Effingham and Chatham Counties that are now in the [far southeastern extension of the] present Eleventh Congressional District but for the need to include additional black population in that district to offset the loss of black population caused by the shift of predominantly black portions of Bibb County in the Second Congressional District which occurred in response to the Department of Justice's March 20th, 1992, objection letter." It conceded further that "[t]o the extent that precincts in the Eleventh Congressional District are split, a substantial reason for their being split was the objective of increasing the black population of that district." And in its brief to this Court, the State concedes that "[i]t is undisputed that Georgia's eleventh is the product of a desire by the General Assembly to create a majority black district." Hence the trial court had little difficulty concluding that the Justice Department "spent months demanding purely race-based revisions to Georgia's redistricting plans, and that Georgia spent months attempting to comply." On this record, we fail to see how the District Court could have reached any conclusion other than that race was the predominant factor in drawing Georgia's Eleventh District; and in any event we conclude the court's finding is not clearly erroneous.

In light of its well-supported finding, the District Court was justified in rejecting the various alternative explanations offered for the district. Although a legislature's compliance with "traditional districting principles such as compactness, contiguity, and respect for political subdivisions" may well suffice to refute a claim of racial gerrymandering, *Shaw*, appellants cannot make such a refutation where, as here, those factors were subordinated to racial objectives. Georgia's Attorney General objected to the Justice Department's demand for three majority-black districts on the ground that to do so the State would have to "violate all reasonable standards of compactness and contiguity." This statement from a state official is powerful evidence that the legislature subordinated traditional districting principles to race when it ultimately enacted a plan creating three majority-black districts, and justified the District Court's finding that "every [objective districting] factor that could realistically be subordinated to racial tinkering in fact suffered that fate."

Nor can the State's districting legislation be rescued by mere recitation of purported communities of interest. The evidence was compelling that there are no tangible communities of interest spanning the hundreds of miles of the Eleventh District. A comprehensive report demonstrated the fractured political, social, and economic interests within the Eleventh District's black population. It is apparent that it was not alleged shared interests but rather the object of maximizing the district's black population and obtaining Justice Department approval that in fact explained the General Assembly's actions. A State is free to recognize communities that have a particular racial makeup, provided its action is directed toward some common thread of relevant interests. "[W]hen members of a racial group live together in one community, a reapportionment plan that concentrates members of the group in one district and excludes them from others may reflect wholly legitimate purposes." *Shaw*. But where the State assumes from a group of voters' race that they "think alike, share the same political interests, and will prefer the same candidates at the polls," it engages in racial stereotyping at odds with equal protection mandates. [*Id.*]

Race was, as the District Court found, the predominant, overriding factor explaining the General Assembly's decision to attach to the Eleventh District various appendages containing dense majority-black populations. As a result, Georgia's congressional redistricting plan cannot be upheld unless it satisfies strict scrutiny, our most rigorous and exacting standard of constitutional review.

III

To satisfy strict scrutiny, the State must demonstrate that its districting legislation is narrowly tailored to achieve a compelling interest. Whether or not in some cases compliance with the [Voting Rights] Act, standing alone, can provide a compelling interest independent of any interest in remedying past discrimination, it cannot do so here. As we suggested in *Shaw*, compliance with federal antidiscrimination laws cannot justify race-based districting where the challenged district was not reasonably necessary under a constitutional reading and application of those laws. The congressional plan challenged here was not required by the Act under a correct reading of the statute.

We do not accept the contention that the State has a compelling interest in complying with whatever preclearance mandates the Justice Department issues. When a state governmental entity seeks to justify race-based remedies to cure the effects of past discrimination, we do not accept the government's mere assertion that the remedial action is required. Rather, we insist on a strong basis in evidence of the harm being remedied. Our presumptive skepticism of all racial classifications prohibits us as well from accepting on its face the Justice Department's conclusion that racial districting is necessary under the Act. Where a State relies on the Department's determination that race-based districting is necessary to comply with the Act, the judiciary retains an independent obligation in adjudicating consequent equal protection challenges to ensure that the State's actions are narrowly tailored to achieve a compelling interest. Were we to accept the Justice Department's objection itself as a compelling interest adequate to insulate racial districting from constitutional review, we would be surrendering to the Executive Branch our role in enforcing the constitutional limits on race-based official action. We may not do so.

For the same reasons, we think it inappropriate for a court engaged in constitutional scrutiny to accord deference to the Justice Department's interpretation of the Act. Although we have deferred to the Department's interpretation in certain statutory cases, we have rejected agency interpretations to which we would otherwise defer where they raise serious constitutional questions. When the Justice Department's interpretation of the Act compels race-based districting, it by definition raises a serious constitutional question and should not receive deference.

Georgia's drawing of the Eleventh District was not required under the Act because there was no reasonable basis to believe that Georgia's earlier enacted plans violated § 5. Wherever a plan is "ameliorative," a term we have used to describe plans increasing the number of majority-minority districts, it cannot violate § 5 unless the new apportionment itself so discriminates on the basis of race or color as to violate the Constitution. Georgia's first and second proposed plans increased the number of majority-black districts from 1 out of 10 (10%) to 2 out of 11 (18.18%). These plans were "ameliorative" and could not have violated § 5's nonretrogression principle. Acknowledging as much, the United States now relies on the fact that the Justice Department may object to a state proposal either on the ground that it has a prohibited purpose or a prohibited effect. The Government justifies its preclearance objections on the ground that the submitted plans violated § 5's purpose element. The key to the Government's position is and always has been that Georgia failed to proffer a nondiscriminatory purpose for its refusal in the first two submissions to take the steps necessary to create a third majority-minority district.

The Government's position is insupportable. Georgia's Attorney General provided a detailed explanation for the State's initial decision not to enact the max-black plan. The District Court accepted this explanation and found an absence of any discriminatory intent. The State's policy of adhering to other districting principles instead of creating as many majority-minority districts as possible does not support an inference that the plan so discriminates on the basis of race or color as to violate the Constitution, and thus cannot provide any basis under §5 for the Justice Department's objection.

[W]e [have] recognized that the purpose of § 5 has always been to insure that no voting-procedure changes would be made that would lead to a retrogression in the position of racial minorities with respect to their effective exercise of the electoral franchise. The Justice Department's maximization policy seems quite far removed from this purpose. We are especially reluctant to conclude that § 5 justifies that policy given the serious constitutional concerns it raises. In *South Carolina v. Katzenbach,* we upheld § 5 as a necessary and constitutional response to some States' "extraordinary stratagem[s] of contriving new rules of various kinds for the sole purpose of perpetuating voting discrimination in the face of adverse federal court decrees." But our belief in *Katzenbach* that the federalism costs exacted by §

5 preclearance could be justified by those extraordinary circumstances does not mean they can be justified in the circumstances of this litigation. And the Justice Department's implicit command that States engage in presumptively unconstitutional race-based districting brings the Act, once upheld as a proper exercise of Congress' authority under § 2 of the Fifteenth Amendment into tension with the Fourteenth Amendment. We need not, however, resolve these troubling and difficult constitutional questions today.

IV

The Act, and its grant of authority to the federal courts to uncover official efforts to abridge minorities' right to vote, has been of vital importance in eradicating invidious discrimination from the electoral process and enhancing the legitimacy of our political institutions. Only if our political system and our society cleanse themselves of that discrimination will all members of the polity share an equal opportunity to gain public office regardless of race. As a Nation we share both the obligation and the aspiration of working toward this end. The end is neither assured nor well served, however, by carving electorates into racial blocs. If our society is to continue to progress as a multi-racial democracy, it must recognize that the automatic invocation of race stereotypes retards that progress and causes continued hurt and injury. It takes a shortsighted and unauthorized view of the Voting Rights Act to invoke that statute, which has played a decisive role in redressing some of our worst forms of discrimination, to demand the very racial stereotyping the Fourteenth Amendment forbids.

Figure 1-5 Appendix A Proposed Eleventh District Under "Max-Black" Plan

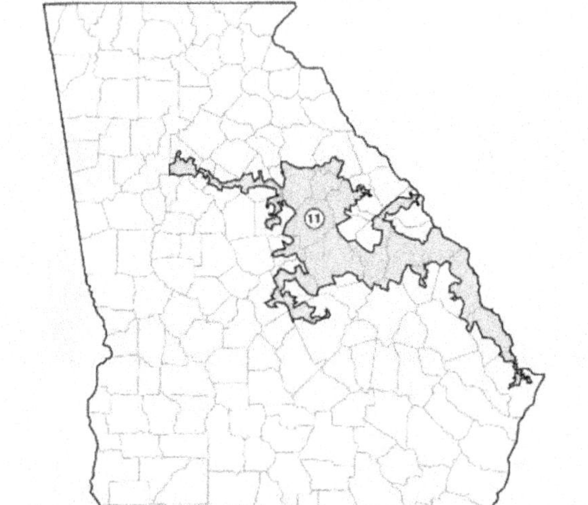

Source: Supreme Court's Appendix to *Miller v. Johnson*, 515 U.S. 900 (1995).

Figure 1-6 Appendix B Current Congressional Districts

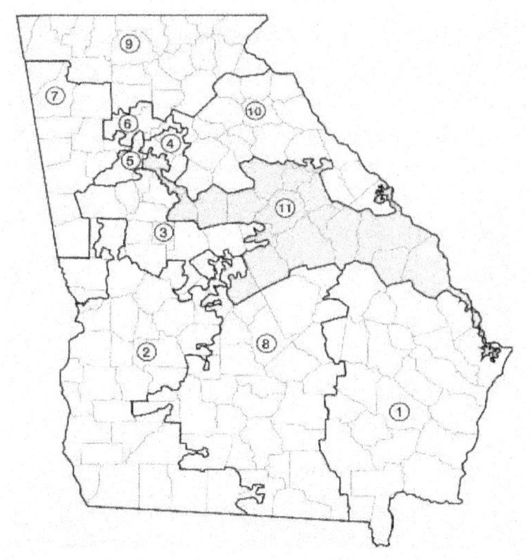

Source: Supreme Court's Appendix to *Miller v. Johnson*, 515 U.S. 900 (1995).

Justice O'CONNOR, concurring.

I understand the threshold standard the Court adopts—that "the legislature subordinated traditional race-neutral districting principles . . . to racial considerations,"—to be a demanding one. To invoke strict scrutiny, a plaintiff must show that the State has relied on race in substantial disregard of customary and traditional districting practices. Those practices provide a crucial frame of reference and therefore constitute a significant governing principle in cases of this kind. The standard would be no different if a legislature had drawn the boundaries to favor some other ethnic group; certainly the standard does not treat efforts to create majority-minority districts *less* favorably than similar efforts on behalf of other groups. Indeed, the driving force behind the adoption of the Fourteenth Amendment was the desire to end legal discrimination against blacks.

Application of the Court's standard does not throw into doubt the vast majority of the Nation's 435 congressional districts, where presumably the States have drawn the boundaries in accordance with their customary districting principles. That is so even though race may well have been considered in the redistricting process. *See Shaw v. Reno.* But application of the Court's standard helps achieve *Shaw*'s basic objective of making extreme instances of gerrymandering subject to meaningful judicial review. I therefore join the Court's opinion.

Justice STEVENS, dissenting.

Our desegregation cases redressed the *exclusion* of black citizens from public facilities reserved for whites. In these cases, in contrast, any voter, black or white, may live in the Eleventh District. What appellees contest is the *inclusion* of too many black voters in the district as drawn. In my view, if appellees allege no vote dilution, that inclusion can cause them no conceivable injury.

The Court's equation of *Shaw* claims with our desegregation decisions is inappropriate for another reason. In each of those cases, legal segregation frustrated the public interest in diversity and tolerance by barring African-Americans from joining whites in the activities at issue. The districting plan here, in contrast, serves the interest in diversity and tolerance by increasing the likelihood that a meaningful number of black representatives will add their voices to legislative debates.

Equally distressing is the Court's equation of traditional gerrymanders, designed to maintain or enhance a dominant group's power, with a dominant group's decision to share its power with a previously underrepresented group. I do not see how a districting plan that favors a politically weak group can violate equal protection. The Constitution does not mandate any form of proportional representation, but it certainly permits a State to adopt a policy that promotes fair representation of different groups.

Justice GINSBURG, with whom Justice STEVENS and Justice BREYER join, and with whom Justice SOUTER joins except as to Part III-B, dissenting.

Today the Court expands the judicial role, announcing that federal courts are to undertake searching review of any district with contours "predominant[ly] motivat[ed]" by race: "[S]trict scrutiny" will be triggered not only when traditional districting practices are abandoned, but also when those practices are "subordinated to"—given less weight than—race. Applying this new "race-as-predominant-factor" standard, the Court invalidates Georgia's districting plan even though Georgia's Eleventh District, the focus of today's dispute, bears the imprint of familiar districting practices. Because I do not endorse the Court's new standard and would not upset Georgia's plan, I dissent.

I

At the outset, it may be useful to note points on which the Court does not divide. First, we agree that federalism and the slim judicial competence to draw district lines weigh heavily against judicial intervention in apportionment decisions; as a rule, the task should remain within the domain of state legislatures. Second, for most of our Nation's history, the franchise has not been enjoyed equally by black citizens and white voters. To redress past wrongs and to avert any recurrence of exclusion of blacks from political processes, federal courts now respond to Equal Protection Clause and Voting Rights Act complaints of state action that dilutes minority voting strength. Third, to meet statutory requirements, state legislatures must sometimes consider race as a factor highly relevant to the drawing of district lines. Finally, state legislatures may recognize communities that have a particular racial or ethnic makeup, even in the absence of any compulsion to do so, in order to account for interests common to or shared by the persons grouped together.

Therefore, the fact that the Georgia General Assembly took account of race in drawing district lines—a fact not in dispute—does not render the State's plan invalid. To offend the Equal Protection Clause, all agree, the legislature had to do more than consider race. How much more, is the issue that divides the Court today.

II

A

The problem in *Shaw* was not the plan architects' consideration of race as relevant in redistricting. Rather, in the Court's estimation, it was the virtual exclusion of other factors from the calculus. Traditional districting practices were cast aside, the Court concluded, with race alone steering placement of district lines.

B

The record before us does not show that race similarly overwhelmed traditional districting practices in Georgia. Although the Georgia General Assembly prominently considered race in shaping the Eleventh District, race did not crowd out all other factors, as the Court found it did in North Carolina's delineation of the *Shaw* district.

In contrast to the snake-like North Carolina district inspected in *Shaw*, Georgia's Eleventh District is hardly "bizarre," "extremely irregular," or "irrational on its face." *Id.* Instead, the Eleventh District's design reflects significant consideration of traditional districting factors (such as keeping political subdivisions intact) and the usual political process of compromise and trades for a variety of nonracial reasons. The district covers a core area in central and eastern Georgia, and its total land area of 6,780 square miles is about average for the State.

Nor does the Eleventh District disrespect the boundaries of political subdivisions. Of the 22 counties in the district, 14 are intact and 8 are divided. That puts the Eleventh District at about the state average in divided counties. Seventy-one percent of the Eleventh District's boundaries track the borders of political subdivisions. Of the State's 11 districts, 5 score worse than the Eleventh District on this criterion, and 5 score better. Eighty-three percent of the Eleventh District's geographic area is composed of intact counties, above average for the State's congressional districts. And notably, the Eleventh District's boundaries largely follow precinct lines.

Evidence at trial similarly shows that considerations other than race went into determining the Eleventh District's boundaries. For a "political reason"—to accommodate the request of an incumbent State Senator regarding the placement of the precinct in which his son lived—the DeKalb County portion of the Eleventh District was drawn to include a particular (largely white) precinct. The corridor through Effingham County was substantially narrowed at the request of a (white) State Representative. In Chatham County, the district was trimmed to exclude a heavily black community in Garden City because a State Representative wanted to keep the city intact inside the neighboring First District. The Savannah extension was configured by "the narrowest means possible" to avoid splitting the city of Port Wentworth.

Georgia's Eleventh District, in sum, is not an outlier district shaped without reference to familiar districting techniques.

C

The Court suggests that it was not Georgia's Legislature, but the U.S. Department of Justice, that effectively drew the lines, and that Department officers did so with nothing but race in mind. Yet the "Max-Black" plan advanced by the Attorney General was not the plan passed by the Georgia General Assembly.

And although the Attorney General refused preclearance to the first two plans approved by Georgia's Legislature, the State was not thereby disarmed; Georgia could have demanded relief from the Department's objections by instituting a civil action in the United States District Court for the District of Columbia, with ultimate review in this Court. Instead of pursuing that avenue, the State chose to adopt the plan here in controversy—a plan the State forcefully defends before us. We should respect Georgia's choice by taking its position as genuine.

D

Along with attention to size, shape, and political subdivisions, the Court recognizes as an appropriate districting principle, "respect for . . . communities defined by actual shared interests." The Court finds no community here, however, because a report in the record showed "fractured political, social, and economic interests within the Eleventh District's black population."

But ethnicity itself can tie people together, as volumes of social science literature have documented—even people with divergent economic interests. For this reason, ethnicity is a significant force in political life.

III

To separate permissible and impermissible use of race in legislative apportionment, the Court orders strict scrutiny for districting plans "predominantly motivated" by race. No longer can a State avoid judicial oversight by giving—as in this case—genuine and measurable consideration to traditional districting practices. Instead, a federal case can be mounted whenever plaintiffs plausibly allege that other factors carried less weight than race. This invitation to litigate against the State seems to me neither necessary nor proper.

A

The Court derives its test from diverse opinions on the relevance of race in contexts distinctly unlike apportionment. The controlling idea, the Court says, is "the simple command [at the heart of the Constitution's guarantee of equal protection] that the Government must treat citizens as individuals, not as simply components of a racial, religious, sexual or national class."

In adopting districting plans, however, States do not treat people as individuals. Apportionment schemes, by their very nature, assemble people in groups. States do not assign voters to districts based on merit or achievement, standards States might use in hiring employees or engaging contractors. Rather, legislators classify voters in groups—by economic, geographical, political, or social characteristics—and then reconcile the competing claims of these groups.

That ethnicity defines some of these groups is a political reality. Until now, no constitutional infirmity has been seen in districting Irish or Italian voters together, for example, so long as the delineation does not abandon familiar apportionment practices. If Chinese-Americans and Russian-Americans may seek and secure group recognition in the delineation of voting districts, then African-Americans should not be dissimilarly treated. Otherwise, in the name of equal protection, we would shut out the very minority group whose history in the United States gave birth to the Equal Protection Clause.

B

Under the Court's approach, judicial review of the same intensity, *i.e.,* strict scrutiny, is in order once it is determined that an apportionment is predominantly motivated by race. It matters not at all, in this new regime, whether the apportionment dilutes or enhances minority voting strength.

Special circumstances justify vigilant judicial inspection to protect minority voters—circumstances that do not apply to majority voters. A history of exclusion from state politics left racial minorities without clout to extract provisions for fair representation in the lawmaking forum. The equal protection rights of minority voters thus could have remained unrealized absent the Judiciary's close surveillance. *Cf. United States v. Carolene Products Co.*, n. 4 (1938) (referring to the "more searching judicial inquiry" that may properly attend classifications adversely affecting "discrete and insular minorities"). The majority, by definition, encounters no such blockage. White voters in Georgia do not lack means to exert strong pressure on their state legislators. The force of their numbers is itself a powerful determiner of what the legislature will do that does not coincide with perceived majority interests.

State legislatures like Georgia's today operate under federal constraints imposed by the Voting Rights Act—constraints justified by history and designed by Congress to make once-subordinated people free and equal citizens. But these federal constraints do not leave majority voters in need of extraordinary judicial solicitude. The Attorney General, who administers the Voting Rights Act's preclearance requirements, is herself a political actor. She has a duty to enforce the law Congress passed, and she is no doubt aware of the political cost of venturing too far to the detriment of majority voters. Majority voters, furthermore, can press the State to seek judicial review if the Attorney General refuses to preclear a plan that the voters favor. Finally, the Act is itself a political measure, subject to modification in the political process.

C

The Court's disposition renders redistricting perilous work for state legislatures. Statutory mandates and political realities may require States to consider race when drawing district lines. But today's decision is a counterforce; it opens the way for federal litigation if "traditional . . . districting principles" arguably were accorded less weight than race. Genuine attention to traditional districting practices and avoidance of bizarre configurations seemed, under *Shaw*, to provide a safe harbor. In view of today's decision, that is no longer the case.

Only after litigation—under either the Voting Rights Act, the Court's new *Miller* standard, or both—will States now be assured that plans conscious of race are safe. Federal judges in large numbers may be drawn into the fray. This enlargement of the judicial role is unwarranted. The reapportionment plan that resulted from Georgia's political process merited this Court's approbation, not its condemnation. Accordingly, I dissent.

NOTES ON *MILLER*

1. Many of the racial gerrymandering cases that the Supreme Court heard in the 1990s emanated from State efforts to secure Section 5 preclearance from the U.S. Department of Justice. Now that preclearance has essentially been rendered a nullity (unless a court orders preclearance as a remedy under Section 3(c)), has the need for racial gerrymandering doctrine been eliminated? (You may wish to review this question after you have considered *Cooper v. Harris.*)

2. Focus for a moment on the rationale for the Court's creation of the racial gerrymandering doctrine. Why does the Court entertain claims of racial gerrymandering? Is it because of harms to individual voters? If so, what are those harms? Is it because of harms to groups of voters? If so, what are those harms? Is it because of harms to candidates? If so, what are those harms? Do any of the answers to these questions provide a sufficient justification for the Court's entry into this particular "political thicket"?

3. *Shaw* seemed to provide a standard for determining whether a redistricting represented a racial gerrymander by centering around the "bizarre" shape of a district. *Miller* changed that analysis by noting that the shape of a district is only one evidentiary factor that goes into the determination as to whether race was the "predominant factor" in the drawing of a district. If race is determined by the court to be a predominant factor then the court proceeds to analyze the district using strict scrutiny.

4. In essence, the *Miller* Court says that the use of race in redistricting is not *ipso facto* unconstitutional. How does one draw the line between what one might call the "run of the mill" use of race in redistricting and the "excessive" or "predominant" use of race in redistricting? Would it be better to develop a clear rule where a redistricting plan would be held unconstitutional if race played *any role at all* in the drawing of a district?

* * *

The twists and turns of the development of the Supreme Court's racial gerrymandering doctrine in the 1990s can be encapsulated in the litigation involving North Carolina's Twelfth Congressional District. That case featured four decisions by a three-judge district court that ended up being reversed by the Supreme Court (an ignominious record if there ever was one!). The first case was *Shaw v. Reno,* which you read about above and involved the creation of a claim of racial gerrymandering based on a bizarrely shaped district. What you are about to read is the fourth opinion in less than a decade from the Supreme Court involving District 12. As you read the case, pay close attention to the history of the litigation and also how this fourth decision might have changed the playing field in relation to the "law" of racial gerrymandering. Consider also the Supreme Court's role in evaluating a district court's factual findings with respect to a redistricting claim.

Easley v. Cromartie

532 U.S. 234 (2001)

Justice BREYER delivered the opinion of the Court.

In this appeal, we review a three-judge District Court's determination that North Carolina's Legislature used race as the "predominant factor" in drawing its

12th Congressional District's 1997 boundaries. The court's findings, in our view, are clearly erroneous. We therefore reverse its conclusion that the State violated the Equal Protection Clause.

I

This "racial districting" litigation is before us for the fourth time. Our first two holdings addressed North Carolina's *former* Congressional District 12, one of two North Carolina congressional districts drawn in 1992 that contained a majority of African-American voters. *See Shaw v. Reno,* (1993) (*Shaw I*); *Shaw v. Hunt,* (1996) (*Shaw II*).

A

In *Shaw I,* the Court considered whether plaintiffs' factual allegation—that the legislature had drawn the former district's boundaries for race-based reasons—if true, could underlie a legal holding that the legislature had violated the Equal Protection Clause. The Court held that it could. It wrote that a violation may exist where the legislature's boundary drawing, though "race neutral on its face," nonetheless can be understood only as an effort to "separate voters into different districts on the basis of race," and where the "separation lacks sufficient justification."

In *Shaw II,* the Court reversed a subsequent three-judge District Court's holding that the boundary-drawing law in question did not violate the Constitution. This Court found that the district's "unconventional," snakelike shape, the way in which its boundaries split towns and counties, its predominately African-American racial makeup, and its history, together demonstrated a deliberate effort to create a "majority-black" district in which race "could not be compromised," not simply a district designed to "protec[t] Democratic incumbents." And the Court concluded that the legislature's use of racial criteria was not justified.

B

Our third holding focused on a new District 12, the boundaries of which the legislature had redrawn in 1997. *Hunt v. Cromartie,* (1999). A three-judge District Court, with one judge dissenting, had granted summary judgment in favor of those challenging the district's boundaries. The court found that the legislature again had "used criteria . . . that are facially race driven," in violation of the Equal Protection Clause. It based this conclusion upon "uncontroverted material facts" showing that the boundaries created an unusually shaped district, split counties and cities, and in particular placed almost all heavily Democratic-registered, predominantly African-American voting precincts, inside the district while locating some heavily Democratic-registered, predominantly white precincts, outside the district. This latter circumstance, said the court, showed that the legislature was trying to maximize new District 12's African-American voting strength, not the district's Democratic voting strength.

This Court reversed. We agreed with the District Court that the new district's shape, the way in which it split towns and counties, and its heavily African-American voting population all helped the plaintiffs' case. But neither that evidence by itself, nor when coupled with the evidence of Democratic registration, was sufficient to show, on summary judgment, the unconstitutional race-based objective that plaintiffs claimed. That is because there was a genuine issue of material fact as to whether the evidence also was consistent with a constitutional political objective, namely, the creation of a safe Democratic seat.

We pointed to the affidavit of an expert witness for defendants, Dr. David W. Peterson. Dr. Peterson offered to show that, because North Carolina's African-American voters are overwhelmingly Democratic voters, one cannot easily distinguish a legislative effort to create a majority-African-American district from a legislative effort to create a safely Democratic district. And he also provided data showing that *registration* did not indicate how voters would actually vote. We agreed that data showing how voters actually behave, not data showing only how those voters are registered, could affect the outcome of this litigation. We concluded that the case was "not suited for summary disposition" and we reversed the District Court.

C

On remand, the parties undertook additional discovery. The three-judge District Court held a 3-day trial. And the court again held (over a dissent) that the legislature had unconstitutionally drawn District 12's new 1997 boundaries. It found that the legislature had tried "(1) [to] cur[e] the [previous district's] constitutional defects" while also "(2) drawing the plan to maintain the existing partisan balance in the State's congressional delegation." It added that to "achieve the second goal," the legislature "drew the new plan (1) to avoid placing two incumbents in the same district and (2) to preserve the partisan core of the existing districts." The court concluded that the "plan as enacted largely reflects these directives." But the court also found "as a matter of fact that the General Assembly . . . used criteria . . . that are facially race driven" without any compelling justification for doing so.

The court based its latter, constitutionally critical, conclusion in part upon the district's snakelike shape, the way in which it split cities and towns, and its heavily African-American (47%) voting population—all matters that this Court had considered when it found summary judgment inappropriate. The court also based this conclusion upon a specific finding—absent when we previously considered this litigation—that the legislature had drawn the boundaries in order "to collect precincts with *high racial identification rather than political identification.*"

This last-mentioned finding rested in turn upon five subsidiary determinations:

(1) that "the legislators excluded many heavily-Democratic precincts from District 12, even when those precincts immediately border the Twelfth and would have established a far more compact district";
(2) that "[a]dditionally, Plaintiffs' expert, Dr. Weber, showed time and again how race trumped party affiliation in the construction of the 12th District and how political explanations utterly failed to explain the composition of the district,";
(3) that Dr. Peterson's testimony was "'unreliable' and not relevant,";
(4) that a legislative redistricting leader, Senator Roy Cooper, had alluded at the time of redistricting "to a need for 'racial and partisan' balance,"; and

(5) that the Senate's redistricting coordinator, Gerry Cohen, had sent Senator Cooper an e-mail reporting that Cooper had "moved Greensboro Black community into the 12th, and now need[ed] to take [about] 60,000 out of the 12th."

The State filed a notice of appeal. And we now reverse.

II

The issue in this case is evidentiary. We must determine whether there is adequate support for the District Court's key findings, particularly the ultimate finding that the legislature's motive was predominantly racial, not political. In making this determination, we are aware that, under *Shaw I* and later cases, the burden of proof on the plaintiffs (who attack the district) is a "demanding one." *Miller v. Johnson* (O'Connor, J., concurring). The Court has specified that those who claim that a legislature has improperly used race as a criterion, in order, for example, to create a majority-minority district, must show at a minimum that the legislature subordinated traditional race-neutral districting principles to racial considerations. Race must not simply have been *a* motivation for the drawing of a majority-minority district, but the *predominant* factor motivating the legislature's districting decision. Plaintiffs must show that a facially neutral law is unexplainable on grounds other than race.

The Court also has made clear that the underlying districting decision is one that ordinarily falls within a legislature's sphere of competence. *Miller*. Hence, the legislature "must have discretion to exercise the political judgment necessary to balance competing interests," and courts must "exercise *extraordinary caution* in adjudicating claims that a State has drawn district lines on the basis of race," *id.* Caution is especially appropriate in this case, where the State has articulated a legitimate political explanation for its districting decision, and the voting population is one in which race and political affiliation are highly correlated.

We also are aware that we review the District Court's findings only for "clear error." In applying this standard, we, like any reviewing court, will not reverse a lower court's finding of fact simply because we would have decided the case differently. Rather, a reviewing court must ask whether, on the entire evidence, it is left with the definite and firm conviction that a mistake has been committed.

Where an intermediate court reviews, and affirms, a trial court's factual findings, this Court will not lightly overturn the concurrent findings of the two lower courts. But in this instance there is no intermediate court, and we are the only court of review. Moreover, the trial here at issue was not lengthy and the key evidence consisted primarily of documents and expert testimony. Credibility evaluations played a minor role. Accordingly, we find that an extensive review of the District Court's findings, for clear error, is warranted. That review leaves us "with the definite and firm conviction" that the District Court's key findings are mistaken.

III

The critical District Court determination—the matter for which we remanded this litigation—consists of the finding that race *rather than* politics *predominantly* explains District 12's 1997 boundaries. That determination rests upon three findings (the district's shape, its splitting of towns and counties, and its high African-American voting population) that we previously found insufficient to support summary judgment. Given the undisputed evidence that racial identification is highly correlated with political affiliation in North Carolina, these facts in and of themselves cannot, as a matter of law, support the District Court's judgment. The District Court rested, however, upon five new subsidiary findings to conclude that District 12's lines are the product of no "mer[e] correlat[ion]," but are instead a result of the predominance of race in the legislature's line-drawing process.

In considering each subsidiary finding, we have given weight to the fact that the District Court was familiar with this litigation, heard the testimony of each witness, and considered all the evidence with care. Nonetheless, we cannot accept the District Court's findings as adequate for reasons which we shall spell out in detail and which we can summarize as follows:

First, the primary evidence upon which the District Court relied for its "race, not politics," conclusion is evidence of voting registration, not voting behavior; and that is precisely the kind of evidence that we said was inadequate the last time this case was before us. Second, the additional evidence to which appellees' expert, Dr. Weber, pointed, and the statements made by Senator Cooper and Gerry Cohen, simply do not provide significant additional support for the District Court's conclusion. Third, the District Court, while not accepting the contrary conclusion of appellants' expert, Dr. Peterson, did not (and as far as the record reveals, could not) reject much of the significant supporting factual information he provided. Fourth, in any event, appellees themselves have provided us with charts summarizing evidence of voting behavior and those charts tend to refute the court's "race, not politics," conclusion.

A

The District Court primarily based its "race, not politics," conclusion upon its finding that "the legislators excluded many heavily-Democratic precincts from District 12, even when those precincts immediately border the Twelfth and would have established a far more compact district." This finding, however—insofar as it differs from the remaining four—rests solely upon evidence that the legislature excluded heavily white precincts with high Democratic Party registration, while including heavily African-American precincts with equivalent, or lower, Democratic Party registration. Indeed, the District Court cites at length figures showing that the legislature included "several precincts with racial compositions of 40 to 100 percent African-American," while excluding certain adjacent precincts "with less than 35 percent African-American population" but which contain between 54% and 76% *registered* Democrats.

As we said before, the problem with this evidence is that it focuses upon party registration, not upon voting behavior. And we previously found the same evidence inadequate because registration figures do not accurately predict preference at the polls. In part this is because white voters registered as Democrats "cross-over" to vote for a Republican candidate more often than do African-Americans, who register and vote Democratic between 95% and 97% of the time.

A legislature trying to secure a safe Democratic seat is interested in Democratic voting behavior. Hence, a legislature may, by placing reliable Democratic precincts within a district without regard to race, end up with a district containing more heavily African-American precincts, but the reasons would be political rather than racial.

B

The District Court wrote that "[a]dditionally, [p]laintiffs' expert, Dr. Weber, showed time and again how race trumped party affiliation in the construction of the 12th District and how political explanations utterly failed to explain the composition of the district." In support of this conclusion, the court relied upon six different citations to Dr. Weber's trial testimony. We have examined each reference.

1

At the first cited pages of the trial transcript, Dr. Weber says that a reliably Democratic voting population of 60% is sufficient to create a safe Democratic seat. Yet, he adds, the legislature created a more-than-60% reliable Democratic voting population in District 12. Hence (we read Dr. Weber to infer), the legislature likely was driven by race, not politics.

The record indicates, however, that, although Dr. Weber is right that District 12 is more than 60% reliably Democratic, it exceeds that figure by very little. Nor did Dr. Weber ask whether other districts, unchallenged by appellees, were significantly less "safe" than was District 12. In fact, the figures the legislature used showed that District 12 would be 63% reliably Democratic. By the same measures, at least two Republican districts (Districts 6 and 10) are 61% reliably Republican. And, as Dr. Weber conceded, incumbents might have urged legislators (trying to maintain a six/six Democrat/Republican delegation split) to make their seats, not 60% safe, but as safe as possible. In a field such as voting behavior, where figures are inherently uncertain, Dr. Weber's tiny calculated percentage differences are simply too small to carry significant evidentiary weight.

2

The District Court cited two parts of the transcript where Dr. Weber testified about a table he had prepared listing all precincts in the six counties, portions of which make up District 12. Dr. Weber said that District 12 contains between 39% and 56% of the precincts (depending on the county) that are more-than-40% reliably Democratic, but it contains almost every precinct with more-than-40% African-American voters. Why, he essentially asks, if the legislature had had politics primarily in mind, would its effort to place reliably Democratic precincts within District 12 not have produced a greater racial mixture?

Dr. Weber's own testimony provides an answer to this question. As Dr. Weber agreed, the precincts listed in the table were at least *40%* reliably Democratic, but virtually all the African-American precincts included in District 12 were *more* than 40% reliably Democratic. Moreover, *none* of the excluded white precincts were *as* reliably Democratic as the African-American precincts that were included in the district. Yet the legislature sought precincts that were reliably Democratic, not precincts that were *40%* reliably Democratic, for obvious political reasons.

Neither does the table specify whether the excluded white-reliably-Democratic precincts were located near enough to District 12's boundaries or each other for the legislature as a practical matter to have drawn District 12's boundaries to have included them, without sacrificing other important political goals. The contrary is suggested by the fact that Dr. Weber's own proposed alternative plan would have pitted two incumbents against each other (Sue Myrick, a Republican from former District 9 and Mel Watt, a Democrat from former District 12). Dr. Weber testified that such a result—"a very competitive race with one of them losing their seat"—was desirable. But the legislature, for political, not racial, reasons, believed the opposite. And it drew its plan to protect incumbents—a legitimate political goal recognized by the District Court.

For these reasons, Dr. Weber's table offers little insight into the legislature's true motive.

3

The next part of the transcript the District Court cited contains Dr. Weber's testimony about a Mecklenburg County precinct (precinct 77) which the legislature split between Districts 9 and 12. Dr. Weber apparently thought that the legislature did not have to split this precinct, placing the more heavily African-American segment within District 12—unless, of course, its motive was racial rather than political. But Dr. Weber simultaneously conceded that he had not considered whether District 9's incumbent Republican would have wanted the whole of precinct 77 left in her own district where it would have burdened her with a significant additional number of reliably Democratic voters. Nor had Dr. Weber "test[ed]" his conclusion that this split helped to show a racial (rather than political) motive, say, by adjusting other boundary lines and determining the political, or other nonracial, consequences of such adjustments.

The maps in evidence indicate that to have placed all of precinct 77 within District 12 would have created a District 12 peninsula that invaded District 9, neatly dividing that latter district in two—a conclusive nonracial reason for the legislature's decision not to do so.

4

The District Court cited Dr. Weber's conclusion that "race is the predominant factor." But this statement of the conclusion is no stronger than the evidence that underlies it.

5

The District Court's final citation is to Dr. Weber's assertion that there are other ways in which the legislature could have created a safely Democratic district without placing so many primarily African-American districts within District 12. And we recognize that *some* such other ways may exist. But, unless the evidence also shows that these hypothetical alternative districts would have better satisfied the legislature's other nonracial political goals as well as traditional nonracial districting principles, this fact alone cannot show an improper legislative motive. After all, the Constitution does not place an *affirmative* obligation upon the legislature to avoid creating districts that turn out to be heavily, even majority, minority. It simply imposes an obligation not to create such districts for predominantly racial, as opposed to political or traditional, districting motivations. And Dr. Weber's testimony does not, at the pages cited, provide evidence of a politically practical alternative plan that the legislature failed to adopt predominantly for racial reasons.

6

We do not see how Dr. Weber's testimony, taken as a whole, could have provided more than minimal support for the District Court's conclusion that race predominantly underlay the legislature's districting decision.

C

[Omitted.]

D

The District Court also relied on two pieces of "direct" evidence of discriminatory intent.

1

The court found that a legislative redistricting leader, Senator Roy Cooper, when testifying before a legislative committee in 1997, had said that the 1997 plan satisfies a "need for 'racial and partisan' balance." The court concluded that the words "racial balance" referred to a 10-to-2 Caucasian/African-American balance in the State's 12-member congressional delegation. Hence, Senator Cooper had admitted that the legislature had drawn the plan with race in mind.

Senator Cooper's full statement reads as follows:

> "Those of you who dealt with Redistricting before realize that you cannot solve each problem that you encounter and everyone can find a problem with this Plan. However, I think that overall it provides for a fair, geographic, racial and partisan balance throughout the State of North Carolina. I think in order to come to an agreement all sides had to give a little bit, but I think we've reached an agreement that we can live with."

We agree that one can read the statement about "racial . . . balance" as the District Court read it—to refer to the current congressional delegation's racial balance. But even as so read, the phrase shows that the legislature considered race, along with other partisan and geographic considerations; and as so read it says little or nothing about whether race played a *predominant* role comparatively speaking.

2

The second piece of "direct" evidence relied upon by the District Court is a February 10, 1997, e-mail sent from Gerry Cohen, a legislative staff member responsible for drafting districting plans, to Senator Cooper and Senator Leslie Winner. Cohen wrote: "I have moved Greensboro Black community into the 12th, and now need to take [about] 60,000 out of the 12th. I await your direction on this."

The reference to race—*i.e.*, "Black community"—is obvious. But the e-mail does not discuss the point of the reference. It does not discuss why Greensboro's African-American voters were placed in the 12th District; it does not discuss the political consequences of failing to do so; it is addressed only to two members of the legislature; and it suggests that the legislature paid less attention to race in respect to the 12th District than in respect to the 1st District, where the e-mail provides a far more extensive, detailed discussion of racial percentages. It is less persuasive than the kinds of direct evidence we have found significant in other redistricting cases. *Miller* (State set out to create majority-minority district). Nonetheless, the e-mail offers some support for the District Court's conclusion.

E

As we have said, we assume that the maps appended to appellees' brief reflect the record insofar as that record describes the relation between District 12's boundaries and reliably Democratic voting behavior. Consequently we shall consider appellees' related claims, made on appeal, that the maps provide significant support for the District Court, in that they show how the legislature might have "swapped" several more heavily African-American District 12 precincts for other less heavily African-American adjacent precincts—without harming its basic "safely Democratic" political objective.

First, appellees suggest, without identifying any specific swap, that the legislature could have brought within District 12 several reliably Democratic, primarily white, precincts in Forsyth County. None of these precincts, however, is more reliably Democratic than the precincts immediately adjacent and within District 12. See Appendix A, *infra* (showing Democratic strength reflected by Republican victories in each precinct). One of them, the Brown/Douglas Recreation Precinct, is heavily African-American. And the remainder form a buffer between the home precinct of Fifth District Representative Richard Burr and the District 12 border, such that their removal from District 5 would deprive Representative Burr of a large portion of his own hometown, making him more vulnerable to a challenge from elsewhere within his district. Consequently the Forsyth County precincts do not significantly help appellees' "race, not politics," thesis.

Second, appellees say that the legislature might have swapped two District 12 Davidson County precincts (Thomasville 1 and Lexington 3) for a District 6 Guilford County precinct (Greensboro 17). Whatever the virtues of such a swap, however, it would have diminished the size of District 12, geographically producing an unusually narrow isthmus linking District 12's north with its south and demographically producing the State's smallest district, deviating by about 1,300 below the legislatively endorsed ideal mean of 552,386 population. Traditional districting considerations consequently militated against any such swap.

Third, appellees suggest that, in Mecklenburg County, two District 12 precincts (Charlotte 81 and LCI-South) be swapped with two District 9 precincts (Charlotte 10 and 21). This suggestion is difficult to evaluate, as the parties provide no map that specifically identifies each precinct in Mecklenburg County by name. Nonetheless, from what we can tell, such a swap would make the district marginally more white (decreasing the African-American population by about 300 persons) while making the shape more questionable, leaving the precinct immediately to the south of Charlotte 81 jutting out into District 9. We are not convinced that this proposal materially advances appellees' claim.

Fourth, appellees argue that the legislature could have swapped two reliably Democratic Greensboro precincts outside District 12 (11 and 14) for four reliably Republican High Point precincts (1, 13, 15, and 19) placed within District 12. The swap would not have improved racial balance significantly, however, for each of the six precincts have an African-American population of less than 35%. Additionally, it too would have altered the shape of District 12 for the worse. And, in any event, the decision to exclude the two Greensboro precincts seems to reflect the legislature's decision to draw boundaries that follow main thoroughfares in Guilford County.

Even if our judgments in respect to a few of these precincts are wrong, a showing that the legislature might have "swapped" a handful of precincts out of a total of 154 precincts, involving a population of a few hundred out of a total population of about half a million, cannot significantly strengthen appellees' case.

IV

We concede the record contains a modicum of evidence offering support for the District Court's conclusion. That evidence includes the Cohen e-mail, Senator Cooper's reference to "racial balance," and to a minor degree, some aspects of Dr. Weber's testimony. The evidence taken together, however, does not show that racial considerations predominated in the drawing of District 12's boundaries. That is because race in this case correlates closely with political behavior. The basic question is whether the legislature drew District 12's boundaries because of race *rather than* because of political behavior (coupled with traditional, nonracial districting considerations). It is not, as the dissent contends, whether a legislature may defend its districting decisions based on a "stereotype" about African-American voting behavior. And given the fact that the party attacking the legislature's decision bears the burden of proving that racial considerations are "dominant and controlling," given the "demanding" nature of that burden of proof, and given the sensitivity, the "extraordinary caution," that district courts must show to avoid treading upon legislative prerogatives, the attacking party has not successfully shown that race, rather than politics, predominantly accounts for the result. The record leaves us with the "definite and firm conviction" that the District Court erred in finding to the contrary. And we do not believe that providing appellees a further opportunity to make their "precinct swapping" arguments in the District Court could change this result.

We can put the matter more generally as follows: In a case such as this one where majority-minority districts (or the approximate equivalent) are at issue and where racial identification correlates highly with political affiliation, the party attacking the legislatively drawn boundaries must show at the least that the legislature could have achieved its legitimate political objectives in alternative ways that are comparably consistent with traditional districting principles. That party must also show that those districting alternatives would have brought about significantly greater racial balance. Appellees failed to make any such showing here. We conclude that the District Court's contrary findings are clearly erroneous. Because of this disposition, we need not address appellants' alternative grounds for reversal.

The judgment of the District Court is

Reversed.

Justice THOMAS, with whom CHIEF JUSTICE [Rehnquist], Justice SCALIA, and Justice KENNEDY join, dissenting.

The issue for the District Court was whether racial considerations were predominant in the design of North Carolina's Congressional District 12. The issue for this Court is simply whether the District Court's factual finding—that racial considerations did predominate—was clearly erroneous. Because I do not believe the court below committed clear error, I respectfully dissent.

I

The Court does cite cases that address the correct standard of review and does couch its conclusion in "clearly erroneous" terms. But these incantations of the correct standard are empty gestures, contradicted by the Court's conclusion that it must engage in "extensive review." In several ways, the Court ignores its role as a reviewing court and engages in its own fact-finding enterprise. First, the Court suggests that there is some significance to the absence of an intermediate court in this action. This cannot be a legitimate consideration. If it were legitimate, we would have mentioned it in prior redistricting cases. After all, in *Miller* and *Shaw*, we also did not have the benefit of intermediate appellate review.

Second, the Court appears to discount clear error review here because the trial was "not lengthy." Even if considerations such as the length of the trial were relevant in deciding how to review factual findings, an assumption about which I have my doubts, these considerations would not counsel against deference in this action. The trial lasted for three days in which the court heard the testimony of 12 witnesses. And quite apart from the total trial time, the District Court sifted through hundreds of pages of deposition testimony and expert analysis, including statistical analysis. It also should not be forgotten that one member of the panel has reviewed the iterations of District 12 since 1992. If one were to calibrate clear error review according to the trier of fact's familiarity with the case, there is simply no question that the court here gained a working knowledge of the facts of this litigation in myriad ways over a period far longer than three days.

Third, the Court downplays deference to the District Court's finding by highlighting that the key evidence was expert testimony requiring no traditional credibility determinations. As a factual matter, the Court overlooks the District Court's express assessment of the legislative redistricting leader's credibility. It is also likely that the court's interpretation of the e-mail written by Gerry Cohen, the primary drafter of District 12, was influenced by its evaluation of Cohen as a witness. And, as a legal matter, the Court's emphasis on the technical nature of the evidence misses the mark. Although we have recognized that particular weight should be given to a trial court's credibility determinations, we have never held that factual findings based on documentary evidence and expert testimony justify "extensive review." Instead, the rationale for deference extends to all determinations of fact because of the trial judge's "expertise" in making such determinations. Accordingly, deference to the fact finder is the rule, not the exception, and I see no reason to depart from this rule in the case before us now.

Finally, perhaps the best evidence that the Court has emptied clear error review of meaningful content in the redistricting context (and the strongest testament to the fact that the District Court was dealing with a complex fact pattern) is the Court's foray into the minutiae of the record. I do not doubt this Court's ability to sift through volumes of facts or to argue *its* interpretation of those facts persuasively. But I do doubt the wisdom, efficiency, increased accuracy, and legitimacy of an extensive review that is any more searching than clear error review. Thus, I would follow our precedents and simply review the District Court's finding for clear error.

II

Reviewing for clear error, I cannot say that the District Court's view of the evidence was impermissible. First, the court relied on objective measures of compactness, which show that District 12 is the most geographically scattered district in North Carolina, to support its conclusion that the district's design was not dictated by traditional districting concerns. Although this evidence was available when we held that summary judgment was inappropriate, we certainly did not hold that it was irrelevant in determining whether racial gerrymandering occurred. On the contrary, we determined that there was a triable issue of fact. Moreover, although we acknowledged "that a district's unusual shape can give rise to an inference of political motivation," we "doubt[ed] that a bizarre shape *equally* supports a political inference and a racial one." Second, the court relied on the expert opinion of Dr. Weber, who interpreted statistical data to conclude that there were Democratic precincts with low black populations excluded from District 12, which would have created a more compact district had they been included.[4] And contrary to the Court's assertion, Dr. Weber did not merely examine the registration data in reaching his conclusions. Dr. Weber explained that he refocused his analysis on *performance.* He did so in response to our concerns, when we reversed the District Court's summary judgment finding, that voter registration might not be the best measure of the Democratic nature of a precinct. This fact was not lost on the District Court, which specifically referred to those pages of the record covering Dr. Weber's analysis of performance.

4. I do not think it necessary to impose a new burden on appellees to show that districting alternatives would have brought about "significantly greater racial balance." I cannot say that it was impermissible for the court to conclude that race predominated in this action even if only a slightly better district could be drawn absent racial considerations. The District Court may reasonably have found that racial motivations predominated in selecting one alternative over another even if the net effect on racial balance was not "significant."

Third, the court credited Dr. Weber's testimony that the districting decisions could not be explained by political motives. In the first instance, I, like the Court, might well have concluded that District 12 was not significantly "safer" than several other districts in North Carolina merely because its Democratic reliability exceeded the optimum by only 3 percent. And I might have concluded that it would make political sense for incumbents to adopt a "the more reliable the better" policy in districting. However, I certainly cannot say that the court's inference from the facts was impermissible.

Finally, the court found that other evidence demonstrated that race was foremost on the legislative agenda: an e-mail from the drafter of the 1992 and 1997 plans to senators in charge of legislative redistricting, the computer capability to draw the district by race, and statements made by Senator Cooper that the legislature was going to be able to avoid *Shaw*'s majority-minority trigger by ending just short of the majority.[8] The e-mail, in combination with the indirect evidence, is evidence ample enough to support the District Court's finding for purposes of clear error review. The drafter of the redistricting plans reported in the bluntest of terms: "I have moved Greensboro Black community into the 12th [District], and now need to take . . . 60,000 out of the 12th [District]." Certainly the District Court was entitled to believe that the drafter was targeting voters and shifting district boundaries purely on the basis of race. The Court tries to belittle the import of this evidence by noting that the e-mail does not discuss *why* blacks were being targeted. However, the District Court was assigned the task of determining *whether,* not *why,* race predominated. As I see it, this inquiry is sufficient to answer the constitutional question because racial gerrymandering offends the Constitution whether the motivation is malicious or benign. It is not a defense that the legislature merely may have drawn the district based on the stereotype that blacks are reliable Democratic voters.

If I were the District Court, I might have reached the same conclusion that the Court does, that "[t]he evidence taken together . . . does not show that racial considerations predominated in the drawing of District 12's boundaries." But I am not the trier of fact, and it is not my role to weigh evidence in the first instance. The only question that this Court should decide is whether the District Court's finding of racial predominance was clearly erroneous. In light of the direct evidence of racial motive and the inferences that may be drawn from the circumstantial evidence, I am satisfied that the District Court's finding was permissible, even if not compelled by the record.

8. The court also relied on the statement of legislative redistricting leader Senator Cooper to the North Carolina Legislature, in which the senator mentioned the goals of geographical, political, and *racial* balance. In isolation, this statement does appear to support only the finding that race was *a* motive. Unlike this Court, however, the District Court had the advantage of listening to and watching Senator Cooper testify. I therefore am in no position to question the court's likely analysis that, although Senator Cooper mentioned all three motives, the predominance of race was apparent. This determination was made all the more reasonable by the fact that the District Court found the senator's claim regarding the "happenstance" final composition of the district to lack credibility in light of the e-mail.

NOTES ON *EASLEY*

1. *Easley* seems to run contrary to the trend that the Court started and continued throughout the 1990s in the racial gerrymandering context. During that decade, when presented with a challenge on racial gerrymandering grounds to a plan drawn by a state legislature, the Court tended to find (or agree with a lower court finding) that a racial gerrymander had occurred.

2. In contrast, *Easley* held that a district court's finding of a racial gerrymander in relation to District 12 was "clearly erroneous." Who has the better of the argument in relation to whether the district court's finding was clearly erroneous: Justice Stephen Breyer for the majority or Justice Clarence Thomas for the dissenters?

3. How is *Easley* different from the racial gerrymandering decisions that came before it? In particular, how is *Easley* different from *Miller*?

4. Given *Easley*, a state presumably would typically defend against a *Shaw* claim by asserting that, as a factual matter, politics rather than race motivated its decision. If you were an attorney representing a plaintiff bringing a *Shaw*-type claim, what evidence would you need to present to survive a motion for summary judgment filed by the state and, ultimately, to prevail after trial? Would you need some sort of "smoking gun" in the form of an email in which the mapmaker admitted that race was the primary motivation for the district's lines? Would even this kind of "smoking gun" be enough? (Why did the email in *Easley* fail in this respect?) Without a "smoking gun" of this type, would it be possible to win a *Shaw*-type case based solely on expert testimony that race, rather than politics, must have been the mapmaker's primary motivation?

* * *

It is interesting to note that while the Supreme Court considered many claims of racial gerrymandering in the 1990s, racial gerrymandering doctrine, in essence, went dormant during the 2000 round of redistricting. Put differently, plaintiffs would allege claims of racial gerrymandering but not prevail. But, as you will see in the following case, *Cooper v. Harris,* racial gerrymandering doctrine re-emerged after the 2010 round of redistricting with a prominent decision that again(!) involved North Carolina's congressional districts.

Cooper v. Harris

137 S. Ct. 1455 (2017)

KAGAN, J., delivered the opinion of the Court, in which THOMAS, GINSBURG, BREYER, and SOTOMAYOR, JJ., joined. THOMAS, J., filed a concurring opinion. ALITO, J., filed an opinion concurring in the judgment in part and dissenting in part, in which ROBERTS, C.J., and KENNEDY, J., joined. GORSUCH, J., took no part in the consideration or decision of the case.

Justice KAGAN delivered the opinion of the Court.

A State may not use race as the predominant factor in drawing district lines unless it has a compelling reason. In this case, a three-judge District Court ruled that North Carolina officials violated that bar when they created two districts whose voting-age populations were majority black. Applying a deferential standard of review to the factual findings underlying that decision, we affirm.

I

A

The Equal Protection Clause of the Fourteenth Amendment limits racial gerrymanders in legislative districting plans. When a voter sues state officials for drawing such race-based lines, our decisions call for a two-step analysis.

First, the plaintiff must prove that race was the predominant factor motivating the legislature's decision to place a significant number of voters within or without a particular district. *Miller v. Johnson* (1995). That entails demonstrating that the legislature subordinated other factors — compactness, respect for political subdivisions, partisan advantage, what have you — to racial considerations. The plaintiff may make the required showing through direct evidence of legislative intent, circumstantial evidence of a district's shape and demographics, or a mix of both.[1]

Second, if racial considerations predominated over others, the design of the district must withstand strict scrutiny. The burden thus shifts to the State to prove that its race-based sorting of voters serves a "compelling interest" and is "narrowly tailored" to that end. This Court has long assumed that one compelling interest is complying with operative provisions of the Voting Rights Act of 1965 (VRA or Act).

Two provisions of the VRA — § 2 and § 5 — are involved in this case. Section 2 prohibits "vote dilution" — brought about, most relevantly here, by the dispersal of a group's members into districts in which they constitute an ineffective minority of voters. Section 5, at the time of the districting in dispute, worked through a different mechanism. Before this Court invalidated its coverage formula, see *Shelby County v. Holder* (2013), that section required certain jurisdictions (including various North Carolina counties) to pre-clear voting changes with the Department of Justice, so as to forestall "retrogression" in the ability of racial minorities to elect their preferred candidates.

When a State invokes the VRA to justify race-based districting, it must show (to meet the "narrow tailoring" requirement) that it had a strong basis in evidence for concluding that the statute required its action. Or said otherwise, the State must establish that it had "good reasons" to think that it would transgress the Act if it did *not* draw race-based district lines. That "strong basis" (or "good reasons") standard gives States "breathing room" to adopt reasonable compliance measures that may prove, in perfect hindsight, not to have been needed.

A district court's assessment of a districting plan, in accordance with the two-step inquiry just described, warrants significant deference on appeal to this Court. We of course retain full power to correct a court's errors of law, at either stage of the

1. A plaintiff succeeds at this stage even if the evidence reveals that a legislature elevated race to the predominant criterion in order to advance other goals, including political ones.

analysis. But the court's findings of fact—most notably, as to whether racial considerations predominated in drawing district lines—are subject to review only for clear error. See *Easley v. Cromartie* (2001). Under that standard, we may not reverse just because we would have decided the matter differently. A finding that is "plausible" in light of the full record—even if another is equally or more so—must govern.

standard of review ↓ deferential

B

This case concerns North Carolina's most recent redrawing of two congressional districts, both of which have long included substantial populations of black voters. In its current incarnation, District 1 is anchored in the northeastern part of the State, with appendages stretching both south and west (the latter into Durham). District 12 begins in the south-central part of the State (where it takes in a large part of Charlotte) and then travels northeast, zig-zagging much of the way to the State's northern border. (Maps showing the districts are included in an appendix to this opinion.) Both have quite the history before this Court.

[The Court recounted the history of racial gerrymandering litigation in the 1990s.]

Under the 2001 map, which went unchallenged in court, neither District 1 nor District 12 had a black voting-age population (called a "BVAP") that was a majority of the whole: The former had a BVAP of around 48%, the latter a BVAP of around 43%. Nonetheless, in five successive general elections conducted in those reconfigured districts, all the candidates preferred by most African-American voters won their contests—and by some handy margins. In District 1, black voters' candidates of choice garnered as much as 70% of the total vote, and never less than 59%. And in District 12, those candidates won with 72% of the vote at the high end and 64% at the low.

Another census, in 2010, necessitated yet another congressional map—the one at issue in this case. State Senator Robert Rucho and State Representative David Lewis, both Republicans, chaired the two committees jointly responsible for preparing the revamped plan. They hired Dr. Thomas Hofeller, a veteran political mapmaker, to assist them in redrawing district lines. Several hearings, drafts, and revisions later, both chambers of the State's General Assembly adopted the scheme the three men proposed.

F

The new map (among other things) significantly altered both District 1 and District 12. The 2010 census had revealed District 1 to be substantially underpopulated: To comply with the Constitution's one-person-one-vote principle, the State needed to place almost 100,000 new people within the district's boundaries. Rucho, Lewis, and Hofeller chose to take most of those people from heavily black areas of Durham, requiring a finger-like extension of the district's western line. With that addition, District 1's BVAP rose from 48.6% to 52.7%. District 12, for its part, had no need for significant total-population changes: It was overpopulated by fewer than 3,000 people out of over 730,000. Still, Rucho, Lewis, and Hofeller decided to reconfigure the district, further narrowing its already snakelike body while adding areas at either end—most relevantly here, in Guilford County. Those changes appreciably shifted the racial composition of District 12: As the district gained some 35,000 African-Americans of voting age and lost some 50,000 whites of that age, its BVAP increased from 43.8% to 50.7%.

II

[Omitted.]

III

[T]he court below found that race furnished the predominant rationale for [District 1's] redesign. And it held that the State's interest in complying with the VRA could not justify that consideration of race. We uphold both conclusions.

A

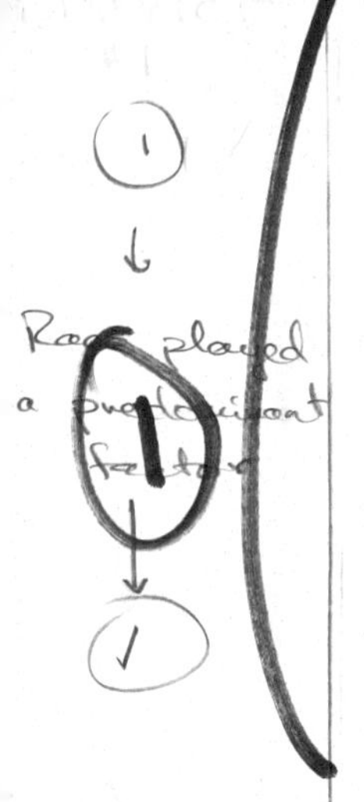

Uncontested evidence in the record shows that the State's mapmakers, in considering District 1, purposefully established a racial target: African-Americans should make up no less than a majority of the voting-age population. Senator Rucho and Representative Lewis were not coy in expressing that goal. They repeatedly told their colleagues that District 1 had to be majority-minority, so as to comply with the VRA. And that objective was communicated in no uncertain terms to the legislators' consultant [Dr. Hofeller.]

Hofeller followed those directions to the letter, such that the 50%-plus racial target had a direct and significant impact on District 1's configuration. In particular, Hofeller moved the district's borders to encompass the heavily black parts of Durham (and only those parts), thus taking in tens of thousands of additional African-American voters. That change and similar ones, made (in his words) to ensure that the district's racial composition would "add[] up correctly," deviated from the districting practices he otherwise would have followed. Hofeller candidly admitted that point: For example, he testified, he sometimes could not respect county or precinct lines as he wished because "the more important thing" was to create a majority-minority district. The result is a district with stark racial borders: Within the same counties, the portions that fall inside District 1 have black populations two to three times larger than the portions placed in neighboring districts.

Faced with this body of evidence—showing an announced racial target that subordinated other districting criteria and produced boundaries amplifying divisions between blacks and whites—the District Court did not clearly err in finding that race predominated in drawing District 1. Indeed, as all three judges recognized, the court could hardly have concluded anything but.

B

The more substantial question is whether District 1 can survive the strict scrutiny applied to racial gerrymanders. As noted earlier, we have long assumed that complying with the VRA is a compelling interest. And we have held that race-based districting is narrowly tailored to that objective if a State had "good reasons" for thinking that the Act demanded such steps.

This Court identified, in *Thornburg v. Gingles*, three threshold conditions for proving vote dilution under § 2 of the VRA. First, a "minority group" must be "sufficiently large and geographically compact to constitute a majority" in some reasonably configured legislative district. Second, the minority group must be "politically cohesive." And third, a district's white majority must "vote [] sufficiently as a bloc" to usually "defeat the minority's preferred candidate." If a State has good reason to think that all the "*Gingles* preconditions" are met, then so too it has good reason to believe that § 2 requires drawing a majority-minority district. But if not, then not.

Here, electoral history provided no evidence that a § 2 plaintiff could demonstrate the third *Gingles* prerequisite—effective white bloc-voting. For most of the twenty years prior to the new plan's adoption, African-Americans had made up less than a majority of District 1's voters; the district's BVAP usually hovered between 46% and 48%. Yet throughout those two decades, as the District Court noted, District 1 was "an extraordinarily safe district for African-American preferred candidates." Those victories (indeed, landslides) occurred because the district's white population did *not* "vote [] sufficiently as a bloc" to thwart black voters' preference; rather, a meaningful number of white voters joined a politically cohesive black community to elect that group's favored candidate. In the lingo of voting law, District 1 functioned, election year in and election year out, as a "crossover" district, in which members of the majority help a "large enough" minority to elect its candidate of choice. So experience gave the State no reason to think that the VRA required it to ramp up District 1's BVAP.

The State counters that, in this context, past performance is no guarantee of future results.

But that reasoning, taken alone, cannot justify North Carolina's race-based redesign of District 1. To have a strong basis in evidence to conclude that § 2 demands such race-based steps, the State must carefully evaluate whether a plaintiff could establish the *Gingles* preconditions—including effective white bloc-voting—in a new district created without those measures. We see nothing in the legislative record that fits that description.

Accordingly, we uphold the District Court's conclusion that North Carolina's use of race as the predominant factor in designing District 1 does not withstand strict scrutiny.

IV

We now look west to District 12, making its fifth (!) appearance before this Court. This time, the district's legality turns, and turns solely, on which of two possible reasons predominantly explains its most recent reconfiguration. The plaintiffs contended at trial that the General Assembly chose voters for District 12, as for District 1, because of their race. According to the State's version of events, Senator Rucho, Representative Lewis, and Dr. Hofeller moved voters in and out of the district as part of a "strictly" political gerrymander, without regard to race. The mapmakers drew their lines, in other words, to "pack" District 12 with Democrats, not African-Americans. After hearing evidence supporting both parties' accounts, the District Court accepted the plaintiffs'.

Getting to the bottom of a dispute like this one poses special challenges for a trial court. In the more usual case alleging a racial gerrymander—where no one has raised a partisanship defense—the court can make real headway by exploring the challenged district's conformity to traditional districting principles, such as compactness and respect for county lines. In *Shaw II*, for example, this Court emphasized the "highly irregular" shape of then-District 12 in concluding that race predominated in its design. But such evidence loses much of its value when the State asserts partisanship as a defense, because a bizarre shape—as of the new District 12—can arise from a "political motivation" as well as a racial one. And crucially, political and racial reasons are capable of yielding similar oddities in a district's boundaries. That is because, of course, "racial identification is highly correlated with political affiliation." *Cromartie II.* As a result of those redistricting realities, a trial court has a formidable task: It must make "a sensitive inquiry" into all "circumstantial and direct evidence of intent" to assess whether the plaintiffs have managed to disentangle race from politics and prove that the former drove a district's lines.[7]

Our job is different—and generally easier. As described earlier, we review a district court's finding as to racial predominance only for clear error, except when the court made a legal mistake. . . .

In light of those principles, we uphold the District Court's finding of racial predominance respecting District 12. The evidence offered at trial, including live witness testimony subject to credibility determinations, adequately supports the conclusion that race, not politics, accounted for the district's reconfiguration. And no error of law infected that judgment: Contrary to North Carolina's view, the District Court had no call to dismiss this challenge just because the plaintiffs did not proffer an alternative design for District 12 as circumstantial evidence of the legislature's intent.

A

Begin with some facts and figures, showing how the redistricting of District 12 affected its racial composition. As explained above, District 12 (unlike District 1) was approximately the right size as it was: North Carolina did not—indeed, could not—much change its total population. But by further slimming the district and adding a couple of knobs to its snakelike body (including in Guilford County), the General Assembly incorporated tens of thousands of new voters and pushed out tens of thousands of old ones. And those changes followed racial lines: To be specific, the new District 12 had 35,000 more African-Americans of voting age and 50,000 fewer whites of that age. (The difference was made up of voters from other racial categories.) Those voter exchanges produced a sizable jump in the district's BVAP, from 43.8% to 50.7%. The Assembly thus turned District 12 (as it did District 1) into a majority-minority district.

[The Court notes that public statements of Rucho and Lewis indicated that racial considerations lay behind District 12's augmented BVAP because of the need

7. As earlier noted, that inquiry is satisfied when legislators have "place[d] a significant number of voters within or without" a district predominantly because of their race, regardless of their ultimate objective in taking that step. So, for example, if legislators use race as their predominant districting criterion with the end goal of advancing their partisan interests—perhaps thinking that a proposed district is more "sellable" as a race-based VRA compliance measure than as a political gerrymander and will accomplish much the same thing—their action still triggers strict scrutiny. In other words, the sorting of voters on the grounds of their race remains suspect even if race is meant to function as a proxy for other (including political) characteristics.

to obtain preclearance under Section 5. The Court also noted that "Hofeller confirmed that intent in both deposition testimony and an expert report." And that the "State's preclearance submission to the Justice Department indicated a similar determination to concentrate black voters in District 12."]

And still there was more: Perhaps the most dramatic testimony in the trial came when Congressman Mel Watt (who had represented District 12 for some 20 years) recounted a conversation he had with Rucho in 2011 about the district's future make-up. According to Watt, Rucho said that "his leadership had told him that he had to ramp the minority percentage in [District 12] up to over 50 percent to comply with the Voting Rights Law."

The State's contrary story—that politics alone drove decisionmaking—came into the trial mostly through Hofeller's testimony. Hofeller explained that Rucho and Lewis instructed him, first and foremost, to make the map as a whole "more favorable to Republican candidates." One agreed-on stratagem in that effort was to pack the historically Democratic District 12 with even more Democratic voters, thus leaving surrounding districts more reliably Republican. To that end, Hofeller recounted, he drew District 12's new boundaries based on political data—specifically, the voting behavior of precincts in the 2008 Presidential election between Barack Obama and John McCain. Indeed, he claimed, he displayed only this data, and no racial data, on his computer screen while mapping the district. Only *after* he drew a politics-based line between those adjacent areas, Hofeller testified, did he "check[]" the racial data and "f[ind] out" that the resulting configuration of District 12 "did not have a [§ 5] issue."

The District Court, however, disbelieved Hofeller's asserted indifference to the new district's racial composition.

Finally, an expert report by Dr. Stephen Ansolabehere lent circumstantial support to the plaintiffs' race-not-politics case. Ansolabehere looked at the six counties overlapping with District 12—essentially the region from which the mapmakers could have drawn the district's population. The question he asked was: Who from those counties actually ended up in District 12? The answer he found was: Only 16% of the region's white registered voters, but 64% of the black ones. Ansolabehere next controlled for party registration, but discovered that doing so made essentially no difference: For example, only 18% of the region's white Democrats wound up in District 12, whereas 65% of the black Democrats did. The upshot was that, regardless of party, a black voter was three to four times more likely than a white voter to cast his ballot within District 12's borders. Those stark disparities led Ansolabehere to conclude that "race, and not party," was "the dominant factor" in District 12's design. His report, as the District Court held, thus tended to confirm the plaintiffs' direct evidence of racial predominance.

The District Court's assessment that all this evidence proved racial predominance clears the bar of clear error review. No doubt other interpretations of that evidence were permissible. Maybe we would have evaluated the testimony differently had we presided over the trial; or then again, maybe we would not have. Either way—and it is only *this* which matters—we are far from having a "definite and firm conviction" that the District Court made a mistake in concluding from the record before it that racial considerations predominated in District 12's design.

B

The State mounts a final, legal rather than factual, attack on the District Court's finding of racial predominance. When race and politics are competing explanations of a district's lines, argues North Carolina, the party challenging the district must introduce a particular kind of circumstantial evidence: "an alternative [map] that achieves the legislature's political objectives while improving racial balance." That is true, the State says, irrespective of what other evidence is in the case—so even if the plaintiff offers powerful direct proof that the legislature adopted the map it did for racial reasons. Because the plaintiffs here (as all agree) did not present such a counter-map, North Carolina concludes that they cannot prevail. The dissent echoes that argument.

We have no doubt that an alternative districting plan, of the kind North Carolina describes, can serve as key evidence in a race-versus-politics dispute. One, often highly persuasive way to disprove a State's contention that politics drove a district's lines is to show that the legislature had the capacity to accomplish all its partisan goals without moving so many members of a minority group into the district. If you were *really* sorting by political behavior instead of skin color (so the argument goes) you would have done—or, at least, could just as well have done—*this.* Such would-have, could-have, and (to round out the set) should-have arguments are a familiar means of undermining a claim that an action was based on a permissible, rather than a prohibited, ground.

But they are hardly the *only* means. Suppose that the plaintiff in a dispute like this one introduced scores of leaked emails from state officials instructing their mapmaker to pack as many black voters as possible into a district, or telling him to make sure its BVAP hit 75%. Based on such evidence, a court could find that racial rather than political factors predominated in a district's design, with or without an alternative map. And so too in cases lacking that kind of smoking gun, as long as the evidence offered satisfies the plaintiff's burden of proof. In *Bush v. Vera,* for example, this Court upheld a finding of racial predominance based on "substantial direct evidence of the legislature's racial motivations"—including credible testimony from political figures and statements made in a § 5 preclearance submission—plus circumstantial evidence that redistricters had access to racial, but not political, data at the "block-by-block level" needed to explain their "intricate" designs. Not a single Member of the Court thought that the absence of a counter-map made any difference. Similarly, it does not matter in this case, where the plaintiffs' introduction of mostly direct and some circumstantial evidence—documents issued in the redistricting process, testimony of government officials, expert analysis of demographic patterns—gave the District Court a sufficient basis, sans any map, to resolve the race-or-politics question.

A plaintiff's task, in other words, is simply to persuade the trial court—without any special evidentiary prerequisite—that race (not politics) was the predominant consideration in deciding to place a significant number of voters within or without a particular district. That burden of proof, we have often held, is "demanding." And because that is so, a plaintiff will sometimes need an alternative map, as a practical matter, to make his case. But in no area of our equal protection law have we forced plaintiffs to submit one particular form of proof to prevail. Nor would it make sense to do so here. The Equal Protection Clause prohibits the unjustified drawing of district lines based on race. An alternative map is merely an evidentiary tool to show that such a substantive violation has occurred; neither its presence nor its absence can itself resolve a racial gerrymandering claim.

North Carolina insists, however, that we have already said to the contrary—more particularly, that our decision in *Cromartie II* imposed a non-negotiable "alternative-map requirement." We there stated:

> "In a case such as this one where majority-minority districts . . . are at issue and where racial identification correlates highly with political affiliation, the party attacking the legislatively drawn boundaries must show at the least that the legislature could have achieved its legitimate political objectives in alternative ways that are comparably consistent with traditional districting principles. That party must also show that those districting alternatives would have brought about significantly greater racial balance."

According to North Carolina, that passage alone settles this case, because it makes an alternative map "essential" to a finding that District 12 (a majority-minority district in which race and partisanship are correlated) was a racial gerrymander. Once again, the dissent says the same.

But the reasoning of *Cromartie II* belies that reading. The Court's opinion nowhere attempts to explicate or justify the categorical rule that the State claims to find there. And given the strangeness of that rule—which would treat a mere form of evidence as the very substance of a constitutional claim—we cannot think that the Court adopted it without any explanation. Still more, the entire thrust of the *Cromartie II* opinion runs counter to an inflexible counter-map requirement. If the Court had adopted that rule, it would have had no need to weigh each piece of evidence in the case and determine whether, taken together, they were "adequate" to show "the predominance of race in the legislature's line-drawing process." But that is exactly what *Cromartie II* did, over a span of 20 pages and in exhaustive detail. Item by item, the Court discussed and dismantled the supposed proof, both direct and circumstantial, of race-based redistricting. All that careful analysis would have been superfluous—that dogged effort wasted—if the Court viewed the absence or inadequacy of a single form of evidence as necessarily dooming a gerrymandering claim.

Rightly understood, the passage from *Cromartie II* had a different and narrower point, arising from and reflecting the evidence offered in that case. The direct evidence of a racial gerrymander, we thought, was extremely weak: We said of one piece that it "says little or nothing about whether race played a predominant role" in drawing district lines; we said of another that it "is less persuasive than the kinds of direct evidence we have found significant in other redistricting cases." Nor did the report of the plaintiffs' expert impress us overmuch: In our view, it "offer[ed] little insight into the legislature's true motive." That left a set of arguments of the would-have-could-have variety. For example, the plaintiffs offered several maps purporting to "show how the legislature might have swapped" some mostly black and mostly white precincts to obtain greater racial balance "without harming [the legislature's] political objective." But the Court determined that none of those proposed exchanges would have worked as advertised—essentially, that the plaintiffs' "you could have redistricted differently" arguments failed on their own terms. Hence emerged the demand quoted above, for maps that would *actually* show what

do not need an alternative map
MAP

the plaintiffs' had not. In a case like *Cromartie II*—that is, one in which the plaintiffs had meager direct evidence of a racial gerrymander and needed to rely on evidence of forgone alternatives—only maps of that kind could carry the day.

But this case is most unlike *Cromartie II,* even though it involves the same electoral district some twenty years on. This case turned not on the possibility of creating more optimally constructed districts, but on direct evidence of the General Assembly's intent in creating the actual District 12, including many hours of trial testimony subject to credibility determinations. That evidence, the District Court plausibly found, itself satisfied the plaintiffs' burden of debunking North Carolina's "it was really politics" defense; there was no need for an alternative map to do the same job. And we pay our precedents no respect when we extend them far beyond the circumstances for which they were designed.

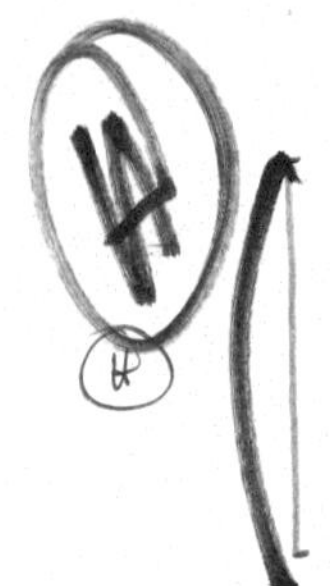

V

Applying a clear error standard, we uphold the District Court's conclusions that racial considerations predominated in designing both District 1 and District 12. For District 12, that is all we must do, because North Carolina has made no attempt to justify race-based districting there. For District 1, we further uphold the District Court's decision that § 2 of the VRA gave North Carolina no good reason to reshuffle voters because of their race. We accordingly affirm the judgment of the District Court.

It is so ordered.

Justice THOMAS, concurring.

I join the opinion of the Court because it correctly applies our precedents under the Constitution and the Voting Rights Act of 1965 (VRA), I write briefly to explain the additional grounds on which I would affirm the three-judge District Court and to note my agreement, in particular, with the Court's clear-error analysis.

As to District 1, I think North Carolina's concession that it created the district as a majority-black district is by itself sufficient to trigger strict scrutiny. I also think that North Carolina cannot satisfy strict scrutiny based on its efforts to comply with § 2 of the VRA. In my view, § 2 does not apply to redistricting and therefore cannot justify a racial gerrymander. *Holder v. Hall.*

As to District 12, I agree with the Court that the District Court did not clearly err when it determined that race was North Carolina's predominant motive in drawing the district. This is the same conclusion I reached when we last reviewed District 12. *Easley v. Cromartie* (*Cromartie II*) (dissenting opinion). The Court reached the contrary conclusion in *Cromartie II* only by misapplying our deferential standard for reviewing factual findings. Today's decision does not repeat *Cromartie II*'s error, and indeed it confines that case to its particular facts. It thus represents a welcome course correction to this Court's application of the clear-error standard.

Justice ALITO, with whom THE CHIEF JUSTICE and Justice KENNEDY join, concurring in the judgment in part and dissenting in part.

A precedent of this Court should not be treated like a disposable household item—say, a paper plate or napkin—to be used once and then tossed in the trash.

But that is what the Court does today in its decision regarding North Carolina's 12th Congressional District: The Court junks a rule adopted in a prior, remarkably similar challenge to this very same congressional district.

In *Easley v. Cromartie* (2001) (*Cromartie II*), the Court considered the constitutionality of the version of District 12 that was adopted in 1997. That district had the same basic shape as the district now before us, and the challengers argued that the legislature's predominant reason for adopting this configuration was race. The State responded that its motive was not race but politics. Its objective, the State insisted, was to create a district in which the Democratic candidate would win. Rejecting that explanation, a three-judge court found that the legislature's predominant motive was racial, specifically to pack African-Americans into District 12. But this Court held that this finding of fact was clearly erroneous.

A critical factor in our analysis was the failure of those challenging the district to come forward with an alternative redistricting map that served the legislature's political objective as well as the challenged version without producing the same racial effects. Noting that race and party affiliation in North Carolina were "highly correlated," we laid down this rule:

> "In a case such as this one . . . , the party attacking the legislatively drawn boundaries must show at the least that the legislature could have achieved its legitimate political objectives in alternative ways that are comparably consistent with traditional districting principles. That party must also show that those districting alternatives would have brought about significantly greater racial balance. Appellees failed to make any such showing here."

Now, District 12 is back before us. After the 2010 census, the North Carolina Legislature, with the Republicans in the majority, drew the present version of District 12. The challengers contend that this version violates equal protection because the predominant motive of the legislature was racial: to pack the district with African-American voters. The legislature responds that its objective was political: to pack the district with Democrats and thus to increase the chances of Republican candidates in neighboring districts.

You might think that the *Cromartie II* rule would be equally applicable in this case, which does not differ in any relevant particular, but the majority executes a stunning about-face. Now, the challengers' failure to produce an alternative map that meets the *Cromartie II* test is inconsequential. It simply "does not matter."

This is not the treatment of precedent that state legislatures have the right to expect from this Court. The failure to produce an alternative map doomed the challengers in *Cromartie II*, and the same should be true now. Partisan gerrymandering is always unsavory, but that is not the issue here. The issue is whether District 12 was drawn predominantly because of race. The record shows that it was not.[1]

I

[Omitted.]

1. I concur in the judgment of the Court regarding Congressional District 1. The State concedes that the district was intentionally created as a majority-minority district. And appellants have not satisfied strict scrutiny.

II

We have repeatedly acknowledged the problem of distinguishing between racial and political motivations in the redistricting context.

The problem arises from the confluence of two factors. The first is the status under the Constitution of partisan gerrymandering. As we have acknowledged, politics and political considerations are inseparable from districting and apportionment, and it is well known that state legislative majorities very often attempt to gain an electoral advantage through that process. Partisan gerrymandering dates back to the founding, and while some might find it distasteful, "[o]ur prior decisions have made clear that a jurisdiction may engage in constitutional political gerrymandering, even if it so happens that the most loyal Democrats happen to be black Democrats and even if the State were *conscious* of that fact." *Cromartie I.*

The second factor is that racial identification is highly correlated with political affiliation in many jurisdictions. This phenomenon makes it difficult to distinguish between political and race-based decisionmaking. If around 90% of African-American voters cast their ballots for the Democratic candidate, as they have in recent elections, a plan that packs Democratic voters will look very much like a plans that packs African-American voters.

A

We addressed this knotty problem in *Cromartie II.*

Cromartie II plainly meant to establish a rule for use in a broad class of cases and not a rule to be employed one time only.

In this case, as in *Cromartie II,* the plaintiffs allege a racial gerrymander, and the State's defense is that political motives explain District 12's boundaries. In such a case, *Cromartie II* instructed, plaintiffs must submit an alternative redistricting map demonstrating that the legislature could have achieved its political goals without the racial effects giving rise to the racial gerrymandering allegation. But in spite of this instruction, plaintiffs in this case failed to submit such a map. Based on what we said in *Cromartie II* about *the same type of claim* involving *the same congressional district,* reversal should be a foregone conclusion. It turns out, however, that the *Cromartie II* rule was good for one use only. Even in a case involving the very same district, it is tossed aside.

B

The alternative-map requirement deserves better. It is a logical response to the difficult problem of distinguishing between racial and political motivations when race and political party preference closely correlate.

There is [an] often-unstated danger where race and politics correlate: that the federal courts will be transformed into weapons of political warfare. Unless courts exercise extraordinary caution in distinguishing race-based redistricting from politics-based redistricting, they will invite the losers in the redistricting process to seek to obtain in court what they could not achieve in the political arena. If the majority party draws districts to favor itself, the minority party can deny the majority its political victory by prevailing on a racial gerrymandering claim. Even if the minority party loses in court, it can exact a heavy price by using the judicial process to engage in political trench warfare for years on end.

Although I do not imply that this is what occurred here, this case *does* reflect what litigation of this sort can look like. This is the *fifth time* that North Carolina's 12th Congressional District has come before this Court since 1993, and we have almost reached a new redistricting cycle without any certainty as to the constitutionality of North Carolina's *current* redistricting map. Given these dangers, *Cromartie II* was justified in crafting an evidentiary rule to prevent false positives.

C

[Omitted.]

III

Even if we set aside the challengers' failure to submit an alternative map, the District Court's finding that race predominated in the drawing of District 12 is clearly erroneous. The State offered strong and coherent evidence that politics, not race, was the legislature's predominant aim, and the evidence supporting the District Court's contrary finding is weak and manifestly inadequate in light of the high evidentiary standard that our cases require challengers to meet in order to prove racial predominance.

Also, evidence shows politics, not race, was motivating factor

[Justice Alito then canvasses the evidence presented in the lower court. Among the facts he cites for his conclusion that politics rather than race predominated in the creation of District 12 are:

- That District 12 retained its same basic shape.
- That Hofeller tried to move Democratic voters into District 12 from surrounding districts to make those surrounding districts more secure for Republicans.
- That retaining the same basic shape and making District 12 more Democratic would inevitably result in black voters being moved into District 12 because of the high correlation between race and partisan preference.
- That some references to and statements about race do not equate with race being the predominant factor in the construction of District 12.]

IV

Reviewing the evidence outlined above, two themes emerge. First, District 12's borders and racial composition are readily explained by political considerations and the effects of the legislature's political strategy on the demographics of District 12. Second, the majority largely ignores this explanation, as did the court below, and instead adopts the most damning interpretation of all available evidence.

The judgment below regarding District 12 should be reversed, and I therefore respectfully dissent.

Figure 1-7

APPENDIX TO OPINION OF THE COURT

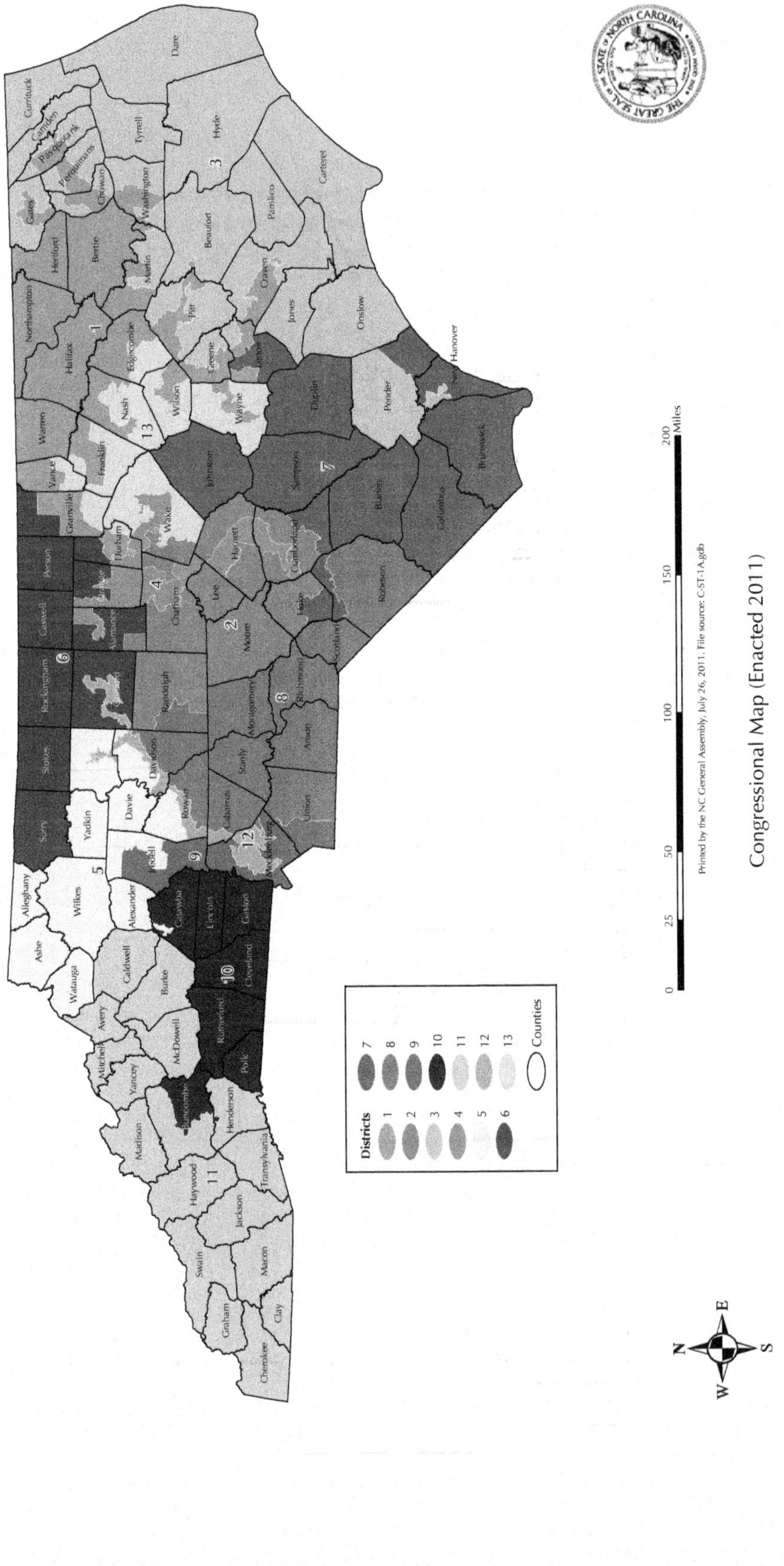
Districts
1
2
3
4
5
6
7
8
9
10
11
12
13
Counties
0 25 50 100 150 200 Miles
Printed by the NC General Assembly, July 26, 2011. File source: C-ST-1A.gdb
Congressional Map (Enacted 2011)
N E S W

Figure 1-8

Appendix to opinion of the Court

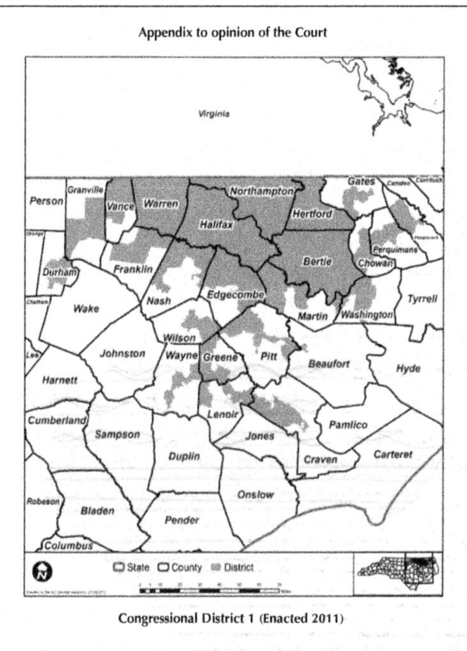

Congressional District 1 (Enacted 2011)

Figure 1-9

Appendix to opinion of the Court

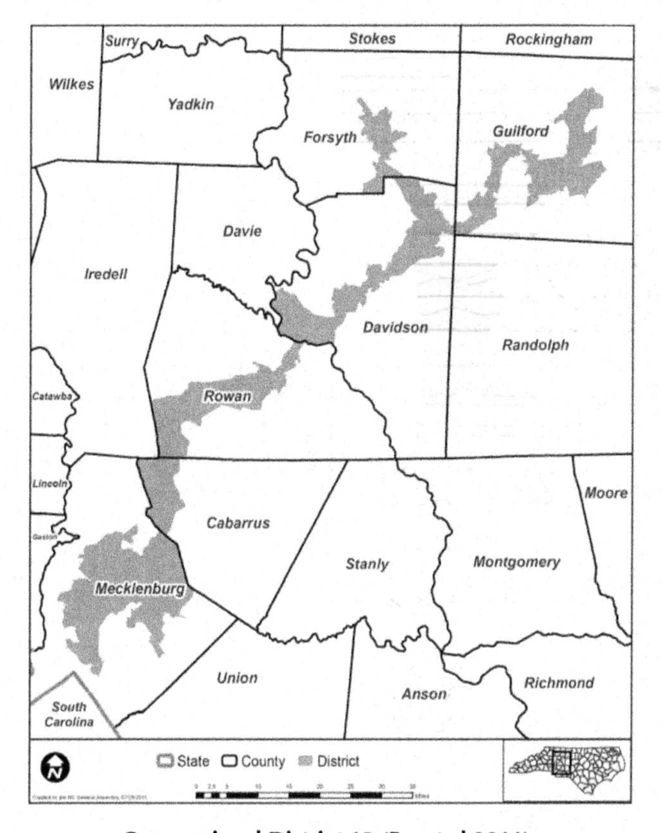

Congressional District 12 (Enacted 2011)

NOTES ON *COOPER*

1. Consider first whether *Cooper* is consistent with *Easley* in relation to its analysis of District 12 with regard to whether race was the predominant factor in its design:

- Is the "clear error" review in *Easley* the same as the "clear error" review of *Cooper*?
- Is the need for an "alternative" map treated the same in *Easley* as in *Cooper*?
- Is the use of race as a proxy for partisan affiliation treated the same in *Easley* as in *Cooper*?

2. Once race is determined to be a predominant factor, the next step of racial gerrymandering doctrine is to determine whether the district meets strict scrutiny—a compelling state interest and narrow tailoring. The *Cooper* majority repeats a mantra the Court has often used in racial gerrymandering cases by "assuming" that compliance with the Voting Rights Act is a compelling state interest. Why does the Court not just *hold* that compliance with the Voting Rights Act is a compelling state interest? What or who could be holding (pun, intended) the Court back?

3. Consider the context in which the racial gerrymandering claims in North Carolina came about. In the 1990s, the litigation involved Republicans who were challenging what everyone agreed were Democratic gerrymanders. In the 2010s, the litigation involved Democrats who were challenging what everyone agreed were Republican gerrymanders. Perhaps this proves that what comes around goes around. But perhaps this proves that the Court might be using racial gerrymandering doctrine as a *sub silentio* tool to attack partisan gerrymandering. (As you will soon see, a claim of unconstitutional partisan gerrymandering has never been successful at the Supreme Court.)

4. The aftermath of *Cooper*. . . . Following the district court opinion, the state was ordered to draw a remedial map. The remedial map (drawn by a Republican legislature) retained the same 10-3 (Republican-Democratic) split from the plan that had been struck down as a racial gerrymander. The new map also "smoothed" out the boundaries of District 1 and District 12 while reducing the black voting age population of each district to, respectively, about 44 percent and 35 percent. A federal trial court then found the remedial map to be an unconstitutional *partisan* gerrymander but that decision was ultimately vacated by the Supreme Court. In September 2019, plaintiffs filed a partisan gerrymandering challenge arguing that the remedial plan violated the *state* constitution. You will read that state court decision in the next section on partisan gerrymandering.

F. PARTISAN GERRYMANDERS

At this point, it should come as no surprise that legislative districts are drawn with the knowledge of how those districts will generally perform in future elections. For instance, in the context of the Voting Rights Act, it is possible to draw a district that will ensure that a certain group of voters will have the ability to control the outcome in a district. As one commentator once described it: "All Districting Is 'Gerrymandering.'" Robert D. Dixon, Jr., *Democratic Representation* 462 (1968).

One of the ways districts can be drawn is to elect members of a certain political party. In the United States, this generally boils down to Democrats drawing districts that advantage (i.e., disproportionately elect) Democrats and Republicans drawing districts that advantage Republicans. In addition, it can also lead to districts being drawn to protect incumbents from both political parties—what might be called an "incumbent gerrymander."

Once we recognize the phenomenon of what is known as "partisan gerrymandering," a few key questions arise. First, does partisan gerrymandering represent a problem? Second, if partisan gerrymandering is a problem, should the courts use the U.S. Constitution to do anything about it? Third, if the courts are not going to tackle the issue using the U.S. Constitution, are there other ways to solve the problem of partisan gerrymandering? All three questions are important, though because this is a casebook about election law litigation, the main focus of our inquiry will be on the second question.

To set the stage for the cases you will be reading, it is helpful to understand the origin of claims of partisan gerrymandering. In the early 1970s, in *Gaffney v. Cummings* (1973), the Court declined to intervene when Democrats and Republicans joined forces to draw lines to create safe seats for each party that would essentially provide for proportional representation for each party.

The next notable decision came in *Davis v. Bandemer*, 478 U.S. 109 (1986). In *Bandemer*, Democrats in Indiana challenged the state's 1981 legislative redistricting as an unconstitutional partisan gerrymander in violation of the Equal Protection Clause. The Court's response to that challenge involved two steps.

First, the Court needed to decide whether it would recognize an Equal Protection claim of unconstitutional partisan gerrymandering. In other words, the Court needed to decide whether a challenge to a redistricting plan as a partisan gerrymander represented a nonjusticiable political question. In *Bandemer*, six justices decided that claims of partisan gerrymandering were not political questions, such that the Court could hear these cases. Thus, starting in 1986, the courts were open for business in relation to the consideration of claims of partisan gerrymandering.

Second, the Court needed to decide the scope of the constitutional right to prevent unconstitutional gerrymandering. Put simply, the Court had to create a framework for deciding which redistricting plans were unconstitutional partisan gerrymanders and then needed to determine whether Indiana's plan was, indeed, such an unconstitutional gerrymander. At this stage, the *Bandemer* Court spoke with a fragmented voice as the justices who thought partisan gerrymandering claims were justiciable could not cobble together a five-justice majority for a particular manageable standard. As a result of the inability to agree on a manageable standard, partisan gerrymandering cases took on a pattern where plaintiffs would bring such claims but the courts would refuse to intervene. In essence, plaintiffs could bring claims of partisan gerrymandering but never win them.

In light of the events post-*Bandemer*, the Court revisited the realm of partisan gerrymandering in the early 2000s in *Vieth v. Jubelirer*, 541 U.S. 267(2004). *Vieth* involved a Republican gerrymander of Pennsylvania's congressional districts and led to a fractured decision. Four members of the Court, led by Justice Scalia, concluded that partisan gerrymandering clams were nonjusticiable. On the opposite end, four members of the Court concluded that partisan gerrymandering claims *were* justiciable and proposed manageable standards. However, those four members proposed three different manageable standards.

Justice Kennedy did not join either of these sides and, therefore, wrote the key opinion in *Vieth*. Justice Kennedy concluded that partisan gerrymandering claims were justiciable. However, he concluded that no judicially manageable standard had yet emerged. In essence, Justice Kennedy kept the door open for claims to be brought in the hope that a judicially manageable standard might emerge in a future case.

Litigation following *Vieth*, thus, was often an exercise in trying to come up with a judicially manageable standard that would satisfy Justice Kennedy. By the middle of the 2010s, lower courts had actually struck down a few redistricting plans as unconstitutional partisan gerrymanders. But Justice Kennedy left the Court in 2018 (he was replaced by Justice Brett Kavanaugh). In the following term, the Court revisited the question of justiciability and manageable standards.

Rucho v. Common Cause

139 S. Ct. 2484 (2019)

Chief Justice Roberts delivered the opinion of the Court.

Voters and other plaintiffs in North Carolina and Maryland challenged their States' congressional districting maps as unconstitutional partisan gerrymanders. The North Carolina plaintiffs complained that the State's districting plan discriminated against Democrats; the Maryland plaintiffs complained that their State's plan discriminated against Republicans. The plaintiffs alleged that the gerrymandering violated the First Amendment, the Equal Protection Clause of the Fourteenth Amendment, the Elections Clause, and Article I, § 2, of the Constitution. The District Courts in both cases ruled in favor of the plaintiffs, and the defendants appealed directly to this Court.

These cases require us to consider once again whether claims of excessive partisanship in districting are "justiciable"—that is, properly suited for resolution by the federal courts. This Court has not previously struck down a districting plan as an unconstitutional partisan gerrymander, and has struggled without success over the past several decades to discern judicially manageable standards for deciding such claims. The districting plans at issue here are highly partisan, by any measure. The question is whether the courts below appropriately exercised judicial power when they found them unconstitutional as well.

I

A

The first case involves a challenge to the congressional redistricting plan enacted by the Republican-controlled North Carolina General Assembly in 2016. The Republican legislators leading the redistricting effort instructed their mapmaker to use political data to draw a map that would produce a congressional delegation of ten Republicans and three Democrats. As one of the two Republicans chairing the redistricting committee stated, "I think electing Republicans is better than electing Democrats. So I drew this map to help foster what I think is better for the country." He further explained that the map was drawn with the aim of electing ten Republicans and three Democrats because he did "not believe it [would be] possible to draw a map with 11 Republicans and 2 Democrats." One Democratic state senator objected that entrenching the 10-3 advantage for Republicans was not "fair, reasonable, [or] balanced" because, as recently as 2012, "Democratic congressional candidates had received more votes on a statewide basis than Republican candidates." The General Assembly was not swayed by that objection and approved the 2016 Plan by a party-line vote.

In November 2016, North Carolina conducted congressional elections using the 2016 Plan, and Republican candidates won 10 of the 13 congressional districts. In the 2018 elections, Republican candidates won nine congressional districts, while Democratic candidates won three. The Republican candidate narrowly prevailed in the remaining district, but the State Board of Elections called a new election after allegations of fraud.

The plaintiffs challenged the 2016 Plan on multiple constitutional grounds. First, they alleged that the Plan violated the Equal Protection Clause of the Fourteenth Amendment by intentionally diluting the electoral strength of Democratic voters. Second, they claimed that the Plan violated their First Amendment rights by retaliating against supporters of Democratic candidates on the basis of their political beliefs. Third, they asserted that the Plan usurped the right of "the People" to elect their preferred candidates for Congress, in violation of the requirement in Article I, § 2, of the Constitution that Members of the House of Representatives be chosen "by the People of the several States." Finally, they alleged that the Plan violated the Elections Clause by exceeding the State's delegated authority to prescribe the "Times, Places and Manner of holding Elections" for Members of Congress.

B

The second case before us is *Lamone v. Benisek*. In 2011, the Maryland Legislature—dominated by Democrats—undertook to redraw the lines of that State's eight congressional districts. The Governor at the time, Democrat Martin O'Malley, led the process. He appointed a redistricting committee to help redraw the map, and asked Congressman Steny Hoyer, who has described himself as a "serial gerrymanderer," to advise the committee. The Governor later testified that his aim was to "use the redistricting process to change the overall composition of Maryland's congressional delegation to 7 Democrats and 1 Republican by flipping" one district. A decision was made to go for the Sixth, which had been held by a Republican for nearly two decades. To achieve the required equal population among districts, only about 10,000 residents needed to be removed from that district. The 2011 Plan accomplished that by moving roughly 360,000 voters out of the Sixth District and moving 350,000 new voters in. Overall, the Plan reduced the number of registered Republicans in the Sixth District by about 66,000 and increased the number of registered Democrats by about 24,000. The map was adopted by a party-line vote. It was used in the 2012 election and succeeded in flipping the Sixth District. A Democrat has held the seat ever since.

In November 2013, three Maryland voters filed this lawsuit. They alleged that the 2011 Plan violated the First Amendment, the Elections Clause, and Article I, § 2, of the Constitution.

II

A

Article III of the Constitution limits federal courts to deciding "Cases" and "Controversies." We have understood that limitation to mean that federal courts can address only questions historically viewed as capable of resolution through the judicial process. In these cases we are asked to decide an important question of constitutional law. But before we do so, we must find that the question is presented in a "case" or "controversy" that is, in James Madison's words, "of a Judiciary Nature."

Chief Justice Marshall famously wrote that it is "the province and duty of the judicial department to say what the law is." *Marbury v. Madison*. Sometimes, however, "the law is that the judicial department has no business entertaining the claim of unlawfulness—because the question is entrusted to one of the political branches or involves no judicially enforceable rights." *Vieth v. Jubelirer* (2004) (plurality opinion). In such a case the claim is said to present a "political question" and to be nonjusticiable—outside the courts' competence and therefore beyond the courts' jurisdiction. *Baker v. Carr* (1962). Among the political question cases the Court has identified are those that lack judicially discoverable and manageable standards for resolving them.

B

Partisan gerrymandering is nothing new. Nor is frustration with it. The practice was known in the Colonies prior to Independence, and the Framers were familiar with it at the time of the drafting and ratification of the Constitution. During the very first congressional elections, George Washington and his Federalist allies accused Patrick Henry of trying to gerrymander Virginia's districts against their candidates—in particular James Madison, who ultimately prevailed over fellow future President James Monroe.

In 1812, Governor of Massachusetts and future Vice President Elbridge Gerry notoriously approved congressional districts that the legislature had drawn to aid the Democratic-Republican Party. The moniker "gerrymander" was born when an outraged Federalist newspaper observed that one of the misshapen districts resembled a salamander.

The Framers addressed the election of Representatives to Congress in the Elections Clause. Art. I, § 4, cl. 1. That provision assigns to state legislatures the power to prescribe the "Times, Places and Manner of holding Elections" for Members of Congress, while giving Congress the power to "make or alter" any such regulations. Whether to give that supervisory authority to the National Government was debated at the Constitutional Convention. When those opposed to such congressional oversight moved to strike the relevant language, Madison came to its defense:

"[T]he State Legislatures will sometimes fail or refuse to consult the common interest at the expense of their local coveniency or prejudices. . . . Whenever the State Legislatures had a favorite measure to carry, they would take care so to mould their regulations as to favor the candidates they wished to succeed." 2 Records of the Federal Convention of 1787, at 240-241.

During the subsequent fight for ratification, the provision remained a subject of debate. Antifederalists predicted that Congress's power under the Elections Clause would allow Congress to make itself "omnipotent," setting the "time" of elections as never or the "place" in difficult to reach corners of the State. Federalists responded that, among other justifications, the revisionary power was necessary to counter state legislatures set on undermining fair representation, including through malapportionment. The Federalists were, for example, concerned that newly developing population centers would be deprived of their proper electoral weight, as some cities had been in Great Britain.

Congress has regularly exercised its Elections Clause power, including to address partisan gerrymandering. The Apportionment Act of 1842, which required single-member districts for the first time, specified that those districts be composed of contiguous territory in an attempt to forbid the practice of the gerrymander. Later statutes added requirements of compactness and equality of population. (Only the single member district requirement remains in place today.) Congress also used its Elections Clause power in 1870, enacting the first comprehensive federal statute dealing with elections as a way to enforce the Fifteenth Amendment. Starting in the 1950s, Congress enacted a series of laws to protect the right to vote through measures such as the suspension of literacy tests and the prohibition of English-only elections.

Appellants suggest that, through the Elections Clause, the Framers set aside electoral issues such as the one before us as questions that only Congress can resolve. We do not agree. In two areas—one-person, one-vote and racial gerrymandering—our cases have held that there is a role for the courts with respect to at least some issues that could arise from a State's drawing of congressional districts.

But the history is not irrelevant. The Framers were aware of electoral districting problems and considered what to do about them. They settled on a characteristic approach, assigning the issue to the state legislatures, expressly checked and balanced by the Federal Congress. As Alexander Hamilton explained, "it will . . . not be denied that a discretionary power over elections ought to exist somewhere. It will, I presume, be as readily conceded that there were only three ways in which this power could have been reasonably modified and disposed: that it must either have been lodged wholly in the national legislature, or wholly in the State legislatures, or primarily in the latter, and ultimately in the former." The Federalist. At no point was there a suggestion that the federal courts had a role to play. Nor was there any indication that the Framers had ever heard of courts doing such a thing.

C

Courts have nevertheless been called upon to resolve a variety of questions surrounding districting. Early on, doubts were raised about the competence of the federal courts to resolve those questions. *See Colegrove v. Green* (1946).

In the leading case of *Baker v. Carr*, voters in Tennessee complained that the State's districting plan for state representatives "debase[d]" their votes, because the plan was predicated on a 60-year-old census that no longer reflected the distribution of population in the State. The Court concluded that the claim of population inequality among districts did not fall into that category [of political questions] because such a claim could be decided under basic equal protection principles.

Another line of challenges to districting plans has focused on race. Laws that explicitly discriminate on the basis of race, as well as those that are race neutral on their face but are unexplainable on grounds other than race, are of course presumptively invalid.

Partisan gerrymandering claims have proved far more difficult to adjudicate. The basic reason is that, while it is illegal for a jurisdiction to depart from the one-person, one-vote rule, or to engage in racial discrimination in districting, a jurisdiction may engage in constitutional political gerrymandering.*

To hold that legislators cannot take partisan interests into account when drawing district lines would essentially countermand the Framers' decision to entrust districting to political entities. The "central problem" is not determining whether a jurisdiction has engaged in partisan gerrymandering. It is "determining when political gerrymandering has gone too far." *Vieth* (plurality opinion).

We first considered a partisan gerrymandering claim in *Gaffney v. Cummings* in 1973. There we rejected an equal protection challenge to Connecticut's redistricting plan, which aimed at a rough scheme of proportional representation of the two major political parties by wiggling and joggling boundary lines to create the appropriate number of safe seats for each party. In upholding the State's plan, we reasoned that districting inevitably has and is intended to have substantial political consequences.

Thirteen years later, in *Davis v. Bandemer*, we addressed a claim that Indiana Republicans had cracked and packed Democrats in violation of the Equal Protection Clause. A majority of the Court agreed that the case was justiciable, but the Court splintered over the proper standard to apply. Four Justices would have required proof of intentional discrimination against an identifiable political group and an actual discriminatory effect on that group. Two Justices would have focused on whether the boundaries of the voting districts have been distorted deliberately and arbitrarily to achieve illegitimate ends. Three Justices, meanwhile, would have held that the Equal Protection Clause simply "does not supply judicially manageable standards for resolving purely political gerrymandering claims." At the end of the day, there was "no 'Court' for a standard that properly should be applied in determining whether a challenged redistricting plan is an unconstitutional partisan political gerrymander." In any event, the Court held that the plaintiffs had failed to show that the plan violated the Constitution.

Eighteen years later, in *Vieth*, the plaintiffs complained that Pennsylvania's legislature ignored all traditional redistricting criteria, including the preservation of local government boundaries, in order to benefit Republican congressional candidates. Justice Scalia wrote for a four-Justice plurality. He would have held that the plaintiffs' claims were nonjusticiable because there was no judicially discernible and manageable standard for deciding them. Justice Kennedy, concurring in the judgment, noted the lack of comprehensive and neutral principles for drawing electoral boundaries and the absence of rules to limit and confine judicial

* [Note the import of what Chief Justice Roberts is saying in this sentence: for the first time, a majority of the Court declared political gerrymandering to be "constitutional."—EDS.]

intervention. He nonetheless left open the possibility that "in another case a standard might emerge." Four Justices dissented.

III

A

In considering whether partisan gerrymandering claims are justiciable, we are mindful of Justice Kennedy's counsel in *Vieth*: Any standard for resolving such claims must be grounded in a "limited and precise rationale" and be "clear, manageable, and politically neutral." An important reason for those careful constraints is that, as a Justice with extensive experience in state and local politics put it, "[t]he opportunity to control the drawing of electoral boundaries through the legislative process of apportionment is a critical and traditional part of politics in the United States." *Bandemer* (opinion of O'Connor, J.). An expansive standard requiring the correction of all election district lines drawn for partisan reasons would commit federal and state courts to unprecedented intervention in the American political process.

As noted, the question is one of degree: How to provide a standard for deciding how much partisan dominance is too much. And it is vital in such circumstances that the Court act only in accord with especially clear standards: "With uncertain limits, intervening courts—even when proceeding with best intentions—would risk assuming political, not legal, responsibility for a process that often produces ill will and distrust." *Vieth* (opinion of Kennedy, J.). If federal courts are to inject themselves into the most heated partisan issues by adjudicating partisan gerrymandering claims, they must be armed with a standard that can reliably differentiate unconstitutional from "constitutional political gerrymandering."

B

Partisan gerrymandering claims rest on an instinct that groups with a certain level of political support should enjoy a commensurate level of political power and influence. Explicitly or implicitly, a districting map is alleged to be unconstitutional because it makes it too difficult for one party to translate statewide support into seats in the legislature. But such a claim is based on a norm that does not exist in our electoral system—statewide elections for representatives along party lines.

Partisan gerrymandering claims invariably sound in a desire for proportional representation. As Justice O'Connor put it, such claims are based on "a conviction that the greater the departure from proportionality, the more suspect an apportionment plan becomes." *Bandemer*. Our cases, however, clearly foreclose any claim that the Constitution requires proportional representation or that legislatures in reapportioning must draw district lines to come as near as possible to allocating seats to the contending parties in proportion to what their anticipated statewide vote will be. See *Mobile v. Bolden* (plurality opinion).

The Founders certainly did not think proportional representation was required. For more than 50 years after ratification of the Constitution, many States elected their congressional representatives through at-large or "general ticket" elections. Such States typically sent single-party delegations to Congress. That meant that a party could garner nearly half of the vote statewide and wind up without any seats in the congressional delegation. The Whigs in Alabama suffered that fate in 1840: their party garnered 43 percent of the statewide vote, yet did not receive a single seat.

Unable to claim that the Constitution requires proportional representation outright, plaintiffs inevitably ask the courts to make their own political judgment about how much representation particular political parties *deserve*—based on the votes of their supporters—and to rearrange the challenged districts to achieve that end. But federal courts are not equipped to apportion political power as a matter of fairness, nor is there any basis for concluding that they were authorized to do so. As Justice Scalia put it for the plurality in *Vieth*:

> 'Fairness' does not seem to us a judicially manageable standard. . . . Some criterion more solid and more demonstrably met than that seems to us necessary to enable the state legislatures to discern the limits of their districting discretion, to meaningfully constrain the discretion of the courts, and to win public acceptance for the courts' intrusion into a process that is the very foundation of democratic decisionmaking.

The initial difficulty in settling on a "clear, manageable and politically neutral" test for fairness is that it is not even clear what fairness looks like in this context. There is a large measure of "unfairness" in any winner-take-all system. Fairness may mean a greater number of competitive districts. Such a claim seeks to undo packing and cracking so that supporters of the disadvantaged party have a better shot at electing their preferred candidates. But making as many districts as possible more competitive could be a recipe for disaster for the disadvantaged party. As Justice White has pointed out, "[i]f all or most of the districts are competitive . . . even a narrow statewide preference for either party would produce an overwhelming majority for the winning party in the state legislature." *Bandemer* (plurality opinion).

On the other hand, perhaps the ultimate objective of a "fairer" share of seats in the congressional delegation is most readily achieved by yielding to the gravitational pull of proportionality and engaging in cracking and packing, to ensure each party its "appropriate" share of "safe" seats. See *Gaffney*. Such an approach, however, comes at the expense of competitive districts and of individuals in districts allocated to the opposing party.

Or perhaps fairness should be measured by adherence to "traditional" districting criteria, such as maintaining political subdivisions, keeping communities of interest together, and protecting incumbents. But protecting incumbents, for example, enshrines a particular partisan distribution. And the natural political geography of a State—such as the fact that urban electoral districts are often dominated by one political party—can itself lead to inherently packed districts. [T]raditional criteria such as compactness and contiguity cannot promise political neutrality when used as the basis for relief. Instead, it seems, a decision under these standards would unavoidably have significant political effect, whether intended or not.

Deciding among just these different visions of fairness (you can imagine many others) poses basic questions that are political, not legal. There are no legal standards discernible in the Constitution for making such judgments, let alone limited and precise standards that are clear, manageable, and politically neutral. Any judicial decision on what is "fair" in this context would be an "unmoored determination" of the sort characteristic of a political question beyond the competence of the federal courts.

And it is only after determining how to define fairness that you can even begin to answer the determinative question: "How much is too much?" At what point does permissible partisanship become unconstitutional? If compliance with traditional districting criteria is the fairness touchstone, for example, how much deviation from those criteria is constitutionally acceptable and how should mapdrawers prioritize competing criteria? Should a court "reverse gerrymander" other parts of a State to counteract "natural" gerrymandering caused, for example, by the urban concentration of one party? If a districting plan protected half of the incumbents but redistricted the rest into head to head races, would that be constitutional? A court would have to rank the relative importance of those traditional criteria and weigh how much deviation from each to allow.

If a court instead focused on the respective number of seats in the legislature, it would have to decide the ideal number of seats for each party and determine at what point deviation from that balance went too far. If a 5-3 allocation corresponds most closely to statewide vote totals, is a 6-2 allocation permissible, given that legislatures have the authority to engage in a certain degree of partisan gerrymandering? Which seats should be packed and which cracked? Or if the goal is as many competitive districts as possible, how close does the split need to be for the district to be considered competitive? Presumably not all districts could qualify, so how to choose? Even assuming the court knew which version of fairness to be looking for, there are no discernible and manageable standards for deciding whether there has been a violation. The questions are unguided and ill suited to the development of judicial standards, and results from one gerrymandering case to the next would likely be disparate and inconsistent.

Appellees contend that if we can adjudicate one-person, one-vote claims, we can also assess partisan gerrymandering claims. But the one-person, one-vote rule is relatively easy to administer as a matter of math. The same cannot be said of partisan gerrymandering claims, because the Constitution supplies no objective measure for assessing whether a districting map treats a political party fairly. It hardly follows from the principle that each person must have an equal say in the election of representatives that a person is entitled to have his political party achieve representation in some way commensurate to its share of statewide support.

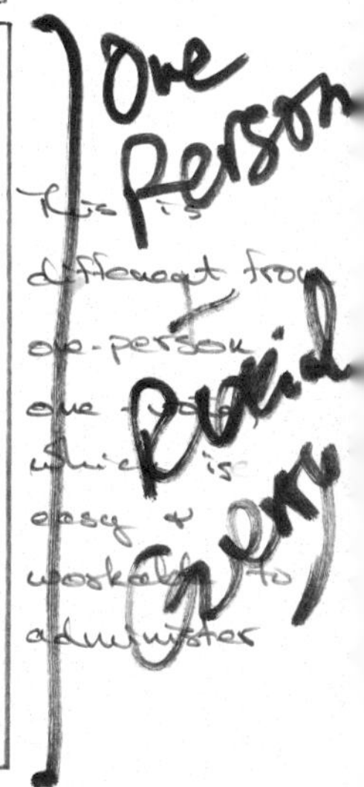

More fundamentally, "vote dilution" in the one-person, one-vote cases refers to the idea that each vote must carry equal weight. In other words, each representative must be accountable to (approximately) the same number of constituents. That requirement does not extend to political parties. It does not mean that each party must be influential in proportion to its number of supporters. [T]his Court is not responsible for vindicating generalized partisan preferences. The Court's constitutionally prescribed role is to vindicate the individual rights of the people appearing before it.[1]

1. The dissent's observation that the Framers viewed political parties "with deep suspicion, as fomenters of factionalism and symptoms of disease in the body politic" is exactly right. Its inference from that fact is exactly wrong. The Framers would have been amazed at a constitutional theory that guarantees a certain degree of representation to political parties.

Nor do our racial gerrymandering cases provide an appropriate standard for assessing partisan gerrymandering. "Nothing in our case law compels the conclusion that racial and political gerrymanders are subject to precisely the same constitutional scrutiny. In fact, our country's long and persistent history of racial discrimination in voting—as well as our Fourteenth Amendment jurisprudence, which always has reserved the strictest scrutiny for discrimination on the basis of race—would seem to compel the opposite conclusion." *Shaw*. Unlike partisan gerrymandering claims, a racial gerrymandering claim does not ask for a fair share of political power and influence, with all the justiciability conundrums that entails. It asks instead for the elimination of a racial classification. A partisan gerrymandering claim cannot ask for the elimination of partisanship.

IV

Appellees and the dissent propose a number of "tests" for evaluating partisan gerrymandering claims, but none meets the need for a limited and precise standard that is judicially discernible and manageable. And none provides a solid grounding for judges to take the extraordinary step of reallocating power and influence between political parties.

A

The *Common Cause* District Court concluded that all but one of the districts in North Carolina's 2016 Plan violated the Equal Protection Clause by intentionally diluting the voting strength of Democrats. In reaching that result the court first required the plaintiffs to prove "that a legislative mapdrawer's predominant purpose in drawing the lines of a particular district was to 'subordinate adherents of one political party and entrench a rival party in power.'" The District Court next required a showing "that the dilution of the votes of supporters of a disfavored party in a particular district—by virtue of cracking or packing—is likely to persist in subsequent elections such that an elected representative from the favored party in the district will not feel a need to be responsive to constituents who support the disfavored party." Finally, after a prima facie showing of partisan vote dilution, the District Court shifted the burden to the defendants to prove that the discriminatory effects are "attributable to a legitimate state interest or other neutral explanation."

The District Court's "predominant intent" prong is borrowed from the racial gerrymandering context. In racial gerrymandering cases, we rely on a "predominant intent" inquiry to determine whether race was, in fact, the reason particular district boundaries were drawn the way they were. If district lines were drawn for the purpose of separating racial groups, then they are subject to strict scrutiny because race-based decisionmaking is inherently suspect. But determining that lines were drawn on the basis of partisanship does not indicate that the districting was improper. A permissible intent—securing partisan advantage—does not become constitutionally impermissible, like racial discrimination, when that permissible intent "predominates."

The District Court tried to limit the reach of its test by requiring plaintiffs to show, in addition to predominant partisan intent, that vote dilution "is likely to persist" to such a degree that the elected representative will feel free to ignore the concerns of the supporters of the minority party. But to allow district courts to strike down apportionment plans on the basis of their prognostications as to the outcome of future elections invites 'findings' on matters as to which neither judges nor anyone else can have any confidence. And the test adopted by the *Common Cause* court requires a far more nuanced prediction than simply who would prevail in future political contests. Judges must forecast with unspecified certainty whether a prospective winner will have a margin of victory sufficient to permit him to ignore the supporters of his defeated opponent (whoever that may turn out to be). Judges not only have to pick the winner—they have to beat the point spread.

The appellees assure us that "the persistence of a party's advantage may be shown through sensitivity testing: probing how a plan would perform under other plausible electoral conditions." Experience proves that accurately predicting electoral outcomes is not so simple, either because the plans are based on flawed assumptions about voter preferences and behavior or because demographics and priorities change over time. In our two leading partisan gerrymandering cases themselves, the predictions of durability proved to be dramatically wrong. In 1981, Republicans controlled both houses of the Indiana Legislature as well as the governorship. Democrats challenged the state legislature districting map enacted by the Republicans. This Court in *Bandemer* rejected that challenge, and just months later the Democrats increased their share of House seats in the 1986 elections. Two years later the House was split 50-50 between Democrats and Republicans, and the Democrats took control of the chamber in 1990. Democrats also challenged the Pennsylvania congressional districting plan at issue in *Vieth.* Two years after that challenge failed, they gained four seats in the delegation, going from a 12-7 minority to an 11-8 majority. At the next election, they flipped another Republican seat.

Even the most sophisticated districting maps cannot reliably account for some of the reasons voters prefer one candidate over another, or why their preferences may change. Voters elect individual candidates in individual districts, and their selections depend on the issues that matter to them, the quality of the candidates, the tone of the candidates' campaigns, the performance of an incumbent, national events or local issues that drive voter turnout, and other considerations. Many voters split their tickets. Others never register with a political party, and vote for candidates from both major parties at different points during their lifetimes. For all of those reasons, asking judges to predict how a particular districting map will perform in future elections risks basing constitutional holdings on unstable ground outside judicial expertise.

It is hard to see what the District Court's third prong—providing the defendant an opportunity to show that the discriminatory effects were due to a "legitimate redistricting objective"—adds to the inquiry. The first prong already requires the plaintiff to prove that partisan advantage predominates. Asking whether a legitimate purpose other than partisanship was the motivation for a particular districting map just restates the question.

B

The District Courts also found partisan gerrymandering claims justiciable under the First Amendment, coalescing around a basic three-part test: proof of intent to burden individuals based on their voting history or party affiliation; an actual burden on political speech or associational rights; and a causal link between the invidious intent and actual burden. Both District Courts concluded that the districting plans at issue violated the plaintiffs' First Amendment right to association. The District Court in North Carolina relied on testimony that, after the 2016 Plan was put in place, the plaintiffs faced "difficulty raising money, attracting candidates, and mobilizing voters to support the political causes and issues such Plaintiffs sought to advance." Similarly, the District Court in Maryland examined testimony that "revealed a lack of enthusiasm, indifference to voting, a sense of disenfranchisement, a sense of disconnection, and confusion," and concluded that Republicans in the Sixth District "were burdened in fundraising, attracting volunteers, campaigning, and generating interest in voting."

To begin, there are no restrictions on speech, association, or any other First Amendment activities in the districting plans at issue. The plaintiffs are free to engage in those activities no matter what the effect of a plan may be on their district.

The plaintiffs' argument is that partisanship in districting should be regarded as simple discrimination against supporters of the opposing party on the basis of political viewpoint. Under that theory, any level of partisanship in districting would constitute an infringement of their First Amendment rights. But as the Court has explained, "[i]t would be idle . . . to contend that any political consideration taken into account in fashioning a reapportionment plan is sufficient to invalidate it." *Gaffney*. The First Amendment test simply describes the act of districting for partisan advantage. It provides no standard for determining when partisan activity goes too far.

As for actual burden, the slight anecdotal evidence found sufficient by the District Courts in these cases shows that this too is not a serious standard for separating constitutional from unconstitutional partisan gerrymandering. The District Courts relied on testimony about difficulty drumming up volunteers and enthusiasm. How much of a decline in voter engagement is enough to constitute a First Amendment burden? How many door knocks must go unanswered? How many petitions unsigned? How many calls for volunteers unheeded? The *Common Cause* District Court held that a partisan gerrymander places an unconstitutional burden on speech if it has more than a "*de minimis*" "chilling effect or adverse impact" on any First Amendment activity. The court went on to rule that there would be an adverse effect "even if the speech of [the plaintiffs] was not *in fact* chilled"; it was enough that the districting plan "makes it easier for supporters of Republican candidates to translate their votes into seats," thereby "enhanc[ing] the[ir] relative voice."

These cases involve blatant examples of partisanship driving districting decisions. But the First Amendment analysis below offers no "clear" and "manageable" way of distinguishing permissible from impermissible partisan motivation. The *Common Cause* court embraced that conclusion, observing that "a judicially manageable framework for evaluating partisan gerrymandering claims need not distinguish an 'acceptable' level of partisan gerrymandering from 'excessive' partisan gerrymandering" because "the Constitution does not authorize state redistricting bodies to engage in such partisan gerrymandering." The decisions below prove the prediction of the *Vieth* plurality that "a First Amendment claim, if it were sustained, would render unlawful *all* consideration of political affiliation in districting," contrary to our established precedent.

C

The dissent proposes using a State's own districting criteria as a neutral baseline from which to measure how extreme a partisan gerrymander is. The dissent would have us line up all the possible maps drawn using those criteria according to the partisan distribution they would produce. Distance from the "median" map would indicate whether a particular districting plan harms supporters of one party to an unconstitutional extent.

As an initial matter, it does not make sense to use criteria that will vary from State to State and year to year as the baseline for determining whether a gerrymander violates the Federal Constitution. The degree of partisan advantage that the Constitution tolerates should not turn on criteria offered by the gerrymanderers themselves. It is easy to imagine how different criteria could move the median map toward different partisan distributions. As a result, the same map could be constitutional or not depending solely on what the mapmakers said they set out to do. That possibility illustrates that the dissent's proposed constitutional test is indeterminate and arbitrary.

Even if we were to accept the dissent's proposed baseline, it would return us to the original unanswerable question (How much political motivation and effect is too much?). Would twenty percent away from the median map be okay? Forty percent? Sixty percent? Why or why not? (We appreciate that the dissent finds all the unanswerable questions annoying, but it seems a useful way to make the point.) The dissent's answer says it all: "This much is too much." That is not even trying to articulate a standard or rule.

The dissent argues that there are other instances in law where matters of degree are left to the courts. True enough. But those instances typically involve constitutional or statutory provisions or common law confining and guiding the exercise of judicial discretion. For example, the dissent cites the need to determine "substantial anticompetitive effect[s]" in antitrust law. That language, however, grew out of the Sherman Act, understood from the beginning to have its origin in the common law and to be familiar in the law of this country prior to and at the time of the adoption of the Act. Judges began with a significant body of law about what constituted a legal violation. In other cases, the pertinent statutory terms draw meaning from related provisions or statutory context. Here, on the other hand, the Constitution provides no basis whatever to guide the exercise of judicial discretion. Common experience gives content to terms such as "substantial risk" or "substantial harm," but the same cannot be said of substantial deviation from a median map. There is no way to tell whether the prohibited deviation from that map should kick in at 25 percent or 75 percent or some other point. The only provision in the Constitution that specifically addresses the matter assigns it to the political branches. See Art. I, § 4, cl. 1.

V

Excessive partisanship in districting leads to results that reasonably seem unjust. But the fact that such gerrymandering is incompatible with democratic principles does not mean that the solution lies with the federal judiciary. We conclude that partisan gerrymandering claims present political questions beyond the reach of the federal courts. Federal judges have no license to reallocate political power between the two

major political parties, with no plausible grant of authority in the Constitution, and no legal standards to limit and direct their decisions. Judicial action must be governed by *standard*, by *rule*, and must be principled, rational, and based upon reasoned distinctions found in the Constitution or laws. Judicial review of partisan gerrymandering does not meet those basic requirements.

Today the dissent essentially embraces the argument that this Court *can* address the problem of partisan gerrymandering because it *must*. That is not the test of our authority under the Constitution; that document instead confines the federal courts to a properly judicial role.

What the appellees and dissent seek is an unprecedented expansion of judicial power. We have never struck down a partisan gerrymander as unconstitutional—despite various requests over the past 45 years. The expansion of judicial authority would not be into just any area of controversy, but into one of the most intensely partisan aspects of American political life. That intervention would be unlimited in scope and duration—it would recur over and over again around the country with each new round of districting, for state as well as federal representatives. Consideration of the impact of today's ruling on democratic principles cannot ignore the effect of the unelected and politically unaccountable branch of the Federal Government assuming such an extraordinary and unprecedented role.

Our conclusion does not condone excessive partisan gerrymandering. Nor does our conclusion condemn complaints about districting to echo into a void. The States, for example, are actively addressing the issue on a number of fronts. In 2015, the Supreme Court of Florida struck down that State's congressional districting plan as a violation of the Fair Districts Amendment to the Florida Constitution. The dissent wonders why we can't do the same. The answer is that there is no "Fair Districts Amendment" to the Federal Constitution. Provisions in state statutes and state constitutions can provide standards and guidance for state courts to apply. (We do not understand how the dissent can maintain that a provision saying that no districting plan "shall be drawn with the intent to favor or disfavor a political party" provides little guidance on the question.) Indeed, numerous other States are restricting partisan considerations in districting through legislation. One way they are doing so is by placing power to draw electoral districts in the hands of independent commissions.* For example, in November 2018, voters in Colorado and Michigan approved constitutional amendments creating multimember commissions that will be responsible in whole or in part for creating and approving district maps for congressional and state legislative districts. Missouri is trying a different

* [Note that in *Arizona State Legislature v. Arizona Independent Redistricting Commission*, 135 S. Ct. 2652 (2015), the Court upheld the Arizona independent redistricting commission that voters adopted through a ballot referendum, taking the redistricting process away from the state legislature. But in that 5-4 decision, Chief Justice Roberts dissented, arguing that the U.S. Constitution allows only the "legislature" to dictate the "times, places, and manner" of regulating congressional elections, and that the people voting in a ballot referendum were not the "legislature." In light of that dissent, think about why Chief Justice Roberts mentions the viability of independent redistricting commissions to solve congressional partisan gerrymandering here in his *Rucho* opinion.—Eds.]

tack. Voters there overwhelmingly approved the creation of a new position—state demographer—to draw state legislative district lines.

Other States have mandated at least some of the traditional districting criteria for their mapmakers. Some have outright prohibited partisan favoritism in redistricting. See Fla. Const., Art. III, § 20(a) ("No apportionment plan or individual district shall be drawn with the intent to favor or disfavor a political party or an incumbent."); Mo. Const., Art. III, § 3 ("Districts shall be designed in a manner that achieves both partisan fairness and, secondarily, competitiveness. 'Partisan fairness' means that parties shall be able to translate their popular support into legislative representation with approximately equal efficiency."); Iowa Code § 42.4(5) (2016) ("No district shall be drawn for the purpose of favoring a political party, incumbent legislator or member of Congress, or other person or group."); Del. Code Ann., Tit. xxix, § 804 (2017) (providing that in determining district boundaries for the state legislature, no district shall "be created so as to unduly favor any person or political party").

As noted, the Framers gave Congress the power to do something about partisan gerrymandering in the Elections Clause. The first bill introduced in the 116th Congress would require States to create 15-member independent commissions to draw congressional districts and would establish certain redistricting criteria, including protection for communities of interest, and ban partisan gerrymandering. H.R. 1, 116th Cong., 1st Sess., §§ 2401, 2411 (2019).

Dozens of other bills have been introduced to limit reliance on political considerations in redistricting. In 2010, H.R. 6250 would have required States to follow standards of compactness, contiguity, and respect for political subdivisions in redistricting. It also would have prohibited the establishment of congressional districts "with the major purpose of diluting the voting strength of any person, or group, including any political party," except when necessary to comply with the Voting Rights Act of 1965. H.R. 6250, 111th Cong., 2d Sess., § 2 (referred to committee).

Another example is the Fairness and Independence in Redistricting Act, which was introduced in 2005 and has been reintroduced in every Congress since. That bill would require every State to establish an independent commission to adopt redistricting plans. The bill also set forth criteria for the independent commissions to use, such as compactness, contiguity, and population equality. It would prohibit consideration of voting history, political party affiliation, or incumbent Representative's residence. H.R. 2642, 109th Cong., 1st Sess., § 4 (referred to subcommittee). We express no view on any of these pending proposals. We simply note that the avenue for reform established by the Framers, and used by Congress in the past, remains open.

***

No one can accuse this Court of having a crabbed view of the reach of its competence. But we have no commission to allocate political power and influence in the absence of a constitutional directive or legal standards to guide us in the exercise of such authority. "It is emphatically the province and duty of the judicial department to say what the law is." *Marbury v. Madison.* In this rare circumstance, that means our duty is to say "this is not law." The judgments are remanded with instructions to dismiss for lack of jurisdiction. *It is so ordered.*

Justice KAGAN, with whom Justice GINSBURG, Justice BREYER, and Justice SOTOMAYOR join, dissenting.

For the first time ever, this Court refuses to remedy a constitutional violation because it thinks the task beyond judicial capabilities.

And not just any constitutional violation. The partisan gerrymanders in these cases deprived citizens of the most fundamental of their constitutional rights: the rights to participate equally in the political process, to join with others to advance political beliefs, and to choose their political representatives. In so doing, the partisan gerrymanders here debased and dishonored our democracy, turning upside-down the core American idea that all governmental power derives from the people. These gerrymanders enabled politicians to entrench themselves in office as against voters' preferences. They promoted partisanship above respect for the popular will. They encouraged a politics of polarization and dysfunction. If left unchecked, gerrymanders like the ones here may irreparably damage our system of government.

And checking them is *not* beyond the courts. The majority's abdication comes just when courts across the country, including those below, have coalesced around manageable judicial standards to resolve partisan gerrymandering claims. Those standards satisfy the majority's own benchmarks. They do not require—indeed, they do not permit—courts to rely on their own ideas of electoral fairness, whether proportional representation or any other. And they limit courts to correcting only egregious gerrymanders, so judges do not become omnipresent players in the political process. But yes, the standards used here do allow—as well they should—judicial intervention in the worst-of-the-worst cases of democratic subversion, causing blatant constitutional harms. In other words, they allow courts to undo partisan gerrymanders of the kind we face today from North Carolina and Maryland. In giving such gerrymanders a pass from judicial review, the majority goes tragically wrong.

I

Maybe the majority errs in these cases because it pays so little attention to the constitutional harms at their core. After dutifully reciting each case's facts, the majority leaves them forever behind, instead immersing itself in everything that could conceivably go amiss if courts became involved. So it is necessary to fill in the gaps. To recount exactly what politicians in North Carolina and Maryland did to entrench their parties in political office, whatever the electorate might think. And to elaborate on the constitutional injury those politicians wreaked, to our democratic system and to individuals' rights. All that will help in considering whether courts confronting partisan gerrymandering claims are really so hamstrung—so unable to carry out their constitutional duties—as the majority thinks.

A

The plaintiffs here challenge two congressional districting plans—one adopted by Republicans in North Carolina and the other by Democrats in Maryland—as unconstitutional partisan gerrymanders. As I relate what happened in those two States, ask yourself: Is this how American democracy is supposed to work?

Start with North Carolina. After the 2010 census, the North Carolina General Assembly, with Republican majorities in both its House and its Senate, enacted a new congressional districting plan. That plan governed the two next national elections. In 2012, Republican candidates won 9 of the State's 13 seats in the U.S. House of Representatives, although they received only 49% of the statewide vote. In 2014, Republican candidates increased their total to 10 of the 13 seats, this time based on 55% of the vote. Soon afterward, a District Court struck down two districts in the plan as unconstitutional racial gerrymanders. The General Assembly, with both chambers still controlled by Republicans, went back to the drawing board to craft the needed remedial state map. And here is how the process unfolded:

- The Republican co-chairs of the Assembly's redistricting committee, Rep. David Lewis and Sen. Robert Rucho, instructed Dr. Thomas Hofeller, a Republican districting specialist, to create a new map that would maintain the 10–3 composition of the State's congressional delegation come what might. Using sophisticated technological tools and precinct-level election results selected to predict voting behavior, Hofeller drew district lines to minimize Democrats' voting strength and ensure the election of 10 Republican Congressmen.
- Lewis then presented for the redistricting committee's (retroactive) approval a list of the criteria Hofeller had employed—including one labeled "Partisan Advantage." That criterion, endorsed by a party-line vote, stated that the committee would make "all reasonable efforts" to construct districts to "maintain the current [10–3] partisan makeup" of the State's congressional delegation.
- Lewis explained the Partisan Advantage criterion to legislators as follows: We are "draw[ing] the maps to give a partisan advantage to 10 Republicans and 3 Democrats because [I] d[o] not believe it['s] possible to draw a map with 11 Republicans and 2 Democrats."
- The committee and the General Assembly later enacted, again on a party-line vote, the map Hofeller had drawn.
- Lewis announced: "I think electing Republicans is better than electing Democrats. So I drew this map to help foster what I think is better for the country."

You might think that judgment best left to the American people. But give Lewis credit for this much: The map has worked just as he planned and predicted. In 2016, Republican congressional candidates won 10 of North Carolina's 13 seats, with 53% of the statewide vote. Two years later, Republican candidates won 9 of 12 seats though they received only 50% of the vote. (The 13th seat has not yet been filled because fraud tainted the initial election.)

Events in Maryland make for a similarly grisly tale. For 50 years, Maryland's 8-person congressional delegation typically consisted of 2 or 3 Republicans and 5 or 6 Democrats. After the 2000 districting, for example, the First and Sixth Districts reliably elected Republicans, and the other districts as reliably elected Democrats. But in the 2010 districting cycle, the State's Democratic leaders, who controlled the governorship and both houses of the General Assembly, decided to press their advantage.

- Governor Martin O'Malley, who oversaw the process, decided (in his own later words) "to create a map that was more favorable for Democrats over the next ten years." Because flipping the First District was geographically next-to-impossible, "a decision was made to go for the Sixth."
- O'Malley appointed an advisory committee as the public face of his effort, while asking Congressman Steny Hoyer, a self-described "serial gerrymanderer," to hire and direct a mapmaker. Hoyer retained Eric Hawkins, an analyst at a political consulting firm providing services to Democrats.
- Hawkins received only two instructions: to ensure that the new map produced 7 reliable Democratic seats, and to protect all Democratic incumbents.
- Using similar technologies and election data as Hofeller, Hawkins produced a map to those specifications. Although new census figures required removing only 10,000 residents from the Sixth District, Hawkins proposed a large-scale population transfer. The map moved about 360,000 voters out of the district and another 350,000 in. That swap decreased the number of registered Republicans in the district by over 66,000 and increased the number of registered Democrats by about 24,000, all to produce a safe Democratic district.
- After the advisory committee adopted the map on a party-line vote, State Senate President Thomas Miller briefed the General Assembly's Democratic caucuses about the new map's aims. Miller told his colleagues that the map would give "Democrats a real opportunity to pick up a seventh seat in the delegation" and that "[i]n the face of Republican gains in redistricting in other states[,] we have a serious obligation to create this opportunity."
- The General Assembly adopted the plan on a party-line vote.

Maryland's Democrats proved no less successful than North Carolina's Republicans in devising a voter-proof map. In the four elections that followed (from 2012 through 2018), Democrats have never received more than 65% of the statewide congressional vote. Yet in each of those elections, Democrats have won (you guessed it) 7 of 8 House seats—including the once-reliably-Republican Sixth District.

B

Now back to the question I asked before: Is that how American democracy is supposed to work? I have yet to meet the person who thinks so.

"Governments," the Declaration of Independence states, "deriv[e] their just Powers from the Consent of the Governed." The Constitution begins: "We the People of the United States." The Gettysburg Address (almost) ends: "[G]overnment of the people, by the people, for the people." If there is a single idea that made our Nation (and that our Nation commended to the world), it is this one: The people are sovereign.

The "power," James Madison wrote, "is in the people over the Government, and not in the Government over the people." Free and fair and periodic elections are the key to that vision. The people get to choose their representatives. And then they get to decide, at regular intervals, whether to keep them. Madison again: "[R]epublican liberty" demands "not only, that all power should be derived from the people; but that those entrusted with it should be kept in dependence on the people." The Federalist No. 57. Members of the House of Representatives, in particular, are supposed to "recollect[] [that] dependence" every day. *Id.* To retain an "intimate sympathy with the people," they must be "compelled to anticipate the moment" when their "exercise of [power] is to be reviewed." *Id.* Election day—next year, and two years later, and two years after that—is what links the people to their representatives, and gives the people their sovereign power. That day is the foundation of democratic governance.

And partisan gerrymandering can make it meaningless. At its most extreme—as in North Carolina and Maryland—the practice amounts to rigging elections. By drawing districts to maximize the power of some voters and minimize the power of others, a party in office at the right time can entrench itself there for a decade or more, no matter what the voters would prefer. Just ask the people of North Carolina and Maryland. The core principle of republican government, this Court has recognized, is that the voters should choose their representatives, not the other way around. Partisan gerrymandering turns it the other way around. By that mechanism, politicians can cherry-pick voters to ensure their reelection. And the power becomes, as Madison put it, "in the Government over the people."

The majority disputes none of this. I think it important to underscore that fact: The majority disputes none of what I have said (or will say) about how gerrymanders undermine democracy. Indeed, the majority concedes (really, how could it not?) that gerrymandering is "incompatible with democratic principles." And therefore what? That recognition would seem to demand a response. The majority offers two ideas that might qualify as such. One is that the political process can deal with the problem—a proposition so dubious on its face that I feel secure in delaying my answer for some time. The other is that political gerrymanders have always been with us. To its credit, the majority does not frame that point as an originalist constitutional argument. After all (as the majority rightly notes), racial and residential gerrymanders were also once with us, but the Court has done something about that fact.[1] The majority's idea instead seems to be that if we have lived with partisan gerrymanders so long, we will survive.

That complacency has no cause. Yes, partisan gerrymandering goes back to the Republic's earliest days. (As does vociferous opposition to it.) But big data and modern technology—of just the kind that the mapmakers in North Carolina and Maryland used—make today's gerrymandering altogether different from the crude linedrawing of the past. Old-time efforts, based on little more than guesses, sometimes led to so-called dummymanders—gerrymanders that went spectacularly wrong. Not likely in today's world. Mapmakers now have access to more granular data about party preference and voting behavior than ever before. County-level voting data has given way to precinct-level or city-block-level data; and increasingly, mapmakers avail themselves of data sets providing wide-ranging information about even individual voters. Just as important, advancements in computing technology

1. And even putting that aside, any originalist argument would have to deal with an inconvenient fact. The Framers originally viewed political parties themselves (let alone their most partisan actions) with deep suspicion, as fomenters of factionalism and "symptom[s] of disease in the body politic." G. Wood, Empire of Liberty: A History of the Early Republic, 1789–1815, p. 140 (2009).

have enabled mapmakers to put that information to use with unprecedented efficiency and precision. While bygone mapmakers may have drafted three or four alternative districting plans, today's mapmakers can generate thousands of possibilities at the touch of a key—and then choose the one giving their party maximum advantage (usually while still meeting traditional districting requirements). The effect is to make gerrymanders far more effective and durable than before, insulating politicians against all but the most titanic shifts in the political tides. These are not your grandfather's—let alone the Framers'—gerrymanders.

The proof is in the 2010 pudding. That redistricting cycle produced some of the most extreme partisan gerrymanders in this country's history. I've already recounted the results from North Carolina and Maryland, and you'll hear even more about those. But the voters in those States were not the only ones to fall prey to such districting perversions. Take Pennsylvania. In the three congressional elections occurring under the State's original districting plan (before the State Supreme Court struck it down), Democrats received between 45% and 51% of the statewide vote, but won only 5 of 18 House seats. Or go next door to Ohio. There, in four congressional elections, Democrats tallied between 39% and 47% of the statewide vote, but never won more than 4 of 16 House seats. (Nor is there any reason to think that the results in those States stemmed from political geography or non-partisan districting criteria, rather than from partisan manipulation.) And gerrymanders will only get worse (or depending on your perspective, better) as time goes on—as data becomes ever more fine-grained and data analysis techniques continue to improve. What was possible with paper and pen—or even with Windows 95—doesn't hold a candle (or an LED bulb?) to what will become possible with developments like machine learning. And someplace along this road, "we the people" become sovereign no longer.

C

Partisan gerrymandering of the kind before us not only subverts democracy (as if that weren't bad enough). It violates individuals' constitutional rights as well. That statement is not the lonesome cry of a dissenting Justice. This Court has recognized extreme partisan gerrymandering as such a violation for many years.

Partisan gerrymandering operates through vote dilution—the devaluation of one citizen's vote as compared to others. A mapmaker draws district lines to "pack" and "crack" voters likely to support the disfavored party. He packs supermajorities of those voters into a relatively few districts, in numbers far greater than needed for their preferred candidates to prevail. Then he cracks the rest across many more districts, spreading them so thin that their candidates will not be able to win. Whether the person is packed or cracked, his vote carries less weight—has less consequence—than it would under a neutrally drawn (non-partisan) map. In short, the mapmaker has made some votes count for less, because they are likely to go for the other party.

That practice implicates the Fourteenth Amendment's Equal Protection Clause. The Fourteenth Amendment, we long ago recognized, "guarantees the opportunity for equal participation by all voters in the election" of legislators. *Reynolds v. Sims.* And that opportunity "can be denied by a debasement or dilution of the weight of a citizen's vote just as effectively as by wholly prohibiting the free exercise of the franchise." Based on that principle, this Court in its one-person-one-vote decisions prohibited creating districts with significantly different populations. A State could not, we explained, thus "dilut[e] the weight of votes because of place of residence." *Id.* The constitutional injury in a partisan gerrymandering case is much the same, except that the dilution is based on party affiliation. In such a case, too, the districters have set out to reduce the weight of certain citizens' votes, and thereby deprive them of their capacity to "full[y] and effective[ly] participat[e] in the political process[]." As Justice Kennedy (in a controlling opinion) once hypothesized: If districters declared that they were drawing a map "so as most to burden [the votes of] Party X's" supporters, it would violate the Equal Protection Clause. *Vieth.* For (in the language of the one-person-one-vote decisions) it would infringe those voters' rights to "equal [electoral] participation." *Reynolds.*

And partisan gerrymandering implicates the First Amendment too. That Amendment gives its greatest protection to political beliefs, speech, and association. Yet partisan gerrymanders subject certain voters to "disfavored treatment"—again, counting their votes for less—precisely because of "their voting history [and] their expression of political views." *Vieth* (opinion of Kennedy, J.). And added to that strictly personal harm is an associational one. Representative democracy is unimaginable without the ability of citizens to band together in support of candidates who espouse their political views. By diluting the votes of certain citizens, the State frustrates their efforts to translate those affiliations into political effectiveness. In both those ways, partisan gerrymanders of the kind we confront here undermine the protections of democracy embodied in the First Amendment.

Though different Justices have described the constitutional harm in diverse ways, nearly all have agreed on this much: Extreme partisan gerrymandering (as happened in North Carolina and Maryland) violates the Constitution. Once again, the majority never disagrees; it appears to accept the principle that each person must have an equal say in the election of representatives. And indeed, without this settled and shared understanding that cases like these inflict constitutional injury, the question of whether there are judicially manageable standards for resolving them would never come up.

II

So the only way to understand the majority's opinion is as follows: In the face of grievous harm to democratic governance and flagrant infringements on individuals' rights—in the face of escalating partisan manipulation whose compatibility with this Nation's values and law no one defends—the majority declines to provide any remedy. For the first time in this Nation's history, the majority declares that it can do nothing about an acknowledged constitutional violation because it has searched high and low and cannot find a workable legal standard to apply.

The majority gives two reasons for thinking that the adjudication of partisan gerrymandering claims is beyond judicial capabilities. First and foremost, the majority says, it cannot find a neutral baseline—one not based on contestable notions of political fairness—from which to measure injury. According to the majority, "[p]artisan gerrymandering claims invariably sound in a desire for proportional representation." But the Constitution does not mandate proportional representation. So, the majority contends, resolving those claims "inevitably" would require courts to decide what is "fair" in the context of districting. They would have "to make their own political judgment about how much representation particular political parties *deserve*" and "to rearrange the challenged districts to achieve that end." And second, the majority argues that even after establishing a baseline, a court would have no way to answer "the determinative question: 'How much is too much?' " No "discernible and manageable" standard is available, the majority claims—and so courts could willy-nilly become embroiled in fixing every districting plan.

I'll give the majority this one—and important—thing: It identifies some dangers everyone should want to avoid. Judges should not be apportioning political power based on their own vision of electoral fairness, whether proportional representation or any other. And judges should not be striking down maps left, right, and center, on the view that every smidgen of politics is a smidgen too much. Respect for state legislative processes—and restraint in the exercise of judicial authority—counsels intervention in only egregious cases.

But in throwing up its hands, the majority misses something under its nose: What it says can't be done *has* been done. Over the past several years, federal courts across the country—including, but not exclusively, in the decisions below—have largely converged on a standard for adjudicating partisan gerrymandering claims (striking down both Democratic and Republican districting plans in the process). And that standard does what the majority says is impossible. The standard does not use any judge-made conception of electoral fairness—either proportional representation or any other; instead, it takes as its baseline a State's *own* criteria of fairness, apart from partisan gain. And by requiring plaintiffs to make difficult showings relating to both purpose and effects, the standard invalidates the most extreme, but only the most extreme, partisan gerrymanders.

Below, I first explain the framework courts have developed, and describe its application in these two cases. Doing so reveals in even starker detail than before how much these partisan gerrymanders deviated from democratic norms. As I lay out the lower courts' analyses, I consider two specific criticisms the majority levels—each of which reveals a saddening nonchalance about the threat such districting poses to self-governance. All of that lays the groundwork for then assessing the majority's more general view, described above, that judicial policing in this area cannot be either neutral or restrained. The lower courts' reasoning, as I'll show, proves the opposite.

A

Start with the standard the lower courts used. The majority disaggregates the opinions below, distinguishing the one from the other and then chopping up each into "a number of 'tests.' " But in doing so, it fails to convey the decisions' most significant—and common—features. Both courts focused on the harm of vote dilution, though the North Carolina court mostly grounded its analysis in the Fourteenth Amendment and the Maryland court in the First. And both courts (like others around the country) used basically the same three-part test to decide whether the plaintiffs had made out a vote dilution claim. As many legal standards do, that test has three parts: (1) intent; (2) effects; and (3) causation. First, the plaintiffs challenging a districting plan must prove that state officials' "predominant purpose" in drawing a district's lines was to entrench [their party] in power by diluting the votes of citizens favoring its rival. Second, the plaintiffs must establish that the lines drawn in fact have the intended effect by "substantially" diluting their votes. And third, if the plaintiffs make those showings, the State must come up with a legitimate, non-partisan justification to save its map.[2] If you are a lawyer, you know that this test looks utterly ordinary. It is the sort of thing courts work with every day.

Turn now to the test's application. First, did the North Carolina and Maryland districters have the predominant purpose of entrenching their own party in power? Here, the two District Courts catalogued the overwhelming direct evidence that they did. To remind you of some highlights: North Carolina's redistricting committee used "Partisan Advantage" as an official criterion for drawing district lines. And from the first to the last, that committee's chair (along with his mapmaker) acted to ensure a 10–3 partisan split, whatever the statewide vote, because he thought that "electing Republicans is better than electing Democrats." For their part, Maryland's Democrats—the Governor, senior Congressman, and State Senate President alike—openly admitted to a single driving purpose: flip the Sixth District from Republican to Democratic. They did not blanch from moving some 700,000 voters into new districts (when one-person-one-vote rules required relocating just 10,000) for that reason and that reason alone.

The majority's response to the District Courts' purpose analysis is discomfiting. The majority does not contest the lower courts' findings; how could it? Instead, the majority says that state officials' intent to entrench their party in power is perfectly "permissible," even when it is the predominant factor in drawing district lines. But that is wrong. True enough, that the intent to inject "political considerations" into districting may not raise any constitutional concerns. In *Gaffney v. Cummings*, for example, we thought it non-problematic when state officials used political data to ensure rough proportional representation between the two parties. And true enough that even the naked purpose to gain partisan advantage may not rise to the level of constitutional notice when it is not the driving force in mapmaking or when the intended gain is slight. See *Vieth* (plurality opinion). But when political actors have a specific and predominant intent to entrench themselves in power by manipulating district lines, that goes too far. Consider again Justice Kennedy's hypothetical of mapmakers who set out to maximally burden (*i.e.*, make count for as little as possible) the votes going to a rival party. Does the majority really think that goal is permissible? But why even bother with hypotheticals? Just consider the purposes here. It cannot be permissible and thus irrelevant, as the majority claims, that state officials have as their purpose the kind of grotesquely gerrymandered map that, according to all this Court has ever said, violates the Constitution.

On to the second step of the analysis, where the plaintiffs must prove that the districting plan substantially dilutes their votes. The majority fails to discuss most of the evidence the District Courts relied on to find that the plaintiffs had done so. But that evidence—particularly from North Carolina—is the key to understanding both the problem these cases present and the solution to it they offer. The evidence

2. Neither North Carolina nor Maryland offered much of an alternative explanation for the evidence that the plaintiffs put forward. Presumably, both States had trouble coming up with something. Like the majority, I therefore pass quickly over this part of the test.

reveals just how bad the two gerrymanders were (in case you had any doubts). And it shows how the same technologies and data that today facilitate extreme partisan gerrymanders also enable courts to discover them, by exposing just how much they dilute votes.

Consider the sort of evidence used in North Carolina first. There, the plaintiffs demonstrated the districting plan's effects mostly by relying on what might be called the "extreme outlier approach." (Here's a spoiler: the State's plan was one.) The approach—which also has recently been used in Michigan and Ohio litigation—begins by using advanced computing technology to randomly generate a large collection of districting plans that incorporate the State's physical and political geography and meet its declared districting criteria, *except for* partisan gain. For each of those maps, the method then uses actual precinct-level votes from past elections to determine a partisan outcome (*i.e.*, the number of Democratic and Republican seats that map produces). Suppose we now have 1,000 maps, each with a partisan outcome attached to it. We can line up those maps on a continuum—the most favorable to Republicans on one end, the most favorable to Democrats on the other.[3] We can then find the median outcome—that is, the outcome smack dab in the center—in a world with no partisan manipulation. And we can see where the State's actual plan falls on the spectrum—at or near the median or way out on one of the tails? The further out on the tail, the more extreme the partisan distortion and the more significant the vote dilution.

Using that approach, the North Carolina plaintiffs offered a boatload of alternative districting plans—all showing that the State's map was an out-out-out-outlier. One expert produced 3,000 maps, adhering in the way described above to the districting criteria that the North Carolina redistricting committee had used, other than partisan advantage. To calculate the partisan outcome of those maps, the expert also used the same election data (a composite of seven elections) that Hofeller had employed when devising the North Carolina plan in the first instance. The results were, shall we say, striking. Every single one of the 3,000 maps would have produced at least one more Democratic House Member than the State's actual map, and 77% would have elected three or four more. A second expert obtained essentially the same results with maps conforming to more generic districting criteria (*e.g.*, compactness and contiguity of districts). Over 99% of that expert's 24,518 simulations would have led to the election of at least one more Democrat, and over 70% would have led to two or three more. Based on those and other findings, the District Court determined that the North Carolina plan substantially dilutes the plaintiffs' votes.[4]

3. As I'll discuss later, this distribution of outcomes provides what the majority says does not exist—a neutral comparator for the State's own plan. It essentially answers the question: In a State with these geographic features and this distribution of voters and this set of districting criteria—but without partisan manipulation—what would happen?

4. The District Court also relied on actual election results (under both the new plan and the similar one preceding it) and on mathematical measurements of the new plan's "partisan asymmetry." Those calculations assess whether supporters of the two parties can translate their votes into representation with equal ease. The court found that the new North Carolina plan led to extreme asymmetry, compared both to plans used in the rest of the country and to plans previously used in the State.

Because the Maryland gerrymander involved just one district, the evidence in that case was far simpler —but no less powerful for that. You've heard some of the numbers before. The 2010 census required only a minimal change in the Sixth District's population—the subtraction of about 10,000 residents from more than 700,000. But instead of making a correspondingly minimal adjustment, Democratic officials reconfigured the entire district. They moved 360,000 residents out and another 350,000 in, while splitting some counties for the first time in almost two centuries. The upshot was a district with 66,000 fewer Republican voters and 24,000 more Democratic ones. In the old Sixth, 47% of registered voters were Republicans and only 36% Democrats. But in the new Sixth, 44% of registered voters were Democrats and only 33% Republicans. That reversal of the district's partisan composition translated into four consecutive Democratic victories, including in a wave election year for Republicans (2014). In what was once a party stronghold, Republicans now have little or no chance to elect their preferred candidate. The District Court thus found that the gerrymandered Maryland map substantially dilutes Republicans' votes.

The majority claims all these findings are mere "prognostications" about the future, in which no one "can have any confidence." But the courts below did not gaze into crystal balls, as the majority tries to suggest. Their findings about these gerrymanders' effects on voters—both in the past and predictably in the future—were evidence-based, data-based, statistics-based. Knowledge-based, one might say. The courts did what anyone would want a decisionmaker to do when so much hangs in the balance. They looked hard at the facts, and they went where the facts led them. They availed themselves of all the information that mapmakers (like Hofeller and Hawkins) and politicians (like Lewis and O'Malley) work so hard to amass and then use to make every districting decision. They refused to content themselves with unsupported and out-of-date musings about the unpredictability of the American voter. They did not bet America's future—as today the majority does—on the idea that maps constructed with so much expertise and care to make electoral outcomes impervious to voting would somehow or other come apart. They looked at the evidence—at the facts about how these districts operated—and they could reach only one conclusion. By substantially diluting the votes of citizens favoring their rivals, the politicians of one party had succeeded in entrenching themselves in office. They had beat democracy.

B

The majority's broadest claim, as I've noted, is that this is a price we must pay because judicial oversight of partisan gerrymandering cannot be "politically neutral" or "manageable." Courts, the majority argues, will have to choose among contested notions of electoral fairness. (Should they take as the ideal mode of districting proportional representation, many competitive seats, adherence to traditional districting criteria, or so forth?) And even once courts have chosen, the majority continues, they will have to decide "[h]ow much is too much?"—that is, how much deviation from the chosen "touchstone" to allow? In answering that question, the majority surmises, they will likely go far too far. So the whole thing is impossible, the majority concludes. To prove its point, the majority throws a bevy of question marks on the page. (I count nine in just two paragraphs.) But it never

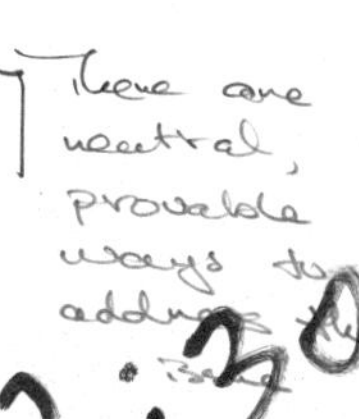

tries to analyze the serious question presented here—whether the kind of standard developed below falls prey to those objections, or instead allows for neutral and manageable oversight. The answer, as you've already heard enough to know, is the latter. That kind of oversight is not only possible; it's been done.

Consider neutrality first. Contrary to the majority's suggestion, the District Courts did not have to—and in fact did not—choose among competing visions of electoral fairness. That is because they did not try to compare the State's actual map to an "ideally fair" one (whether based on proportional representation or some other criterion). Instead, they looked at the difference between what the State did and what the State would have done if politicians hadn't been intent on partisan gain. Or put differently, the comparator (or baseline or touchstone) is the result not of a judge's philosophizing but of the State's own characteristics and judgments. The effects evidence in these cases accepted as a given the State's physical geography (*e.g.*, where does the Chesapeake run?) and political geography (*e.g.*, where do the Democrats live on top of each other?). So the courts did not, in the majority's words, try to "counteract 'natural' gerrymandering caused, for example, by the urban concentration of one party." Still more, the courts' analyses used the State's own criteria for electoral fairness—except for naked partisan gain. Under their approach, in other words, the State selected its own fairness baseline in the form of its other districting criteria. All the courts did was determine how far the State had gone off that track because of its politicians' effort to entrench themselves in office.

The North Carolina litigation well illustrates the point. The thousands of randomly generated maps I've mentioned formed the core of the plaintiffs' case that the North Carolina plan was an "extreme[] outlier." Those maps took the State's political landscape as a given. In North Carolina, for example, Democratic voters are highly concentrated in cities. That fact was built into all the maps; it became part of the baseline. On top of that, the maps took the State's legal landscape as a given. They incorporated the State's districting priorities, excluding partisanship. So in North Carolina, for example, all the maps adhered to the traditional criteria of contiguity and compactness. But the comparator maps in another State would have incorporated different objectives—say, the emphasis Arizona places on competitive districts or the requirement Iowa imposes that counties remain whole. The point is that the assemblage of maps, reflecting the characteristics and judgments of the State itself, creates a neutral baseline from which to assess whether partisanship has run amok. Extreme outlier as to what? As to the other maps the State could have produced given its unique political geography and its chosen districting criteria. *Not* as to the maps a judge, with his own view of electoral fairness, could have dreamed up.

The Maryland court lacked North Carolina's fancy evidence, but analyzed the gerrymander's effects in much the same way—not as against an ideal goal, but as against an *ex ante* baseline. To see the difference, shift gears for a moment and compare Maryland and Massachusetts—both of which (aside from Maryland's partisan gerrymander) use traditional districting criteria. In those two States alike, Republicans receive about 35% of the vote in statewide elections. But the political geography of the States differs. In Massachusetts, the Republican vote is spread evenly across the State; because that is so, districting plans (using traditional criteria of contiguity and compactness) consistently lead to an all-Democratic congressional delegation. By contrast, in Maryland, Republicans are clumped—into the Eastern Shore (the First District) and the Northwest Corner (the old Sixth). Claims of partisan gerrymandering in those two States could come out the same way if judges, à la the majority, used their own visions of fairness to police districting plans; a judge in each State could then insist, in line with proportional representation, that 35% of the vote share entitles citizens to around that much of the delegation. But those suits would not come out the same if courts instead asked: What would have happened, given the State's natural political geography and chosen districting criteria, had officials not indulged in partisan manipulation? And that is what the District Court in Maryland inquired into. The court did not strike down the new Sixth District because a judicial ideal of proportional representation commanded another Republican seat. It invalidated that district because the quest for partisan gain made the State override *its own* political geography and districting criteria. So much, then, for the impossibility of neutrality.

The majority's sole response misses the point. According to the majority, "it does not make sense to use" a State's own (non-partisan) districting criteria as the baseline from which to measure partisan gerrymandering because those criteria "will vary from State to State and year to year." But that is a virtue, not a vice—a feature, not a bug. Using the criteria the State itself has chosen at the relevant time prevents any judicial predilections from affecting the analysis—exactly what the majority claims it wants. At the same time, using those criteria enables a court to measure just what it should: the extent to which the pursuit of partisan advantage—by these legislators at this moment—has distorted the State's districting decisions. Sure, different non-partisan criteria could result, as the majority notes, in different partisan distributions to serve as the baseline. But that in itself raises no issue: Everyone agrees that state officials using non-partisan criteria (*e.g.*, must counties be kept together? should districts be compact?) have wide latitude in districting. The problem arises only when legislators or mapmakers substantially deviate from the baseline distribution by manipulating district lines for partisan gain. So once again, the majority's analysis falters because it equates the demand to eliminate partisan gerrymandering with a demand for a single partisan distribution—the one reflecting proportional representation. But those two demands are different, and only the former is at issue here.

The majority's "how much is too much" critique fares no better than its neutrality argument. How about the following for a first-cut answer: This much is too much. By any measure, a map that produces a greater partisan skew than any of 3,000 randomly generated maps (all with the State's political geography and districting criteria built in) reflects "too much" partisanship. Think about what I just said: The absolute worst of 3,001 possible maps. The *only one* that could produce a 10–3 partisan split even as Republicans got a bare majority of the statewide vote. And again: How much is too much? This much is too much: A map that without any evident non-partisan districting reason (to the contrary) shifted the composition of a district from 47% Republicans and 36% Democrats to 33% Republicans and 42% Democrats. A map that in 2011 was responsible for the largest partisan swing of a congressional district in the country. Even the majority acknowledges that "[t]hese cases involve blatant examples of partisanship driving districting decisions." If the majority had done nothing else, it could have set the line here. How much is too much? At the least, any gerrymanders as bad as these.

And if the majority thought that approach too case-specific, it could have used the lower courts' general standard—focusing on "predominant" purpose and "substantial" effects—without fear of indeterminacy. I do not take even the majority to claim that courts are incapable of investigating whether legislators mainly intended to seek partisan advantage. That is for good reason. Although purpose inquiries carry certain hazards (which courts must attend to), they are a common form of analysis in constitutional cases. See, *e.g.*, *Miller v. Johnson*. Those inquiries would be no harder here than in other contexts.

Nor is there any reason to doubt, as the majority does, the competence of courts to determine whether a district map "substantially" dilutes the votes of a rival party's supporters from the everything-but-partisanship baseline described above. (Most of the majority's difficulties here really come from its idea that ideal visions set the baseline. But that is double-counting—and, as already shown, wrong to boot.) [T]he law is full of instances where a judge's decision rests on estimating rightly some matter of degree—including the substantiality of risk or harm. The majority is wrong to think that these laws typically (let alone uniformly) further confine and guide judicial decisionmaking. They do not, either in themselves or through "statutory context." To the extent additional guidance has developed over the years (as under the Sherman Act), courts themselves have been its author—as they could be in this context too. And contrary to the majority's suggestion, courts all the time make judgments about the substantiality of harm without reducing them to particular percentages. If courts are no longer competent to do so, they will have to relinquish, well, substantial portions of their docket.

And the combined inquiry used in these cases set the bar high, so that courts could intervene in the worst partisan gerrymanders, but no others. Or to say the same thing, so that courts could intervene in the kind of extreme gerrymanders that nearly every Justice for decades has thought to violate the Constitution. Illicit purpose was simple to show here only because politicians and mapmakers thought their actions could not be attacked in court. They therefore felt free to openly proclaim their intent to entrench their party in office. But if the Court today had declared that behavior justiciable, such smoking guns would all but disappear. Even assuming some officials continued to try implementing extreme partisan gerrymanders,[5] they would not brag about their efforts. So plaintiffs would have to prove the intent to entrench through circumstantial evidence—essentially showing that no other explanation (no geographic feature or non-partisan districting objective) could explain the districting plan's vote dilutive effects. And that would be impossible unless those effects were even more than substantial—unless mapmakers had packed and cracked with abandon in unprecedented ways. As again, they did here. That the two courts below found constitutional violations does not mean their tests were unrigorous; it means that the conduct they confronted was constitutionally appalling—by even the strictest measure, inordinately partisan.

The majority, in the end, fails to understand both the plaintiffs' claims and the decisions below. Everything in today's opinion assumes that these cases grew out of

5. A decision of this Court invalidating the North Carolina and Maryland gerrymanders would of course have curbed much of that behavior. In districting cases no less than others, officials respond to what this Court determines the law to sanction.

a "desire for proportional representation" or, more generally phrased, a "fair share of political power." And everything in it assumes that the courts below had to (and did) decide what that fair share would be. But that is not so. The plaintiffs objected to one specific practice—the extreme manipulation of district lines for partisan gain. Elimination of that practice could have led to proportional representation. Or it could have led to nothing close. What was left after the practice's removal could have been fair, or could have been unfair, by any number of measures. That was not the crux of this suit. The plaintiffs asked only that the courts bar politicians from entrenching themselves in power by diluting the votes of their rivals' supporters. And the courts, using neutral and manageable—and eminently legal—standards, provided that (and only that) relief. This Court should have cheered, not overturned, that restoration of the people's power to vote.

III

This Court has long understood that it has a special responsibility to remedy violations of constitutional rights resulting from politicians' districting decisions. Over 50 years ago, we committed to providing judicial review in that sphere, recognizing as we established the one-person-one-vote rule that "our oath and our office require no less." *Reynolds*. Of course, our oath and our office require us to vindicate all constitutional rights. But the need for judicial review is at its most urgent in cases like these. For here, politicians' incentives conflict with voters' interests, leaving citizens without any political remedy for their constitutional harms. Those harms arise because politicians want to stay in office. No one can look to them for effective relief.

The majority disagrees, concluding its opinion with a paean to congressional bills limiting partisan gerrymanders. "Dozens of [those] bills have been introduced," the majority says. One was "introduced in 2005 and has been reintroduced in every Congress since." And might be reintroduced until the end of time. Because what all these *bills* have in common is that they are not *laws*. The politicians who benefit from partisan gerrymandering are unlikely to change partisan gerrymandering. And because those politicians maintain themselves in office through partisan gerrymandering, the chances for legislative reform are slight.

No worries, the majority says; it has another idea. The majority notes that voters themselves have recently approved ballot initiatives to put power over districting in the hands of independent commissions or other non-partisan actors. Some Members of the majority, of course, once thought such initiatives unconstitutional. See *Arizona State Legislature* (Roberts, C.J., dissenting). But put that aside. Fewer than half the States offer voters an opportunity to put initiatives to direct vote; in all the rest (including North Carolina and Maryland), voters are dependent on legislators to make electoral changes (which for all the reasons already given, they are unlikely to do). And even when voters have a mechanism they can work themselves, legislators often fight their efforts tooth and nail. Look at Missouri. There, the majority touts a voter-approved proposal to turn districting over to a state demographer. But before the demographer had drawn a single line, Members of the state legislature had introduced a bill to start undoing the change. I'd put better odds on that bill's passage than on all the congressional proposals the majority cites.

The majority's most perplexing "solution" is to look to state courts. "[O]ur conclusion," the majority states, does not "condemn complaints about districting to echo into a void": Just a few years back, "the Supreme Court of Florida struck down that State's congressional districting plan as a violation" of the State Constitution. And indeed, the majority might have added, the Supreme Court of Pennsylvania last year did the same thing. But what do those courts know that this Court does not? If they can develop and apply neutral and manageable standards to identify unconstitutional gerrymanders, why couldn't we?[6]

We could have, and we should have. The gerrymanders here—and they are typical of many—violated the constitutional rights of many hundreds of thousands of American citizens. Those voters (Republicans in the one case, Democrats in the other) did not have an equal opportunity to participate in the political process. Their votes counted for far less than they should have because of their partisan affiliation. When faced with such constitutional wrongs, courts must intervene: "It is emphatically the province and duty of the judicial department to say what the law is." *Marbury v. Madison.* That is what the courts below did. Their decisions are worth a read. They (and others that have recently remedied similar violations) are detailed, thorough, painstaking. They evaluated with immense care the factual evidence and legal arguments the parties presented. They used neutral and manageable and strict standards. They had not a shred of politics about them. Contra the majority, this *was* law.

That is not to deny, of course, that these cases have great political consequence. They do. Among the *amicus* briefs here is one from a bipartisan group of current and former Members of the House of Representatives. They describe all the ways partisan gerrymandering harms our political system—what they call "a cascade of negative results." These artificially drawn districts shift influence from swing voters to party-base voters who participate in primaries; make bipartisanship and pragmatic compromise politically difficult or impossible; and drive voters away from an ever more dysfunctional political process. Last year, we heard much the same from current and former state legislators. In their view, partisan gerrymandering has "sounded the death-knell of bipartisanship," creating a legislative environment that is "toxic" and "tribal." Gerrymandering, in short, helps create the polarized political system so many Americans loathe.

And gerrymandering is, as so many Justices have emphasized before, antidemocratic in the most profound sense. In our government, all political power flows from the people. And that means, as Alexander Hamilton once said, "that the people should choose whom they please to govern them." 2 Debates on the

6. Contrary to the majority's suggestion, state courts do not typically have more specific "standards and guidance" to apply than federal courts have. The Pennsylvania Supreme Court based its gerrymandering decision on a constitutional clause providing only that "elections shall be free and equal" and no one shall "interfere to prevent the free exercise of the right of suffrage." And even the Florida "Free Districts Amendment," which the majority touts, says nothing more than that no districting plan "shall be drawn with the intent to favor or disfavor a political party." If the majority wants the kind of guidance that will keep courts from intervening too far in the political sphere, that Amendment does not provide it: The standard is in fact a good deal less exacting than the one the District Courts below applied. In any event, only a few States have a constitutional provision like Florida's, so the majority's state-court solution does not go far.

Constitution 257. But in Maryland and North Carolina they cannot do so. In Maryland, election in and election out, there are 7 Democrats and 1 Republican in the congressional delegation. In North Carolina, however the political winds blow, there are 10 Republicans and 3 Democrats. Is it conceivable that someday voters will be able to break out of that prefabricated box? Sure. But everything possible has been done to make that hard. To create a world in which power does not flow from the people because they do not choose their governors.

Of all times to abandon the Court's duty to declare the law, this was not the one. The practices challenged in these cases imperil our system of government. Part of the Court's role in that system is to defend its foundations. None is more important than free and fair elections. With respect but deep sadness, I dissent.

POLICY

NOTES ON *RUCHO v. COMMON CAUSE*

1. We have created a "Political Gerrymandering Hypothetical" (see below) to illustrate how political gerrymandering can work. A key point is that it is possible for the political party in control of the mapmaking process to draw the lines so that it retains control of a majority of legislative seats even after it becomes the minority party in terms of voter popularity. Thus, in the hypothetical, if the Democrats control the districting process, they can gerrymander to assure themselves of six safe seats (out of ten total), even though a shift in public opinion causes Republicans to gain a 55 to 45 percent majority statewide (550,000 Rs; 450,000 Ds). Basically, the idea is to "pack" or concentrate Republicans into fewer districts, so that these Republicans have "wasted" extra votes in these districts (in other words, especially large majorities there), enabling the Democrats to effectively spread themselves over enough districts to control a majority.

Political Gerrymandering Hypothetical

Rs	550,000
Ds	450,000
Total	1,000,000

Need to create 10 Districts

Option A			Option B		
District	Rs	Ds	District	Rs	Ds
1	10	90	1	30	70
2	20	80	2	30	70
3	20	80	3	30	70
4	40	60	4	40	60
5	60	40	5	40	60
6	60	40	6	40	60
7	80	20	7	70	30

2:45

Option A			Option B		
District	Rs	Ds	District	Rs	Ds
8	80	20	8	90	10
9	90	10	9	90	10
10	90	10	10	90	10
T	550	450	T	550	450
6 safe R seats			6 safe D seats		

Assume Option A is more compact and better protects city and county boundaries. Should a court find Option B unconstitutional?

2. The legal question in *Rucho* is: When, if ever, does it violate the U.S. Constitution for a state's mapmaking authority to engage in this kind of political gerrymandering?

3. The majority says that Congress, if it wished, could prohibit the gerrymandering of congressional districts. Does it seem likely Congress would do so? And even if it did, would not the majority also invoke the political question doctrine to reject judicial consideration of an Equal Protection Clause challenge to the political gerrymandering of a *state* legislature?

4. Why is Chief Justice Roberts unwilling to subject claims of *political* gerrymandering to judicial scrutiny, when he is willing to subject claims of *racial* gerrymandering to judicial scrutiny? Is the difference in the applicable constitutional standard, the cultural difference between race and party affiliation, a combination of these two, or something else?

5. As we saw with *Shaw*, *Miller*, and *Easley*, the constitutional standard applicable to claims of *racial* gerrymanders is hardly the model of precision: Race must not *predominate* in the drawing of district lines; the consideration of race in districting cannot be *excessive*. Why is it not "judicially manageable" for the courts to implement the same standard with respect to *political* gerrymandering claims? Wouldn't it be just as easy (or equally difficult) for the courts to determine whether the desire for partisan advantage *predominated* the districting process, or was *excessive*, as for the courts to ascertain whether there was *too much* consideration of race?

6. Were you convinced that Justice Kagan has found a judicially manageable standard?

7. In the 2010 redistricting cycle, several states, including California and Arizona, used independent redistricting commissions comprised of citizens to redraw the state's maps. The goal was to minimize partisanship in the redistricting process. Is this the best solution to the perceived problem or can we still rely on state courts to remedy the most egregious partisan gerrymanders? If independent commissions are the best solution, how should such commissions be designed?

8. In a sense, *Rucho* did not change things much in relation to partisan gerrymandering claims at the Supreme Court, which had never recognized a judicially manageable standard, but it did put a stop to the lower courts stepping in just as lower courts had begun to coalesce around a test. Yet the political party that loses the redistricting battle in the legislature will still likely try to reverse (or at least

mitigate) its loss. This reality leads political parties to channel their energies into other types of legal challenges. In other words, the existing legal framework forces the political losers of redistricting battles to challenge redistricting plans using one person, one vote, the Voting Rights Act, or constitutional doctrines related to race and redistricting. Consider some of the cases you have read where the Court has found constitutional violations, such as *Karcher v. Daggett* (one person, one vote involving a Democratic gerrymander) and *Cooper v. Harris* (racial gerrymandering involving a Republican gerrymander). In reality, are the results in these cases really partisan gerrymandering holdings in disguise?

* * *

Up to this point, we have been addressing only the role of the federal constitution in relation to partisan gerrymandering. But there is another possible avenue for the judiciary to constrain partisan gerrymandering. Indeed, one might more accurately say that there are 50 possible avenues for the judiciary to address partisan gerrymandering—each state has its own constitution and judicial branch.

The lack of intervention in this arena by the federal courts using the federal constitution may create opportunities for state courts to intervene using state constitutions. This state-level oversight could occur through interpretations of existing state constitutional provisions or through amendments to state constitutions that compel state judiciaries to police partisan gerrymandering.

Note that when reading the next case, you are already somewhat familiar with the redistricting plan at issue. Following the district court opinion in the racial gerrymandering case of *Cooper v. Harris,* the state was ordered to draw a remedial map. The remedial map (drawn by a Republican legislature) retained the same 10-3 (Republican-Democratic) split from the plan that had been struck down as a racial gerrymander. The new map also "smoothed" out the boundaries of District 1 and District 12 while reducing the black voting age population of each district to, respectively, about 44 percent and 35 percent. A federal trial court then found the remedial map to be an unconstitutional *partisan* gerrymander but that decision was ultimately vacated by the Supreme Court. In September 2019, plaintiffs filed a partisan gerrymandering challenge arguing that the remedial plan violated the *state* constitution.

Harper v. Lewis

State of North Carolina, Wake County

In the General Court of Justice Superior Court Division

19 CVS 012667

THIS MATTER came on for hearing on October 24, 2019, before the undersigned three-judge panel upon Plaintiffs' Motion for Preliminary Injunction, filed September 30, 2019.

PROCEDURAL HISTORY

On February 19, 2016, the current North Carolina congressional districts (hereinafter "2016 congressional districts") were established by an act of the General Assembly, as a result of litigation in federal court over the congressional districts originally drawn in 2011. On September 27, 2019, Plaintiffs filed a verified complaint in Superior Court, Wake County, seeking a declaration that the 2016 congressional districts violate the rights of Plaintiffs and all Democratic voters in North Carolina under the North Carolina Constitution's Free Elections Clause, Art. I, § 10; Equal Protection Clause, Art. I, § 19; and Freedom of Speech and Freedom of Assembly Clauses, Art. I, §§ 12 & 14. Plaintiffs seek to enjoin the future use of the 2016 congressional districts.

The Court, having considered the pleadings, motions, briefs and arguments of the parties, supplemental materials submitted by the parties, pertinent case law, and the record proper and court file, hereby finds and concludes, for the purposes of this Order, as follows.

POLITICAL QUESTION DOCTRINE

Legislative Defendants contend Plaintiffs' claims—challenges to the validity of and act of the General Assembly that apportions or redistricts the congressional districts of this State—present non-justiciable political questions. Such claims are within the statutorily provided jurisdiction of this three-judge panel, N.C.G.S. § 1-267.1, and the Court concludes that partisan gerrymandering claims specifically present justiciable issues, as distinguished from non-justiciable political questions. Such claims fall within the broad, default category of constitutional cases our courts are empowered and obliged to decide on the merits, and not within the narrow category of exceptional cases covered by the political question doctrine. Indeed, as the Supreme Court of the United States recently explained, partisan gerrymandering claims are not "condemn[ed] . . . to echo in the void," because although the federal courthouse doors may be closed, "state constitutions can provide standards and guidance for state courts to apply." *Rucho v. Common Cause* (2019).

APPLICABLE LEGAL STANDARDS

At its most basic level, partisan gerrymandering is defined as: "the drawing of legislative district lines to subordinate adherents of one political party and entrench a rival party in power." *Ariz. State Legislature v. Ariz. Indep. Redistricting Comm'n* (2016). Partisan gerrymandering operates through vote dilution—the devaluation of one citizen's vote as compared to others. A mapmaker draws district lines to "pack" and "crack" voters likely to support the disfavored party.

Plaintiffs claim the 2016 congressional districts are partisan gerrymanders that violate the rights of Plaintiffs and all Democratic voters in North Carolina under the North Carolina Constitution's Free Elections Clause, Art. I, §10; Equal Protection Clause, Art. I, § 19; and Freedom of Speech and Freedom of Assembly Clauses, Art. I, §§ 12 & 14. Extreme partisan gerrymandering violates each of these provisions of the North Carolina Constitution.

Free Elections Clause

The North Carolina Constitution, in the Declaration of Rights, Article I, § 10, declares that "[a]ll elections shall be free." Our Supreme Court has long recognized the fundamental role of the will of the people in our democratic government: "Our government is founded on the will of the people. Their will is expressed by the ballot." *People ex rel. Van Bokkelen v. Canaday* (1875). In particular, our Supreme Court has directed that in construing provisions of the Constitution, "we should keep in mind that this is a government of the people, in which the will of the people—the majority—legally expressed, must govern." *State ex rel. Quinn v. Lattimore,* (1897). Therefore, our Supreme Court continued, because elections should express the will of the people, it follows that "all acts providing for elections, should be liberally construed, that tend to promote a fair election or expression of this popular will." *Id.* "[F]air and honest elections are to prevail in this state." *McDonald v. Morrow* (1896). Moreover, in giving meaning to the Free Elections Clause, this Court's construction of the words contained therein must therefore be broad to comport with the following Supreme Court mandate: "We think the object of all elections is to ascertain, fairly and truthfully, the will of the people—the qualified voters." *Hill v. Skinner* (1915).

As such, the meaning of the Free Elections Clause is that elections must be conducted freely and honestly to ascertain, fairly and truthfully, the will of the people. In contrast, extreme partisan gerrymandering—namely redistricting plans that entrench politicians in power, that evince a fundamental distrust of voters by serving the self-interest of political parties over the public good, and that dilute and devalue votes of some citizens compared to others—is contrary to the fundamental right of North Carolina citizens to have elections conducted freely and honestly to ascertain, fairly and truthfully, the will of the people.

Equal Protection Clause

The Equal Protection Clause of the North Carolina Constitution guarantees to all North Carolinians that "[n]o person shall be denied the equal protection of the laws." N.C. Const., art. I, § 19. Our Supreme Court has held that North Carolina's Equal Protection Clause protects "the fundamental right of each North Carolinian to *substantially equal voting power.*" *Stephenson v. Bartlett* (2002). "It is well settled in this State that 'the right to vote *on equal terms* is a fundamental right.'" *Id.*

Although the North Carolina Constitution provides greater protection for voting rights than the federal Equal Protection Clause, our courts use the same test as federal courts in evaluating the constitutionality of challenged classifications under an equal protection analysis. Generally, this test has three parts: (1) intent, (2) effects, and (3) causation. First, the plaintiffs challenging a districting plan must prove that state officials' "predominant purpose" in drawing district lines was to "entrench [their party] in power" by diluting the votes of citizens favoring their rival. *Ariz. State Legis.* Second, the plaintiffs must establish that the lines drawn in fact have the intended effect by "substantially" diluting their votes. Finally, if the plaintiffs make those showings, the State must provide a legitimate, non-partisan justification (i.e., that the impermissible intent did not cause the effect) to preserve its map. *Rucho* (Kagan, J., dissenting).

Generally, partisan gerrymandering runs afoul of the State's obligation to provide all persons with equal protection of law because, by seeking to diminish the electoral power of supporters of a disfavored party, a partisan gerrymander treats individuals who support candidates of one political party less favorably than individuals who support candidates of another party.

As such, extreme partisan gerrymandering runs afoul of the North Carolina Constitution's guarantee that no person shall be denied the equal protection of the laws.

Freedom of Speech and Freedom of Assembly Clauses

The Freedom of Speech Clause in Article I, § 14 of the North Carolina Constitution provides that "[f]reedom of speech and of the press are two of the great bulwarks of liberty and therefore shall never be restrained." The Freedom of Assembly Clause in Article I, §12 provides, in relevant part, that "[t]he people have a right to assemble together to consult for their common good, to instruct their representatives, and to apply to the General Assembly for redress of grievances."

There is no right more basic in our democracy than the right to participate in electing our political leaders—including, of course, the right to vote. Political belief and association constitute the core of those activities protected by the First Amendment. In North Carolina, the right to assembly encompasses the right of association. Moreover, citizens form parties to express their political beliefs and to assist others in casting votes in alignment with those beliefs. And for elections to express the popular will, the right to assemble and consult for the common good must be guaranteed.

It is axiomatic that the government may not infringe on protected activity based on the individual's viewpoint. The guarantee of free expression stands against attempts to disfavor certain subjects or viewpoints. Viewpoint discrimination is *most* insidious where the targeted speech is political; "in the context of political speech, . . . [b]oth history and logic" demonstrate the perils of permitting the government to "identif[y] certain preferred speakers" while burdening the speech of "disfavored speakers." *Citizens United v. FEC* (2010).

The government may not burden the speech of some elements of our society in order to enhance the relative voice of others in electing officials. The government also may not retaliate based on protected speech and expression. Courts carefully guard against retaliation by the party in power. When patronage or retaliation restrains citizens' freedoms of belief and association, it is at war with the deeper traditions of democracy embodied in the First Amendment.

When a legislature engages in extreme partisan gerrymandering, it identifies certain preferred speakers (e.g. Republican voters) while targeting certain disfavored speakers (e.g. Democratic voters) because of disagreement with the views they express when they vote. Then, disfavored speakers are packed and cracked into legislative districts with the aim of diluting their votes and, in cracked districts, ensuring that these voters are significantly less likely, in comparison to favored voters, to be able to elect a candidate who shares their views. Moreover, a legislature that engages in extreme partisan gerrymandering burdens the associational rights of disfavored voters to "instruct their representatives, and to apply to the General Assembly for redress of grievances."N.C. Const. art. I, § 12. As such, extreme partisan gerrymandering runs afoul of these important guarantees in the North Carolina Constitution of the freedom of speech and the right of the people of our State to assemble together to consult for their common good, to instruct their representatives, and to apply to the General Assembly for redress of grievances.

INJUNCTIVE RELIEF

It is well settled in this State that the courts have the power, and it is their duty in proper cases, to declare an act of the General Assembly unconstitutional—but it must be plainly and clearly the case. If there is any reasonable doubt, it will be resolved in favor of the lawful exercise of their powers by the representatives of the people.

The purpose of a preliminary injunction is ordinarily to preserve the *status quo* pending trial on the merits. Its issuance is a matter of discretion to be exercised by the hearing judge after a careful balancing of the equities. A preliminary injunction is an extraordinary remedy and will issue only (1) if a plaintiff is able to show *likelihood* of success on the merits of his case and (2) if a plaintiff is likely to sustain irreparable loss unless the injunction is issued, or if, in the opinion of the Court, issuance is necessary for the protection of a plaintiff's rights during the course of litigation. When assessing the preliminary injunction factors, the trial judge should engage in a balancing process, weighing potential harm to the plaintiff if the injunction is not issued against the potential harm to the defendant if injunctive relief is granted. In effect, the harm alleged by the plaintiff must satisfy a standard of relative substantiality as well as irreparability.

Status Quo

The 2011 congressional districts, enacted by the General Assembly on July 28, 2011, were struck down as unconstitutional racial gerrymanders and ordered to be redrawn on February 5, 2016. *See Harris v. McCrory,* 159 F. Supp. 3d 600, 627 (M.D.N.C. 2016). As a result, the 2016 congressional districts were then enacted by the General Assembly on February 19, 2016. N.C. Sess. Laws 2016-1. Plaintiffs' challenge to the 2016 congressional districts is a challenge to S.L. 2016-1 as enacted; hence, the status quo which Plaintiffs desire to preserve is the existing state of affairs prior to the enactment of S.L.2016-1.

Therefore, the existing state of affairs—i.e., the status quo—prior to the enactment of S.L. 2016-1 was the period in which no lawful congressional district map for North Carolina existed absent the enactment of a remedial map by the General Assembly.

Plaintiffs are Likely to Succeed on the Merits

Quite notably in this case, the 2016 congressional districts have already been the subject of years-long litigation in federal court arising from challenges to the districts on partisan gerrymandering grounds. As such, there is a detailed record of both the partisan intent and the intended partisan effects of the 2016 congressional districts drawn with the aid of Dr. Thomas Hofeller and enacted by the General Assembly.

For instance, Dr. Hofeller was directed by legislators to use political data—precinct-level election results from all statewide elections, excluding presidential elections, dating back to January 1, 2008—in drawing the remedial plan, and was further instructed to use that political data to draw a map that would maintain the existing partisan makeup of the state's congressional delegation, which, as elected under the racially gerrymandered plan, included 10 Republicans and 3 Democrats.

As another example, the redistricting committee approved several criteria for the map-drawing process, including the use of past election data (i.e., "Political Data") and another labeled "Partisan Advantage," which was defined as: "The partisan makeup of the congressional delegation under the enacted plan is 10 Republicans and 3 Democrats. The Committee shall make reasonable efforts to construct districts in the 2016 Contingent Congressional Plan to maintain the current partisan makeup of North Carolina's congressional delegation." In explaining these two criteria, Representative David Lewis acknowledged freely that this would be a political gerrymander, which he maintained was not against the law, while also going on to state that he "propose[d] that [the Committee] draw the maps to give a partisan advantage to 10 Republicans and 3 Democrats because [he] d[id] not believe it[would be] possible to draw a map with 11 Republicans and 2 Democrats."

Moreover, when drawing the 2016 congressional districts, Dr. Hofeller used an aggregate variable he created to predict partisan performance all while constantly aware of the partisan characteristics of each county, precinct, and VTD.

Finally, the redistricting committee, and ultimately the General Assembly as a whole, approved the 2016 congressional districts by party-line vote.

In light of the above, this Court agrees with Plaintiffs and finds there is a substantial likelihood that Plaintiffs will prevail on the merits of this action by showing beyond a reasonable doubt that the 2016 congressional districts are extreme partisan gerrymanders in violation of the North Carolina Constitution's Free Elections Clause, Art. I, § 10; Equal Protection Clause, Art. I, § 19; and Freedom of Speech and Freedom of Assembly Clauses, Art. I, §§ 12 &14.

Plaintiffs Will Suffer Irreparable Loss Unless the Injunction Is Issued

The loss to Plaintiffs' fundamental rights guaranteed by the North Carolina Constitution will undoubtedly be irreparable if congressional elections are allowed to proceed under the 2016 congressional districts. As discussed above, Plaintiffs' have shown a likelihood of succeeding on the merits of their claims that these districts violate multiple fundamental rights guaranteed by the North Carolina Constitution. And as Defendants have emphasized, the 2020 primary elections for these congressional districts—the final congressional elections of this decade before the 2020 census and subsequent decennial redistricting—are set to be held in March of 2020 with the filing period beginning December 2, 2019.

As such, this Court finds that Plaintiffs are likely to sustain irreparable loss to their fundamental rights guaranteed by the North Carolina Constitution unless the injunction is issued, and likewise, issuance is necessary for the continued protection of Plaintiffs' fundamental rights guaranteed by the North Carolina Constitution during the course of the litigation.

A Balancing of the Equities Weighs in Favor of Plaintiffs

On one hand, Legislative Defendants contend a general harm to them will result from issuing the injunction because the General Assembly will be prevented from effectuating an act of the General Assembly. On the other hand, Plaintiffs' and all North Carolinians' fundamental rights guaranteed by the North Carolina Constitution will be irreparably lost, as discussed above, if the injunction is not granted. Simply put, the people of our State will lose the opportunity to participate in congressional elections conducted freely and honestly to ascertain, fairly and truthfully, the will of the people. The Court finds that this specific harm to Plaintiffs absent issuance of the injunction outweighs the potential harm to Legislative Defendants if the injunction is granted.

Defendants also contend the issuance of the injunction will result in disruption, confusion, and uncertainty in the electoral process for them, candidates, election officials, and the voting public. But, again, such a proffered harm does not outweigh the specific harm to Plaintiffs from the irreparable loss of their fundamental rights guaranteed by the North Carolina Constitution. Moreover, while State Defendants would prefer not to move elections or otherwise change the current schedule for the 2020 congressional primary election, they recognize that proceeding under the 2016 congressional districts "would require the Board to administer an election that violates the constitutional rights of North Carolina voters" and acknowledge that the election schedule can be changed if necessary. State Defs. Response Brief at 2. In that vein, State Defendants agree with Plaintiffs that "it would be appropriate for this Court to issue an injunction that relieves the Board of any duty to administer elections using an unconstitutionally gerrymandered congressional redistricting plan." *Id.*

Finally, Defendants contend Plaintiffs simply waited too long to bring their challenge to the 2016 congressional districts in state court. Plaintiffs, however, filed this action in state court only a matter of months after litigation reached its conclusion in federal court, at a time still prior to the candidate filing period. While the timing of Plaintiffs' action does weigh against Plaintiffs, the Court does not find that the timing of Plaintiffs' filing of this action should bar them from seeking equitable relief in the form of the requested preliminary injunction.

Consequently, after weighing the potential harm to Plaintiffs if the injunction is not issued against the potential harm to Defendants if injunctive relief is granted, this Court concludes the balance of the equities weighs in Plaintiffs' favor. Indeed, the harm alleged by Plaintiffs is both substantial and irreparable should congressional elections in North Carolina proceed under the 2016 congressional districts.

CONCLUSION

Under these circumstances, the Court, in its discretion and after a careful balancing of the equities, concludes that the requested injunctive relief shall issue in regard to the 2016 congressional districts.

This Court recognizes the significance and the urgency of the issues presented by this litigation, particularly when considering the impending 2020 congressional primary elections and all accompanying deadlines, details, and logistics. This Court also is mindful of its responsibility not to disturb an act of the General

Assembly unless it plainly and clearly, without any reasonable doubt, runs counter to a constitutional limitation or prohibition. For these reasons, the Court will, upon the forthcoming filing of Plaintiffs' motion for summary judgment, provide for an expedited schedule so that Plaintiffs' dispositive motion may be heard prior to the close of the filing period for the 2020 primary election.

This Court observes that the consequences, as argued by Defendants, resulting from a delay in the congressional primary—e.g., decreased voter turnout, additional costs and labor for the State Board of Elections—would be both serious and probable should the primary schedule be adjusted as a result of this Order and Plaintiffs' ultimate success on the merits of this action. But as discussed above, should Plaintiffs prevail through motion or trial, these consequences pale in comparison to voters of our State proceeding to the polls to vote, yet again, in congressional elections administered pursuant to maps drawn in violation of the North Carolina Constitution.

This Court, however, notes that these disruptions to the election process need not occur, nor may an expedited schedule for summary judgment or trial even be needed, should the General Assembly, on its own initiative, act immediately and with all due haste to enact new congressional districts. This Court does not presume, at this early stage of this litigation, to have any authority to compel the General Assembly to commence a process of enacting new Congressional districts, and this Court recognizes that such a decision is wholly within the discretion of a coequal branch of government. The General Assembly, however, has recently shown it has the capacity to enact new legislative districts in a short amount of time in a transparent and bipartisan manner, and that the resulting legislative districts, having been approved by this Court, are districts that are more likely to achieve the constitutional objective of allowing for elections to be conducted more freely and honestly to ascertain, fairly and truthfully, the will of the people. *See Common Cause v. Lewis*, 18-CVS-014001 (N.C. Sup. Ct., October 28, 2019). The Court respectfully urges the General Assembly to adopt an expeditious process, as it did in response to this Court's mandate in the September 3, 2019, Judgment in *Common Cause v. Lewis*, that ensures full transparency and allows for bipartisan participation and consensus to create new congressional districts that likewise seek to achieve this fundamental constitutional objective.

Accordingly, the Court, in its discretion and for good cause shown, hereby ORDERS that Plaintiffs' motion for preliminary injunction is GRANTED as follows:

1. Legislative Defendants and State Defendants, their officers, agents, servants, employees and attorneys and any person in active concert or participation with them are hereby enjoined from preparing for or administering the 2020 primary and general elections for congressional districts under the 2016 congressional districts established by S.L.2016-1.

SO ORDERED, this the 28th day of October, 2019.

NOTES ON *HARPER*

1. As you read in *Rucho*, the U.S. Supreme Court has taken the position that political gerrymandering claims are nonjusticiable because there is no judicially

manageable standard by which to analyze them. Does the opinion from the North Carolina state court provide support for that nonjusticiability position, or does the North Carolina opinion provide an effective counterargument to that position?

2. Note how easily and, perhaps, casually the state court strikes down an act of the state legislature. Does that mean partisan gerrymandering claims are actually quite simple to adjudicate? Or, alternatively, does that mean state courts should not be trusted to adjudicate these claims?

3. Consider another approach to state court intervention. In 2010, Florida voters approved an amendment to the Florida Constitution that required the Supreme Court of Florida to review redistricting plans drawn by the state legislature. That constitutional amendment reads as follows:

> **SECTION 21. Standards for establishing legislative district boundaries.—** In establishing legislative district boundaries:
> (a) No apportionment plan or district shall be drawn with the intent to favor or disfavor a political party or an incumbent; and districts shall not be drawn with the intent or result of denying or abridging the equal opportunity of racial or language minorities to participate in the political process or to diminish their ability to elect representatives of their choice; and districts shall consist of contiguous territory.
> (b) Unless compliance with the standards in this subsection conflicts with the standards in subsection (a) or with federal law, districts shall be as nearly equal in population as is practicable; districts shall be compact; and districts shall, where feasible, utilize existing political and geographical boundaries.
> (c) The order in which the standards within subsections (a) and (b) of this section are set forth shall not be read to establish any priority of one standard over the other within that subsection.

Florida Constitution, Art. III, Sec. 21.

Note that Florida's provision directs that there can be "*no* . . . *intent* to favor or disfavor a political party or an incumbent" (emphasis added). The Florida Supreme Court has interpreted this standard as different from a standard that tries to determine whether a partisan gerrymander has "gone too far" and noted that "there is no accepted level of improper [partisan] intent." *In re Senate Joint Resolution of Legislative Apportionment 1176*, 80 So. 3d 597, 616-17 (Fla. 2012). Is Florida's process for judicial intervention better than North Carolina's in that the voters recently and explicitly authorized judicial intervention? Is Florida's substantive standard for adjudicating such claims better in that it allows for no partisan intent rather than trying to determine whether partisan intent has gone too far?

G. *BRINGING IT ALL TOGETHER*

You have separately seen and considered the primary constitutional doctrines and statutory provisions that govern redistricting. It should come as no surprise, however, that modern redistricting cases often involve arguments not just about one of these issues but several of them. To assess your understanding of these doctrines, consider the following problem that is loosely based on an actual case.

A REDISTRICTING PROBLEM

San Juan County, Utah, (hereinafter the "County") is located in the far southeastern corner of the State. It occupies a huge expanse—it is the largest county in the State and borders more counties than any other county in the United States. The County is governed by a three-member County Commission. The three commissioners are elected from single-member districts.

As of the 2010 Census, the County had a population of 14,746, of whom 8,847 (60%) are Navajo. The County's citizen voting age population is 9,732, of whom 5,060 (52%) are Navajo. The Navajo are an American Indian tribe, and they are unquestionably eligible to bring any of the various legal claims we have discussed in this Part of the casebook. There is also a history of discrimination against members of American Indiana tribes, as Utah did not allow most American Indian tribe members to vote until 1957.

The political affiliations of voters in the County are what you might expect. White voters in the County are overwhelmingly Republican, like the rest of the State of Utah. Members of the Navajo community are overwhelmingly Democrats. In essence, whites in the County are more than 95 percent Republican and members of the Navajo community are more than 95 percent Democrat.

In the mid-1980s, the County was sued under Section 2 of the Voting Rights Act. At the time, the County elected its three commissioners at-large with a majority-vote requirement from numbered positions, as it had since the County's creation in 1880. In the mid-1980s, the County was about 40 percent Navajo and no Navajo person had ever won election to the County Commission, although several had sought the office.

The County settled the Section 2 lawsuit and entered into a consent decree that could be enforced by the federal district court. The consent decree created three single-member districts. One of those districts, District 3, was entirely comprised of a geographic area in the southern part of the County that makes up the Navajo Reservation. In other words, the boundaries of District 3 were coterminous with the boundaries of the Navajo Reservation. At the time it was originally constructed, District 3 was 88 percent Navajo. At the first election under the new system, District 3 elected a Commissioner who was Navajo and a Democrat, and District 3 has elected a Navajo, Democrat as its Commissioner ever since. Districts 1 and 2, which each had about 25 percent Navajo population at the time they were originally constructed, have always elected Commissioners who are white and Republican.

The County did not redistrict after the 1990 Census; nor did it redistrict after the 2000 Census.

After the 2010 Census data was released, members of the Navajo community requested that the County Commission engage in redistricting for the first time in more than 25 years. The Navajo community proposed a redistricting plan, called the NAVMAX plan, with the following demographics:

	Total Pop.	Navajo Total Pop. (%)	Total VAP	Navajo VAP (%)
District 1	5,020	3,514 (70%)	3,126	2,017 (65%)
District 2	4,937	4,076 (83%)	3,127	2,340 (75%)
District 3	4,789	1,257 (26%)	3,479	703 (20%)
Totals	**14,746**	**8,847**	**9,732**	**5,060**

Figure 1-10 is a map of the NAVMAX plan:

Figure 1-10

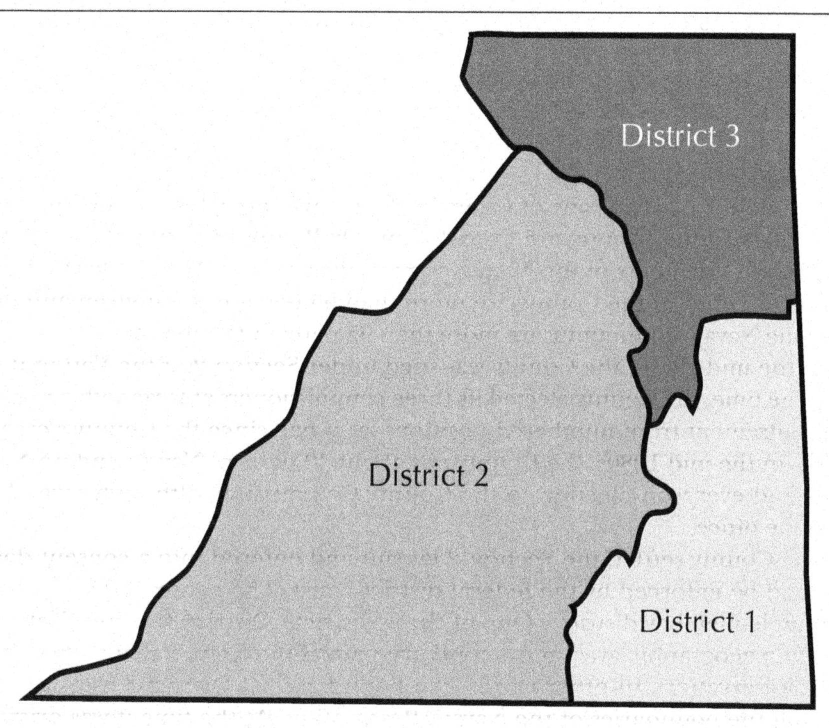

Two white, Republican, incumbent members of the County Commission proposed another plan called COUNTYPLAN. COUNTYPLAN made *absolutely no changes* to the boundaries of current District 3. It also made almost no changes to current Districts 1 and 2—merely shifting two very lightly populated voting precincts from District 1 to District 2. COUNTYPLAN did not split any cities, towns, or voting precincts.

The demographics of COUNTYPLAN were as follows:

	Total Pop.	Navajo Total Pop. (%)	Total VAP	Navajo VAP (%)
District 1	5,347	2,037 (38%)	3,465	1,029 (30%)
District 2	4,450	2,008 (45%)	3,440	1,304 (38%)
District 3	4,949	4,802 (97%)	2,827	2,727 (96%)
Total	**14,746**	**8,847**	**9,732**	**5,060**

Figure 1-11 is a map of COUNTYPLAN.

Figure 1-11

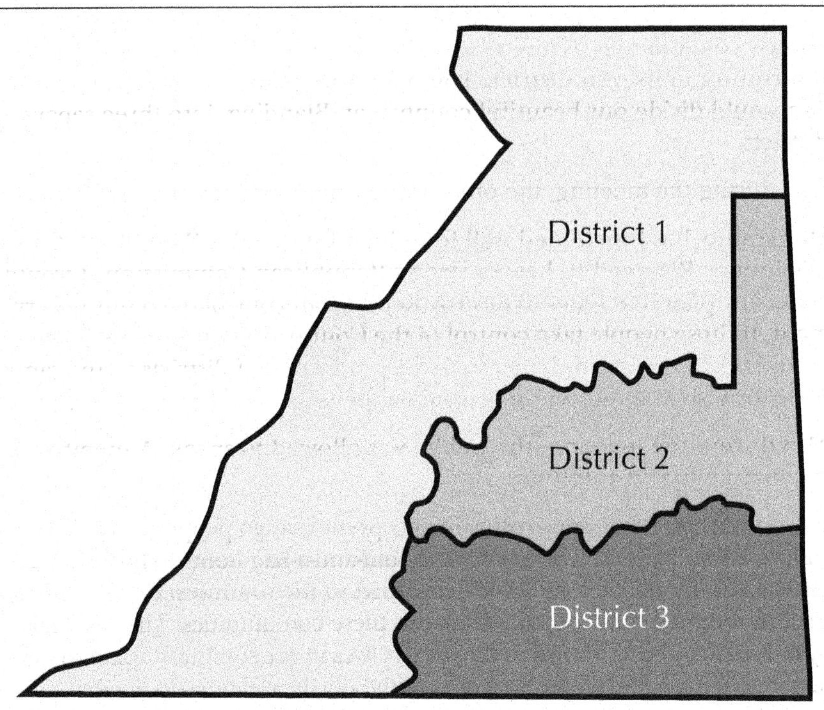

The Navajo community presented its NAVMAX plan at a meeting of the County Commissioners in 2012. The meeting was packed with hundreds of County citizens. Members of the Navajo community turned out in large numbers to urge the County Commissioners to redistrict and adopt the NAVMAX plan. Members of the white community turned out in large numbers to urge the County Commissioners to basically retain the status quo.

The County Commissioners rejected the NAVMAX plan on a 2-1 vote with the lone Navajo Commissioner voting in favor of the NAVMAX plan and the two white Commissioners voting against. The County Commissioners then adopted COUNTYPLAN (previously described above) on a 2-1 vote with the sole Navajo Commissioner voting against COUNTYPLAN.

During the meeting at which COUNTYPLAN was adopted, the Navajo Commissioner said as follows:

> The time has come for the Navajo community to be recognized. We have waited far too long to get our fair representation in County politics. We have presented a map that is fair and that succeeds in drawing two majority-Navajo districts that will allow Navajo citizens to elect their candidates of choice. I urge the County Commission to adopt the NAVMAX map.

During the same meeting, one white Commissioner said as follows:

> There is no need to redistrict. We settled a lawsuit more than 25 years ago. That lawsuit provided the Navajo community with the representation it

> deserves. There is no reason to revisit the consent agreement. Our lines comply with all applicable federal laws and to change the lines would be dangerous and potentially in violation of the consent decree.
>
> The NAVMAX plan is bad for the community. The current map reflects communities of interest, including keeping the area in the Navajo reservation in its own district. The NAVMAX plan would undo that and also would divide our beautiful county seat, Blanding, into three separate districts.

Also during the meeting, the other white Commissioner said as follows:

> Our county has functioned well for a long time under Republican Commissioners. We need to keep a strong Republican Commission. I would reject any plan that seeks to destroy Republican control of county government. If those people take control of the County Commission, the County will go down the drain. We have to keep the current districts in the same basic form so as to prevent this from happening.

Also during the meeting, the public was allowed to speak. A member of the Navajo community said as follows:

> The current plan is a monstrosity that keeps the Navajo people down. District 1 is incredibly large. It takes more than four-and-a-half hours to travel the 250 miles from the northeast end of the district to the southwest end of the district. And there is nothing that connects these communities. The vast majority of the Navajo population in the district lives in the southwest while the vast majority of the white population lives in the north. We must do better.

By some accounts, the current white Commissioner in District 1 has represented the interests of the Navajo community. She has lobbied the state and federal governments on behalf of the Navajo community. She helped secure federal funds for a recently completed multimillion-dollar project in Oljeto (a Navajo community) that paved a 12-mile road to the community center. In 2006, fires at Navajo Mountain (another Navajo community) contaminated the community's water source and water-treatment tank, and the District 1 commissioner was instrumental in getting immediate help to unplug the ash and silt from the water supplies and has worked on a multi-year pipeline project that will bring water to the area.

In the County, there are socioeconomic differences between the Navajo and white communities.

- 34% of whites have a college degree compared to 5% of Navajos.
- 10% of whites have lived in poverty during the last year compared to 40% of Navajos.
- 30% of white household incomes are above $75,000 whereas 30% of Navajo household incomes are below $10,000. (The median household income for whites is double that of Navajos—$50,000 compared to $25,000.)
- The percentage of Navajos who reported no earnings from employment during the past year was double that of whites (60% compared to 30%).

The Navajo community has recently brought a lawsuit against the County in federal district court. There is no question that the lawsuit has been properly brought (i.e., there are no procedural issues, such as standing, that are in question).

Question A: You represent the Navajo community. Based upon what you have learned in Part I, write a brief that argues why the County's plan should be declared invalid.

Question B: You represent the County. Based upon what you have learned in Part I, write a brief that argues why the County's plan should be upheld.

SUMMARY OF THE LAW OF LEGISLATIVE DISTRICTING

The law of redistricting is complex and multifaceted. Those charged with drawing lines must think about legal considerations at almost every turn, as the "losers" in redistricting have numerous potential legal challenges at their disposal. Yet those who bring legal challenges to redistricting plans also face hurdles of their own, as the courts always seem cognizant of the hazards that lie in the "political thicket."

We began by noting that redistricting has four separate areas (plus Section 5 of the Voting Rights Act) and it makes sense to briefly recap from a very macro-level where the law stands and where it might be headed:

- One person, one vote is a firmly established doctrine that amounts to a first principle for redistricting actors to consider. Future cases are likely to focus on litigants arguing for a stricter or looser interpretation of the one person, one vote principle rather than for a wholesale dismantling of the doctrine.
- Racial vote dilution under the Constitution and Section 2 of the Voting Rights Act will likely be a dynamic area with continued disputes over the role of the Court and the level of representation that must be provided to minority groups to meet constitutional and statutory dictates. Section 2 may become even more important given the Court's decision in *Shelby County* that, essentially, eliminated Section 5 preclearance (absent further congressional action). Constitutional claims may also see renewed vitality as successful constitutional claims can be used to re-trigger the preclearance requirement using Section 3(c) of the Voting Rights Act.
- Section 5 of the Voting Rights Act has been effectively nullified by the Court's *Shelby County* decision declaring that the coverage formula is unconstitutional. The Court's decision has led to: (1) calls for Congress to pass legislation creating a new coverage formula; (2) litigants attempting to reinstate preclearance using Section 3(c); and (3) the channeling of issues that originally would have been handled by Section 5 preclearance into Section 2 litigation.
- Racial gerrymandering doctrine was a very active doctrine in the 1990s, went dormant in the 2000 redistricting cycle, but has reappeared in the 2010 cycle.
- Political gerrymandering claims are now dead at the federal level. Future action that attempts to curb partisan gerrymandering is now directed at legislative or referendum/initiative proposals aimed at substituting independent redistricting commissions for legislative control over redistricting, through litigation seeking to have state courts limit partisan gerrymandering through interpretations of state constitutions, or by indirect attacks using one of the other redistricting doctrines.

PART II

THE LAW OF NOMINATING CANDIDATES

INTRODUCTION

A major challenge for any electoral process is winnowing the field of potential candidates from many to few to eventually a winner. When several candidates seek the same office, what are the proper legal rules for choosing nominees to appear on a general election ballot? This is a common issue: early presidential debates often have a crowded stage with up to ten candidates—and that's just for either the Democratic or Republican Party!

In the 2020 presidential election, over twenty Democrats declared for the presidency; for the first presidential debate, the Democratic National Committee had to hold two separate debates on consecutive nights with ten candidates each, and still several candidates were left off of the debate stage for not having enough support in the polls or not securing a sufficient number of small donations. In 2016, seventeen Republican candidates participated in at least one presidential debate, and there were still twelve candidates actively campaigning as of the Iowa Caucus on February 1, 2016, the first chance for voters to express a preference.

There were also third-party and independent candidates for President in 2016, including former Republican-turned-Libertarian Gary Johnson, Jill Stein of the Green Party, and former Republican-turned-independent Evan McMullin. Perhaps the most famous third-party candidate in recent memory was Ralph Nader, who ran as the Green Party nominee in 2000 and as an independent in 2004. Nader may have been a major factor in the 2000 presidential election: Had his supporters in Florida voted instead for Democrat Al Gore, there would have been no recount controversy between Gore and George W. Bush that year: Gore would have won Florida and therefore the presidency. (Of course, it is possible that supporters of Nader would not have voted at all.) Each presidential election also contains an array of minor-party candidates unlikely to draw any significant support, including those from the Constitution, Prohibition, Socialist, and Socialist Workers parties.

In the United States, we divide the winnowing process into two basic stages: first, primaries, and second, the general election. We do this for presidential elections as well as for other contests (gubernatorial, congressional, state legislative, mayoral, and so forth). But the primary process for presidential elections, because of its uniquely national scope, is quite different from primaries for all other races. Take, for example, the election for governor of any state. The primary process for that election will generally consist of a single date, confined to that single state, and the winner of the party primaries will be placed on the ballot for the general election, along with any third-party or independent candidates who qualify for the ballot through some means other than conducting a party primary (usually by complying with a signature requirement).

The primary process for presidential elections, however, is not so simple. The winner of any state's presidential primary does not necessarily end up on the general election ballot in that state or any other. (Think of the early primaries that Democrats Bernie Sanders or Pete Buttigieg won in 2020, or the votes cast for Republican Ted Cruz in 2016, and yet none of them were on the ballot in the general election.) Instead, presidential primaries (and caucuses) elect delegates to National Party conventions, which nominate candidates based on the total number of delegates for each candidate within the party. The party nominees, in turn, become candidates on the general election ballot, along with the third-party and independent candidates who qualify through other means.

Whether in its simpler form for gubernatorial (and other nonpresidential) elections, or in its more complicated form for presidential elections, the primary process raises important constitutional questions. To what extent can the government, state or federal, regulate these primaries? Or, conversely, to what extent do the political parties control these primaries, immune from governmental regulation, by virtue of their rights to political association protected by the First Amendment? As we shall see, the U.S. Supreme Court has struggled with these questions ever since challenges arose, in what are known as the "White Primary" cases, to the discriminatory exclusion of African Americans from Democratic Party primaries in the South during the post-Reconstruction era of segregation.

In addition to the rights of political parties, the ballot access cases raise further questions: Is there a constitutional right to be a candidate? And when can a state exclude someone from running for office? Finally, from a policy perspective, is the party primary system the best way to winnow the field from many to few to one? What about a top-two system, where all candidates from all parties run in the same primary and the top two vote recipients move on to the general election? Would ranked choice voting—where voters can list the candidates in order of preference—make more sense when there are multiple candidates? How about approval voting, used for St. Louis local elections in 2021, in which voters "approve" as many or as few candidates in the primary as they wish, and the two candidates with the most approval votes then move on to the general election?

This part of the case book considers the laws for nominating candidates. How have the Court's decisions impacted the "many to few to one" process? We first discuss rules governing the primary process, and then we analyze issues involving ballot access for general elections. When reading this material, consider the clash of values and rights between the various stakeholders: voter, major and minor political parties, independent candidates, and the state and federal governments. Also pay attention to whose rights come out on top in the constitutional analysis. Finally, consider what type of nomination system makes the most sense for American democracy.

Before going further, it may be useful to define a few terms regarding different types of primaries that you will see mentioned in the cases:

- **Closed primary:** Only registered members of the party may participate.
- **Semi-closed primary:** Registered party members and independents (voters not registered as a member of any party) may participate.
- **Open primary:** Any voter may participate in the party's primary, but they must vote in the same party's primary in any given year; they can't switch back and forth between the parties.
- **Blanket primary**: Voters can choose one party for one office and a different party for another office; they could, for example, vote in the Democratic primary for governor and the Republican primary for secretary of state. The Supreme Court struck down this system as unconstitutional in *California Democratic Party v. Jones*, 530 U.S. 567 (2000).
- **Top-two primary:** All candidates appear on the same ballot regardless of party and all voters may vote in that primary; the top two vote recipients, regardless of party, move on to the general election; Alaska has adopted a similar **top-four primary**, in which the top four vote recipients move on to the general election, with Ranked Choice Voting then used in that general election to select the winner.
- **Ranked Choice Voting:** Voters rank-order the candidates in order of preference, designating their first choice, second choice, and so on. When tallying the results to determine the winner, if no one has received a majority, the candidate with the fewest first-place votes is eliminated and voters who selected that candidate as their first preference have their second choice count instead. The process repeats itself until a candidate has over 50% of the vote.

THE WHITE PRIMARY CASES: POLITICAL PARTIES AS STATE ACTORS SUBJECT TO THE U.S. CONSTITUTION

The so-called "White Primary Cases" from the 1940s and 1950s, *Smith v. Allwright*, 321 U.S. 649 (1944), and *Terry v. Adams*, 345 U.S. 461 (1953), were cases in which both the political party and the state government were in agreement that they wanted to exclude African Americans from the right to vote in primary elections. (At least, the state government wanted to permit the Democratic Party to make this choice for itself. Earlier, the state law itself had banned African Americans from participating in Democratic Party primaries.) The U.S. Supreme Court, however, held that the U.S. Constitution's prohibition on race discrimination with respect to voting trumped the wishes of both the party and the state.

The White Primary Cases were decided on the ground that the primary election was an integral component of the overall electoral process leading up to the general election. Texas law required the Democratic Party to nominate its candidates through a primary election. Texas law also heavily regulated the internal operations of the Democratic Party, including the means by which its officers were chosen. These regulations, according to the Court, made the Party "an agency of the state in so far as it determines the participants in a primary election." *Smith v. Allwright*, 321 U.S. at 663. That is, the Democratic Party was a "state actor" with respect to how it ran its primary.

Is this an accurate description of how political parties operate? Are they public or private organizations? In the White Primary Cases, the Court in essence said that the way the Democratic Party in Texas operated made it tantamount to an arm of the state, satisfying the state action doctrine. Therefore, the Democratic Party was subject to the U.S. Constitution and its equal protection mandate. The Court was influenced in part by the fact that whoever won the Democratic Party primary in Texas in the 1940s and 1950s also, as a practical matter, had a lock on the general election. Consequently, the Court thought it essential to eliminate race discrimination in the primary election to vindicate the right to vote. This right, the Court said, "is not to be nullified by a state through casting its electoral process in a form which permits a private organization to practice racial discrimination in the election." *Id.* at 664.

It seems clear under the rationale of the White Primary Cases that a political party is a state actor when the party's nominee usually wins the general election and the party is excluding people on the basis of race. But how far does that principle extend? What if there were a political party called the American Christian Party and its internal governing rules denied membership to anyone unwilling to swear an oath that they are Christians? If a voter or candidate challenged that exclusion as unconstitutional religious discrimination, analogous to the unconstitutional racial discrimination in the White Primary Cases, would the claim prevail? If not, why not? Because religion is different than race? Or because the American Christian Party is (presumably) a minor party, in contrast to the Democratic Party? (If either major political party today required its members to swear allegiance to "Judeo-Christian values," would that membership requirement be constitutionally permissible?) Think about what arguments you would make to analyze these hypotheticals in light of the cases that follow. Also consider how these next few cases are different, constitutionally, from the White Primary Cases. Do primaries belong to the political party, the government, or both?

A. *POLITICAL PARTY VERSUS THE STATE*

In 2008, a dispute arose over whether the national Democratic Party would seat the delegates from Florida and Michigan at the 2008 National Convention. Those states had decided to hold their presidential primaries in January, earlier than the national party's rules allowed, to enhance their influence in the selection of the party's nominee. (National Party rules dictate when states may hold their presidential primaries, stipulating that New Hampshire shall have the first primary and Iowa shall have the first caucus. Florida and Michigan scheduled their primaries for after these states but still before National Party rules permitted.) As a "punishment," the National Party threatened either not to seat delegates from those states or to give them reduced voting power at the National Convention. Hillary Clinton, who had won those states' Democratic primaries, sought to require the National Party to seat the delegates at the Convention. A federal court eventually ruled that the DNC had a First Amendment right to exclude delegates chosen contrary to DNC rules. *See Nelson v. Dean*, 528 F. Supp. 2d 1271 (N.D. Fla. 2007). Once the primary process concluded and it became clear that Barack Obama would have enough delegates to win the Democratic nomination for president, however, the DNC agreed to seat all of the Florida and Michigan delegates with full voting power.

The Supreme Court had previously decided a case from Wisconsin that resembles in many ways the 2008 dispute over the delegates from Florida and Michigan. As you read the following case, note two distinctions between it and the 2008 dispute: First, the Wisconsin case did not involve the date on which the state's primary was held, but instead entailed the rules for who could vote in the state's primary—and the state law's mandate to the party's convention delegates to follow the results of the primary. Second, unlike Wisconsin, neither Florida nor Michigan took legal action in 2008 to try to force the Democratic Party to seat its delegates with full voting power; instead, individual voters who supported Hillary Clinton attempted (unsuccessfully) to sue the Democratic Party on the ground that it was violating their constitutionally protected voting rights. Consequently, as you read this Wisconsin case, ask yourself how either of these two distinctions (or both in combination) affect its status as precedent in a potential future dispute over the date of a state's primary, especially one brought by individual voters who seek full representation for their delegates at the National Convention. To what extent are the national party's rules paramount over a state's desire to regulate its primary process?

Democratic Party of the United States v. Wisconsin ex rel. La Follette

450 U.S. 107 (1981)

Justice STEWART delivered the opinion of the Court.

The charter of the appellant Democratic Party of the United States (National Party) provides that delegates to its National Convention shall be chosen through procedures in which only Democrats can participate. The question on this appeal is whether Wisconsin may successfully insist that its delegates to the Convention be seated, even though those delegates are chosen through a process that includes a binding state preference primary election in which voters do not declare their party affiliation. The Wisconsin Supreme Court held that the National Convention is bound by the Wisconsin primary election results, and cannot refuse to seat the delegates chosen in accord with Wisconsin law.

I

Rule 2A of the Democratic Selection Rules for the 1980 National Convention states: "Participation in the delegate selection process in primaries or caucuses shall be restricted to Democratic voters only who publicly declare their party preference and have that preference publicly recorded."

The election laws of Wisconsin allow non-Democrats—including members of other parties and independents—to vote in the Democratic primary without regard to party affiliation and without requiring a public declaration of party preference. The voters in Wisconsin's "open" primary express their choice among Presidential candidates for the Democratic Party's nomination; they do not vote for delegates to the National Convention. Delegates to the National Convention are chosen separately, after the primary, at caucuses of persons who have stated their affiliation with the Party. But these delegates, under Wisconsin law, are bound to vote at the National Convention in accord with the results of the open primary election. Accordingly, while Wisconsin's open Presidential preference primary does not itself violate National Party rules, the State's mandate that the results of the primary shall determine the allocation of votes cast by the State's delegates at the National Convention does.

[The Wisconsin Supreme Court ruled that the National Party had to seat the Wisconsin delegates at the National Convention because the state's system of selecting delegates is constitutional and binding on the National Party. The National Party appealed.]

II

Rule 2A can be traced to efforts of the National Party to study and reform its nominating procedures and internal structure after the 1968 Democratic National Convention. The Convention, the Party's highest governing authority, directed the Democratic National Committee (DNC) to establish a Commission on Party Structure and Delegate Selection. This Commission concluded that a major problem faced by the Party was that rank-and-file Party members had been underrepresented at its Convention, and that the Party should "find methods which would guarantee every American who claims a stake in the Democratic Party the opportunity to make his judgment felt in the presidential nominating process." The Commission stressed that Party nominating procedures should be as open and accessible as possible to all persons who wished to join the Party, but expressed the concern that "a full opportunity for all Democrats to participate is diluted if members of other political parties are allowed to participate in the selection of delegates to the Democratic National Convention."

III

The question in this case is not whether Wisconsin may conduct an open primary election if it chooses to do so, or whether the National Party may require Wisconsin to limit its primary election to publicly declared Democrats. Rather, the question is whether, once Wisconsin has opened its Democratic Presidential preference primary to voters who do not publicly declare their party affiliation, it may then bind the National Party to honor the binding primary results, even though those results were reached in a manner contrary to National Party rules.

The Wisconsin Supreme Court considered the question before it to be the constitutionality of the "open" feature of the state primary election law, as such. Concluding that the open primary serves compelling state interest by encouraging voter participation, the court held the state open primary constitutionally valid. Upon this issue, the Wisconsin Supreme Court may well be correct. In any event there is no need to question its conclusion here. For the rules of the National Party do not challenge the authority of a State to conduct an open primary, so long as it is not binding on the National Party Convention. The issue is whether the State may compel the National Party to seat a delegation chosen in a way that violates the rules of the Party. And this issue was resolved, we believe, in *Cousins v. Wigoda* (1975).

In *Cousins* the Court reviewed the decision of an Illinois court holding that state law exclusively governed the seating of a state delegation at the 1972 Democratic National Convention, and enjoining the National Party from refusing to seat delegates selected in a manner in accord with state law although contrary to National Party rules. Certiorari was granted "to decide the important question . . . whether the [a]ppellate [c]ourt was correct in according primacy to state law over the National Political Party's rules in the determination of the qualifications and eligibility of delegates to the Party's National Convention." The Court reversed the state judgment, holding that "Illinois' interest in protecting the integrity of its electoral process cannot be deemed compelling in the context of the selection of delegates to the National Party Convention." That disposition controls here.

The *Cousins* Court relied upon the principle that "[t]he National Democratic Party and its adherents enjoy a constitutionally protected right of political association." This First Amendment freedom to gather in association for the purpose of advancing shared beliefs is protected by the Fourteenth Amendment from infringement by any State. And the freedom to associate for the common advancement of political beliefs necessarily presupposes the freedom to identify the people who constitute the association, and to limit the association to those people only.* Here, the members of the National Party, speaking through their rules, chose to define their associational rights by limiting those who could participate in the processes leading to the selection of delegates to their National Convention. On several occasions this Court has recognized that the inclusion of persons unaffiliated with a political party may seriously distort its collective decisions — thus impairing the party's essential functions — and that political parties may accordingly protect themselves from intrusion by those with adverse political principles. In *Rosario v. Rockefeller*, for example, the Court sustained the constitutionality of a requirement — there imposed by a state statute — that a voter enroll in the party of his choice at least 30 days before the general election in order to vote in the next party primary. The purpose of that statute was "to inhibit party 'raiding,' whereby voters in sympathy with one party designate themselves as voters of another party so as to influence or determine the results of the other party's primary."

The State argues that its law places only a minor burden on the National Party. The National Party argues that the burden is substantial, because it prevents the Party from "screen[ing] out those whose affiliation is . . . slight, tenuous, or fleeting," and that such screening is essential to build a more effective and responsible

* [Re-read this sentence, as it contains an important principle of law regarding the freedom of association under the First Amendment. — Eds]

Party. But it is not for the courts to mediate the merits of this dispute. For even if the State were correct, a State, or a court, may not constitutionally substitute its own judgment for that of the Party. A political party's choice among the various ways of determining the makeup of a State's delegation to the party's national convention is protected by the Constitution.

IV

We must consider, finally, whether the State has compelling interests that justify the imposition of its will upon the appellants. "Neither the right to associate nor the right to participate in political activities is absolute." The State asserts a compelling interest in preserving the overall integrity of the electoral process, providing secrecy of the ballot, increasing voter participation in primaries, and preventing harassment of voters. But all those interests go to the conduct of the Presidential preference primary—not to the imposition of voting requirements upon those who, in a separate process, are eventually selected as delegates. Therefore, the interests advanced by the State do not justify its substantial intrusion into the associational freedom of members of the National Party.

V

The State has a substantial interest in the manner in which its elections are conducted, and the National Party has a substantial interest in the manner in which the delegates to its National Convention are selected. But these interests are not incompatible, and to the limited extent they clash in this case, both interests can be preserved. The National Party rules do not forbid Wisconsin to conduct an open primary. But if Wisconsin does open its primary, it cannot require that Wisconsin delegates to the National Party Convention vote there in accordance with the primary results, if to do so would violate Party rules. Since the Wisconsin Supreme Court has declared that the National Party cannot disqualify delegates who are bound to vote in accordance with the results of the Wisconsin open primary, its judgment is reversed.

Justice POWELL, with whom Justice BLACKMUN and Justice REHNQUIST join, dissenting.

Under Wisconsin law, the Wisconsin delegations to the Presidential nominating conventions of the two major political parties are required to cast their votes in a way that reflects the outcome of the State's "open" primary election. That election is conducted without advance party registration or any public declaration of party affiliation, thus allowing any registered voter to participate in the process by which the Presidential preferences of the Wisconsin delegation to the Democratic National Convention are determined. The question in this case is whether, in light of the National Party's rule that only publicly declared Democrats may have a voice in the nomination process, Wisconsin's open primary law infringes the National Party's First Amendment rights of association. Because I believe that this law does not impose a substantial burden on the associational freedom of the National Party, and actually promotes the free political activity of the citizens of Wisconsin, I dissent.

I

The Wisconsin open primary law was enacted in 1903. It was amended two years later to apply to Presidential nominations. As the Wisconsin Supreme Court described in its opinion below:

> "The primary was aimed at stimulating popular participation in politics thereby ending boss rule, corruption, and fraudulent practices which were perceived to be part of the party caucus or convention system. Robert M. La Follette, Sr., supported the primary because he believed that citizens should nominate the party candidates; that the citizens, not the party bosses, could control the party by controlling the candidate selection process; and that the candidates and public officials would be more directly responsible to the citizens."

II

The analysis in this kind of First Amendment case has two stages. If the law can be said to impose a burden on the freedom of association, then the question becomes whether this burden is justified by a compelling state interest. The Court in this case concludes that the Wisconsin law burdens associational freedoms. It then appears to acknowledge that the interests asserted by Wisconsin are substantial, but argues that these interests "go to the conduct of the Presidential preference primary—not to the imposition of voting requirements upon those who, in a separate process, are eventually selected as delegates." In my view, however, any burden here is not constitutionally significant, and the State has presented at least a formidable argument linking the law to compelling state interests.

A

In analyzing the burden imposed on associational freedoms in this case, the Court treats the Wisconsin law as the equivalent of one regulating delegate selection, and, relying on *Cousins v. Wigoda*, concludes that any interference with the National Party's accepted delegate-selection procedures impinges on constitutionally protected rights. It is important to recognize, however, that the facts of this case present issues that differ considerably from those we dealt with in *Cousins*.

In *Cousins*, we reversed a determination that a state court could interfere with the Democratic Convention's freedom to select one delegation from the State of Illinois over another. At issue in the case was the power of the National Party to reject a delegation chosen in accordance with state law because the State's delegate-selection procedures violated party rules regarding participation of minorities, women, and young people, as well as other matters. The state court had ordered the Convention to seat the delegation chosen under state law, rather than the delegation preferred by the Convention itself. In contrast with the direct state regulation of the delegate-selection process at issue in *Cousins*, this case involves a state statutory scheme that regulates delegate selection only indirectly. Under Wisconsin law, the "method of selecting the delegates or alternates [is] determined by the state party organization." Wisconsin simply mandates that each delegate selected, by whatever procedure, must be pledged to represent a candidate who has won in the state primary election the right to delegate votes at the Convention.

In evaluating the constitutional significance of this relatively minimal state regulation of party membership requirements, I am unwilling—at least in the context of a claim by one of the two major political parties—to conclude that every conflict between state law and party rules concerning participation in the nomination process creates a burden on associational rights. Instead, I would look closely at the nature of the intrusion, in light of the nature of the association involved, to see whether we are presented with a real limitation on First Amendment freedoms.

It goes without saying that nomination of a candidate for President is a principal function performed by a national political party, and Wisconsin has, to an extent, regulated the terms on which a citizen may become a "member" of the group of people permitted to influence that decision. If appellant National Party were an organization with a particular ideological orientation or political mission, perhaps this regulation would present a different question. In such a case, the state law might well open the organization to participation by persons with incompatible beliefs and interfere with the associational rights of its founders.

The Democratic Party, however, is not organized around the achievement of defined ideological goals. Instead, the major parties in this country "have been characterized by a fluidity and overlap of philosophy and membership." *Rosario v. Rockefeller* (1973) (Powell, J., dissenting). It can hardly be denied that this party generally has been composed of various elements reflecting most of the American political spectrum. The Party does take positions on public issues, but these positions vary from time to time, and there never has been a serious effort to establish for the Party a monolithic ideological identity by excluding all those with differing views. As a result, it is hard to see what the Democratic Party has to fear from an open primary plan. Wisconsin's law may influence to some extent the outcome of a primary contest by allowing participation by voters who are unwilling to affiliate with the Party publicly. It is unlikely, however, that this influence will produce a delegation with preferences that differ from those represented by a substantial number of delegates from other parts of the country. Moreover, it seems reasonable to conclude that, insofar as the major parties do have ideological identities, an open primary merely allows relatively independent voters to cast their lot with the party that speaks to their present concerns. By attracting participation by relatively independent-minded voters, the Wisconsin plan arguably may enlarge the support for a party at the general election.

It is significant that the Democratic Party of Wisconsin, which represents those citizens of Wisconsin willing to take part publicly in Party affairs, is here *defending* the state law. Moreover, the National Party's apparent concern that the outcome of the Wisconsin Presidential primary will be skewed cannot be taken seriously when one considers the alternative delegate-selection methods that are acceptable to the Party under its rules. Delegates pledged to various candidates may be selected by a caucus procedure involving a small minority of Party members, as long as all participants in the process are publicly affiliated. While such a process would eliminate "crossovers," it would be at least as likely as an open primary to reflect inaccurately the views of a State's Democrats. In addition, the National Party apparently is quite willing to accept public affiliation immediately before primary voting, which some States permit. As Party affiliation becomes this easy for a voter to change in order to participate in a particular primary election, the difference between open and closed primaries loses its practical significance.

In sum, I would hold that the National Party has failed to make a sufficient showing of a burden on its associational rights.

B

The Court does not dispute that the State serves important interests by its open primary plan. Instead the Court argues that these interests are irrelevant because they do not support a requirement that the outcome of the primary be binding on delegates chosen for the convention. This argument, however, is premised on the unstated assumption that a nonbinding primary would be an adequate mechanism for pursuing the state interests involved. This assumption is unsupportable because the very purpose of a Presidential primary, as enunciated as early as 1903 when Wisconsin passed its first primary law, was to give control over the nomination process to individual voters. Wisconsin cannot do this, and still pursue the interests underlying an open primary, without making the open primary binding.

III

The history of state regulation of the major political parties suggests a continuing accommodation of the interests of the parties with those of the States and their citizens. In the process, "the States have evolved comprehensive, and in many respects complex, election codes regulating in most substantial ways, with respect to both federal and state elections, the time, place, and manner of holding primary and general elections, the registration and qualifications of voters, and the selection and qualification of candidates." Today, the Court departs from this process of accommodation. It does so, it seems to me, by upholding a First Amendment claim by one of the two major parties without any serious inquiry into the extent of the burden on associational freedoms and without due consideration of the countervailing state interests.

NOTES ON *DEMOCRATIC PARTY v. WISCONSIN*

1. The Court in *Wisconsin* relies on *Cousins v. Wigoda*, 419 U.S. 477 (1975), which involved a dispute over the rules for selecting delegates to the Democratic National Convention in 1972. In that case, the National Party chose to seat one slate of delegates from Illinois (who supported George McGovern) over another slate (who supported Chicago Mayor Richard Daley). The McGovern slate was selected according to the National Party's new rules, while the Daley slate conformed with state law. The Court declared that "[t]he National Democratic Party and its adherents enjoy a constitutionally protected right of political association" and held that Illinois's law must yield to the party's desire to seat delegates in accordance with its own rules. Several Justices in *Cousins* (including Justice Stewart, who wrote the majority opinion in *Wisconsin*) wrote separately to object to the Court's "unnecessarily broad language." How does the holding in *Cousins* relate to the holding in *Wisconsin*? Did the *Wisconsin* Court narrow this holding?

2. What does this case say about the primacy of political parties' associational rights under the First Amendment? One takeaway seems to be that the rights of national political parties are paramount over state laws regarding the internal processes of the nomination process.

3. Who or what is a political party? Is it the voters? The candidates? The party leaders? Of these groups, whose interests does the majority of the Court find to be paramount in *Wisconsin*? A political party is, of course, a coalition of all of these groups, but it seems that the national party's wishes, as dictated by party leaders, wins out in the constitutional analysis.

4. Is Justice Powell correct in *Wisconsin* that the Democratic Party is not "organized around the achievement of defined ideological goals"? Would Justice Powell rule differently if this was the "Lower Taxes Party"? Perhaps. Does it make sense to have one set of rules for the major political parties (Democrats and Republicans) and different rules for the minor parties? Even if Justice Powell accurately described the Democratic Party of the early 1980s, is his description still accurate in today's highly polarized environment? Assuming the answer is no, then does that fact undercut his analysis?

5. In a 2008 case, *New York State Board of Elections v. López Torres*, 552 U.S. 196 (2008), the Court found that there is no constitutional requirement that a candidate have a "fair shot" at securing a party's nomination. New York has a particularly complex statutory scheme for nominating candidates for judicial office, which involved a requirement that a candidate obtain thousands of signatures in a short time period, and then lobby hundreds of delegates in the two weeks after the primary election to choose that candidate at the nominating convention. Political parties could more easily navigate this system given their pre-existing apparatuses through county chairs. An "outsider" candidate challenged this system as violating her right to a fair opportunity at the nomination. The Court, per Justice Scalia, ruled that the First Amendment does not contain any mandate that a party give a candidate a "fair shot." Thus, party leaders can dictate how they wish to select their nominees. As Justice Scalia wrote, "The First Amendment creates an open marketplace where ideas, most especially political ideas, may compete without government interference. It does not call on the federal courts to manage the market by preventing too many buyers from settling upon a single product." In the clash between a candidate and the party, then, the party's First Amendment associational rights win out.

B. *WASHINGTON'S "TOP-TWO" PRIMARY AND THE LIMITS OF PARTY AUTONOMY*

Insofar as the *Wisconsin* case from 1981 signaled that the U.S. Supreme Court would protect vigorously a political party's autonomy from interfering state legislation, that signal became even stronger in *California Democratic Party v. Jones*, 530 U.S. 567 (2000). In *Jones*, the Court relied heavily on the *Wisconsin* precedent to hold that a state may not use a so-called "blanket" primary where doing so would deprive a party of its freedom to nominate the candidate of its own choice for the general election. A blanket primary is one in which a voter can choose any candidate from any party for any office on the ballot. Think of it as an "open primary on steroids": In an "open" primary, the voter can choose whichever party he or she wants that day, but must vote from only among that party's candidates for all of the races on the ballot; by contrast, in a blanket primary, the voter can choose one of the Democratic candidates for president, one of the Republican candidates for governor, go back to one of the Democratic candidates for senator, then back to one of the Republican candidates for House representative, and so forth.

The flaw that the U.S. Supreme Court found in California's version of the blanket primary was that the top vote-recipient from each party for each office moved on to the general election as the nominee of the political party with which they were affiliated in the primary. Thus, voters who were not party members and who had voted for a different party's candidate for a different office could have a significant say in selecting the party's nominee. Had voting for the party's candidate for each office been confined solely to party members, a different primary candidate might have been the winner. In the Court's judgment, this interference with the party's autonomy to identify its own nominee for the general election violated the First Amendment. But the Court pointed out how a state could achieve the goals of a blanket primary without violating the First Amendment: Simply make it a *nonpartisan* blanket primary, in which the top two vote-recipients move on to the general election ballot (making it a kind of run-off election) but without identifying either of these general election candidates as the official nominee of a political party.

In the wake of *Jones*, the State of Washington modified its own version of the blanket primary to comply with the Court's instructions. But were the modifications sufficient? That's the subject of the next case.

Washington State Grange v. Washington State Republican Party

552 U.S. 442 (2008)

Justice THOMAS delivered the opinion of the Court.

In 2004, voters in the State of Washington passed an initiative changing the State's primary election system. The People's Choice Initiative of 2004, or Initiative 872 (I-872), provides that candidates for office shall be identified on the ballot by their self-designated "party preference"; that voters may vote for any candidate; and that the top two votegetters for each office, regardless of party preference, advance to the general election. The Court of Appeals for the Ninth Circuit held I-872 facially invalid as imposing an unconstitutional burden on state political parties' First Amendment rights. Because I-872 does not on its face impose a severe burden on political parties' associational rights, and because respondents' arguments to the contrary rest on factual assumptions about voter confusion that can be evaluated only in the context of an as-applied challenge, we reverse.

I

For most of the past century, Washington voters selected nominees for state and local offices using a blanket primary.[1] From 1935 until 2003, the State used a blanket primary that placed candidates from all parties on one ballot and allowed voters to select a candidate from any party. Under this system, the candidate who won a plurality of votes within each major party became that party's nominee in the general election. California used a nearly identical primary in its own elections until our decision in *California Democratic Party v. Jones* (2000).

In *Jones*, four political parties challenged California's blanket primary, arguing that it unconstitutionally burdened their associational rights by forcing them to associate with voters who did not share their beliefs. We agreed and struck down the blanket primary as inconsistent with the First Amendment. In so doing, we emphasized the importance of the nomination process as "the crucial juncture at which the appeal to common principles may be translated into concerted action, and hence to political power in the community." We observed that a party's right to exclude is central to its freedom of association, and is never "more important than in the process of selecting its nominee." California's blanket primary, we concluded, severely burdened the parties' freedom of association because it forced them to allow nonmembers to participate in selecting the parties' nominees. That the parties retained the right to endorse their preferred candidates did not render the burden any less severe, as "[t]here is simply no substitute for a party's selecting its own candidates."

Because California's blanket primary severely burdened the parties' associational rights, we subjected it to strict scrutiny, carefully examining each of the state interests offered by California in support of its primary system. We rejected as illegitimate three of the asserted interests: "producing elected officials who better represent the electorate," "expanding candidate debate beyond the scope of partisan concerns," and ensuring "the right to an effective vote" by allowing nonmembers of a party to vote in the majority party's primary in "safe" districts. We concluded that the remaining interests—promoting fairness, affording voters greater choice, increasing voter participation, and protecting privacy—were not compelling on the facts of the case. Even if they were, the partisan California primary was not narrowly tailored to further those interests because a nonpartisan blanket primary, in which the top two votegetters advance to the general election regardless of party affiliation, would accomplish each of those interests without burdening the parties' associational rights. The nonpartisan blanket primary had "all the characteristics of the partisan blanket primary, save the constitutionally crucial one: Primary voters [were] not choosing a party's nominee."

After our decision in *Jones* the Court of Appeals for the Ninth Circuit struck down Washington's primary as "materially indistinguishable from the California

1. The term "blanket primary" refers to a system in which "any person, regardless of party affiliation, may vote for a party's nominee." *California Democratic Party v. Jones* (2000). A blanket primary is distinct from an "open primary," in which a person may vote for any party's nominees, but must choose among that party's nominees for all offices, and the more traditional "closed primary" in which "only persons who are members of the political party . . . can vote on its nominee," *id.*

scheme." The Washington State Grange promptly proposed I-872 as a replacement. It passed with nearly 60% of the vote and became effective in December 2004.

Under I-872, all elections for "partisan offices" are conducted in two stages: a primary and a general election. To participate in the primary, a candidate must file a "declaration of candidacy" form, on which he declares his "major or minor party preference, or independent status." Each candidate and his party preference (or independent status) is in turn designated on the primary election ballot. A political party cannot prevent a candidate who is unaffiliated with, or even repugnant to, the party from designating it as his party of preference. In the primary election, voters may select "any candidate listed on the ballot, regardless of the party preference of the candidates or the voter."

The Court of Appeals noted a "constitutionally significant distinction between ballots and other vehicles for political expression," reasoning that the risk of perceived association is particularly acute when ballots include party labels because such labels are typically used to designate candidates' views on issues of public concern. And it determined that the State's interests underlying I-872 were not sufficiently compelling to justify the severe burden on the parties' association. Concluding that the provisions of I-872 providing for the party-preference designation on the ballot were not severable, the court struck down I-872 in its entirety. We granted certiorari, to determine whether I-872, on its face, violates the political parties' associational rights.

II

Respondents object to I-872 not in the context of an actual election, but in a facial challenge. Under *United States* v. *Salerno* (1987), a plaintiff can only succeed in a facial challenge by "establish[ing] that no set of circumstances exists under which the Act would be valid," i.e., that the law is unconstitutional in all of its applications. While some Members of the Court have criticized the *Salerno* formulation, all agree that a facial challenge must fail where the statute has a plainly legitimate sweep. Washington's primary system survives under either standard, as we explain below. In determining whether a law is facially invalid, we must be careful not to go beyond the statute's facial requirements and speculate about "hypothetical" or "imaginary" cases. The State has had no opportunity to implement I-872, and its courts have had no occasion to construe the law in the context of actual disputes arising from the electoral context, or to accord the law a limiting construction to avoid constitutional questions. Exercising judicial restraint in a facial challenge frees the Court not only from unnecessary pronouncement on constitutional issues, but also from premature interpretations of statutes in areas where their constitutional application might be cloudy.

Facial challenges are disfavored for several reasons. Claims of facial invalidity often rest on speculation. As a consequence, they raise the risk of "premature interpretation of statutes on the basis of factually barebones records." *Sabri* v. *United States* (2004). Facial challenges also run contrary to the fundamental principle of judicial restraint that courts should neither "anticipate a question of constitutional law in advance of the necessity of deciding it nor formulate a rule of constitutional law broader than is required by the precise facts to which it is to be applied." *Ashwander v. TVA* (1936) (Brandeis, J., concurring). Finally, facial challenges threaten to short circuit the democratic process by preventing laws embodying the will of the people from being implemented in a manner consistent with the Constitution. We must keep in mind that "[a] ruling of unconstitutionality frustrates the intent of the elected representatives of the people." *Ayotte v. Planned Parenthood of Northern New Eng.* (2006). It is with these principles in view that we turn to the merits of respondents' facial challenge to I-872.

A

Election regulations that impose a severe burden on associational rights are subject to strict scrutiny, and we uphold them only if they are "narrowly tailored to serve a compelling state interest." If a statute imposes only modest burdens, however, then "the State's important regulatory interests are generally sufficient to justify reasonable, nondiscriminatory restrictions" on election procedures. *Anderson v. Celebrezze* (1983). "Accordingly, we have repeatedly upheld reasonable, politically neutral regulations that have the effect of channeling expressive activity at the polls." *Burdick v. Takushi* (1992).*

The parties do not dispute these general principles; rather, they disagree about whether I-872 severely burdens respondents' associational rights. That disagreement begins with *Jones.* Petitioners argue that the I-872 primary is indistinguishable from the alternative *Jones* suggested would be constitutional. In *Jones* we noted that a nonpartisan blanket primary, where the top two votegetters proceed to the general election regardless of their party, was a less restrictive alternative to California's system because such a primary does not nominate candidates.

That question is now squarely before us. Respondents argue that I-872 is unconstitutional under *Jones* because it has the same "constitutionally crucial" infirmity that doomed California's blanket primary: it allows primary voters who are unaffiliated with a party to choose the party's nominee. Respondents claim that candidates who progress to the general election under I-872 will become the *de facto* nominees of the parties they prefer, thereby violating the parties' right to choose their own standard-bearers, and altering their messages.

The flaw in this argument is that, unlike the California primary, the I-872 primary does not, by its terms, choose parties' nominees. The essence of nomination—the choice of a party representative—does not occur under I-872. The law never refers to the candidates as nominees of any party, nor does it treat them as such. To the contrary, the election regulations specifically provide that the primary "does not serve to determine the nominees of a political party but serves to winnow the number of candidates to a final list of two for the general election." The top two candidates from the primary election proceed to the general election regardless of their party preferences. Whether parties nominate their own candidates outside the state-run primary is simply irrelevant. In fact, parties may now nominate candidates by whatever mechanism they

* [This paragraph lays out the common test the Court employs for constitutional challenges to the right to vote, with a threshold question involving the severity of the burden to determine the level of scrutiny to apply. You'll see this standard again in other cases in this case book.—EDS.]

choose because I-872 repealed Washington's prior regulations governing party nominations.[7]

Respondents counter that, even if the I-872 primary does not actually choose parties' nominees, it nevertheless burdens their associational rights because voters will assume that candidates on the general election ballot are the nominees of their preferred parties. This brings us to the heart of respondents' case—and to the fatal flaw in their argument. At bottom, respondents' objection to I-872 is that voters will be confused by candidates' party-preference designations. Respondents' arguments are largely variations on this theme. Thus, they argue that even if voters do not assume that candidates on the general election ballot are the nominees of their parties, they will at least assume that the parties associate with, and approve of, them. This, they say, compels them to associate with candidates they do not endorse, alters the messages they wish to convey, and forces them to engage in counterspeech to disassociate themselves from the candidates and their positions on the issues.

We reject each of these contentions for the same reason: They all depend, not on any facial requirement of I-872, but on the possibility that voters will be confused as to the meaning of the party-preference designation. But respondents' assertion that voters will misinterpret the party-preference designation is sheer speculation. It "depends upon the belief that voters can be 'misled' by party labels. But [o]ur cases reflect a greater faith in the ability of individual voters to inform themselves about campaign issues." *Tashjian v. Republican Party of Conn.* (1986). There is simply no basis to presume that a well-informed electorate will interpret a candidate's party-preference designation to mean that the candidate is the party's chosen nominee or representative or that the party associates with or approves of the candidate. This strikes us as especially true here, given that it was the voters of Washington themselves, rather than their elected representatives, who enacted I-872.

Of course, it is *possible* that voters will misinterpret the candidates' party-preference designations as reflecting endorsement by the parties. [But this case involves] a facial challenge, and we cannot strike down I-872 on its face based on the mere possibility of voter confusion. Because respondents brought their suit as a facial challenge, we have no evidentiary record against which to assess their assertions that voters will be confused. Indeed, because I-872 has never been implemented, we do not even have ballots indicating how party preference will be displayed. It stands to reason that whether voters will be confused by the party-preference designations will depend in significant part on the form of the ballot. The Court of Appeals assumed that the ballot would not place abbreviations like "D" and "R," or "Dem." and "Rep." after the names of candidates, but would instead

7. It is true that parties may no longer indicate their nominees on the ballot, but that is unexceptionable: The First Amendment does not give political parties a right to have their nominees designated as such on the ballot. *See Timmons v. Twin Cities Area New Party* (1997) ("We are unpersuaded, however, by the party's contention that it has a right to use the ballot itself to send a particularized message, to its candidate and to the voters, about the nature of its support for the candidate"). Parties do not gain such a right simply because the State affords candidates the opportunity to indicate their party preference on the ballot. "Ballots serve primarily to elect candidates, not as forums for political expression." *Id.*

"clearly state that a particular candidate 'prefers' a particular party." It thought that even such a clear statement did too little to eliminate the risk of voter confusion.

But we see no reason to stop there. As long as we are speculating about the form of the ballot—and we can do no more than speculate in this facial challenge—we must, in fairness to the voters of the State of Washington who enacted I-872 and in deference to the executive and judicial officials who are charged with implementing it, ask whether the ballot could conceivably be printed in such a way as to eliminate the possibility of widespread voter confusion and with it the perceived threat to the First Amendment.

It is not difficult to conceive of such a ballot. For example, petitioners propose that the actual I-872 ballot could include prominent disclaimers explaining that party preference reflects only the self-designation of the candidate and not an official endorsement by the party. They also suggest that the ballots might note preference in the form of a candidate statement that emphasizes the candidate's personal determination rather than the party's acceptance of the candidate, such as "my party preference is the Republican Party." Additionally, the State could decide to educate the public about the new primary ballots through advertising or explanatory materials mailed to voters along with their ballots.[8] We are satisfied that there are a variety of ways in which the State could implement I-872 that would eliminate any real threat of voter confusion. And without the specter of widespread voter confusion, respondents' arguments about forced association and compelled speech fall flat.

Our conclusion that these implementations of I-872 would be consistent with the First Amendment is fatal to respondents' facial challenge. Each of their arguments rests on factual assumptions about voter confusion, and each fails for the same reason: In the absence of evidence, we cannot assume that Washington's voters will be misled. That factual determination must await an as-applied challenge. On its face, I-872 does not impose any severe burden on respondents' associational rights.

B

Because we have concluded that I-872 does not severely burden respondents, the State need not assert a compelling interest. The State's asserted interest in providing voters with relevant information about the candidates on the ballot is easily sufficient to sustain I-872. *See Anderson* ("There can be no question about the legitimacy of the State's interest in fostering informed and educated expressions of the popular will in a general election").

Respondents ask this Court to invalidate a popularly enacted election process that has never been carried out. Immediately after implementing regulations were enacted, respondents obtained a permanent injunction against the enforcement of I-872. The First Amendment does not require this extraordinary and precipitous nullification of the will of the people. Because I-872 does not on its face provide for the nomination of candidates or compel political parties to associate with

8. Washington counties have broad authority to conduct elections entirely by mail ballot rather than at in-person polling places. As a result, over 90% of Washington voters now vote by mail. [Washington now conducts all of its elections entirely through vote-by-mail.—Eds.]

parties, and no good reason to wait until Washington has undermined its political parties to declare that it is forbidden to do so.

B

The Chief Justice would wait to see if the law is implemented in a manner that no more harms political parties than allowing a person to state that he "like[s] Campbell's soup" would harm the Campbell Soup Company. It is hard to know how to respond. First and most fundamentally, there is simply no comparison between statements of "preference" for an expressive association and statements of "preference" for soup. The robust First Amendment freedom to associate belongs only to groups "engage[d] in 'expressive association,'" *Dale*. The Campbell Soup Company does not exist to promote a message, and "there is only minimal constitutional protection of the freedom of commercial association," *Roberts v. United States Jaycees* (1984) (O'Connor, J., concurring in part and concurring in judgment).

Second, I assuredly do not share The Chief Justice's view that the First Amendment will be satisfied so long as the ballot "is designed in such a manner that no reasonable voter would believe that the candidates listed there are nominees or members of, or otherwise associated with, the parties the candidates claimed to 'prefer.'" To begin with, it seems to me quite impossible for the ballot to satisfy a reasonable voter that the candidate is not "associated with" the party for which he has expressed a preference. He has associated himself with the party by his very expression of a preference—and that indeed is the whole purpose of allowing the preference to be expressed. If all the Chief Justice means by "associated with" is that the candidate "does not speak on the party's behalf or with the party's approval," none of my analysis in this opinion relies upon that misperception, nor upon the misperception that the candidate is a member or the nominee of the party. Avoiding those misperceptions is far from enough. Is it enough to say on the ballot that a notorious and despised racist who says that the party is his choice does not speak with the party's approval? Surely not. His unrebutted association of that party with his views distorts the image of the party nonetheless. And the fact that the candidate who expresses a "preference" for one or another party is shown not to be the nominee of that party does not deprive him of the boost from the party's reputation which the party wishes to confer only on its nominee. The Chief Justice claims that "the content of the ballots in the pertinent respect is yet to be determined." I disagree. We know all we need to know about the form of ballot. When pressed, Washington's Attorney General assured us at oral argument that the ballot will not say whether the party for whom the candidate expresses a preference claims or disavows him. (Of course it will not, for that would enable the party expression that it is the very object of this legislation to impair.)

And finally, while The Chief Justice earlier expresses his awareness that the special character of the ballot is what makes these cases different, his Campbell's Soup example seems to forget that. If we must speak in terms of soup, Washington's law is like a law that encourages Oscar the Grouch (Sesame Street's famed bad-taste resident of a garbage can) to state a "preference" for Campbell's at every point of sale, while barring the soup company from disavowing his endorsement, or indeed using its name at all, in those same crucial locations. Reserving the most critical communications forum for statements of "preference" by a potentially distasteful speaker alters public perceptions of the entity that is "preferred"; and when this privileged connection undermines not a company's ability to identify and promote soup but an expressive association's ability to identify and promote its message and its standard bearer, the State treads on the constitutionally protected freedom of association.

The majority opinion and The Chief Justice's concurrence also endorse a wait-and-see approach on the grounds that it is not yet evident how the law will affect voter perception of the political parties. But contrary to the Court's suggestion, it is not incumbent on the political parties to adduce "evidence" that forced association affects their ability to advocate for their candidates and their causes. We have never put expressive groups to this perhaps-impossible task. Rather, we accept their own assessments of the matter. It does not take a study to establish that when statements of party connection are the sole information listed next to candidate names on the ballot, those statements will affect voters' perceptions of what the candidate stands for, what the party stands for, and whom they should elect.

III

The right to associate for the election of candidates is fundamental to the operation of our political system, and state action impairing that association bears a heavy burden of justification. Washington's electoral system permits individuals to appropriate the parties' trademarks, so to speak, at the most crucial stage of election, thereby distorting the parties' messages and impairing their endorsement of candidates. The State's justification for this (to convey a "modicum of relevant information") is not only weak but undeserving of credence. We have here a system which, like the one it replaced, does not merely refuse to assist, but positively impairs, the legitimate role of political parties. I dissent from the Court's conclusion that the Constitution permits this sabotage.

Chief Justice ROBERTS, with whom Justice ALITO joins, concurring.

I share Justice Scalia's concern that permitting a candidate to identify his political party preference on an official election ballot—regardless of whether the candidate is endorsed by the party or is even a member—may effectively force parties to accept candidates they do not want, amounting to forced association in violation of the First Amendment.

I do think, however, that whether voters *perceive* the candidate and the party to be associated is relevant to the constitutional inquiry. Our other forced-association cases indicate as much. In *Boy Scouts of America v. Dale* (2000), we said that Dale's presence in the Boy Scouts would "force the organization to send a message . . . [to] the world" that the Scouts approved of homosexuality. In other words, accepting Dale would lead outsiders to believe the Scouts endorsed homosexual conduct. Largely for that reason, we held that the First Amendment entitled the Scouts to exclude Dale. Similarly, in *Hurley v. Irish-American Gay, Lesbian and Bisexual Group of Boston, Inc.* (1995), we allowed the organizers of Boston's St. Patrick's Day Parade to exclude a pro-gay rights float because the float's presence in the parade might create the impression that the organizers agreed with the float-sponsors' message.

Voter perceptions matter, and if voters do not actually believe the parties and the candidates are tied together, it is hard to see how the parties' associational rights are adversely implicated. After all, individuals frequently claim to favor this or that political party; these preferences, without more, do not create an unconstitutional forced association.

What makes these cases different, as Justice Scalia explains, is the place where the candidates express their party preferences: on the ballot. And what makes the ballot "special" is precisely the effect it has on voter impressions. But because respondents brought this challenge before the State of Washington had printed ballots for use under the new primary regime, we have no idea what those ballots will look like. Petitioners themselves emphasize that the content of the ballots in the pertinent respect is yet to be determined.

If the ballot is designed in such a manner that no reasonable voter would believe that the candidates listed there are nominees or members of, or otherwise associated with, the parties the candidates claimed to "prefer," the I-872 primary system would likely pass constitutional muster. I cannot say on the present record that it would be impossible for the State to design such a ballot. Assuming the ballot is so designed, voters would not regard the listed candidates as "party" candidates, any more than someone saying "I like Campbell's soup" would be understood to be associated with Campbell's. Voters would understand that the candidate does not speak on the party's behalf or with the party's approval. On the other hand, if the ballot merely lists the candidates' preferred parties next to the candidates' names, or otherwise fails clearly to convey that the parties and the candidates are not necessarily associated, the I-872 system would not survive a First Amendment challenge.

Justice Scalia complains that "[i]t is hard to know how to respond" to such mistaken views, but he soldiers on nonetheless. He would hold that a party is burdened by a candidate's statement of preference even if no reasonable voter believes from the ballot that the party and the candidate are associated. I take his point to be that a particular candidate's "endorsement" of a party might alter the party's message, and this violates the party's freedom of association.

But there is no general right to stop an individual from saying, "I prefer this party," even if the party would rather he not. Normally, the party protects its message in such a case through responsive speech of its own. What makes this case different of course is that the State controls the content of the ballot, which we have never considered a public forum. Neither the candidate nor the party dictates the message conveyed by the ballot. In such a case, it is important to know what the ballot actually says—both about the candidate and about the party's association with the candidate. It is possible that no reasonable voter in Washington State will regard the listed candidates as members of, or otherwise associated with, the political parties the candidates claim to prefer. Nothing in my analysis requires the parties to produce studies regarding voter perceptions on this score, but I would wait to see what the ballot says before deciding whether it is unconstitutional.

Still, I agree with Justice Scalia that the history of the challenged law suggests the State is not particularly interested in devising ballots that meet these constitutional requirements. But this record simply does not allow us to say with certainty that the election system created by I-872 is unconstitutional. Accordingly, I agree with the Court that respondents' present challenge to the law must fail, and I join the Court's opinion.

NOTES ON *WASHINGTON STATE GRANGE*

1. Much of Justice Thomas's majority opinion focuses on the difference between facial and as-applied challenges. In a facial challenge, the plaintiff is claiming that the law is unconstitutional in every instance, regardless of how it operates with respect to that plaintiff specifically. In an as-applied challenge, by contrast, the plaintiff is asserting only that the law is unconstitutional as it affects that plaintiff (and

those similarly situated). That is, a facial challenge is a challenge to the law in its entirety. An as-applied challenge is narrower, as a court could rule the law unconstitutional with respect to that plaintiff but not to others with different circumstances. Why is the difference so significant here? Should the plaintiffs have waited for an actual election to challenge the law so there was evidence on how the law operated? What sort of evidence might they need to bring a successful as-applied challenge? One implication of this opinion might be that the political party must suffer a potential constitutional violation for at least one election before it can secure judicial relief.

2. Does a designation that a candidate "Prefers Democratic Party" really tell a voter that the affiliation is only one way? How do most voters decide who to vote for in down-ballot elections? Many voters use political party affiliation as a useful proxy. This decision therefore puts a lot of faith in voters' knowledge that a party does not endorse a candidate even if the candidate prefers the party. Is it realistic to expect voters to understand this distinction? On the other hand, perhaps a top-two primary is useful for branches of one of the major parties, such as the Tea Party movement. A candidate could prefer "Tea Party" instead of "Republican Party" to indicate his or her specific views.

Figure 2-1

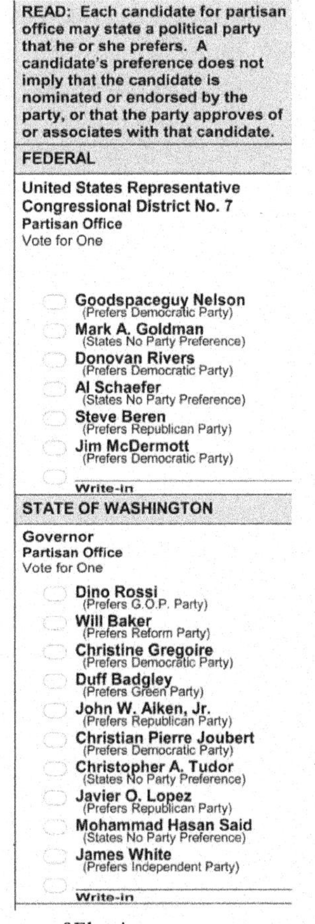

READ: Each candidate for partisan office may state a political party that he or she prefers. A candidate's preference does not imply that the candidate is nominated or endorsed by the party, or that the party approves of or associates with that candidate.

FEDERAL

United States Representative
Congressional District No. 7
Partisan Office
Vote for One

Goodspaceguy Nelson (Prefers Democratic Party)
Mark A. Goldman (States No Party Preference)
Donovan Rivers (Prefers Democratic Party)
Al Schaefer (States No Party Preference)
Steve Beren (Prefers Republican Party)
Jim McDermott (Prefers Democratic Party)
Write-in

STATE OF WASHINGTON

Governor
Partisan Office
Vote for One

Dino Rossi (Prefers G.O.P. Party)
Will Baker (Prefers Reform Party)
Christine Gregoire (Prefers Democratic Party)
Duff Badgley (Prefers Green Party)
John W. Aiken, Jr. (Prefers Republican Party)
Christian Pierre Joubert (Prefers Democratic Party)
Christopher A. Tudor (States No Party Preference)
Javier O. Lopez (Prefers Republican Party)
Mohammad Hasan Said (States No Party Preference)
James White (Prefers Independent Party)
Write-in

Source: King County, (WA) Department of Elections.

3. Figure 2-1 on the previous page is a copy of part of the "sample ballot" that King County, Washington distributed to voters before the 2008 election. This is the ballot the Department of Elections designed in the wake of Washington's new top-two law. Does seeing the ballot alter your views on whether it would confuse voters about a political party's endorsement of a candidate?

4. Imagine you represent the Democratic Party. Tucker Carlson, a noted conservative television host, decides to run for office in Washington State and declares his party preference for the ballot as Democratic Party, perhaps to take away votes from the "true" Democrats in the election. What would you advise the party to do?

5. Does this decision pull back on the seeming primacy of political parties from *Democratic Party v. Wisconsin*? Can you reconcile the two cases?

6. In 2010, taking advantage of the *Washington State Grange* decision, California adopted its own version of the top-two primary (as distinct from its earlier blanket primary invalidated in *California Democratic Party v. Jones*). Because California is the nation's largest state (and is especially multicultural in its demographics), politicians and pundits have watched the state closely to see how the top-two primary operates there, and whether the combined experience of California and Washington serves as a catalyst for adopting this reform in other states. Louisiana, too, uses a top-two system, as does Nebraska for its nonpartisan state legislative races. Supporters of a top-two primary argue that the system increases the likelihood that more moderate candidates will move on to the general election; opponents say that the system can cut out the political minority as well as third-party or independent candidates. But there's also a concern from political parties that control an area: for instance, in 2018, some California Democrats were concerned that if there were many Democrats and only two Republicans running in a heavily Democratic district, the Democratic candidates would split the Democratic vote and the two Republicans would secure enough votes to move on to the general election. Though this outcome did not occur, the top-two system introduces this possibility.

Meanwhile, a three-judge panel of the Ninth Circuit unanimously upheld California's top-two primary against a First Amendment challenge. *Chamness v. Brown*, 722 F.3d 1110 (9th Cir. 2013). In that case, a candidate unaffiliated with any political party complained that the California law only gave him the option of stating "No Party Designation" on the primary ballot, rather than the label "Independent," which he preferred. The court held that because the ballot belonged to the state, and because the label "Independent" might cause confusion with the "American Independent" party (one of the six political parties qualified for party designation under California's law), the state's rule was a reasonable regulation. The candidate of course remained free to describe himself as an "Independent" in his own campaign communications.

7. In November 2020, Alaska voters narrowly approved an initiative to adopt a top-four open primary system. All candidates run on the same ballot in the primary and the top four vote recipients move on to the general election. The state then uses Ranked Choice Voting for the general election. An opponent brought suit against the measure in state court; although that case has not been resolved as of the writing of this book, courts in other states have rejected challenges to Ranked Choice Voting, as discussed later in this Part.

C. *INVITING NONMEMBERS TO THE PARTY (OR AT LEAST TO ITS PRIMARY)*

As *California Democratic Party* and *Washington State Grange* show, often a political party does not want to permit nonmembers to affect the choice of which candidate from the party carries the party's banner in the general election. In 2008, for example, some Democrats feared that—after John McCain clinched the Republican nomination but the battle for the Democratic nomination between Barack Obama and Hillary Clinton waged on in states like Ohio—Republicans would "cross-over" or "raid" the remaining Democratic Party primaries to vote for Clinton because they thought she would be easier for McCain to beat in the general election. Whatever its motive, the cross-over vote in Ohio may have contributed to the prolonged fight between Obama and Clinton, which could have used up Obama's resources before he won the nomination and entered the general election campaign.

Sometimes, however, political parties like to welcome nonmembers to vote in their primaries. The strategy is to appeal to centrist voters early, so that the party's nominees are not chosen solely by its "base" and thus are less likely to be polarizing choices in November. In *Tashjian v. Republican Party of Connecticut*, 479 U.S. 208 (1986), Connecticut law mandated a "closed" primary in that state, meaning that only party members were permitted to vote in a party's primary. The Republican Party in the state wanted to permit independents to vote in its primary and thus sued to invalidate the state law on First Amendment grounds. The party prevailed in the U.S. Supreme Court.

The reach of *Tashjian* as precedent was the focus of this important case, which failed to produce a clear majority opinion. Pay special attention to Justice O'Connor's concurrence, asking yourself why she and Justice Breyer refused to join Justice Thomas's opinion in full, and how their disagreement might prove significant in future litigation.

Clingman v. Beaver

544 U.S. 581 (2005)

Justice Thomas delivered the opinion of the Court, except as to Part II-A.

Oklahoma has a semi-closed primary system, in which a political party may invite only its own party members and voters registered as Independents to vote in the party's primary. [Members of other political parties are excluded.] The Court of Appeals held that this system violates the right to freedom of association of the Libertarian Party of Oklahoma (LPO) and several Oklahomans who are registered members of the Republican and Democratic parties. We hold that it does not.

I

In May 2000, the LPO notified the secretary of the Oklahoma State Election Board that it wanted to open its upcoming primary to all registered Oklahoma voters, without regard to their party affiliation. [T]he secretary agreed as to Independent voters, but not as to voters registered with other political parties. The LPO and several Republican and Democratic voters then sued for declaratory and injunctive relief . . . , alleging that Oklahoma's semi-closed primary law unconstitutionally burdens their First Amendment right to freedom of political association.

II

The Constitution grants States "broad power to prescribe the 'Time, Places and Manner of holding Elections for Senators and Representatives,' Art. I, §4, cl. 1, which power is matched by state control over the election process for state offices." *Tashjian v. Republican Party of Conn.* (1986). We have held that the First Amendment, among other things, protects the right of citizens "to band together in promoting among the electorate candidates who espouse their political views." *California Democratic Party v. Jones* (2000). Regulations that impose severe burdens on associational rights must be narrowly tailored to serve a compelling state interest. However, when regulations impose lesser burdens, "a State's important regulatory interests will usually be enough to justify reasonable, nondiscriminatory restrictions."

In *Tashjian*, this Court struck down, as inconsistent with the First Amendment, a closed primary system that prevented a political party from inviting Independent voters to vote in the party's primary. This case presents a question that *Tashjian* left open: whether a State may prevent a political party from inviting registered voters of other parties to vote in its primary. As *Tashjian* acknowledged, opening a party's primary "to all voters, including members of other parties, . . . raise[s] a different combination of considerations." We are persuaded that any burden Oklahoma's semi-closed primary imposes is minor and justified by legitimate state interests.

A

[Plurality, Justice THOMAS joined by Chief Justice REHNQUIST, Justice SCALIA, and Justice KENNEDY.]

At the outset, we note that Oklahoma's semi-closed primary system is unlike other laws this Court has held to infringe associational rights. Oklahoma has not sought through its electoral system to discover the names of the LPO's members; to interfere with the LPO by restricting activities central to its purpose; to disqualify the LPO from public benefits or privileges; or to compel the LPO's association with unwanted members or voters. The LPO is free to canvass the electorate, enroll or exclude potential members, nominate the candidate of its choice, and engage in the same electoral activities as every other political party in Oklahoma. Oklahoma merely prohibits the LPO from leaving the selection of its candidates to people who are members of another political party. Nothing prevents members of other parties from switching their registration to the LPO or to Independent status.[2] The

2. Respondents argue, for the first time before this Court, that Oklahoma election statutes other than [the statute at issue requiring the semi-closed primary] make it difficult for voters to disaffiliate from their parties of first choice and register as Libertarians or Independents (either of which would allow them to vote in the LPO primary). [Because respondents raised this argument for the first time in their merits brief to this Court,] we decline to consider this aspect of respondents' challenge.

question is whether the Constitution requires that voters who are registered in other parties be allowed to vote in the LPO's primary.

In other words, the Republican and Democratic voters who have brought this action do not want to associate with the LPO, at least not in any formal sense. They wish to remain registered with the Republican, Democratic, or Reform parties, and yet to assist in selecting the Libertarian Party's candidates for the general election. Their interest is in casting a vote for a Libertarian candidate in a particular primary election, rather than in banding together with fellow citizens committed to the LPO's political goals and ideas. And the LPO is happy to have their votes, if not their membership on the party rolls.

However, a voter who is unwilling to disaffiliate from another party to vote in the LPO's primary forms little "association" with the LPO—nor the LPO with him. That same voter might wish to participate in numerous party primaries, or cast ballots for several candidates, in any given race. The issue is not "dual associations," but seemingly boundless ones. "If the concept of freedom of association is extended" to a voter's every desire at the ballot box, "it ceases to be of any analytic use." *Tashjian* (Scalia, J., dissenting).

But even if Oklahoma's semi-closed primary system burdens an associational right, the burden is less severe than others this Court has upheld as constitutional. For instance, in *Timmons*, we considered a Minnesota election law prohibiting multiparty, or "fusion," candidacies in which a candidate appears on the ballot as the nominee of more than one party. Minnesota's law prevented the New Party, a minor party under state law, from putting forward the same candidate as a major party. The New Party challenged the law as unconstitutionally burdening its associational rights. This Court concluded that the burdens imposed by Minnesota's law—"though not trivial—[were] not severe."

The burdens were not severe because the New Party and its members remained free to govern themselves internally and to communicate with the public as they wished. Minnesota had neither regulated the New Party's internal decision-making process, nor compelled it to associate with voters of any political persuasion. The New Party and its members simply could not nominate as their candidate any of "those few individuals who both have already agreed to be another party's candidate and also, if forced to choose, themselves prefer that other party."

The same reasons underpinning our decision in *Timmons* show that Oklahoma's semi-closed primary system burdens the LPO only minimally. As in *Timmons*, Oklahoma's law does not regulate the LPO's internal processes, its authority to exclude unwanted members, or its capacity to communicate with the public. And just as in *Timmons*, in which Minnesota conditioned the party's ability to nominate the candidate of its choice on the candidate's willingness to disaffiliate from another political party, Oklahoma conditions the party's ability to welcome a voter into its primary on the voter's willingness to dissociate from his current party of choice. If anything, it is "[t]he moment of choosing the party's nominee" that matters far more, for that is "the crucial juncture at which the appeal to common principles may be translated into concerted action, and hence to political power in the community," *Jones*. If a party may be prevented from associating with the candidate of its choice—its desired "standard bearer"—because that candidate refuses to disaffiliate from another political party, a party may also be prevented from associating with a voter who refuses to do the same.

B

Respondents argue that this case is no different from *Tashjian*. According to respondents, the burden imposed by Oklahoma's semi-closed primary system is no less severe than the burden at issue in *Tashjian*, and hence we must apply strict scrutiny as we did in *Tashjian*. We disagree. At issue in *Tashjian* was a Connecticut election statute that required voters to register with a political party before participating in its primary. The State's Republican Party, having adopted a rule that allowed Independent voters to participate in its primary, contended that Connecticut's closed primary infringed its right to associate with Independent voters. Applying strict scrutiny, this Court found that the interests Connecticut advanced to justify its ban were not compelling, and thus that the State could not constitutionally prevent the Republican Party from inviting into its primary willing Independent voters.

Respondents' reliance on *Tashjian* is unavailing. As an initial matter, *Tashjian* applied strict scrutiny with little discussion of the magnitude of the burdens imposed by Connecticut's closed primary on parties' and voters' associational rights. But not every electoral law that burdens associational rights is subject to strict scrutiny. Instead, as our cases since *Tashjian* have clarified, strict scrutiny is appropriate only if the burden is severe. In *Tashjian* itself, Independent voters could join the Connecticut Republican Party as late as the day before the primary. As explained above, requiring voters to register with a party prior to participating in the party's primary minimally burdens voters' associational rights.

Nevertheless, *Tashjian* is distinguishable.* Oklahoma's semi-closed primary imposes an even less substantial burden than did the Connecticut closed primary at issue in *Tashjian*. In *Tashjian*, this Court identified two ways in which Connecticut's closed primary limited citizens' freedom of political association. The first and most important was that it required Independent voters to affiliate publicly with a party to vote in its primary. That is not true in this case. At issue here are voters who have *already* affiliated publicly with one of Oklahoma's political parties. These voters need not register as Libertarians to vote in the LPO's primary; they need only declare themselves Independents, which would leave them free to participate in any party primary that is open to registered Independents.

The second and less important burden imposed by Connecticut's closed primary system was that political parties could not "broaden opportunities for joining . . . by their own act, without any intervening action by potential voters." *Tashjian*. Voters also had to act by registering themselves in a particular party. That is equally true of Oklahoma's semi-closed primary system: Voters must register as Libertarians or Independents to participate in the LPO's primary. However, *Tashjian* did not characterize this burden alone as severe, and with good reason. Many electoral regulations, including voter registration generally, require that voters take some action to participate in the primary process. Election laws invariably "affec[t]—at least to some degree—the individual's right to vote and his right to associate with others for political ends." *Anderson v. Celebrezze* (1983).

* [How do you think Justice Thomas would have voted in *Tashjian*? (He was not on the Court yet.) As you read this section, think about whether his attempt to distinguish that case is persuasive.—Eds]

These minor barriers between voter and party do not compel strict scrutiny. To deem ordinary and widespread burdens like these severe would subject virtually every electoral regulation to strict scrutiny, hamper the ability of States to run efficient and equitable elections, and compel federal courts to rewrite state electoral codes.* The Constitution does not require that result, for it is beyond question "that States may, and inevitably must, enact reasonable regulations of parties, elections, and ballots to reduce election- and campaign-related disorder." *Timmons.* Oklahoma's semi-closed primary system does not severely burden the associational rights of the state's citizenry.

C

When a state electoral provision places no heavy burden on associational rights, "a State's important regulatory interests will usually be enough to justify reasonable, nondiscriminatory restrictions." *Timmons.* Here, Oklahoma's semi-closed primary advances a number of regulatory interests that this Court recognizes as important: It preserves political parties as viable and identifiable interest groups; enhances parties' electioneering and party-building efforts; and guards against party raiding and "sore loser" candidacies by spurned primary contenders.

First, [t]he LPO wishes to open its primary to registered Republicans and Democrats, who may well vote in numbers that dwarf the roughly 300 registered LPO voters in Oklahoma. If the LPO is permitted to open its primary to all registered voters regardless of party affiliation, the candidate who emerges from the LPO primary may be "unconcerned with, if not . . . hostile to," the political preferences of the majority of the LPO's members. It does not matter that the LPO is willing to risk the surrender of its identity in exchange for electoral success. Oklahoma's interest is independent and concerns the integrity of its primary system. The State wants to "avoid primary election outcomes which would tend to confuse or mislead the general voting population to the extent [it] relies on party labels as representative of certain ideologies."

Moreover, this Court has found that in facilitating the effective operation of a democratic government, a state might reasonably classify voters or candidates according to political affiliations. But for that classification to mean much, Oklahoma must be allowed to limit voters' ability to roam among parties' primaries. The purpose of party registration is to provide a minimal demonstration by the voter that he has some "commitment" to the party in whose primary he wishes to participate. That commitment is lessened if party members may retain their registration in one party while voting in another party's primary. Opening the LPO's primary to all voters not only would render the LPO's *imprimatur* an unreliable index of its candidate's actual political philosophy, but it also would make registered party affiliations significantly less meaningful in the Oklahoma primary election system. Oklahoma reasonably has concluded that opening the LPO's primary to all voters regardless of party affiliation would undermine the crucial role of political parties in the primary process.

* [This is a very important sentence that is cited frequently in future case law.—Eds.]

Second, Oklahoma's semi-closed primary system, by retaining the importance of party affiliation, aids in parties' electioneering and party-building efforts. It is common experience that direct solicitation of party members—by mail, telephone, or face-to-face contact, and by the candidates themselves or by their active supporters—is part of any primary election campaign. Yet parties' voter turnout efforts depend in large part on accurate voter registration rolls.

When voters are no longer required to disaffiliate before participating in other parties' primaries, voter registration rolls cease to be an accurate reflection of voters' political preferences. And without registration rolls that accurately reflect likely or potential primary voters, parties risk expending precious resources to turn out party members who may have decided to cast their votes elsewhere. If encouraging citizens to vote is an important state interest, then Oklahoma is entitled to protect parties' ability to plan their primaries for a stable group of voters.

Third, Oklahoma has an interest in preventing party raiding, or "the organized switching of blocs of voters from one party to another in order to manipulate the outcome of the other party's primary election." *Anderson*. For example, if the outcome of the Democratic Party primary were not in doubt, Democrats might vote in the LPO primary for the candidate most likely to siphon off votes from the Republican candidate in the general election. Or a Democratic primary contender who senses defeat might launch a "sore loser" candidacy by defecting to the LPO primary, taking with him loyal Democratic voters, and thus undermining the Democratic Party in the general election. Oklahoma has an interest in "temper[ing] the destabilizing effects" of precisely this sort of "party-splintering and excessive factionalism." *Timmons*. Oklahoma's semi-closed primary system serves that interest by discouraging voters from temporarily defecting from another party to vote in the LPO primary. While the State's interest will not justify "unreasonably exclusionary restrictions," we have "repeatedly upheld reasonable, politically neutral regulations" like Oklahoma's semi-closed primary law. [*Id.*]

III

[Omitted.]

. . .

Oklahoma remains free to allow the LPO to invite registered voters of other parties to vote in its primary. But the Constitution leaves that choice to the democratic process, not to the courts. The judgment of the Court of Appeals is reversed, and the case is remanded for further proceedings.

Justice O'CONNOR, with whom Justice BREYER joins except as to Part III, concurring in part and concurring in the judgment.

I join the Court's opinion except for Part II-A. Although I agree with most of the Court's reasoning, I write separately to emphasize two points. First, I think respondents' claim implicates important associational interests, and I see no reason to minimize those interests to dispose of this case. Second, I agree with the Court that only Oklahoma's semi-closed primary law is properly before us, that standing alone it imposes only a modest, nondiscriminatory burden on respondents' associational rights, and that this burden is justified by the State's legitimate regulatory interests. I note, however, that there are some grounds for concern that other state laws may unreasonably restrict voters' ability to change party registration so as to participate in the Libertarian Party of Oklahoma's (LPO) primary. A realistic assessment of regulatory burdens on associational rights would, in an appropriate case, require examination of the cumulative effects of the State's overall scheme governing primary elections; and any finding of a more severe burden would trigger more probing review of the justifications offered by the State.

I

Nearly every State in the Nation now mandates that political parties select their candidates for national or statewide office by means of primary elections. Primaries constitute both a crucial juncture in the electoral process, and a vital forum for expressive association among voters and political parties. It is here that the parties invite voters to join in selecting their standard bearers. The outcome is pivotal, of course, for it dictates the range of choices available at—and often the presumptive winner of—the general election.

"No right is more precious in a free country than that of having a voice in the election of those who make the laws under which, as good citizens, we must live," *Wesberry v. Sanders*, and the right to associate with the political party of one's choice is an integral part of this basic constitutional freedom. The Court has repeatedly reaffirmed that the First and Fourteenth Amendments protect the rights of voters and parties to associate through primary elections. Indeed, constitutional protection of associational rights is especially important in this context because the aggregation of votes is, in some sense, the essence of the electoral process. To have a meaningful voice in this process, the individual voter must join together with like-minded others at the polls. And the choice of who will participate in selecting a party's candidate obviously plays a critical role in determining both the party's message and its prospects of success in the electoral contest.

The majority questions whether the LPO and voters registered with another party have any constitutionally cognizable interest in associating with one another through the LPO's primary. Its doubts on this point appear to stem from two implicit premises: first, that a voter forms a cognizable association with a political party only by registering with that party; and second, that a voter can only form a cognizable association with one party at a time. Neither of these premises is sound, in my view. As to the first, registration with a political party surely may signify an important personal commitment, which may be accompanied by faithful voting and even activism beyond the polls. But for many voters, registration serves principally as a mandatory (and perhaps even ministerial) prerequisite to participation in the party's primaries. The act of casting a ballot in a given primary may, for both the voter and the party, constitute a form of association that is at least as important as the act of registering. The fact that voting is episodic does not, in my judgment, undermine its associational significance; it simply reflects the special character of the electoral process, which allows citizens to join together at regular intervals to shape government through the choice of public officials.

As to the question of dual associations, I fail to see why registration with one party should negate a voter's First Amendment interest in associating with a second party. We surely would not say, for instance, that a registered Republican or Democrat has no protected interest in associating with the Libertarian Party by attending meetings or making political contributions. The validity of voters' and parties' interests in dual associations seems particularly clear where minor parties are concerned. For example, a voter may have a longstanding affiliation with a major party that she wishes to maintain, but she may nevertheless have a substantial interest in associating with a minor party during particular election cycles or in elections for particular offices. The voter's refusal to disaffiliate from the major party may reflect her abiding commitment to that party (which is not necessarily inconsistent with her desire to associate with a second party), the objective costs of disaffiliation or both. The minor party, for its part, may have a significant interest in augmenting its voice in the political process by associating with sympathetic members of the major parties.

None of this is to suggest that the State does not have a superseding interest in restricting certain forms of association. We have never questioned, for example, the States' authority to restrict voters' public registration to a single party or to limit each voter to participating in a single party's primary. But the fact that a State's regulatory authority may ultimately trump voters' or parties' associational interests in a particular context is no reason to dismiss the validity of those interests. As a more general matter, I question whether judicial inquiry into the genuineness, intensity, or duration of a given voter's association with a given party is a fruitful way to approach constitutional challenges to regulations like the one at issue here. Primary voting is an episodic and sometimes isolated act of association, but it is a vitally important one and should be entitled to some level of constitutional protection. Accordingly, where a party invites a voter to participate in its primary and the voter seeks to do so, we should begin with the premise that there are significant associational interests at stake. From this starting point, we can then ask to what extent and in what manner the State may justifiably restrict those interests.

II

[Omitted.]

III

In briefing and oral argument before this Court, respondents raise for the first time the claim that Oklahoma's semi-closed primary law severely burdens their associational rights not through the law's own operation, but rather because *other* state laws make it quite difficult for voters to reregister as Independents or Libertarians so as to participate in the LPO primary. Respondents characterize Oklahoma's regulatory scheme as follows.

Partisan primaries in Oklahoma are held on the last Tuesday in July of each even-numbered year. To field a party candidate in an election, the LPO must obtain "recognized" party status. This requires it to submit, no later than May 1 of any even-numbered year (*i.e.*, any election year), a petition with the signatures of registered voters equal to at least five percent of the total votes cast in the most recent gubernatorial or Presidential election. The State Election Board then has 30 days to determine whether the petition is sufficient. The LPO has attained recognized party status in this fashion in every Presidential election year since 1980. However, unless the party's candidate receives at least 10 percent of the total votes cast for

Governor or President in the general election (which no minor party has been able to do in any State in recent history), it loses recognized party status. To regain party status, the group must go through the petition process again.

When a party loses its recognized status, as the LPO has after every general election in which it has participated, the affiliation of any voter registered with the party is changed to Independent. As the District Court noted, "it is highly likely that the ranks of independents, and, indeed, of registered Republicans and Democrats, contain numerous voters who sympathize with the LPO but who simply do not wish to go through the motions of re-registering every time they are purged from the rolls." And the Republican and Democratic parties in Oklahoma, as it turns out, do not permit voters registered as Independents to participate in their primaries.

Most importantly, according to respondents, the deadline for changing party affiliation makes it quite difficult for the LPO to invite voters to reregister in order to participate in its primary. Assuming the LPO submits its petition for recognized party status on the May 1 deadline, the State has until May 31 to determine whether party status will be conferred. But in order to participate in the LPO primary, a voter registered with another party must change her party affiliation to Independent or Libertarian no later than June 1. Moreover, no candidate for office is permitted officially to declare her candidacy with the State Election Board until the period between the first Monday in June and the next succeeding Wednesday.

If this characterization of state law is accurate, a registered Democrat or Republican sympathetic to the LPO or to an LPO candidate in a given election year would seem to face a genuine dilemma. On the one hand, she may stick with her major party registration and forfeit the opportunity to participate in the LPO primary. Alternatively, she may reregister as a Libertarian or Independent, thus forfeiting her opportunity to participate in the major party primary, though no candidate will have officially declared yet and the voter may not yet know whether the LPO will even be permitted to conduct a primary. Moreover, she must make this choice roughly eight weeks before the primaries, at a time when most voters have not yet even tuned in to the election, much less decided upon a candidate. That might pose a special difficulty for voters attracted to minor party candidates, for whom support may not coalesce until comparatively late in the election cycle.

Throughout the proceedings in the lower courts, which included a full bench trial before the District Court, respondents made no attempt to challenge these other electoral requirements or to argue that they were relevant to respondents' challenge to the semi-closed primary law. The lower courts, accordingly, gave little or no consideration to how these various regulations interrelate or operate in practice, nor did the State seek to justify them. Given this posture, I agree with the Court that it would be neither proper nor prudent for us to rule on the reformulated claim that respondents now urge.

Nevertheless, respondents' allegations are troubling, and, if they had been properly raised, the Court would want to examine the *cumulative* burdens imposed by the *overall* scheme of electoral regulations upon the rights of voters and parties to associate through primary elections. A panoply of regulations, each apparently defensible when considered alone, may nevertheless have the combined effect of severely restricting participation and competition. Even if each part of a regulatory regime might be upheld if challenged separately, one or another of these parts might have to fall if the overall scheme unreasonably curtails associational freedoms. Oklahoma's requirement that a voter register as an Independent or a

Libertarian in order to participate in the LPO's primary is not itself unduly onerous; but that is true only to the extent that the State provides reasonable avenues through which a voter can change her registration status. The State's regulations governing changes in party affiliation are not properly before us now. But if it were shown, in an appropriate case, that such regulations imposed a weighty or discriminatory restriction on voters' ability to participate in the LPO's or some other party's primary, then more probing scrutiny of the State's justifications would be required.

Justice STEVENS, with whom Justice GINSBURG joins, and with whom Justice SOUTER joins as to Parts I, II, and III, dissenting.

The Court's decision today diminishes the value of two important rights protected by the First Amendment: the individual citizen's right to vote for the candidate of her choice and a political party's right to define its own mission.

I

In rejecting the individual respondents' claims, the majority focuses on their associational interests. While the voters in this case certainly have an interest in associating with the LPO, they are primarily interested in voting for a particular candidate, who happens to be in the LPO. Indeed, I think we have lost sight of the principal purpose of a primary: to nominate a candidate for office.

Because our recent cases have focused on the associational interest of voters, rather than the right to vote itself, it is important to identify three basic precepts. First, it is clear that the right to vote includes the right to vote in a primary election. When the State makes the primary an integral part of the procedure of choice, every eligible citizen's right to vote should receive the same protection as in the general election. Second, the right to vote, whether in the primary or the general election, is the right to vote for the candidate of one's choice. Finally, in assessing burdens on that right—burdens that are not limited to absolute denial of the right—we should focus on the realities of the situation, not on empty formalism.

Here, the impact of the Oklahoma statute on the voters' right to vote for the candidate of their choosing is not a mere "burden"; it is a prohibition. By virtue of the fact that their preferred candidate is a member of a different party, respondents are absolutely precluded from voting for him or her in the primary election. It is not an answer that the voters could participate in another primary (*i.e.*, the primary for the party with which they are registered) since the individual for whom they wish to vote is not a candidate in that primary.

This is not to say that voters have an absolute right to participate in whatever primary they desire. For instance, the parties themselves have a strong associational interest in determining which individuals may vote in their primaries, and that interest will normally outweigh the interest of the uninvited voter. But in the ordinary case the State simply has no interest in classifying voters by their political party and in limiting the elections in which voters may participate as a result of that classification. Just as we held in *Reynolds* that all voters of a State stand in the same relation to the State regardless of where they live, and that the State must thus not make their vote count more or less depending upon that factor, so too do citizens stand in the same relation *to the State* regardless of the political party to which they belong. The State may thus not deny them participation in a primary of a party that seeks their participation absent a state interest of overriding importance.

II

In addition to burdening the individual respondent's right to vote, the Oklahoma scheme places a heavy burden on the LPO's associational rights. While Oklahoma permits independent voters to participate in the LPO's primary elections, it refuses to allow registered Republicans or Democrats to do so. That refusal has a direct impact on the LPO's selection of candidates for public office, the importance of which cannot be overstated. A primary election plays a critical role in enabling a party to disseminate its message to the public. It is through its candidates that a party is able to give voice to its political views, to engage other candidates on important issues of the day, and to affect change in the government of our society. Our cases "vigorously affirm the special place the First Amendment reserves for, and the special protection it accords, the process by which a political party selects a standard bearer who best represents the party's ideologies and preferences." [*Jones.*]

The LPO's desire to include Democrats and Republicans is undoubtedly informed by the fact that, given the stringent requirements of Oklahoma law, the LPO ceases to become a formally recognized party after each election cycle, and its members automatically revert to being independents. Because the LPO routinely loses its status as a recognized party, many voters who might otherwise register as Libertarians instead register as Democrats or Republicans. Thus, the LPO's interest in inviting registered Republicans and Democrats to participate in the selection of its standard-bearer has even greater force than did the Republican Party's desire to invite independents to associate with it in *Tashjian.*

III

As justification for the State's abridgment of the constitutionally protected interests asserted by the LPO and the voters, the majority relies on countervailing state interests that are either irrelevant or insignificant. Neither separately nor in the aggregate do these interests support the Court's decision.

First, the Court makes the remarkable suggestion that by opening up its primary to Democrats and Republicans, the LPO will be saddled with so many non-libertarian voters that the ultimate candidate will not be, in any sense, "libertarian." But the LPO is *seeking* the crossover voting of Republicans and Democrats. Rightly or wrongly, the LPO feels that the best way to produce a viable candidate is to invite voters from other parties to participate in its primary. That may dilute what the Court believes to be the core of the Libertarian philosophy, but it is no business of the State to tell a political party what its message should be, how it should select its candidates, or how it should form coalitions to ensure electoral success.

Second, the majority expresses concern that crossover voting may create voter confusion. This paternalistic concern is belied by the District Court's finding that no significant voter confusion would occur.

Third, the majority suggests that crossover voting will impair the State's interest in properly classifying candidates and voters. As an empirical matter, a crossover voter may have a lesser commitment to the party with which he is registered if he votes in another party's primary. Nevertheless, the State does not have a valid interest in defining what it means to be a Republican or a Democrat, or in attempting to ensure the political orthodoxy of party members simply for the convenience of those parties. Even if participation in the LPO's primary causes a voter to be a less committed "Democrat" or "Republican" (a proposition I reject), the dilution of that commitment does not justify abridgment of the fundamental rights at issue in this case. While party identity is important in our political system, it should not be immunized from the risk of change.

Fourth, the majority argues that opening up the LPO primary to members of the Republican and Democratic parties might interfere with electioneering and party-building efforts. It is clear, of course, that the majority here is concerned only with the Democratic and Republican parties, since party building is precisely what the LPO is attempting to accomplish. Nevertheless, that concern is misplaced. Even if, as the majority claims, the Republican and Democratic voter rolls, mailing lists, and phone banks are not as accurate as they would otherwise be, the administrative inconvenience of the major parties does not outweigh the right to vote or the associational interests of those voters and the LPO. At its core, this argument is based on a fear that the LPO might be successful in convincing Democratic or Republican voters to participate more fully in the LPO. Far from being a compelling interest, it is an impermissible one.

Finally, the majority warns against the possibility of raiding by which voters of another party maliciously vote in a primary in order to change the outcome of the primary, either to nominate a particularly weak candidate, a "sore-loser" candidate, or a candidate who would siphon votes from another party. The District Court, whose factual findings are entitled to substantial deference, found as a factual and legal matter that the State's argument concerning raiding was "unpersuasive."

Even if raiding were a possibility, however, the state interests are remote. The possibility of harm to the LPO itself is insufficient to overcome the LPO's associational rights. If the LPO is willing to take the risk that its party may be "hijacked" by individuals who hold views opposite to their own, the State has little interest in second-guessing the LPO's decision.

With respect to the possibility that Democratic or Republican voters might raid the LPO to the detriment of their own or another party, neither the State nor the majority has identified any evidence that voters are sufficiently organized to achieve such a targeted result. Such speculation is not, in my view, sufficient to override the real and acknowledged interest of the LPO and the voters who wish to participate in its primary.[11]

In the end, the balance of interests clearly favors the LPO and those voters who wish to participate in its primary. The associational interests asserted—the right to select a standard bearer that the party thinks has the best chance of success, the ability to associate at the crucial juncture of selecting a candidate, and the desire

11. The flimsy character of the state interests in this case confirms my view that today's decision rests primarily on a desire to protect the two-party system. In *Jones*, the Court concluded that the associational interests of the parties trumped state interests that were much more compelling than those asserted in this case. Here, by contrast, where the associational interests are being asserted by a minor party rather than by one of the dominant parties, the Court has reversed course and rejected those associational interests as insubstantial compared to the interests asserted by the State.

to reach out to voters of other parties—are substantial and undoubtedly burdened by Oklahoma's statutory scheme. Any doubt about that fact is clearly answered by *Tashjian*. On the other side, the interests asserted by the State are either entirely speculative or simply protectionist measures that benefit the parties in power. No matter what the standard, they simply do not outweigh the interests of the LPO and its voters.

IV

The Libertarian Party of Oklahoma is not the only loser in this litigation. Other minor parties and voters who have primary allegiance to one party but sometimes switch their support to rival candidates are also harmed by this decision. In my judgment, however, the real losers include all participants in the political market. Decisions that give undue deference to the interest in preserving the two-party system, like decisions that encourage partisan gerrymandering, enhance the likelihood that so-called "safe districts" will play an increasingly predominant role in the electoral process. Primary elections are already replacing general elections as the most common method of actually determining the composition of our legislative bodies. The trend can only increase the bitter partisanship that has already poisoned some of those bodies that once provided inspiring examples of courteous adversary debate and deliberation.

The decision in this case, like the misguided decisions in *Timmons* and *Jones*, attaches overriding importance to the interest in preserving the two-party system. In my view, there is over a century of experience demonstrating that the two major parties are fully capable of maintaining their own positions of dominance in the political marketplace without any special assistance from the state governments that they dominate or from this Court. Whenever they receive special advantages, the offsetting harm to independent voters may be far more significant than the majority recognizes.

Because the Court's holding today has little to support it other than a naked interest in protecting the two major parties, I respectfully dissent.

NOTES ON *CLINGMAN*

1. Is *Clingman* distinguishable from *Tashjian*? Note that the majority in *Clingman* strongly suggests that *Tashjian* was incorrect, but it still attempts to distinguish rather than overrule *Tashjian*.

2. Justice Thomas states, "[t]o deem ordinary and widespread burdens like these severe would subject virtually every electoral regulation to strict scrutiny, hamper the ability of States to run efficient and equitable elections, and compel federal courts to rewrite state electoral codes." Subsequent courts have relied heavily on this statement to uphold state election regulations. Is he going too far? Is he giving states too much power to regulate the electoral process? Or is he correct that states need wide leeway in running elections and that applying strict scrutiny would entail too much judicial oversight?

3. What do the different opinions suggest about the role of the major political parties versus minor political parties? Is there a thumb on the scale in favor of the Republican and Democratic parties? If so, is this acceptable?

4. What does Justice O'Connor's opinion suggest about the proper way to craft a challenge to a state's election rules? In 2007, the Oklahoma Court of Appeals rejected the LPO's challenge to Oklahoma's ballot access rules that require an "unrecognized" political party to obtain signatures of at least 5 percent of the total votes cast in the previous general election by May 31 of an election year. The court found that the laws were not "*unreasonably* restrictive, severe, or discriminatory." Libertarian Political Org. of Oklahoma v. Clingman, 162 P.3d 948 (Okl. Ct. Civ. App.2007).

D. THE GENERAL ELECTION BALLOT

In the cases that we have read so far in Part II of this book, the disputes have concerned the rules governing primary elections—and the consequences of those rules for the placement of a candidate's name on the general election ballot. The next set of cases in Part II cover disputes over the rules for the general election ballot.

We first consider "independent" candidates on the general election ballot who are not affiliated with any political party. Although the focus of presidential elections is typically on the Democratic and Republican nominees, most years there are also independent or third-party candidates on the general election ballot. What rules govern ballot access for these candidates? That is, to what extent can a state limit ballot access for independent candidates in an effort to ward off "sore loser" candidacies for those candidates who embark on the political primary process, see the writing on the wall that they will not secure the party's nomination, and decide to mount an independent candidacy? The next case considers these questions—and provides a framework for analyzing future ballot access and right-to-vote cases. Pay particular attention to the balancing test that Justice Stevens announces in this case.

Anderson v. Celebrezze

460 U.S. 780 (1983)

Justice STEVENS delivered the opinion of the Court.

On April 24, 1980, petitioner John Anderson announced that he was an independent candidate for the office of President of the United States. Thereafter, his supporters—by gathering the signatures of registered voters, filing required documents, and submitting filing fees—were able to meet the substantive requirements for having his name placed on the ballot for the general election in November 1980 in all 50 States and the District of Columbia. On April 24, however, it was already too late for Anderson to qualify for a position on the ballot in Ohio and certain other states because the statutory deadlines for filing a statement of candidacy had already passed. The question presented by this case is whether Ohio's early filing deadline placed an unconstitutional burden on the voting and associational rights of Anderson's supporters.

The facts are not in dispute. On May 16, 1980, Anderson's supporters tendered a nominating petition containing approximately 14,500 signatures and a statement of candidacy to respondent Celebrezze, the Ohio Secretary of State. These documents would have entitled Anderson to a place on the ballot if they had been filed on or before March 20, 1980. Respondent refused to accept the petition solely because it had not been filed within the time required by §3513.257 of the Ohio Revised Code. Three days later Anderson and three voters, two registered in Ohio and one in New Jersey, commenced this action in the United States District Court for the Southern District of Ohio, challenging the constitutionality of Ohio's early filing deadline for independent candidates. The District Court granted petitioners' motion for summary judgment and ordered respondent to place Anderson's name on the general election ballot.

The Secretary of State promptly appealed and unsuccessfully requested expedited review in both the Court of Appeals and this Court, but apparently did not seek to stay the District Court's order. The election was held while the appeal was pending. In Ohio Anderson received 254,472 votes, or 5.9 percent of the votes cast; nationally, he received 5,720,060 votes or approximately 6.6 percent of the total.

The Court of Appeals reversed. It held that Ohio's early deadline "ensures that voters making the important choice of their next president have the opportunity for a careful look at the candidates, a chance to see how they withstand the close scrutiny of a political campaign."

In other litigation brought by Anderson challenging early filing deadlines in Maine and Maryland, the Courts of Appeals for the First and Fourth Circuits affirmed District Court judgments ordering Anderson's name placed on the ballot. The conflict among the Circuits on an important question of constitutional law led us to grant certiorari. We now reverse.

I

After a date toward the end of March, even if intervening events create unanticipated political opportunities, no independent candidate may enter the Presidential race and seek to place his name on the Ohio general election ballot. Thus the direct impact of Ohio's early filing deadline falls upon aspirants for office. Nevertheless, as we have recognized, "the rights of voters and the rights of candidates do not lend themselves to neat separation; laws that affect candidates always have at least some theoretical, correlative effect on voters." *Bullock v. Carter* (1972). Our primary concern is with the tendency of ballot access restrictions "to limit the field of candidates from which voters might choose." Therefore, "[i]n approaching candidate restrictions, it is essential to examine in a realistic light the extent and nature of their impact on voters."

Although [the] rights of voters are fundamental, not all restrictions imposed by the States on candidates' eligibility for the ballot impose constitutionally-suspect burdens on voters' rights to associate or to choose among candidates. We have recognized that, "as a practical matter, there must be a substantial regulation of elections if they are to be fair and honest and if some sort of order, rather than chaos, is to accompany the democratic processes." *Storer v. Brown* (1974). To achieve these necessary objectives, States have enacted comprehensive and sometimes complex election codes. Each provision of these schemes, whether it governs the registration and qualifications of voters, the selection and eligibility of candidates, or the voting process itself, inevitably affects — at least to some degree — the individual's right to vote and his right to associate with others for political ends. Nevertheless, the state's important regulatory interests are generally sufficient to justify reasonable, nondiscriminatory restrictions.[9]

Constitutional challenges to specific provisions of a State's election laws therefore cannot be resolved by any "litmus-paper test" that will separate valid from invalid restrictions. Instead, a court must resolve such a challenge by an analytical process that parallels its work in ordinary litigation. It must first consider the character and magnitude of the asserted injury to the rights protected by the First and Fourteenth Amendments that the plaintiff seeks to vindicate. It then must identify and evaluate the precise interests put forward by the State as justifications for the burden imposed by its rule. In passing judgment, the Court must not only determine the legitimacy and strength of each of those interests; it also must consider the extent to which those interests make it necessary to burden the plaintiff's rights. Only after weighing all these factors is the reviewing court in a position to decide whether the challenged provision is unconstitutional. The results of this evaluation will not be automatic; as we have recognized, there is "no substitute for the hard judgments that must be made." *Storer v. Brown.**

II

An early filing deadline may have a substantial impact on independent-minded voters. In election campaigns, particularly those which are national in scope, the candidates and the issues simply do not remain static over time. Various candidates rise and fall in popularity; domestic and international developments bring new issues to center stage and may affect voters' assessments of national problems. Such developments will certainly affect the strategies of candidates who have already entered the race; they may also create opportunities for new candidacies. Yet Ohio's filing deadline prevents persons who wish to be independent candidates from entering the significant political arena established in the State by a Presidential election campaign — and creating new political coalitions of Ohio voters — at any time after mid-to-late March. At this point developments in campaigns for the major-party nominations have only begun, and the major parties will not adopt their nominees and platforms for another five months. Candidates and supporters within the major parties thus have the political advantage of continued flexibility; for independents, the inflexibility imposed by the March filing deadline is a correlative disadvantage because of the competitive nature of the electoral process.

9. We have upheld generally-applicable and evenhanded restrictions that protect the integrity and reliability of the electoral process itself. The State has the undoubted right to require candidates to make a preliminary showing of substantial support in order to qualify for a place on the ballot, because it is both wasteful and confusing to encumber the ballot with the names of frivolous candidates.

* [We encourage you to re-read this paragraph, as it provides an important balancing test used in future cases. — EDS.]

If the State's filing deadline were later in the year, a newly-emergent independent candidate could serve as the focal point for a grouping of Ohio voters who decide, after mid-March, that they are dissatisfied with the choices within the two major parties. As we recognized in *Williams v. Rhodes* (1968), "Since the principal policies of the major parties change to some extent from year to year, and since the identity of the likely major party nominees may not be known until shortly before the election, this disaffected 'group' will rarely if ever be a cohesive or identifiable group until a few months before the election." Indeed, several important third-party candidacies in American history were launched after the two major parties staked out their positions and selected their nominees at national conventions during the summer. But under [Ohio law], a late-emerging Presidential candidate outside the major parties, whose positions on the issues could command widespread community support, is excluded from the Ohio general election ballot. The "Ohio system thus denies the 'disaffected' not only a choice of leadership but a choice on the issues as well." *Williams v. Rhodes.*

Not only does the challenged Ohio statute totally exclude any candidate who makes the decision to run for President as an independent after the March deadline. It also burdens the signature-gathering efforts of independents who decide to run in time to meet the deadline. When the primary campaigns are far in the future and the election itself is even more remote, the obstacles facing an independent candidate's organizing efforts are compounded. Volunteers are more difficult to recruit and retain, media publicity and campaign contributions are more difficult to secure, and voters are less interested in the campaign.

It is clear, then, that the March filing deadline places a particular burden on an identifiable segment of Ohio's independent-minded voters. As our cases have held, it is especially difficult for the State to justify a restriction that limits political participation by an identifiable political group whose members share a particular viewpoint, associational preference, or economic status.

A burden that falls unequally on new or small political parties or on independent candidates impinges, by its very nature, on associational choices protected by the First Amendment. It discriminates against those candidates and—of particular importance—against those voters whose political preferences lie outside the existing political parties. By limiting the opportunities of independent-minded voters to associate in the electoral arena to enhance their political effectiveness as a group, such restrictions threaten to reduce diversity and competition in the marketplace of ideas. Historically political figures outside the two major parties have been fertile sources of new ideas and new programs; many of their challenges to the status quo have in time made their way into the political mainstream. In short, the primary values protected by the First Amendment—"a profound national commitment to the principle that debate on public issues should be uninhibited, robust, and wide-open," *New York Times Co. v. Sullivan*—are served when election campaigns are not monopolized by the existing political parties.

Furthermore, in the context of a Presidential election, state-imposed restrictions implicate a uniquely important national interest. For the President and the Vice President of the United States are the only elected officials who represent all the voters in the Nation. Moreover, the impact of the votes cast in each State is affected by the votes cast for the various candidates in other States. Thus in a Presidential election a State's enforcement of more stringent ballot access requirements, including filing deadlines, has an impact beyond its own borders.[20] Similarly, the State has a less important interest in regulating Presidential elections than statewide or local elections, because the outcome of the former will be largely determined by voters beyond the State's boundaries. This Court, striking down a state statute unduly restricting the choices made by a major party's Presidential nominating convention, observed that such conventions serve "the pervasive national interest in the selection of candidates for national office, and this national interest is greater than any interest of an individual State." *Cousins v. Wigoda.* The Ohio filing deadline challenged in this case does more than burden the associational rights of independent voters and candidates. It places a significant state-imposed restriction on a nationwide electoral process.

III

The State identifies three separate interests that it seeks to further by its early filing deadline for independent Presidential candidates: voter education, equal treatment for partisan and independent candidates, and political stability. We now examine the legitimacy of these interests and the extent to which the March filing deadline serves them.

Voter Education

There can be no question about the legitimacy of the State's interest in fostering informed and educated expressions of the popular will in a general election. Moreover, the Court of Appeals correctly identified that interest as one of the concerns that motivated the Framers' decision not to provide for direct popular election of the President. We are persuaded, however, that the State's important and legitimate interest in voter education does not justify the specific restriction on participation in a Presidential election that is at issue in this case.

The passage of time since the Constitutional Convention in 1787 has brought about two changes that are relevant to the reasonableness of Ohio's statutory requirement that independents formally declare their candidacy at least seven months in advance of a general election. First, although it took days and often weeks for even the most rudimentary information about important events to be transmitted from one part of the country to another in 1787, today even trivial details about national candidates are instantaneously communicated nationwide in both verbal and visual form. Second, although literacy was far from universal in 18th-century America, today the vast majority of the electorate not only is literate but is informed on a day-to-day basis about events and issues that affect election choices and about the ever-changing popularity of individual candidates. In the modern world it is somewhat unrealistic to suggest that it takes more than seven

20. In approximately two-thirds of the States and the District of Columbia, filing deadlines for independent Presidential candidates occur in August or September. The deadlines in a number of other States are in June or July. Anderson was barred by early filing deadlines in Ohio and four other States; he succeeded in obtaining court orders requiring placement on the ballot in all five.

months to inform the electorate about the qualifications of a particular candidate simply because he lacks a partisan label.

Our cases reflect a greater faith in the ability of individual voters to inform themselves about campaign issues. In *Dunn v. Blumstein* (1972), the Court considered the validity of a Tennessee statute requiring residence in the State for one year and in the county for three months as a prerequisite for registration to vote. The Court held the statute unconstitutional, specifically rejecting the argument that the requirements were justified by the State's interest in voter education.

This reasoning applies with even greater force to a Presidential election, which receives more intense publicity. Nor are we persuaded by the State's assertion that, unless a candidate actually files a formal declaration of candidacy in Ohio by the March deadline, Ohio voters will not realize that they should pay attention to his candidacy. The validity of this asserted interest is undermined by the State's willingness to place major-party nominees on the November ballot even if they never campaigned in Ohio.

It is also by no means self-evident that the interest in voter education is served at all by a requirement that independent candidates must declare their candidacy before the end of March in order to be eligible for a place on the ballot in November. Had the requirement been enforced in Ohio, petitioner Anderson might well have determined that it would be futile for him to allocate any of his time and money to campaigning in that State. The Ohio electorate might thereby have been denied whatever benefits his participation in local debates could have contributed to an understanding of the issues. A State's claim that it is enhancing the ability of its citizenry to make wise decisions by restricting the flow of information to them must be viewed with some skepticism.

Equal Treatment

We also find no merit in the State's claim that the early filing deadline serves the interest of treating all candidates alike. It is true that a candidate participating in a primary election must declare his candidacy on the same date as an independent. But both the burdens and the benefits of the respective requirements are materially different, and the reasons for requiring early filing for a primary candidate are inapplicable to independent candidates in the general election.

The consequences of failing to meet the statutory deadline are entirely different for party primary participants and independents. The name of the nominees of the Democratic and Republican parties will appear on the Ohio ballot in November even if they did not decide to run until after Ohio's March deadline had passed, but the independent is simply denied a position on the ballot if he waits too long.[26] Thus, under Ohio's scheme, the major parties may include all events preceding their national conventions in the calculus that produces their respective nominees and campaign platforms, but the independent's judgment must be based on a history that ends in March.

26. It is true, of course, that Ohio permits "write-in" votes for independents. We have previously noted that this opportunity is not an adequate substitute for having the candidate's name appear on the printed ballot.

The early filing deadline for a candidate in a party's primary election is adequately justified by administrative concerns. Seventy-five days appears to be a reasonable time for processing the documents submitted by candidates and preparing the ballot. The primary date itself must be set sufficiently in advance of the general election; furthermore, a Presidential preference primary must precede the national convention, which is regularly held during the summer. Finally, the successful participant in a party primary generally acquires the automatic support of an experienced political organization; in the Presidential contest he obtains the support of convention delegates.

Neither the administrative justification nor the benefit of an early filing deadline is applicable to an independent candidate. Ohio does not suggest that the March deadline is necessary to allow petition signatures to be counted and verified or to permit November general election ballots to be printed.[28] In addition, the early deadline does not correspond to a potential benefit for the independent, as it does for the party candidate. After filing his statement of candidacy, the independent does not participate in a structured intraparty contest to determine who will receive organizational support; he must develop support by other means. In short, "equal treatment" of partisan and independent candidates simply is not achieved by imposing the March filing deadline on both. As we have written, "[s]ometimes the grossest discrimination can lie in treating things that are different as though they were exactly alike." *Jenness v. Fortson* (1971).

Political Stability

The State's brief explains that the State has a substantial interest in protecting the two major political parties from "damaging intraparty feuding." According to the State, a candidate's decision to abandon efforts to win the party primary and to run as an independent "can be very damaging to state political party structure." Anderson's decision to run as an independent, the State argues, threatened to "splinter" the Ohio Republican party "by drawing away its activists to work in his 'independent' campaign."

Ohio's asserted interest in political stability amounts to a desire to protect existing political parties from competition—competition for campaign workers, voter support, and other campaign resources—generated by independent candidates who have previously been affiliated with the party. Our evaluation of this interest is guided by two of our prior cases, *Williams v. Rhodes* and *Storer v. Brown*.

In *Williams v. Rhodes* we squarely held that protecting the Republican and Democratic parties from external competition cannot justify the virtual exclusion of other political aspirants from the political arena. Thus in *Williams v. Rhodes* we

28. Respondent conceded in the District Court that the nominating petitions filed on March 20 remain unprocessed in his office until June 15, when he transmits them to county boards of election. The boards do not begin to verify the signatures until the period July 1 to July 15. Finally, the Secretary of State does not certify the names of Presidential candidates, including independents, for inclusion on the ballot until late August, after the party nominating conventions. According to the District Court, based on the stipulated facts, it appears that no more than 75 days are necessary to perform these tasks.

concluded that First Amendment values outweighed the State's interest in protecting the two major political parties.

On the other hand, in *Storer v. Brown* we upheld two California statutory provisions that restricted access by independent candidates to the general election ballot. Under California law, a person could not run as an independent in November if he had been defeated in a party primary that year or if he had been registered with a political party within one year prior to that year's primary election. We stated that "California apparently believes with the Founding Fathers that splintered parties and unrestrained factionalism may do significant damage to the fabric of government," and that destruction of "the political stability of the system of the State" could have "profound consequences for the entire citizenry." Further, we approved the State's goals of discouraging "independent candidacies prompted by short-range political goals, pique, or personal quarrel."

Ohio's challenged restriction is substantially different from the California provisions upheld in *Storer*. As we have noted, the early filing deadline does discriminate against independents. And the deadline is neither a "sore loser" provision nor a disaffiliation statute. Furthermore, it is important to recognize that *Storer* upheld the State's interest in avoiding political fragmentation in the context of elections wholly within the boundaries of California. The State's interest in regulating a nationwide Presidential election is not nearly as strong; no State could singlehandedly assure "political stability" in the Presidential context. The Ohio deadline does not serve any state interest in "maintaining the integrity of the various routes to the ballot" for the Presidency, because Ohio's Presidential preference primary does not serve to narrow the field for the general election. A major party candidate who loses the Ohio primary, or who does not even run in Ohio, may nonetheless appear on the November general election ballot as the party's nominee. In addition, the national scope of the competition for delegates at the Presidential nominating conventions assures that "intraparty feuding" will continue until August.

More generally, the early filing deadline is not precisely drawn to protect the parties from "intraparty feuding," whatever legitimacy that state goal may have in a Presidential election. If the deadline is designed to keep intraparty competition within the party structure, its coverage is both too broad and too narrow. It is true that in this case §3513.257 was applied to a candidate who had previously competed in party primaries and then sought to run as an independent. But the early deadline applies broadly to independent candidates who have not been affiliated in the recent past with any political party. On the other hand, as long as the decision to run is made before the March deadline, Ohio does not prohibit independent candidacies by persons formerly affiliated with a political party, or currently participating in intraparty competition in other States—regardless of the effect on the political party structure.

We conclude that Ohio's March filing deadline for independent candidates for the office of President of the United States cannot be justified by the State's asserted interest in protecting political stability.

IV

We began our inquiry by noting that our primary concern is not the interest of candidate Anderson, but rather, the interests of the voters who chose to associate together to express their support for Anderson's candidacy and the views he espoused. Under any realistic appraisal, the "extent and nature" of the burdens Ohio has placed on the voters' freedom of choice and freedom of association, in an election of nationwide importance, unquestionably outweigh the State's minimal interest in imposing a March deadline.

The judgment of the Court of Appeals is *Reversed.*

Justice REHNQUIST, with whom Justice WHITE, Justice POWELL, and Justice O'CONNOR join, dissenting.

Article II of the Constitution provides that "[e]ach State shall appoint, in such Manner as the Legislature thereof may direct, a Number of Electors" who shall select the President of the United States. U.S. Const., art. II, §1, cl. 2. This provision, one of few in the Constitution that grants an express plenary power to the States, conveys "the broadest power of determination" and "[i]t recognizes that [in the election of a President] the people act through their representatives in the legislature, and *leaves it to the legislature exclusively to define the method of effecting the object.*"

In exercising this power, the Ohio legislature has provided alternative routes to its general election ballot for capture of Ohio's Presidential electoral votes. *Political parties* can earn the right to field a Presidential candidate in the general election in one of two ways. Parties that obtained at least 5% of the vote in the preceding gubernatorial or Presidential election are automatically entitled to have a candidate on the general election ballot. Other political parties are required to file 120 days before the primary election (in 1980 the date was February 4) a statement of intent to participate in the primary, together with petitions containing signatures of voters equal to 1% of the votes cast in the last gubernatorial or Presidential election (in 1980 approximately 28,000 signatures would have been required).

Ohio also offers *candidates* different routes to the general election ballot. Should a candidate decide to seek the nomination of a political party participating in Ohio's primary election by capturing delegate votes for the party's national convention, the candidate must file a declaration of candidacy and a nominating petition bearing signatures from 1,000 members of the party; the filing must occur no later than the 75th day before the first Tuesday after the first Monday in June of the election year (in 1980 the date was March 20). Of course, because a political party has earned the right to put on the ballot a candidate chosen at its national convention, a candidate seeking the nomination of that party could forgo the Ohio primary process and, if he should win at the national convention, still be placed on the ballot as a party candidate. If a candidate chooses to run as a nonparty candidate, he must file, by the same date as a party candidate participating in the primary, a statement of candidacy and a nominating petition bearing the signatures of 5,000 qualified voters. Since a nonparty candidate does not participate in a national convention, obviously he cannot benefit from the routes made available to political parties.

Today the Court holds that the filing deadline for nonparty candidates in this statutory scheme violated the First Amendment rights of 1980 Presidential hopeful John Anderson and Anderson's supporters. Certainly, absent a court injunction ordering that his name be placed on the ballot, Anderson and his supporters would have been injured by Ohio's ballot access requirements; by failing to comply with the filing deadline for nonparty candidates Anderson would have been excluded from Ohio's 1980 general election ballot.[1] But the Constitution does not require that a State allow any particular Presidential candidate to be on its ballot, and so long as the Ohio ballot access laws are rational and allow nonparty candidates reasonable access to the general election ballot, this Court should not interfere with Ohio's exercise of its Article II, §1, cl. 2 power. Since I believe that the Ohio laws meet these criteria, I dissent.

On the record before us, the effect of the Ohio filing deadline is quite easily summarized: it requires that a candidate, who has already decided to run for President, decide by March 20 which route his candidacy will take. He can become a nonparty candidate by filing a nominating petition with 5,000 signatures and assure himself a place on the general election ballot. Or, he can become a party candidate and take his chances in securing a position on the general election ballot by seeking the nomination of a party's national convention. Anderson chose the latter route and submitted in a timely fashion his nominating petition for Ohio's Republican Primary. Then, realizing that he had no chance for the Republican nomination, Anderson sought to change the form of this candidacy. The Ohio filing deadline prevented him from making this change. Quite clearly, rather than prohibiting him from seeking the Presidency, the filing deadline only prevented Anderson from having two shots at it in the same election year.

Refusing to own up to the conflict its opinion creates with *Storer*, the Court tries to distinguish it[.] "Ohio's asserted interest in political stability," says the Court, "amounts to a desire to protect existing political parties from competition." But this simply is not the case. The Ohio filing deadline in no way makes it "virtually impossible" for new parties or nonparty candidates to secure a position on the general election ballot. It does require early decisions. But once a decision is made, there is no claim that the additional requirements for new parties and nonparty candidates are too burdensome. In fact, past experience has shown otherwise. What the Ohio filing deadline prevents is a candidate such as Anderson from seeking a party nomination and then, finding that he is rejected by the party, bolting from the party to form an independent candidacy. This is precisely the same behavior that California sought to prevent by the disaffiliation statute this Court upheld in *Storer*.

The Court makes other attempts to distinguish this case from the obviously similar *Storer* case. The Court says Ohio has no interest in preventing "intraparty feuding" because by the nature of the Presidential nominating conventions " 'intraparty feuding' will continue until August."[4] This is certainly no different than the

1. Anderson would not have been totally excluded from participating in the general election since Ohio allows for "write-in" candidacies. The Court suggests, however, that this is of no relevance because a write-in procedure "is not an adequate substitute for having the candidate's name appear on the printed ballot." Until today the Court had not squarely so held and in fact in earlier decisions the Court had treated the availability of write-in candidacies as quite relevant. *See Storer v. Brown*.

4. The Court seeks comfort from the idea that the filing deadline is not a "sore loser" statute which prevents a candidate who is defeated in a primary from running as an independent candidate. But the effect of the deadline in this case is much the same. Under the Court's approach, so long as a candidate pulls out of his party race before the votes of the party are counted, he must be recognized as a "newly-emergent independent candidate" whose candidacy is created by a dramatic change in national events. To the contrary, I submit that such a candidate is no more than a "sore loser" who ducked out before putting his popularity to the vote of his party.

situation in *Storer.* Essentially all of the battles for party nominations in California would have taken place during the 12 months before the party primaries; the period during which an independent candidate had to be disaffiliated with any party.

The Court further notes that "*Storer* upheld the State's interest in avoiding political fragmentation in the context of elections wholly within the boundaries of California. The State's interest in regulating a nationwide Presidential election is not nearly as strong." The Court's characterization of the election simply is incorrect. The Ohio general election in 1980, among other things, was for the appointment of Ohio's representatives to the Electoral College. U.S. Const., art. II, §1, cl. 2. The Court throughout its opinion fails to come to grips with this fact. While Ohio may have a lesser interest in who is ultimately selected by the Electoral College, its interest in who is supported by its own Presidential electors must be at least as strong as its interest in electing other representatives. While the Presidential electors may serve a short term and may speak only one time on behalf of the voters they represent, their role in casting Ohio's electoral votes for a President may be second to none in importance.

The point the Court misses is that in cases like this and *Storer,* we have never required that States meet some kind of "narrowly tailored" standard in order to pass constitutional muster. In reviewing election laws like Ohio's filing deadline, we have said before that a court's job is to ensure that the State "in no way freezes the status quo, but implicitly recognizes the potential fluidity of American political life." *Jenness v. Fortson.* If it does not freeze the status quo, then the State's laws will be upheld if they are "tied to a particularized legitimate purpose, and [are] in no sense invidious or arbitrary." *Rosario v. Rockefeller.* The Court tries to avoid the rules set forth in some of these cases, saying that such rules were "applicable only to party primaries" and that "this case involves restrictions on access to the general election ballot." The fallacy in this reasoning is quite apparent: one cannot restrict access to the primary ballot without also restricting access to the general election ballot. As the Court said in *Storer v. Brown*: "The direct party primary in California is not merely an exercise or warm-up for the general election but an integral part of the entire election process, the initial stage in a two-stage process by which the people choose their public officers. It functions to winnow out and finally reject all but the chosen candidates."

The Ohio filing deadline easily meets the test described above. In the interest of the "stability of its political system," Ohio must be "free to assure itself that [a nonparty] candidate is a serious contender, *truly independent,* and with a satisfactory level of community support." *Storer v. Brown.* This interest alone is sufficient to support Ohio ballot access laws which require that candidates for Presidential electors choose their route early, thus preventing a person who has decided to run for a party nomination from switching to a nonparty candidacy after he discovers that he is not the favorite of his party. But this is not the only interest furthered by Ohio's laws.

Ohio maintains that requiring an early declaration of candidacy gives its voters a better opportunity to take a careful look at the candidates and see how they withstand the close scrutiny of a political campaign. The Court does not dispute the legitimacy of this interest. But the Court finds that "the State's important and legitimate interest in voter education does not justify the specific restriction on participation in a Presidential election that is at issue in this case." The Court explains that "[i]n the modern world it is somewhat unrealistic to suggest that it takes more than seven months to inform the electorate about the qualifications of a particular candidate. . . . Our cases reflect a greater faith in the ability of individual voters to inform themselves about campaign issues."

I cannot agree with the suggestion that the early deadline reflects a lack of "faith" in the voters. That Ohio wants to give its voters as much time as possible to gather information on the potential candidates would seem to lead to the contrary conclusion. There is nothing improper about wanting as much time as possible in which to evaluate all available information when making an important decision. Besides, the Court's assertion that it does not take seven months to inform the electorate is difficult to explain in light of the fact that Anderson allowed himself some 19 months to complete this task; and we are all well aware that Anderson's decision to make an early go of it is not atypical.

Ohio also has an interest in assisting its citizens in apportioning their resources among various candidates running for the Presidency. The supply of resources needed for operating a political campaign is limited; this is especially true of two of the most important commodities, money and volunteers. By doing its best to present the field of candidates by Spring, right at the time that campaigns begin to intensify, Ohio allows those of its citizens who want to provide support other than voting adequate time to decide how to divide up that support. While the Court does not give attention to this interest, it is certainly a legitimate one and an important one in terms of the effective campaigning of Presidential candidates.

The Court's decision in this case is not necessary for the protection of like-minded voters who want to support an independent candidate; Ohio laws already protect such voters. This case presents a completely different story. John Anderson decided some 19 months before the 1980 general election to run for President. He decided to run as a Republican Party candidate. When Anderson sought to get on the Ohio ballot after the March 20 deadline, he was not a "newly-emergent independent candidate" whose candidacy had been created by dramatic changes in the election campaign. He was a party candidate who saw impending rejection by his party and rather than throw his support to the party's candidate or some other existing candidacy, Anderson wanted to bolt and have a second try.

The Court's opinion protects this particular kind of candidate—an individual who decides well in advance to become a Presidential candidate, decides which route to follow in seeking a position on the general election ballot, and, after seeing his hopes turn to ashes, wants to try another route. The Court's opinion draws no line; I presume that a State must wait until all party nominees are chosen and then allow all unsuccessful party candidates to refight their party battles by forming an "independent" candidacy. I find nothing in the Constitution which requires this result. For this reason I would affirm the judgment of the Court of Appeals.

NOTES ON *ANDERSON*

1. *Anderson* presents the initial "balancing of interests" framework that, along with *Burdick v. Takushi* (presented next), eventually became known as the "severe burden" test. This was one of the first indications that laws restricting voting rights would not necessarily require strict scrutiny review.

2. Note that the Court construes the plaintiffs' claims as challenging the law's impact on voters, even though the law does not regulate voters directly. Are laws impacting candidates tantamount to laws burdening voters? We will consider later whether there is a constitutional right to be a candidate, separate from the rights of voters who may support that candidate.

3. Justice Stevens discusses the "practical difficulties" independent candidates face, particularly in gathering signatures and seeking money early in the campaign season. Justice Rehnquist responds that Anderson himself did not actually face any problems because he was able to obtain the signatures and finance a robust campaign. To what extent should the practical realities of the situation before the Court play into the analysis? Is it more important to consider the facts of that case, the rule to apply in the future, or the theoretical underpinnings of the analysis? In some ways this debate foreshadows the discussion of facial and as-applied challenges in more recent cases such as *Washington State Grange* (presented earlier in this Part) and *Crawford v. Marion County Election Board* (presented in Part IV of this book).

4. Justice Stevens categorizes the state interests as voter education, equal treatment between candidates, and political stability. Are these legitimate state interests? If so, why does Justice Stevens strike down the law? How is the early filing deadline tailored to these interests?

5. Is Justice Stevens' opinion faithful to the constitutional grant of authority to states to determine how to choose their presidential electors? Justice Rehnquist focuses his dissent on this constitutional provision; Justice Stevens largely ignores it.

6. Note also how Justice Rehnquist construes the early filing deadline: it primarily serves as a sore loser law. Is that true?

E. CANDIDATE *v.* STATE: THE PURPOSE OF THE BALLOT

Anderson gave us a "balancing of the interests" test for construing constitutional challenges to rules on candidate access to the ballot and, in turn, challenges involving the constitutional right to vote. We next examine two U.S. Supreme Court cases that refine the framework for analyzing ballot access cases: The first of these two cases involves a state's prohibition against "write-in" candidates, while the second involves the desire of candidates to be listed on the ballot as the nominee of more than one political party. In both cases, the state prevails against the claim that these laws governing the content of the state's general election ballot violate the First Amendment rights of candidates and their supporters. As you read these cases, consider the purpose of the ballot. Does a ballot have a First Amendment expressive component or is it just a utilitarian method of selecting a winner? In addition, do these ballot access rules contribute to the fact that third party candidates rarely win? To what extent are these ballot access rules simply mechanisms—supported by the Democratic and Republican Parties—to sustain the two-party system and entrench themselves in power? Should the Court uphold as constitutional a ballot access rule that has, as its purpose, the preservation of the two-party system? Finally, pay attention to how *Burdick v. Takushi* refined the standard from *Anderson v. Celebrezze* into a two-part judicial test for analyzing burdens on the constitutional right to vote (and the rights of voters to support candidates of their choosing).

Burdick v. Takushi

504 U.S. 428 (1992)

Justice WHITE delivered the opinion of the Court.

The issue in this case is whether Hawaii's prohibition on write-in voting unreasonably infringes upon its citizens' rights under the First and Fourteenth Amendments. Petitioner contends that the Constitution requires Hawaii to provide for the casting, tabulation, and publication of write-in votes. The Court of Appeals for the Ninth Circuit disagreed, holding that the prohibition, taken as part of the State's comprehensive election scheme, does not impermissibly burden the right to vote. We affirm.

I

[Omitted.]

II

Petitioner proceeds from the erroneous assumption that a law that imposes any burden upon the right to vote must be subject to strict scrutiny. Our cases do not so hold.

It is beyond cavil that "voting is of the most fundamental significance under our constitutional structure." *Illinois Bd. of Elections v. Socialist Workers Party* (1979). It does not follow, however, that the right to vote in any manner and the right to associate for political purposes through the ballot are absolute. The Constitution provides that States may prescribe "[t]he Times, Places and Manner of holding Elections for Senators and Representatives," Art. I, §4, cl. 1, and the Court therefore has recognized that States retain the power to regulate their own elections. Common sense, as well as constitutional law, compels the conclusion that government must play an active role in structuring elections; "as a practical matter, there must be a substantial regulation of elections if they are to be fair and honest and if some sort of order, rather than chaos, is to accompany the democratic processes." *Storer v. Brown* (1974).

Election laws will invariably impose some burden upon individual voters. Each provision of a code, "whether it governs the registration and qualifications of voters, the selection and eligibility of candidates, or the voting process itself, inevitably affects—at least to some degree—the individual's right to vote and his right to associate with others for political ends." *Anderson v. Celebrezze* (1983). Consequently, to subject every voting regulation to strict scrutiny and to require that the regulation be narrowly tailored to advance a compelling state interest, as petitioner suggests, would tie the hands of States seeking to assure that elections are operated equitably and efficiently. Accordingly, the mere fact that a State's system "creates barriers . . . tending to limit the field of candidates from which voters might choose . . . does not of itself compel close scrutiny." *Bullock v. Carter* (1972).

Instead, as the full Court agreed in *Anderson*, a more flexible standard applies. A court considering a challenge to a state election law must weigh "the character and magnitude of the asserted injury to the rights protected by the First and Fourteenth Amendments that the plaintiff seeks to vindicate" against "the precise interests put forward by the State as justifications for the burden imposed by its rule," taking into consideration "the extent to which those interests make it necessary to burden the plaintiff's rights."

Under this standard, the rigorousness of our inquiry into the propriety of a state election law depends upon the extent to which a challenged regulation burdens First and Fourteenth Amendment rights. Thus, as we have recognized when those rights are subjected to "severe" restrictions, the regulation must be "narrowly drawn to advance a state interest of compelling importance." *Norman v. Reed* (1992). But when a state election law provision imposes only "reasonable, nondiscriminatory restrictions" upon the First and Fourteenth Amendment rights of voters, "the State's important regulatory interests are generally sufficient to justify" the restrictions.*

A

There is no doubt that the Hawaii election laws, like all election regulations, have an impact on the right to vote, but it can hardly be said that the laws at issue here unconstitutionally limit access to the ballot by party or independent candidates or unreasonably interfere with the right of voters to associate and have candidates of their choice placed on the ballot. Indeed, petitioner understandably does not challenge the manner in which the State regulates candidate access to the ballot.

To obtain a position on the November general election ballot, a candidate must participate in Hawaii's open primary, in which all registered voters may choose in which party primary to vote. The State provides three mechanisms through which a voter's candidate-of-choice may appear on the primary ballot.

[The Court discussed the three mechanisms, which included filing a party petition with enough signatures for new parties, filing nominating papers for candidates for "established" parties, and appearing on the designated nonpartisan ballot and receiving 10 percent of the primary vote to advance to the general election.]

Although Hawaii makes no provision for write-in voting in its primary or general elections, the system outlined above provides for easy access to the ballot until the cutoff date for the filing of nominating petitions, two months before the primary. Consequently, any burden on voters' freedom of choice and association is borne only by those who fail to identify their candidate of choice until days before the primary.

Because he has characterized this as a voting rights rather than ballot access case, petitioner submits that the write-in prohibition deprives him of the

* [We encourage you to re-read these paragraphs, as they form the basis of the crucial *Anderson-Burdick* test still used for the constitutional right to vote.—Eds.]

opportunity to cast a meaningful ballot, conditions his electoral participation upon the waiver of his First Amendment right to remain free from espousing positions that he does not support, and discriminates against him based on the content of the message he seeks to convey through his vote. At bottom, he claims that he is entitled to cast and Hawaii required to count a "protest vote" for Donald Duck, and that any impediment to this asserted "right" is unconstitutional.

Petitioner's argument is based on two flawed premises. First, in *Bullock v. Carter*, we minimized the extent to which voting rights cases are distinguishable from ballot access cases, stating that "the rights of voters and the rights of candidates do not lend themselves to neat separation." Second, the function of the election process is "to winnow out and finally reject all but the chosen candidates," not to provide a means of giving vent to "short-range political goals, pique, or personal quarrel[s]." *Storer.* Attributing to elections a more generalized expressive function would undermine the ability of States to operate elections fairly and efficiently.

Accordingly, we have repeatedly upheld reasonable, politically neutral regulations that have the effect of channeling expressive activity at the polls. Petitioner offers no persuasive reason to depart from these precedents. Reasonable regulation of elections *does not* require voters to espouse positions that they do not support; it *does* require them to act in a timely fashion if they wish to express their views in the voting booth. And there is nothing content based about a flat ban on all forms of write-in ballots.

The appropriate standard for evaluating a claim that a state law burdens the right to vote is set forth in *Anderson.* Applying that standard, we conclude that, in light of the adequate ballot access afforded under Hawaii's election code, the State's ban on write-in voting imposes only a limited burden on voters' rights to make free choices and to associate politically through the vote.

B

We turn next to the interests asserted by Hawaii to justify the burden imposed by its prohibition of write-in voting. Because we have already concluded that the burden is slight, the State need not establish a compelling interest to tip the constitutional scales in its direction. Here, the State's interests outweigh petitioner's limited interest in waiting until the eleventh hour to choose his preferred candidate.

Hawaii's interest in "avoid[ing] the possibility of unrestrained factionalism at the general election," *Munro v. Socialist Workers Party* (1986), provides adequate justification for its ban on write-in voting in November. The primary election is "an integral part of the entire election process," and the State is within its rights to reserve "[t]he general election ballot . . . for major struggles . . . [and] not a forum for continuing intraparty feuds." *Storer.* The prohibition on write-in voting is a legitimate means of averting divisive sore-loser candidacies. Hawaii further promotes the two-stage, primary-general election process of winnowing out candidates by permitting the unopposed victors in certain primaries to be designated office-holders. This focuses the attention of voters upon contested races in the general election. This would not be possible, absent the write-in voting ban.

Hawaii also asserts that its ban on write-in voting at the primary stage is necessary to guard against "party raiding." *Tashjian.* Party raiding is generally defined as "the organized switching of blocs of voters from one party to another in order to manipulate the outcome of the other party's primary election." *Anderson.* Petitioner suggests that, because Hawaii conducts an open primary, this is not a cognizable interest. We disagree. While voters may vote on any ticket in Hawaii's primary, the State requires that party candidates be "member[s] of the party," and prohibits candidates from filing "nomination papers both as a party candidate and as a nonpartisan candidate." Hawaii's system could easily be circumvented in a party primary election by mounting a write-in campaign for a person who had not filed in time or who had never intended to run for election. It could also be frustrated at the general election by permitting write-in votes for a loser in a party primary or for an independent who had failed to get sufficient votes to make the general election ballot. The State has a legitimate interest in preventing these sorts of maneuvers, and the write-in voting ban is a reasonable way of accomplishing this goal.

We think these legitimate interests asserted by the State are sufficient to outweigh the limited burden that the write-in voting ban imposes upon Hawaii's voters.

III

[Omitted.]

Justice KENNEDY, with whom Justice BLACKMUN and Justice STEVENS join, dissenting.

The record demonstrates the significant burden that Hawaii's write-in ban imposes on the right of voters such as petitioner to vote for the candidates of their choice. In the election that triggered this lawsuit, petitioner did not wish to vote for the one candidate who ran for state representative in his district. Because he could not write in the name of a candidate he preferred, he had no way to cast a meaningful vote. Petitioner's dilemma is a recurring, frequent phenomenon in Hawaii because of the State's ballot access rules and the circumstance that one party, the Democratic Party, is predominant. It is critical to understand that petitioner's case is not an isolated example of a restriction on the free choice of candidates. The very ballot access rules the Court cites as mitigating his injury in fact compound it system wide.

The majority suggests that it is easy for new parties to petition for a place on the primary ballot because they must obtain the signatures of only one percent of the State's registered voters. This ignores the difficulty presented by the early deadline for gathering these signatures: 150 days (5 months) before the primary election. Meeting this deadline requires considerable organization at an early stage in the election, a condition difficult for many small parties to meet.

If the party petition is unsuccessful or not completed in time, or if a candidate does not wish to be affiliated with a party, he may run as an independent. While the requirements to get on the nonpartisan ballot are not onerous (15 to 25 signatures, 60 days before the primary), the non-partisan ballot presents voters with a difficult choice. This is because each primary voter can choose only a single ballot for all offices. Hence, a voter who wishes to vote for an independent candidate for one office must forgo the opportunity to vote in an established party primary in every other race. Since there might be no independent candidates for most of the other offices, in practical terms the voter who wants to vote for one independent candidate forfeits the right to participate in the selection of candidates for all other offices. This rule, the very ballot access rule that the Court finds to be curative, in fact presents a substantial disincentive for voters to select the nonpartisan ballot. A voter who wishes to vote for a third-party candidate for only one particular office faces a similar disincentive to select the third party's ballot.

The dominance of the Democratic Party magnifies the disincentive because the primary election is dispositive in so many races. In effect, a Hawaii voter who wishes to vote for any independent candidate must choose between doing so and participating in what will be the dispositive election for many offices. This dilemma imposes a substantial burden on voter choice. It explains also why so few independent candidates secure enough primary votes to advance to the general election. As the majority notes, only eight independent candidates have succeeded in advancing to the general election in the past 10 years. That is, less than one independent candidate per year on average has in fact run in a general election in Hawaii.

Aside from constraints related to ballot access restrictions, the write-in ban limits voter choice in another way. Write-in voting can serve as an important safety mechanism in those instances where a late-developing issue arises or where new information is disclosed about a candidate late in the race. In these situations, voters may become disenchanted with the available candidates when it is too late for other candidates to come forward and qualify for the ballot. The prohibition on write-in voting imposes a significant burden on voters, forcing them either to vote for a candidate whom they no longer support or to cast a blank ballot. Write-in voting provides a way out of the quandary, allowing voters to switch their support to candidates who are not on the official ballot. Even if there are other mechanisms to address the problem of late-breaking election developments (unsuitable candidates who win an election can be recalled), allowing write-in voting is the only way to preserve the voters' right to cast a meaningful vote in the general election.

Timmons v. Twin Cities Area New Party

520 U.S. 351 (1997)

Chief Justice REHNQUIST delivered the opinion of the Court.

Most States prohibit multiple-party, or "fusion," candidacies for elected office.[1] The Minnesota laws challenged in this case prohibit a candidate from appearing on the ballot as the candidate of more than one party. We hold that such a prohibition does not violate the First and Fourteenth Amendments to the United States Constitution.

Respondent is a chartered chapter of the national New Party. Petitioners are Minnesota election officials. In April 1994, Minnesota State Representative Andy Dawkins was running unopposed in the Minnesota Democratic-Farmer-Labor Party's (DFL) primary. That same month, New Party members chose Dawkins as their candidate for the same office in the November 1994 general election. Neither

1. "Fusion," also called "cross-filing" or "multiple-party nomination," is "the electoral support of a single set of candidates by two or more parties." Argersinger, "A Place on the Ballot": Fusion Politics and Antifusion Laws, 85 Am. Hist. Rev. 287, 288 (1980); *see alsoTwin Cities Area New Party v. McKenna* (8th Cir. 1996) (Fusion is "the nomination by more than one political party of the same candidate for the same office in the same general election").

Dawkins nor the DFL objected, and Dawkins signed the required affidavit of candidacy for the New Party. Minnesota, however, prohibits fusion candidacies. Because Dawkins had already filed as a candidate for the DFL's nomination, local election officials refused to accept the New Party's nominating petition.

The New Party filed suit in United States District Court, contending that Minnesota's antifusion laws violated the party's associational rights under the First and Fourteenth Amendments. The District Court granted summary judgment for the state defendants[.]

The Court of Appeals reversed. We granted certiorari and now reverse.

Fusion was a regular feature of Gilded Age American politics. Particularly in the West and Midwest, candidates of issue-oriented parties like the Grangers, Independents, Greenbackers, and Populists often succeeded through fusion with the Democrats, and vice versa. Republicans, for their part, sometimes arranged fusion candidacies in the South, as part of a general strategy of encouraging and exploiting divisions within the dominant Democratic Party.

Fusion was common in part because political parties, rather than local or state governments, printed and distributed their own ballots. These ballots contained only the names of a particular party's candidates, and so a voter could drop his party's ticket in the ballot box without even knowing that his party's candidates were supported by other parties as well. But after the 1888 presidential election, which was widely regarded as having been plagued by fraud, many States moved to the "Australian ballot system." Under that system, an official ballot, containing the names of all the candidates legally nominated by all the parties, was printed at public expense and distributed by public officials at polling places. By 1896, use of the Australian ballot was widespread. During the same period, many States enacted other election-related reforms, including bans on fusion candidacies. Minnesota banned fusion in 1901. This trend has continued and, in this century, fusion has become the exception, not the rule. Today, multiple-party candidacies are permitted in just a few States, and fusion plays a significant role only in New York.

The First Amendment protects the right of citizens to associate and to form political parties for the advancement of common political goals and ideas.

On the other hand, it is also clear that States may, and inevitably must, enact reasonable regulations of parties, elections, and ballots to reduce election- and campaign-related disorder.

When deciding whether a state election law violates First and Fourteenth Amendment associational rights, we weigh the character and magnitude of the burden the State's rule imposes on those rights against the interests the State contends justify that burden, and consider the extent to which the State's concerns make the burden necessary. Regulations imposing severe burdens on plaintiffs' rights must be narrowly tailored and advance a compelling state interest. Lesser burdens, however, trigger less exacting review, and a State's important regulatory interests will usually be enough to justify reasonable, nondiscriminatory restrictions. No bright line separates permissible election-related regulation from unconstitutional infringements on First Amendment freedoms.*

* [Here is another good recitation of the Court's judicial test for the constitutional right to vote.—Eds.]

The New Party's claim that it has a right to select its own candidate is uncontroversial, so far as it goes. That is, the New Party, and not someone else, has the right to select the New Party's "standard bearer." It does not follow, though, that a party is absolutely entitled to have its nominee appear on the ballot as that party's candidate. A particular candidate might be ineligible for office, unwilling to serve, or, as here, another party's candidate. That a particular individual may not appear on the ballot as a particular party's candidate does not severely burden that party's associational rights.

The New Party relies on *Eu v. San Francisco County Democratic Central Comm.* (1989) and *Tashjian v. Republican Party of Conn.* (1986). In *Eu*, we struck down California election provisions that prohibited political parties from endorsing candidates in party primaries and regulated parties' internal affairs and structure. And in *Tashjian*, we held that Connecticut's closed-primary statute, which required voters in a party primary to be registered party members, interfered with a party's associational rights by limiting "the group of registered voters whom the Party may invite to participate in the basic function of selecting the Party's candidates." But while *Tashjian* and *Eu* involved regulation of political parties' internal affairs and core associational activities, Minnesota's fusion ban does not. The ban, which applies to major and minor parties alike, simply precludes one party's candidate from appearing on the ballot, as that party's candidate, if already nominated by another party. Respondent is free to try to convince Representative Dawkins to be the New Party's, not the DFL's, candidate. Whether the party still wants to endorse a candidate who, because of the fusion ban, will not appear on the ballot as the party's candidate, is up to the party.

The Court of Appeals also held that Minnesota's laws "keep the New Party from developing consensual political alliances and thus broadening the base of public participation in and support for its activities." The burden on the party was, the court held, severe because "[h]istory shows that minor parties have played a significant role in the electoral system where multiple party nomination is legal, but have no meaningful influence where multiple party nomination is banned." In the view of the Court of Appeals, Minnesota's fusion ban forces members of the New Party to make a "no-win choice" between voting for "candidates with no realistic chance of winning, defect[ing] from their party and vot[ing] for a major party candidate who does, or declin[ing] to vote at all."

But Minnesota has not directly precluded minor political parties from developing and organizing. Nor has Minnesota excluded a particular group of citizens, or a political party, from participation in the election process. The New Party remains free to endorse whom it likes, to ally itself with others, to nominate candidates for office, and to spread its message to all who will listen.

The Court of Appeals emphasized its belief that, without fusion-based alliances, minor parties cannot thrive. This is a predictive judgment which is by no means self-evident.[9] But, more importantly, the supposed benefits of fusion to

9. Between the First and Second World Wars, for example, various radical, agrarian, and labor-oriented parties thrived, without fusion, in the Midwest. One of these parties, Minnesota's Farmer-Labor Party, displaced the Democratic Party as the Republicans' primary opponent in Minnesota during the 1930's. As one historian has noted: "The Minnesota

minor parties do not require that Minnesota permit it. Many features of our political system — *e.g.*, single-member districts, "first past the post" elections, and the high costs of campaigning — make it difficult for third parties to succeed in American politics. But the Constitution does not require States to permit fusion any more than it requires them to move to proportional-representation elections or public financing of campaigns.

The New Party contends that the fusion ban burdens its "right . . . to communicate its choice of nominees on the ballot on terms equal to those offered other parties, and the right of the party's supporters and other voters to receive that information," and insists that communication on the ballot of a party's candidate choice is a "critical source of information for the great majority of voters . . . who . . . rely upon party 'labels' as a voting guide."

It is true that Minnesota's fusion ban prevents the New Party from using the ballot to communicate to the public that it supports a particular candidate who is already another party's candidate. In addition, the ban shuts off one possible avenue a party might use to send a message to its preferred *candidate* because, with fusion, a candidate who wins an election on the basis of two parties' votes will likely know more — if the parties' votes are counted separately — about the particular wishes and ideals of his constituency. We are unpersuaded, however, by the party's contention that it has a right to use the ballot itself to send a particularized message, to its candidate and to the voters, about the nature of its support for the candidate. Ballots serve primarily to elect candidates, not as forums for political expression. Like all parties in Minnesota, the New Party is able to use the ballot to communicate information about itself and its candidate to the voters, so long as that candidate is not already someone else's candidate. The party retains great latitude in its ability to communicate ideas to voters and candidates through its participation in the campaign, and party members may campaign for, endorse, and vote for their preferred candidate even if he is listed on the ballot as another party's candidate.

In sum, Minnesota's laws do not restrict the ability of the New Party and its members to endorse, support, or vote for anyone they like. The laws do not directly limit the party's access to the ballot. They are silent on parties' internal structure, governance, and policymaking. Instead, these provisions reduce the universe of potential candidates who may appear on the ballot as the party's nominee only by ruling out those few individuals who both have already agreed to be another party's candidate and also, if forced to choose, themselves prefer that other party. They also limit, slightly, the party's ability to send a message to the voters and to

Farmer-Labor Party elected its candidates to the governorship on four occasions, to the U.S. Senate in five elections, and to the U.S. House in twenty-five campaigns. . . . Never less than Minnesota's second strongest party, in 1936 Farmer-Laborites dominated state politics. . . . The Farmer-Labor Party was a success despite its independence of America's two dominant national parties and despite the sometimes bold anticapitalist rhetoric of its platforms." It appears that factionalism within the Farmer-Labor Party, the popular successes of New Deal programs and ideology, and the gradual movement of political power from the States to the National Government contributed to the party's decline. Eventually, a much-weakened Farmer-Labor Party merged with the Democrats, forming what is now Minnesota's Democratic-Farmer-Labor Party, in 1944.

its preferred candidates. We conclude that the burdens Minnesota imposes on the party's First and Fourteenth Amendment associational rights—though not trivial—are not severe.

The Court of Appeals determined that Minnesota's fusion ban imposed "severe" burdens on the New Party's associational rights, and so it required the State to show that the ban was narrowly tailored to serve compelling state interests. We disagree; given the burdens imposed, the bar is not so high. Instead, the State's asserted regulatory interests need only be "sufficiently weighty to justify the limitation" imposed on the party's rights. Nor do we require elaborate, empirical verification of the weightiness of the State's asserted justifications.

The Court of Appeals acknowledged Minnesota's interests in avoiding voter confusion and overcrowded ballots, preventing party splintering and disruptions of the two-party system, and being able to clearly identify the election winner. Minnesota argues here that its fusion ban is justified by its interests in avoiding voter confusion, promoting candidate competition (by reserving limited ballot space for opposing candidates), preventing electoral distortions and ballot manipulations, and discouraging party splintering and "unrestrained factionalism."

States certainly have an interest in protecting the integrity, fairness, and efficiency of their ballots and election processes as means for electing public officials. Petitioners contend that a candidate or party could easily exploit fusion as a way of associating his or its name with popular slogans and catchphrases. For example, members of a major party could decide that a powerful way of "sending a message" via the ballot would be for various factions of that party to nominate the major party's candidate as the candidate for the newly-formed "No New Taxes," "Conserve Our Environment," and "Stop Crime Now" parties. In response, an opposing major party would likely instruct its factions to nominate that party's candidate as the "Fiscal Responsibility," "Healthy Planet," and "Safe Streets" parties' candidate.

Whether or not the putative "fusion" candidates' names appeared on one or four ballot lines, such maneuvering would undermine the ballot's purpose by transforming it from a means of choosing candidates to a billboard for political advertising. The New Party responds to this concern, ironically enough, by insisting that the State could avoid such manipulation by adopting more demanding ballot-access standards rather than prohibiting multiple-party nomination. However, as we stated above, because the burdens the fusion ban imposes on the party's associational rights are not severe, the State need not narrowly tailor the means it chooses to promote ballot integrity. The Constitution does not require that Minnesota compromise the policy choices embodied in its ballot-access requirements to accommodate the New Party's fusion strategy.

Relatedly, petitioners urge that permitting fusion would undercut Minnesota's ballot-access regime by allowing minor parties to capitalize on the popularity of another party's candidate, rather than on their own appeal to the voters, in order to secure access to the ballot. That is, voters who might not sign a minor party's nominating petition based on the party's own views and candidates might do so if they viewed the minor party as just another way of nominating the same person nominated by one of the major parties. Thus, Minnesota fears that fusion would enable minor parties, by nominating a major party's candidate, to bootstrap their way to major-party status in the next election and circumvent the State's nominating-petition requirement for minor parties. The State surely has a valid interest in making sure that minor and third parties who are granted access to the ballot are bona fide and actually supported, on their own merits, by those who have provided the statutorily required petition or ballot support.

States also have a strong interest in the stability of their political systems. This interest does not permit a State to completely insulate the two-party system from minor parties' or independent candidates' competition and influence; nor is it a paternalistic license for States to protect political parties from the consequences of their own internal disagreements. That said, the States' interest permits them to enact reasonable election regulations that may, in practice, favor the traditional two-party system, and that temper the destabilizing effects of party-splintering and excessive factionalism. The Constitution permits the Minnesota Legislature to decide that political stability is best served through a healthy two-party system. And while an interest in securing the perceived benefits of a stable two-party system will not justify unreasonably exclusionary restrictions, States need not remove all of the many hurdles third parties face in the American political arena today.

We conclude that the burdens Minnesota's fusion ban imposes on the New Party's associational rights are justified by "correspondingly weighty" valid state interests in ballot integrity and political stability. In deciding that Minnesota's fusion ban does not unconstitutionally burden the New Party's First and Fourteenth Amendment rights, we express no views on the New Party's policy-based arguments concerning the wisdom of fusion. It may well be that, as support for new political parties increases, these arguments will carry the day in some States' legislatures. But the Constitution does not require Minnesota, and the approximately 40 other States that do not permit fusion, to allow it. The judgment of the Court of Appeals is reversed.

Justice STEVENS, with whom Justice GINSBURG joins, and with whom Justice SOUTER joins as to Parts I and II, dissenting.

The Court's conclusion that the Minnesota statute prohibiting multiple-party candidacies is constitutional rests on three dubious premises: (1) that the statute imposes only a minor burden on the Party's right to choose and to support the candidate of its choice; (2) that the statute significantly serves the State's asserted interests in avoiding ballot manipulation and factionalism; and (3) that, in any event, the interest in preserving the two-party system justifies the imposition of the burden at issue in this case. I disagree with each of these premises.

I

The members of a recognized political party unquestionably have a constitutional right to select their nominees for public office and to communicate the identity of their nominees to the voting public. Both the right to choose and the right to advise voters of that choice are entitled to the highest respect.

The Minnesota statutes place a significant burden on both of those rights. The Court's recital of burdens that the statute does not inflict on the Party does nothing to minimize the severity of the burdens that it does impose. The fact that the Party may nominate its second choice surely does not diminish the significance of a restriction that denies it the right to have the name of its first choice appear on the ballot. Nor does the point that it may use some of its limited resources to publicize the fact that its first choice is the nominee of some other party provide an adequate substitute for the message that is conveyed to every person who actually votes when a party's nominees appear on the ballot.

As to the first point, the State contends that the fusion ban in fact limits by only a few candidates the range of individuals a party may nominate, and that the burden is therefore quite small. But the *number* of candidates removed from the Party's reach cannot be the determinative factor. The ban leaves the Party free to nominate any eligible candidate except the particular "standard bearer who best represents the party's ideologies and preferences."

The State next argues that—instead of nominating a second-choice candidate—the Party could remove itself from the ballot altogether, and publicly endorse the candidate of another party. But the right to be on the election ballot is precisely what separates a political party from any other interest group. The Court relies on the fact that the Party remains free "to spread its message to all who will listen" through forums other than the ballot. Given the limited resources available to most minor parties, and the less-than-universal interest in the messages of third parties, it is apparent that the Party's message will, in this manner, reach a much smaller audience than that composed of all voters who can read the ballot in the polling booth.

In this case, and presumably in most cases, the burden of a statute of this kind is imposed upon the members of a minor party, but its potential impact is much broader. Popular candidates like Andy Dawkins sometimes receive nationwide recognition. Fiorello LaGuardia, Earl Warren, Ronald Reagan, and Franklin D. Roosevelt are names that come readily to mind as candidates whose reputations and political careers were enhanced because they appeared on election ballots as fusion candidates. A statute that denied a political party the right to nominate any of those individuals for high office simply because he had already been nominated by another party would, in my opinion, place an intolerable burden on political expression and association.

II

Minnesota argues that the statutory restriction on the Party's right to nominate the candidate of its choice is justified by the State's interests in avoiding voter confusion, preventing ballot clutter and manipulation, encouraging candidate competition, and minimizing intraparty factionalism. None of these rationales can support the fusion ban because the State has failed to explain how the ban actually serves the asserted interests.

I believe that the law significantly abridges First Amendment freedoms and that the State therefore must shoulder a correspondingly heavy burden of justification if the law is to survive judicial scrutiny. But even accepting the majority's view that the burdens imposed by the law are not weighty, the State's asserted interests must at least bear some plausible relationship to the burdens it places on political parties. Although the Court today suggests that the State does not have to support its asserted justifications for the fusion ban with evidence that they have any empirical validity, we have previously required more than a bare assertion that some particular state interest is served by a burdensome election requirement. While the State describes some imaginative theoretical sources of voter confusion that could result from fusion candidacies, in my judgment the argument that the burden on First Amendment interests is justified by this concern is meritless and severely underestimates the intelligence of the typical voter.

The State's concern about ballot manipulation, readily accepted by the majority, is similarly farfetched. The possibility that members of the major parties will begin to create dozens of minor parties with detailed, issue-oriented titles for the sole purpose of nominating candidates under those titles is entirely hypothetical. The majority dismisses out-of-hand the Party's argument that the risk of this type of ballot manipulation and crowding is more easily averted by maintaining reasonably stringent requirements for the creation of minor parties. In fact, though, the Party's point merely illustrates the idea that a State can place some kinds—but not every kind—of limitation on the abilities of small parties to thrive. If the State wants to make it more difficult for any group to achieve the legal status of being a political party, it can do so within reason and still not run up against the First Amendment. But once the State has established a standard for achieving party status, forbidding an acknowledged party to put on the ballot its chosen candidate clearly frustrates core associational rights.[5]

The State argues that the fusion ban promotes political stability by preventing intraparty factionalism and party raiding. States do certainly have an interest in maintaining a stable political system. But the State has not convincingly articulated how the fusion ban will prevent the factionalism it fears. Unlike the law at issue in *Storer v. Brown*, for example, this law would not prevent sore-loser candidates from defecting with a disaffected segment of a major party and running as an opposition candidate for a newly formed minor party. Nor does this law, like those aimed at requiring parties to show a modicum of support in order to secure a place on the election ballot, prevent the formation of numerous small parties. Indeed, the activity banned by Minnesota's law is the formation of coalitions, not the division and dissension of "splintered parties and unrestrained factionalism."

As for the State's argument that the fusion ban encourages candidate competition, this claim treats "candidates" as fungible goods, ignoring entirely each party's interest in nominating not just any candidate, but the candidate who best represents the party's views. Minnesota's fusion ban simply cannot be justified with reference to this or any of the above-mentioned rationales. I turn, therefore, to what appears to be the true basis for the Court's holding—the interest in preserving the two-party system.

III

In most States, perhaps in all, there are two and only two major political parties. It is not surprising, therefore, that most States have enacted election laws that impose burdens on the development and growth of third parties. The law at issue

5. A second "ballot manipulation" argument accepted by the majority is that minor parties will attempt to "capitalize on the popularity of another party's candidate, rather than on their own appeal to the voters, in order to secure access to the ballot." What the majority appears unwilling to accept is that *Andy Dawkins was the Party's chosen candidate.* The Party was not trying to capitalize on his status as someone else's candidate, but to identify him as their own choice.

in this case is undeniably such a law. The fact that the law was both intended to disadvantage minor parties and has had that effect is a matter that should weigh against, rather than in favor of, its constitutionality.

Our jurisprudence in this area reflects a certain tension: On the one hand, we have been clear that political stability is an important state interest and that incidental burdens on the formation of minor parties are reasonable to protect that interest; on the other, we have struck down state elections laws specifically because they give "the two old, established parties a decided advantage over any new parties struggling for existence," *Williams v. Rhodes* (1968). Between these boundaries, we have acknowledged that there is "no litmus-paper test for separating those restrictions that are valid from those that are invidious. . . . The rule is not self-executing and is no substitute for the hard judgments that must be made." *Storer.*

Nothing in the Constitution prohibits the States from maintaining single-member districts with winner-take-all voting arrangements. And these elements of an election system do make it significantly more difficult for third parties to thrive. But these laws are different in two respects from the fusion bans at issue here. First, the method by which they hamper third-party development is not one that impinges on the associational rights of those third parties; minor parties remain free to nominate candidates of their choice, and to rally support for those candidates. The small parties' relatively limited likelihood of ultimate success on election day does not deprive them of the right to try. Second, the establishment of single-member districts correlates directly with the States' interests in political stability. Systems of proportional representation, for example, may tend toward factionalism and fragile coalitions that diminish legislative effectiveness. In the context of fusion candidacies, the risks to political stability are extremely attenuated. Of course, the reason minor parties so ardently support fusion politics is because it allows the parties to build up a greater base of support, as potential minor party members realize that a vote for the smaller party candidate is not necessarily a "wasted" vote. Eventually, a minor party might gather sufficient strength that—were its members so inclined—it could successfully run a candidate not endorsed by any major party, and legislative coalition building will be made more difficult by the presence of third-party legislators. But the risks to political stability in that scenario are speculative at best.

In some respects, the fusion candidacy is the best marriage of the virtues of the minor party challenge to entrenched viewpoints and the political stability that the two-party system provides. The fusion candidacy does not threaten to divide the legislature and create significant risks of factionalism, which is the principal risk proponents of the two-party system point to. But it does provide a means by which voters with viewpoints not adequately represented by the platforms of the two major parties can indicate to a particular candidate that—in addition to his support for the major party views—he should be responsive to the views of the minor party whose support for him was demonstrated where political parties demonstrate support—on the ballot.

The strength of the two-party system—and of each of its major components—is the product of the power of the ideas, the traditions, the candidates, and the voters that constitute the parties. It demeans the strength of the two-party system to assume that the major parties need to rely on laws that discriminate against independent voters and minor parties in order to preserve their positions of power. Indeed, it is a central theme of our jurisprudence that the entire electorate, which necessarily includes the members of the major parties, will benefit from robust competition in ideas and governmental policies that "is at the core of our electoral process and of the First Amendment freedoms." *Anderson.*

In my opinion legislation that would otherwise be unconstitutional because it burdens First Amendment interests and discriminates against minor political parties cannot survive simply because it benefits the two major parties. Accordingly, I respectfully dissent.

Justice SOUTER, dissenting.
[Omitted.]

NOTES ON *BURDICK* AND *TIMMONS*

1. Note the common themes between these two cases: In both cases, the Court weighs the burdens on the individual and political party with the state's interests; both cases discuss the role and purpose of the ballot (as a form of expression or simply to allow the state to winnow the candidates and decide the race); in both cases the concern of favoring the two-party system plays a prominent role in the analysis; and in both cases the Court elevates the state's interests in regulating a free and fair election over the burdens imposed on voters and political parties.

2. Note also the continuing refinement of the proper level of scrutiny for a law that impacts electoral rights. The majority in *Burdick* states, "to subject every voting regulation to strict scrutiny and to require that the regulation be narrowly tailored to advance a compelling state interest, as petitioner suggests, would tie the hands of States seeking to assure that elections are operated equitably and efficiently." Is this a sound rationale for rejecting strict scrutiny and employing a balancing test dependent on the "burdens" the law imposes? The "severe burden" framework from both *Burdick* and *Anderson v. Celebrezze* is often referred to as the "*Anderson-Burdick* balancing test." We will see this test employed again in many of the cases in Part IV of this case book.

3. Make sure to understand the state's asserted interests for the law in each case. Do you consider these interests sufficient to sustain the laws?

4. What is the role of a ballot? Should it be to allow parties and voters to engage in a particular expression, or is it merely for the purpose of deciding who wins a race?

5. Should the state be allowed to create rules that favor the two-party system? What does this say about the role of minor parties in our democracy? Is this just a function of entrenchment?

F. THE RIGHTS OF CANDIDATES

The cases above demonstrate that the rights of candidates and the rights of the candidates' supporters are intertwined, and that the Supreme Court will construe a ballot access restriction as an infringement on voters' rights to select a candidate of their choice. But what rules dictate whether a person is even eligible to be a candidate for a particular office?

The U.S. Constitution dictates specific eligibility requirements for candidates for federal office. To be President, an individual must be at least thirty-five years old, a natural born citizen, and a resident of the U.S. for fourteen years. U.S. CONST. art. II, § 1. During the 2016 presidential election, there was some question as to whether Republican Ted Cruz would be eligible under the natural born citizen clause: Cruz was born in Canada and is a citizen by virtue of his mother being a U.S. citizen (Cruz's father was born in Cuba). Numerous lawsuits were filed but none were successful. In addition, the Illinois Board of Elections declared that Cruz is a natural born citizen "by virtue of being born in Canada to his mother who was a U.S. citizen at the time of his birth" and that he "did not have to take any steps to go through a naturalization process at some point after birth." *See* Chad Merda, *Illinois election board: Ted Cruz is a natural-born citizen*, CHICAGO SUN-TIMES, Feb. 4, 2016.

To be eligible for the U.S. Senate, a candidate must be at least thirty years old, a citizen of the U.S. for at least nine years, and be an "inhabitant" of the state when elected. U.S. CONST. art. I, § 3. To be a member of the U.S. House of Representatives, a person must be at least twenty-five years old, a citizen of the U.S. for at least seven years, and be an "inhabitant" of the state when elected. U.S. CONST. art. I, § 2. Note that a member of the House need not live in the district that he or she represents; there are a handful of members of Congress who actually live outside of their districts, although that fact can harm a candidate politically if voters view the person as an "outsider."

And that's it. A state may not impose additional eligibility requirements for federal office. Indeed, the U.S. Supreme Court struck down a state-imposed term limit law that forbade candidates from running for re-election if they had served a certain number of terms in Congress. Justice Stevens, writing for a 5-4 Court, explained, "state imposed restrictions . . . violate a [fundamental principle of our representative democracy]: that the right to choose representatives belongs not to the States, but to the people." *U.S. Term Limits, Inc. v. Thornton*, 514 U.S. 779, 820–21 (1995). In the wake of the 2016 presidential election, when Republican Donald Trump refused to publicly release his personal tax returns, some states considered whether to impose a ballot access requirement on future presidential candidates to release their tax returns. Would this kind of law pass constitutional muster? How would you distinguish *U.S. Term Limits*? Under Article II of the Constitution, states have plenary authority to determine how to award their Electoral College votes as they see fit. Does this fact make a difference?

Although the U.S. Constitution sets out specific eligibility rules for federal office—and essentially forbids states from adding their own additional requirements—states can impose other eligibility requirements for state offices. Do candidates themselves have a constitutional right to be a candidate in the face of these rules? What eligibility requirements may states impose on candidates? The next two cases analyze those questions.

Clements v. Fashing

457 U.S. 957 (1982)

Justice REHNQUIST delivered the opinion of the Court with respect to Parts I, II, and V, and delivered an opinion with respect to Parts III and IV, in which THE CHIEF JUSTICE, Justice POWELL, and Justice O'CONNOR joined.

Appellees in this case challenge two provisions of the Texas Constitution that limit a public official's ability to become a candidate for another public office. The primary question in this appeal is whether these provisions violate the Equal Protection Clause of the Fourteenth Amendment.

I

Article III, § 19, of the Texas Constitution provides:

> "No judge of any court, Secretary of State, Attorney General, clerk of any court of record, or any person holding a lucrative office under the United States, or this State, or any foreign government shall during the term for which he is elected or appointed, be eligible to the Legislature."

Section 19 renders an officeholder ineligible for the Texas Legislature if his current term of office will not expire until after the legislative term to which he aspires begins. Resignation is ineffective to avoid § 19 if the officeholder's current term of office overlaps the term of the legislature to which he seeks election. In other words, § 19 requires an officeholder to complete his current term of office before he may be eligible to serve in the legislature.

II

[Omitted.]

III

The Equal Protection Clause allows the States considerable leeway to enact legislation that may appear to affect similarly situated people differently. Legislatures are ordinarily assumed to have acted constitutionally. Under traditional equal protection principles, distinctions need only be drawn in such a manner as to bear some rational relationship to a legitimate state end. Classifications are set aside only if they are based solely on reasons totally unrelated to the pursuit of the State's goals and only if no grounds can be conceived to justify them. We have departed from traditional equal protection principles only when the challenged statute places burdens upon "suspect classes" of persons or on a constitutional right that is deemed to be "fundamental."

Thus, we must first determine whether the provisions challenged in this case deserve "scrutiny" more vigorous than that which the traditional principles would require.

Far from recognizing candidacy as a "fundamental right," we have held that the existence of barriers to a candidate's access to the ballot "does not of itself compel close scrutiny." *Bullock v. Carter* (1972). "In approaching candidate restrictions, it is essential to examine in a realistic light the extent and nature of their impact on voters." *Id.* In assessing challenges to state election laws that restrict access to the ballot, this Court has not formulated a "litmus-paper test for separating those restrictions that are valid from those that are invidious under the Equal Protection Clause." *Storer v. Brown* (1974). Decision in this area of constitutional adjudication is a matter of degree, and involves a consideration of the facts and circumstances behind the law, the interests the State seeks to protect by placing restrictions on candidacy, and the nature of the interests of those who may be burdened by the restrictions.

Our ballot access cases, however, do focus on the degree to which the challenged restrictions operate as a mechanism to exclude certain classes of candidates from the electoral process. The inquiry is whether the challenged restriction unfairly or unnecessarily burdens the "availability of political opportunity." This Court has departed from traditional equal protection analysis in recent years in two essentially separate, although similar, lines of ballot access cases.

One line of ballot access cases involves classifications based on wealth. Economic status is not a measure of a prospective candidate's qualifications to hold elective office, and a filing fee alone is an inadequate test of whether a candidacy is serious or spurious. Clearly, the challenged provisions in the instant case involve neither filing fees nor restrictions that invidiously burden those of lower economic status. This line of cases, therefore does not support a departure from the traditional equal protection principles.

The second line of ballot access cases involves classification schemes that impose burdens on new or small political parties or independent candidates. These cases involve requirements that an independent candidate or minor party demonstrate a certain level of support among the electorate before the minor party or candidate may obtain a place on the ballot. In these cases, the Court has emphasized that the States have important interests in protecting the integrity of their political processes from frivolous or fraudulent candidacies, in ensuring that their election processes are efficient, in avoiding voter confusion caused by an overcrowded ballot, and in avoiding the expense and burden of run-off elections. To this end, the Court has upheld reasonable level-of-support requirements and classifications that turn on the political party's success in prior elections. The Court has recognized, however, that such requirements may burden First Amendment interests in ensuring freedom of association, as these requirements classify on the basis of a candidate's association with particular political parties. Consequently, the State may not act to maintain the "status quo" by making it virtually impossible for any but the two major parties to achieve ballot positions for their candidates.

The provisions of the Texas Constitution challenged in this case do not contain any classification that imposes special burdens on minority political parties or independent candidates. The burdens placed on those candidates subject to § 19 . . . in no way depend upon political affiliation or political viewpoint.

Not all ballot access restrictions require "heightened" equal protection scrutiny. The Court, for example, applied traditional equal protection principles to uphold a classification scheme that denied absentee ballots to inmates in jail awaiting trial. *McDonald v. Board of Election Comm'rs* (1969). Thus, it is necessary to examine the provisions in question in terms of the extent of the burdens that they place on the candidacy of current holders of public office.

IV

A

The issue in this case . . . is whether § 19 may be applied to a Justice of the Peace in a manner consistent with the Equal Protection Clause.

Section 19 merely prohibits officeholders from cutting short their current term of office in order to serve in the legislature. In Texas, the term of office for a Justice of the Peace is four years, while legislative elections are held every two years. Therefore, § 19 simply requires [the plaintiff] to complete his 4-year term as Justice of the Peace before he may be eligible for the legislature. At most, therefore, [the plaintiff] must wait two years—one election cycle—before he may run as a candidate for the legislature.

In establishing a maximum "waiting period" of two years for candidacy by a Justice of the Peace for the legislature, § 19 places a *de minimis* burden on the political aspirations of a *current* officeholder. Section 19 discriminates neither on the basis of political affiliation nor on any factor not related to a candidate's qualifications to hold political office. Unlike filing fees or the level-of-support requirements, § 19 in no way burdens access to the political process by those who are outside the "mainstream" of political life. In this case, § 19 burdens only a candidate who has successfully been elected to one office, but whose political ambitions lead him to pursue a seat in the Texas Legislature.

A "waiting period" is hardly a significant barrier to candidacy. Section 19 clearly rests on a rational predicate. That provision furthers Texas' interests in maintaining the integrity of the State's Justices of the Peace. By prohibiting candidacy for the legislature until completion of one's term of office, § 19 seeks to ensure that a Justice of the Peace will neither abuse his position nor neglect his duties because of his aspirations for higher office. The demands of a political campaign may tempt a Justice of the Peace to devote less than his full time and energies to the responsibilities of his office. A campaigning Justice of the Peace might be tempted to render decisions and take actions that might serve more to further his political ambitions than the responsibilities of his office. The State's interests are especially important with regard to judicial officers. It is a serious accusation to charge a judicial officer with making a politically motivated decision. By contrast, it is to be expected that a legislator will vote with due regard to the views of his constituents.

Texas has a legitimate interest in discouraging its Justices of the Peace from vacating their current terms of office. By requiring Justices of the Peace to complete their current terms of office, the State has eliminated one incentive to vacate one's office prior to the expiration of the term. The State may act to avoid the difficulties that accompany interim elections and appointments.

B

[Omitted.]

V

As an alternative ground to support the judgments of the courts below, appellees contend that § 19 violate[s] the First Amendment. Our analysis of appellees' challenge under the Equal Protection Clause disposes of this argument. We have concluded that the burden on appellees' First Amendment interests in candidacy are so insignificant that the classifications of § 19 . . . may be upheld consistent with traditional equal protection principles. The State's interests in this regard are sufficient to warrant the *de minimis* interference with appellees' interests in candidacy.

These provisions in no way restrict appellees' ability to participate in the political campaigns of third parties. They limit neither political contributions nor expenditures. They do not preclude appellees from holding an office in a political party. Consistent with § 19, appellees may distribute campaign literature and may make speeches on behalf of a candidate.

Neither the Equal Protection Clause nor the First Amendment authorizes this Court to review in cases such as this the manner in which a State has decided to govern itself. Constitutional limitations arise only if the classification scheme is invidious or if the challenged provision significantly impairs interests protected by the First Amendment. Our view of the wisdom of a state constitutional provision may not color our task of constitutional adjudication.

Justice STEVENS, concurring in part and concurring in the judgment.
[Omitted.]

Justice BRENNAN, with whom Justice MARSHALL and Justice BLACKMUN join, and with whom Justice WHITE joins as to Part I, dissenting.

I

Putting to one side the question of the proper level of equal protection scrutiny to be applied to these restrictions on candidacy for public office, I find it clear that no genuine justification exists that might support the classifications embodied in . . . Art. III, § 19.

The State seeks to justify [the] provision on the basis of its interest in discouraging abuse of office and neglect of duties by current officeholders campaigning for higher office during their terms. The plurality posits an additional justification not asserted by the State for § 19: That section also discourages certain officeholders "from vacating their current terms of office." But neither the State nor the plurality offers any justification for *differential* treatment of various classes of officeholders, and the search for such justification makes clear that the classifications embodied in these provisions lack any meaningful relationship to the State's asserted or supposed interests.

II

I also believe that Art. III, § 19, violates the First Amendment. The Court dismisses this contention by stating that this provision is a more limited restriction on political activities of public employees than we have upheld in prior cases. But none of our precedents presented a restriction on campaigning that applied even *after* an official had resigned from public office or to officials who did not serve in the regulating government. Moreover, the Court does not go on to address what is for me the crucial question: What justification does the State have for this restriction and how does this provision address the State's asserted interests?

It is clear to me that Art. III, § 19 is not narrowly tailored to conform to the State's asserted interests. Nor does it further those interests in a meaningful way. Section 19 bars the candidacy of a wide class of state, federal, and foreign officeholders. The offices enumerated in § 19 include the judges of all courts, the Secretary of State, the Attorney General, the clerks of any court of record, and all persons holding any "lucrative" office under the United States, Texas, or any foreign government. Section 19 by its terms would bar, for example, a retired United States District Court Judge, appointed for life, whose District was outside of Texas, from running for the Texas State Legislature.

In many of its applications § 19 has absolutely *no* connection to Texas' interest in how Texas public officials perform their current duties. This provision applies to persons holding office under the United States or any foreign government and would thus bar a person holding *federal* office from resigning from that office and running for the Texas Legislature. Even with respect to persons who are currently Texas public officials, § 19 continues to operate after their resignations from current positions have taken effect and their responsibility to the Texas electorate has ceased. A provision directed only at Texas officeholders, that gave those officeholders a choice between resigning and serving out their current terms would serve all of the asserted state interests; yet Texas has inexplicably chosen this far more restrictive alternative.

Because the Court finds neither an equal protection nor a First Amendment violation in either of these restrictions on candidacy, I respectfully dissent.

Maksym v. Board of Election Commissioners of the City of Chicago

242 Ill.2d 303 (Ill. S. Ct. 2011)

Justice THOMAS delivered the judgment of the court, with opinion.

The petitioners, Walter P. Maksym, Jr., and Thomas L. McMahon, filed written objections to the candidacy of the respondent, Rahm Emanuel (the candidate), who seeks to be a candidate for mayor of the City of Chicago in the municipal general election to be held on February 22, 2011. After an evidentiary hearing, the Board of Election Commissioners of the City of Chicago (the Board) dismissed the objections and ruled that the candidate was entitled to have his name included on the ballot as a mayoral candidate. The petitioners sought judicial review in the circuit court of Cook County, which confirmed the decision of the Board. The petitioners appealed, and the appellate court reversed the circuit court's judgment, set aside the Board's decision, and ordered that the candidate's name be excluded (or, if necessary, removed) from the ballot for Chicago's February 22, 2011, mayoral election. [This appeal followed.]

The candidate was born in Chicago and, in December 1998, purchased a Chicago home (the Hermitage House), which he still owns. The candidate lived with his family in that home from 1998 through January 2009. On January 2, 2009, the candidate, who had up to then served as a member of the United States House of Representatives elected from the district that included the Hermitage House, resigned his office in order to serve in Washington, D.C., as Chief of Staff to the President of the United States. After traveling to Washington, D.C., he and his spouse purchased additional land adjoining their Chicago property.

From January through May 2009, the candidate lived in an "in-law apartment" in Washington, D.C., while his family remained in the Hermitage House. From

June 2009 until October 1, 2010, the candidate, and his family, lived in a Washington, D.C., house (the Woodley House) that was leased for the term spanning June 1, 2009, through June 30, 2011. The family received their mail at the Woodley House and moved most of their clothes and personal belongings to Washington, D.C. They did, however, leave behind at the Hermitage House several larger household items, including televisions, a piano, and a bed, as well as several personal possessions such as family heirlooms and books. The candidate's Hermitage House was leased to another family for the term of September 1, 2009, through June 30, 2011.

At all relevant times, including the time he was in Washington, D.C., the candidate continued to pay property taxes for the Hermitage House, continued to hold an Illinois driver's license listing the Hermitage House as his address, continued to list the Hermitage House address on his personal checks, and continued to vote with the Hermitage House as his registered voting address. He did, however, pay income tax in 2009 and 2010 to both Washington, D.C., and Illinois.

On October 1, 2010, the candidate resigned his position of Chief of Staff to the President of the United States and entered into a lease to live in an apartment located on Milwaukee Avenue in Chicago from October 1, 2010, through June 30, 2011. He has lived in that apartment since October 1, 2010. In his testimony, the candidate explained that he had always expected to serve as Chief of Staff to the President for approximately 18 to 24 months before returning to live in the Hermitage House.

From these facts, the Board concluded that the candidate met the qualification for candidacy, contained in subsection 3.1–10–5(a) of the Illinois Municipal Code, mandating that he had "resided in" Chicago for the one year preceding the February 22, 2011, mayoral election. The Board noted that the objectors and candidate agreed that "residence" in this context means "permanent abode," and that two elements are required for a permanent abode: (1) physical presence; and (2) an intent to remain there as a permanent abode. The Board cited case law establishing that, once a permanent abode is established, residence continues until abandoned. The Board concluded that the objectors had failed to establish that the candidate abandoned his residence, basing its conclusion on the evidence that the candidate maintained significant contacts with Chicago, intended to return to Chicago and to the Hermitage House, and had lived in Washington, D.C., solely for the purpose of working for the President.

[The court of appeals] ultimately determined that, as used in section 3.1–10–5(a), "resided in" does *not* refer to a permanent abode, but rather where a person "actually live[s]" or "actually reside[s]." However, the court never explained what it meant by these terms, other than to say that the candidate does not qualify as a resident if this definition is used.

ANALYSIS

Before proceeding to the merits, we wish to emphasize that, until just a few days ago, the governing law on this question had been settled in this State for going on 150 years. In *Smith v. People ex rel. Frisbie* (1867), this court was faced with a question remarkably similar to that which is before us today. Smith, a longtime resident of Illinois, had been appointed a circuit judge by the governor of Illinois, and a *quo warranto* action was brought to remove Smith from that office on the grounds that he had not been an Illinois resident "for at least five years next preceding . . . his appointment," as the Illinois Constitution then required. In support of their action, the objectors pointed to the fact that Smith had moved with his family to Tennessee for eight months during the relevant five-year residency period.

In concluding that Smith's eight-month sojourn to Tennessee did not result in an abandonment of his established Illinois residency, this court explained that, once established, "residence is lost . . . by a union of intention and acts" and that "the intention in many cases will be inferred from the surrounding circumstances." This court then examined the "surrounding circumstances" and found that (1) Smith frequently declared that his move to Tennessee was only an experiment; (2) just two months after arriving in Tennessee, Smith expressed a desire to return to Illinois as soon as became feasible; (3) Smith at no time expressed an unqualified intention to remain in Tennessee; (4) Smith declined to vote in a Tennessee election because "he desired to do no act by which he would lose his citizenship in [Illinois]"; (5) he refused to sell his Illinois law books prior to his move, saying that "he would probably return, and would then need them in his [Illinois law] practice"; and (6) he "only rented his [Illinois] residence when he left." This evidence, the court concluded, was insufficient to "establish a presumption of loss of residence."

Thus, from April 1867 through January 24 of this year, the principles governing the question before us were settled. Things changed, however, when the appellate court below issued its decision and announced that it was no longer bound by any of the law cited above, including this court's decision in *Smith,* but was instead free to craft its own original standard for determining a candidate's residency. Thus, our review of the appellate court's decision in this case begins not where it should, with an assessment of whether the court accurately applied established Illinois law to the particular facts, but with an assessment of whether the appellate court was justified in tossing out 150 years of settled residency law in favor of its own preferred standard. We emphatically hold that it was not.

The *Smith* principles control this case, plain and simple. With the sole exception of the prescribed time period, the provision at issue in *Smith* is identical to the one at issue here. Both provide that, in order to be eligible for public office, a person must reside in the relevant jurisdiction for some period "next preceding the election or appointment." And in both cases, the sole issue presented is whether the person seeking to hold the office in question had abandoned his Illinois residency by virtue of an extended relocation to another part of the country. In answering that question in *Smith,* this court explained that, once established, "residence is lost . . . by a union of intention and acts" and that "the intention in many cases will be inferred from the surrounding circumstances." The court then examined the surrounding circumstances, including both Smith's words and Smith's actions, to determine whether Smith had abandoned his Illinois residency. Ultimately, the court concluded that he had not. In every relevant way, the analysis that this court employed in *Smith* is the very analysis that the hearing officer, the Board, and the circuit court below employed, and they were correct in doing so. *Smith* has never been overruled, and it is directly on point.

For two reasons, the appellate court concluded that *Smith* was not controlling authority in this case. Neither of these reasons is convincing. First, the court noted that, because *Smith* involved a *quo warranto* action [to remove a current officeholder], the burden of proof on the objecting party was higher (clear and convincing) than it is for the objectors in this case (preponderance of the evidence). While this is undeniably true, we fail to see how it renders *Smith's* residency analysis irrelevant, as burden of proof does not impact *what* a party must prove, but only *how well* the party must prove it. The appellate court's other basis for rejecting *Smith* was its determination that, "although the supreme court's discussion in *Smith* was based nominally on principles of residence, it appears from its analysis that it actually applied concepts of domicile." In other words, the appellate court concluded that *Smith* is not binding because this court did not know what it was talking about when it wrote it.

The issue in this case is whether the candidate met the statutory requirements to run for and hold elected municipal office, as set forth in section 3.1–10–5(a) of the Municipal Code. That section states, in relevant part:

> "A person is not eligible for an elective municipal office unless that person is a qualified elector of the municipality and has resided in the municipality at least one year next preceding the election or appointment. . . ."

For present purposes, the critical question is what does this section mean by "reside[ ] in"? This presents a question of statutory interpretation, which is a question of law subject to *de novo* review and the rules governing our inquiry are familiar. Our primary goal when interpreting the language of a statute is to ascertain and give effect to the intent of the legislature. The plain language of a statute is the best indication of the legislature's intent. Where the statutory language is clear and unambiguous, we will enforce it as written and will not read into it exceptions, conditions, or limitations that the legislature did not express.

As *Smith* demonstrates, this court very early on announced the principles that would inform residency analysis in the context of eligibility to hold public office. And since *Smith,* this court has consistently applied similar residency principles in a variety of other contexts, most especially in the context of voting. From these cases, several well-settled principles emerge. First, to *establish* residency, two elements are required: (1) physical presence, and (2) an intent to remain in that place as a permanent home. Second, once residency is established, the test is no longer physical presence but rather abandonment. Indeed, once a person has *established* residence, he or she can be physically absent from that residence for months or even years without having abandoned it:

> "[T]he shortest absence, if at the time intended as a permanent abandonment, is sufficient, although the party may soon afterwards change his intention; while, on the other hand, an absence for months, or even years, if all the while intended as a mere temporary absence for some temporary purpose, to be followed by a resumption of the former residence, will not be an abandonment." *Kreitz v. Behrensmeyer* (Ill. 1888).

Stated differently, a residence is not lost "by temporary removal with the intention to return, or even with a conditional intention of acquiring a new residence, but when one abandons his home and takes up his residence in another county or election district." *Clark v. Quick* (Ill. 1941). Third, both the establishment and the abandonment of a residence is principally a question of intent. Fourth, and finally, once a residence has been established, the presumption is that it continues, and the burden of proof is on the contesting party to show that it has been abandoned.

In Illinois, the legal meaning of residence has been settled for well over 100 years, not only in the very context that section 3.1–10–5(a) concerns (see *Smith*), but in virtually every other setting in which this court has construed a legal residency requirement. There is absolutely no indication anywhere in the Municipal Code that the legislature intended residency in section 3.1–10–5(a) to mean anything other than this well-settled meaning.

Of course, the appellate court did not see the statutory question this way. But its reasons for departing from over 100 years of settled residency law are hardly compelling and deserve only brief attention. First, as already noted, the appellate court asserts that this court "has at least once noted the distinction between candidate and voter residency requirements." In support, the appellate court cites to this court's 1960 pronouncement that the residency requirements set forth in the Municipal Code "'differentiate[d] between "electors" and those persons who may qualify for municipal office.'" (quoting *People ex rel. Moran v. Teolis* (Ill. 1960)). The intended implication, of course, is that this court has a history of defining residency differently as between candidates and electors. What the appellate court fails to mention is that the cited portion of *Moran* was referring solely to the statutory *time periods* in the respective local residency requirements (*i.e.*, 30 days for electors, one year for candidates), a "distinction" that appears on the face of the statute and says nothing about *how*, as opposed to *how long*, residency must be established.

By way of final thought on this question, we wish to point out that, while this court's traditional definition of residence may be plugged into the Municipal Code without creating any ambiguity or confusion, the appellate court's new and undefined standard promises just the opposite. Although adopting a previously unheard-of test for residency that would have applied to all future municipal elections, the court made no attempt to explain what its standard means. The only hint given by the appellate court is that, whatever its standard means, this candidate did not satisfy it. The appellate court never explained what it meant by "actually reside" or "actually live." Indeed, as its discussion of section 3.1–10–5(d) reflects, the entire appellate court opinion can be read as nothing more than an extended exercise in question begging, in which the appellate court sets forth the question to be answered as what it means to "reside" and concludes that it means to have "actually resided."

The difficulty of applying such a standard is immediately apparent. For instance, consider a Chicago resident who owns a second home in Florida and typically spends a month there every winter. Where is that person "actually living" or "actually residing" during the month when he or she is at the second home? Is such a person ineligible for municipal office unless he or she sleeps at the Chicago house every night for the year preceding the election? Is there a time limit with this test? Would a week at the second home be short enough but two months be too long? What about a Chicago resident whose job requires him to spend extended periods of time out of the country every year? Where is such a person "actually living" or "actually residing" when out of the country? Assuming without deciding that the appellate court was correct that the government service exception does not apply to candidates, consider the example of Representatives in Congress who often spend four to five days a week in Washington, D.C. If a Representative from a Chicago congressional district owns a condominium in Washington, D.C., where is that representative "actually living" or "actually residing" when Congress is in session? Under the majority's test, would the candidate have been ineligible to run for mayor even during the time he was serving in Congress? The same confusion would arise with respect to State Representatives or State Senators who must spend considerable amounts of time in Springfield. Applying the traditional test of residency to all of the above examples leads to the commonsense conclusion that all would remain Chicago residents even when away. Under the appellate court's test, considerable doubt would arise as to whether *any* of these people could meet a residency test that requires one year of "actually living" or "actually residing" in the municipality. Once the practical implications of adopting a standard for residence that means "actually lives" or "actually resides" are considered, one can readily appreciate why such a standard has never been adopted and why the standard used in Illinois has endured for well over a century.

So where does all of this leave us? It leaves us convinced that, when determining whether a candidate for public office has "resided in" the municipality at least one year next preceding the election or appointment, the principles that govern are identical to those embodied in *Smith* and consistently applied in the context of determining whether a voter has "resided in" this state and in the election district 30 days next preceding any election. Thus, in assessing whether the candidate has *established* residency, the two required elements are: (1) physical presence, and (2) an intent to remain in that place as a permanent home. Once residency is established, the test is no longer physical presence but rather abandonment, the presumption is that residency continues, and the burden of proof is on the contesting party to show that residency has been abandoned. Both the establishment and abandonment of a residence is largely a question of intent, and while intent is shown primarily from a candidate's acts, a candidate is absolutely competent to testify as to his intention, though such testimony is not necessarily conclusive.

[B]ecause it is uncontested that the candidate was a Chicago resident at least until January 2, 2009, when he resigned his office as Representative from the Fifth Congressional District of Illinois, the Board correctly determined that the relevant question was *not* whether the candidate had *established* residency in Chicago, but rather whether the objectors had proved by a preponderance of the evidence that the candidate had *abandoned* that residency at any time during the one-year period before the February 22, 2011, election. Only when abandonment is proven is residence lost. On the question of abandonment, a party's intention is controlling. Intention is determined both by a person's declarations and his acts. A person's declarations of intent are not conclusive and may be disproved by his acts. Once a residence has been established the presumption is that it continues, and the burden of proof is on the party claiming that it has been changed.

The objectors claim that, once a person rents out a residence, he or she has abandoned it as a matter of law. This is obviously incorrect, as it is directly contrary to *Smith*. Indeed, *Smith* makes clear that rental is merely one factor to consider in determining abandonment and the terms of the rental and the circumstances surrounding it must be considered. For instance, if an Illinois resident accepts a permanent job with an out-of-state corporation, purchases a house in a new state, moves his or her family into the new house, moves all of his or her belongings out of the old house and into the new one, and then rents out the old house on a one-year lease with a right to renew, it clearly could be said that this was an abandonment of the Illinois residency. By contrast, the Board did not believe that this rental showed abandonment when the candidate took a position as Chief of Staff to the President of the United States (an inherently temporary position of national service), merely rented in Washington, D.C., left many personal belongings in the Chicago residence, and ensured that the lease term for the Chicago house ended at the same time as the lease on the Washington, D.C., house. The Board determined that, in this situation, the rental did not show abandonment of the residence. This conclusion was well supported by the evidence and was not clearly erroneous.

So there will be no mistake, let us be entirely clear. This court's decision is based on the following and *only on the following:* (1) what it means to be a resident for election purposes was clearly established long ago, and Illinois law has been consistent on the matter since at least the 19th Century; (2) the novel standard adopted by the appellate court majority is without any foundation in Illinois law; (3) the Board's factual findings were not against the manifest weight of the evidence; and (4) the Board's decision was not clearly erroneous.

Justices FREEMAN and BURKE, specially concurring:

We join in the majority's decision to reverse the judgment of the appellate court. We do not, however, agree with the majority's reasoning.

The result in this case is in no way as clear-cut as the majority makes it out to be. The majority states that, in Illinois, "the legal meaning of residence has been settled for well over 100 years, not only in the very context that section 3.1–10–5(a) concerns, but in virtually every other setting in which this court has construed a legal residency requirement." This is simply not true.

As this court has noted, the legal term "residence" does not "have a fixed and constant meaning"

The majority bases its decision entirely on *Smith* (1867). As the appellate court correctly noted, the outcome in that decision turned solely on intent, a principle that is consistent with the legal concept of domicile. Unfortunately, *Smith* was not this court's last pronouncement on the issue. Later decisions, namely *Pope v. Board of Election Commissioners* (1938), *Park v. Hood* (1940), and *Clark v. Quick* (1941), each define residence in terms of domicile *plus* a permanent abode. In other words, under these cases, intent alone is not enough to establish residency.

Suffice it to say, therefore, that this court has not always spoken clearly on what is meant by residency, and the majority should acknowledge this fact. This is why both sides in this dispute can contend that their respective positions are supported by decades of precedent. Indeed, contrary to the majority's assertions, the only thing that is well established in this case is the confusion that has existed on this subject. The majority today now makes clear that residency for all purposes is the equivalent of domicile. The majority, therefore, should overrule those portions of *Pope*, *Park*, and *Clark* which hold to the contrary.

It is for this reason that the tone taken by the majority today is unfortunate. Because our own case law was, until today, unclear, it is unfair of the majority to state that the appellate court majority "toss[ed] out 150 years of settled residency law," adopted a "previously unheard-of test for residency," or was engaged in a "mysterious" analysis. In order to properly address the parties' arguments, the appellate court had to reconcile this court's conflicting pronouncements on the question of residency. That court did the best it could without the benefit of a supreme court opinion which clarified the standards. By refusing to acknowledge the role our own case law has played in creating the dispute before us, the majority unwittingly adds credence to the inflammatory statements contained in the dissenting opinion below.

Spirited debate plays an essential role in legal discourse. But the majority opinion here and the appellate dissent cross the line. Inflammatory accusations serve only to damage the integrity of the judiciary and lessen the trust which the public places in judicial opinions. The present case, one of obvious public interest, raises difficult questions regarding the legal concept of residency about which reasonable minds may differ. Indeed, as noted above, the meaning of the term "residency" has puzzled attorneys and judges since the term first appeared in the statute books. The majority and dissenting appellate court opinions illustrate the confusion that has long existed on this issue, which is the very reason for the difficulty in discerning what the General Assembly meant when it used the words "has resided in" in section 3.1–10–5(a) of the Illinois Municipal Code. There is no reason for the majority here to cast aspersions on the appellate court's motivations.

NOTES ON *CLEMENTS* AND *MAKSYM*

1. What do you make of the constitutional analysis in *Clements*? The Court finds that there is no constitutional right to be a candidate and therefore applies rational basis review to an equal protection clause challenge. Is this the correct approach? What about the voters who would support the candidates that Texas law bars from office? Do they have a constitutional right to have a candidate they support appear on the ballot?

2. As *Maksym* demonstrates, state law can have specific eligibility rules—such as a residency requirement—for state offices. But often those rules themselves are subject to judicial interpretation. In a challenge over a candidate's residency, the factual record matters quite a bit. That said, courts generally seem reluctant to remove an otherwise-eligible candidate from the ballot, preferring to allow the voters themselves to determine if someone's absence from the area makes that person unsuitable for the office. But that raises another question: why have a residency requirement at all? Or conversely, should the U.S. Constitution require residency in the district for members of Congress?

3. What do you make of the *Maksym* majority's attitude toward the court of appeals? Was it appropriate, or do you agree with the concurrence that it went too far? Why do you think the court of appeals ruled in the way it did? Perhaps the inherent politics of the dispute (and the candidate at issue) made a difference—but does that make it ok?

G. *RANKED CHOICE VOTING*

Several jurisdictions have adopted a different kind of winnowing process for the selection of nominees and winners called Ranked Choice Voting. Under this system, voters rank-order their preferences among all of the candidates—noting, for example, that they like Foley 1st, Pitts 2nd, Douglas 3rd, and so on, up to as many or as few candidates as they would like. (A voter could express a preference for only one candidate, of course, or could rank all or only some of them.) If a candidate receives more than 50 percent of the first-place votes, they win. If not, then the candidate with the fewest first-place votes is eliminated, and voters who selected that candidate have their second choice count instead. The process continues until a candidate has over 50 percent of the vote. In this way, Ranked Choice Voting ensures that a winning candidate actually receives a majority—not just a plurality—of the vote, at least when considering the second or third choices of voters whose first choice has been eliminated. Proponents say that the system avoids the prospect of a voter having to choose between the "lessor of two evils," instead allowing them to designate their ranked preferences among the candidates. They also say that campaigns are more positive: instead of throwing mud at their opponent (which might turn off their supporters), a candidate might send a message that "even if you like a different candidate as your number one choice, perhaps you might rank me as number two!" Finally, advocates say that Ranked Choice Voting is cheaper because jurisdictions need run only one election instead of a subsequent runoff election. It is possible to use Ranked Choice Voting for a party primary or for a general election; in a primary, the winning candidate would simply move on to the general election.

Ranked Choice Voting was used decades ago in places like Cincinnati, but its modern resurgence began in San Francisco in 2002. Then places like Minneapolis, St. Paul, Santa Fe, Oakland, and Portland, Maine adopted the system for their local elections. New York City adopted it for mayoral elections as well. Maine used Ranked Choice Voting statewide for the 2018 midterm election and the 2020 presidential election. The idea is therefore growing. Even the Academy Awards use Ranked Choice Voting to determine the Best Picture winner.

Opponents have argued that Ranked Choice Voting is unconstitutional, but courts have rejected these arguments so far. The next case, on San Francisco's law (which it termed "Instant Runoff Voting"), offers a clear explanation of why. Pay attention to the constitutional claims that opponents made and why the courts rejected those arguments.

Dudum v. Arntz

640 F.3d 1098 (9th Cir. 2011)

Berzon, Circuit Judge:

In 1873, Charles Lutwidge Dodgson, better known by his pen name, Lewis Carroll, spotted what he took to be an "extraordinary injustice": using simple plurality voting to determine the winners of elections. Dodgson, celebrated for his whimsical classics *Alice's Adventures in Wonderland* and *Through the Looking Glass,* was also a mathematician who developed election systems—meaning, simply, methods for translating preferences, or votes, into winners of elections. Dodgson disliked simple plurality voting because, in fields with several candidates, it can elect a candidate who receives the most first-place votes but is strongly *disfavored* by a majority of the electorate. Dodgson's innovative election systems were designed to remedy that limitation, and are still praised today because they tend to elect candidates with widespread electoral support.

While Dodgson preferred his systems to simple plurality voting, he recognized that his innovations were themselves imperfect. In a letter accompanying one of his pamphlets, Dodgson lamented: "A really scientific method for arriving at the result which is, on the whole, most satisfactory to a body of electors, seems to be still a desideratum."

Over a century later, Dodgson's wish remains unfulfilled. No perfect election system has been devised. Nonetheless, some governmental entities continue to experiment with innovative methods for electing candidates. At issue here is one such system, used by San Francisco for the election of certain city officials.

FACTUAL AND PROCEDURAL HISTORY

In March 2002, San Francisco voters approved a ballot measure, Proposition A, amending the City Charter to adopt a new electoral system for certain municipal elections. Before adoption of Proposition A, most city officials were selected in a two-round election: The city first held a general election. Then, unless one candidate won an outright majority in the first-round election, the two candidates who had garnered the most votes faced each other in a runoff election. Proposition A implemented instant runoff voting ("IRV") to replace the two-round runoff election system for the following city offices: Mayor, Sheriff, District Attorney, City Attorney, Treasurer, Assessor-Recorder, Public Defender, and members of the Board of Supervisors.

IRV allows voters to rank, in order of preference, candidates for a single office. The Department of Elections (the "Department") then tabulates the voters' preferences as follows: First, all first-choice rankings indicated on the ballots are counted. If a candidate wins a majority of these first-choice votes, he wins the election. If not, the candidate who received the fewest first-choice votes is "eliminated," meaning that that candidate cannot win the election. The second-choice votes on the ballots that had selected the eliminated candidate are then distributed to those voters' second-choice candidates. Some candidates' vote totals, as a result, now reflect a combination of first- and second-choice votes. If all candidates ranked by a voter are eliminated, that voters' ballot is "exhausted," meaning that it is not recounted as the tabulation continues. As long as no candidate receives a majority of the votes from the "continuing" ballots—that is, the nonexhausted ballots—the process of eliminating candidates, transferring preferences, and "exhausting" ballots repeats. A candidate is declared elected when he receives a majority of the operative votes on the "continuing" ballots.

San Francisco's Charter provides that IRV ballots are to allow voters to rank a number of candidates equal to the total number of candidates running in an election. For instance, if ten candidates are running for mayor, then voters are to be able to rank all ten of them. But the Charter also provides that if the voting system or equipment used by the Department cannot "feasibly accommodate" ranking that many choices, the Director of Elections can limit the number of candidates voters may rank to no fewer than three. We refer to this variant as "restricted IRV."

As it has turned out, in all of the City's IRV elections since Proposition A passed, the Department has restricted the number of rankings on each ballot to three. San Francisco maintains, and the plaintiffs, several San Francisco voters (collectively "Dudum"), do not dispute, that this choice is one of necessity: The voting machines currently in use are not equipped to tabulate unlimited rankings; cost and logistical concerns make accommodating the unlimited option untenable; and providing a ballot on which voters may rank every candidate in a large field could result in confusion, voter error, and inaccuracies in vote calculation.*

The Department makes publicly available on its website tables showing the election results for the City's past IRV elections. These tables tally the total ballots cast in each election; provide synopses of vote distribution during the tabulation process and of the final votes attributed to each candidate; and show the numbers of ballots "exhausted" as the tabulations proceeded. These tables provide helpful illustrations of how restricted IRV has worked in practice.

Dudum filed suit in federal court seeking injunctive relief against San Francisco and its election officials. Principally, Dudum maintains that when more than four candidates run for a particular office, the restricted IRV system precludes some groups of voters from participating to the same extent as others. That argument is premised on an analogy: It would be unconstitutional, Dudum asserts, to prevent qualified voters from casting ballots in a runoff election; "exhausting" the ballot of a voter who would have ranked more than three candidates if allowed to do so, Dudum contends, is no different. Dudum also points out that the City's Charter declares that "exhausted" ballots are "*not counted* in further stages of the tabulation," and argues that not including the votes of certain voters in the later tabulation stages once all three of their chosen candidates have been eliminated is similar to disenfranchisement of those voters, and so unconstitutional. In support of those arguments, Dudum points to several recent elections in which significant numbers of ballots were "exhausted" before tabulation was completed, sometimes in numbers greater than the final margin of victory. Dudum maintains that as a result of the mandatory "exhaustion" feature and its impact, the restricted IRV system violates the First Amendment, the Equal Protection and Due Process clauses of the Fourteenth Amendment, and the Civil Rights Act, 42 U.S.C. §1983. He requests declaratory and injunctive relief prohibiting the City from using the system in future elections.

Agreeing that material facts are not in dispute, the parties filed cross-motions for summary judgment. The district court granted summary judgment for the City on all claims. Dudum appealed.

* [San Francisco has since adopted a voting mechanism to allow voters to rank up to 10 candidates.—EDS.]

DISCUSSION

A. Overview

As a way of "structuring elections," San Francisco's IRV system is fairly innovative in the context of American elections, yet has a historied pedigree. First developed in the 1870s by W.R. Ware, a professor at the Massachusetts Institute of Technology, instant runoff systems have been used in the United States and elsewhere at various times since then. Australia, Ireland, and London use IRV for certain elections, and several U.S. cities use versions of the restricted IRV system at issue here, including Oakland and Berkeley, California, and Minneapolis, Minnesota, among others.

Like all electoral systems, including widely-used systems such as plurality voting and two-round runoff elections, IRV offers a package of potential advantages and disadvantages. Dodgson's disappointed "desideratum" observation, made in 1877, remains true. For instance, in the familiar simple plurality system, sometimes called "first-past-the-post" elections, voters chose one candidate, and the winner is the candidate with the most votes. Plurality voting is widely used in the United States for single-office elections, including races for mayors and governors. Plurality voting has the benefit of simplicity: It is easy for voters to use, and also easy for voters to understand how their votes are tabulated and the winning candidate determined. Plurality voting also avoids the expense and burden of holding a runoff election.

But the system has less auspicious features as well. In contests with several candidates, it privileges candidates with a robust and organized core of support, even if they are strongly disapproved of by most of the electorate. Likewise, plurality voting allows a candidate to win with a small minority of the total votes cast when many candidates are on the ballot.

A two-round runoff system, sometimes called a "double-ballot" election, similarly has both significant strengths and troublesome weaknesses. In such a system, long used in many local elections and in some state races, voters select a single candidate in the first round of voting, much like plurality voting. If no candidate receives a majority of the vote, a second round of voting is held, in which voters choose between the two candidates who received the highest number of votes in the first round. Two-round runoff systems result in the election of candidates with majority support of those voters who turn out for the second election.

That majority support, however, is misleading in some respects. When the second- and third-place candidates, or second-, third-, and fourth-place candidates, are relatively close in a first-round election, a runoff scheme can arbitrarily eliminate a candidate who might otherwise have won the election at the runoff stage. Also, an elected candidate will likely receive support from voters who strongly preferred candidates eliminated in the first-round election, as voters may choose between the two candidates left standing on a "lesser of two evils" basis. And, of course, the system requires the expense and burden of holding two separate elections, and results in two different, albeit overlapping, electorate pools, the relative sizes of which can be affected by the choice of dates for the runoff round.

Unrestricted and restricted IRV systems eliminate the need for a separate runoff and ordinarily will result in the election of a candidate with more widespread support than would simple plurality voting. IRV systems also tend to produce fewer votes cast only for losing candidates—in academic parlance, "wasted votes"—than does straight plurality voting, because votes that would otherwise be cast for losing candidates can be redistributed to candidates with a chance of winning. Likewise, IRV systems allow the voters more say over who they want to represent them: if it is not to be their first choice, then they can choose a second.

Under restricted or unrestricted IRV, a candidate who did not receive the most number of first-choice votes can be elected. Whether that feature is a disadvantage or an advantage is, of course, debatable. Where, for instance, there is no candidate with a majority, and the vote spread between the top plurality candidates is small, the more nuanced IRV systems can be seen as better tests of the depth of voter support for each candidate than a simple first-past-the-post plurality system. Additionally, while both IRV systems allow voters to rank their preferences, neither system allows voters to *reconsider* their choices after seeing which candidates have a chance of winning. In other words, voters must submit their preferences before polls close, and, even though they might have chosen differently with more specific information about other voters' selections, they are not provided an opportunity to revise their choices. A two-round runoff system, in contrast, provides voters that opportunity through a new round of balloting in a runoff election. Finally, both IRV systems are unfamiliar to many voters, and so some voters might not entirely understand how their votes will affect the election.

Moreover, all voting systems in elections with more than two candidates can be manipulated through strategic voting. In a plurality voting scheme, a voter might choose a candidate who is not his first-choice preference, but who he believes has a realistic chance of winning. In a two-round runoff system, a voter might cast a vote in the first-stage election for a weak candidate, so that his actual first-choice candidate will face that weak candidate in the runoff. The risk of strategic voting exists in IRV but is less severe than in plurality voting or the first stage of a runoff election: Voters are more free to vote their true preferences, because they face less of a threat of having their votes entirely "wasted" on unsuccessful candidates.

In sum, restricted IRV, like every election system, offers a menu of benefits and limitations. But that observation does not mean it is a constitutionally acceptable system, so we now turn to Dudum's constitutional objections to the City's restricted IRV system.

B. The Burden on Voters

Dudum concentrates on challenging the three-rank restriction aspect of San Francisco's system. We consider below the characteristics of restricted IRV Dudum does challenge, to determine the degree to which those features burden voters' constitutional rights, if at all, and if so, whether the burdens are so severe as to trigger strict scrutiny.

1

Dudum first contends that the treatment accorded "exhausted" ballots as the vote tabulation proceeds under the City's restricted IRV scheme is akin to prohibiting certain voters from voting in an election, and so imposes a severe, or at least a serious, burden on voters' constitutional rights. To support that characterization, Dudum points out that IRV replaced a two-round runoff system, and that explanations of how IRV works often analogize the successive vote calculation steps to a series of elections. For instance, the supervisors who supported adoption of Proposition A stated in their official ballot argument that "[t]he 'instant' runoff works much like December's 'delayed' runoff."

But the analogy is just that—an analogy. Upon examination, the analogy is off the mark in describing the real impacts of restricted IRV on voters' opportunities to cast ballots.

In actuality, all voters participating in a restricted IRV election are afforded a single and equal opportunity to express their preferences for three candidates; voters can use all three preferences, or fewer if they choose. Most notably, once the polls close and calculations begin, no new *votes* are cast. To determine the winner of the election based on that single set of votes cast, restricted IRV uses an algorithm. The ballots, each representing three or fewer preferences, are the initial inputs; the sequence of calculations mandated by restricted IRV is used to arrive at a single output—one winning candidate. The series of calculations required by the algorithm to produce the winning candidate are simply steps of a single tabulation, not separate rounds of voting.

In contrast, a two-round runoff system involves at least two rounds of voting, or *inputs,* explaining why it is sometimes referred to as a "double-ballot" election. For instance, in a two-round runoff system, even if a voter's chosen candidate in the first round successfully proceeds to the runoff election, that voter is still afforded an opportunity in the runoff election to select a different candidate, or not to vote at all. In a restricted IRV system, in contrast, if that voter chooses a successful candidate in one round, he is *not* afforded the opportunity to switch his vote to a different candidate as the tabulation progresses. That is so because restricted IRV considers only one round of inputs, i.e., votes.

Restricted IRV, of course, can be used *in place of* a two-round runoff election, which is what occurred in San Francisco and explains why the city supervisors compared the two. But restricted IRV does not *replicate* a two-round runoff system because, as we just explained, in two-round runoffs, voters cast ballots twice—that is, make and record their choices twice—whereas IRV allows only one chance to vote.

Dudum's contention that restricted IRV threatens to exclude some voters from *voting* is therefore incorrect. The contention sidesteps the basic fact that there is only one round of voting in restricted IRV.

2

Dudum tries a second tack: He maintains that the tabulation scheme under San Francisco's system burdens voters' constitutional rights to vote by effectively discarding, rather than counting, the votes from "exhausted" ballots.

In support of this characterization, Dudum points to the text of two provisions in the San Francisco Charter: First, according to the Charter, voters whose ballots are "exhausted" do not have their ballots "counted in further stages of the tabulation." Second, a candidate wins the election when he receives "a majority of the votes from the continuing ballots," meaning the nonexhausted ballots. *Id.* §13.102(c) & (d) (emphasis added). Dudum reads this text as meaning that "exhausted" ballots are discarded, and so not counted, in determining the election's ultimate outcome.

An examination of how restricted IRV works, however, indicates that the supposed inequity Dudum has identified is one of surface appearances and semantics, not substance. The algorithm used to determine the winner in an election conducted pursuant to the City's IRV system can be elaborated so that the outcome is mathematically identical, yet the features forming the basis of Dudum's characterization of the system as not counting some votes disappear. In essence, a more complete explication of the tabulation process demonstrates that "exhausted" ballots *are* counted in the election, they are simply counted as votes for losing candidates, just as if a voter had selected a losing candidate in a plurality or runoff election.

In other words, even though last-place candidates could no longer mathematically win the election, and could not obtain further votes, one could clutter the tabulation process by showing their votes on the tabulation tables even after they had been proven incapable of prevailing. The winner could then be defined as the candidate who receives a plurality of the *total votes cast* (including votes cast for candidates mathematically eliminated in prior stages), as long as he also receives a majority of the votes cast for candidates who were not mathematically eliminated previously. This "show your work" alternative—to quote many high school teachers—is more cumbersome than San Francisco's actual tabulation regime, but it accomplishes precisely the same result. As pertinent to Dudum's challenge, the rephrasing makes explicit what is implicit in the current scheme: "Exhausted" ballots *are* counted in the election, they are just counted for losing candidates in the tally of total votes. In the terms used by election experts, these are "wasted" votes, not because they aren't counted, but because they were cast for candidates not ultimately elected.

3

Dudum's final contention regarding the voting burden imposed by the restricted IRV system is that San Francisco's restricted IRV system is nonetheless unconstitutional because it results in the *dilution* of certain votes. Specifically, Dudum maintains that "some voters—those who vote for continuing candidates—only have one vote counted in 'the election'; other voters, however, have votes counted for three different candidates." Therefore, the argument goes, the City's IRV system violates the equal protection guarantee of "one person, one vote." At its core, Dudum's argument is that some voters are literally allowed more than one vote (i.e., they may cast votes for their first-, second-, and third-choice candidates), while others are not.

Once again, Dudum's contention mischaracterizes the actual operation of San Francisco's restricted IRV system and so cannot prevail. In fact, the option to rank multiple *preferences* is not the same as providing additional *votes,* or more heavily-weighted votes, relative to other votes cast. Each ballot is counted as no more than one vote at each tabulation step, whether representing the voters' first-choice candidate or the voters' second- or third-choice candidate, and each vote attributed to a candidate, whether a first-, second- or third-rank choice, is afforded the same mathematical weight in the election. The ability to rank multiple candidates simply provides a chance to have several preferences recorded and counted *sequentially,* not at once.

Dudum's vote dilution argument fails, because the ability to rank preferences sequentially does not affect the ultimate weight accorded any vote cast in the election.

Therefore, *if* the characteristics of the City's system Dudum has identified impose any burdens on the right to vote, they are minimal at best. For the sake of completeness, we shall assume *some* burden is imposed, however limited, and so consider whether the restricted IRV system serves governmental interests sufficient to justify that minimal at best burden under the flexible balancing analysis. *See, e.g., Burdick.*

C. The Governmental Interests

Because restricted IRV does not impose severe burdens on voting rights, we do not apply strict scrutiny. And here, the City's "important regulatory interests" are more than substantial enough to justify the minimal at best burdens imposed by the City's chosen system.

1

Dudum challenges only the three-candidate limitation, not IRV generally. In light of that limited challenge, one would expect Dudum to argue that the interests advanced by the City *in favor of the three-candidate restriction* are inadequate. But Dudum does not contest those specific justifications. Instead, he argues that the interests advanced in favor of IRV *generally* can be served just as well by either a plurality system or a two-round runoff scheme. Dudum's logic seems to be that if the three-candidate limit imposes a burden on voting rights, and if the City maintains that it cannot eliminate that restriction, then restricted IRV should be compared to election systems whose constitutionality is not in question.

In the end, then, Dudum is effectively asking the court to choose between electoral systems (i.e., between restricted IRV, plurality voting, or two-round runoff elections). As explained, however, electoral systems serve diverse interests with various degrees of success. That is why, absent a truly serious burden on voting rights, it is the job of democratically-elected representatives to weigh the pros and cons of various [election] systems.

2

The City advances several interests justifying the minimal at best burdens of which Dudum complains. Some of those interests concern the three-candidate restriction, and some support IRV as compared to the two-round runoff system it replaced.

First, the City adduces evidence that (1) the current voting machines cannot process ballots allowing unlimited ranking, and (2) permitting voters to rank more than three candidates might exceed the memory capacity of the machines now in use. The City maintains that the state certification necessary for new voting software or hardware or for redesigned ballots could take months or years, so allowing unlimited choices would disrupt the City's preparation for upcoming elections. Moreover, contends the City, (1) because some elections include many candidates, allowing unlimited rankings would require either extremely large, confusing ballots or multiple ballots for each voter; (2) multiple ballots could lead to calculation errors; and (3) in testing, voters regarded ballots offering four choices as confusing. Notably, Dudum introduced no evidence suggesting that San Francisco *could* conduct unrestricted elections without running into the problems identified, and does not now argue that the City's interests are inadequate to justify the three-candidate restriction.

Assuming for the moment the constitutional validity of IRV systems generally, then, the three-candidate restriction furthers important interests in maintaining the orderly administration of San Francisco's elections and in avoiding voter confusion.

We could stop there, as Dudum purports to challenge only the three-rank restriction, not IRV generally. But even if we expand the comparative inquiry to other election systems, as Dudum would have us do, his challenge fares no better.

The City points to evidence that restricted IRV will save money compared to a two-round runoff system (the election system in place prior to IRV), as each runoff election costs the City between $1.5 million and $3 million. The interest in alleviating the costs and administrative burdens of conducting additional elections can be "a legitimate state objective" that also justifies the use of IRV, given the minimal at best burdens the system imposes on voters' constitutional rights to vote.

Further, restricted IRV advances the City's legitimate interests in providing voters an opportunity to express nuanced voting preferences and electing candidates with strong plurality support. Unlike a two-round runoff election, restricted IRV will not always produce a candidate with majority support. But restricted IRV also does not limit voters' choices to only two candidates, and so it allows voters to express a wider range of preferences. Moreover, in practice, the ability to express more nuanced preferences means that candidates with *greater* plurality support (although not necessarily majority support) tend to be elected, as compared to a traditional plurality system.

In sum, we have no difficulty holding that these important governmental interests are more than sufficient to outweigh the extremely limited burdens—if any—that the restricted IRV features Dudum challenges impose upon San Francisco's voters.

CONCLUSION

If the aspects of the City's restricted IRV scheme Dudum challenges impose any burdens on voters' constitutional rights to vote, they are minimal at best. Moreover, the City has advanced valid, sufficiently-important interests to justify using its system. We, of course, express no views on the wisdom of using IRV, restricted IRV, or any other electoral method. There is no perfect election system, and our search for one would prove no more successful than a hunt for the mythical snark. Happily, we are not required to engage in any such endeavor. We hold only that Dudum has not established that the City's chosen system is unconstitutional. Affirmed.

NOTES ON *DUDUM* AND RANKED CHOICE VOTING

1. What was the plaintiff's primary constitutional challenge? In thinking about the one person, one vote principle from the redistricting cases in Part I, do you agree that Ranked Choice Voting/Instant Runoff Voting does not place more weight on some voters' ballots as compared to others? Does it dilute the strength of some votes by not allowing a plurality winner?

2. Maine's adoption of Ranked Choice Voting (RCV) has generated a lot of litigation, especially as it was the first state to implement the system statewide. Some of those challenges involved state constitutional law and whether a people's initiative could constitutionally adopt Ranked Choice Voting for state elections. The Maine Supreme Judicial Court said it could not, as the state constitution requires plurality winners for those offices, thereby limiting the use of Ranked Choice Voting to federal and local elections. *Opinion of the Justices*, 162 A.3d 188, 193, *as revised* (Sept. 19, 2017) (Me. 2017). Next, the Maine Republican Party asserted that requiring it to use RCV for its party primaries violated its First Amendment associational rights, but the federal district court rejected the argument. The court found that RCV "does not regulate who may participate in a primary or intrude on the Maine Republican Party's internal governance or processes, [and therefore] its effect on Maine's primary process does not impose a severe or heavy burden on the Maine Republican Party's associational right." The court also found that Maine had a sufficiently weighty interest in adopting this voting system for primary elections. *Maine Republican Party v. Dunlap*, No. 1:18-cv-001 (D. Me. May 29, 2018). Further, in a post-election challenge by the winner of the plurality of votes but not the ranked choice votes in a congressional election, a court rejected the claim that RCV is unconstitutional. The plaintiffs asserted that the U.S. Constitution requires "that all ballots be counted in a single round and that the candidate with the plurality of votes is the winner," but the court found that the Constitution does not require plurality winners. The court noted that "both majority and plurality standards have historical antecedents in American politics." In rejecting the plaintiff's claim that RCV violates the Fourteenth Amendment, the court held that "Maine's RCV system is designed to enable every voter the opportunity to express a preference, and be counted, with respect to the candidates most likely to win the election." *Baber v. Dunlap*, NO.1:18-CV-465 (D. Me. Nov. 15, 2018). The system therefore did not deprive anyone of casting an effective ballot.

3. What do you think of Ranked Choice Voting as a matter of election policy? Opponents say that the system is too confusing for voters and makes it possible for a candidate with few first-place votes to ultimately win an election based on their more widespread selection as a second or third place choice; the winner could therefore be a candidate who most people did not favor the most. Advocates point to the ability of a Ranked Choice Voting system to nominate or elect a consensus candidate who enjoys the support of the majority of the electorate, even if they are not the first choice of a majority. They also say that Ranked Choice Voting reduces costs and creates more positive campaigns. Those virtues, in turn, might increase turnout. Which side is correct? What are the hurdles to the adoption of Ranked Choice Voting either for local or statewide elections? How would Ranked Choice Voting alter presidential elections?

SUMMARY OF THE LAW OF NOMINATING CANDIDATES

The cases in this Part had several overarching themes. Among them included:

- Discerning the best way to go from "many to few to one" in selecting a party nominee (or independent candidate) and then eventual winner
- Determining the permissible requirements for ballot access

- Employing the severe burden test to determine the proper level of scrutiny—which often ultimately decided the constitutionality of the law under review
- The concern of entrenchment and the protection of the two major political parties
- The constitutional rights of a candidate to run for office and the rights of voters who want to support a candidate
- The spreading adoption of Ranked Choice Voting as an alternative method to select either primary winners or the overall winner in a general election.

The cases showed that major political parties have a robust First Amendment right to freedom of association and have wide discretion in choosing the method for selecting their nominees. In addition, national political parties seem to have more discretion than state political parties, especially when the issue involves party autonomy. But we also found that states have wide leeway to enact regulations for ballot access—such as imposing write-in bans (*Burdick*), antifusion laws (*Timmons*), and signature requirements for independent candidates (*Anderson*)—so long as the burdens are not too severe and there are legitimate state interests. We learned about different kinds of primaries: open, closed (*Tashjian*), semi-closed (*Clingman v. Beaver*), and top two (*Washington State Grange*). We studied a political party's interest in avoiding party raiding and sore loser candidacies, and the way in which these interests impact the constitutionality of ballot access rules. We discussed the difference between facial and as-applied challenges in litigation involving election laws (most poignantly discussed in *Washington State Grange*). We saw that candidates do not have constitutional rights, independent of voters, to be a candidate (*Clements v. Fashing*), and that the factual record matters a great deal to eligibility challenges (*Maksym*). Through it all, we realized that in many of these cases it is difficult to locate a reconciling principle beyond determining the severity of the burden and weighing that burden against the importance of the state's interests.

Therefore, one of the more important aspects of this material to master is the *Anderson-Burdick* "severe burden" test and how courts employ (or, some might say, manipulate) it to determine the level of scrutiny. We will see courts use this test again in issues involving election administration in Part IV. You should also consider the clash between stakeholders in this area: candidates and their supporters, state political parties, national political parties, minor parties, and the state in its regulation of the political process. We see, in cases such as *Democratic Party v. Wisconsin*, that the Court highly values a political party's right to associational autonomy. But this right is not absolute, as the *Washington State Grange* and *Clingman* decisions demonstrate, as in both cases the state was allowed greater leeway to regulate the political process. With respect to independent candidates securing ballot access for the general election, the Court requires the path to the ballot to be open, but states can impose modest constraints such as reasonable signature requirements. Once again, then, we circle back to the application of the "severe burden" balancing test in an attempt to reconcile this area of law.

PART III

The Law of Campaign Practices

INTRODUCTION

Now that we have defined a constituency to elect a person through redistricting and determined how a candidate appears on the ballot, the next step in the electoral process is running the campaign. This involves two main topics: (1) laws involving the conduct of the campaign itself (such as campaign ads, last-minute campaigning at the polls, or even more egregious efforts to persuade a voter to cast a ballot for a particular candidate, such as financial inducements); and (2) laws about the regulation of money used to pay for campaign activities, or (in other words) campaign finance.

During the most recent election cycles, there have been many allegations of campaign practices that seemed to push the limits of permissible activity. There were reports of flyers distributed to poor, largely African-American communities claiming that Election Day had been moved to Wednesday (the day after the actual Election Day). There were also reports of unlawful "vote buying" across the country. The past few election cycles have also entailed evidence of misinformation and unfounded and unsupported allegations of massive election fraud. Beyond illegal or untoward campaign activities, every election entails questions regarding the permissible scope of advertising, campaigning, and get-out-the-vote efforts. And, of course, there is the question of foreign interference in U.S. elections and how to combat that concern.

On the campaign finance front, the past few years have been extremely volatile. The amount of money in politics has skyrocketed as the Supreme Court has struck down various campaign finance limitations. In part as a result of the Supreme Court's 2010 decision in *Citizens United v. FEC*, the 2010 midterm elections were the most expensive in history. The 2012 general election surpassed this record. 2016 was even more expensive, but 2020 then crushed that record, with over $14 billion spent nationwide on the presidential and congressional elections—more than double the amount of money spent in 2016.*

* The line between "campaign" regulations, addressed in this Part of the book, and "voting" regulations, addressed in Part IV, is inevitably blurry at the margins. For example, the regulation of campaign activities that occur at polling places on Election Day itself could be considered in either category. The same can be said of laws that prohibit the payment of a financial inducement in exchange for the promise to vote for a particular candidate. We

Throughout the materials in this Part, consider the manner in which courts allow federal or state governments to regulate campaign practices. To what extent are there limits on the ability of candidates and campaigns to interact with voters? When does a plea to vote become harassing? How does the constitutional right to vote conflict with the First Amendment right to freedom of speech, and what falls under the rubric of allowed "speech" for campaign purposes? In justifying their laws, the federal and state governments usually point to interests in election integrity, ensuring open and equal access to the ballot, and limiting corruption and fraud. When are these interests sufficient? As in the other Parts of this book, there are usually no easy answers, and the analysis depends largely on the clash of rights between stakeholders in the electoral arena.

A. FALSE OR MISLEADING CAMPAIGN ADS

Few would dispute that our politics have become extremely vitriolic. Negative ads are a routine part of campaigns. In fact, studies have demonstrated that "going negative" often works in a campaign, especially to make up ground in a close race. Negative ads can depress turnout: even if a negative ad does not convince a voter to support a candidate, it can lead voters to become apathetic and not show up at all. Do states have an interest in promoting civil discourse during elections by regulating the kinds of permissible campaign advertisements? Is limiting misleading or even downright false campaign statements consistent with the First Amendment rights of candidates? When does an advertisement cross the line from being a fair attack on an opponent's record to being inaccurate or even a lie, and is there anything a state can do about advertisements that go too far? The next set of cases explore these issues. The cases demonstrate that most judicial interpretation of the First Amendment makes it hard for states to regulate false campaign ads, though there are forceful arguments in dissent.

As a backdrop to these cases, you should know that the U.S. Supreme Court has permitted the punishment of intentional or reckless falsehoods in the context of defamation law, which is designed to protect against injury to reputation. In fact, there are examples of candidates suing their opponents for defamation after an election based on a false statement during the campaign. Should the same First Amendment (freedom of speech) standard apply when the state is asserting the different interest of protecting the electoral process? Defamation law is inapplicable when a candidate lies about facts relevant to a policy issue ("Gas prices tripled in the last three years"—when in fact they rose by only 30 percent), or when candidates falsely inflate their own records ("I received the Medal of Honor for bravery under fire in the Iraq War"—when in fact the candidate never saw combat). That

have chosen to include these particular topics in Part III, rather than Part IV, because we want to focus attention in this Part on the extent to which the law may constrain candidates and their campaigns from attempting to influence a voter's choice. In Part IV, by contrast, we focus on the regulation of casting and counting ballots even when there is no issue concerning improper influence on the voter's free electoral choice.

is, based on well-settled doctrine, a defamation lawsuit is unavailable for false statements about a policy matter or when the candidate lies about him or herself. But defamation suits are possible when a candidate lies about his or her opponent. Yet those suits typically occur after the election and do not limit the falsehood influencing the electorate. Should states be able to regulate this speech ahead of Election Day to ensure voters have the most accurate information possible when making their choices?

As you read these next cases, consider whether the First Amendment should distinguish among types of campaign falsehoods for the purpose of a candidate's potential liability. Moreover, what sorts of punishments would be permissible for the state to impose if and when a court finds a speaker liable for a false or misleading campaign ad? For example, would it be permissible for a court to disqualify a candidate from holding office, or only to impose a modest fine? Finally, if you conclude that campaign ads should be entirely protected from liability, except in the context of a defamation lawsuit, are there any other steps that the government can take in an effort to protect the public from the intentional lies of unscrupulous politicians?

Rickert v. State Public Disclosure Commission

168 P.3d 826 (Wash. 2007)

J.M. JOHNSON, J.

The United States and Washington Constitutions both protect the right of free speech, and political speech is the core of that right. The notion that a censorship scheme like RCW 42.17.530(1)(a) [the statute at issue in this case, as described below] may be constitutionally enforced by a government agency erroneously "presupposes [that] the State possesses an independent right to determine truth and falsity in political debate." *State ex rel. Pub. Disclosure Comm'n v. 119 Vote No! Comm.* (Wash. 1998) (plurality opinion). Yet, "'[t]he very purpose of the First Amendment is to foreclose public authority from assuming a guardianship of the public mind.'" *Id.*(quoting *Meyer v. Grant* (1988)). This court has previously agreed that state censorship is not allowed: "The State cannot 'substitute its judgment as to how best to speak for that of speakers and listeners; free and robust debate cannot thrive if directed by the government.'" *Id.* (quoting *Riley v. Nat'l Fed'n of Blind, Inc.* (1988)). The present case provides an opportunity to vigorously reaffirm the law on this vital constitutional issue.

FACTS AND PROCEDURAL HISTORY

In 2002, Ms. Rickert challenged incumbent Senator Tim Sheldon in the election for state senator from Washington's 35th Legislative District. During the campaign, Ms. Rickert sponsored a mailing that included a brochure comparing her positions to those of Senator Sheldon. In part, the brochure stated that Ms. Rickert "[s]upports social services for the most vulnerable of the state's citizens." By way of comparison, the brochure stated that Senator Sheldon "voted to close a facility for the developmentally challenged in his district." In response to the latter statement, Senator Sheldon filed a complaint with the Public Disclosure Commission (PDC), alleging a violation of RCW 42.17.530(1)(a).

RCW 42.17.530(1) provides, in relevant part:

> It is a violation of this chapter for a person to sponsor with actual malice:
>
> (a) Political advertising or an electioneering communication that contains a false statement of material fact about a candidate for public office. However, this subsection (1)(a) does not apply to statements made by a candidate or the candidate's agent about the candidate himself or herself.

"Actual malice" means "to act with knowledge of falsity or with reckless disregard as to truth or falsity." RCW 42.17.020(1). A violation of RCW 42.17.530(1)(a) must be proven by clear and convincing evidence. RCW 42.17.530(2).

The PDC held a hearing regarding Senator Sheldon's complaint on July 29, 2003, months after Senator Sheldon handily defeated Ms. Rickert in the 2002 election. The PDC found that Ms. Rickert's brochure contained two false statements: "(a) Senator Sheldon voted to close the Mission Creek Youth Camp, and (b) . . . Mission Creek was a facility for the developmentally challenged." Additionally, the PDC concluded that the statements were material, that Ms. Rickert sponsored the brochure with actual malice, and that her violation of RCW 42.17.530(1)(a) had been established by clear and convincing evidence. The PDC imposed a $1,000 penalty on Ms. Rickert.

The superior court affirmed the PDC's final order. Ms. Rickert then appealed to the Court of Appeals, which reversed. The Court of Appeals held that RCW 42.17.530(1)(a) violates the First Amendment because it cannot survive strict scrutiny. We agree and, accordingly, affirm.

ANALYSIS

A. RCW 42.17.530(1)(A) Extends to Protected Speech, Hence, Strict Scrutiny Applies

"[T]he First Amendment 'has its fullest and most urgent application' to speech uttered during a campaign for political office." *Burson v. Freeman* (1992) (plurality opinion). Accordingly, any statute that purports to regulate such speech based on its content is subject to strict scrutiny. Under this standard, the State must demonstrate that RCW 42.17.530(1)(a) is necessary to serve a compelling state interest and that it is narrowly drawn to achieve that end.

The text of RCW 42.17.530(1)(a) suggests that the legislature may have intended to limit the scope of its prohibition to the unprotected category of political defamation speech identified by the United States Supreme Court in *New York Times Co. v. Sullivan* (1964). However, as correctly noted by the Court of Appeals, "[U]nder *New York Times*, only *defamatory* statements . . . are not constitutionally protected speech." Because RCW 42.17.530(1)(a) does not require proof of the defamatory nature of the statements it prohibits, its reach is not limited to the very narrow category of unprotected speech identified in *New York Times* and its progeny. Thus, RCW 42.17.530(1)(a) extends to protected political speech and strict scrutiny must apply.

B. RCW 42.17.530(1)(A) Cannot Survive Strict Scrutiny

1. Protecting candidates is not a compelling government interest here, and RCW 42.17.530(1)(a) is not narrowly tailored to further that interest

The plain language of RCW 42.17.530(1)(a) provides that the law's purpose is "to provide protection for candidates for public office." [T]he State claims that it may prohibit false statements of fact contained in political advertisements. However, this claim presupposes the State possesses an independent right to determine truth and falsity in political debate, a proposition fundamentally at odds with the principles embodied in the First Amendment. Moreover, it naively assumes that the government is capable of correctly and consistently negotiating the thin line between fact and opinion in political speech. Yet, political speech is usually as much opinion as fact. ("Spinning" is a common term used to describe putting different perspectives on facts.) Every person must be his own watchman for truth, because the forefathers did not trust any government to separate the truth from the false for us.

Particularly relevant here is the fundamental First Amendment principle forbidding censorship or coerced silence in the context of political debate. "The First Amendment exists precisely to protect against laws . . . which suppress ideas and inhibit free discussion of governmental affairs." [Court of Appeals' decision] Hence, the Sedition Act of 1798, which censored speech about government, has been subject to nearly unanimous historical condemnation. For similar reasons, RCW 42.17.530(1)(a) is deserving of condemnation, lacks a compelling justification, and thus must be declared unconstitutional.

The Supreme Court has recognized a legitimate, and at times compelling, interest in "compensating private individuals for wrongful injury to reputation." *Gertz v. Robert Welch, Inc.* (1974). However, this interest cannot justify a government-enforced censorship scheme like RCW 42.17.530(1)(a). The statute may protect candidates from criticism, but it has no mechanism for compensation for damage to reputations. More importantly, there is no requirement that the statements subject to sanction under RCW 42.17.530(1)(a) be of the kind that tend to cause harm to an individual's reputation, i.e., defamatory.

In sum, the interest asserted by the legislature—protecting political candidates (including themselves)—is not a compelling interest in support of RCW 42.17.530(1)(a). Accordingly, the statute fails under strict scrutiny.

2. Preserving the integrity of elections is not a compelling government interest here, and RCW 42.17.530(1)(a) is not narrowly tailored to further that interest

At argument below and before this court, the PDC suggests that preserving the integrity of the election process is the primary government interest furthered by RCW 42.17.530(1)(a). However, this was not the interest asserted by the legislature in enacting RCW 42.17.530(1)(a). Under strict scrutiny, a law burdening speech may not be upheld for any conceivable purpose but must be evaluated according to its actual purpose. Thus, it is arguably inappropriate to even consider the PDC's argument based on this belated, alternative interest.

Even assuming it were proper to consider a state interest asserted for the first time at argument, the PDC's claim still fails. The government may have a compelling interest in preventing direct harm to elections. However, that interest is not advanced in any significant manner by prosecuting Ms. Rickert, and other similarly situated individuals, under RCW 42.17.530(1)(a). Rather, the PDC's claim that it must prohibit arguably false, but nondefamatory, statements about political candidates to save our elections conflicts with the fundamental principles of the First Amendment. Therefore, "preserving the integrity of the election process" cannot be deemed a compelling interest in the context of a scheme like RCW 42.17.530(1)(a).

Furthermore, even if such an interest were valid, RCW 42.17.530(1)(a) would remain unconstitutional because it is not narrowly tailored. The statute is underinclusive because it does not apply to many statements that pose an equal threat to the State's alleged interest in protecting elections. Specifically, the statute exempts all statements made by a candidate (or his supporters) about himself. Basically, a candidate is free to lie about himself, while an opponent will be sanctioned. Yet, "[t]he PDC presents no compelling reason why a candidate would be less likely to deceive the electorate on matters concerning him- or herself and [thus] compromise the integrity of the elections process." [Court of Appeals' decision.]

In sum, RCW 42.17.530(1)(a)'s exemption for candidates' false speech about themselves demonstrates that the statute is not narrowly tailored to serve the State's alleged interest in preserving the integrity of elections. Because RCW 42.17.530(1)(a) is not narrowly tailored, the statute cannot survive under strict scrutiny.

3. The faulty procedural mechanisms of RCW 42.17.530(1)(a) confirm that the law is not narrowly tailored and, thus, fails under strict scrutiny

RCW 42.17.530(1)(a) is also fatally flawed due to its enforcement procedures, which are likely to have a chilling effect on speech. These procedural defects further indicate that the statute is not the least restrictive alternative to achieve the compelling interests it allegedly furthers. Ultimately, these defects support the conclusion that any statute permitting censorship by a group of unelected government officials is inherently unconstitutional.

The members of the PDC, the administrative body that enforces RCW 42.17.530(1)(a), are appointed by the governor, a political officer. This group of unelected individuals is empowered not only to review alleged false statements made in political campaigns but also to impose sanctions. Finally, there is no requirement that a reviewing court conduct an independent, de novo review as to whether there is clear and convincing evidence the respondent uttered the statements with actual malice.

The chilling effects resulting from this procedural scheme are manifest. A sitting governor may appoint a majority of the PDC's members. When this same governor seeks reelection, the governor's own appointees will decide whether to sanction the speech of campaign opponents. The campaign opponents will not be guaranteed a jury trial or independent, de novo judicial review. The mere threat of such a process will chill political speech. Likewise, the prospect of such a proceeding justifiably undermines the public's confidence in the propriety of Washington's electoral process—the very interest which the PDC purports to serve. Because of the risks to liberty inherent in RCW 42.17.530(1)(a)'s enforcement mechanisms, the statute cannot survive strict scrutiny.

CONCLUSION

Our constitutional election system already contains the solution to the problem that RCW 42.17.530(1)(a) is meant to address. "In a political campaign, a candidate's factual blunder is unlikely to escape the notice of, and correction by, the erring candidate's political opponent. The preferred First Amendment remedy of 'more speech, not enforced silence,' thus has special force." *Brown v. Hartlage* (1982) (quoting *Whitney v. California* (1927) (Brandeis, J., concurring)). In other words, the best remedy for false or unpleasant speech is more speech, not less speech. The importance of this constitutional principle is illustrated by the very real threats to liberty posed by allowing an unelected government censor like the PDC to act as an arbiter of truth.

In the case at bar, Ms. Rickert made knowingly false or reckless statements about Senator Sheldon, a man with an outstanding reputation. Senator Sheldon and his (many) supporters responded to Ms. Rickert's false statements with the truth. As a consequence, Ms. Rickert's statements appear to have had little negative impact on Senator Sheldon's successful campaign and may even have increased his vote. *See* [Court of Appeals' decision] (noting that "Senator Sheldon was reelected . . . by approximately 79 percent of the vote."). Were there injury to Senator Sheldon's reputation, compensation would be available through a defamation action. As it is, Ms. Rickert was singled out by the PDC for punishment, six months after the election, based on statements that had no apparent impact on the government interests allegedly furthered by the statute. That the statute may be applied in such a manner proves that it is fatally flawed under the First Amendment.

There can be no doubt that false personal attacks are too common in political campaigns, with wide-ranging detrimental consequences. However, government censorship such as RCW 42.17.530(1)(a) is not a constitutionally permitted remedy. We hold that this statute, which allows a government agency to censor political speech, is unconstitutional and affirm the decision of the Court of Appeals.

We concur: Charles W. Johnson, Susan Owens, Richard B. Sanders.

JJ. Alexander, C.J. concurring.
[Omitted.]

Madsen, J. dissenting.

The impression left by the majority's rhetoric, that oppressive government regulation is at issue in this case, is simply wrong. When cases decided by the United States Supreme Court are properly applied, it is obvious that RCW 42.17.530(1)(a) infringes on no First Amendment rights.

Unfortunately, the majority's decision is an invitation to lie with impunity. The majority opinion advances the efforts of those who would turn political campaigns into contests of the best stratagems of lies and deceit, to the end that honest discourse and honest candidates are lost in the maelstrom. The majority does no service to the people of Washington when it turns the First Amendment into a shield for the "unscrupulous . . . and skillful" liar to use knowingly false statements as an "effective political tool" in election campaigns. *See Garrison v. Louisiana* (1964). It is little wonder that so many view political campaigns with distrust and cynicism.

The majority is wrong when it says that state government cannot constitutionally regulate truth or falsity of political speech. No such blanket rule exists under the First Amendment. There is no question that the First and Fourteenth Amendments embody our "profound national commitment to the principle that debate on public issues should be uninhibited, robust, and wide-open, and that it may well include vehement, caustic, and sometimes unpleasantly sharp attacks on government and public officials." *New York Times Co. v. Sullivan* (1964). But it is equally true that the use of calculated falsehood is not constitutionally protected. "Neither the intentional lie nor the careless error materially advances society's interest in 'uninhibited, robust, and wide-open' debate on public issues." *Gertz v. Robert Welch, Inc.* (1974) (quoting *New York Times*).

The United States Supreme Court has made it absolutely clear that the deliberate lie in political debate has no protected place under the First Amendment because such lies do not advance the free political process but rather subvert it[.]

The majority's premise that there can be no regulation of political speech whatsoever cannot be squared with the United States Supreme Court's conclusion that under the First Amendment:

> *Calculated falsehood falls into that class of utterances which "are no essential part of any exposition of ideas, and are of such slight social value as a step to truth that any benefit that may be derived from them is clearly outweighed by the social interest in order and morality. . . ."* *Chaplinsky v. New Hampshire* [(1942)]. Hence the knowingly false statement and the false statement made with reckless disregard of the truths do not enjoy constitutional protection.

[*Garrison*] (emphasis added).

The majority is also wrong when it asserts that the only time that a false statement about a candidate for office can be burdened is when the statement constitutes civil defamation, actionable in tort law. This premise is no more accurate than the majority's conclusion that government cannot regulate political speech by proscribing the known lie.

Because the majority declines to follow precedent holding that false statements under the actual malice standard are not protected speech, it engages in a strict scrutiny analysis of RCW 42.17.530(1)(a)'s constitutionality. However, if the actual malice standard is met the speech falls within a class of speech that is not constitutionally protected. Therefore, a statute that proscribes speech under this standard does not have to meet the strict scrutiny/compelling governmental interest test that applies to statutes regulating protected political speech.

Further, the majority refuses to recognize that the actual malice standard is an exceedingly high standard to meet. Most political speech does not even approach being subject to regulation under this standard; the standard prohibits only the very worst untruths—those made with knowledge of their falsity or with reckless disregard to truth or falsity. In addition, the burden of proof is also high—proof must be by clear and convincing evidence. The actual malice standard is deliberately difficult to satisfy, precisely because free speech rights are at issue. Therefore, much nuanced speech, and all speech that constitutes opinion rather than fact, will simply fall short of it.

Finally, while the majority would prefer that no entity have authority to make final decisions on whether speech may be regulated and whether any regulations that are enacted conform to First Amendment requirements, this authority is constitutionally vested in the courts. Under RCW 42.17.530(1) the courts will continue to act as the final arbiter of any administrative decision.

Ultimately, the majority's claim of government censorship does not reflect the statute or the legislature's attempt to prohibit unprotected speech. Accordingly, I dissent.

The calculated falsehood in the course of an election campaign can distort the electoral process by misinforming the voters and so interfere with the process "upon which democracy is based." William P. Marshall, *False Campaign Speech and the First Amendment*, 153 U. Pa. L. Rev. 285, 294 (2004). As Marshall notes, and quoted above, using the known lie as a tool is at odds with the premises of democratic government and the orderly way in which change is to be effected. False statements can lower the quality of campaign discourse and debate, generating response to the attacks rather than engagement on major issues. False advertising also may give rise to or exacerbate voter alienation and distrust of the political process.

In light of these interests, there is no reason to treat the calculated falsehood with any greater protection in the context of a campaign than the Court said is constitutionally required in a defamation action involving a public official or public figure and a matter of public concern, or in the other contexts where it has applied the standard. These interests justify the actual malice standard in the context of political campaigns. They also warrant the conclusion that the calculated lie about a candidate for office during an election campaign is not subject to correction only through more speech or only through private defamation actions.

I believe that the actual malice standard is both a necessary and a sufficient standard for regulating false campaign speech.

In sum, RCW 42.17.530(1)(a) prohibits false statements of facts that are material to the election campaign. By limiting the statute's reach to facts, the legislature has avoided unconstitutionally infringing on opinions and ideas.

The majority, however, finds constitutional infirmity in the fact that the statute does not apply to statements made by a candidate, or his or her agent, about the candidate. In the course of its erroneous strict scrutiny analysis the majority agrees with Ms. Rickert's contention that the statute is not narrowly tailored because it does not apply to such statements.

Here, the basis for the discrimination consists entirely of the reasons that the calculated falsehood may be proscribed, and therefore no significant danger of viewpoint discrimination exists. As explained, lies about public officials are clearly outweighed by "'the social interest in order and morality,'" *Garrison* (quoting *Chaplinsky*), because they undermine the integrity and reliability of the election process, distort the political process through untrue and inaccurate speech that misinforms the voters and so interferes with the democratic process and the orderly way that change should be effected, lower the quality of campaign discourse and debate by generating response to the attacks rather than engagement on major issues, lead to public cynicism and apathy toward the electoral process, and cause or increase voter alienation and distrust of the political process. These reasons "have special force" when the statements are made about a candidate for office (not including false statements by a candidate about himself or herself).

The majority also finds unconstitutionality in the procedural aspects of the statute because liability under the statute is determined by an administrative agency rather than a jury. Aside from the majority's general disparaging remarks about nonelected officials and its unwarranted claims of censorship, the thrust of the majority's dissatisfaction is that the Public Disclosure Commission determines in the first instance whether there is a violation and, the majority says, there is no requirement that a reviewing court conduct an independent, de novo review, assessing whether the actual malice standard was satisfied. The majority says, in fact, that "[t]he campaign opponents will not be guaranteed . . . independent, de novo judicial review."

Whether RCW 42.17.530 (or any other statute) expressly provides for independent, de novo judicial review, such review unquestionably applies as a matter of constitutional law. A court is required to "make an independent examination of the whole record, so as to assure [itself] that the judgment does not constitute a forbidden intrusion on the field of free expression." *Bose* [*Corp. v. Consumers Union* (1984)]. The independent review rule is "a rule of federal constitutional law." [*Id.*] Thus, irrespective of whether there is a statutory requirement for independent, de novo judicial review, the *Constitution* mandates such review. Accordingly, the absence of a statutory provision for independent judicial review does not chill free speech rights as the majority asserts.

CONCLUSION

I would reverse the Court of Appeals' holding that RCW 42.17.530(1)(a) is facially unconstitutional. The statute accurately sets forth the *New York Times* standard for determining that certain false statements are not protected speech under the First Amendment, and this standard may constitutionally be applied to regulate candidates' speech during election campaigns.

I dissent.

We concur: Tom CHAMBERS, Mary E. FAIRHURST, Bobbe J. BRIDGE, JJ.

Susan B. Anthony List v. Driehaus

814 F.3d 466 (6th Cir. 2016)

COLE, Chief Judge.

Susan B. Anthony List ("SBA List") and the Coalition Opposed to Additional Spending and Taxes ("COAST") sued the Ohio Elections Commission ("Commission") and various state officials, alleging that Ohio's political false-statements laws, Ohio Rev. Code § 3517.21(B)(9)–(10), violate the First and Fourteenth Amendments. The district court agreed and entered summary judgment and a permanent injunction in favor of SBA List and COAST. Because the laws are content-based restrictions that burden core protected political speech and are not narrowly tailored to achieve the state's interest in promoting fair elections, we affirm.

I. FACTUAL BACKGROUND AND PROCEDURAL HISTORY

A. Ohio's Political False-Statements Laws

Ohio's political false-statements laws prohibit persons from disseminating false information about a political candidate in campaign materials during the campaign season "knowing the same to be false or with reckless disregard of whether it was false or not, if the statement is designed to promote the election, nomination, or defeat of the candidate." The statutes specifically prohibit false statements about a candidate's voting record, but are not limited to that. "Campaign materials" are broadly defined as, but not limited to, "sample ballots, an advertisement on radio or television or in a newspaper or periodical, a public speech, [or] press release."

Any person, including the Secretary of State or a Board of Elections official, may file a complaint with the Commission alleging a violation of the political false-statements laws. For a complaint filed shortly before an election, there is a three-step process to be convicted of the crime of making a political false statement. First, a panel of the Commission conducts a preliminary probable cause hearing based on the complaint and issues a public finding. If the panel finds probable cause, the complaint proceeds to an adjudicatory hearing before the full Commission. If, after the adjudicatory hearing, the Commission finds by clear and convincing evidence that a party violated the political false-statements laws, it may refer the case to a prosecutor. If convicted in subsequent state court proceedings, first-time violators may be sentenced up to six months in prison or fined up to $5,000. For complaints filed after an election, more than sixty days before a primary election, or more than ninety days before a general election, there is no probable cause hearing and the complaint proceeds directly to an adjudicatory hearing.

B. Litigation

In 2010, then-Congressman Steven Driehaus filed a complaint with the Commission alleging that SBA List violated Ohio's political false-statements laws by issuing a press release accusing him of voting for "taxpayer-funded abortion" by voting for the Affordable Care Act. A panel of the Commission issued a probable cause finding that SBA List violated the law.

SBA List responded by filing suit against Driehaus and various state officials in the Southern District of Ohio. That case was consolidated with a similar case that COAST filed, adding the Commission as a defendant, based on its desire to make similar accusations against Driehaus in a mass email. On remand [from the U.S. Supreme Court, which held that the case was ripe for review], the district court granted SBA List's and COAST's motions for summary judgment, holding that Ohio's political false-statements laws were content-based restrictions that fail strict scrutiny review. The Commission appeals.

II. STANDARD OF REVIEW

[Omitted.]

III. ANALYSIS

A. Whether We Are Bound By Sixth Circuit Precedent

As an initial matter, the Commission argues we are bound by our decision in *Pestrak v. Ohio Elections Commission* (6th Cir. 1991), which held that Ohio's political false-statements laws were constitutional on their face and, for the most part, in their enforcement.

But the Supreme Court's decision in *United States v. Alvarez* (2012), most clearly abrogates *Pestrak*'s reasoning. In *Alvarez,* the Supreme Court struck down the Stolen Valor Act, a law that prohibited persons from falsely claiming they won the Congressional Medal of Honor, regardless of if the false statement was made knowingly.

Alvarez abrogates *Pestrak's* holding that knowing false speech merits no constitutional protection. In *Pestrak,* we determined that, on their face, Ohio's political false-statements laws were constitutional because "false speech, even political speech, does not merit constitutional protection if the speaker knows of the falsehood or recklessly disregards the truth." However, in *Alvarez* the Supreme Court unanimously rejected the "categorical rule . . . that false statements receive no First Amendment protection." This undermines *Pestrak* 's fundamental premise that false statements, without more, deserve no constitutional protection.

Finally, *Alvarez* confirms that the First Amendment protects the "civic duty" to engage in public debate, with a preference for counteracting lies with more accurate information, rather than by restricting lies.

B. Level of Scrutiny

1. Burdening Core Speech

[Omitted.]

2. Content-Based Prohibitions

The Supreme Court's 2015 decision in *Reed v. Town of Gilbert* sought to clarify the level of review due to certain speech prohibitions. That test focused on whether a law was content-based at all, rather than the type of content the law targeted. The *Reed* Court held that strict scrutiny is the appropriate level of review when a law governs any "specific subject matter . . . even if it does not discriminate among viewpoints within that subject matter." Content-based laws "are presumptively unconstitutional and may be justified only if the government proves that they are narrowly tailored to serve compelling state interests." *Reed.* Ohio's political false-statements laws only govern speech about political candidates during an election. Thus, they are content-based restrictions focused on a specific subject matter and are subject to strict scrutiny.

C. Constitutional Analysis

Laws subject to strict scrutiny are presumptively unconstitutional and can only survive if they (1) serve a compelling state interest and (2) are narrowly tailored to achieve that interest.

Here, Ohio's interests in preserving the integrity of its elections, protecting "voters from confusion and undue influence," and "ensuring that an individual's right to vote is not undermined by fraud in the election process" are compelling. *Burson v. Freeman* (1992); *see also McIntyre v. Ohio Elections Commission* (1995) (Ohio's interest in preventing fraud and libel "carries special weight during election campaigns when false statements, if credited, may have serious adverse consequences for the public at large."). But Ohio's laws do not meet the second requirement: being narrowly tailored to protect the integrity of Ohio's elections. Thus, this is not such a "rare case" that survives strict scrutiny.

The Commission argues that Ohio's political false-statements laws should receive the less-exacting intermediate scrutiny. It did not address SBA List's and COAST's argument that the law is subject to strict scrutiny. Therefore, it is not surprising that the Commission's arguments are insufficient to survive strict scrutiny. Ohio's laws do not pass constitutional muster because they are not narrowly tailored in their (1) timing, (2) lack of a screening process for frivolous complaints, (3) application to non-material statements, (4) application to commercial intermediaries, and (5) over-inclusiveness and under-inclusiveness.

First, the timing of Ohio's administrative process does not necessarily promote fair elections. While the laws provide an expedited timeline for complaints filed within a certain number of days before an election, complaints filed outside this timeframe are free to linger for six months. Even when a complaint is expedited, there is no guarantee the administrative or criminal proceedings will conclude before the election or within time for the candidate's campaign to recover from any false information that was disseminated. Indeed, candidates filing complaints against their political opponents count on the fact that "an ultimate decision on the merits will be deferred until after the relevant election." [citing amicus brief at Supreme Court]. A final finding that occurs *after* the election does not preserve the integrity of the election. On the other hand, in many cases, "a preelection probable-cause finding . . . itself may be viewed [by the electorate] as a sanction by the State" that "triggers 'profound' political damage, even before a final [Commission] adjudication." [citing two different amicus briefs]. The timing of Ohio's process is not narrowly tailored to promote fair elections.

Second, Ohio fails to screen out frivolous complaints prior to a probable cause hearing. While this permits a panel of the Commission to review and reach a probable cause conclusion on complaints as quickly as possible, it also provides frivolous complainants an audience and requires purported violators to respond to a potentially frivolous complaint. "Because the universe of potential complainants is not restricted to state officials who are constrained by explicit guidelines or ethical obligations, there is a real risk of complaints from, for example, political opponents." [citing Supreme Court's prior decision in this case]. There is no process for screening out frivolous complaints or complaints that, on their face, only complain of non-actionable statements, such as opinions. Indeed, some complainants use the law's process "to gain a campaign advantage without ever having to prove the falsity of a statement . . . tim[ing] their submissions to achieve maximum disruption . . . forc[ing political opponents] to divert significant time and resources . . . in the crucial days leading up to an election." [citing amicus brief at Supreme Court]. The potential for attorney's fees and the costs for frivolous complaints does not save the law because this finding of frivolity does not occur until *after* a probable cause finding or a full adjudicatory hearing. The process of designating a panel, permitting parties to engage in motion practice, and having a panel conduct a probable cause review for plainly frivolous or non-actionable complaints is not narrowly tailored to preserve fair elections.

Third, Ohio's laws apply to *all* false statements, including non-material statements. Though the Commission argues that the political false-statements laws require that the false statement be material, no such requirement exists on the law's face, nor has either party cited any case in which courts have imputed a materiality requirement to the political false-statements laws. Thus, influencing an election by lying about a political candidate's shoe size or vote on whether to continue a congressional debate is just as actionable as lying about a candidate's party affiliation or vote on an important policy issue, such as the Affordable Care Act. Further, the law prohibits false statements regarding a political candidate—even outside the political arena—so long as the statement is "designed to promote the election, nomination, or defeat of the candidate," and is made in broadly defined "campaign materials." Penalizing non-material statements, particularly those made outside the political arena, is not narrowly tailored to preserve fair elections.

Fourth, Ohio's laws apply to anyone who advertises, "post[s], publish[es], circulate[s], distribute[s], or otherwise disseminate[s]" false political speech. Such a broad prohibition "applies not only to the speaker of the false statement but also to commercial intermediates like the company that was supposed to erect SBA List's billboard in 2010." [Citation omitted.] Conducting hearings against or prosecuting a billboard company executive, who was simply the messenger, is not narrowly tailored to preserve fair elections.

Fifth, the law is both over-inclusive and underinclusive. Causing damage to a campaign that ultimately may not be in violation of the law, through a preliminary probable cause ruling, does not preserve the integrity of the elections and in fact undermines the state's interest in promoting fair elections. At the same time, the law may not timely penalize those who violate it, nor does it provide for campaigns that are the victim of potentially damaging false statements. "[A] law cannot be regarded as protecting an interest of the highest order, and thus as justifying a restriction on truthful speech, when it leaves appreciable damage to that supposedly vital interest unprohibited." *Reed.* Though Ohio's interests "are assuredly legitimate, we are not persuaded that they justify [such an] extremely broad prohibition." *McIntyre.* Indeed, courts have consistently erred on the side of permitting more political speech than less. *See, e.g., Alvarez.*

Finally, Ohio's political false-statements laws have similar features to another Ohio election law that the Supreme Court found unconstitutional. In *McIntyre,* the Supreme Court struck down Ohio's election law prohibiting anonymous leafleting because its prohibitions included non-material statements that were "not even arguably false or misleading," made by candidates, campaign supporters, and "individuals acting independently and using only their own modest resources," whether made "on the eve of an election, when the opportunity for reply is limited," or months in advance. Ohio's political false-statements laws have all of the same flaws. Such glaring oversteps are not narrowly tailored to preserve fair elections.

Other courts to evaluate similar laws post-*Alvarez* have reached the same conclusion. [citing cases from Minnesota, Massachusetts, and Washington that struck down similar laws].

IV. CONCLUSION

Ohio's political false-statements laws are content-based restrictions targeting core political speech that are not narrowly tailored to serve the state's admittedly compelling interest in conducting fair elections. Accordingly, we affirm the district court's judgment finding the laws unconstitutional.

NOTES ON *RICKERT* AND *SUSAN B. ANTHONY*

1. The Supreme Court recognized the First Amendment protection for false or misleading speech in *New York Times v. Sullivan*, 376 U.S. 254 (1964). The First Amendment protection of campaign speech is quite extensive because it is based on the premise that there is "a profound national commitment to the principle that debate on public issues should be uninhibited, robust, and wide-open, and that it may well include vehement, caustic, and sometimes unpleasantly sharp attacks on government and public officials." Thus, the First Amendment protects negligently made false statements during a campaign. Similarly, if a statement is made with a good-faith belief of its truthfulness, it receives constitutional protection.

2. As the court in *Susan B. Anthony* explained, the Supreme Court has even given First Amendment protection for outright lies. In *United States v. Alvarez*, 132 S. Ct. 2537 (2012), the Supreme Court struck down the "Stolen Valor Act," which made it a crime to lie about receiving the Congressional Medal of Honor. The defendant was a board member of a local water board and lied during a public meeting about receiving the Medal of Honor. The Court rejected the government's argument that the law was needed to protect the sanctity of the nation's highest military award.

3. What do you think of the majority's formulation in *Rickert* of the proper remedy for false ads: more speech? Is this really the right solution? In 2016, *Politico* had a headline asking, "Are Clinton and Trump the Biggest Liars Ever to Run for President?" and *Politifact* named Donald Trump's collective falsehoods its "Lie of the Year" for 2015. During the final presidential debate between Trump and Democratic nominee Hillary Clinton in 2016, Trump claimed that the State Department had lost $6 billion while Clinton was Secretary of State. Clinton immediately refuted this assertion as false. But these examples raise the question: Does "more speech" help to counter the blatant lie once it is out there? Doesn't the lie by itself do sufficient damage to voters' perceptions of the candidates? Can the government—or another actor—do anything about it so that voters' choices are based on truthful information?

4. Do negative ads have an adverse effect on the political tenor of a campaign? Why do candidates go negative? Obviously, they think it works, and political science research bears this belief out—to an extent. There are a ton of studies on the effects of negative campaign ads and some of the findings contradict each other. One common belief is that negative ads both harm the person being attacked and lower turnout rates of voters who might otherwise support that candidate. But there is also some evidence that attack ads could backfire. Given all of this research, what role, if any, should a legislature play in regulating campaign speech? Of course, any standard the legislature chooses would need to be enforced by bureaucrats or

judges; can they be entirely impartial between competing candidates? In addition, might legislatures and executives enact incumbent-friendly laws—such as Washington's regime of allowing the governor's appointees to determine the truthfulness of campaign statements during the governor's re-election campaign—in an effort to entrench themselves?

5. Does the decision in *Susan B. Anthony* mean that a state can never try to regulate a false campaign ad? The court held that the Ohio law was not narrowly tailored. Can you think of a way to craft a narrower law that might satisfy the First Amendment?

6. What about lies regarding the election process itself? Would a law that forbids lies about Election Day—e.g., a flyer that says "Given high projected turn out, Republicans should vote on Tuesday and Democrats vote on Wednesday"—pass First Amendment scrutiny?

B. LAST-MINUTE AND HARASSING CAMPAIGN TACTICS AT THE POLLS

What happens when the exercise of First Amendment rights clashes with the fundamental right to vote? The next case presents the question of whether a state may create a "campaign-free" zone around a polling place.

During the days leading up to Election Day, streets and sidewalks sometimes become cluttered with campaign signs. In some states, campaign workers set up tables outside of the polls to disseminate literature on their candidates. Political parties might hand out a "sample ballot" with their preferred choices for voters to follow as they vote. Candidates themselves often spend time at the busiest polling places shaking hands and seeking last-minute support. In the next case, *Burson v. Freeman,* Tennessee sought to give voters a reprieve from these campaign messages—as well as other more overt forms of campaigning—directly around the polling site. The underlying purpose, according to the state, was to protect the right to vote and to limit fraud and intimidation.

Indeed, the United States has a long history of actual or perceived election fraud. This case provides a detailed explanation for the main reason behind secret balloting: to limit the possibility of undue influence or intimidation infiltrating the voting process. In the early days of our democracy, political parties printed ballots listing their nominees, and voters simply took the party's ballot they preferred with them to the polls. Concerns about vote buying and fraud led most states to adopt the "Australian" ballot, in which the government prints the ballot of all parties' nominees and voters make their selections via secret ballot. Does a campaign-free zone serve the same purposes as a secret ballot?

Further, given the state's interest in rooting out fraud, is the restriction on campaigning near the polls consistent with a candidate's First Amendment right to disseminate a political message? Consider how the Supreme Court reconciles the right to vote with the right to freedom of speech in this case. Then think about whether this case is consistent with a ban on political apparel inside the polling place, which is the issue in *Mansky,* the case that follows *Burson.*

Figure 3-1

Reprinted with permission from the *Ann Arbor Chronicle*.

As Figure 3-1 shows, polling places often become cluttered with campaign signs. The law at question in *Burson v. Freeman* attempted to limit this kind of campaigning outside of the polls.

Burson v. Freeman

504 U.S. 191 (1992)

Justice Blackmun announced the judgment of the Court and delivered an opinion, in which Chief Justice Rehnquist, Justice White, and Justice Kennedy join.

Twenty-six years ago, this Court struck down a state law that made it a crime for a newspaper editor to publish an editorial on election day urging readers to vote in a particular way. *Mills v. Alabama* (1966). While the Court did not hesitate to denounce the statute as an "obvious and flagrant abridgment" of First Amendment rights, it was quick to point out that its holding "in no way involve[d] the extent of a State's power to regulate conduct in and around the polls in order to maintain peace, order and decorum there[.]" [*Id.*]

Today, we confront the issue carefully left open in *Mills*. The question presented is whether a provision of the Tennessee Code, which prohibits the solicitation of votes and the display or distribution of campaign materials within 100 feet of the entrance to a polling place, violates the First and Fourteenth Amendments.

I

The State of Tennessee has carved out an election-day "campaign-free zone" through § 2-7-111(b) of its election code. That section reads in pertinent part:

> "Within the appropriate boundary as established in subsection (a) [100 feet from the entrances], and the building in which the polling place is located, the display of campaign posters, signs or other campaign materials, distribution of campaign materials, and solicitation of votes for or against any person or political party or position on a question are prohibited." Tenn. Code Ann. § 2-7-111(b) (Supp. 1991).

Violation of § 2-7-111(b) is a Class C misdemeanor punishable by a term of imprisonment not greater than 30 days or a fine not to exceed $50, or both. Tenn. Code Ann. §§ 2-19-119 and 40-35-111(e)(3) (1990).

II

Respondent Mary Rebecca Freeman has been a candidate for office in Tennessee, has managed local campaigns, and has worked actively in statewide elections. In 1987, she was the treasurer for the campaign of a city-council candidate in Metropolitan Nashville-Davidson County.

Asserting that §§ 2-7-111(b) and 2-19-119 limited her ability to communicate with voters, respondent brought a facial challenge to these statutes in Davidson County Chancery Court. She sought a declaratory judgment that the provisions were unconstitutional under both the United States and the Tennessee Constitutions. She also sought a permanent injunction against their enforcement.

The Chancellor ruled that the statutes did not violate the United States or Tennessee Constitutions and dismissed respondent's suit. He determined that § 2-7-111(b) was a content-neutral and reasonable time, place, and manner restriction; that the 100-foot boundary served a compelling state interest in protecting voters from interference, harassment, and intimidation during the voting process; and that there was an alternative channel for respondent to exercise her free speech rights outside the 100-foot boundary.

The Tennessee Supreme Court, by a 4-to-1 vote, reversed. The court first held that § 2-7-111(b) was content based "because it regulates a specific subject matter, the solicitation of votes and the display or distribution of campaign materials, and a certain category of speakers, campaign workers." The court then held that such a content-based statute could not be upheld unless (i) the burden placed on free speech rights is justified by a compelling state interest and (ii) the means chosen bear a substantial relation to that interest and are the least intrusive to achieve the State's goals. While the Tennessee Supreme Court found that the State unquestionably had shown a compelling interest in banning solicitation of voters and distribution of campaign materials within the polling place itself, it concluded that the State had not shown a compelling interest in regulating the premises around the polling place. Accordingly, the court held that the 100-foot limit was not narrowly tailored to protect the demonstrated interest. The court also held that the statute was not the least restrictive means to serve the State's interests. The court found less restrictive the current Tennessee statutes prohibiting interference with an election or the use of violence or intimidation to prevent voting. Finally, the court noted that if the State were able to show a compelling interest in preventing congestion and disruption at the entrances to polling places, a shorter radius "might perhaps pass constitutional muster."

Because of the importance of the issue, we granted certiorari. We now reverse the Tennessee Supreme Court's judgment that the statute violates the First Amendment of the United States Constitution.

III

The Tennessee statute implicates three central concerns in our First Amendment jurisprudence: regulation of political speech, regulation of speech in a public forum, and regulation based on the content of the speech. The speech restricted by § 2-7-111(b) obviously is political speech. [T]his Court has recognized that "the First Amendment 'has its fullest and most urgent application' to speech uttered during a campaign for political office." *Eu v. San Francisco Cty. Democratic Central Comm.* (1989) (quoting *Monitor Patriot Co. v. Roy* (1971)).

The second important feature of § 2-7-111(b) is that it bars speech in quintessential public forums. These forums include those places "which by long tradition or by government fiat have been devoted to assembly and debate," such as parks, streets, and sidewalks. *Perry Ed. Assn. v. Perry Local Educators' Assn.* (1983). At the same time, however, expressive activity, even in a quintessential public forum, may interfere with other important activities for which the property is used. Accordingly, this Court has held that the government may regulate the time, place, and manner of the expressive activity, so long as such restrictions are content neutral, are narrowly tailored to serve a significant governmental interest, and leave open ample alternatives for communication.

The Tennessee restriction under consideration, however, is not a facially content-neutral time, place, or manner restriction. Whether individuals may exercise their free speech rights near polling places depends entirely on whether their speech is related to a political campaign. The statute does not reach other categories of speech, such as commercial solicitation, distribution, and display. This Court has held that the First Amendment's hostility to content-based regulation extends not only to a restriction on a particular viewpoint, but also to a prohibition of public discussion of an entire topic.

As a facially content-based restriction on political speech in a public forum, § 2-7-111(b) must be subjected to exacting scrutiny: The State must show that the "regulation is necessary to serve a compelling state interest and that it is narrowly drawn to achieve that end." *Perry Ed. Assn. v. Perry Local Educators' Assn.*

Despite the ritualistic ease with which we state this now-familiar standard, its announcement does not allow us to avoid the truly difficult issues involving the First Amendment. Perhaps foremost among these serious issues are cases that force us to reconcile our commitment to free speech with our commitment to other constitutional rights embodied in government proceedings. *See, e.g., Sheppard v. Maxwell* (1966) (outlining restrictions on speech of trial participants that courts may impose to protect an accused's right to a fair trial). This case presents us with a particularly difficult reconciliation: the accommodation of the right to engage in political discourse with the right to vote—a right at the heart of our democracy.

IV

Tennessee asserts that its campaign-free zone serves two compelling interests. First, the State argues that its regulation serves its compelling interest in protecting the right of its citizens to vote freely for the candidates of their choice. Second, Tennessee argues that its restriction protects the right to vote in an election conducted with integrity and reliability.

The interests advanced by Tennessee obviously are compelling ones. This Court has recognized that the "right to vote freely for the candidate of one's choice is of the essence of a democratic society." *Reynolds v. Sims* (1964). Indeed,

> "[n]o right is more precious in a free country than that of having a voice in the election of those who make the laws under which, as good citizens, we must live. Other rights, even the most basic, are illusory if the right to vote is undermined." *Wesberry v. Sanders* (1964).

Accordingly, this Court has concluded that a State has a compelling interest in protecting voters from confusion and undue influence.

The Court also has recognized that a State "indisputably has a compelling interest in preserving the integrity of its election process." [*Eu.*] The Court thus has "upheld generally applicable and evenhanded restrictions that protect the integrity and reliability of the electoral process itself." *Anderson v. Celebrezze* (1983) (collecting cases). In other words, it has recognized that a State has a compelling interest in ensuring that an individual's right to vote is not undermined by fraud in the election process.

To survive strict scrutiny, however, a State must do more than assert a compelling state interest—it must demonstrate that its law is necessary to serve the asserted interest. While we readily acknowledge that a law rarely survives such scrutiny, an examination of the evolution of election reform, both in this country and abroad, demonstrates the necessity of restricted areas in or around polling places.

During the colonial period, many government officials were elected by the *viva voce* method or by the showing of hands, as was the custom in most parts of Europe. That voting scheme was not a private affair, but an open, public decision, witnessed by all and improperly influenced by some. The opportunities that the *viva voce* system gave for bribery and intimidation gradually led to its repeal.

Within 20 years of the formation of the Union, most States had incorporated the paper ballot into their electoral system. Initially, this paper ballot was a vast improvement. Individual voters made their own handwritten ballots, marked them in the privacy of their homes, and then brought them to the polls for counting. But the effort of making out such a ballot became increasingly more complex and cumbersome.

Wishing to gain influence, political parties began to produce their own ballots for voters. These ballots were often printed with flamboyant colors, distinctive designs, and emblems so that they could be recognized at a distance. State attempts to standardize the ballots were easily thwarted—the vote buyer could simply place a ballot in the hands of the bribed voter and watch until he placed it in the polling box. Thus, the evils associated with the earlier *viva voce* system reinfected the election process; the failure of the law to secure secrecy opened the door to bribery[6] and intimidation.[7]

Approaching the polling place under this system was akin to entering an open auction place. As the elector started his journey to the polls, he was met by various party ticket peddlers "who were only too anxious to supply him with their party tickets." Evans, [*A History of the Australia Ballot System in the United States* (1917), at] 9. Often the competition became heated when several such peddlers found an uncommitted or wavering voter. Sham battles were frequently engaged in to keep away elderly and timid voters of the opposition.

The problems with voter intimidation and election fraud that the United States was experiencing were not unique. Several other countries were attempting to work out satisfactory solutions to these same problems. Some Australian provinces adopted a series of reforms intended to secure the secrecy of an elector's vote. The most famous feature of the Australian system was its provision for an official ballot, encompassing all candidates of all parties on the same ticket. But this was not the only measure adopted to preserve the secrecy of the ballot. The Australian system also provided for the erection of polling booths (containing several voting compartments) open only to election officials, two "scrutinees" for each candidate, and electors about to vote.

The Australian system was enacted in England in 1872 after a study by the committee of election practices identified Australia's ballot as the best possible remedy for the existing situation. Belgium followed England's example in 1877. Like the Australian provinces, both England and Belgium excluded the general public from the entire polling room.

After several failed attempts to adopt the Australian system in Michigan and Wisconsin, the Louisville, Kentucky, municipal government, the Commonwealth of Massachusetts, and the State of New York adopted the Australian system in 1888. The Louisville law prohibited all but voters, candidates or their agents, and electors from coming within 50 feet of the voting room inclosure. The Louisville law also provided that candidates' agents within the restricted area "were not allowed

6. One writer described the conditions as follows: "This sounds like exaggeration, but it is truth; and these are facts so notorious that no one acquainted with the conduct of recent elections now attempts a denial—that the raising of colossal sums for the purpose of bribery has been rewarded by promotion to the highest offices in the Government; that systematic organization for the purchase of votes, individually and in blocks, at the polls, has become a recognized factor in the machinery of the parties; that the number of voters who demand money compensation for their ballots has grown greater with each recurring election." J. Gordon, The Protection of Suffrage 13 (1891) (quoted in Evans 11).Evans reports that the bribery of voters in Indiana in 1880 and 1888 was sufficient to determine the results of the election and that "[m]any electors, aware that the corrupt element was large enough to be able to turn the election, held aloof altogether."

7. According to a report of a committee of the 46th Congress, men were frequently marched or carried to the polls in their employers' carriages. They were then furnished with ballots and compelled to hold their hands up with their ballots in them so they could easily be watched until the ballots were dropped into the box. S. Rep. No. 497, 46th Cong., 2d Sess., 9-10 (1880).

to persuade, influence, or intimidate any one in the choice of his candidate, or to attempt doing so. . . ." Wigmore [*The Australian Ballot System Embodied in the Legislation of Various Countries* (1889)]. The Massachusetts and New York laws differed somewhat from the previous Acts in that they excluded the general public only from the area encompassed within a guardrail constructed six feet from the voting compartments. This modification was considered an improvement because it provided additional monitoring by members of the general public and independent candidates, who in most States were not allowed to be represented by separate inspectors. Otherwise, "in order to perpetrate almost every election fraud it would only be necessary to buy up the election officers of the other party." *Id.* Finally, New York also prohibited any person from "electioneering on election day within any polling-place, or within one hundred feet of any polling place." *Id.*

The success achieved through these reforms was immediately noticed and widely praised. One commentator remarked of the New York law of 1888:

> "We have secured secrecy; and intimidation by employers, party bosses, police officers, saloonkeepers and others has come to an end.
>
> "In earlier times our polling places were frequently, to quote the litany, 'scenes of battle, murder, and sudden death.' This also has come to an end, and until nightfall, when the jubilation begins, our election days are now as peaceful as our Sabbaths.
>
> "The new legislation has also rendered impossible the old methods of frank, hardy, straightforward and shameless bribery of voters at the polls." W. Ivins, The Electoral System of the State of New York, Proceedings of the 29th Annual Meeting of the New York State Bar Association (1906).

The triumphs of 1888 set off a rapid and widespread adoption of the Australian system in the United States. By 1896, almost 90 percent of the States had adopted the Australian system. This accounted for 92 percent of the national electorate.

The roots of Tennessee's regulation can be traced back to two provisions passed during this period of rapid reform. Tennessee passed the first relevant provision in 1890 as part of its switch to an Australian system. In its effort to "secur[e] the purity of elections," Tennessee provided that only voters and certain election officials were permitted within the room where the election was held or within 50 feet of the entrance. The Act did not provide any penalty for violation and applied only in the more highly populated counties and cities.

The second relevant provision was passed in 1901 as an amendment to Tennessee's "Act to preserve the purity of elections, and define and punish offenses against the elective franchise." The original Act, passed in 1897, made it a misdemeanor to commit various election offenses, including the use of bribery, violence, or intimidation in order to induce a person to vote or refrain from voting for any particular person or measure. The 1901 amendment made it a misdemeanor for any person, except the officers holding the elections, to approach nearer than 30 feet to any voter or ballot box. This provision applied to all Tennessee elections.

These two laws remained relatively unchanged until 1967, when Tennessee added yet another proscription to its secret ballot law. This amendment prohibited the distribution of campaign literature "on the same floor of a building, or within one hundred (100) feet thereof, where an election is in progress."

In 1972, the State enacted a comprehensive code to regulate the conduct of elections. The code included a section that proscribed the display and the distribution of campaign material and the solicitation of votes within 100 feet of the entrance to a polling place. The 1972 "campaign-free zone" is the direct precursor of the restriction challenged in the present litigation.

Today, all 50 States limit access to the areas in or around polling places. The National Labor Relations Board also limits activities at or near polling places in union-representation elections.

In sum, an examination of the history of election regulation in this country reveals a persistent battle against two evils: voter intimidation and election fraud. After an unsuccessful experiment with an unofficial ballot system, all 50 States, together with numerous other Western democracies, settled on the same solution: a secret ballot secured in part by a restricted zone around the voting compartments. We find that this widespread and time-tested consensus demonstrates that some restricted zone is necessary in order to serve the States' compelling interests in preventing voter intimidation and election fraud.

Respondent and the dissent advance three principal challenges to this conclusion. First, respondent argues that restricted zones are overinclusive because States could secure these same compelling interests with statutes that make it a misdemeanor to interfere with an election or to use violence or intimidation to prevent voting. We are not persuaded. Intimidation and interference laws fall short of serving a State's compelling interests because they "deal with only the most blatant and specific attempts" to impede elections. *Cf. Buckley v. Valeo* (1976) (existence of bribery statute does not preclude need for limits on contributions to political campaigns). Moreover, because law enforcement officers generally are barred from the vicinity of the polls to avoid any appearance of coercion in the electoral process, many acts of interference would go undetected. These undetected or less than blatant acts may nonetheless drive the voter away before remedial action can be taken.

Second, respondent and the dissent argue that Tennessee's statute is underinclusive because it does not restrict other types of speech, such as charitable and commercial solicitation or exit polling, within the 100-foot zone. We agree that distinguishing among types of speech requires that the statute be subjected to strict scrutiny. We do not, however, agree that the failure to regulate all speech renders the statute fatally underinclusive. In fact, as one early commentator pointed out, allowing members of the general public access to the polling place makes it more difficult for political machines to buy off all the monitors. *See* Wigmore. But regardless of the need for such additional monitoring, there is, as summarized above, ample evidence that political candidates have used campaign workers to commit voter intimidation or electoral fraud. In contrast, there is simply no evidence that political candidates have used other forms of solicitation or exit polling to commit such electoral abuses. States adopt laws to address the problems that confront them. The First Amendment does not require States to regulate for problems that do not exist.

Finally, the dissent argues that we confuse history with necessity. Yet the dissent concedes that a secret ballot was necessary to cure electoral abuses. Contrary to the dissent's contention, the link between ballot secrecy and some restricted zone surrounding the voting area is not merely timing—it is common sense. The only way to preserve the secrecy of the ballot is to limit access to the area around the voter.

Accordingly, we hold that *some* restricted zone around the voting area is necessary to secure the State's compelling interest.

The real question then is *how large* a restricted zone is permissible or sufficiently tailored. Respondent and the dissent argue that Tennessee's 100-foot boundary is not narrowly drawn to achieve the State's compelling interest in protecting the right to vote. We disagree.

As a preliminary matter, the long, uninterrupted and prevalent use of these statutes makes it difficult for States to come forward with the sort of proof the dissent wishes to require. The majority of these laws were adopted originally in the 1890s, long before States engaged in extensive legislative hearings on election regulations. The prevalence of these laws, both here and abroad, then encouraged their reenactment without much comment. The fact that these laws have been in effect for a long period of time also makes it difficult for the States to put on witnesses who can testify as to what would happen without them. Finally, it is difficult to isolate the exact effect of these laws on voter intimidation and election fraud. Voter intimidation and election fraud are successful precisely because they are difficult to detect.

Furthermore, because a government has such a compelling interest in securing the right to vote freely and effectively, this Court never has held a State "to the burden of demonstrating empirically the objective effects on political stability that [are] produced" by the voting regulation in question. *Munro v. Socialist Workers Party* (1986).[11] Elections vary from year to year, and place to place. It is therefore difficult to make specific findings about the effects of a voting regulation. Moreover, the remedy for a tainted election is an imperfect one. Rerunning an election would have a negative impact on voter turnout. Thus, requiring proof that a 100-foot boundary is perfectly tailored to deal with voter intimidation and election fraud

> "would necessitate that a State's political system sustain some level of damage before the legislature could take corrective action. Legislatures, we think, should be permitted to respond to potential deficiencies in the electoral process with foresight rather than reactively, provided that the response is reasonable and does not *significantly impinge* on constitutionally protected rights." *Id.* (emphasis added).

We do not think that the minor geographic limitation prescribed by § 2-7-111(b) constitutes such a significant impingement. Thus, we simply do not view the question whether the 100-foot boundary line could be somewhat tighter as a question of "constitutional dimension." *Id.* Reducing the boundary to 25 feet, as suggested by the Tennessee Supreme Court, is a difference only in degree, not a less restrictive alternative in kind. As was pointed out in the dissenting opinion in

11. This modified "burden of proof" does not apply to all cases in which there is a conflict between First Amendment rights and a State's election process—instead, it applies only when the First Amendment right threatens to interfere with the act of voting itself, *i.e.*, cases involving voter confusion from overcrowded ballots, like *Munro*, or cases such as this one, in which the challenged activity physically interferes with electors attempting to cast their ballots. Thus, for example, States must come forward with more specific findings to support regulations directed at intangible "influence," such as the ban on election-day editorials struck down in *Mills v. Alabama* (1966).

the Tennessee Supreme Court, it "takes approximately 15 seconds to walk 75 feet." The State of Tennessee has decided that these last 15 seconds before its citizens enter the polling place should be their own, as free from interference as possible. We do not find that this is an unconstitutional choice.[13]

At some measurable distance from the polls, of course, governmental regulation of vote solicitation could effectively become an impermissible burden akin to the statute struck down in *Mills v. Alabama* (1966). In reviewing challenges to specific provisions of a State's election laws, however, this Court has not employed any " 'litmus-paper test' that will separate valid from invalid restrictions." *Anderson v. Celebrezze.* Accordingly, it is sufficient to say that in establishing a 100-foot boundary, Tennessee is on the constitutional side of the line.

In conclusion, we reaffirm that it is the rare case in which we have held that a law survives strict scrutiny. This, however, is such a rare case. Here, the State, as recognized administrator of elections, has asserted that the exercise of free speech rights conflicts with another fundamental right, the right to cast a ballot in an election free from the taint of intimidation and fraud. A long history, a substantial consensus, and simple common sense show that some restricted zone around polling places is necessary to protect that fundamental right. Given the conflict between these two rights, we hold that requiring solicitors to stand 100 feet from the entrances to polling places does not constitute an unconstitutional compromise.

The judgment of the Tennessee Supreme Court is reversed, and the case is remanded for further proceedings not inconsistent with this opinion.

Justice THOMAS took no part in the consideration or decision of this case.

Justice KENNEDY, concurring.

[T]here is a narrow area in which the First Amendment permits freedom of expression to yield to the extent necessary for the accommodation of another constitutional right. Voting is one of the most fundamental and cherished liberties in our democratic system of government. The State is not using this justification to suppress legitimate expression.

Justice SCALIA, concurring in the judgment.

If the category of "traditional public forum" is to be a tool of analysis rather than a conclusory label, it must remain faithful to its name and derive its content

13. Respondent also raises two more specific challenges to the tailoring of the Tennessee statute. First, she contends that there may be some polling places so situated that the 100-foot boundary falls in or on the other side of a highway. Second, respondent argues that the inclusion of quintessential public forums in some campaign-free zones could result in the prosecution of an individual for driving by in an automobile with a campaign bumper sticker. At oral argument, petitioner denied that the statute would reach this latter, inadvertent conduct, since this would not constitute "display" of campaign material. In any event, these arguments are "as applied" challenges that should be made by an individual prosecuted for such conduct. If successful, these challenges would call for a limiting construction rather than a facial invalidation. In the absence of any factual record to support respondent's contention that the statute has been applied to reach such circumstances, we do not entertain the challenges in this case.

from *tradition*. Because restrictions on speech around polling places on election day are as venerable a part of the American tradition as the secret ballot, Tenn. Code Ann. § 2-7-111 does not restrict speech in a traditional public forum, and the "exacting scrutiny" that the plurality purports to apply, is inappropriate. Instead, I believe that § 2-7-111, though content-based, is constitutional because it is a reasonable, viewpoint-neutral regulation of a nonpublic forum.

Justice STEVENS, with whom Justice O'CONNOR and Justice SOUTER join, dissenting.

The speech and conduct prohibited in the campaign-free zone created by Tenn. Code Ann. § 2-7-111 is classic political expression. Therefore, I fully agree with the plurality that Tennessee must show that its " 'regulation is necessary to serve a compelling state interest and that it is narrowly drawn to achieve that end.' " I do not agree, however, that Tennessee has made anything approaching such a showing.

I

Statutes creating campaign-free zones outside polling places serve two quite different functions—they protect orderly access to the polls and they prevent last-minute campaigning. There can be no question that the former constitutes a compelling state interest and that, in light of our decision in *Mills v. Alabama* (1966), the latter does not. Accordingly, a State must demonstrate that the particular means it has fashioned to ensure orderly access to the polls do not unnecessarily hinder last-minute campaigning.

Campaign-free zones are noteworthy for their broad, antiseptic sweep. The Tennessee zone encompasses at least 30,000 square feet around each polling place; in some States, such as Kentucky and Wisconsin, the radius of the restricted zone is 500 feet—silencing an area of over 750,000 square feet. Even under the most sanguine scenario of participatory democracy, it is difficult to imagine voter turnout so complete as to require the clearing of hundreds of thousands of square feet simply to ensure that the path to the polling-place door remains open and that the curtain that protects the secrecy of the ballot box remains closed.

The fact that campaign-free zones cover such a large area in some States unmistakably identifies censorship of election-day campaigning as an animating force behind these restrictions. That some States have no problem maintaining order with zones of 50 feet or less strongly suggests that the more expansive prohibitions are not necessary to maintain access and order. Indeed, on its face, Tennessee's statute appears informed by political concerns. Although the statute initially established a 100-foot zone, it was later amended to establish a 300-foot zone in 12 of the State's 95 counties. As the State Attorney General observed, "there is not a rational basis" for this special treatment, for there is no "discernable reason why an extension of the boundary . . . is necessary in" those 12 counties.

Moreover, the Tennessee statute does not merely regulate conduct that might inhibit voting; it bars the simple "display of campaign posters, signs, or other campaign materials." § 2-7-111(b). Bumper stickers on parked cars and lapel buttons on pedestrians are taboo. The notion that such sweeping restrictions on speech are necessary to maintain the freedom to vote and the integrity of the ballot box borders on the absurd.

The evidence introduced at trial to demonstrate the necessity for Tennessee's campaign-free zone was exceptionally thin. Although the State's sole witness explained the need for special restrictions *inside* the polling place itself, she offered no justification for a ban on political expression *outside* the polling place. On this record it is far from surprising that the Tennessee Supreme Court—which surely is more familiar with the State's electoral practices and traditions than we are—concluded that the 100-foot ban outside the polling place was not justified by regulatory concerns. This conclusion is bolstered by Tennessee law, which indicates that normal police protection is completely adequate to maintain order in the area more than *10* feet from the polling place.

Perhaps in recognition of the poverty of the record, the plurality—without briefing, or legislative or judicial factfinding—looks to history to assess whether Tennessee's statute is in fact necessary to serve the State's interests.

This analysis is deeply flawed; it confuses history with necessity, and mistakes the traditional for the indispensable. The plurality's reasoning combines two logical errors: First, the plurality assumes that a practice's long life itself establishes its necessity; and second, the plurality assumes that a practice that was once necessary remains necessary until it is ended.

With regard to the first, the fact that campaign-free zones were, as the plurality indicates, introduced as part of a broader package of electoral reforms does not demonstrate that such zones were *necessary*. The abuses that affected the electoral system could have been cured by the institution of the secret ballot and by the heightened regulation of the polling place alone, without silencing the political speech *outside* the polling place.[4] In my opinion, more than mere timing is required to infer necessity from tradition.

We have never regarded tradition as a proxy for necessity where necessity must be demonstrated. To the contrary, our election-law jurisprudence is rich with examples of traditions that, though longstanding, were later held to be unnecessary. For example, "[m]ost of the early Colonies had [poll taxes]; many of the States have had them during much of their histories. . . ." *Harper v. Virginia Bd. of Elections* (1966) (Harlan, J., dissenting). Similarly, substantial barriers to candidacy, such as stringent petition requirements, see *Williams v. Rhodes* (1968), property-ownership requirements, see *Turner v. Fouche* (1970), and onerous filing fees, see *Lubin v. Panish* (1974), were all longstanding features of the electoral labyrinth.

Never have we indicated that tradition was synonymous with necessity.

Even if we assume that campaign-free zones were once somehow "necessary," it would not follow that, 100 years later, those practices remain necessary. Much in our political culture, institutions, and practices has changed since the turn of the century: Our elections are far less corrupt, far more civil, and far more democratic today than 100 years ago. These salutary developments have substantially

4. The plurality's suggestion that "[t]he only way to preserve the secrecy of the ballot is to limit access to the area around the voter" is specious. First, there are obvious and simple means of preserving voter secrecy (*e.g.*, opaque doors or curtains on the voting booth) that do not involve the suppression of political speech. Second, there is no disagreement that the restrictions on campaigning *within the polling place* are constitutional; the issue is not whether the State may limit access to the "area *around the voter*" but whether the State may limit speech in the area *around the polling place.*

eliminated the need for what is, in my opinion, a sweeping suppression of core political speech.

Although the plurality today blithely dispenses with the need for factual findings to determine the necessity of "traditional" restrictions on speech, courts that have made such findings with regard to other campaign-free zones have, without exception, found such zones unnecessary. [Citing cases.] All of these courts, having received evidence on this issue, were far better situated than we are to assess the contemporary necessity of campaign-free zones. All of these courts concluded that such suppression of expression is unnecessary, suggesting that such zones were something of a social atavism. To my mind, this recent history, developed in the context of an adversarial search for the truth, indicates that, whatever the original historical basis for campaign-free zones may have been, their continued "necessity" has not been established. Especially when we deal with the First Amendment, when the reason for a restriction disappears, the restriction should as well.

II

In addition to sweeping too broadly in its reach, Tennessee's campaign-free zone selectively prohibits speech based on content. Within the zone, § 2-7-111 silences all campaign-related expression, but allows expression on any other subject: religious, artistic, commercial speech, even political debate and solicitation concerning issues or candidates not on the day's ballot. Indeed, as I read it, § 2-7-111 does not prohibit exit polling, which surely presents at least as great a potential interference with orderly access to the polls as does the distribution of campaign leaflets, the display of campaign posters, or the wearing of campaign buttons. This discriminatory feature of the statute severely undercuts the credibility of its purported law-and-order justification.

Tennessee's content-based discrimination is particularly problematic because such a regulation will inevitably favor certain groups of candidates. As the testimony in this case illustrates, several groups of candidates rely heavily on last-minute campaigning. Candidates with fewer resources, candidates for lower visibility offices, and "grassroots" candidates benefit disproportionately from last-minute campaigning near the polling place.

Access to, and order around, the polls would be just as threatened by the congregation of citizens concerned about a local environmental issue not on the ballot as by the congregation of citizens urging election of their favored candidate. Similarly, assuming that disorder immediately outside the polling place could lead to the commission of errors or the perpetration of fraud, such disorder could just as easily be caused by a religious dispute sparked by a colporteur as by a campaign-related dispute sparked by a campaign worker. In short, Tennessee has failed to point to any legitimate interest that would justify its selective regulation of campaign-related expression.

III

[Omitted.]

IV

In my opinion, the presence of campaign workers outside a polling place is, in most situations, a minor nuisance. But we have long recognized that " 'the fact that society may find speech offensive is not a sufficient reason for suppressing it.' " *Hustler Magazine, Inc. v. Falwell* (1988). Although we often pay homage to the electoral process, we must be careful not to confuse sanctity with silence. The hubbub of campaign workers outside a polling place may be a nuisance, but it is also the sound of a vibrant democracy.

In silencing that sound, Tennessee "trenches upon an area in which the importance of First Amendment protections is 'at its zenith.' " *Meyer v. Grant* (1988). For that reason, Tennessee must shoulder the burden of demonstrating that its restrictions on political speech are no broader than necessary to protect orderly access to the polls. It has not done so.

I therefore respectfully dissent.

NOTES ON *BURSON*

1. The Supreme Court in *Burson* upheld a content-based restriction on speech to effectuate the right to vote in an unimpeded manner. Can you reconcile this decision with the Court's more recent pronouncements on the value of campaign speech? Would this case survive the reasoning from *United States v. Alvarez* (2012), which struck down a ban on outright lies?

2. How large of a campaign-free zone is too large? The Court in *Burson* upheld Tennessee's 100-foot buffer. What about a 200-foot buffer? 300 feet? Just before the 2014 election a district court invalidated Kentucky's 300-foot campaign free zone, which did not exempt speech on private property, finding that the law was overbroad. The Sixth Circuit stayed the ruling for the 2014 election but ultimately affirmed the decision. *See Russell v. Lundergan-Grimes* (6th Cir. 2015). The state then enacted a regulation to impose a 100-foot buffer. Missouri's campaign-free zone is one of the smallest, at 25 feet. Alabama has a 30-foot buffer requirement. On the other end of the scale, Louisiana has a 600-foot campaign free zone that exempts campaign speech on private property.

3. What about other kinds of seemingly harassing campaign activity, such as automated robocalls? In September 2019, the Ninth Circuit struck down Montana's ban on political robocalls. The Court found that "Regulating robocalls based on the content of their messaging presents a more severe threat to First Amendment freedoms than regulating their time, place and manner. In particular, prohibiting political robocalls strikes at the heart of the First Amendment (and) disproportionately disadvantages political candidates with fewer resources." *Victory Processing v. Fox* (9th Cir. 2019). In 2020, the Supreme Court considered a case involving the Telephone Consumer Protection Act, which prohibits robocalls to cell phones. The law, however, exempted robocalls made to collect a debt owed to the U.S. government. The Court found that the government debt exemption was content based and could not survive strict scrutiny review. But the majority severed that provision of the law from the rest of the TCPA, meaning that the ban

on political robocalls to cell phones remains. *Barr v. American Association of Political Consultants, Inc.* (2020).

C. REGULATING CONDUCT INSIDE THE POLLING PLACE

The Court in *Burson* recounted how U.S. states and localities adopted the "Australian" secret ballot in an effort to root out fraud, intimidation, and vote buying. Protecting the integrity of electoral processes is often a key consideration in promulgating an election law.

But *Burson* involved a regulation of campaigning *outside* of the polling place. What about regulations of voter conduct inside the polling place, such as wearing a t-shirt of a candidate on the ballot? Is there a concern of undue influence from a voter who might wear, say, a pro-Trump "MAGA" (Make America Great Again) hat into the polling place? The Supreme Court considered that question in 2018 in *Minnesota Voters Alliance v. Mansky*.

Burson also focused on the concern of election fraud and vote buying. Should a state impose regulations at the polls to ward off this threat? Some states have banned "ballot selfies," or the practice of voters taking a picture of their ballot, perhaps to post on social media. On the one hand, ballot selfies could help to improve turnout as voters encourage their friends and family members to participate on Election Day. They are, in essence, a form of campaign speech. On the other hand, ballot selfies are an easy way to prove how someone voted, which vote buyers will want to verify before paying for a vote. Does a ban on ballot seflies violate the First Amendment? The courts of appeals have split on the question, as demonstrated below. How do you think the Supreme Court will rule when faced with this issue?

Minnesota Voters Alliance v. Mansky

138 S. Ct. 1876 (2018)

Chief Justice ROBERTS delivered the opinion of the Court.

Under Minnesota law, voters may not wear a political badge, political button, or anything bearing political insignia inside a polling place on Election Day. The question presented is whether this ban violates the Free Speech Clause of the First Amendment.

I

A

Today, Americans going to their polling places on Election Day expect to wait in a line, briefly interact with an election official, enter a private voting booth, and cast an anonymous ballot. Little about this ritual would have been familiar to a voter in the mid-to-late nineteenth century. For one thing, voters typically deposited privately prepared ballots at the polls instead of completing official ballots onsite. These pre-made ballots often took the form of "party tickets"—printed slates of candidate selections, often distinctive in appearance, that political parties distributed to their supporters and pressed upon others around the polls.

The physical arrangement confronting the voter was also different. The polling place often consisted simply of a "voting window" through which the voter would hand his ballot to an election official situated in a separate room with the ballot box. As a result of this arrangement, "the actual act of voting was usually performed in the open," frequently within view of interested onlookers.

As documented in *Burson v. Freeman* (1992), "[a]pproaching the polling place under this system was akin to entering an open auction place." The room containing the ballot boxes was "usually quiet and orderly," but "[t]he public space outside the window . . . was chaotic." Electioneering of all kinds was permitted. Crowds would gather to heckle and harass voters who appeared to be supporting the other side. Indeed, "[u]nder the informal conventions of the period, election etiquette required only that a 'man of ordinary courage' be able to make his way to the voting window."

By the late nineteenth century, States began implementing reforms to address these vulnerabilities and improve the reliability of elections. Between 1888 and 1896, nearly every State adopted the secret ballot. Because voters now needed to mark their state-printed ballots on-site and in secret, voting moved into a sequestered space where the voters could "deliberate and make a decision in . . . privacy." In addition, States enacted "viewpoint-neutral restrictions on election-day speech" in the immediate vicinity of the polls. *Burson.* Today, all 50 States and the District of Columbia have laws curbing various forms of speech in and around polling places on Election Day.

Minnesota's such law contains three prohibitions, only one of which is challenged here. *See* Minn. Stat. § 211B.11(1). The first sentence of § 211B.11(1) forbids any person to "display campaign material, post signs, ask, solicit, or in any manner try to induce or persuade a voter within a polling place or within 100 feet of the building in which a polling place is situated" to "vote for or refrain from voting for a candidate or ballot question." The second sentence prohibits the distribution of "political badges, political buttons, or other political insignia to be worn at or about the polling place." The third sentence—the "political apparel ban"—states that a "political badge, political button, or other political insignia may not be worn at or about the polling place." Versions of all three prohibitions have been on the books in Minnesota for over a century.

There is no dispute that the political apparel ban applies only within the polling place, and covers articles of clothing and accessories with "political insignia" upon them. Minnesota election judges—temporary government employees working the polls on Election Day—have the authority to decide whether a particular item falls within the ban. If a voter shows up wearing a prohibited item, the election judge is to ask the individual to conceal or remove it. If the individual refuses, the election judge must allow him to vote, while making clear that the incident "will be recorded and referred to appropriate authorities." Violators are subject to an administrative process before the Minnesota Office of Administrative Hearings, which, upon finding a violation, may issue a reprimand or impose a civil penalty. That administrative body may also refer the complaint to the county attorney for prosecution as a petty misdemeanor; the maximum penalty is a $300 fine.

B

[The plaintiffs, which includes Minnesota Voters Alliance (MVA)]—calling themselves "Election Integrity Watch" (EIW)—planned to have supporters wear buttons to the polls printed with the words "Please I.D. Me," a picture of an eye, and a telephone number and web address for EIW. (Minnesota law does not require individuals to show identification to vote.) One of the individual plaintiffs also planned to wear a "Tea Party Patriots" shirt.

As alleged in the plaintiffs' amended complaint and supporting declarations, some voters associated with EIW ran into trouble with the ban on Election Day. One individual was asked to cover up his Tea Party shirt. Another refused to conceal his "Please I.D. Me" button, and an election judge recorded his name and address for possible referral. And petitioner Cilek—who was wearing the same button and a T-shirt with the words "Don't Tread on Me" and the Tea Party Patriots logo—was twice turned away from the polls altogether, then finally permitted to vote after an election judge recorded his information.

II

The First Amendment prohibits laws "abridging the freedom of speech." Minnesota's ban on wearing any "political badge, political button, or other political insignia" plainly restricts a form of expression within the protection of the First Amendment.

But the ban applies only in a specific location: the interior of a polling place. It therefore implicates our " 'forum based' approach for assessing restrictions that the government seeks to place on the use of its property." [Citation omitted.]

A polling place in Minnesota qualifies as a nonpublic forum. It is, at least on Election Day, government-controlled property set aside for the sole purpose of voting. Rules strictly govern who may be present, for what purpose, and for how long. And while the four-Justice plurality in *Burson* and Justice Scalia's concurrence in the judgment parted ways over whether the public sidewalks and streets surrounding a polling place qualify as a nonpublic forum, neither opinion suggested that the interior of the building was anything but.

We therefore evaluate MVA's First Amendment challenge under the nonpublic forum standard. The text of the apparel ban makes no distinction based on the speaker's political persuasion, so MVA does not claim that the ban discriminates on the basis of viewpoint on its face. The question accordingly is whether Minnesota's ban on political apparel is "reasonable in light of the purpose served by the forum": voting.

III

A

We first consider whether Minnesota is pursuing a permissible objective in prohibiting voters from wearing particular kinds of expressive apparel or accessories while inside the polling place. The natural starting point for evaluating a First Amendment challenge to such a restriction is this Court's decision in *Burson*, which upheld a Tennessee law imposing a 100-foot campaign-free zone around polling place entrances. The plurality found that the law withstood even the strict scrutiny applicable to speech restrictions in traditional public forums.

MVA disputes the relevance of *Burson* to Minnesota's apparel ban. On MVA's reading, *Burson* considered only "active campaigning" outside the polling place by campaign workers and others trying to engage voters approaching the polls. Minnesota's law, by contrast, prohibits what MVA characterizes as "passive, silent" self-expression by voters themselves when voting. MVA also points out that the plurality focused on the extent to which the restricted zone combated "voter intimidation and election fraud,"—concerns that, in MVA's view, have little to do with a prohibition on certain types of voter apparel.

[W]e see no basis for rejecting Minnesota's determination that some forms of advocacy should be excluded from the polling place, to set it aside as "an island of calm in which voters can peacefully contemplate their choices." [citing state's brief]. Casting a vote is a weighty civic act, akin to a jury's return of a verdict, or a representative's vote on a piece of legislation. It is a time for choosing, not campaigning. The State may reasonably decide that the interior of the polling place should reflect that distinction.

[On Election Day,] [m]embers of the public are brought together at that place, at the end of what may have been a divisive election season, to reach considered decisions about their government and laws. The State may reasonably take steps to ensure that partisan discord not follow the voter up to the voting booth, and distract from a sense of shared civic obligation at the moment it counts the most. That interest may be thwarted by displays that do not raise significant concerns in other situations.

Thus, in light of the special purpose of the polling place itself, Minnesota may choose to prohibit certain apparel there because of the message it conveys, so that voters may focus on the important decisions immediately at hand.

B

But the State must draw a reasonable line. Although there is no requirement of narrow tailoring in a nonpublic forum, the State must be able to articulate some sensible basis for distinguishing what may come in from what must stay out. Here, the unmoored use of the term "political" in the Minnesota law, combined with haphazard interpretations the State has provided in official guidance and representations to this Court, cause Minnesota's restriction to fail even this forgiving test.

Again, the statute prohibits wearing a "political badge, political button, or other political insignia." It does not define the term "political." And the word can be expansive. It can encompass anything "of or relating to government, a government, or the conduct of governmental affairs," Webster's Third New International Dictionary 1755 (2002), or anything "[o]f, relating to, or dealing with the structure or affairs of government, politics, or the state," American Heritage Dictionary 1401 (3d ed. 1996). Under a literal reading of those definitions, a button or T-shirt merely imploring others to "Vote!" could qualify.

The State argues that the apparel ban should not be read so broadly. According to the State, the statute does not prohibit "any conceivably 'political' message" or cover "all 'political' speech, broadly construed." Instead, the State interprets the ban to proscribe "only words and symbols that an objectively reasonable observer would perceive as conveying a message about the electoral choices at issue in [the] polling place."

At the same time, the State argues that the category of "political" apparel is not limited to campaign apparel. After all, the reference to "campaign material" in the first sentence of the statute—describing what one may not "display" in the buffer zone as well as inside the polling place—implies that the distinct term "political" should be understood to cover a broader class of items. As the State's counsel explained to the Court, Minnesota's law "expand[s] the scope of what is prohibited from campaign speech to additional political speech."

For specific examples of what is banned under its standard, the State points to the 2010 Election Day Policy—which it continues to hold out as authoritative guidance regarding implementation of the statute. The first three examples in the Policy are clear enough: items displaying the name of a political party, items displaying the name of a candidate, and items demonstrating "support of or opposition to a ballot question."

But the next example—"[i]ssue oriented material designed to influence or impact voting" raises more questions than it answers. What qualifies as an "issue"? The answer, as far as we can tell from the State's briefing and argument, is any subject on which a political candidate or party has taken a stance. For instance, the Election Day Policy specifically notes that the "Please I.D. Me" buttons are prohibited. But a voter identification requirement was not on the ballot in 2010, so a Minnesotan would have had no explicit "electoral choice" to make in that respect. The buttons were nonetheless covered, the State tells us, because the Republican candidates for Governor and Secretary of State had staked out positions on whether photo identification should be required.

A rule whose fair enforcement requires an election judge to maintain a mental index of the platforms and positions of every candidate and party on the ballot is not reasonable. Candidates for statewide and federal office and major political parties can be expected to take positions on a wide array of subjects of local and national import. Would a "Support Our Troops" shirt be banned, if one of the candidates or parties had expressed a view on military funding or aid for veterans? What about a "# MeToo" shirt, referencing the movement to increase awareness of sexual harassment and assault? At oral argument, the State indicated that the ban would cover such an item if a candidate had "brought up" the topic.

The next broad category in the Election Day Policy—any item "promoting a group with recognizable political views"—makes matters worse. The State construes the category as limited to groups with "views" about "the issues confronting voters in a given election." The State does not, however, confine that category to groups that have endorsed a candidate or taken a position on a ballot question.

Any number of associations, educational institutions, businesses, and religious organizations could have an opinion on an "issue[] confronting voters in a given election." For instance, the American Civil Liberties Union, the AARP, the World Wildlife Fund, and Ben & Jerry's all have stated positions on matters of public concern. If the views of those groups align or conflict with the position of a candidate or party on the ballot, does that mean that their insignia are banned? Take another example: In the run-up to the 2012 election, Presidential candidates of both major parties issued public statements regarding the then-existing policy of the Boy Scouts of America to exclude members on the basis of sexual orientation. Should a Scout leader in 2012 stopping to vote on his way to a troop meeting have been asked to cover up his uniform?

The State emphasizes that the ban covers only apparel promoting groups whose political positions are sufficiently "well-known." But that requirement, if anything, only increases the potential for erratic application. Well known by whom? The State tells us the lodestar is the "typical observer" of the item. But that measure may turn in significant part on the background knowledge and media consumption of the particular election judge applying it.

The State's "electoral choices" standard, considered together with the nonexclusive examples in the Election Day Policy, poses riddles that even the State's top lawyers struggle to solve. A shirt declaring "All Lives Matter," we are told, could be "perceived" as political. How about a shirt bearing the name of the National Rifle Association? Definitely out. That said, a shirt displaying a rainbow flag could be worn "unless there was an issue on the ballot" that "related somehow . . . to gay rights." A shirt simply displaying the text of the Second Amendment? Prohibited. But a shirt with the text of the First Amendment? "It would be allowed."

Election judges "have the authority to decide what is political" when screening individuals at the entrance to the polls. We do not doubt that the vast majority of election judges strive to enforce the statute in an evenhanded manner, nor that some degree of discretion in this setting is necessary. But that discretion must be guided by objective, workable standards. Without them, an election judge's own politics may shape his views on what counts as "political." And if voters experience or witness episodes of unfair or inconsistent enforcement of the ban, the State's interest in maintaining a polling place free of distraction and disruption would be undermined by the very measure intended to further it.

That is not to say that Minnesota has set upon an impossible task. Other States have laws proscribing displays (including apparel) in more lucid terms. See, e.g., Cal. Elec. Code Ann. § 319.5 (prohibiting "the visible display . . . of information that advocates for or against any candidate or measure," including the "display of a candidate's name, likeness, or logo," the "display of a ballot measure's number, title, subject, or logo," and "[b]uttons, hats," or "shirts" containing such information); Tex. Elec. Code Ann. § 61.010(a) (prohibiting the wearing of "a badge, insignia, emblem, or other similar communicative device relating to a candidate, measure, or political party appearing on the ballot, or to the conduct of the election"). We do not suggest that such provisions set the outer limit of what a State may proscribe, and do not pass on the constitutionality of laws that are not before us. But we do hold that if a State wishes to set its polling places apart as areas free of partisan discord, it must employ a more discernible approach than the one Minnesota has offered here.

Justice SOTOMAYOR, with whom Justice BREYER joins, dissenting.

I agree with the Court that "[c]asting a vote is a weighty civic act" and that "State[s] may reasonably take steps to ensure that partisan discord not follow the voter up to the voting booth," including by "prohibit[ing] certain apparel [in polling places] because of the message it conveys." I disagree, however, with the Court's decision to declare Minnesota's political apparel ban unconstitutional on its face because, in its view, the ban is not "capable of reasoned application," when the Court has not first afforded the Minnesota state courts " 'a reasonable opportunity to pass upon' " and construe the statute. [Citation omitted.] I would certify this case to the Minnesota Supreme Court for a definitive interpretation of the political apparel ban under Minn. Stat. § 211B.11(1), which likely would obviate the hypothetical line-drawing problems that form the basis of the Court's decision today.

[Remainder of dissent omitted.]

Rideout v. Gardner

838 F.3d 65 (1st Cir. 2016)

LYNCH, Circuit Judge.

In 2014, New Hampshire amended a statute meant to avoid vote buying and voter intimidation by newly forbidding citizens from photographing their marked ballots and publicizing such photographs. While the photographs need not show the voter, they often do and are commonly referred to as "ballot selfies." The statute imposes a fine of up to $1,000 for a violation of the prohibition. See N.H. Rev. Stat. Ann. § 659:35, IV; id. § 651:2, IV(a).

Three New Hampshire citizens who are under investigation for violation of the revised statute, and who are represented by the American Civil Liberties Union of New Hampshire, challenged the statute's constitutionality. The district court held that the statute is a content-based restriction of speech that on its face violates the First Amendment. The New Hampshire Secretary of State appeals, arguing that the statute is justified as a prophylactic measure to prevent new technology from facilitating future vote buying and voter coercion. We affirm on the narrower ground that the statute as amended fails to meet the test for intermediate scrutiny under the First Amendment and that the statute's purposes cannot justify the restrictions it imposes on speech.

I

In 2014, the New Hampshire legislature revised [the relevant statute] as follows:

> No voter shall allow his or her ballot to be seen by any person with the intention of letting it be known how he or she is about to vote or how he or she has voted except as provided in RSA 659:20 [which allows voters who need assistance marking a ballot to receive such assistance]. This prohibition shall include taking a digital image or photograph of his or her marked ballot and distributing or sharing the image via social media or by any other means.

The legislative history of the bill does not contain any corroborated evidence of vote buying or voter coercion in New Hampshire during the twentieth and twenty-first centuries. Representative Mary Till, who authored the House Committee on Election Law's statement of intent for the bill, provided the sole anecdotal allegation of vote buying. She asserted:

> I was told by a Goffstown resident that he knew for a fact that one of the major parties paid students from St[.] Anselm's $50 to vote in the 2012 election. I don't know whether that is true or not, but I do know that if I were going to pay someone to vote a particular way, I would want proof that they actually voted that way.

[Plaintiff] Rideout, a member of the New Hampshire House of Representatives and a Selectman for Lancaster, New Hampshire, took a photograph of his ballot, which showed that he had voted for himself and other Republican candidates in the September 9, 2014 primary. Later that day, he posted the ballot selfie on his Twitter feed and on his House of Representatives Facebook page. He then explained in an interview with the Nashua Telegraph, published on September 11, 2014, that he took and posted the photograph online "to make a statement," and that he thought section 659:35, I was "unconstitutional."

II

The First Amendment, which applies to the States through the Fourteenth Amendment, provides that "Congress shall make no law . . . abridging the freedom of speech." Standards to evaluate justifications by the state of a restriction on speech turn, inter alia, on whether the restriction focuses on content, that is, if it applies to "particular speech because of the topic discussed or the idea or message expressed." *Reed v. Town of Gilbert* (2015). "This commonsense meaning of the phrase 'content based' requires a court to consider whether a regulation of speech 'on its face' draws distinctions based on the message a speaker conveys." *Id.* Content-based regulations are subject to strict scrutiny, which requires the government to demonstrate "a compelling interest and . . . narrow[] tailor[ing] to achieve that interest." *Id.* Narrow tailoring in the strict scrutiny context requires the statute to be "the least restrictive means among available, effective alternatives." *Ashcroft v. Am. Civil Liberties Union* (2004).

In contrast, content-neutral regulations require a lesser level of justification. These laws do not apply to speech based on or because of the content of what has been said, but instead "serve[] purposes unrelated to the content of expression." *Ward v. Rock Against Racism* (1989). "The principal inquiry in determining content neutrality . . . is whether the government has adopted a regulation of speech because of disagreement with the message it conveys. The government's purpose is the controlling consideration. A regulation that serves purposes unrelated to the context of expression is deemed neutral. . . ." *Id.* Content-neutral restrictions are subject to intermediate scrutiny, which demands that the law be "narrowly tailored to serve a significant governmental interest." *Id.* "[U]nlike a content-based restriction of speech, [a content-neutral regulation] 'need not be the least restrictive or least intrusive means of' serving the government's interests." *McCullen v. Coakley* (2014).

We reach the conclusion that the statute at issue here is facially unconstitutional even applying only intermediate scrutiny. [T]here is a substantial mismatch between New Hampshire's objectives and the ballot-selfie prohibition in section 659:35, I.

In order to survive intermediate scrutiny, section 659:35, I must be "narrowly tailored to serve a significant governmental interest." *McCullen.* Though content-neutral laws "need not be the least restrictive or least intrusive means of serving the government's interests, the government still 'may not regulate expression in such a manner that a substantial portion of the burden on speech does not serve to advance its goals,'" *Id.* The statute fails this standard.

Secretary Gardner essentially concedes that section 659:35, I does not respond to a present "'actual problem' in need of solving." *Brown v. Entm't Merchs. Ass'n*

(2011). Instead, he argues that the statute serves prophylactically to "preserve the secrecy of the ballot" from potential future vote buying and voter coercion, because ballot selfies make it easier for voters to prove how they voted. He characterizes the amendment in section 659:35, I as a natural update of the older version of the statute, done in response to the development of "modern technology, such as digital photography and social media," which may facilitate a future rise in vote buying and voter intimidation schemes.

As the district court noted, the prevention of vote buying and voter coercion is unquestionably "compelling in the abstract." But intermediate scrutiny is not satisfied by the assertion of abstract interests. Broad prophylactic prohibitions that fail to "respond[] precisely to the substantive problem which legitimately concerns" the State cannot withstand intermediate scrutiny.

Digital photography, the internet, and social media are not unknown quantities—they have been ubiquitous for several election cycles, without being shown to have the effect of furthering vote buying or voter intimidation. As the plaintiffs note, "small cameras" and digital photography "have been in use for at least 15 years," and New Hampshire cannot identify a single complaint of vote buying or intimidation related to a voter's publishing a photograph of a marked ballot during that period. Indeed, Secretary Gardner has admitted that New Hampshire has not received any complaints of vote buying or voter intimidation since at least 1976, nor has he pointed to any such incidents since the nineteenth century.

Secretary Gardner also highlights scattered examples of cases involving vote buying from other American jurisdictions. But Secretary Gardner admits that "there is no evidence that digital photography [of a ballot shared with others by a voter] played a[ny] role in any of the examples" he cites. A few recent instances of vote buying in other states do not substantiate New Hampshire's asserted interest in targeting vote buying through banning the publication of ballot selfies.

Secretary Gardner tries to anchor the state interest for section 659:35, I on *Burson v. Freeman* (1992), which held that Tennessee had a compelling interest in banning "the solicitation of votes and the display or distribution of campaign materials within 100 feet of the entrance to a polling place." *Burson* is obviously distinguishable. The discussion in *Burson* of the long history of regulating polling places and the location of elections makes clear that the interest at stake in *Burson* centered on the protection of physical election spaces from interference and coercion. The plurality acknowledged in *Burson* that two competing interests had to be balanced: the right to speak on political issues and the right to be free from coercion or fraud at the polling place.

The intrusion on the voters' First Amendment rights is much greater here than that involved in *Burson*. Section 659:35, I does not secure the immediate physical site of elections, but instead controls the use of imagery of marked ballots, regardless of where, when, and how that imagery is publicized.

But even accepting the possibility that ballot selfies will make vote buying and voter coercion easier by providing proof of how the voter actually voted, the statute still fails for lack of narrow tailoring.

New Hampshire has "too readily forgone options that could serve its interests just as well, without substantially burdening" legitimate political speech. *McCullen*. At least two different reasons show that New Hampshire has not attempted to tailor its solution to the potential problem it perceives. First, the prohibition on ballot selfies reaches and curtails the speech rights of all voters, not just those motivated to cast a particular vote for illegal reasons. New Hampshire does so in the name of trying to prevent a much smaller hypothetical pool of voters who, New Hampshire fears, may try to sell their votes. New Hampshire admits that no such vote-selling market has in fact emerged. And to the extent that the State hypothesizes this will make intimidation of some voters more likely, that is no reason to infringe on the rights of all voters.

Second, the State has not demonstrated that other state and federal laws prohibiting vote corruption are not already adequate to the justifications it has identified. As the district court observed, there are less restrictive alternatives available:

> [T]he state has an obviously less restrictive way to address any concern that images of completed ballots will be used to facilitate vote buying and voter coercion: it can simply make it unlawful to use an image of a completed ballot in connection with vote buying and voter coercion schemes.

The restriction affects voters who are engaged in core political speech, an area highly protected by the First Amendment. Ballot selfies have taken on a special communicative value: they both express support for a candidate and communicate that the voter has in fact given his or her vote to that candidate.

New Hampshire may not impose such a broad restriction on speech by banning ballot selfies in order to combat an unsubstantiated and hypothetical danger. We repeat the old adage: "a picture is worth a thousand words."

Silberberg v. Board of Elections of the State of New York

272 F. Supp. 3d 454 (S.D.N.Y. 2017)

CASTEL, Senior District Judge:

N.Y. Elec. Law § 17-130(10), first enacted in 1890 as part of the Australian ballot movement, provides that "[a]ny person who . . . [s]hows his ballot after it is prepared for voting, to any person so as to reveal the contents . . . is guilty of a misdemeanor." The language of this statute and the purpose for its enactment—combating vote buying and voter intimidation by depriving the perpetrator of a means by which to verify his target's compliance—sweep within their reach the act of taking a ballot selfie at a polling place and posting it to a social media site. Posting a photograph of one's marked ballot to social media is indisputably a potent form of political speech, presumptively entitled to protection under the First Amendment.

For reasons to be explained, the statute as applied to ballot selfies survives strict scrutiny. The State of New York has a compelling interest in preventing vote buying and voter coercion. The State's interest in the integrity of its elections is paramount. The law is also narrowly tailored, for a law prohibiting the display a marked ballot only for the purpose of vote buying or coercion would be ineffective.

Alternatively, the Court finds that the statute is a reasonable, viewpoint neutral restriction of speech within a non-public forum.

BACKGROUND AND EVIDENCE

I. Procedural History

[Omitted.]

DISCUSSION

[I and II Omitted.]

III. N.Y. Elec. Law § 17-130(10) Survives Strict Scrutiny

A. N.Y. Elec. Law § 17-130(10) Furthers a Compelling State Interest

i. Burson

"[A] State 'indisputably has a compelling interest in preserving the integrity of its election process.' . . . In other words, . . . a State has a compelling interest in ensuring that an individual's right to vote is not undermined by fraud in the election process." *Burson v. Freeman* (1992). A state has a further compelling interest in "protecting voters from confusion and undue influence." *Id.*

In *Burson*, the Supreme Court upheld against a First Amendment challenge a Tennessee law that prohibited certain campaign related speech, including the display of campaign materials, such as signs or posters, or the solicitation of votes for or against a person, political party, or position on a question, within 100 feet of the entrance to a polling site. This statute, first enacted in slightly different form in 1890, was intended to combat the same evils that the 1890 New York statute was intended to combat; vote buying and voter intimidation.

[T]he Supreme Court in *Burson* emphasized that the Tennessee law in question was only one piece of the Australian ballot reforms in that state, which also included secret, standardized ballots. The Court noted that these provisions worked in tandem to combat voter fraud.

Though the Supreme Court in *Burson* did not directly face a challenge to the part of the Tennessee Australian ballot reforms that mandated secret ballots, the Supreme Court's analysis made clear the necessity of the secret ballot to the reforms as a whole, which were necessary to remedy the evils of vote buying and voter coercion, which undermine the integrity of elections and which the state has a compelling interest to protect.

ii. N.Y. Elec. Law § 17-130(10) was Designed to Combat Election Fraud.

The same concerns regarding vote buying and voter intimidation that prompted the adoption of the Australian ballot reforms nationwide, as well as the enactment in 1890 of the specific Tennessee statute at issue in *Burson*, motivated the enactment of N.Y. Elec. Law § 17-130(10) that same year. The evidence at trial supports the conclusion that in New York, prior to the enactment of the statute, vote buying and voter intimidation were rampant. Preventing these evils and upholding the integrity of New York's elections is a compelling state interest.

After New York's adoption of the Australian ballot reforms vote buying and voter intimidation virtually disappeared. Yet they did not disappear completely—a handful of vote buying schemes have been uncovered in the last several years. A federal prosecution in this district against the perpetrators of a vote buying scheme is still ongoing.

The lack of evidence of widespread vote buying and voter intimidation in contemporary New York elections does not mean that the state no longer has a compelling interest in preventing these evils. As the Supreme Court has observed, "it is difficult to isolate the exact effect of these laws on voter intimidation and election fraud. Voter intimidation and election fraud are successful precisely because they are difficult to detect." *Burson.*

N.Y. Elec. Law § 17-130(10) was adopted in substantially the same form 127 years ago and has been in effect ever since. Defendants are thus limited in their ability to present evidence of what would happen if the statute were stricken or its application limited to a person-to-person showing of a marked ballot. Defendants have convincingly demonstrated that secret ballots remain critical to combating vote buying and voter intimidation.

Plaintiffs urge this Court to follow *Rideout v. Gardner*, where the First Circuit, in upholding the district court's injunction against the enforcement of a New Hampshire statute updated in 2014 to specifically prohibit the sharing via social media of a digital photograph of a marked ballot, found that the statute did not address an "actual problem in need of solving." In that case, decided on summary judgment, virtually no specific evidence was presented regarding vote buying or voter intimidation in New Hampshire. In the present case, ample evidence has been presented regarding vote buying and voter intimidation in New York, both historic and contemporary. And New Hampshire is not New York City. New York elections were bought and sold for decades before the introduction of the Australian ballot reforms. The statute was an appropriate response to the political corruption in New York in 1890 and is a valid measure today to prevent that history from repeating itself.

B. N.Y. Elec. Law § 17-130(10) is Narrowly Tailored

For the statute as applied to ballot selfies to survive strict scrutiny the state must demonstrate not only that the law serves a compelling state interest, but also that the law is narrowly tailored to serve that interest. To make this showing, the state must "prove that the proposed alternatives will not be as effective as the challenged statute." Because speech must not be restricted further than necessary to achieve the state's interest, the statute must be "the least restrictive alternative that can be used to achieve that goal." In other words, the statute will be struck down if the government does not prove that "the challenged regulation is the least restrictive means among available, effective alternatives."

Vote buying and voter intimidation are against the law. However, these crimes, in and of themselves, are very difficult to detect. A key way to disrupt this kind of voter fraud is to prevent would-be vote buyers and intimidators from verifying their targets' compliance. Viewing a photograph of an individual along with their marked ballot is an especially efficacious way to verify that the individual in the photograph voted consistent with the marked ballot in the photo, as such a photograph would be more difficult to fake.

Plaintiffs argue that the statute is overinclusive because it criminalizes the posting of photographs of marked ballots to social media by individuals who are not involved in a vote buying scheme or any other kind of voter fraud. Plaintiffs allege that the least restrictive means of upholding the state's compelling interest in the integrity of elections is to criminalize vote buying and voter intimidation. The

Supreme Court rejected a similar argument with respect to the 100–foot restricted zone around polling sites in *Burson*, finding that "[i]ntimidation and interference laws fall short of serving a State's compelling interests because they deal with only the most blatant and specific attempts to impede elections." Likewise, history and common sense teach that prohibiting vote buying and voter intimidation are unlikely to be a particularly effective means to combat these evils so long as the perpetrators may verify their target's votes. It was in fact the failure of such laws that prompted the Australian ballot reforms in the first place.

Next, plaintiffs argue that the statute does not effectively prevent vote buyers or intimidators from verifying their targets' votes because photographs of marked ballots could be transmitted privately rather than posted publically [sic], and these transmissions would be virtually impossible to detect. Thus, plaintiffs argue, the prohibition on the display of a photograph of a marked ballot does not in any way prevent vote buying or voter intimidation beyond the criminal statutes prohibiting such behavior directly.

While at first glance it appears intuitive that an individual engaged in a vote buying scheme would not publically [sic] post a ballot selfie on social media for fear of detection, closer examination reveals that in reality, the opposite is true. A vote buyer or voter intimidator who wishes to verify his targets' votes is presented with a dilemma—the electronic transmittal of a photograph of a marked ballot will almost invariably leave some sort of electronic record. In order to eliminate an electronic trail, the perpetrator might command that the photograph be posted to social media, where anyone can see it. Using this tactic, the perpetrators of election fraud would leave virtually no evidence of their misdeeds and authorities would have little hope of apprehending them, especially in the likely event that posting ballot selfies increases in popularity absent this law.

Plaintiffs put forth no alternative that would be as effective in restricting the ability of individuals or entities who would commit election fraud from ensuring that their targets complied with their instructions, and the Court is aware of none. As described, any law prohibiting only the posting to social media of photographs of marked ballots for fraudulent purposes would allow the posting of marked ballots in general to proliferate, thus giving cover to those who would use these photographs to fraudulently alter elections.

C. Social Coercion

N.Y. Elec. Law § 17-130(10) is narrowly tailored to serve the compelling government interest of preventing vote buying and voter intimidation, and thus survives strict scrutiny. Separately, though not unrelatedly, the law is narrowly tailored to serve the compelling government interest in maintaining the integrity of the election process by preventing employers and other groups and organizations from exercising more subtle forms coercion on their members to enforce orthodoxy in voting.

Defendants argue that the potential for coercion by employers, unions, and other groups represents a serious threat to the integrity of elections in New York. Such coercion, they argue, is difficult to address through laws that prohibit threating [sic] to inflict harm or loss on a voter to influence voting behavior.

Employers and other organizations have many ways of enforcing various kinds of orthodoxy among their employees and members. Currently, an employer or group's power to enforce political orthodoxy among its members ends at the entrance to the voting booth. Without the prohibition on displaying a photograph of one's marked ballot, the protection gained from secret voting will disappear, and employers, unions, political groups, or religious organizations will be able to pressure individual members to produce photographs of ballots marked in support of the organization's preferences, or face suspicion that the person has acted in an unorthodox manner.

This social pressure that could be brought to bear could be both direct and indirect, subtle and open. Members could be pressured to produce such photographs in private, to management, or leaders of the organization, or to post them publically [sic] on a group social media page. For many voters, ballot secrecy must be required by law for voting in secret to even be an option.

Easy cases, such as an employer firing an employee for failure to post may be reached by a narrower law. But private associations and groups would be much harder to police. More subtle sanctions, such as the disapprobation of other individuals in the organization, or the possibility of being shunned by group members, or even entire communities, would be difficult to address. The state has a compelling interest in ensuring that citizens are allowed to vote their conscience. Secrecy in voting allows the voter to engage in the act of voting free from the judgement of others.

IV. N.Y. Elec. Law § 17-130(10) is a Permissible Content–Based Restriction of Speech in a Non–Public Forum

[Omitted.]

CONCLUSION

Because plaintiffs have failed to show that N.Y. Elec. Law § 17-130(10) . . . abridge[s] their rights under the First and Fourteenth Amendments, their claims are dismissed.

NOTES ON *MANSKY, RIDEOUT,* AND *SILBERBERG*

1. The Supreme Court in *Mansky* struck down Minnesota's law on wearing political apparel at the polling place as essentially overbroad. But would a narrower law achieve Minnesota's goals of avoiding coercion and intimidation at the polls? Is it even possible to write a narrower provision? Are poll workers in the best position to determine if a particular shirt or hat is "too" political?

2. The courts in *Rideout* and *Silberberg* come out in opposite ways on the constitutionality of a ban on ballot selfies. Which court had the better argument? Are these laws content based or content neutral? Are they necessary to avoid the potential of vote buying? Were you convinced by the way the New York court distinguished the New Hampshire case in saying that New York elections are fundamentally different from New Hampshire elections? Given the Supreme Court's decisions in *Burson* and *Mansky*, how do you expect the Court to rule when faced with a challenge to a ballot selfie law?

3. How does a vote buying scheme actually work? Obviously the vote buyer wants to ensure that the vote seller is voting as directed. Sometimes those involved

enlist poll workers to ensure that voters cast their ballots for the candidate that is buying their votes, or have poll workers manipulate the machines to change votes after the voters leave. A recent judicial opinion sheds some light on how this happens:

> Political candidates pooled money to buy votes and to pay "vote haulers" to deliver voters whose votes could be bought. In order to be paid, voters had to vote for a particular set of candidates, known as a "slate" or "ticket." To ensure that these voters actually voted for the correct slate, co-conspiring election officers and poll workers reviewed voters' ballots—a practice known in this case as "voting the voter." Once the proper slate was confirmed, a token (such as a raffle ticket) or marking was given to the voters to confirm that they did in fact vote for the proper slate. Voters with the token or marking were then paid by members of the conspiracy in a location away from the polls. Conspirators retained lists of voters to avoid double payments and to keep track of whose votes could be bought in ensuing elections.
>
> In addition to hiring vote haulers, defendants allegedly utilized other methods of buying votes. Absentee voting and voter-assistance forms helped minimize the difficulty of checking paid voters' ballots. In the latter case, co-conspiring poll workers were permitted to be in the voting booth under the pretext that they were assisting voters; in reality, co-conspiring poll workers were confirming that voters chose the proper slates. When electronic voting machines were introduced to Clay County in the 2006 election, the conspiracy both stole and bought votes. To steal votes, conspirators, typically poll workers, purposefully misinformed voters that they did not need to click "cast ballot" on a screen that appeared after voters had selected candidates for whom they wished to vote. Co-conspiring poll workers would enter the voting booth after the voter exited and change the electronic ballot to reflect the slate before finally casting the ballot.

United States v. Adams, 722 F.3d 788 (6th Cir. 2013).

Are criminal laws sufficient to deter vote buying of this kind? The court in *Adams* reversed the defendants' criminal convictions based on errors the district court made in admitting certain evidence.

D. *CAMPAIGN FINANCE*

Political campaigns are expensive. The amount of money spent for political campaigns has continued to skyrocket. Observers thought that the 2016 election cycle's record-breaking spending was unprecedented, but then candidates, campaigns, and political organizations spent double that amount in 2020. Spending on presidential and congressional races in 2020 topped $14.4 billion, and that doesn't even include state races! As the costs to run for office have increased, so too has a candidate's need to solicit and spend money to stay viable.

Where do candidates find this money? The main sources are the candidate's own pockets (if the candidate is wealthy enough); political parties, individual voters, or organized interest groups sympathetic to the candidate's views; and (where applicable) the public itself through public financing. Moreover, outside groups (and even corporations) may spend money on their own electioneering communications to support or oppose a candidate. The cases in this section are organized loosely around the concept of who is spending the money: candidates, individuals, political parties, corporations and unions, the public through public financing, and political action committees (PACs), which are nonprofit organizations created to be generally independent of candidates and which engage in electioneering activities. Consider the way in which the rules differ for different kinds of political actors.

In addition to focusing on the *who*, it is important to consider *what* the actors are doing with their money. As you will see, the Supreme Court has made a fundamental conceptual distinction between *donations* to a candidate, a political party, or a PAC, and *independent expenditures* to advocate for or against a candidate's election, which are separate from the candidate's own spending. (This distinction will become clearer as you read the Court's cases.) But even within the realm of independent spending to support or oppose a candidate, there is the further distinction between *express advocacy*, which explicitly declares its support or opposition to a candidate's election, and *issue advocacy*, which discusses issues of public policy and might even mention the name of a candidate—thereby seeming implicitly to support or oppose the candidate's election—but without an explicit statement of electoral advocacy. Moreover, because the distinction between federal and state elections matters for campaign finance law, in some contexts it is important to know whether a political party has paid for activities that specifically benefit their federal candidates or, instead, has paid for campaign activities that benefit both their federal and state candidates.

With increased money in campaigns comes concerns about potential corruption or undue influence of those who contribute. Might a politician favor those who contributed to his or her campaign when passing legislation? Will those who give money have greater access to influence the politician? Does the increase of money in politics mean that only wealthy individuals, or those backed by wealthy groups, have a chance to win?

Enter Congress and state legislatures, which have sought to regulate this area. Since the 1970s, in response to the egregious and well-documented corruption that occurred as part of President Nixon's efforts to win reelection in 1972 (usually referred to as "Watergate," although the break-in of the Democratic Party's headquarters at the Watergate Hotel was just one piece of the overall corruption), Congress became more active in passing laws that place parameters around the use of money in politics. In particular, Congress has sought to impose limits on the amount of money individuals can contribute, the amount candidates can spend, and the amount individuals or groups not affiliated with a campaign may spend (independent expenditures). Generally, Congress has espoused the goals of eliminating corruption or the appearance of corruption, ensuring political actors cannot circumvent valid campaign finance restrictions, and equalizing the opportunities for electoral success by reducing the skyrocketing cost of campaigns. As you read through the cases, consider to what extent courts deem these interests valid. We start with the seminal case in this area, *Buckley v. Valeo.*

1. *The* Buckley *Foundation*

The United States has regulated campaign finance for over a century. In 1907, Congress passed the Tillman Act, which prohibited corporations from contributing to national political campaigns. Congress followed with additional regulation through the Federal Corrupt Practices Act of 1925, the Hatch Act of 1939 (and its amendments in 1940), and the Taft-Hartley Act of 1947. All of these laws sought to regulate spending in campaigns for federal office. But none provided a comprehensive solution, and in practice there was little regulation of money in campaigns. As the Federal Election Commission (the federal agency that administers campaign finance laws for federal elections) explained, "The campaign finance provisions of all of these laws were largely ignored . . . because none provided an institutional framework to administer their provisions effectively. The laws had other flaws as well. For example, spending limits applied only to committees active in two or more States. Further, candidates could avoid the spending limit and disclosure requirements altogether because a candidate who claimed to have no knowledge of spending on his behalf was not liable under the 1925 [Federal Corrupt Practices] Act." *See* The Federal Election Commission: The First 10 Years, 1975-1985.

Congress, perceiving abuses in the financing of campaigns and concerned about the rising costs of campaigning, enacted the Federal Election Campaign Act (FECA) of 1971. Congress found, in passing FECA, that "the unchecked rise in campaign expenditures coupled with the absence of limitations on contributions and expenditures, has increased the dependence of candidates on special interest groups and large contributors. Under the present law the impression persists that a candidate can buy an election by simply spending large sums in a campaign." FECA itself was substantially amended just a few years later, after the Watergate abuses showed that the original version of the statute was inadequate to achieve its anticorruption goals.

For our purposes, FECA introduced three major changes to the financing of campaigns. First, the law imposed a limit on how much individuals could contribute to campaigns. Second, FECA set limits on independent expenditures—money not given to a campaign, and spent without any coordination with the campaign, but still advocating for a certain result. In essence, a contribution is writing a check to the campaign itself; an independent expenditure is spending your own money directly on campaign activities, such as buying your own billboard or ad in support of a candidate or issue. Finally, the law imposed disclosure requirements.

Opponents of the law immediately challenged these aspects of FECA. The Supreme Court's decision, upholding the contribution limits and disclosure requirements but striking down the independent expenditure limitations, forms the foundation for today's campaign finance regime. As you read *Buckley*, consider the way in which the analysis for contributions as opposed to independent expenditures is or should be different. Also note how the Court deems campaign spending a form of "speech" that requires robust First Amendment protection.

Buckley v. Valeo

424 U.S. 1 (1976)

PER CURIAM.

These appeals present constitutional challenges to the key provisions of the Federal Election Campaign Act of 1971 (Act), as amended in 1974.

The statutes at issue summarized in broad terms, contain the following provisions: individual political contributions are limited to $1,000 to any single candidate per election, with an overall annual limitation of $25,000 by any contributor;* independent expenditures by individuals and groups "relative to a clearly identified candidate" are limited to $1,000 a year; campaign spending by candidates for various federal offices and spending for national conventions by political parties are subject to prescribed limits.

I. CONTRIBUTION AND EXPENDITURE LIMITATIONS

The intricate statutory scheme adopted by Congress to regulate federal election campaigns includes restrictions on political contributions and expenditures that apply broadly to all phases of and all participants in the election process. The major contribution and expenditure limitations in the Act prohibit individuals from contributing more than $25,000 in a single year or more than $1,000 to any single candidate for an election campaign and from spending more than $1,000 a year "relative to a clearly identified candidate." Other provisions restrict a candidate's use of personal and family resources in his campaign and limit the overall amount that can be spent by a candidate in campaigning for federal office.

The constitutional power of Congress to regulate federal elections is well established and is not questioned by any of the parties in this case. Thus, the critical constitutional questions presented here go not to the basic power of Congress to legislate in this area, but to whether the specific legislation that Congress has enacted interferes with First Amendment freedoms. . . .

A. General Principles

The Act's contribution and expenditure limitations operate in an area of the most fundamental First Amendment activities. Discussion of public issues and debate on the qualifications of candidates are integral to the operation of

* [The contribution limits are indexed for inflation; for the 2020 election, the contribution limit for individuals was $2,800 per candidate per election (with primary and general elections counted separately, meaning that an individual could give a total of $5,600 to candidates who win the primary and go on to the general election). This amount includes in-kind contributions; the total amount of actual money given and in-kind contributions, such as for services provided, cannot exceed $2,800 per election. Individuals may also give to the national, state, or local parties, with separate ceilings for these contributions. There are also contribution limits that apply to political action committees. To see a chart listing these limits, visit https://www.fec.gov/help-candidates-and-committees/candidate-taking-receipts/contribution-limits/.—EDS.]

the system of government established by our Constitution. The First Amendment affords the broadest protection to such political expression in order "to assure (the) unfettered interchange of ideas for the bringing about of political and social changes desired by the people." *Roth v. United States* (1957). Although First Amendment protections are not confined to "the exposition of ideas," "there is practically universal agreement that a major purpose of that Amendment was to protect the free discussion of governmental affairs. . . . of course includ(ing) discussions of candidates. . . ." *Mills v. Alabama* (1966). This no more than reflects our "profound national commitment to the principle that debate on public issues should be uninhibited, robust, and wide-open," *New York Times Co. v. Sullivan* (1964). In a republic where the people are sovereign, the ability of the citizenry to make informed choices among candidates for office is essential, for the identities of those who are elected will inevitably shape the course that we follow as a nation. As the Court observed in *Monitor Patriot Co. v. Roy* (1971), "it can hardly be doubted that the constitutional guarantee has its fullest and most urgent application precisely to the conduct of campaigns for political office."

It is with these principles in mind that we consider the primary contentions of the parties with respect to the Act's limitations upon the giving and spending of money in political campaigns. Appellees contend that what the Act regulates is conduct, and that its effect on speech and association is incidental at most. Appellants respond that contributions and expenditures are at the very core of political speech, and that the Act's limitations thus constitute restraints on First Amendment liberty that are both gross and direct.

Some forms of communication made possible by the giving and spending of money involve speech alone, some involve conduct primarily, and some involve a combination of the two. Yet this Court has never suggested that the dependence of a communication on the expenditure of money operates itself to introduce a nonspeech element or to reduce the exacting scrutiny required by the First Amendment.

Even if the categorization of the expenditure of money as conduct were accepted, the limitations challenged here . . . involve "suppressing communication." The interests served by the Act include restricting the voices of people and interest groups who have money to spend and reducing the overall scope of federal election campaigns. Although the Act does not focus on the ideas expressed by persons or groups subject to its regulations, it is aimed in part at equalizing the relative ability of all voters to affect electoral outcomes by placing a ceiling on expenditures for political expression by citizens and groups.

A restriction on the amount of money a person or group can spend on political communication during a campaign necessarily reduces the quantity of expression by restricting the number of issues discussed, the depth of their exploration, and the size of the audience reached.[18] This is because virtually every means of communicating ideas in today's mass society requires the expenditure of money. The distribution of the humblest handbill or leaflet entails printing, paper, and

18. Being free to engage in unlimited political expression subject to a ceiling on expenditures is like being free to drive an automobile as far and as often as one desires on a single tank of gasoline.

circulation costs. Speeches and rallies generally necessitate hiring a hall and publicizing the event. The electorate's increasing dependence on television, radio, and other mass media for news and information has made these expensive modes of communication indispensable instruments of effective political speech.

The expenditure limitations contained in the Act represent substantial rather than merely theoretical restraints on the quantity and diversity of political speech. The $1,000 ceiling on spending "relative to a clearly identified candidate" would appear to exclude all citizens and groups except candidates, political parties, and the institutional press from any significant use of the most effective modes of communication. Although the Act's limitations on expenditures by campaign organizations and political parties provide substantially greater room for discussion and debate, they would have required restrictions in the scope of a number of past congressional and Presidential campaigns and would operate to constrain campaigning by candidates who raise sums in excess of the spending ceiling.

By contrast with a limitation upon expenditures for political expression, a limitation upon the amount that any one person or group may contribute to a candidate or political committee entails only a marginal restriction upon the contributor's ability to engage in free communication. A contribution serves as a general expression of support for the candidate and his views, but does not communicate the underlying basis for the support. The quantity of communication by the contributor does not increase perceptibly with the size of his contribution, since the expression rests solely on the undifferentiated, symbolic act of contributing. At most, the size of the contribution provides a very rough index of the intensity of the contributor's support for the candidate. A limitation on the amount of money a person may give to a candidate or campaign organization thus involves little direct restraint on his political communication, for it permits the symbolic expression of support evidenced by a contribution but does not in any way infringe the contributor's freedom to discuss candidates and issues. While contributions may result in political expression if spent by a candidate or an association to present views to the voters, the transformation of contributions into political debate involves speech by someone other than the contributor.

Given the important role of contributions in financing political campaigns, contribution restrictions could have a severe impact on political dialogue if the limitations prevented candidates and political committees from amassing the resources necessary for effective advocacy. There is no indication, however, that the contribution limitations imposed by the Act would have any dramatic adverse effect on the funding of campaigns and political associations. The overall effect of the Act's contribution ceilings is merely to require candidates and political committees to raise funds from a greater number of persons and to compel people who would otherwise contribute amounts greater than the statutory limits to expend such funds on direct political expression, rather than to reduce the total amount of money potentially available to promote political expression.

The Act's contribution and expenditure limitations also impinge on protected associational freedoms. Making a contribution, like joining a political party, serves to affiliate a person with a candidate. In addition, it enables like-minded persons to pool their resources in furtherance of common political goals. The Act's contribution ceilings thus limit one important means of associating with a candidate or committee, but leave the contributor free to become a member of any political association and to assist personally in the association's efforts on behalf of candidates. And the Act's contribution limitations permit associations and candidates to aggregate large sums of money to promote effective advocacy. By contrast, the Act's $1,000 limitation on independent expenditures "relative to a clearly identified candidate" precludes most associations from effectively amplifying the voice of their adherents, the original basis for the recognition of First Amendment protection of the freedom of association. *See NAACP v. Alabama* [(1958)].

In sum, although the Act's contribution and expenditure limitations both implicate fundamental First Amendment interests, its expenditure ceilings impose significantly more severe restrictions on protected freedoms of political expression and association than do its limitations on financial contributions.

B. Contribution Limitations

1. The $1,000 Limitation on Contributions by Individuals and Groups to Candidates and Authorized Campaign Committees

Section 608(b) provides, with certain limited exceptions, that "no person shall make contributions to any candidate with respect to any election for Federal office which, in the aggregate, exceed $1,000." The $1,000 ceiling applies regardless of whether the contribution is given to the candidate, to a committee authorized in writing by the candidate to accept contributions on his behalf, or indirectly via earmarked gifts passed through an intermediary to the candidate. The restriction applies to aggregate amounts contributed to the candidate for each election with primaries, run-off elections, and general elections counted separately, and all Presidential primaries held in any calendar year treated together as a single election campaign.

Appellants contend that the $1,000 contribution ceiling unjustifiably burdens First Amendment freedoms, employs overbroad dollar limits, and discriminates against candidates opposing incumbent officeholders. We address each of these claims of invalidity in turn.

(a)

As the general discussion in Part I-A indicated, the primary First Amendment problem raised by the Act's contribution limitations is their restriction of one aspect of the contributor's freedom of political association. In view of the fundamental nature of the right to associate, governmental "action which may have the effect of curtailing the freedom to associate is subject to the closest scrutiny." *NAACP v. Alabama.* Yet, it is clear that "(n)either the right to associate nor the right to participate in political activities is absolute." *CSC v. Letter Carriers* (1973). Even a "'significant interference' with protected rights of political association" may be sustained if the State demonstrates a sufficiently important interest and employs means closely drawn to avoid unnecessary abridgment of associational freedoms.

Appellees argue that the Act's restrictions on large campaign contributions are justified by three governmental interests. [T]he primary interest served by the limitations and, indeed, by the Act as a whole, is the prevention of corruption and the appearance of corruption spawned by the real or imagined coercive influence of large financial contributions on candidates' positions and on their actions if elected to office. Two "ancillary" interests underlying the Act are also allegedly furthered by the $1,000 limits on contributions. First, the limits serve to mute the voices of affluent persons and groups in the election process and thereby to equalize the relative ability of all citizens to affect the outcome of elections.[26] Second, it is argued, the ceilings may to some extent act as a brake on the skyrocketing cost of political campaigns and thereby serve to open the political system more widely to candidates without access to sources of large amounts of money.

It is unnecessary to look beyond the Act's primary purpose to limit the actuality and appearance of corruption resulting from large individual financial contributions in order to find a constitutionally sufficient justification for the $1,000 contribution limitation. Under a system of private financing of elections, a candidate lacking immense personal or family wealth must depend on financial contributions from others to provide the resources necessary to conduct a successful campaign. The increasing importance of the communications media and sophisticated mass-mailing and polling operations to effective campaigning make the raising of large sums of money an ever more essential ingredient of an effective candidacy. To the extent that large contributions are given to secure a political quid pro quo from current and potential office holders, the integrity of our system of representative democracy is undermined. Although the scope of such pernicious practices can never be reliably ascertained, the deeply disturbing examples surfacing after the 1972 election demonstrate that the problem is not an illusory one.

Of almost equal concern as the danger of actual quid pro quo arrangements is the impact of the appearance of corruption stemming from public awareness of the opportunities for abuse inherent in a regime of large individual financial contributions. Congress could legitimately conclude that the avoidance of the appearance of improper influence is also critical if confidence in the system of representative Government is not to be eroded to a disastrous extent.

Appellants contend that the contribution limitations must be invalidated because bribery laws and narrowly drawn disclosure requirements constitute a less restrictive means of dealing with "proven and suspected quid pro quo arrangements." But laws making criminal the giving and taking of bribes deal with only the most blatant and specific attempts of those with money to influence governmental action. And while disclosure requirements serve many salutary purposes, Congress was surely entitled to conclude that disclosure was only a partial measure, and that contribution ceilings were a necessary legislative concomitant to deal with the reality or appearance of corruption inherent in a system permitting unlimited financial contributions, even when the identities of the contributors and the amounts of their contributions are fully disclosed.

The Act's $1,000 contribution limitation focuses precisely on the problem of large campaign contributions the narrow aspect of political association where the actuality and potential for corruption have been identified while leaving persons free to engage in independent political expression, to associate actively through volunteering their services, and to assist to a limited but nonetheless substantial extent in supporting candidates and committees with financial resources.

26. Contribution limitations alone would not reduce the greater potential voice of affluent persons and well-financed groups, who would remain free to spend unlimited sums directly to promote candidates and policies they favor in an effort to persuade voters.

Significantly, the Act's contribution limitations in themselves do not undermine to any material degree the potential for robust and effective discussion of candidates and campaign issues by individual citizens, associations, the institutional press, candidates, and political parties.

We find that, under the rigorous standard of review established by our prior decisions, the weighty interests served by restricting the size of financial contributions to political candidates are sufficient to justify the limited effect upon First Amendment freedoms caused by the $1,000 contribution ceiling.

(b)

Appellants' first overbreadth challenge to the contribution ceilings rests on the proposition that most large contributors do not seek improper influence over a candidate's position or an officeholder's action. Although the truth of that proposition may be assumed, it does not undercut the validity of the $1,000 contribution limitation. Not only is it difficult to isolate suspect contributions, but, more importantly, Congress was justified in concluding that the interest in safeguarding against the appearance of impropriety requires that the opportunity for abuse inherent in the process of raising large monetary contributions be eliminated.

A second, related overbreadth claim is that the $1,000 restriction is unrealistically low because much more than that amount would still not be enough to enable an unscrupulous contributor to exercise improper influence over a candidate or officeholder, especially in campaigns for statewide or national office. While the contribution limitation provisions might well have been structured to take account of the graduated expenditure limitations for congressional and Presidential campaigns, Congress' failure to engage in such fine tuning does not invalidate the legislation. If it is satisfied that some limit on contributions is necessary, a court has no scalpel to probe, whether, say, a $2,000 ceiling might not serve as well as $1,000. Such distinctions in degree become significant only when they can be said to amount to differences in kind.

(c)

Apart from these First Amendment concerns, appellants argue that the contribution limitations work such an invidious discrimination between incumbents and challengers that the statutory provisions must be declared unconstitutional on their face. In considering this contention, it is important at the outset to note that the Act applies the same limitations on contributions to all candidates regardless of their present occupations, ideological views, or party affiliations. Absent record evidence of invidious discrimination against challengers as a class, a court should generally be hesitant to invalidate legislation which on its face imposes evenhanded restrictions.

There is no such evidence to support the claim that the contribution limitations in themselves discriminate against major-party challengers to incumbents. Challengers can and often do defeat incumbents in federal elections. Major-party challengers in federal elections are usually men and women who are well known and influential in their community or State. Often such challengers are themselves incumbents in important local, state, or federal offices. Statistics in the record indicate that major-party challengers as well as incumbents are capable of raising large sums for campaigning. Indeed, a small but nonetheless significant number of challengers have in recent elections outspent their incumbent rivals. And, to the extent that incumbents generally are more likely than challengers to attract very large contributions, the Act's $1,000 ceiling has the practical effect of benefiting challengers as a class. Contrary to the broad generalization drawn by the appellants, the practical impact of the contribution ceilings in any given election will clearly depend upon the amounts in excess of the ceilings that, for various reasons, the candidates in that election would otherwise have received and the utility of these additional amounts to the candidates. To be sure, the limitations may have a significant effect on particular challengers or incumbents, but the record provides no basis for predicting that such adventitious factors will invariably and invidiously benefit incumbents as a class. Since the danger of corruption and the appearance of corruption apply with equal force to challengers and to incumbents, Congress had ample justification for imposing the same fundraising constraints upon both.

In view of these considerations, we conclude that the impact of the Act's $1,000 contribution limitation on major-party challengers and on minor-party candidates does not render the provision unconstitutional on its face.

2. The $5,000 Limitation on Contributions by Political Committees

Section 608(b)(2) permits certain committees, designated as "political committees," to contribute up to $5,000 to any candidate with respect to any election for federal office. In order to qualify for the higher contribution ceiling, a group must have been registered with the [Federal Election] Commission as a political committee for not less than six months, have received contributions from more than 50 persons, and, except for state political party organizations, have contributed to five or more candidates for federal office. Appellants argue that these qualifications unconstitutionally discriminate against ad hoc organizations in favor of established interest groups and impermissibly burden free association. The argument is without merit. Rather than undermining freedom of association, the basic provision enhances the opportunity of bona fide groups to participate in the election process, and the registration, contribution, and candidate conditions serve the permissible purpose of preventing individuals from evading the applicable contribution limitations by labeling themselves committees.

3. Limitations on Volunteers' Incidental Expenses

[Omitted.]

4. The $25,000 Limitation on Total Contributions During any Calendar Year

[Omitted. The Supreme Court overruled this portion of *Buckley* in *McCutcheon v. FEC* (2014), presented below.]

C. Expenditure Limitations

The Act's expenditure ceilings impose direct and substantial restraints on the quantity of political speech. The most drastic of the limitations restricts individuals and groups . . . to an expenditure of $1,000 "relative to a clearly identified candidate during a calendar year." Other expenditure ceilings limit spending by candidates, their campaigns, and political parties in connection with election campaigns.

It is clear that a primary effect of these expenditure limitations is to restrict the quantity of campaign speech by individuals, groups, and candidates. The restrictions, while neutral as to the ideas expressed, limit political expression "at the core of our electoral process and of the First Amendment freedoms." *Williams v. Rhodes* (1968).

1. The $1,000 Limitation on Expenditures "Relative to a Clearly Identified Candidate"

Section 608(e)(1) provides that "(n)o person may make any expenditure . . . relative to a clearly identified candidate during a calendar year which, when added to all other expenditures made by such person during the year advocating the election or defeat of such candidate, exceeds $1,000." [45] The plain effect of § 608(e)(1) is to prohibit all individuals, who are neither candidates nor owners of institutional press facilities, and all groups, except political parties and campaign organizations, from voicing their views "relative to a clearly identified candidate" through means that entail aggregate expenditures of more than $1,000 during a calendar year. The provision, for example, would make it a federal criminal offense for a person or association to place a single one-quarter page advertisement "relative to a clearly identified candidate" in a major metropolitan newspaper.

Before examining the interests advanced in support of § 608(e)(1)'s expenditure ceiling, consideration must be given to appellants' contention that the provision is unconstitutionally vague. Close examination of the specificity of the statutory limitation is required where, as here, the legislation imposes criminal penalties in an area permeated by First Amendment interests. The test is whether the language of § 608(e)(1) affords the "(p)recision of regulation (that) must be the touchstone in an area so closely touching our most precious freedoms." *NAACP v. Button* [(1963)].

The key operative language of the provision limits "any expenditure . . . relative to a clearly identified candidate." Although "expenditure," "clearly identified," and "candidate" are defined in the Act, there is no definition clarifying what expenditures are "relative to" a candidate. The use of so indefinite a phrase as "relative to" a candidate fails to clearly mark the boundary between permissible and impermissible speech, unless other portions of § 608(e)(1) make sufficiently explicit the range of expenditures covered by the limitation. The section prohibits "any expenditure . . . relative to a clearly identified candidate during a calendar year which, when added to all other expenditures . . . *advocating the election or defeat of such candidate*, exceeds, $1,000." This context clearly permits, if indeed it does not require, the phrase "relative to" a candidate to be read to mean "advocating the election or defeat of" a candidate.

But while such a construction of § 608(e)(1) refocuses the vagueness question, the distinction between discussion of issues and candidates and advocacy of election or defeat of candidates may often dissolve in practical application. Candidates,

45. The statute provides some limited exceptions [including] "any news story, commentary, or editorial distributed through the facilities of any broadcasting station, newspaper, magazine, or other periodical publication, unless such facilities are owned or controlled by any political party, political committee, or candidate."

especially incumbents, are intimately tied to public issues involving legislative proposals and governmental actions. Not only do candidates campaign on the basis of their positions on various public issues, but campaigns themselves generate issues of public interest.

The constitutional deficiencies can be avoided only by reading § 608(e)(1) as limited to communications that include explicit words of advocacy of election or defeat of a candidate. This is the reading of the provision suggested by the non-governmental appellees in arguing that "(f)unds spent to propagate one's views on issues without expressly calling for a candidate's election or defeat are thus not covered." We agree that in order to preserve the provision against invalidation on vagueness grounds, § 608(e)(1) must be construed to apply only to expenditures for communications that in express terms advocate the election or defeat of a clearly identified candidate for federal office.[52]

We turn then to the basic First Amendment question whether § 608(e)(1), even as thus narrowly and explicitly construed, impermissibly burdens the constitutional right of free expression.

The discussion in Part I-A explains why the Act's expenditure limitations impose far greater restraints on the freedom of speech and association than do its contribution limitations. The markedly greater burden on basic freedoms caused by § 608(e)(1) thus cannot be sustained simply by invoking the interest in maximizing the effectiveness of the less intrusive contribution limitations. Rather, the constitutionality of § 608(e)(1) turns on whether the governmental interests advanced in its support satisfy the exacting scrutiny applicable to limitations on core First Amendment rights of political expression.

We find that the governmental interest in preventing corruption and the appearance of corruption is inadequate to justify § 608(e)(1)'s ceiling on independent expenditures. First, assuming, arguendo, that large independent expenditures pose the same dangers of actual or apparent quid pro quo arrangements as do large contributions, § 608(e)(1) does not provide an answer that sufficiently relates to the elimination of those dangers. Unlike the contribution limitations' total ban on the giving of large amounts of money to candidates, § 608(e)(1) prevents only some large expenditures. So long as persons and groups eschew expenditures that in express terms advocate the election or defeat of a clearly identified candidate, they are free to spend as much as they want to promote the candidate and his views. The exacting interpretation of the statutory language necessary to avoid unconstitutional vagueness thus undermines the limitation's effectiveness as a loophole-closing provision by facilitating circumvention by those seeking to exert improper influence upon a candidate or office-holder. It would naively underestimate the ingenuity and resourcefulness of persons and groups desiring to buy influence to believe that they would have much difficulty devising expenditures that skirted the restriction on express advocacy of election or defeat but nevertheless benefited the candidate's campaign. Yet no substantial societal interest would be served by a loophole-closing provision designed

52. This construction would restrict the application of § 608(e)(1) to communications containing express words of advocacy of election or defeat, such as "vote for," "elect," "support," "cast your ballot for," "Smith for Congress," "vote against," "defeat," "reject."

to check corruption that permitted unscrupulous persons and organizations to expend unlimited sums of money in order to obtain improper influence over candidates for elective office.

Second, quite apart from the shortcomings of § 608(e)(1) in preventing any abuses generated by large independent expenditures, the independent advocacy restricted by the provision does not presently appear to pose dangers of real or apparent corruption comparable to those identified with large campaign contributions. The parties defending § 608(e)(1) contend that it is necessary to prevent would-be contributors from avoiding the contribution limitations by the simple expedient of paying directly for media advertisements or for other portions of the candidate's campaign activities. They argue that expenditures controlled by or coordinated with the candidate and his campaign might well have virtually the same value to the candidate as a contribution and would pose similar dangers of abuse. Yet such controlled or coordinated expenditures are treated as contributions rather than expenditures under the Act. Section 608(b)'s contribution ceilings rather than § 608(e)(1)'s independent expenditure limitation prevent attempts to circumvent the Act through prearranged or coordinated expenditures amounting to disguised contributions. By contrast, § 608(e)(1) limits expenditures for express advocacy of candidates made totally independently of the candidate and his campaign. Unlike contributions, such independent expenditures may well provide little assistance to the candidate's campaign and indeed may prove counterproductive. The absence of prearrangement and coordination of an expenditure with the candidate or his agent not only undermines the value of the expenditure to the candidate, but also alleviates the danger that expenditures will be given as a quid pro quo for improper commitments from the candidate. Rather than preventing circumvention of the contribution limitations, §608(e)(1) severely restricts all independent advocacy despite its substantially diminished potential for abuse.

While the independent expenditure ceiling thus fails to serve any substantial governmental interest in stemming the reality or appearance of corruption in the electoral process, it heavily burdens core First Amendment expression. Advocacy of the election or defeat of candidates for federal office is no less entitled to protection under the First Amendment than the discussion of political policy generally or advocacy of the passage or defeat of legislation.

It is argued, however, that the ancillary governmental interest in equalizing the relative ability of individuals and groups to influence the outcome of elections serves to justify the limitation on express advocacy of the election or defeat of candidates imposed by § 608(e)(1)'s expenditure ceiling. But the concept that government may restrict the speech of some elements of our society in order to enhance the relative voice of others is wholly foreign to the First Amendment, which was designed "to secure 'the widest possible dissemination of information from diverse and antagonistic sources,'" and "'to assure unfettered interchange of ideas for the bringing about of political and social changes desired by the people.'" *New York Times Co. v. Sullivan.* The First Amendment's protection against governmental abridgment of free expression cannot properly be made to depend on a person's financial ability to engage in public discussion.

For the reasons stated, we conclude that § 608(e)(1)'s independent expenditure limitation is unconstitutional under the First Amendment.[56]

2. Limitation on Expenditures by Candidates from Personal or Family Resources

The Act also sets limits on expenditures by a candidate "from his personal funds, or the personal funds of his immediate family, in connection with his campaigns during any calendar year." These ceilings vary from $50,000 for Presidential or Vice Presidential candidates to $35,000 for senatorial candidates, and $25,000 for most candidates for the House of Representatives.

[For essentially the same reasons that the independent expenditure limitation is unconstitutional, we] hold that § 608(a)'s restriction on a candidate's personal expenditures is unconstitutional.

3. Limitations on Campaign Expenditures

Section 608(c) places limitations on overall campaign expenditures by candidates seeking nomination for election and election to federal office.

No governmental interest that has been suggested is sufficient to justify the restriction on the quantity of political expression imposed by § 608(c)'s campaign expenditure limitations. The major evil associated with rapidly increasing campaign expenditures is the danger of candidate dependence on large contributions. The interest in alleviating the corrupting influence of large contributions is served by the Act's contribution limitations and disclosure provisions rather than by § 608(c)'s campaign expenditure ceilings.

The campaign expenditure ceilings appear to be designed primarily to serve the governmental interests in reducing the allegedly skyrocketing costs of political campaigns. [T]he mere growth in the cost of federal election campaigns in and of itself provides no basis for governmental restrictions on the quantity of campaign spending and the resulting limitation on the scope of federal campaigns.

For these reasons we hold that § 608(c) is constitutionally invalid.

In sum, the provisions of the Act that impose a $1,000 limitation on contributions to a single candidate, a $5,000 limitation on contributions by a political committee to a single candidate, and a $25,000 limitation on total contributions by an individual during any calendar year, are constitutionally valid. These limitations, along with the disclosure provisions, constitute the Act's primary weapons against the reality or appearance of improper influence stemming from the dependence of candidates on large campaign contributions. The contribution ceilings thus serve the basic governmental interest in safeguarding the integrity of the electoral process without directly impinging upon the rights of individual citizens

56. The Act exempts most elements of the institutional press, limiting only expenditures by institutional press facilities that are owned or controlled by candidates and political parties. But, whatever differences there may be between the constitutional guarantees of a free press and of free speech, it is difficult to conceive of any principled basis upon which to distinguish § 608(e)(1)'s limitations upon the public at large and similar limitations imposed upon the press specifically. [Footnote relocated.—Eds.]

and candidates to engage in political debate and discussion. By contrast, the First Amendment requires the invalidation of the Act's independent expenditure ceiling, its limitation on a candidate's expenditures from his own personal funds, and its ceilings on overall campaign expenditures. These provisions place substantial and direct restrictions on the ability of candidates, citizens, and associations to engage in protected political expression, restrictions that the First Amendment cannot tolerate.

Mr. Chief Justice BURGER, concurring in part and dissenting in part.

The contribution limitations infringe on First Amendment liberties and suffer from the same infirmities that the Court correctly sees in the expenditure ceilings.

More broadly, the Court's result does violence to the intent of Congress in this comprehensive scheme of campaign finance. By dissecting the Act bit by bit, and casting off vital parts, the Court fails to recognize that the whole of this Act is greater than the sum of its parts. Congress intended to regulate all aspects of federal campaign finances, but what remains after today's holding leaves no more than a shadow of what Congress contemplated. I question whether the residue leaves a workable program.

CONTRIBUTION AND EXPENDITURE LIMITS

I agree fully with that part of the Court's opinion that holds unconstitutional the limitations the Act puts on campaign expenditures which "place substantial and direct restrictions on the ability of candidates, citizens, and associations to engage in protected political expression, restrictions that the First Amendment cannot tolerate." Yet when it approves similarly stringent limitations on contributions, the Court ignores the reasons it finds so persuasive in the context of expenditures. For me contributions and expenditures are two sides of the same First Amendment coin.

[THE STATUTE AS A WHOLE]

I cannot join in the attempt to determine which parts of the Act can survive review here. The statute as it now stands is unworkable and inequitable.

Given the unfortunate record of past attempts to draw distinctions of this kind, it is not too much to predict that the Court's holding will invite avoidance, if not evasion of the intent of the Act, with "independent" committees undertaking "unauthorized" activities in order to escape the limits on contributions.

Mr. Justice WHITE, concurring in part and dissenting in part.

I am in agreement with the Court's judgment upholding the limitations on contributions. I dissent, however, from the Court's view that the expenditure limitations violate the First Amendment.

It would make little sense to me, and apparently made none to Congress, to limit the amounts an individual may give to a candidate or spend with his approval but fail to limit the amounts that could be spent on his behalf. Yet the Court permits the former while striking down the latter limitation. No more than $1,000 may be given to a candidate or spent at his request or with his approval or cooperation; but otherwise, apparently, a contributor is to be constitutionally protected in spending unlimited amounts of money in support of his chosen candidate or candidates.

I would take the word of those who know that limiting independent expenditures is essential to prevent transparent and widespread evasion of the contribution limits.

It is also important to restore and maintain public confidence in federal elections. It is critical to obviate or dispel the impression that federal elections are purely and simply a function of money, that federal offices are bought and sold or that political races are reserved for those who have the facility and the stomach for doing whatever it takes to bring together those interests, groups, and individuals that can raise or contribute large fortunes in order to prevail at the polls.

As with the campaign expenditure limits, Congress was entitled to determine that personal wealth ought to play a less important role in political campaigns than it has in the past. Nothing in the First Amendment stands in the way of that determination.

For these reasons I respectfully dissent from the Court's [decision striking down the independent expenditure limitation, the total campaign expenditure limitation, and the limitation on the amount of money that a candidate or his family may spend on his campaign.]

Mr. Justice MARSHALL, concurring in part and dissenting in part.

I join in all of the Court's opinion except Part I-C-2, which deals with 18 U.S.C. § 608(a) (1970 ed., Supp. IV). That section limits the amount a candidate may spend from his personal funds, or family funds under his control, in connection with his campaigns during any calendar year. The Court invalidates § 608(a) as violative of the candidate's First Amendment rights.

To be sure, § 608(a) affects the candidate's exercise of his First Amendment rights. But unlike the other expenditure limitations contained in the Act and invalidated by the Court, the limitations on expenditures by candidates from personal resources contained in § 608(a) need never prevent the speaker from spending another dollar to communicate his ideas. Section 608(a) imposes no overall limit on the amount a candidate can spend; it simply limits the "contribution" a candidate may make to his own campaign. The candidate remains free to raise an unlimited amount in contributions from others. So long as the candidate does not contribute to his campaign more than the amount specified in § 608(a), and so long as he does not accept contributions from others in excess of the limitations imposed by § 608(b), he is free to spend without limit on behalf of his campaign.

The Court views "(t)he ancillary interest in equalizing the relative financial resources of candidates" as the relevant rationale for § 608(a), and deems that interest insufficient to justify § 608(a). In my view the interest is more precisely the interest in promoting the reality and appearance of equal access to the political arena. [This provision] emerges not simply as a device to reduce the natural advantage of the wealthy candidate, but as a provision providing some symmetry to a regulatory scheme that otherwise enhances the natural advantage of the wealthy. I therefore respectfully dissent from the Court's invalidation of § 608(a).

Mr. Justice REHNQUIST, concurring in part and dissenting in part. [Omitted; Justice Rehnquist dissented on an aspect of the majority's opinion dealing with minor political parties and independent candidates.]

Mr. Justice BLACKMUN, concurring in part and dissenting in part. [Omitted; same position as C.J. Burger.]

NOTES ON *BUCKLEY*

1. Count the votes: Seven Justices (all but Burger and Blackmun) voted to uphold the contribution limitations; eight Justices (all but White) voted to strike down the independent expenditure limitations.

2. Is spending money on elections a form of "speech" that the First Amendment must protect? Though some may argue that money is not inherently expressive by itself, the "money equals speech" proposition from *Buckley* is generally well-settled. But need it be so? Are there any arguments against construing campaign spending as speech? Money facilitates speech, but is it speech itself? *Buckley* might be dependent on the proposition that spending money is itself expressive activity that the First Amendment protects, but it also could rely on the notion that money is critically instrumental to the production and dissemination of expression—including books, films, or any other medium of expression. Which, if either, is a better justification for the decision? Would the First Amendment tolerate limits on spending money for speech unrelated to campaigns—for example, money to produce Hollywood movies or TV shows (even ones with political themes, such as "The West Wing" or "Veep?")? Or would the First Amendment tolerate limits on the amount of money a newspaper could spend to report on, and editorialize about, politics? If not, then why might the First Amendment permit spending limits with respect to campaign-specific speech? Is the answer that it is simply unfair to allow a wealthy candidate (or those with wealthy backers) to drown out non-wealthy candidates? After all, there is a finite pie when it comes to campaign advertising space, though perhaps internet advertising mitigates this concern. Either way, pay attention to the "equalization" rationale in the development of the case law that follows.

3. Is there a clear line between contributions and independent expenditures? One potential problem arises if a candidate controls someone else's expenditures that purport to be independent but in fact are not. Suppose an individual says to a candidate, "Rather than donate money directly to your campaign for you to spend, tell me how you'd like me to use my money to support your candidacy." This would be an obvious end-run around the contribution limit. Consequently, FECA deems such "coordinated expenditures" to be "contributions" and thus to fall within the contribution limitations. In other words, "independent" expenditures must truly be independent of the campaign, making them the speaker's own speech. But what if, without direct coordination, candidates are able to signal to their outside supporters what kinds of ads they would like to be run through independent expenditures? In the current era of the Internet and the 24-hour news cycle, this kind of signaling may be much easier than in the past. Campaigns will put up stock footage of their candidate for anyone to use and even publish a list of key talking points. In the past few presidential elections, all of the spending by the

so-called "super PACs" was supposed to be independent and uncoordinated with a candidate's own campaign (more on "super PACs" later), but is the "independence" of this spending entirely a fiction? If so, has the fundamental conceptual distinction in *Buckley* between contributions and independent expenditures completely broken down?

4. One recurring theme of those who oppose campaign finance regulations is that they are unnecessary because criminal sanctions and disclosure laws can handle corruption or the appearance of corruption. As the majority in *Buckley* notes, however, Congress determined that more direct regulations are required. Keep this debate in mind as you move through the material that follows.

5. Note Chief Justice Burger's prediction that political operatives will still be able to spend large amounts of money on political campaigns regardless of FECA's contribution limitations, particularly by channeling money through independent expenditures. Put differently, if one goal of contribution limitations is to reduce the amount of money in politics, that plainly has not occurred, as campaigns have become more and more expensive. Is this a problem of our electoral system or a virtue?

2. *"Soft Money" and Political Party Spending*

After almost three decades under the FECA system, Congress realized that candidates and political parties had found ways around FECA's contribution limitations. Part of the culprit was the Federal Election Commission's "allocation" regime, which construed political parties' mixed-purpose activities—generic party activities such as get-out-the-vote drives that benefit both the party and federal candidates—as not constituting "contributions" under FECA. Parties were allowed to raise and spend unlimited amounts of this so-called "soft money," which is money not expressly directed solely at the election or defeat of a federal candidate. That is, "soft money" was considered "nonfederal" because it was not tied explicitly to the election of a federal candidate and therefore was raised outside of the limits and prohibitions of federal campaign finance law. Of course, however, many party-building "nonfederal" purposes have a significant effect on federal candidates. For example, voter turnout efforts for the political party in general obviously help that party's federal candidates, but money spent on those activities did not "count" as contributions under federal law. In addition, there was a tremendous rise in unlimited "issue advertising" that omitted the use of "magic words" (expressly advocating the election or defeat of a candidate) so as not to fall within FECA's regulation. Congress sought to close both of these loopholes in the Bipartisan Campaign Reform Act of 2002 (BCRA), sometimes referred to as McCain-Feingold after its two main sponsors, Republican Senator John McCain of Arizona and Democratic Senator Russ Feingold of Wisconsin. The most significant portions of BCRA banned the national political parties from raising or spending "soft money" and limited corporate and union independent expenditures.

The next case presents the initial constitutional challenge to BCRA and its consideration of the Act's various limitations on soft money. Later, in *Citizens United*, we will analyze BCRA's prohibition on "electioneering communication" by corporations and unions.

The Court ruled, 5-4, to uphold the soft money limitations, with the more "liberal" Justices (along with Justice O'Connor) in the majority. By contrast, Justice Kennedy in dissent would have struck down the soft money ban as an unconstitutional expenditure limitation. One of the main disputes between the majority and the dissent in this case is whether a soft money ban is more like a contribution limitation or an expenditure limitation. As we know from *Buckley*, a contribution limitation receives a lower level of scrutiny than an independent expenditure limitation, which is generally unconstitutional.

As you are reading this case, pay attention to the discussion of the rise of "soft money" in elections. Where does this money come from? Was the goal of BCRA's soft money regulations simply to limit the influence of political parties in how they can spend money? Indeed, the most significant part of BCRA Title I is § 323(a), which prohibits National Party committees and their agents from soliciting, receiving, directing, or spending any soft money. What is the governmental interest in this provision? Is it trying to root out the same type of corruption that the government sought to eliminate in *Buckley*? Or has the conception of corruption shifted? In particular, think about the Court's construction of Congress's main interest in passing BCRA: to eliminate corruption and the appearance of corruption in campaigns. Should "corruption" have a broad or narrow definition? How do the majority and dissenting opinions differ in their definitions of corruption? Congress also had a further goal of anticircumvention: the desire to create rules to ensure that candidates and political parties cannot circumvent valid contribution limitations, that is, to close loopholes in the law. Is that ever possible, or will politicians always find ways around the rules?

Finally, consider what Congress was really trying to do here: (1) prevent the corruption of candidates (or its appearance) through soft money gifts to parties; and (2) limit campaign spending by corporations, unions, and wealthy individuals on both sides of the aisle, again in the name of preventing corruption or the appearance of corruption. The majority states that limiting donations from wealthy individuals and groups will increase the number of donors a candidate or party must solicit, thus opening up the campaign to many more people. Moreover, Congress determined—based in part on evidence in the years after *Buckley*—that large donations to incumbents create an unacceptably high risk of corruption or at least the appearance of corruption. Is the dissent's response to this evidence to deny it factually, or instead to argue that officeholders inevitably will become beholden to financial interests and that this influence-peddling is a necessary offspring of First Amendment freedom?

McConnell v. FEC

540 U.S. 93 (2003)†

Justice STEVENS and Justice O'CONNOR delivered the opinion of the Court with respect to BCRA Titles I and II.*

† [Disclosure: One of the casebook authors served as a consultant to the attorneys representing Senators McCain and Feingold and the other legislative sponsors of the statute, who were Intervenor-Defendants in the case.—EDS.]

* Justice SOUTER, Justice GINSBURG, and Justice BREYER join this opinion in its entirety.

The Bipartisan Campaign Reform Act of 2002 (BCRA), contains a series of amendments to the Federal Election Campaign Act of 1971 (FECA or Act), and other portions of the United States Code, that are challenged in these cases. In this opinion we discuss Titles I and II of BCRA. [What follows here is the Court's discussion of the background of BCRA and its legal analysis of Title I, the "soft money" part of the statute. We have omitted the portion of the Court's opinion addressing Title II and the "electioneering communications" part of the statute, as the Court overruled that portion of *McConnell* in 2010 in *Citizens United v. FEC.*]

I

BCRA is the most recent federal enactment designed to purge national politics of what was conceived to be the pernicious influence of "big money" campaign contributions.

Three important developments in the years after our decision in *Buckley* persuaded Congress that further legislation was necessary to regulate the role that corporations, unions, and wealthy contributors play in the electoral process. As a preface to our discussion of the specific provisions of BCRA, we comment briefly on the increased importance of "soft money," the proliferation of "issue ads," and the disturbing findings of a Senate investigation into campaign practices related to the 1996 federal elections.

Soft Money

Under FECA, "contributions" must be made with funds that are subject to the Act's disclosure requirements and source and amount limitations. Such funds are known as "federal" or "hard" money. FECA defines the term "contribution," however, to include only the gift or advance of anything of value "made by any person for the purpose of influencing any election for *Federal* office." 2 U.S.C. § 431(8)(A)(i) (emphasis added). Donations made solely for the purpose of influencing state or local elections are therefore unaffected by FECA's requirements and prohibitions. As a result, prior to the enactment of BCRA, federal law permitted corporations and unions, as well as individuals who had already made the maximum permissible contributions to federal candidates, to contribute "nonfederal money"—also known as "soft money"—to political parties for activities intended to influence state or local elections.

Shortly after *Buckley* was decided, questions arose concerning the treatment of contributions intended to influence both federal and state elections. Although a literal reading of FECA's definition of "contribution" would have required such activities to be funded with hard money, the FEC ruled that political parties could fund mixed-purpose activities—including get-out-the-vote drives and generic party advertising—in part with soft money. In 1995 the FEC concluded that the parties could also use soft money to defray the costs of "legislative advocacy media advertisements," even if the ads mentioned the name of a federal candidate, so long as they did not expressly advocate the candidate's election or defeat.

As the permissible uses of soft money expanded, the amount of soft money raised and spent by the national political parties increased exponentially. Of the two major parties' total spending, soft money accounted for 5% ($21.6 million) in 1984, 11% ($45 million) in 1988, 16% ($80 million) in 1992, 30% ($272 million) in 1996, and 42% ($498 million) in 2000. The national parties transferred large amounts of their soft money to the state parties, which were allowed to use a larger percentage of soft money to finance mixed-purpose activities under FEC rules. In the year 2000, for example, the national parties diverted $280 million—more than half of their soft money—to state parties.

Many contributions of soft money were dramatically larger than the contributions of hard money permitted by FECA. For example, in 1996 the top five corporate soft-money donors gave, in total, more than $9 million in nonfederal funds to the two national party committees. In the most recent election cycle the political parties raised almost $300 million—60% of their total soft-money fundraising—from just 800 donors, each of which contributed a minimum of $120,000. Moreover, the largest corporate donors often made substantial contributions to both parties. Such practices corroborate evidence indicating that many corporate contributions were motivated by a desire for access to candidates and a fear of being placed at a disadvantage in the legislative process relative to other contributors, rather than by ideological support for the candidates and parties.

The solicitation, transfer, and use of soft money thus enabled parties and candidates to circumvent FECA's limitations on the source and amount of contributions in connection with federal elections.

Issue Advertising

In *Buckley* we construed FECA's disclosure and reporting requirements, as well as its expenditure limitations, "to reach only funds used for communications that expressly advocate the election or defeat of a clearly identified candidate." As a result of that strict reading of the statute, the use or omission of "magic words" such as "Elect John Smith" or "Vote Against Jane Doe" marked a bright statutory line separating "express advocacy" from "issue advocacy." Express advocacy was subject to FECA's limitations and could be financed only using hard money. The political parties, in other words, could not use soft money to sponsor ads that used any magic words, and corporations and unions could not fund such ads out of their general treasuries. So-called issue ads, on the other hand, not only could be financed with soft money, but could be aired without disclosing the identity of, or any other information about, their sponsors.

While the distinction between "issue" and express advocacy seemed neat in theory, the two categories of advertisements proved functionally identical in important respects. Both were used to advocate the election or defeat of clearly identified federal candidates, even though the so-called issue ads eschewed the use of magic words. Little difference existed, for example, between an ad that urged viewers to "vote against Jane Doe" and one that condemned Jane Doe's record on a particular issue before exhorting viewers to "call Jane Doe and tell her what you think." Indeed, campaign professionals testified that the most effective campaign ads, like the most effective commercials for products such as Coca-Cola, should, and did, avoid the use of the magic words.

Because FECA's disclosure requirements did not apply to so-called issue ads, sponsors of such ads often used misleading names to conceal their identity. "Citizens for Better Medicare," for instance, was not a grassroots organization of citizens, as its name might suggest, but was instead a platform for an association of drug manufacturers. And "Republicans for Clean Air," which ran ads in the 2000

Republican Presidential primary, was actually an organization consisting of just two individuals—brothers who together spent $25 million on ads supporting their favored candidate.

While the public may not have been fully informed about the sponsorship of so-called issue ads, the record indicates that candidates and officeholders often were. A former Senator confirmed that candidates and officials knew who their friends were and "sometimes suggest[ed] that corporations or individuals make donations to interest groups that run 'issue ads.'" As with soft-money contributions, political parties and candidates used the availability of so-called issue ads to circumvent FECA's limitations, asking donors who contributed their permitted quota of hard money to give money to nonprofit corporations to spend on "issue" advocacy.

Senate Committee Investigation

In 1998 the Senate Committee on Governmental Affairs issued a six-volume report summarizing the results of an extensive investigation into the campaign practices in the 1996 federal elections. The report gave particular attention to the effect of soft money on the American political system, including elected officials' practice of granting special access in return for political contributions.

The committee's principal findings relating to Democratic Party fundraising were set forth in the majority's report, while the minority report primarily described Republican practices. The two reports reached consensus, however, on certain central propositions. They agreed that the "soft money loophole" had led to a "meltdown" of the campaign finance system that had been intended "to keep corporate, union and large individual contributions from influencing the electoral process." One Senator stated that "the hearings provided overwhelming evidence that the twin loopholes of soft money and bogus issue advertising have virtually destroyed our campaign finance laws, leaving us with little more than a pile of legal rubble."

The report was critical of both parties' methods of raising soft money, as well as their use of those funds. It concluded that both parties promised and provided special access to candidates and senior Government officials in exchange for large soft-money contributions. The committee majority described the White House coffees that rewarded major donors with access to President Clinton, and the courtesies extended to an international businessman named Roger Tamraz, who candidly acknowledged that his donations of about $300,000 to the DNC and to state parties were motivated by his interest in gaining the Federal Government's support for an oil-line project in the Caucasus. The minority described the promotional materials used by the RNC's two principal donor programs, "Team 100" and the "Republican Eagles," which promised "special access to high-ranking Republican elected officials, including governors, senators, and representatives." One fundraising letter recited that the chairman of the RNC had personally escorted a donor on appointments that "turned out to be very significant in legislation affecting public utility holding companies" and made the donor "a hero in his industry."

In 1996 both parties began to use large amounts of soft money to pay for issue advertising designed to influence federal elections. The committee found such ads highly problematic for two reasons. Since they accomplished the same purposes as express advocacy (which could lawfully be funded only with hard money), the ads enabled unions, corporations, and wealthy contributors to circumvent protections that FECA was intended to provide. Moreover, though ostensibly independent of the candidates, the ads were often actually coordinated with, and controlled by, the campaigns. The ads thus provided a means for evading FECA's candidate contribution limits.

The report also emphasized the role of state and local parties. While the FEC's allocation regime permitted national parties to use soft money to pay for up to 40% of the costs of both generic voter activities and issue advertising, they allowed state and local parties to use larger percentages of soft money for those purposes. For that reason, national parties often made substantial transfers of soft money to "state and local political parties for 'generic voter activities' that in fact ultimately benefit[ed] federal candidates because the funds for all practical purposes remain[ed] under the control of the national committees." The report concluded that "[t]he use of such soft money thus allow[ed] more corporate, union treasury, and large contributions from wealthy individuals into the system."

The report discussed potential reforms, including a ban on soft money at the national and state party levels and restrictions on sham issue advocacy by nonparty groups. The majority expressed the view that a ban on the raising of soft money by national party committees would effectively address the use of union and corporate general treasury funds in the federal political process only if it required that candidate-specific ads be funded with hard money. The minority similarly recommended the elimination of soft-money contributions to political parties from individuals, corporations, and unions, as well as "reforms addressing candidate advertisements masquerading as issue ads."

II

In BCRA, Congress enacted many of the committee's proposed reforms. BCRA's central provisions are designed to address Congress' concerns about the increasing use of soft money and issue advertising to influence federal elections. Title I regulates the use of soft money by political parties, officeholders, and candidates.

III

Title I is Congress' effort to plug the soft-money loophole. The cornerstone of Title I is new FECA § 323(a), which prohibits national party committees and their agents from soliciting, receiving, directing, or spending any soft money. In short, § 323(a) takes national parties out of the soft-money business.

Plaintiffs mount a facial First Amendment challenge to new FECA § 323, as well as challenges based on the Elections Clause, U.S. Const., Art. I, § 4, principles of federalism, and the equal protection component of the Due Process Clause. We address these challenges in turn.

A

In *Buckley* and subsequent cases, we have subjected restrictions on campaign expenditures to closer scrutiny than limits on campaign contributions. In these cases we have recognized that contribution limits, unlike limits on expenditures, "entai[l] only a marginal restriction upon the contributor's ability to engage in free communication."

Because the communicative value of large contributions inheres mainly in their ability to facilitate the speech of their recipients, we have said that contribution limits impose serious burdens on free speech only if they are so low as to "preven[t] candidates and political committees from amassing the resources necessary for effective advocacy."

Like the contribution limits we upheld in *Buckley*, § 323's restrictions have only a marginal impact on the ability of contributors, candidates, officeholders, and parties to engage in effective political speech. Complex as its provisions may be, § 323, in the main, does little more than regulate the ability of wealthy individuals, corporations, and unions to contribute large sums of money to influence federal elections, federal candidates, and federal officeholders.

Plaintiffs contend that we must apply strict scrutiny to § 323 because many of its provisions restrict not only contributions but also the spending and solicitation of funds raised outside of FECA's contribution limits. But for purposes of determining the level of scrutiny, it is irrelevant that Congress chose in § 323 to regulate contributions on the demand rather than the supply side. The relevant inquiry is whether the mechanism adopted to implement the contribution limit, or to prevent circumvention of that limit, burdens speech in a way that a direct restriction on the contribution itself would not. That is not the case here.

For example, while § 323(a) prohibits national parties from receiving or spending nonfederal money, and § 323(b) prohibits state party committees from spending nonfederal money on federal election activities, neither provision in any way limits the total amount of money parties can spend. Rather, they simply limit the source and individual amount of donations. That they do so by prohibiting the spending of soft money does not render them expenditure limitations.

Section 323 thus shows "due regard for the reality that solicitation is characteristically intertwined with informative and perhaps persuasive speech seeking support for particular causes or for particular views." *Schaumburg v. Citizens for a Better Environment* (1980). The fact that party committees and federal candidates and officeholders must now ask only for limited dollar amounts or request that a corporation or union contribute money through its PAC in no way alters or impairs the political message "intertwined" with the solicitation. And rather than chill such solicitations, the restriction here tends to increase the dissemination of information by forcing parties, candidates, and officeholders to solicit from a wider array of potential donors. As with direct limits on contributions, therefore, § 323's spending and solicitation restrictions have only a marginal impact on political speech.

Finally, plaintiffs contend that the type of associational burdens that § 323 imposes are fundamentally different from the burdens that accompanied *Buckley*'s contribution limits, and merit the type of strict scrutiny we have applied to attempts to regulate the internal processes of political parties. *E.g., California Democratic Party v. Jones* (2000). In making this argument, plaintiffs greatly exaggerate the effect of § 323, contending that it precludes *any* collaboration among national, state, and local committees of the same party in fundraising and electioneering activities. We do not read the provisions in that way. Section 323 merely subjects a greater percentage of contributions to parties and candidates to FECA's source and amount limitations. *Buckley* has already acknowledged that such limitations "leave the contributor free to become a member of any political association and to assist personally in the association's efforts on behalf of candidates." The modest impact that § 323 has on the ability of committees within a party to associate with each other does not independently occasion strict scrutiny. None of this is to suggest that the alleged associational burdens imposed on parties by § 323 have no place in the First Amendment analysis; it is only that we account for them in the application, rather than the choice, of the appropriate level of scrutiny.

With these principles in mind, we apply the less rigorous scrutiny applicable to contribution limits to evaluate the constitutionality of new FECA § 323. Because the five challenged provisions of § 323 implicate different First Amendment concerns, we discuss them separately. We are mindful, however, that Congress enacted § 323 as an integrated whole to vindicate the Government's important interest in preventing corruption and the appearance of corruption.

New FECA § 323(a)'s Restrictions on National Party Committees

The core of Title I is new FECA § 323(a), which provides that "national committee[s] of a political party . . . may not solicit, receive, or direct to another person a contribution, donation, or transfer of funds or any other thing of value, or spend any funds, that are not subject to the limitations, prohibitions, and reporting requirements of this Act." 2 U.S.C. § 441i(a)(1) (Supp. 2003). The prohibition extends to "any officer or agent acting on behalf of such a national committee, and any entity that is directly or indirectly established, financed, maintained, or controlled by such a national committee." § 441i(a)(2).

The main goal of § 323(a) is modest. In large part, it simply effects a return to the scheme that was approved in *Buckley* and that was subverted by the creation of the FEC's allocation regime, which permitted the political parties to fund federal electioneering efforts with a combination of hard and soft money. Under that allocation regime, national parties were able to use vast amounts of soft money in their efforts to elect federal candidates. Consequently, as long as they directed the money to the political parties, donors could contribute large amounts of soft money for use in activities designed to influence federal elections. New § 323(a) is designed to put a stop to that practice.

1. Governmental Interests Underlying New FECA § 323(a)

The Government defends § 323(a)'s ban on national parties' involvement with soft money as necessary to prevent the actual and apparent corruption of federal candidates and officeholders. Our cases have made clear that the prevention of corruption or its appearance constitutes a sufficiently important interest to justify political contribution limits. We have not limited that interest to the elimination of cash-for-votes exchanges. In *Buckley*, we expressly rejected the argument that antibribery laws provided a less restrictive alternative to FECA's contribution limits, noting that such laws "deal[t] with only the most blatant and specific attempts of those with money to influence governmental action." Thus, "[i]n speaking of 'improper influence' and 'opportunities for abuse' in addition to '*quid pro quo* arrangements,' we [have] recognized a concern not confined to bribery of public officials, but extending to the broader threat from politicians too compliant with the wishes of large contributors." [*Nixon v. Shrink Missouri Government PAC* (2000)]; *see also* [*FEC v. Colorado Republican Campaign Committee* (2001) (*Colorado II*)] (acknowledging that corruption extends beyond explicit cash-for-votes agreements to "undue influence on an officeholder's judgment").

Of "almost equal" importance has been the Government's interest in combating the appearance or perception of corruption engendered by large campaign contributions. Take away Congress' authority to regulate the appearance of undue influence and "the cynical assumption that large donors call the tune could jeopardize the willingness of voters to take part in democratic governance." *Shrink Missouri.* And because the First Amendment does not require Congress to ignore the fact that candidates, donors, and parties test the limits of the current law, these interests have been sufficient to justify not only contribution limits themselves, but laws preventing the circumvention of such limits.

The idea that large contributions to a national party can corrupt or, at the very least, create the appearance of corruption of federal candidates and officeholders is neither novel nor implausible. For nearly 30 years, FECA has placed strict dollar limits and source restrictions on contributions that individuals and other entities can give to national, state, and local party committees for the purpose of influencing a federal election. The premise behind these restrictions has been, and continues to be, that contributions to a federal candidate's party in aid of that candidate's campaign threaten to create—no less than would a direct contribution to the candidate—a sense of obligation. This is particularly true of contributions to national parties, with which federal candidates and officeholders enjoy a special relationship and unity of interest. This close affiliation has placed national parties in a unique position, "whether they like it or not," to serve as "agents for spending on behalf of those who seek to produce obligated officeholders." *Colorado II.*

The question for present purposes is whether large *soft-money* contributions to national party committees have a corrupting influence or give rise to the appearance of corruption. Both common sense and the ample record in these cases confirm Congress' belief that they do. [T]he FEC's allocation regime has invited widespread circumvention of FECA's limits on contributions to parties for the purpose of influencing federal elections. Under this system, corporate, union, and wealthy individual donors have been free to contribute substantial sums of soft money to the national parties, which the parties can spend for the specific purpose of influencing a particular candidate's federal election. It is not only plausible, but likely, that candidates would feel grateful for such donations and that donors would seek to exploit that gratitude.

The evidence in the record shows that candidates and donors alike have in fact exploited the soft-money loophole, the former to increase their prospects of election and the latter to create debt on the part of officeholders, with the national parties serving as willing intermediaries. Thus, despite FECA's hard-money limits on direct contributions to candidates, federal officeholders have commonly asked donors to make soft-money donations to national and state committees solely in order to assist federal campaigns, including the officeholder's own. Parties kept tallies of the amounts of soft money raised by each officeholder, and "the amount of money a Member of Congress raise[d] for the national political party committees often affect[ed] the amount the committees g[a]ve to assist the Member's campaign." Donors often asked that their contributions be credited to particular candidates, and the parties obliged, irrespective of whether the funds were hard or soft. National party committees often teamed with individual candidates' campaign committees to create joint fundraising committees, which enabled the candidates to take advantage of the party's higher contribution limits while still allowing donors to give to their preferred candidate. Even when not participating directly in the fundraising, federal officeholders were well aware of the identities of the donors: National party committees would distribute lists of potential or actual donors, or donors themselves would report their generosity to officeholders.

For their part, lobbyists, CEOs, and wealthy individuals alike all have candidly admitted donating substantial sums of soft money to national committees not on ideological grounds, but for the express purpose of securing influence over federal officials.

Particularly telling is the fact that, in 1996 and 2000, more than half of the top 50 soft-money donors gave substantial sums to *both* major national parties, leaving room for no other conclusion but that these donors were seeking influence, or avoiding retaliation, rather than promoting any particular ideology.

The evidence from the federal officeholders' perspective is similar. For example, one former Senator described the influence purchased by nonfederal donations as follows:

> "Too often, Members' first thought is not what is right or what they believe, but how it will affect fundraising. Who, after all, can seriously contend that a $100,000 donation does not alter the way one thinks about—and quite possibly votes on—an issue? . . . When you don't pay the piper that finances your campaigns, you will never get any more money from that piper. Since money is the mother's milk of politics, you never want to be in that situation." [Lower court opinion] (quoting declaration of former Sen. Alan Simpson).

Plaintiffs argue that without concrete evidence of an instance in which a federal officeholder has actually switched a vote (or, presumably, evidence of a specific instance where the public believes a vote was switched), Congress has not shown that there exists real or apparent corruption. But the record is to the contrary. The evidence connects soft money to manipulations of the legislative calendar, leading to Congress' failure to enact, among other things, generic drug legislation, tort reform, and tobacco legislation. To claim that such actions do not change legislative outcomes surely misunderstands the legislative process.*

More importantly, plaintiffs conceive of corruption too narrowly. Our cases have firmly established that Congress' legitimate interest extends beyond preventing simple cash-for-votes corruption to curbing "undue influence on an officeholder's judgment, and the appearance of such influence." *Colorado II.* Many of the "deeply disturbing examples" of corruption cited by this Court in *Buckley* to justify

* [The Court based its factual determination in this paragraph, at least in part, on evidence contained in a sealed, undisclosed record of specific instances in which soft-money contributions to political parties affected the legislative behavior of Members of Congress. Even though the Court could not discuss this evidence in detail, it seems plausible that it was influential in persuading Justice O'Connor, who had been skeptical of the government's position at oral argument—but who herself had been a member of Arizona's state legislature before becoming a judge and thus appreciated the risk of improper financial influence on legislative behavior—to provide the fifth vote to uphold the constitutionality of BCRA's soft-money provisions.—EDS.]

FECA's contribution limits were not episodes of vote buying, but evidence that various corporate interests had given substantial donations to gain access to high-level government officials. Even if that access did not secure actual influence, it certainly gave the "appearance of such influence."

The record in the present case is replete with similar examples of national party committees peddling access to federal candidates and officeholders in exchange for large soft-money donations.

Despite this evidence and the close ties that candidates and officeholders have with their parties, Justice Kennedy would limit Congress' regulatory interest *only* to the prevention of the actual or apparent *quid pro quo* corruption "inherent in" contributions made directly to, contributions made at the express behest of, and expenditures made in coordination with, a federal officeholder or candidate. Regulation of any other donation or expenditure—regardless of its size, the recipient's relationship to the candidate or officeholder, its potential impact on a candidate's election, its value to the candidate, or its unabashed and explicit intent to purchase influence—would, according to Justice Kennedy, simply be out of bounds. This crabbed view of corruption, and particularly of the appearance of corruption, ignores precedent, common sense, and the realities of political fundraising exposed by the record in this litigation.

In sum, there is substantial evidence to support Congress' determination that large soft-money contributions to national political parties give rise to corruption and the appearance of corruption.

2. *New FECA § 323(a)'s Restriction on Spending and Receiving Soft Money*

Plaintiffs and Chief Justice [Rehnquist] contend that § 323(a) is impermissibly overbroad because it subjects *all* funds raised and spent by national parties to FECA's hard-money source and amount limits, including, for example, funds spent on purely state and local elections in which no federal office is at stake. Such activities, Chief Justice [Rehnquist] asserts, pose "little or no potential to corrupt . . . federal candidates and officeholders." This observation is beside the point. Section 323(a), like the remainder of § 323, regulates contributions, not activities. As the record demonstrates, it is the close relationship between federal officeholders and the national parties, as well as the means by which parties have traded on that relationship, that have made all large soft-money contributions to national parties suspect.

Given this close connection and alignment of interests, large soft-money contributions to national parties are likely to create actual or apparent indebtedness on the part of federal officeholders, regardless of how those funds are ultimately used.

This close affiliation has also placed national parties in a position to sell access to federal officeholders in exchange for soft-money contributions that the party can then use for its own purposes. Access to federal officeholders is the most valuable favor the national party committees are able to give in exchange for large donations. The fact that officeholders comply by donating their valuable time indicates either that officeholders place substantial value on the soft-money contribution themselves, without regard to their end use, or that national committees are able to exert considerable control over federal officeholders. Either way, large soft-money donations to national party committees are likely to buy donors preferential access to federal officeholders no matter the ends to which their contributions are eventually put. Congress had sufficient grounds to regulate the appearance of undue influence associated with this practice. The Government's strong interests in preventing corruption, and in particular the appearance of corruption, are thus sufficient to justify subjecting all donations to national parties to the source, amount, and disclosure limitations of FECA.

3. New FECA § 323(a)'s Restriction on Soliciting or Directing Soft Money

[The Court rejected the Plaintiffs' contention that § 323(a)'s prohibition on National Parties' soliciting or directing soft-money contributions was substantially overbroad. The Court explained that National Party committees could still solicit hard money, and that officers of National Parties could still solicit soft money in their individual capacities. "A national committee is likely to respond favorably to a donation made at its request regardless of whether the recipient is the committee itself or another entity."]

4. New FECA § 323(a)'s Application to Minor Parties

[The Court rejected the argument that § 323(a) is substantially overbroad because it impermissibly infringes the speech and associational rights of minor parties who are unlikely to pose a threat of corruption. The Court explained, "the relevance of the interest in avoiding actual or apparent corruption is not a function of the number of legislators a given party manages to elect. It applies as much to a minor party that manages to elect only one of its members to federal office as it does to a major party whose members make up a majority of Congress."]

5. New FECA § 323(a)'s Associational Burdens

[The Court rejected the Plaintiffs' argument that "§ 323(a) is unconstitutional because it impermissibly interferes with the ability of national committees to associate with state and local committees," reasoning that even under § 323(a) National and state party officers can still engage in "joint planning and electioneering activity."]

Accordingly, we reject the plaintiffs' First Amendment challenge to new FECA § 323(a).

New FECA § 323(b)'s Restrictions on State and Local Party Committees

In constructing a coherent scheme of campaign finance regulation, Congress recognized that, given the close ties between federal candidates and state party committees, BCRA's restrictions on national committee activity would rapidly become ineffective if state and local committees remained available as a conduit for soft-money donations. Section 323(b) is designed to foreclose wholesale evasion of § 323(a)'s anticorruption measures by sharply curbing state committees' ability to use large soft-money contributions to influence federal elections. The core of § 323(b) is a straightforward contribution regulation: It prevents donors from contributing nonfederal funds to state and local party committees to help finance "Federal election activity." 2 U.S.C. § 441i(b)(1). The term "Federal election activity" encompasses four distinct categories of electioneering: (1) voter registration activity during the 120 days preceding a regularly scheduled federal election; (2) voter identification, get-out-the-vote (GOTV), and generic campaign activity[54] that is

54. Generic campaign activity promotes a political party rather than a specific candidate. 2 U.S.C. § 431(21).

"conducted in connection with an election in which a candidate for Federal office appears on the ballot"; (3) any "public communication" that "refers to a clearly identified candidate for Federal office" and "promotes," "supports," "attacks," or "opposes" a candidate for that office; and (4) the services provided by a state committee employee who dedicates more than 25% of his or her time to "activities in connection with a Federal election." §§ 431(20)(A)(i)-(iv). The Act explicitly excludes several categories of activity from this definition: public communications that refer solely to nonfederal candidates; contributions to nonfederal candidates; state and local political conventions; and the cost of grassroots campaign materials like bumper stickers that refer only to state candidates. All activities that fall within the statutory definition must be funded with hard money.

1. Governmental Interests Underlying New FECA § 323(b)

We begin by noting that, in addressing the problem of soft-money contributions to state committees, Congress both drew a conclusion and made a prediction. Its conclusion, based on the evidence before it, was that the corrupting influence of soft money does not insinuate itself into the political process solely through national party committees. Rather, state committees function as an alternate avenue for precisely the same corrupting forces. Indeed, both candidates and parties already ask donors who have reached the limit on their direct contributions to donate to state committees. There is at least as much evidence as there was in *Buckley* that such donations have been made with the intent—and in at least some cases the effect—of gaining influence over federal officeholders. Section 323(b) thus promotes an important governmental interest by confronting the corrupting influence that soft-money donations to political parties already have.

Congress also made a prediction. Having been taught the hard lesson of circumvention by the entire history of campaign finance regulation, Congress knew that soft-money donors would react to § 323(a) by scrambling to find another way to purchase influence. It was neither novel nor implausible for Congress to conclude that political parties would react to § 323(a) by directing soft-money contributors to the state committees, and that federal candidates would be just as indebted to these contributors as they had been to those who had formerly contributed to the national parties. We "must accord substantial deference to the predictive judgments of Congress," *Turner Broadcasting System, Inc. v. FCC* (1994) (plurality opinion), particularly when, as here, those predictions are so firmly rooted in relevant history and common sense. Preventing corrupting activity from shifting wholesale to state committees and thereby eviscerating FECA clearly qualifies as an important governmental interest.

2. New FECA § 323(b)'s Tailoring

Plaintiffs argue that even if some legitimate interest might be served by § 323(b), the provision's restrictions are unjustifiably burdensome and therefore cannot be considered "closely drawn" to match the Government's objectives.

Plaintiffs assert that § 323(b) represents a new brand of pervasive federal regulation of state-focused electioneering activities that cannot possibly corrupt or appear to corrupt federal officeholders and thus goes well beyond Congress' concerns about the corruption of the federal electoral process. We disagree.

It is true that § 323(b) captures some activities that affect state campaigns for nonfederal offices. But these are the same sorts of activities that already were covered by the FEC's pre-BCRA allocation rules, and thus had to be funded in part by hard money, because they affect federal as well as state elections. As a practical matter, BCRA merely codifies the principles of the FEC's allocation regime while at the same time justifiably adjusting the formulas applicable to these activities in order to restore the efficacy of FECA's longtime statutory restriction—approved by the Court and eroded by the FEC's allocation regime—on contributions to state and local party committees for the purpose of influencing federal elections.

The first two categories of "Federal election activity," voter registration efforts, and voter identification, GOTV, and generic campaign activities conducted in connection with a federal election, clearly capture activity that benefits federal candidates. Common sense dictates, and it was "undisputed" below, that a party's efforts to register voters sympathetic to that party directly assist the party's candidates for federal office. It is equally clear that federal candidates reap substantial rewards from any efforts that increase the number of like-minded registered voters who actually go to the polls.

The record also makes quite clear that federal officeholders are grateful for contributions to state and local parties that can be converted into GOTV-type efforts.

Because voter registration, voter identification, GOTV, and generic campaign activity all confer substantial benefits on federal candidates, the funding of such activities creates a significant risk of actual and apparent corruption. Section 323(b) is a reasonable response to that risk. Its contribution limitations are focused on the subset of voter registration activity that is most likely to affect the election prospects of federal candidates: activity that occurs within 120 days before a federal election. Appropriately, in implementing this subsection, the FEC has categorically excluded all activity that takes place during the run up to elections when no federal office is at stake. The prohibition on the use of soft money in connection with these activities is therefore closely drawn to meet the sufficiently important governmental interests of avoiding corruption and its appearance.

"Public communications" that promote or attack a candidate for federal office—the third category of "Federal election activity," § 301(20)(A)(iii)—also undoubtedly have a dramatic effect on federal elections. Such ads were a prime motivating force behind BCRA's passage. As explained below, any public communication that promotes or attacks a clearly identified federal candidate directly affects the election in which he is participating. The record on this score could scarcely be more abundant. Given the overwhelming tendency of public communications, as carefully defined in § 301(20)(A)(iii), to benefit directly federal candidates, we hold that application of § 323(b)'s contribution caps to such communications is also closely drawn to the anticorruption interest it is intended to address.

As for the final category of "Federal election activity," § 301(20)(A)(iv), we find that Congress' interest in preventing circumvention of § 323(b)'s other restrictions justifies the requirement that state and local parties spend federal funds to pay the salary of any employee spending more than 25% of his or her compensated time on activities in connection with a federal election. In the absence of this provision, a party might use soft money to pay for the equivalent of a full-time employee engaged in federal electioneering, by the simple expedient of dividing the federal workload among multiple employees. Plaintiffs have suggested no reason for us to strike down this provision. Accordingly, we give "deference to [the] congressional determination of the need for [this] prophylactic rule." [*Fed. Election Comm'n v.*] *National Conservative Political Action Comm* [(1985)].

We accordingly conclude that § 323(b), on its face, is closely drawn to match the important governmental interests of preventing corruption and the appearance of corruption.

New FECA § 323(d)'s Restrictions on Parties' Solicitations for, and Donations to, Tax-Exempt Organizations

1. New FECA § 323(d)'s Regulation of Solicitations

[The Court upheld the restriction on parties soliciting donations to third-party tax-exempt organizations as preventing circumvention of Title I's limits on contributions of soft money to national, state, and local party committees. "Section 323(d)'s solicitation restriction is closely drawn to prevent political parties from using tax-exempt organizations as soft-money surrogates."]

2. New FECA § 323(d)'s Regulation of Donations

[The Court upheld the prohibition of national, state, and local party committees from making or directing donations to tax-exempt organizations, again explaining that the regulation served to prevent circumvention of § 323(a)'s anti-solicitation restrictions. However, the Court construed this provision to apply only to donations of funds not raised in compliance with cFECA, not hard money. If political parties could direct soft-money donations to tax-exempt organizations but could not raise their own soft money, they would just do so through organizations that support the party and its candidates, thereby thwarting § 323(a).]

New FECA § 323(e)'s Restrictions on Federal Candidates and Officeholders

[The Court upheld § 323(e), which regulates the raising and soliciting of soft money by federal candidates and officeholders, as a valid anticircumvention measure. "Without some restriction on solicitations, federal candidates and officeholders could easily avoid FECA's contribution limits by soliciting funds from large donors and restricted sources to like-minded organizations engaging in federal election activities."]

New FECA § 323(f)'s Restrictions on State Candidates and Officeholders

[The Court upheld the BCRA's restriction on candidates for local office, or state or local officeholders, from spending soft money to fund "public communications" that refer to a candidate for federal office. The Court explained that this provision is geared toward preventing the circumvention of valid contribution limits.]

B

[Omitted.]

C

Finally, plaintiffs argue that Title I violates the equal protection component of the Due Process Clause of the Fifth Amendment because it discriminates against political parties in favor of special interest groups such as the National Rifle Association, American Civil Liberties Union, and Sierra Club. As explained earlier, BCRA imposes numerous restrictions on the fundraising abilities of political parties, of which the soft-money ban is only the most prominent. Interest groups, however, remain free to raise soft money to fund voter registration, GOTV activities, mailings, and broadcast advertising (other than electioneering communications). We conclude that this disparate treatment does not offend the Constitution.

As an initial matter, we note that BCRA actually favors political parties in many ways. Most obviously, party committees are entitled to receive individual contributions that substantially exceed FECA's limits on contributions to nonparty political committees; individuals can give $25,000 to political party committees whereas they can give a maximum of $5,000 to nonparty political committees. In addition, party committees are entitled in effect to contribute to candidates by making coordinated expenditures, and those expenditures may greatly exceed the contribution limits that apply to other donors.

More importantly, however, Congress is fully entitled to consider the real-world differences between political parties and interest groups when crafting a system of campaign finance regulation. Interest groups do not select slates of candidates for elections. Interest groups do not determine who will serve on legislative committees, elect congressional leadership, or organize legislative caucuses. Political parties have influence and power in the Legislature that vastly exceeds that of any interest group. As a result, it is hardly surprising that party affiliation is the primary way by which voters identify candidates, or that parties in turn have special access to and relationships with federal officeholders. Congress' efforts at campaign finance regulation may account for these salient differences. Taken seriously, plaintiffs' equal protection arguments would call into question not just Title I of BCRA, but much of the pre-existing structure of FECA as well. We therefore reject those arguments.

[Based on the foregoing reasoning, the Court rejected the plaintiffs' facial challenge to BCRA's soft-money provisions.]

McCONNELL v. FEC DISSENTS

As you read the dissents* in this case, keep a few things in mind:

(1) What definition of "corruption" do the dissents embrace?
(2) What is the role of a political party in relation to its candidates?
(3) What is the relationship between national and state parties, and does BCRA unconstitutionally infringe on state parties' rights?
(4) To what extent is BCRA an incumbent-protection measure? (5) Is a law like BCRA needed to ferret out "bad" money in politics?

---

* [The dissents have been re-ordered to aid comprehension. — EDS.]

Justice KENNEDY, dissenting in part with respect to BCRA Title I, [in which Chief Justice REHNQUIST and Justice SCALIA joined in relevant part].

The First Amendment guarantees our citizens the right to judge for themselves the most effective means for the expression of political views and to decide for themselves which entities to trust as reliable speakers. Significant portions of Titles I and II of the Bipartisan Campaign Reform Act of 2002 (BCRA or Act) constrain that freedom. These new laws force speakers to abandon their own preference for speaking through parties and organizations. And they provide safe harbor to the mainstream press, suggesting that the corporate media alone suffice to alleviate the burdens the Act places on the rights and freedoms of ordinary citizens.

Today's decision upholding these laws purports simply to follow *Buckley v. Valeo* (1976) and to abide by *stare decisis*; but the majority, to make its decision work, must abridge free speech where *Buckley* did not. *Buckley* did not authorize Congress to decide what shapes and forms the national political dialogue is to take. To reach today's decision, the Court surpasses *Buckley*'s limits and expands Congress' regulatory power. In so doing, it replaces discrete and respected First Amendment principles with new, amorphous, and unsound rules, rules which dismantle basic protections for speech.

Our precedents teach, above all, that Government cannot be trusted to moderate its own rules for suppression of speech. The dangers posed by speech regulations have led the Court to insist upon principled constitutional lines and a rigorous standard of review. The majority now abandons these distinctions and limitations.

I. TITLE I AND COORDINATION PROVISIONS

Even a cursory review of the speech and association burdens these laws create makes their First Amendment infirmities obvious:

Title I bars individuals with shared beliefs from pooling their money above limits set by Congress to form a new third party.

Title I bars national party officials from soliciting or directing soft money to state parties for use on a state ballot initiative. This is true even if no federal office appears on the same ballot as the state initiative.

A national party's mere involvement in the strategic planning of fundraising for a state ballot initiative risks a determination that the national party is exercising "indirect control" of the state party. If that determination is made, the state party must abide by federal regulations. And this is so even if the federal candidate on the ballot, if there is one, runs unopposed or is so certain of election that the only voter interest is in the state and local campaigns.

Title I compels speech. Party officials who want to engage in activity such as fundraising must now speak magic words to ensure the solicitation cannot be interpreted as anything other than a solicitation for hard, not soft, money.

Title I prohibits the national parties from giving any sort of funds to nonprofit entities, even federally regulated hard money, and even if the party hoped to sponsor the interest group's exploration of a particular issue in advance of the party's addition of it to their platform.

By express terms, Title I imposes multiple different forms of spending caps on parties, candidates, and their agents.

A. Constitutionally Sufficient Interest

In *Buckley*, the Court held that one, and only one, interest justified the significant burden on the right of association involved there: eliminating, or preventing, actual corruption or the appearance of corruption stemming from contributions to candidates.

In parallel, *Buckley* concluded the expenditure limitations in question were invalid because they did not advance that same interest.

Thus, though *Buckley* subjected expenditure limits to strict scrutiny and contribution limits to less exacting review, it held neither could withstand constitutional challenge unless it was shown to advance the anticorruption interest. In these consolidated cases, unless *Buckley* is to be repudiated, we must conclude that the regulations further that interest before considering whether they are closely drawn or narrowly tailored. If the interest is not advanced, the regulations cannot comport with the Constitution, quite apart from the standard of review.

Buckley made clear, by its express language and its context, that the corruption interest only justifies regulating candidates' and officeholders' receipt of what we can call the "*quids*" in the *quid pro quo* formulation. The Court rested its decision on the principle that campaign finance regulation that restricts speech without requiring proof of particular corrupt action withstands constitutional challenge only if it regulates conduct posing a demonstrable *quid pro quo* danger[.]

Placing *Buckley*'s anticorruption rationale in the context of the federal legislative power yields the following rule: Congress' interest in preventing corruption provides a basis for regulating federal candidates' and officeholders' receipt of *quids*, whether or not the candidate or officeholder corruptly received them. Conversely, the rule requires the Court to strike down campaign finance regulations when they do not add regulation to "actual or apparent *quid pro quo* arrangements."

The Court ignores these constitutional bounds and in effect interprets the anticorruption rationale to allow regulation not just of "actual or apparent *quid pro quo* arrangements," but of any conduct that wins goodwill from or influences a Member of Congress. It is not that there is any quarrel between this opinion and the majority that the inquiry since *Buckley* has been whether certain conduct creates "undue influence." On that we agree. The very aim of *Buckley*'s standard, however, was to define undue influence by reference to the presence of *quid pro quo* involving the officeholder. The Court, in contrast, concludes that access, without more, proves influence is undue. Access, in the Court's view, has the same legal ramifications as actual or apparent corruption of officeholders. This new definition of corruption sweeps away all protections for speech that lie in its path.

The majority also ignores that in *Buckley*, and ever since, those party contributions that have been subject to congressional limit were not general party-building contributions but were only contributions used to influence particular elections. That is, they were contributions that flowed to a particular candidate's benefit, again posing a *quid pro quo* danger.

Access in itself, however, shows only that in a general sense an officeholder favors someone or that someone has influence on the officeholder. There is no basis, in law or in fact, to say favoritism or influence in general is the same as corrupt favoritism or influence in particular.

The generic favoritism or influence theory articulated by the Court is at odds with standard First Amendment analyses because it is unbounded and susceptible to no limiting principle. Any given action might be favored by any given person, so by the Court's reasoning political loyalty of the purest sort can be prohibited.

Though the majority cites common sense as the foundation for its definition of corruption, in the context of the real world only a single definition of corruption has been found to identify political corruption successfully and to distinguish good political responsiveness from bad—that is *quid pro quo*. Favoritism and influence are not, as the Government's theory suggests, avoidable in representative politics. It is in the nature of an elected representative to favor certain policies, and, by necessary corollary, to favor the voters and contributors who support those policies. It is well understood that a substantial and legitimate reason, if not the only reason, to cast a vote for, or to make a contribution to, one candidate over another is that the candidate will respond by producing those political outcomes the supporter favors. Democracy is premised on responsiveness. *Quid pro quo* corruption has been, until now, the only agreed upon conduct that represents the bad form of responsiveness and presents a justiciable standard with a relatively clear limiting principle: Bad responsiveness may be demonstrated by pointing to a relationship between an official and a *quid*.

The majority attempts to mask its extension of *Buckley* under claims that BCRA prevents the appearance of corruption, even if it does not prevent actual corruption, since some assert that any donation of money to a political party is suspect. Under *Buckley*'s holding that Congress has a valid "interest in stemming the reality or appearance of corruption," however, the inquiry does not turn on whether some persons assert that an appearance of corruption exists. Rather, the inquiry turns on whether the Legislature has established that the regulated conduct has inherent corruption potential, thus justifying the inference that regulating the conduct will stem the appearance of real corruption. *Buckley* was guided and constrained by this analysis. In striking down expenditure limits the Court in *Buckley* did not ask whether people thought large election expenditures corrupt, because clearly at that time many persons, including a majority of Congress and the President, did. Instead, the Court asked whether the Government had proved that the regulated conduct, the expenditures, posed inherent *quid pro quo* corruption potential.

From that it follows that the Court today should not ask, as it does, whether some persons, even Members of Congress, conclusorily assert that the regulated conduct appears corrupt to them. Following *Buckley*, it should instead inquire whether the conduct now prohibited inherently poses a real or substantive *quid pro quo* danger, so that its regulation will stem the appearance of *quid pro quo* corruption.

1. New FECA §§ 323(a), (b), (d), and (f)

Sections 323(a), (b), (d), and (f), cannot stand because they do not add regulation to conduct that poses a demonstrable *quid pro quo* danger. They do not further *Buckley*'s corruption interest.

The majority, with a broad brush, paints § 323(a) as aimed at limiting contributions possessing federal officeholder corruption potential. From there it would justify § 323's remaining provisions as necessary complements to ensure the national parties cannot circumvent § 323(a)'s prohibitions. The broad brush approach fails, however, when the provisions are reviewed under *Buckley*'s proper definition of corruption potential.

On its face § 323(a) does not regulate federal candidates' or officeholders' receipt of *quids* because it does not regulate contributions to, or conduct by, candidates or officeholders.

The realities that underlie the statute, furthermore, do not support the majority's interpretation. Before BCRA's enactment, parties could only use soft money for a candidate's "benefit" (*e.g.*, through issue ads, which all parties now admit may influence elections) independent of that candidate. And, as discussed later, § 323(e) validly prohibits federal candidate and officeholder solicitation of soft money party donations. Section 323(a), therefore, only adds regulation to soft money party donations not solicited by, or spent in coordination with, a candidate or officeholder.

These donations (noncandidate or officeholder solicited soft money party donations that are independently spent) do not pose the *quid pro quo* dangers that provide the basis for restricting protected speech. Though the government argues § 323(a) does regulate federal candidates' and officeholders' receipt of *quids*, it bases its argument on this flawed reasoning:

(1) "[F]ederal elected officeholders are inextricably linked to their political parties,"
(2) All party receipts must be connected to, and must create, corrupt donor favoritism among these officeholders.
(3) Therefore, regulation of party receipts equals regulation of *quids* to the party's officeholders.

The reasoning is flawed because the Government's reasoning only establishes the first step in its chain of logic: that a party is a proxy for its candidates generally. It does not establish the second step: that as a proxy for its candidates generally, *all* moneys the party receives (not just candidate solicited-soft money donations, or donations used in coordinated activity) represent *quids* for all the party's candidates and officeholders.

The piece of record evidence the Government puts forward on this score comes by way of deposition testimony from former Senator Simon and Senator Feingold. Senator Simon reported an unidentified colleague indicated frustration with Simon's opposition to legislation that would benefit a party contributor on the grounds that " 'we've got to pay attention to who is buttering our bread' " and testified he did not think there was any question " 'this' " (*i.e.*, "donors getting their way") was why the legislation passed. Senator Feingold, too, testified an unidentified colleague suggested he support the legislation because " 'they [*i.e.*, the donor] just gave us [*i.e.*, the party] $100,000.' "

That evidence in fact works against the Government. These two testifying Senators expressed disgust toward the favoring of a soft money giver, and not the good will one would have expected under the Government's theory. That necessarily undercuts the inference of corruption the Government would have us draw from the evidence.

Even more damaging to the Government's argument from the testimony is the absence of testimony that the Senator who allegedly succumbed to corrupt influence had himself solicited soft money from the donor in question. Equally, there is no indication he simply favored the company with his vote because it had, without any involvement from him, given funds to the party to which he belonged. This fact is crucial. If the Senator himself had been the solicitor of the soft money funds in question, the incident does nothing more than confirm that Congress' efforts at campaign finance reform ought to be directed to conduct that implicates *quid pro quo* relationships. Only if there was some evidence that the officeholder had not solicited funds from the donor could the Court extrapolate from this episode that general party contributions function as *quids*, inspiring corrupt favoritism among party members. The episode is the single one of its type reported in the record and does not seem sufficient basis for major incursions into settled practice. Given the Government's claim that the corrupt favoritism problem is widespread, its inability to produce more than a single instance purporting to illustrate the point demonstrates the Government has not fairly characterized the general attitudes of Members towards soft money donors from whom they have not solicited.

In light of all this, § 323(a) has no valid anticorruption interest. The anticircumvention interests the Government offers in defense of §§ 323(b), (d), and (f) must also fall with the interests asserted to justify § 323(a). Any anticircumvention interest can be only as compelling as the interest justifying the underlying regulation.

None of these other sections has an independent justifying interest.

When one recognizes that §§ 323(a), (b), (d), and (f) do not serve the interest the anticorruption rationale contemplates, Title I's entirety begins to look very much like an incumbency protection plan. The controlling point, of course, is the practical burden on challengers. That the prohibition applies to both incumbents and challengers in no way establishes that it burdens them equally in that regard. Name recognition and other advantages held by incumbents ensure that as a general rule incumbents will be advantaged by the legislation the Court today upholds.

The Government identifies no valid anticorruption interest justifying §§ 323(a), (b), (d), and (f). The very nature of the restrictions imposed by these provisions makes one all the more skeptical of the Court's explanation of the interests at stake. These provisions cannot stand under the First Amendment.

2. New FECA § 323(e)

Ultimately, only one of the challenged Title I provisions satisfies *Buckley*'s anticorruption rationale and the First Amendment's guarantee. It is § 323(e). This provision is the sole aspect of Title I that is a direct and necessary regulation of federal candidates' and officeholders' receipt of *quids*. Section 323(e) governs "candidate[s], individual[s] holding Federal office, agent[s] of a candidate or an individual holding Federal office, or an entity directly or indirectly established, financed, maintained or controlled by or acting on behalf of 1 or more candidates or individuals holding Federal office." These provisions, and the regulations that follow, limit candidates' and their agents' solicitation of soft money. The regulation of a candidate's receipt of funds furthers a constitutionally sufficient interest. More difficult, however, is the question whether regulation of a candidate's solicitation of funds also furthers this interest if the funds are given to another.

I agree with the Court that the broader solicitation regulation does further a sufficient interest. The making of a solicited gift is a *quid* both to the recipient of the money and to the one who solicits the payment (by granting his request). Rules governing candidates' or officeholders' solicitation of contributions are, therefore, regulations governing their receipt of *quids*. This regulation fits under *Buckley*'s anticorruption rationale.

B. Standard of Review

It is common ground between the majority and this opinion that a speech-suppressing campaign finance regulation, even if supported by a sufficient Government interest, is unlawful if it cannot satisfy our designated standard of review. In *Buckley*, we applied "closely drawn" scrutiny to contribution limitations and strict scrutiny to expenditure limitations. Against that backdrop, the majority assumes that because *Buckley* applied the rationale in the context of contribution and expenditure limits, its application gives Congress and the Court the capacity to classify any challenged campaign finance regulation as either a contribution or an expenditure limit. Thus, it first concludes Title I's regulations are contributions limits and then proceeds to apply the lesser scrutiny.

Though the majority's analysis denies it, Title I's dynamics defy this facile, initial classification.

Title I's provisions prohibit the receipt of funds; and in most instances, but not all, this can be defined as a contribution limit. They prohibit the spending of funds; and in most instances this can be defined as an expenditure limit. They prohibit the giving of funds to nonprofit groups; and this falls within neither definition as we have ever defined it. Finally, they prohibit fundraising activity; and the parties dispute the classification of this regulation (the challengers say it is core political association, while the Government says it ultimately results only in a limit on contribution receipts).

The majority's classification overlooks these competing characteristics and exchanges *Buckley*'s substance for a formulaic caricature of it. Despite the parties' and the majority's best efforts on both sides of the question, it ignores reality to force these regulations into one of the two legal categories as either contribution or expenditure limitations. Instead, these characteristics seem to indicate Congress has enacted regulations that are neither contribution nor expenditure limits, or are perhaps both at once.

Even if the laws could be classified in broad terms as only contribution limits, as the majority is inclined to do, that still leaves the question what "contribution limits" can include if they are to be upheld under *Buckley*. *Buckley*'s application of a less exacting review to contribution limits must be confined to the narrow category of money gifts that are directed, in some manner, to a candidate or officeholder. Any broader definition of the category contradicts *Buckley*'s *quid pro quo* rationale and overlooks *Buckley*'s language, which contemplates limits on contributions to a candidate or campaign committee in explicit terms.

The Court, it must be acknowledged, both in *Buckley* and on other occasions, has described contribution limits due some more deferential review in less than precise terms. At times it implied that donations to political parties would also qualify as contributions whose limitation too would be subject to less exacting review.

These seemingly conflicting statements are best reconciled by reference to *Buckley*'s underlying rationale for applying less exacting review. In a similar, but more imperative, sense proper application of the standard of review to regulations that are neither contribution nor expenditure limits (nor which are both at once) can only be determined by reference to that rationale.

Buckley's underlying rationale is this: Less exacting review applies to Government regulations that "significantly interfere" with First Amendment rights of association. But any regulation of speech or associational rights creating "markedly greater interference" than such significant interference receives strict scrutiny.

The majority makes *Buckley*'s already awkward and imprecise test all but meaningless in its application. If one is viewing BCRA through *Buckley*'s lens, as the majority purports to do, one must conclude the Act creates markedly greater associational burdens than the significant burden created by contribution limitations and, unlike contribution limitations, also creates significant burdens on speech itself. While BCRA contains federal contribution limitations, which significantly burden association, it goes even further. The Act entirely reorders the nature of relations between national political parties and their candidates, between national political parties and state and local parties, and between national political parties and nonprofit organizations.

The many and varied aspects of Title I's regulations impose far greater burdens on the associational rights of the parties, their officials, candidates, and citizens than do regulations that do no more than cap the amount of money persons can contribute to a political candidate or committee. The evidence shows that national parties have a long tradition of engaging in essential associational activities, such as planning and coordinating fundraising with state and local parties, often with respect to elections that are not federal in nature. This strengthens the conclusion that the regulations now before us have unprecedented impact. It makes impossible, moreover, the contrary conclusion—which the Court's standard of review determination necessarily implies—that BCRA's soft money regulations will not much change the nature of association between parties, candidates, nonprofit groups, and the like. Similarly, Title I now compels speech by party officials. These officials must be sure their words are not mistaken for words uttered in their official capacity or mistaken for soliciting prohibited soft, and not hard, money. Few interferences with the speech, association, and free expression of our people are greater than attempts by Congress to say which groups can or cannot advocate a cause, or how they must do it.

Congress has undertaken this comprehensive reordering of association and speech rights in the name of enforcing contribution limitations. Here, however, as in *Buckley*, "[t]he markedly greater burden on basic freedoms caused by [BCRA's pervasive regulation] cannot be sustained simply by invoking the interest in maximizing the effectiveness of the less intrusive contribution limitations." BCRA fundamentally alters, and thereby burdens, protected speech and association throughout our society. Strict scrutiny ought apply to review of its constitutionality. Under strict scrutiny, the congressional scheme, for the most part, cannot survive. This is all but acknowledged by the Government, which fails even to argue that strict scrutiny could be met.

1. New FECA § 323(e)

Because most of the Title I provisions discussed so far do not serve a compelling or sufficient interest, the standard of review analysis is only dispositive with respect to new FECA § 323(e). As to § 323(e), I agree with the Court that this provision withstands constitutional scrutiny.

Section 323(e) is directed solely to federal candidates and their agents; it does not ban all solicitation by candidates, but only their solicitation of soft money contributions; and it incorporates important exceptions to its limits (candidates may receive, solicit, or direct funds that comply with hard money standards; candidates may speak at fundraising events; candidates may solicit or direct unlimited funds to organizations not involved with federal election activity; and candidates may solicit or direct up to $20,000 per individual per year for organizations involved with certain federal election activity (*e.g.*, GOTV, voter registration)). These provisions help ensure that the law is narrowly tailored to satisfy First Amendment requirements. For these reasons, I agree § 323(e) is valid.

2. New FECA §§ 323(a), (b), (d), and (f)

Though these sections do not survive even the first test of serving a constitutionally valid interest, it is necessary as well to examine the vast overbreadth of the remainder of Title I, so the import of the majority's holding today is understood. Sections 323(a), (b), (d), and (f), are not narrowly tailored, cannot survive strict scrutiny, and cannot even be considered closely drawn, unless that phrase is emptied of all meaning.

First, the sections all possess fatal overbreadth. By regulating conduct that does not pose *quid pro quo* dangers, they are incursions on important categories of protected speech by voters and party officials.

[Justice Kennedy discussed each of the sections in turn. Section 323(a), he asserted, is overbroad because it regulates all National Parties, even if they do not present candidates in federal elections, and even during odd-numbered years that have only state and local elections. Section 323(b), he asserted, reaches speech by the state parties on nonfederal issues, such as a state or local party saying, "The Democratic slate for state assembly opposes President Bush's tax policy . . . Elect the Republican slate to tell Washington, D.C. we don't want higher taxes." Section 323(b), he noted, also is overbroad because it proscribes the use of soft money for all state party voter registration efforts occurring within 120 days of a federal election, meaning that "the vagaries of election timing, not any real interest related to corruption, will control whether state parties can spend nonfederally regulated funds on ballot efforts." Sections 323(d) and 323(f), according to Justice Kennedy, also are not narrowly tailored.]

Compared to the narrowly tailored effort of § 323(e), which addresses in direct and specific terms federal candidates' and officeholders' quest for dollars, these sections cast a wide net not confined to the critical categories of federal candidate or officeholder involvement. They are not narrowly tailored; they are not closely drawn; they flatly violate the First Amendment; and even if they do encompass some speech that poses a regulable *quid pro quo* danger, that little assurance does not justify or permit a regime which silences so many legitimate voices in this protected sphere.

Chief Justice REHNQUIST, dissenting with respect to BCRA Title I, [in which Justice SCALIA and KENNEDY joined].

Although I join Justice Kennedy's opinion in full, I write separately to highlight my disagreement with the Court on Title I of the [BCRA].

I

The issue presented by Title I is not, as the Court implies, whether Congress can permissibly regulate campaign contributions to candidates, *de facto* or otherwise, or seek to eliminate corruption in the political process. Rather, the issue is whether Congress can permissibly regulate much speech that has no plausible connection to candidate contributions or corruption to achieve those goals. Under our precedent, restrictions on political contributions implicate important First Amendment values and are constitutional only if they are "closely drawn" to reduce the corruption of federal candidates or the appearance of corruption. *Buckley v. Valeo.* Because, in reality, Title I is much broader than the Court allows, regulating a good deal of speech that does *not* have the potential to corrupt federal candidates and officeholders, I dissent.

The linchpin of Title I, new FECA § 323(a), prohibits national political party committees from "solicit[ing]," "receiv[ing]," "direct[ing] to another person," and "spend[ing]" *any* funds not subject to federal regulation, even if those funds are used for nonelection related activities. [Section] 323(a) does not regulate only donations given to influence a particular federal election; it regulates *all donations* to national political committees, no matter the use to which the funds are put.

The Court attempts to sidestep the unprecedented breadth of this regulation by stating that the "close relationship between federal officeholders and the national parties" makes all donations to the national parties "suspect." But a close association with others, especially in the realm of political speech, is not a surrogate for corruption; it is one of our most treasured First Amendment rights. The Court's willingness to impute corruption on the basis of a relationship greatly infringes associational rights and expands Congress' ability to regulate political speech. And there is nothing in the Court's analysis that limits congressional regulation to national political parties. In fact, the Court relies in part on this closeness rationale to regulate *nonprofit organizations.* Who knows what association will be deemed too close to federal officeholders next. When a donation to an organization has no potential to corrupt a federal officeholder, the relationship between the officeholder and the organization is simply irrelevant.

The Court fails to recognize that the national political parties are exemplars of political speech at all levels of government, in addition to effective fundraisers for federal candidates and officeholders. For sure, national political party committees exist in large part to elect federal candidates, but they also promote coordinated political messages and participate in public policy debates unrelated to federal elections, promote, even in off-year elections, state and local candidates and seek to influence policy at those levels, and increase public participation in the electoral process.

As these activities illustrate, political parties often foster speech crucial to a healthy democracy, and fulfill the need for like-minded individuals to band together and promote a political philosophy. When political parties engage in pure political speech that has little or no potential to corrupt their federal candidates and officeholders, the Government cannot constitutionally burden their speech any more than it could burden the speech of individuals engaging in these same activities. Notwithstanding the Court's citation to the numerous abuses of FECA, under any definition of "exacting scrutiny," the means chosen by Congress, restricting all donations to national parties no matter the purpose for which they are given or are used, are not "closely drawn to avoid unnecessary abridgment of associational freedoms." *Buckley*.

BCRA's overinclusiveness is not limited to national political parties. To prevent the circumvention of the ban on the national parties' use of nonfederal funds, BCRA extensively regulates state parties, primarily state elections, and state candidates. For example, new FECA § 323(b) prohibits state parties from using nonfederal funds for general partybuilding activities such as voter registration, voter identification, and get out the vote for state candidates even if federal candidates are not mentioned. New FECA § 323(d) prohibits state and local political party committees, like their national counterparts, from soliciting and donating "any funds" to nonprofit organizations such as the National Rifle Association or the National Association for the Advancement of Colored People (NAACP). And, new FECA § 323(f) requires a state gubernatorial candidate to abide by federal funding restrictions when airing a television ad that tells voters that, if elected, he would oppose the President's policy of increased oil and gas exploration within the State because it would harm the environment.

Although these provisions are more focused on activities that may *affect* federal elections, there is scant evidence in the record to indicate that federal candidates or officeholders are corrupted or would appear corrupted by donations for these activities. Nonetheless, the Court concludes that because these activities *benefit* federal candidates and officeholders, or prevent the circumvention of pre-existing or contemporaneously enacted restrictions, it must defer to the predictive judgments of Congress.

Yet the Court cannot truly mean what it says. Newspaper editorials and political talk shows *benefit* federal candidates and officeholders every bit as much as a generic voter registration drive conducted by a state party; there is little doubt that the endorsement of a major newspaper *affects* federal elections, and federal candidates and officeholders are surely "grateful," for positive media coverage. I doubt, however, the Court would seriously contend that we must defer to Congress' judgment if it chose to reduce the influence of political endorsements in federal elections. *SeeMiami Herald Publishing Co. v. Tornillo* (1974) (holding unconstitutional a state law that required newspapers to provide "right to reply" to any candidate who was personally or professionally assailed in order to eliminate the "abuses of bias and manipulative reportage" by the press).

It is also true that any circumvention rationale ultimately must rest on the circumvention itself leading to the corruption of federal candidates and officeholders. All political speech that is not sifted through federal regulation circumvents the regulatory scheme to some degree or another, and thus by the Court's standard would be a "loophole" in the current system. Unless the Court would uphold federal regulation of all funding of political speech, a rationale dependent on circumvention alone will not do. By untethering its inquiry from corruption or the appearance of corruption, the Court has removed the touchstone of our campaign finance precedent and has failed to replace it with any logical limiting principle.

But such an untethering is necessary to the Court's analysis. Only by using amorphous language to conclude a federal interest, however vaguely defined, exists can the Court avoid the obvious fact that new FECA §§ 323(a), (b), (d), and (f) are vastly overinclusive. Any campaign finance law aimed at reducing corruption will almost surely affect federal elections or prohibit the circumvention of federal law, and if broad enough, most laws will generally reduce some appearance of corruption. Indeed, it is precisely because broad laws are likely to nominally further a legitimate interest that we require Congress to tailor its restrictions; requiring all federal candidates to self-finance their campaigns would surely reduce the appearance of donor corruption, but it would hardly be constitutional. In allowing Congress to rely on general principles such as affecting a federal election or prohibiting the circumvention of existing law, the Court all but eliminates the "closely drawn" tailoring requirement and meaningful judicial review.

No doubt Congress was convinced by the many abuses of the current system that something in this area must be done. Its response, however, was too blunt. Many of the abuses described by the Court involve donations that were made for the "purpose of influencing a federal election," and thus are already regulated. Congress could have sought to have the existing restrictions enforced or to enact other restrictions that are "closely drawn" to its legitimate concerns. But it should not be able to broadly restrict political speech in the fashion it has chosen. Today's decision, by not requiring tailored restrictions, has significantly reduced the protection for political speech having little or nothing to do with corruption or the appearance of corruption.

Justice THOMAS, dissenting with respect to BCRA Title I, [in which Justice SCALIA joined].

[T]he Court today upholds what can only be described as the most significant abridgment of the freedoms of speech and association since the Civil War. With breathtaking scope, the [BCRA] directly targets and constricts core political speech. In response to this assault on the free exchange of ideas and with only the slightest consideration of the appropriate standard of review or of the Court's traditional role of protecting First Amendment freedoms, the Court has placed its *imprimatur* on these unprecedented restrictions. The very "purpose of the First Amendment [is] to preserve an uninhibited marketplace of ideas in which truth will ultimately prevail." *Red Lion Broadcasting Co. v. FCC* (1969). Yet today the fundamental principle that "the best test of truth is the power of the thought to get itself accepted in the competition of the market," *Abrams v. United States* (1919) (Holmes, J., dissenting), is cast aside in the purported service of preventing "corruption," or the mere "appearance of corruption." *Buckley v. Valeo.*

I

A

"[C]ampaign finance laws are subject to strict scrutiny," *Federal Election Comm'n v. Beaumont* (Thomas, J., dissenting), and thus Title I must satisfy that demanding standard even if it were (incorrectly) conceived of as nothing more than a contribution limitation. [A]s I have previously noted, it is unclear why "[b]ribery laws

[that] bar precisely the *quid pro quo* arrangements that are targeted here" and "disclosure laws" are not "less restrictive means of addressing [the government's] interest in curtailing corruption." *Shrink Missouri.*

The joint opinion not only continues the errors of *Buckley v. Valeo*, by applying a low level of scrutiny to contribution ceilings, but also builds upon these errors by expanding the anticircumvention rationale beyond reason.

Rather than permit this never-ending and self-justifying process, I would require that the Government explain why proposed speech restrictions are needed in light of actual Government interests, and, in particular, why the bribery laws are not sufficient.

B

But Title I falls even on the joint opinion's terms. A donation to a political party is a clumsy method by which to influence a candidate, as the party is free to spend the donation however it sees fit, and could easily spend the money as to provide no help to the candidate. And, a soft-money donation to a party will be of even less benefit to a candidate, "because of legal restrictions on how the money may be spent." Brief for FEC. It follows that the defendants bear an especially heavy empirical burden in justifying Title I.

The evidence cited by the joint opinion does not meet this standard and would barely suffice for anything more than rational-basis review. The first category of the joint opinion's evidence is evidence that "federal officeholders have commonly asked donors to make soft-money donations to national and state committees solely in order to assist federal campaigns, including the officeholder's own." But to the extent that donors and federal officeholders have collaborated so that donors could give donations to a national party committee "for the purpose of influencing any election for Federal office," the alleged soft-money donation is in actuality a regular "contribution" as already defined and regulated by FECA. Neither the joint opinion nor the defendants present evidence that enforcement of pre-BCRA law has proved to be impossible, ineffective, or even particularly difficult.

The second category is evidence that "lobbyists, CEOs, and wealthy individuals" have "donat[ed] substantial sums of soft money to national committees not on ideological grounds, but for the express purpose of securing influence over federal officials." Even if true (and the cited evidence consists of nothing more than vague allegations of wrongdoing), it is unclear why existing bribery laws could not address this problem. Again, neither the joint opinion nor the defendants point to evidence that the enforcement of bribery laws has been or would be ineffective. If the problem has been clear and widespread, as the joint opinion suggests, I would expect that convictions, or at least prosecutions, would be more frequent.

The joint opinion also places a substantial amount of weight on the fact that "in 1996 and 2000, more than half of the top 50 soft-money donors gave substantial sums to *both* major national parties," and suggests that this fact "leav[es] room for no other conclusion but that these donors were seeking influence, or avoiding retaliation, rather than promoting any particular ideology." But that is not necessarily the case. The two major parties are not perfect ideological opposites, and supporters or opponents of certain policies or ideas might find substantial overlap between the two parties. If donors feel that both major parties are in general agreement over an issue of importance to them, it is unremarkable that such donors show support for both parties. This commonsense explanation surely belies the joint opinion's too-hasty conclusion drawn from a relatively innocent fact.

Justice SCALIA, [dissenting with report to Title I].

This is a sad day for the freedom of speech. Who could have imagined that the same Court which, within the past four years, has sternly disapproved of restrictions upon such inconsequential forms of expression as virtual child pornography, tobacco advertising, dissemination of illegally intercepted communications, and sexually explicit cable programming, would smile with favor upon a law that cuts to the heart of what the First Amendment is meant to protect: the right to criticize the government. For that is what the most offensive provisions of this legislation are all about. We are governed by Congress, and this legislation prohibits the criticism of Members of Congress by those entities most capable of giving such criticism loud voice: national political parties and corporations, both of the commercial and the not-for-profit sort. It forbids national-party use of "soft" money to fund "issue ads" that incumbents find so offensive.

To be sure, the legislation is evenhanded: It similarly prohibits criticism of the candidates who oppose Members of Congress in their reelection bids. But as everyone knows, this is an area in which evenhandedness is not fairness. If *all* electioneering were evenhandedly prohibited, incumbents would have an enormous advantage. Likewise, if incumbents and challengers are limited to the same quantity of electioneering, incumbents are favored. In other words, any restriction upon a type of campaign speech that is equally available to challengers and incumbents tends to favor incumbents.

Beyond that, however, the present legislation targets for prohibition certain categories of campaign speech that are particularly harmful to incumbents. Is it accidental, do you think, that incumbents raise about three times as much "hard money"—the sort of funding generally not restricted by this legislation—as do their challengers? Or that lobbyists (who seek the favor of incumbents) give 92 percent of their money in "hard" contributions? And is it mere happenstance, do you estimate, that national-party funding, which is severely limited by the Act, is more likely to assist cash-strapped challengers than flush-with-hard-money incumbents? Was it unintended, by any chance, that incumbents are free personally to receive some soft money and even to solicit it for other organizations, while national parties are not? See new FECA §§ 323(a) and (e).

This litigation is about preventing criticism of the government. I cannot say for certain that many, or some, or even any, of the Members of Congress who voted for this legislation did so not to produce "fairer" campaigns, but to mute criticism of their records and facilitate reelection. Indeed, I will stipulate that all those who voted for BCRA believed they were acting for the good of the country. There remains the problem of the Charlie Wilson Phenomenon, named after Charles Wilson, former president of General Motors, who is supposed to have said during the Senate hearing on his nomination as Secretary of Defense that "what's good for General Motors is good for the country." Those in power, even giving them the benefit of the greatest good will, are inclined to believe that what is good for them is good for the country. Whether in prescient recognition of the Charlie Wilson Phenomenon, or out of fear of good old-fashioned, malicious, self-interested manipulation, "[t]he fundamental approach of the First Amendment . . . was to assume the worst, and to rule the regulation of political speech 'for fairness' sake' simply out of bounds." *Austin* [*v. Michigan Chamber of Commerce* (1990)] (Scalia, J., dissenting). Having abandoned that approach to a limited extent in *Buckley*, we abandon it much further today.

We will unquestionably be called upon to abandon it further still in the future. The most frightening passage in the lengthy floor debates on this legislation is the following assurance given by one of the cosponsoring Senators to his colleagues:

"This is a modest step, it is a first step, it is an essential step, but it does not even begin to address, in some ways, the fundamental problems that exist with the hard money aspect of the system." 148 Cong. Rec. S2101 (Mar. 20, 2002) (statement of Sen. Feingold).

The system indeed. The first instinct of power is the retention of power, and, under a Constitution that requires periodic elections, that is best achieved by the suppression of election-time speech. We have witnessed merely the second scene of Act I of what promises to be a lengthy tragedy. In scene 3 the Court, having abandoned most of the First Amendment weaponry that *Buckley* left intact, will be even less equipped to resist the incumbents' writing of the rules of political debate. The federal election campaign laws, which are already (as today's opinions show) so voluminous, so detailed, so complex, that no ordinary citizen dare run for office, or even contribute a significant sum, without hiring an expert adviser in the field, can be expected to grow more voluminous, more detailed, and more complex in the years to come—and always, always, with the objective of reducing the excessive amount of speech.

NOTES ON *McCONNELL v. FEC*

1. Notice the different constructions of "corruption" between the majority and dissenting opinions. The majority defined corruption broadly to encompass the securing of *access* to elected officials in exchange for soft-money contributions. The dissents, by contrast, limit "corruption" to quid-pro-quo arrangements. Which is more consistent with today's political realities? Does the First Amendment, whether from an originalist or a philosophically sound perspective, compel choosing one over the other?

2. Justice Kennedy and the other dissenters question the strength of the government's evidence. Is it possible for the public to evaluate the dispute between the Justices on this point, given the fact that the key relevant evidence was kept secret in the sealed record in the case? Did the dissenters deny the facts as the majority understood them, or instead did the dissenters simply disagree about the constitutional implications of those facts?

3. Justice Thomas obviously thinks *Buckley* was incorrectly decided and that Congress should not be able to impose contribution limits. Instead, he believes that bribery and disclosure laws can root out undue influence. Is he correct? Keep this debate in mind for the *Citizens United* discussion later in this Part.

4. Justice Scalia's opinion concurring in part and dissenting in part addressed (in a portion we omitted) what he termed "fallacious" propositions that he saw supporters of BCRA explicitly or implicitly endorsing: that "money is not speech," that

"pooling money is not speech," and that "speech by corporations can be abridged." The last proposition relates more to BCRA's "electioneering communications" provision, discussed below in *Citizens United.* What about the first two? Is spending money a form of speech, and is there (or should there be) a First Amendment right to pool money together to influence the political process?

5. The soft-money holdings of *McConnell* secured only a five-Justice majority (including Justice O'Connor). Justice Alito, who was appointed to replace Justice O'Connor, has been a lot more conservative on campaign finance issues than Justice O'Connor. Are the soft-money holdings therefore vulnerable to overruling? The Court rejected an invitation to do so in *Republican National Committee (RNC) v. FEC* (2010), but perhaps the Court's unwillingness in that case was just a matter of timing. (The Court did not write an opinion but simply summarily affirmed the lower court.) The Court had already overruled a huge portion of *McConnnell* in *Citizens United* when *RNC v. FEC* arrived at its doorstep, and maybe the Court did not have the stomach for overruling the soft-money part of *McConnell* so quickly thereafter. But after *Citizens United,* and with a changed composition of the Court, will a majority be ready to adopt the dissent's view of the soft-money issue and its narrow definition of corruption?

6. Some scholars have suggested that the soft money ban has weakened the political parties too much, leading to the rise of factions within the parties. More polarized candidates and lawmakers are less beholden to the party leadership, the argument goes, because they do not need to rely on the party as much for soft money expenditures for their campaigns. Weakened political parties, in turn, have caused greater factions within Congress itself. If this is true, does it suggest that Congress's goals in banning soft money have backfired?

3. *Political Parties and "Coordinated" Expenditures*

In *Buckley* and *McConnell,* the Court explained that when a candidate coordinates with a political party, the resulting expenditure is deemed to be a "coordinated" expenditure and therefore becomes subject to the contribution limitations of the law. That is, unlimited (and unregulated) independent expenditures must truly be independent—at least in theory. As the Court explained in *Buckley,* designating coordinated expenditures as contributions is required to ensure that candidates cannot circumvent the valid contribution limitations simply by funneling their spending through political parties.

Moreover, in *Colorado Republican Fed. Campaign Comm. v. FEC* (1996) ("*Colorado I*"), the Court held that political parties may spend unlimited amounts in support of a candidate (that is, make unlimited independent expenditures) so long as that spending is truly independent. The Court thus sustained an as-applied challenge to the portion of the law that limited political parties' independent expenditures. But in *FEC v. Colorado Republican Fed. Campaign Comm.* (2001) ("*Colorado II*"), the Court rejected a facial challenge to the law and found that "a party's coordinated expenditures, unlike expenditures truly independent, may be restricted to minimize circumvention of contribution limits." Given these two holdings, political parties have created internal units, separated from their operations that work directly with their candidates, so that these separate units may engage in unlimited "independent expenditures" in support of their candidates. Political parties have spent hundreds of millions of dollars in independent expenditures in recent elections.

Joseph Cao was a Member of Congress from Louisiana who was running for reelection in 2008. The Republican National Committee sought to run its own ad supporting Cao's candidacy but wanted to coordinate with Cao regarding the best timing for the ad. Could the party do so without having the ad be considered a regulated "coordinated" expenditure? That is the topic of this next case, from the United States Court of Appeals for the Fifth Circuit. Notice how the court considers coordination—including the test it uses—and the response from the dissent.

In re Cao

619 F.3d 410 (5th Cir. 2010) (en banc)

W. Eugene Davis and Benavides, Circuit Judges:

The challenges raised in the present case require this court to decide whether certain provisions of the Federal Election Campaign Act ("FECA" or "the Act") of 1971 violate the Plaintiffs' right to free speech under the First Amendment. Applying Supreme Court precedent, we conclude that each of the challenged FECA provisions constitutes a constitutionally permissible regulation of political parties' campaign contributions and coordinated expenditures. Accordingly, we find that none of the challenged provisions unconstitutionally infringe upon the rights of the Plaintiffs to engage in political debate and discussion.

I

Plaintiff Anh "Joseph" Cao is the United States Representative for the Second Congressional District of Louisiana, and Plaintiff Republican National Committee ("RNC") is the national political party committee of the Republican Party. Generally, the Plaintiffs challenge the statutory provisions limiting the RNC's contributions to, and expenditures made in coordination with, Cao's 2008 congressional campaign.

[T]he district court began by discussing the general contribution and expenditure limitations FECA places on political parties. Specifically examining how FECA affected the RNC's contributions and expenditures related to the 2008 Cao campaign, the district court then found that the RNC spent all of the $42,100 it was allowed to spend on coordinated expenditures under the Party Expenditure Provision, 2 U.S.C. § 441a(d)(2)(3),[5] and reached its $5,000 contribution limit under § 441a(a)(2)(A). Additionally, the district court found that the RNC would have spent additional money on speech expressly advocating the election of Cao had it been permitted to spend beyond FECA limitations.

5. [Section 441a(d)(2)(3), the "Party Expenditure Provision," provides limits on the amount political parties may expend in connection with the general election campaign of candidates for various offices.—Eds.]

[The district court certified four constitutional questions to the en banc court of appeals under the procedure outlined in 2 U.S.C. § 437h.]

II

This appeal requires us to address the intersection of congressional campaign finance reform with the fundamental right to free speech under the First Amendment. Since the landmark decision of *Buckley v. Valeo* (1976), the Supreme Court on a number of occasions has evaluated the limitations that the First Amendment imposes on the Government's ability to preserve the integrity of the democratic election process through its regulation of campaign expenditures and contributions made to federal candidates.

In . . . articulating the constitutional distinction between contributions and expenditures, the Court [in *Buckley*] carefully distinguished independent expenditures from those expenditures that are "prearranged or coordinated" with a particular candidate. Following the terminology used in FECA, the *Buckley* Court considered that for purposes of First Amendment scrutiny, "prearranged or coordinated expenditures" are constitutionally equivalent to contributions. According to the Court, it followed that coordinated expenditures are subject to the same limitations and scrutiny that apply to contributions. Although the facts of the challenge and nature of the Court's analysis in *Buckley* gave the Court no reason to specifically address the level of scrutiny for coordinated expenditures, the *Buckley* Court implicitly recognized that limitations on coordinated expenditures would be, like contribution limitations, subject to a lower level of constitutional scrutiny than limitations on independent expenditures.

III

The second question certified to the en banc court asks:

> Do the expenditure and contribution limits and contribution provision in 2 U.S.C. §§ 441a(a)(23), 441a(a)(2)(A), and 441a(a)(7)(B)(i) violate the First Amendment rights of one or more of [the] plaintiffs as applied to coordinated communications that convey the basis for the expressed support?

This question arose out of the RNC's desire to spend in excess of the amount allowed for coordinated campaign expenditures under the Party Expenditure Provision. Particularly, the RNC wanted to expend its funds to run a radio advertisement in support of Cao (hereinafter "the Cao ad"). The proposed Cao ad said:

> Why We Support Cao
>
> The Republican National Committee has long stood for certain core principles, which we believe are the fundamentals of good government. When it comes to the issues of lower taxes, individual freedoms and a strong national defense, we need leaders who will stand with the American people and defend those issues.
>
> We need leaders who understand that our economy is in a recession, our individual freedoms are constantly under attack and we continue to fight the global war on terrorism to keep our families safe.

> Joseph Cao understands and fights for those issues. And, that is why we ask you to join us in supporting him on December 6. It's important for Louisiana and important for the country.

The RNC wanted to coordinate with the Cao campaign as to the "best timing" for the Cao ad. However, the RNC's involvement with the Cao campaign amounted to coordination, and the RNC already had spent the entire amount it was allowed to spend on coordinated campaign expenditures under FECA. Therefore, the RNC concluded that it could not coordinate with the Cao campaign to run the Cao ad without violating FECA. Ultimately, the RNC chose to not expend its funds to air the Cao ad and brought this challenge to FECA's restrictions on coordinated expenditures.

Because we are a court of error and only decide issues the parties bring to us, it is important at the outset to identify the RNC's sole argument on this certified question. The RNC argues and only argues that §§ 441a(d)(2)(3), 441a(a)(2)(A), and 441a(a)(7)(B)(i) violate its First Amendment rights because the provisions regulate the RNCs "own speech." The RNC asserts that its own speech may not be regulated, regardless of whether the speech is coordinated. "Own speech" is defined by the RNC as speech that is "attributable" to the RNC and includes speech the candidate writes and decides how the speech is to be disseminated. In other words, the RNC argues that speech it adopts is attributed to it and therefore exempt from regulation regardless of the extent of coordination with the candidate.

To evaluate the merit of the Plaintiffs' expansive "own speech" argument, we return to *Buckley v. Valeo*, the first case to discuss coordinated expenditures under FECA. In *Buckley*, the Supreme Court examined, *inter alia*, then-18 U.S.C. § 608(e)(1) which limited individuals' ability to make independent expenditures. The Government argued that Congress could restrict independent expenditures because independent expenditures could be used to circumvent contribution limits. The *Buckley* Court rejected the Government's argument. In finding that independent expenditures could not be regulated, the Court compared § 608(e)(1) with § 608(b), the provision that regulated expenditures coordinated with a candidate. The *Buckley* Court stated:

> . . . [C]ontrolled or coordinated expenditures are treated as contributions rather than expenditures under the Act. Section 608(b)'s contribution ceilings rather than §608(e)(1)'s independent expenditure limitation prevent attempts to circumvent the Act through prearranged or coordinated expenditures amounting to disguised contributions. By contrast, §608(e)(1) limits expenditures for express advocacy of candidates made totally independently of the candidate and his campaign. Unlike contributions, such independent expenditures may well provide little assistance to the candidate's campaign and indeed may prove counterproductive. The absence of prearrangement and coordination of an expenditure with the candidate or his agent not only undermines the value of the expenditure to the candidate, but also alleviates the danger that expenditures will be given as a quid pro quo for improper commitments from the candidate.

Thus, the *Buckley* Court concluded that although Congress was unable to regulate individuals' independent expenditures, Congress could regulate individuals' coordinated expenditures.

Building on and embracing its analysis in *Buckley*, the Court in *Colorado I* and *Colorado II* further examined the limitations on coordinated and independent expenditures as applied to political parties. In *Colorado I*, the Colorado Republican Party ("CRP") brought an as-applied challenge to the Party Expenditure Provision arguing that restricting a party's independent expenditures was unconstitutional. The *Colorado I* Court followed the *Buckley* rationale and found that "the constitutionally significant fact . . . is the lack of coordination between the candidate and the source of the expenditure." *Colorado I.* In holding that the restraint on an independent expenditure was unconstitutional, the Court distinguished between coordinated expenditures and independent expenditures, stating:

> . . . [T]he Court's cases have found a "fundamental constitutional difference between money spent to advertise one's views independently of the candidate's campaign and money contributed to the candidate to be spent on his campaign." . . . [R]easonable contribution limits directly and materially advance the Government's interest in preventing exchanges of large financial contributions for political favors.
>
> . . . [L]imitations on independent expenditures are less directly related to preventing corruption, since "the absence of prearrangement and coordination of an expenditure with the candidate . . . not only undermines the value of the expenditure to the candidate, but also alleviates the danger that expenditures will be given as a quid pro quo for improper commitments from the candidate."

Thus, the *Colorado I* Court found that the Party Expenditure Provision was unconstitutional as applied to the CRP's independent expenditures.

In *Colorado I*, the CRP also raised a facial challenge to the application of the Party Expenditure Provision to coordinated expenditures. The *Colorado I* Court remanded this facial challenge because the lower courts had not considered the issue. The remanded issue of whether Congress could restrict coordinated expenditures reached the Supreme Court five years later as *Colorado II*. After analyzing its precedents in *Buckley* and *Colorado I*, the *Colorado II* Court found that "a party's coordinated expenditures, unlike expenditures truly independent, may be restricted to minimize circumvention of contribution limits." In examining whether coordinated expenditures could be restricted, the Court applied the intermediate scrutiny standard announced in *Buckley*: the restriction must be closely drawn to match a important government interest. The Court found that Congress could regulate coordinated expenditures as contributions because of the sufficiently important governmental interest in preventing the potential for political corruption by circumvention of campaign finance laws. The Court stated:

> There is no significant functional difference between a party's coordinated expenditure and a direct party contribution to the candidate, and there is good reason to expect that a party's right of unlimited coordinated spending would attract increased contributions to parties to finance exactly that kind of spending. Coordinated expenditures of money donated to a party are tailor-made to undermine contribution limits. Therefore the choice here is not, as in *Buckley* and *Colorado I*, between a limit on pure contributions and pure expenditures. The choice is between limiting contributions

> and limiting expenditures whose special value as expenditures is also the source of their power to corrupt. Congress is entitled to its choice.

Though the *Colorado II* Court unambiguously found the application of the Party Expenditure Provision to coordinated expenditures to be facially constitutional, the Plaintiffs argue that "*Colorado II* expressly left open the as-applied question of whether parties' own speech may be limited as contributions."

Assuming that the *Colorado II* Court left open the possibility for an as-applied challenge to the Party Expenditure Provision's application to coordinated spending, the facts and arguments in the instant case do not present this court with that question. Acceptance of the Plaintiffs' "own speech" argument would effectively eviscerate the Supreme Court's holding in *Colorado II*, which dealt only with coordinated expenditures. The Court in *Colorado II* expressly recognized that Congress has the power to regulate coordinated expenditures in order to combat circumvention of the contribution limits and political corruption.

The *Colorado II* Court stated:

> . . . [T]he question is whether experience under the present law confirms a serious threat of abuse from the unlimited coordinated party spending as the Government contends. It clearly does. Despite years of enforcement of the challenged limits, substantial evidence demonstrates how candidates, donors, and parties test the limits of the current law, and it shows beyond serious doubt how contribution limits would be eroded if inducement to circumvent them were enhanced by declaring parties' coordinated spending wide open.

If this court were to accept the Plaintiffs' exceedingly broad argument, we would be reaching a conclusion inconsistent with the *Colorado II* Court's teaching that coordinated expenditures may be restricted. The RNC's sole argument throughout has been that there is no limit to its claim that Congress cannot regulate a party's own speech regardless of the degree of coordination with the candidate. The district court succinctly identified the Plaintiffs' argument: "Plaintiffs claim that a party coordinated communication disclosed as paid for by the party is the party's 'own speech' even if a candidate indicates in the communication that he has approved the message." Moreover, "Plaintiffs claim that a party coordinated communication disclosed as having been paid for by the party is the party's 'own speech' even if the candidate or her campaign actually creates the communication and passes it along to the party." Thus, under the Plaintiffs' standard, all coordinated expenditures paid for and adopted by the party would be considered a party's own speech and not subject to restriction. As demonstrated above, the *Colorado II* Court, as well as the Court's earlier cases, clearly held that coordinated expenditures may be restricted to prevent circumvention and corruption.

We find the *Colorado II* Court's concern with corruption particularly important since, in the present case, the Plaintiffs admit that they themselves have already taken steps to circumvent the Act's individual donor contribution limits. The district court found that "[t]he RNC encourages its candidates to tell their 'maxed out' donors to contribute to the RNC." Representative Cao confirmed in his deposition this behavior by the RNC. "Congressman Cao has personally suggested to donors who had given the maximum amount to his campaign that they could also contribute to the party." [Citation to district court's opinion.] Furthermore, the district court found that "the party has shared [its] donor list" with its federal candidates, and that "[t]he sharing of information also happens in the other direction[, since the party] receives information from federal candidates about who has contributed to their campaigns." The district court also found that "the RNC organizes 'fulfillment' events to which individuals who have made a large contribution to the RNC of a specified amount are invited" so that they can have special access to federal lawmakers. The *Colorado II* Court warned that "[i]f the effectiveness of party spending could be enhanced by limitless coordination, the ties of straitened candidates to prosperous ones and, vicariously, to large donors would be reinforced as well." The above facts demonstrate the potential corruption and abuse that concerned *Colorado II.*

Colorado II certainly left open the possibility for an as-applied challenge to the Party Expenditure Provision as it applies to coordinated expenditures; it is well-established that the facial upholding of a law does not prevent future as-applied challenges. However, simply characterizing the challenge as an as-applied challenge does [not] make it one. "While rejection of a facial challenge to a statute does not preclude all as-applied attacks, surely it precludes one resting upon the same asserted principle of law." *Penry v. Lynaugh* (1989) (Scalia, J., dissenting).

The argument raised by the Plaintiffs in this case rests not on a sufficiently developed factual record, but rather, on the same general principles rejected by the Court in *Colorado II,* namely the broad position that coordinated expenditures may not be regulated. Finding for the Plaintiffs would require us to hold that Congress cannot limit a party's expenditures on a campaign ad, the content of which the party adopts, regardless of the degree of coordination with the candidate. Because such a conclusion would effectually overrule all restrictions on coordinated expenditures, the RNC's argument must fail in light of *Colorado II.*

The Plaintiffs' "own speech" argument cannot be reconciled with *Colorado II.* As such, we find that the expenditure and contribution limits and contribution provision in 2 U.S.C. §§ 441a(a)(2)(3), 441a(a)(2)(A), and 441a(a)(7)(B)(I) do not violate the First Amendment rights of one or more of the Plaintiffs as applied to coordinated communications that convey the basis for the party's expressed support.

IV

The principal disagreement we have with the dissents is over the scope of Plaintiffs' argument with respect to the constitutionality of contribution restrictions relative to coordinated expenditures. Based on the record, briefs and oral argument, we have explained above why we conclude that the only issue Plaintiffs presented to us for decision is whether the RNC's "own speech" is subject to regulation and restriction under FECA. As we read Chief Judge Jones's dissent, she agrees that *Colorado II* answers this question and authorizes regulation of RNC's own speech generally. Chief Judge Jones's principal argument is that Plaintiffs also presented for decision whether the Act can constitutionally restrict expenditures for the Cao Ad involved in this case when that ad was coordinated between the RNC and the candidate as to "timing only."

[The majority recounts its determination, based on the briefs and oral argument, that the Plaintiffs conceded that the ad in question amounted to a coordinated expenditure.]

Even if we further consider that Plaintiffs made and did not abandon the argument that the coordination between the candidate and the party was de minimis, based on the stipulation and admission of counsel the coordination cannot be considered de minimis. At oral argument, Plaintiffs' counsel conceded that the RNC intended to coordinate the Cao Ad with Cao not only with regard to timing, but also by providing Cao with advance knowledge of the Cao Ad's content.

This "content awareness" stipulation has significance that the dissents completely overlook. For instance, given advance knowledge of the Cao Ad's content, if Cao approved of the content and found it favorable to his campaign, he may have told or requested the RNC to run the ad frequently during prime hours. If Cao disapproved of the Cao Ad's content and found it unfavorable to his campaign, he may have told or requested the party to run it infrequently during off hours, or perhaps not at all. This degree of coordination of campaign expenditures contrasts sharply with the Supreme Court's functional definition of independent expenditures. Whereas the Supreme Court has explained that an independent expenditure representing the party's own views may at times work against the candidate's interests, timing-plus-content-awareness coordination may ensure that a party's message virtually always works in the candidate's favor.

For these reasons we cannot agree with Chief Judge Jones's conclusion that "there is no functional difference between the Cao Ad and a constitutionally protected independent expenditure." As we have explained above, knowledge of content plus timing coordination makes a huge difference relative to the benefit of the ad to the candidate that the dissent fails to recognize—namely, the candidate's ability to direct approved content for maximum impact and redirect disapproved content for minimum impact on his campaign.

This type of coordinated activity, moreover, implicates the same corruption and circumvention concerns of the *Colorado II* Court. Therefore, based on what we know of the extent of the proposed coordination on this scant record, it is reasonable to infer that the coordination of the Cao Ad between the candidate and the party as to timing with the candidate's prior knowledge of the ad's content would amount to a coordinated expenditure subject to restriction under *Colorado II*.

JONES, Chief Judge, concurring in part and dissenting in part:

The first object of the First Amendment is to protect robust political debate that underpins free citizens' ability to govern ourselves. "Speech is an essential mechanism of democracy, for it is the means to hold officials accountable to the people. . . . The First Amendment has its fullest and most urgent application to speech uttered during a campaign for political office." *Citizens United v. FEC* (2010). Yet the majority hold that Congress may forbid a political party from broadcasting an advertisement explaining why the party supports its own congressional candidate merely because the advertisement was coordinated with the candidate as to timing.

We dissent. The Cao Ad cannot be suppressed by the FEC on the facts before us.

Substantively, the majority['s] analysis, flawed by its overbroad premises, ultimately begs the primary question before us—at what point does "coordination" between a candidate and a political party transform the party's communicative speech into a mere "contribution" subject to strict dollar limits? This question was left open by the Supreme Court. *Colorado II* (2001). In light of subsequent Supreme Court decisions, courts must begin to deal with it.

I. A Narrow Fact-Based Challenge Is Before the Court

Despite the majority's contentions, the court is obliged to address the facts that have actually been presented—specifically, whether this particular ad can be regulated as a de facto contribution even though the coordination regarded solely the timing of its broadcast.

It is important to stress just how minimal was the level of coordination. When the Supreme Court has interpreted the term "coordinated expenditures," it described a spectrum, at one end of which political parties would simply foot the candidate's bills. The present scenario stands at the other end.

The ad was produced and approved by the RNC, on its own initiative, without any input from Cao. Cao and the RNC intended to cooperate only as to the timing of the ad. Timing constituted the only coordination. There is no evidence that Cao suggested, instigated or requested the ad. There is no evidence that he or his campaign wrote it or provided their views on its content. There is no evidence that the ad might have caused Cao to spend his campaign funds any differently. Thus, whether or not such de minimis coordination allows the Cao Ad to be banned as a "coordinated expenditure" is before the court for decision.

II. The Court Must Address Narrow Issues First

[Omitted.]

III. Evaluating Cao's As-Applied Challenge

In this as-applied attack on the coordinated expenditure limit that would ban broadcast of the Cao Ad, this court must first determine the appropriate level of scrutiny and then evaluate the evidence concerning the government's regulation. Two levels of scrutiny govern campaign finance regulations: strict scrutiny and, unique to campaign finance jurisprudence, "closely drawn" scrutiny. *Buckley v. Valeo* (1976). The former has been applied to candidates' speech and independent expenditures, while the latter applies to contributions and facially to "coordinated expenditures." Which standard pertains to the government's regulation of the Cao Ad depends on whether the ad is core political speech or a functional contribution. This court is not bound by the government's simply labeling the speech "coordinated[.]"

Buckley held that contributions to a candidate may be regulated, because contributions, unlike communicative independent expenditures, express merely a general support for a candidate. The FECA defines contributions as including "expenditures made by any person in cooperation, consultation, or concert, with, or at the request or suggestion of, a candidate." 2 U.S.C. § 441a(a)(7)(B)(i). While the Supreme Court has placed great importance on whether speech is coordinated, and thus regarded as a contribution, it has offered no guidance except to acknowledge that the sweeping term "coordinated expenditures" covers a wide range of activities with varying constitutional attributes:

> The principal opinion in *Colorado I* noted that coordinated expenditures "share some of the constitutionally relevant features of independent expenditures." But it also observed that "many [party coordinated expenditures] are . . . virtually indistinguishable from simple contributions." Coordinated spending by a party, in other words, covers a spectrum of activity, as does coordinated spending by other political actors.

Colorado II.

There is no doubt that, standing alone, the Cao Ad is core political speech. The Cao Ad is more than "a general expression of support for the candidate." *Buckley*. The ad expressly advocates for Cao, "communicate[s] the underlying basis for [the RNC's] support," and increases "the quantity of communication." [*Id.*]

Further, the ad hews closely to the independent expenditure side of the spectrum. The RNC independently produced the Cao Ad without input from Cao; the RNC created the ad at its own initiative; the RNC planned the ad's message; the RNC produced the ad; the RNC approved the final version of the ad; and the RNC decided to air the ad. Like the ads in *Colorado I*, the Cao Ad "was developed by the [party] independently and not pursuant to any general or particular understanding with a candidate." *Colorado I*. It unambiguously "reflects [the RNC's] members' views about the philosophical and governmental matters that bind them together [and] also seeks to convince others to join those members in a practical democratic task, the task of creating a government that voters can instruct and hold responsible for subsequent success or failure." [*Id.*]

At the opposite end of the coordination spectrum are instances in which a party simply pays its candidate's bills. Apparently rejecting the spectrum approach, the FEC asserts that the Cao Ad is functionally the same as a cash contribution to the candidate. This is inaccurate. The critical differences between the Cao Ad and a direct contribution or "footing the candidate's bills" include the ad's initiator, message, quality, ultimate source of approval, and decision to air. The Cao Ad is not "virtually identical" to one that Cao might produce. Further, despite the timing coordination, the ads "may well provide little assistance to the candidate's campaign and indeed may prove counterproductive." *Buckley*. Because the party decides to create and air the ad of its own initiative, the candidate cannot depend on it. The candidate will not know whether the ad is effective. If the ad is useful to the candidate, then it is useful only because the interests of the party and the candidate coincide. On all these grounds, there is no significant functional difference between the Cao Ad and a constitutionally protected independent expenditure.

Compared with the *Colorado II* pronouncement that the coordinated expenditure limits are facially valid, this case presents the narrow question whether de minimis coordination transforms otherwise constitutionally protected core political speech into something less. We believe it does not. Because the Cao Ad represents core political speech, it should be evaluated under the traditional strict scrutiny test. Alternatively, even if "closely drawn" scrutiny is required because of *Colorado II*, the Cao Ad cannot be subjected to dollar limits.

A. Applying Strict Scrutiny

That a statute has been held facially valid does not answer whether it may be constitutionally applied in a specific circumstance. Instead "[a] court applying strict scrutiny must ensure that a compelling interest supports each application of a statute restricting speech." [*FEC v. Wisconsin Right to Life, Inc.* (2007) (*WRTL*).] Moreover, the government bears the burden to demonstrate that the law is constitutional as applied to plaintiffs' speech.

The government contends that regulating timing-only coordination furthers its compelling interest in preventing corruption or its appearance or circumvention of the contribution limits. The FEC also argues that an expansive definition of "coordination" is necessary to ensure that it can regulate all coordinated expenditures that truly are de facto contributions.

The import of [the Supreme Court's precedents] is clear. Even if the record afforded some support for regulating timing-only coordination, which it does not, it clearly does not support treating the Cao Ad as the "functional equivalent" of a mere monetary contribution. The expressive content of the ad prevents that. In addition, the risk of circumvention of campaign contribution limits is not appreciably greater here than it is with "independent" expenditures. The candidate lacks control or influence over the initiation, production, and content of the party ad. The party decides whether or not an ad will be made, what it will say, what it will look like, and whether it will air. The candidate may or may not approve of the ad or find it useful.

Consequently, this expenditure will be useful to the candidate only to the extent that his and the party's interests coincide. Should the candidate "encourage" donors to give money to the party, he cannot be certain whether these party donations will be more useful to him than an independent expenditure. Without some link of candidate control or influence, neither the quid pro quo corruption nor appearance of corruption that justifies contribution limits can occur.

The FEC essentially argues . . . that expansive definitions of coordination and coordinated expenditures are needed to ensure that coordinating solely the broadcast timing of the party's ad does not circumvent the rule against coordinated expenditures which in turn helps to prevent circumvention of contribution limits which culminates in preventing quid pro quo corruption or the appearance of such corruption. It is an overly broad approach that here sweeps up protected speech.

B. Applying "Closely Drawn" Scrutiny

Even if the regulation of the Cao Ad must be evaluated under *Buckley*'s "closely drawn" standard because of its de minimis coordination, the government still must affirmatively demonstrate some sufficiently important interest—preventing corruption, the appearance of corruption, or circumvention. The government remains obliged to present evidence that the interest applies to the facts before us. Not to require some level of proof by the government would allow censorship of the party's ad based on nothing more than the general proof offered to sustain the statute's facial validity in *Colorado II*.

The FEC offered no evidence or argument that coordination of the Cao Ad as to broadcast timing will appreciably increase the risk or appearance of corruption or circumvention of contribution limits. Overall, the record evidence proves that money plays a primary role in political campaigns, that parties and party leaders are significantly involved in political fund-raising, and that independent groups have played an increasing role in recent years. More money than ever is being raised, and election advertising has become more important and more of a science than ever before. Frequently, this money, whether it travels through campaigns, parties, or independent groups, opens up opportunities for access to candidates and politicians. In short, despite FECA, as amended by McCain-Feingold, money and politics remain inextricably linked, and may be more entangled than they were at the time of FECA's passage.

None of this, however, demonstrates that the specific type of coordination at issue in this case, concerning the timing of otherwise-independent expenditures, has any propensity to increase quid pro quo corruption or the appearance of corruption or to promote circumvention of contribution limits. Indeed, the voluminous evidentiary record contains only a few, incidental references to timing coordination. For example, a campaign finance expert opines that "Giving candidates a direct say in whether, when, and how often a party's speech is broadcast essentially gives them a direct say in the content of what the voters get to hear." Content, however, is not at issue in this case. A former politician states that party advertisements in the final days of a campaign can make the difference between winning and losing. Coordination is hardly necessary to draw that conclusion. One campaign consultant complained that "the clutter on television during the last few weeks of the campaign really prevented our message from getting through as clearly as we would have liked." No doubt. What is absent from the record is any discussion or evaluation (let alone evidence) on whether timing coordination increases the risk of corruption or its appearance. Instead, the record simply includes blanket conclusions that any coordination increases the risk.

In contrast, the general evidence demonstrating risks of circumvention presented in *Colorado II* involved situations where the candidate retained real control over the party's coordinated expenditures. Candidates controlled the message and its presentation and, ultimately, approved of those coordinated expenditures. Here, Cao had no influence over the RNC's speech save what time it would air. The candidate does not even have input into whether or on what stations the ad will air, only when it will air, and he cannot be certain that the party will heed his advice. If there is any heightened possibility of corruption or circumvention in this arrangement, the government has not pointed to it, and we ought not to invent some conceivable interest that the government itself is unable to articulate or prove.

Nor, in this instance, are entirely uncoordinated expenditures an adequate alternative to minimally coordinated speech. The record demonstrates that FEC's coordination-regulation regime prevents party leaders from exercising any degree of control over their party's advertisements in support of a candidate. Because party leaders inevitably associate with candidates, to avoid the taint of coordination parties must establish "independent expenditure programs" staffed by hired consultants who are responsible for all aspects of the party's communications, from polling and research to writing the scripts, but for the topline budget. In effect, a party has no control over its own message. The party leaders must make a Hobson's choice between talking to their own candidates and controlling their own party's message. The government justifies this regime by reference to the risk of "circumvention." But by prohibiting speech subject to de minimis coordination, the FEC severely abridges parties' constitutionally protected right to engage in independent expenditures—in other words, to speak in public in support of their own candidates.

"Closely drawn" scrutiny has to mean something when applied to censorship of core political speech. Where the government cannot demonstrate a compelling interest, and the effect of regulation in this case is to ban the Cao Ad, the regulation cannot be "closely drawn."

IV. The Majority Opinion

[Omitted.]

V. Conclusion

The constitutional rules governing campaign finance law are presently in a state of flux, but there is a clear trend favoring the protection of political speech. [T]he Supreme Court has, in measured steps, protected political speech while leaving the scaffolding of *Buckley* in place. It has cast aside both recently enacted speech restrictions and decades-old speech restrictions. Lower courts have conformed to this trend.

In each of those instances, the Supreme Court has demanded, to justify banning speech, that the government provide strong evidence of a compelling interest in preventing the appearance or occurrence of corruption. Where there is uncertainty about the government's interest, "the First Amendment requires us to err on the side of protecting political speech rather than suppressing it." *WRTL*. [T]he Cao Ad is core political speech. The RNC wishes to coordinate with Cao on its broadcast timing, but the Supreme Court has never spoken on what degree of contact makes expressive political speech "coordinated" such that it may be suppressed. The Supreme Court's recent decisions demand much more from the government than it has presented here—essentially nothing. Even if the government were to meet its burden, it seems inconceivable that in this country founded on the hope and reality of free and open political debate, otherwise independent political speech could be banned because its speakers have asked a candidate, "When do we air the ad?"

It is not our place to revisit whether the government may generally regulate coordinated expenditures. Still less is it our place to approve the banning of a specific political ad simply because the Court has held that when coordinated expenditures are generally analogous to paying the candidate's bills, they may be regulated. But when it comes to defining what speech qualifies as coordinated expenditures subject to such regulation—the issue we do have to decide—we should follow Chief Justice Roberts's admonition in *WRTL*:

> [W]e give the benefit of the doubt to speech, not censorship. The First Amendment's command that "Congress shall make no law . . . abridging the freedom of speech" demands at least that.

We respectfully dissent.

BROWN CLEMENT, Circuit Judge, concurring in part and dissenting in part:

I join the Chief Judge's dissent because I believe the Party Expenditure Provision cannot be constitutionally applied to the Cao ad. I write separately to note that I would go further than the Chief Judge in fashioning a standard that protects political speech that is not the functional equivalent of a campaign contribution.

I see no reason that timing alone makes any difference in the constitutional analysis, and question whether a de minimis standard provides a line bright enough to avoid chilling protected speech through the threat of an enforcement action. The Supreme Court has drawn the relevant distinction between an expenditure and a contribution: a contribution "serves as a general expression of support for the candidate and his views," while an expenditure "communicate[s] the underlying basis for the support." *Buckley v. Valeo* (1976). The Court has also identified the goal of the anti-coordination rules: preventing circumvention of the contribution limits by expenditures that amount to simply paying a candidate's bills. A "timing only" standard does nothing to capture the difference between these two constitutionally distinct forms of communication. The same could be said of other standards based on the manner of coordination, such as medium (radio versus television); venue (the local Spanish-language channel versus the soft rock channel); or region (the Lower Ninth Ward versus Uptown New Orleans).

Likewise, a de minimis standard is difficult to apply and interpret. The FEC would be required to develop extensive regulations drawing lines between de minimis and prohibited coordination. Courts attempting to adjudicate the application of these regulations to specific factual situations would find themselves drawn into similar hair splitting. Litigants would be forced to respond to extensive discovery on the substance of their contacts with the candidate. A speaker contemplating engaging in speech such as the Cao ad would face a "burdensome, expert-driven inquiry, with an indeterminate result." *WRTL* (2007). Despite the best intentions of such a standard, "it will unquestionably chill a substantial amount of political speech." *Id.*

What does make a difference in the constitutional analysis, however, is coordination as to the content of the ad. The Cao ad is the RNC's own speech, expressing its views on political issues, and identifying Cao as a candidate who supports those views. Cao did not provide input on its content and was not asked to provide his consent to run the ad. If he had, that would indeed raise a suspicion that the parties were attempting to circumvent the rules against coordination so that the RNC could pay the bill for Cao's speech—the evil at which the coordination rules are aimed.

Accordingly, I would propose a two-pronged standard that is "content-driven," rather than one that turns on the degree of coordination. Specifically, I would propose the following: An advertisement is functionally identical to a contribution only if it is susceptible of no other reasonable interpretation than as a general expression of support for the candidate, and the ad was not generated by the candidate. Under this standard, the speaker could only take refuge in the safe harbor of a content-driven standard if the speech conveys the underlying basis of the support, and was not merely adopted speech indistinguishable from paying a candidate's advertising bills. This approach . . . is clear, objective, and content-driven, and because it is relatively simple for both speakers and regulators to understand and apply, will not chill speech through the threat of litigation. It limits discovery to a factual issue that is relatively easy to ascertain, i.e., whether the ad was generated by or its content approved by the candidate or the political party. It references the fundamental distinction the Court drew between contributions and expenditures in *Buckley*, and exempts from its protection expenditures that amount to a party merely paying a candidate's bills. The standard would also align more closely than other possible standards with the actual definition of a coordinated expenditure, which prohibits spending "*at the request or suggestion of*, a candidate." 2 U.S.C. § 441a(a)(7)(B)(I) (emphasis added).

Applying this standard, the Cao ad is not functionally identical to a campaign contribution. The ad was generated by the RNC. It expresses not merely the kind of generalized sentiment—"Vote for Joseph Cao"—that the Court has described as the hallmark of a contribution, but expresses the RNC's view on important matters of public concern and urges a vote for Cao because he shares the same views. While the "takeaway" message of this advertisement may be one urging support for Cao, the message is anchored and inspired not by the RNC's support for Cao, but by Cao's support for the views expressed by the RNC. The ad thus communicates the underlying basis for the support, making it more like an expenditure protected by strict scrutiny. This is far from the archetypal coordination described in *Buckley*: effectively paying a candidate's advertising bills. The Cao ad can reasonably be interpreted as something other than a general expression of support for a candidate and was not generated by Cao, and as such, strict scrutiny should apply to laws regulating this ad.

The Court has emphasized that political parties have the First Amendment right to speak on political issues and explicitly acknowledged that coordinated expenditures "share some of the constitutionally relevant features of independent expenditures." *Colorado I*. Speech that articulates a set of political views and explains the speaker's support of a candidate in terms of that candidate's endorsement of those views—i.e., speech that conveys the underlying basis of support—is speech that implicates the strongest and most compelling First Amendment interests.

In any case dealing with campaign finance law it is easy to mystify oneself—and one's audience—with talk of "coordination," "circumvention," "functional equivalent," and the like. These bland phrases mask the import of the absolutist position the majority has taken today. The standard I have proposed makes distinctions and is consistent with the Court's often difficult precedents in this area, but it proceeds from a fairly simple impulse: If the First Amendment means anything, it means that political speech is not the same thing as paying a candidate's bills for travel, or salaries, or for hamburgers and balloons. In this case, a group of citizens has banded together to express their views on important public matters. Congress has abridged their freedom to do so. This the Constitution does not permit. I respectfully dissent.

NOTES ON *CAO*

1. Do coordinated expenditures pose the same kind of corruption concern as contributions? Put differently, if political parties and candidates can coordinate as to timing and discuss the content of the party's ad, will this open the door to circumvention of valid contribution limits? That, in essence, is the crux of the debate: Is the coordinated expenditure limitation a needed measure for anticircumvention?

2. Notice how the majority and dissents are in essence talking past each other about what is even in dispute. At oral argument and in postargument briefs, the

Republican Party emphatically conceded that it was not challenging whether this ad was a coordinated ad. They made this concession by stipulating that discussion of the timing of the ad with Cao would qualify the ad as a coordinated expenditure. Why do you think the plaintiffs conceded this point? Was this a wise strategy? And should this concession preclude the court from deciding whether the Cao Ad qualifies as a coordinated expenditure (the majority's position), or, as Chief Judge Jones posits, can the court resolve whether this ad is still "core political speech" that the First Amendment protects?

3. What do you think of the standard Judge Clement proposes? As a lower court of appeals judge, is she in a position to suggest such a standard? More importantly, is there a meaningful way to distinguish between a political party's "own speech" and speech that it coordinates with a candidate? Put differently, is there a way to distinguish "good" coordination from "bad" coordination?

4. The legality of spending by nominally independent entities will likely be fodder for litigation in the coming years. During the 2016 presidential election campaign, both Hillary Clinton and Donald Trump had several "independent" organizations that supported their candidacies. The 2020 election between Trump and Joe Biden was no different. These political action committees, known as Super PACs, were created in the wake of the Supreme Court's decision in *Citizens United* (discussed below), and their purpose was to make only independent expenditures (that is, not on behalf of or coordinated with the candidate or campaign) for their "own" electioneering. Should this activity be considered "coordinated" spending? Note that former aides of both candidates created the Super PACs to support those candidacies. In theory, none of the Super PACs coordinated their spending with the campaigns they supported. Is it realistic to think that the former aides, who were personally close to each candidate, were not discussing their campaign strategies or spending initiatives with the campaign? How should the Federal Election Commission or the courts determine if this kind of spending is "coordinated" and therefore should be subject to the expenditure limitations of federal law? If you were a lawyer for one of these Super PACs, what kinds of "walls" or other strategies would you advise to ensure that the spending is not considered "coordinated"? (We will revisit these issues at the end of this Part after the *Speech Now* case.)

4. *Corporate and Union Independent Expenditures*

The Supreme Court's 2010 opinion in *Citizens United v. FEC* was probably the most controversial decision since *Bush v. Gore* (which we will read in Part IV of this book), and perhaps even more so. This case considered the constitutionality of BCRA's ban on corporations and unions using money from their general treasuries to fund their own campaign ads.

The opinion spanned 183 pages. We will consider the opinion in three parts. First, we will look at Justice Kennedy's majority opinion for five Justices (the typical "conservatives"—Roberts, Scalia, Kennedy, Thomas, and Alito). Second, we will read Justice Stevens's lengthy dissent for the four traditionally "liberal" Justices (Stevens, Breyer, Ginsburg, and Sotomayor). Finally, later in this Part, we will consider a portion of Justice Kennedy's majority opinion and Justice Thomas's dissent with respect to the law's disclosure and disclaimer requirements.

Some background may be useful before reading the opinions. Congress first prohibited corporations from making contributions to candidates in 1907 in the Tillman Act. As Justice Stevens says in his dissent in *Citizens United*, Congress was concerned with "the enormous power corporations had come to wield in federal elections, with the accompanying threat of both actual corruption and a public perception of corruption" and "a respect for the interest of shareholders and members in preventing the use of their money to support candidates they opposed." In 1947, Congress passed the Taft-Hartley Act, which extended the prohibition on corporate support of candidates to include independent expenditures.

As you know, Congress banned individuals from making more than $1,000 of independent expenditures in FECA, and the Court in *Buckley* struck down that provision as unconstitutional. Federal law (beginning with the Taft-Hartley Act of 1947) also included a separate ban on corporate and union independent expenditures, but the Court did not consider that provision in *Buckley*.

The Court subsequently rendered several opinions on laws involving corporate independent expenditure bans. In *First Nat. Bank of Boston v. Bellotti* (1978), by a 5-4 vote, the Court struck down a Massachusetts law that criminalized a corporate expenditure advocating the adoption or defeat of a referendum or other ballot question submitted directly to the voters. The particular ballot question in the case concerned whether to raise taxes, and the bank wanted to spend its money to broadcast ads opposing this measure. In essence, the Court said that Massachusetts could not limit corporate independent expenditures in ballot initiative campaigns because there was little concern about corruption in that type of election. The Court did not address whether the state could ban corporate independent expenditures for candidate elections.

Then, in *Federal Election Comm'n v. Massachusetts Citizens for Life, Inc.* (1986) (*MCFL*), the Court carved out an as-applied exception to FECA's ban on corporate independent expenditures, determining that it could not validly apply to nonprofit corporations that (1) were formed for the sole purpose of promoting political ideas, (2) did not engage in business activities, and (3) did not accept contributions from for-profit corporations or labor unions. The Court determined that this type of nonprofit organization did not pose a danger of corruption that would justify the ban, or at least that the First Amendment interests in permitting this type of entity to engage in the advocacy outweighed whatever risks of corruption the express electoral activity might create.

In *Austin v. Michigan Chamber of Commerce* (1990) (5-4), the Court upheld a Michigan law that banned corporations from using their general treasury funds to make independent expenditures. The case involved the Michigan Chamber of Commerce, which could not qualify for the First Amendment protection identified in *MCFL* because the Chamber accepted funds from for-profit business corporations. The majority opinion in *Austin* was concerned with the ability of business corporations to use the wealth they aggregated from their business activities, with the benefit of the corporate form, to unduly influence public debate over which candidates deserve election to public office. *Austin* was widely recognized as a major decision that permitted the regulation of campaign finance in the interest of protecting the perceived integrity of the electoral process. Opponents of *Austin*, including Justices Kennedy and Scalia dissenting in that case, saw it as anathema to the free marketplace of political ideas—in which corporations as much as individual citizens, in their view, are entitled to participate.

The next major development was the passage of BCRA in 2003. As the *Citizens United* opinion explains, that law prohibited corporations and unions from using their general treasury funds to make "electioneering communications" within 30 days of a primary or 60 days of a general election. In this respect, BCRA extended the prohibition in Taft-Hartley from the narrower category of express electoral advocacy (considered by some at the time to be limited to ads containing specific "magic words" like "Vote for" or "Vote against") to the broader category of "electioneering communications" as defined in the new statute. Part of the facial challenge to BCRA in *McConnell* (which you read above regarding soft money) included an argument that the electioneering communications ban was unconstitutional. The Court upheld the law on its face, by an unexpected 5-4 vote (with Justice O'Connor providing the key fifth vote for the majority even though she had dissented in *Austin*), and Justice Kennedy writing a vigorous dissent.

Then, in *Federal Election Comm'n v. Wisconsin Right to Life, Inc.* (2007) (*WRTL*), the Court sustained an as-applied challenge to the law. The Court determined that the law could not apply validly to a nonprofit corporation's "issue advocacy." The Court stated that the "electioneering communication" ban could apply only to "express advocacy," which the Court defined as an ad that is "susceptible of no reasonable interpretation other than as an appeal to vote for or against a specific candidate." Thus, the opinion in *WRTL* significantly narrowed the scope of BCRA's ban on corporate independent expenditures, saying that it applied only to a corporation's "express ads" and not to their "issue ads," thereby essentially confining the statutory prohibition to what was enacted in the 1947 Taft-Hartley law rather than the broader BCRA formulation. This set up the Court's decision in *Citizens United*, in which it sustained a facial challenge to the law as violating the First Amendment, thus overruling *Austin* as well as a portion of *McConnell* and rendering the Taft-Hartley law (and not just BCRA) unconstitutional as written.

Citizens United originally was another attempt to chip away at the law incrementally through an as-applied challenge, at least as the lawyers who filed the complaint initially intended. The plaintiff nonprofit corporation, which had aired a "video-on-demand" film critical of Hillary Clinton at the time she was running for President in 2008, sought to create another exception similar to the one from *MCFL* or *WRTL*. The Court heard oral argument in the case in March 2009. On the last day of the Term, the Supreme Court declined to issue an opinion and instead set the case for a new oral argument for September 2009 (before the new Term was to start). To prepare for the re-argument, the Court asked the parties to file additional briefs on whether it should overrule its decisions in *Austin* and *McConnell*. The Court therefore signaled that it would consider the broader question of the statute's facial constitutionality, instead of whether it should merely create another narrow as-applied exception. The re-argument was Justice Sotomayor's first case on the Court. It was also Elena Kagan's first argument as Solicitor General (and first ever court argument in any case) before she eventually became a Justice a year later.

What changed between *Austin* (decided in 1990), *McConnell* (decided in 2003), and the Court's consideration of *Citizens United* in 2009? Supporters of the majority's decision would note that *Austin* and *McConnell* were simply wrong from the start and that the Court merely corrected its error. Cynics of the decision might counter that the personnel on the Court changed; in particular, Justice Alito, who voted with the majority in *Citizens United* to strike down the law, replaced Justice O'Connor, who had voted to uphold the law in *McConnell*.

Also in the background of this case was the Supreme Court's decision the year before in *Caperton v. Massey Coal*, in which it ruled, 5-4, that the failure of an elected judge to recuse himself from a case that involved one of his main donors "created a constitutionally intolerable probability of actual bias." *Caperton v. A.T. Massey Coal Co.* (2009). This case was not about federal campaign finance law but still provided some insights on the Court's views regarding independent expenditures and their actual or apparent corrupting influence. The donor had contributed the maximum amount to the judge's campaign for the West Virginia Supreme Court and also had given almost $2.5 million to a "527 organization" (a tax-exempt political group that is technically unaffiliated with a candidate) that ran ads targeting the judge's opponent. That is, the donor helped to fund independent expenditures that assisted the judge in his election. The Court found that the judge's failure to recuse in a case involving the donor's company raised a specter of *quid pro quo* corruption, even if there was no evidence that the judge's vote in the case was because of the favorable expenditures. Thus, the Court recognized that independent expenditures could bring about an appearance of corruption, at least when it involved a judicial election. But this was a due process case about the appearance of fairness in litigation based on donations to a judge, not the rights of an individual or corporation to make those independent expenditures. The remedy in *Caperton* was not to limit the expenditures themselves but to require the judge to recuse. Justice Kennedy authored the majority opinion, joined by the four typically "liberal" Justices; he also wrote the majority opinion (joined by the four "conservatives") in *Citizens United* that invalidated the independent expenditure limitation. Essentially, then, Justice Kennedy's vote made the difference in requiring recusal in *Caperton* but striking down the independent expenditure limitation in *Citizens United*. Given that Justice Kennedy wrote both opinions, think about how he might reconcile these views.

As you are reading *Citizens United*, be sure to understand the government's main arguments and why the Court rejects them. What were the justifications behind the law? Why were they insufficient? Also consider the implications of the holding: that corporations and unions have a similar First Amendment right to freedom of speech as do individuals in the political arena. What impact will this have on campaigns? Then consider Justice Stevens's response in his dissent. Was there a narrower ground to resolve this dispute? Were the government's stated interests valid? Did the government make any strategic mistakes in arguing this case? Finally, consider the role of stare decisis. Was the Court justified in overruling precedents that were only seven (*McConnell*) and twenty (*Austin*) years old?

Citizens United v. FEC

558 U.S. 310 (2010)

Justice KENNEDY delivered the opinion of the Court.

Federal law prohibits corporations and unions from using their general treasury funds to make independent expenditures for speech defined as an "electioneering communication" or for speech expressly advocating the election or defeat of a candidate. 2 U.S.C. § 441b. Limits on electioneering communications were upheld in *McConnell v. Federal Election Comm'n* (2003). The holding of *McConnell* rested to a large extent on an earlier case, *Austin v. Michigan Chamber of Commerce* (1990). *Austin* had held that political speech may be banned based on the speaker's corporate identity.

In this case we are asked to reconsider *Austin* and, in effect, *McConnell.* It has been noted that "*Austin* was a significant departure from ancient First Amendment principles," *Federal Election Comm'n v. Wisconsin Right to Life, Inc.* (2007) *(WRTL)* (Scalia, J., concurring in part and concurring in judgment). We agree with that conclusion and hold that *stare decisis* does not compel the continued acceptance of *Austin.* The Government may regulate corporate political speech through disclaimer and disclosure requirements, but it may not suppress that speech altogether.

I

A

Citizens United is a nonprofit corporation [with] an annual budget of about $12 million. Most of its funds are from donations by individuals; but, in addition, it accepts a small portion of its funds from for-profit corporations.

In January 2008, Citizens United released a film entitled *Hillary: The Movie.* We refer to the film as *Hillary.* It is a 90-minute documentary about then-Senator Hillary Clinton, who was a candidate in the Democratic Party's 2008 Presidential primary elections. *Hillary* mentions Senator Clinton by name and depicts interviews with political commentators and other persons, most of them quite critical of Senator Clinton. *Hillary* was released in theaters and on DVD, but Citizens United wanted to increase distribution by making it available through video-on-demand.

Video-on-demand allows digital cable subscribers to select programming from various menus, including movies, television shows, sports, news, and music. The viewer can watch the program at any time and can elect to rewind or pause the program. In December 2007, a cable company offered, for a payment of $1.2 million, to make *Hillary* available on a video-on-demand channel called "Elections '08." Some video-on-demand services require viewers to pay a small fee to view a selected program, but here the proposal was to make *Hillary* available to viewers free of charge.

B

Before the Bipartisan Campaign Reform Act of 2002 (BCRA), federal law prohibited—and still does prohibit—corporations and unions from using general treasury funds to [either (1)] make direct contributions to candidates or [(2) make] independent expenditures that expressly advocate the election or defeat of a candidate, through any form of media, in connection with certain qualified federal elections. 2 U.S.C. § 441b (2000 ed.); *see McConnell*; *Federal Election Comm'n v. Massachusetts Citizens for Life, Inc.* (*MCFL*) (1986). BCRA § 203 amended § 441b to prohibit [the use of corporate or union general treasury funds to be used for] any "electioneering communication" as well. 2 U.S.C. § 441b(b)(2) (2006 ed.). An electioneering communication is defined as "any broadcast, cable, or satellite communication" that "refers to a clearly identified candidate for Federal office" and is made within 30 days of a primary or 60 days of a general election. § 434(f)(3)(A). The Federal Election Commission's (FEC) regulations further define an electioneering communication as a communication that is "publicly distributed." 11 CFR § 100.29(a)(2) (2009). "In the case of a candidate for nomination for President . . . *publicly distributed* means" that the communication "[c]an be received by 50,000 or more persons in a State where a primary election . . . is being held within 30 days." § 100.29(b)(3)(ii). Corporations and unions are barred from using their general treasury funds for express advocacy or electioneering communications. They may establish, however, a "separate segregated fund" (known as a political action committee, or PAC) for these purposes. 2 U.S.C. § 441b(b)(2). The moneys received by the segregated fund are limited to donations from stockholders and employees of the corporation or, in the case of unions, members of the union.

C

Citizens United wanted to make *Hillary* available through video-on-demand within 30 days of the 2008 primary elections. It feared, however, that both the film and the ads would be covered by § 441b's ban on corporate-funded independent expenditures, thus subjecting the corporation to civil and criminal penalties under § 437g. In December 2007, Citizens United sought declaratory and injunctive relief against the FEC. It argued that (1) § 441b is unconstitutional as applied to *Hillary*; and (2) BCRA's disclaimer and disclosure requirements, BCRA §§ 201 and 311, are unconstitutional as applied to *Hillary* and to three ads for the movie.

II

Before considering whether *Austin* should be overruled, we first address whether Citizens United's claim that § 441b cannot be applied to *Hillary* may be resolved on other, narrower grounds.

A

[Omitted.]

B

[Omitted.]

C

Citizens United contends that § 441b should be invalidated as applied to movies shown through video-on-demand, arguing that this delivery system has a lower risk of distorting the political process than do television ads. On what we might call conventional television, advertising spots reach viewers who have chosen a channel or a program for reasons unrelated to the advertising. With video-on-demand, by contrast, the viewer selects a program after taking "a series of affirmative steps": subscribing to cable; navigating through various menus; and selecting the program.

While some means of communication may be less effective than others at influencing the public in different contexts, any effort by the Judiciary to decide which means of communications are to be preferred for the particular type of message and speaker would raise questions as to the courts' own lawful authority. Substantial questions would arise if courts were to begin saying what means of speech should be preferred or disfavored. And in all events, those differentiations might soon prove to be irrelevant or outdated by technologies that are in rapid flux.

Courts, too, are bound by the First Amendment. We must decline to draw, and then redraw, constitutional lines based on the particular media or technology used to disseminate political speech from a particular speaker. It must be noted, moreover, that this undertaking would require substantial litigation over an extended time, all to interpret a law that beyond doubt discloses serious First Amendment flaws. The interpretive process itself would create an inevitable, pervasive, and serious risk of chilling protected speech pending the drawing of fine distinctions that, in the end, would themselves be questionable.

D

Citizens United also asks us to carve out an exception to § 441b's expenditure ban for nonprofit corporate political speech funded overwhelmingly by individuals. As an alternative to reconsidering *Austin,* the Government also seems to prefer this approach. This line of analysis, however, would be unavailing.

In *MCFL,* the Court found unconstitutional § 441b's restrictions on corporate expenditures as applied to nonprofit corporations that were formed for the sole purpose of promoting political ideas, did not engage in business activities, and did not accept contributions from for-profit corporations or labor unions. Citizens United does not qualify for the *MCFL* exemption, however, since some funds used to make the movie were donations from for-profit corporations.

The Government suggests we could [extend *MCFL* to nonprofits that receive only a negligible amount of funds from for-profit corporations]. If the Court decided to create a *de minimis* exception to *MCFL,* the result would be to allow for-profit corporate general treasury funds to be spent for independent expenditures that support candidates. There is no principled basis for doing this without rewriting *Austin*'s holding that the Government can restrict corporate independent expenditures for political speech.

Though it is true that the Court should construe statutes as necessary to avoid constitutional questions, [here this approach] would be difficult to take in view of the language of the statute. In addition to those difficulties the Government's suggestion is troubling for still another reason. The Government does not say that it agrees with the interpretation it wants us to consider. *See* Supp. Brief for Appellee 3, n. 1 ("Some courts" have implied a *de minimis* exception, and "appellant would appear to be covered by these decisions"). Presumably it would find textual difficulties in this approach too. The Government, like any party, can make arguments in the alternative; but it ought to say if there is merit to an alternative proposal instead of merely suggesting it. This is especially true in the context of the First Amendment. As the Government stated, this case "would require a remand" to apply a *de minimis* standard. Tr. of Oral Arg. 39 (Sept. 9, 2009). Applying this standard would thus require case-by-case determinations. But archetypical political speech would be chilled in the meantime. " 'First Amendment freedoms need breathing space to survive.' " *WRTL* (opinion of Roberts, C.J.) (quoting *NAACP v. Button* (1963)). We decline to adopt an interpretation that requires intricate case-by-case determinations to verify whether political speech is banned, especially if we are convinced that, in the end, this corporation has a constitutional right to speak on this subject.

E

As the foregoing analysis confirms, the Court cannot resolve this case on a narrower ground without chilling political speech, speech that is central to the meaning and purpose of the First Amendment. It is not judicial restraint to accept an unsound, narrow argument just so the Court can avoid another argument with broader implications. Indeed, a court would be remiss in performing its duties were it to accept an unsound principle merely to avoid the necessity of making a broader ruling. Here, the lack of a valid basis for an alternative ruling requires full consideration of the continuing effect of the speech suppression upheld in *Austin*.

III

The First Amendment provides that "Congress shall make no law . . . abridging the freedom of speech." The law before us is an outright ban, backed by criminal sanctions. Section 441b makes it a felony for all corporations—including nonprofit advocacy corporations—either to expressly advocate the election or defeat of candidates or to broadcast electioneering communications within 30 days of a primary election and 60 days of a general election. Thus, the following acts would all be felonies under § 441b: The Sierra Club runs an ad, within the crucial phase of 60 days before the general election, that exhorts the public to disapprove of a Congressman who favors logging in national forests; the National Rifle Association publishes a book urging the public to vote for the challenger because the incumbent U.S. Senator supports a handgun ban; and the American Civil Liberties Union creates a Web site telling the public to vote for a Presidential candidate in light of that candidate's defense of free speech. These prohibitions are classic examples of censorship.

Section 441b is a ban on corporate speech notwithstanding the fact that a PAC created by a corporation can still speak. A PAC is a separate association from the corporation. So the PAC exemption from § 441b's expenditure ban does not allow corporations to speak. Even if a PAC could somehow allow a corporation to speak—and it does not—the option to form PACs does not alleviate the First Amendment problems with § 441b. PACs are burdensome alternatives; they are expensive to administer and subject to extensive regulations. For example, every PAC must appoint a treasurer, forward donations to the treasurer promptly, keep detailed records of the identities of the persons making donations, preserve receipts for three years, and file an organization statement and report changes to this information within 10 days.

PACs have to comply with these regulations just to speak. This might explain why fewer than 2,000 of the millions of corporations in this country have PACs. PACs, furthermore, must exist before they can speak. Given the onerous restrictions, a corporation may not be able to establish a PAC in time to make its views known regarding candidates and issues in a current campaign.

Section 441b's prohibition on corporate independent expenditures is thus a ban on speech. As a "restriction on the amount of money a person or group can spend on political communication during a campaign," that statute "necessarily reduces the quantity of expression by restricting the number of issues discussed, the depth of their exploration, and the size of the audience reached." *Buckley v. Valeo* (1976). Were the Court to uphold these restrictions, the Government could repress speech by silencing certain voices at any of the various points in the speech process. If § 441b applied to individuals, no one would believe that it is merely a time, place, or manner restriction on speech. Its purpose and effect are to silence entities whose voices the Government deems to be suspect.

Speech is an essential mechanism of democracy, for it is the means to hold officials accountable to the people. The right of citizens to inquire, to hear, to speak, and to use information to reach consensus is a precondition to enlightened self-government and a necessary means to protect it. The First Amendment "'has its fullest and most urgent application' to speech uttered during a campaign for political office." *Eu v. San Francisco County Democratic Central Comm.* (1989) (quoting *Monitor Patriot Co. v. Roy* (1971)).

For these reasons, political speech must prevail against laws that would suppress it, whether by design or inadvertence. Laws that burden political speech are "subject to strict scrutiny," which requires the Government to prove that the restriction "furthers a compelling interest and is narrowly tailored to achieve that interest." *WRTL* (opinion of Roberts, C.J.). While it might be maintained that political speech simply cannot be banned or restricted as a categorical matter, the quoted language from *WRTL* provides a sufficient framework for protecting the relevant First Amendment interests in this case. We shall employ it here.

Premised on mistrust of governmental power, the First Amendment stands against attempts to disfavor certain subjects or viewpoints. Prohibited, too, are restrictions distinguishing among different speakers, allowing speech by some but not others. *See First Nat. Bank of Boston v. Bellotti* (1978). As instruments to censor, these categories are interrelated: Speech restrictions based on the identity of the speaker are all too often simply a means to control content.

Quite apart from the purpose or effect of regulating content, moreover, the Government may commit a constitutional wrong when by law it identifies certain preferred speakers. By taking the right to speak from some and giving it to others, the Government deprives the disadvantaged person or class of the right to use speech to strive to establish worth, standing, and respect for the speaker's voice. The Government may not by these means deprive the public of the right and privilege to determine for itself what speech and speakers are worthy of consideration. The First Amendment protects speech and speaker, and the ideas that flow from each.

The Court has upheld a narrow class of speech restrictions that operate to the disadvantage of certain persons, but these rulings were based on an interest in allowing governmental entities to perform their functions. *See, e.g., Bethel School Dist. No. 403 v. Fraser* (1986) (protecting the "function of public school education"); *Jones v. North Carolina Prisoners' Labor Union, Inc.* (1977) (furthering "the legitimate penological objectives of the corrections system"); *Parker v. Levy* (1974) (ensuring "the capacity of the Government to discharge its [military] responsibilities"); *Civil Service Comm'n v. Letter Carriers* (1973) ("[F]ederal service should depend upon meritorious performance rather than political service"). The corporate independent expenditures at issue in this case, however, would not interfere with governmental functions, so these cases are inapposite.* These precedents stand only for the proposition that there are certain governmental functions that cannot operate without some restrictions on particular kinds of speech. By contrast, it is inherent in the nature of the political process that voters must be free to obtain information from diverse sources in order to determine how to cast their votes. At least before *Austin*, the Court had not allowed the exclusion of a class of speakers from the general public dialogue.

We find no basis for the proposition that, in the context of political speech, the Government may impose restrictions on certain disfavored speakers. Both history and logic lead us to this conclusion.

A

1

The Court has recognized that First Amendment protection extends to corporations. *Bellotti.* This protection has been extended by explicit holdings to the context of political speech. Under the rationale of these precedents, political speech does not lose First Amendment protection "simply because its source is a corporation." *Bellotti.* The Court has thus rejected the argument that political speech of corporations or other associations should be treated differently under the First Amendment simply because such associations are not "natural persons." [*Id.*]

[The Court discussed some of its previous cases that touched upon this issue, but none had dealt directly with the constitutional question regarding a ban on corporate independent expenditures. In most of these cases, a separate concurring or dissenting opinion had mentioned that those Justices would reach the constitutional issues.]

2

[The Court discussed in detail two of its prior cases relating to this issue. In *Buckley v. Valeo*, the Court struck down an independent expenditure ban. The *Buckley* Court, however, "did not consider § 610's separate ban on corporate and union independent expenditures. Had § 610 been challenged in the wake of *Buckley*, however, it could not have been squared with the reasoning and analysis of that precedent."

Four months after *Buckley* was decided, Congress recodified § 610's corporate and union expenditure ban at 2 U.S.C. § 441b, which is the precursor to the law being challenged in *Citizens United.*

Shortly after deciding *Buckley*, the Court in *First Nat. Bank of Boston v. Bellotti* (1978) struck down a state-law prohibition on corporate independent expenditures

* [Ask yourself whether the Court would distinguish a case involving a corporation with particularly extensive ties to the government; for example, a banking corporation that is a member of the Federal Reserve system, or a defense contractor that depends on the military for most of its revenues. *Cf. Lebron v. National Railroad Passenger Corporation* (1995) (holding that Amtrak, although technically a corporation, counts as part of the federal government for First Amendment purposes). *Lebron* also explores the history of governmental corporations and explains why they must be treated to a functional rather than a formalistic analysis under the First Amendment.—Eds.]

related to referenda (as opposed to candidate elections). "*Bellotti* did not address the constitutionality of the State's ban on corporate independent expenditures to support candidates. In our view, however, that restriction would have been unconstitutional under *Bellotti*'s central principle: that the First Amendment does not allow political speech restrictions based on a speaker's corporate identity."]

3

Thus the law stood until *Austin*. *Austin* "uph[eld] a direct restriction on the independent expenditure of funds for political speech for the first time in [this Court's] history." [*Austin v. Michigan Chamber of Commerce* (1990)] (Kennedy, J., dissenting). There, the Michigan Chamber of Commerce sought to use general treasury funds to run a newspaper ad supporting a specific candidate. Michigan law, however, prohibited corporate independent expenditures that supported or opposed any candidate for state office. A violation of the law was punishable as a felony. The Court sustained the speech prohibition.

To bypass *Buckley* and *Bellotti*, the *Austin* Court identified a new governmental interest in limiting political speech: an antidistortion interest. *Austin* found a compelling governmental interest in preventing "the corrosive and distorting effects of immense aggregations of wealth that are accumulated with the help of the corporate form and that have little or no correlation to the public's support for the corporation's political ideas."

B

The Court is thus confronted with conflicting lines of precedent: a pre-*Austin* line that forbids restrictions on political speech based on the speaker's corporate identity and a post-*Austin* line that permits them. No case before *Austin* had held that Congress could prohibit independent expenditures for political speech based on the speaker's corporate identity. Before *Austin* Congress had enacted legislation for this purpose, and the Government urged the same proposition before this Court [but never] did the Court adopt the proposition.

In its defense of the corporate-speech restrictions in § 441b, the Government notes the antidistortion rationale on which *Austin* and its progeny rest in part, yet it all but abandons reliance upon it. It argues instead that two other compelling interests support *Austin*'s holding that corporate expenditure restrictions are constitutional: an anticorruption interest and a shareholder-protection interest. We consider the three points in turn.

1

As for *Austin*'s antidistortion rationale, the Government does little to defend it. And with good reason, for the rationale cannot support § 441b.

If the First Amendment has any force, it prohibits Congress from fining or jailing citizens, or associations of citizens, for simply engaging in political speech. If the antidistortion rationale were to be accepted, however, it would permit Government to ban political speech simply because the speaker is an association that has taken on the corporate form. The Government contends that *Austin* permits it to ban corporate expenditures for almost all forms of communication stemming from a corporation. If *Austin* were correct, the Government could prohibit a corporation from expressing political views in media beyond those presented here, such as by printing books. The Government responds "that the FEC has never applied this statute to a book," and if it did, "there would be quite [a] good as-applied challenge." Tr. of Oral Arg. 65 (Sept. 9, 2009). This troubling assertion of brooding governmental power cannot be reconciled with the confidence and stability in civic discourse that the First Amendment must secure.

Political speech is "indispensable to decisionmaking in a democracy, and this is no less true because the speech comes from a corporation rather than an individual." *Bellotti.* This protection for speech is inconsistent with *Austin*'s antidistortion rationale. *Austin* sought to defend the antidistortion rationale as a means to prevent corporations from obtaining " 'an unfair advantage in the political marketplace' " by using " 'resources amassed in the economic marketplace.' " *Austin* (quoting *MCFL*). But *Buckley* rejected the premise that the Government has an interest "in equalizing the relative ability of individuals and groups to influence the outcome of elections." *Buckley* was specific in stating that "the skyrocketing cost of political campaigns" could not sustain the governmental prohibition. The First Amendment's protections do not depend on the speaker's "financial ability to engage in public discussion." [*Id.*]

Either as support for its antidistortion rationale or as a further argument, the *Austin* majority undertook to distinguish wealthy individuals from corporations on the ground that "[s]tate law grants corporations special advantages—such as limited liability, perpetual life, and favorable treatment of the accumulation and distribution of assets." This does not suffice, however, to allow laws prohibiting speech. "It is rudimentary that the State cannot exact as the price of those special advantages the forfeiture of First Amendment rights." *Id.* (Scalia, J., dissenting).

It is irrelevant for purposes of the First Amendment that corporate funds may "have little or no correlation to the public's support for the corporation's political ideas." *Id.* (majority opinion). All speakers, including individuals and the media, use money amassed from the economic marketplace to fund their speech. The First Amendment protects the resulting speech, even if it was enabled by economic transactions with persons or entities who disagree with the speaker's ideas.

Austin's antidistortion rationale would produce the dangerous, and unacceptable, consequence that Congress could ban political speech of media corporations. Media corporations are now exempt from § 441b's ban on corporate expenditures. *See* 2 U.S.C. §§ 431(9)(B)(i), 434(f)(3)(B)(i). Yet media corporations accumulate wealth with the help of the corporate form, the largest media corporations have "immense aggregations of wealth," and the views expressed by media corporations often "have little or no correlation to the public's support" for those views. *Austin.* Thus, under the Government's reasoning, wealthy media corporations could have their voices diminished to put them on par with other media entities. There is no precedent for permitting this under the First Amendment.

The media exemption discloses further difficulties with the law now under consideration. There is no precedent supporting laws that attempt to distinguish between corporations which are deemed to be exempt as media corporations and those which are not. "We have consistently rejected the proposition that the institutional press has any constitutional privilege beyond that of other speakers." *Id.* (Scalia, J., dissenting). With the advent of the Internet and the decline of print and broadcast media, moreover, the line between the media and others who wish to comment on political and social issues becomes far more blurred.

The law's exception for media corporations is, on its own terms, all but an admission of the invalidity of the antidistortion rationale. And the exemption results in a further, separate reason for finding this law invalid: Again by its own terms, the law exempts some corporations but covers others, even though both have the need or the motive to communicate their views. The exemption applies to media corporations owned or controlled by corporations that have diverse and substantial investments and participate in endeavors other than news. So even assuming the most doubtful proposition that a news organization has a right to speak when others do not, the exemption would allow a conglomerate that owns both a media business and an unrelated business to influence or control the media in order to advance its overall business interest. At the same time, some other corporation, with an identical business interest but no media outlet in its ownership structure, would be forbidden to speak or inform the public about the same issue. This differential treatment cannot be squared with the First Amendment.

Austin interferes with the "open marketplace" of ideas protected by the First Amendment. It permits the Government to ban the political speech of millions of associations of citizens. *See* Statistics of Income 2 (5.8 million for-profit corporations filed 2006 tax returns). Most of these are small corporations without large amounts of wealth. *See* Supp. Brief for Chamber of Commerce of the United States of America as *Amicus Curiae* 1, 3 (96% of the 3 million businesses that belong to the U.S. Chamber of Commerce have fewer than 100 employees); M. Keightley, Congressional Research Service Report for Congress, Business Organizational Choices: Taxation and Responses to Legislative Changes 10 (2009) (more than 75% of corporations whose income is taxed under federal law, see 26 U.S.C. § 301, have less than $1 million in receipts per year). This fact belies the Government's argument that the statute is justified on the ground that it prevents the "distorting effects of immense aggregations of wealth." *Austin.* It is not even aimed at amassed wealth.

The purpose and effect of this law is to prevent corporations, including small and nonprofit corporations, from presenting both facts and opinions to the public. This makes *Austin*'s antidistortion rationale all the more an aberration. "[T]he First Amendment protects the right of corporations to petition legislative and administrative bodies." *Bellotti.* Corporate executives and employees counsel Members of Congress and Presidential administrations on many issues, as a matter of routine and often in private. An *amici* brief filed on behalf of Montana and 25 other States notes that lobbying and corporate communications with elected officials occur on a regular basis. When that phenomenon is coupled with § 441b, the result is that smaller or nonprofit corporations cannot raise a voice to object when other corporations, including those with vast wealth, are cooperating with the Government. That cooperation may sometimes be voluntary, or it may be at the demand of a Government official who uses his or her authority, influence, and power to threaten corporations to support the Government's policies. Those kinds of interactions are often unknown and unseen. The speech that § 441b forbids, though, is public, and all can judge its content and purpose. References to massive corporate treasuries should not mask the real operation of this law. Rhetoric ought not obscure reality.

Even if § 441b's expenditure ban were constitutional, wealthy corporations could still lobby elected officials, although smaller corporations may not have the resources to do so. And wealthy individuals and unincorporated associations can spend unlimited amounts on independent expenditures. Yet certain disfavored associations of citizens—those that have taken on the corporate form—are penalized for engaging in the same political speech.

When Government seeks to use its full power, including the criminal law, to command where a person may get his or her information or what distrusted source he or she may not hear, it uses censorship to control thought. This is unlawful. The First Amendment confirms the freedom to think for ourselves.

2

What we have said also shows the invalidity of other arguments made by the Government. For the most part relinquishing the antidistortion rationale, the Government falls back on the argument that corporate political speech can be banned in order to prevent corruption or its appearance. In *Buckley*, the Court found this interest "sufficiently important" to allow limits on contributions but did not extend that reasoning to expenditure limits. When *Buckley* examined an expenditure ban, it found "that the governmental interest in preventing corruption and the appearance of corruption [was] inadequate to justify [the ban] on independent expenditures."

With regard to large direct contributions, *Buckley* reasoned that they could be given "to secure a political *quid pro quo*," and that "the scope of such pernicious practices can never be reliably ascertained." The practices *Buckley* noted would be covered by bribery laws, *see, e.g.*, 18 U.S.C. § 201, if a *quid pro quo* arrangement were proved. The Court, in consequence, has noted that restrictions on direct contributions are preventative, because few if any contributions to candidates will involve *quid pro quo* arrangements. The *Buckley* Court, nevertheless, sustained limits on direct contributions in order to ensure against the reality or appearance of corruption. That case did not extend this rationale to independent expenditures, and the Court does not do so here.

"The absence of prearrangement and coordination of an expenditure with the candidate or his agent not only undermines the value of the expenditure to the candidate, but also alleviates the danger that expenditures will be given as a *quid pro quo* for improper commitments from the candidate." *Buckley* (independent expenditures have a "substantially diminished potential for abuse"). Limits on independent expenditures, such as § 441b, have a chilling effect extending well beyond the Government's interest in preventing *quid pro quo* corruption. The anticorruption interest is not sufficient to displace the speech here in question. Indeed, 26 States do not restrict independent expenditures by for-profit corporations. The Government does not claim that these expenditures have corrupted the political process in those States.

When *Buckley* identified a sufficiently important governmental interest in preventing corruption or the appearance of corruption, that interest was limited to *quid pro quo* corruption. The fact that speakers may have influence over or access to elected officials does not mean that these officials are corrupt:

> "Favoritism and influence are not . . . avoidable in representative politics. It is in the nature of an elected representative to favor certain policies,

and, by necessary corollary, to favor the voters and contributors who support those policies. It is well understood that a substantial and legitimate reason, if not the only reason, to cast a vote for, or to make a contribution to, one candidate over another is that the candidate will respond by producing those political outcomes the supporter favors. Democracy is premised on responsiveness." *McConnell* (opinion of Kennedy, J.).

Reliance on a "generic favoritism or influence theory . . . is at odds with standard First Amendment analyses because it is unbounded and susceptible to no limiting principle." *Id.*

The appearance of influence or access, furthermore, will not cause the electorate to lose faith in our democracy. By definition, an independent expenditure is political speech presented to the electorate that is not coordinated with a candidate. The fact that a corporation, or any other speaker, is willing to spend money to try to persuade voters presupposes that the people have the ultimate influence over elected officials. This is inconsistent with any suggestion that the electorate will refuse " 'to take part in democratic governance' " because of additional political speech made by a corporation or any other speaker. *McConnell.*

The *McConnell* record was "over 100,000 pages" long, yet it "does not have any direct examples of votes being exchanged for . . . expenditures." [Citation to lower court opinion] (opinion of Kollar-Kotelly, J.). This confirms *Buckley*'s reasoning that independent expenditures do not lead to, or create the appearance of, *quid pro quo* corruption. In fact, there is only scant evidence that independent expenditures even ingratiate. Ingratiation and access, in any event, are not corruption. The BCRA record establishes that certain donations to political parties, called "soft money," were made to gain access to elected officials. This case, however, is about independent expenditures, not soft money. When Congress finds that a problem exists, we must give that finding due deference; but Congress may not choose an unconstitutional remedy. If elected officials succumb to improper influences from independent expenditures; if they surrender their best judgment; and if they put expediency before principle, then surely there is cause for concern. We must give weight to attempts by Congress to seek to dispel either the appearance or the reality of these influences. The remedies enacted by law, however, must comply with the First Amendment; and, it is our law and our tradition that more speech, not less, is the governing rule. An outright ban on corporate political speech during the critical preelection period is not a permissible remedy. Here Congress has created categorical bans on speech that are asymmetrical to preventing *quid pro quo* corruption.

3

The Government contends further that corporate independent expenditures can be limited because of its interest in protecting dissenting shareholders from being compelled to fund corporate political speech. This asserted interest, like *Austin*'s antidistortion rationale, would allow the Government to ban the political speech even of media corporations. Assume, for example, that a shareholder of a corporation that owns a newspaper disagrees with the political views the newspaper expresses. Under the Government's view, that potential disagreement could give the Government the authority to restrict the media corporation's political speech.

The First Amendment does not allow that power. There is, furthermore, little evidence of abuse that cannot be corrected by shareholders "through the procedures of corporate democracy." *Bellotti.*

Those reasons are sufficient to reject this shareholder-protection interest; and, moreover, the statute is both underinclusive and overinclusive. As to the first, if Congress had been seeking to protect dissenting shareholders, it would not have banned corporate speech in only certain media within 30 or 60 days before an election. A dissenting shareholder's interests would be implicated by speech in any media at any time. As to the second, the statute is overinclusive because it covers all corporations, including nonprofit corporations and for-profit corporations with only single shareholders. As to other corporations, the remedy is not to restrict speech but to consider and explore other regulatory mechanisms. The regulatory mechanism here, based on speech, contravenes the First Amendment.

4

We need not reach the question whether the Government has a compelling interest in preventing foreign individuals or associations from influencing our Nation's political process. *Cf.* 2 U.S.C. § 441e (contribution and expenditure ban applied to "foreign national[s]"). Section 441b is not limited to corporations or associations that were created in foreign countries or funded predominately by foreign shareholders. Section 441b therefore would be overbroad even if we assumed, *arguendo,* that the Government has a compelling interest in limiting foreign influence over our political process.*

C

For the reasons above, it must be concluded that *Austin* was not well reasoned. *Austin* is [further] undermined by experience since its announcement. Political speech is so ingrained in our culture that speakers find ways to circumvent campaign finance laws. Our Nation's speech dynamic is changing, and informative voices should not have to circumvent onerous restrictions to exercise their First Amendment rights. Speakers have become adept at presenting citizens with sound bites, talking points, and scripted messages that dominate the 24-hour news cycle. Corporations, like individuals, do not have monolithic views. On certain topics corporations may possess valuable expertise, leaving them the best equipped to point out errors or fallacies in speech of all sorts, including the speech of candidates and elected officials.

Rapid changes in technology—and the creative dynamic inherent in the concept of free expression—counsel against upholding a law that restricts political speech in certain media or by certain speakers. Today, 30-second television ads

* [This paragraph was the basis of the dispute between President Barack Obama and Justice Alito at Obama's 2010 State of the Union address. Obama stated that the Court's decision would "open the floodgates for special interests—including foreign companies—to spend without limit in our elections," and Alito visibly mouthed "not true." This set off a vigorous debate regarding whether the President should criticize a Supreme Court decision during the State of the Union speech with the Justices sitting in the front row.—Eds.]

may be the most effective way to convey a political message. Soon, however, it may be that Internet sources, such as blogs and social networking Web sites, will provide citizens with significant information about political candidates and issues. Yet, § 441b would seem to ban a blog post expressly advocating the election or defeat of a candidate if that blog were created with corporate funds. The First Amendment does not permit Congress to make these categorical distinctions based on the corporate identity of the speaker and the content of the political speech.

Due consideration leads to this conclusion: *Austin* should be and now is overruled. We return to the principle established in *Buckley* and *Bellotti* that the Government may not suppress political speech on the basis of the speaker's corporate identity. No sufficient governmental interest justifies limits on the political speech of nonprofit or for-profit corporations.

D

Austin is overruled, so it provides no basis for allowing the Government to limit corporate independent expenditures. As the Government appears to concede, overruling *Austin* "effectively invalidate[s] not only BCRA Section 203, but also 2 U.S.C. 441b's prohibition on the use of corporate treasury funds for express advocacy." Brief for Appellee 33, n. 12. Section 441b's restrictions on corporate independent expenditures are therefore invalid and cannot be applied to *Hillary*.

Given our conclusion we are further required to overrule the part of *McConnell* that upheld BCRA § 203's extension of § 441b's restrictions on corporate independent expenditures. The *McConnell* Court relied on the antidistortion interest recognized in *Austin* to uphold a greater restriction on speech than the restriction upheld in *Austin*, and we have found this interest unconvincing and insufficient. This part of *McConnell* is now overruled.

IV

[This Part of the opinion considered the disclosure and disclaimer requirements and is presented below.]

V

When word concerning the plot of the movie *Mr. Smith Goes to Washington* reached the circles of Government, some officials sought, by persuasion, to discourage its distribution. Under *Austin*, though, officials could have done more than discourage its distribution—they could have banned the film. After all, it, like *Hillary*, was speech funded by a corporation that was critical of Members of Congress.* *Mr. Smith Goes to Washington* may be fiction and caricature; but fiction and caricature can be a powerful force.

* [The Court's claim that under *Austin* Congress could have banned the movie *Mr. Smith Goes to Washington* is incorrect or at least very misleading. This movie did not cross the line from *Bellotti* to *Austin*, from "issue" advocacy to "express candidate" advocacy. Therefore, the movie would have been protected under *Bellotti* even if *Austin* remained good law.—Eds.]

Modern day movies, television comedies, or skits on Youtube.com might portray public officials or public policies in unflattering ways. Yet if a covered transmission during the blackout period creates the background for candidate endorsement or opposition, a felony occurs solely because a corporation, other than an exempt media corporation, has made the "purchase, payment, distribution, loan, advance, deposit, or gift of money or anything of value" in order to engage in political speech. 2 U.S.C. § 431(9)(A)(i). Speech would be suppressed in the realm where its necessity is most evident: in the public dialogue preceding a real election. Governments are often hostile to speech, but under our law and our tradition it seems stranger than fiction for our Government to make this political speech a crime. Yet this is the statute's purpose and design.

Some members of the public might consider *Hillary* to be insightful and instructive; some might find it to be neither high art nor a fair discussion on how to set the Nation's course; still others simply might suspend judgment on these points but decide to think more about issues and candidates. Those choices and assessments, however, are not for the Government to make. "The First Amendment underwrites the freedom to experiment and to create in the realm of thought and speech. Citizens must be free to use new forms, and new forums, for the expression of ideas. The civic discourse belongs to the people, and the Government may not prescribe the means used to conduct it." *McConnell* (opinion of Kennedy, J.).

The judgment of the District Court is reversed with respect to the constitutionality of 2 U.S.C. § 441b's restrictions on corporate independent expenditures.

Citizens United v. FEC Dissent

Justice STEVENS, with whom Justice GINSBURG, Justice BREYER, and Justice SOTOMAYOR join, concurring in part and dissenting in part.

The real issue in this case concerns how, not if, the appellant may finance its electioneering. Citizens United is a wealthy nonprofit corporation that runs a political action committee (PAC) with millions of dollars in assets. Under the Bipartisan Campaign Reform Act of 2002 (BCRA), it could have used those assets to televise and promote *Hillary: The Movie* wherever and whenever it wanted to. It also could have spent unrestricted sums to broadcast *Hillary* at any time other than the 30 days before the last primary election. Neither Citizens United's nor any other corporation's speech has been "banned." All that the parties dispute is whether Citizens United had a right to use the funds in its general treasury to pay for broadcasts during the 30-day period. The notion that the First Amendment dictates an affirmative answer to that question is, in my judgment, profoundly misguided. Even more misguided is the notion that the Court must rewrite the law relating to campaign expenditures by *for-profit* corporations and unions to decide this case.

The basic premise underlying the Court's ruling is its iteration, and constant reiteration, of the proposition that the First Amendment bars regulatory distinctions based on a speaker's identity, including its "identity" as a corporation. While that glittering generality has rhetorical appeal, it is not a correct statement of the law. Nor does it tell us when a corporation may engage in electioneering that some of its shareholders oppose. It does not even resolve the specific question whether

Citizens United may be required to finance some of its messages with the money in its PAC. The conceit that corporations must be treated identically to natural persons in the political sphere is not only inaccurate but also inadequate to justify the Court's disposition of this case.

In the context of election to public office, the distinction between corporate and human speakers is significant. Although they make enormous contributions to our society, corporations are not actually members of it. They cannot vote or run for office. Because they may be managed and controlled by nonresidents, their interests may conflict in fundamental respects with the interests of eligible voters. The financial resources, legal structure, and instrumental orientation of corporations raise legitimate concerns about their role in the electoral process. Our lawmakers have a compelling constitutional basis, if not also a democratic duty, to take measures designed to guard against the potentially deleterious effects of corporate spending in local and national races.

Although I concur in the Court's decision to sustain BCRA's disclosure provisions and join Part IV of its opinion, I emphatically dissent from its principal holding.[1]

I

The Court's ruling threatens to undermine the integrity of elected institutions across the Nation. The path it has taken to reach its outcome will, I fear, do damage to this institution. Before turning to the question whether to overrule *Austin* and part of *McConnell*, it is important to explain why the Court should not be deciding that question.

Narrower Grounds

Consider just three of the narrower grounds of decision that the majority has bypassed. First, the Court could have ruled, on statutory grounds, that a feature-length film distributed through video-on-demand does not qualify as an "electioneering communication" under § 203 of BCRA, 2 U.S.C. § 441b. BCRA defines that term to encompass certain communications transmitted by "broadcast, cable, or satellite." § 434(f)(3)(A). When Congress was developing BCRA, the video-on-demand medium was still in its infancy, and legislators were focused on a very different sort of programming: short advertisements run on television or radio. The sponsors of BCRA acknowledge that the FEC's implementing regulations do not clearly apply to video-on-demand transmissions. *See* Brief for Senator John McCain et al. as *Amici Curiae*. In light of this ambiguity, the distinctive characteristics of video-on-demand, and "[t]he elementary rule . . . that every reasonable construction must be resorted to, in order to save a statute from unconstitutionality," *Hooper*

1. Specifically, Part I addresses the procedural history of the case and the narrower grounds of decision the majority has bypassed. Part II addresses *stare decisis*. Part III addresses the Court's assumptions that BCRA "bans" corporate speech, that identity-based distinctions may not be drawn in the political realm, and that *Austin* and *McConnell* were outliers in our First Amendment tradition. Part IV addresses the Court's treatment of the anticorruption, antidistortion, and shareholder protection rationales for regulating corporate electioneering. [Footnote relocated.—Eds.]

v. California (1895), the Court could have reasonably ruled that § 203 does not apply to *Hillary*.

Second, the Court could have expanded the *MCFL* exemption to cover § 501(c)(4) nonprofits that accept only a *de minimis* amount of money from for-profit corporations. Citizens United professes to be such a group: Its brief says it "is funded predominantly by donations from individuals who support [its] ideological message." Brief for Appellant. Numerous Courts of Appeal have held that *de minimis* business support does not, in itself, remove an otherwise qualifying organization from the ambit of *MCFL*. This Court could have simply followed their lead.

Finally, let us not forget Citizens United's as-applied constitutional challenge. Precisely because Citizens United looks so much like the *MCFL* organizations we have exempted from regulation, while a feature-length video-on-demand film looks so unlike the types of electoral advocacy Congress has found deserving of regulation, this challenge is a substantial one. As the appellant's own arguments show, the Court could have easily limited the breadth of its constitutional holding had it declined to adopt the novel notion that speakers and speech acts must always be treated identically—and always spared expenditures restrictions—in the political realm. Yet the Court nonetheless turns its back on the as-applied review process that has been a staple of campaign finance litigation since *Buckley v. Valeo* (1976).

This brief tour of alternative grounds on which the case could have been decided is not meant to show that any of these grounds is ideal, though each is perfectly "valid" (majority opinion).[16] It is meant to show that there were principled, narrower paths that a Court that was serious about judicial restraint could have taken. There was also the straightforward path: applying *Austin* and *McConnell*, just as the District Court did in holding that the funding of Citizens United's film can be regulated under them. The only thing preventing the majority from affirming the District Court, or adopting a narrower ground that would retain *Austin*, is its disdain for *Austin*.

II

The final principle of judicial process that the majority violates is the most transparent: *stare decisis*. I am not an absolutist when it comes to *stare decisis*, in the campaign finance area or in any other. No one is. But if this principle is to do any meaningful work in supporting the rule of law, it must at least demand a significant justification, beyond the preferences of five Justices, for overturning settled doctrine. "[A] decision to overrule should rest on some special reason

16. The Chief Justice finds our discussion of these narrower solutions "quite perplexing" because we suggest that the Court should "latch on to one of them in order to avoid reaching the broader constitutional question," without doing the same ourselves. There is nothing perplexing about the matter, because we are not similarly situated to our colleagues in the majority. We do not share their view of the First Amendment. Our reading of the Constitution would not lead us to strike down any statutes or overturn any precedents in this case, and we therefore have no occasion to practice constitutional avoidance or to vindicate Citizens United's as-applied challenge. Each of the arguments made above is surely at least as strong as the statutory argument the Court accepted in last year's Voting Rights Act case, *Northwest Austin Municipal Util. Dist. No. One v. Holder* (2009).

over and above the belief that a prior case was wrongly decided." *Planned Parenthood of Southeastern Pa. v. Casey* (1992). No such justification exists in this case, and to the contrary there are powerful prudential reasons to keep faith with our precedents.

The Court's central argument for why *stare decisis* ought to be trumped is that it does not like *Austin.* The opinion "was not well reasoned," our colleagues assert, and it conflicts with First Amendment principles. This, of course, is the Court's merits argument, the many defects in which we will soon consider. I am perfectly willing to concede that if one of our precedents were dead wrong in its reasoning or irreconcilable with the rest of our doctrine, there would be a compelling basis for revisiting it. But neither is true of *Austin,* as I explain at length in Parts III and IV [of this dissent], and restating a merits argument with additional vigor does not give it extra weight in the *stare decisis* calculus.

In the end, the Court's rejection of *Austin* and *McConnell* comes down to nothing more than its disagreement with their results. Virtually every one of its arguments was made and rejected in those cases, and the majority opinion is essentially an amalgamation of resuscitated dissents. The only relevant thing that has changed since *Austin* and *McConnell* is the composition of this Court. Today's ruling thus strikes at the vitals of *stare decisis,* "the means by which we ensure that the law will not merely change erratically, but will develop in a principled and intelligible fashion" that "permits society to presume that bedrock principles are founded in the law rather than in the proclivities of individuals." *Vasquez v. Hillery* (1986).

III

The novelty of the Court's procedural dereliction and its approach to *stare decisis* is matched by the novelty of its ruling on the merits. The ruling rests on several premises. First, the Court claims that *Austin* and *McConnell* have "banned" corporate speech. Second, it claims that the First Amendment precludes regulatory distinctions based on speaker identity, including the speaker's identity as a corporation. Third, it claims that *Austin* and *McConnell* were radical outliers in our First Amendment tradition and our campaign finance jurisprudence. Each of these claims is wrong.

The So-Called "Ban"

Pervading the Court's analysis is the ominous image of a "categorical ba[n]" on corporate speech. Indeed, the majority invokes the specter of a "ban" on nearly every page of its opinion. This characterization is highly misleading, and needs to be corrected.

In fact it already has been. Our cases have repeatedly pointed out that, "[c]ontrary to the [majority's] critical assumptions," the statutes upheld in *Austin* and *McConnell* do "not impose an *absolute* ban on all forms of corporate political spending." *Austin; see also McConnell.* For starters, both statutes provide exemptions for PACs, separate segregated funds established by a corporation for political purposes. "The ability to form and administer separate segregated funds," we observed in *McConnell,* "has provided corporations and unions with a constitutionally sufficient opportunity to engage in express advocacy. That has been this Court's unanimous view."

Under BCRA, any corporation's "stockholders and their families and its executive or administrative personnel and their families" can pool their resources to finance electioneering communications. 2 U.S.C. § 441b(b)(4)(A)(i). A significant and growing number of corporations avail themselves of this option; during the most recent election cycle, corporate and union PACs raised nearly a billion dollars. Administering a PAC entails some administrative burden, but so does complying with the disclaimer, disclosure, and reporting requirements that the Court today upholds, and no one has suggested that the burden is severe for a sophisticated for-profit corporation. To the extent the majority is worried about this issue, it is important to keep in mind that we have no record to show how substantial the burden really is, just the majority's own unsupported factfinding. Like all other natural persons, every shareholder of every corporation remains entirely free under *Austin* and *McConnell* to do however much electioneering she pleases outside of the corporate form. The owners of a "mom & pop" store can simply place ads in their own names, rather than the store's. If ideologically aligned individuals wish to make unlimited expenditures through the corporate form, they may utilize an *MCFL* organization that has policies in place to avoid becoming a conduit for business or union interests.

The laws upheld in *Austin* and *McConnell* leave open many additional avenues for corporations' political speech.

At the time Citizens United brought this lawsuit, the only types of speech that could be regulated under § 203 were: (1) broadcast, cable, or satellite communications; (2) capable of reaching at least 50,000 persons in the relevant electorate; (3) made within 30 days of a primary or 60 days of a general federal election; (4) by a labor union or a non-*MCFL*, nonmedia corporation; (5) paid for with general treasury funds; and (6) susceptible of no reasonable interpretation other than as an appeal to vote for or against a specific candidate. The category of communications meeting all of these criteria is not trivial, but the notion that corporate political speech has been "suppress[ed] . . . altogether," that corporations have been "exclu[ded] . . . from the general public dialogue," or that a work of fiction such as *Mr. Smith Goes to Washington* might be covered, is nonsense.

In many ways, then, § 203 functions as a source restriction or a time, place, and manner restriction. It applies in a viewpoint-neutral fashion to a narrow subset of advocacy messages about clearly identified candidates for federal office, made during discrete time periods through discrete channels. In the case at hand, all Citizens United needed to do to broadcast *Hillary* right before the primary was to abjure business contributions or use the funds in its PAC, which by its own account is "one of the most active conservative PACs in America."

So let us be clear: Neither *Austin* nor *McConnell* held or implied that corporations may be silenced; the FEC is not a "censor"; and in the years since these cases were decided, corporations have continued to play a major role in the national dialogue. Laws such as § 203 target a class of communications that is especially likely to corrupt the political process, that is at least one degree removed from the views of individual citizens, and that may not even reflect the views of those who pay for it. Such laws burden political speech, and that is always a serious matter, demanding careful scrutiny. But the majority's incessant talk of a "ban" aims at a straw man.

Identity-Based Distinctions

[Justice Stevens discounted the majority's argument that Congress cannot make distinctions based on the speaker, especially as between individuals and corporations.]

Our First Amendment Tradition

A third fulcrum of the Court's opinion is the idea that *Austin* and *McConnell* are radical outliers, "aberration[s]," in our First Amendment tradition. The Court has it exactly backwards. It is today's holding that is the radical departure from what had been settled First Amendment law.

[Discussion omitted.]

IV

Having explained why this is not an appropriate case in which to revisit *Austin* and *McConnell* and why these decisions sit perfectly well with "First Amendment principles," I come at last to the interests that are at stake. The majority recognizes that *Austin* and *McConnell* may be defended on anticorruption, antidistortion, and shareholder protection rationales. It badly errs both in explaining the nature of these rationales, which overlap and complement each other, and in applying them to the case at hand.

The Anticorruption Interest

Undergirding the majority's approach to the merits is the claim that the only "sufficiently important governmental interest in preventing corruption or the appearance of corruption" is one that is "limited to *quid pro quo* corruption." This is the same "crabbed view of corruption" that was espoused by Justice Kennedy in *McConnell* and squarely rejected by the Court in that case. While it is true that we have not always spoken about corruption in a clear or consistent voice, the approach taken by the majority cannot be right, in my judgment. It disregards our constitutional history and the fundamental demands of a democratic society.

On numerous occasions we have recognized Congress' legitimate interest in preventing the money that is spent on elections from exerting an " 'undue influence on an officeholder's judgment' " and from creating " 'the appearance of such influence,' " beyond the sphere of *quid pro quo* relationships. [*McConnell*]. Corruption can take many forms. Bribery may be the paradigm case. But the difference between selling a vote and selling access is a matter of degree, not kind. And selling access is not qualitatively different from giving special preference to those who spent money on one's behalf. Corruption operates along a spectrum, and the majority's apparent belief that *quid pro quo* arrangements can be neatly demarcated from other improper influences does not accord with the theory or reality of politics. It certainly does not accord with the record Congress developed in passing BCRA, a record that stands as a remarkable testament to the energy and ingenuity with which corporations, unions, lobbyists, and politicians may go about scratching each other's backs—and which amply supported Congress' determination to target a limited set of especially destructive practices.

Quid Pro Quo Corruption

There is no need to take my side in the debate over the scope of the anticorruption interest to see that the Court's merits holding is wrong. Even under the majority's "crabbed view of corruption," *McConnell*, the Government should not lose this case.

"The importance of the governmental interest in preventing [corruption through the creation of political debts] has never been doubted." *Bellotti*. Even in the cases that have construed the anticorruption interest most narrowly, we have never suggested that such *quid pro quo* debts must take the form of outright vote buying or bribes, which have long been distinct crimes. Rather, they encompass the myriad ways in which outside parties may induce an officeholder to confer a legislative benefit in direct response to, or anticipation of, some outlay of money the parties have made or will make on behalf of the officeholder. It has likewise never been doubted that "[o]f almost equal concern as the danger of actual *quid pro quo* arrangements is the impact of the appearance of corruption." *Id.* A democracy cannot function effectively when its constituent members believe laws are being bought and sold.

In theory, our colleagues accept this much. As applied to BCRA § 203, however, they conclude "[t]he anticorruption interest is not sufficient to displace the speech here in question."

The legislative and judicial proceedings relating to BCRA generated a substantial body of evidence suggesting that, as corporations grew more and more adept at crafting "issue ads" to help or harm a particular candidate, these nominally independent expenditures began to corrupt the political process in a very direct sense. The sponsors of these ads were routinely granted special access after the campaign was over; "candidates and officials knew who their friends were[.]" *McConnell*. Many corporate independent expenditures, it seemed, had become essentially interchangeable with direct contributions in their capacity to generate *quid pro quo* arrangements. In an age in which money and television ads are the coin of the campaign realm, it is hardly surprising that corporations deployed these ads to curry favor with, and to gain influence over, public officials.

The majority appears to think it decisive that the BCRA record does not contain "direct examples of votes being exchanged for . . . expenditures." It would have been quite remarkable if Congress had created a record detailing such behavior by its own Members. Proving that a specific vote was exchanged for a specific expenditure has always been next to impossible: Elected officials have diverse motivations, and no one will acknowledge that he sold a vote. Yet, even if "[i]ngratiation and access . . . are not corruption" themselves, they are necessary prerequisites to it; they can create both the opportunity for, and the appearance of, *quid pro quo* arrangements. The influx of unlimited corporate money into the electoral realm also creates new opportunities for the mirror image of *quid pro quo* deals: threats, both explicit and implicit. Starting today, corporations with large war chests to deploy on electioneering may find democratically elected bodies becoming much more attuned to their interests. The majority both misreads the facts and draws the wrong conclusions when it suggests that BCRA record provides "only scant evidence that independent expenditures . . . ingratiate," and that, "in any event," none of it matters.

[T]he consequences of today's holding will not be limited to the legislative or executive context. The majority of the States select their judges through popular elections. At a time when concerns about the conduct of judicial elections have reached a fever pitch, the Court today unleashes the floodgates of corporate and union general treasury spending in these races. Perhaps "*Caperton* motions" [seeking recusal of a Judge who received contributions or significant independent expenditures from a party in a suit before that Judge] will catch some of the worst abuses. This will be small comfort to those States that, after today, may no longer have the ability to place modest limits on corporate electioneering even if they believe such limits to be critical to maintaining the integrity of their judicial systems.

***Austin* and Corporate Expenditures**

Just as the majority gives short shrift to the general societal interests at stake in campaign finance regulation, it also overlooks the distinctive considerations raised by the regulation of *corporate* expenditures. The majority fails to appreciate that *Austin*'s antidistortion rationale is itself an anticorruption rationale, tied to the special concerns raised by corporations. Understood properly, "antidistortion" is simply a variant on the classic governmental interest in protecting against improper influences on officeholders that debilitate the democratic process. It is manifestly not just an "equalizing" ideal in disguise.

1. Antidistortion

The fact that corporations are different from human beings might seem to need no elaboration, except that the majority opinion almost completely elides it. *Austin* set forth some of the basic differences. Unlike natural persons, corporations have "limited liability" for their owners and managers, "perpetual life," separation of ownership and control, "and favorable treatment of the accumulation and distribution of assets . . . that enhance their ability to attract capital and to deploy their resources in ways that maximize the return on their shareholders' investments." [*Austin*]. Unlike voters in U.S. elections, corporations may be foreign controlled. Unlike other interest groups, business corporations have been "effectively delegated responsibility for ensuring society's economic welfare"; they inescapably structure the life of every citizen. " '[T]he resources in the treasury of a business corporation,' " furthermore, " 'are not an indication of popular support for the corporation's political ideas.' " [*Austin*] (quoting *MCFL*). " 'They reflect instead the economically motivated decisions of investors and customers. The availability of these resources may make a corporation a formidable political presence, even though the power of the corporation may be no reflection of the power of its ideas.' " [*Id.* (quoting *MCFL*)].

It might also be added that corporations have no consciences, no beliefs, no feelings, no thoughts, no desires. Corporations help structure and facilitate the activities of human beings, to be sure, and their "personhood" often serves as a useful legal fiction. But they are not themselves members of "We the People" by whom and for whom our Constitution was established.

It is an interesting question "who" is even speaking when a business corporation places an advertisement that endorses or attacks a particular candidate.

Presumably it is not the customers or employees, who typically have no say in such matters. It cannot realistically be said to be the shareholders, who tend to be far removed from the day-to-day decisions of the firm and whose political preferences may be opaque to management. Perhaps the officers or directors of the corporation have the best claim to be the ones speaking, except their fiduciary duties generally prohibit them from using corporate funds for personal ends. Some individuals associated with the corporation must make the decision to place the ad, but the idea that these individuals are thereby fostering their self-expression or cultivating their critical faculties is fanciful. It is entirely possible that the corporation's electoral message will *conflict* with their personal convictions. Take away the ability to use general treasury funds for some of those ads, and no one's autonomy, dignity, or political equality has been impinged upon in the least.

"[C]orporate participation" in elections, any business executive will tell you, "is more transactional than ideological." Supp. Brief for Committee for Economic Development as *Amicus Curiae*. In this transactional spirit, some corporations have affirmatively urged Congress to place limits on their electioneering communications. These corporations fear that officeholders will shake them down for supportive ads, that they will have to spend increasing sums on elections in an ever-escalating arms race with their competitors, and that public trust in business will be eroded. A system that effectively forces corporations to use their shareholders' money both to maintain access to, and to avoid retribution from, elected officials may ultimately prove more harmful than beneficial to many corporations. It can impose a kind of implicit tax.

In short, regulations such as § 203 and the statute upheld in *Austin* impose only a limited burden on First Amendment freedoms not only because they target a narrow subset of expenditures and leave untouched the broader "public dialogue," but also because they leave untouched the speech of natural persons. Recognizing the weakness of a speaker-based critique of *Austin*, the Court places primary emphasis not on the corporation's right to electioneer, but rather on the listener's interest in hearing what every possible speaker may have to say. The Court's central argument is that laws such as § 203 have " 'deprived [the electorate] of information, knowledge and opinion vital to its function,' " and this, in turn, "interferes with the 'open marketplace' of ideas protected by the First Amendment."

There are many flaws in this argument. If the overriding concern depends on the interests of the audience, surely the public's perception of the value of corporate speech should be given important weight. That perception today is the same as it was a century ago when Theodore Roosevelt delivered the speeches to Congress that, in time, led to the limited prohibition on corporate campaign expenditures that is overruled today. The distinctive threat to democratic integrity posed by corporate domination of politics was recognized at "the inception of the republic" and "has been a persistent theme in American political life" ever since. It is only certain Members of this Court, not the listeners themselves, who have agitated for more corporate electioneering.

Austin recognized that there are substantial reasons why a legislature might conclude that unregulated general treasury expenditures will give corporations "unfai[r] influence" in the electoral process and distort public debate in ways that undermine rather than advance the interests of listeners. The legal structure of corporations allows them to amass and deploy financial resources on a scale few natural persons can match. The structure of a business corporation, furthermore, draws a line between the corporation's economic interests and the political preferences of the individuals associated with the corporation; the corporation must engage the electoral process with the aim "to enhance the profitability of the company, no matter how persuasive the arguments for a broader or conflicting set of priorities," Brief for American Independent Business Alliance as *Amicus Curiae.* In a state election such as the one at issue in *Austin,* the interests of nonresident corporations may be fundamentally adverse to the interests of local voters. Consequently, when corporations grab up the prime broadcasting slots on the eve of an election, they can flood the market with advocacy that bears "little or no correlation" to the ideas of natural persons or to any broader notion of the public good. [*Austin*]. The opinions of real people may be marginalized. "The expenditure restrictions of [2 U.S.C.] § 441b are thus meant to ensure that competition among actors in the political arena is truly competition among ideas." *MCFL.*

In addition to this immediate drowning out of noncorporate voices, there may be deleterious effects that follow soon thereafter. Corporate "domination" of electioneering can generate the impression that corporations dominate our democracy. When citizens turn on their televisions and radios before an election and hear only corporate electioneering, they may lose faith in their capacity, as citizens, to influence public policy. A Government captured by corporate interests, they may come to believe, will be neither responsive to their needs nor willing to give their views a fair hearing. The predictable result is cynicism and disenchantment: an increased perception that large spenders "call the tune" and a reduced "willingness of voters to take part in democratic governance." *McConnell.* To the extent that corporations are allowed to exert undue influence in electoral races, the speech of the eventual winners of those races may also be chilled. Politicians who fear that a certain corporation can make or break their reelection chances may be cowed into silence about that corporation. On a variety of levels, unregulated corporate electioneering might diminish the ability of citizens to "hold officials accountable to the people" and disserve the goal of a public debate that is "uninhibited, robust, and wide-open," *New York Times Co. v. Sullivan* (1964). At the least, I stress again, a legislature is entitled to credit these concerns and to take tailored measures in response.

The majority's unwillingness to distinguish between corporations and humans similarly blinds it to the possibility that corporations' "war chests" and their special "advantages" in the legal realm may translate into special advantages in the market for legislation. When large numbers of citizens have a common stake in a measure that is under consideration, it may be very difficult for them to coordinate resources on behalf of their position. The corporate form, by contrast, "provides a simple way to channel rents to only those who have paid their dues, as it were. If you do not own stock, you do not benefit from the larger dividends or appreciation in the stock price caused by the passage of private interest legislation." Sitkoff, *Corporate Political Speech, Political Extortion, and the Competition for Corporate Charters,* 69 U. Chi. L. Rev. 1103, 1113 (2002). Corporations, that is, are uniquely equipped to seek laws that favor their owners, not simply because they have a lot of money but because of their legal and organizational structure. Remove all restrictions on their electioneering, and the door may be opened to a type of rent seeking that is "far more destructive" than what noncorporations are capable of. It is for reasons such as these that our campaign finance jurisprudence has long appreciated that "the 'differing structures and purposes' of different entities 'may require different forms of regulation in order to protect the integrity of the electoral process.'" [*Federal Election Comm'n v. National Right to Work Committee* (1982) (*NRWC*)].

The Court's facile depiction of corporate electioneering assumes away all of these complexities. Our colleagues ridicule the idea of regulating expenditures based on "nothing more" than a fear that corporations have a special "ability to persuade," as if corporations were our society's ablest debaters and viewpoint-neutral laws such as § 203 were created to suppress their best arguments. In their haste to knock down yet another straw man, our colleagues simply ignore the fundamental concerns of the *Austin* Court and the legislatures that have passed laws like § 203: to safeguard the integrity, competitiveness, and democratic responsiveness of the electoral process. All of the majority's theoretical arguments turn on a proposition with undeniable surface appeal but little grounding in evidence or experience, "that there is no such thing as too much speech."[74] If individuals in our society had infinite free time to listen to and contemplate every last bit of speech uttered by anyone, anywhere; and if broadcast advertisements had no special ability to influence elections apart from the merits of their arguments (to the extent they make any); and if legislators always operated with nothing less than perfect virtue; then I suppose the majority's premise would be sound. In the real world, we have seen, corporate domination of the airwaves prior to an election may decrease the average listener's exposure to relevant viewpoints, and it may diminish citizens' willingness and capacity to participate in the democratic process.

None of this is to suggest that corporations can or should be denied an opportunity to participate in election campaigns or in any other public forum (much less that a work of art such as *Mr. Smith Goes to Washington* may be banned), or to deny that some corporate speech may contribute significantly to public debate. What it shows, however, is that *Austin*'s "concern about corporate domination of the political process," reflects more than a concern to protect governmental interests outside of the First Amendment. It also reflects a concern to *facilitate* First Amendment values by preserving some breathing room around the electoral "marketplace" of ideas, the marketplace in which the actual people of this Nation determine how they will govern themselves. The majority seems oblivious to the simple truth that laws such as § 203 do not merely pit the anticorruption interest against the First Amendment, but also pit competing First Amendment values against each other. There are, to be sure, serious concerns with any effort to balance the First Amendment rights of speakers against the First Amendment rights of listeners. But when the speakers in question are not real people and when the appeal to "First Amendment principles" depends almost entirely on the listeners' perspective, it becomes necessary to consider how listeners will actually be affected.

In critiquing *Austin*'s antidistortion rationale and campaign finance regulation more generally, our colleagues place tremendous weight on the example of media

74. Of course, no presiding person in a courtroom, legislature, classroom, polling place, or family dinner would take this hyperbole literally.

corporations. Yet it is not at all clear that *Austin* would permit § 203 to be applied to them. The press plays a unique role not only in the text, history, and structure of the First Amendment but also in facilitating public discourse; as the *Austin* Court explained, "media corporations differ significantly from other corporations in that their resources are devoted to the collection of information and its dissemination to the public." Our colleagues have raised some interesting and difficult questions about Congress' authority to regulate electioneering by the press, and about how to define what constitutes the press. *But that is not the case before us.* Section 203 does not apply to media corporations, and even if it did, Citizens United is not a media corporation. There would be absolutely no reason to consider the issue of media corporations if the majority did not invent the theory that legislatures must eschew all "identity"-based distinctions and treat a local nonprofit news outlet exactly the same as General Motors.[75] This calls to mind George Berkeley's description of philosophers: "[W]e have first raised a dust and then complain we cannot see." Principles of Human Knowledge/Three Dialogues (R. Woolhouse ed. 1988).

The Court's blinkered and aphoristic approach to the First Amendment may well promote corporate power at the cost of the individual and collective self-expression the Amendment was meant to serve. It will undoubtedly cripple the ability of ordinary citizens, Congress, and the States to adopt even limited measures to protect against corporate domination of the electoral process. Americans may be forgiven if they do not feel the Court has advanced the cause of self-government today.

2. Shareholder Protection

There is yet another way in which laws such as § 203 can serve First Amendment values. Interwoven with *Austin*'s concern to protect the integrity of the electoral process is a concern to protect the rights of shareholders from a kind of coerced speech: electioneering expenditures that do not "reflec[t] [their] support." When corporations use general treasury funds to praise or attack a particular candidate for office, it is the shareholders, as the residual claimants, who are effectively footing the bill. Those shareholders who disagree with the corporation's electoral message may find their financial investments being used to undermine their political convictions.

The PAC mechanism, by contrast, helps assure that those who pay for an electioneering communication actually support its content and that managers do not use general treasuries to advance personal agendas. It " 'allows corporate political participation without the temptation to use corporate funds for political influence, quite possibly at odds with the sentiments of some shareholders or members.' " *McConnell*. A rule that privileges the use of PACs thus does more than facilitate the

75. Under the majority's view, the legislature is thus damned if it does and damned if it doesn't. If the legislature gives media corporations an exemption from electioneering regulations that apply to other corporations, it violates the newly minted First Amendment rule against identity-based distinctions. If the legislature does not give media corporations an exemption, it violates the First Amendment rights of the press. The only way out of this invented bind: no regulations whatsoever.

political speech of like-minded shareholders; it also curbs the rent seeking behavior of executives and respects the views of dissenters. *Austin*'s acceptance of restrictions on general treasury spending "simply allows people who have invested in the business corporation for purely economic reasons"—the vast majority of investors, one assumes—"to avoid being taken advantage of, without sacrificing their economic objectives." Winkler, *Beyond* Bellotti, 32 Loyola (LA) L. Rev. 133, 201 (1998).

The concern to protect dissenting shareholders and union members has a long history in campaign finance reform. It provided a central motivation for the Tillman Act in 1907 and subsequent legislation, and it has been endorsed in a long line of our cases. Indeed, we have unanimously recognized the governmental interest in "protect[ing] the individuals who have paid money into a corporation or union for purposes other than the support of candidates from having that money used to support political candidates to whom they may be opposed." *NRWC.*

The Court dismisses this interest on the ground that abuses of shareholder money can be corrected "through the procedures of corporate democracy" and, it seems, through Internet-based disclosures.[76] I fail to understand how this addresses the concerns of dissenting union members, who will also be affected by today's ruling, and I fail to understand why the Court is so confident in these mechanisms. By "corporate democracy," presumably the Court means the rights of shareholders to vote and to bring derivative suits for breach of fiduciary duty. In practice, however, many corporate lawyers will tell you that "these rights are so limited as to be almost nonexistent," given the internal authority wielded by boards and managers and the expansive protections afforded by the business judgment rule. Modern technology may help make it easier to track corporate activity, including electoral advocacy, but it is utopian to believe that it solves the problem. Most American households that own stock do so through intermediaries such as mutual funds and pension plans, which makes it more difficult both to monitor and to alter particular holdings. Studies show that a majority of individual investors make no trades at all during a given year. Moreover, if the corporation in question operates a PAC, an investor who sees the company's ads may not know whether they are being funded through the PAC or through the general treasury.

If and when shareholders learn that a corporation has been spending general treasury money on objectionable electioneering, they can divest. Even assuming that they reliably learn as much, however, this solution is only partial. The injury to the shareholders' expressive rights has already occurred; they might have preferred to keep that corporation's stock in their portfolio for any number of economic reasons; and they may incur a capital gains tax or other penalty from selling their shares, changing their pension plan, or the like. The shareholder protection

76. I note that, among the many other regulatory possibilities it has left open, ranging from new versions of § 203 supported by additional evidence of *quid pro quo* corruption or its appearance to any number of tax incentive or public financing schemes, today's decision does not require that a legislature rely solely on these mechanisms to protect shareholders. Legislatures remain free in their incorporation and tax laws to condition the types of activity in which corporations may engage, including electioneering activity, on specific disclosure requirements or on prior express approval by shareholders or members.

rationale has been criticized as underinclusive, in that corporations also spend money on lobbying and charitable contributions in ways that any particular shareholder might disapprove. But those expenditures do not implicate the selection of public officials, an area in which "the interests of unwilling . . . corporate shareholders [in not being] forced to subsidize that speech" "are at their zenith." *Austin*. And in any event, the question is whether shareholder protection provides a basis for regulating expenditures in the weeks before an election, not whether additional types of corporate communications might similarly be conditioned on voluntariness.

Recognizing the limits of the shareholder protection rationale, the *Austin* Court did not hold it out as an adequate and independent ground for sustaining the statute in question. Rather, the Court applied it to reinforce the antidistortion rationale, in two main ways. First, the problem of dissenting shareholders shows that even if electioneering expenditures can advance the political views of some members of a corporation, they will often compromise the views of others. Second, it provides an additional reason, beyond the distinctive legal attributes of the corporate form, for doubting that these "expenditures reflect actual public support for the political ideas espoused." The shareholder protection rationale, in other words, bolsters the conclusion that restrictions on corporate electioneering can serve both speakers' and listeners' interests, as well as the anticorruption interest. And it supplies yet another reason why corporate expenditures merit less protection than individual expenditures.

V

Today's decision is backwards in many senses. It elevates the majority's agenda over the litigants' submissions, broad constitutional theories over narrow statutory grounds, individual dissenting opinions over precedential holdings, assertion over tradition, absolutism over empiricism, rhetoric over reality. Our colleagues have arrived at the conclusion that *Austin* must be overruled and that § 203 is unconstitutional only after mischaracterizing both the reach and rationale of those authorities, and after bypassing or ignoring rules of judicial restraint used to cabin the Court's lawmaking power. Their conclusion that the societal interest in avoiding corruption and the appearance of corruption does not provide an adequate justification for regulating corporate expenditures on candidate elections relies on an incorrect description of that interest, along with a failure to acknowledge the relevance of established facts and the considered judgments of state and federal legislatures over many decades.

In a democratic society, the longstanding consensus on the need to limit corporate campaign spending should outweigh the wooden application of judge-made rules. The majority's rejection of this principle "elevate[s] corporations to a level of deference which has not been seen at least since the days when substantive due process was regularly used to invalidate regulatory legislation thought to unfairly impinge upon established economic interests." *Bellotti* (White, J., dissenting). At bottom, the Court's opinion is thus a rejection of the common sense of the American people, who have recognized a need to prevent corporations from undermining self-government since the founding, and who have fought against the distinctive corrupting potential of corporate electioneering since the days of Theodore Roosevelt. It is a strange time to repudiate that common sense. While American democracy is imperfect, few outside the majority of this Court would have thought its flaws included a dearth of corporate money in politics.

I would affirm the judgment of the District Court.

CITIZENS UNITED v. FEC CONCURRENCES

The concurrences in this case sought largely to respond to Justice Stevens's dissent. Chief Justice Roberts wrote to explain why overruling recent precedent was required in this case. Justice Scalia wrote to respond to Justice Stevens's argument regarding the "Original Understandings" of the First Amendment (which we largely omitted from his opinion above). We have included a few paragraphs from each concurrence just so you have a flavor of the arguments.

Chief Justice ROBERTS, with whom Justice ALITO joins, concurring.

The Government urges us in this case to uphold a direct prohibition on political speech. It asks us to embrace a theory of the First Amendment that would allow censorship not only of television and radio broadcasts, but of pamphlets, posters, the Internet, and virtually any other medium that corporations and unions might find useful in expressing their views on matters of public concern. Its theory, if accepted, would empower the Government to prohibit newspapers from running editorials or opinion pieces supporting or opposing candidates for office, so long as the newspapers were owned by corporations—as the major ones are. First Amendment rights could be confined to individuals, subverting the vibrant public discourse that is at the foundation of our democracy.

It is only because the majority rejects Citizens United's statutory claim that it proceeds to consider the group's various constitutional arguments, beginning with its narrowest claim (that *Hillary* is not the functional equivalent of express advocacy) and proceeding to its broadest claim (that *Austin* should be overruled).

The dissent advocates an approach to addressing Citizens United's claims that I find quite perplexing. It presumably agrees with the majority that Citizens United's narrower statutory and constitutional arguments lack merit—otherwise its conclusion that the group should lose this case would make no sense. Despite agreeing that these narrower arguments fail, however, the dissent argues that the majority should nonetheless latch on to one of them in order to avoid reaching the broader constitutional question of whether *Austin* remains good law. It even suggests that the Court's failure to adopt one of these concededly meritless arguments is a sign that the majority is not "serious about judicial restraint."

This approach is based on a false premise: that our practice of avoiding unnecessary (and unnecessarily broad) constitutional holdings somehow trumps our obligation faithfully to interpret the law. It should go without saying, however, that we cannot embrace a narrow ground of decision simply because it is narrow; it must also be right.

The Court properly rejects that theory, and I join its opinion in full. The First Amendment protects more than just the individual on a soapbox and the lonely pamphleteer. I write separately to address the important principles of judicial restraint and *stare decisis* implicated in this case.

[*S*]*tare decisis* is neither an "inexorable command," *Lawrence v. Texas* (2003), nor "a mechanical formula of adherence to the latest decision," *Helvering v. Hallock* (1940), especially in constitutional cases. If it were, segregation would be legal, minimum wage laws would be unconstitutional, and the Government could wiretap ordinary criminal suspects without first obtaining warrants. As the dissent properly notes, none of us has viewed *stare decisis* in such absolute terms.

Stare decisis is instead a "principle of policy." *Helvering.* When considering whether to reexamine a prior erroneous holding, we must balance the importance of having constitutional questions *decided* against the importance of having them *decided right.* As Justice Jackson explained, this requires a "sober appraisal of the disadvantages of the innovation as well as those of the questioned case, a weighing of practical effects of one against the other." Jackson, Decisional Law and *Stare Decisis,* 30 A.B.A.J. 334 (1944).

In conducting this balancing, we must keep in mind that *stare decisis* is not an end in itself. It is instead "the means by which we ensure that the law will not merely change erratically, but will develop in a principled and intelligible fashion." *Vasquez v. Hillery* (1986). Its greatest purpose is to serve a constitutional ideal—the rule of law. It follows that in the unusual circumstance when fidelity to any particular precedent does more to damage this constitutional ideal than to advance it, we must be more willing to depart from that precedent.

[Chief Justice Roberts then discussed why he believed the balancing required the Court to overrule *Austin.*]

Justice SCALIA, with whom Justice ALITO joins, and with whom Justice THOMAS joins in part, concurring.

I write separately to address Justice Stevens' discussion of "*Original Understandings.*" This section of the dissent purports to show that today's decision is not supported by the original understanding of the First Amendment. The dissent attempts this demonstration, however, in splendid isolation from the text of the First Amendment. It never shows why "the freedom of speech" that was the right of Englishmen did not include the freedom to speak in association with other individuals, including association in the corporate form. To be sure, in 1791 (as now) corporations could pursue only the objectives set forth in their charters; but the dissent provides no evidence that their speech in the pursuit of those objectives could be censored.

Instead of taking this straightforward approach to determining the Amendment's meaning, the dissent embarks on a detailed exploration of the Framers' views about the "role of corporations in society." The Framers didn't like corporations, the dissent concludes, and therefore it follows (as night the day) that corporations had no rights of free speech. Of course the Framers' personal affection or disaffection for corporations is relevant only insofar as it can be thought to be reflected in the understood meaning of the text they enacted—not, as the dissent suggests, as a freestanding substitute for that text. But the dissent's distortion of proper analysis is even worse than that. Though faced with a constitutional text that makes no distinction between types of speakers, the dissent feels no necessity to provide even an isolated statement from the founding era to the effect that corporations are *not* covered, but places the burden on petitioners to bring forward statements showing that they *are* ("there is not a scintilla of evidence to support the notion that anyone believed [the First Amendment] would preclude regulatory distinctions based on the corporate form").

. . .

Historical evidence relating to the textually similar clause "the freedom of . . . the press" also provides no support for the proposition that the First Amendment excludes conduct of artificial legal entities from the scope of its protection. The freedom of "the press" was widely understood to protect the publishing activities of individual editors and printers. But these individuals often acted through newspapers, which (much like corporations) had their own names, outlived the individuals who had founded them, could be bought and sold, were sometimes owned by more than one person, and were operated for profit. Their activities were not stripped of First Amendment protection simply because they were carried out under the banner of an artificial legal entity. And the notion which follows from the dissent's view, that modern newspapers, since they are incorporated, have free-speech rights only at the sufferance of Congress, boggles the mind.[6]

. . .

But to return to, and summarize, my principal point, which is the conformity of today's opinion with the original meaning of the First Amendment. The Amendment is written in terms of "speech," not speakers. Its text offers no foothold for excluding any category of speaker, from single individuals to partnerships of individuals, to unincorporated associations of individuals, to incorporated associations of individuals—and the dissent offers no evidence about the original meaning of the text to support any such exclusion. We are therefore simply left with the question whether the speech at issue in this case is "speech" covered by the First Amendment. No one says otherwise. A documentary film critical of a potential Presidential candidate is core political speech, and its nature as such does not change simply because it was funded by a corporation. Nor does the character of that funding produce any reduction whatever in the "inherent worth of the speech" and "its capacity for informing the public," *First Nat. Bank of Boston v. Bellotti* (1978). Indeed, to exclude or impede corporate speech is to muzzle the principal agents of the modern free economy. We should celebrate rather than condemn the addition of this speech to the public debate.

6. The dissent seeks to avoid this conclusion (and to turn a liability into an asset) by interpreting the Freedom of the Press Clause to refer to the institutional press (thus demonstrating, according to the dissent, that the Founders "did draw distinctions—explicit distinctions—between types of 'speakers,' or speech outlets or forms"). It is passing strange to interpret the phrase "the freedom of speech, or of the press" to mean, not everyone's right to speak or publish, but rather everyone's right to speak or the institutional press's right to publish. No one thought that is what it meant.

5. Contribution Limitations

INDIVIDUAL CONTRIBUTION LIMITS

As you are well aware, in *Buckley* and subsequent cases the Supreme Court upheld the ability of Congress to enact contribution limitations to prevent corruption or the appearance of corruption. Is there a level of contributions that is so de minimis as not to raise a corruption concern? Moreover, might setting a contribution limit at an extremely low level raise First Amendment problems in that the limitation in essence precludes donors from having any "voice" in politics or thwarts candidates from having any chance to campaign effectively? The next two cases address these issues in the context of state campaign finance laws. Note that—having won a challenge to independent expenditure limitations for corporations (in *Citizens United*, discussed above), the "antiregulation" movement is now setting its sights on eliminating any regulation of contributions. How successful are they likely to be?

As you are reading these cases, keep the following issues in mind: (1) Is *Buckley*'s holding regarding contributions sustainable? (2) Is there a guiding principle on what level of contribution limits are too low? (3) Must contribution limitations be indexed to inflation? (4) What kind of evidence must plaintiffs present to demonstrate that contribution limits are too low? Notice also that these cases are in some ways outliers in that the courts apply the "lower" level of scrutiny for contribution limitations but still strike down both laws.

Randall v. Sorrell

548 U.S. 230 (2006)

Justice Breyer announced the judgment of the Court and delivered an opinion, in which The Chief Justice joins, and in which Justice Alito joins except as to Parts II-B-1 and II-B-2.

We here consider the constitutionality of a Vermont campaign finance statute that limits both (1) the amounts that candidates for state office may spend on their campaigns (expenditure limitations) and (2) the amounts that individuals, organizations, and political parties may contribute to those campaigns (contribution limitations). Vt. Stat. Ann., Tit. 17, § 2801 et seq. (2002). We hold that both sets of limitations are inconsistent with the First Amendment. Well-established precedent makes clear that the expenditure limits violate the First Amendment. The contribution limits are unconstitutional because in their specific details (involving low maximum levels and other restrictions) they fail to satisfy the First Amendment's requirement of careful tailoring. That is to say, they impose burdens upon First Amendment interests that (when viewed in light of the statute's legitimate objectives) are disproportionately severe.

I

A

Prior to 1997, Vermont's campaign finance law imposed no limit upon the amount a candidate for state office could spend. It did, however, impose limits upon the amounts that individuals, corporations, and political committees could contribute to the campaign of such a candidate. Individuals and corporations could contribute no more than $1,000 to any candidate for state office. Political committees, excluding political parties, could contribute no more than $3,000. The statute imposed no limit on the amount that political parties could contribute to candidates.

In 1997, Vermont enacted a more stringent campaign finance law, [Act 64,] the statute at issue here.

Act 64 . . . imposes strict contribution limits. The amount any single individual can contribute to the campaign of a candidate for state office during a "two-year general election cycle" [(which encompasses the primary and general elections)] is limited as follows: governor, lieutenant governor, and other statewide offices, $400; state senator, $300; and state representative, $200. Unlike its expenditure limits, Act 64's contribution limits are not indexed for inflation.

A political committee is subject to these same limits. So is a political party, defined broadly to include "any subsidiary, branch or local unit" of a party, as well as any "national or regional affiliates" of a party (taken separately or together). § 2801(5). Thus, for example, the statute treats the local, state, and national affiliates of the Democratic Party as if they were a single entity and limits their total contribution to a single candidate's campaign for governor (during the primary and the general election together) to $400.

The Act also imposes a limit of $2,000 upon the amount any individual can give to a political party during a 2-year general election cycle.

The Act defines "contribution" broadly in approximately the same way it defines "expenditure." Any expenditure made on a candidate's behalf counts as a contribution to the candidate if it is "intentionally facilitated by, solicited by or approved by" the candidate. §§ 2809(a), (c). And a party expenditure that "primarily benefits six or fewer candidates who are associated with the" party is "presumed" to count against the party's contribution limits. §§ 2809(a), (d).

There are a few exceptions. A candidate's own contributions to the campaign and those of the candidate's family fall outside the contribution limits. Volunteer services do not count as contributions. Nor does the cost of a meet-the-candidate function, provided that the total cost for the function amounts to $100 or less.

B

[Omitted.]

II

[The Court struck down the expenditure limitation in Vermont's law as violating the First Amendment. The Court rejected the state's invitation to overrule the part of *Buckley* that struck down FECA's independent expenditure limits and ruled that *Buckley* is indistinguishable from this case with respect to independent expenditures.]

III

We turn now to a more complex question, namely, the constitutionality of Act 64's contribution limits. The parties, while accepting *Buckley*'s approach, dispute whether, despite *Buckley*'s general approval of statutes that limit campaign contributions, Act 64's contribution limits are so severe that in the circumstances its particular limits violate the First Amendment.

A

As with the Act's expenditure limits, we begin with *Buckley*. In that case, the Court upheld the $1,000 contribution limit before it. *Buckley* recognized that contribution limits, like expenditure limits, "implicate fundamental First Amendment interests," namely, the freedoms of "political expression" and "political association." But, unlike expenditure limits (which "necessarily reduc[e] the quantity of expression by restricting the number of issues discussed, the depth of their exploration, and the size of the audience reached,") contribution limits "involv[e] little direct restraint on" the contributor's speech. They do restrict "one aspect of the contributor's freedom of political association," namely, the contributor's ability to support a favored candidate, but they nonetheless "permi[t] the symbolic expression of support evidenced by a contribution," and they do "not in any way infringe the contributor's freedom to discuss candidates and issues."

Consequently, the Court wrote, contribution limitations are permissible as long as the Government demonstrates that the limits are "closely drawn" to match a "sufficiently important interest." It found that the interest advanced in the case, "prevent[ing] corruption" and its "appearance," was "sufficiently important" to justify the statute's contribution limits.

The Court also found that the contribution limits before it were "closely drawn." It recognized that, in determining whether a particular contribution limit was "closely drawn," the amount, or level, of that limit could make a difference. Indeed, it wrote that "contribution restrictions could have a severe impact on political dialogue if the limitations prevented candidates and political committees from amassing the resources necessary for effective advocacy." But the Court added that such "distinctions in degree become significant only when they can be said to amount to differences in kind." Pointing out that it had " 'no scalpel to probe, whether, say, a $2,000 ceiling might not serve as well as $1,000,' " the Court found "no indication" that the $1,000 contribution limitations imposed by the Act would have "any dramatic adverse effect on the funding of campaigns." It therefore found the limitations constitutional.

B

Following *Buckley*, we must determine whether Act 64's contribution limits prevent candidates from "amassing the resources necessary for effective [campaign] advocacy"; whether they magnify the advantages of incumbency to the point where they put challengers to a significant disadvantage; in a word, whether they are too low and too strict to survive First Amendment scrutiny. In answering these questions, we recognize, as *Buckley* stated, that we have " 'no scalpel to probe' " each possible contribution level. We cannot determine with any degree of exactitude the precise restriction necessary to carry out the statute's legitimate objectives. In practice, the legislature is better equipped to make such empirical judgments, as legislators have "particular expertise" in matters related to the costs and nature of running for office. *McConnell.* Thus ordinarily we have deferred to the legislature's determination of such matters.

Nonetheless, as *Buckley* acknowledged, we must recognize the existence of some lower bound. At some point the constitutional risks to the democratic electoral process become too great. After all, the interests underlying contribution limits, preventing corruption and the appearance of corruption, "directly implicate the integrity of our electoral process." *McConnell.* Yet that rationale does not simply mean "the lower the limit, the better." That is because contribution limits that are too low can also harm the electoral process by preventing challengers from mounting effective campaigns against incumbent officeholders, thereby reducing democratic accountability. Were we to ignore that fact, a statute that seeks to regulate campaign contributions could itself prove an obstacle to the very electoral fairness it seeks to promote. Thus, we see no alternative to the exercise of independent judicial judgment as a statute reaches those outer limits. And, where there is strong indication in a particular case, i.e., danger signs, that such risks exist (both present in kind and likely serious in degree), courts, including appellate courts, must review the record independently and carefully with an eye toward assessing the statute's "tailoring," that is, toward assessing the proportionality of the restrictions.

We find those danger signs present here. As compared with the contribution limits upheld by the Court in the past, and with those in force in other States, Act 64's limits are sufficiently low as to generate suspicion that they are not closely drawn. The Act sets its limits per election cycle, which includes both a primary and a general election. Thus, in a gubernatorial race with both primary and final election contests, the Act's contribution limit amounts to $200 per election per candidate (with significantly lower limits for contributions to candidates for State Senate and House of Representatives). These limits apply both to contributions from individuals and to contributions from political parties, whether made in cash or in expenditures coordinated (or presumed to be coordinated) with the candidate.

These limits are well below the limits this Court upheld in *Buckley.* Indeed, in terms of real dollars (i.e., adjusting for inflation), the Act's $200 per election limit on individual contributions to a campaign for governor is slightly more than one-twentieth of the limit on contributions to campaigns for federal office before the Court in *Buckley.*

Moreover, considered as a whole, Vermont's contribution limits are the lowest in the Nation. Act 64 limits contributions to candidates for statewide office (including governor) to $200 per candidate per election. We have found no State that imposes a lower per election limit. Indeed, we have found only seven States that impose limits on contributions to candidates for statewide office at or below $500 per election, more than twice Act 64's limit.* We are aware of no State that imposes a limit on contributions from political parties to candidates for statewide office lower than Act 64's $200 per candidate per election limit. Similarly, we have found only three States that have limits on contributions to candidates for state legislature below Act 64's $150 and $100 per election limits.** And we are aware of no

* [These states are Arizona, Colorado, Florida, Maine, Massachusetts, Montana, South Dakota.—Eds.]

** [These states are Arizona, Montana, and South Dakota.—Eds.]

State that has a lower limit on contributions from political parties to state legislative candidates.

Finally, Vermont's limit is well below the lowest limit this Court has previously upheld, the limit of $1,075 per election (adjusted for inflation every two years) for candidates for Missouri state auditor. [*Nixon v. Shrink Missouri Government PAC* (2000)]. The comparable Vermont limit of roughly $200 per election, not adjusted for inflation, is less than one-sixth of Missouri's current inflation-adjusted limit ($1,275).

In sum, Act 64's contribution limits are substantially lower than both the limits we have previously upheld and comparable limits in other States. These are danger signs that Act 64's contribution limits may fall outside tolerable First Amendment limits. We consequently must examine the record independently and carefully to determine whether Act 64's contribution limits are "closely drawn" to match the State's interests.

C

Our examination of the record convinces us that, from a constitutional perspective, Act 64's contribution limits are too restrictive. We reach this conclusion based not merely on the low dollar amounts of the limits themselves, but also on the statute's effect on political parties and on volunteer activity in Vermont elections. Taken together, Act 64's substantial restrictions on the ability of candidates to raise the funds necessary to run a competitive election, on the ability of political parties to help their candidates get elected, and on the ability of individual citizens to volunteer their time to campaigns show that the Act is not closely drawn to meet its objectives. In particular, five factors together lead us to this decision.

First, the record suggests, though it does not conclusively prove, that Act 64's contribution limits will significantly restrict the amount of funding available for challengers to run competitive campaigns. For one thing, the petitioners' expert, Clark Bensen, conducted a race-by-race analysis of the 1998 legislative elections (the last to take place before Act 64 took effect) and concluded that Act 64's contribution limits would have reduced the funds available in 1998 to Republican challengers in competitive races in amounts ranging from 18% to 53% of their total campaign income.

For another thing, the petitioners' expert witnesses produced evidence and analysis showing that Vermont political parties (particularly the Republican Party) "target" their contributions to candidates in competitive races, that those contributions represent a significant amount of total candidate funding in such races, and that the contribution limits will cut the parties' contributions to competitive races dramatically. Their statistics showed that the party contributions accounted for a significant percentage of the total campaign income in those races. And their studies showed that Act 64's contribution limits would cut the party contributions by between 85% (for the legislature on average) and 99% (for governor).

The respondents did not contest these figures. Rather, they presented evidence that focused, not upon strongly contested campaigns, but upon the funding amounts available for the average campaign. The respondents' expert, Anthony Gierzynski, concluded, for example, that Act 64 would have a "minimal effect on . . . candidates' ability to raise funds." But he rested this conclusion upon his finding that "only a small proportion of" all contributions to all campaigns for state office "made during the last three elections would have been affected by the new limits."

The respondents' evidence leaves the petitioners' evidence unrebutted in certain key respects. That is because the critical question concerns not simply the average effect of contribution limits on fundraising but, more importantly, the ability of a candidate running against an incumbent officeholder to mount an effective challenge. And information about average races, rather than competitive races, is only distantly related to that question, because competitive races are likely to be far more expensive than the average race.

Rather, the petitioners' studies, taken together with low average Vermont campaign expenditures and the typically higher costs that a challenger must bear to overcome the name-recognition advantage enjoyed by an incumbent, raise a reasonable inference that the contribution limits are so low that they may pose a significant obstacle to candidates in competitive elections. Information about average races does not rebut that inference. Consequently, the inference amounts to one factor (among others) that here counts against the constitutional validity of the contribution limits.

Second, Act 64's insistence that political parties abide by exactly the same low contribution limits that apply to other contributors threatens harm to a particularly important political right, the right to associate in a political party.

The Act applies its $200 to $400 limits—precisely the same limits it applies to an individual—to virtually all affiliates of a political party taken together as if they were a single contributor. That means, for example, that the Vermont Democratic Party, taken together with all its local affiliates, can make one contribution of at most $400 to the Democratic gubernatorial candidate, one contribution of at most $300 to a Democratic candidate for State Senate, and one contribution of at most $200 to a Democratic candidate for the State House of Representatives. The Act includes within these limits not only direct monetary contributions but also expenditures in kind: stamps, stationery, coffee, doughnuts, gasoline, campaign buttons, and so forth. Indeed, it includes all party expenditures "intended to promote the election of a specific candidate or group of candidates" as long as the candidate's campaign "facilitate[s]," "solicit[s]," or "approve[s]" them. §§ 2809(a), (c). And a party expenditure that "primarily benefits six or fewer candidates who are associated with the" party is "presumed" to count against the party's contribution limits. § 2809(d).

In addition to the negative effect on "amassing funds" that we have described, the Act would severely limit the ability of a party to assist its candidates' campaigns by engaging in coordinated spending on advertising, candidate events, voter lists, mass mailings, even yard signs. And, to an unusual degree, it would discourage those who wish to contribute small amounts of money to a party, amounts that easily comply with individual contribution limits. Suppose that many individuals do not know Vermont legislative candidates personally, but wish to contribute, say, $20 or $40, to the State Republican Party, with the intent that the party use the money to help elect whichever candidates the party believes would best advance its ideals and interests—the basic object of a political party. Or, to take a more extreme example, imagine that 6,000 Vermont citizens each want to give $1 to the State Democratic Party because, though unfamiliar with the details of the individual races, they would like to make a small financial contribution to the goal of electing a Democratic state legislature. And further imagine that the party believes control of the legislature will depend on the outcome of three (and only three) House races. The Act prohibits the party from giving $2,000 (of the $6,000) to each of its candidates in those pivotal races. Indeed, it permits the party to give no more than $200 to each candidate, thereby thwarting the aims of the 6,000 donors from making a meaningful contribution to state politics by giving a small amount of money to the party they support. Thus, the Act would severely inhibit collective political activity by preventing a political party from using contributions by small donors to provide meaningful assistance to any individual candidate.

We consequently agree with the District Court that the Act's contribution limits "would reduce the voice of political parties" in Vermont to a "whisper." And we count the special party-related harms that Act 64 threatens as a further factor weighing against the constitutional validity of the contribution limits.

Third, the Act's treatment of volunteer services aggravates the problem. Like its federal statutory counterpart, the Act excludes from its definition of "contribution" all "services provided without compensation by individuals volunteering their time on behalf of a candidate." Vt. Stat. Ann., Tit. 17, § 2801(2) (2002). But the Act does not exclude the expenses those volunteers incur, such as travel expenses, in the course of campaign activities. The Act's broad definitions would seem to count those expenses against the volunteer's contribution limit, at least where the spending was facilitated or approved by campaign officials. And, unlike the Federal Government's treatment of comparable requirements, the State has not (insofar as we are aware) created an exception excluding such expenses.

The absence of some such exception may matter in the present context, where contribution limits are very low. That combination, low limits and no exceptions, means that a gubernatorial campaign volunteer who makes four or five round trips driving across the State performing volunteer activities coordinated with the campaign can find that he or she is near, or has surpassed, the contribution limit. So too will a volunteer who offers a campaign the use of her house along with coffee and doughnuts for a few dozen neighbors to meet the candidate, say, two or three times during a campaign. Such supporters will have to keep careful track of all miles driven, postage supplied (500 stamps equals $200), pencils and pads used, and so forth. And any carelessness in this respect can prove costly, perhaps generating a headline, "Campaign laws violated," that works serious harm to the candidate.

These sorts of problems are unlikely to affect the constitutionality of a limit that is reasonably high. But Act 64's contribution limits are so low, and its definition of "contribution" so broad, that the Act may well impede a campaign's ability effectively to use volunteers, thereby making it more difficult for individuals to associate in this way. Again, the very low limits at issue help to transform differences in degree into difference in kind. And the likelihood of unjustified interference in the present context is sufficiently great that we must consider the lack of tailoring in the Act's definition of "contribution" as an added factor counting against the constitutional validity of the contribution limits before us.

Fourth, unlike the contribution limits we upheld in *Shrink*, Act 64's contribution limits are not adjusted for inflation. Its limits decline in real value each year. Indeed, in real dollars the Act's limits have already declined by about 20% ($200 in 2006 dollars has a real value of $160.66 in 1997 dollars). A failure to index limits means that limits which are already suspiciously low will almost inevitably become too low over time. It means that future legislation will be necessary to stop that almost inevitable decline, and it thereby imposes the burden of preventing the decline upon incumbent legislators who may not diligently police the need for changes in limit levels to ensure the adequate financing of electoral challenges.

Fifth, we have found nowhere in the record any special justification that might warrant a contribution limit so low or so restrictive as to bring about the serious associational and expressive problems that we have described. Rather, the basic justifications the State has advanced in support of such limits are those present in *Buckley*. The record contains no indication that, for example, corruption (or its appearance) in Vermont is significantly more serious a matter than elsewhere. Indeed, other things being equal, one might reasonably believe that a contribution of, say, $250 (or $450) to a candidate's campaign was less likely to prove a corruptive force than the far larger contributions at issue in the other campaign finance cases we have considered.

These five sets of considerations, taken together, lead us to conclude that Act 64's contribution limits are not narrowly tailored. Rather, the Act burdens First Amendment interests by threatening to inhibit effective advocacy by those who seek election, particularly challengers; its contribution limits mute the voice of political parties; they hamper participation in campaigns through volunteer activities; and they are not indexed for inflation. Vermont does not point to a legitimate statutory objective that might justify these special burdens. We understand that many, though not all, campaign finance regulations impose certain of these burdens to some degree. We also understand the legitimate need for constitutional leeway in respect to legislative line-drawing. But our discussion indicates why we conclude that Act 64 in this respect nonetheless goes too far. It disproportionately burdens numerous First Amendment interests, and consequently, in our view, violates the First Amendment.

[T]he judgment of the Court of Appeals is reversed, and the cases are remanded for further proceedings.

It is so ordered.

Justice ALITO, concurring in part and concurring in the judgment.
[Omitted.]

Justice KENNEDY, concurring in the judgment.
[Omitted.]

Justice THOMAS, with whom Justice SCALIA joins, concurring in the judgment.

[Justice Thomas indicated that he would overrule *Buckley*'s holding with respect to contribution limitations, stating that there is no meaningful distinction between a contribution and an independent expenditure. He would thus subject both contribution and expenditure limitations to strict scrutiny review.]

Justice STEVENS, dissenting.

[Justice Stevens stated that he would overrule *Buckley*'s holding with respect to independent expenditures and allow Congress to regulate them. Justice Stevens noted the "fundraising straitjacket" that the lack of independent expenditure limitations engenders.]

Justice SOUTER, with whom Justice GINSBURG joins, and with whom Justice STEVENS joins as to Parts II and III, dissenting.

In 1997, the Legislature of Vermont passed Act 64 after a series of public hearings persuaded legislators that rehabilitating the State's political process required campaign finance reform. A majority of the Court today decides that the expenditure and contribution limits enacted are irreconcilable with the Constitution's guarantee of free speech. I would adhere to the Court of Appeals's decision to remand for further enquiry bearing on the limitations on candidates' expenditures, and I think the contribution limits satisfy controlling precedent. I respectfully dissent.

I

[Omitted.]

II

I believe the Court of Appeals correctly rejected the challenge to the contribution limits. Low though they are, one cannot say that "the contribution limitation[s are] so radical in effect as to render political association ineffective, drive the sound of a candidate's voice below the level of notice, and render contributions pointless." *Nixon v. Shrink Missouri Government PAC* (2000).

To place Vermont's contribution limits beyond the constitutional pale, therefore, is to forget not only the facts of *Shrink*, but also our self-admonition against second-guessing legislative judgments about the risk of corruption to which contribution limits have to be fitted. And deference here would surely not be overly complaisant. Vermont's legislators themselves testified at length about the money that gets their special attention, see Legislative Findings (finding that "[s]ome candidates and elected officials, particularly when time is limited, respond and give access to contributors who make large contributions in preference to those who make small or no contributions"); [Lower court opinion] (testimony of Elizabeth Ready: "If I have only got an hour at night when I get home to return calls, I am much more likely to return [a donor's] call than I would [a non-donor's]. . . . [W]hen you only have a few minutes to talk, there are certain people that get access" (alterations in original)). The record revealed the amount of money the public sees as suspiciously large. And testimony identified the amounts high enough to pay for effective campaigning in a State where the cost of running tends to be on the low side.

Still, our cases do not say deference should be absolute. We can all imagine dollar limits that would be laughable, and per capita comparisons that would be meaningless because aggregated donations simply could not sustain effective campaigns. The plurality thinks that point has been reached in Vermont, and in particular that the low contribution limits threaten the ability of challengers to run effective races against incumbents. Thus, the plurality's limit of deference is substantially a function of suspicion that political incumbents in the legislature set low contribution limits because their public recognition and easy access to free publicity will effectively augment their own spending power beyond anything a challenger can muster. The suspicion is, in other words, that incumbents cannot be trusted to set fair limits, because facially neutral limits do not in fact give challengers an even break. But this received suspicion is itself a proper subject of suspicion. The petitioners offered, and the plurality invokes, no evidence that the risk of a pro-incumbent advantage has been realized. The Legislature of Vermont evidently tried to account for the realities of campaigning in Vermont, and I see no evidence of constitutional miscalculation sufficient to dispense with respect for its judgments.

III

Four issues of detail call for some attention, the first being the requirement that a volunteer's expenses count against the person's contribution limit. The plurality certainly makes out the case that accounting for these expenses will be a colossal nuisance, but there is no case here that the nuisance will noticeably limit volunteering, or that volunteers whose expenses reach the limit cannot continue with their efforts subject to charging their candidates for the excess. Granted, if the provisions for contribution limits were teetering on the edge of unconstitutionality, Act 64's treatment of volunteers' expenses might be the finger-flick that gives the fatal push, but it has no greater significance than that.

Second, the failure of the Vermont law to index its limits for inflation is even less important. This challenge is to the law as it is, not to a law that may have a different impact after future inflation if the state legislature fails to bring it up to economic date.

Third, subjecting political parties to the same contribution limits as individuals does not condemn the Vermont scheme. What we said in *Federal Election Comm'n v. Colorado Republican Federal Campaign Comm.* (2001), dealing with regulation of coordinated expenditures, goes here, too. The capacity and desire of parties to make large contributions to competitive candidates with uphill fights are shared by rich individuals, and the risk that large party contributions would be channels to evade individual limits cannot be eliminated. Nor are these reasons to support the party limits undercut by claims that the restrictions render parties impotent, for the parties are not precluded from uncoordinated spending to benefit their candidates. That said, I acknowledge the suggestions in the petitioners' briefs that such restrictions in synergy with other influences weakening party power would justify a wholesale reexamination of the situation of party organization today. But whether such a comprehensive reexamination belongs in courts or only in legislatures is not an issue presented by these cases.

[Justice Souter's fourth point here is omitted.]

IV

Because I would not pass upon the constitutionality of Vermont's expenditure limits prior to further enquiry into their fit with the problem of fundraising demands on candidates, and because I do not see the contribution limits as depressed to the level of political inaudibility, I respectfully dissent.

Foster v. Dilger

Civil Action No. 3:10-41 (E.D. Ky. 2010)

DANNY C. REEVES, District Judge.

Plaintiffs Benjamin Foster and Edward Britton have filed a Motion for a Preliminary Injunction. Plaintiffs argue that Kentucky Revised Statutes ("KRS") § 121.150(6) is unconstitutional and Defendant Dilger and the Kentucky Registry of Election Finance ("Registry") should be enjoined from enforcing the statute's limits on contributions by individuals. For the following reasons, the motion will be granted.

I. BACKGROUND AND FINDINGS OF FACT

Plaintiffs are individuals who wish to contribute more than $100 to local school board election campaigns, but cannot do so for fear of criminal prosecution. At the current time, a donor may not contribute more than $100 to each school board candidate. The pertinent portion of KRS § 121.150(6) states:

> No person, permanent committee, or contributing organization shall contribute more than one thousand dollars ($1,000) to any one (1) candidate, campaign committee, political issues committee, nor anyone acting on their behalf, in any one (1) election; except that no person shall contribute more than one hundred dollars ($100) and no permanent committee or contributing organization shall contribute more than two hundred dollars ($200) to any one (1) school board candidate, his campaign committee, nor anyone acting on their behalf, in any one (1) election.

A violation of KRS § 121.150(6) carries a criminal penalty. Plaintiffs claim that the provision limiting donations to candidates for school board unconstitutionally violates their First Amendment rights of expression and association.

The most salient facts in this case are those from Jefferson County. In Jefferson County, campaigns for school board have become increasingly expensive as a result of large independent expenditures by the Jefferson County Teachers Association ("JCTA"). In 2008, JCTA spent nearly $150,000 in support of a single candidate. Plaintiffs highlighted numerous other races where JCTA spent well over $100,000 in support of individual candidates. In contrast, candidates who rely on individual donations must raise support in $100 increments. The Registry confirmed that the overwhelming majority of candidates raise less than $3,000 per campaign from individual donors. Plaintiffs argue that the $100 limit is unconstitutional because, when viewed in contrast with the increasing amounts of independent expenditures and cost of campaigns, it drives the candidate's voice below the point of notice and effectively nullifies their ability to mount a campaign based on individual donations.

II. ANALYSIS

A. Preliminary Injunction Standard

The Sixth Circuit has developed a well-settled, four-factor test to direct the Court's inquiry. The Court should consider: (1) whether there is a strong or substantial likelihood of success on the merits; (2) whether an injunction is necessary to prevent irreparable harm to the plaintiff; (3) whether granting the injunction will cause harm to others, including the defendant; and (4) whether the public interest favors granting the injunction.

B. Irreparable Injury

Plaintiffs correctly contend that they will suffer irreparable harm if the Court does not enjoin enforcement of KRS § 121.150(6). The violation of an individual's constitutional guarantees is intolerable and undoubtably causes irreparable injury. The Supreme Court has recognized that "the loss of First Amendment freedoms, for even minimal periods of time, unquestionably constitutes irreparable injury." *Elrod v. Burns* (1976). If KRS § 121.150(6) does in fact violate Plaintiffs' constitutional freedom of association or speech, allowing its continued operation would cause Plaintiffs irreparable harm.

C. Likelihood of Success on the Merits

The question then becomes whether KRS § 121.150(6) violates Plaintiffs' constitutional right or, in other words, whether Plaintiffs are likely to succeed on the merits of their challenge. After considering the respective arguments, the Court concludes that the Plaintiffs have shown a substantial likelihood of success on their constitutional challenge.

1. Standard of Scrutiny

The initial issue in determining whether Plaintiffs are likely to succeed on the merits is what standard of scrutiny should be applied to the provision they challenge. Under Supreme Court precedent, there is a distinction between the standard of scrutiny applied to regulations of campaign expenditures and those limiting campaign contributions. *Buckley v. Valeo* (1976). Despite Plaintiffs' contention that this distinction is "dubious" and "meaningless," both the Supreme Court and Sixth Circuit have continued to apply it in their holdings. While limits on expenditures are subject to strict scrutiny, limits on contributions are subject to "less rigorous scrutiny," *McConnell.* Contribution limits must be "closely drawn to match a sufficiently important [governmental] interest." [citation omitted] (quoting *McConnell*). KRS § 121.150(6) limits direct contributions. Therefore, to withstand constitutional scrutiny, the regulation must be closely drawn to a sufficiently important governmental interest.

2. The Government's Interest

Defendant asserts that the regulation's purpose is to prevent corruption or the appearance of corruption. This interest is clearly important. The Court in *Citizens United* explained that the anti-corruption rationale is limited to the prevention of actual quid pro quo corruption or the appearance of such. *Citizens United* (2010). Defendant has provided a sufficiently important justification for KRS § 121.150(6), because it is intended to prevent quid pro quo corruption or the appearance of such corruption.

3. Whether the Regulation is "Closely Drawn" to Prevent Quid Pro Quo Corruption

While there is little doubt about the sufficiency of the government's interest, the question becomes whether KRS § 121.150(6) is closely drawn to achieve its stated purpose. A statute is closely drawn when its enforcement does not substantially burden an individual's rights more than is necessary to further the government's legitimate interests.

Plaintiffs contend that the $100 limit is so small that it impermissibly burdens Plaintiffs' associational rights more than is necessary to simply prevent corruption. This argument has substantial merit. While the Court has held that the dollar amount of a contribution "need not be 'fine tuned,'" *Nixon* [*v. Shrink Missouri Government PAC* (2000)] (citing *Buckley*), there is a point at which a limit is so low as to effectively abridge an individual contributor's associational rights. The Court in *Nixon* recognized that some limits may be "so radical in effect as to render political association ineffective, drive the sound of a candidate's voice below the level of notice, and render contributions pointless." The issue, the Court held, "must go to the power to mount a campaign with all the dollars likely to be forthcoming."

Plaintiffs have produced evidence which shows a substantial likelihood that the statute's $100 limit is so low as to make individual contributors' political association ineffective.

At the outset, a regulation limiting contributions over $100 cannot be per se too low. The Sixth Circuit approved a $100 contribution limit for the City of Akron's municipal elections. *Frank v. City of Akron* (6th Cir. 2002). However, the Sixth Circuit's holding in *Frank* is distinguishable from the case at bar. The amendment to the City of Akron's charter limited contributions for elections in one locality: Akron. The court explained that the limit did not fall below the *Nixon* threshold because it did not inhibit candidates from accumulating substantial war chests. The limit did not drive the voice of the candidate below notice because candidates in Akron elections rarely used mass media or television in the way candidates in larger campaigns did. The court found the $100 limit closely drawn to prevent quid pro quo corruption in the Akron municipal elections.

The same cannot be said for a $100 limit for all school board elections across the Commonwealth. Other courts have considered equally low limits and found that they were not "closely drawn." *See Russel v. Burris* (8th Cir. 1998) (striking down contribution limits of $100 and $300 for statewide candidates); *Carver v. Nixon* (8th Cir. 1995) (striking down a system of tiered contribution limits based on the size of the district, where districts with fewer than 100,000 residents were subject to a $100 contribution limit); *Nat'l Black Police Ass'n v. Dist. of Columbia Bd. of Elections and Ethics* (D.D.C. 1996) (holding a $100 contribution limit for mayoral elections unconstitutional).

Defendants have not shown that any of the factors which distinguished *Frank* from this line of precedents are present in this case. First, Jefferson County is significantly larger than the City of Akron. Campaigns in Jefferson County have become increasingly expensive and candidates who rely on individual donations cannot compete. Well-funded candidates regularly utilize expensive mass-media to support their campaigns. Large independent expenditures have driven up the costs of campaigns and made it unrealistic to mount a campaign based solely on individual contributions. The facts which the court found persuasive in *Frank* do not apply to school board elections in counties such as Jefferson County. Plaintiffs' constitutional rights are in danger because KRS § 121.150(6)'s $100 limit threatens to make their individual contributions, and political association, absolutely ineffective. As the *Nixon* court stated, the issue is the power to mount a campaign with the dollars likely to be forthcoming. Here, the Plaintiffs have shown that mounting a campaign on individual contributions is nearly impossible in Jefferson County. Defendant argues that in smaller counties, such as Clay County or Breathitt County, raising the limit to $1,000 is imprudent because that amount "could buy contributors considerable influence." They demonstrate the tailoring problem precisely. While a $100 limit may be necessary to prevent quid pro quo corruption in smaller counties, a $100 contribution is insignificant in Jefferson County. If the purpose is to prevent quid pro quo corruption, the potential for such corruption at a particular dollar amount cannot be the same in every county of every size statewide. The charter amendment in *Frank* was upheld because it was closely drawn to the need to prevent corruption in a particular city election. The Registry has not provided evidence to show that a limit as low as $100 is closely drawn to prevent quid pro quo in places such as Jefferson County. In those counties, such a limit is so low as to nullify Plaintiffs' associational exercise.

Based upon the foregoing analysis, the Plaintiffs have made a sufficient showing that they have a substantial likelihood of success on the merits of their constitutional challenge.

D. Injury to Others

Defendant argues that the Registry and other candidates for school board will be harmed by the granting of a preliminary injunction. He asserts that an injunction will harm the Registry because the Registry has already printed materials outlining the current guidelines and changing the guidelines would cause confusion and expense. Defendant also argues other candidates will be injured who had "planned their campaign strategies taking into account the $100 contribution limit." The Court does not find either of these arguments persuasive.

The harm and difficulty of changing a regulation cannot be said to outweigh the violation of constitutional rights it perpetuates. It would be far worse that an election continue under an unconstitutional regime than the Registry experience difficulty or expense in altering that regime. Further, it is unlikely any individual candidate will be harmed by an injunction. First, the Defendant has offered no proof to support his contention that all candidates have built their campaign strategies around $100 limits. Second, the change in regulations will apply to all candidates. No one candidate will suddenly be on stronger footing than another. All will be allowed to solicit $1,000 donations. It is unlikely that the availability of an extra $900 per donor, by being able to solicit $1,000 rather than $100, will cause harm to an individual candidate. When the potential harm to Plaintiffs is the violation of their constitutional rights and the potential harms to Defendant and others are small, the balance of hardships weighs in favor of granting the injunction.

E. The Public Interest

"It is in the public interest not to perpetuate the unconstitutional application of a statute." *Martin-Marietta Corp. v. Bendix Corp.* (6th Cir. 1982). Every citizen of Kentucky, not just the individual plaintiffs, has a constitutionally-protected interest in political association. When a statute potentially violates that interest, the public interest weighs in favor of enjoining its enforcement. Here, Plaintiffs have met their burden of showing that they have a substantial likelihood of success on the merits of their challenge, and the public interest weighs in favor of enjoining the continued enforcement of the potentially unconstitutional provision.

F. Scope of Injunction

When a court confronts a constitutional flaw in a statute, the court should "fit the solution to the problem" and enjoin only the unconstitutional applications while leaving the other applications in force. *Ayotte v. Planned Parenthood* (2006). Accordingly, there is no need for the Court to enjoin the enforcement of KRS § 121.150(6) altogether. The Court will limit the scope of its injunction to the enforcement of the $100 contribution limit for individual donors to school board campaigns. The $1,000 limit on contributions stands and now governs campaigns for school board as well.

III. CONCLUSION

Plaintiffs have met their burden of showing that a preliminary injunction is proper. They have proven that their constitutional right of association is in danger and that they will suffer irreparable harm if the Court does not issue an injunction. They have also demonstrated a substantial likelihood of success on the merits of their constitutional challenge to KRS § 121.150(6). They have further shown that an injunction would not cause undue harm to others and that the public interest supports an injunction. For these reasons, it is hereby

Ordered that Plaintiffs' Motion for a Preliminary Injunction is granted. The Court preliminarily enjoins the Registry from enforcing KRS § 121.150(6)'s $100 contribution limit in school board campaigns or prosecuting individuals for contributing amounts above that limit.

[Note: The court eventually converted its preliminary injunction to a permanent injunction and entered a declaratory judgment that KRS § 121.150(6)'s $100 contribution limit for school board campaigns violates the First Amendment.]

NOTES ON *RANDALL* AND *FOSTER*

1. Note how the analyses in these cases are extremely fact-specific. The courts thus far have eschewed bright-line rules in the contribution context, instead explaining that the constitutionality of a contribution limitation will depend largely on the context of the elections in the particular jurisdiction. But ask yourself whether the analysis will be the same in the future in light of the changed composition of the Court, with Justice Alito replacing Justice O'Connor, Justice Kavanaugh replacing Justice Kennedy, and Justice Barrett replacing Justice Ginsburg, and the consequent rightward shift of the Court on campaign finance regulation.

2. The *Buckley* Court seemed to suggest that contribution limitations are usually valid because they must meet only a lower ("closely drawn") level of scrutiny. Given that both courts struck down contribution limitations under that "lower" threshold, do these cases call that holding into question? Note that other lower courts have generally upheld contribution limitations under closely drawn scrutiny. That is, most contribution limitations are probably constitutional, so long as they are not so low as to actually preclude a candidate from mounting a successful campaign.

3. In a portion of *Randall* that we omitted, the Court invalidated Vermont's expenditure limitations, refusing the state's invitation to overrule *Buckley*. It also disagreed with Vermont's alternative argument for imposing an expenditure limitation: to reduce the amount of time candidates must spend raising money. Vermont asserted that, without an expenditure limitation, candidates would have to spend more time raising money to combat the expenditures against them and therefore less time meeting voters. The Court rejected this rationale, saying that a desire to protect a candidate's time from fundraising did not undermine *Buckley*'s reasoning regarding the First Amendment implications of an expenditure limitation.

4. *Foster* is also a good illustration of how the preliminary injunction standard operates in the context of an election law dispute. This standard comes up frequently in election litigation, especially as an election draws near.

5. Imagine you are in the Kentucky legislature. What kind of bill would you propose to maintain a sufficiently low contribution limit for school board elections but still follow the *Foster* court's requirements? Put more broadly, what is the best way to tailor a contribution limitation?

***

AGGREGATE CONTRIBUTION LIMITS

In addition to limiting the size of a contribution that an individual may give to a single candidate, federal law also limited the total contributions an individual could give to all candidates or political committees during a two-year election cycle. Under the Federal Election Campaign Act (FECA) (as subsequently amended), an individual could contribute a total of $48,600 to all federal candidates combined, and a total of $74,600 to all noncandidate political committees such as national or state political parties or PACs, during a two-year election cycle. (The aggregate contribution limits were indexed for inflation.) *See* 2 U.S.C. § 441a. These aggregate limits represented the total cap of all contributions; the law also imposed base contribution limits for individual donations (in 2020, set at $2,800 per election to a federal candidate, $10,000 per year to a state or local political party, $35,500 per year to a national political party committee, $106,500 to other national party committee accounts such as for inauguration expenses or election recounts, and $5,000 per year to any other political committee).

The aggregation limits, however, did not apply to so-called "Super PACs," which promise to make only independent expenditures rather than contributions of their own to candidates. In the wake of *Citizens United* and *Speech Now* (to be addressed later in this Part), the Federal Election Commission decided not to enforce any limits on the amount of money individuals may give to these Super

PACs, which in turn are free to spend as much as they wish on express advocacy to support a candidate.

The Court in *Buckley* had upheld FECA's original aggregate contribution limits but did not provide much explanation. Here is the crux of the analysis from *Buckley*:

> The over-all [contribution] ceiling does impose an ultimate restriction upon the number of candidates and committees with which an individual may associate himself by means of financial support. But this quite modest restraint upon protected political activity serves to prevent evasion of the [individual] contribution limitation by a person who might otherwise contribute massive amounts of money to a particular candidate through the use of unearmarked contributions to political committees likely to contribute to that candidate, or huge contributions to the candidate's political party. The limited, additional restriction on associational freedom imposed by the over-all ceiling is thus no more than a corollary of the basic individual contribution limitation that we have found to be constitutionally valid.

Buckley v. Valeo (1976).

The Supreme Court revisited the aggregate contribution limitation in 2014 in *McCutcheon v. FEC*, reversing this portion of *Buckley* by a 5-4 vote and striking down the limit on the total amount an individual may give to all candidates during an election cycle. As you read this case, think about what the majority's reasoning suggests regarding Congress's ability to regulate the flow of money in politics. Does the ability of wealthy individuals to spread their money to as many candidates as they want undermine the effectiveness of contribution limits to quell corruption or its appearance, especially given that candidates may give money from their campaign accounts to other candidates? Does this decision suggest that the individual contribution ban might fall as well in the near future?

McCutcheon v. FEC

572 U.S. 185 (2014)

Chief Justice Roberts announced the judgment of the Court and delivered an opinion, in which Justice Scalia, Justice Kennedy, and Justice Alito join.

The statute at issue in this case imposes two types of limits on campaign contributions. The first, called base limits, restricts how much money a donor may contribute to a particular candidate or committee. 2 U.S.C. § 441a(a)(1). The second, called aggregate limits, restricts how much money a donor may contribute in total to all candidates or committees. § 441a(a)(3).

This case does not involve any challenge to the base limits, which we have previously upheld as serving the permissible objective of combatting corruption. The Government contends that the aggregate limits also serve that objective, by preventing circumvention of the base limits. We conclude, however, that the aggregate limits do little, if anything, to address that concern, while seriously restricting participation in the democratic process. The aggregate limits are therefore invalid under the First Amendment.

I

A

The base limits restrict how much money a donor may contribute to any particular candidate or committee; the aggregate limits have the effect of restricting how many candidates or committees the donor may support, to the extent permitted by the base limits.

B

[Omitted.]

II

A

[Omitted.]

B

1

The parties and *amici curiae* spend significant energy debating whether the line that *Buckley* drew between contributions and expenditures should remain the law. Notwithstanding the robust debate, we see no need in this case to revisit *Buckley*'s distinction between contributions and expenditures and the corollary distinction in the applicable standards of review. *Buckley* held that the Government's interest in preventing *quid pro quo* corruption or its appearance was "sufficiently important"; we have elsewhere stated that the same interest may properly be labeled "compelling," so that the interest would satisfy even strict scrutiny. Moreover, regardless whether we apply strict scrutiny or *Buckley*'s "closely drawn" test [for contribution limitations], we must assess the fit between the stated governmental objective and the means selected to achieve that objective. Or to put it another way, if a law that restricts political speech does not "avoid unnecessary abridgement" of First Amendment rights, *Buckley*, it cannot survive "rigorous" review.

Because we find a substantial mismatch between the Government's stated objective and the means selected to achieve it, the aggregate limits fail even under the "closely drawn" test. We therefore need not parse the differences between the two standards in this case.

2

Buckley treated the constitutionality of the $25,000 aggregate limit as contingent upon that limit's ability to prevent circumvention of the $1,000 base limit, describing the aggregate limit as "no more than a corollary" of the base limit. The Court determined that circumvention could occur when an individual legally contributes "massive amounts of money to a particular candidate through the use of unearmarked contributions" to entities that are themselves likely to contribute to the candidate. For that reason, the Court upheld the $25,000 aggregate limit.

Although *Buckley* provides some guidance, we think that its ultimate conclusion about the constitutionality of the aggregate limit in place under FECA does not control here. *Buckley* spent a total of three sentences analyzing that limit; in fact, the opinion pointed out that the constitutionality of the aggregate limit "ha[d] not been separately addressed at length by the parties." We are now asked to address appellants' direct challenge to the aggregate limits in place under BCRA. BCRA is a different statutory regime, and the aggregate limits it imposes operate against a distinct legal backdrop.

Most notably, statutory safeguards against circumvention have been considerably strengthened since *Buckley* was decided, through both statutory additions and the introduction of a comprehensive regulatory scheme. With more targeted anti-circumvention measures in place today, the indiscriminate aggregate limits under BCRA appear particularly heavy-handed.

The intricate regulatory scheme that the Federal Election Commission has enacted since *Buckley* . . . limits the opportunities for circumvention of the base limits via "unearmarked contributions to political committees likely to contribute" to a particular candidate. Although the earmarking provision was in place when *Buckley* was decided, the FEC has since added regulations that define earmarking broadly. For example, the regulations construe earmarking to include any designation, "whether direct or indirect, express or implied, oral or written." The regulations specify that an individual who has contributed to a particular candidate may not also contribute to a single-candidate committee for that candidate. Nor may an individual who has contributed to a candidate also contribute to a political committee that has supported or anticipates supporting the same candidate, if the individual knows that "a substantial portion [of his contribution] will be contributed to, or expended on behalf of," that candidate.

Given the foregoing, this case cannot be resolved merely by pointing to three sentences in *Buckley* that were written without the benefit of full briefing or argument on the issue. We are confronted with a different statute and different legal arguments, at a different point in the development of campaign finance regulation. Appellants' substantial First Amendment challenge to the system of aggregate limits currently in place thus merits our plenary consideration.

III

Buckley acknowledged that aggregate limits at least diminish an individual's right of political association. As the Court explained, the "overall $25,000 ceiling does impose an ultimate restriction upon the number of candidates and committees with which an individual may associate himself by means of financial support." But the Court characterized that restriction as a "quite modest restraint upon protected political activity." We cannot agree with that characterization. An aggregate limit on *how many* candidates and committees an individual may support through contributions is not a "modest restraint" at all. The Government may no more restrict how many candidates or causes a donor may support than it may tell a newspaper how many candidates it may endorse.

To put it in the simplest terms, the aggregate limits prohibit an individual from fully contributing to the primary and general election campaigns of ten or more candidates, even if all contributions fall within the base limits Congress views as adequate to protect against corruption. The individual may give up to $5,200 each to nine candidates, but the aggregate limits constitute an outright ban on further contributions to any other candidate (beyond the additional $1,800 that may be spent before reaching the $48,600 aggregate limit). At that point, the limits deny the individual all ability to exercise his expressive and associational rights by contributing to someone who will advocate for his policy preferences. A donor must limit the number of candidates he supports, and may have to choose which of several policy concerns he will advance—clear First Amendment harms that the dissent never acknowledges.

It is no answer to say that the individual can simply contribute less money to more people. To require one person to contribute at lower levels than others because he wants to support more candidates or causes is to impose a special burden on broader participation in the democratic process. And as we have recently admonished, the Government may not penalize an individual for "robustly exercis[ing]" his First Amendment rights. *Davis v. Federal Election Comm'n* (2008).

The First Amendment burden is especially great for individuals who do not have ready access to alternative avenues for supporting their preferred politicians and policies. In the context of base contribution limits, *Buckley* observed that a supporter could vindicate his associational interests by personally volunteering his time and energy on behalf of a candidate. Such personal volunteering is not a realistic alternative for those who wish to support a wide variety of candidates or causes. Other effective methods of supporting preferred candidates or causes without contributing money are reserved for a select few, such as entertainers capable of raising hundreds of thousands of dollars in a single evening.

The dissent faults this focus on "the individual's right to engage in political speech," saying that it fails to take into account "the public's interest" in "collective speech." This "collective" interest is said to promote "a government where laws reflect the very thoughts, views, ideas, and sentiments, the expression of which the First Amendment protects."

But there are compelling reasons not to define the boundaries of the First Amendment by reference to such a generalized conception of the public good. First, the dissent's "collective speech" reflected in laws is of course the will of the majority, and plainly can include laws that restrict free speech. The whole point of the First Amendment is to afford individuals protection against such infringements. The First Amendment does not protect the government, even when the government purports to act through legislation reflecting "collective speech."

Second, the degree to which speech is protected cannot turn on a legislative or judicial determination that particular speech is useful to the democratic process. The First Amendment does not contemplate such ad hoc balancing of relative social costs and benefits.

Third, our established First Amendment analysis already takes account of any "collective" interest that may justify restrictions on individual speech. Under that accepted analysis, such restrictions are measured against the asserted public interest (usually framed as an important or compelling governmental interest). As explained below, we do not doubt the compelling nature of the "collective" interest in preventing corruption in the electoral process. But we permit Congress to pursue that interest only so long as it does not unnecessarily infringe an individual's right to freedom of speech; we do not truncate this tailoring test at the outset.

IV

A

With the significant First Amendment costs for individual citizens in mind, we turn to the governmental interests asserted in this case. This Court has identified only one legitimate governmental interest for restricting campaign finances: preventing corruption or the appearance of corruption. We have consistently rejected attempts to suppress campaign speech based on other legislative objectives. No matter how desirable it may seem, it is not an acceptable governmental objective to "level the playing field," or to "level electoral opportunities," or to "equaliz[e] the financial resources of candidates." [Citations omitted.] The First Amendment prohibits such legislative attempts to "fine-tun[e]" the electoral process, no matter how well intentioned.

As we framed the relevant principle in *Buckley*, "the concept that government may restrict the speech of some elements of our society in order to enhance the relative voice of others is wholly foreign to the First Amendment."

Moreover, while preventing corruption or its appearance is a legitimate objective, Congress may target only a specific type of corruption—"*quid pro quo* " corruption. As *Buckley* explained, Congress may permissibly seek to rein in "large contributions [that] are given to secure a political *quid pro quo* from current and potential office holders." In addition to "actual *quid pro quo* arrangements," Congress may permissibly limit "the appearance of corruption stemming from public awareness of the opportunities for abuse inherent in a regime of large individual financial contributions" to particular candidates

Spending large sums of money in connection with elections, but not in connection with an effort to control the exercise of an officeholder's official duties, does not give rise to such *quid pro quo* corruption. Nor does the possibility that an individual who spends large sums may garner "influence over or access to" elected officials or political parties. And because the Government's interest in preventing the appearance of corruption is equally confined to the appearance of *quid pro quo* corruption, the Government may not seek to limit the appearance of mere influence or access. See *Citizens United.*

The dissent advocates a broader conception of corruption and would apply the label to any individual contributions above limits deemed necessary to protect "collective speech." Thus, under the dissent's view, it is perfectly fine to contribute $5,200 to nine candidates but somehow corrupt to give the same amount to a tenth.

It is fair to say that we have not always spoken about corruption in a clear or consistent voice. The definition of corruption that we apply today, however, has firm roots in *Buckley* itself. The Court in that case upheld base contribution limits because they targeted "the danger of actual *quid pro quo* arrangements" and "the impact of the appearance of corruption stemming from public awareness" of such a system of unchecked direct contributions. *Buckley* simultaneously rejected limits on spending that was less likely to "be given as a *quid pro quo* for improper commitments from the candidate." In any event, this case is not the first in which the debate over the proper breadth of the Government's anticorruption interest has been engaged. *Citizens United.*

The line between *quid pro quo* corruption and general influence may seem vague at times, but the distinction must be respected in order to safeguard basic

First Amendment rights. In addition, "[i]n drawing that line, the First Amendment requires us to err on the side of protecting political speech rather than suppressing it." *Federal Election Comm'n v. Wisconsin Right to Life* (2007).

The dissent laments that our opinion leaves only remnants of FECA and BCRA that are inadequate to combat corruption. Such rhetoric ignores the fact that we leave the base limits undisturbed.[6] Those base limits remain the primary means of regulating campaign contributions—the obvious explanation for why the aggregate limits received a scant few sentences of attention in *Buckley*.[7]

B

When the Government restricts speech, the Government bears the burden of proving the constitutionality of its actions. Here, the Government seeks to carry that burden by arguing that the aggregate limits further the permissible objective of preventing *quid pro quo* corruption.

The difficulty is that once the aggregate limits kick in, they ban all contributions of *any* amount. But Congress's selection of a $5,200 base limit indicates its belief that contributions of that amount or less do not create a cognizable risk of corruption. If there is no corruption concern in giving nine candidates up to $5,200 each, it is difficult to understand how a tenth candidate can be regarded as corruptible if given $1,801, and all others corruptible if given a dime. And if there is no risk that additional candidates will be corrupted by donations of up to $5,200, then the Government must defend the aggregate limits by demonstrating that they prevent circumvention of the base limits.

As an initial matter, there is not the same risk of *quid pro quo* corruption or its appearance when money flows through independent actors to a candidate, as when a donor contributes to a candidate directly. When an individual contributes to a candidate, a party committee, or a PAC, the individual must by law cede control over the funds. The Government admits that if the funds are subsequently re-routed to a particular candidate, such action occurs at the initial recipient's discretion—not the donor's. As a consequence, the chain of attribution grows longer, and any credit must be shared among the various actors along the way. For those reasons, the risk of *quid pro quo* corruption is generally applicable only to "the narrow category of money gifts that are directed, in some manner, to a candidate or officeholder." *McConnell* (opinion of Kennedy, J.).

Buckley nonetheless focused on the possibility that "unearmarked contributions" could eventually find their way to a candidate's coffers. Even accepting the

6. The fact that this opinion does not address the base limits also belies the dissent's concern that we have silently overruled the Court's holding in *McConnell v. Federal Election Comm'n* (2003). At issue in *McConnell* was BCRA's extension of the base limits to so-called "soft money"—previously unregulated contributions to national party committees. Our holding about the constitutionality of the aggregate limits clearly does not overrule *McConnell's* holding about "soft money."

7. It would be especially odd to regard aggregate limits as essential to enforce base limits when state campaign finance schemes typically include base limits but not aggregate limits. Just eight of the 38 States that have imposed base limits on contributions from individuals to candidates have also imposed aggregate limits (excluding restrictions on a specific subset of donors).

validity of *Buckley*'s circumvention theory, it is hard to see how a candidate today could receive a "massive amount[] of money" that could be traced back to a particular contributor uninhibited by the aggregate limits. The Government offers a series of scenarios in support of that possibility. But each is sufficiently implausible that the Government has not carried its burden of demonstrating that the aggregate limits further its anticircumvention interest.

The primary example of circumvention, in one form or another, envisions an individual donor who contributes the maximum amount under the base limits to a particular candidate, say, Representative Smith. Then the donor also channels "massive amounts of money" to Smith through a series of contributions to PACs that have stated their intention to support Smith.

Various earmarking and antiproliferation rules disarm this example. Importantly, the donor may not contribute to the most obvious PACs: those that support only Smith. Nor may the donor contribute to the slightly less obvious PACs that he knows will route "a substantial portion" of his contribution to Smith.

The donor must instead turn to other PACs that are likely to give to Smith. When he does so, however, he discovers that his contribution will be significantly diluted by all the contributions from others to the same PACs. After all, the donor cannot give more than $5,000 to a PAC and so cannot dominate the PAC's total receipts, as he could when *Buckley* was decided. He cannot retain control over his contribution, direct his money "in any way" to Smith, or even *imply* that he would like his money to be recontributed to Smith. His salience as a Smith supporter has been diminished, and with it the potential for corruption.

It is not clear how many candidates a PAC must support before our dedicated donor can avoid being tagged with the impermissible knowledge that "a substantial portion" of his contribution will go to Smith. But imagine that the donor is one of ten equal donors to a PAC that gives the highest possible contribution to Smith. The PAC may give no more than $2,600 per election to Smith. Of that sum, just $260 will be attributable to the donor intent on circumventing the base limits. Thus far he has hardly succeeded in funneling "massive amounts of money" to Smith.

But what if this donor does the same thing via, say, 100 different PACs? His $260 contribution will balloon to $26,000, ten times what he may contribute directly to Smith in any given election.

This 100-PAC scenario is highly implausible. In the first instance, it is not true that the individual donor will necessarily have access to a sufficient number of PACs to effectuate such a scheme. There are many PACs, but they are not limitless. For the 2012 election cycle, the FEC reported about 2,700 nonconnected PACs (excluding PACs that finance independent expenditures only). And not every PAC that supports Smith will work in this scheme: For our donor's pro rata share of a PAC's contribution to Smith to remain meaningful, the PAC must be funded by only a small handful of donors. The antiproliferation rules, which were not in effect when *Buckley* was decided, prohibit our donor from creating 100 pro-Smith PACs of his own, or collaborating with the nine other donors to do so.

Moreover, if 100 PACs were to contribute to Smith and few other candidates, and if specific individuals like our ardent Smith supporter were to contribute to each, the FEC could weigh those "circumstantial factors" to determine whether to deem the PACs affiliated. The FEC's analysis could take account of a "common or overlapping membership" and "similar patterns of contributions or contributors," among other considerations. The FEC has in the past initiated enforcement proceedings against contributors with such suspicious patterns of PAC donations.

On a more basic level, it is hard to believe that a rational actor would engage in such machinations. In the example described, a dedicated donor spent $500,000—donating the full $5,000 to 100 different PACs—to add just $26,000 to Smith's campaign coffers. That same donor, meanwhile, could have spent unlimited funds on independent expenditures on behalf of Smith. Indeed, he could have spent his entire $500,000 advocating for Smith, without the risk that his selected PACs would choose not to give to Smith, or that he would have to share credit with other contributors to the PACs.

We have said in the context of independent expenditures that "'[t]he absence of prearrangement and coordination of an expenditure with the candidate or his agent . . . undermines the value of the expenditure to the candidate.'" *Citizens United* (quoting *Buckley*). But probably not by 95 percent. And at least from the *donor's* point of view, it strikes us as far more likely that he will want to see his full $500,000 spent on behalf of his favored candidate—even if it must be spent independently—rather than see it diluted to a small fraction so that it can be contributed directly by someone else.

These scenarios, along with others that have been suggested, are either illegal under current campaign finance laws or divorced from reality. The three examples posed by the dissent are no exception. The dissent does not explain how the large sums it postulates can be legally rerouted to a particular candidate, why most state committees would participate in a plan to redirect their donations to a candidate in another State, or how a donor or group of donors can avoid regulations prohibiting contributions to a committee "with the knowledge that a substantial portion" of the contribution will support a candidate to whom the donor has already contributed.

Buckley upheld aggregate limits only on the ground that they prevented channeling money to candidates beyond the base limits. The absence of such a prospect today belies the Government's asserted objective of preventing corruption or its appearance. The improbability of circumvention indicates that the aggregate limits instead further the impermissible objective of simply limiting the amount of money in political campaigns.

C

Quite apart from the foregoing, the aggregate limits violate the First Amendment because they are not "closely drawn to avoid unnecessary abridgment of associational freedoms." *Buckley*. In the First Amendment context, fit matters. Even when the Court is not applying strict scrutiny, we still require "a fit that is not necessarily perfect, but reasonable; that represents not necessarily the single best disposition but one whose scope is 'in proportion to the interest served,' . . . that employs not necessarily the least restrictive means but . . . a means narrowly tailored to achieve the desired objective." [Citations omitted.] Here, because the statute is poorly tailored to the Government's interest in preventing circumvention of the base limits, it impermissibly restricts participation in the political process.

1

The Government argues that the aggregate limits are justified because they prevent an individual from giving to too many initial recipients who might subsequently recontribute a donation. After all, only recontributed funds can conceivably give rise to circumvention of the base limits. Yet all indications are that many types of recipients have scant interest in regifting donations they receive.

Experience suggests that the vast majority of contributions made in excess of the aggregate limits are likely to be retained and spent by their recipients rather than rerouted to candidates.

Based on what we can discern from experience, the indiscriminate ban on all contributions above the aggregate limits is disproportionate to the Government's interest in preventing circumvention. The Government has not given us any reason to believe that parties or candidates would dramatically shift their priorities if the aggregate limits were lifted. Absent such a showing, we cannot conclude that the sweeping aggregate limits are appropriately tailored to guard against any contributions that might implicate the Government's anticircumvention interest.

2

Importantly, there are multiple alternatives available to Congress that would serve the Government's anticircumvention interest, while avoiding "unnecessary abridgment" of First Amendment rights.

The most obvious might involve targeted restrictions on transfers among candidates and political committees. There are currently no such limits on transfers among party committees and from candidates to party committees. Perhaps for that reason, a central concern of the District Court, the Government, multiple *amici curiae,* and the dissent has been the ability of party committees to transfer money freely. If Congress agrees that this is problematic, it might tighten its permissive transfer rules. Doing so would impose a lesser burden on First Amendment rights, as compared to aggregate limits that flatly ban contributions beyond certain levels.

One possible option for restricting transfers would be to require contributions above the current aggregate limits to be deposited into segregated, nontransferable accounts and spent only by their recipients. Such a solution would address the same circumvention possibilities as the current aggregate limits, while not completely barring contributions beyond the aggregate levels. In addition (or as an alternative), if Congress believes that circumvention is especially likely to occur through creation of a joint fundraising committee, it could require that funds received through those committees be spent by their recipients (or perhaps it could simply limit the size of joint fundraising committees). Such alternatives to the aggregate limits properly refocus the inquiry on the delinquent actor: the recipient of a contribution within the base limits, who then routes the money in a manner that undermines those limits.

Other alternatives might focus on earmarking. Many of the scenarios that the Government and the dissent hypothesize involve at least implicit agreements to circumvent the base limits—agreements that are already prohibited by the earmarking rules. The FEC might strengthen those rules further by, for example, defining how many candidates a PAC must support in order to ensure that "a substantial portion" of a donor's contribution is not rerouted to a certain candidate.

We do not mean to opine on the validity of any particular proposal. The point is that there are numerous alternative approaches available to Congress to prevent circumvention of the base limits.

D

Finally, disclosure of contributions minimizes the potential for abuse of the campaign finance system. Disclosure requirements are in part "justified based on a governmental interest in 'provid[ing] the electorate with information' about the sources of election-related spending." *Citizens United* (quoting *Buckley*). They may also "deter actual corruption and avoid the appearance of corruption by exposing large contributions and expenditures to the light of publicity." *Id.* Disclosure requirements burden speech, but—unlike the aggregate limits—they do not impose a ceiling on speech. For that reason, disclosure often represents a less restrictive alternative to flat bans on certain types or quantities of speech.

With modern technology, disclosure now offers a particularly effective means of arming the voting public with information. Reports and databases are available on the FEC's Web site almost immediately after they are filed, supplemented by private entities such as OpenSecrets.org and FollowTheMoney.org. Because massive quantities of information can be accessed at the click of a mouse, disclosure is effective to a degree not possible at the time *Buckley*, or even *McConnell*, was decided.

V

[Omitted.]

***

The Government has a strong interest, no less critical to our democratic system, in combatting corruption and its appearance. We have, however, held that this interest must be limited to a specific kind of corruption—*quid pro quo* corruption—in order to ensure that the Government's efforts do not have the effect of restricting the First Amendment right of citizens to choose who shall govern them. For the reasons set forth, we conclude that the aggregate limits on contributions do not further the only governmental interest this Court accepted as legitimate in *Buckley*. They instead intrude without justification on a citizen's ability to exercise "the most fundamental First Amendment activities." *Buckley*.

Justice THOMAS, concurring in the judgment.

I adhere to the view that this Court's decision in *Buckley v. Valeo* denigrates core First Amendment speech and should be overruled.

[Justice Thomas explained why he believes the Court was wrong in *Buckley* to separate contributions from independent expenditures.]

In sum, what remains of *Buckley* is a rule without a rationale. Contributions and expenditures are simply "two sides of the same First Amendment coin," and our efforts to distinguish the two have produced mere "word games" rather than any cognizable principle of constitutional law. *Buckley* (Burger, C.J., concurring in part and dissenting in part). For that reason, I would overrule *Buckley* and subject the aggregate limits in BCRA to strict scrutiny, which they would surely fail.

For these reasons, I concur only in the judgment.

Justice BREYER, with whom Justice GINSBURG, Justice SOTOMAYOR, and Justice KAGAN join, dissenting.

Nearly 40 years ago in *Buckley v. Valeo*, this Court considered the constitutionality of laws that imposed limits upon the overall amount a single person can contribute to all federal candidates, political parties, and committees taken together. The Court held that those limits did not violate the Constitution.

Today a majority of the Court overrules this holding. It is wrong to do so. Its conclusion rests upon its own, not a record-based, view of the facts. Its legal analysis is faulty: It misconstrues the nature of the competing constitutional interests at stake. It understates the importance of protecting the political integrity of our governmental institutions. It creates a loophole that will allow a single individual to contribute millions of dollars to a political party or to a candidate's campaign. Taken together with *Citizens United*, today's decision eviscerates our Nation's campaign finance laws, leaving a remnant incapable of dealing with the grave problems of democratic legitimacy that those laws were intended to resolve.

I

[Omitted.]

II

The plurality's first claim—that large aggregate contributions do not "give rise" to "corruption"—is plausible only because the plurality defines "corruption" too narrowly. It . . . defines *quid pro quo* corruption to mean no more than "a direct exchange of an official act for money"—an act akin to bribery. It adds specifically that corruption does *not* include efforts to "garner 'influence over or access to' elected officials or political parties."

This critically important definition of "corruption" is inconsistent with the Court's prior case law (with the possible exception of *Citizens United*). It is virtually impossible to reconcile with this Court's decision in *McConnell*, upholding the Bipartisan Campaign Reform Act of 2002 (BCRA). And it misunderstands the constitutional importance of the interests at stake. In fact, constitutional interests—indeed, First Amendment interests—lie on both sides of the legal equation.

A

In reality, as the history of campaign finance reform shows and as our earlier cases on the subject have recognized, the anticorruption interest that drives Congress to regulate campaign contributions is a far broader, more important interest than the plurality acknowledges. It is an interest in maintaining the integrity of our public governmental institutions. And it is an interest rooted in the Constitution and in the First Amendment itself.

Consider at least one reason why the First Amendment protects political speech. Speech does not exist in a vacuum. Rather, political communication seeks to secure government action. A politically oriented "marketplace of ideas" seeks to form a public opinion that can and will influence elected representatives.

This is not a new idea. Eighty-seven years ago, Justice Brandeis wrote that the First Amendment's protection of speech was "essential to effective democracy." *Whitney v. California* (1927) (concurring opinion).

Accordingly, the First Amendment advances not only the individual's right to engage in political speech, but also the public's interest in preserving a democratic order in which collective speech *matters.*

What has this to do with corruption? It has everything to do with corruption. Corruption breaks the constitutionally necessary "chain of communication" between the people and their representatives. It derails the essential speech-to-government-action tie. Where enough money calls the tune, the general public will not be heard. Insofar as corruption cuts the link between political thought and political action, a free marketplace of political ideas loses its point. That is one reason why the Court has stressed the constitutional importance of Congress' concern that a few large donations not drown out the voices of the many. See, *e.g., Buckley.*

The upshot is that the interests the Court has long described as preventing "corruption" or the "appearance of corruption" are more than ordinary factors to be weighed against the constitutional right to political speech. Rather, they are interests rooted in the First Amendment itself. They are rooted in the constitutional effort to create a democracy responsive to the people — a government where laws reflect the very thoughts, views, ideas, and sentiments, the expression of which the First Amendment protects. Given that end, we can and should understand campaign finance laws as resting upon a broader and more significant constitutional rationale than the plurality's limited definition of "corruption" suggests. We should see these laws as seeking in significant part to strengthen, rather than weaken, the First Amendment. To say this is not to deny the potential for conflict between (1) the need to permit contributions that pay for the diffusion of ideas, and (2) the need to limit payments in order to help maintain the integrity of the electoral process. But that conflict takes place within, not outside, the First Amendment's boundaries.

B

[Omitted.]

C

[Omitted.]

D

III

The plurality invalidates the aggregate contribution limits for a second reason. It believes they are no longer needed to prevent contributors from circumventing federal limits on direct contributions to individuals, political parties, and political action committees. Other "campaign finance laws," combined with "experience" and "common sense," foreclose the various circumvention scenarios that the Government hypothesizes. Accordingly, the plurality concludes, the aggregate limits provide no added benefit.

The plurality is wrong. Here, as in *Buckley*, in the absence of limits on aggregate political contributions, donors can and likely will find ways to channel millions of dollars to parties and to individual candidates, producing precisely the kind of "corruption" or "appearance of corruption" that previously led the Court to hold aggregate limits constitutional. Those opportunities for circumvention will also produce the type of corruption that concerns the plurality today. The methods for using today's opinion to evade the law's individual contribution limits are complex, but they are well known, or will become well known, to party fundraisers. I shall describe three.

A

Example One: Gifts for the Benefit of the Party. Campaign finance law permits each individual to give $64,800 over two years to a national party committee. The two major political parties each have three national committees. Federal law also entitles an individual to give $20,000 to a state party committee over two years. Each major political party has 50 such committees. Those individual limits mean that, in the absence of any aggregate limit, an individual could legally give to the Republican Party or to the Democratic Party about $1.2 million over two years. To make it easier for contributors to give gifts of this size, each party could create a "Joint Party Committee," comprising all of its national and state party committees. The titular heads could be the Speaker of the House of Representatives and the Minority Leader of the House. A contributor could then write a single check to the Joint Party Committee—and its staff would divide the funds so that each constituent unit receives no more than it could obtain from the contributor directly ($64,800 for a national committee over two years, $20,000 for a state committee over the same). Before today's decision, the total size of Rich Donor's check to the Joint Party Committee was capped at $74,600—the aggregate limit for donations to political parties over a 2-year election cycle. After today's decision, Rich Donor can write a single check to the Joint Party Committee in an amount of about $1.2 million.

Will political parties seek these large checks? Why not? The recipient national and state committees can spend the money to buy generic party advertisements, say television commercials or bumper stickers saying "Support Republicans," "Support Democrats," or the like. They also can transfer the money to party committees in battleground States to increase the chances of winning hotly contested seats. *See* § 441a(a)(4) (permitting national or state political committees to make unlimited "transfers" to other committees "of the same political party").

Will party officials and candidates solicit these large contributions from wealthy donors? Absolutely. Such contributions will help increase the party's power, as well as the candidate's standing among his colleagues.

Will elected officials be particularly grateful to the large donor, feeling obliged to provide him special access and influence, and perhaps even a *quid pro quo* legislative favor? That is what we have previously believed. *See McConnell.*

Example Two: Donations to Individual Candidates (The $3.6 Million Check). The first example significantly *understates* the problem. That is because federal election law also allows a single contributor to give $5,200 to each party candidate over a 2-year election cycle (assuming the candidate is running in both a primary and a general election). There are 435 party candidates for House seats and 33 party candidates for Senate seats in any given election year. That makes an additional $2.4 million in allowable contributions. Thus, without an aggregate limit, the law will permit a wealthy individual to write a check, over a 2-year election cycle, for $3.6 million—all to benefit his political party and its candidates.

As I have just said, without any aggregate limit, the law will allow Rich Donor to write a single check to, say, the Smith Victory Committee, for up to $3.6 million. This check represents the total amount that the contributor could contribute to all of the participants in the Committee over a 2-year cycle. The Committee would operate under an agreement that provides a formula for the allocation of fundraising proceeds among its constituent units. And that "formula" would divide the proceeds so that no committee or candidate receives more than it could have received from Rich Donor directly—$64,800, $20,000, or $5,200.

So what is wrong with that? The check is considerably larger than *Example One*'s check. But is there anything else wrong? The answer is yes, absolutely. The law will also permit a party and its candidates to shift most of Rich Donor's contributions to a *single* candidate, say Smith. Here is how:

The law permits each candidate and each party committee in the Smith Victory Committee to write Candidate Smith a check directly. For his primary and general elections combined, they can write checks of up to $4,000 (from each candidate's authorized campaign committee) and $10,000 (from each state and national committee). This yields a potential $1,872,000 (from candidates) plus $530,000 (from party committees). Thus, the law permits the candidates and party entities to redirect $2.37 million of Rich Donor's $3.6 million check to Candidate Smith. It also permits state and national committees to contribute to Smith's general election campaign through making coordinated expenditures—in amounts that range from $46,600 to $2.68 million for a general election (depending upon the size of Smith's State and whether he is running for a House or Senate seat).

The upshot is that Candidate Smith can receive at least $2.37 million and possibly the full $3.6 million contributed by Rich Donor to the Smith Victory Committee, even though the funds must first be divided up among the constituent units before they can be rerouted to Smith. Nothing requires the Smith Victory Committee to explain in advance to Rich Donor all of the various transfers that will take place, and nothing prevents the entities in the Committee from informing the donor and the receiving candidate after the fact what has transpired. Accordingly, the money can be donated and rerouted to Candidate Smith without the donor having violated the base limits or any other FEC regulation.

If this does not count as evasion of the base limits, what does? Present aggregate limits confine the size of any individual gift to $123,200. Today's opinion creates a loophole measured in the millions.

Example Three: Proliferating Political Action Committees (PACs). Campaign finance law prohibits an individual from contributing (1) more than $5,200 to any candidate in a federal election cycle, and (2) more than $5,000 to a PAC in a calendar year. It also prohibits (3) any PAC from contributing more than $10,000 to any candidate in an election cycle. But the law does not prohibit an individual from contributing (within the current $123,200 biannual aggregate limit) $5,000 to each of an unlimited total number of PACs. And there, so to speak, lies the rub.

Here is how, without any aggregate limits, a party will be able to channel $2 million from each of ten Rich Donors to each of ten Embattled Candidates.

Groups of party supporters—individuals, corporations, or trade unions—create 200 PACs. Each PAC claims it will use the funds it raises to support several candidates from the party, though it will favor those who are most endangered. Over a 2-year election cycle, Rich Donor One gives $10,000 to each PAC ($5,000 per year)—yielding $2 million total. Rich Donor 2 does the same. So, too, do the other eight Rich Donors. This brings their total donations to $20 million, disbursed among the 200 PACs. Each PAC will have collected $100,000, and each can use its money to write ten checks of $10,000—to each of the ten most Embattled Candidates in the party (over two years). Every Embattled Candidate, receiving a $10,000 check from 200 PACs, will have collected $2 million.

The upshot is that ten Rich Donors will have contributed $2 million each, and ten Embattled Candidates will have collected $2 million each. In this example, unlike *Example Two,* the recipient candidates may not know which of the ten Rich Donors is personally responsible for the $2 million he or she receives. But the recipient candidate is highly likely to know who the ten Rich Donors are, and to feel appropriately grateful.

B

The plurality believes that the three scenarios I have just depicted either pose no threat, or cannot or will not take place. [But] a candidate who solicits a multimillion dollar check for his party will be deeply grateful to the checkwriter, and surely could reward him with a *quid pro quo* favor. The plurality discounts the scenarios depicted in *Example Two* and *Example Three* because it finds such circumvention tactics "illegal under current campaign finance laws," " implausible," or "divorced from reality." But they are not.

The plurality's view depends in large part upon its claim that since this Court decided *Buckley* in 1976, changes in either statutory law or in applicable regulations have come to make it difficult, if not impossible, for these circumvention scenarios to arise. Hence, it concludes, there is no longer a need for aggregate contribution limits. But a closer examination of the five legal changes to which the plurality points makes clear that those changes cannot effectively stop the abuses that I have depicted.

[Justice Breyer considered the five legal changes in detail, explaining that they would not prevent the circumvention demonstrated in his three examples.]

Using these entities, candidates, parties, and party supporters can transfer and, we are told, have transferred large sums of money to specific candidates, thereby avoiding the base contribution limits in ways that Examples Two and Three help demonstrate. They have done so without drawing FEC prosecution—at least not according to my (and apparently the plurality's) search of publicly available records. In the real world, the methods of achieving circumvention are more subtle and more complex than our stylized *Examples Two* and *Three* depict. And persons have used these entities to channel money to candidates without any individual breaching the current aggregate $123,200 limit. The plurality now removes that limit, thereby permitting wealthy donors to make aggregate contributions not of $123,200, but of several millions of dollars. If the FEC regulation has failed to plug a small hole, how can it possibly plug a large one?

IV

[Omitted.]

V

The District Court in this case, holding that *Buckley* foreclosed McCutcheon's constitutional challenge to the aggregate limits, granted the Government's motion to dismiss the complaint prior to a full evidentiary hearing. If the plurality now believes the District Court was wrong, then why does it not return the case for the further evidentiary development which has not yet taken place?

Without further development of the record . . . I fail to see how the plurality can now find grounds for overturning *Buckley*. The justification for aggregate contribution restrictions is strongly rooted in the need to assure political integrity and ultimately in the First Amendment itself. The threat to that integrity posed by the risk of special access and influence remains real. Even taking the plurality on its own terms and considering solely the threat of *quid pro quo* corruption (*i.e.*, money-for-votes exchanges), the aggregate limits are a necessary tool to stop circumvention. And there is no basis for finding a lack of "fit" between the threat and the means used to combat it, namely the aggregate limits.

The plurality reaches the opposite conclusion. The result, as I said at the outset, is a decision that substitutes judges' understandings of how the political process works for the understanding of Congress; that fails to recognize the difference between influence resting upon public opinion and influence bought by money alone; that overturns key precedent; that creates huge loopholes in the law; and that undermines, perhaps devastates, what remains of campaign finance reform.

With respect, I dissent.

NOTES ON *McCUTCHEON*

1. Notice the continuing debate among the two wings of the Court on the proper definition of "corruption" in the campaign finance context. Who has the better argument? Should the Court define corruption narrowly to reach only direct *quid pro quo* arrangements, as the plurality suggests, or is the dissent correct that corruption in politics should have a broader meaning?

2. Does the plurality make a convincing argument as to why it must overrule the portion of *Buckley* that considered aggregate contribution limits? The plurality focuses on the fact that the *Buckley* Court did not seem to consider the issue much, as *Buckley* had disposed of it in just three sentences as a corollary to its decision to uphold the individual contribution limits. Is that a sufficient reason to overturn a holding that was almost 40 years old?

3. The dissent (and the lower court) believed that politicians and wealthy donors would find ways to work around limits to funnel as much money as possible to their preferred candidates. The plurality disputes this assertion as mere speculation. Are political committees likely to operate in the sophisticated ways that Justice Breyer contemplates? And even if they are likely to do so, does each successive level of pass-through minimize the potential of *quid pro quo* corruption, as Chief Justice Roberts claims?

4. The plurality suggests numerous policies that Congress or the FEC could adopt to close potential loopholes in campaign finance laws. Do you think these policies would work? Is Congress likely to pass them?

5. What do you make of Justice Thomas's continued insistence that there is no meaningful distinction between independent expenditures and contribution limitations and that strict scrutiny should apply to all campaign finance regulations? Senator Mitch McConnell filed an amicus brief in this case urging the Court to apply strict scrutiny to all contribution limits, which would open the door for the Court to overturn the portion of *Buckley* that upheld the individual (base) contribution limitations. The plurality declines this invitation, though Justice Thomas agrees. The dissent does not engage in this argument, but what do you think it might say in response? That issue, of course, may come up in a future case, especially one that challenges individual contribution limits directly.

6. *Congress's Attempts to Limit Foreign Interference in U.S. Elections*

Congress has long been concerned about foreign individuals attempting to influence an American election. In BCRA, Congress outlawed foreign nationals from making campaign contributions or independent expenditures in U.S. elections. In the important case of *Bluman v. FEC* (2012), a three-judge district court panel upheld this portion of BCRA. The U.S. Supreme Court summarily affirmed the decision without an opinion, which means it has some (though perhaps not full) precedential weight. Note that now-Justice Kavanaugh authored the opinion of the three-judge district court.

As you are reading this case, note how the court distinguishes *Citizens United*. Recall that in *Citizens United*, the Supreme Court held that the First Amendment does not allow Congress to make distinctions based on the identity of the speaker, but the Court issued an important caveat: "We need not reach the question whether the Government has a compelling interest in preventing foreign individuals or associations from influencing our Nation's political process. [The independent expenditure ban] is not limited to corporations or associations that were created in foreign countries or funded predominately by foreign shareholders. [The provision] therefore would be overbroad even if we assumed, *arguendo*, that the Government has a compelling interest in limiting foreign influence over our political process." *Citizens United v. FEC* (2010). This section caused a rift between President Barack Obama and Justice Samuel Alito at the 2010 State of the Union address, which Obama delivered shortly after the Court decided *Citizens United*. Obama stated that the Court's decision would "open the floodgates for special interests—including foreign companies—to spend without limit in our elections," and Alito visibly mouthed "not true."

The *Bluman* court takes on the question directly. Are you convinced by the court's analytical distinction between the holding of *Citizens United* and its application to foreign nationals? What does the decision say about who comprises the political community that may participate in American democracy? What's the court's conception of self-governance? And what do you make of the Supreme Court summarily affirming this decision?

Note also that this decision is separate from two major issues surrounding the 2016 and 2020 elections: Russian interference through social media campaigns and infiltration of voter registration databases in 2016, and President Trump's solicitation of Ukraine to investigate his 2020 Democratic rival, Joe Biden. The notes after *Bluman* discuss these issues in more detail.

Bluman v. FEC

800 F. Supp. 2d 281 (D.D.C. 2011) (three-judge court)

KAVANAUGH, Circuit Judge:

Plaintiffs are foreign citizens who temporarily live and work in the United States. They are neither U.S. citizens nor lawful permanent residents; rather, they are lawfully in the United States on temporary work visas. Although they are not U.S. citizens and are in this country only temporarily, plaintiffs want to participate in the U.S. campaign process. They seek to donate money to candidates in U.S. federal and state elections, to contribute to national political parties and outside political groups, and to make expenditures expressly advocating for and against the election of candidates in U.S. elections. Plaintiffs are barred from doing so, however, by federal statute.

In this suit, plaintiffs argue that the federal ban on their proposed activities is unconstitutional. Plaintiffs contend, in particular, that foreign citizens lawfully resident in the United States have a right under the First Amendment to the United States Constitution to contribute to candidates and political parties and to make express-advocacy expenditures.

The Supreme Court has long held that the government (federal, state, and local) may exclude foreign citizens from activities that are part of democratic self-government in the United States. For example, the Supreme Court has ruled that the government may bar aliens from voting, serving as jurors, working as police or probation officers, or teaching at public schools. Under those precedents, the federal ban at issue here readily passes constitutional muster.

LEGAL BACKGROUND

As political campaigns grew more expensive in the latter half of the 20th Century, especially with the advent of costly television advertising, money became more important to the campaign process—in terms of both contributions to candidates and political parties and expenditures advocating for or against candidates. As money became more important to the election process, concern grew that foreign entities and citizens might try to influence the outcome of U.S. elections. In 1966, Congress sought to limit foreign influence over American elections by prohibiting agents of foreign governments and entities from making contributions to candidates. In 1974, Congress expanded that ban and barred contributions to candidates from all "foreign nationals," defined as all foreign citizens except lawful permanent residents of the United States.

But those restrictions did not eliminate the possibility of foreign citizens influencing American elections by, for example, soft-money donations to political parties as opposed to direct contributions to candidates. Activities by foreign citizens in the 1996 election cycle sparked public controversy and an extensive investigation by the Senate Committee on Governmental Affairs. The Committee found that foreign citizens had used soft-money contributions to political parties to essentially buy access to American political officials. It also found that the Chinese government had made an effort to "influence U.S. policies and elections through, among other means, financing election campaigns."In response, Congress eventually passed and President George W. Bush signed legislation [called BCRA] that, among many other things, strengthened the prohibition on foreign financial involvement in American elections. This new Act expanded the ban on foreign nationals' financial influence on elections by banning foreign nationals both from making expenditures and from making contributions to political parties, thus supplementing the pre-existing ban on foreign nationals making contributions to candidates.

The relevant provision of the statute as amended in 2002 reads:

> **(a) Prohibition**
>
> It shall be unlawful for—
>
> (1) a foreign national, directly or indirectly, to make—
>
> (A) a contribution or donation of money or other thing of value, or to make an express or implied promise to make a contribution or donation, in connection with a Federal, State, or local election;
>
> (B)a contribution or donation to a committee of a political party; or
>
> (C) an expenditure, independent expenditure, or disbursement for an electioneering communication; or
>
> (2) a person to solicit, accept, or receive a contribution or donation described in subparagraph (A) or (B) of paragraph (1) from a foreign national.

2 U.S.C. § 441e(a). The statute continues to define "foreign national" to include all foreign citizens except those who have been admitted as lawful permanent residents.

This statute, as we interpret it, does not bar foreign nationals from issue advocacy—that is, speech that does not expressly advocate the election or defeat of a specific candidate.

FACTUAL AND PROCEDURAL BACKGROUND

The plaintiffs in this suit—Benjamin Bluman and Asenath Steiman—are foreign citizens who live and work in the United States on temporary visas. Bluman is a Canadian citizen who has lawfully resided in the United States since November 2009 on a temporary work visa. From September 2006 to June 2009, he lawfully resided in the United States on a temporary student visa while attending law school. His current visa will allow him to stay in the country until November 2012, at which time he plans to apply for a second three-year term. He is an associate at a law firm in New York City.

Bluman wants to contribute to three candidates: Representative Jay Inslee of Washington; Diane Savino, a New York state senator; and President Obama. He also wants to print flyers supporting President Obama's reelection and to distribute them in Central Park.

Steiman is a dual citizen of Canada and Israel. She has a temporary visa authorizing her to live and work in the United States for a period of three years, through June 2012, but that term could be extended for up to seven years. She is a medical resident at a hospital in New York.

Steiman wants to contribute money to Senator Tom Coburn; a yet-to-be-determined candidate for the Republican nomination for President in 2012; the National Republican Senatorial Committee; and the Club for Growth, an independent organization that advocates with respect to certain issues and candidates.

All of plaintiffs' desired activities are barred by 2 U.S.C. § 441e(a) as amended in 2002 [by BCRA].

DISCUSSION

I. Standard of Scrutiny

[T]he debate over the level of scrutiny is ultimately not decisive here because we conclude that § 441e(a) passes muster even under strict scrutiny. Therefore, we may assume for the sake of argument that § 441e(a)'s ban on political contributions and expenditures by foreign nationals is subject to strict scrutiny.

II. The Merits

[T]his case raises a preliminary and foundational question about the definition of the American political community and, in particular, the role of foreign citizens in the U.S. electoral process.

We know from more than a century of Supreme Court case law that foreign citizens in the United States enjoy many of the same constitutional rights that U.S. citizens do. For example, aliens are generally entitled to the same rights as U.S. citizens in the criminal process, among several other areas.

But we also know from Supreme Court case law that foreign citizens may be denied certain rights and privileges that U.S. citizens possess. For example, the Court has ruled that government may bar foreign citizens from voting, serving as jurors, working as police or probation officers, or working as public school teachers. Beyond that, the Constitution itself of course bars foreign citizens from holding certain offices.

In those many decisions, the Supreme Court has drawn a fairly clear line: The government may exclude foreign citizens from activities "intimately related to the process of democratic self-government."As the Court has written, "a State's historical power to exclude aliens from participation in its democratic political institutions [is] part of the sovereign's obligation to preserve the basic conception of a political community." In other words, the government may reserve "participation in its democratic political institutions" for citizens of this country. When reviewing a statute barring foreign citizens from serving as probation officers, the Court explained that the "exclusion of aliens from basic governmental processes is not a deficiency in the democratic system but *a necessary consequence of the community's process of political self-definition*." Upholding a statute barring aliens from teaching in public schools, the Court reasoned that the "distinction between citizens and aliens, though ordinarily irrelevant to private activity, is *fundamental to the definition and government of a State* . . . . It is because of this special significance of citizenship that governmental entities, when exercising the functions of government, have wider latitude in limiting the participation of noncitizens." *Ambach v. Norwick* (1979). And in upholding a ban on aliens serving as police officers, the Court stated that, "although we extend to aliens the right to education and public welfare, along with the ability to earn a livelihood and engage in licensed professions, the right to govern is reserved to citizens." *Foley v. Connelie* (1978).We read these cases to set forth a straightforward principle: It is fundamental to the definition of our national political community that foreign citizens do not have a constitutional right to participate in, and thus may be excluded from, activities of democratic self-government. It follows, therefore, that the United States has a compelling interest for purposes of First Amendment analysis in limiting the participation of foreign citizens in activities of American democratic self-government, and in thereby preventing foreign influence over the U.S. political process.[I]t is undisputed that the government may bar foreign citizens from voting and serving as elected officers. It follows that the government may bar foreign citizens (at least those who are not lawful permanent residents of the United States) from participating in the campaign process that seeks to influence how voters will cast their ballots in the elections. Those limitations on the activities of foreign citizens are of a piece and are all "part of the sovereign's obligation to preserve the basic conception of a political community." *Foley*. Our task here is made simpler because the Supreme Court has deemed the activities of democratic self-government to include functions as unrelated to the electoral process as teaching in public schools and serving as police and probation officers. In our view, spending money to influence voters and finance campaigns is at least as (and probably far more) closely related to democratic self-government than serving as a probation officer or public schoolteacher. Thus, our conclusion here follows almost *a fortiori* from those cases.

For their part, plaintiffs concede that the government may bar foreign citizens *abroad* from making contributions or express-advocacy expenditures in U.S. elections. They thus concede that the government may make distinctions based on the foreign identity of the speaker when the speaker is abroad. Plaintiffs contend, however, that the government may not impose the same restrictions on foreign citizens who are lawfully present in the United States on a temporary visa. We disagree.

Although the Supreme Court has never squarely addressed the issue presented in this case, the only four justices who spoke to the question in *Citizens United* indicated that the government obviously has the power to bar foreign nationals from making campaign contributions and expenditures. Justice Stevens wrote for those four justices:

> The Government routinely places special restrictions on the speech rights of students, prisoners, members of the Armed Forces, foreigners, and its own employees. . . . Although we have not reviewed them directly, we have never cast doubt on laws that place special restrictions on campaign spending by foreign nationals. The Court all but confesses that a categorical approach to speaker identity is untenable when it acknowledges that Congress might be allowed to take measures aimed at "preventing foreign individuals or associations from influencing our Nation's political process."Such measures have been a part of U.S. campaign finance law for

> many years. The notion that Congress might lack the authority to distinguish foreigners from citizens in the regulation of electioneering would certainly have surprised the Framers, whose obsession with foreign influence derived from a fear that foreign powers and individuals had no basic investment in the well-being of the country.

Citizens United (Stevens, J., concurring in part and dissenting in part). For Justices Stevens, Ginsburg, Breyer, and Sotomayor, it was plain—indeed, beyond rational debate—that the government may bar foreign contributions and expenditures. To be sure, the other five Justices did not have occasion to expressly address this issue in *Citizens United,* but the majority's analysis in *Citizens United* certainly was not in conflict with Justice Stevens's conclusion on this particular question about foreign influence. Indeed, in our view, the majority opinion in *Citizens United* is entirely consistent with a ban on foreign contributions and expenditures. And we find the force of Justice Stevens's statement to be a telling and accurate indicator of where the Supreme Court's jurisprudence stands on the question of foreign contributions and expenditures.

Plaintiffs try in various ways to overcome the relevant Supreme Court precedents. First, they acknowledge that they do not have the right to vote in U.S. elections, but they contend that the right to *speak* about elections is different from the right to *participate* in elections. But in this case, that is not a clear dichotomy. When an expressive act is directly targeted at influencing the outcome of an election, it is both speech and participation in democratic self-government. Spending money to contribute to a candidate or party or to expressly advocate for or against the election of a political candidate is participating in the process of democratic self-government.

Plaintiffs further contend that § 441e(a)'s restrictions on contributions and expenditures cannot be justified by the longstanding ban on foreign citizens voting in U.S. elections because the statutory restrictions here are not tied to the right to vote. But that argument misunderstands the compelling interest that is at stake. The statute does not serve a compelling interest in limiting the participation of *non-voters* in the activities of democratic self-government; it serves the compelling interest of limiting the participation of *non-Americans* in the activities of democratic self-government. A statute that excludes foreign nationals from political spending is therefore tailored to achieve that compelling interest.

Plaintiffs also point out that many groups of people who are not entitled to vote may nonetheless make contributions and expenditures related to elections—for example, minors, American corporations, and citizens of states or municipalities other than the state or municipality of the elective office. But minors, American corporations, and citizens of other states and municipalities are all members of the American political community. By contrast, the Supreme Court has said that "[a]liens are by definition those outside of this community." The compelling interest that justifies Congress in restraining foreign nationals' participation in American elections—namely, preventing foreign influence over the U.S. government—does not apply equally to minors, corporations, and citizens of other states and municipalities. It is long established that the government's legislative and regulatory prerogatives are at their apex in matters pertaining to alienage. It is hardly surprising, therefore, that a law that is justified as applied to aliens may not be justified as applied to citizens of the United States, or entities made up of such citizens. Thus, the fact that those other non-voting groups of U.S. citizens are free to contribute and make expenditures does not mean that foreign nationals are similarly entitled.

Plaintiffs argue that the statute, as a measure designed to limit foreign influence over American self-government, is underinclusive and not narrowly tailored because it does not prohibit contributions and expenditures by lawful permanent residents. But as Members of Congress stated when rejecting a proposal to include lawful permanent residents in § 441e(a)'s prohibition, Congress may reasonably conclude that lawful permanent residents of the United States stand in a different relationship to the American political community than other foreign citizens do. Lawful permanent residents have a long-term stake in the flourishing of American society, whereas temporary resident foreign citizens by definition have only a short-term interest in the national community. Temporary resident foreign citizens by definition have primary loyalty to other national political communities, many of which have interests that compete with those of the United States. Apart from that, lawful permanent residents share important rights and obligations with citizens; for example, lawful permanent residents may—and do, in large numbers—serve in the United States military. In those two ways—their indefinite residence in the United States and their eligibility for military service—lawful permanent residents can be viewed as more similar to citizens than they are to temporary visitors, and thus Congress's decision to exclude them from the ban on foreign nationals' contributions and expenditures does not render the statute underinclusive. In fact, one might argue that Congress's carve-out for lawful permanent residents makes the statute more narrowly tailored to the precise interest that it is designed to serve—namely, minimizing *foreign* participation in and influence over American self-government.

Plaintiffs also suggest that Congress's ban on foreign participation in the campaign process is the product of jingoistic sentiment in the United States Congress and thus should not be accepted by the courts. To begin with, Congress's most recent legislation on this issue was based on a factual record collected in the aftermath of the 1996 elections and Congress's genuine concern about foreign influences on U.S. elections. It bears mentioning, moreover, that plaintiffs' home countries—Israel and Canada—and many other democratic countries impose similar restraints on political spending by foreign citizens. To be sure, the United States protects speech and expression more than most (perhaps more than all) foreign countries do, and U.S. courts should not be bound by foreign nations' practices when analyzing constitutional issues such as this. But as the examples of Canada and Israel help show, distinguishing citizens from non-citizens in this context is hardly unusual or deserving of scorn; rather, it is part of a common international understanding of the meaning of sovereignty and shared concern about foreign influence over elections.[4]

4. Our holding means, of course, that foreign corporations are likewise barred from making contributions and expenditures prohibited by 2 U.S.C. § 441e(a). Because this case concerns individuals, we have no occasion to analyze the circumstances under which a corporation may be considered a foreign corporation for purposes of First Amendment analysis. [Footnote relocated.—EDS.]

[W]e note three important limits to our holding in this case. First, we do not here decide whether Congress could constitutionally extend the current statutory ban to lawful permanent residents who have a more significant attachment to the United States than the temporary resident plaintiffs in this case. Any such extension would raise substantial questions not raised by this case. Second, we do not decide whether Congress could prohibit foreign nationals from engaging in speech other than contributions to candidates and parties, express-advocacy expenditures, and donations to outside groups to be used for contributions to candidates and parties and express-advocacy expenditures. Plaintiffs express concern, for example, that a ruling against them here would green-light Congress to impose bans on lobbying by aliens temporarily in this country. They similarly express concern that Congress might bar them from issue advocacy and speaking out on issues of public policy. Our holding does not address such questions, and our holding should not be read to support such bans. Third, we caution the government that seeking criminal penalties for violations of this provision—which requires that the defendant act "willfully"—will require proof of the defendant's knowledge of the law. There are many aliens in this country who no doubt are unaware of the statutory ban on foreign *expenditures,* in particular.

NOTES ON *BLUMAN*

1. What is then-Judge Kavanaugh's conception of democracy? Do you think the Supreme Court (of which he is now a member) would agree? The Court has robustly protected First Amendment rights: Does that extend only to American citizens, at least for political campaigns?

2. Some cities, such as San Francisco and Takoma Park, Maryland, allow non-citizens to vote in local or school board elections. Is that practice contrary to the court's formulation of self-governance? Or is voting for local offices different, especially if voters have adopted that practice in a local referendum? Would a constitutional challenge to non-citizen voting in local elections succeed?

3. U.S. officials uncovered evidence showing that Russia interfered in the 2016 U.S. election, in two key ways. First, Russia infiltrated several states' voter registration databases, although there is no evidence that Russia changed any information. Second, Russia engaged in a disinformation campaign, especially on social media, to sow discord among the American electorate and ultimately to support the election of Donald Trump. There is no evidence that Russia interfered with the actual operation of Election Day. With all of that said, what should the United States do about the threat of foreign interference in U.S. elections? In October 2018, the U.S. House of Representatives passed a bill that would forbid candidates from communicating about their campaign with foreign governments and would require campaigns to report any offers of foreign assistance. Is that enough? Only Democrats voted in favor of the bill, with Republicans suggesting that it was unnecessary and would violate the First Amendment. How could Congress make the proposal bipartisan? And how would the First Amendment analysis play out if the law passes and it is challenged in court?

Social media companies like Facebook and Twitter, where a lot of the Russian interference occurred in 2016, have come under fire to reject foreign advertising money and provide stronger disclosure of the sources of ads or other sponsored content. Congress held hearings and filed legislation to regulate political ads on social media. The companies, fearing federal oversight, then "voluntarily" changed their policies on political ads on their platforms. Have the changes been enough? Would congressional regulation of political ads on Facebook or Twitter violate the First Amendment?

Notably, the concern of foreign interference did not disappear in 2020: Evidence suggests that both Russia and Iran attempted to influence the U.S. election that year, although it does not appear that either country sought to change vote totals.

4. The first impeachment of Donald Trump in 2019 and his ultimate acquittal in the Senate in early 2020 raised a slightly different issue of foreign involvement in U.S. elections. Evidence demonstrated that President Trump sought the assistance of Ukrainian President Volodymyr Zelensky to dig up dirt on Joe Biden, who was running for the Democratic presidential nomination in 2020. During a phone call in July 2019, President Trump essentially asked President Zelensky to assist in an investigation of Hunter Biden, Joe Biden's son, who served on the board of directors of Burisma Holdings, a Ukrainian energy company. Evidence showed that Trump even implied that he would withhold aid to Ukraine and would refuse a White House visit for President Zelensky unless Zelensky cooperated. There were, of course, a lot more details and permutations of this scandal. Democrats (and Republican Senator Mitt Romney, the only Republican who voted to convict in this first impeachment) found that Trump had essentially engaged in an unlawful quid pro quo arrangement and had abused his office to help support his re-election by seeking the assistance of a foreign government to harm his ultimate rival in 2020. Republicans (besides Romney) either said that Trump's conduct was a permissible exercise of his authority to regulate foreign affairs or found that, while potentially improper, it was not enough to warrant impeachment and conviction. (Trump himself said that the key phone call between himself and Zelensky was "perfect.")

Most legal analysts would likely agree that Trump's conduct seemed to violate federal law, which makes it a crime for any person "to solicit, accept, or receive a contribution or donation" from a "foreign national," with "contribution" to include "other thing of value . . . in connection with a Federal, State, or local election." 52 U.S.C. § 30121. Information on a political rival is included within "other thing of value." Yet the Department of Justice has a policy not to indict or prosecute a sitting president. In addition, some might argue that the statute forbidding a candidate from seeking foreign assistance itself violates the First Amendment. What does *Bluman* suggest about that question? *Bluman* was about a foreign national's desire to participate in American democracy. Is the question different if an American candidate solicits help from a foreign national?

Thus, there are several levels of analysis to consider on this topic: Can Congress limit foreign nationals from participating in American democracy? What can Congress do about false or misleading political ads on social media, especially if those ads come from outside the United States? How should our democracy deal with a sitting president who seeks assistance from a foreign government, ostensibly as part of the president's foreign affairs powers, but potentially in a way that can help that president's re-election?

Moreover, this inquiry is separate from the general question of election integrity, which became a further issue in the 2020 election after the COVID-19 pandemic required a major expansion of mail-in voting and a faction of the Republican Party criticized the process as rife with fraud (despite zero evidence that expanded mail-in voting created significant fraud). Donald Trump's refusal to concede the 2020 presidential election because of this alleged fraud (for which there was no evidentiary support), of course, led to the insurrection at the U.S. Capitol on January 6, 2021. Although that incident did not involve foreign interference, this discussion shows how the issues of election integrity are intertwined.

How American democracy responds to all of these threats (real or imagined) — and what it can do given First Amendment principles — could have a lasting influence for years to come.

7. *Public Financing*

In an effort to reduce the amount of outside money in campaigns and to try to equalize the opportunity for nonwealthy candidates to compete, both Congress and some state legislatures have passed public financing regimes. Typically, to accept public funds, a candidate must agree to certain conditions, such as a cap on the amount of money their campaigns will raise in contributions or will spend on campaigning.

Congress adopted a public financing system for presidential candidates in FECA. Ever notice the check box on your federal tax form to designate $3 of your tax money to the "presidential election campaign"? That money does not increase your tax liability but simply directs $3 of your taxes to the public money that presidential candidates can use, if they opt-in to public financing. But by opting in, presidential candidates agree to limit their overall spending. In the early 1980s, around 25 percent of Americans checked the box to designate $3 of their taxes to this fund, but that number has dwindled to just about 6 percent of taxpayers who have checked the box in recent years.* Presidential candidates, too, have shied away from public financing recently. In 2008, Republican candidate John McCain took public funds but the winner, Democrat Barack Obama, refused the funds, choosing instead to raise more money on his own. Both major party candidates in 2012 — Obama and Republican Mitt Romney — refused public financing. Both raised well more than the $91.2 million they would have received in public funds. Neither Hillary Clinton nor Donald Trump used public funding in 2016. Trump and Joe Biden also refused public financing in 2020.

The Supreme Court upheld the federal public financing scheme in *Buckley*. The Court noted that the public financing system "is a congressional effort, not to abridge, restrict, or censor speech, but rather to use public money to facilitate and enlarge public discussion and participation in the electoral process, goals vital to a self-governing people. Thus, [public financing] furthers, not abridges, pertinent First Amendment values." *Buckley v. Valeo* (1976).

* *See* Andrew Flowers, *A Checkbox on Your Tax Return Helped Kill Public Campaign Funding*, FiveThirtyEight, April 9, 2015, https://fivethirtyeight.com/features/a-checkbox-on-your-tax-return-helped-kill-public-campaign-funding.

There is no public financing available for congressional candidates. But Congress tried to minimize the influence of a wealthy candidate self-funding his or her campaign in BCRA. The law included what has been termed the "Millionaire's Amendment": If a candidate spent more than $350,000 of his or her personal funds on the campaign, an opponent who was not spending that much in personal funds could collect up to three times the normal contribution amount. Essentially, the "Millionaire's Amendment" raised the contribution limit for candidates who faced wealthy opponents who were self-financing their own campaign. The Court struck down this provision in *Davis v. FEC* (2008). The Court held that the increased contribution cap for a non–self-financed candidate unconstitutionally forced a self-financed candidate "to choose between the First Amendment right to engage in unfettered political speech and subjection to discriminatory fundraising limitations."

Arizona had a similar triggering mechanism, but instead of increasing the contribution limits, it actually gave the publicly financed candidate more state money for the campaign if a privately financed candidate spent over a certain amount. Was that provision unconstitutional under the Court's decision in *Davis*, or were there unique features of the Arizona system that would allow it to pass constitutional muster? That question is the subject of the next case. As you are reading, note the strong divide between the majority and dissent. What is the point of public financing systems? Are they viable if rich candidates can devote their personal wealth to being elected? That is, why would a candidate ever accept public financing (and the accompanying strings on contribution limits) if they know a wealthy candidate will be able to raise and spend as much as he or she wants? Does this mean that less-wealthy candidates have no shot at winning an election? Also note the continued adherence to the anticorruption rationale that the Court requires to sustain a campaign finance regulation. Finally, why are the opinions so pointed and caustic toward each other? Are the two sides exhibiting incompatible worldviews regarding the financing of elections?

Arizona Free Enterprise Club's Freedom Club PAC v. Bennett

564 U.S. 721(2011)

Chief Justice Roberts delivered the opinion of the Court.

Under Arizona law, candidates for state office who accept public financing can receive additional money from the State in direct response to the campaign activities of privately financed candidates and independent expenditure groups. Once a set spending limit is exceeded, a publicly financed candidate receives roughly one dollar for every dollar spent by an opposing privately financed candidate. The publicly financed candidate also receives roughly one dollar for every dollar spent by independent expenditure groups to support the privately financed candidate, or to oppose the publicly financed candidate. We hold that Arizona's matching funds scheme substantially burdens protected political speech without serving a compelling state interest and therefore violates the First Amendment.

I

A

The Arizona Citizens Clean Elections Act, passed by initiative in 1998, created a voluntary public financing system to fund the primary and general election campaigns of candidates for state office. All eligible candidates for Governor, secretary of state, attorney general, treasurer, superintendent of public instruction, the corporation commission, mine inspector, and the state legislature (both the House and Senate) may opt to receive public funding. Eligibility is contingent on the collection of a specified number of five-dollar contributions from Arizona voters, and the acceptance of certain campaign restrictions and obligations. Publicly funded candidates must agree, among other things, to limit their expenditure of personal funds to $500; participate in at least one public debate; adhere to an overall expenditure cap; and return all unspent public moneys to the State.

In exchange for accepting these conditions, participating candidates are granted public funds to conduct their campaigns. In many cases, this initial allotment may be the whole of the State's financial backing of a publicly funded candidate. But when certain conditions are met, publicly funded candidates are granted additional "equalizing" or matching funds.

Matching funds are available in both primary and general elections. In a primary, matching funds are triggered when a privately financed candidate's expenditures, combined with the expenditures of independent groups made in support of the privately financed candidate or in opposition to a publicly financed candidate, exceed the primary election allotment of state funds to the publicly financed candidate. During the general election, matching funds are triggered when the amount of money a privately financed candidate receives in contributions, combined with the expenditures of independent groups made in support of the privately financed candidate or in opposition to a publicly financed candidate, exceed the general election allotment of state funds to the publicly financed candidate. A privately financed candidate's expenditures of his personal funds are counted as contributions for purposes of calculating matching funds during a general election.

Once matching funds are triggered, each additional dollar that a privately financed candidate spends during the primary results in one dollar in additional state funding to his publicly financed opponent (less a 6% reduction meant to account for fundraising expenses). During a general election, every dollar that a candidate receives in contributions—which includes any money of his own that a candidate spends on his campaign—results in roughly one dollar in additional state funding to his publicly financed opponent. In an election where a privately funded candidate faces multiple publicly financed candidates, one dollar raised or spent by the privately financed candidate results in an almost one dollar increase in public funding to each of the publicly financed candidates.

Once the public financing cap is exceeded, additional expenditures by independent groups can result in dollar-for-dollar matching funds as well. Spending by independent groups on behalf of a privately funded candidate, or in opposition to a publicly funded candidate, results in matching funds. Independent expenditures made in support of a publicly financed candidate can result in matching funds for other publicly financed candidates in a race. The matching funds provision is not activated, however, when independent expenditures are made in opposition to a privately financed candidate. Matching funds top out at two times the initial authorized grant of public funding to the publicly financed candidate.

Under Arizona law, a privately financed candidate may raise and spend unlimited funds, subject to state-imposed contribution limits and disclosure requirements. Contributions to candidates for statewide office are limited to $840 per contributor per election cycle and contributions to legislative candidates are limited to $410 per contributor per election cycle.

An example may help clarify how the Arizona matching funds provision operates. Arizona is divided into 30 districts for purposes of electing members to the State's House of Representatives. Each district elects two representatives to the House biannually. In the last general election, the number of candidates competing for the two available seats in each district ranged from two to seven. Arizona's Fourth District had three candidates for its two available House seats. Two of those candidates opted to accept public funding; one candidate chose to operate his campaign with private funds.

In that election, if the total funds contributed to the privately funded candidate, added to that candidate's expenditure of personal funds and the expenditures of supportive independent groups, exceeded $21,479—the allocation of public funds for the general election in a contested State House race—the matching funds provision would be triggered. At that point, a number of different political activities could result in the distribution of matching funds. For example:

- If the privately funded candidate spent $1,000 of his own money to conduct a direct mailing, each of his publicly funded opponents would receive $940 ($1,000 less the 6% offset).
- If the privately funded candidate held a fundraiser that generated $1,000 in contributions, each of his publicly funded opponents would receive $940.
- If an independent expenditure group spent $1,000 on a brochure expressing its support for the privately financed candidate, each of the publicly financed candidates would receive $940 directly.
- If an independent expenditure group spent $1,000 on a brochure opposing one of the publicly financed candidates, but saying nothing about the privately financed candidate, the publicly financed candidates would receive $940 directly.
- If an independent expenditure group spent $1,000 on a brochure supporting one of the publicly financed candidates, the other publicly financed candidate would receive $940 directly, but the privately financed candidate would receive nothing.
- If an independent expenditure group spent $1,000 on a brochure opposing the privately financed candidate, no matching funds would be issued.

A publicly financed candidate would continue to receive additional state money in response to fundraising and spending by the privately financed candidate and independent expenditure groups until that publicly financed candidate received a total of $64,437 in state funds (three times the initial allocation for a State House race).[3]

B

[Omitted.]

II

"Discussion of public issues and debate on the qualifications of candidates are integral to the operation" of our system of government. *Buckley v. Valeo* (1976). As a result, the First Amendment " 'has its fullest and most urgent application' to speech uttered during a campaign for political office." *Eu v. San Francisco County Democratic Central Comm.* (1989) (quoting *Monitor Patriot Co. v. Roy* (1971)). "Laws that burden political speech are" accordingly "subject to strict scrutiny, which requires the Government to prove that the restriction furthers a compelling interest and is narrowly tailored to achieve that interest." *Citizens United v. Federal Election Comm'n* (2010).

Although the speech of the candidates and independent expenditure groups that brought this suit is not directly capped by Arizona's matching funds provision, those parties contend that their political speech is substantially burdened by the state law in the same way that speech was burdened by the law we recently found invalid in *Davis v. Federal Election Comm'n* (2008). In *Davis*, we considered a First Amendment challenge to the so-called "Millionaire's Amendment" of the Bipartisan Campaign Reform Act of 2002. Under that Amendment, if a candidate for the United States House of Representatives spent more than $350,000 of his personal funds, "a new, asymmetrical regulatory scheme [came] into play." The opponent of the candidate who exceeded that limit was permitted to collect individual contributions up to $6,900 per contributor—three times the normal contribution limit of $2,300. The candidate who spent more than the personal funds limit remained subject to the original contribution cap. Davis argued that this scheme "burden[ed] his exercise of his First Amendment right to make unlimited expenditures of his personal funds because" doing so had "the effect of enabling his opponent to raise more money and to use that money to finance speech that counteract[ed] and thus diminishe[d] the effectiveness of Davis' own speech."

In addressing the constitutionality of the Millionaire's Amendment, we acknowledged that the provision did not impose an outright cap on a candidate's personal expenditures. We nonetheless concluded that the Amendment was unconstitutional because it forced a candidate "to choose between the First Amendment right to engage in unfettered political speech and subjection to discriminatory fundraising limitations." Any candidate who chose to spend more than $350,000 of his own money was forced to "shoulder a special and potentially significant burden" because that choice gave fundraising advantages to the candidate's adversary.

3. Maine and North Carolina have both passed matching funds statutes that resemble Arizona's law. Minnesota, Connecticut, and Florida have also adopted matching funds provisions, but courts have enjoined the enforcement of those schemes after concluding that their operation violates the First Amendment.

We determined that this constituted an "unprecedented penalty" and "impose[d] a substantial burden on the exercise of the First Amendment right to use personal funds for campaign speech," and concluded that the Government had failed to advance any compelling interest that would justify such a burden.

A

1

The logic of *Davis* largely controls our approach to this case. Much like the burden placed on speech in *Davis*, the matching funds provision "imposes an unprecedented penalty on any candidate who robustly exercises [his] First Amendment right[s]." Under that provision, "the vigorous exercise of the right to use personal funds to finance campaign speech" leads to "advantages for opponents in the competitive context of electoral politics."

Once a privately financed candidate has raised or spent more than the State's initial grant to a publicly financed candidate, each personal dollar spent by the privately financed candidate results in an award of almost one additional dollar to his opponent. That plainly forces the privately financed candidate to "shoulder a special and potentially significant burden" when choosing to exercise his First Amendment right to spend funds on behalf of his candidacy. If the law at issue in *Davis* imposed a burden on candidate speech, the Arizona law unquestionably does so as well.

The penalty imposed by Arizona's matching funds provision is different in some respects from the penalty imposed by the law we struck down in *Davis*. But those differences make the Arizona law more constitutionally problematic, not less. First, the penalty in *Davis* consisted of raising the contribution limits for one of the candidates. The candidate who benefited from the increased limits still had to go out and raise the funds. He may or may not have been able to do so. The other candidate, therefore, faced merely the possibility that his opponent would be able to raise additional funds, through contribution limits that remained subject to a cap. And still the Court held that this was an "unprecedented penalty," a "special and potentially significant burden" that had to be justified by a compelling state interest—a rigorous First Amendment hurdle. Here the benefit to the publicly financed candidate is the direct and automatic release of public money. That is a far heavier burden than in *Davis*.

Second, depending on the specifics of the election at issue, the matching funds provision can create a multiplier effect. In the Arizona Fourth District House election previously discussed, if the spending cap were exceeded, each dollar spent by the privately funded candidate would result in an additional dollar of campaign funding to each of that candidate's publicly financed opponents. In such a situation, the matching funds provision forces privately funded candidates to fight a political hydra of sorts. Each dollar they spend generates two adversarial dollars in response. Again, a markedly more significant burden than in *Davis*.

Third, unlike the law at issue in *Davis*, all of this is to some extent out of the privately financed candidate's hands. Even if that candidate opted to spend less than the initial public financing cap, any spending by independent expenditure groups to promote the privately financed candidate's election—regardless whether such support was welcome or helpful—could trigger matching funds. What is more, that state money would go directly to the publicly funded candidate to use as he saw fit. That disparity in control—giving money directly to a publicly financed candidate, in response to independent expenditures that cannot be coordinated with the privately funded candidate—is a substantial advantage for the publicly funded candidate. That candidate can allocate the money according to his own campaign strategy, which the privately financed candidate could not do with the independent group expenditures that triggered the matching funds.

2

Arizona, the Clean Elections Institute, and the United States offer several arguments attempting to explain away the existence or significance of any burden imposed by matching funds. None is persuasive.

Arizona contends that the matching funds provision is distinguishable from the law we invalidated in *Davis*. The State correctly points out that our decision in *Davis* focused on the asymmetrical contribution limits imposed by the Millionaire's Amendment. But that is not because—as the State asserts—the reach of that opinion is limited to asymmetrical contribution limits. It is because that was the particular burden on candidate speech we faced in *Davis*. And whatever the significance of the distinction in general, there can be no doubt that the burden on speech is significantly greater in this case than in *Davis*: That means that the law here—like the one in *Davis*—must be justified by a compelling state interest.

The State argues that the matching funds provision actually results in more speech by "increas[ing] debate about issues of public concern" in Arizona elections and "promot[ing] the free and open debate that the First Amendment was intended to foster." In the State's view, this promotion of First Amendment ideals offsets any burden the law might impose on some speakers.

Not so. Any increase in speech resulting from the Arizona law is of one kind and one kind only—that of publicly financed candidates. The burden imposed on privately financed candidates and independent expenditure groups reduces their speech; "restriction[s] on the amount of money a person or group can spend on political communication during a campaign necessarily reduces the quantity of expression." *Buckley*. Thus, even if the matching funds provision did result in more speech by publicly financed candidates and more speech in general, it would do so at the expense of impermissibly burdening (and thus reducing) the speech of privately financed candidates and independent expenditure groups. This sort of "beggar thy neighbor" approach to free speech—"restrict[ing] the speech of some elements of our society in order to enhance the relative voice of others"—is "wholly foreign to the First Amendment." *Id.*

The State correctly asserts that the candidates and independent expenditure groups "do not . . . claim that a single lump sum payment to publicly funded candidates," equivalent to the maximum amount of state financing that a candidate can obtain through matching funds, would impermissibly burden their speech. The State reasons that if providing all the money up front would not burden speech, providing it piecemeal does not do so either. And the State further argues that such incremental administration is necessary to ensure that public funding is not under- or over-distributed.

These arguments miss the point. It is not the amount of funding that the State provides to publicly financed candidates that is constitutionally problematic in this case. It is the manner in which that funding is provided—in direct response to the political speech of privately financed candidates and independent expenditure groups. And the fact that the State's matching mechanism may be more efficient than other alternatives—that it may help the State in "finding the sweet-spot" or "fine-tuning" its financing system to avoid a drain on public resources—is of no moment; "the First Amendment does not permit the State to sacrifice speech for efficiency." *Riley v. National Federation of Blind of N.C., Inc.* (1988).

B

Because the Arizona matching funds provision imposes a substantial burden on the speech of privately financed candidates and independent expenditure groups, "that provision cannot stand unless it is 'justified by a compelling state interest,'" *id.* (quoting *Massachusetts Citizens for Life*).

There is a debate between the parties in this case as to what state interest is served by the matching funds provision. The privately financed candidates and independent expenditure groups contend that the provision works to "level[] electoral opportunities" by equalizing candidate "resources and influence." The State and the Clean Elections Institute counter that the provision "furthers Arizona's interest in preventing corruption and the appearance of corruption."

1

There is ample support for the argument that the matching funds provision seeks to "level the playing field" in terms of candidate resources. The clearest evidence is of course the very operation of the provision: It ensures that campaign funding is equal, up to three times the initial public funding allotment. The text of the Citizens Clean Elections Act itself confirms this purpose. The statutory provision setting up the matching funds regime is titled "Equal funding of candidates." Ariz. Rev. Stat. Ann. § 16-952. The Act refers to the funds doled out after the Act's matching mechanism is triggered as "equalizing funds." See §§ 16-952(C)(4), (5). And the regulations implementing the matching funds provision refer to those funds as "equalizing funds" as well. *See* Citizens Clean Elections Commission, Ariz. Admin. Rule R2-20-113.[10]

We have repeatedly rejected the argument that the government has a compelling state interest in "leveling the playing field" that can justify undue burdens on political speech. In *Davis*, we stated that discriminatory contribution limits meant to "level electoral opportunities for candidates of different personal wealth" did not serve "a legitimate government objective," let alone a compelling one. And in *Buckley*, we held that limits on overall campaign expenditures could not be justified by a purported government "interest in equalizing the financial resources of

10. Prior to oral argument in this case, the Citizens Clean Elections Commission's Web site stated that "'The Citizens Clean Elections Act was passed by the people of Arizona in 1998 to level the playing field when it comes to running for office.'" AFEC Brief 10, n. 3 (quoting http://www.azcleanelections.gov/about-us/get-involved.aspx). The Web site now says that "The Citizens Clean Elections Act was passed by the people of Arizona in 1998 to restore citizen participation and confidence in our political system." [Footnote relocated.—Eds.]

candidates." After all, equalizing campaign resources "might serve not to equalize the opportunities of all candidates, but to handicap a candidate who lacked substantial name recognition or exposure of his views before the start of the campaign." *Id.*

"Leveling the playing field" can sound like a good thing. But in a democracy, campaigning for office is not a game. It is a critically important form of speech. The First Amendment embodies our choice as a Nation that, when it comes to such speech, the guiding principle is freedom—the "unfettered interchange of ideas"—not whatever the State may view as fair. [*Id.*]

2

As already noted, the State and the Clean Elections Institute disavow any interest in "leveling the playing field." They instead assert that the "Equal funding of candidates" provision serves the State's compelling interest in combating corruption and the appearance of corruption.

Burdening a candidate's expenditure of his own funds on his own campaign does not further the State's anticorruption interest. Indeed, we have said that "reliance on personal funds reduces the threat of corruption" and that "discouraging [the] use of personal funds[] disserves the anticorruption interest." *Davis.* That is because "the use of personal funds reduces the candidate's dependence on outside contributions and thereby counteracts the coercive pressures and attendant risks of abuse" of money in politics. *Buckley.* The matching funds provision counts a candidate's expenditures of his own money on his own campaign as contributions, and to that extent cannot be supported by any anticorruption interest.

Arizona already has some of the most austere contribution limits in the United States. Arizona also has stringent fundraising disclosure requirements. In the face of such ascetic contribution limits, strict disclosure requirements, and the general availability of public funding, it is hard to imagine what marginal corruption deterrence could be generated by the matching funds provision.

III

"[T]here is practically universal agreement that a major purpose of" the First Amendment "was to protect the free discussion of governmental affairs," "includ[ing] discussions of candidates." *Buckley.* That agreement "reflects our 'profound national commitment to the principle that debate on public issues should be uninhibited, robust, and wide-open.'" [*Id.*] (quoting *New York Times Co. v. Sullivan* (1964)). True when we said it and true today. Laws like Arizona's matching funds provision that inhibit robust and wide-open political debate without sufficient justification cannot stand.

Justice KAGAN, with whom Justice GINSBURG, Justice BREYER, and Justice SOTOMAYOR join, dissenting.

Imagine two States, each plagued by a corrupt political system. In both States, candidates for public office accept large campaign contributions in exchange for the promise that, after assuming office, they will rank the donors' interests ahead of all others. As a result of these bargains, politicians ignore the public interest, sound public policy languishes, and the citizens lose confidence in their government.

Recognizing the cancerous effect of this corruption, voters of the first State, acting through referendum, enact several campaign finance measures previously approved by this Court. They cap campaign contributions; require disclosure of substantial donations; and create an optional public financing program that gives candidates a fixed public subsidy if they refrain from private fundraising. But these measures do not work. Individuals who "bundle" campaign contributions become indispensable to candidates in need of money. Simple disclosure fails to prevent shady dealing. And candidates choose not to participate in the public financing system because the sums provided do not make them competitive with their privately financed opponents. So the State remains afflicted with corruption.

Voters of the second State, having witnessed this failure, take an ever-so-slightly different tack to cleaning up their political system. They too enact contribution limits and disclosure requirements. But they believe that the greatest hope of eliminating corruption lies in creating an effective public financing program, which will break candidates' dependence on large donors and bundlers. These voters realize, based on the first State's experience, that such a program will not work unless candidates agree to participate in it. And candidates will participate only if they know that they will receive sufficient funding to run competitive races. So the voters enact a program that carefully adjusts the money given to would-be officeholders, through the use of a matching funds mechanism, in order to provide this assurance. The program does not discriminate against any candidate or point of view, and it does not restrict any person's ability to speak. In fact, by providing resources to many candidates, the program creates more speech and thereby broadens public debate. And just as the voters had hoped, the program accomplishes its mission of restoring integrity to the political system. The second State rids itself of corruption.

A person familiar with our country's core values—our devotion to democratic self-governance, as well as to "uninhibited, robust, and wide-open" debate, *New York Times Co. v. Sullivan* (1964)—might expect this Court to celebrate, or at least not to interfere with, the second State's success. But today, the majority holds that the second State's system—the system that produces honest government, working on behalf of all the people—clashes with our Constitution. The First Amendment, the majority insists, requires us all to rely on the measures employed in the first State, even when they have failed to break the stranglehold of special interests on elected officials.

I disagree. The First Amendment's core purpose is to foster a healthy, vibrant political system full of robust discussion and debate. Nothing in Arizona's anti-corruption statute, the Arizona Citizens Clean Elections Act, violates this constitutional protection. To the contrary, the Act promotes the values underlying both the First Amendment and our entire Constitution by enhancing the "opportunity for free political discussion to the end that government may be responsive to the will of the people." *Id.* I therefore respectfully dissent.

I

A

[P]ublic financing systems today dot the national landscape. Almost one-third of the States have adopted some form of public financing, and so too has the Federal Government for presidential elections. The federal program—which offers presidential candidates a fixed public subsidy if they abstain from private fundraising—originated in the campaign finance law that Congress enacted in 1974 on the heels of the Watergate scandal. Congress explained at the time that the "potentia[l] for abuse" inherent in privately funded elections was "all too clear." S. Rep. No. 93-689, p. 4 (1974).

We declared the presidential public financing system constitutional in *Buckley v. Valeo.* Congress, we stated, had created the program "for the 'general welfare'—to reduce the deleterious influence of large contributions on our political process," as well as to "facilitate communication by candidates with the electorate, and to free candidates from the rigors of fundraising." We thus gave state and municipal governments the green light to adopt public financing systems along the presidential model.

But this model, which distributes a lump-sum grant at the beginning of an election cycle, has a significant weakness: It lacks a mechanism for setting the subsidy at a level that will give candidates sufficient incentive to participate, while also conserving public resources. Public financing can achieve its goals only if a meaningful number of candidates receive the state subsidy, rather than raise private funds. But a public funding program must be voluntary to pass constitutional muster, because of its restrictions on contributions and expenditures. And candidates will choose to sign up only if the subsidy provided enables them to run competitive races. If the grant is pegged too low, it puts the participating candidate at a disadvantage: Because he has agreed to spend no more than the amount of the subsidy, he will lack the means to respond if his privately funded opponent spends over that threshold. So when lump-sum grants do not keep up with campaign expenditures, more and more candidates will choose not to participate.[1] But if the subsidy is set too high, it may impose an unsustainable burden on the public fisc. At the least, hefty grants will waste public resources in the many state races where lack of competition makes such funding unnecessary.

The difficulty, then, is in finding the Goldilocks solution—not too large, not too small, but just right. And this in a world of countless variables—where the amount of money needed to run a viable campaign against a privately funded candidate depends on, among other things, the district, the office, and the election cycle. A state may set lump-sum grants district-by-district, based on spending in past elections; but even that approach leaves out many factors—including the resources of the privately funded candidate—that alter the competitiveness of a seat from one election to the next. In short, the dynamic nature of our electoral system makes ex ante predictions about campaign expenditures almost impossible. And that creates a chronic problem for lump-sum public financing programs, because inaccurate estimates produce subsidies that either dissuade candidates from participating or waste taxpayer money. And so States have made adjustments to the lump-sum scheme that we approved in *Buckley*, in attempts to more effectively reduce corruption.

1. The problem is apparent in the federal system. In recent years, the number of presidential candidates opting to receive public financing has declined because the subsidy has not kept pace with spending by privately financed candidates. The last election cycle offers a stark example: Then-candidate Barack Obama raised $745.7 million in private funds in 2008, in contrast with the $105.4 million he could have received in public funds.

B

[Omitted.]

II

Arizona's statute does not impose a "restriction" or "substantia[l] burde[n]" on expression. [Citation to majority opinion.] The law has quite the opposite effect: It subsidizes and so produces more political speech. We recognized in *Buckley* that, for this reason, public financing of elections "facilitate[s] and enlarge[s] public discussion," in support of First Amendment values. And what we said then is just as true today. Except in a world gone topsy-turvy, additional campaign speech and electoral competition is not a First Amendment injury.

A

At every turn, the majority tries to convey the impression that Arizona's matching fund statute is of a piece with laws prohibiting electoral speech. The majority invokes the language of "limits," "bar[s]," and "restraints." It equates the law to a "restrictio[n] on the amount of money a person or group can spend on political communication during a campaign." It insists that the statute "restrict[s] the speech of some elements of our society" to enhance the speech of others. And it concludes by reminding us that the point of the First Amendment is to protect "against unjustified government restrictions on speech."

There is just one problem. Arizona's matching funds provision does not restrict, but instead subsidizes, speech. By enabling participating candidates to respond to their opponents' expression, the statute expands public debate, in adherence to "our tradition that more speech, not less, is the governing rule." *Citizens United.* What the law does—all the law does—is fund more speech.

This suit, in fact, may merit less attention than any challenge to a speech subsidy ever seen in this Court. In the usual First Amendment subsidy case, a person complains that the government declined to finance his speech, while bankrolling someone else's; we must then decide whether the government differentiated between these speakers on a prohibited basis—because it preferred one speaker's ideas to another's. But the candidates bringing this challenge do not make that claim—because they were never denied a subsidy. Arizona, remember, offers to support any person running for state office. Petitioners here refused that assistance. So they are making a novel argument: that Arizona violated their First Amendment rights by disbursing funds to other speakers even though they could have received (but chose to spurn) the same financial assistance. Some people might call that *chutzpah.*

Indeed, what petitioners demand is essentially a right to quash others' speech through the prohibition of a (universally available) subsidy program. Petitioners are able to convey their ideas without public financing—and they would prefer the field to themselves, so that they can speak free from response. To attain that goal, they ask this Court to prevent Arizona from funding electoral speech—even though that assistance is offered to every state candidate, on the same (entirely unobjectionable) basis. And this Court gladly obliges.

If an ordinary citizen, without the hindrance of a law degree, thought this result an upending of First Amendment values, he would be correct. [T]o invalidate a statute that restricts no one's speech and discriminates against no idea—that only provides more voices, wider discussion, and greater competition in elections—is to undermine, rather than to enforce, the First Amendment.

B

The majority has one, and only one, way of separating this case from *Buckley* and our other, many precedents involving speech subsidies. According to the Court, the special problem here lies in Arizona's matching funds mechanism, which the majority claims imposes a "substantia[l] burde[n]" on a privately funded candidate's speech.

[D]oes [the supposed effect of the matching provision in leading a privately funded candidate to stop spending in an election] count as a severe burden on expression? By the measure of our prior decisions—which have upheld campaign reforms with an equal or greater impact on speech—the answer is no.

Number one: *Any* system of public financing, including the lump-sum model upheld in *Buckley*, imposes a similar burden on privately funded candidates. Suppose Arizona were to do what all parties agree it could under *Buckley*—provide a single upfront payment (say, $150,000) to a participating candidate, rather than an initial payment (of $50,000) plus 94% of whatever his privately funded opponent spent, up to a ceiling (the same $150,000). That system would "diminis[h] the effectiveness" of a privately funded candidate's speech at least as much, and in the same way: It would give his opponent, who presumably would not be able to raise that sum on his own, more money to spend. And so too, a lump-sum system may deter speech. A person relying on private resources might well choose not to enter a race at all, because he knows he will face an adequately funded opponent. And even if he decides to run, he likely will choose to speak in different ways—for example, by eschewing dubious, easy-to-answer charges—because his opponent has the ability to respond. Indeed, privately funded candidates may well find the lump-sum system more burdensome than Arizona's (assuming the lump is big enough). Pretend you are financing your campaign through private donations. Would you prefer that your opponent receive a guaranteed, upfront payment of $150,000, or that he receive only $50,000, with the possibility—a possibility that you mostly get to control—of collecting another $100,000 somewhere down the road? Me too. That's the first reason the burden on speech cannot command a different result in this case than in *Buckley*.

Number two: Our decisions about disclosure and disclaimer requirements show the Court is wrong. Like a disclosure rule, the matching funds provision may occasionally deter, but "impose[s] no ceiling" on electoral expression. [*Citizens United.*]

Number three: Any burden that the Arizona law imposes does not exceed the burden associated with contribution limits, which we have also repeatedly upheld. I doubt I have to reiterate that the Arizona statute imposes no restraints on any expressive activity. So the majority once again has no reason here to reach a different result.

In this way, our campaign finance cases join our speech subsidy cases in supporting the constitutionality of Arizona's law. Both sets of precedents are in accord that a statute funding electoral speech in the way Arizona's does imposes no First Amendment injury.

C

The majority thinks it has one case on its side—*Davis v. Federal Election Comm'n*—and it pegs everything on that decision. But *Davis* relies on principles that fit securely within our First Amendment law and tradition—most unlike today's opinion.

Under the First Amendment, the similarity between *Davis* and this case matters far less than the differences. Here is the similarity: In both cases, one candidate's campaign expenditure triggered . . . something. Now here are the differences: In *Davis*, the candidate's expenditure triggered a discriminatory speech restriction, which Congress could not otherwise have imposed consistent with the First Amendment; by contrast, in this case, the candidate's expenditure triggers a non-discriminatory speech subsidy, which all parties agree Arizona could have provided in the first instance. In First Amendment law, that difference makes a difference—indeed, it makes all the difference.

But what of the trigger mechanism—in *Davis*, as here, a candidate's campaign expenditures? That, after all, is the only thing that this case and *Davis* share. If *Davis* had held that the trigger mechanism itself violated the First Amendment, then the case would support today's holding. But *Davis* said nothing of the kind. It made clear that the trigger mechanism could not rescue the discriminatory contribution limits from constitutional invalidity; that the limits went into effect only after a candidate spent substantial personal resources rendered them no more permissible under the First Amendment. But *Davis* did not call into question the trigger mechanism itself. Indeed, *Davis* explained that Congress could have used that mechanism to activate a non-discriminatory (i.e., across-the-board) increase in contribution limits; in that case, the Court stated, "Davis' argument would plainly fail." The constitutional infirmity in *Davis* was not the trigger mechanism, but rather what lay on the other side of it—a discriminatory speech restriction.

III

For all these reasons, the Court errs in holding that the government action in this case substantially burdens speech and so requires the State to offer a compelling interest. But in any event, Arizona has come forward with just such an interest, explaining that the Clean Elections Act attacks corruption and the appearance of corruption in the State's political system. The majority's denigration of this interest—the suggestion that it either is not real or does not matter—wrongly prevents Arizona from protecting the strength and integrity of its democracy.

A

Our campaign finance precedents leave no doubt: Preventing corruption or the appearance of corruption is a compelling government interest. And so too, these precedents are clear: Public financing of elections serves this interest.

And that interest justifies the matching funds provision at issue because it is a critical facet of Arizona's public financing program. The provision is no more than a disbursement mechanism; but it is also the thing that makes the whole Clean Elections Act work. As described earlier, public financing has an Achilles heel—the difficulty of setting the subsidy at the right amount. Too small, and the grant will not attract candidates to the program; and with no participating candidates, the program can hardly decrease corruption. Too large, and the system becomes unsustainable, or at the least an unnecessary drain on public resources. But finding the sweet-spot is near impossible because of variation, across districts and over time, in the political system. Enter the matching funds provision, which takes an ordinary lump-sum amount, divides it into thirds, and disburses the last two of these (to the extent necessary) via a self-calibrating mechanism. That provision is just a fine-tuning of the lump-sum program approved in *Buckley*—a fine-tuning, it bears repeating, that prevents no one from speaking and discriminates against no message. But that fine-tuning can make the difference between a wholly ineffectual program and one that removes corruption from the political system.[12] If public financing furthers a compelling interest—and according to this Court, it does—then so too does the disbursement formula that Arizona uses to make public financing effective. The one conclusion follows directly from the other.

B

The majority instead devotes most of its energy to trying to show that "level[ing] the playing field," not fighting corruption, was the State's real goal. But the majority's distaste for "leveling" provides no excuse for striking down Arizona's law.

1

For starters, the Court has no basis to question the sincerity of the State's interest in rooting out political corruption. As I have just explained, that is the interest the State has asserted in this Court; it is the interest predominantly expressed in the "findings and declarations" section of the statute; and it is the interest universally understood (stretching back to Teddy Roosevelt's time) to support public financing of elections. As against all this, the majority claims to have found three smoking guns that reveal the State's true (and nefarious) intention to level the playing field. But the only smoke here is the majority's, and it is the kind that goes with mirrors.

The majority first observes that the matching funds provision is titled " 'Equal funding of candidates' " and that it refers to matching grants as " 'equalizing funds.' " Well, yes. The statute provides for matching funds (above and below certain thresholds); a synonym for "match" is "equal"; and so the statute uses that

12. For this reason, the majority is quite wrong to say that the State's interest in combating corruption does not support the matching fund provision's application to a candidate's expenditure of his own money or to an independent expenditure. The point is not that these expenditures themselves corrupt the political process. Rather, Arizona includes these, as well as all other, expenditures in the program to ensure that participating candidates receive the funds necessary to run competitive races—and so to attract those candidates in the first instance. That is in direct service of the State's anti-corruption interest.

term. In sum, the statute describes what the statute does. But the relevant question here (according to the majority's own analysis) is why the statute does that thing—otherwise said, what interest the statute serves. The State explains that its goal is to prevent corruption, and nothing in the Act's descriptive terms suggests any other objective.

Next, the majority notes that the Act allows participating candidates to accept private contributions if (but only if) the State cannot provide the funds it has promised (for example, because of a budget crisis). That provision, the majority argues, shows that when push comes to shove, the State cares more about "leveling" than about fighting corruption. But this is a plain misreading of the law. All the statute does is assure participating candidates that they will not be left in the lurch if public funds suddenly become unavailable. That guarantee helps persuade candidates to enter the program by removing the risk of a state default. And so the provision directly advances the Act's goal of combating corruption.

Finally, the Court remarks in a footnote that the Clean Elections Commission's website once stated that the "'Act was passed by the people of Arizona . . . to level the playing field.'" I can understand why the majority does not place much emphasis on this point. Some members of the majority have ridiculed the practice of relying on subsequent statements by legislators to demonstrate an earlier Congress's intent in enacting a statute. *See, e.g.*, *Sullivan v. Finkelstein* (1990) (Scalia, J., concurring in part); *United States v. Hayes* (2009) (Roberts, C.J., dissenting). Yet here the majority makes a much stranger claim: that a statement appearing on a government website in 2011 (written by who-knows-whom?) reveals what hundreds of thousands of Arizona's voters sought to do in 1998 when they enacted the Clean Elections Act by referendum. Just to state that proposition is to know it is wrong.

So the majority has no evidence—zero, none—that the objective of the Act is anything other than the interest that the State asserts, the Act proclaims, and the history of public financing supports: fighting corruption.

2

[Omitted.]

IV

[Omitted. Justice Kagan ended her dissent by saying: "Truly, democracy is not a game. I respectfully dissent."]

NOTES ON *ARIZONA FREE ENTERPRISE v. BENNETT*

1. In a part of Justice Kagan's dissent that we omitted, she recounted the evidence of massive corruption in Arizona's politics. Before enacting the public financing scheme that was the subject of this case, Arizona had passed, by referendum, a contribution limitation. Five years after the implementation of that campaign finance regulation, Arizona suffered "the worst public corruption scandal in its history," in which nearly 10 percent of the state's legislators were caught accepting campaign contributions or bribes in exchange for favorable legislative votes. Following that scandal the voters of Arizona passed the public financing/matching system. Should this history make a difference in the analysis?

2. Do public finance regimes root out corruption or the appearance of corruption? Both sides seem to be in agreement here that they can—as they allow candidates to forgo relying on wealthy donors. So what is the split among the Justices? Is there any way to craft a "trigger" to alter the campaign finance rules that can pass First Amendment scrutiny? Imagine you are a legislator in Arizona who supports this kind of law. What kind of new bill might you propose to respond to the Court's concerns in this case but still achieve the state's goals?

3. To what extent are public funding programs such as Arizona's a valid response to entrenchment—the concern that incumbents will naturally favor policies to help their own electoral chances to keep themselves in office? That is, a public financing regime might help "outside" candidates remain viable against well-financed and wealthy incumbents. The people of Arizona, in approving a referendum for public financing, were likely concerned about entrenchment. Should the Court have considered this potential rationale?

4. In recent years some localities have experimented with various public financing mechanisms for local elections. New York City, for instance, offers a matching funds program for candidates for local office. By opting in and agreeing to various spending limits and audits, candidates will receive a match of $8 for every $1 they raise from New York City residents, up to a limit for each contribution. As the website for the New York City system, notes, "A $10 contribution from a NYC resident to a participating candidate in the 2021 election could be worth as much as $90 to their campaign." Seattle offers an even more innovative program. The city mails every Seattle voter four $25 vouchers for residents to then give to candidates who have opted-in to public financing. Candidates thus campaign not only for votes but also for these "Democracy Vouchers," and the amount of public funds they receive is dependent on how many Democracy Vouchers they can collect. The city pays for the system through a property tax. Plaintiffs challenged the tax, arguing that it abridged their First Amendment rights by forcing them essentially to pay for speech with which they disagreed, but the Washington Supreme Court rejected the challenge. The court noted that "[t]he tax at issue here does not alter, abridge, restrict, censor, or burden speech. On the contrary, the Democracy Voucher Program 'facilitate[s] and enlarge[s] public discussion and participation in the electoral process.' *Buckley*. The program resembles other content-neutral ways the government facilitates political speech, for example, when the government distributes voters' pamphlets." *Elster v. City of Seattle* (Wash. 2019). Other cities, such as Austin, Texas, have indicated interest in adopting a similar Democracy Vouchers program.

8. *Disclosure and Disclaimer Requirements*

Along with limits on expenditures and contributions, the third main pillar of campaign finance law that has seen the most judicial activity is disclosure and disclaimer requirements. Once again, *Buckley* provides the foundation. Part of the Federal Election Campaign Act imposed various disclosure and disclaimer requirements on those who spent money on elections. The goal, as in the other parts of FECA, was to reduce the pernicious influence of money in politics, and in addition to shed light on who was spending on campaigns.

Congress first passed a campaign finance disclosure law in 1910. It then broadened the disclosure requirements in 1925 as part of the Federal Corrupt Practices Act. However, as the Court notes in *Buckley*, these disclosure provisions were "widely circumvented." Congress therefore made the disclosure requirements in FECA more robust. Those opposed to FECA challenged these disclosure provisions along with the other parts of the Act.

The government asserted three main interests in supporting disclosure laws. First, there is an informational interest: giving voters information about the source of political funding. Second, there is the familiar "corruption or the appearance of corruption" rationale. Third, disclosure laws can help to detect violations of valid contribution limitations. As you are reading this portion of *Buckley*, think about why the Court expanded the permissible justifications for disclosure laws, as opposed to its narrower construction of the required governmental interests for contribution and expenditure laws.

Then consider whether—with the shifting landscape of campaign finance law, most notably from *Citizens United*—the Court might now construe disclosure laws more strictly. Are the same three justifications listed above still valid governmental interests in the wake of *Citizens United*? As you will see, the Court rejected a constitutional attack to BCRA's disclaimer and disclosure laws in *Citizens United*. What does this suggest about the scope of campaign finance regulation moving forward?

Buckley v. Valeo

424 U.S. 1 (1976)

PER CURIAM

II. REPORTING AND DISCLOSURE REQUIREMENTS

Unlike the limitations on contributions and expenditures imposed by 18 U.S.C. § 608, the disclosure requirements of the Act, 2 U.S.C. § 431 et seq. are not challenged by appellants as per se unconstitutional restrictions on the exercise of First Amendment freedoms of speech and association. Indeed, appellants argue that "narrowly drawn disclosure requirements are the proper solution to virtually all of the evils Congress sought to remedy." The particular requirements embodied in the Act are attacked as overbroad both in their application to minor-party and independent candidates and in their extension to contributions as small as $11 or $101. Appellants also challenge the provision for disclosure by those who make independent contributions and expenditures. The Court of Appeals found no constitutional infirmities in the provisions challenged here. We affirm the determination on overbreadth and hold that § 434(e), if narrowly construed, also is within constitutional bounds.

The Act presently under review replaced all prior disclosure laws. Its primary disclosure provisions impose reporting obligations on "political committees" and candidates. "Political committee" is defined in § 431(d) as a group of persons that receives "contributions" or makes "expenditures" of over $1,000 in a calendar year. "Contributions" and "expenditures" are defined in lengthy parallel provisions. Both definitions focus on the use of money or other objects of value "for the purpose of . . . influencing" the nomination or election of any person to federal office. § 431(e)(1), (f)(1).

Each political committee is required to register with the Commission, and to keep detailed records of both contributions and expenditures. These records must include the name and address of everyone making a contribution in excess of $10, along with the date and amount of the contribution. If a person's contributions aggregate more than $100, his occupation and principal place of business are also to be included. These files are subject to periodic audits and field investigations by the Commission.

Each committee and each candidate also is required to file quarterly reports. The reports are to contain detailed financial information, including the full name, mailing address, occupation, and principal place of business of each person who has contributed over $100 in a calendar year, as well as the amount and date of the contributions. They are to be made available by the Commission "for public inspection and copying." § 438(a)(4). Every candidate for federal office is required to designate a "principal campaign committee," which is to receive reports of contributions and expenditures made on the candidate's behalf from other political committees and to compile and file these reports, together with its own statements, with the Commission.

Every individual or group, other than a political committee or candidate, who makes "contributions" or "expenditures" of over $100 in a calendar year "other than by contribution to a political committee or candidate" is required to file a statement with the Commission. Any violation of these record-keeping and reporting provisions is punishable by a fine of not more than $1,000 or a prison term of not more than a year, or both.

A. General Principles

Unlike the overall limitations on contributions and expenditures, the disclosure requirements impose no ceiling on campaign-related activities. But we have repeatedly found that compelled disclosure, in itself, can seriously infringe on privacy of association and belief guaranteed by the First Amendment.

We long have recognized that significant encroachments on First Amendment rights of the sort that compelled disclosure imposes cannot be justified by a mere showing of some legitimate governmental interest. Since *NAACP v. Alabama* [(1958)] we have required that the subordinating interests of the State must survive exacting scrutiny. We also have insisted that there be a "relevant correlation" or "substantial relation" between the governmental interest and the information required to be disclosed. [Citations omitted.] This type of scrutiny is necessary even if any deterrent effect on the exercise of First Amendment rights arises, not through direct government action, but indirectly as an unintended but inevitable result of the government's conduct in requiring disclosure.

The strict test established by *NAACP v. Alabama* is necessary because compelled disclosure has the potential for substantially infringing the exercise of First Amendment rights. But we have acknowledged that there are governmental interests sufficiently important to outweigh the possibility of infringement, particularly when the "free functioning of our national institutions" is involved. *Communist Party v. Subversive Activities Control Bd.* (1961).

The governmental interests sought to be vindicated by the disclosure requirements are of this magnitude. They fall into three categories. First, disclosure provides the electorate with information "as to where political campaign money comes from and how it is spent by the candidate" in order to aid the voters in evaluating those who seek federal office. It allows voters to place each candidate in the political spectrum more precisely than is often possible solely on the basis of party labels and campaign speeches. The sources of a candidate's financial support also alert the voter to the interests to which a candidate is most likely to be responsive and thus facilitate predictions of future performance in office.

Second, disclosure requirements deter actual corruption and avoid the appearance of corruption by exposing large contributions and expenditures to the light of publicity. This exposure may discourage those who would use money for improper purposes either before or after the election. A public armed with information about a candidate's most generous supporters is better able to detect any post-election special favors that may be given in return. And, as we recognized in *Burroughs v. United States* [(1934)], Congress could reasonably conclude that full disclosure during an election campaign tends "to prevent the corrupt use of money to affect elections." In enacting these requirements it may have been mindful of Mr. Justice Brandeis' advice:

> "Publicity is justly commended as a remedy for social and industrial diseases. Sunlight is said to be the best of disinfectants; electric light the most efficient policeman." [80]

Third, and not least significant, recordkeeping, reporting, and disclosure requirements are an essential means of gathering the data necessary to detect violations of the contribution limitations described above.

The disclosure requirements, as a general matter, directly serve substantial governmental interests. In determining whether these interests are sufficient to justify the requirements we must look to the extent of the burden that they place on individual rights.

It is undoubtedly true that public disclosure of contributions to candidates and political parties will deter some individuals who otherwise might contribute. In some instances, disclosure may even expose contributors to harassment or retaliation. These are not insignificant burdens on individual rights, and they must be weighed carefully against the interests which Congress has sought to promote by this legislation. In this process, we note and agree with appellants' concession that disclosure requirements certainly in most applications appear to be the least restrictive means of curbing the evils of campaign ignorance and corruption that Congress found to exist.

B. Application to Minor Parties and Independents

[Omitted.]

80. L. Brandeis, Other People's Money 62 (National Home Library Foundation ed. 1933).

C. Section 434(E)

Section 434(e) requires "(e)very person (other than a political committee or candidate) who makes contributions or expenditures" aggregating over $100 in a calendar year "other than by contribution to a political committee or candidate" to file a statement with the Commission. Unlike the other disclosure provisions, this section does not seek the contribution list of any association. Instead, it requires direct disclosure of what an individual or group contributes or spends.

1. The Role of § 434(e)

The Court of Appeals upheld § 434(e) as necessary to enforce the independent-expenditure ceiling imposed by 18 U.S.C. § 608(e)(1). It said:

> "If . . . Congress has both the authority and a compelling interest to regulate independent expenditures under section 608(e), surely it can require that there be disclosure to prevent misuse of the spending channel."

We have found that § 608(e)(1) unconstitutionally infringes upon First Amendment rights. If the sole function of § 434(e) were to aid in the enforcement of that provision, it would no longer serve any governmental purpose.

But the two provisions are not so intimately tied. The legislative history on the function of § 434(e) is bare, but it was clearly intended to stand independently of § 608(e)(1). It was enacted with the general disclosure provisions in 1971 as part of the original Act, while § 608(e)(1) was part of the 1974 amendments. Like the other disclosure provisions, § 434(e) could play a role in the enforcement of the expanded contribution and expenditure limitations included in the 1974 amendments, but it also has independent functions. Section 434(e) is part of Congress' effort to achieve "total disclosure" by reaching "every kind of political activity" in order to insure that the voters are fully informed and to achieve through publicity the maximum deterrence to corruption and undue influence possible. The provision is responsive to the legitimate fear that efforts would be made, as they had been in the past, to avoid the disclosure requirements by routing financial support of candidates through avenues not explicitly covered by the general provisions of the Act.

2. Vagueness Problems

In its effort to be all-inclusive, however, the provision raises serious problems of vagueness, particularly treacherous where, as here, the violation of its terms carries criminal penalties and fear of incurring these sanctions may deter those who seek to exercise protected First Amendment rights.

Section 434(e) applies to "(e)very person . . . who makes contributions or expenditures." "Contributions" and "expenditures" are defined in parallel provisions in terms of the use of money or other valuable assets "for the purpose of . . . influencing" the nomination or election of candidates for federal office. It is the ambiguity of this phrase that poses constitutional problems.

In enacting the legislation under review Congress addressed broadly the problem of political campaign financing. It wished to promote full disclosure of campaign-oriented spending to insure both the reality and the appearance of the purity and openness of the federal election process. Our task is to construe "for the purpose of . . . influencing," incorporated in § 434(e) through the definitions of "contributions" and "expenditures," in a manner that precisely furthers this goal.

In Part I we discussed what constituted a "contribution" for purposes of the contribution limitations set forth in 18 U.S.C. § 608(b). We construed that term to include not only contributions made directly or indirectly to a candidate, political party, or campaign committee, and contributions made to other organizations or individuals but earmarked for political purposes, but also all expenditures placed in cooperation with or with the consent of a candidate, his agents, or an authorized committee of the candidate. The definition of "contribution" in § 431(e) for disclosure purposes parallels the definition in Title 18 almost word for word, and we construe the former provision as we have the latter. So defined, "contributions" have a sufficiently close relationship to the goals of the Act, for they are connected with a candidate or his campaign.

When we attempt to define "expenditure" in a similarly narrow way we encounter line-drawing problems of the sort we faced in 18 U.S.C. § 608(e)(1). Although the phrase, "for the purpose of . . . influencing" an election or nomination, differs from the language used in § 608(e)(1), it shares the same potential for encompassing both issue discussion and advocacy of a political result. The general requirement that "political committees" and candidates disclose their expenditures could raise similar vagueness problems, for "political committee" is defined only in terms of amount of annual "contributions" and "expenditures," and could be interpreted to reach groups engaged purely in issue discussion. The lower courts have construed the words "political committee" more narrowly. To fulfill the purposes of the Act they need only encompass organizations that are under the control of a candidate or the major purpose of which is the nomination or election of a candidate. Expenditures of candidates and of "political committees" so construed can be assumed to fall within the core area sought to be addressed by Congress. They are, by definition, campaign related.

But when the maker of the expenditure is not within these categories when it is an individual other than a candidate or a group other than a "political committee" the relation of the information sought to the purposes of the Act may be too remote. To insure that the reach of § 434(e) is not impermissibly broad, we construe "expenditure" for purposes of that section in the same way we construed the terms of § 608(e) to reach only funds used for communications that expressly advocate the election or defeat of a clearly identified candidate. This reading is directed precisely to that spending that is unambiguously related to the campaign of a particular federal candidate.

In summary, § 434(e), as construed, imposes independent reporting requirements on individuals and groups that are not candidates or political committees only in the following circumstances: (1) when they make contributions earmarked for political purposes or authorized or requested by a candidate or his agent, to some person other than a candidate or political committee, and (2) when they make expenditures for communications that expressly advocate the election or defeat of a clearly identified candidate.

Unlike 18 U.S.C. § 608(e)(1), § 434(e), as construed, bears a sufficient relationship to a substantial governmental interest. As narrowed, § 434(e), like § 608(e)(1), does not reach all partisan discussion for it only requires disclosure of those expenditures that expressly advocate a particular election result. This might have been fatal if the only purpose of § 434(e) were to stem corruption or its appearance by closing a loophole in the general disclosure requirements. But the disclosure provisions, including § 434(e), serve another, informational interest, and even as construed § 434(e) increases the fund of information concerning those who support the candidates. It goes beyond the general disclosure requirements to shed the light of publicity on spending that is unambiguously campaign related but would not otherwise be reported because it takes the form of independent expenditures or of contributions to an individual or group not itself required to report the names of its contributors. By the same token, it is not fatal that § 434(e) encompasses purely independent expenditures uncoordinated with a particular candidate or his agent. The corruption potential of these expenditures may be significantly different, but the informational interest can be as strong as it is in coordinated spending, for disclosure helps voters to define more of the candidates' constituencies.

D. Thresholds

[Omitted.]

In summary, we find no constitutional infirmities in the recordkeeping, reporting, and disclosure provisions of the Act.

Citizens United v. FEC

558 U.S. 310 (2010)

Justice KENNEDY's majority opinion on disclaimer and disclosure portion of BCRA:*

IV

A

Citizens United next challenges BCRA's disclaimer and disclosure provisions as applied to *Hillary* and three advertisements for the movie. Under BCRA § 311, televised electioneering communications funded by anyone other than a candidate must include a disclaimer that " '_______ is responsible for the content of this advertising.' " 2 U.S.C. § 441d(d)(2). The required statement must be made in a "clearly spoken manner," and displayed on the screen in a "clearly readable manner" for at least four seconds. It must state that the communication "is not authorized by any candidate or candidate's committee"; it must also display the name and address (or Web site address) of the person or group that funded the advertisement. § 441d(a)(3). Under BCRA § 201, any person who spends more than $10,000 on electioneering communications within a calendar year must file a disclosure statement with the FEC. That statement must identify the person making the expenditure, the amount of the expenditure, the election to which the communication was directed, and the names of certain contributors.

* [This portion of the opinion garnered eight votes: all but Justice Thomas agreed with Justice Kennedy's decision regarding the disclosure and disclaimer requirements —EDS.].

Disclaimer and disclosure requirements may burden the ability to speak, but they "impose no ceiling on campaign-related activities," *Buckley*, and "do not prevent anyone from speaking," *McConnell*. The Court has subjected these requirements to "exacting scrutiny," which requires a "substantial relation" between the disclosure requirement and a "sufficiently important" governmental interest. *Buckley*.

In *Buckley*, the Court explained that disclosure could be justified based on a governmental interest in "provid[ing] the electorate with information" about the sources of election-related spending. The *McConnell* Court applied this interest in rejecting facial challenges to BCRA §§ 201 and 311. There was evidence in the record that independent groups were running election-related advertisements "while hiding behind dubious and misleading names." The Court therefore upheld BCRA §§ 201 and 311 on the ground that they would help citizens "make informed choices in the political marketplace." [*Id.*]

Although both provisions were facially upheld, the Court acknowledged that as-applied challenges would be available if a group could show a "reasonable probability'" that disclosure of its contributors' names "will subject them to threats, harassment, or reprisals from either Government officials or private parties." *Id.*

For the reasons stated below, we find the statute valid as applied to the ads for the movie and to the movie itself.

B

Citizens United sought to broadcast one 30-second and two 10-second ads to promote *Hillary*. Under FEC regulations, a communication that "[p]roposes a commercial transaction" was not subject to 2 U.S.C. § 441b's restrictions on corporate or union funding of electioneering communications. 11 CFR § 114.15(b)(3)(ii). The regulations, however, do not exempt those communications from the disclaimer and disclosure requirements in BCRA §§ 201 and 311.

Citizens United argues that the disclaimer requirements in § 311 are unconstitutional as applied to its ads. It contends that the governmental interest in providing information to the electorate does not justify requiring disclaimers for any commercial advertisements, including the ones at issue here. We disagree. The ads fall within BCRA's definition of an "electioneering communication": They referred to then-Senator Clinton by name shortly before a primary and contained pejorative references to her candidacy. The disclaimers required by § 311 "provid[e] the electorate with information," *McConnell*, and "insure that the voters are fully informed" about the person or group who is speaking, *Buckley*; *see also Bellotti* ("Identification of the source of advertising may be required as a means of disclosure, so that the people will be able to evaluate the arguments to which they are being subjected"). At the very least, the disclaimers avoid confusion by making clear that the ads are not funded by a candidate or political party.

Citizens United argues that § 311 is underinclusive because it requires disclaimers for broadcast advertisements but not for print or Internet advertising. It asserts that § 311 decreases both the quantity and effectiveness of the group's speech by forcing it to devote four seconds of each advertisement to the spoken disclaimer. We rejected these arguments in *McConnell*. And we now adhere to that decision as it pertains to the disclosure provisions.

As a final point, Citizens United claims that, in any event, the disclosure requirements in § 201 must be confined to speech that is the functional equivalent of express advocacy. We reject this contention. The Court has explained that disclosure is a less restrictive alternative to more comprehensive regulations of speech. In *Buckley*, the Court upheld a disclosure requirement for independent expenditures even though it invalidated a provision that imposed a ceiling on those expenditures. In *McConnell*, three Justices who would have found § 441b to be unconstitutional nonetheless voted to uphold BCRA's disclosure and disclaimer requirements. *McConnell* (opinion of Kennedy, J., joined by Rehnquist, C.J., and Scalia, J.). And the Court has upheld registration and disclosure requirements on lobbyists, even though Congress has no power to ban lobbying itself. *United States v. Harriss* (1954) (Congress "has merely provided for a modicum of information from those who for hire attempt to influence legislation or who collect or spend funds for that purpose"). For these reasons, we reject Citizens United's contention that the disclosure requirements must be limited to speech that is the functional equivalent of express advocacy.

Citizens United also disputes that an informational interest justifies the application of § 201 to its ads, which only attempt to persuade viewers to see the film. Even if it disclosed the funding sources for the ads, Citizens United says, the information would not help viewers make informed choices in the political marketplace. This is similar to the argument rejected above with respect to disclaimers. Even if the ads only pertain to a commercial transaction, the public has an interest in knowing who is speaking about a candidate shortly before an election. Because the informational interest alone is sufficient to justify application of § 201 to these ads, it is not necessary to consider the Government's other asserted interests.

Last, Citizens United argues that disclosure requirements can chill donations to an organization by exposing donors to retaliation. Some *amici* point to recent events in which donors to certain causes were blacklisted, threatened, or otherwise targeted for retaliation. In *McConnell*, the Court recognized that § 201 would be unconstitutional as applied to an organization if there were a reasonable probability that the group's members would face threats, harassment, or reprisals if their names were disclosed. The examples cited by *amici* are cause for concern. Citizens United, however, has offered no evidence that its members may face similar threats or reprisals. To the contrary, Citizens United has been disclosing its donors for years and has identified no instance of harassment or retaliation.

Shareholder objections raised through the procedures of corporate democracy can be more effective today because modern technology makes disclosures rapid and informative. A campaign finance system that pairs corporate independent expenditures with effective disclosure has not existed before today. It must be noted, furthermore, that many of Congress' findings in passing BCRA were premised on a system without adequate disclosure. With the advent of the Internet, prompt disclosure of expenditures can provide shareholders and citizens with the information needed to hold corporations and elected officials accountable for their positions and supporters. Shareholders can determine whether their corporation's political speech advances the corporation's interest in making profits, and citizens can see whether elected officials are " 'in the pocket' of so-called moneyed interests." *McConnell* (opinion of Scalia, J.). The First Amendment protects political speech; and disclosure permits citizens and shareholders to react to the speech of corporate entities in a proper way. This transparency enables the electorate to make informed decisions and give proper weight to different speakers and messages.

C

For the same reasons we uphold the application of BCRA §§ 201 and 311 to the ads, we affirm their application to *Hillary*. We find no constitutional impediment to the application of BCRA's disclaimer and disclosure requirements to a movie broadcast via video-on-demand. And there has been no showing that, as applied in this case, these requirements would impose a chill on speech or expression.

Justice THOMAS, concurring in part and dissenting in part.

I join all but Part IV of the Court's opinion.

Political speech is entitled to robust protection under the First Amendment. Section 203 of the Bipartisan Campaign Reform Act of 2002 (BCRA) has never been reconcilable with that protection. By striking down § 203, the Court takes an important first step toward restoring full constitutional protection to speech that is "indispensable to the effective and intelligent use of the processes of popular government." *McConnell* (Thomas, J., concurring in part, concurring in judgment in part, and dissenting in part). I dissent from Part IV of the Court's opinion, however, because the Court's constitutional analysis does not go far enough. The disclosure, disclaimer, and reporting requirements in BCRA §§ 201 and 311 are also unconstitutional.

Congress may not abridge the "right to anonymous speech" based on the "simple interest in providing voters with additional relevant information," *id.* (quoting *McIntyre v. Ohio Elections Comm'n* (1995)). In continuing to hold otherwise, the Court misapprehends the import of "recent events" that some *amici* describe "in which donors to certain causes were blacklisted, threatened, or otherwise targeted for retaliation." The Court properly recognizes these events as "cause for concern," but fails to acknowledge their constitutional significance. In my view, *amici*'s submissions show why the Court's insistence on upholding §§ 201 and 311 will ultimately prove as misguided (and ill fated) as was its prior approval of § 203.

Before the 2008 Presidential election, a "newly formed nonprofit group . . . plann[ed] to confront donors to conservative groups, hoping to create a chilling effect that will dry up contributions." Luo, Group Plans Campaign Against G.O.P. Donors, N.Y. Times, Aug. 8, 2008, p. A15. Its leader, "who described his effort as 'going for the jugular,'" detailed the group's plan to send a "warning letter . . . alerting donors who might be considering giving to right-wing groups to a variety of potential dangers, including legal trouble, public exposure and watchdog groups digging through their lives."

These instances of retaliation sufficiently demonstrate why this Court should invalidate mandatory disclosure and reporting requirements. But *amici* present evidence of yet another reason to do so—the threat of retaliation from *elected officials*. For example, a candidate challenging an incumbent state attorney general reported that some members of the State's business community feared donating to his campaign because they did not want to cross the incumbent; in his words, "'I go to so many people and hear the same thing: "I sure hope you beat [the incumbent], but I can't afford to have my name on your records. He might come after me next." ' " Strassel, Challenging Spitzerism at the Polls, Wall Street Journal, Aug. 1, 2008, p. A11. The incumbent won reelection in 2008.

My point is to demonstrate — using real-world, recent examples — the fallacy in the Court's conclusion that "[d]isclaimer and disclosure requirements . . . impose no ceiling on campaign-related activities, and do not prevent anyone from speaking." Of course they do. Disclaimer and disclosure requirements enable private citizens and elected officials to implement political strategies *specifically calculated* to curtail campaign-related activity and prevent the lawful, peaceful exercise of First Amendment rights.

The Court nevertheless insists that as-applied challenges to disclosure requirements will suffice to vindicate those speech rights, as long as potential plaintiffs can "show a reasonable probability that disclosure . . . will subject them to threats, harassment, or reprisals from either Government officials or private parties." But the Court's opinion itself proves the irony in this compromise. In correctly explaining why it must address the facial constitutionality of § 203, the Court recognizes that "[t]he First Amendment does not permit laws that force speakers to. . . seek declaratory rulings before discussing the most salient political issues of our day," that as-applied challenges to § 203 "would require substantial litigation over an extended time" and result in an "interpretive process [that] itself would create an inevitable, pervasive, and serious risk of chilling protected speech pending the drawing of fine distinctions that, in the end, would themselves be questionable," that "a court would be remiss in performing its duties were it to accept an unsound principle merely to avoid the necessity of making a broader ruling," and that avoiding a facial challenge to § 203 "would prolong the substantial, nation-wide chilling effect" that § 203 causes. This logic, of course, applies equally to as-applied challenges to §§ 201 and 311.

Irony aside, the Court's promise that as-applied challenges will adequately protect speech is a hollow assurance. Now more than ever, §§ 201 and 311 will chill protected speech because "the advent of the Internet" enables "prompt disclosure of expenditures," which "provide[s]" political opponents "with the information needed" to intimidate and retaliate against their foes. Thus, "disclosure permits citizens . . . to react to the speech of [their political opponents] in a proper" — or undeniably *improper* — "way" long before a plaintiff could prevail on an as-applied challenge.

I cannot endorse a view of the First Amendment that subjects citizens of this Nation to death threats, ruined careers, damaged or defaced property, or pre-emptive and threatening warning letters as the price for engaging in "core political speech, the primary object of First Amendment protection." *McConnell* (Thomas, J., concurring in part, concurring in judgment in part, and dissenting in part). Accordingly, I respectfully dissent from the Court's judgment upholding BCRA §§ 201 and 311.

* * *

The D.C. Circuit has issued two important decisions on campaign finance disclosure since *Citizens United*. What do these cases suggest about how plaintiffs should proceed in challenging disclosure requirements? *SpeechNow* presents the D.C. Circuit's understanding of *Citizens United*; another portion of the decision (which we will consider below) opens the door to unlimited contributions to Super PACs, or political committees that engage only in independent expenditures. The second case, *CREW*, recognizes the potential problems that arise from new court interpretations of campaign finance law. The Federal Election Commission had issued an interpretation of the disclosure rules under federal law, but the rules did not apply to many activities—until the Court in *Citizens United* allowed for increased independent expenditures and the D.C. Circuit's decision in *SpeechNow* allowed for unlimited contributions to organizations that engage only in independent expenditures. Consider whether the FEC's older interpretation of the disclosure requirements makes sense in light of these more recent cases. Notice also that *CREW* involves administrative law principles, not the First Amendment.

SpeechNow.org v. FEC

599 F.3d 686 (D.C. Cir. 2010) (en banc)

SENTELLE, Chief Judge:

David Keating is president of an unincorporated nonprofit association, SpeechNow.org (SpeechNow), that intends to engage in express advocacy supporting candidates for federal office who share his views on First Amendment rights of free speech and freedom to assemble. In January 2008, the Federal Election Committee (FEC) issued a draft advisory opinion concluding that under the Federal Election Campaign Act (FECA), SpeechNow would be required to organize as a "political committee" as defined by 2 U.S.C. § 431(4) and would be subject to all the requirements and restrictions concomitant with that designation. Keating and four other individuals availed themselves of 2 U.S.C. § 437h, under which an individual may seek declaratory judgment to construe the constitutionality of any provision of FECA. As required by that provision, the district court certified the constitutional questions directly to this court for en banc determination. Thereafter, the Supreme Court decided *Citizens United v. FEC* (2010), which resolves this appeal. In accordance with that decision, we hold that the contribution limits of 2 U.S.C. § 441a(a)(1)(C) and 441a(a)(3) are unconstitutional as applied to individuals' contributions to SpeechNow. However, we also hold that the reporting requirements of 2 U.S.C. §§ 432, 433, and 434(a) and the organizational requirements of 2 U.S.C. § 431(4) and 431(8) can constitutionally be applied to SpeechNow.

I. BACKGROUND

SpeechNow is an unincorporated nonprofit association registered as a "political organization" under § 527 of the Internal Revenue Code. Its purpose is to promote the First Amendment rights of free speech and freedom to assemble by expressly advocating for federal candidates whom it views as supporting those rights and against those whom it sees as insufficiently committed to those rights. It intends to acquire funds solely through donations by individuals. SpeechNow further intends to operate exclusively through "independent expenditures." FECA defines "independent expenditures" as expenditures "expressly advocating the election or defeat of a clearly identified candidate" that are "not made in concert or cooperation with or at the request or suggestion of such candidate, the candidate's authorized political committee, or their agents, or a political party committee or its agents." 2 U.S.C. § 431(17). SpeechNow has five members, two of whom are plaintiffs in this case: David Keating, who is also SpeechNow's president and treasurer, and Edward Crane. Keating makes the operational decisions for SpeechNow, including in which election campaigns to run advertisements, which candidates to support or oppose, and all administrative decisions.

Believing that subjecting SpeechNow to all the restrictions imposed on political committees would be unconstitutional, SpeechNow and the five individual plaintiffs filed a complaint in the district court requesting declaratory relief against the FEC.

The district court made findings of fact, and certified to this court five questions:

[Questions 1 through 3 are related to the contribution and expenditure limitations and are discussed below in the reading on PACs.]

4. Whether the organizational, administrative, and continuous reporting requirements set forth in 2 U.S.C. §§ 432, 433, and 434(a) violate the First Amendment by requiring David Keating, SpeechNow.org's president and treasurer, to register SpeechNow.org as a political committee, to adopt the organizational structure of a political committee, and to comply with the continuous reporting requirements that apply to political committees.
5. Whether 2 U.S.C. §§ 431(4) and 431(8) violate the First Amendment by requiring David Keating, SpeechNow.org's president and treasurer, to register SpeechNow.org as a political committee and comply with the organizational and continuous reporting requirements for political committees before SpeechNow.org has made any expenditures or broadcast any advertisements.

Under FECA, a political committee is "any committee, club, association, or other group of persons" that receives contributions of more than $1000 in a year or makes expenditures of more than $1000 in a year. 2 U.S.C. § 431(4). A political committee . . . must comply with all applicable recordkeeping and reporting requirements of 2 U.S.C. §§ 432, 433, and 434(a). Under those sections, if the FEC regulates SpeechNow as a political committee, SpeechNow would be required to, among other things: appoint a treasurer; maintain a separately designated bank account; keep records for three years that include the name and address of any person who makes a contribution in excess of $50; keep records for three years that include the date, amount, and purpose of any disbursement and the name and address of the recipient; register with the FEC within ten days of becoming a political committee; file with the FEC quarterly or monthly reports during the calendar year of a general election detailing cash on hand, total contributions, the identification of each person who contributes an annual aggregate amount of more than $200, independent expenditures, donations to other political committees, any other disbursements, and any outstanding debts or obligations; file a pre-election report and a post-election report detailing the same; file semiannual or monthly reports with the same information during years without a general election; and file a written statement in order to terminate the committee.

II. ANALYSIS

A. Contribution Limits (Certified Questions 1-3)

[Omitted here. This portion of the opinion is included below in the unit on PACs.]

B. Organizational and Reporting Requirements (Certified Questions 4 & 5)

Disclosure requirements also burden First Amendment interests because "compelled disclosure, in itself, can seriously infringe on privacy of association and belief." *Buckley*. However, in contrast with limiting a person's ability to spend money on political speech, disclosure requirements "impose no ceiling on campaign-related activities," *id.*, and "do not prevent anyone from speaking," *McConnell*. Because disclosure requirements inhibit speech less than do contribution and expenditure limits, the Supreme Court has not limited the government's acceptable interests to anti-corruption alone. Instead, the government may point to any "sufficiently important" governmental interest that bears a "substantial relation" to the disclosure requirement. *Citizens United*. Indeed, the Court has approvingly noted that "disclosure is a less restrictive alternative to more comprehensive regulations of speech." [*Id.*]

The Supreme Court has consistently upheld organizational and reporting requirements against facial challenges. In *Buckley*, the Court upheld FECA's disclosure requirements, including the requirements of §§ 432, 433, and 434(a) at issue here, based on a governmental interest in "provid[ing] the electorate with information" about the sources of political campaign funds, not just the interest in deterring corruption and enforcing anti-corruption measures. In *McConnell*, the Court upheld similar requirements for organizations engaging in electioneering communications for the same reasons. *Citizens United* upheld disclaimer and disclosure requirements for electioneering communications as applied to Citizens United, again citing the government's interest in providing the electorate with information. And while the Court in *Davis v. FEC* found that a certain disclosure requirement violated the First Amendment, it only did so because that disclosure triggered the application of an unconstitutional provision which imposed asymmetrical contribution limits on candidates based on how much of their personal funds they planned to spend. Because the asymmetrical limits were unconstitutional, there was no justification for the disclosure requirement.

Plaintiffs do not disagree that the government may constitutionally impose reporting requirements, and SpeechNow intends to comply with the disclosure requirements that would apply even if it were not a political committee. *See* 2 U.S.C. § 434(c) (reporting requirements for individuals or groups that are not political committees that make independent expenditures); § 441d (disclaimer requirements for independent expenditures and electioneering communications). Instead, plaintiffs argue that the additional burden that would be imposed on SpeechNow if it were required to comply with the organizational and reporting requirements applicable to political committees is too much for the First Amendment to bear. We disagree.

SpeechNow, as we have said, intends to comply with the disclosure requirements applicable to those who make independent expenditures but are not organized as political committees. Those disclosure requirements include, for example, reporting much of the same data on contributors that is required of political committees; information about each independent expenditure, such as which candidate the expenditure supports or opposes; reporting within 24 hours expenditures of $1000 or more made in the twenty days before an election; and reporting within 48 hours any expenditures or contracts for expenditures of $10,000 or more made at any other time.

Because SpeechNow intends only to make independent expenditures, the additional reporting requirements that the FEC would impose on SpeechNow if it were a political committee are minimal. Indeed, at oral argument, plaintiffs conceded that "the reporting is not really going to impose an additional burden" on SpeechNow. Oral Arg. Tr. at 14 ("Judge Sentelle: So, just calling you a [PAC] and not making you do anything except the reporting is not really going to impose an additional burden on you right? . . . Mr. Simpson: I think that's true. Yes."). Nor do the organizational requirements that SpeechNow protests, such as designating a treasurer and retaining records, impose much of an additional burden upon SpeechNow, especially given the relative simplicity with which SpeechNow intends to operate.

Neither can SpeechNow claim to be burdened by the requirement to organize as a political committee as soon as it receives $1000, as required by the definition of "political committee," 2 U.S.C. § 431(4), 431(8), rather than waiting until it expends $1000. Plaintiffs argue that such a requirement forces SpeechNow to comply with the burdens of political committees without knowing if it is going to have enough money to make its independent expenditures. This is a specious interpretation of the facts before us. As the district court found, SpeechNow already has $121,700 in planned contributions from plaintiffs alone, with dozens more individuals claiming to want to donate. SpeechNow can hardly compare itself to "ad hoc groups that want to create themselves on the spur of the moment," as plaintiffs attempted at oral argument. In addition, plaintiffs concede that in practice the burden is substantially the same to *any* group whether the FEC imposes reporting requirements at the point of the money's receipt or at the point of its expenditure. A group raising money for political speech will, we presume, always hope to raise enough to make it worthwhile to spend it. Therefore, groups would need to collect and keep the necessary data on contributions even before an expenditure is made; it makes little difference to the burden of compliance *when* the group must comply as long as it anticipates complying at some point.

We cannot hold that the organizational and reporting requirements are unconstitutional. If SpeechNow were not a political committee, it would not have to report contributions made exclusively for administrative expenses. But the public has an interest in knowing who is speaking about a candidate and who is funding that speech, no matter whether the contributions were made towards administrative expenses or independent expenditures. Further, requiring disclosure of such information deters and helps expose violations of other campaign finance restrictions, such as those barring contributions from foreign corporations or individuals. These are sufficiently important governmental interests to justify requiring SpeechNow to organize and report to the FEC as a political committee.

We therefore answer the last two certified questions in the negative. The FEC may constitutionally require SpeechNow to comply with 2 U.S.C. §§ 432, 433, and 434(a), and it may require SpeechNow to start complying with those requirements as soon as it becomes a political committee under the current definition of § 431(4).

Citizens for Responsibility and Ethics in Washington (Crew) v. FEC

971 F.3d 340 (D.C. Cir. 2020)

SRINIVASAN, Chief Judge:

In recent election cycles, billions of dollars have been spent on political advertisements known as "independent expenditures," or IEs. IEs expressly urge the election or defeat of an identified candidate but without coordination with any candidate. Most IEs are made by organizations that fund their activities with donations.

Some of those donations must be publicly disclosed under a Federal Election Commission Rule. The Rule's disclosure obligation is relatively narrow, however, requiring an IE-making organization to disclose a contribution only if it is earmarked to support a *particular* IE. Under the Rule, then, IE makers need not disclose any donors who give with the intent of *generally* supporting IEs, without an intent to support a specific one.

The plaintiffs here, led by Citizens for Responsibility and Ethics in Washington (CREW), claim that the narrow reach of the Rule's disclosure obligation is inconsistent with the Federal Election Campaign Act. As CREW reads the statute, it requires an IE maker to disclose any contributor who gives $200 in the aggregate, without regard to any intent to support IEs or a specific IE. At a minimum, CREW argues, donating to generally support the making of IEs suffices to come within the statute's disclosure obligations.

CREW brought an enforcement complaint before the Commission alleging that a well-known IE-making entity, Crossroads GPS, had violated the Rule by failing to disclose certain contributors. The Commission dismissed the complaint, finding that none of the relevant donors had intended to support a specific IE and that their contributions therefore fell outside the Rule's disclosure obligation.

CREW then brought this action in the district court, seeking to have the Rule's circumscribed disclosure mandate declared invalid as inconsistent with the statute. The district court agreed with CREW and held that the Rule conflicts with the plain terms of the statute's broader disclosure requirements. We read the statute the same way and thus affirm the district court's decision.

I

A

The Federal Election Campaign Act (FECA) requires public disclosures by groups and individuals that engage in certain election-related activities. One such activity is the making of "independent expenditures," or IEs. An IE is a payment that (i) goes toward "expressly advocating the election or defeat of a clearly identified candidate" and (ii) "is not made in concert or cooperation with or at the request or suggestion of such candidate," a political committee, or their agents. The FECA imposes disclosure obligations on any entity (other than political committees, which are separately regulated) that makes over $250 worth of IEs in a calendar year. Among those disclosure obligations is a requirement that IE makers (we use the term to exclude political committees) provide information about at least some of the contributions they receive. The FECA defines a "contribution" as a donation "made by any person for the purpose of influencing any election for Federal office."

Two relevant FECA provisions call for IE makers to disclose information about contributions. First, 52 U.S.C. § 30104(c)(1) states that IE makers "shall file a statement containing the information required under subsection (b)(3)(A) for all contributions received." The cross-referenced subsection (b)(3)(A) imposes disclosure obligations on political committees, requiring them to "identif[y] each . . . person . . . who makes a contribution to the reporting committee during the reporting period, whose contribution or contributions have an aggregate amount or value in excess of $200 within the calendar year . . . together with the date and amount of any such contribution." Second, subsection 30104(c)(2)(C) separately requires IE makers to disclose "each person who made a contribution in excess of $200 . . . for the purpose of furthering an independent expenditure."

Both of those provisions, which we will refer to by shorthand as FECA (c)(1) and (c)(2)(C), were enacted in 1980. Shortly thereafter, the Federal Election Commission issued implementing regulations. As relevant here, one of those regulations requires IE makers to disclose contributors only if they "made a contribution . . . for the purpose of furthering *the reported* independent expenditure." As a result, whereas FECA (c)(2)(C) requires disclosure of contributions "made for the purpose of furthering *an* independent expenditure," the Commission Rule requires disclosure only of contributions "made for the purpose of furthering *the reported* independent expenditure." The Rule is also silent as to the separate disclosure obligation set forth in FECA (c)(1).

B

For many years, those disclosure obligations operated in relative obscurity. Before 2010, a separate FECA provision generally prohibited corporations and unions from making IEs or contributing to support IEs. As a result of that ban, IEs made up a small portion of overall election-related spending. And most IEs were made not by individuals, who would have been subject to the Rule, but by political committees.

Things changed, though, following the Supreme Court's decision striking down the FECA's prohibition on corporate and union IE activity, *Citizens United*, and our court's follow-on decision invalidating the FECA's limits on contributions to political committees as applied to "super PACs," i.e., committees whose sole function is to make IEs, *SpeechNow.org v. FEC* (D.C. Cir. 2010). After those 2010 decisions, overall IE spending exploded: nearly $1.4 billion worth of IEs were made during the 2016 election cycle, compared to $143.7 million in the 2008 cycle and $63.9 million in the 2004 cycle. IE spending is now dominated by organized entities, such as super PACs and 501(c)(4) social welfare organizations, rather than individuals.

Owing in part to the Rule's narrow disclosure obligation, a significant amount of IE spending now comes from organizations that do not disclose their contributors. In fact, more IEs were made by such entities during the 2016 election cycle ($174.8 million) than the total amount of IEs made during the 2008 cycle ($143.7 million). What is more, the same non-disclosing entities also contribute millions to political committees, such as super PACs, in order to further those committees' political activities, including IEs. And while those political committees must disclose their contributors, that reveals little when a contributor is an entity that need not identify its own underlying donors. In that way, entities subject to the Rule can serve as a kind of pass-through, non-disclosure vehicle.

C

Crossroads GPS is one such entity. Since its creation as a 501(c)(4) social welfare organization in 2010, Crossroads has made over $100 million worth of IEs and over $75 million in contributions to other IE-making entities. Crossroads has not disclosed a single contribution in any of its reports to the Commission.

In 2012, the plaintiffs in this case, led by CREW, sought to uncover the identities of some of Crossroads's contributors. Relying on news reports about a Crossroads fundraiser in Tampa, CREW brought an administrative complaint before the Commission. The complaint asserted that Crossroads had improperly failed to disclose certain contributors connected to the fundraiser.

After Crossroads responded to CREW's allegations, the Commission's Office of General Counsel (OGC) prepared a report with its factual and legal conclusions. OGC's account of the facts explained that the Tampa event, which had been co-hosted by Crossroads, contained two separate pitches for donations.

OGC "recommend[ed] that the Commission find no reason to believe that Crossroads violated" the FECA or the Rule by failing to disclose the donors' identities. As OGC read the Rule, it "appears to require an express link between the receipt and the independent expenditure," such that the "donation[] [is] tied to a specific" IE.

The Commissioners deadlocked 3-3 on OGC's recommendations. Adhering to their typical practice when there is no majority decision, the Commissioners voted unanimously to dismiss the administrative complaint. Because a majority of the Commission did not offer a Statement of Reasons for its dismissal, the OGC memorandum recommending dismissal became the Commission's controlling statement.

D

CREW then brought this action against the Commission in the United States District Court for the District of Columbia. CREW's complaint included three counts, each containing a claim under the FECA and a claim under the Administrative Procedure Act. First, CREW alleged that the Commission's dismissal of the complaint was arbitrary and capricious because there was ample record evidence that the contributions at issue were intended to support specific IEs, as required by the Rule. Second, CREW asserted that the Commission's reliance on the Rule was contrary to law because the regulation conflicts with FECA (c)(2)(C). Third, CREW alleged that the Commission's failure to apply the disclosure obligation in FECA (c)(1) was contrary to law.

After permitting Crossroads to intervene to defend the Commission's decision, the court granted summary judgment for CREW. Applying the Chevron framework, the court declared the Rule inconsistent with both FECA (c)(1) and (c)(2)(C). As a result, the Commission's decision, which had relied on the Rule to dismiss the complaint, was contrary to law.

II

[Omitted.]

III

We come to the heart of the matter: whether the Rule's requirement that IE makers disclose only those contributions aimed at supporting a specific IE can be squared with FECA (c)(1) and (c)(2)(C). Our analysis is governed by *Chevron U.S.A. Inc. v. Nat. Res. Def. Council, Inc.* (1984), under which we accept an agency's reasonable construction of an ambiguous statutory provision. Yet "under *Chevron,* we owe [the Commission's] interpretation of the law no deference unless, after employing traditional tools of statutory construction, we find ourselves unable to discern Congress's meaning." *SAS Inst., Inc. v. Iancu* (2018). "If the intent of Congress is clear, that is the end of the matter." *Chevron.*

That is the case here. The Rule conflicts with the FECA's unambiguous terms twice over. First, the Rule disregards (c)(1)'s requirement that IE makers disclose each donation from contributors who give more than $200, regardless of any connection to IEs eventually made. Second, by requiring disclosure only of donations linked to a particular IE, the Rule impermissibly narrows (c)(2)(C)'s requirement that contributors be identified if their donations are "made for the purpose of furthering *an* independent expenditure."

A

We first consider FECA (c)(1). It states that any person who makes over $250 worth of IEs in a calendar year "shall file a statement containing the information required under subsection (b)(3)(A) for all contributions received by such person."

The language of (c)(1) yields a straightforward interpretation. Any IE maker who surpasses the $250 trigger must "file a statement containing" certain "information." That "information" is found in subsection (b)(3)(A), which governs the disclosure obligations of political committees. Subsection (b)(3)(A) requires "the identification of each . . . person (other than a political committee) who makes a contribution to the reporting committee during the reporting period, whose contribution or contributions have an aggregate amount or value in excess of $200 within the calendar year . . . together with the date and amount of any such contribution." That "information," according to (c)(1), must be disclosed "for all contributions received by" the IE maker. Putting it all together, (c)(1)'s meaning is apparent: any entity (excluding political committees) that makes over $250 worth of IEs in a calendar year must disclose the name of every donor who has given the entity over $200 in the aggregate in "contributions," along with the date and amount of each of those contributions.

The Supreme Court [has] interpreted FECA (c)(1) in that way. In *FEC v. Mass. Citizens for Life, Inc.* (*MCFL*) (1986), the Supreme Court carved out a narrow exception to the then-existing ban on corporate IEs, allowing IEs to be made by nonprofit corporations organized for the purpose of promoting political ideas. The Commission urged the Court against doing so in order to prevent opening the door to "massive undisclosed political spending." The Court responded by noting that MCFL and similar entities remained subject to subsection 30104(c)'s disclosure obligations. Among those was (c)(1), which, according to the Court, requires entities making IEs to "identify all contributors who annually provide in the aggregate $200 in funds intended to influence elections."

The lack of ambiguity in (c)(1) draws further confirmation from Crossroads's inability to present a plausible alternative reading. Crossroads proposes understanding (c)(1) as a generalized opening statement that merely instructs an IE maker to file a report, without specifying any of the report's underlying contents. According to that reading, (c)(2) then supplies *all* the information that must be disclosed. That account of Congress's intent falls short for several reasons.

First, it is incompatible with the statutory text. Crossroads admits that (c)(1) requires disclosing "the information required under subsection (b)(3)(A)." But according to Crossroads, that language only calls for disclosing the date and amount of any contribution already required to be disclosed by (c)(2)(C). Subsection (c)(1)'s cross-reference to subsection (b)(3)(A), in other words, would pull in only the "date and amount" language of the latter subsection. Nothing in (c)(1), though, cabins the information required to be disclosed in that way. Rather, (c)(1) refers generally to "the information required under subsection (b)(3)(A)," not *some* of the information required under (b)(3)(A). And (b)(3)(A) in turn requires "identification of each . . . person . . . whose contribution or contributions have an aggregate amount or value in excess of $200." Indeed, that information—i.e., the name of any such person—is the *first* and principal item of information listed in (b)(3)(A), yet Crossroads's reading would leave that information out of the required disclosure, while leaving in supplemental date-and-amount information mentioned later in (b)(3)(A).

Crossroads looks for support for its reading in subsection 30104(c)'s title, which reads as follows: "Statements by other than political committees; filing; contents; indices of expenditures." Connecting each clause to a different subsection, Crossroads claims that "filing" refers to (c)(1), "contents" to (c)(2), and "indices" to (c)(3). As a result, Crossroads urges, subsection (c)(1) merely contains a filing obligation. But "[t]he plain meaning of a statute cannot be limited by its title," especially when, as here, the "provisions in [the] statute do not . . . align with its title." *Nat'l Ctr. for Mfg. Scis. v. Dep't of Defense* (D.C. Cir. 2000).

In its reply brief, Crossroads advanced an alternative argument tied to the meaning of "contribution." Although the FECA defines "contribution" to include "any [donation] made by any person for the purpose of influencing any election for Federal office," Crossroads insists that *Buckley* imposed a narrowing construction for purposes of subsection 30104(c): a donation made for the purpose of furthering IEs. The upshot of that argument is that, even if (c)(1) mandates disclosure of all "contributors" who give over $200 in the aggregate, the universe of donors covered by the term "contributor" entirely overlaps with the reach of (c)(2)(C), such that the only donors who count are those who give "for the purpose of furthering an independent expenditure."

Crossroads, however, misreads *Buckley*. Rather than limit the term "contribution" to donations earmarked to support IEs, *Buckley* stated more broadly that the term covers any donation "earmarked for political purposes." To the same effect, ten years later, *MCFL* similarly read the term "contribution" as used in subsection 30104(c) to cover "funds intended to influence elections."

Crossroads's final argument about (c)(1) is that the Commission was entitled to adopt a limiting construction to avoid constitutional concerns. In Crossroads's view, requiring disclosure of all persons who donate over $200 for political purposes to any entity that makes over $250 in IEs "impos[es] . . . burdens on core political speech that are clearly not necessary." Crossroads Brief.

The Rule, though, does not limit disclosure to contributions intended to support IEs generally. Instead, it requires a link to a particular expenditure. Even if there were a First Amendment problem to be avoided, then, the narrowing construction embodied in the Rule goes much further than Crossroads thinks necessary. The Rule cannot, therefore, be justified on avoidance grounds. Accordingly, we have no occasion to decide any constitutional question concerning (c)(1), or to delineate the precise scope of its requirement to disclose all donations "made . . . for the purpose of influencing any election for Federal office."

In sum, FECA (c)(1) unambiguously requires an entity making over $250 in IEs to disclose the name of any contributor whose contributions during the relevant reporting period total $200, along with the date and amount of each contribution. The Rule does not require such disclosures, and yet it purports to implement (c)(1). The Rule therefore is invalid.

B

The Rule is also contrary to (c)(2)(C). That provision requires "the identification of each person who made a contribution in excess of $200 to the [IE maker] which was made for the purpose of furthering an independent expenditure." The Rule, however, requires disclosure of the identity only of persons whose contributions were "made for the purpose of furthering *the reported* independent expenditure." (emphasis added). The Rule thus exempts from disclosure any contribution intended to support IEs in general, rather than a particular IE.

That contravenes the plain meaning of the phrase, "for the purpose of furthering an independent expenditure," which naturally reads more broadly than referring only to a particular IE. If we were confronted with a statute that covered grants "made for the purpose of furthering *an* infrastructure project" or transactions "made for the purpose of furthering *a* fraudulent scheme," we would assume that Congress intended to reach *any* such project or scheme. So too here: FECA (c)(2)(C) is naturally read to cover contributions intended to support any IE made by the recipient.

As was the case with (c)(1), our reading accords with . . . the Supreme Court's understanding of the statute in *MCFL*. In *MCFL*, the Court stated that, under subsection (c)(2)(C), IE makers are "bound to identify all persons making contributions over $200 who request that the money be used for independent expenditures."

Dictionary definitions of the word "an" fortify our reading. According to the Oxford English Dictionary, the indefinite articles "a" and "an" are used when "referring to something not specifically identified . . . but [instead] treated as one of a class: one, some, any." Dictionaries from the period in which (c)(2)(C) was enacted are in agreement.

Crossroads argues that the pre-1979 FECA did not require disclosure of contributions generally intended to support IEs, and points to legislative history suggesting that the 1979 Amendments did not expand the information to be reported as compared with previous versions of the Act. Because the language of (c)(2)(C) is clear, however, we have no warrant to look to the legislative history. At any rate, the 1976 version of the FECA is ambiguous as to whether contributions generally intended to support IEs, but not earmarked to support a particular IE, needed to be disclosed. Crossroads points to disclosure forms used by the Commission at the time, in an effort to show that the Commission did not require disclosure of contributions intended to support IEs generally. The forms, though, do not tell us what Congress intended in 1976, let alone what Congress intended in 1979.

Crossroads next observes that Congress did not disapprove the Rule when it was submitted for legislative review in 1980 (as required by the FECA), and it has never amended subsection 30104(c) despite having made several changes to related provisions of the FECA. Therefore, Crossroads submits, Congress has ratified the Rule's approach to implementing subsection 30104(c).

We disagree. By all accounts, disclosure under 30104(c) was barely an issue until 2010, much less one we may assume would have drawn Congress's attention. Until the decisions in *Citizens United* and *SpeechNow.org*, IEs made up a relatively small slice of election-related spending. An even smaller portion of overall IEs were subject to 30104(c), which is limited to IEs produced by entities other than political committees. And those IEs were usually made by individuals, not organizations soliciting contributions from others. As a result, the fact that Congress did not block the Rule in 1980, or countermand it when enacting new laws such as the Bipartisan Campaign Reform Act of 2002, is not probative of Congressional intent vis-à-vis the Rule.

Finally, Crossroads argues that our interpretations of FECA (c)(1) and (c)(2)(C) render the two provisions entirely duplicative and thus must be erroneous. While it is true that every contributor who must be identified under (c)(2)(C) must also be disclosed under (c)(1), that does not make the two subsections completely coextensive or render (c)(2)(C) superfluous. FECA (c)(2)(C) still calls for providing information that (c)(1) does not—namely, whether a disclosed "contribution" was intended to support IEs or instead aimed only at supporting the recipient's other election-related activities. There is then no reason to refrain from giving the terms of (c)(2)(C) their natural reading. And because (c)(2)(C), on that reading, establishes a broader disclosure mandate than the Rule ostensibly implementing it, the Rule is invalid.

NOTES ON DISCLOSURE LAWS

1. What do these cases say about the landscape of disclaimer and disclosure laws? Are they the only hope for any sort of campaign finance "reform" given the Court's recent decisions, which otherwise deregulate this area?

2. Disclosure laws may be the next major political battlefield in campaign finance. After *Citizens United*, Democrats in Congress proposed a new disclosure

law, the DISCLOSE Act (Democracy is Stronger by Casting Light on Spending in Elections Act). The law was intended to strengthen disclosure requirements for corporate campaign contributions and place limits on political contributions from foreign corporations. The law also would have required CEOs and heads of interest groups to appear on camera in a political ad to endorse the group's message. Senate Republicans succeeded in blocking the bill, claiming it would have violated corporations' and other groups' free speech rights. But Democrats won control of both Houses of Congress and the presidency in 2020. In addition to voting rights reform, they have proposed overhauling the campaign finance system, including through new disclosure requirements. The hurdles, of course, are both political and legal: Do they have the votes to pass a law to further regulate campaign finance, and even if they do, would a new law pass constitutional muster?

3. Although not in the campaign finance context, the Court in *Doe v. Reed* (2010) upheld the public disclosure of the names of those who signed a petition to place a referendum on the ballot. Relying in part on the discussion of disclosure laws in *Buckley* and *Citizen United,* the Court held that public disclosure of petition signatures is tied to the government's compelling interest in achieving "transparency and accountability in the electoral process." The Court explained that the public disclosure of signatures helps to preserve the integrity of the election, particularly because it makes it easier to ferret out fraudulent or invalid signatures. The Court left the door open to an as-applied challenge to public disclosure if there was actual evidence of harassment from the disclosure.

4. Assume you represent an individual or entity that opposes disclosure laws. How might you present your argument in light of the courts' decisions in these cases? What kind of evidence must you gather?

9. *Super PACs*

One of the most significant aspects of the post-*Citizens United* climate is the rise of "outside" groups spending money on politics. According to the website OpenSecrets.org, the 2012 election cycle saw outside groups, from both sides of the aisle, spend over $1.2 billion, often through political action committees (PACs). That number increased to over $1.6 billion during the 2016 election. But that paled in comparison to 2020, which saw outside spending top $3.2 billion.

PACs have existed for years. A PAC is an organization of individuals that is created, generally independent of a particular candidate, for the purpose of engaging in political advocacy. Under federal law, PACs must register, file certain disclosures, and are subject to other restrictions. The question after *Citizens United* was whether various campaign finance regulations, such as contribution limits, still applied to these organizations. In *SpeechNow,* the D.C. Circuit considered the application of *Citizens United* to organizations created solely to make independent expenditures during a campaign—often referred to as a Super PAC. (In this respect, a Super PAC is different from a conventional PAC, often created to channel contributions to particular candidates. A Super PAC, by contrast, promises to make no contributions to, or coordinated expenditures with, any candidate.) You read above that the court in *SpeechNow* upheld disclosure obligations on independent expenditure-only groups. The portion of the case that you will read below is considered to be the most important analysis to date on funding restrictions as applied to outside advocacy groups. FECA, which by its own terms does not distinguish between conventional PACs and Super PACs, limits permissible contributions to PACs to $5,000. But what about the applicability of this $5,000 limit to Super PACs? As long as a Super PAC makes no contributions of its own, should it not be able to receive as much money as its donors wish to give it—as a means of collectively engaging in the right to make unlimited independent expenditures (as upheld in *Citizens United*)? At least that's the argument considered in the case; can you formulate a counterargument?

Moreover, PACs have additional limitations and reporting requirements, as compared to nonprofit organizations that are not designated as "political organizations." In the second case below, *Real Truth*, we will consider how the Federal Election Commission (FEC) designates a group as a "political organization." As you are reading, think about the best way to determine if a group is "political enough" to fall under the FEC's regulations. Also ask yourself whether it is better to have clearly defined or more context-specific rules for this question.

SpeechNow.org v. FEC

599 F.3d 686 (D.C. Cir. 2010) (en banc)

SENTELLE, Chief Judge:

[You have already read part of this opinion above, in the unit on disclosure laws. A portion of the beginning of the opinion is also included here for context.]

SpeechNow is an unincorporated nonprofit association registered as a "political organization" under § 527 of the Internal Revenue Code. Its purpose is to promote the First Amendment rights of free speech and freedom to assemble by expressly advocating for federal candidates whom it views as supporting those rights and against those whom it sees as insufficiently committed to those rights. It intends to acquire funds solely through donations by individuals. SpeechNow further intends to operate exclusively through "independent expenditures." FECA defines "independent expenditures" as expenditures "expressly advocating the election or defeat of a clearly identified candidate" that are "not made in concert or cooperation with or at the request or suggestion of such candidate, the candidate's authorized political committee, or their agents, or a political party committee or its agents." SpeechNow has five members, two of whom are plaintiffs in this case: David Keating, who is also SpeechNow's president and treasurer, and Edward Crane. Keating makes the operational decisions for SpeechNow, including in which election campaigns to run advertisements, which candidates to support or oppose, and all administrative decisions.

Though it has not yet begun operations, SpeechNow has made plans both for fundraising and for making independent expenditures. All five of the individual plaintiffs—Keating, Crane, Fred Young, Brad Russo, and Scott Burkhardt—are prepared to donate to SpeechNow. Keating proposes to donate $5500. Crane proposes to donate $6000. Young, who is otherwise unaffiliated with SpeechNow, proposes to donate $110,000. Russo and Burkhardt want to make donations of $100 each. In addition, as of August 2008, seventy-five other individuals had indicated on

SpeechNow's website that they were interested in making donations. As for expenditures, SpeechNow planned ads for the 2008 election cycle against two incumbent candidates for federal office who, in the opinion of SpeechNow, did not sufficiently support First Amendment rights. These ads would have cost around $12,000 to produce. Keating intended to place the ads so that the target audience would view the ads at least ten times, which would have cost around $400,000. As SpeechNow never accepted any donations, it never produced or ran these ads. However, SpeechNow intends to run similar ads for the 2010 election cycle if it is not subject to the contribution limits of § 441a(a) at issue in this case.

Believing that subjecting SpeechNow to all the restrictions imposed on political committees would be unconstitutional, SpeechNow and the five individual plaintiffs filed a complaint in the district court requesting declaratory relief against the FEC.

The district court made findings of fact, and certified to this court five questions:

1. Whether the contribution limits contained in 2 U.S.C. §§ 441a(a)(1)(C) and 441a(a)(3) violate the First Amendment by preventing David Keating, SpeechNow.org's president and treasurer, from accepting contributions to Speech Now.org in excess of the limits contained in §§ 441a(a)(1)(C) and 441a(a)(3).
2. Whether the contribution limit mandated by 2 U.S.C. § 441a(a)(1)(C) violates the First Amendment by preventing the individual plaintiffs from making contributions to SpeechNow.org in excess of $5000 per calendar year.
3. Whether the biennial aggregate contribution limit mandated by 2 U.S.C. § 441a(a)(3) violates the First Amendment by preventing Fred Young from making contributions to SpeechNow.org that would exceed his individual biennial aggregate limit.

[Questions 4 and 5 relate to the disclosure provisions and are discussed above in the unit on disclosure.]

Under FECA, a political committee is "any committee, club, association, or other group of persons" that receives contributions of more than $1000 in a year or makes expenditures of more than $1000 in a year. Once a group is so designated, contributions to the committee are restricted by 2 U.S.C. § 441a(a)(1)(C) and 441a(a)(3). The first provision limits an individual's contribution to a political committee to $5000 per calendar year; the second limits an individual's total contributions to all political committees to $69,900 biennially.[2]

2. Subject to exceptions not here relevant, FECA defines "contributions" as "any gift, subscription, loan, advance, or deposit of money or anything of value made by any person for the purpose of influencing any election for Federal office." 2 U.S.C. § 431(8)(A)(i). Again subject to exceptions, the Act defines "expenditure" as "any purchase, payment, distribution, loan, advance, deposit, or gift of money or anything of value, made by any person for the purpose of influencing any election for Federal office; and [] a written contract, promise, or agreement to make an expenditure." 2 U.S.C. § 431(9)(A)(i)-(ii).

II. ANALYSIS

A. Contribution Limits (Certified Questions 1-3)

The First Amendment mandates that "Congress shall make no law . . . abridging the freedom of speech." In *Buckley v. Valeo*, the Supreme Court held that, although contribution limits do encroach upon First Amendment interests, they do not encroach upon First Amendment interests to as great a degree as expenditure limits. In *Buckley*, the Supreme Court first delineated the differing treatments afforded contribution and expenditure limits. In that case, the Court struck down limits on an individual's expenditures for political advocacy, but upheld limits on contributions to political candidates and campaigns. In making the distinction, the Court emphasized that in "contrast with a limitation upon expenditures for political expression, a limitation upon the amount that any one person or group may contribute to a candidate or political committee entails only a marginal restriction upon the contributor's ability to engage in free communication." However, contribution limits still do implicate fundamental First Amendment interests.

When the government attempts to regulate the financing of political campaigns and express advocacy through contribution limits, therefore, it must have a countervailing interest that outweighs the limit's burden on the exercise of First Amendment rights. Thus a "contribution limit involving significant interference with associational rights must be closely drawn to serve a sufficiently important interest." *Davis v. FEC* (2008) (quoting *McConnell v. FEC* (2003)). The Supreme Court has recognized only one interest sufficiently important to outweigh the First Amendment interests implicated by contributions for political speech: preventing corruption or the appearance of corruption. The Court has rejected each of the few other interests the government has, at one point or another, suggested as a justification for contribution or expenditure limits. Equalization of differing viewpoints is not a legitimate government objective. *Davis*. An informational interest in "identifying the sources of support for and opposition to" a political position or candidate is not enough to justify the First Amendment burden. *Citizens Against Rent Control v. City of Berkeley* (1981). And, though this rationale would not affect an unincorporated association such as SpeechNow, the Court has also refused to find a sufficiently compelling governmental interest in preventing "the corrosive and distorting effects of immense aggregations of wealth that are accumulated with the help of the corporate form." *Citizens United.*

Given this precedent, the only interest we may evaluate to determine whether the government can justify contribution limits as applied to SpeechNow is the government's anticorruption interest. Because of the Supreme Court's recent decision in *Citizens United v. FEC*, the analysis is straightforward. There, the Court held that the government has no anti-corruption interest in limiting independent expenditures.[3]

Citizens United involved a nonprofit corporation that in January 2008 produced a film that was highly critical of then-Senator Hillary Clinton, a candidate in the Democratic Party's 2008 Presidential primary elections. The film was, "in

3. Of course, the government still has an interest in preventing quid pro quo corruption. However, after *Citizens United*, independent expenditures do not implicate that interest.

essence, . . . a feature-length negative advertisement that urges viewers to vote against Senator Clinton for President." As such, the film was subject to the restrictions of 2 U.S.C. § 441b. That provision made it unlawful for any corporation or union to use general treasury funds to make independent expenditures as defined by 2 U.S.C. § 431(17) or expenditures for speech defined as "electioneering communications," which are certain types of political ads aired shortly before an election or primary, 2 U.S.C. § 434(f)(3). The Supreme Court declared this expenditure ban unconstitutional, holding that corporations may not be prohibited from spending money for express political advocacy when those expenditures are independent from candidates and uncoordinated with their campaigns.

The independence of independent expenditures was a central consideration in the Court's decision. By definition, independent expenditures are "not made in concert or cooperation with or at the request or suggestion of such candidate, the candidate's authorized political committee, or their agents, or a political party committee or its agents." 2 U.S.C. § 431(17). As the *Buckley* Court explained when it struck down a limit on independent expenditures, "[t]he absence of prearrangement and coordination of an expenditure with the candidate or his agent . . . alleviates the danger that expenditures will be given as a quid pro quo for improper commitments from the candidate." However, the *Buckley* Court left open the possibility that the future might bring data linking independent expenditures to corruption or the appearance of corruption. The Court merely concluded that independent expenditures "do [] not presently appear to pose dangers of real or apparent corruption comparable to those identified with large campaign contributions."

Over the next several decades, Congress and the Court gave little further guidance respecting *Buckley*'s reasoning that a lack of coordination diminishes the possibility of corruption. Just a few months after *Buckley*, Congress codified a ban on corporations' independent expenditures at 2 U.S.C. § 441b. In 1978, in *First National Bank of Boston v. Bellotti*, the Court "struck down a state-law prohibition on corporate independent expenditures related to referenda," but did not "address the constitutionality of the State's ban on corporate independent expenditures to support candidates." *Citizens United*. Though the *Bellotti* Court sweepingly rejected "the proposition that speech that otherwise would be within the protection of the First Amendment loses that protection simply because its source is a corporation," it limited the implications of that rejection by opining in a footnote that "Congress might well be able to demonstrate the existence of a danger of real or apparent corruption in independent expenditures by corporations to influence candidate elections." Then, in *Austin*, the Court expressly upheld a Michigan law that prohibited corporate independent expenditures. And in *McConnell*, the Court relied on *Austin* to uphold the Bipartisan Campaign Reform Act of 2002's (BCRA's) extension of § 441b's ban on corporate expenditures to electioneering communications.

The *Citizens United* Court reevaluated this line of cases and found them to be incompatible with *Buckley*'s original reasoning. The Court overruled *Austin* and the part of *McConnell* that upheld BCRA's amendments to § 441b. More important for this case, the Court did so by expressly deciding the question left open by the footnoted caveat in *Bellotti*. The Court stated, "[W]e now conclude that independent expenditures, including those made by corporations, do not give rise to corruption or the appearance of corruption." *Citizens United*.

The Court came to this conclusion by looking to the definition of corruption and the appearance of corruption. For several decades after *Buckley*, the Court's analysis of the government's anti-corruption interest revolved largely around the "hallmark of corruption," "financial quid pro quo: dollars for political favors." However, in a series of cases culminating in *McConnell*, the Court expanded the definition to include "the appearance of undue influence" created by large donations given for the purpose of "buying access." The *McConnell* Court concluded that limiting the government's anticorruption interest to preventing quid pro quo was a "crabbed view of corruption, and particularly of the appearance of corruption" that "ignores precedent, common sense, and the realities of political fundraising." The *Citizens United* Court retracted this view of the government's interest, saying that "[t]he fact that speakers may have influence over or access to elected officials does not mean that these officials are corrupt." The Court returned to its older definition of corruption that focused on quid pro quo, saying that "[i]ngratiation and access . . . are not corruption." Therefore, without any evidence that independent expenditures "lead to, or create the appearance of, quid pro quo corruption," and only "scant evidence" that they even ingratiate, the Court concluded that independent expenditures do not corrupt or create the appearance of corruption.

In light of the Court's holding as a matter of law that independent expenditures do not corrupt or create the appearance of quid pro quo corruption, contributions to groups that make only independent expenditures also cannot corrupt or create the appearance of corruption. The Court has effectively held that there is no corrupting "quid" for which a candidate might in exchange offer a corrupt "quo."

Given this analysis from *Citizens United*, we must conclude that the government has no anti-corruption interest in limiting contributions to an independent expenditure group such as SpeechNow. This simplifies the task of weighing the First Amendment interests implicated by contributions to SpeechNow against the government's interest in limiting such contributions. Thus, we do not need to quantify to what extent contributions to SpeechNow are an expression of core political speech. We do not need to answer whether giving money is speech per se, or if contributions are merely symbolic expressions of general support, or if it matters in this case that just one person, David Keating, decides what the group will say. All that matters is that the First Amendment cannot be encroached upon for naught.

At oral argument, the FEC insisted that *Citizens United* does not disrupt *Buckley*'s longstanding decision upholding contribution limits. This is literally true. But, as *Citizens United* emphasized, the limits upheld in *Buckley* were limits on contributions made directly to candidates. Limits on direct contributions to candidates, "unlike limits on independent expenditures, have been an accepted means to prevent quid pro quo corruption." *Citizens United.*

The FEC argues that the analysis of *Citizens United* does not apply because that case involved an expenditure limit while this case involves a contribution limit. Alluding to the divide between expenditure limits and contribution limits established by *Buckley*, the FEC insists that contribution limits are subject to a lower standard of review than expenditure limits, so that "what may be insufficient to justify an expenditure limit may be sufficient to justify a contribution limit." Plaintiffs, on the other hand, argue that *Citizens United* stands for the proposition that "burdensome laws trigger strict scrutiny." We do not find it necessary to decide whether the logic of *Citizens United* has any effect on the standard of review generally afforded contribution limits. The *Citizens United* Court avoided "reconsider[ing] whether contribution limits should be subjected to rigorous First Amendment scrutiny," and so do we. Instead, we return to what we have said before: because *Citizens United* holds that independent expenditures do not corrupt or give the appearance of corruption as a matter of law, then the government can have no anti-corruption interest in limiting contributions to independent expenditure-only organizations. No matter which standard of review governs contribution limits, the limits on contributions to SpeechNow cannot stand.

We therefore answer in the affirmative each of the first three questions certified to this Court. The contribution limits of 2 U.S.C. § 441a(a)(1)(C) and 441a(a)(3) violate the First Amendment by preventing plaintiffs from donating to SpeechNow in excess of the limits and by prohibiting SpeechNow from accepting donations in excess of the limits. We should be clear, however, that we only decide these questions as applied to contributions to SpeechNow, an independent expenditure-only group. Our holding does not affect, for example, § 441a(a)(3)'s limits on direct contributions to candidates.

The Real Truth About Abortion, Inc. v. FEC

681 F.3d 544 (4th Cir. 2012)

NIEMEYER, Circuit Judge:

The Real Truth About Abortion, Inc. (formerly known as The Real Truth About Obama, Inc.), a Virginia non-profit corporation organized under § 527 of the Internal Revenue Code to provide "accurate and truthful information about the public policy positions of Senator Barack Obama," commenced this action against the Federal Election Commission and the Department of Justice, contending that it was "chilled" from posting information about then-Senator Obama because of the vagueness of a Commission regulation and a Commission policy relating to whether Real Truth has to make disclosures or is a "political committee" (commonly referred to as a political action committee or PAC). Real Truth asserts that it is not subject to regulation but fears the Commission could take steps to regulate it because of the vagueness of 11 C.F.R. § 100.22(b) and the policy of the Commission to determine whether an organization is a PAC by applying the "major purpose" test on a case-by-case basis. It alleges that the regulation and policy are unconstitutionally broad and vague, both facially and as applied to it, in violation of the First and Fifth Amendments.

On cross-motions for summary judgment, the district court found both the regulation and the policy constitutional. And, applying the "exacting scrutiny" standard applicable to disclosure provisions, we affirm.

I

Real Truth was organized on July 24, 2008, as an "issue-[advocacy] '527' organization" under § 527 of the Internal Revenue Code. In its IRS filing, Real Truth stated that its purpose was to provide truthful information about the public positions taken by Senator Barack Obama but that it would not "expressly advocate the election or defeat" of any political candidate or "make any contribution" to a candidate.

Within a few days of its incorporation, Real Truth commenced this action challenging . . . the Commission's regulations implementing the Federal Election Campaign Act ("FECA")—11 C.F.R. § 100.22(b) (defining when a communication expressly advocates the election or defeat of a clearly identified candidate). In addition, Real Truth challenged the Commission's policy of determining PAC status by using a "major purpose" test on a case-by-case basis. It asserted that these regulations and the policy were unconstitutional, facially and as applied, in that they were overbroad and vague, in violation of the First and Fifth Amendments to the Constitution.

[T]he district court granted summary judgment to the Commission and the Department of Justice, holding that 11 C.F.R. § 100.22(b) and the Commission's case-by-case policy for determining whether an organization was a PAC were constitutional, both facially and as applied to Real Truth. More particularly, the court found that § 100.22(b) was consistent with the "appeal-to-vote" test articulated in *Federal Election Commission v. Wisconsin Right to Life, Inc.* (2007), and that the Commission was entitled to use a multifactor approach on a case-by-case basis for determining PAC status because "ascertaining an organization's single major purpose is an inherently comparative task and requires consideration of the full range of an organization's activities."

II

At the outset, we address Real Truth's contention that, in reviewing the Commission's regulation and policy, we should apply the strict scrutiny standard. Real Truth argues that the regulation and policy place onerous burdens on speech similar to the burdens to which the Supreme Court applied strict scrutiny in *Citizens United.*

The Commission contends instead that because the challenged regulation and policy only implicate disclosure requirements and do not restrict either campaign activities or speech, we should apply the less stringent "exacting scrutiny" standard. Under this standard, the government must demonstrate only a "substantial relation" between the disclosure requirement and "sufficiently important government interest."

Regulation 100.22(b), which Real Truth challenges as too broad and vague, implements the statutory definition of "independent expenditure," 2 U.S.C. § 431(17), which in turn determines whether a person must make disclosures as required by 2 U.S.C. § 434(c). The definition could also contribute to the determination of whether Real Truth is a PAC because it is an organization with expenditures of more than $1,000, which would impose not only disclosure requirements, but also organizational requirements. Similarly, the Commission's policy for applying the "major purposes" test to organizations, which Real Truth also challenges, would also determine whether Real Truth is a PAC, again implicating disclosure and organizational requirements.

Such disclosure and organizational requirements, however, are not as burdensome on speech as are limits imposed on campaign activities or limits imposed on contributions to and expenditures by campaigns. Indeed, the Supreme Court has noted that "disclosure requirements certainly in most applications appear to be the least restrictive means of curbing the evils of campaign ignorance and corruption that Congress found to exist." *Buckley v. Valeo.* Accordingly, an intermediate level of scrutiny known as "exacting scrutiny" is the appropriate standard to apply in reviewing provisions that impose disclosure requirements, such as the regulation and policy.

In sum, we conclude that even after *Citizens United*, it remains the law that provisions imposing disclosure obligations are reviewed under the intermediate scrutiny level of "exacting scrutiny." We will accordingly review the Commission's regulation 100.22(b) and its policy for determining the major purpose of an organization under the exacting scrutiny standard.

III

Turning to the challenge of 11 C.F.R. § 100.22, Real Truth contends that the regulation's second definition of "expressly advocating," as contained in subsection (b), is fatally broader and more vague than the restrictions imposed on the definition of "expressly advocating" by *Buckley*.

Regulation 100.22 defines "expressly advocating" as the term is used in 2 U.S.C. § 431(17), which in turn defines "independent expenditure" as an expenditure by a person "*expressly advocating* the election or defeat of a clearly identified candidate" and not made by or in coordination with a candidate or political party. (Emphasis added.) Subsection (a) defines "expressly advocating" in the manner stated by the Supreme Court in *Buckley* and thus includes communications that use phrases "which in context can have no other reasonable meaning than to urge the election or defeat" of a candidate, 11 C.F.R. § 100.22(a)—words such as "vote for," "elect," "defeat," or "reject," which are often referred to as the express advocacy "magic words." *See McConnell v. Fed. Election Comm'n.* Subsection (b), on the other hand, defines "expressly advocating" more contextually, without using the "magic words." This subsection, which is the subject of Real Truth's challenge, provides in relevant part:

> Expressly advocating means any communication that—
> (b) When taken as a whole and with limited reference to external events, such as the proximity to the election, could only be interpreted by a reasonable person as containing advocacy of the election or defeat of one or more clearly identified candidate(s) because—
> (1) The electoral portion of the communication is unmistakable, unambiguous, and suggestive of only one meaning; and
> (2) Reasonable minds could not differ as to whether it encourages actions to elect or defeat one or more clearly identified candidate(s) or encourages some other kind of action.

A

Real Truth first challenges § 100.22(b) as facially overbroad. The Commission's approach of defining "expressly advocating" with the magic words of *Buckley* in subsection (a) and with their functional equivalent in subsection (b) was upheld by the Supreme Court in considering a facial over-breadth challenge to the BCRA, which included a provision defining express advocacy for purposes of electioneering communications. *See McConnell.* In rejecting the challenge, the *McConnell* Court noted that *Buckley*'s narrow construction of the FECA to require express advocacy was a function of the vagueness of the original statutory definition of "expenditure," not an absolute First Amendment imperative. The Court accordingly held that Congress could permissibly regulate not only communications containing the "magic words" of *Buckley*, but also communications that were "the functional equivalent" of express advocacy.

Later, in *Federal Election Commission v. Wisconsin Right to Life, Inc.* (2007), the Chief Justice's controlling opinion further elaborated on the meaning of *McConnell*'s "functional equivalent" test. The Chief Justice held that where an "ad is susceptible of no reasonable interpretation other than as an appeal to vote for or against a specific candidate," it could be regulated in the same manner as express advocacy. The Chief Justice explicitly rejected the argument, raised by Justice Scalia's concurring opinion, that the only permissible test for express advocacy is a magic words test.

Contrary to Real Truth's assertions, *Citizens United* also supports the Commission's use of a functional equivalent test in defining "express advocacy." In the course of striking down FECA's spending prohibitions on certain corporate election expenditures, the *Citizens United* majority first considered whether those regulations applied to the communications at issue in the case. Using *Wisconsin Right to Life*'s "functional equivalent" test, the Court concluded that one advertisement—Hillary: The Movie—qualified as the functional equivalent of express advocacy because it was "in essence . . . a feature-length negative advertisement that urges viewers to vote against Senator [Hillary] Clinton for President." But more importantly for our decision, the Court also upheld BCRA's disclosure requirements for all electioneering communications—including those that are not the functional equivalent of express advocacy. In this portion of the opinion, joined by eight Justices, the Court explained that because disclosure "is a less restrictive alternative to more comprehensive regulations of speech," mandatory disclosure requirements are constitutionally permissible even if ads contain no direct candidate advocacy and "only pertain to a commercial transaction." If mandatory disclosure requirements are permissible when applied to ads that merely mention a federal candidate, then applying the same burden to ads that go further and are the functional equivalent of express advocacy cannot automatically be impermissible.

B

In addition to its overbreadth argument, Real Truth argues that even if express advocacy is not limited to communications using *Buckley*'s magic words, § 100.22(b) is nonetheless unconstitutionally vague. Here again, however, Real Truth's arguments run counter to an established Supreme Court precedent. The language of § 100.22(b) is consistent with the test for the "functional equivalent of express advocacy" that was adopted in *Wisconsin Right to Life*, a test that the controlling opinion specifically stated was not "impermissibly vague." Moreover, just as the "functional equivalent" test is objective, so too is the similar test contained in § 100.22(b).

Both standards are also restrictive, in that they limit the application of the disclosure requirements solely to those communications that, in the estimation of any reasonable person, would constitute advocacy. Although it is true that the language of § 100.22(b) does not exactly mirror the functional equivalent definition in *Wisconsin Right to Life*—e.g., § 100.22(b) uses the word "suggestive" while *Wisconsin Right to Life* used the word "susceptible"—the differences between the two tests are not meaningful. Indeed, the test in § 100.22(b) is likely narrower than the one articulated in *Wisconsin Right to Life,* since it requires a communication to have an "electoral portion" that is "unmistakable" and "unambiguous."

The Supreme Court has routinely recognized that because disclosure requirements occasion a lesser burden on speech, it is constitutionally permissible to require disclosure for a wider variety of speech than mere electioneering. *Citizens United* only confirmed the breadth of Congress' power in this regard.

C

At bottom, we conclude that § 100.22(b) is constitutional, facially and as applied to Real Truth's intended advertisements. The regulation is consistent with the test developed in *Wisconsin Right to Life* and is not unduly vague.

IV

Finally, Real Truth contends that the Commission's policy for applying the "major purpose" test in determining whether an organization is a PAC is unconstitutional because it "weigh[s] various vague and overbroad factors with undisclosed weight." It maintains that the only permissible methods of analyzing PAC status are (1) examining an organization's expenditures to see if campaign-related speech amounts to 50% of all expenditures; or (2) reviewing "the organization's central purpose revealed by its organic documents."

The FECA defines a "political committee" or PAC, as we have called it, as any "committee, club, association, or other group of persons" that makes more than $1,000 in political expenditures or receives more than $1,000 in contributions during a calendar year. The terms "expenditures" and "contributions" are in turn defined to encompass any spending or fundraising "for the purpose of influencing any election for Federal office."

In *Buckley,* the Supreme Court concluded that defining PACs "only in terms of amounts of annual 'contributions' and 'expenditures'" might produce vagueness issues. Accordingly, the Court limited the applicability of FECA's PAC requirements to organizations controlled by a candidate or whose "major purpose" is the nomination or election of candidates. An organization that is not controlled by a candidate must therefore register as a PAC if its contributions or expenditures exceed $1,000 and its "major purpose" is the nomination or election of a federal candidate.

Following *Buckley,* the Commission adopted a policy of determining PAC status on a case-by-case basis. Under this approach, the Commission first considers a group's political activities, such as spending on a particular electoral or issue-advocacy campaign, and then it evaluates an organization's "major purpose," as revealed by that group's public statements, fundraising appeals, government filings, and organizational documents.

In March 2004, the Commission published a Notice of Proposed Rulemaking that, among other things, requested comments on whether the Commission should adopt a regulatory definition of "political committee" or PAC. After receiving public comments and holding several hearings, the Commission issued a Final Rule stating that it would not alter its existing method of determining PAC status.

When the Commission's decision not to adopt a statutory definition of a PAC was challenged in [the D.C. district] court, the court rejected the plaintiffs' request to require the Commission to commence a new rulemaking. It found, however, that the Commission had "failed to present a reasoned explanation for its decision" to regulate § 527 organizations through case-by-case adjudication rather than a rulemaking. Therefore, it remanded the case to the Commission "to explain its decision or institute a new rulemaking."

The Commission responded in February 2007 by publishing in the Federal Register a "Supplemental Explanation and Justification," as part of the 2007 Notice, where it gave notice of its decision not to promulgate a new definition of "political committee" and discussed the reasons it would not do so but instead would continue to apply a case-by-case approach. The Commission stated that "[a]pplying the major purpose doctrine . . . requires the flexibility of a case-by-case analysis of an organization's conduct that is incompatible with a one-size-fits-all rule." The 2007 Notice also "explain[ed] the framework for establishing political committee status under FECA" and "discusse[d] several recently resolved administrative matters that provide considerable guidance to all organizations regarding . . . political committee status."

Although *Buckley* did create the major purpose test, it did not mandate a particular methodology for determining an organization's major purpose. And thus the Commission was free to administer FECA political committee regulations either through categorical rules or through individualized adjudications.

We conclude that the Commission had good and legal reasons for taking the approach it did. The determination of whether the election or defeat of federal candidates for office is the major purpose of an organization, and not simply *a* major purpose, is inherently a comparative task, and in most instances it will require weighing the importance of some of a group's activities against others. As the district court noted in upholding the case-by-case approach in *Shays v. Federal Election Commission* (D.D.C. 2007)

> an organization . . . may engage in many non-electoral activities so that determining its major purpose requires a very close examination of various activities and statements. Or an organization may be engaging in substantial amounts of both federal and non-federal electoral activity, again requiring a detailed analysis of its various activities.

The necessity of a contextual inquiry is supported by judicial decisions applying the major purpose test, which have used the same fact-intensive analysis that the Commission has adopted.

Real Truth's argument that the major purpose test requires a bright-line, two-factor test relies heavily on *Massachusetts Citizens for Life.* But [this case] can[not] bear the weight Real Truth ascribes to it. In *Massachusetts Citizens for Life,* the Court suggested in dicta (inasmuch as Massachusetts Citizens for Life was not a PAC) that an organization's independent spending could "become so extensive that the organization's major purpose may be regarded as campaign activity." This statement indicates that the amount of independent spending is a relevant factor in determining PAC status, but it does not imply that the Commission may only consider spending. Indeed, the Court in *Massachusetts Citizens for Life* implicitly endorsed the Commission's approach when it examined the entire record to conclude that the plaintiff did not satisfy the "major purpose" test.

Thus, although cases since *Buckley* have indicated that certain facts may be particularly relevant when assessing an organization's major purpose, those decisions do not foreclose the Commission from using a more comprehensive methodology.

Despite Real Truth's protestations, we see little risk that the Commission's existing major purpose test will chill political expression. In the First Amendment context, a statute may be found overbroad if a "substantial number of [the statute's] applications are unconstitutional, judged in relation to the statute's plainly legitimate sweep." *United States v. Stevens* (2010) (quoting *Wash. State Grange v. Wash. State Republican Party* (2008)). Real Truth has failed to explain why the Commission's test would prevent any party from speaking, especially in view of the fact that the application of the test to find that an organization is a PAC would subject the organization only to "minimal" reporting and organizational obligations.

We should note that the class of speakers who would be subject to FECA's PAC regulations would be significantly smaller than the totality of groups that speak on political subjects. In most cases the Commission would only begin to consider a group's "major purpose" after confirming that the group had either made $1,000 in expenditures or received more than $1,000 in contributions. The expenditure or contribution threshold means that some groups whose "major purpose" was indisputably the nomination or election of federal candidates would not be designated PACs.

And even if an organization were to find itself subject to a major-purpose investigation, that investigation would not necessarily be an intrusive one. Much of the information the Commission would consider would already be available in that organization's government filings or public statements. If additional information were required, the Commission's Federal Register notices, advisory opinions, and other policy documents would provide the organization with ample guidance as to the criteria the Commission might consider.

At bottom, we conclude that the Commission, in its policy, adopted a sensible approach to determining whether an organization qualifies for PAC status. And more importantly the Commission's multi-factor major-purpose test is consistent with Supreme Court precedent and does not unlawfully deter protected speech. Accordingly, we find the policy constitutional.

NOTES ON *SPEECHNOW* AND *REAL TRUTH*

1. Does the decision in *SpeechNow* inextricably flow from *Citizens United*? The court in *SpeechNow* says that *Citizens United* stated "as a matter of law" that independent expenditures do not lead to corruption. But is that an accurate reading of *Citizens United*? Or was the Court in *Citizens United* instead making a factual determination that independent expenditures usually do not lead to corruption, but that the law might be valid if there is evidence of *quid pro quo* corruption based on

independent expenditures? In a challenge to a Montana law prohibiting corporate independent expenditures, the Montana Supreme Court upheld the law and ruled that Montana's unique history of corporate corruption distinguished *Citizens United* as a factual matter. The Supreme Court issued a 5-4 summary reversal, holding that *Citizens United* applies to Montana. *American Tradition Partnership v. Bullock* (2012).

2. Think about the real-world implications of the decision in *Real Truth*. Can an organization ever be secure that it is or is not subject to FECA's regulations? Is the "major purpose" test clear enough that you would be able to advise a client regarding whether it must comply? If the "major purpose" test is too murky, how would you revise it? What are the pitfalls of having a stricter test? Presumably, organizations would go right up to the line of whatever that test is before they fell under the regulation's strictures. Which is better in this area: bright-line rules or context-specific tests?

3. As a result of the decision in *SpeechNow*, new organizations began to pop up, beginning for the 2010 midterms and 2012 presidential election cycles: Super PACs. A Super PAC is an independent expenditure-only organization. In essence, it is a political committee that is separate from a candidate and exists solely to make independent expenditures. Technically speaking, Super PACs are completely separate from political candidates; in reality, most Super PACs are aligned with a particular candidate even though there is no formal "coordination." During the 2020 election season, there were almost 2,300 Super PACs, which made over $2 billion in independent expenditures; the website OpenSecrets.org classified 56 percent of that spending as supporting "conservative" viewpoints and 42.7 percent as supporting "liberal" viewpoints.

4. How should the Federal Election Commission and the courts determine if a Super PAC's spending qualifies as an independent expenditure or instead is being coordinated with a campaign? The FEC's website, citing the relevant regulation, provides that a payment for a communication is "coordinated" if it is "made in cooperation, consultation or concert with, or at the request or suggestion of, a candidate, a candidate's authorized committee or their agents, or a political party committee or its agents." Is this standard helpful? The FEC has also created a three-part test to determine if a communication is "coordinated," all three of which must be satisfied for the communication to be coordinated and therefore subject to BCRA's contribution limitations. First, under the "payment" prong, the communication simply needs to be paid for by someone other than the candidate or political party committee. Second, under the "content" prong, the communication essentially must be about the candidate or the campaign. Finally, under the "conduct" prong, the person paying for the communication and the candidate or campaign must have some interaction, such as having substantial discussions between the entity paying for the ad and the candidate or campaign about the content or timing of the ad, or employing the same vendor when that vendor uses material information it has learned about the campaign's plans or activities in the creation, production, or distribution of the ad. Does this adequately capture the kind of communications that the Constitution allows the government to limit? For a detailed explanation of the three-prong test, visit the FEC's website at https://www.fec.gov/help-candidates-and-committees/candidate-taking-receipts/

coordinated-communications. *See also* 11 C.F.R. § 109.21. Note that some of these regulations themselves have been the subject of judicial decisions, meaning that the law in this area is still ever-changing.

A NOTE ON "DARK MONEY"

Sometimes donors do not want to disclose that they are spending money to help a candidate or cause. Tax laws and campaign finance laws can help them essentially "hide" their identity, giving rise to what some have termed "dark money."After both *Citizens United* and *SpeechNow*, some political operatives who wanted to keep their donors secret created new political groups, organizing them as tax-exempt 501(c)(4) entities. Under this provision of the tax code, 501(c)(4) groups need not disclose the identity of their donors. The section defines an eligible organization as "civic leagues, social welfare organizations, and local associations of employees." Generally accepted guidance is that an organization falls within the definition of a "social welfare organization" so long as its primary purpose—that is, at least 50 percent of its activities—is nonpolitical, i.e., related to social welfare. Yet there is often little scrutiny of whether these groups' activities are at least half nonpolitical, and some will even dissolve after an election and before they must certify their activities to the IRS to sustain their nonprofit status.

Most Super PACs are organized under Section 527 and must disclose their donors. But they can take donations from 501(c)(4) organizations that need not disclose their own donors. Thus, an individual who wishes to hide their political spending can donate to a 501(c)(4) organization. That 501(c)(4) group can then donate to the Super PAC. When the Super PAC discloses its donors as part of its FEC filing, it will simply show as its donor the 501(c)(4) "social welfare" group, and not the actual individuals behind the money. (This same process can occur for 501(c)(5) "labor and agricultural organizations" and 501(c)(6) "business leagues.") Dark money spending is significant. OpenSecrets.org reported that the 2020 election saw over $1 billion of dark money spending. Reversing a prior trend, in which dark money spending has traditionally favored Republicans, Democratic groups dominated dark money expenditures in both the 2018 and 2020 elections. But Republicans have still benefited immensely: OpenSecrets.org also noted that conservative billionaires Charles and David Koch (often known as the "Koch Brothers") have spent hundreds of millions of dollars over the past decade on political races throughout the country using a network of dark money groups.

Do you think Congress is likely to address the issue of dark money in the future? Of course, any requirement that 501(c)(4) organizations disclose all of their donors could make it harder for some charities to raise money; some people do not want to publicly disclose their charitable giving. But even if Congress acted, would the Supreme Court uphold a robust disclosure regime for all political spending, even requiring the disclosure of individuals who give to a group which in turn gives to a political organization? That is the crux of the issue, which is likely to see further developments in the coming years.

SUMMARY OF THE LAW OF CAMPAIGN PRACTICES

We have woven our way through the intricacies of the law of campaign practices, which has covered campaign ads, limits to campaign activities, and campaign finance. The recurring themes of the cases included:

- The clash of the First Amendment right to free speech with the desire to regulate false or misleading campaign ads, and the corresponding degree of regulation permissible to achieve better discourse in campaigning.
- A discussion of the best ways to ferret out improper or illegal campaign practices, such as stopping "harassment" at the polls and limiting "ballot selfies."
- The push-and-pull of regulating money in politics, and in particular, the proper definition of "corruption" in this area.
- The emerging issues regarding public financing, disclosure, and PACs.

Specifically regarding campaign finance, we saw that the cases usually turn on both the type of money spent (contribution or independent expenditure), as well as who is spending it (the candidate, political party, individual, corporation or union, the public through public financing, or a political organization such as a PAC). The key question is whether the money spent would lead to actual or apparent corruption, defined (at least for the current majority of the Supreme Court) solely as *quid pro quo* corruption. Spending money on elections is a form of speech, so it receives constitutional protection under the First Amendment. But legislatures have an interest in limiting (to an extent) the improper influence of money in politics.

Current doctrine provides that legislatures cannot limit any kind of independent expenditures, as those are "independent" of any candidate and therefore cannot lead to a sufficient risk of corruption or the appearance of corruption, which is the only valid governmental interest to justify constraints on the freedom to engage in such electoral advocacy. These laws must pass strict scrutiny review. Contribution limits are usually tolerable, to an extent, as courts review them under the lower "exacting scrutiny" standard. But they cannot be so low as to preclude any effective political expression. Disclosure laws are usually valid, again under close scrutiny. Public financing regimes cannot treat candidates unequally, even if the candidates have preexisting unequal resources. There is also a continuing debate regarding the level of coordination allowed between candidates and so-called "outside" groups such as PACs. As the doctrine reveals, this is an ever-changing field, especially as campaigns become even more expensive. If anything, then, this unit demonstrated the extent to which courts can influence greatly the ways in which campaigns are run.

PART IV
THE LAW OF VOTING

INTRODUCTION

We now reach the last portion of our journey through the election cycle: casting and counting the ballots. This Part deals with the myriad aspects involved in actually voting for a candidate and tallying the results. Many of the issues discussed in this Part fall under the umbrella of "election administration," but the doctrine encompasses more than just the nuts-and-bolts of running an election. There are constitutional considerations regarding the right to vote, political concerns about how to register voters and run the polls—both with early voting and on Election Day—and practical aspects of resolving an election that goes into overtime.

The issues in this Part are sometimes the most contested, often appearing on the front pages of newspapers as an election nears. We will consider, for example, voter purges of registration lists, photo ID laws, and postelection disputes—including *Bush v. Gore* as well as all the litigation and disputes over the 2020 presidential election. The fights over the voting process are continuing in the aftermath of the 2020, as state legislatures consider cutting back voting opportunities used during the unprecedented pandemic election. How the judiciary will respond to whatever laws ultimately are enacted is very much unsettled at the time this edition goes to press, as is what new voting rights laws Congress might enact (with or without eliminating the Senate filibuster).

As you are reading this material, consider the following:

- What is the proper judicial test for the constitutional right to vote?
- Should we allow partisan operatives to run our elections? If so, is the judiciary an effective check?
- To what extent are the rules of election administration too incumbent-friendly, and should that concern us?
- How can we avoid another postelection meltdown?
- How should we resolve these postelection disputes?

Many of the cases in this Part come from the last six presidential election cycles (2000, 2004, 2008, 2012, 2016, and 2020), meaning that the law in this area is both recent and ever-changing. The Law of Voting will likely continue to prove tumultuous in the years ahead. Although there are few clear answers, by the end of this Part you will at least have a better grasp on what has been the judiciary's role in the voting process.

A. *VOTER ELIGIBILITY*

1. *Foundations*

The "right to vote" is not explicitly enumerated within the federal Constitution. In addition, the federal Constitution did not originally constrain a state's choice about which of its citizens were entitled to vote in state elections. Indeed, the Constitution piggybacked on state law to determine who was eligible to vote for U.S. House of Representatives: "The electors in each state shall have the qualifications requisite for the electors of the most numerous branch of the state legislature."*

Nor was the Fourteenth Amendment originally understood to constrain a state's choice concerning the qualifications necessary for voting. In *Minor v. Happersett*, 88 U.S. 162 (1874), decided just six years after the Fourteenth Amendment's ratification, the Supreme Court specifically rejected the claim that the Fourteenth Amendment required states to extend voting rights equally to women and men. Instead, it was thought necessary to add more amendments to the federal Constitution to limit a state's ability to differentiate among citizens in determining who may exercise the right to vote. Thus, the Fifteenth Amendment prohibits states from denying the right to vote "on account of race," while the Nineteenth Amendment explicitly did what *Minor v. Happersett* refused: give women the same voting rights as men.

Moreover, the Twenty-Fourth Amendment, ratified in 1964, prohibits a state from making the payment of a poll tax a prerequisite to voting in an election for *federal* office, although by its terms it imposes no constraint on poll taxes as a prerequisite for voting in an election for *state* office. The Twenty-Sixth Amendment, ratified in 1971, prohibits a state from making age a barrier to voting for any citizen at least 18 years old.

In light of this history, and specifically the intentionally limited language of the Twenty-Fourth Amendment, how do you understand the following case, *Harper v. Virginia Bd. of Elections*, which in 1966—just two years after the Twenty-Fourth Amendment's adoption—interpreted the Fourteenth Amendment to prohibit states from making the payment of a poll tax a prerequisite for voting in a *state* election? Is *Harper* a legitimate exercise of constitutional *interpretation*, or instead an illegitimate act of constitutional *amendment* undertaken by the Supreme Court unilaterally (without following the amendment process in Article V of the federal Constitution)?

Whatever your view of *Harper*, it seems here to stay for the foreseeable future. (Is there any reason to doubt that in light of the increased number of self-proclaimed "originalists" on the U.S. Supreme Court? At the moment, the balance of power on the Court seems controlled by more pragmatic conservatives, Chief Justice Roberts and Justice Kavanaugh, rather than by originalist purists, and thus a longstanding precedent like *Harper* seems safe from overruling no matter how

* The Seventeenth Amendment contains this same language with respect to U.S. Senate elections.

contrary to originalism it might be. But who knows for sure?) As the case after *Harper*, *Kramer v. Union Free School Dist. No. 15*, demonstrates, *Harper* was part of a series of cases that the Warren Court decided in the 1960s concerning the right to vote. These cases, which included the "one person, one vote" doctrine of *Reynolds v. Sims* and related reapportionment decisions, gave voting rights strict federal constitutional protections. The U.S. Supreme Court, even as it has become successively more conservative, has repeatedly reaffirmed—and even extended—the Warren Court's voting rights jurisprudence. As you will see, *Bush v. Gore* cites *Harper* and *Reynolds* as the key precedents for its own Equal Protection holding. Thus, unlike some Warren Court precedents in other areas of constitutional law, few Court-watchers think that *Harper* (or *Kramer*) is vulnerable to overruling—although the Court may tinker with the application of these precedents (as the Court arguably did in the voter ID case you will soon read).

Harper v. Virginia State Board of Elections

383 U.S. 663 (1966)

[Virginia law imposed a $1.50 annual poll tax on all citizens of voting age. Failure to pay the poll tax disqualified a person from voting. The revenue from the tax was used to pay for public schools and other local government functions. Suit was brought in federal district court to declare the poll tax unconstitutional under the Equal Protection Clause of the Fourteenth Amendment. The suit was dismissed on the authority of *Breedlove v. Suttles*, 302 U.S. 277 (1937), which had rejected an Equal Protection challenge to a state poll tax. Plaintiffs appealed directly to the Supreme Court.]

Justice DOUGLAS delivered the opinion of the Court.

We conclude that a State violates the Equal Protection Clause whenever it makes the affluence of the voter or payment of any fee an electoral standard. Voter qualifications have no relation to wealth nor to paying or not paying this or any other tax.

Long ago in *Yick Wo v. Hopkins* (1886), the Court referred to "the political franchise of voting" as a "fundamental political right, because preservative of all rights." Recently in *Reynolds v. Sims* (1964), we said, "Undoubtedly, the right of suffrage is a fundamental matter in a free and democratic society. Especially since the right to exercise the franchise in a free and unimpaired manner is preservative of other basic civil and political rights, any alleged infringement of the right of citizens to vote must be carefully and meticulously scrutinized." There we were considering charges that voters in one part of the State had greater representation per person in the State Legislature than voters in another part of the State. We concluded: "A citizen, a qualified voter, is no more nor no less so because he lives in the city or on the farm."

We say the same whether the citizen, otherwise qualified to vote, has $1.50 in his pocket or nothing at all, pays the fee or fails to pay it. The principle that denies the State the right to dilute a citizen's vote on account of his economic status or other such factors by analogy bars a system which excludes those unable to pay a fee to vote or who fail to pay.

It is argued that a State may exact fees from citizens for many different kinds of licenses; that if it can demand from all an equal fee for a driver's license, it can demand from all an equal poll tax for voting. But we must remember that the interest of the State, when it comes to voting, is limited to the power to fix qualifications. Wealth, like race, creed, or color, is not germane to one's ability to participate intelligently in the electoral process. Lines drawn on the basis of wealth or property, like those of race, are traditionally disfavored. To introduce wealth or payment of a fee as a measure of a voter's qualifications is to introduce a capricious or irrelevant factor. The degree of the discrimination is irrelevant. In this context that is, as a condition of obtaining a ballot the requirement of fee paying causes an "invidious" discrimination that runs afoul of the Equal Protection Clause. Levy "by the poll," as stated in *Breedlove v. Suttles* is an old familiar form of taxation; and we say nothing to impair its validity so long as it is not made a condition to the exercise of the franchise. *Breedlove v. Suttles* sanctioned its use as "a prerequisite of voting." To that extent the *Breedlove* case is overruled.

We agree, of course, with Mr. Justice Holmes that the Due Process Clause of the Fourteenth Amendment "does not enact Mr. Herbert Spencer's Social Statics" (*Lochner v. People of State of New York* [(1905)]). Likewise, the Equal Protection Clause is not shackled to the political theory of a particular era. In determining what lines are unconstitutionally discriminatory, we have never been confined to historic notions of equality, any more than we have restricted due process to a fixed catalogue of what was at a given time deemed to be the limits of fundamental rights. Notions of what constitutes equal treatment for purposes of the Equal Protection Clause do change. This Court in 1896 held that laws providing for separate public facilities for white and Negro citizens did not deprive the latter of the equal protection and treatment that the Fourteenth Amendment commands. *Plessy v. Ferguson* [(1896)]. When, in 1954 more than a half-century later we repudiated the "separate-but-equal" doctrine of *Plessy* as respects public education we stated: "In approaching this problem, we cannot turn the clock back to 1868 when the Amendment was adopted, or even to 1896 when *Plessy v. Ferguson* was written." *Brown v. Board of Education* [(1954)].

We have long been mindful that where fundamental rights and liberties are asserted under the Equal Protection Clause, classifications which might invade or restrain them must be closely scrutinized and carefully confined. *See, e.g., Skinner v. State of Oklahoma,* [(1942)].

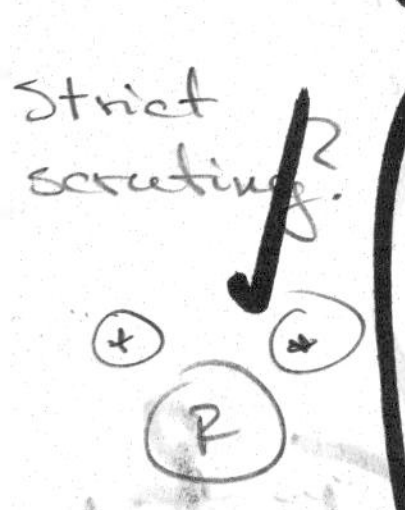

Those principles apply here. For to repeat, wealth or fee paying has, in our view, no relation to voting qualifications; the right to vote is too precious, too fundamental to be so burdened or conditioned.

Reversed.

Mr. Justice HARLAN, whom Mr. Justice STEWART joins, dissenting.

The final demise of state poll taxes, already totally proscribed by the Twenty-Fourth Amendment with respect to federal elections and abolished by the States themselves in all but four States with respect to state elections,[8] is perhaps in itself not of great moment. But that fact that the coup de grace has been administered

8. Alabama, Mississippi, Texas, and Virginia.

by this Court instead of being left to the affected States or to the federal political process should be a matter of continuing concern to all interested in maintaining the proper role of this tribunal under our scheme of government.

My disagreement with the present decision is that in holding the Virginia poll tax violative of the Equal Protection Clause the Court has departed from long-established standards governing the application of that clause.

The Equal Protection Clause prevents States from arbitrarily treating people differently under their laws. Whether any such differing treatment is to be deemed arbitrary depends on whether or not it reflects an appropriate differentiating classification among those affected; the clause has never been thought to require equal treatment of all persons despite differing circumstances. The test evolved by this Court for determining whether an asserted justifying classification exists is whether such a classification can be deemed to be founded on some rational and otherwise constitutionally permissible state policy. This standard reduces to a minimum the likelihood that the federal judiciary will judge state policies in terms of the individual notions and predilections of its own members, and until recently it has been followed in all kinds of "equal protection" cases.

Reynolds v. Sims, among its other breaks with the past, also marked a departure from these traditional and wise principles. Unless its "one man, one vote" thesis of state legislative apportionment is to be attributed to the unsupportable proposition that "Equal Protection" simply means indiscriminate equality, it seems inescapable that what *Reynolds* really reflected was but this Court's own views of how modern American representative government should be run. For it can hardly be thought that no other method of apportionment may be considered rational.

[T]oday in holding unconstitutional state poll taxes and property qualifications for voting and overruling *Breedlove v. Suttles*, the Court [continues] the highly subjective judicial approach manifested by *Reynolds*. In substance the Court's analysis of the equal protection issue goes no further than to say that the electoral franchise is "precious" and "fundamental," and to conclude that "(t)o introduce wealth or payment of a fee as a measure of a voter's qualifications is to introduce a capricious or irrelevant factor." These are of course captivating phrases, but they are wholly inadequate to satisfy the standard governing adjudication of the equal protection issue: Is there a rational basis for Virginia's poll tax as a voting qualification? I think the answer to that question is undoubtedly "yes."

Property qualifications and poll taxes have been a traditional part of our political structure. [W]ith property qualifications, it is only by fiat that it can be said, especially in the context of American history, that there can be no rational debate as to their advisability. Most of the early Colonies had them; many of the States have had them during much of their histories; and, whether one agrees or not, arguments have been and still can be made in favor of them. For example, it is certainly a rational argument that payment of some minimal poll tax promotes civic responsibility, weeding out those who do not care enough about public affairs to pay $1.50 or thereabouts a year for the exercise of the franchise. It is also arguable, indeed it was probably accepted as sound political theory by a large percentage of Americans through most of our history, that people with some property have a deeper stake in community affairs, and are consequently more responsible, more educated, more knowledgeable, more worthy of confidence, than those without means, and that the community and Nation would be better managed if the franchise were restricted to such citizens. Nondiscriminatory and fairly applied literacy tests, upheld by this Court in *Lassiter v. Northampton County Board of Elections* (1959), find justification on very similar grounds.

These viewpoints, to be sure, ring hollow on most contemporary ears. Their lack of acceptance today is evidenced by the fact that nearly all of the States, left to their own devices, have eliminated property or poll-tax qualifications; by the cognate fact that Congress and three-quarters of the States quickly ratified the Twenty-Fourth Amendment.

Property and poll-tax qualifications, very simply, are not in accord with current egalitarian notions of how a modern democracy should be organized. It is of course entirely fitting that legislatures should modify the law to reflect such changes in popular attitudes. However, it is all wrong, in my view, for the Court to adopt the political doctrines popularly accepted at a particular moment of our history and to declare all others to be irrational and invidious, barring them from the range of choice by reasonably minded people acting through the political process. It was not too long ago that Mr. Justice Holmes felt impelled to remind the Court that the Due Process Clause of the Fourteenth Amendment does not enact the laissez-faire theory of society, *Lochner v. People of State of New York.* The times have changed, and perhaps it is appropriate to observe that neither does the Equal Protection Clause of that Amendment rigidly impose upon America an ideology of unrestrained egalitarianism.

Mr. Justice BLACK, dissenting.

[Justice Black dissented for essentially the same reasons that Justices Harlan and Stewart did. He added these points:]

All voting laws treat some persons differently from others in some respects. Some bar a person from voting who is under 21 years of age; others bar those under 18. Some bar convicted felons or the insane, and some have attached a freehold or other property qualification for voting. And in *Lassiter v. Northampton Election Board* (1959)], this Court held that state laws which disqualified the illiterate from voting did not violate the Equal Protection Clause. [I]t is clear that some discriminatory voting qualifications can be imposed without violating the Equal Protection Clause.

Another reason for my dissent from the Court's judgment and opinion is that it seems to be using the old "natural-law-due-process formula" to justify striking down state laws as violations of the Equal Protection Clause. I have heretofore had many occasions to express my strong belief that there is no constitutional support whatever for this Court to use the Due Process Clause as though it provided a blank check to alter the meaning of the Constitution as written so as to add to it substantive constitutional changes which a majority of the Court at any given time believes are needed to meet present-day problems. If basic changes as to the respective powers of the state and national governments are needed, I prefer to let those changes be made by amendment as Article V of the Constitution provides. For a majority of this Court to undertake that task, whether purporting to do so under the Due Process or the Equal Protection Clause amounts, in my judgment, to an exercise of power the Constitution makers with foresight and wisdom refused to give the Judicial Branch of the Government.

The Court denies that it is using the "natural-law-due-process formula." I find no statement in the Court's opinion, however, which advances even a plausible argument as to why the alleged discriminations which might possibly be effected by

Virginia's poll tax law are "irrational," "unreasonable," "arbitrary," or "invidious" or have no relevance to a legitimate policy which the State wishes to adopt. The Court gives no reason at all to discredit the long-standing beliefs that making the payment of a tax a prerequisite to voting is an effective way of collecting revenue and that people who pay their taxes are likely to have a far greater interest in their government. The Court's failure to give any reasons to show that these purposes of the poll tax are "irrational," "unreasonable," "arbitrary," or "invidious" is a pretty clear indication to me that none exist. I can only conclude that the primary, controlling, predominate, if not the exclusive reason for declaring the Virginia law unconstitutional is the Court's deep-seated hostility and antagonism, which I share, to making payment of a tax a prerequisite to voting.

The Court's justification for consulting its own notions rather than following the original meaning of the Constitution, as I would, apparently is based on the belief of the majority of the Court that for this Court to be bound by the original meaning of the Constitution is an intolerable and debilitating evil; that our Constitution should not be "shackled to the political theory of a particular era," and that to save the country from the original Constitution the Court must have constant power to renew it and keep it abreast of this Court's more enlightening theories of what is best for our society. It seems to me that this is an attack not only on the great value of our Constitution itself but also on the concept of a written constitution which is to survive through the years as originally written unless changed through the amendment process which the Framers wisely provided. Moreover, when a "political theory" embodied in our Constitution becomes outdated, it seems to me that a majority of the nine members of this Court are not only without constitutional power but are far less qualified to choose a new constitutional political theory than the people of this country proceeding in the manner provided by Article V.

The people have not found it impossible to amend their Constitution to meet new conditions. The Equal Protection Clause itself is the product of the people's desire to use their constitutional power to amend the Constitution to meet new problems. Moreover, the people, in § 5 of the Fourteenth Amendment, designated the governmental tribunal they wanted to provide additional rules to enforce the guarantees of that Amendment. The branch of Government they chose was not the Judicial Branch but the Legislative. I have no doubt at all that Congress has the power under § 5 to pass legislation to abolish the poll tax in order to protect the citizens of this country if it believes that the poll tax is being used as a device to deny voters equal protection of the laws.

Kramer v. Union Free School District No. 15

395 U.S. 621 (1969)

Mr. Chief Justice WARREN delivered the opinion of the Court.

In this case we are called on to determine whether § 2012 of the New York Education Law is constitutional. The legislation provides that in certain New York school districts residents who are otherwise eligible to vote in state and federal elections may vote in the school district election only if they (1) own (or lease) taxable real property within the district, or (2) are parents (or have custody of) children enrolled in the local public schools. Appellant, a bachelor who neither owns nor leases taxable real property, filed suit in federal court claiming that § 2012 denied him equal protection of the laws in violation of the Fourteenth Amendment. With one judge dissenting, a three-judge District Court dismissed appellant's complaint. Finding that § 2012 does violate the Equal Protection Clause of the Fourteenth Amendment, we reverse.

At the outset, it is important to note what is not at issue in this case. The requirements of § 2012 that school district voters must (1) be citizens of the United States, (2) be bona fide residents of the school district, and (3) be at least 21 years of age are not challenged. Appellant agrees that the States have the power to impose reasonable citizenship, age, and residency requirements on the availability of the ballot. The sole issue in this case is whether the additional requirements of § 2012, which prohibit some district residents who are otherwise qualified by age and citizenship from participating in district meetings and school board elections, violate equal protection.

"In determining whether or not a state law violates the Equal Protection Clause, we must consider the facts and circumstances behind the law, the interests which the State claims to be protecting, and the interests of those who are disadvantaged by the classification." *Williams v. Rhodes* (1968). And, in this case, we must give the statute a close and exacting examination. "(S)ince the right to exercise the franchise in a free and unimpaired manner is preservative of other basic civil and political rights, any alleged infringement of the right of citizens to vote must be carefully and meticulously scrutinized." *Reynolds v. Sims* (1964). This careful examination is necessary because statutes distributing the franchise constitute the foundation of our representative society. Any unjustified discrimination in determining who may participate in political affairs or in the selection of public officials undermines the legitimacy of representative government.

Thus, state apportionment statutes, which may dilute the effectiveness of some citizens' votes, receive close scrutiny from this Court. No less rigid an examination is applicable to statutes denying the franchise to citizens who are otherwise qualified by residence and age. Statutes granting the franchise to residents on a selective basis always pose the danger of denying some citizens any effective voice in the governmental affairs which substantially affect their lives. Therefore, if a challenged state statute grants the right to vote to some bona fide residents of requisite age and citizenship and denies the franchise to others, the Court must determine whether the exclusions are necessary to promote a compelling state interest.

And, for these reasons, the deference usually given to the judgment of legislators does not extend to decisions concerning which resident citizens may participate in the election of legislators and other public officials. Those decisions must be carefully scrutinized by the Court to determine whether each resident citizen has, as far as is possible, an equal voice in the selections. Accordingly, when we are reviewing statutes which deny some residents the right to vote, the general presumption of constitutionality afforded state statutes and the traditional approval given state classifications if the Court can conceive of a "rational basis" for the distinctions made are not applicable. *See Harper v. Virginia State Bd. of Elections* (1966). The presumption of constitutionality and the approval given "rational" classifications in other types of enactments are based on an assumption that the institutions of state government are structured so as to represent fairly all the people. However, when the challenge to the statute is in effect a challenge of this basic assumption, the assumption can no longer serve as the basis for presuming constitutionality. And, the assumption is no less under attack because the legislature which decides who may participate at the various levels of political choice is fairly elected. Legislation which delegates decision making to bodies elected by only a portion of those eligible to vote for the legislature can cause unfair representation. Such legislation can exclude a minority of voters from any voice in the decisions just as effectively as if the decisions were made by legislators the minority had no voice in selecting.

The need for exacting judicial scrutiny of statutes distributing the franchise is undiminished simply because, under a different statutory scheme, the offices subject to election might have been filled through appointment. States do have latitude in determining whether certain public officials shall be selected by election or chosen by appointment and whether various questions shall be submitted to the voters. In fact, we have held that where a county school board is an administrative, not legislative, body, its members need not be elected. *Sailors v. Kent County Bd. of Education* (1967). However, "once the franchise is granted to the electorate, lines may not be drawn which are inconsistent with the Equal Protection Clause of the Fourteenth Amendment." *Harper.*

Nor is the need for close judicial examination affected because the district meetings and the school board do not have "general" legislative powers. Our exacting examination is not necessitated by the subject of the election; rather, it is required because some resident citizens are permitted to participate and some are not. For example, a city charter might well provide that the elected city council appoint a mayor who would have broad administrative powers. Assuming the council were elected consistent with the commands of the Equal Protection Clause, the delegation of power to the mayor would not call for this Court's exacting review. On the other hand, if the city charter made the office of mayor subject to an election in which only some resident citizens were entitled to vote, there would be presented a situation calling for our close review.

Besides appellant and others who similarly live in their parents' homes, the statute also disenfranchises the following persons (unless they are parents or guardians of children enrolled in the district public school): senior citizens and others living with children or relatives; clergy, military personnel, and others who live on tax-exempt property; boarders and lodgers; parents who neither own nor lease qualifying property and whose children are too young to attend school; parents who neither own nor lease qualifying property and whose children attend private schools.

Appellant asserts that excluding him from participation in the district elections denies him equal protection of the laws. He contends that he and others of his class are substantially interested in and significantly affected by the school meeting decisions. All members of the community have an interest in the quality and structure of public education, appellant says, and he urges that "the decisions taken by local boards . . . may have grave consequences to the entire population." Appellant also argues that the level of property taxation affects him, even though he does not own property, as property tax levels affect the price of goods and services in the community.

We turn therefore to question whether the exclusion is necessary to promote a compelling state interest. First appellees argue that the State has a legitimate interest in limiting the franchise in school district elections to "members of the community of interest"—those "primarily interested in such elections." Second, appellees urge that the State may reasonably and permissibly conclude that "property taxpayers" (including lessees of taxable property who share the tax burden through rent payments) and parents of the children enrolled in the district's schools are those "primarily interested" in school affairs.

We do not understand appellees to argue that the State is attempting to limit the franchise to those "subjectively concerned" about school matters. Rather, they appear to argue that the State's legitimate interest is in restricting a voice in school matters to those "directly affected" by such decisions. The State apparently reasons that since the schools are financed in part by local property taxes, persons whose out-of-pocket expenses are "directly" affected by property tax changes should be allowed to vote. Similarly, parents of children in school are thought to have a "direct" stake in school affairs and are given a vote.

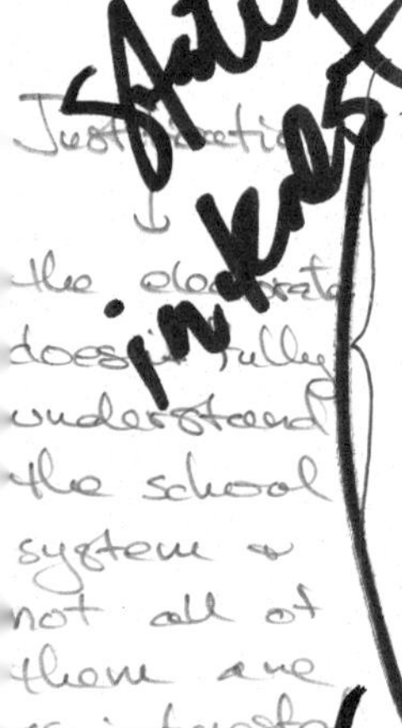

Appellees argue that it is necessary to limit the franchise to those "primarily interested" in school affairs because "the ever increasing complexity of the many interacting phases of the school system and structure make it extremely difficult for the electorate fully to understand the whys and wherefores of the detailed operations of the school system." Appellees say that many communications of school boards and school administrations are sent home to the parents through the district pupils and are "not broadcast to the general public"; thus, nonparents will be less informed than parents. Further, appellees argue, those who are assessed for local property taxes (either directly or indirectly through rent) will have enough of an interest "through the burden on their pocketbooks, to acquire such information as they may need."

We need express no opinion as to whether the State in some circumstances might limit the exercise of the franchise to those "primarily interested" or "primarily affected." Of course, we therefore do not reach the issue of whether these particular elections are of the type in which the franchise may be so limited. For, assuming, arguendo, that New York legitimately might limit the franchise in these school district elections to those "primarily interested in school affairs," close scrutiny of the § 2012 classifications demonstrates that they do not accomplish this purpose with sufficient precision to justify denying appellant the franchise.

Whether classifications allegedly limiting the franchise to those resident citizens "primarily interested" deny those excluded equal protection of the laws depends, inter alia, on whether all those excluded are in fact substantially less interested or affected than those the statute includes. In other words, the classifications must be tailored so that the exclusion of appellant and members of his class is necessary to achieve the articulated state goal.[14] Section 2012 does not meet the exacting standard of precision we require of statutes which selectively distribute the franchise. The classifications in § 2012 permit inclusion of many persons who

14. Of course, if the exclusions are necessary to promote the articulated state interest, we must then determine whether the interest promoted by limiting the franchise constitutes a compelling state interest. We do not reach that issue in this case.

have, at best, a remote and indirect interest, in school affairs and, on the other hand, exclude others who have a distinct and direct interest in the school meeting decisions.[15]

Nor do appellees offer any justification for the exclusion of seemingly interested and informed residents—other than to argue that the § 2012 classifications include those "whom the State could understandably deem to be the most intimately interested in actions taken by the school board," and urge that "the task of . . . balancing the interest of the community in the maintenance of orderly school district elections against the interest of any individual in voting in such elections should clearly remain with the Legislature." But the issue is not whether the legislative judgments are rational. A more exacting standard obtains. The issue is whether the § 2012 requirements do in fact sufficiently further a compelling state interest to justify denying the franchise to appellant and members of his class. The requirements of § 2012 are not sufficiently tailored to limiting the franchise to those "primarily interested" in school affairs to justify the denial of the franchise to appellant and members of his class.

Mr. Justice STEWART, with whom Mr. Justice BLACK, and Mr. Justice HARLAN join, dissenting.

[T]he appellant explicitly concedes, as he must, the validity of voting requirements relating to residence, literacy, and age. Yet he argues—and the Court accepts the argument—that the voting qualifications involved here somehow have a different constitutional status. I am unable to see the distinction.

Clearly a State may reasonably assume that its residents have a greater stake in the outcome of elections held within its boundaries than do other persons. Likewise, it is entirely rational for a state legislature to suppose that residents, being generally better informed regarding state affairs than are nonresidents, will be more likely than nonresidents to vote responsibly. And the same may be said of legislative assumptions regarding the electoral competence of adults and literate persons on the one hand, and of minors and illiterates on the other. It is clear, of course, that lines thus drawn can not infallibly perform their intended legislative function. Just as illiterate people may be intelligent voters, nonresidents or minors might also in some instances be interested, informed, and intelligent participants in the electoral process. Persons who commute across a state line to work may well have a great stake in the affairs of the State in which they are employed; some college students under 21 may be both better informed and more passionately interested in political affairs than many adults. But such discrepancies are the inevitable concomitant of the line-drawing that is essential to law making. So long as the classification is rationally related to a permissible legislative end, therefore—as are residence, literacy, and age requirements imposed with respect to voting—there is no denial of equal protection.

15. For example, appellant resides with his parents in the school district, pays state and federal taxes and is interested in and affected by school board decisions; however, he has no vote. On the other hand, an uninterested unemployed young man who pays no state or federal taxes, but who rents an apartment in the district, can participate in the election.

Thus judged, the statutory classification involved here seems to me clearly to be valid. New York has made the judgment that local educational policy is best left to those persons who have certain direct and definable interests in that policy: those who are either immediately involved as parents of school children or who, as owners or lessees of taxable property are burdened with the local cost of funding school district operations. True, persons outside those classes may be genuinely interested in the conduct of a school district's business—just as commuters from New Jersey may be genuinely interested in the outcome of a New York City election. But unless this Court is to claim a monopoly of wisdom regarding the sound operation of school systems in the 50 States, I see no way to justify the conclusion that the legislative classification involved here is not rationally related to a legitimate legislative purpose.

With good reason, the Court does not really argue the contrary. Instead, it strikes down New York's statute by asserting that the traditional equal protection standard is inapt in this case, and that a considerably stricter standard—under which classifications relating to "the franchise" are to be subjected to "exacting judicial scrutiny"—should be applied. But the asserted justification for applying such a standard cannot withstand analysis.

The Court is quite explicit in explaining why it believes this statute should be given "close scrutiny":

> "The presumption of constitutionality and the approval given 'rational' classifications in other types of enactments are based on an assumption that the institutions of state government are structured so as to represent fairly all the people. However, when the challenge to the statute is in effect a challenge of this basic assumption, the assumption can no longer serve as the basis for presuming constitutionality." (Footnote omitted.)

I am at a loss to understand how such reasoning is at all relevant to the present case. The voting qualifications at issue have been promulgated, not by Union Free School District No. 15, but by the New York State Legislature, and the appellant is of course fully able to participate in the election of representatives in that body. There is simply no claim whatever here that the state government is not "structured so as to represent fairly all the people," including the appellant.

Nor is there any other jurisdiction for imposing the Court's "exacting" equal protection test. This case does not involve racial classifications, which in light of the genesis of the Fourteenth Amendment have traditionally been viewed as inherently "suspect." And this statute is not one that impinges upon a constitutionally protected right, and that consequently can be justified only by a "compelling" state interest. For "the Constitution of the United States does not confer the right of suffrage upon any one. . . ." *Minor v. Happerset* [(1875)].

In any event, it seems to me that under any equal protection standard, short of a doctrinaire insistence that universal suffrage is somehow mandated by the Constitution, the appellant's claim must be rejected. First of all, it must be emphasized despite the Court's undifferentiated references to what it terms "the franchise" that we are dealing here, not with a general election, but with a limited, special purpose

Statute satisfies RB

Appellant can vote for those who oversee the school board, the Legislature

This is not an important election

election.[9] The appellant is eligible to vote in all state, local, and federal elections in which general governmental policy is determined. He is fully able, therefore, to participate not only in the processes by which the requirements for school district voting may be changed, but also in those by which the levels of state and federal financial assistance to the District are determined. He clearly is not locked into any self-perpetuating status of exclusion from the electoral process.

Secondly, the appellant is of course limited to asserting his own rights, not the purported rights of hypothetical childless clergymen or parents of preschool children, who neither own nor rent taxable property. The appellant's status is merely that of a citizen who says he is interested in the affairs of his local public schools. If the Constitution requires that he must be given a decision-making role in the governance of those affairs, then it seems to me that any individual who seeks such a role must be given it.

This will open the doors for everyone to vote

2. *Discrimination in Voting Rights Based on Age or Mental Infirmity*

Just how extensive is the federal constitutional protection of the right to vote? Would it limit a state's power to deny the right to vote to individuals adjudicated to be mentally incompetent, by reason of either severe mental retardation or severe mental illness? *See, e.g.*, *In Matter of Absentee Ballots Cast by Five Residents of Trenton Psychiatric Hospital*, 750 A.2d 790 (2000) (Superior Court of New Jersey, Appellate Division). This issue is not merely theoretical. It has increasingly practical importance in the specific context of senility and voting by nursing home patients, as the large "baby boomer" generation becomes elderly. Obviously a sensitive subject, the question still must be asked whether the Fourteenth Amendment would limit a state's effort to prevent ballots cast on behalf of mentally incompetent nursing home residents, who might be manipulated by staff or others to vote in ways they would not want or do not understand. Conversely, voting rights groups are becoming increasingly assertive about the right of the cognitively impaired to cast a ballot. *See* Paula Span, *Having Dementia Doesn't Mean You Can't Vote*, N.Y. TIMES (Oct. 14, 2020); ABA, *Assisting Cognitively Impaired Individuals with Voting: a Quick Guide*, https://www.americanbar.org/content/dam/aba/administrative/law_aging/2020-voting-guide.pdf.

A related but separate issue arose during the pandemic election of 2020: Some states have laws that permit voters over a certain age to cast an absentee ballot just because of their age, while younger voters need a different justification under

9. Special-purpose governmental authorities such as water, lighting, and sewer districts exist in various sections of the country, and participation in such districts is undoubtedly limited in many instances to those who partake of the agency's services and are assessed for its expenses. The constitutional validity of such a policy is, it seems to me, unquestionable. And while it is true, as the appellant argues, that a school system has a more pervasive influence in the community than do most other such special-purpose authorities, I cannot agree that that difference in degree presents anything approaching a distinction of constitutional dimension.

state law to cast an absentee ballot (illness, disability, or business travel, for example). Is this differential access to an absentee ballot based solely on age a form of unconstitutional discrimination, either under the Equal Protection Clause of the Fourteenth Amendment or the Twenty-Sixth Amendment? The latter amendment, adopted during the Vietnam War (based on a belief that it was unfair to deny soldiers the right to vote), explicitly provides: "The right of citizens of the United States, who are eighteen years of age or older, to vote shall not be denied or abridged by the United States or by any State on account of age."

In litigation leading up to the November 2020 election, both the Fifth and Seventh Circuits rejected claims that this kind of law violates the Twenty-Sixth Amendment. The Seventh Circuit quickly dismissed the claim, stating "the fundamental right to vote means the ability to cast a ballot, but not the right to do so in a voter's preferred manner, such as by mail." *Tully v. Okeson*, 977 F.3d 608, 613 (7th Cir. 2020). The Seventh Circuit rejected the analogy that to deny women or Blacks the same right to cast an absentee ballot as men or Whites means that age-based discrimination accessing an absentee ballot must be equally unconstitutional, given that the Twenty-Sixth Amendment functions similarly to the Fifteenth and Nineteenth Amendments:

> Plaintiffs retort that this conclusion is wrong because hypothetical laws similarly restricting the ability of African Americans or women or the poor to vote by mail would violate the Fifteenth, Nineteenth, and Twenty-Fourth Amendments, respectively. Plaintiffs are correct that such laws could be subject to heightened scrutiny for "operat[ing] to the peculiar disadvantage of a suspect class." *Mass. Bd. of Ret. v. Murgia*, 427 U.S. 307, 312 (1976). But this scrutiny would come from the Fourteenth Amendment's Equal Protection Clause. *Am. Party of Tex. v. White*, 415 U.S. 767, 795 (1974) ("[P]ermitting absentee voting by some classes of voters and denying the privilege to other classes . . . is an arbitrary discrimination violative of the *Equal Protection Clause.*" (emphasis added)). It would *not* come from the Fifteenth, Nineteenth, or Twenty-Fourth Amendments because Plaintiffs' hypothetical laws do not implicate the right to vote. Plaintiffs' rebuttal thus bears no weight.

The Fifth Circuit essentially reached the same conclusion, but its reasoning was much more elaborate; here's just an excerpt:

> To abridge is "[t]o reduce or diminish." Evaluating whether there has been a *denial* of a right will rarely involve a comparison. On the other hand, "[i]t makes no sense to suggest that a voting practice 'abridges' the right to vote without some baseline with which to compare the practice." *Reno v. Bossier Parish Sch. Bd.*, 528 U.S. 320, 334 (2000).
>
> The plaintiffs insist that an abridgment occurs any time a new election law makes voting more difficult for one age group than it is for another. Under that construct, when Texas in 1975 legislated a privilege for older voters to cast absentee votes without needing to claim a reason such as being out of the county, it abridged younger voters' rights even though no change was made as to them. In essence, a new baseline for voting arises with each new election rule. If some category of voters

has more limited rights after the change in comparison to other categories, an abridgement has occurred.

Our first reaction is that this seems an implausible reading of "abridge." Conceptually, plaintiffs are converting the Twenty-Sixth Amendment into the positive assertion that voting rights must be identical for all age groups at all times. Any indulgence solely for one age group of voters would fail; voters of all ages must get the same indulgence. The Amendment, though, is a prohibition against adopting rules based on age that deny or abridge the rights voters already have. Indeed, neither the Twenty-Sixth Amendment nor the related amendments we have been discussing are written in terms of granting a positive right to vote. Instead, they each are phrased in the negative, namely, that the right to vote shall not be denied or abridged based on the relevant reason. More consistent with the text of the Twenty-Sixth Amendment is for us to evaluate whether younger voters' rights were reduced by the addition of a privilege for older voters.

The point just made, though, needs to take into account a possible exception. We return to the *Bossier Parish* decision concerning the Fifteenth Amendment. The Court stated that "abridging" for purposes of the Fifteenth Amendment refers to discrimination more generally, not just to retrogression. That certainly makes sense, as litigation under the Fifteenth Amendment went far beyond just challenging recent changes but sought to dismantle longstanding discrimination in voting.

Even if this concept applies to the Twenty-Sixth Amendment, *i.e.*, that abridging goes beyond just looking at the change but also at the validity of the state's voting rules generally, we see no basis to hold that Texas's absentee-voting rules as a whole are something that ought not to be.

Rejecting the plaintiffs' arguments, we hold that an election law abridges a person's right to vote for the purposes of the Twenty-Sixth Amendment only if it makes voting *more difficult* for that person than it was before the law was enacted or enforced. As the Court has held, the "core meaning" of "abridge" is to "shorten," and shortening "necessarily entails a comparison." *Bossier Parish*, 528 U.S. at 333-34. Abridgment of the right to vote applies to laws that place a barrier or prerequisite to voting, or otherwise make it more difficult to vote, relative to the baseline.

On the other hand, a law that makes it *easier* for others to vote does not abridge any person's right to vote for the purposes of the Twenty-Sixth Amendment. That is not to say that a state may always enact such a law, but it does not violate the Twenty-Sixth Amendment.

Sophisticated attempts to circumvent this rule could arise. The Supreme Court, though, has these constitutional amendments "nullif[y] sophisticated as well as simple-minded modes of impairing the right guaranteed." *See Forssenius*, 380 U.S. at 540-41, 85 S. Ct. 1177 (quotation marks omitted). Courts will be able to respond properly to any artful efforts.

Texas Democratic Party v. Abbott, 978 F.3d 168, 188-92 (5th Cir. 2020), *cert. denied*, 141 S. Ct. 1124, 208 L. Ed. 2d 562 (2021).

Neither the Seventh nor Fifth Circuit opinions provoked a dissent, and for procedural reasons neither addressed the parallel claim of unconstitutional age discrimination under the Fourteenth Amendment. (The Seventh Circuit considered the discrimination under the rational basis test, finding the discrimination rational, but refused to consider whether heightened scrutiny applied either because voting rights were involved or because the discrimination was based on age, or both.) Do you find the reasoning of these two courts persuasive? Do you think the Supreme Court would affirm if it were to consider the issue? If the American people wanted to give all voters an equal right to cast an absentee ballot regardless of age, what constitutional language should be employed beyond the text of the Twenty-Sixth Amendment?

3. Felon Disenfranchisement

Historically, most states have denied the right to vote to their citizens who have been convicted of a felony, at least during the time in which they are serving their prison sentence.* As a result, more than 5 million U.S. citizens, who otherwise would be qualified to vote, are ineligible to do so.** Because of growing concern about the effects of "mass incarceration" and the racially disparate impact of the nation's criminal justice system, the widespread practice of felon disenfranchisement has come under attack in the past decade, and the trend has developed to reverse these longstanding policies.

The federal Constitution, in section two of the Fourteenth Amendment, explicitly permits states to deny their citizens the right to vote because of a felony conviction. The U.S. Supreme Court has specifically confirmed this point of constitutional law. *Richardson v. Ramirez*, 418 U.S. 24 (1974). The Court has also made clear that a state may not adopt a felony disenfranchisement rule for the *purpose* of denying equal opportunities to vote on the basis of race; that kind of intentional racial discrimination would violate both the Fifteenth Amendment and the Equal Protection Clause of the Fourteenth Amendment. But the Court has not specifically considered whether the racially discriminatory *effect* of a felon disenfranchisement law violates section 2 of the Voting Rights Act. The lower federal courts, however, have treated felon disenfranchisement laws immune from invalidation under the "results" test of VRA's section 2 (although there has been considerable disagreement among lower-court judges on this point, including the proper analysis to apply). The leading case on this point follows; *see also Simmons v. Galvin*, 575 F.3d 24, 41 (1st Cir. 2009); *Farrakhan v. Gregoire*, 623 F.3d 990 (9th Cir. 2010) (en banc); *Johnson v. Governor*, 405 F.3d 2014 (11th Cir. 2005).

* Only Maine, Vermont, and D.C. do not disenfranchise felons even while they are serving their prison term. The National Conference of State Legislatures (NCSL) collects the relevant laws: https://www.ncsl.org/research/elections-and-campaigns/felon-voting-rights.aspx.

** https://www.sentencingproject.org/issues/voting-rights/.

Hayden v. Pataki

449 F.3d 305 (2d Cir. 2006) (en banc)

José A. Cabranes, Circuit Judge.

We have granted en banc review in order to decide whether plaintiffs can state a claim for violation of Section 2 of the Voting Rights Act ("VRA"), 42 U.S.C. § 1973, based on allegations that a New York State statute that disenfranchises currently incarcerated felons and parolees, N.Y. Election Law § 5-106, results in unlawful vote denial and vote dilution.

We hold that the Voting Rights Act does not encompass these felon disenfranchisement provisions. Our holding is based on our conclusion that Congress did not intend or understand the Voting Rights Act to encompass such felon disenfranchisement statutes, that application of the Voting Rights Act to felon disenfranchisement statutes such as these would alter the constitutional balance between the States and the Federal Government, and that Congress at the very least did not clearly indicate that it intended the Voting Rights Act to alter the federal balance in this way.

I

Plaintiffs' amended complaint challenges "New York State's discriminatory practice of denying suffrage to persons who are incarcerated or on parole for a felony conviction and the resulting discriminatory impact that such denial of suffrage has on Blacks and Latinos in the State." Plaintiffs allege both vote denial and vote dilution claims under Section 2 of the Voting Rights Act.

[T]he District Court grant[ed] defendants' motion for judgment on the pleadings and dismiss[ed] all of plaintiffs' claims. [We affirm.]

II

A. Statutory Provisions

Section 5-106 of the New York Election Law provides that no person convicted of a felony "shall have the right to register for or vote at any election" unless he has been pardoned, his maximum sentence of imprisonment has expired, or he has been discharged from parole.

Felon disenfranchisement has a long history in New York. The New York State Constitution of 1821 authorized the state legislature to enact laws disenfranchising those convicted of "infamous crimes." The state legislature passed such a law the next year. This law, as revised, has been in effect in the State ever since. It was modified in 1971 to provide that those convicted of felonies would automatically regain the right to vote once their maximum sentence had been served or they had been discharged from parole. In 1973, New York again amended the statute to ensure that felons were only disenfranchised if they were sentenced to a term of imprisonment and not if they were sentenced to fines, probation, or conditional discharge.

Section 2 of the Voting Rights Act provides: "No voting qualification or prerequisite to voting or standard, practice, or procedure shall be imposed or applied by any State or political subdivision in a manner which results in a denial or abridgement of the right of any citizen of the United States to vote on account of race or color." 42 U.S.C. § 1973(a). Section 1973(b), originally enacted in 1982, states, in relevant part, that "[a] violation of subsection (a) . . . is established if, based on the totality of circumstances, it is shown that . . . members [of protected minority groups] have less opportunity than other members of the electorate to participate in the political process and to elect representatives of their choice."

The current language of § 1973 was enacted by Congress as part of the Voting Rights Act Amendments of 1982, largely in response to the Supreme Court's decision in *City of Mobile v. Bolden* (1980). In *Bolden,* a plurality of the Court held that racially neutral state action violates § 1973 only if it is motivated by a discriminatory purpose. The amended version of § 1973 eliminates this "discriminatory purpose" requirement and, instead, prohibits any voting qualification or standard that "results" in the denial of the right to vote "on account of" race.

B

[Omitted.]

C. Vote Denial

We confront the question whether the VRA applies to a claim that a prisoner disenfranchisement statute such as § 5-106, acting in combination with historic racial discrimination allegedly afflicting the New York criminal justice system as well as society at large, results in the denial to Black and Latino prisoners of the right to vote "on account of race or color." [W]e must first determine whether the Act applies to such statutes at all. If the VRA does not encompass such statutes, that would end our inquiry; if, conversely, we conclude that it may apply to felon disenfranchisement laws, we would then need to evaluate such an interpretation of the VRA in light of its implications for our constitutional jurisprudence and the structure of our federal system.

We thus consider the scope of § 1973. There is no question that the language of § 1973 is extremely broad—any "voting qualification or prerequisite to voting or standard, practice, or procedure" that adversely affects the right to vote—and could be read to include felon disenfranchisement provisions if the phrase is read without the benefit of context and background assumptions supplied by other statutory and Constitutional wording, by history, and by the manifestations of intent by Congress at the time of the VRA's enactment and thereafter.

We are not convinced that the use of broad language in the statute necessarily means that the statute is unambiguous with regard to its application to felon disenfranchisement laws. In any event, our interpretation of a statute is not in all circumstances limited to any apparent "plain meaning." As Justice Holmes has observed, "[i]t is said that when the meaning of language is plain we are not to resort to evidence in order to raise doubts. That is rather an axiom of experience than a rule of law, and does not preclude consideration of persuasive evidence if it exists." *Boston Sand & Gravel Co. v. United States* (1928). Here, there are persuasive reasons to believe that Congress did not intend to include felon disenfranchisement provisions within the coverage of the Voting Rights Act, and we must therefore look beyond the plain text of the statute in construing the reach of its provisions. These reasons include (1) the explicit approval given such laws in the Fourteenth Amendment; (2) the long history and continuing prevalence of felon disenfranchisement provisions throughout the United States; (3) the statements in the House and Senate Judiciary Committee Reports and on the Senate floor explicitly excluding felon disenfranchisement laws from provisions of the statute; (4) the absence of any affirmative consideration of felon disenfranchisement laws during either the 1965 passage of the Act or its 1982 revision; (5) the introduction thereafter of bills specifically intended to include felon disenfranchisement provisions within the VRA's coverage; (6) the enactment of a felon disenfranchisement statute for the District of Columbia by Congress soon after the passage of the Voting Rights Act; and (7) the subsequent passage of statutes designed to facilitate the removal of convicted felons from the voting rolls. We therefore conclude that § 1973 was not intended to—and thus does not—encompass felon disenfranchisement provisions.

D. Felon Disenfranchisement

The starting point for our analysis is the explicit approval given felon disenfranchisement provisions in the Constitution. Section 2 of the Fourteenth Amendment provides that "when the right to vote at any [federal] election . . . is denied to any of the male inhabitants of [a] State . . . or in any way abridged, *except for participation in rebellion, or other crime,* the basis of representation therein shall be reduced. . . ." U.S. CONST. amend. XIV, § 2 (emphasis added). The Supreme Court has ruled that, as a result of this language, felon disenfranchisement provisions are presumptively constitutional. *Richardson v. Ramirez* (1974) (rejecting a nonracial Equal Protection challenge to the felon disenfranchisement provision of California's constitution).

Indeed, the practice of disenfranchising those convicted of crimes is of ancient origin. Professor Mirjan R. Damaska of the Yale Law School, among others, has recounted that in ancient Athens, the penalty for certain crimes was placement in a state of "infamy," which entailed the loss of those rights that enabled a citizen to participate in public affairs, such as the rights to vote, to attend assemblies, to make speeches, and to hold public office. Mirjan R. Damaska, *Adverse Legal Consequences of Conviction and their Removal: A Comparative Study,* 59 J. Crim. L., Criminology & Police Sci. 347, 351 (1968). The Roman Republic also employed infamy as a penalty for those convicted of crimes involving moral turpitude. *Id.*

Similar laws disenfranchising felons were adopted in the American Colonies and the Early American Republic as well. [E]leven state constitutions adopted between 1776 and 1821 prohibited or authorized the legislature to prohibit exercise of the franchise by convicted felons, and twenty-nine states had such provisions when the Fourteenth Amendment was adopted in 1868. Today, likewise, every state except Maine and Vermont disenfranchises felons. As the Eleventh Circuit noted, "considering the prevalence of felon disenfranchisement [provisions] in every region of the country since the Founding, it seems unfathomable that Congress would silently amend the Voting Rights Act in a way that would affect them." *Johnson* [*v. Gov. of State of Florida* (11th Cir. 2005) (en banc)]. We now proceed to determine whether Congress in fact intended to do so.

E. Congressional Intent in the Voting Rights Act

The Voting Rights Act "was designed by Congress to banish the blight of racial discrimination in voting, which has infected the electoral process in parts of our country for nearly a century." *South Carolina v. Katzenbach* (1966). It is indisputable that the Congress intended "to give the Act the broadest possible scope." *Allen v. State Bd. of Elections* (1969).

We do not believe that this general intent answers the specific question regarding whether the Act covers felon disenfranchisement laws, as it is equally indisputable that Congress did not explicitly consider felon disenfranchisement laws to be covered by the Act and indeed affirmatively stated that such laws were *not* implicated by provisions of the statute. In discussing Section 4(c) of the Voting Rights Act, which banned any "test or device" that limited the ability to vote to those individuals with "good moral character," the Senate Judiciary Committee Report stated that the provision "would not result in the proscription of the frequent requirement of States and political subdivisions that an applicant for voting or registration for voting be free of conviction of a felony or mental disability." S. Rep. No. 89-162, at 24 (1965), *see also* H.R. Rep. No. 89-439, at 25-26 (1965), ("This subsection does not proscribe a requirement of a State or any political subdivision of a State that an applicant for voting or registration for voting be free of conviction of a felony or mental disability."). Senator Joseph D. Tydings of Maryland "emphasize[d]" on the Senate floor that Section 4(c) was not intended to prohibit "a requirement that an applicant for voting or registration for voting be free of conviction of a felony or mental disability. Those grounds for disqualification are objective, easily applied, and do not lend themselves to fraudulent manipulation." 111 Cong. Rec. S8366 (daily ed. April 23, 1965).

Though these statements were made in the context of a particular VRA provision not at issue here—the provision banning any "test or device"—it is apparent to us that Congress's effort to highlight the exclusion of felon disenfranchisement laws from a VRA provision that otherwise would likely be read to invalidate such laws is indicative of its broader intention to exclude such laws from the reach of the statute. Indeed, the emphatic language chosen to provide assurance that felon disenfranchisement laws remain unaffected by the statute suggests that these statements be read to indicate that "*not even this section* applies to felon disenfranchisement laws," rather than "*this section* does not apply to felon disenfranchisement laws, but other sections might," as plaintiffs argue.

Further indications that Congress in 1965 did not intend or understand the Voting Rights Act (or its subsequent amendments) to apply to felon disenfranchisement provisions come from the unsuccessful attempts in the early 1970s to amend the statute to apply to such provisions. Following hearings by the House Judiciary Committee in 1972 to address "The Problems of the Ex-Offender," several notable proponents of the VRA jointly introduced a bill designed "[t]o amend the Voting Rights Act of 1970 to prohibit the States from denying the right to vote in Federal elections to former criminal offenders who have not been convicted of any offense related to voting or elections and who are not confined in a correctional institution." H.R. 15049, 92d Cong. (1972). The bill was thus expressly intended to *amend* the Voting Rights Act to encompass the very laws that plaintiffs in the instant case insist were already covered by the 1965 Act. Apparently, no further action was taken on this bill.

In the next Congress, in 1973, Representative Kastenmeier, a supporter of the Voting Rights Act of 1965 and a "principal architect" of the re-authorization of the Voting Rights Act in 1968 as well as the enactment of the Civil Rights Act of 1964, introduced a new bill with the identical text. H.R. 9020, 93d Cong. (1973). A hearing on the proposed bill was entirely predicated on the understanding that the Voting Rights Act did not cover felon disenfranchisement laws. Accordingly, the hearing focused on whether such an amendment to the VRA would be constitutional and whether it was sound policy. None of the Representatives who spoke at the hearing so much as intimated that the proposed bill was made unnecessary by the fact that the statute already encompassed felon disenfranchisement laws.

The proposed bills of 1972 and 1973 thus reveal that the law was not understood by those most familiar with it to encompass felon disenfranchisement provisions. Furthermore, because these proposed bills only sought to add Voting Rights Act coverage to those who were no longer "confined in a correctional institution," it is yet more implausible that the Voting Rights Act was understood to apply to prisoner disenfranchisement statutes.

In this regard, it is also telling that during this same period, Congress affirmatively enacted a felon disenfranchisement statute in the District of Columbia, over which it had plenary power before the conferral of "home rule" in 1974. It is highly implausible that shortly after passing a statute (the VRA) purportedly intended to limit such laws, Congress would have enacted for its local jurisdiction a new statute doing exactly what it had supposedly forbidden on a national level.

The 1982 amendment of the Voting Rights Act also gives no indication that the law is to apply to felon disenfranchisement provisions. Congress's intention in amending § 1973 was to target those electoral laws, practices, and procedures that resulted in diluting the strength of the votes of members of racial and ethnic minorities but did not on their face deny any individuals the vote. The addition of § 1973(b) further demonstrates that Congress's particular focus was these vote-diluting practices. Section 1973(b) provides that a violation of the VRA can be established if "the political processes leading to nomination or election in the State or political subdivision are not equally open to participation" by members of a protected class of citizens such that "its members have less opportunity than other members of the electorate to participate in the political process and to elect representatives of their choice." 42 U.S.C. § 1973(b). There is no question that incarcerated persons cannot "fully participate in the political process"—they cannot petition, protest, campaign, travel, freely associate, or raise funds. It follows that Congress did not have this subpopulation in mind when the VRA section at issue took its present form in 1982.

Subsequent Congressional actions provide additional evidence that Congress has not understood the Voting Rights Act to cover felon disenfranchisement laws. For example, the National Voter Registration Act, enacted in 1993, explicitly provides for "criminal conviction" as a basis upon which voters' names may be removed from lists of eligible voters. The Help America Vote Act of 2002 directs States to remove disenfranchised felons from their lists of those eligible to vote in federal elections. Finally, a number of bills have been proposed in the past several years that would limit States' ability to disenfranchise felons. These bills further indicate that Congress itself continues to assume that the Voting Rights Act does not apply to felon disenfranchisement provisions.

In light of this wealth of persuasive evidence that Congress has never intended to extend the coverage of the Voting Rights Act to felon disenfranchisement provisions, we deem this one of the "rare cases [in which] the literal application of a statute will produce a result demonstrably at odds with the intentions of its drafters." *United States v. Ron Pair Enters., Inc.* (1989). We accordingly construe the statute to not encompass felon disenfranchisement laws.

III

A. Clear Statement Rule

Our decision not to apply § 1973 to felon disenfranchisement provisions is confirmed and supported by the operation of the clear statement rule (also known as the "plain statement rule"), a canon of interpretation which requires Congress to make its intent "unmistakably clear" when enacting statutes that would alter the usual constitutional balance between the Federal Government and the States. *Gregory v. Ashcroft* (1991).

For the clear statement rule to apply here in defendants' favor, we would therefore need to conclude (1) that applying § 1973 to prisoner disenfranchisement laws would alter the constitutional balance between the States and the Federal Government and (2) that Congress has not made its intention to alter that balance *unmistakably clear.*

B. Threshold Question: Does the Clear Statement Rule Apply?

Given the "sensitive topic" at issue, we would expect Congress to have specified that felon disenfranchisement provisions are covered by the Voting Rights Act if that were its intent.

C. Application of the Clear Statement Rule

In applying the clear statement rule, we must first decide whether bringing felon disenfranchisement laws within the scope of the Voting Rights Act would "alter the usual constitutional balance between the States and the Federal Government." *Gregory*. As a preliminary matter, plaintiffs argue that the application of the Voting Rights Act to felon disenfranchisement provisions could not affect the "federal balance" because that balance was already changed by the passage of the Fourteenth and Fifteenth Amendments, and the sole task of the Voting Rights Act is to effectuate those constitutional provisions. We do not find this argument persuasive, for, while it undoubtedly rings true for the Voting Rights Act in general, Section 2 of the Fourteenth Amendment explicitly leaves the federal balance intact with regard to felon disenfranchisement laws specifically. Therefore, extending the coverage of the Voting Rights Act to these provisions would introduce a change in the federal balance not contemplated by the framers of the Fourteenth Amendment.

D. Has Congress Made a Clear Statement?

[O]ur review of the legislative history of both the 1965 enactment and 1982 revision of the Voting Rights Act as well as our examination of other proposed legislation on this issue compel us to conclude that Congress unquestionably did not manifest an "unmistakably clear" intent to include felon disenfranchisement laws under the VRA. As a result, we hold that the requirements of the clear statement rule are not met, and we will accordingly not construe the Voting Rights Act to reach these laws.

* * *

Accordingly, we conclude that plaintiffs' vote denial claim, which seeks to challenge New York's prisoner disenfranchisement statute under the Voting Rights Act, must be dismissed.

IV

Vote Dilution Claim

[P]laintiffs have also raised a vote dilution claim based on "the disproportionate disfranchisement under New York State Election Law § 5-106(2) of Black and Latino persons who are incarcerated or on parole for a felony conviction." In light of our conclusion that the Voting Rights Act does not encompass felon disenfranchisement provisions and that plaintiffs thus cannot state a vote denial claim under the statute, it is clear that plaintiffs also cannot state a claim for vote dilution based on the assertion that the denial of the vote to incarcerated felons and parolees dilutes the voting strength of minority communities. Accordingly, this claim is likewise dismissed.

John M. WALKER, Jr., Chief Judge, concurring, with whom Judge JACOB joins.

[E]ven if Section 2 of the VRA applies to Section 5-106 and no contrary congressional intent were evident, then I believe that, as applied, the VRA would be unconstitutional because Congress would have exceeded its enforcement power under the Reconstruction Amendments. As the majority demonstrates, the case can be resolved without reaching this issue, but I believe it provides yet another sound basis for rejecting the dissent's position. [This concurrence then applied the "congruence and proportionality" test to conclude that bringing felon disenfranchisement statutes with the scope of the VRA would be beyond congressional power.]

STRAUB, Circuit Judge, with whom Judge SACK joins, concurring in part and concurring in judgment.

We concur in the result reached by the majority and in its reasoning that the evidence of legislative intent weighs decisively against applying the Voting Rights Act to New York Election Law § 5-106. We do not join in any holding that a clear statement rule applies here, as we believe such a rule, in addition to being unnecessary to the disposition of this case, would be inappropriate in the voting rights context.

CALABRESI, Circuit Judge, dissenting.

The majority opinion is learned, thoroughly researched, well-written, and restrained but it is almost totally irrelevant to the question presented in this case. The majority demonstrates beyond peradventure that Congress did not intend the

Voting Rights Act to prohibit felon disenfranchisement *categorically,* as that statute *categorically* prohibits, for instance, the use of literacy tests and "good moral character" requirements in certain jurisdictions. And if the plaintiffs were, in fact, arguing that the Voting Rights Act erects a *per se* ban on felon disenfranchisement, I would readily join the majority. But, of course, this is not the plaintiffs' position. Rather, they contend that the Voting Rights Act prohibits felon disenfranchisement laws *that result in the denial or dilution of voting rights on the basis of race.* Their complaint alleges that New York Election Law § 5-106 has precisely this result, and we are bound to accept this allegation as the gospel truth for purposes of New York's motion for judgment on the pleadings. Nothing in the majority opinion—nor, for that matter, in the concurrences—gives a single reason to suggest that Congress did not intend the Voting Rights Act to do what its plain language says and bar felon disenfranchisement statutes *that result in racial discrimination.* I, therefore, see no basis for depriving the plaintiffs of the right to prove their allegations.

I

The majority makes much of legislative history showing that Congress did not intend § 4(c) to forbid felon disenfranchisement. True enough. Felon disenfranchisement is *not* prohibited in the absence of a showing that it brings about discriminatory results. But the statements in legislative history that felon disenfranchisement is not banned by § 4(c) cannot be taken to imply a wholesale carve-out that exempts felon disenfranchisement from Voting Rights Act scrutiny altogether, as the majority asserts. The fact that race-neutral felon disenfranchisement is permissible under § 4(c) tells us nothing at all about whether § 2 allows *racially discriminatory* felon disenfranchisement. And the language of § 2(a) makes perfectly plain that such discriminatory disenfranchisement *is* barred.

The majority also tells us that some members of Congress tried, unsuccessfully, to amend the Voting Rights Act "to prohibit the States from denying the right to vote in Federal elections to former criminal offenders who have not been convicted of any offense related to voting or elections and who are not confined in a correctional institution." Once again, this does indeed imply that the Voting Rights Act does not, of itself, prohibit *all* felon disenfranchisement—a fact that no one disputes. How the majority moves from the fact that Congress declined to proscribe *race-neutral* felon disenfranchisement to the conclusion that Congress intended to exempt *racially discriminatory* felon disenfranchisement from the coverage of the Voting Rights Act is beyond me. It is perfectly clear that voting practices and procedures that are not *per se* impermissible under the Voting Rights Act—at-large voting and multi-member districts, for instance—violate the statute when they produce discriminatory results. And so it is with felon disenfranchisement laws. The majority has shown that some members of Congress thought felon disenfranchisement to be so inimical to voting rights as to try to forbid the practice even in the absence of discriminatory effects. The idea that such congressional efforts somehow imply the existence of a "safe harbor" for felon disenfranchisement statutes that *do* result in racially discriminatory denials or dilutions of voting rights is, it seems to me, risible.

Nor do subsequent enactments that presuppose the validity of felon disenfranchisement laws (*e.g.,* a provision of the Help America Vote Act of 2002), or bills that seek to limit felon disenfranchisement (*e.g.*, the Ex-Offenders Voting Rights Act of 2005), suggest in the slightest that Congress understands *discriminatory* felon disenfranchisement to be consistent with the Voting Rights Act.

Still, the majority concludes, largely based on the statutory history recounted above, that "the Voting Rights Act does not apply to felon disenfranchisement provisions." What is behind this remarkable decision to buck text, context, and legislative history in order to insulate a particular racially discriminatory practice from an anti-discrimination rule of general applicability?

II

I believe the majority opinion [is] motivated in large part by skepticism that Congress could have intended the result that the plaintiffs urge. But it is important here, in talking about congressional intent, to distinguish between the enacting Congress and the current Congress. It is, of course, the legislative intent of the enacting Congress—not the current Congress—that is controlling. And I see no reason to think that the 97th Congress, which was responsible for the "dramatic substantive transformation" of the Voting Rights Act in 1982, meant the expansive prohibition of discriminatory results it enacted to apply in any other way than precisely as written. The fact that the 109th Congress in the year 2006, if asked, might very well choose not to invalidate felon disenfranchisement laws that produce discriminatory results in no way indicates that the very different Congress of a generation ago made, or would now make, the same choice.

Sotomayor, Circuit Judge, dissenting.

It is plain to anyone reading the Voting Rights Act that it applies to all "voting qualification[s]." And it is equally plain that § 5-106 disqualifies a group of people from voting. These two propositions should constitute the entirety of our analysis. Section 2 of the Act by its unambiguous terms subjects felony disenfranchisement and all other voting qualifications to its coverage.

The duty of a judge is to follow the law, not to question its plain terms. I do not believe that Congress wishes us to disregard the plain language of any statute or to invent exceptions to the statutes it has created. The majority's "wealth of persuasive evidence" that Congress intended felony disenfranchisement laws to be immune from scrutiny under § 2 of the Act includes not a single legislator actually saying so. But even if Congress had doubts about the wisdom of subjecting felony disenfranchisement laws to the results test of § 2, I trust that Congress would prefer to make any needed changes itself, rather than have courts do so for it.

Katzmann, Circuit Judge, dissenting.

[I]f I saw clear evidence in the authoritative legislative history that the Congress that enacted it intended to exclude felon disenfranchisement policies from its reach, I would so construe it. But when we look to the authoritative legislative history, we find complete silence as to whether Congress intended to exclude felon disenfranchisement policies from its reach. Surely, the silence of enacting legislators cannot overcome the unambiguous and broadly worded provisions of a statute that was meant to apply to a multitude of state policies not specifically enumerated in its text.

B.D. Parker, Jr., Circuit Judge, dissenting.

The majority concludes that felon disenfranchisement laws are immune from VRA scrutiny, no matter how discriminatory the effects of those laws might be. No one disputes that states have the right to disenfranchise felons: § 2 of the Fourteenth Amendment makes that clear. But the fact that felon disenfranchisement statutes may sometimes be constitutional does not mean they are always constitutional. In any event, this case is largely about the Fifteenth, not the Fourteenth Amendment. Section 1 of the Fifteenth Amendment makes it clear that states may not disenfranchise on the basis of race. Section 2 of the VRA, as amended in 1982, also makes it clear that states may not disenfranchise on the basis of race, *even unintentionally.*

[VRA] § 4 and § 2(a) employ starkly different language that dramatically distinguishes their scope. Section 4's use of the narrow terms "any test or device," is not comparable to § 2(a)'s use of the broad language "[n]o voting qualification or prerequisite to voting or standard, practice, or procedure." Second, § 4 and § 2 serve separate functions and operate differently. Section 4 imposes an outright ban on tests or devices, while § 2(a) creates a "results" test, which requires investigating and weighing numerous factors. Given this outright ban, one can understand why Congress would want to narrow the category of voting mechanisms falling under § 4(c) relative to § 2(a), where a plaintiff need only demonstrate discriminatory results. Third, the legislative history of one provision enacted in 1965 (§ 4) has nothing to say about Congress's intentions when amending a different provision (§ 2), seventeen years later in 1982. Equivocal fragments from legislative history should not obscure the fact that, from its inception and particularly through its amendment in 1982, Congress intended that § 2, unlike § 4, be given the broadest possible reach, as the text it chose makes clear.

For several reasons, the clear statement rule does not apply. First, for it to apply, ambiguity must exist, and § 2(a) is unambiguous. Second, even if VRA § 2(a) were ambiguous, the clear statement rule would still not apply because the provision is broadly worded, and the rule does not apply to broadly worded remedial statutes. Congress used language in § 2 that was deliberately broad and generic. Congress could hardly have been expected to have enumerated every conceivable voting qualification, prerequisite, practice, or procedure to which the statute could apply in the text, or even the legislative history, of § 2(a). To do so would have left the states free to devise new means to discriminate that were not listed. To hold that Congress did not intend the VRA to cover felon disenfranchisement statutes is to hold that Congress actually intended to allow some forms of race-based voter disenfranchisement. Such a result I find improbable—indeed inconceivable.

Third, the clear statement rule cannot be justified by contending that unless it is applied, the VRA would improperly interfere with "sensitive domains" such as the core state function of regulating the franchise. This contention overlooks the quite obvious fact that the very purpose of the VRA was to impose Congressional regulation on the traditional state function of regulating voting. *See Lopez v. Monterey County* (1999) ("In short, the Voting Rights Act, by its nature, intrudes on state sovereignty. The Fifteenth Amendment permits this intrusion, however"). Felon disenfranchisement is no more a core state function than any of these examples.

Fourth, while it is correct that the states possess the primary authority for defining and enforcing the criminal law, the short and conclusive answer is that

New York Election Law § 5-106 is not a criminal law. It is a voting law found in New York's Election code, not among its criminal laws. As Judge Friendly pointed out, "[d]epriving convicted felons of the franchise is not a punishment but rather is a nonpenal exercise of the power to regulate the franchise." *Green v. Bd. of Elections* (2d Cir. 1967).

Fifth, the clear statement rule is particularly inappropriate in the context of the VRA, which was enacted and amended pursuant to Congress's powers under *both* the Fourteenth *and* Fifteenth Amendments. Contrary to the suggestion of some members of this Court, the seismic shift created by the Fourteenth and Fifteenth Amendments clearly altered the federal-state balance in an attempt to address a truly compelling national interest namely, reducing racial discrimination perpetuated by the states. Indeed, these Amendments "were specifically designed as an expansion of federal power and an intrusion on state sovereignty." *Gregory*. In sum, any shift in the federal-state balance of power that would purportedly result from applying VRA § 2 to New York Election Law § 5-106 would not occur as a result of the resolution of this case. That shift occurred more than 130 years ago when the Reconstruction Amendments were passed and ratified.

[Moreover], were a clear statement required, VRA § 2(a) supplies it. Since § 2(a) covers all voting qualifications, it indisputably covers felon disenfranchisement laws like New York Election Law § 5-106. If anything is clear from the legislative history of the VRA it is that Congress intended to eliminate all race-based disfranchisement, no matter the means by which it was achieved.

[Finally], Judge Walker's view that Congress lacks the authority to reach felon disenfranchisement statutes that result in the denial of the right to vote on account of race is wrong. To adopt that view is to conclude that there are some forms of race-based voter discrimination that are beyond Congress's reach, a proposition that is not correct.

FELON DISENFRANCHISEMENT IN FLORIDA

The most significant development concerning felon disenfranchisement law in recent years occurred in Florida. That state had an especially high rate of citizens denied the right to vote because of a felony conviction (10.4% in 2012). Because of the state's large population, and because the disenfranchisement caused by the state's law imposed an especially disproportionate burden on the state's Black citizens (23% of Black Floridians denied the right to vote), Florida's version of felon disenfranchisement had the most racially discriminatory consequence in the entire nation.* Florida's voters, in a ballot initiative called Amendment 4, voted to repeal the state's felon disenfranchisement law. But, as you will read in the next case, the state's legislature intervened to block—at least to some extent—the effect of the electorate's decision. In response to this legislative intervention, a group of affected citizens sued, and the following major Eleventh Circuit decision resulted.

* William E. Gibson, *Florida Leads U.S. in Barring Ex-Felons from Voting*, ORLANDO SENTINEL, July 13, 2012, A3.

Jones v. Governor of Florida

975 F.3d 1016 (11th Cir. 2020)

William PRYOR, Chief Judge, delivered the opinion of the Court, in which NEWSOM, BRANCH, GRANT, LUCK, and LAGOA, Circuit Judges, joined, except with respect to Part III-B-2, in which only NEWSOM and LAGOA, Circuit Judges, joined.

William PRYOR, Chief Judge:

Florida has long followed the common practice of excluding those who commit serious crimes from voting. But in 2018, the people of Florida approved a historic amendment to their state constitution to restore the voting rights of thousands of convicted felons. They imposed only one condition: before regaining the right to vote, felons must complete *all* the terms of their criminal sentences, including imprisonment, probation, and payment of any fines, fees, costs, and restitution. We must decide whether the financial terms of that condition violate the Constitution.

Several felons sued to challenge the requirement that they pay their fines, fees, costs, and restitution before regaining the right to vote. They complained that this requirement violates the Equal Protection Clause of the Fourteenth Amendment as applied to felons who cannot afford to pay the required amounts and that it imposes a tax on voting in violation of the Twenty-Fourth Amendment, that the laws governing felon reenfranchisement and voter fraud are void for vagueness, and that Florida has denied them procedural due process by adopting requirements that make it difficult for them to determine whether they are eligible to vote. The district court entered a permanent injunction that allows any felon who is unable to pay his fines or restitution or who has failed for any reason to pay his court fees and costs to register and vote. Because the felons failed to prove a violation of the Constitution, we reverse the judgment of the district court and vacate the challenged portions of its injunction.

BACKGROUND

In 2018, the people of Florida amended their constitution to restore the voting rights of some felons. Amendment 4 began as a voter initiative that appeared on the general election ballot in November 2018. The amendment provides that "any disqualification from voting arising from a felony conviction shall terminate, and voting rights shall be restored upon completion of all terms of sentence including parole or probation." Fla. Const. art. VI, § 4(a). It does not apply to felons convicted of murder or a felony sexual offense. *Id.* § 4(a)-(b). The amendment passed with about 65 percent of the vote, just over the required 60-percent threshold. *See id.* art. XI, § 5(e).

Shortly after Amendment 4 took effect, the Florida Legislature enacted a statute, Senate Bill 7066, to implement the amendment. This statute defined the phrase "[c]ompletion of all terms of sentence" in Amendment 4 to mean any portion of a sentence contained in the sentencing document, including imprisonment, probation, restitution, fines, fees, and costs. Fla. Stat. § 98.0751(2)(a). The Supreme Court of Florida later agreed with that interpretation and ruled that the phrase "all terms of sentence" includes all financial obligations imposed as part of a criminal sentence. *Advisory Opinion to the Governor re: Implementation of Amendment 4* (Fla. 2020).

To vote in Florida, a person must submit a registration form. The form requires registrants to affirm that they are not a convicted felon or that, if they are, their right to vote has been restored. Florida does not require felons to prove that they have completed their sentences during the registration process. The State allows felons to request an advisory opinion on eligibility before registration, and any felon who registers in reliance on an opinion is immune from prosecution. If the registration form is complete and the Division of Elections determines that the registrant is a real person, it adds the person to the voter registration system. If the State later obtains "credible and reliable" information establishing that the person has a felony conviction and has not completed all the terms of his sentence, the person is subject to removal from the voter rolls. *See* Fla. Stat. § 98.075(5). But any such felon is considered a registered voter, and before removal from the voter registration system, he is entitled to notice—including "a copy of any documentation upon which [his] potential ineligibility is based"—and a hearing, as well as *de novo* judicial review of an adverse eligibility determination. *Id.* §§ 98.075(7), 98.0755.

At the time of trial, Florida had received 85,000 registrations from felons who believe they were reenfranchised by Amendment 4. State law requires that those registrations be screened for, among other things, the voters' failure to complete the terms of their sentences including financial obligations. *Id.* § 98.0751. Florida has yet to complete its screening of any of the registrations. Until it does, it will not have credible and reliable information supporting anyone's removal from the voter rolls, and all 85,000 felons will be entitled to vote. *See id.* §§ 98.075(5) and (7).

Several felons sued Florida officials to challenge the requirement that they pay their fines, fees, costs, and restitution before regaining the right to vote. Among other provisions, they alleged that the reenfranchisement laws violate the Equal Protection and Due Process Clauses of the Fourteenth Amendment and the Twenty-Fourth Amendment.

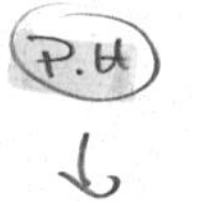

The district court entered a preliminary injunction in favor of the felons because it concluded they were likely to succeed on their claim under the Equal Protection Clause. It ruled that requiring felons to complete all financial terms of their sentences before regaining the right to vote was unconstitutional wealth discrimination as applied to felons unable to pay the required amounts. The preliminary injunction ordered the officials not to prevent the plaintiff felons from registering or voting based solely on their inability to pay any outstanding financial obligations in their sentences.

A panel of this Court affirmed the preliminary injunction on interlocutory appeal. *Jones v. Governor of Fla.* (11th Cir. 2020). The panel held that the decision to condition reenfranchisement on the completion of "all terms of sentence" violated the Equal Protection Clause as applied to indigent felons who cannot afford to pay their fines, fees, costs, and restitution. *Id.* It reached this conclusion by applying heightened scrutiny on the ground that Amendment 4 and Senate Bill 7066 discriminate on the basis of wealth. *Id.* at 817. It also suggested in dicta that the laws may fail even rational basis review. *Id.* at 809, 817.

The district court certified a class and a subclass of felons for purposes of final injunctive and declaratory relief. *See* Fed. R. Civ. P. 23(b)(2). The class comprises "all persons who would be eligible to vote in Florida but for unpaid financial obligations." The subclass comprises "all persons who would be eligible to vote in Florida but for unpaid financial obligations that the person asserts the person is genuinely unable to pay."

After a trial on the merits, the district court ruled that Amendment 4 and Senate Bill 7066 violate the Equal Protection Clause as applied to felons who cannot afford to complete their sentences. It applied heightened scrutiny to reach that conclusion based on the panel decision in the earlier appeal, and it alternatively ruled that the laws failed even rational basis review as applied to felons who are unable to pay the required amounts. The district court also ruled that Amendment 4 and Senate Bill 7066 impose a "tax" on voting by requiring felons to pay court fees and costs imposed in their sentences in violation of the Twenty-Fourth Amendment.

The district court did not decide whether Florida's reenfranchisement laws violate the Due Process Clause. It stated that there was "considerable force" to the arguments that the relevant laws are void for vagueness and deny the felons procedural due process. It found that felons are sometimes unable to determine the amount of financial obligations imposed in their sentences or the total amount they have paid toward all related obligations. The amount of financial obligations imposed in a sentence is usually clear from the judgment, which can be obtained from the county of conviction. But many felons no longer have copies of their judgments, and some counties may lack records for older convictions. When judgments contain both misdemeanor and felony offenses, it may not be immediately clear whether all financial obligations were imposed only for a disqualifying felony offense. The district court did not decide whether these facts established a violation of the Due Process Clause, but it stated that its remedy for the other constitutional violations would eliminate any due process concerns.

The district court awarded declaratory and injunctive relief. It declared Amendment 4 and Senate Bill 7066 unconstitutional insofar as they prohibit otherwise-eligible felons who are "genuinely unable to pay" their financial obligations from voting, require felons to pay "amounts that are unknown and cannot be determined with diligence" to regain their voting rights, and require any felons "to pay fees and costs as a condition of voting." It enjoined any defendant from taking steps to enforce those requirements. But it did not enjoin the requirement that felons pay "a determinable amount of fines and restitution as a condition of voting" if they can afford to do so.

The district court also imposed new procedures to govern the registration and voting process for felons. Its injunction required the Secretary of State to publish a form to request an advisory opinion from the Division of Elections regarding the existence and amount of any outstanding fines or restitution that could render a felon ineligible to vote. The form allowed requesters to check a box that stated, "I believe I am unable to pay the required amount." If the Division failed to respond to a request within 21 days and if the requester checked the box, the injunction required that the requester be allowed to vote.

The Governor and the Secretary of State appealed. They petitioned this Court for initial hearing en banc and moved to stay most aspects of the permanent injunction pending appeal. We granted both requests.

III. DISCUSSION

We divide our discussion in three parts. We first explain that Amendment 4 and Senate Bill 7066 do not violate the Equal Protection Clause. Next, we explain why the laws do not impose a tax on voting in violation of the Twenty-Fourth Amendment. Finally, we reject the arguments that the challenged laws are void for vagueness and that Florida has denied the felons due process.

A. Amendment 4 and Senate Bill 7066 Do Not Violate the Equal Protection Clause.

This appeal requires us to consider what limits the Equal Protection Clause places on the selective *restoration* of felons' voting rights. By conditioning reenfranchisement on the completion of all terms of sentence, Florida has decided to restore some felons to the franchise but not others. The felons challenge the classification Florida has drawn between felons who have completed all their terms of sentence, including financial terms, and those who have not. They argue that this classification violates the Equal Protection Clause as applied to felons who have completed all other terms of sentence but cannot afford to pay their fines, fees, costs, and restitution.

Under the Equal Protection Clause, classifications that neither implicate fundamental rights nor proceed along suspect lines are subject to rational basis review. *See, e.g., Heller v. Doe ex rel. Doe* (1993). Whatever may be true of the right to vote generally, felons "cannot complain about their loss of a fundamental right to vote because felon disenfranchisement is explicitly permitted under the terms of *Richardson*." *Harvey v. Brewer* (9th Cir. 2010) (O'Connor, J.). If the right of felons to vote were fundamental, every law that distinguished between different groups of felons in granting or denying access to the franchise would be subject to "exacting judicial scrutiny." *Kramer v. Union Free Sch. Dist. No. 15* (1969). But the Constitution does not put States to an all-or-nothing choice when it comes to deciding whether felons may vote.

States may restrict voting by felons in ways that would be impermissible for other citizens. For example, no one doubts that a State could not require citizens never convicted of a crime to serve a term of confinement or supervision to access the franchise. Such a requirement would have "no relation to voting qualifications" and so would be invalid under the Equal Protection Clause. *Harper v. Va. Bd. of Elections* (1966). But States may unquestionably require felons to complete their terms of imprisonment and parole before regaining the right to vote. The reason for this difference is clear: requiring felons to complete their sentences is directly related to voting qualifications because imprisonment and parole are imposed as punishment for the crimes by which felons forfeited their right to vote.

Although States enjoy significant discretion in distributing the franchise to felons, it is not unfettered. A State may not rely on suspect classifications in this area any more than in other areas of legislation. But absent a suspect classification that independently warrants heightened scrutiny, laws that govern felon disenfranchisement and reenfranchisement are subject to rational basis review. Every other Circuit to consider the question has reached the same conclusion.

The only classification at issue is between felons who have completed all terms of their sentences, including financial terms, and those who have not. This classification does not turn on membership in a suspect class: the requirement that felons complete their sentences applies regardless of race, religion, or national origin. Because this classification is not suspect, we review it for a rational basis only.

In the earlier appeal from the preliminary injunction, the panel elided this analysis and applied "some form of heightened scrutiny" on the ground that Amendment 4 and Senate Bill 7066 invidiously discriminate based on wealth. That decision was wrong. To reiterate, Florida withholds the franchise from *any* felon, regardless of wealth, who has failed to complete *any* term of his criminal sentence—financial or otherwise. It does not single out the failure to complete financial terms for special treatment. And in any event, wealth is not a suspect classification. Outside of narrow circumstances, laws that burden the indigent are subject only to rational basis review. *See M.L.B. v. S.L.J.* (1996).

To justify its application of heightened scrutiny, the panel relied on Supreme Court precedents governing poll taxes, *Harper*, poverty-based imprisonment, *e.g.*, *Bearden v. Georgia* (1983); and access to judicial proceedings, *e.g.*, *Griffin v. Illinois* (1956). The felons ask us to affirm the permanent injunction based on these same decisions. But none of these precedents, alone or in combination, requires heightened scrutiny for the decision to condition reenfranchisement on the full completion of a criminal sentence.

Consider first *Harper*, which invalidated a $1.50 poll tax under the Equal Protection Clause. This poll tax applied to the Virginia electorate generally; any voter who wished to cast a ballot in a state election had to pay the tax. Although States have the power to set voter qualifications, the Court explained that the Equal Protection Clause "restrains the States from fixing voter qualifications which invidiously discriminate." Because poll taxes bear "no relation" to voter qualifications, the Court concluded that Virginia had "introduce[d] a capricious or irrelevant factor" by requiring voters to pay the tax. Under *Harper*, it is a per se violation of the Equal Protection Clause for a State to "make[] the affluence of the voter or payment of any fee an electoral standard."

Amendment 4 and Senate Bill 7066 are markedly different from the poll tax in *Harper*. They do not make affluence or the payment of a fee an "electoral standard." They instead impose a different electoral standard: to regain the right to vote, felons, rich and poor, must complete all terms of their criminal sentences. Unlike the poll tax in *Harper*, that requirement is highly relevant to voter qualifications. It promotes full rehabilitation of returning citizens and ensures full satisfaction of the punishment imposed for the crimes by which felons forfeited the right to vote. That criminal sentences often include financial obligations does not make this requirement a "capricious or irrelevant factor." Monetary provisions of a sentence are no less a part of the penalty that society imposes for a crime than terms of imprisonment. Indeed, some felons face substantial monetary penalties but little or no prison time.

Because the financial obligations at issue are directly related to legitimate voter qualifications, *Harper* is inapplicable. The felons' contrary reading of *Harper* would call into question *any* law that made voting more expensive for some people than others, even if the additional cost were directly tied to valid voter qualifications.

Harper also proves too much to help the felons, which is further evidence that it does not apply. *Harper* held that the Virginia poll tax was unconstitutional *regardless* of whether a voter could pay the tax; it did not matter whether a voter "ha[d] $1.50 in his pocket or nothing at all, pa[id] the fee or fail[ed] to pay it." But no one doubts that the Equal Protection Clause allows Florida to require felons who are *able* to complete the financial terms of their sentences to do so. If completing the financial terms of a sentence were truly "irrelevant" to voter qualifications, Florida could not require *any* felons to satisfy that requirement as a condition of voting. The watered-down version of *Harper* that the felons would have us apply ignores the crucial distinction between poll taxes and Florida's reenfranchisement law: poll taxes are *never* relevant to voter qualifications, but laws that require the completion of a criminal sentence are. The per se rule of *Harper* does not apply to voting requirements that are related to legitimate voter qualifications, even if some voters must pay to comply with the requirement.

In addition to *Harper*, the panel in the earlier appeal relied on two other lines of Supreme Court precedent to apply heightened scrutiny. These decisions represent limited exceptions to the general rule that rational basis review applies to claims of wealth discrimination. They do not apply here.

[Analysis of non-election precedents omitted.]

We hold that rational basis review applies, and overrule the contrary holding by the panel in the earlier appeal from the preliminary injunction.

A classification survives rational basis review if it is rationally related to some legitimate government interest, and two interests are relevant here. Florida unquestionably has an interest in disenfranchising convicted felons, even those who have completed their sentences. But Amendment 4 and Senate Bill 7066 also reflect a different, related interest. They advance Florida's interest in *restoring* felons to the electorate after justice has been done and they have been fully rehabilitated by the criminal justice system. The policy Florida has adopted reflects the "more modern view" described in *Richardson* that "it is essential to the process of rehabilitating the ex-felon that he be returned to his role in society as a fully participating citizen when he has completed the serving of his term." The twin interests in disenfranchising those who disregard the law and restoring those who satisfy the demands of justice are both legitimate goals for a State to advance. The question is whether the classification Florida has adopted between felons who have completed their full sentences and those who have not is rationally related to those interests.

The dissenters suggest that Florida's only possible interests are in punishment and debt collection, and that narrow view leads them to conclude that Senate Bill 7066 is irrational. The dissenters dismiss our view that Florida also has an interest in restoring rehabilitated felons to the electorate as "an *ipse dixit* . . . [that] merely restates what the law does." But it is not unusual for a policy to directly achieve an objective itself. And we do not think it is unnatural to find state interests broader than punishment and revenue-raising in a reenfranchisement law.

In deciding whether Florida's classification is rational, we are mindful that our review is extremely narrow. *See FCC v. Beach Commc'ns, Inc.* (1993) ("This standard of review is a paradigm of judicial restraint."). We must uphold the classification unless the felons "negative every conceivable basis which might support it." *Id.* at 315, 113 S. Ct. 2096 (internal quotation marks omitted). For this reason, the Supreme Court "hardly ever strikes down a policy as illegitimate under rational basis scrutiny." *Trump v. Hawaii* (2018). In the rare instances when it has done so,

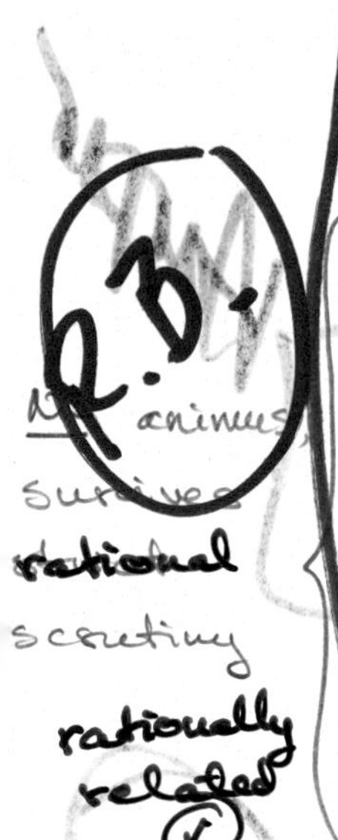

"a common thread has been that the laws at issue lack any purpose other than a 'bare desire to harm a politically unpopular group.'" *Id.* (alteration adopted) (quoting *U.S. Dep't of Agric. v. Moreno* (1973)); *see also Romer v. Evans* (1996); *City of Cleburne v. Cleburne Living Ctr.* (1985). There is no evidence that any kind of animus toward indigent felons motivated Florida voters and legislators to condition reenfranchisement on the completion of all terms of sentence. After all, the voters of Florida made it easier for the vast majority of felons—who are disproportionately indigent—to regain their voting rights. So we must uphold their choice if there is any conceivable basis that could justify it. *See Heller*, 509 U.S. at 319, 113 S. Ct. 2637 ("[R]ational-basis review . . . is not a license for courts to judge the wisdom, fairness, or logic of legislative choices." (internal quotation marks omitted)).

Under this deferential standard, we readily conclude that Florida's classification survives scrutiny. The people of Florida could rationally conclude that felons who have completed all terms of their sentences, including paying their fines, fees, costs, and restitution, are more likely to responsibly exercise the franchise than those who have not. If a State may decide that those who commit serious crimes are presumptively unfit for the franchise, it may also conclude that those who have completed their sentences are the best candidates for reenfranchisement.

To be sure, the line Florida drew might be imperfect. The classification may exclude some felons who would responsibly exercise the franchise and include others who are arguably less deserving. But Florida was not required "to draw the perfect line nor even to draw a line superior to some other line it might have drawn." *Armour v. City of Indianapolis* (2012). The Constitution requires only "a rational line." *Id.*

The classification is rational for other reasons too. Before extending the franchise to even more felons, Florida may have wished to test the waters by reenfranchising only those who complete their full sentences. Under rational basis review, "reform may take one step at a time." *Williamson v. Lee Optical of Okla., Inc.* (1955). The State need not "strike at all evils at the same time or in the same way," *Semler v. Or. State Bd. of Dental Exam'rs* (1935), and "[a] statute is not invalid under the Constitution because it might have gone farther than it did," *Roschen v. Ward* (1929). Although "every reform that benefits some more than others may be criticized for what it fails to accomplish," that reality does not invalidate the measure under the Equal Protection Clause. *San Antonio Indep. Sch. Dist. v. Rodriguez* (1973).

Confusion about Florida's voter registration system and the record before the district court leads the dissenters to conclude that Senate Bill 7066 "does not 'rationally' further the goal of re-enfranchising felons," a goal the dissent acknowledges only "[f]or the sake of argument." The dissenters purport to prove that conclusion with a smoking gun: "the fact that Florida had restored voting rights to 0 felons as of the time of trial." But that "fact" is not true. Once a felon submits a facially complete registration form and Florida determines that he is a real person, he is added to the voting rolls as a registered voter; he is not then required to prove that he has completed his sentence. To be sure, Florida attempts to identify "registered voters" with felony convictions whose rights have not been restored and, after securing "credible and reliable" information, initiates the process of removing them from the voter registration system. But at the time of trial, 85,000 felons had submitted facially complete voter registration forms, and Florida had not yet been able to find information justifying the removal of *any* of them from the voting rolls. Until it does, *all* 85,000 are entitled to vote. The dissenters' contention that state officials' implementation of Amendment 4 has prevented any felons from benefitting from the amendment is false. Eighty-five thousand felons are now registered voters, and each one will remain so unless Florida meets its self-imposed burden of gathering the information necessary to prove his ineligibility. Our dissenting colleagues quibble with our assertion that all of these registered voters are "entitled to vote," but they point to no evidence that any of the 85,000 voters will be unable to cast a ballot in an upcoming election.

The felons argue that Florida rendered its classification irrational by adopting the "every dollar" method for determining when a sentence is complete, but this argument misunderstands rational basis review. If the relationship between a State's interest and its means of achieving it is "at least debatable," then it survives scrutiny. The "every dollar" policy is at least arguably related to Florida's interest in reenfranchising only those felons who have paid their debt to society and been fully rehabilitated. It ensures that no felons will be reenfranchised unless they have paid amounts equal to those imposed in their criminal sentences. Florida could rationally define "completion" of a sentence in this manner to help ensure that felons who enrolled in payment plans pay no more to complete their sentences than felons who paid their fines, fees, costs, and restitution immediately.

The reasoning of the district court and the panel in the earlier appeal bore no resemblance to rational basis review. Their first error was to assess the rationality of Florida's classification by asking only whether it was rational to prohibit *these plaintiffs* from voting.) A legislative classification "may be based on rational speculation unsupported by evidence." *Beach Commc'ns,* 508 U.S. at 315, 113 S. Ct. 2096. For that reason, a law may be rational "even if in a particular case [it] appears to discriminate irrationally." *In re Wood* (11th Cir. 1989); *see also Beller v. Middendorf* (9th Cir. 1980) (Kennedy, J.) ("Nearly any statute which classifies people may be irrational as applied in particular cases.").

The second error of the district court and the panel in the earlier appeal was to assume that the law would be rational if most felons could eventually pay their fines, fees, costs, and restitution but irrational if a substantial number could not. The proportion of felons who can eventually complete their sentences has no bearing on whether it is rational to conclude that felons who *do* complete their sentences—whatever their number—are generally more deserving of reenfranchisement than those who do not. The district court and the panel in the earlier appeal reached a contrary conclusion only by disregarding settled law. The dissenters echo that flawed reasoning when they contend that any law that would leave a substantial portion of felons unable to benefit from Amendment 4 is "a nullification of the will of the electorate." But the face of the amendment makes clear that Florida voters do not share the dissenters' view that it is unjust to tell some criminals that they have incurred debts to society that will never be repaid. *See* Fla. Const. art. VI, § 4(b) (denying automatic reenfranchisement to felony sex offenders and murderers). In fact, it is the dissenters who would nullify the will of the Florida electorate by reenfranchising felons whom voters clearly would not have expected to benefit from Amendment 4, including a named plaintiff who jointly owes $59 million in restitution for conspiracy to commit insurance and wire fraud.

Florida's voters intended only to reenfranchise felons who have been fully rehabilitated, and Senate Bill 7066 drew a rational line in pursuit of that goal.

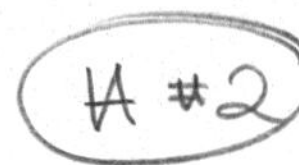

B. Amendment 4 and Senate Bill 7066 Do Not Violate the Twenty-Fourth Amendment.

Ratified in 1964, the Twenty-Fourth Amendment to the Constitution forbids taxes on voting in federal elections:

> The right of citizens of the United States to vote in any primary or other election for President or Vice President, for electors for President or Vice President, or for Senator or Representative in Congress, shall not be denied or abridged by the United States or any State by reason of failure to pay any poll tax or other tax.

The felons argue that Florida has denied them the right to vote by reason of their failure to pay court fees and costs imposed in their criminal sentences, which they contend are an "other tax" under the Twenty-Fourth Amendment. They do not argue that fines and restitution are taxes, and for good reason. Fines, which are paid to the government as punishment for a crime, and restitution, which compensates victims of crime, are not taxes under any fair reading of that term.

The felons' argument presents two questions: first, whether fees and costs imposed in a criminal sentence are taxes under the Twenty-Fourth Amendment; and second, if fees and costs are taxes, whether Florida has denied the right to vote "by reason of" the failure to pay fees and costs.

1. Court Costs and Fees Are Not Taxes.

The term "tax" is a broad one, but it does not cover all monetary exactions imposed by the government. The Supreme Court has long distinguished taxes from *penalties* in a variety of contexts. This distinction was well established when the Twenty-Fourth Amendment was adopted, and it continues to define the outer limits of the term "tax" today. In short, if a government exaction is a penalty, it is not a tax.

"The difference between a tax and a penalty is sometimes difficult to define," but at least one principle is clear. The Supreme Court has explained in multiple contexts that "if the concept of penalty means anything, it means punishment for an unlawful act or omission." Court fees and costs imposed in a criminal sentence fall within this definition: they are part of the State's punishment for a crime. They are not taxes.

The functional analysis used in *National Federation of Independent Business* supports our conclusion that the fees and costs in this appeal are penalties, not taxes. The Court explained that exactions imposed only on those who knowingly violate the law are suggestive of a penalty; not a tax. The Court also stressed that using a "criminal prosecution" to collect an exaction is "suggestive of a punitive sanction." And the Court reasoned that an exaction is likely a tax when the behavior to which it applies is lawful. Here, by contrast, fees and costs are imposed only on those who, following criminal prosecution for their unlawful acts, are subject to the punitive and rehabilitative powers of a Florida court. The characteristic features of penalties that the Court noted were absent in *National Federation of Independent Business* are present here.

To be sure, one purpose of fees and costs is to raise revenue, but that does not transform them from criminal punishment into a tax. Every financial penalty raises revenue for the government, sometimes considerable revenue. In addition to costs and fees, Florida uses criminal fines to fund both its courts and general government operations, but that additional purpose does not make them taxes. Nor does the fact that many fees and costs do not vary based on the severity of the offense render them nonpunitive. Some punishments, like disenfranchisement, are imposed on all felons alike regardless of the severity of their crimes. Because court costs and fees are legitimate parts of a criminal *sentence*—that is, part of the debt to society that felons must pay for their crimes—there is no basis to regard them as a tax. We hold that fees and costs imposed in a criminal sentence are not taxes under the Twenty-Fourth Amendment, and we reject the felons' Twenty-Fourth Amendment argument on that basis.

2. Florida Does Not Deny the Right to Vote "by Reason of" Failure to Pay a Tax.

States may deny all felons the right to vote but may not, consistent with the Twenty-Fourth Amendment, discriminate among felons by extending the franchise to some felons while denying it to others by reason of their failure to pay a tax. The Twenty-Fourth Amendment, like the Fifteenth and Nineteenth Amendments before it and the later Twenty-Sixth Amendment, applies whenever the State sets a voter qualification that extends the right to vote to some persons but denies it to others on a prohibited basis. The Twenty-Fourth Amendment plainly applies to felon reenfranchisement. The only remaining question is whether Florida denies some felons the right to vote "by reason of" their failure to pay a poll tax or other tax.

The felons are correct in one respect: just as it would plainly violate the other amendments to reenfranchise only white, male, or 30-year old felons, it would also violate the Twenty-Fourth Amendment to reenfranchise only felons who pay a poll tax—that is, a tax on the franchise itself. But the felons overlook one important difference between the Twenty-Fourth Amendment and the other amendments: the language it uses to describe the relationship between the denial of the right to vote and the prohibited basis of that denial.

Consider the text of all four voting-rights amendments. The Fifteenth Amendment says that the right to vote may not be denied "*on account of* race, color, or previous condition of servitude." U.S. Const. amend. XV, § 1 (emphasis added). The Nineteenth Amendment says that this right may not be denied "*on account of* sex." *Id.*, amend. XIX (emphasis added). And the Twenty-Sixth Amendment says that it may not be denied to citizens age 18 or older "*on account of* age." *Id.*, amend. XXVI, § 1 (emphasis added). In contrast, the Twenty-Fourth Amendment alone uses the phrase "by reason of" instead of "on account of."

A material variation in language suggests a variation in meaning. So the text of the Constitution creates an inference that the right to vote stands in a different relationship to race, sex, and age than it does to the nonpayment of taxes. To understand this difference in meaning, one should begin with the meanings of the Fifteenth and Nineteenth Amendments, both of which were well established when the Twenty-Fourth Amendment was ratified. With an understanding of those amendments in place, evidence surrounding the ratification of the Twenty-Fourth

Amendment makes clear that the difference in language reflects a difference in meaning.

The Fifteenth and Nineteenth Amendments are best understood to forbid any voter qualification that makes race or sex a but-for cause of the denial of the right to vote. The relationship between the right to vote and a person's race is the most thoroughly discussed in Supreme Court precedent, and the but-for causation principle is clear in that context. Race is never a permissible criterion for determining the scope of the franchise. And this understanding extends to the Nineteenth Amendment's prohibition of sex-based voter qualifications.

The Fifteenth Amendment's prohibition on accounting for race as a voter qualification is absolute. This prohibition is powerful enough to "remove . . . or render inoperative" any suffrage provision in a state constitution that refers to race, even in the absence of implementing legislation by Congress. The amendment has similar bite even when States impose discriminatory voting qualifications by facially neutral means.

To be sure, our nation failed to achieve the egalitarian goal of the Fifteenth Amendment to any significant degree until Congress used its power under section 2 of the amendment to enact the Voting Rights Act of 1965. But the amendment established a powerful baseline: States must set voter qualifications without any regard to race. The Fifteenth Amendment does not subject race-based voter qualifications to strict scrutiny—they are per se unconstitutional.

The Nineteenth Amendment forbids the use of sex as a voter qualification in the same way.

By the time Congress proposed the Twenty-Fourth Amendment in 1962, the Fifteenth and Nineteenth Amendments, which provided that the right to vote could not be denied or abridged "on account of race" or "on account of sex," were clearly and correctly understood to prevent the States from making a person's eligibility to vote turn in any way on race or sex. Under the Fifteenth and Nineteenth Amendments, a but-for-causation test like the one the felons propose accurately reflects the constitutional rule. When a State sets a voter qualification that would allow a person to vote but for the person's race or sex, it violates the Constitution.

But the Twenty-Fourth Amendment did not adopt the language of the Fifteenth and Nineteenth Amendments wholesale. The Twenty-Fourth Amendment prohibits States from denying the right vote "by reason of" the failure to pay a tax, not "on account of" it. If possible, that different language should be given a different meaning. Interpreting the phrase "by reason of" only as a synonym for "on account of" violates well-established principles of textual interpretation.

Because the phrase "by reason of" cannot refer only to but-for causation, it is necessary to consider other possible meanings. Focusing on the main word in that phrase yields an answer: the Twenty-Fourth Amendment prohibits denials of the right to vote for which the failure to pay a tax is not only the but-for cause, but also the *reason* for the State's action.

The word "reason" has multiple commonly used subsenses. For example, "reason" may refer to an "expression or statement offered . . . as a justification of an act or procedure" or a "consideration, motive, or judgment . . . leading to an action or course of action; a rational ground or motive." *Id.* This justification-based subsense controls the meaning of "by reason of" in the Twenty-Fourth Amendment.

Under this subsense, the Twenty-Fourth Amendment prohibits denials of the right to vote motivated by a person's failure to pay a tax. It does not prohibit every voting requirement with any causal relationship to the payment of a tax. If a State establishes a legitimate voter qualification for constitutionally legitimate reasons, it does not violate the Twenty-Fourth Amendment—even if the qualification sometimes denies the right to vote because a person failed to pay a tax. To take the most obvious example, a requirement that voters have no felony convictions is lawful even if the but-for cause of a felony conviction is the failure to pay taxes. The Twenty-Fourth Amendment does not forbid the disenfranchisement of tax felons.

C. Florida Has Not Violated the Due Process Clause.

Although the district court did not decide whether Florida's reenfranchisement laws violate the Due Process Clause, part of its injunction cannot be justified by any of its other rulings. The district court declared Amendment 4 and Senate Bill 7066 unconstitutional as applied to felons who cannot determine the amount of their outstanding financial obligations with diligence, and it created a process under which felons could request an opinion from the Division of Elections stating their total amount of outstanding fines and restitution. The injunction allowed any felon who did not receive an answer within 21 days to register and vote, and it prohibited the defendants from causing or assisting in the prosecution of any persons who registered or voted under this process. The felons ask us to affirm these aspects of the injunction on the grounds that the relevant Florida laws are void for vagueness and deny them procedural due process.

We first address the vagueness challenge. To register to vote in Florida, a person must affirm that he is not disqualified from voting because of a felony conviction. And it is a crime for a person to "willfully submit[] any false voter registration information," Fla. Stat. § 104.011(2), or to "willfully vote[] at any election" "knowing he or she is not a qualified elector," *id.* § 104.15. The felons argue these criminal laws are void for vagueness because Senate Bill 7066 makes it difficult or impossible for some felons to determine whether they are eligible to vote.

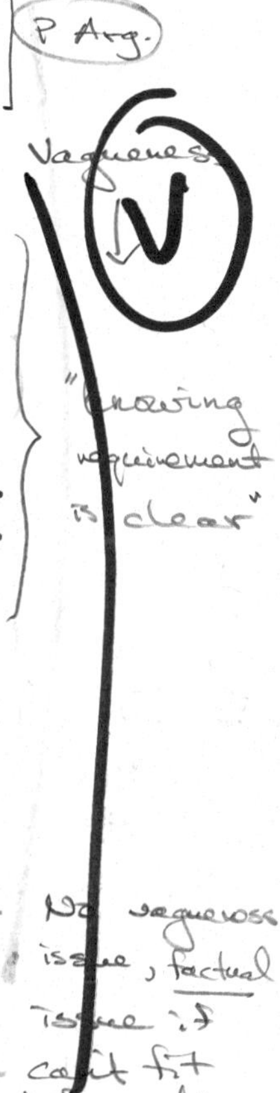

The challenged laws are not vague. Felons and law enforcement can discern from the relevant statutes exactly what conduct is prohibited: a felon may not vote or register to vote if he *knows* that he has failed to complete all terms of his criminal sentence. *See* Fla. Stat. §§ 104.011(2), 104.15, 98.0751(1)-(2). This clear standard, which includes a scienter requirement, provides fair notice to prospective voters and "limit[s] prosecutorial discretion."

The felons' real complaint is that it is sometimes difficult to determine whether a felon has completed the financial terms of his sentence. They offer examples of felons who cannot locate their criminal judgments, cannot determine which financial obligations were imposed for felony as opposed to misdemeanor offenses, or do not know how much they have paid toward their financial obligations. But these concerns arise not from a vague law but from factual circumstances that sometimes make it difficult to determine whether an incriminating fact exists. These difficulties in proving the facts that determine a felon's eligibility to vote cast no doubt on the clarity of the requirement that felons neither register nor vote if they *know* they have not satisfied the financial obligations imposed in their sentences. Because there is no uncertainty about "what fact must be proved" to convict a defendant under these statutes, the laws are not vague.

The felons argue that the State's "every dollar" policy makes the challenged laws vague, but that policy only *narrows* the scope of criminal liability. The challenged laws forbid felons to register or vote if they know they have failed to complete their sentences. And the policy adopts one of the narrowest possible constructions of "failing to complete" a sentence. Under the policy, a felon fails to complete the financial terms of his sentence only if his total payments toward *all* obligations related to his sentence—even financing costs that accrue after sentencing—are *less* than the amount imposed in his sentence. This narrowing construction mitigates vagueness concerns instead of enhancing them: a felon cannot reasonably think he has "completed" his terms of sentence if the total amount he has paid toward *all* related obligations is less than the amount included in his sentence. And only felons in this category are ineligible to vote under the "every dollar" policy.

The felons also argue that Florida has denied them procedural due process. *See Mathews v. Eldridge* (1976). They assert a liberty interest in the right to vote and argue that Florida has deprived them of that interest without adequate process. We may assume that the right to vote is a liberty interest protected by the Due Process Clause. Even so, this argument fails because any deprivation of that right was accomplished through the legislative process and the process for adopting a constitutional amendment, which provide more than adequate procedures for the adoption of generally applicable rules regarding voter qualifications.

The felons were deprived of the right to vote through legislative action, not adjudicative action. Under its Constitution, Florida deprives all felons of the right to vote upon conviction. And even if we accept the argument that Amendment 4 and Senate Bill 7066 deprive felons of the right to vote by conditioning reenfranchisement on the completion of all terms of sentence, those laws also qualify as legislative acts. The legislative and constitutional-amendment processes gave the felons all the process they were due before Florida deprived them of the right to vote and conditioned the restoration of that right on completion of their sentences.

The felons complain that it is sometimes difficult to ascertain the facts that determine eligibility to vote under Amendment 4 and Senate Bill 7066, but this complaint is only another version of the vagueness argument we have already rejected. The Due Process Clause does not require States to provide individual process to help citizens learn the facts necessary to comply with laws of general application.

To avail themselves of the *Mathews v. Eldridge* framework, the felons were obliged to prove a deprivation of liberty based on *adjudicative* action. But the felons do not challenge any individual voter-eligibility determinations that could qualify as adjudicative action, so *Mathews* does not apply. And in any event, Florida provides registered voters with adequate process before an individual determination of ineligibility. Before being removed from the voter registration system, voters are entitled to predeprivation notice and a hearing. Fla. Stat. § 98.075(5), (7). And any voter who is dissatisfied with the result is entitled to *de novo* review of the removal decision in state court. *Id.* § 98.0755. These procedures provide more than adequate process to guard against erroneous ineligibility determinations. *See Mathews*, 424 U.S. at 333-35, 96 S. Ct. 893.

The injunction the district court entered looks nothing like a remedy for a denial of due process. It does not require additional procedures for any existing adjudicative action that deprives felons of a liberty interest in voting. Instead, it *creates* an adjudicative process to aid felons in complying with nonvague laws of general application. States are certainly free to establish such a process—indeed, Florida has done so through its preregistration advisory-opinion process and accompanying immunity from criminal prosecution. But the notion that due process *mandates* this kind of procedure in the absence of any adjudicative action is unprecedented. The injunction did not remedy any denial of due process, so we cannot affirm it on that ground.

A fundamental confusion in this litigation has been the notion that the Due Process Clause somehow makes Florida responsible not only for giving felons notice of the standards that determine their eligibility to vote but also for locating and providing felons with the *facts* necessary to determine whether they have completed their financial terms of sentence. The Due Process Clause imposes no such obligation. States are constitutionally entitled to set legitimate voter qualifications through laws of general application and to require voters to comply with those laws through their own efforts. So long as a State provides adequate procedures to challenge individual determinations of ineligibility—as Florida does—due process requires nothing more.

IV. CONCLUSION

We **REVERSE** the judgment of the district court and **VACATE** the challenged portions of its injunction.

William PRYOR, Chief Judge, joined by LAGOA, Circuit Judge, concurring:

I write separately to explain a difficult truth about the nature of the judicial role. Our dissenting colleagues predict that our decision will not be "viewed as kindly by history" as the voting-rights decisions of our heroic predecessors. But the "heroism" that the Constitution demands of judges—modeled so well by our predecessors—is that of "devotion to the rule of law and basic morality." Our duty is not to reach the outcomes we think will please whoever comes to sit on the court of human history. The Constitution instead tasks us with "administering the rule of law in courts of limited jurisdiction," which means that we must respect the political decisions made by the people of Florida and their officials within the bounds of our Supreme Law, regardless of whether we agree with those decisions. And in the end, as our judicial oath acknowledges, we will answer for our work to the Judge who sits outside of human history.

JORDAN, Circuit Judge, joined by WILSON, MARTIN, and JILL PRYOR, Circuit Judges, dissenting.

> *"Failure to pay court fines and fees should never result in the deprivation of fundamental rights, including the right to vote."*

AMERICAN BAR ASSOCIATION, RESOLUTION: TEN GUIDELINES ON COURT FINES AND FEES, GUIDELINE 5 (AUG. 2018).

In 2018 Florida's voters, by a 64.55% super-majority, enacted Amendment 4 to allow felons to vote "upon completion of all terms of sentence including parole or probation." Since then, the Florida legislature has decreed, *see* Fla. Stat. § 98.0751, and the Florida Supreme Court has ruled, *see Advisory Opinion to Governor re Implementation of Amendment 4, The Voting Restoration Amendment* (Fla. 2020), that Amendment 4 requires felons to satisfy legal financial obligations ("LFOs") before being allowed to vote.

But if anyone thought that Florida really cared about collecting unpaid LFOs—whether for crime victims or for its own coffers—that pretense was laid bare at trial, which was held after we affirmed the district court's preliminary injunction.

The evidence showed, and the district court found, that since the passage of Amendment 4 Florida has demonstrated a "staggering inability to administer" its LFO requirement. That is an understatement. Florida cannot tell felons—the great majority of whom are indigent—how much they owe, has not completed screening a single felon registrant for unpaid LFOs, has processed 0 out of 85,000 pending registrations of felons (that's not a misprint—it really is 0), and has come up with conflicting (and uncodified) methods for determining how LFO payments by felons should be credited. To demonstrate the magnitude of the problem, Florida has not even been able to tell the 17 named plaintiffs in this case what their outstanding LFOs are. So felons who want to satisfy the LFO requirement are unable to do so, and will be prevented from voting in the 2020 elections and far beyond. Had Florida wanted to create a system to obstruct, impede, and impair the ability of felons to vote under Amendment 4, it could not have come up with a better one.

Incredibly, and sadly, the majority says that Florida has complied with the Constitution. So much is profoundly wrong with the majority opinion that it is difficult to know where to begin. But one must start somewhere, so I will first turn to the facts, those "stubborn things," which though proven at trial and unchallenged on appeal, are generally relegated to the dustbin in the majority opinion.

I

The majority proceeds as though the reality on the ground does not matter, but the record tells a different story. After an eight-day bench trial, the district court issued a 125-page opinion containing the following findings of fact—none of which Florida challenges on appeal.

1. "[T]he overwhelming majority of felons who have not paid their LFOs in full, but who are otherwise eligible to vote, are genuinely unable to pay the required amount, and thus, under Florida's pay-to-vote system, will be barred from voting solely because they lack sufficient funds."
2. "[M]any felons do not know, and some have no way to find out, the amount of LFOs included in a judgment."
3. Even if a felon knows that he owes LFOs, "[d]etermining the amount that has been paid on an LFO presents an even greater difficulty" and "is often impossible."
4. In many cases, "probably most," felons cannot pay their outstanding balance without being required to pay additional fees that were not included in their sentence.

5. In the 18 months since Amendment 4 was adopted by Florida voters, Florida has not completed screening *even a single registrant* for unpaid LFOs, and it has processed 0 out of 85,000 pending registrations of felons.
6. "It is likely that if the State's pay-to-vote system remains in place, some citizens who are eligible to vote, based on the Constitution or even on the state's own view of the law, will choose not to risk prosecution and thus will not vote." In other words, the district court found that it is likely that the lack of clarity about LFO obligations will likely deter eligible felons from voting, out of fear that they will be prosecuted if they vote and then later find out that they were not in fact eligible.

With these facts in mind, I turn to the plaintiffs' equal protection, due process, and Twenty-Fourth Amendment claims.

II

In my view, we correctly ruled in *Jones I*, 950 F.3d at 817-25, that heightened scrutiny should apply to the plaintiffs' equal protection claim. But even if heightened scrutiny does not apply, the district court properly concluded that Florida's LFO scheme fails rational basis review.

A

We held in *Jones I* that "heightened scrutiny applies . . . because we are faced with a narrow exception to traditional rational basis review: the creation of a wealth classification that punishes those genuinely unable to pay fees, fines, and restitution more harshly than those able to pay—that is, it punishes more harshly solely on account of wealth—by withholding access to the ballot box." *Jones I*, 950 F.3d at 809. I wholeheartedly agree.

1

Harper indicates that heightened scrutiny should apply here. The majority seeks to avoid the application of *Harper* by asserting that, unlike the poll tax in that case, the LFO requirement "do[es] not make affluence or the payment of a fee an 'electoral standard.'" Instead, the majority asserts, the LFO requirement makes completing all terms of a sentence an "electoral standard," which is "highly relevant to voter qualifications."

The record reflects, and the district court found, that hundreds of thousands of felons would be eligible to vote but for their inability to pay LFOs. *See Jones II*, 462 F.Supp.3d at 1203 ("Florida has adopted a system under which nearly a million otherwise-eligible citizens will be allowed to vote only if they pay an amount of money."). As in *Harper*, the LFO requirement makes "affluence" the electoral standard, even though "[v]oter qualifications have no relation to wealth[.]" *Harper*, 383 U.S. at 666, 86 S.Ct. 1079. Given the importance of voting in our political system, *Harper*, *Griffin*, and *Bearden* call for heightened scrutiny. *Cf.* John Hart Ely, Democracy and Distrust 87 (1980) (advocating a "participation-oriented" and "representation-reinforcing" approach to judicial review).

2

Heightened scrutiny also applies for another reason—the right to vote is indisputably fundamental. *See, e.g., Yick Wo v. Hopkins* (1886) (voting "is regarded as a fundamental political right . . . preservative of all rights"); *Reynolds v. Sims* (1964) ("Undoubtedly, the right of suffrage is a fundamental matter in a free and democratic society."). And even if voting is not fundamental for felons who are re-enfranchised, it is certainly a critically important right that demands a searching analysis.

The majority contends that felons do not have a fundamental right to vote because felon disenfranchisement is permitted under *Richardson v. Ramirez* (1974). That contention is too simplistic, and "amounts to an analytical trick." Although *Richardson* interpreted § 2 of the Fourteenth Amendment to permit states to disenfranchise felons, it did not address what level of scrutiny would or should apply if a state chose to re-enfranchise felons but conditioned re-enfranchisement on their ability to pay LFOs. *Richardson* cannot control an issue it did not confront (or even discuss).

C

Though I would review the LFO requirement under heightened scrutiny, my bottom-line position does not turn on what level of scrutiny applies. Even under rational basis review, the district court correctly held that the LFO requirement violates equal protection.

1

As every student of constitutional law knows, the Supreme Court has not always applied rational basis review with the same level of "bite." The more important the interest at stake, the more demanding rational basis review becomes.

The majority applies the most deferential form of rational basis review. But if heightened scrutiny does not apply under the *Griffin-Bearden-Harper* line of cases, the fact that voting rights are being denied due to indigency at least warrants a more exacting form of rational basis review. The right to vote—even if not considered fundamental for felons who are re-enfranchised—is certainly an important one in our democracy, and it should not be lumped together with other state-created benefits that lack similar institutional significance.

The majority also says—incorrectly I think—that an as-applied challenge is inappropriate under rational basis review. In *Cleburne v. Cleburne Living Center* (1985), the Supreme Court reviewed, under rational basis, a zoning ordinance that required a special use permit for the operation of a group home for the mentally disabled. It found the ordinance unconstitutional "as applied" in that case. *See id.* at 447, 105 S. Ct. 3249 (stating that reviewing the zoning ordinance as applied "is the preferred course of adjudication since it enables courts to avoid making unnecessarily broad constitutional judgments"). The majority may not like *Cleburne*, but it is not for us to choose which Supreme Court cases we are bound by.

Reviewing statutes as applied to indigents, moreover, seems to be typical in wealth discrimination cases where due process and equal protection guarantees intersect. For instance, in *Griffin*, the Supreme Court evaluated whether a state statute requiring defendants to pay for transcripts needed for an appeal could be applied "so as to deny adequate appellate review to the poor while granting such review to all others." *See* 351 U.S. at 18, 76 S. Ct. 585. It did not (as the majority would have us do here) ask whether a state may require payment for transcripts generally.

The district court found "that the mine-run of felons affected by the pay-to-vote requirement are genuinely unable to pay," and Florida does not challenge this finding on appeal. Though the majority says a "substantial number" of felons being unable to pay LFOs does not make the scheme irrational, the district court found that "the *overwhelming majority* of felons who have not paid their LFOs in full, but who are otherwise eligible to vote, are genuinely unable to pay[.]" *Jones II,* 462 F. Supp. 3d at 1219 (emphasis added). How can a system that seeks to encourage felons to pay LFOs be rational if the vast majority are simply *unable* to pay?

2

Rational basis review is deferential to government action, but it is not "toothless." Under the rational basis standard, a law that distinguishes between different groups does not violate equal protection if "there is a rational relationship between the disparity of treatment and some legitimate governmental purpose." The rational basis test thus has two prongs: (1) the law must further a legitimate state interest; *and* (2) there must be "a rational relationship between the government's objective and the means it has chosen to achieve it."

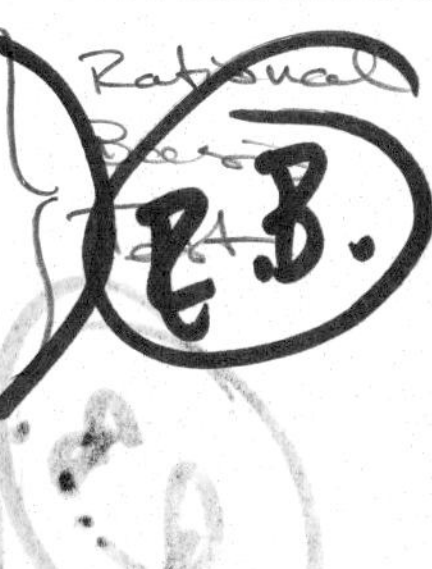

Florida asserts that it has an interest in ensuring "that *all* felons complete *all* terms of sentence to repay their debt to society," or in other words, "in enforcing the punishments it has imposed for violations of its criminal laws." Appellants' Initial En Banc Br. at 35. *See also id.* at 38 (describing the state's interest "in demanding a full measure of justice from every felon"). The majority somewhat re-frames Florida's goals, stating that "two interests are relevant here": Florida's "interest in disenfranchising convicted felons" and its related "interest in *restoring* felons to the electorate after justice has been done and they have been fully rehabilitated[.]"

Disenfranchising felons, however, is not the goal of Amendment 4. Quite the opposite, Amendment 4 automatically restored voting rights to felons who completed all the terms of their sentences. Nor was disenfranchisement the purpose of § 98.0751, which implemented Amendment 4 and is titled "Restoration of voting rights; termination of ineligibility subsequent to a felony conviction." Framing Florida's goal as *reenfranchising* felons who have completed the terms of their sentences is an *ipse dixit*—it merely restates what the law does, rather than provide an interest furthered by the LFO requirement.

For the sake of argument, however, let's assume the legitimacy of each of the asserted state interests. If we do that, "[t]he only remaining question is whether [Florida] achieved its purpose in a patently arbitrary or irrational way." *U.S. R.R. Ret. Bd. v. Fritz* (1980). In my view, the answer to that question is yes.

I will start with whether the LFO requirement rationally furthers the goals articulated by the majority. Though Florida may disenfranchise felons under *Richardson,* or choose to re-enfranchise only some felons, it cannot draw arbitrary lines between those felons it re-enfranchises and those it does not.

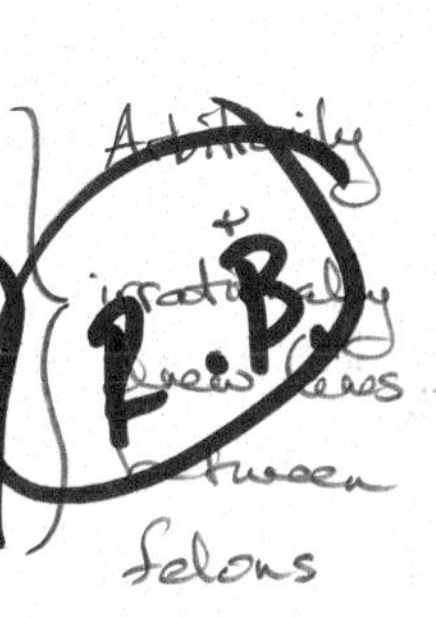

Re-enfranchising felons who complete the terms of their sentences—except for those who are *unable* to pay LFOs—"amounts to nothing 'more than a naked assertion that [a felon's] poverty by itself,' is a sufficient reason to disqualify the felon from regaining the right to participate in the exercise of democracy." The majority bases its entire rational basis analysis on the proposition that felons cannot intelligently exercise the franchise—the right to vote—unless they have fully paid their LFOs. But as *Harper* teaches, a felon's wealth has no bearing on whether he is qualified to vote. The notion that the indigent cannot be rehabilitated due solely to their inability to pay is non-sensical.

Critically, the fact that Florida had restored voting rights to 0 felons as of the time of trial indicates that this scheme does not "rationally" further the goal of reenfranchising felons. Instead, it shows that Florida's organs of government are doing their best to slowly but surely suffocate Amendment 4.

The majority says that even though their registrations have not been screened, "all 85,000 [registered] felons will be entitled to vote." It also seems to suggest that felons may go ahead and register, as "[o]nce a felon submits a facially complete registration form . . . , he is added to the voting rolls as a registered voter; he is not then required to prove that he has completed his sentence." *Id.* at 1035. But these statements overlook the critical fact that Florida has kept tens of thousands of felons in voting limbo, not knowing their LFO status (and therefore not knowing their eligibility to vote).

Should felons choose to vote after registering, and then later find out that they are not in fact eligible to vote, they may be subject to prosecution. Even the Director of the Division of Elections acknowledged at trial that if she "were in the voter's position, [she doesn't] know that [she] would be swearing under oath if [she] wasn't sure about" her eligibility. She agreed that requiring felons to affirm their eligibility to vote in their registration forms "is certainly a challenge . . . and that's why [the Division] offered up the advisory opinion to see if that would give them some cover." *Id.* To make matters more treacherous for felons, there is no good-faith safe harbor to protect those who register and vote, but later turn out to be mistaken about their eligibility.

Unlike the majority, Florida does not assert that felons should go ahead and vote once they register, instead arguing that it "has an interest in avoiding having felons presumed eligible to vote before an investigation can reasonably be completed, as that would pose a substantial risk of authorizing *ineligible* felons to vote." Appellants' En Banc Reply Br. at 32. If the majority's suggestion that felons can simply vote once they register (without knowing whether they have actually satisfied their LFO requirements) were accurate, that would belie Florida's contention (adopted by the majority) that the purpose of the LFO-requirement is to ensure that felons cannot vote until they complete all terms of their sentences.

3

Florida, as noted, maintains that the LFO scheme advances its interest in "*all* felons complet[ing] *all* terms of sentence," or in enforcing the punishments it imposes. To the extent that Florida's interest is in punishment, as we explained in *Jones I*, the LFO scheme punishes indigent felons "more harshly than those who committed precisely the same crime. . . . And this punishment is linked not to their culpability, but rather to the exogenous fact of their wealth." *Jones I*, 950 F.3d at 812. This cannot be rational.

If Florida's interest is in felons repaying their full debts to society, requiring indigent felons to pay LFOs before regaining the right to vote does not actually aid in collections.

The district court's undisputed factual findings show that Florida often cannot tell felons how much they owe. If Florida cannot inform felons about the amount of LFOs they have outstanding—information which they must have in order to satisfy their obligations—how can this system possibly encourage or incentivize felons to complete the terms of their sentences? There is no answer, because no answer is possible.

III

The LFO requirement violates due process because Florida does not provide felons with adequate notice of their eligibility to vote. Contrary to the majority's assertion, the LFO requirement is not merely "legislative," and it is subject to a procedural due process challenge. Figuring out whether felons have paid their LFOs is adjudicative, for the Division of Elections is tasked with both conducting an individualized assessment of a felon's LFOs and determining whether they have been satisfied.

Finally, § 98.0751 is unconstitutionally vague. It does not provide sufficient standards for how to determine whether a felon has satisfied the LFO requirement, resulting in arbitrary application.

A

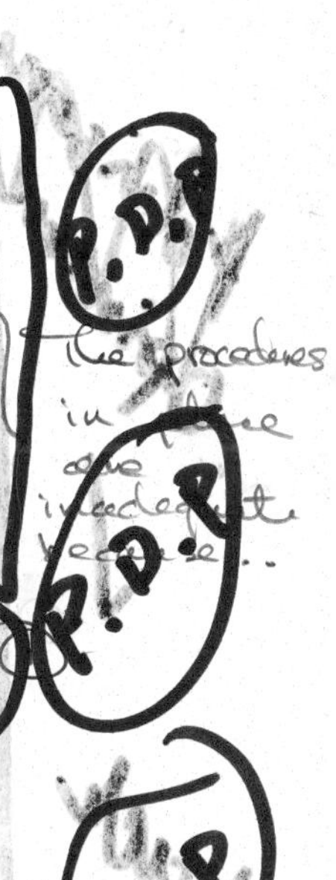

Though the Constitution permits states to disenfranchise felons, Florida's citizens chose through Amendment 4 to provide a right to vote for felons who have completed all terms of their sentences, thereby creating a liberty interest. And when a state chooses to create a liberty interest, "the Due Process Clause requires fair procedures for its vindication."

Before a state can deprive a person of a liberty or property interest, due process obligates it to provide him with adequate notice.

A Florida statute, § 98.075(7), outlines the procedures for removal from the voter rolls, including notice of the registered voter's ineligibility and an opportunity to request a hearing. But these procedures fall constitutionally short for several reasons.

First, the procedures set forth in § 98.075(7) do not come into play until *after* the Division of Elections begins to screen registrants, determines that they are ineligible to vote, and seeks to remove them from the voter rolls. As the district court found, and Florida does not contest, the Division of Elections has processed 0 out of 85,000 pending registrations of felons. So, for those 85,000 registrants—and all those who will surely follow—the statutory requirement of notice and a hearing is completely illusory. Those appalling numbers, unfortunately, mean nothing to Florida or to the majority.

Second, should any of these 85,000 registrants choose to vote in the upcoming election—as they may believe, in good faith, they have a right to do—they risk criminal prosecution if they turn out to be wrong about their eligibility. Given Florida's lack of clarity regarding how to calculate outstanding LFOs, this will surely be the case for at least some felons. The truth is that many of these registrants will not vote to avoid the risk of prosecution, even if they are in fact eligible, creating a de facto denial of the franchise.

Third, there is no procedure for a felon to determine his eligibility to vote *before* registering—even though the voter registration form requires registrants to sign an oath affirming that they are qualified to vote. Florida says that felons who wish to vote may access their records through the county clerk's office or call clerks to obtain information. But the record belies that claim, and reflects that such inquiries are usually fruitless. As discussed earlier, the evidence at trial showed that the state's records are often inconsistent or incomplete, clerks are often unhelpful, counties do not maintain records of payments (including collection or payment plan fees), and the state often maintains no records of restitution. Understandably, the district court found that "[t]rying to obtain accurate information" by contacting the supervisor of elections or clerk of court "will almost never work."

Fourth, if a felon registers based on the belief that he is eligible to vote, and then turns out to be wrong, he may be prosecuted for making a false affirmation in connection with voting. Florida downplays this risk, proclaiming that felons should rest assured that they will not be convicted if they registered in good faith because willfulness must be shown to prove a violation of Fla. Stat. § 104.011. But that comforting assurance—tactically made for an advantage in litigation—is useless, as it does not tell us how the state's prosecutors will choose to prosecute possible or alleged violations of the law. Felons should not have to register in the hope that a jury will later find good faith should they be prosecuted.

B

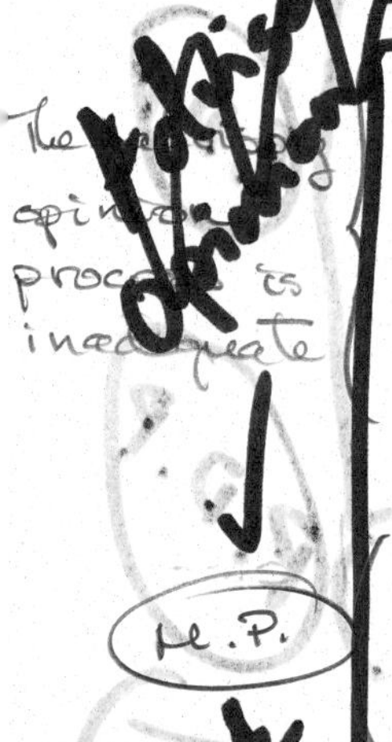

The Director of the Division of Elections testified that, to avoid risk of prosecution, a felon may request an advisory opinion. Under Fla. Stat. § 106.23(2), any person who relies on an advisory opinion in good faith will be immune from prosecution. But that statute does not make clear that the advisory opinion process is available to any individual with questions about his or her eligibility to vote. The statute, moreover, sets no time frame for when the Division must provide an advisory opinion. Tellingly, the Director could not say how long it would take to obtain an advisory opinion, other than to generally state that it could take a week or months. To make matters worse, the Division's own website does not provide guidance on what a request for an advisory opinion should include. Florida's lack of good faith in the 18 months since the passage of Amendment 4 is undeniable and palpable. What Florida is really unhappy about is that the district court's advisory opinion process will actually require it to work, to do its job, within a specified time-frame.

Although it was the Director of the Division of Elections who suggested the advisory opinion procedure at trial, Florida now incredibly argues that "[t]he district court offered no legal basis for charging *the State* with the responsibility of providing felons with information about their own unfulfilled criminal sentences and any payments that they themselves have made toward them." The majority seems to adopt this argument, stating that the Due Process Clause does not make Florida responsible for "locating and providing felons with the *facts* necessary to determine whether they have completed their financial terms of sentence."

This is a remarkable holding. I know of no cases (or other authorities) that say or hold that a state can impose a condition for the exercise of a right or privilege, and then refuse to explain to a person what the condition consists of or how to satisfy it. To the contrary, §§ 98.075(5) and 98.0751(3)(a)—Florida's own laws—obligate the Division of Elections to make initial eligibility determinations, and §§ 98.075(7) and 98.0751(3)(b) charge County Supervisors of Elections with making the ultimate determination of eligibility. Federal law likewise requires states to inform applicants of voter eligibility requirements. *See* 52 U.S.C. § 20507(a)(5)(A). How can Florida make eligibility determinations without figuring out the amount of LFOs that a felon has outstanding? Florida cannot choose to condition the right to vote on payment of LFOs and then throw up its hands and refuse to tell potential voters how to fulfill that condition.

To put this in some perspective, imagine a state that requires, as a condition of renewing drivers' licenses and vehicle registrations, that drivers pay all outstanding citations for parking/traffic infractions. A driver goes to his county agency and is told that he may have some unpaid citations. He asks for information about the citations and their respective amounts so that he can verify their accuracy and pay whatever is outstanding. But the clerk tells him that the state can't give him the information because the debt for the citations has been sold to third-party collection agencies; those agencies charge certain fees (which vary by agency and year) on top of the citation amounts; and the county has no way of knowing what those fees are or what amounts have been paid or credited. The clerk tries to call other state agencies (and some of the collection agencies) to get answers, but to no avail, and tells the driver he will have to figure everything out on his own. So the driver has to leave without his license and car registration, and will need to risk driving in violation of the law—and face arrest—in order to get to work, take his children to school, and carry out the other tasks of daily life. Would this state of affairs be constitutionally permissible? Of course not.

Assuming Florida ever gets around to processing felons' registrations—something I have significant doubts about given the record in this case—those who it believes are ineligible would presumably receive notice under § 98.075(7). That statute does not, however, require the County Supervisor of Elections to disclose in the notice the amount of LFOs that a felon owes. *See* § 98.075(7)(a)(1)(a) (providing that the notice must include a "statement of the basis for the registered voter's potential ineligibility," but not requiring a specific determination of the amount of LFOs owed). And the record reflects that Florida often will be unable to determine that amount itself.

Even if felons could be saddled with the initial burden of trying to figure out their LFO status, it is Florida—and only Florida—which has the information and the ability to provide the ultimate answer to the felons' inquiries. There is no third-party aggregator of data to whom the felons can turn.

C

The majority rejects the plaintiffs' due process argument because, it says, any deprivation of their right to vote "was accomplished through the legislative process and the process for adopting a constitutional amendment[.]" It is true that "[w]hen the legislature passes a law which affects a general class of persons, those persons have all received procedural process—the legislative process." But the majority ignores the necessary adjudicative phase of the re-enfranchisement process under Florida's own laws.

On its face, § 98.0751 sets forth an adjudicative process for determining felons' eligibility to vote. It explains that "[t]he department shall obtain and review information pursuant to s. 98.075(5) related to a person who registers to vote and make an initial determination on whether such information is credible and reliable regarding whether the person is eligible," and that "[u]pon making an initial determination of the credibility and reliability of such information, the department shall forward such information to the supervisor of elections pursuant to s. 98.075." § 98.0751(3)(a). It further provides that "[a] local supervisor of elections shall verify and make a final determination pursuant to s. 98.075 regarding whether the person who registers to vote is eligible," and that "the supervisor of elections may request additional assistance from the department in making the final determination, if necessary." § 98.0751(3)(b)-(c).

As these provisions make clear, determining eligibility to vote under Florida law requires evaluating past facts, including the amount of LFOs a felon was ordered to pay, and then calculating the amount that has already been paid (and where or to whom the payments are credited). This requires a number of adjudicative decisions—e.g., deciding whether LFOs are linked to misdemeanor or felony convictions if a felon has both, deciding whether to employ the actual-balance or every-dollar method, and deciding what evidence is enough to prove a payment has been made.

Under Supreme Court and Eleventh Circuit precedent, this process is undeniably individual and adjudicatory. Indeed, Florida's procedure for determining whether registrants should be removed from the voter rolls is similar to schemes that the Supreme Court has reviewed in other due process cases involving the denial of a state-created benefit. *See, e.g., Goldberg v. Kelly* (1970) (reviewing whether a state's procedure for terminating public assistance payments violated procedural due process); *Mathews v. Eldridge* (1976) (reviewing whether the procedure for terminating Social Security disability benefit payments complied with due process).

D

The due process problems do not end there. The Supreme Court has told us that a law may be vague for two independent reasons: "First, it may fail to provide the kind of notice that will enable ordinary people to understand what conduct it prohibits; second, it may authorize and even encourage arbitrary and discriminatory enforcement." *Chicago v. Morales* (1999). In my view, § 98.0751 is impermissibly vague for the latter reason—it fails to "provide explicit standards" on how to implement the LFO requirement so as to avoid "arbitrary and discriminatory" application.

The majority says that the law itself is not vague, and instead felons are just uncertain about "factual circumstances" regarding their eligibility to vote. But these "factual circumstances" are the whole ballgame, and not merely insignificant details. In any event, it is not just felons who are confused about whether they have satisfied the terms of their sentences. Because the Division of Elections has not provided any guidance to County Supervisors of Elections on how to implement the LFO requirement, they too are "left guessing" as to how to impose it. And a "wrong guess" here results in "severe consequences": the wrongful denial of the right to vote, or an arrest for a voting violation.

What a great system Florida has set up. If the stakes were not so high, it would be laughable and deserving of a Dave Barry article lampooning the state's bureaucratic incompetence and malfeasance.

IV

The Twenty-Fourth Amendment, ratified in 1964, provides that the right to vote "shall not be denied or abridged by the United States or any State by reason of failure to pay any poll tax or other tax." This straightforward language confirms the principle that "a tax on the right to vote is constitutionally indefensible."

A

Fees and costs routinely imposed on criminal defendants—in operation and in substance—constitute an "other tax" under the Twenty-Fourth Amendment.

B

The majority says that these fees and costs are penalties, and not fines, because they are linked to culpability and are not imposed on defendants who are acquitted. Although they are also imposed on those who plead no contest and/or have their adjudication of guilt withheld, the majority emphasizes that under Florida law defendants who withhold their adjudication or plead no contest may be subject to punishment. The majority's contention that these fees and costs are punitive, however, is belied by the fact that they bear no relation to the crimes charged, as "a defendant adjudged guilty of a violent offense ordinarily is assessed the same amount as a defendant who is charged with a comparatively minor nonviolent offense, denies guilt, pleads no-contest, and is not adjudged guilty."

But even if there is some incidental punitive purpose for these fees and costs, that does not change the undeniable fact that their *primary* purpose is the raising of revenue. And Supreme Court precedent tells us that it is the primary purpose that matters.

The fees and costs here serve primarily to raise revenue for the state, and therefore are taxes. As one of the *amici* correctly explain, "[t]he mere fact of antecedent criminal conviction does not change a 'tax' to something else." Amicus Br. of Tax & Constitutional Law Professors at 13 (noting that if hypothetically Florida imposed an income tax of 10% on individuals convicted of crimes, and prohibited felons from voting if they failed to pay the tax, that would violate the Twenty-Fourth Amendment). I could not have put it any better.

C

Several colleagues in Part III.B.2 advocate for a narrow reading of the Twenty-Fourth Amendment by arguing that the phrase "by reason of" in the Amendment is different in meaning than the phrase "on account of" in the Fifteenth, Nineteenth, and Twenty-Sixth Amendments. As Part III.B.2 does not even garner a plurality of the judges in the majority, I am unsure why this linguistic exegesis is necessary. But given the number of pages dedicated to this contention, I will take a moment to point out its deficiencies.

A straightforward textual analysis shows that "by reason of" has the same meaning as "on account of." Indeed, our colleagues acknowledge that dictionaries from the time the Twenty-Fourth Amendment was drafted define the phrases "by reason of" and "on account of" by reference to each other. But rather than confront the inevitable conclusion—that the two phrases are synonymous—our colleagues instead say that this means the dictionary definitions "are of limited value." What they are saying, I think, is that they do not like the result of a simple textual analysis, and therefore feel free to go beyond the text's common understanding because that understanding is not helpful to their position. If that is textualism, textualism is a mirage.

This analytical move is surprising given the current emphasis placed on public understanding of the words used in constitutional text.

Rather than rely on these consistent definitions of the phrase "by reason of," our colleagues isolate the word "reason" and then select a definition of that one word to define the entire phrase. But "reason," when used in a phrase, cannot be read in isolation because the "text must be construed as a whole."

The fees and costs Florida imposes "exact[] a price for the privilege of exercising the franchise." That is exactly what the framers of the Twenty-Fourth Amendment sought to prevent.

V

Our predecessor, the former Fifth Circuit, has been rightly praised for its landmark decisions on voting rights in the 1950s and 1960s. I doubt that today's decision—which blesses Florida's neutering of Amendment 4—will be viewed as kindly by history.

B. *VOTER REGISTRATION AND IDENTIFICATION*

1. *Historical Overview and the Basis of State and Federal Power*

Since the presidential election of 2000, which was extraordinarily close and controversial, the United States has undertaken an extensive reexamination of many of its rules that govern the casting of ballots. Most of these rules are enacted by state legislatures, rather than by Congress, although Congress has imposed some constraints on the voting rules that states may adopt.

Much of this legislative reform has been motivated by a genuine desire to improve the voting process. But some appears to derive from partisan desires to tilt the electoral playing field in a way that would favor one party's candidates, or the other's, over their competitors. Right or wrong, there is a widespread perception among political professionals that Democrats generally favor voting rules that make it easier to cast ballots even at the risk that some of those ballots may be illegitimate, while Republicans prefer voting rules that make it tougher to cast an invalid ballot but also make it harder for eligible voters to cast their valid ballots. There is even the cynical view that some Republican politicians would like to impose more rigorous voting requirements solely to reduce turnout among certain groups of voters, like minorities and lower-income individuals, who tend to vote for Democrats—while, conversely, Democratic politicians would like to reduce the barriers to casting a ballot simply because doing so would make it more likely for Democrats to win elections. The partisan fights over the rules of the voting process have intensified, and become nastier, over the last decade and consequently have been dubbed "The Voting Wars."*

If we take a historical perspective, however, these voting wars are nothing new. The two dominant political parties have been fighting over the rules for casting ballots for just about as long as our political system has had two dominant political parties, which is to say for almost as long as the Republic has been in existence. In the nineteenth century, the fight initially was over whether there would be voter registration requirements. With the expansion of the franchise associated with the removal of property qualifications, there became increasing pressure to adopt requirements that potential voters register in advance of the day on which they would be entitled to cast their ballots. Poll workers could use the registration lists to ensure that individuals arriving at the polling place to cast ballots were indeed eligible to vote. Opponents of the new registration requirements argued that they were unconstitutional (under state constitutional provisions) on the ground that the obligation to register in advance added an extra eligibility prerequisite inconsistent with the constitutional specification of the entitlement to the franchise. (In other words, if the state constitution said that all male citizens over the age of 21 were entitled to vote, then opponents of the new registration requirement said that it was an extra limitation on the franchise not specified in the state constitution.) State courts generally rejected this argument on the ground that the registration requirement was not a limitation on who was eligible to vote, but instead a regulation of the method by which eligible voters exercised the franchise. As you will see, this longstanding distinction figures prominently in a new case from the U.S. Supreme Court, *Arizona v. Intertribal Council*, which is a major statement delineating the relationship of state and federal power over the regulation of the voting process.

Another aspect of the current voting wars echoes old historical patterns. In the early twentieth century, registration rules were used to make it more difficult for recent immigrants to become registered. Requirements to register in person, rather than by mail, or even limiting the opportunity to register to a single day, were particularly onerous for workers whose jobs did not give them the flexibility to go register during working hours. And especially in the South, a whole variety of practices were developed to prevent African Americans from voting. In Part I, we saw that the drawing of legislative districts can be manipulated to curtail

* *See* Richard L. Hasen, The Voting Wars: From Florida 2000 to the Next Meltdown (2012).

the influence of African-American voters. But other outright barriers, like literacy tests, were erected during the Jim Crow era to disenfranchise African Americans.

The impotency of the Fifteenth Amendment in protecting against these racially discriminatory measures was best illustrated by *Giles v. Harris*, 189 U.S. 475 (1903), in which Justice Oliver Wendell Holmes (writing for the Court) refused to grant injunctive relief to stop even blatantly overt and systematic discrimination against African Americans in the registration of new voters in Alabama. Justice Holmes said that if the racial discrimination was as systematic as the plaintiffs alleged, then the federal judiciary would be powerless to remedy the wrong unless it took over control of the state's entire voting apparatus—something the Supreme Court in 1903 was unprepared to undertake. Today one can understand *Giles* only by recognizing that, after the abandonment of Reconstruction in the last decades of the nineteenth century, there was no national will to protect African Americans from the renewed thoroughgoing subjugation of Jim Crow.

The Voting Rights Act of 1965, arguably the greatest of all the achievements of the Civil Rights movement, resulted in great strides being made in enfranchising African Americans. It did so, at least in part, by banning literacy tests—first in the places where discrimination against African Americans was most rampant, and then nationwide. The Voting Rights Act (VRA) also included Section 5 preclearance, which served as a check on election administration changes that would discriminate against African Americans and language minorities in the jurisdictions (mostly in the South and Southwest) covered by Section 5.

Yet we saw in Part I of this book that the Supreme Court, in *Shelby County v. Holder*, rendered Section 5 dormant. One of the major unanswered questions of the current voting wars is the extent to which the remainder of the VRA will be effective in preventing any newly erected barriers to casting ballots that are racially discriminatory in either intent or effect. *Shelby County* left standing Section 2 of the VRA, which prohibits any voting "practice" or "procedure" that "results in a denial or abridgement of the right of any citizen of the United States to vote on account of race." But this statutory text will not necessarily be broadly interpreted. Instead, the federal judiciary is still in the process of developing a standard for determining when a voting rule that imposes a differentially heavier burden on minority voters is a violation of the results test of the VRA's Section 2.

The number one issue over which the current voting wars have been fought is voter identification—what sort of evidence should voters be required to present when they cast their ballots to demonstrate who they are? Voter identification is closely related to voter registration, as *Arizona v. Intertribal Council* will show. There is arguably no need to register in advance if voters can show up at the polls on Election Day with adequate proof of their identity, which establishes their eligibility to vote. Indeed, several states have adopted this policy, which is usually called Election Day Registration, because citizens can register and vote at the same time on Election Day.

Conversely, if citizens establish their eligibility when they register, then arguably the identification requirement can be less onerous when they show up to cast their ballot on Election Day. In this situation, they do not need to prove their eligibility all over again; they only need to confirm that they are the same person who previously registered. In the twentieth century, after registering in advance had become a widespread requirement, it was often thought adequate for voters simply to sign their names in a poll book listing registered voters. This signature, when checked against the one on file, would confirm the identity of the registered voter. Since 2000, however, there has been increasing sentiment that some additional documentary proof of identity should be required when a voter casts a ballot. *Crawford v. Marion County Election Board,* which we will read after *Arizona v. Intertribal Council,* concerns how strict or lenient this identification requirement should be.

But first let's examine the basic question of how and when voters establish the fundamental eligibility requirement of citizenship. Should it be sufficient for voters simply to sign a statement, under penalty of perjury (or the equivalent) that they are in fact U.S. citizens? Or should voters be required to show documentary proof of their citizenship, such as a birth certificate or naturalization papers? And, if so, when? Is it better to have the voters present this documentary proof of citizenship when they register in advance? Or should voters be required to bring this documentary proof of citizenship with them to the polls on Election Day?

Arizona enacted a law that requires documentary proof of citizenship at the time of registration. Arguably, this law is less onerous than one that would require the same documentary proof of citizenship at the time of voting. But the legal question arose whether Arizona's law conflicted with the National Voter Registration Act (NVRA), which Congress passed in 1993 (and which is often colloquially called the "Motor Voter" law). And if Arizona's law does conflict with the federal statute, which one must give way under the federal Constitution—specifically, the Elections Clause of Article I, Section 4? These were the legal and constitutional questions that the U.S. Supreme Court addressed in the following, potentially far-reaching case.

Arizona v. Inter Tribal Council of Arizona, Inc.

133 S. Ct. 2247 (2013)

Justice SCALIA delivered the opinion of the Court.

The National Voter Registration Act [NVRA] requires States to "accept and use" a uniform federal form to register voters for federal elections. The contents of that form (colloquially known as the Federal Form) are prescribed by a federal agency, the Election Assistance Commission. The Federal Form developed by the EAC does not require documentary evidence of citizenship; rather, it requires only that an applicant aver, under penalty of perjury, that he is a citizen. Arizona law requires voter-registration officials to "reject" any application for registration, including a Federal Form, that is not accompanied by concrete evidence of citizenship. The question is whether Arizona's evidence-of-citizenship requirement, as applied to Federal Form applicants, is pre-empted by the Act's mandate that States "accept and use" the Federal Form.

I

Over the past two decades, Congress has erected a complex superstructure of federal regulation atop state voter-registration systems. The NVRA "requires States to provide simplified systems for registering to vote in *federal* elections." *Young v. Fordice* (1997). The Act requires each State to permit prospective voters to "register to vote in elections for Federal office" by any of three methods: simultaneously with a driver's license application, in person, or by mail.

This case concerns registration by mail. Section 1973gg-4 requires States to "accept and use" a standard federal registration form. The Election Assistance Commission is invested with rulemaking authority to prescribe the contents of that Federal Form. The EAC is explicitly instructed, however, to develop the Federal Form "in consultation with the chief election officers of the States." The Federal Form thus contains a number of state-specific instructions, which tell residents of each State what additional information they must provide and where they must submit the form. *See* National Mail Voter Registration Form.* Each state-specific instruction must be approved by the EAC before it is included on the Federal Form.

To be eligible to vote under Arizona law, a person must be a citizen of the United States. This case concerns Arizona's efforts to enforce that qualification. In 2004, Arizona voters adopted Proposition 200, a ballot initiative designed in part "to combat voter fraud by requiring voters to present proof of citizenship when they register to vote and to present identification when they vote on election day." *Purcell v. Gonzalez* (2006). Proposition 200 amended the State's election code to require county recorders to "reject any application for registration that is not accompanied by satisfactory evidence of United States citizenship." Ariz. Rev. Stat. Ann. §16-166(F). The proof-of-citizenship requirement is satisfied by (1) a photocopy of the applicant's passport or birth certificate, (2) a driver's license number, if the license states that the issuing authority verified the holder's U.S. citizenship, (3) evidence of naturalization, (4) tribal identification, or (5) "[o]ther documents or methods of proof . . . established pursuant to the Immigration Reform and Control Act of 1986." The EAC did not grant Arizona's request to include this new requirement among the state-specific instructions for Arizona on the Federal Form. Consequently, the Federal Form includes a statutorily required attestation, subscribed to under penalty of perjury, that an Arizona applicant meets the State's voting requirements (including the citizenship requirement), but does not require concrete evidence of citizenship.

[P]laintiffs [sued] seeking to enjoin the voting provisions of Proposition 200. A panel of the Ninth Circuit [ruled] that "Proposition 200's documentary proof of citizenship requirement conflicts with the NVRA's text, structure, and purpose." The en banc Court of Appeals agreed.

II

The Elections Clause, Art. I, § 4, cl. 1, provides:

> "The Times, Places and Manner of holding Elections for Senators and Representatives, shall be prescribed in each State by the Legislature thereof; but the Congress may at any time by Law make or alter such Regulations, except as to the places of chusing [*sic*] Senators."

* *Available at* http://www.eac.gov/assets/1/Documents/Federal%20Voter%Registration_1209_en9242012.pdf.

The Clause empowers Congress to pre-empt state regulations governing the "Times, Places and Manner" of holding congressional elections. The question here is whether the federal statutory requirement that States "accept and use" the Federal Form pre-empts Arizona's state-law requirement that officials "reject" the application of a prospective voter who submits a completed Federal Form unaccompanied by documentary evidence of citizenship.

A

The Elections Clause has two functions. Upon the States it imposes the duty ("*shall* be prescribed") to prescribe the time, place, and manner of electing Representatives and Senators; upon Congress it confers the power to alter those regulations or supplant them altogether. This grant of congressional power was the Framers' insurance against the possibility that a State would refuse to provide for the election of representatives to the Federal Congress.

The Clause's substantive scope is broad. "Times, Places, and Manner," we have written, are "comprehensive words," which "embrace authority to provide a complete code for congressional elections," including, as relevant here and as petitioners do not contest, regulations relating to "registration." *Smiley v. Holm* (1932). In practice, the Clause functions as "a default provision; it invests the States with responsibility for the mechanics of congressional elections, but only so far as Congress declines to pre-empt state legislative choices." *Foster v. Love* (1997). The power of Congress over the "Times, Places and Manner" of congressional elections "is paramount, and may be exercised at any time, and to any extent which it deems expedient; and so far as it is exercised, and no farther, the regulations effected supersede those of the State which are inconsistent therewith." *Ex parte Siebold* (1880).

B

The straightforward textual question here is whether Ariz. Rev. Stat. Ann. § 16-166(F), which requires state officials to "reject" a Federal Form unaccompanied by documentary evidence of citizenship, conflicts with the NVRA's mandate that Arizona "accept and use" the Federal Form. If so, the state law, "so far as the conflict extends, ceases to be operative." *Siebold.* In Arizona's view, these seemingly incompatible obligations can be read to operate harmoniously: The NVRA, it contends, requires merely that a State receive the Federal Form willingly and use that form as one element in its (perhaps lengthy) transaction with a prospective voter.

Taken in isolation, the mandate that a State "accept and use" the Federal Form is fairly susceptible of two interpretations. It might mean that a State must accept the Federal Form as a complete and sufficient registration application; or it might mean that the State is merely required to receive the form willingly and use it *somehow* in its voter registration process. Both readings — "receive willingly" and "accept as sufficient" — are compatible with the plain meaning of the word "accept." *See* 1 Oxford English Dictionary 70 (2d ed. 1989) ("To take or receive (a thing offered) willingly"; "To receive as sufficient or adequate"); Webster's New International Dictionary 14 (2d ed. 1954) ("To receive (a thing offered to or thrust upon one) with a consenting mind"; "To receive with favor; to approve"). And we take it as self-evident that the "elastic" verb "use," read in isolation, is broad enough to encompass Arizona's preferred construction. In common parlance, one might say that a restaurant accepts and uses credit cards even though it requires customers to show matching identification when making a purchase.

"Words that can have more than one meaning are given content, however, by their surroundings." *Whitman v. American Trucking Assns., Inc.* (2001). And reading "accept" merely to denote willing receipt seems out of place in the context of an official mandate to accept and use something for a given purpose. The implication of such a mandate is that its object is to be accepted *as sufficient* for the requirement it is meant to satisfy. For example, a government *diktat* that "civil servants shall accept government IOUs for payment of salaries" does not invite the response, "sure, we'll accept IOUs—if you pay us a ten percent down payment in cash." Many federal statutes contain similarly phrased commands, and they contemplate more than mere willing receipt.[3]

Arizona's reading is also difficult to reconcile with neighboring provisions of the NVRA. Section 1973gg-6(a)(1)(B) provides that a State shall "ensure that any eligible applicant is registered to vote in an election . . . if the *valid voter registration form* of the applicant is postmarked" not later than a specified number of days before the election. (Emphasis added.) Yet Arizona reads the phrase "accept and use" in § 1973gg-4(a)(1) as permitting it to *reject* a completed Federal Form if the applicant does not submit additional information required by state law. That reading can be squared with Arizona's obligation under § 1973gg-6(a)(1) only if a completed Federal Form is not a "valid voter registration form," which seems unlikely. The statute empowers the EAC to create the Federal Form, requires the EAC to prescribe its contents within specified limits, and requires States to "accept and use" it. It is improbable that the statute envisions a completed copy of the form it takes such pains to create as being anything less than "valid."

The Act also authorizes States, "*[i]n addition to* accepting and using the" Federal Form, to create their own, state-specific voter-registration forms, which can be used to register voters in both state and federal elections. (Emphasis added). These state-developed forms may require information the Federal Form does not. (For example, unlike the Federal Form, Arizona's registration form includes Proposition 200's proof-of-citizenship requirement.) This permission works in tandem with the requirement that States "accept and use" the Federal Form. States retain the flexibility to design and use their own registration forms, but the Federal Form provides a backstop: No matter what procedural hurdles a State's own form imposes, the Federal Form guarantees that a simple means of registering to vote in federal elections will be available.[4] Arizona's reading would permit a State to demand of

3. The dissent accepts that a State may not impose additional requirements that render the Federal Form *entirely* superfluous; it would require that the State "us[e] the form as a meaningful part of the registration process." The dissent does not tell us precisely how large a role for the Federal Form suffices to make it "meaningful": One step out of two? Three? Ten? There is no easy answer, for the dissent's "meaningful part" standard is as indeterminate as it is atextual. [Footnote relocated.—EDS.]

4. In the face of this straightforward explanation, the dissent maintains that it would be "nonsensical" for a less demanding federal form to exist alongside a more demanding state form. But it is the dissent's alternative explanation for § 1973gg-4(a)(2) that makes no sense. The "purpose" of the Federal Form, it claims, is "to facilitate interstate voter registration

Federal Form applicants every additional piece of information the State requires on its state-specific form. If that is so, the Federal Form ceases to perform any meaningful function, and would be a feeble means of "increas[ing] the number of eligible citizens who register to vote in elections for Federal office." § 1973gg(b).

Finally, Arizona appeals to the presumption against pre-emption sometimes invoked in our Supremacy Clause cases. *See, e.g., Gregory v. Ashcroft* (1991). Where it applies, "we start with the assumption that the historic police powers of the States were not to be superseded by the Federal Act unless that was the clear and manifest purpose of Congress." *Rice v. Santa Fe Elevator Corp.* (1947). That rule of construction rests on an assumption about congressional intent: that "Congress does not exercise lightly" the "extraordinary power" to "legislate in areas traditionally regulated by the States." *Gregory*. We have never mentioned such a principle in our Elections Clause cases. *Siebold*, for example, simply said that Elections Clause legislation, "so far as it extends and conflicts with the regulations of the State, necessarily supersedes them." There is good reason for treating Elections Clause legislation differently: The assumption that Congress is reluctant to pre-empt does not hold when Congress acts under that constitutional provision, which empowers Congress to "make or alter" state election regulations. Art. I, § 4, cl. 1. When Congress legislates with respect to the "Times, Places and Manner" of holding congressional elections, it *necessarily* displaces some element of a pre-existing legal regime erected by the States. Because the power the Elections Clause confers is none other than the power to pre-empt, the reasonable assumption is that the statutory text accurately communicates the scope of Congress's pre-emptive intent. Moreover, the federalism concerns underlying the presumption in the Supremacy Clause context are somewhat weaker here. Unlike the States' "historic police powers," the States' role in regulating congressional elections—while weighty and worthy of respect—has always existed subject to the express qualification that it "terminates according to federal law." *Buckman Co. v. Plaintiffs' Legal Comm.* (2001). In sum, there is no compelling reason not to read Elections Clause legislation simply to mean what it says.

We conclude that the fairest reading of the statute is that a state-imposed requirement of evidence of citizenship not required by the Federal Form is inconsistent with the NVRA's mandate that States "accept and use" the Federal Form. If this reading prevails, the Elections Clause requires that Arizona's rule give way.

We note, however, that while the NVRA forbids States to demand that an applicant submit additional information beyond that required by the Federal Form, it does not preclude States from "deny[ing] registration based on information in their possession establishing the applicant's ineligibility." Brief for United States as *Amicus Curiae* 24. The NVRA clearly contemplates that not every submitted Federal

drives. Thanks to the federal form, volunteers distributing voter registration materials at a shopping mall in Yuma can give a copy of the same form to every person they meet without attempting to distinguish between residents of Arizona and California." But in the dissent's world, a volunteer in Yuma would have to give every prospective voter not only a Federal Form, but also a separate set of either Arizona- or California-specific instructions detailing the additional information the applicant must submit to the State. In ours, every eligible voter can be assured that if he does what the Federal Form says, he will be registered. The dissent therefore provides yet another compelling reason to interpret the statute our way.

Form will result in registration. *See* § 1973gg-7(b)(1) (Federal Form "may require only" information "necessary to enable the appropriate State election official to *assess the eligibility of the applicant*" (emphasis added)); § 1973gg-6(a)(2) (States must require election officials to "send notice to each applicant of the disposition of the application").

III

Arizona contends, however, that its construction of the phrase "accept and use" is necessary to avoid a conflict between the NVRA and Arizona's constitutional authority to establish qualifications (such as citizenship) for voting. Arizona is correct that the Elections Clause empowers Congress to regulate *how* federal elections are held, but not *who* may vote in them.* The Constitution prescribes a straightforward rule for the composition of the federal electorate. Article I, § 2, cl. 1, provides that electors in each State for the House of Representatives "shall have the Qualifications requisite for Electors of the most numerous Branch of the State Legislature," and the Seventeenth Amendment adopts the same criterion for senatorial elections. One cannot read the Elections Clause as treating implicitly what these other constitutional provisions regulate explicitly. "It is difficult to see how words could be clearer in stating what Congress can control and what it cannot control. Surely nothing in these provisions lends itself to the view that voting qualifications in federal elections are to be set by Congress." *Oregon v. Mitchell* (1970) (Harlan, J., concurring in part and dissenting in part).[8]

Prescribing voting qualifications, therefore, "forms no part of the power to be conferred upon the national government" by the Elections Clause, which is "expressly restricted to the regulation of the *times,* the *places,* and the *manner* of elections." The Federalist No. 60, at 371 (A. Hamilton). This allocation of authority sprang from the Framers' aversion to concentrated power. A Congress empowered to regulate the qualifications of its own electorate, Madison warned, could "by

* [The statement in this sentence and the ones that follow—which stipulate that Congress may dictate *how* elections are run but not *who* may vote in them—are extremely important, in that they delineate the balance of power between the federal and state governments in promulgating election regulations. In essence, Justice Scalia is saying that Congress has some, but not complete, authority and that states also have significant power. —Eds.]

8. In *Mitchell,* the judgment of the Court was that Congress could compel the States to permit 18-year-olds to vote in federal elections. Of the five Justices who concurred in that outcome, only Justice Black was of the view that congressional power to prescribe this age qualification derived from the Elections Clause, while four Justices relied on the Fourteenth Amendment, *id.* (opinion of Douglas, J.), (joint opinion of Brennan, White, and Marshall, JJ.). That result, which lacked a majority rationale, is of minimal precedential value here. Five Justices took the position that the Elections Clause did *not* confer upon Congress the power to regulate voter qualifications in federal elections. *Mitchell* (opinion of Douglas, J.), (opinion of Harlan, J.), (opinion of Stewart, J., joined by Burger, C.J., and Blackmun, J.). (Justices Brennan, White, and Marshall did not address the Elections Clause.) This last view, which commanded a majority in *Mitchell,* underlies our analysis here. Five Justices also agreed that the Fourteenth Amendment did not empower Congress to impose the 18-year-old-voting mandate. *See Mitchell* (opinion of Black, J.), (opinion of Harlan, J.), (opinion of Stewart, J.).

degrees subvert the Constitution." 2 Records of the Federal Convention of 1787, p. 250 (M. Farrand rev. 1966). At the same time, by tying the federal franchise to the state franchise instead of simply placing it within the unfettered discretion of state legislatures, the Framers avoided "render[ing] too dependent on the State governments that branch of the federal government which ought to be dependent on the people alone." The Federalist No. 52, at 326 (J. Madison).

Since the power to establish voting requirements is of little value without the power to enforce those requirements, Arizona is correct that it would raise serious constitutional doubts if a federal statute precluded a State from obtaining the information necessary to enforce its voter qualifications.[9] If, but for Arizona's interpretation of the "accept and use" provision, the State would be precluded from obtaining information necessary for enforcement, we would have to determine whether Arizona's interpretation, though plainly not the best reading, is at least a possible one. *Cf. Crowell v. Benson* (1932) (the Court will "ascertain whether a construction of the statute *is fairly possible* by which the [constitutional] question may be avoided" (emphasis added)). Happily, we are spared that necessity, since the statute provides another means by which Arizona may obtain information needed for enforcement.

Section 1973gg-7(b)(1) of the Act provides that the Federal Form "may require only such identifying information (including the signature of the applicant) and other information (including data relating to previous registration by the applicant), as is necessary to enable the appropriate State election official to assess the eligibility of the applicant and to administer voter registration and other parts of the election process." At oral argument, the United States expressed the view that the phrase "may require only" in § 1973gg-7(b)(1) means that the EAC "*shall require* information that's necessary, but may only require that information." (emphasis added). That is to say, § 1973gg-7(b)(1) acts as both a ceiling and a floor with respect to the contents of the Federal Form. We need not consider the Government's contention that despite the statute's statement that the EAC "may" require on the Federal Form information "necessary to enable the appropriate State election official to assess the eligibility of the applicant," other provisions of the Act indicate that such action is statutorily required. That is because we think that—by analogy to the rule of statutory interpretation that avoids questionable constitutionality—validly conferred discretionary executive authority is properly exercised (as the Government has proposed) to avoid serious constitutional doubt. That is to say, it is surely permissible if not requisite for the Government to say that necessary information which *may* be required *will* be required.

Since, pursuant to the Government's concession, a State may request that the EAC alter the Federal Form to include information the State deems necessary to determine eligibility, and may challenge the EAC's rejection of that request in a suit under the Administrative Procedure Act, no constitutional doubt is raised by giving the "accept and use" provision of the NVRA its fairest reading. That alternative means of enforcing its constitutional power to determine voting qualifications

9. In their reply brief, petitioners suggest for the first time that "registration is itself a qualification to vote." We resolve this case on the theory on which it has hitherto been litigated: that *citizenship* (not registration) is the voter qualification Arizona seeks to enforce.

remains open to Arizona here. In 2005, the EAC divided 2-to-2 on the request by Arizona to include the evidence-of-citizenship requirement among the state-specific instructions on the Federal Form, which meant that no action could be taken. Arizona did not challenge that agency action (or rather inaction) by seeking APA review in federal court, but we are aware of nothing that prevents Arizona from renewing its request.[10] Should the EAC's inaction persist, Arizona would have the opportunity to establish in a reviewing court that a mere oath will not suffice to effectuate its citizenship requirement and that the EAC is therefore under a nondiscretionary duty to include Arizona's concrete evidence requirement on the Federal Form. Arizona might also assert (as it has argued here) that it would be arbitrary for the EAC to refuse to include Arizona's instruction when it has accepted a similar instruction requested by Louisiana.

We hold that 42 U.S.C. § 1973gg-4 precludes Arizona from requiring a Federal Form applicant to submit information beyond that required by the form itself. Arizona may, however, request anew that the EAC include such a requirement among the Federal Form's state-specific instructions, and may seek judicial review of the EAC's decision under the Administrative Procedure Act.

The judgment of the Court of Appeals is affirmed.

Justice Kennedy, concurring in part and concurring in the judgment.

The opinion for the Court insists on stating a proposition that, in my respectful view, is unnecessary for the proper disposition of the case and is incorrect in any event. The Court concludes that the normal "starting presumption that Congress does not intend to supplant state law" does not apply here because the source of congressional power is the Elections Clause and not some other provision of the Constitution.

There is no sound basis for the Court to rule, for the first time, that there exists a hierarchy of federal powers so that some statutes pre-empting state law must be interpreted by different rules than others, all depending upon which power Congress has exercised.

Whether the federal statute concerns congressional regulation of elections or any other subject proper for Congress to address, a court must not lightly infer a congressional directive to negate the States' otherwise proper exercise of their sovereign power. This case illustrates the point. The separate States have a continuing, essential interest in the integrity and accuracy of the process used to select both state and federal officials. The States pay the costs of holding these elections, which for practical reasons often overlap so that the two sets of officials are selected at the same time, on the same ballots, by the same voters. It seems most doubtful to me

10. The EAC currently lacks a quorum—indeed, the Commission has not a single active Commissioner. If the EAC proves unable to act on a renewed request, Arizona would be free to seek a writ of mandamus to "compel agency action unlawfully withheld or unreasonably delayed." 5 U.S.C. § 706(1). It is a nice point, which we need not resolve here, whether a court can compel agency action that the agency itself, for lack of the statutorily required quorum, is incapable of taking. If the answer to that is no, Arizona might then be in a position to assert a constitutional right to demand concrete evidence of citizenship apart from the Federal Form.

to suggest that States have some lesser concern when what is involved is their own historic role in the conduct of elections. [To the contrary,] the State's undoubted interest in the regulation and conduct of elections must be taken into account and ought not to be deemed by this Court to be a subject of secondary importance.

Here, in my view, the Court is correct to conclude that the National Voter Registration Act of 1993 is unambiguous in its pre-emption of Arizona's statute. For this reason, I concur in the judgment and join all of the Court's opinion except its discussion of the presumption against pre-emption.

Justice THOMAS, dissenting.

I think that both the plain text and the history of the Voter Qualifications Clause, U.S. CONST., Art. I, § 2, cl. 1, and the Seventeenth Amendment authorize States to determine the qualifications of voters in federal elections, which necessarily includes the related power to determine whether those qualifications are satisfied. To avoid substantial constitutional problems created by interpreting § 1973gg-4(a)(1) to permit Congress to effectively countermand this authority, I would construe the law as only requiring Arizona to accept and use the form as part of its voter registration process, leaving the State free to request whatever additional information it determines is necessary to ensure that voters meet the qualifications it has the constitutional authority to establish.

The United States argues that Congress has the authority under Article I, § 4, "to set the rules for voter registration in federal elections." Neither the text nor the original understanding of Article I, § 4, supports that position.

Prior to the Constitution's ratification, the phrase "manner of election" was commonly used in England, Scotland, Ireland, and North America to describe the entire election process. Natelson, The Original Scope of the Congressional Power to Regulate Elections, 13 U. Pa. J. Constitutional L. 1, 10-18 (2010). But there are good reasons for concluding that Article I, § 4's use of "Manner" is considerably more limited. The Constitution does not use the word "Manner" in isolation; rather, "after providing for qualifications, times, and places, the Constitution described the residuum as 'the Manner of holding Elections.' This precise phrase seems to have been newly coined to denote a subset of traditional 'manner' regulation." Consistent with this view, during the state ratification debates, the "Manner of holding Elections" was construed to mean the circumstances under which elections were held and the mechanics of the actual election. *See* 4 Debates in the Several State Conventions on the Adoption of the Federal Constitution 71 (J. Elliot 2d ed. 1863) (hereafter Elliot's Debates) ("The power over the manner of elections does not include that of saying who shall vote . . . the power over the manner only enables them to determine *how* those electors shall elect—whether by ballot, or by vote, or by any other way" (John Steele at the North Carolina ratification debates)). The text of the Times, Places and Manner Clause, therefore, cannot be read to authorize Congress to dictate voter eligibility to the States.

Respondents and the United States point out that *Smiley v. Holm* (1932), mentioned "registration" in a list of voting-related subjects it believed Congress could regulate under Article I, § 4. *Id.* (listing "notices, *registration,* supervision of voting, protection of voters, prevention of fraud and corrupt practices, counting of votes, duties of inspectors and canvassers, and making and publication of election returns" (emphasis added). But that statement was dicta because *Smiley* involved congressional redistricting, not voter registration. Cases since *Smiley* have similarly not addressed the issue of voter qualifications but merely repeated the word "registration" without further analysis.

It is, thus, difficult to maintain that the Times, Places and Manner Clause gives Congress power beyond regulating the casting of ballots and related activities, even as a matter of precedent.

I would interpret § 1973gg-4(a)(1) to avoid the constitutional problems discussed above.

I cannot, therefore, adopt the Court's interpretation that § 1973gg-4(a)(1)'s "accept and use" provision requires states to register anyone who completes and submits the form. Arizona sets citizenship as a qualification to vote, and it wishes to verify citizenship, as it is authorized to do under Article 1, § 2. It matters not whether the United States has specified one way in which *it* believes Arizona might be able to verify citizenship; Arizona has the independent constitutional authority to verify citizenship in the way it deems necessary. By requiring Arizona to register people who have not demonstrated to Arizona's satisfaction that they meet its citizenship qualification for voting, the NVRA, as interpreted by the Court, would exceed Congress' powers under Article I, § 4, and violate Article 1, § 2.

Fortunately, Arizona's alternative interpretation of § 1973gg-4(a)(1) avoids this problem. It is plausible that Arizona "accept[s] and use[s]" the federal form under § 1973gg-4(a)(1) so long as it receives the form and considers it as part of its voter application process. Given States' exclusive authority to set voter qualifications and to determine whether those qualifications are met, I would hold that Arizona may request whatever additional information it requires to verify voter eligibility.

I would not require Arizona to seek approval for its registration requirements from the Federal Government, for, as I have shown, the Federal Government does not have the constitutional authority to withhold such approval. Accordingly, it does not have the authority to command States to seek it. As a result, the majority's proposed solution does little to avoid the serious constitutional problems created by its interpretation.

Justice ALITO, dissenting.

The Court reads an ambiguous federal statute in a way that brushes aside the constitutional authority of the States and produces truly strange results.

Under the Constitution, the States, not Congress, have the authority to establish the qualifications of voters in elections for Members of Congress. The States also have the default authority to regulate federal voter registration. Exercising its right to set federal voter qualifications, Arizona, like every other State, permits only U.S. citizens to vote in federal elections, and Arizona has concluded that this requirement cannot be effectively enforced unless applicants for registration are required to provide proof of citizenship. According to the Court, however, the National Voter Registration Act of 1993 (NVRA) deprives Arizona of this authority. I do not think that this is what Congress intended.

I also doubt that Congress meant for the success of an application for voter registration to depend on which of two valid but substantially different registration forms the applicant happens to fill out and submit, but that is how the Court reads the NVRA. The Court interprets one provision, 42 U.S.C. § 1973gg-6(a)(1)(B), to mean that, if an applicant fills out the federal form, a State must register the applicant without requiring proof of citizenship. But the Court does not question Arizona's authority under another provision of the NVRA, § 1973gg-4(a)(2), to create its own application form that demands proof of citizenship; nor does the Court dispute Arizona's right to refuse to register an applicant who submits that form without the requisite proof. I find it very hard to believe that this is what Congress had in mind.

These results are not required by the NVRA. Proper respect for the constitutional authority of the States demands a clear indication of a congressional intent to pre-empt state laws enforcing voter qualifications. And while the relevant provisions of the Act are hardly models of clarity, their best reading is that the States need not treat the federal form as a complete voter registration application.

I would begin by applying a presumption against pre-emption of the Arizona law requiring voter registration applicants to submit proof of citizenship. Under the Elections Clause, the States have the authority to specify the times, places, and manner of federal elections except to the extent that Congress chooses to provide otherwise. And in recognition of this allocation of authority, it is appropriate to presume that the States retain this authority unless Congress has clearly manifested a contrary intent. The presumption against pre-emption applies with full force when Congress legislates in a "field which the States have traditionally occupied," and the NVRA was the first significant federal regulation of voter registration enacted under the Elections Clause since Reconstruction.

The NVRA does not come close to manifesting the clear intent to pre-empt that we should expect to find when Congress has exercised its Elections Clause power in a way that is constitutionally questionable. Indeed, even if neither the presumption against pre-emption nor the canon of constitutional avoidance applied, the better reading of the Act would be that Arizona is free to require those who use the federal form to supplement their applications with proof of citizenship.

I agree with the Court that the phrase "accept and use," when read in isolation, is ambiguous, but I disagree with the Court's conclusion that § 1973gg-4(a)(1)'s use of that phrase means that a State must treat the federal form as a complete application and must either grant or deny registration without requiring that the applicant supply additional information. Instead, I would hold that a State "accept[s] and use [s]" the federal form so long as it uses the form as a meaningful part of the registration process.

The Court begins its analysis of § 1973gg-4(a)(1)'s context by examining unrelated uses of the word "accept" elsewhere in the United States Code. But a better place to start is to ask what it normally means to "accept and use" an application form. When the phrase is used in that context, it is clear that an organization can "accept and use" a form that it does not treat as a complete application. For example, many colleges and universities accept and use the Common Application for Undergraduate College Admission but also require that applicants submit various additional forms or documents. Similarly, the Social Security Administration undoubtedly "accepts and uses" its Social Security card application form even though someone applying for a card must also prove that he or she is a citizen or has a qualifying immigration status. As such examples illustrate, when an organization says that it "accepts and uses" an application form, it does not necessarily mean that the form constitutes a complete application.

Although § 1973gg-4(a)(1) forbids States from requiring applicants who use the federal form to submit a duplicative state form, nothing in that provision's text prevents Arizona from insisting that federal form applicants supplement their applications with additional information.

That understanding of § 1973gg-4(a)(1) is confirmed by § 1973gg-4(a)(2), which allows States to design and use their own voter registration forms "[i]n addition to accepting and using" the federal form. The Act clearly permits States to require proof of citizenship on their own forms, *see* §§ 1973gg-4(a)(2) and 1973gg-7(b)—a step that Arizona has taken and that today's decision does not disturb. Thus, under the Court's approach, whether someone can register to vote in Arizona without providing proof of citizenship will depend on the happenstance of which of two alternative forms the applicant completes. That could not possibly be what Congress intended; it is as if the Internal Revenue Service issued two sets of personal income tax forms with different tax rates.

We could avoid this nonsensical result by holding that the Act lets the States decide for themselves what information "is necessary . . . to assess the eligibility of the applicant"—both by designing their own forms and by requiring that federal form applicants provide supplemental information when appropriate. The Act's provision for state forms shows that the purpose of the federal form is not to supplant the States' authority in this area but to facilitate interstate voter registration drives. Thanks to the federal form, volunteers distributing voter registration materials at a shopping mall in Yuma can give a copy of the same form to every person they meet without attempting to distinguish between residents of Arizona and California. The federal form was meant to facilitate voter registration drives, not to take away the States' traditional authority to decide what information registrants must supply.[3]

The Court purports to find support for its contrary approach in § 1973gg-6(a)(1)(B), which says that a State must "ensure that any eligible applicant is registered to vote in an election . . . if the valid voter registration form of the applicant is postmarked" within a specified period. The Court understands § 1973gg-6(a)(1)(B) to mean that a State must register an eligible applicant if he or she submits a "valid voter registration form." But when read in context, that provision simply identifies the time within which a State must process registration applications; it says nothing about whether a State may require the submission of supplemental information. The Court's more expansive interpretation of § 1973gg-6(a)(1)(B) sneaks in a qualification that is nowhere to be found in the text. The Court takes pains to say that a State need not register an applicant who properly completes and submits a federal form but is known by the State to be ineligible. But the Court takes the position that a State may not demand that an

3. The Court argues that the federal form would not accomplish this purpose under my interpretation because "a volunteer in Yuma would have to give every prospective voter not only a Federal Form, but also a separate set of either Arizona- or California-specific instructions." But this is exactly what Congress envisioned. Eighteen of the federal form's 23 pages are state-specific instructions.

applicant supply any additional information to confirm voting eligibility. Nothing in § 1973gg-6(a)(1)(B) supports this distinction.

What is a State to do if it has reason to doubt an applicant's eligibility but cannot be sure that the applicant is ineligible? Must the State either grant or deny registration without communicating with the applicant? Or does the Court believe that a State may ask for additional information in individual cases but may not impose a categorical requirement for all applicants? If that is the Court's position, on which provision of the NVRA does it rely? The Court's reading of § 1973gg-6(a)(1)(B) is atextual and makes little sense.

Properly interpreted, the NVRA permits Arizona to require applicants for federal voter registration to provide proof of eligibility.

QUESTIONS ON ARIZONA v. INTER TRIBAL COUNCIL

1. How important is the Court's qualification that Arizona can ask the U.S. Election Assistance Commission to include the documentation-of-citizenship requirement as part of the Federal Form? If the EAC denied that request, would the NVRA then be unconstitutional as-applied for interfering with Arizona's constitutional authority to set the basic requirements for voter eligibility? Or can Arizona adequately enforce its citizenship eligibility requirement by other means?

2. Is the debate between Justices Scalia and Kennedy over whether there should be a "presumption against preemption" under the Elections Clause of practical, or only theoretical, significance?

3. What do you make of the fact that Justices Scalia and Roberts, two of the Court's conservative members, joined the Court's four liberals to make up the majority opinion (and with Kennedy also joining almost all of it), leaving the case essentially a 7-2 split?

4. Virtually every state constitution includes an explicit grant of the right to vote to its state citizens. As Justice Scalia explains, the Election Clause contemplates the states determining voter eligibility. What role does this suggest state courts should play in construing their state constitutional provisions? Should they follow U.S. Supreme Court guidance on the question or give their state constitutions some kind of independent interpretation? If the latter, what factors should go into the meaning of the state constitutional right to vote?

2. *Voter Identification and Equal Protection*

From the media's treatment of the voting wars, one might think that the issue of voter identification (ID) is purely dichotomous, like an on-off switch—either you are for it or against it, and there are no middle-ground positions. But that simplistic view is grossly inaccurate. Even a signature is a form of identification, and thus anyone who believes that voters should be required to sign a poll register when they go to cast their ballots is in favor of at least one form of voter identification. At the other end of the spectrum, conversely, supporting a strict requirement that only one particular type of identification—for example, a photo ID issued by a state's department of motor vehicles—as a satisfactory prerequisite to casting a countable ballot is a very different view on the voter identification issue. In between these two polar positions, there are lots of different points on the spectrum concerning what different forms of ID might suffice—like bank statements or utility bills or library cards, and the like—and what is the consequence of not being able to present an ID at the time of casting one's ballot. For example, some states permit voters without an ID to sign an affidavit as an alternative; other states do not permit this affidavit option.

Congress weighed in on this debate in a limited way in the Help America Vote Act of 2002 (HAVA), requiring identification of first-time voters who register to vote by mail. But Congress permitted a wide range of documents (including pay checks or bank statements) to satisfy this limited federal voter ID requirement. Apart from this requirement, Congress has otherwise left the issue to the states—assuming, of course, that voter ID rules do not discriminate on the basis of race in violation of the federal Voting Rights Act (an issue that is under litigation in Texas and may end up being further litigated in other places). The states have responded by enacting various different types of voter ID laws, some much stricter than others.

The Supreme Court was involved in the voter ID debate in the following case, although the Court was fractured in deciding it, with the nine Justices splintering into three groups of three: the plurality (Stevens, with Roberts and Kennedy), a concurrence (Scalia, with Thomas and Alito), and the dissenters (Breyer, Souter, and Ginsburg, in two separate dissents). As you wade through the opinions, ask yourself what is the relationship of this case to the canonical voter eligibility cases of *Harper* and *Kramer*. Is voter identification a form of voting qualification, like the payment of a poll tax in *Harper*, since an individual is ineligible to cast a ballot that counts if the individual fails to provide the required ID? In fact, is a voter ID rule actually a kind of unconstitutional poll tax, in violation of *Harper* itself, if it costs the individual money to obtain the ID (or, to complicate the issue, as you will see soon, if it costs the individual money to obtain an underlying document, like a birth certificate, to obtain the necessary voter ID)? Or, alternatively, as long as a voter ID rule does not operate as a wealth qualification in violation of *Harper*, then is a voter ID rule really not an eligibility requirement at all, but just a procedure the voter must follow—like going to the voter's correct polling place to cast a ballot, or signing the poll book before voting? (This division between eligibility requirements, on the one hand, and "manner of voting" rules, on the other, tracks the distinction the Court drew in *Arizona v. Intertribal Council.*)

These questions raise more broadly the issue of what standard of review the Court should apply to a voter ID rule. As you will see, the Justices diverge on this issue. Is that because they differ on how to think about the voter ID rule specifically, or do they have a more general jurisprudential disagreement about the role of the federal judiciary in voting cases (a disagreement we have seen before, and will see again in cases that have nothing to do with voter ID itself)? Similarly, are some of the Justices more faithful to the legacy of *Harper* and *Kramer* than others, or are they all on board with *Harper* and *Kramer* as far as those precedents go, but the Justices just diverge as they move farther along the journey of adjudicating voting rights cases?

A few more things to think about as you read this very important case: (1) Why is Justice Stevens, usually a "liberal," grouped here with Roberts and Kennedy, who are usually more conservative than Stevens? (2) To what extent does it matter that this case involved a "facial" rather than "as-applied" challenge (and what difference might this distinction make in future cases)? (3) How important is the factual debate over the extent to which "voter fraud" exists and might be thwarted by voter ID rules (in other words, how often do individuals attempt to cast ballots pretending to be someone they are not, such that an ID rule would stop them from doing so)? (4) As a factual matter, how many persons does a voter ID law actually disenfranchise?

Crawford v. Marion County Election Board

553 U.S. 181 (2008)

Justice STEVENS announced the judgment of the Court and delivered an opinion in which THE CHIEF JUSTICE and Justice KENNEDY join.

At issue is the constitutionality of an Indiana statute requiring citizens voting in person on election day, or casting a ballot in person at the office of the circuit court clerk prior to election day, to present photo identification issued by the government.

Referred to as either the "Voter ID Law" or "SEA 483," the statute applies to in-person voting at both primary and general elections. The requirement does not apply to absentee ballots submitted by mail, and the statute contains an exception for persons living and voting in a state-licensed facility such as a nursing home. A voter who is indigent or has a religious objection to being photographed may cast a provisional ballot that will be counted only if she executes an appropriate affidavit before the circuit court clerk within 10 days following the election. A voter who has photo identification but is unable to present that identification on election day may file a provisional ballot that will be counted if she brings her photo identification to the circuit county clerk's office within 10 days. No photo identification is required in order to register to vote, and the State offers free photo identification to qualified voters able to establish their residence and identity.

We are persuaded that the District Court and the Court of Appeals correctly concluded that the evidence in the record is not sufficient to support a facial attack on the validity of the entire statute, and thus affirm.

I

In *Harper v. Virginia Bd. of Elections* (1966), the Court held that Virginia could not condition the right to vote in a state election on the payment of a poll tax of $1.50. We rejected the dissenters' argument that the interest in promoting civic responsibility by weeding out those voters who did not care enough about public affairs to pay a small sum for the privilege of voting provided a rational basis for the tax. Applying a stricter standard, we concluded that a State "violates the Equal Protection Clause of the Fourteenth Amendment whenever it makes the affluence

of the voter or payment of any fee an electoral standard." We used the term "invidiously discriminate" to describe conduct prohibited under that standard. Although the State's justification for the tax was rational, it was invidious because it was irrelevant to the voter's qualifications. Thus, under the standard applied in *Harper*, even rational restrictions on the right to vote are invidious if they are unrelated to voter qualifications. In *Anderson v. Celebrezze*, however, we confirmed the general rule that "evenhanded restrictions that protect the integrity and reliability of the electoral process itself" are not invidious and satisfy the standard set forth in *Harper*. Rather than applying any "litmus test" that would neatly separate valid from invalid restrictions, we concluded that a court must identify and evaluate the interests put forward by the State as justifications for the burden imposed by its rule, and then make the "hard judgment" that our adversary system demands.

Later, in *Burdick v. Takushi* (1992), we applied *Anderson*'s standard for "reasonable, nondiscriminatory restrictions" and upheld Hawaii's prohibition on write-in voting despite the fact that it prevented a significant number of "voters from participating in Hawaii elections in a meaningful manner." *Id.* (Kennedy, J., dissenting). We reaffirmed *Anderson*'s requirement that a court evaluating a constitutional challenge to an election regulation weigh the asserted injury to the right to vote against the "precise interests put forward by the State as justifications for the burden imposed by its rule." (quoting *Anderson*).[8]

In neither [*Anderson*] nor *Burdick* did we identify any litmus test for measuring the severity of a burden that a state law imposes on a political party, an individual voter, or a discrete class of voters. However slight that burden may appear, as *Harper* demonstrates, it must be justified by relevant and legitimate state interests sufficiently weighty to justify the limitation.

II

The State has identified several state interests that arguably justify the burdens that SEA 483 imposes on voters and potential voters. While petitioners argue that the statute was actually motivated by partisan concerns and dispute both the significance of the State's interests and the magnitude of any real threat to those interests, they do not question the legitimacy of the interests the State has identified. Each is unquestionably relevant to the State's interest in protecting the integrity and reliability of the electoral process.

The first is the interest in deterring and detecting voter fraud. The State has a valid interest in participating in a nationwide effort to improve and modernize election procedures that have been criticized as antiquated and inefficient. The State also argues that it has a particular interest in preventing voter fraud in response to a problem that is in part the product of its own maladministration—namely,

8. Contrary to Justice Scalia's suggestion, our approach remains faithful to *Anderson* and *Burdick*. The *Burdick* opinion was explicit in its endorsement and adherence to *Anderson* and repeatedly cited *Anderson*. To be sure, *Burdick* rejected the argument that strict scrutiny applies to all laws imposing a burden on the right to vote; but in its place, the Court applied the "flexible standard" set forth in *Anderson*. *Burdick* surely did not create a novel "deferential 'important regulatory interests' standard."

that Indiana's voter registration rolls include a large number of names of persons who are either deceased or no longer live in Indiana. Finally, the State relies on its interest in safeguarding voter confidence. Each of these interests merits separate comment.

Election Modernization

[N]either HAVA nor NVRA required Indiana to enact SEA 483, but they do indicate that Congress believes that photo identification is one effective method of establishing a voter's qualification to vote and that the integrity of elections is enhanced through improved technology.

Voter Fraud

The only kind of voter fraud that SEA 483 addresses is in-person voter impersonation at polling places. The record contains no evidence of any such fraud actually occurring in Indiana at any time in its history. Moreover, petitioners argue that provisions of the Indiana Criminal Code punishing such conduct as a felony provide adequate protection against the risk that such conduct will occur in the future. It remains true, however, that flagrant examples of such fraud in other parts of the country have been documented throughout this Nation's history by respected historians and journalists,[11] that occasional examples have surfaced in recent years, and that Indiana's own experience with fraudulent voting in the 2003 Democratic primary for East Chicago Mayor—though perpetrated using absentee ballots and not in-person fraud—demonstrate that not only is the risk of voter fraud real but that it could affect the outcome of a close election.

There is no question about the legitimacy or importance of the State's interest in counting only the votes of eligible voters. Moreover, the interest in orderly administration and accurate recordkeeping provides a sufficient justification for carefully identifying all voters participating in the election process. While the most effective method of preventing election fraud may well be debatable, the propriety of doing so is perfectly clear.

[T]he State argues that the inflation of its voter rolls provides further support for its enactment of SEA 483. Even though Indiana's own negligence may have contributed to the serious inflation of its registration lists when SEA 483 was enacted, the fact of inflated voter rolls does provide a neutral and nondiscriminatory reason supporting the State's decision to require photo identification.

11. One infamous example is the New York City elections of 1868. William (Boss) Tweed set about solidifying and consolidating his control of the city. One local tough who worked for Boss Tweed, "Big Tim" Sullivan, insisted that his "repeaters" (individuals paid to vote multiple times) have whiskers:

> "When you've voted 'em with their whiskers on, you take 'em to a barber and scrape off the chin fringe. Then you vote 'em again with the side lilacs and a mustache. Then to a barber again, off comes the sides and you vote 'em a third time with the mustache. If that ain't enough and the box can stand a few more ballots, clean off the mustache and vote 'em plain face. That makes every one of 'em good for four votes." A. Callow, The Tweed Ring 210 (1966) (quoting M. Werner, Tammany Hall 439 (1928)).

Safeguarding Voter Confidence

Finally, the State contends that it has an interest in protecting public confidence "in the integrity and legitimacy of representative government." While that interest is closely related to the State's interest in preventing voter fraud, public confidence in the integrity of the electoral process has independent significance, because it encourages citizen participation in the democratic process. As the Carter-Baker Report [a bipartisan report conducted by former President Jimmy Carter and former Secretary of State James Baker] observed, the "electoral system cannot inspire public confidence if no safeguards exist to deter or detect fraud or to confirm the identity of voters."

III

A photo identification requirement imposes some burdens on voters that other methods of identification do not share. For example, a voter may lose his photo identification, may have his wallet stolen on the way to the polls, or may not resemble the photo in the identification because he recently grew a beard. Burdens of that sort arising from life's vagaries, however, are neither so serious nor so frequent as to raise any question about the constitutionality of SEA 483; the availability of the right to cast a provisional ballot provides an adequate remedy for problems of that character.

The burdens that are relevant to the issue before us are those imposed on persons who are eligible to vote but do not possess a current photo identification that complies with the requirements of SEA 483. The fact that most voters already possess a valid driver's license, or some other form of acceptable identification, would not save the statute under our reasoning in *Harper*, if the State required voters to pay a tax or a fee to obtain a new photo identification. But just as other States provide free voter registration cards, the photo identification cards issued by Indiana's BMV are also free. For most voters who need them, the inconvenience of making a trip to the BMV, gathering the required documents, and posing for a photograph surely does not qualify as a substantial burden on the right to vote, or even represent a significant increase over the usual burdens of voting.[17]

Both evidence in the record and facts of which we may take judicial notice, however, indicate that a somewhat heavier burden may be placed on a limited number of persons. They include elderly persons born out-of-state, who may have difficulty obtaining a birth certificate; persons who because of economic or other personal limitations may find it difficult either to secure a copy of their birth certificate or to assemble the other required documentation to obtain a state-issued identification; homeless persons; and persons with a religious objection to being photographed. If we assume, as the evidence suggests, that some members of these classes were registered voters when SEA 483 was enacted, the new identification requirement may have imposed a special burden on their right to vote.

17. To obtain a photo identification card a person must present at least one "primary" document, which can be a birth certificate, certificate of naturalization, U.S. veterans photo identification, U.S. military photo identification, or a U.S. passport. Indiana, like most States, charges a fee for obtaining a copy of one's birth certificate. This fee varies by county and is currently between $3 and $12. Some States charge substantially more.

The severity of that burden is, of course, mitigated by the fact that, if eligible, voters without photo identification may cast provisional ballots that will ultimately be counted. To do so, however, they must travel to the circuit court clerk's office within 10 days to execute the required affidavit. It is unlikely that such a requirement would pose a constitutional problem unless it is wholly unjustified. And even assuming that the burden may not be justified as to a few voters, that conclusion is by no means sufficient to establish petitioners' right to the relief they seek in this litigation.

IV

Given the fact that petitioners have advanced a broad attack on the constitutionality of SEA 483, seeking relief that would invalidate the statute in all its applications, they bear a heavy burden of persuasion. Only a few weeks ago we held that the Court of Appeals for the Ninth Circuit had failed to give appropriate weight to the magnitude of that burden when it sustained a preelection, facial attack on a Washington statute regulating that State's primary election procedures. *Washington State Grange v. Washington State Republican Party* (2008). Our reasoning in that case applies with added force [here].

Petitioners ask this Court, in effect, to perform a unique balancing analysis that looks specifically at a small number of voters who may experience a special burden under the statute and weighs their burdens against the State's broad interests in protecting election integrity. Petitioners urge us to ask whether the State's interests justify the burden imposed on voters who cannot afford or obtain a birth certificate and who must make a second trip to the circuit court clerk's office after voting. But on the basis of the evidence in the record it is not possible to quantify either the magnitude of the burden on this narrow class of voters or the portion of the burden imposed on them that is fully justified.

First, the evidence in the record does not provide us with the number of registered voters without photo identification. Further, the evidence does not provide any concrete evidence of the burden imposed on voters who currently lack photo identification. [Also,] although it may not be a completely acceptable alternative, the elderly in Indiana are able to vote absentee without presenting photo identification.

The record says virtually nothing about the difficulties faced by either indigent voters or voters with religious objections to being photographed. The record does contain the affidavit of one homeless woman who has a copy of her birth certificate, but was denied a photo identification card because she did not have an address. But that single affidavit gives no indication of how common the problem is.

In sum, we cannot conclude that the statute imposes "excessively burdensome requirements" on any class of voters. *See Storer v. Brown* (1974).[20] A facial challenge

20. While it is true that obtaining a birth certificate carries with it a financial cost, the record does not provide even a rough estimate of how many indigent voters lack copies of their birth certificates. Supposition based on extensive Internet research is not an adequate substitute for admissible evidence subject to cross-examination in constitutional adjudication.

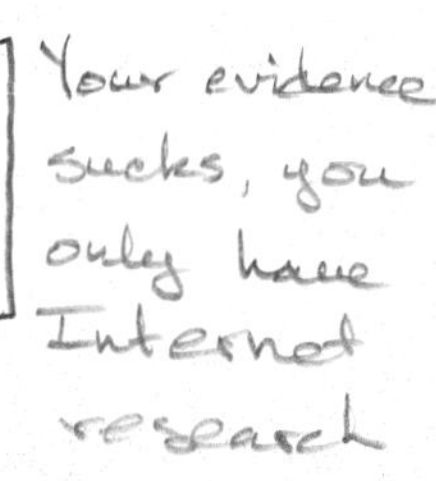

must fail where the statute has a plainly legitimate sweep. When we consider only the statute's broad application to all Indiana voters we conclude that it "imposes only a limited burden on voters' rights." *Burdick*. The precise interests advanced by the State are therefore sufficient to defeat petitioners' facial challenge to SEA 483.

Finally we note that petitioners have not demonstrated that the proper remedy—even assuming an unjustified burden on some voters—would be to invalidate the entire statute. When evaluating a neutral, nondiscriminatory regulation of voting procedure, "[w]e must keep in mind that a ruling of unconstitutionality frustrates the intent of the elected representatives of the people." *Ayotte v. Planned Parenthood of Northern New Eng.* [(2006)].

V

In their briefs, petitioners stress the fact that all of the Republicans in the General Assembly voted in favor of SEA 483 and the Democrats were unanimous in opposing it. It is fair to infer that partisan considerations may have played a significant role in the decision to enact SEA 483. If such considerations had provided the only justification for a photo identification requirement, we may also assume that SEA 483 would suffer the same fate as the poll tax at issue in *Harper*.

But if a nondiscriminatory law is supported by valid neutral justifications, those justifications should not be disregarded simply because partisan interests may have provided one motivation for the votes of individual legislators. The state interests identified as justifications for SEA 483 are both neutral and sufficiently strong to require us to reject petitioners' facial attack on the statute. The application of the statute to the vast majority of Indiana voters is amply justified by the valid interest in protecting "the integrity and reliability of the electoral process." *Anderson*.

Justice SCALIA, with whom Justice THOMAS and Justice ALITO join, concurring in the judgment.

The lead opinion assumes petitioners' premise that the voter-identification law "may have imposed a special burden on" some voters, but holds that petitioners have not assembled evidence to show that the special burden is severe enough to warrant strict scrutiny. That is true enough, but for the sake of clarity and finality (as well as adherence to precedent), I prefer to decide these cases on the grounds that petitioners' premise is irrelevant and that the burden at issue is minimal and justified.

To evaluate a law respecting the right to vote—whether it governs voter qualifications, candidate selection, or the voting process—we use the approach set out in *Burdick v. Takushi* (1992). This calls for application of a deferential "important regulatory interests" standard for nonsevere, nondiscriminatory restrictions, reserving strict scrutiny for laws that severely restrict the right to vote. The lead opinion resists the import of *Burdick* by characterizing it as simply adopting "the balancing approach" of *Anderson v. Celebrezze* (1983). Although *Burdick* liberally quoted *Anderson*, *Burdick* forged *Anderson*'s amorphous "flexible standard" into something resembling an administrable rule. Since *Burdick*, we have repeatedly reaffirmed the primacy of its two-track approach. "[S]trict scrutiny is appropriate only if the burden is severe." [*Clingman v. Beaver*, (2005).] Thus, the first step is to decide whether a challenged law severely burdens the right to vote. Ordinary and widespread burdens, such as those requiring "nominal effort" of everyone, are not severe. Burdens are severe if they go beyond the merely inconvenient.

Of course, we have to identify a burden before we can weigh it. The Indiana law affects different voters differently, but what petitioners view as the law's several light and heavy burdens are no more than the different impacts of the single burden that the law uniformly imposes on all voters. To vote in person in Indiana, everyone must have and present a photo identification that can be obtained for free. The State draws no classifications, let alone discriminatory ones, except to establish optional absentee and provisional balloting for certain poor, elderly, and institutionalized voters and for religious objectors. Nor are voters who already have photo identifications exempted from the burden, since those voters must maintain the accuracy of the information displayed on the identifications, renew them before they expire, and replace them if they are lost.

The Indiana photo-identification law is a generally applicable, nondiscriminatory voting regulation, and our precedents refute the view that individual impacts are relevant to determining the severity of the burden it imposes. Indeed, *Clingman*'s holding that burdens are not severe if they are ordinary and widespread would be rendered meaningless if a single plaintiff could claim a severe burden.

Insofar as our election-regulation cases rest upon the requirements of the Fourteenth Amendment, weighing the burden of a nondiscriminatory voting law upon each voter and concomitantly requiring exceptions for vulnerable voters would effectively turn back decades of equal-protection jurisprudence. A voter complaining about such a law's effect on him has no valid equal-protection claim because, without proof of discriminatory intent, a generally applicable law with disparate impact is not unconstitutional. *See, e.g., Washington v. Davis* (1976). The Fourteenth Amendment does not regard neutral laws as invidious ones, even when their burdens purportedly fall disproportionately on a protected class. A fortiori it does not do so when, as here, the classes complaining of disparate impact are not even protected.

Even if I thought that *stare decisis* did not foreclose adopting an individual-focused approach, I would reject it as an original matter. This is an area where the dos and don'ts need to be known in advance of the election, and voter-by-voter examination of the burdens of voting regulations would prove especially disruptive. A case-by-case approach naturally encourages constant litigation. Very few new election regulations improve everyone's lot, so the potential allegations of severe burden are endless. A State reducing the number of polling places would be open to the complaint it has violated the rights of disabled voters who live near the closed stations. Indeed, it may even be the case that some laws already on the books are especially burdensome for some voters.

That sort of detailed judicial supervision of the election process would flout the Constitution's express commitment of the task to the States. It is for state legislatures to weigh the costs and benefits of possible changes to their election codes, and their judgment must prevail unless it imposes a severe and unjustified overall burden upon the right to vote, or is intended to disadvantage a particular class. Judicial review of their handiwork must apply an objective, uniform standard that will enable them to determine, ex ante, whether the burden they impose is too severe.

The lead opinion's record-based resolution of these cases, which neither rejects nor embraces the rule of our precedents, provides no certainty, and will embolden litigants who surmise that our precedents have been abandoned. There is no good reason to prefer that course.

***

The universally applicable requirements of Indiana's voter-identification law are eminently reasonable. The burden of acquiring, possessing, and showing free photo identification is simply not severe, because it does not even represent a significant increase over the usual burdens of voting. And the State's interests are sufficient to sustain that minimal burden. That should end the matter. That the State accommodates some voters by permitting (not requiring) the casting of absentee or provisional ballots, is an indulgence—not a constitutional imperative that falls short of what is required.

Justice SOUTER, with whom Justice GINSBURG joins, dissenting.

Indiana's "Voter ID Law" threatens to impose nontrivial burdens on the voting right of tens of thousands of the State's citizens, and a significant percentage of those individuals are likely to be deterred from voting. The statute is unconstitutional under the balancing standard of *Burdick v. Takushi* (1992): a State may not burden the right to vote merely by invoking abstract interests, be they legitimate, or even compelling, but must make a particular, factual showing that threats to its interests outweigh the particular impediments it has imposed. The State has made no such justification here, and as to some aspects of its law, it has hardly even tried.

I

Voting-rights cases raise two competing interests, the one side being the fundamental right to vote. The Judiciary is obliged to train a skeptical eye on any qualification of that right. *See Reynolds*.

As against the unfettered right, however, lies the "[c]ommon sense, as well as constitutional law . . . that government must play an active role in structuring elections; as a practical matter, there must be a substantial regulation of elections if they are to be fair and honest and if some sort of order, rather than chaos, is to accompany the democratic processes." *Burdick*.

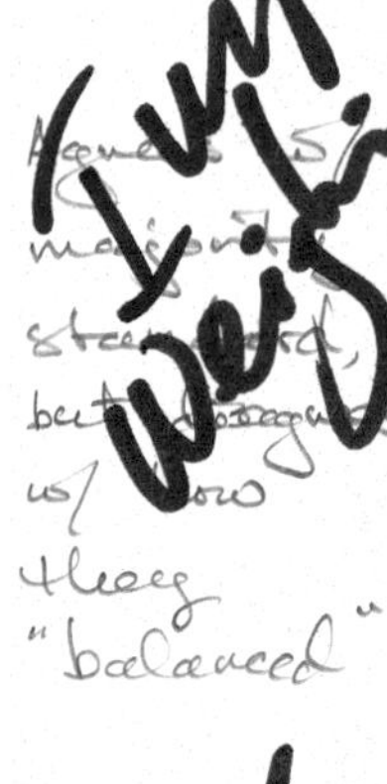

Given the legitimacy of interests on both sides, we have avoided pre-set levels of scrutiny in favor of a sliding-scale balancing analysis: the scrutiny varies with the effect of the regulation at issue. And whatever the claim, the Court has long made a careful, ground-level appraisal both of the practical burdens on the right to vote and of the State's reasons for imposing those precise burdens.

The lead opinion does not disavow these basic principles. But I think it does not insist enough on the hard facts that our standard of review demands.

II

A

The first set of burdens shown in these cases is the travel costs and fees necessary to get one of the limited variety of federal or state photo identifications needed to cast a regular ballot under the Voter ID Law. The travel is required for the personal visit to the BMV, which is demanded of anyone applying for a driver's license or non-driver photo identification. Poor, old, and disabled voters who do not drive a car may find the trip prohibitive.[4]

The burden of traveling to a more distant BMV office rather than a conveniently located polling place is probably serious for many of the individuals who lack photo identification. They almost certainly will not own cars, and public transportation in Indiana is fairly limited.

For those voters who can afford the roundtrip, a second financial hurdle appears: in order to get photo identification for the first time, they need to present "a birth certificate, a certificate of naturalization, U.S. veterans photo identification, U.S. military photo identification, or a U.S. passport." As the lead opinion says, the two most common of these documents come at a price: Indiana counties charge anywhere from $3 to $12 for a birth certificate (and in some other States the fee is significantly higher), and that same price must usually be paid for a first-time passport, since a birth certificate is required to prove U.S. citizenship by birth. The total fees for a passport are up to about $100. As with the travel costs, these fees are far from shocking on their face, but in the *Burdick* analysis it matters that both the travel costs and the fees are disproportionately heavy for, and thus disproportionately likely to deter, the poor, the old, and the immobile.

B

To be sure, Indiana has a provisional-ballot exception to the ID requirement for individuals the State considers "indigent" as well as those with religious objections to being photographed, and this sort of exception could in theory provide a way around the costs of procuring an ID. But Indiana's chosen exception does not amount to much relief.

[T]o have the provisional ballot counted, a voter must appear in person before the circuit court clerk or county election board within 10 days of the election, to sign an affidavit attesting to indigency or religious objection to being photographed (or to present an ID at that point). Forcing these people to travel to the county seat every time they try to vote is particularly onerous.

4. The State asserts that the elderly and disabled are adequately accommodated through their option to cast absentee ballots, and so any burdens on them are irrelevant. There are crucial differences between the absentee and regular ballot. Voting by absentee ballot leaves an individual without the possibility of receiving assistance from poll workers, and thus increases the likelihood of confusion and error. More seriously, Indiana law "treats absentee voters differently from the way it treats Election Day voters," in the important sense that "an absentee ballot may not be recounted in situations where clerical error by an election officer rendered it invalid." *Horseman v. Keller*, 841 N.E.2d 164, 171 (Ind. 2006). The State itself notes that "election officials routinely reject absentee ballots on suspicion of forgery." The record indicates that voters in Indiana are not unaware of these risks. It is one thing (and a commendable thing) for the State to make absentee voting available to the elderly and disabled; but it is quite another to suggest that, because the more convenient but less reliable absentee ballot is available, the State may freely deprive the elderly and disabled of the option of voting in person.

That the need to travel to the county seat each election amounts to a high hurdle is shown in the results of the 2007 municipal elections in Marion County, to which Indiana's Voter ID Law applied. Thirty-four provisional ballots were cast, but only two provisional voters made it to the County Clerk's Office within the 10 days. All 34 of these aspiring voters appeared at the appropriate precinct; 33 of them provided a signature, and every signature matched the one on file; and 26 of the 32 voters whose ballots were not counted had a history of voting in Marion County elections.

C

Indiana's Voter ID Law thus threatens to impose serious burdens on the voting right, and the next question under *Burdick* is whether the number of individuals likely to be affected is significant as well. Record evidence and facts open to judicial notice answer yes.

Although the District Court found that petitioners failed to offer any reliable empirical study of numbers of voters affected, we may accept that court's rough calculation that 43,000 voting-age residents lack the kind of identification card required by Indiana's law.

The State, in fact, shows no discomfort with the District Court's finding that an "estimated 43,000 individuals" (about 1% of the State's voting-age population) lack a qualifying ID. If the State's willingness to take that number is surprising, it may be less so in light of the District Court's observation that "several factors . . . suggest the percentage of Indiana's voting age population with photo identification is actually lower than 99%," a suggestion in line with national surveys showing roughly 6-10% of voting-age Americans without a state-issued photo-identification card.

The upshot is this. Tens of thousands of voting-age residents lack the necessary photo identification. A large proportion of them are likely to be in bad shape economically.[25] The Voter ID Law places hurdles in the way of either getting an ID or of voting provisionally, and they translate into nontrivial economic costs. There is accordingly no reason to doubt that a significant number of state residents will be discouraged or disabled from voting.

Thus, petitioners' case is clearly strong enough to prompt more than a cursory examination of the State's asserted interests. And the fact that Indiana's photo identification requirement is one of the most restrictive in the country makes a critical examination of the State's claims all the more in order.

25. Studies in other States suggest that the burdens of an ID requirement may also fall disproportionately upon racial minorities. *See* Overton, *Voter Identification,* 105 Mich. L. Rev. 631, 659 (2007) ("In 1994, the U.S. Department of Justice found that African-Americans in Louisiana were four to five times less likely than white residents to have government-sanctioned photo identification"); *id.*, at 659-660 (describing June 2005 study by the Employment and Training Institute at the University of Wisconsin-Milwaukee, which found that while 17% of voting-age whites lacked a valid driver's license, 55% of black males and 49% of black females were unlicensed, and 46% of Latino males and 59% of Latino females were similarly unlicensed).

III

Because the lead opinion finds only "limited" burdens on the right to vote, it avoids a hard look at the State's claimed interests. As the lead opinion sees it, the State has offered four related concerns that suffice to justify the Voter ID Law: modernizing election procedures, combating voter fraud, addressing the consequences of the State's bloated voter rolls, and protecting public confidence in the integrity of the electoral process. On closer look, however, it appears that the first two (which are really just one) can claim modest weight at best, and the latter two if anything weaken the State's case.

A

1

There is no denying the abstract importance, the compelling nature, of combating voter fraud. But it takes several steps to get beyond the level of abstraction here.

To begin with, requiring a voter to show photo identification before casting a regular ballot addresses only one form of voter fraud: in-person voter impersonation. The photo ID requirement leaves untouched the problems of absentee-ballot fraud, which (unlike in-person voter impersonation) is a documented problem in Indiana; of registered voters voting more than once (but maintaining their own identities) in different counties or in different States; of felons and other disqualified individuals voting in their own names; of vote buying; or, for that matter, of ballot-stuffing, ballot miscounting, voter intimidation, or any other type of corruption on the part of officials administering elections.

[Moreover,] the State has not come across a single instance of in-person voter impersonation fraud in all of Indiana's history. The State responds to the want of evidence with the assertion that in-person voter impersonation fraud is hard to detect. But this is like saying the "man who wasn't there" is hard to spot, and to know whether difficulty in detection accounts for the lack of evidence one at least has to ask whether in-person voter impersonation is (or would be) relatively harder to ferret out than other kinds of fraud (*e.g.*, by absentee ballot) which the State has had no trouble documenting. The answer seems to be no; there is reason to think [according to the relevant federal agency] that "impersonation of voters is . . . the most likely type of fraud to be discovered." U.S. Election Assistance Commission, Election Crimes: An Initial Report and Recommendations for Future Study 9 (Dec. 2006).

2

For that matter, the deterrence argument can do only so much work, since photo identification is itself hardly a failsafe against impersonation. Indiana knows this, and that is why in 2007 the State began to issue redesigned driver's licenses with digital watermarking. The State has made this shift precisely because, in the words of its BMV, "visual inspection is not adequate to determine the authenticity" of driver's licenses. Indeed, the BMV explains that the digital watermarks (which can be scanned using equipment that, so far, Indiana does not use at polling places) is needed to "tak[e] the guesswork out of inspection." So, at least until polling places have the machines and special software to scan the new driver's licenses, and until all the licenses with the older designs expire, Indiana's law does no more than assure that any in-person voter fraud will take place with fake IDs, not attempted signature forgery.

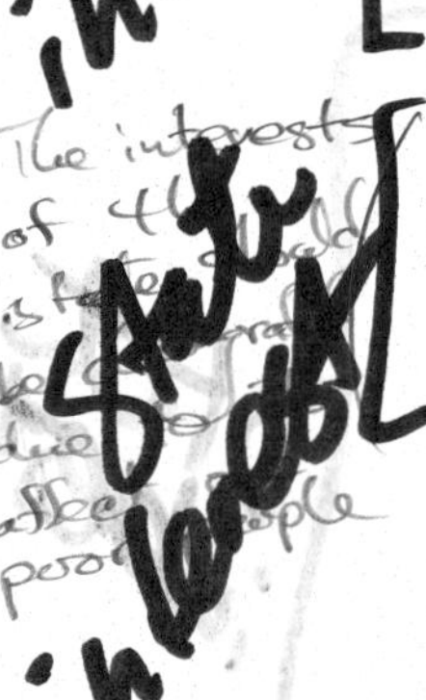

Despite all this, I will readily stipulate that a State has an interest in responding to the risk (however small) of in-person voter impersonation. But the ultimate valuation of the particular interest a State asserts has to take account of evidence against it as well as legislative judgments for it (certainly when the law is one of the most restrictive of its kind), and on this record it would be unreasonable to accord this assumed state interest more than very modest significance.

3

What is left of the State's claim must be downgraded further for one final reason: regardless of the interest the State may have in adopting a photo identification requirement as a general matter, that interest in no way necessitates the particular burdens the Voter ID Law imposes on poor people and religious objectors. Individuals unable to get photo identification are forced to travel to the county seat every time they wish to exercise the franchise, and they have to get there within 10 days of the election. Nothing about the State's interest in fighting voter fraud justifies this requirement of a post-election trip to the county seat instead of some verification process at the polling places.

In briefing this Court, the State responds by pointing to an interest in keeping lines at polling places short. But this argument fails on its own terms, for whatever might be the number of individuals casting a provisional ballot, the State could simply allow voters to sign the indigency affidavit at the polls subject to review there after the election.

Indeed, the State's argument more than fails; it backfires, in implicitly conceding that a not-insignificant number of individuals will need to rely on the burdensome provisional-ballot mechanism. What is more, as the District Court found, the Voter ID Law itself actually increases the likelihood of delay at the polls. Since any minor discrepancy between a voter's photo identification card and the registration information may lead to a challenge, "the opportunities for presenting challenges ha[ve] increased as a result of the photo identification requirements." [District court opinion.]

B

The State's asserted interests in modernizing elections and combating fraud are decidedly modest; at best, they fail to offset the clear inference that thousands of Indiana citizens will be discouraged from voting. The two remaining justifications, meanwhile, actually weaken the State's case.

[Justice Souter addresses Indiana's contention that it imposed the Voter ID law in part in response to its own failure to maintain accurate voter registration lists.]

How any of this can justify restrictions on the right to vote is difficult to say. The State is simply trying to take advantage of its own wrong: if it is true that the

State's fear of in-person voter impersonation fraud arises from its bloated voter checklist, the answer to the problem is in the State's own hands.

The State's final justification, its interest in safeguarding voter confidence, similarly collapses. The problem with claiming this interest lies in its connection to the bloated voter rolls; the State has come up with nothing to suggest that its citizens doubt the integrity of the State's electoral process, except its own failure to maintain its rolls. The answer to this problem is not to burden the right to vote, but to end the official negligence.

It should go without saying that none of this is to deny States' legitimate interest in safeguarding public confidence. It is simply not plausible to assume here, with no evidence of in-person voter impersonation fraud in a State, and very little of it nationwide, that a public perception of such fraud is nevertheless "inherent" in an election system providing severe criminal penalties for fraud and mandating signature checks at the polls.

C

If more were needed to condemn this law, our own precedent would provide it, for the calculation revealed in the Indiana statute crosses a line when it targets the poor and the weak. The State's requirements here, that people without cars travel to a motor vehicle registry and that the poor who fail to do that get to their county seats within 10 days of every election, translate into unjustified economic burdens uncomfortably close to the outright $1.50 fee we struck down 42 years ago [in *Harper*]. Like that fee, the onus of the Indiana law is illegitimate just because it correlates with no state interest so well as it does with the object of deterring poorer residents from exercising the franchise.

Justice Breyer, dissenting.

I believe the statute is unconstitutional because it imposes a disproportionate burden upon those eligible voters who lack a driver's license or other statutorily valid form of photo ID. I share the general view of the lead opinion insofar as it holds that the Constitution does not *automatically* forbid Indiana from enacting a photo ID requirement. I cannot agree, however, with Justice Stevens' or Justice Scalia's assessment of the burdens imposed by the statute. The Carter-Baker Commission *conditioned* its recommendation upon the States' willingness to ensure that the requisite photo IDs "be easily available and issued free of charge" and that the requirement be "phased in" over two federal election cycles, to ease the transition. Indiana's law fails to satisfy these aspects of the Commission's recommendation.

By way of contrast, two other States—Florida and Georgia—have put into practice photo ID requirements significantly less restrictive than Indiana's. Under the Florida law, the range of permissible forms of photo ID is substantially greater than in Indiana. Moreover, a Florida voter who lacks photo ID may cast a provisional ballot at the polling place that will be counted if the State determines that his signature matches the one on his voter registration form.

Georgia restricts voters to a more limited list of acceptable photo IDs than does Florida, but accepts in addition to proof of voter registration a broader range of underlying documentation than does Indiana. While Indiana allows only certain groups such as the elderly and disabled to vote by absentee ballot, in Georgia *any* voter may vote absentee without providing any excuse, and (except where required by federal law) need not present a photo ID in order to do so. Finally, neither Georgia nor Florida insists, as Indiana does, that indigent voters travel each election cycle to potentially distant places for the purposes of signing an indigency affidavit.

NOTE ON VOTER ID LAWS SINCE *CRAWFORD*

Voter ID has continued to be a hotly contested issues since *Crawford,* in both federal and state courts, and applied to both in-person and absentee voting. We will focus specifically on the longstanding controversy over Wisconsin's version of voter ID, which has involved the Seventh Circuit and the local federal courts in the state for many years—with litigation flaring up during each presidential election year, because Wisconsin has become a pivotal Electoral College battle-ground. But before we consider ongoing litigation over voter ID, and the specific role that courts play as local election officials prepare to administer an upcoming election, we need to examine the implication of *Crawford* for the *Anderson-Burdick* balancing test as it applies to a wide range of election administration issues.

ANDERSON-BURDICK-CRAWFORD APPLIED TO VARIOUS ELECTION ADMINISTRATION ISSUES

The lower federal courts have spent more than a decade applying the *Anderson-Burdick* balancing test, as supplemented by *Crawford,* to a myriad of voting rules, from the maintenance of voter registration lists to the requirements for casting absentee or provisional ballots. One conceptual question that has arisen is whether evaluating the burden on voting under *Anderson-Burdick* balancing should take account of changes in law, comparing a voter's access to the ballot both before and after the challenged law was adopted, or instead only whether the current law—without regard to what the rule was in the past—imposes a burden on the opportunity to cast a ballot. This issue arose most clearly in the context to the following challenge to Ohio's decision to cut back the number of days it made available for early voting. Had the resulting number of days not been less than what was offered previously, there is no doubt that the challenge to the law under *Anderson-Burdick* would have failed: 29 of days of early voting would not have qualified as a burden under *Anderson-Burdick* balancing. But compared to what Ohio had offered before, it was a curtailment in the opportunity to cast a ballot. Should that matter? Here's what the Sixth Circuit had to say on this subject:

Ohio Democratic Party v. Husted

834 F.3d 620 (2016)

McKEAGUE, Circuit Judge.

This case presents yet another appeal asking the federal courts to become entangled, as overseers and micromanagers, in the minutiae of state election processes. No one denies that our Constitution, in defining the relationship between the people and the government, establishes certain fundamental rights—including the right to vote—that warrant vigilant enforcement. But our Constitution also defines the relationship between spheres of government, state and federal, and their responsibilities for protecting the rights of the people. The genius of this balance of power is no less deserving of vigilant respect.

Ohio is a national leader when it comes to early voting opportunities. The state election regulation at issue allows early in-person voting for 29 days before Election Day. This is really quite generous. The law is facially neutral; it offers early voting to everyone. The Constitution does not require *any* opportunities for early voting and as many as thirteen states offer just one day for voting: Election Day. Moreover, the subject regulation is the product of a bipartisan recommendation, as amended pursuant to a subsequent litigation settlement. It is the product of collaborative processes, not unilateral overreaching by the political party that happened to be in power. Yet, plaintiffs complain that allowance of 29 days of early voting does not suffice under federal law. They insist that Ohio's prior accommodation—35 days of early voting, which also created a six-day "Golden Week" opportunity for same-day registration and voting—established a federal floor that Ohio may add to but never subtract from. This is an astonishing proposition.

Nearly a third of the states offer no early voting. Adopting plaintiffs' theory of disenfranchisement would create a "one-way ratchet" that would discourage states from ever increasing early voting opportunities, lest they be prohibited by federal courts from later modifying their election procedures in response to changing circumstances. Further, while the challenged regulation may slightly diminish the convenience of registration and voting, it applies even-handedly to all voters, and, despite the change, Ohio continues to provide generous, reasonable, and accessible voting options to all Ohioans. The issue is not whether some voter somewhere would benefit from six additional days of early voting or from the opportunity to register and vote at the same time. Rather, the issue is whether the challenged law results in a cognizable injury under the Constitution. We conclude that it does not.

Federal judicial remedies, of course, are necessary where a state law impermissibly infringes the fundamental right to vote. No such infringement having been shown in this case, judicial restraint is in order. Proper deference to state legislative authority requires that Ohio's election process be allowed to proceed unhindered by the federal courts. Accordingly, and for the reasons more fully set forth below, we REVERSE the decision of the district court insofar as it declared the subject regulation invalid and enjoined its implementation.

I. BACKGROUND

A. Procedural History

This is an appeal by State of Ohio officials from a district court judgment declaring a state election regulation invalid as violative of equal. The law, known as Senate Bill 238, amends Ohio Revised Code § 3509.01 to allow early in-person voting for a period of 29 days before Election Day. The court enjoined enforcement of S.B. 238, thereby effectively restoring Ohio's preexisting 35-day early in-person voting period.

B. Voting in Ohio

A brief review of recent voting regulation history in Ohio provides context. In 2004, Ohio permitted absentee ballots only if registered voters asserted one of several "excuses." *See* Ohio Rev. Code § 3509.02(A)(1)-(8) (2004). The timeline for voting by absentee ballot was generous: a voter could pick up a ballot 35 days before Election Day, the first five of which extended into Ohio's voter registration period (which ended 30 days before an election). Thus, Ohio maintained a five-day overlap of its registration period and its absentee voting period, allowing residents armed with a proper excuse to both register and vote (absentee) on the same day. This "same-day registration" window became known in Ohio as "Golden Week."

The 2004 presidential election brought special challenges to Ohio's general voting apparatus. Among other problems, Ohio voters faced long lines and wait-times that, at some polling places, stretched into the early morning of the following day. Largely in response to this experience, Ohio refined its absentee voting system in 2005 to permit early voting without need of an excuse. Ohio residents enjoying the freedom of this "no-fault" or "no excuse" system could vote absentee by mail or in person ("early in-person" or "EIP" voting) at their convenience. Ohio retained its preexisting absentee voting time frame.

Until 2012, each of Ohio's 88 county boards of elections retained the discretion to implement its own schedule for early in-person absentee voting. Varying schedules resulted. To remedy the inconsistencies, a task force from the Ohio Association of Election Officials (OAEO), a bipartisan association of election officials, proposed adoption of a uniform 21-day early in-person voting schedule, under which the period for "early" or "absentee" voting would start nine days *after* the end of the voter registration period.

In 2012, Ohio passed a law based on the OAEO recommendation, but repealed it after the law became subject to a referendum. In 2013, another bipartisan task force recommended that absentee voting not be allowed until the day after the registration period closed, establishing an early voting time frame of 29 days instead of the previously recommended 21 days. On February 19, 2014, Ohio passed S.B. 238, amending Ohio Rev. Code § 3509.01 to make the first day of early absentee voting—whether early in-person or by mail—the day after the close of voter registration. This amendment effectively eliminated Golden Week and the possibility of same-day registration.

Shortly before the 2014 election, the NAACP and other groups challenged S.B. 238. Though a panel of this court upheld a preliminary injunction preventing implementation of the law, the Supreme Court stayed the injunction, and the panel subsequently vacated its decision for mootness. Thus, the 2014 election took place with S.B. 238 in full effect. After the election, the parties to *NAACP* reached a settlement under which Ohio added another Sunday of early in-person voting as well as additional evening hours, and the plaintiffs voluntarily dismissed their claim challenging the 29-day voting period.

This brings us to the present action. After *NAACP* settled, plaintiffs in this action, the Ohio Democratic Party, the Democratic Party of Cuyahoga County, the Montgomery County Democratic Party, and three individuals (collectively referred to as "plaintiffs" or the "Democratic Parties"), evidently finding the settlement negotiated by the NAACP to be unsatisfactory, challenged S.B. 238 (as modified per settlement) and other Ohio laws as violating the Equal Protection Clause. Despite subsequently acknowledging that "Ohio's national leadership in voting opportunities is to be commended,", the district court held that S.B. 238 violated the Equal Protection Clause based largely on what it called the "highly persuasive" reasoning of this court's since-vacated ruling upholding a preliminary injunction in *NAACP*.

Regarding plaintiffs' equal protection challenge, the district court concluded that S.B. 238 imposed a "modest" (i.e., "more than minimal but less than significant") disparate burden on African Americans. The "numerous opportunities to cast a ballot in Ohio, including vot[ing] by mail, in person on Election Day, and on other EIP voting days" were deemed insufficient to mitigate the burden. Although Ohio allows numerous and convenient registration options (including registration by mail), more than four weeks of absentee voting, and more than three weeks of early in-person voting, the district court acknowledged that there are minimal postage costs associated with voting by mail and accepted what it characterized as "anecdotal evidence" that "African Americans are distrustful of voting by mail" to conclude that voting by mail may not be a suitable alternative to early in-person voting for many African-Americans. The court concluded that, despite Ohio's generous voting options, S.B. 238's modification of Ohio's early voting schedule resulted in a disparate burden on some African-American voters. And despite accepting the legitimacy of Ohio's asserted interests (preventing fraud, decreasing costs, reducing administrative burdens, and enhancing voter confidence, the court held they did not justify the modest burdens imposed by the law.

II. EQUAL PROTECTION

A. Framework

When a constitutional challenge to an election regulation calls us to resolve a dispute concerning these competing interests, we apply the so-called *Anderson-Burdick* framework, an analysis arising from the Supreme Court's holdings in *Anderson v. Celebrezze* (1983), and *Burdick v. Takushi* (1992). The *Anderson-Burdick* framework involves the following considerations:

> [T]he court must first consider the character and magnitude of the asserted injury to the rights protected by the [Constitution] that the plaintiff seeks to vindicate. Second, it must identify and evaluate the precise interests put forward by the State as justifications for the burden imposed by its rule. Finally, it must determine the legitimacy and strength of each of those interests and consider the extent to which those interests make it necessary to burden the plaintiff's rights.

Though the touchstone of *Anderson-Burdick* is its flexibility in weighing competing interests, the "rigorousness of our inquiry into the propriety of a state election law depends upon the extent to which a challenged regulation burdens First and Fourteenth Amendment rights." *Burdick*, 504 U.S. at 434, 112 S. Ct. 2059. This flexible balancing approach is not totally devoid of guidelines. If a state imposes "severe restrictions" on a plaintiff's constitutional rights (here, the right to vote), its regulations survive only if "narrowly drawn to advance a state interest of compelling importance." *Id.* On the other hand, "minimally burdensome and

nondiscriminatory" regulations are subject to a "less-searching examination closer to rational basis" and "'the State's important regulatory interests are generally sufficient to justify the restrictions.'" *Ohio Council 8 Am. Fed'n of State v. Husted* (6th Cir. 2016) (citing *Hargett*, 767 F.3d at 546, and quoting *Burdick*, 504 U.S. at 434, 112 S. Ct. 2059). Regulations falling somewhere in between—i.e., regulations that impose a more-than-minimal but less-than-severe burden—require a "flexible" analysis, "weighing the burden on the plaintiffs against the state's asserted interest and chosen means of pursuing it." *Hargett*, 767 F.3d at 546.

Because plaintiffs have advanced a broad attack on the constitutionality of S.B. 238, "seeking relief that would invalidate the statute in all its applications, they bear a heavy burden of persuasion." *Crawford*, 553 U.S. at 200, 128 S. Ct. 1610 (Stevens, J., op.). Because we conclude that S.B. 238 results, at most, in a minimal disparate burden on some African Americans' right to vote, and because the State's legitimate interests are "sufficiently weighty" to justify this minimal burden, S.B. 238 easily survives plaintiffs' equal protection challenge.

B. Disparate Burden on African-American Voters

1. District Court's Characterization

The first step in evaluating the plaintiffs' equal protection challenge requires us to identify the "character and magnitude" of the burden on African-American voters as a result of the challenged law. The district court identified the burden imposed on some African Americans' right to vote by considering the *changes* effected by S.B. 238, rather than by examining Ohio's election regime as a whole. The court found that operation of S.B. 238 resulted in a disparate burden on some African Americans as a function of two changes: "(1) by reducing the overall [early in-person] voting period, and (2) by eliminating the opportunity for [same-day registration]."

Regarding the reduction of the early in-person voting period, the district court discerned a burden after accepting three simple premises: (1) that tens of thousands of people voted during Golden Week in both 2008 and 2012 and are likely to do so in the upcoming 2016 election; (2) that S.B. 238's elimination of Golden Week requires that "[i]ndividuals who would have voted during Golden Week in future elections must now vote on other days during the early voting period, vote absentee by mail, vote on Election Day, or not vote at all;" and (3) because African Americans have shown a preference for voting early in person (and during Golden Week) at a rate higher than other voters, the "elimination of the extra days for EIP voting provided by Golden Week will disproportionately burden African Americans." The district court further noted that beginning early in-person voting after the registration period eliminated "same-day registration," meaning that "voters must now register and vote at separate times, which increases the 'cost of voting,' especially for socioeconomically disadvantaged groups." That is, the court recognized that "it may be more difficult for voters with time, resource, transportation, and childcare restraints to make two separate trips to register and vote, and Golden Week allowed individuals to do both at once." *Id.* The district court concluded that, because "African Americans in particular are more likely to be subject to economic, transportation, time, and childcare constraints," they "disproportionately make up the group that benefits the most from [same-day registration], and the elimination of that opportunity burdens their right to vote." Taking the reduction in early in-person voting days and the elimination of same-day registration together, the district court characterized the changes effected by S.B. 238 as imposing a "modest" burden on African Americans' right to vote.

2. Defining the Burden

As a threshold matter, we note that the district court's characterization of the resultant burden as "modest" is not a factual finding, but a legal determination subject to de novo review. Inasmuch as the State does not challenge the district court's findings of fact, we evaluate de novo the district court's application of legal principles to those subsidiary facts in characterizing the burden made out by those facts.

The undisputed factual record shows that it's easy to vote in Ohio. Very easy, actually. Viewing S.B. 238 as one component of Ohio's progressive voting system, and considering the many options that remain available to Ohio voters, even accepting the district court's focus on the *changes* wrought by S.B. 238, the removal of Golden Week can hardly be deemed to impose a true "burden" on any person's right to vote. At worst, it represents a withdrawal or contraction of just one of many conveniences that have generously facilitated voting participation in Ohio. This is especially apparent when Ohio's voting practices are compared to those of other states.

Ohio's early voting system, as amended by S.B. 238, is one of the more generous in the nation. The State's 29-day early voting period is currently the tenth-longest among all the states. When compared to the thirteen states (including two other states in our circuit, Kentucky and Michigan) that do not permit *any* early in-person voting days, an Ohioan's path to voting is open and easy, *not* burdensome. And S.B. 238's withdrawal of the convenience of same-day registration is hardly obstructive; it merely brings Ohio into line with thirty-eight other states that require registration *before* an individual may vote. Ironically, if Ohio had never expanded access to absentee ballots in the first place and maintained early voting systems similar to Michigan's or Kentucky's (permitting no early in-person voting), it would have avoided this challenge altogether. Instead, "it is [Ohio's] willingness to go further than many States in extending the absentee voting privileges . . . that has provided [plaintiffs] with a basis for arguing that the provisions operate in an invidiously discriminatory fashion to deny them a *more convenient* method of exercising the franchise." *McDonald*, 394 U.S. at 810-11, 89 S. Ct. 1404 (emphasis added). It's as if plaintiffs disregard the Constitution's clear mandate that the states (and not the courts) establish election protocols, instead reading the document to require all states to maximize voting convenience. Under this conception of the federal courts' role, little stretch of imagination is needed to fast-forward and envision a regime of judicially-mandated voting by text message or Tweet (assuming of course, that cell phones and Twitter handles are not disparately possessed by identifiable segments of the voting population).

The district court ignored Ohio's national leadership in affording privileged voting opportunities, believing that comparison of Ohio's early-voting system to that of other states was irrelevant under *Anderson-Burdick*. We fail to see the merit in wearing blinders. While comparisons with the laws and experience of other states may not be determinative of a challenged law's constitutionality, to ignore such information as irrelevant is to needlessly forfeit a potentially valuable tool in construing and applying "equal protection of the laws," a constitutional standard applicable to *all* the states. Forfeiting such a tool would artificially constrict the court's vision and deny reality: courts routinely examine the burden resulting from a state's regulation with the experience of its neighboring states. *See Frank v. Walker* (7th Cir. 2014) (comparing Wisconsin's voter-ID statute to Indiana's).

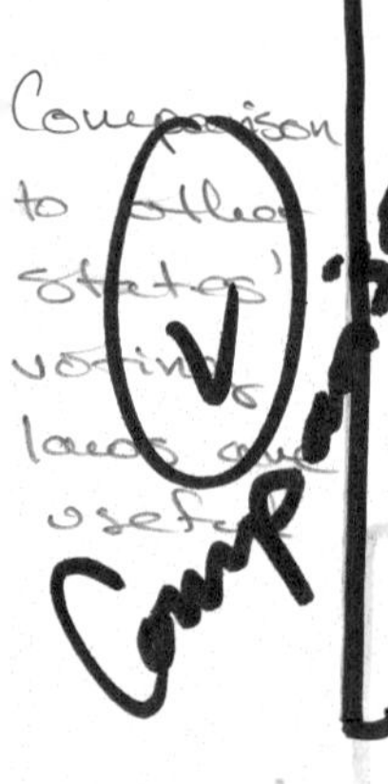

We certainly recognize that different states may offer different justifications for the existence or absence of early in-person voting or same-day registration, and do not suggest that Ohio may escape challenges to election regulations simply by pointing to the least accommodating state and saying, "We do it better." Rather, we reject the notion that such comparisons are irrelevant, as they provide a contextual basis for determining whether the "burden" said to fall here disproportionately on some African-American voters is properly characterized as non-existent, or minimal, or slight, or limited, or modest, or significant, or enormous, or severe. And besides, Ohio is not simply arguing its practices are better. Instead, State officials are defending a liberal absentee voting practice that *facilitates* participation by all members of the voting public, including those in "socioeconomically disadvantaged groups," of whatever race or ethnic background, in a manner more accommodating than the practices of most other states, by affording a "no-questions-asked" right to an absentee ballot and a litany of ways to use it.

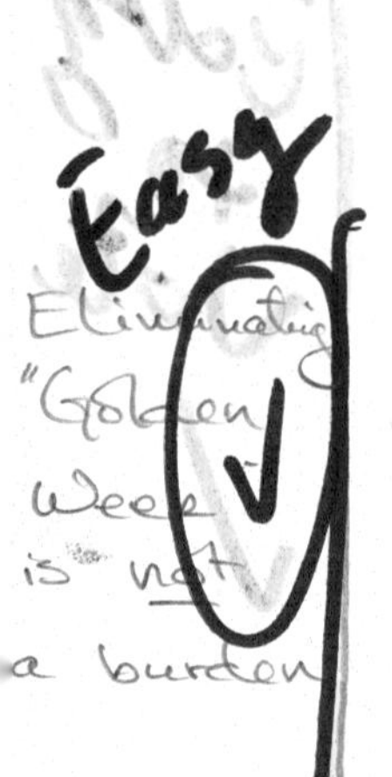

Thus, in evaluating the magnitude of the "burden," we find that elimination of Golden Week is a small part of what remains, objectively viewed, a generous early voting schedule. The notion that S.B. 238's elimination of same day registration disparately imposes anything more than a "minimal" burden on some African Americans ignores the abundant and convenient alternatives that remain for all Ohioans who wish to vote.

Consider the numerous options available to all Ohio voters, including African Americans, to conveniently cast a ballot before Election Day. The State's use of "no-excuse" absentee ballots provides any interested resident the chance to cast a ballot more than *four weeks* before Election Day by mail, and more than *three weeks* before Election Day if a voter prefers to do so in person. Ohio Rev. Code § 3509.01. Moreover, this early in-person voting schedule includes two Saturdays, two Sundays, and ten days when voting is permitted until either 6:00 p.m. or 7:00 p.m.—for voters who are "distrustful of voting by mail," who are assisted by "Souls to the Polls" initiatives, who struggle to find time away from "hourly wage jobs,", or who merely prefer to save on postage. And these accommodations are a *direct result* of the settlement reached in *NAACP* which was specifically designed to accommodate voters in Ohio's African-American communities.

The district court placed inordinate weight on its finding that some African-American voters *may prefer* voting on Sundays, or avoiding the mail, or saving on postage, or voting after a nine-to-five work day. To the extent S.B. 238 may be viewed as impacting such preferences, its "burden" clearly results more from a "matter of choice rather than a state-created obstacle." *Frank*, 768 F.3d at 749. The Equal Protection Clause, as applied under the *Anderson-Burdick* framework, simply cannot be reasonably understood as demanding recognition and accommodation of such variable personal preferences, even if the preferences are shown to be shared in higher numbers by members of certain identifiable segments of the voting public.

We also conclude that the elimination of same-day registration and the resulting need for Ohioans to register and vote on separate occasions is, at most, minimally burdensome. Like voting before Election Day, Ohio also makes registration easy. Registration forms are conveniently distributed throughout its communities at the 88 boards of elections offices as well as many other locations, including "local libraries, at many of the municipal city halls, high schools"—and can even be printed from county websites. And if this isn't enough, the Secretary of State mailed absentee ballot applications to almost every registered voter in the state in the past two elections and plans to do so in the 2016 election. Thus, even without Golden Week, Ohio's registration and voting processes afford abundant opportunity for all Ohio voters, of whatever racial or ethnic background, to register and exercise their right to vote.

It's no surprise then, that the Supreme Court in *Crawford* rejected an analogous challenge to an undeniably more burdensome law based on this sort of "burden of making a second trip to vote" argument. The Court held that first going to the Bureau of Motor Vehicles *and then* casting a ballot was ultimately no more "burdensome" than the usual challenges of voting. Scrounging up a birth certificate, making a trip to the BMV, and obtaining a photo ID surely cannot be considered less "burdensome" than submitting one of Ohio's virtually ubiquitous registration cards (which can be mailed back, dropped off in person, or returned by another) and enjoying the convenience of a no-excuse early absentee voting on any one of Ohio's *twenty-nine* voting days.

Therefore, viewing S.B. 238 objectively under the *Anderson-Burdick* framework in a manner consonant with the Court's most recent application of the framework in *Crawford*, we see a regulation that can only be characterized as minimally burdensome on the right of some African-American voters. Beyond evidence that African Americans may use early in-person voting at higher rates than other voters and may therefore be theoretically disadvantaged by reduction of the early voting period, the record does not establish that S.B. 238—as opposed to non-state-created circumstances—*actually makes voting harder* for African Americans. Plaintiffs do not point to any individual who, post-S.B. 238, will be precluded from voting. Without sufficient evidence to "quantify either the magnitude of the burden on this narrow class of voters or the portion of the burden that is fully justified," the *Crawford* Court refused to accept bare assertions that "a small number of voters . . . may experience a special burden" and instead looked to the statute's "broad application" to all state voters in concluding that the law imposed "only a limited burden on voters' rights."

Considering the generally applicable and non-discriminatory nature of S.B. 238 in light of Ohio's generous absentee voting system, a system which provides extensive opportunities for all voters, including African Americans, to cast their ballots short of coming out on Election Day, we hold that S.B. 238 results only in a minimal burden on African Americans' right to vote. We therefore reject the district court's conclusion that S.B. 238 imposes a "modest" burden. We next look to the State's interests in adopting the regulation.

C. State's Interests

Because S.B. 238 is minimally burdensome and nondiscriminatory, we apply a deferential standard of review akin to rational basis and Ohio need only advance

"important regulatory interests" to satisfy the *Anderson-Burdick* analysis. Here, the interests advanced by the State are analogous to, and even better substantiated than those accepted as sufficient in *Crawford.* It follows that the State's present interests pass muster under *Anderson-Burdick*: they justify the minimal burden potentially visited on some African-American voters as a result of S.B. 238. However, even if we were to accept the district court's characterization of the burden as "modest," which may conceivably trigger a slightly less deferential review under the "flexible" *Anderson-Burdick* framework, Ohio's proffered interests are still "sufficiently weighty" to justify it.

Ohio contends S.B. 238 serves four legitimate interests: "(1) preventing voter fraud; (2) reducing costs; (3) reducing administrative burdens; and (4) increasing voter confidence and preventing voter confusion." The district court rejected Ohio's justifications, noting that "while they may be legitimate," the State's "insufficient evidence" shows they are "minimal, unsupported, or not accomplished by S.B. 238." The district court demanded too much. For regulations that are not unduly burdensome, the *Anderson-Burdick* analysis never requires a state to actually *prove* "the sufficiency of the 'evidence.'" *Munro v. Socialist Workers Party* (1986) (explaining that a contrary rule would "would invariably lead to endless court battles over the sufficiency of the 'evidence'"). Rather, at least with respect to a minimally burdensome regulation triggering rational-basis review, we accept a justification's sufficiency as a "legislative fact" and defer to the findings of Ohio's legislature so long as its findings are reasonable. *See Frank*, 768 F.3d at 750; *see also Munro*, 479 U.S. at 195-96, 107 S. Ct. 533.

Voter Fraud and Public Confidence. Ohio first justifies S.B. 238 by asserting that it decreases the opportunity for voter fraud arising from same-day registration during Golden Week. The district court discounted Ohio's interest in combating potential fraud because, "while the general opinion evidence [showed] that Golden Week increases the opportunity for voter fraud . . . actual instances of voter fraud during Golden Week are extremely rare" and "[t]his very limited evidence of voter fraud is insufficient to justify the modest burden imposed by S.B. 238." But we do not "require elaborate, empirical verification of the weightiness of the State's asserted justifications." *Timmons v. Twin Cities Area New Party* (1997). Moreover, such a view is totally irreconcilable with *Crawford*, which upheld an unquestionably *more burdensome* regulation requiring all in-person voters in Indiana to maintain and present "photo identification issued by the government" even where the "record contain[ed] no evidence of any such fraud actually occurring in Indiana at any time in its history." *Crawford*, 553 U.S. at 194-96, 128 S. Ct. 1610 (Stevens, J., op.). The Court had "no question about the legitimacy or importance of the State's interest in counting only the votes of eligible voters," and because "the risk of voter fraud [is] real [and] . . . could affect the outcome of a close election," the Court declined to examine Indiana's total lack of evidence that the photo identification law would actually preclude fraud in the way it was designed to.

Here, Ohio offers inconclusive, but concrete evidence of voter fraud during Golden Week's same-day registration period. Under *Crawford*'s teaching, working to achieve that goal is a "sufficiently weighty" interest to justify the minimal burden experienced by some African-American voters. Running in tandem with the State's interest in preventing voter fraud is its closely related, but independently significant justification for eliminating same-day registration: safeguarding public confidence by eliminating "even appearances of fraud." The *Crawford* court accepted this justification as practically self-evidently true, observing that a state's "electoral system cannot inspire public confidence if no safeguards exist to deter or detect fraud or to confirm the identity of voters." Unlike the district court, we adhere to *Crawford*'s approach and conclude that the State's purpose of preventing potential fraud and promoting public confidence is in furtherance of legitimate and important regulatory interests.

The district court was not only dissatisfied with Ohio's evidence, but also with Ohio's method of combatting potential fraud. Part of the State's fraud-based rationale arose from the bipartisan OAEO recommendation that early voting begin only after the close of registration, because overlapping registration and voting periods were deemed to constitute "the greatest time for voter fraud to occur." S.B. 238 addressed this concern by eliminating Golden Week's same-day registration. The district court, again relying on our vacated decision in *NAACP*, 768 F.3d at 547, attacked the efficacy of eliminating same-day registration in targeting potential fraud by pointing to a hypothetical voter who could still register to vote 30 days before the election and then return to cast an early in-person ballot on the 29th day before the election—in theory, voting before the board of elections completed its mail verification process.

Yet, our task (especially with respect to minimally burdensome laws) is neither to craft the "best" approach, nor "to impose our own idea of democracy upon the Ohio state legislature." *Libertarian Party*, 462 F.3d at 587. Rather, we simply call balls and strikes and apply a generous strike zone when the state articulates legitimate and reasonable justifications for minimally burdensome, non-discriminatory election regulations. Given the weight afforded to State measures targeting potential fraud (even without evidentiary support) in *Crawford*; and given the Court's hesitation to scrutinize the regulation's fraud-fighting effectiveness, we accept Ohio's goal of reducing potential voter fraud as an "important regulatory interest" sufficient to justify the minimal burden identified in this case. Moreover, Ohio offers additional justifications.

Administrative Burdens. Asserting that its boards of elections are extremely busy with finalizing ballots, running ballots through voting machines for "logic and accuracy testing," processing the registration wave that arrives near the close of registration, and recruiting and training poll workers, Ohio justifies S.B. 238 as reflecting a realization of the need to balance early-voting options with the burdens on boards of elections. Again, the district court rejected the State's justification because the "only evidence in support of that notion [was] that in 2010, the Ohio Association of Election Officials [OAEO] task force, aware of these administrative concerns, recommended that early voting begin twenty-one days before Election Day" and the State failed to prove that the boards would be "unable to manage" the administrative burdens and costs associated with Golden Week.

Again, the district court demanded too much. We agree rather with the Supreme Court that legislatures "should be permitted to respond to potential deficiencies in the electoral process with foresight rather than reactively." *Munro*, 479 U.S. at 195, 107 S. Ct. 533. Requiring that a "[s]tate's political system sustain some level of damage before the legislature could take corrective action" is neither practical, nor constitutionally compelled. *Id.*[8] Again, we note that S.B. 238 is minimally burdensome and facially non-discriminatory, and is therefore not violative of equal protection if it advances "important regulatory interests." Ohio's proffered interests of preventing voter fraud, increasing voter confidence by eliminating appearances of voter fraud, and easing administrative burdens on boards of elections are undoubtedly "important regulatory interests." The State's interests thus provide ample justification. We hold that plaintiffs have failed to establish their "heavy constitutional burden" of demonstrating that S.B. 238 is unconstitutional.

As a final note, the district court failed to consider *Crawford* when evaluating Ohio's interests due to its nearly wholesale reliance on our vacated decision in *NAACP*, which went to great lengths to distinguish *Crawford*'s ready acceptance of voter fraud and voter confidence as sufficient justifications for a regulation that imposed only a "limited burden on voter's rights." To the extent it relied on our now-vacated decision, the district court erred. *NAACP* is a different case, as S.B. 238 at that time still included the Secretary of State's Directive 2014-17 that "eliminate[ed] all evening voting hours for non-presidential elections and [] provid[ed] only one Sunday of [early in-person] voting." *NAACP* therefore analyzed Ohio's law as one imposing a burden that was "significant although not severe," requiring *more justification* than the "modest" burden the district court identified in this case, an interest we here hold to be minimal. The district court therefore used *NAACP* as an imperfect legend, and applied it to a different map. Its reliance on the vacated *NAACP* decision was not sound. Moreover, the vacated opinion in *NAACP* evinced a certain dissatisfaction with the *Crawford* Court's ruling and a preference for the view of dissenting Justices. To the extent the district court, by relying on *NAACP*, effectively resuscitated reasoning at odds with the holding of *Crawford*, the district court ignored a fundamental of our "hierarchical judicial system," which precludes a lower court from "declar[ing] a statute unconstitutional just because [it] thinks . . . that the dissent was right and the majority wrong." *Frank*, 768 F.3d at 750.

"When evaluating a neutral, nondiscriminatory regulation of voting procedure, '[w]e must keep in mind that [a] ruling of unconstitutionality frustrates the intent of the elected representatives of the people.'" *Crawford*, 553 U.S. at 203, 128 S. Ct. 1610 (Stevens, J., op). Plaintiffs prefer that we adopt a broad rule that any expansion of voting rights must remain on the books forever. Such a rule would have a chilling effect on the democratic process: states would have little incentive to pass bills expanding voting access if, once in place, they could never be modified in a way that might arguably burden some segment of the voting population's right to vote. Accepting the "long recognized . . . role of the States as laboratories for devising solutions to difficult legal problems," *Arizona State Legislature v. Arizona Indep. Redistricting Comm'n* (2015), we hold that imposing such a one-way ratchet is incompatible with the "flexible" *Anderson-Burdick* framework.

8. The same is true regarding the district court's outright rejection of Ohio's cost savings arguments. Though saving tens of thousands of dollars may be a "minimal" benefit when compared to the overall election budgets, we reject the district court's dubious and blanket proposition that "where *more than minimal* burdens on voters are established, the State must demonstrate that such costs would actually be burdensome." *Id.* at 6176 (citing *NAACP*, 768 F.3d at 548) (emphasis added). Fiscal responsibility, even if only incrementally served, is undeniably a legitimate and reasonable legislative purpose.

Applying *Anderson-Burdick* to S.B. 238, we hold that the State's justifications easily outweigh and sufficiently justify the minimal burden that some voters may experience. Accordingly, plaintiffs' equal protection challenge fails.

III. VOTING RIGHTS ACT

[Omitted.]

IV. CONCLUSION

Accordingly, we conclude that S.B. 238, affording abundant and convenient opportunities for all Ohioans to exercise their right to vote, is well within the constitutionally granted prerogative and authority of the Ohio Legislature to regulate state election processes. It does not run afoul of the Equal Protection Clause, as interpreted and applied to voting regulations in the most instructive decisions of the Supreme Court. The district court's award of declaratory and injunctive relief invalidating and enjoining enforcement of S.B. 238 must be **VACATED** and its judgment must be **REVERSED**.

STRANCH, Circuit Judge, dissenting.

Before addressing the governing law in light of the extensive record before us, I need to address the assumptions that frame the majority's opinion. This case is portrayed as an improper intrusion of the federal courts "as overseers and micromanagers, in the minutiae of state election processes." I disagree.

I. DISTRICT COURT RECORD AND DECISION

I begin with the extensive record made in the district court. For example, an expert analysis of individual level data based on census blocks within three of the largest counties in Ohio—which contain nearly two-fifths of the state's minority population—found that "the rate which African Americans used EIP voting in 2010 and 2014 was slightly higher than the white rate," and that the "usage rates of *Golden week specifically* were far higher among African Americans than among whites in both 2008 and 2012." The Golden Week usage rates in 2008 for 100% homogeneous black census blocks was 3.514 times higher than 100% white blocks. In 2012, the Golden Week usage rate was 5.186 times higher for homogeneous black blocks. The district court also noted the expert evidence that African Americans are "more likely to be subject to economic, transportation, time, and childcare constraints that increase the cost of voting." "[R]elative to whites," the district court found, "African Americans in Ohio are less likely to work in professional and managerial jobs; are more likely to work in service and sales jobs, including hourly wage jobs; have lower incomes; are nearly three times more likely to live in poverty; and are more than two and a half times more likely to live in a neighborhood in which more than 20% of the residents are in poverty."

The court's review of the record evidence evincing these disparities led it to conclude

> that the cost of voting is therefore generally higher for African Americans, as they are less likely to be able to take time off of work, find childcare, and secure reliable transportation to the polls. Moreover, greater levels

> of transience may result in more frequent changes of address, which in turn requires individuals to update their registration more frequently. SDR [same-day registration] provided an opportunity to do so and vote at the same time. As such, African Americans disproportionately make up the group that benefits the most from SDR, and the elimination of that opportunity burdens their right to vote.

[T]he majority opinion's blithe assertion "that it's easy to vote in Ohio. Very easy, actually" . . . is problematic for [this] reason—the district court's finding that Ohio law imposes some burden on the right of African Americans to vote in Ohio indicates that how "easy" it is to vote under Ohio's new regime bears some small but definable relationship to the color of your skin.

II. EQUAL PROTECTION

The majority argues that de novo review applies to the district court's conclusion that elimination of Golden Week imposes a "modest" burden on the right of African American's to vote. Neither our precedent nor that of our sister Circuits supports this argument.

In *Obama for America v. Husted* (6th Cir. 2012) (*OFA*), we applied clear error review to a district court's determination that an Ohio law restricting early in-person voting placed a "burden on Plaintiffs [that] was 'particularly high' because their members, supporters, and constituents represent a large percentage of those who participated in early voting in past elections." We held that "[b]ased on the evidence in the record, this conclusion was not clearly erroneous." *Id. OFA* involved an appeal from a district court's grant of a preliminary injunction and, accordingly, we reviewed the court's legal conclusions de novo and its factual determinations for clear error. *See id.* at 428. The same standard applies where, as here, a party appeals following a bench trial. Consequently, it is clear error review we must apply to the district court's finding that the elimination of Golden Week imposes a more than minimal but less than significant burden on African Americans' right to vote in Ohio.

None of the cases cited by the majority dictates our standard of review here. Rather, as in *OFA* (and *NAACP*), we are limited to reviewing for clear error the district court's finding based on record evidence that S.B. 238's "elimination of Golden Week imposes a modest burden—which the Court defines as a more than minimal but less than significant burden—on the right to vote of African Americans." Our sister Circuits agree. The Fourth and Fifth Circuits have applied clear error review to the findings made by district courts in similar challenges under the Fourteenth Amendment.

Applying the correct standard reveals that the district court's finding of a modest burden under the *Anderson-Burdick* test is more than plausible—it is well-supported by the record. The district court extensively reviewed and relied upon expert and anecdotal evidence in the record before concluding that "this evidence of the effects of the reduction in EIP voting days and the elimination of SDR demonstrates that S.B. 238 imposes a modest, as well as a disproportionate, burden on African Americans' right to vote."

In arguing under the standard it proposes, the majority seeks to rely on voting systems in other states as an important "contextual basis" for determining whether the burden of S.B. 238 falls disproportionately on African Americans. But the usefulness of that contextual information depends on whether the many variable methods for voting in each system line up. Certain types of voting processes, like early voting, "do[] not necessarily play the same role in all jurisdictions in ensuring that certain groups of voters are actually able to vote" and as a result, "the same law may impose a significant burden in one state and only a minimal burden in the other." *NAACP*, 768 F.3d at 546. Simply stating that Ohio's early voting system is "one of the more generous in the nation" provides little helpful information. It fails, for example, to account for the rate at which early voting is actually used by different populations, let alone how the voting options in other states might impact the comparison. In most respects, this issue is local and dependent on the particular circumstances of Ohio's law and its population. Analysis of the burden that S.B. 238 places on Ohio voters thus necessarily entails engaging with the factual record. The majority opinion fails to perform that essential work.

The majority opinion next seeks to recast African American voters' reliance on EIP and SDR as mere "personal preference." This is based on surmise, not record evidence. So, too, is its conclusory assertion that "[a]t worst," the elimination of Golden Week "represents a withdrawal or contraction of just one of many conveniences that have generously facilitated voting participation in Ohio." The record in this case shows that the State of Ohio instituted no fault early voting in 2005 not as a generous convenience but as a necessary tool "to remedy the manifold problems experienced during the 2004 election," "including extremely long lines at the polls" and other "election administration problems." As the Fourth Circuit recently concluded in a similar vote denial case and as this record supports, "socioeconomic disparities establish that no mere 'preference' led African Americans to disproportionately use early voting[and] same-day registration[.]" "Registration and voting tools may be a simple 'preference' for many white [voters]," the Fourth Circuit recognized, "but for many African Americans they are a necessity."

The majority opinion again relies on assumptions about voting preferences to conclude that the record evidence that African Americans use early voting at higher rates than other voters may make them "theoretically disadvantaged" by reductions in early voting. There is nothing theoretical about the disadvantage found by the district court. Using an extensive record, the district court determined that S.B. 238's changes to early voting and same day voter registration impose a modest and disproportionate burden on African Americans' right to vote. The majority points to no clear error by the district court on the record. I would affirm its finding because it satisfies the correct standard of review.

The majority opinion, however, rejects the district court's decision that S.B. 238 imposes a "modest" burden and, based on its chosen standard of de novo review, concludes that it is a "minimal burden." Building on that error, it applies a deferential standard of review akin to rational basis and presumes that *Crawford* both applies and resolves this case.

This series of conclusions relies on standards of review not applicable to this case. First, *Crawford* arose in a different context because it was an appeal from a summary judgment order, not a bench trial. Second, the case is factually distinct in essential ways because there the Court "held only that the lower courts 'correctly concluded that the evidence in the record [was] not sufficient to support a facial attack on the validity of the entire statute' under the constitutional *Anderson-Burdick* framework." *Crawford* concerned a facial challenge to a voter identification law, but the summary judgment record in that case "(1) did not quantify the voters without qualifying ID, (2) provided no 'concrete evidence of the burden imposed on voters who currently lack photo identification,' and (3) said 'virtually nothing about the difficulties faced by . . . indigent voters.'" In other words, "[t]he petitioners in *Crawford* had not presented any evidence in the record that even estimated the number of individuals who lacked identification cards. Nor did the affidavits or depositions in the record of lower-income individuals or elderly voters in *Crawford* substantiate that they in fact faced difficulties in obtaining identification cards." *NAACP*, 768 F.3d at 544 (citation omitted). Thus, "on the basis of the record that ha[d] been made in th[at] litigation," the Court could not "conclude that the statute impose[d] excessively burdensome requirements."

Here, by contrast, the record is replete with specific evidence supporting the plaintiffs' claims and the district court's conclusion regarding the amount of burden imposed by the elimination of Golden Week. Over the course of a ten-day bench trial, the district court weighed evidence from eight expert witnesses and nineteen lay witnesses, from statistical analyses to testimony of Get Out the Vote efforts, ultimately making determinations of credibility that led to its conclusion that S.B. 238 disproportionately burdens African Americans. The record in this case provides ample evidence by which the district court could "quantify . . . the magnitude of the burden" on African American voters. I would also affirm the district court's application of *Anderson*-Burdick balancing and the court's resulting conclusion that the State has failed to present sufficient evidence to show that its specific (as opposed to abstract) interests justify the burden that eliminating Golden Week imposes on African American voters.

The majority opinion argues that the overarching question with respect to plaintiffs' equal protection claim in this case is whether Ohio may experiment with expanding and contracting voting regulations. Of course it may. The question is whether it may do so in a way that disparately impacts a protected group without sufficient justification by a relevant and legitimate state interest. Because I agree with the district court that Ohio's revised S.B. 238 improperly burdens the right to vote of African American citizens of Ohio and constitutes a violation of equal protection, I respectfully dissent.

IV. CONCLUSION

I would affirm the very limited injunction issued by the district court on the basis that S.B. 238's elimination of Golden Week, reducing early in-person voting and same day registration, is a violation of equal protection. The district court applied the correct constitutional test and its decision is fully supported by the extensive record resulting from its ten day bench trial. The charge that this appeal—and apparently many others—intrude upon the right of the states to run their own election process is both unfounded and antiquated. Our American society and legal system now recognize that appropriate scrutiny is essential to protection of the fundamental right to vote. The scrutiny applied by the district court was proper and in accord with governing precedent. I therefore respectfully dissent.

THE VOTING RIGHTS ACT AND CLAIMS OF VOTE DENIAL UNDER SECTION 2

In 2021, the Supreme Court issued a major opinion on the use of Section 2 of the Voting Rights Act to challenge an election rule or procedure as discriminating on the basis of race with respect to the casting and counting of ballots—the kinds of issues addressed in Part IV of this book. This category of Section 2 cases, which had been percolating in the lower federal courts before the Supreme Court agreed to address the issue, had come to be called "vote denial" claims to distinguish them from "vote dilution" claims in the context of redistricting. But the term "vote denial" is something of a misnomer, as it too narrowly describes the applicable category: State rules and procedures that abridge the right to vote, even if they do not outright deny electoral participation, are subject to Section 2 if they are racially discriminatory. For example, a state law that limits the time available for voting in a racially discriminatory way is potentially violative of Section 2 even if it does not deny anyone the right to vote. With this caveat about nomenclature, the term "vote denial" remains a useful shorthand to differentiate this category from "vote dilution" cases under Section 2.

As we saw in Part I, the Court had long applied Section 2 to claims of vote dilution in the redistricting context. In those cases, the Court had crafted a test to determine if a district's map would dilute the strength of minority voters and make it harder for them to elect candidates of their choice. In this 2021 case, plaintiffs argued that two Arizona laws would make it disproportionately harder for minorities, compared to non-minority voters, to cast a ballot that will count. One provision said that no one (with some exceptions such as for postal workers, family members, and caregivers) may collect and return another person's ballot, a practice which opponents term "ballot harvesting." The other provision said that a vote cast in the wrong precinct—if, for instance, the person does not reside within the precinct's boundaries and therefore casts a provisional ballot—would not count. In the language of Section 2 of the Voting Rights Act, the plaintiffs argued that these two rules would "result[] in a denial or abridgement of the right of any citizen of the United States to vote on account of race or color" because they gave minorities "less opportunity than other members of the electorate to participate in the political process and to elect representatives of their choice."

The district court upheld the laws in a narrow opinion, as did a three-judge panel of the Ninth Circuit, but the en banc Ninth Circuit reversed, finding that the laws violated Section 2 of the Voting Rights Act. The Supreme Court then reversed the Ninth Circuit in this important case. The question of the legality of these two Arizona provisions is much less important than the test the six-justice majority set out for future Section 2 vote denial claims. Pay close attention to the five "guideposts" Justice Alito offers. Where does he come up with these "guideposts"?

Brnovich v. Democratic National Committee

141 S. Ct. 2321 (2021)

Justice ALITO delivered the opinion of the Court.

In these cases, we are called upon for the first time to apply § 2 of the Voting Rights Act of 1965 to regulations that govern how ballots are collected and counted. Arizona law generally makes it very easy to vote. All voters may vote by mail or in person for nearly a month before election day, but Arizona imposes two restrictions that are claimed to be unlawful. First, in some counties, voters who choose to cast a ballot in person on election day must vote in their own precincts or else their ballots will not be counted. Second, mail-in ballots cannot be collected by anyone other than an election official, a mail carrier, or a voter's family member, household member, or caregiver. After a trial, a District Court upheld these rules, as did a panel of the United States Court of Appeals for the Ninth Circuit. But an en banc court, by a divided vote, found them to be unlawful. It relied on the rules' small disparate impacts on members of minority groups, as well as past discrimination dating back to the State's territorial days. And it overturned the District Court's finding that the Arizona Legislature did not adopt the ballot-collection restriction for a discriminatory purpose. We now hold that the en banc court misunderstood and misapplied § 2 and that it exceeded its authority in rejecting the District Court's factual finding on the issue of legislative intent.

I

A

Congress enacted the landmark Voting Rights Act of 1965 in an effort to achieve at long last what the Fifteenth Amendment had sought to bring about 95 years earlier: an end to the denial of the right to vote based on race.

Despite the ratification of the Fifteenth Amendment, the right of African-Americans to vote was heavily suppressed for nearly a century. States employed a variety of notorious methods, including poll taxes, literacy tests, property qualifications, white primar[ies], and grandfather clause[s]. Challenges to some blatant efforts reached this Court and were held to violate the Fifteenth Amendment.

Invoking the power conferred by § 2 of the Fifteenth Amendment, Congress enacted the Voting Rights Act (VRA) to address this entrenched problem. The Act and its amendments in the 1970s specifically forbade some of the practices that had been used to suppress black voting. Sections 4 and 5 of the VRA imposed special requirements for States and subdivisions where violations of the right to vote had been severe. And § 2 addressed the denial or abridgment of the right to vote in any part of the country.

As originally enacted, § 2 closely tracked the language of the Amendment it was adopted to enforce. Section 2 stated simply that "[n]o voting qualification or prerequisite to voting, or standard, practice, or procedure shall be imposed or applied by any State or political subdivision to deny or abridge the right of any citizen of the United States to vote on account of race or color." Unlike other provisions of the VRA, § 2 attracted relatively little attention during the congressional debates and was "little-used" for more than a decade after its passage. But during the same period, this Court considered several cases involving "vote-dilution" claims asserted under the Equal Protection Clause of the Fourteenth Amendment. In these and later vote-dilution cases, plaintiffs claimed that features of legislative districting plans, including the configuration of legislative districts and the use of multi-member districts, diluted the ability of particular voters to affect the outcome of elections.

A few years later, the question whether a VRA § 2 claim required discriminatory purpose or intent came before this Court in *Mobile v. Bolden* (1980). The plurality opinion for four Justices concluded first that § 2 of the VRA added nothing to the protections afforded by the Fifteenth Amendment. The plurality then observed that prior decisions "ha[d] made clear that action by a State that is racially neutral on its face violates the Fifteenth Amendment only if motivated by a discriminatory purpose." The obvious result of those premises was that facially neutral voting practices violate § 2 only if motivated by a discriminatory purpose.

Shortly after *Bolden* was handed down, Congress amended § 2 of the VRA. The oft-cited Report of the Senate Judiciary Committee accompanying the 1982 Amendment stated that the amendment's purpose was to repudiate *Bolden* and establish a new vote-dilution test. . . . The bill that was initially passed by the House of Representatives included what is now § 2(a). In place of the phrase "to deny or abridge the right . . . to vote on account of race or color," the amendment substituted "in a manner which results in a denial or abridgement of the right . . . to vote on account of race or color." H

The House bill "originally passed. . . under a loose understanding that § 2 would prohibit all discriminatory 'effects' of voting practices, and that intent would be 'irrelevant,'" but "[t]his version met stiff resistance in the Senate." The House and Senate compromised, and the final product included language proposed by Senator Dole. What is now § 2(b) was added, and that provision sets out what must be shown to prove a § 2 violation. It requires consideration of "the totality of circumstances" in each case and demands proof that "the political processes leading to nomination or election in the State or political subdivision are not equally open to participation" by members of a protected class "in that its members have less opportunity than other members of the electorate to participate in the political process and to elect representatives of their choice."

B

The present dispute concerns two features of Arizona voting law, which generally makes it quite easy for residents to vote. All Arizonans may vote by mail for 27 days before an election using an "early ballot." No special excuse is needed, and any voter may ask to be sent an early ballot automatically in future elections. In addition, during the 27 days before an election, Arizonans may vote in person at an early voting location in each county. And they may also vote in person on election day.

Each county is free to conduct election-day voting either by using the traditional precinct model or by setting up "voting centers." Voting centers are equipped to provide all voters in a county with the appropriate ballot for the precinct in which they are registered, and this allows voters in the county to use whichever vote center they prefer.

The regulations at issue in this suit govern precinct-based election-day voting and early mail-in voting. Voters who choose to vote in person on election day in a county that uses the precinct system must vote in their assigned precincts. If a voter goes to the wrong polling place, poll workers are trained to direct the voter to the right location. If a voter finds that his or her name does not appear on the register at what the voter believes is the right precinct, the voter ordinarily may cast a provisional ballot. That ballot is later counted if the voter's address is determined to be within the precinct. But if it turns out that the voter cast a ballot at the wrong precinct, that vote is not counted.

For those who choose to vote early by mail, Arizona has long required that "[o]nly the elector may be in possession of that elector's unvoted early ballot." In 2016, the state legislature enacted House Bill 2023 (HB 2023), which makes it a crime for any person other than a postal worker, an elections official, or a voter's caregiver, family member, or household member to knowingly collect an early ballot—either before or after it has been completed.

In 2016, the Democratic National Committee and certain affiliates brought this suit and named as defendants (among others) the Arizona attorney general and secretary of state in their official capacities. Among other things, the plaintiffs claimed that both the State's refusal to count ballots cast in the wrong precinct and its ballot-collection restriction "adversely and disparately affect Arizona's American Indian, Hispanic, and African American citizens," in violation of § 2 of the VRA. In addition, they alleged that the ballot-collection restriction was "enacted with discriminatory intent" and thus violated both § 2 of the VRA and the Fifteenth Amendment.

After a 10-day bench trial, the District Court made extensive findings of fact and rejected all the plaintiffs' claims. The court first found that the out-of-precinct policy "has no meaningfully disparate impact on the opportunities of minority voters to elect" representatives of their choice. The percentage of ballots invalidated under this policy was very small (0.15% of all ballots cast in 2016) and decreasing, and while the percentages were slightly higher for members of minority groups, the court found that this disparity "does not result in minorities having unequal access to the political process." The court also found that the plaintiffs had not proved that the policy "causes minorities to show up to vote at the wrong precinct at rates higher than their non-minority counterparts," and the court noted that the plaintiffs had not even challenged "the manner in which Arizona counties allocate and assign polling places or Arizona's requirement that voters re-register to vote when they move."

The District Court similarly found that the ballot collection restriction is unlikely to "cause a meaningful inequality in the electoral opportunities of minorities." Rather, the court noted, the restriction applies equally to all voters and "does not impose burdens beyond those traditionally associated with voting." The court observed that the plaintiffs had presented no records showing how many voters had previously relied on now-prohibited third-party ballot collectors and that the plaintiffs also had "provided no quantitative or statistical evidence" of the percentage of minority and non-minority voters in this group.

Finally, the court found that the ballot-collection law had not been enacted with discriminatory intent. "[T]he majority of H.B. 2023's proponents," the court found, "were sincere in their belief that ballot collection increased the risk of early voting fraud, and that H.B. 2023 was a necessary prophylactic measure to bring early mail ballot security in line with in-person voting." The court added that "some individual legislators and proponents were motivated in part by partisan interests." But it distinguished between partisan and racial motives, while recognizing that "racially polarized voting can sometimes blur the lines."

A divided panel of the Ninth Circuit affirmed, but an en banc court reversed.

II

[W]e think it prudent to make clear at the beginning that we decline in these cases to announce a test to govern all VRA § 2 claims involving rules, like those at issue here, that specify the time, place, or manner for casting ballots. Each of the parties advocated a different test, as did many amici and the courts below. In a brief filed in December in support of petitioners, the Department of Justice proposed one such test but later disavowed the analysis in that brief. The Department informed us, however, that it did not disagree with its prior conclusion that the two provisions of Arizona law at issue in these cases do not violate § 2 of the Voting Rights Act. All told, no fewer than 10 tests have been proposed. But as this is our first foray into the area, we think it sufficient for present purposes to identify certain guideposts that lead us to our decision in these cases.

III

A

We start with the text of VRA § 2. It now provides:

> "(a) No voting qualification or prerequisite to voting or standard, practice, or procedure shall be imposed or applied by any State or political subdivision in a manner which results in a denial or abridgement of the right of any citizen of the United States to vote on account of race or color, or in contravention of the guarantees set forth in section 10303(f)(2) of this title, as provided in subsection (b).
>
> "(b) A violation of subsection (a) is established if, based on the totality of circumstances, it is shown that the political processes leading to nomination or election in the State or political subdivision are not equally open to participation by members of a class of citizens protected by subsection (a) in that its members have less opportunity than other members of the electorate to participate in the political process and to elect representatives of their choice. The extent to which members of a protected class have been elected to office in the State or political subdivision is one circumstance which may be considered: Provided, That nothing in this section establishes a right to have members of a protected class elected in numbers equal to their proportion in the population." 52 U.S.C. § 10301.

[B]ecause this is our first § 2 time, place, or manner case, a fresh look at the statutory text is appropriate. Today, our statutory interpretation cases almost always start with a careful consideration of the text, and there is no reason to do otherwise here.

B

Section 2(b) states that § 2 is violated only where "the political processes leading to nomination or election" are not "*equally open* to participation" by members of the relevant protected group "*in that its members have less opportunity* than other members of the electorate to participate in the political process and to elect representatives of their choice." (Emphasis added.)

The key requirement is that the political processes leading to nomination and election (here, the process of voting) must be "equally open" to minority and non-minority groups alike, and the most relevant definition of the term "open," as used in § 2(b), is "without restrictions as to who may participate," Random House Dictionary of the English Language 1008 (J. Stein ed. 1966), or "requiring no special status, identification, or permit for entry or participation," Webster's Third New International Dictionary 1579 (1976).

What § 2(b) means by voting that is not "equally open" is further explained by this language: "in that its members have less opportunity than other members of the electorate to participate in the political process and to elect representatives of their choice." The phrase "in that" is "used to specify the respect in which a statement is true." Thus, equal openness and equal opportunity are not separate requirements. Instead, equal opportunity helps to explain the meaning of equal openness. And the term "opportunity" means, among other things, "a combination of circumstances, time, and place suitable or favorable for a particular activity or action."

Putting these terms together, it appears that the core of § 2(b) is the requirement that voting be "equally open." The statute's reference to equal "opportunity" may stretch that concept to some degree to include consideration of a person's ability to use the means that are equally open. But equal openness remains the touchstone.

C

One other important feature of § 2(b) stands out. The provision requires consideration of "the totality of circumstances." Thus, any circumstance that has a logical bearing on whether voting is "equally open" and affords equal "opportunity" may be considered. We will not attempt to compile an exhaustive list, but several important circumstances should be mentioned.

1

1. First, the size of the burden imposed by a challenged voting rule is highly relevant. The concepts of "open[ness]" and "opportunity" connote the absence of obstacles and burdens that block or seriously hinder voting, and therefore the size of the burden imposed by a voting rule is important. After all, every voting rule imposes a burden of some sort. Voting takes time and, for almost everyone, some travel, even if only to a nearby mailbox. Casting a vote, whether by following the directions for using a voting machine or completing a paper ballot, requires compliance with certain rules. But because voting necessarily requires some effort and compliance with some rules, the concept of a voting system that is "equally open" and that furnishes an equal "opportunity" to cast a ballot must tolerate the "usual burdens of voting." *Crawford v. Marion County Election Bd.* (2008) Mere inconvenience cannot be enough to demonstrate a violation of § 2.

2. For similar reasons, the degree to which a voting rule departs from what was standard practice when § 2 was amended in 1982 is a relevant consideration. Because every voting rule imposes a burden of some sort, it is useful to have benchmarks with which the burdens imposed by a challenged rule can be compared. The burdens associated with the rules in widespread use when § 2 was adopted are therefore useful in gauging whether the burdens imposed by a challenged rule are sufficient to prevent voting from being equally "open" or furnishing an equal "opportunity" to vote in the sense meant by § 2. Therefore, it is relevant that in 1982 States typically required nearly all voters to cast their ballots in person on election day and allowed only narrow and tightly defined categories of voters to cast absentee ballots. We doubt that Congress intended to uproot facially neutral time, place, and manner regulations that have a long pedigree or are in widespread use in the United States. We have no need to decide whether adherence to, or a return to, a 1982 framework is necessarily lawful under § 2, but the degree to which

a challenged rule has a long pedigree or is in widespread use in the United States is a circumstance that must be taken into account.

3. The size of any disparities in a rule's impact on members of different racial or ethnic groups is also an important factor to consider. Small disparities are less likely than large ones to indicate that a system is not equally open. To the extent that minority and non-minority groups differ with respect to employment, wealth, and education, even neutral regulations, no matter how crafted, may well result in some predictable disparities in rates of voting and noncompliance with voting rules. But the mere fact there is some disparity in impact does not necessarily mean that a system is not equally open or that it does not give everyone an equal opportunity to vote. The size of any disparity matters. And in assessing the size of any disparity, a meaningful comparison is essential. What are at bottom very small differences should not be artificially magnified.

4. Next, courts must consider the opportunities provided by a State's entire system of voting when assessing the burden imposed by a challenged provision. This follows from § 2(b)'s reference to the collective concept of a State's "political processes" and its "political process" as a whole. Thus, where a State provides multiple ways to vote, any burden imposed on voters who choose one of the available options cannot be evaluated without also taking into account the other available means.

5. Finally, the strength of the state interests served by a challenged voting rule is also an important factor that must be taken into account. As noted, every voting rule imposes a burden of some sort, and therefore, in determining "based on the totality of circumstances" whether a rule goes too far, it is important to consider the reason for the rule. Rules that are supported by strong state interests are less likely to violate § 2.

One strong and entirely legitimate state interest is the prevention of fraud. Fraud can affect the outcome of a close election, and fraudulent votes dilute the right of citizens to cast ballots that carry appropriate weight. Fraud can also undermine public confidence in the fairness of elections and the perceived legitimacy of the announced outcome. . . .

Ensuring that every vote is cast freely, without intimidation or undue influence, is also a valid and important state interest. This interest helped to spur the adoption of what soon became standard practice in this country and in other democratic nations the world round: the use of private voting booths. *See Burson v. Freeman* (1992).

2

[Omitted.]

D

The interpretation set out above follows directly from what § 2 commands: consideration of "the totality of circumstances" that have a bearing on whether a State makes voting "equally open" to all and gives everyone an equal "opportunity" to vote. The dissent, by contrast, would rewrite the text of § 2 and make it turn almost entirely on just one circumstance—disparate impact. That is a radical project, and the dissent strains mightily to obscure its objective.

Recall that the version originally passed by the House did not contain § 2(b) and was thought to prohibit any voting practice that had "discriminatory effects," loosely defined. That is the freewheeling disparate-impact regime the dissent wants to impose on the States. But the version enacted into law includes § 2(b), and that subsection directs us to consider "the totality of circumstances," not, as the dissent would have it, the totality of just one circumstance. There is nothing to the dissent's charge that we are departing from the statutory text by identifying some of those considerations.

We have listed five relevant circumstances and have explained why they all stem from the statutory text and have a bearing on the determination that § 2 requires. The dissent does not mention a single additional consideration, and it does its best to push aside all but one of the circumstances we discuss.

With all other circumstances swept away, all that remains in the dissent's approach is the size of any disparity in a rule's impact on members of protected groups. As we have noted, differences in employment, wealth, and education may make it virtually impossible for a State to devise rules that do not have some disparate impact. But under the dissent's interpretation of § 2, any "statistically significant" disparity—wherever that is in the statute—may be enough to take down even facially neutral voting rules with long pedigrees that reasonably pursue important state interests.

Section 2 of the Voting Rights Act provides vital protection against discriminatory voting rules, and no one suggests that discrimination in voting has been extirpated or that the threat has been eliminated. But § 2 does not deprive the States of their authority to establish non-discriminatory voting rules, and that is precisely what the dissent's radical interpretation would mean in practice. The dissent is correct that the Voting Rights Act exemplifies our country's commitment to democracy, but there is nothing democratic about the dissent's attempt to bring about a wholesale transfer of the authority to set voting rules from the States to the federal courts.

IV

A

In light of the principles set out above, neither Arizona's out-of-precinct rule nor its ballot-collection law violates § 2 of the VRA. Arizona's out-of-precinct rule enforces the requirement that voters who choose to vote in person on election day must do so in their assigned precincts. Having to identify one's own polling place and then travel there to vote does not exceed the "usual burdens of voting." *Crawford*. On the contrary, these tasks are quintessential examples of the usual burdens of voting.

The burdens of identifying and traveling to one's assigned precinct are also modest when considering Arizona's "political processes" as a whole. The Court of Appeals noted that Arizona leads other States in the rate of votes rejected on the ground that they were cast in the wrong precinct, and the court attributed this to frequent changes in polling locations, confusing placement of polling places, and high levels of residential mobility. But even if it is marginally harder for Arizona voters to find their assigned polling places, the State offers other easy ways to vote. Any voter can request an early ballot without excuse. Any voter can ask to be placed on the permanent early voter list so that an early ballot will be mailed automatically. Voters may drop off their early ballots at any polling place, even one to which they are not assigned. And for nearly a month before election day, any voter can vote in person at an early voting location in his or her county. The availability of those options likely explains why out-of-precinct votes on election day make up such a small and apparently diminishing portion of overall ballots cast—0.47% of all ballots in the 2012 general election and just 0.15% in 2016.

Next, the racial disparity in burdens allegedly caused by the out-of-precinct policy is small in absolute terms. The District Court accepted the plaintiffs' evidence that, of the Arizona counties that reported out-of-precinct ballots in the 2016 general election, a little over 1% of Hispanic voters, 1% of African-American voters, and 1% of Native American voters who voted on election day cast an out-of-precinct ballot. For non-minority voters, the rate was around 0.5%. A policy that appears to work for 98% or more of voters to whom it applies—minority and non-minority alike—is unlikely to render a system unequally open.

The Court of Appeals' decision also failed to give appropriate weight to the state interests that the out-of-precinct rule serves. Not counting out-of-precinct votes induces compliance with the requirement that Arizonans who choose to vote in-person on election day do so at their assigned polling places. And as the District Court recognized, precinct-based voting furthers important state interests. It helps to distribute voters more evenly among polling places and thus reduces wait times. It can put polling places closer to voter residences than would a more centralized voting-center model. In addition, precinct-based voting helps to ensure that each voter receives a ballot that lists only the candidates and public questions on which he or she can vote, and this orderly administration tends to decrease voter confusion and increase voter confidence in elections. It is also significant that precinct-based voting has a long pedigree in the United States.

Section 2 does not require a State to show that its chosen policy is absolutely necessary or that a less restrictive means would not adequately serve the State's objectives. In light of the modest burdens allegedly imposed by Arizona's out-of-precinct policy, the small size of its disparate impact, and the State's justifications, we conclude the rule does not violate § 2 of the VRA.

B

HB 2023 likewise passes muster under the results test of § 2. Arizonans who receive early ballots can submit them by going to a mailbox, a post office, an early ballot drop box, or an authorized election official's office within the 27-day early voting period. They can also drop off their ballots at any polling place or voting center on election day, and in order to do so, they can skip the line of voters waiting to vote in person. Making any of these trips—much like traveling to an assigned polling place—falls squarely within the heartland of the "usual burdens of voting." *Crawford*. And voters can also ask a statutorily authorized proxy—a family member, a household member, or a caregiver—to mail a ballot or drop it off at any time within 27 days of an election.

Arizona also makes special provision for certain groups of voters who are unable to use the early voting system. Every county must establish a special election board to serve voters who are "confined as the result of a continuing illness or physical disability," are unable to go to the polls on election day, and do not wish to cast an early vote by mail. At the request of a voter in this group, the board will deliver a ballot in person and return it on the voter's behalf. Arizona law also requires employers to give employees time off to vote when they are otherwise scheduled to work certain shifts on election day.

The plaintiffs were unable to provide statistical evidence showing that HB 2023 had a disparate impact on minority voters. Instead, they called witnesses who testified that third-party ballot collection tends to be used most heavily in disadvantaged communities and that minorities in Arizona—especially Native Americans—are disproportionately disadvantaged. But from that evidence the District Court could conclude only that prior to HB 2023's enactment, "minorities generically were more likely than non-minorities to return their early ballots with the assistance of third parties." How much more, the court could not say from the record. Neither can we. And without more concrete evidence, we cannot conclude that HB 2023 results in less opportunity to participate in the political process.

Even if the plaintiffs had shown a disparate burden caused by HB 2023, the State's justifications would suffice to avoid § 2 liability. "A State indisputably has a compelling interest in preserving the integrity of its election process." *Purcell v. Gonzalez* (2006). Limiting the classes of persons who may handle early ballots to those less likely to have ulterior motives deters potential fraud and improves voter confidence.

The Court of Appeals thought that the State's justifications for HB 2023 were tenuous in large part because there was no evidence that fraud in connection with early ballots had occurred in Arizona. But prevention of fraud is not the only legitimate interest served by restrictions on ballot collection. [T]hird-party ballot collection can lead to pressure and intimidation. And it should go without saying that a State may take action to prevent election fraud without waiting for it to occur and be detected within its own borders. Section 2's command that the political processes remain equally open surely does not demand that "a State's political system sustain some level of damage before the legislature [can] take corrective action." *Munro* (1986). Fraud is a real risk that accompanies mail-in voting even if Arizona had the good fortune to avoid it. Election fraud has had serious consequences in other States. For example, the North Carolina Board of Elections invalidated the results of a 2018 race for a seat in the House of Representatives for evidence of fraudulent mail-in ballots. The Arizona Legislature was not obligated to wait for something similar to happen closer to home.

As with the out-of-precinct policy, the modest evidence of racially disparate burdens caused by HB 2023, in light of the State's justifications, leads us to the conclusion that the law does not violate § 2 of the VRA.

V

We also granted certiorari to review whether the Court of Appeals erred in concluding that HB 2023 was enacted with a discriminatory purpose. The District Court found that it was not and appellate review of that conclusion is for clear error

The District Court's finding on the question of discriminatory intent had ample support in the record.

We are more than satisfied that the District Court's interpretation of the evidence is permissible. The spark for the debate over mail-in voting may well have been provided by one Senator's enflamed partisanship, but partisan motives are not the same as racial motives. *See Cooper v. Harris* (2017). The District Court noted that the voting preferences of members of a racial group may make the former look like the latter, but it carefully distinguished between the two. And while the District Court recognized that the "racially-tinged" video helped spur the debate about ballot collection, it found no evidence that the legislature as a whole was imbued with racial motives.

The Court of Appeals did not dispute the District Court's assessment of the sincerity of HB 2023's proponents. It even agreed that some members of the legislature had a "sincere, though mistaken, non-race-based belief that there had been fraud in third-party ballot collection, and that the problem needed to be addressed." The Court of Appeals nevertheless concluded that the District Court committed clear error by failing to apply a " 'cat's paw' " theory sometimes used in employment discrimination cases. A "cat's paw" is a "dupe" who is "used by another to accomplish his purposes." A plaintiff in a "cat's paw" case typically seeks to hold the plaintiff's employer liable for "the animus of a supervisor who was not charged with making the ultimate [adverse] employment decision." The "cat's paw" theory has no application to legislative bodies. The theory rests on the agency relationship that exists between an employer and a supervisor, but the legislators who vote to adopt a bill are not the agents of the bill's sponsor or proponents. Under our form of government, legislators have a duty to exercise their judgment and to represent their constituents. It is insulting to suggest that they are mere dupes or tools.

* * *

Arizona's out-of-precinct policy and HB 2023 do not violate § 2 of the VRA, and HB 2023 was not enacted with a racially discriminatory purpose.

Justice GORSUCH, with whom Justice THOMAS joins, concurring.
[Omitted.]

Justice KAGAN, with whom Justice BREYER and Justice SOTOMAYOR join, dissenting.

If a single statute represents the best of America, it is the Voting Rights Act. It marries two great ideals: democracy and racial equality. And it dedicates our country to carrying them out. Section 2, the provision at issue here, guarantees that members of every racial group will have equal voting opportunities. Citizens of every race will have the same shot to participate in the political process and to elect representatives of their choice. They will all own our democracy together—no one more and no one less than any other.

If a single statute reminds us of the worst of America, it is the Voting Rights Act. Because it was—and remains—so necessary. Because a century after the Civil War was fought, at the time of the Act's passage, the promise of political equality remained a distant dream for African American citizens. Because States and localities continually "contriv[ed] new rules," mostly neutral on their face but discriminatory in operation, to keep minority voters from the polls. Because "Congress had reason to suppose" that States would "try similar maneuvers in the future"—"pour[ing] old poison into new bottles" to suppress minority votes. Because Congress has been proved right.

The Voting Rights Act is ambitious, in both goal and scope. When President Lyndon Johnson sent the bill to Congress, ten days after John Lewis led marchers across the Edmund Pettus Bridge, he explained that it was "carefully drafted to meet its objective—the end of discrimination in voting in America." He was right about how the Act's drafting reflected its aim. "The end of discrimination in voting" is a far-reaching goal. And the Voting Rights Act's text is just as far-reaching. A later amendment, adding the provision at issue here, became necessary when this Court construed the statute too narrowly. And in the last decade, this Court assailed the Act again, undoing its vital Section 5. *See Shelby County v. Holder* (2013). But Section 2 of the Act remains, as written, as expansive as ever—demanding that every citizen of this country possess a right at once grand and obvious: the right to an equal opportunity to vote.

Today, the Court undermines Section 2 and the right it provides. The majority fears that the statute Congress wrote is too "radical"—that it will invalidate too many state voting laws. So the majority writes its own set of rules, limiting Section 2 from multiple directions. Wherever it can, the majority gives a cramped reading to broad language. And then it uses that reading to uphold two election laws from Arizona that discriminate against minority voters. I could say—and will in the following pages—that this is not how the Court is supposed to interpret and apply statutes. But that ordinary critique woefully undersells the problem. What is tragic here is that the Court has (yet again) rewritten—in order to weaken—a statute that stands as a monument to America's greatness, and protects against its basest impulses. What is tragic is that the Court has damaged a statute designed to bring about "the end of discrimination in voting." I respectfully dissent.

[Because of space constraints, we have omitted most of Justice Kagan's lengthy and thorough dissent. But we encourage you to read the dissent in full when you have the chance.]

NOTES ON *BRNOVICH*

1. Many voting rights advocates were fearful of this case going to the Supreme Court at all, believing that the conservative Court majority would cabin the reach of Section 2. They thought that the Democratic National Committee and its allies never should have brought the case in the first place (or at least should not have appealed the district court decision that upheld the laws), as the two laws at issue were not particularly draconian (at least as compared to other voting rules that states were adopting). It turns out that they were likely right: the Court's new test may make it much harder for plaintiffs to win future Section 2 vote denial claims. This debate raises an important question about litigation strategy: is it sometimes better not to challenge a mildly harmful law, or should plaintiffs challenge anything that might harm the right to vote?

2. Where does Justice Alito find the five "guideposts" or "circumstances" that should govern Section 2 vote denial cases? Does each of them make sense? Consider the second one, about a rule's pedigree and whether it existed in 1982, when Congress amended the VRA. Should the fact that a rule is long-standing be a factor in determining liability in future VRA challenges if the law *now* results in a disparate impact? How much should a state's concern about election integrity allow a rule that might have a slight burden on minority voters?

3. How should voting rights plaintiffs respond to this decision? Are the five guideposts workable or do they just place the thumb on the scale of states too much? Should voting rights plaintiffs abandon challenges under Section 2 and instead focus on other avenues, such as state constitutions and state courts?

4. Notice how Justice Alito uses prior cases such as *Crawford* to justify both the minimal burdens a voter must overcome and a state's interests in regulating the voting process. *Brnovich* seems to build upon the notion from *Crawford* that states can enact rules that impose minimal burdens in an effort to root out the potential of voter fraud—even if there is no actual evidence that massive voter fraud exists.

C. *"ELECTION EVE" LITIGATION: THE* PURCELL *PRINCIPLE*

The leading case concerning "election eve" litigation is *Purcell v. Gonzales*, 549 U.S. 1 (2006). We have already read a later phase of the same lawsuit as *Purcell v. Gonzales*: *Arizona v. Intertribal Council*, about the validity of Arizona's requirement that voters prove their citizenship when they register to vote, was the subsequent substantive decision on the merits long after the preliminary procedural ruling in *Purcell v. Gonzales*. Thus, *Purcell* illustrates how different substantive issues can be intertwined with similar procedural issues. Indeed, after reading *Purcell* itself, we will consider some additional "election eve" litigation that concerned other types of substantive issues, including Wisconsin's voter ID law.

Purcell v. Gonzalez

549 U.S. 1 (2006)

PER CURIAM.

The State of Arizona and officials from four of its counties seek relief from an interlocutory injunction entered by a two-judge motions panel of the Court of Appeals for the Ninth Circuit. We construe the filings of the State and the county officials as petitions for certiorari; we grant the petitions; and we vacate the order of the Court of Appeals.

I

In 2004, Arizona voters approved Proposition 200. The measure sought to combat voter fraud by requiring voters to present proof of citizenship when they register to vote and to present identification when they vote on election day.

The election procedures implemented to effect Proposition 200 do not necessarily result in the turning away of qualified, registered voters by election officials for lack of proper identification. A voter who arrives at the polls on election day without identification may cast a provisional ballot. For that ballot to be counted, the voter is allowed five business days to return to a designated site and present proper identification. In addition, any voter who knows he or she cannot secure identification within five business days of the election has the option to vote before election day during the early voting period. The State has determined that, because there is adequate time during the early voting period to compare the voters' signatures on the ballot with their signatures on the registration rolls, voters need not present identification if voting early.

In the District Court the plaintiffs in this action are residents of Arizona; Indian tribes; and various community organizations. In May 2006, these plaintiffs brought suit challenging Proposition 200's identification requirements. On September 11, 2006, the District Court denied their request for a preliminary injunction, but it did not at that time issue findings of fact or conclusions of law. These findings were important because resolution of legal questions in the Court of Appeals required evaluation of underlying factual issues.

The plaintiffs appealed the denial, and the Clerk of the Court of Appeals set a briefing schedule that concluded on November 21, two weeks after the upcoming November 7 election. The plaintiffs then requested an injunction pending appeal. Pursuant to the Court of Appeals' rules, the request for an injunction was assigned to a two-judge motions/screening panel. On October 5, after receiving lengthy written responses from the State and the county officials but without oral argument, the panel issued a four-sentence order enjoining Arizona from enforcing Proposition 200's provisions pending [appeal]. The Court of Appeals offered no explanation or justification for its order.

Despite the time-sensitive nature of the proceedings and the pendency of a request for emergency relief in the Court of Appeals, the District Court did not issue its findings of fact and conclusions of law until October 12. It then concluded that "plaintiffs have shown a possibility of success on the merits of some of their arguments but the Court cannot say that at this stage they have shown a strong likelihood." The District Court then found the balance of the harms and the public interest counseled in favor of denying the injunction.

II

"A State indisputably has a compelling interest in preserving the integrity of its election process." *Eu v. San Francisco County Democratic Central Comm.* (1989). Confidence in the integrity of our electoral processes is essential to the functioning of our participatory democracy. Voter fraud drives honest citizens out of the democratic process and breeds distrust of our government. Voters who fear their legitimate votes will be outweighed by fraudulent ones will feel disenfranchised. "[T]he right of suffrage can be denied by a debasement or dilution of the weight of a citizen's vote just as effectively as by wholly prohibiting the free exercise of the franchise." *Reynolds v. Sims* (1964). Countering the State's compelling interest in preventing voter fraud is the plaintiffs' strong interest in exercising the "fundamental political right" to vote. *Dunn v. Blumstein* (1972). Although the likely effects of Proposition 200 are much debated, the possibility that qualified voters might be turned away from the polls would caution any district judge to give careful consideration to the plaintiffs' challenges.

Faced with an application to enjoin operation of voter identification procedures just weeks before an election, the Court of Appeals was required to weigh, in addition to the harms attendant upon issuance or nonissuance of an injunction, considerations specific to election cases and its own institutional procedures. Court orders affecting elections, especially conflicting orders, can themselves result in voter confusion and consequent incentive to remain away from the polls. As an election draws closer, that risk will increase. So, the Court of Appeals may have deemed this consideration to be grounds for prompt action. Furthermore, it might have given some weight to the possibility that the nonprevailing parties would want to seek en banc review. In the Ninth Circuit that procedure, involving voting by all active judges and an en banc hearing by a court of 15, can consume further valuable time. These considerations, however, cannot be controlling here. It was still necessary, as a procedural matter, for the Court of Appeals to give deference to the discretion of the District Court. We find no indication that it did so, and we conclude this was error.

Although at the time the Court of Appeals issued its order the District Court had not yet made factual findings to which the Court of Appeals owed deference, by failing to provide any factual findings or indeed any reasoning of its own the Court of Appeals left this Court in the position of evaluating the Court of Appeals' bare order in light of the District Court's ultimate findings. There has been no explanation given by the Court of Appeals showing the ruling and findings of the District Court to be incorrect. In view of the impending election, the necessity for clear guidance to the State of Arizona, and our conclusion regarding the Court of Appeals' issuance of the order, we vacate the order of the Court of Appeals.

We underscore that we express no opinion here on the correct disposition, after full briefing and argument, of the appeals from the District Court's September 11 order or on the ultimate resolution of these cases. As we have noted, the facts in these cases are hotly contested, and "[n]o bright line separates permissible election-related regulation from unconstitutional infringements." *Timmons v. Twin Cities Area New Party* (1997). Given the imminence of the election and the inadequate time to resolve the factual disputes, our action today shall of necessity allow the election to proceed without an injunction suspending the voter identification rules.

The order of the Court of Appeals is vacated, and the cases are remanded for further proceedings consistent with this opinion.

Frank v. Walker

819 F.3d 384 (7th Cir. 2016)

EASTERBROOK, Circuit Judge.

In 2011 Wisconsin enacted a statute requiring voters to present photographic identification. A federal district judge found that the statute violates the Constitution as well as the Voting Rights Act and enjoined its application across the board. We reversed that decision. 768 F.3d 744 (7th Cir. 2014).

One of the two sets of plaintiffs asked the district court to take up some issues that it had not previously resolved. But the district court declined to address plaintiffs' principal argument—that some persons qualified to vote are entitled to relief because they face daunting obstacles to obtaining acceptable photo ID. The court ruled that all arguments relating to the difficulty of obtaining photo ID were before this court in 2014 and that our mandate leaves no room for further debate. Plaintiffs appeal this part of the district court's decision, contending that the judge misunderstood the scope of our mandate.

Plaintiffs want relief for three classes of persons: (1) eligible voters unable to obtain acceptable photo ID with reasonable expense and effort because of name mismatches or other errors in birth certificates or other necessary documents; (2) eligible voters who need a credential from some other agency (such as the Social Security Administration) that will not issue the credential unless Wisconsin's Department of Motor Vehicles first issues a photo ID, which the DMV won't do until the other credential has been obtained; (3) eligible voters who need a document that no longer exists (such as a birth certificate issued by an agency whose records have been lost in a fire). We refer to these three categories collectively as inability to obtain a qualifying photo ID with reasonable effort, though the gastonette in category (2) and the loss of documents in category (3) may amount to impossibility rather than just difficulty. Plaintiffs maintain that preventing persons in these categories from voting for the rest of their lives would violate the Constitution, as understood in decisions such as *Anderson v. Celebrezze* (1983), and *Burdick v. Takushi* (1992).

The scope of an appellate mandate depends on what the court decided—and we did not decide that persons unable to get a photo ID with reasonable effort lack a serious grievance. The district court had held in 2014 that, because *some* voters face undue difficulties in obtaining acceptable photo IDs, Wisconsin could not require *any* voter to present a photo ID. And the district judge had included in the set of people encountering undue difficulty many who could get a state-issued photo ID but disliked the hassle. For example, the judge thought that persons who lack birth certificates but could get them on request, and those who have birth certificates but have not used them to get a state-issued photo ID, were among those facing undue difficulties.

We reversed that injunction as incompatible with *Crawford v. Marion County Election Board* (2008), in which the Supreme Court held that Indiana's voter-ID statute is valid notwithstanding the same sort of critiques the district court leveled against Wisconsin's. In *Crawford* the lead opinion concluded: "For most voters who need them, the inconvenience of making a trip to the [department of motor vehicles], gathering the required documents, and posing for a photograph surely does not qualify as a substantial burden on the right to vote, or even represent a significant increase over the usual burdens of voting." 553 U.S. at 198. The Court added that an across-the-board injunction would be improper because "[t]he application of the statute to the vast majority of Indiana voters is amply justified" (*id.* at 2040). That is equally true in Wisconsin, we held. It followed that the burden some voters faced could not prevent the state from applying the law generally.

The argument plaintiffs now present is different. Instead of saying that inconvenience for some voters means that no one needs photo ID, plaintiffs contend that high hurdles for some persons eligible to vote entitle those particular persons to relief. Plaintiffs' approach is potentially sound if even a single person eligible to vote is unable to get acceptable photo ID with reasonable effort. The right to vote is personal and is not defeated by the fact that 99% of other people can secure the necessary credentials easily. Plaintiffs now accept the propriety of requiring photo ID from persons who already have or can get it with reasonable effort, while endeavoring to protect the voting rights of those who encounter high hurdles. This is compatible with our opinion and mandate, just as it is compatible with *Crawford.*

Indeed, one may understand plaintiffs as seeking for Wisconsin the sort of safety net that Indiana has had from the outset. A person seeking to vote in Indiana who contends that despite effort he has been unable to obtain a complying photo ID for financial or religious reasons may file an affidavit to that effect and have his vote provisionally counted. No one contended in this court in 2014 that such an accommodation was essential to the validity of Indiana's law, and neither our opinion nor the Supreme Court's decision in *Crawford* forecloses such an argument. Wisconsin's rules for casting provisional ballots, unlike those of Indiana, require a voter who does not present an acceptable photo ID at the polling place to present such an ID by the end of the week. Wis. Stat. § 6.97. Under Wisconsin's current law, people who do not have qualifying photo ID thus cannot vote, even if it is impossible for them to get such an ID. Plaintiffs want relief from that prohibition, not from the general application of Act 23 to the millions of persons who have or readily can get qualifying photo ID.

Because the district court did not address the substance of plaintiffs' argument, we do not do so either. After the record closed in the district court, the Supreme Court of Wisconsin instructed state officials not to condition issuance of voting identification on any person's failure to obtain documents for which a governmental agency requires a fee. The state's administrative agencies may have made other adjustments since the end of discovery. The district court should permit the parties to explore how the state's system works today before taking up plaintiffs' remaining substantive contentions.

[*Next phase of the same ligitation:* After the Seventh Circuit sent the case back to the district court, that court essentially ordered that any voter who asserted a difficulty with obtaining a voter ID would be exempt from the statute's requirement. The Seventh Circuit once again reversed, holding that the district court had construed the scope of a winning as-applied claim too broadly.]

Before Frank H. Easterbrook, Circuit Judge Michael S. Kanne, Circuit Judge Diane S. Sykes, Circuit Judge.

The injunction entered by the district court on July 19, 2016, is stayed pending appeal. Applying the standards of *Nken v. Holder* (2009), we conclude both that the district court's decision is likely to be reversed on appeal and that disruption of the state's electoral system in the interim will cause irreparable injury.

Our most recent decision in this case concluded that anyone who is eligible to vote in Wisconsin, but cannot obtain a qualifying photo ID with reasonable effort, is entitled to an accommodation that will permit him or her to cast a ballot. *Frank v. Walker* (7th Cir. 2016). On remand, the district court concluded that at least some voters fall in this category, notwithstanding the most recent revisions to the procedures that Wisconsin uses to issue photo IDs. But instead of attempting to identify these voters, or to identify the kinds of situations in which the state's procedures fall short, the district court issued an injunction that permits any registered voter to declare by affidavit that reasonable effort would not produce a photo ID—even if the voter has never tried to secure one, and even if by objective standards the effort needed would be reasonable (and would succeed).

The district court's injunction allows any registered voter to check a box stating a reason why reasonable effort would not produce a qualifying photo ID. The boxes include lack of necessary documents (apparently including situations in which the person has not tried to obtain them), "work", "family responsibilities", and "other"—and the voter can put anything in the "other" box, including a belief that spending a single minute to obtain a qualifying photo ID is not reasonable. The injunction adds that state officials are forbidden to dispute or question any reason the registered voter gives. Yet the Supreme Court held in *Crawford v. Marion County Election Board* (2008), that "the inconvenience of making a trip to the [department of motor vehicles], gathering the required documents, and posing for a photograph surely does not qualify as a substantial burden on the right to vote, or even represent a significant increase over the usual burdens of voting." A given voter's disagreement with this approach does not show that requiring one trip to a governmental office is unreasonable.

Because the district court has not attempted to distinguish genuine difficulties of the kind our opinion mentioned, or any other variety of substantial obstacle to voting, from any given voter's unwillingness to make the effort that the Supreme Court has held that a state can require, there is a substantial likelihood that the injunction will be reversed on appeal.

[Meanwhile, in addition to this particular *Frank v. Walker* lawsuit over Wisconsin's voter ID law, a second suit was filed that challenged the new ID law among a variety of changes to Wisconsin's voting laws: *One Wisconsin Institute v. Thomsen.* The judge in this second case issued a narrower injunction against the ID law in those circumstances involving winning as-applied challenges; essentially, this injunction required individuals actually harmed by the ID law to take steps to attempt to get a valid ID, compared to the injunction in *Frank v. Walker,* which permitted an individual merely to assert that it would be difficult for that voter to obtain an ID. The en banc Seventh Circuit, signaling its agreement with this narrower, declined to entertain en banc review in advance of a panel decision on the merits of this narrower injunction (Aug. 29, 2016).]

Before WOOD, Chief Judge, and POSNER, FLAUM, EASTERBROOK, KANNE, ROVNER, WILLIAMS, SYKES, and HAMILTON, Circuit Judges.

PER CURIAM.

Before us are two sets of appeals and cross-appeals, each of which concerns Wisconsin's law requiring voters to have qualifying photo identification. In each matter, one originating in the Eastern District of Wisconsin and the other in the Western District of Wisconsin, the plaintiffs have petitioned for initial review en banc. We have consolidated their petitions for the purposes of this order. The plaintiffs argue that only initial en banc treatment will permit a decision in time for the court's conclusions to be put into effect for the election upcoming in November 2016. It is questionable whether action on that schedule is feasible, given that Wisconsin will start printing absentee ballots at the end of this month. We will assume for the sake of argument, however, that this obstacle alone is not enough to deny the petitions.

There is a more important concern, however, which has to do with the regularity of the judicial process. Whether this court should try to resolve the parties' disputes on such a short schedule depends in part on whether qualified electors will be unable to vote under Wisconsin's current procedures. In evaluating that question, we must take account of the conclusions reached by the district court in the Western District of Wisconsin in *One Wisconsin Institute, Inc. v. Thomsen* (July 29, 2016). The Eastern District of Wisconsin concluded that every registered voter should be allowed to vote if he or she signs an affidavit stating that obtaining a qualifying photo ID would be unreasonably hard. A panel of this court has stayed that order. *Frank v. Walker* (Aug. 10, 2016). The Western District, by contrast, declined to adopt the affidavit procedure but required Wisconsin to reform its ID Petition

Process (IDPP), revised in May in response to this court's decision in *Frank v. Walker* (7th Cir. 2016) (*Frank II*).

Frank II held that "[t]he right to vote is personal and is not defeated by the fact that 99% of other people can secure the necessary credentials easily", and that the state may not frustrate this right for any eligible person by making it unreasonably difficult to obtain a qualifying photo ID. The district court in *One Wisconsin Institute* concluded from this that an eligible voter who submits materials sufficient to initiate the IDPP is entitled to a credential valid for voting, unless readily available information shows that the petitioner is not a qualified elector. The court in *One Wisconsin Institute* also held that the state must inform the general public that those who enter the IDPP will promptly receive a credential valid for voting, unless readily available information shows that the petitioner is not a qualified elector entitled to such a credential. This court denied the State's motion to stay the Western District's injunction pending appeal.

The State assures us that the temporary credentials required in the *One Wisconsin Institute* decision will indeed be available to all qualified persons who seek them: "[T]he State has already voluntarily accommodated any concerns relating to the November 2016 election. Specifically, Wisconsin has enacted a rule that requires the Division of Motor Vehicles ('DMV') to mail *automatically* a free photo ID to anyone who comes to DMV one time and initiates the free ID process. No one must present documents, that, for some, have proved challenging to acquire; no one must show a birth certificate, proof of citizenship, and the like" (emphasis in original).

Given the State's representation that "initiation" of the IDPP means only that the voter must show up at a DMV with as much as he or she has, and that the State will not refuse to recognize the "initiation" of the process because a birth certificate, proof of citizenship, Social Security card, or other particular document is missing, we conclude that the urgency needed to justify an initial en banc hearing has not been shown. Our conclusion depends also on the State's compliance with the district court's second criterion, namely, that the State adequately inform the general public that those who enter the IDPP will promptly receive a credential for voting, unless it is plain that they are not qualified. The Western District has the authority to monitor compliance with its injunction, and we trust that it will do so conscientiously between now and the November 2016 election.

On these understandings, the petitions for initial hearing en banc are DENIED.

[On Oct. 13, 2016, the judge in *One Wisconsin Institute v. Thomsen* ordered the state to do a better job training its workers to comply with the safety-net requirements and to report back to the court on its progress with this training.]

One Wisconsin Institute, Inc. v. Thomsen

09/28/2020

James D. Peterson, District Judge

These consolidated cases involve challenges to Wisconsin's ID petition process (IDPP), which is how Wisconsin residents obtain an ID valid for voting if they don't have the required documentation. The question before the court now is what relief is needed to alleviate unreasonable burdens on those who need to obtain an ID though the IDPP before the November 3 general election. The court will direct the Wisconsin Election Commission and the Department of Transportation to make modest changes to their policy on distributing new and replacement temporary IDs and to provide targeted outreach to potential voters who are most likely to need the IDPP. The court will defer decisions on more fundamental reforms to the IDPP until after the general election is certified.

BACKGROUND

This court concluded in 2016 that the IDPP imposes unreasonable burdens on the right to vote, so the court directed defendants to implement certain reforms. *See One Wisconsin Inst., Inc. v. Thomsen* (W.D. Wis. 2016). But because the 2016 presidential election was looming, the court stayed its order on long-term reforms and directed defendants to take interim measures to: (1) "allow anyone who enters the IDPP to get a receipt that will serve as a valid ID for the November 2016 election," and (2) inform the public about the IDPP.

The case was then appealed, and the Court of Appeals for the Seventh Circuit issued its decision on June 29, 2020. *See Luft v. Evers* (7th Cir. 2020). The court of appeals didn't rule on the constitutionality of the IDPP because "[t]he district court acted on a record assembled years ago," and the state represented that it had made changes to the IDPP since 2016. So the court of appeals directed this court to take a fresh look at the process to determine whether "every eligible voter can get a qualifying photo ID with reasonable effort." *Id.* at 679.

The court held a hearing via videoconference on the parties' motions on September 25 and issued an oral ruling, denying defendants' motion for summary judgment, granting some preliminary relief to plaintiffs, denying other requests, and deferring other issues until after the election. This order will summarize the court's reasoning and conclusions.

ANALYSIS

The court is in much the same position now as it was in 2016, except now there is even less time before the impending general election. As it did in 2016, the court will focus on the factors that might prevent qualified electors from casting their ballots in the upcoming election. This approach will provide relief where it's needed most without causing confusion by changing the rules for voters or poll workers.

A. Defendants' Motion for Summary Judgment

Defendants' position is that they are entitled to summary judgment because eligible voters can obtain a voting-compliant ID by "mak[ing] a trip to the DMV and fill[ing] out simple application forms." This argument is referring to the receipts voters receive while their ID petitions are pending. Because those receipts can be used as a voter ID, defendants say that there is no undue burden on the right to vote. The court considered and rejected this argument in 2016 because the receipts are temporary and petitioners must still convince the DMV to exercise its discretion to issue a long-term ID. *One Wisconsin Inst., Inc. v. Thomsen* (W.D. Wis.

2016). "[Q]ualified electors are entitled to vote as a matter of constitutional right, not merely by the grace of the executive branch of the state government." *Id.*

Defendants point to nothing in *Luft* suggesting that the temporary receipts satisfy the state's constitutional duties. After all, the state was already using the receipts in 2016, so there would have been no reason to require further proceedings if the court of appeals believed that no more was required.

It is true that defendants have refined the process so that temporary receipts are now automatically renewed every 60 days until a petition is granted or denied. This alleviates some burden on petitioners, but plaintiffs point to examples of petitioners who continue to get "stuck" in the process for months or even years through no fault of their own while they wait for state officials to exercise their discretion. Defendants do not acknowledge that group of petitioners in their opening brief, even though those petitioners were the focus of the court's 2016 decision.

Plaintiffs lay the blame for the continued problems on the way the IDPP is implemented, most notably that the state fails to adhere to its own standard that a petition should be granted if it is "more likely than not" that the petitioner is eligible to vote. Instead, plaintiffs say, the state continues searching for more corroborating documentation, subjecting petitioners to unreasonable demands for information and leaving them in a state of limbo indefinitely, even after it becomes clear that petitioners are qualified.

The parties dispute the extent and causes of some petitioners' continued difficulties in obtaining a long-term ID. But the court is persuaded that the evidence cited by plaintiffs is sufficient to show that there are genuine issues of fact on the question whether qualified electors continue to face unreasonable burdens on their right to vote. So the court will deny defendants' motion for summary judgment.

B. Plaintiffs' Motions for a Preliminary Injunction

The ultimate question before the court is whether "every eligible voter can get a qualifying photo ID with reasonable effort." *Luft*, 963 F.3d at 679. To obtain a preliminary injunction, a plaintiff must show that: (1) it will suffer irreparable harm without the relief; (2) traditional legal remedies would be inadequate; and (3) it has some likelihood of prevailing on the merits of its claims. If a plaintiff makes such a showing, the court proceeds to a balancing analysis, where the court must weigh the harm the denial of the preliminary injunction would cause the plaintiff against the harm to the defendant if the court were to grant it. For the reasons given in the previous section, the court concludes that plaintiffs have shown some prospects of success on the merits. And, should any voter fail to receive a voting credential before the election, they would suffer irreparable harm by missing the chance to vote in the election.

The court will focus on two narrow issues: (1) removing unreasonable barriers to voting in the general election for those petitioners with pending or new applications in the IDPP; (2) providing public education about the IDPP to those who need it most.

As for the first category, the court will order the following. For eligible voters who submit an IDPP application between October 19 and November 2, 2020, defendants must send the temporary receipt by overnight mail. For already-issued temporary receipts that expire between October 19 and November 2, 2020, defendants may use First Class or Priority Mail to send replacement receipts if they are placed in the mail by October 9. Otherwise, replacement receipts for those expiring between October 19 and November 2, 2020, must be sent by overnight mail.

The United States Postal Service is continuing to face challenges with timely delivery. The court's order, which represents only a modest change to defendants' current policies, is necessary to help minimize the risk that eligible voters will be left without a valid credential on election day. Defendants haven't identified any harm they will suffer from this requirement, so the public interest and the balance of harms favors this approach. *See* Boardman Decl., ¶ 9 (acknowledging that "DMV could overnight mail IDPP receipts beginning October 19").

Plaintiffs seek more relief related to the temporary receipts, including individualized outreach to petitioners, allowing the use of expired receipts, and allowing voters without a receipt to use an affidavit instead. But plaintiffs haven't shown that such relief is narrowly tailored to alleviate unreasonable burdens on the right to vote, so the court declines to impose those additional requirements, some of which would requiring retraining of poll workers and could lead to confusion at the polls.

As for public education efforts, plaintiffs seek a wide variety of relief, including mailings to all Wisconsin residents who are eligible to vote but don't have an ID, expanded outreach, and changes to any publication, website, or mailing that mentions the voter ID requirement. The court is not persuaded that these measures are constitutionally required or that plaintiffs will be irreparably harmed without them.

Both this court and the court of appeals directed defendants to engage in certain public education efforts in 2016. But at the time, the IDPP was still relatively new, and its operation was in flux, as the state continued making changes. Plaintiffs presented persuasive evidence in 2016 that the state was providing inaccurate information about the IDPP and that even state employees responsible for providing information to the public about the IDPP were uninformed.

The IDPP has now been in place for several years, so the need for intensive public education is diminished. The court has reviewed Administrator Wolfe's declaration explaining the Commission's outreach efforts, and the court concludes that they are adequate for the most part. But plaintiffs have identified two discrete areas that require improvement.

First, plaintiffs have pointed out problems with outreach to underserved communities. For example, the Commission was still providing information on its website stating that homeless individuals needed a birth certificate in order to vote. Defendants acknowledged the mistake during the September 25 hearing, explaining that the website has since been updated. But the misinformation is evidence that more outreach to the homeless is needed. Plaintiffs have agreed to provide a list of homeless service organizations and their contact information to defendants and the court by Wednesday, October 30. If the court approves the list, defendants will send their digital "voter outreach toolkit" to the specified organizations. Defendants will also obtain from KW2 (a media consultant for the Commission) a list of minority media organizations, and the Commission will include those organizations on its press distribution list.

Second, plaintiffs pointed to a lack of information about IDPP available at polling places. For example, when voters submit a provisional ballot, they are not informed how to obtain an ID through the IDPP. Lack of a qualifying ID is one of the reasons that a voter may need to cast a provisional ballot, so the court is persuaded that information about the IDPP should be readily available at the polls. Administrator Wolfe acknowledged during the hearing that voters casting a provisional ballot could be given the already-prepared "palm card," a one-page information sheet that clearly and succinctly explains how a voter enters the IDPP and what the voter can expect after initiating the process. Wolfe also said that she could direct municipal clerks to post a copy of the palm card at polling places. The court will direct defendants to take both actions.

Although the election is near, the limited relief ordered by the court doesn't implicate the so-called *Purcell* principle, under which "lower federal courts should ordinarily not alter the election rules on the eve of an election." The purpose of the *Purcell* principle is to avoid "judicially created confusion." In this case, the court isn't altering any election rules; rather, the court's order is directed at ensuring that eligible voters know what the rules are and can exercise their established rights. Ensuring prompt receipt of voting credentials and informing the public about the IDPP should minimize confusion, not increase it.

The court finds that the relief ordered is necessary to avoid irreparable harm to petitioners, that plaintiffs are likely to succeed in showing that their right to vote will be unreasonably burdened without the relief, and that the public interest favors granting the relief.

PURCELL AND THE PANDEMIC: THE EXTRAORDINARY ELECTION YEAR OF 2020

As 2020 began, that year's presidential election was already shaping up to be one of the most contentious—and litigated—in U.S. history. President Trump, running for reelection, has been impeached by the House of Representatives, and was on trial in the Senate, for his efforts to get Ukraine to investigate his potential (and eventual) opponent, Joe Biden. Voting rights plaintiffs already had begun to file lawsuits seeking to make it easier to cast ballots that would count.

Then, the coronavirus pandemic struck, shutting the country down in March, including the presidential primaries that were underway. Litigation over voting rules—especially vote by mail, which election officials were emphasizing as a safe way to vote in the midst of a public health crisis, but which President Trump was opposing based on a fear of fraud—exploded. The U.S. Supreme Court inevitably became involved, starting in April with the Wisconsin primary and a case concerning a lower court's adjustment of the state's deadline for returning mailed ballots.

EMERGENCY LITIGATION DURING THE PRIMARIES

Republican National Committee, v. Democratic National Committee

140 S.Ct. 1205 (2020)

PER CURIAM.

The application for stay presented to Justice Kavanaugh and by him referred to the Court is granted. The District Court's order granting a preliminary injunction is stayed to the extent it requires the State to count absentee ballots postmarked after April 7, 2020.

Wisconsin has decided to proceed with the elections scheduled for Tuesday, April 7. The wisdom of that decision is not the question before the Court. The question before the Court is a narrow, technical question about the absentee ballot process. In this Court, all agree that the deadline for the municipal clerks to receive absentee ballots has been extended from Tuesday, April 7, to Monday, April 13. That extension, which is not challenged in this Court, has afforded Wisconsin voters several extra days in which to mail their absentee ballots. The sole question before the Court is whether absentee ballots now must be mailed and postmarked by election day, Tuesday, April 7, as state law would necessarily require, or instead may be mailed and postmarked after election day, so long as they are received by Monday, April 13. Importantly, in their preliminary injunction motions, the plaintiffs did not ask that the District Court allow ballots mailed and postmarked after election day, April 7, to be counted. That is a critical point in the case. Nonetheless, five days before the scheduled election, the District Court unilaterally ordered that absentee ballots mailed and postmarked after election day, April 7, still be counted so long as they are received by April 13. Extending the date by which ballots may be cast by voters—not just received by the municipal clerks but cast by voters—for an additional six days after the scheduled election day fundamentally alters the nature of the election. And again, the plaintiffs themselves did not even ask for that relief in their preliminary injunction motions. Our point is not that the argument is necessarily forfeited, but is that the plaintiffs themselves did not see the need to ask for such relief. By changing the election rules so close to the election date and by affording relief that the plaintiffs themselves did not ask for in their preliminary injunction motions, the District Court contravened this Court's precedents and erred by ordering such relief. This Court has repeatedly emphasized that lower federal courts should ordinarily not alter the election rules on the eve of an election. See *Purcell v. Gonzalez* (2006) (*per curiam*).

The unusual nature of the District Court's order allowing ballots to be mailed and postmarked after election day is perhaps best demonstrated by the fact that the District Court had to issue a subsequent order enjoining the public release of any election results for six days after election day. In doing so, the District Court in essence enjoined nonparties to this lawsuit. It is highly questionable, moreover, that this attempt to suppress disclosure of the election results for six days after election day would work. And if any information were released during that time, that would gravely affect the integrity of the election process. The District Court's order suppressing disclosure of election results showcases the unusual nature of the District Court's order allowing absentee ballots mailed and postmarked after election day to be counted. And all of that further underscores the wisdom of the *Purcell* principle, which seeks to avoid this kind of judicially created confusion.

The dissent is quite wrong on several points. First, the dissent entirely disregards the critical point that the plaintiffs themselves did not ask for this additional relief in their preliminary injunction motions. Second, the dissent contends that this Court should not intervene at this late date. The Court would prefer not to do so, but when a lower court intervenes and alters the election rules so close to the election date, our precedents indicate that this Court, as appropriate, should correct that error. Third, the dissent refers to voters who have not yet received their absentee ballots. But even in an ordinary election, voters who request an absentee ballot at the deadline for requesting ballots (which was this past Friday in this case) will usually receive their ballots on the day before or day of the election, which in this case would be today or tomorrow. The plaintiffs put forward no probative evidence in the District Court that these voters here would be in a substantially different position from late-requesting voters in other Wisconsin elections with respect to the timing of their receipt of absentee ballots. In that regard, it bears mention that absentee voting has been underway for many weeks, and 1.2 million Wisconsin voters have requested and have been sent their absentee ballots, which is about five times the number of absentee ballots requested in the 2016 spring election. Fourth, the dissent's rhetoric is entirely misplaced and completely overlooks the fact that the deadline for receiving ballots was already extended to accommodate Wisconsin voters, from April 7 to April 13. Again, that extension has the effect of extending the date for a voter to mail the ballot from, in effect, Saturday, April 4, to Tuesday, April 7. That extension was designed to ensure that the voters of Wisconsin can cast their ballots and have their votes count. That is the relief that the plaintiffs actually requested in their preliminary injunction motions. The District Court on its own ordered yet an additional extension, which would allow voters to mail their ballots after election day, which is extraordinary relief and would fundamentally alter the nature of the election by allowing voting for six additional days after the election.

Therefore, subject to any further alterations that the State may make to state law, in order to be counted in this election a voter's absentee ballot must be either (i) postmarked by election day, April 7, 2020, and received by April 13, 2020, at 4:00 p.m., or (ii) hand-delivered as provided under state law by April 7, 2020, at 8:00 p.m.

The Court's decision on the narrow question before the Court should not be viewed as expressing an opinion on the broader question of whether to hold the election, or whether other reforms or modifications in election procedures in light of COVID-19 are appropriate. That point cannot be stressed enough.

Justice GINSBURG, with whom Justice BREYER, Justice SOTOMAYOR, and Justice KAGAN join, dissenting.

The District Court, acting in view of the dramatically evolving COVID-19 pandemic, entered a preliminary injunction to safeguard the availability of absentee voting in Wisconsin's spring election. This Court now intervenes at the eleventh hour to prevent voters who have timely requested absentee ballots from casting their votes. I would not disturb the District Court's disposition, which the Seventh Circuit allowed to stand.

I

A

Wisconsin's spring election is scheduled for tomorrow, Tuesday, April 7, 2020. At issue are the presidential primaries, a seat on the Wisconsin Supreme Court, three seats on the Wisconsin Court of Appeals, over 100 other judgeships, over 500 school board seats, and several thousand other positions.

In the weeks leading up to the election, the COVID-19 pandemic has become a "public health crisis." As of April 2, Wisconsin had 1,550 confirmed cases of

COVID-19 and 24 deaths attributable to the disease, "with evidence of increasing community spread." On March 24, the Governor ordered Wisconsinites to stay at home until April 24 to slow the spread of the disease.

Because gathering at the polling place now poses dire health risks, an unprecedented number of Wisconsin voters—at the encouragement of public officials—have turned to voting absentee. About one million more voters have requested absentee ballots in this election than in 2016. Accommodating the surge of absentee ballot requests has heavily burdened election officials, resulting in a severe backlog of ballots requested but not promptly mailed to voters.

B

Several weeks ago, plaintiffs—comprising individual Wisconsin voters, community organizations, and the state and national Democratic parties—filed three [federal-court] lawsuits against members of the Wisconsin Elections Commission. The plaintiffs sought several forms of relief, all aimed at easing the effects of the COVID-19 pandemic on the upcoming election.

After holding an evidentiary hearing, the District Court issued a preliminary injunction on April 2. The court concluded that the existing deadlines for absentee voting would unconstitutionally burden Wisconsin citizens' right to vote [under *Anderson-Burdick* analysis]. To alleviate that burden, the court entered a twofold remedy. First, the District Court extended the deadline for voters to request absentee ballots from April 2 to April 3. Second, the District Court extended the deadline for election officials to receive completed absentee ballots. Previously, Wisconsin law required that absentee ballots be received by 8 p.m. on election day, April 7; under the preliminary injunction, the ballots would be accepted until 4 p.m. on April 13, regardless of the postmark date. The District Court also enjoined members of the Elections Commission and election inspectors from releasing any report of polling results before the new absentee-voting deadline, April 13.

Although the members of the Wisconsin Elections Commission did not challenge the preliminary injunction, the intervening defendants applied to the Seventh Circuit for a partial stay. Of the twofold remedy just described, the stay applicants challenged only the second aspect, the extension of the deadline for returning absentee ballots. On April 3, the Seventh Circuit declined to modify the absentee-ballot deadline. The same applicants then sought a partial stay in this Court, which the Court today grants.

II

A

The Court's order requires absentee voters to postmark their ballots by election day, April 7—*i.e.*, tomorrow—even if they did not receive their ballots by that date. That is a novel requirement. Recall that absentee ballots were originally due back to election officials on April 7, which the District Court extended to April 13. Neither of those deadlines carried a postmark-by requirement.

While I do not doubt the good faith of my colleagues, the Court's order, I fear, will result in massive disenfranchisement. A voter cannot deliver for postmarking a ballot she has not received. Yet tens of thousands of voters who timely requested ballots are unlikely to receive them by April 7, the Court's postmark deadline. Rising concern about the COVID-19 pandemic has caused a late surge in absentee-ballot requests. The Court's suggestion that the current situation is not "substantially different" from "an ordinary election" boggles the mind. Some 150,000 requests for absentee ballots have been processed since Thursday, state records indicate. The surge in absentee-ballot requests has overwhelmed election officials, who face a huge backlog in sending ballots. As of Sunday morning, 12,000 ballots reportedly had not yet been mailed out. It takes days for a mailed ballot to reach its recipient—the postal service recommends budgeting a week—even without accounting for pandemic-induced mail delays. It is therefore likely that ballots mailed in recent days will not reach voters by tomorrow; for ballots not yet mailed, late arrival is all but certain. Under the District Court's order, an absentee voter who receives a ballot after tomorrow could still have voted, as long as she delivered it to election officials by April 13. Now, under this Court's order, tens of thousands of absentee voters, unlikely to receive their ballots in time to cast them, will be left quite literally without a vote.

This Court's intervention is thus ill advised, especially so at this late hour. See *Purcell v. Gonzalez* (2006) (*per curiam*). Election officials have spent the past few days establishing procedures and informing voters in accordance with the District Court's deadline. For this Court to upend the process—a day before the April 7 postmark deadline—is sure to confound election officials and voters.

B

What concerns could justify consequences so grave? The Court's order first suggests a problem of forfeiture, noting that the plaintiffs' written preliminary-injunction motions did not ask that ballots postmarked after April 7 be counted. But unheeded by the Court, although initially silent, the plaintiffs specifically requested that remedy at the preliminary-injunction hearing in view of the ever-increasing demand for absentee ballots.

Second, the Court's order cites *Purcell*, apparently skeptical of the District Court's intervention shortly before an election. Never mind that the District Court was reacting to a grave, rapidly developing public health crisis. If proximity to the election counseled hesitation when the District Court acted several days ago, this Court's intervention today—even closer to the election—is all the more inappropriate.

Third, the Court notes that the District Court's order allowed absentee voters to cast ballots after election day. If a voter already in line by the poll's closing time can still vote, why should Wisconsin's absentee voters, already in line to receive ballots, be denied the franchise? According to the stay applicants, election-distorting gamesmanship might occur if ballots could be cast after initial results are published. But obviating that harm, the District Court enjoined the publication of election results before April 13, the deadline for returning absentee ballots, and the Wisconsin Elections Commission directed election officials not to publish results before that date.

The concerns advanced by the Court and the applicants pale in comparison to the risk that tens of thousands of voters will be disenfranchised. Ensuring an opportunity for the people of Wisconsin to exercise their votes should be our paramount concern.

***

The majority of this Court declares that this case presents a "narrow, technical question." That is wrong. The question here is whether tens of thousands of Wisconsin citizens can vote safely in the midst of a pandemic. Under the District Court's order, they would be able to do so. Even if they receive their absentee ballot in the days immediately following election day, they could return it. With the majority's stay in place, that will not be possible. Either they will have to brave the polls, endangering their own and others' safety. Or they will lose their right to vote, through no fault of their own. That is a matter of utmost importance—to the constitutional rights of Wisconsin's citizens, the integrity of the State's election process, and in this most extraordinary time, the health of the Nation.

PREPARING FOR THE NOVEMBER 3 GENERAL ELECTION

During the summer and fall of 2020, election officials all around the country scrambled to prepare for the November 3 general election. They recognized the need to provide both safe in-person voting opportunities for those preferring to cast ballots at the polls—especially as concerns over the reliability of the U.S. Postal Service intensified—and increased availability of vote by mail for those counting on that option because of the pandemic. The U.S. Supreme Court adopted the posture of upholding the decisions that state and local election officials made on these issues, rejecting attempts to challenge those decisions from both the left and the right.

For instance, in Alabama and South Carolina federal district courts required states to adjust voting rules in ways that their officials had rejected. In Alabama, officials refused to provide curbside voting. In South Carolina, officials retained the state's witness requirement for absentee ballots. In both states, the federal district courts granted injunctions to force the states to change the rules in the ways the plaintiffs requested. In each case, a majority of the U.S. Supreme Court stayed the injunction, rendering it inoperable for the election. *Merrill v. People First of Alabama,* 141 S. Ct. 25 (2020); *Andino v. Middleton,* 141 S. Ct. 9 (2020).

In Rhode Island, by contrast, state officials agreed to suspend that state's witness rule for absentee voting. The Republican Party objected to that agreement, and when the First Circuit refused to block the agreement, the Republicans asked the Supreme Court to do so. But the Supreme Court, in a 6-3 order, refused as well. (The three most conservative justices—Thomas, Alito, and Gorsuch—would have granted the GOP's stay application.) *RNC v. Common Cause Rhode Island,* 41 S. Ct. 206 (2020). In its brief unsigned order, the Court majority explained:

> Unlike *Merrill v. People First of Alabama,* and other similar cases where a State defends its own law, here the state election officials support the challenged decree, and no state official has expressed opposition. Under this circumstance, the applicants lack a cognizable interest in the State's ability to enforce its duly enacted laws. The status quo is one in which the challenged requirement has not been in effect, given the rules used in Rhode Island's last election, and many Rhode Island voters may well hold that belief.

Pennsylvania posed a special challenge for the U.S. Supreme Court. The state had come to be a key Electoral College battleground, upon which the fight for the presidency might hinge. Unlike other battleground states, however, Pennsylvania's own supreme court was dominated by Democrats and had a record of decisions based on state constitutional law favorable to Democrats and opposed by Republicans. Most prominently, in 2018 the state supreme court had ruled gerrymandering a violation of the state constitution, invalidating the state's GOP-gerrymandered congressional districts.

On September 17, 2020, the Pennsylvania Supreme Court by a 4-3 vote extended the deadline for submitting absentee ballots in the November 3 election by three days. The state's statute set the deadline at 8 p.m. on election day itself. But the majority opinion of the state supreme court relied on the state constitution to grant the Pennsylvania Democratic Party's request for an extension of the deadline, over the objection of Pennsylvania Republicans.

Pennsylvania Democratic Party v. Boockvar

238 A.3d 345 (2020)

Petitioner presents this Court with an as-applied challenge to the Election Code's deadline for receiving ballots ("received-by deadline"), which requires mail-in and absentee ballots to be returned to Boards no later than 8:00 p.m. on Election Day. It contends that strict enforcement of this deadline, in light of the current COVID-19 pandemic and alleged delays in mail delivery by the USPS, will result in extensive voter disenfranchisement in violation of the Pennsylvania Constitution's Free and Equal Elections Clause, [which] provides that "[e]lections shall be free and equal; and no power, civil or military, shall at any time interfere to prevent the free exercise of the right to suffrage." Petitioner interprets this provision as forbidding the Boards from interfering with the right to vote by failing to act in a timely manner so as to allow electors to participate in the election through mail-in voting.

Petitioner recounts this Commonwealth's recent experience during the June Primary. It emphasizes that, during the Primary, the Boards were inundated with over 1.8 million requests for mail-in ballots, rather than the expected 80,000-100,000, due in large part to the COVID-19 pandemic, which caused many voters to be wary of congregating in polling places. Petitioner asserts that "[t]his crush of applications created massive disparities in the distribution and return of mail-in ballots."

It explains that, while some Boards were able to process the requests within the statutory requirements established by Act 77,[16] other boards, especially those in areas hard-hit by the pandemic, were unable to provide electors with ballots in time for the electors to return their ballot in accord with the statutory deadline. Indeed, it avers that in Delaware County, thousands of ballots were "not mailed out until the night" of the Primary, making timely return impossible. Bucks County apparently experienced similar delays.

16. Act 77, *inter alia*, requires Boards to verify an applicant's submitted information to determine whether the applicant is "qualified to receive an official mail-in ballot." 25 P.S. § 3150.12b(a). After approving an application, the Election Code, as amended by Act 77, instructs that "the board shall deliver or mail official mail-in ballots to the additional electors within 48 hours." 25 P.S. § 3150.15.

In light of the lessons learned from the June Primary, Petitioner asserts that a statewide remedy is now necessary for the General Election. Moreover, it emphasizes that a statewide order from this Court early in the election process would reduce voter confusion, as compared to the last-minute county-by-county relief granted during the Primary to address emergency situations.

Petitioner avers that the difficulties encountered by Boards processing the ballot applications prior to the June Primary will only be exacerbated in the November General Election. It emphasizes the continued grip of the pandemic, and a potential second wave of infections, which will result in more electors seeking to exercise their right to vote by mail. Additionally, it recognizes the undisputed fact that heavily contested Presidential elections involve substantially greater voter participation than largely uncontested primaries, further observing that "[i]t is normal in elections with significant public attention for there to be a flood of registrations received right before deadlines." It highlights that the Secretary estimates that 3 million electors will seek mail-in or absentee ballots for the General Election in contrast to the 1.5 million votes cast by mail at the Primary, and the pre-pandemic assumption of 80,000-100,000 absentee and mail-in ballots.

Petitioner asserts that the overwhelming demand on the Boards will be exacerbated by delays in the USPS mail delivery system. Petitioner observes that historically the law presumed that a document placed in a mail collection box would be delivered within three days of placement, rather than the current two to five day delivery expectation of the USPS. Petitioner avers that substantial delivery delays have resulted from a combination of recent operational changes at the USPS and decreased staffing caused by the pandemic. It emphasizes that the USPS recently warned that there is a "significant risk" that Pennsylvania voters who submit timely ballot requests will not have sufficient time to complete and return their ballot to meet the Election Code's received-by deadline.

Petitioner avers that this Court has the authority to act to protect electors' right to cast their ballot, as protected by Pennsylvania's Free and Equal Elections Clause. It emphasizes that " '[c]ourt[s] possess broad authority to craft meaningful remedies' when 'regulations of law . . . impair the right of suffrage.' "*Id.* at 48-49 (quoting *League of Women Voters of Pa.*, 178 A.3d at 809, 822) (alterations in original). It observes that courts have exercised that authority to provide equitable relief to voters faced with natural disasters that impede their right to vote. As an example, Petitioner highlights the Commonwealth Court's actions in *In re General Election-1985* (1987), in which the court affirmed a two-week suspension in an election where severe flooding prevented electors from safely voting due to "circumstances beyond their control." Petitioner asserts that Pennsylvania electors in the November General Election similarly face a threat to their ability to vote due to no fault of their own, but instead due to a perfect storm combining the dramatic increase in requested ballots due to the COVID-19 pandemic and the inability of the USPS to meet the delivery standards required by the Election Code.

Accordingly, Petitioner asks this Court to grant an injunction ordering the Respondent to "lift the deadline in the Election Code across the state in a uniform standard to allow any ballot postmarked by 8 p.m. on Election Night to be counted if it is received by 5:00 p.m. on Tuesday, November 10. Recognizing that the Secretary recommends a three-day extension, Petitioner counters that "[a] 7-day extension to the ballot receipt deadline is consistent with the USPS's recommendation to the Secretary that voters should mail their ballots to Boards no later than October 27, 2020," which is seven days prior to Election Day. While it acknowledges that a seven-day extension could impact other post-election deadlines, it asserts that this Court has the authority to alter those deadlines to be consistent with the relief granted in this case.

The Secretary sought extraordinary jurisdiction to allow this Court to resolve the various challenges to the mail-in ballot process in an orderly and timely fashion before the impending General Election, where she estimates more than three million Pennsylvanians will exercise their right to vote by mail.

Significantly, the USPS General Counsel's Letter opined that "certain deadlines for requesting and casting mail-in ballots are incongruous with the Postal Service's delivery standards," providing for 2-5 day delivery for domestic First Class Mail and 3-10 day delivery for domestic Marketing Mail. As the parties recognize, the Election Code designates October 27, 2020, as the last day for electors to request a mail-in ballot. Even if a county board were to process and mail a ballot the next day by First Class Mail on Wednesday, October 28th, according to the delivery standards of the USPS, the voter might not receive the ballot until five days later on Monday, November 2nd, resulting in the impossibility of returning the ballot by mail before Election Day, Tuesday November 3rd. The USPS General Counsel's Letter, instead, advised that voters should mail their ballots no later than October 27, 2020 in order to meet the received-by deadline. "This mismatch [between the USPS's delivery standards and the Election Code deadlines] creates a risk that ballots requested near the deadline under state law will not be returned by mail in time to be counted under [Pennsylvania's Election Code]."

In light of the information contained in the USPS General Counsel's Letter, the Secretary concludes that a temporary extension of the Election Code's received-by deadline is necessary for the upcoming General Election to ensure a free and equal election as protected by Article I, Section 5 of the Pennsylvania Constitution. The Secretary specifically asks that this Court order an extension of the deadline to allow the counting of any ballot postmarked by Election Day and received on or before the third day after Election Day, which is November 6, 2020.[20] The Secretary deems a three-day extension of the deadline, rather than the seven-day extension sought by Petitioner, to be sufficient to address the potential delay in mailing while also not disrupting other elements of election administration.

The Secretary emphasizes that the remedy sought here is not the invalidation of the Election Code's received-by deadline, but rather the grant of equitable

20. She specifically recommends that the Court "order that ballots mailed by voters by 8:00 p.m. on Election Day be counted if they are otherwise valid and received by the county boards of election by November 6, 2020. Ballots received within this period that lack a postmark or other proof of mailing, or for which the postmark or other proof of mailing is illegible, should enjoy a presumption that they were mailed by Election Day." We observe that this proposal therefore requires that all votes be cast by Election Day but does not disenfranchise a voter based upon the absence or illegibility of a USPS postmark that is beyond the control of the voter once she places her ballot in the USPS delivery system.

relief to extend temporarily the deadline to address "mail-delivery delays during an on-going public health disaster." She emphasizes that the statutory deadline would remain unchanged for future elections.

The Secretary observes that courts have previously granted temporary equitable relief to address natural disasters, given that neither the Election Code nor the Constitution "provides any procedure to follow when a natural disaster creates an emergency situation that interferes with an election." She argues that the current pandemic is equivalent to other natural disasters and that it necessitates the requested extension of the Election Code's received-by deadline for mail-in ballots.

In contrast, Respondent contends that Petitioner asks this Court to rewrite the plain language of Act 77 and to substitute its preferred ballot deadline for the statutory deadline that resulted from the legislative compromise during the bi-partisan enactment of Act 77.

Judicial restraint, according to Respondent, is especially necessary in regard to election law, where this Court has long recognized that "[t]he power to regulate elections is a legislative one, and has been exercised by the General Assembly since the foundation of the government." Indeed, it observes that the United States Constitution dictates that "[t]he Times, Places, and Manner of holding Elections for Senators and Representatives, shall be prescribed in each state by the Legislature thereof," subject to directives of Congress, and that "[e]ach State shall appoint, in such Manner as the Legislature thereof may direct," electors for President and Vice President. U.S. Const. art. II, § 1, cl. 2. Respondent highlights special concerns relevant to Presidential elections, emphasizing that " '[w]ith respect to a Presidential election,' state courts must 'be mindful of the legislature's role under Article II in choosing the manner of appointing electors.' " Respondent's Supplemental Brief at 20 (quoting *Bush v. Gore* (2000) (Rehnquist, C.J., concurring)).

On the merits, Respondent asserts that the plain language of the Election Code setting the deadline for submission of ballots by 8:00 p.m. on Election Day does not violate the Free and Equal Elections Clause but instead provides "a neutral, evenhanded rule that applies to all Pennsylvania voters equally." It emphasizes that numerous courts, including this Court during the June Primary, have upheld the application of mail-in deadlines during the COVID-19 pandemic.

Respondent additionally rejects the Secretary's assertion that the deadline should be extended based upon the threat of mail delays. It avers that these concerns are "speculative at best." Moreover, it contends that "given Pennsylvania's unparalleled and generous absentee and mail-in voting period, any voter's inability to cast a timely ballot is not caused by the Election Day received-by deadline but instead by their own failure to take timely steps to effect completion and return of their ballot."

In his statement, Postmaster General Louis DeJoy addressed public accusations that the implementation of various cost-saving reforms had allegedly resulted in delays in mail delivery that threatened the timely delivery of election mail. While disputing the validity of the accusations, the Postmaster General provided the following commitments relating to the delivery of election mail:

> [R]etail hours at Post Offices won't be changed, and mail processing equipment and blue collection boxes won't be removed during this period. No mail processing facilities will be closed and we have terminated

> the pilot program that began in July that expedited carrier departures to their delivery routes, without plans to extend or expand it. To clear up any confusion, overtime has, and will continue to be, approved as needed. Finally, effective October 1, 2020, we will engage standby resources in all areas of our operations, including transportation, to satisfy any unforeseen demand for the election.

Respondent emphasizes that Postmaster General DeJoy also asserted that the "USPS has not changed [its] delivery standards, [its] processing, [its] rules, or [its] prices for Election Mail[,]" and that it "can, and will, handle the volume of Election Mail [it] receive[s]."

Finally, Respondent argues that moving the received-by deadline until after Election Day would undermine the federal designation of a uniform Election Day, as set forth in three federal statutes, specifically 3 U.S.C. § 1 ("The electors of President and Vice President shall be appointed, in each State, on the Tuesday next after the first Monday in November, every fourth year succeeding every election of a President and Vice President"); 2 U.S.C. § 7 ("The Tuesday next after the 1st Monday in November, in every even numbered year, is established as the day for the election, in each of the States and Territories of the United States, of Representatives and Delegates to the Congress commencing on the 3d day of January next thereafter."); and 2 U.S.C. § 1 ("At the regular election held in any State next preceding the expiration of the term for which any Senator was elected to represent such State in Congress is regularly by law to be chosen, a United States Senator from said State shall be elected by the people thereof for a term commencing on the 3d day of January next thereafter.").

We are not asked to interpret the statutory language establishing the received-by deadline for mail-in ballots. Indeed, there is no ambiguity regarding the deadline set by the General Assembly:

> **Deadline.**—Except as provided under 25 Pa.C.S. § 3511 (relating to receipt of voted ballot [by military and overseas voters]), a completed mail-in ballot must be received in the office of the county board of elections no later than eight o'clock P.M. on the day of the primary or election.

25 P.S. § 3150.16(c). Moreover, we are not asked to declare the language facially unconstitutional as there is nothing constitutionally infirm about a deadline of 8:00 p.m. on Election Day for the receipt of ballots. The parties, instead, question whether the application of the statutory language to the facts of the current unprecedented situation results in an as-applied infringement of electors' right to vote.

In considering this issue, we reiterate that the Free and Equal Elections Clause of the Pennsylvania Constitution requires that "all aspects of the electoral process, to the greatest degree possible, be kept open and unrestricted to the voters of our Commonwealth, and, also, conducted in a manner which guarantees, to the greatest degree possible, a voter's right to equal participation in the electoral process for the selection of his or her representatives in government." *League of Women Voters*, 178 A.3d at 804. Nevertheless, we also recognize that "the state may enact substantial regulation containing reasonable, non-discriminatory restrictions to ensure honest and fair elections that proceed in an orderly and efficient manner." *Banfield v. Cortes* (2015) (internal citation and quotation marks omitted).

As we have recently seen, an orderly and efficient election process can be crucial to the protection of a voter's participation in that process. Indeed, the struggles of our most populous counties to avoid disenfranchising voters while processing the overwhelming number of pandemic-fueled mail-in ballot applications during the 2020 Primary demonstrates that orderly and efficient election processes are essential to safeguarding the right to vote. An elector cannot exercise the franchise while her ballot application is awaiting processing in a county election board nor when her ballot is sitting in a USPS facility after the deadline for ballots to be received.

We are fully cognizant that a balance must be struck between providing voters ample time to request mail-in ballots, while also building enough flexibility into the election timeline to guarantee that ballot has time to travel through the USPS delivery system to ensure that the completed ballot can be counted in the election. Moreover, we recognize that the determination of that balance is fully enshrined within the authority granted to the Legislature under the United States and Pennsylvania Constitutions.

Nevertheless, we find the Commonwealth Court's rationale in *In re General Election-1985* germane to the current challenge to the application of the ballot received-by deadline. In that case, the court recognized that, while neither the Constitution nor the Election Code specified "any procedure to follow when a natural disaster creates an emergency situation that interferes with an election," courts could look to the direction of 25 P.S. § 3046. [That section] provides courts of common pleas the power, on the day of an election, to decide "matters pertaining to the election as may be necessary to carry out the intent" of the Election Code, which the Commonwealth Court properly deemed to include providing "an equal opportunity for all eligible electors to participate in the election process," which in that case necessitated delaying the election during a flood.

We have no hesitation in concluding that the ongoing COVID-19 pandemic equates to a natural disaster. Moreover, the effects of the pandemic threatened the disenfranchisement of thousands of Pennsylvanians during the 2020 Primary, when several of the Commonwealth's county election boards struggled to process the flow of mail-in ballot applications for voters who sought to avoid exposure to the virus. It is beyond cavil that the numbers of mail-in ballot requests for the Primary will be dwarfed by those applications filed during the upcoming highly-contested Presidential Election in the midst of the pandemic where many voters are still wary of congregating in crowded locations such as polling places. We acknowledge that the Secretary has estimated that nearly three million Pennsylvanians will apply for mail-in applications, in contrast to the 1.5 million cast during the Primary.

In light of these unprecedented numbers and the near-certain delays that will occur in Boards processing the mail-in applications, we conclude that the timeline built into the Election Code cannot be met by the USPS's current delivery standards, regardless of whether those delivery standards are due to recent changes in the USPS's logistical procedures or whether the standards are consistent with what the General Assembly expected when it enacted Act 77. In this regard, we place stock in the USPS's General Counsel's expression that his client could be unable to meet Pennsylvania's statutory election calendar. The Legislature enacted an extremely condensed timeline, providing only seven days between the last date to request a mail-in ballot and the last day to return a completed ballot. While it may be feasible under normal conditions, it will unquestionably fail under the strain of COVID-19 and the 2020 Presidential Election, resulting in the disenfranchisement of voters.

Under our Extraordinary Jurisdiction, this Court can and should act to extend the received-by deadline for mail-in ballots to prevent the disenfranchisement of voters. We have previously recognized that, in enforcing the Free and Equal Elections Clause, this "Court possesses broad authority to craft meaningful remedies when required." We additionally conclude that voters' rights are better protected by addressing the impending crisis at this point in the election cycle on a statewide basis rather than allowing the chaos to brew, creating voter confusion regarding whether extensions will be granted, for how long, and in what counties. Instead, we act now to allow the Secretary, the county election boards, and most importantly, the voters in Pennsylvania to have clarity as to the timeline for the 2020 General Election mail-in ballot process.

After consideration, we adopt the Secretary's informed recommendation of a three-day extension of the absentee and mail-in ballot received-by deadline to allow for the tabulation of ballots mailed by voters via the USPS and postmarked by 8:00 p.m. on Election Day to reduce voter disenfranchisement resulting from the conflict between the Election Code and the current USPS delivery standards, given the expected number of Pennsylvanians opting to use mail-in ballots during the pandemic.[26] We observe that this extension provides more time for the delivery of ballots while also not requiring alteration of the subsequent canvassing and reporting dates necessary for the Secretary's final reporting of the election results. In so doing, we emphasize that the Pennsylvania's election laws currently accommodate the receipt of certain ballots after Election Day, as it allows the tabulation of military and overseas ballots received up to seven days after Election Day. We conclude that this extension of the received-by deadline protects voters' rights while being least at variance with Pennsylvania's permanent election calendar, which we respect and do not alter lightly, even temporarily.

Chief Justice SAYLOR, dissenting

I respectfully dissent concerning the extension of the deadline for receiving mail-in ballots.

Relative to the deadline for receiving mail-in ballots, I join Justice Donohue's dissenting opinion, as this most closely hews to the express legislative intent that the election be concluded by 8:00 p.m. on election night.

26. We likewise incorporate the Secretary's recommendation addressing ballots received within this period that lack a postmark or other proof of mailing, or for which the postmark or other proof of mailing is illegible. Accordingly, in such cases, we conclude that a ballot received on or before 5:00 p.m. on November 6, 2020, will be presumed to have been mailed by Election Day unless a preponderance of the evidence demonstrates that it was mailed after Election Day. We emphasize that voters utilizing the USPS must cast their ballots prior to 8:00 p.m. on Election Day, like all voters, including those utilizing drop boxes. We refuse, however, to disenfranchise voters for the lack or illegibility of a postmark resulting from the USPS processing system, which is undeniably outside the control of the individual voter.

Finally, although the majority decision appears to be designed to accommodate only ballots actually mailed on Election Day or before, the majority does not so much as require a postmark. This substantially increases the likelihood of confusion, as well as the possibility that votes will be cast after 8:00 p.m. on Election Day, thus greatly undermining a pervading objective of the General Assembly.

Justice MUNDY joins this opinion.

Justice DONOHUE, dissenting.

I agree that Petitioners are entitled to relief, but I distance myself from the Majority's analysis to reach this conclusion as well as the specific relief granted. Petitioners base their request for relief on the infringement of the rights afforded by Article 1, Section 5 of the Pennsylvania Constitution, our Free and Equal Elections Clause.

Petitioners and the Secretary seek equitable relief in the form of an order permitting non-compliance with the received-by provision in Act 77 during the COVID-19 pandemic. I am not as comfortable as the Majority with the ability of this Court to exercise equitable powers in election matters. Because they are inherently political, elections are appropriately regulated by the political branch. As such, out of respect for legislatures and for the sake of regularity and orderliness in the election process, the supreme courts of our sister states have routinely held that courts cannot exercise equitable powers to mitigate harsh results in derogation of legislative requirements for strict compliance with election-related deadlines.

Given the deadlines set for the request of and subsequent return of ballots, considered in light of the pandemic and current lagging USPS service standards (which are highly unlikely to improve significantly before Election Day), there is a strong likelihood that voters who wait until the last day to apply for a mail-in or absentee ballot will be disenfranchised, as their mail-in ballots will not be delivered by Election Day and thus will not be counted. Thus, the short seven-day window set forth in Sections 3150.12a(a) and 3150.16(c) of Act 77 constitutes an interference with the free exercise of the right to vote as guaranteed by our Free and Equal Elections Clause. The evidentiary linchpin for establishing the unconstitutionality of the seven-day time frame was correspondence from Thomas J. Marshall, General Counsel and Executive Vice President for the USPS, to Secretary Boockvar dated July 29, 2020 advising that the current service standards for delivery of First Class Mail is two to five days, and cautioning that Pennsylvania's application and return deadlines for mail-in ballots are such that despite prompt actions by voters, the ballots may "not be returned in time to be counted."

The role of the judiciary when a meritorious constitutional challenge is brought "includes the obligation to vindicate" the constitutional rights at issue, and in doing so courts have wide latitude to craft an appropriate remedy." Where, as here, "a legislatively unforeseen constitutional problem requires modification of a statutory provision as applied," the United States Supreme Court has admonished courts to look to legislative intent when devising a remedy.

Petitioners recommend that the "received by" date be moved from Election Day to seven days after Election Day, so long as the mailing is postmarked by Election Day. In *Crossey* (and here), Secretary Boockvar believes that moving the received-by day forward by three days is sufficient, and that Petitioners' longer time period would in fact interfere with other important functions that must take place after Election Day. In crafting a remedy for an as-applied constitutional violation, a court's duty is to effectuate the intent of the General Assembly to the extent possible and to otherwise not disrupt the statutory scheme. In light of these principles, I do not believe that either of the parties' recommended remedies provide the appropriate solution.

There is no reasonable reading of the statute that would lead to the conclusion that the Tuesday before Election Day was of any institutional importance. Instead, the clear legislative intent was that all ballots were to be cast by 8:00 p.m. on Election Day, the termination of the balloting process. It cannot be viewed as a coincidence that the closing of the polls terminating in-person voting and the receipt of mail-in ballots were designated by the statute to be the same. The last date on which applications for ballots would be accepted was tied to an assumption that a timely vote could be cast before the only meaningful milestone, Election Day. As a result, the remedy to best effectuate the legislative intent before the intervening circumstances is to move back, i.e., make earlier, the final date on which applications for mail-in ballots may be submitted to the county boards of elections. I would accept Secretary Boockvar's opinion that three additional days will substantially correct the problem. However, moving back by three days the deadline for the receipt of applications by the boards of elections would result in that deadline falling on Saturday. Instead, to reflect normal business days, the deadline for receipt of the application by the boards of election should be moved to Friday, October 23, 2020. The received-by date for the ballot by the boards of elections, Election Day by 8:00 p.m., should remain unchanged.

As required when remedying an as-applied constitutional defect, this remedy is the least disruptive to the enacted statutory scheme. The problem to be remedied here is that the seven-day period to complete the mail-in vote process has been rendered unworkable by the current extraordinary circumstances. I have no doubt that the statute was intended to accommodate the realities as they existed when Act 77 was enacted. It is unconstitutional as applied to the November 2020 general election because of current realities.

For these reasons, in connection with the November 2020 general election only, the deadline for requesting a ballot should be moved to Friday, October 23, 2020. The legislative choice of Election Day at 8:00 p.m. should remain intact.

Republican Party of Pennsylvania v. Boockvar

141 S. Ct. 1 (2020)

[The day after the Pennsylvania Supreme Court issued this decision, Justice Ruth Bader Ginsburg died, leaving the U.S. Supreme Court with only eight members until Justice Amy Coney Barrett took her seat on October 27. During this interim, the Pennsylvania Republican Party asked the Court to stay the state court's decision. On October 19, the Court split 4-4, which had the effect of denying the request. The Court's order noted that the conservatives—Thomas, Alito, Gorsuch, and Kavanaugh—would have granted the stay. Thus, Chief Justice Roberts joined the Court's remaining liberals (Breyer, Sotomayor, and Kagan) to leave the state court order in effect.

[With Justice Barrett arriving at the Court, the Republicans renewed their request that the Court consider the case. (Their renewal came in the form of a motion to expedite consideration of their petition for a writ of certiorari.) But on October 28, the Court denied that renewed request. The Court's order noted that Justice Barrett did not participate in the decision. Justice Alito, joined by Justice Thomas and Gorsuch (but notably not Justice Kavanaugh), issued the following statement:]

The Court's handling of the important constitutional issue raised by this matter has needlessly created conditions that could lead to serious post-election problems. The Supreme Court of Pennsylvania has issued a decree that squarely alters an important statutory provision enacted by the Pennsylvania Legislature pursuant to its authority under the Constitution of the United States to make rules governing the conduct of elections for federal office. See Art. I, § 4, cl. 1; Art. II, § 1, cl. 2; *Bush v. Palm Beach County Canvassing Bd.* (2000) (*per curiam*). In a law called Act 77, the legislature permitted all voters to cast their ballots by mail but unambiguously required that all mailed ballots be received by 8 p.m. on election day. It also specified that if this provision was declared invalid, much of the rest of Act 77, including its liberalization of mail-in voting, would be void. Act 77, § 11. The legislature subsequently made it clear that, in its judgment, the COVID-19 pandemic did not call for any change in the election-day deadline. In a law enacted in March 2020, the legislature addressed election-related issues caused by the pandemic, but it chose not to amend the deadline for the receipt of mailed ballots.

In the face of Act 77's deadline, the Pennsylvania Supreme Court, by a vote of four to three, decreed that mailed ballots need not be received by election day. Instead, it imposed a different rule: Ballots are to be treated as timely if they are postmarked on or before election day and are received within three days thereafter. In addition, the court ordered that a ballot with no postmark or an illegible postmark must be regarded as timely if it is received by that same date. The court expressly acknowledged that the statutory provision mandating receipt by election day was unambiguous and that its abrogation of that rule was not based on an interpretation of the statute. It further conceded that the statutory deadline was constitutional on its face, but it claimed broad power to do what it thought was needed to respond to a "natural disaster," and it justified its decree as necessary to protect voters' rights under the Free and Equal Elections Clause of the State Constitution.

A month ago, the Republican Party of Pennsylvania and the Pennsylvania Senate leaders asked this Court to stay the Pennsylvania Supreme Court's decision pending the filing and disposition of a petition for certiorari. They argued that the state court decision violated the previously cited constitutional provisions, as well as the federal statute setting a uniform date for federal elections. Respondent, Democratic Party of Pennsylvania (DPP), agreed that the constitutionality of the State Supreme Court's decision was a matter of national importance and urged us to grant review and to decide the issue before the election. Instead of doing what either party sought, the Court simply denied the stay. Although there were four votes to enter a stay, the application failed by an equally divided vote. Now, in a last ditch attempt to prevent the election in Pennsylvania from being conducted under a cloud, we have been asked to grant a petition for a writ of certiorari, to expedite review, and to decide the constitutional question prior to the election.

It would be highly desirable to issue a ruling on the constitutionality of the State Supreme Court's decision before the election. That question has national importance, and there is a strong likelihood that the State Supreme Court decision violates the Federal Constitution. The provisions of the Federal Constitution conferring on state legislatures, not state courts, the authority to make rules governing federal elections would be meaningless if a state court could override the rules adopted by the legislature simply by claiming that a state constitutional provision gave the courts the authority to make whatever rules it thought appropriate for the conduct of a fair election.

For these reasons, the question presented by the Pennsylvania Supreme Court's decision calls out for review by this Court—as both the State Republican and Democratic Parties agreed when the former applied for a stay. But I reluctantly conclude that there is simply not enough time at this late date to decide the question before the election.

That does not mean, however, that the state court decision must escape our review. Although the Court denies the motion to expedite, the petition for certiorari remains before us, and if it is granted, the case can then be decided under a shortened schedule. In addition, the Court's denial of the motion to expedite is not a denial of a request for this Court to order that ballots received after election day be segregated so that if the State Supreme Court's decision is ultimately overturned, a targeted remedy will be available. Petitioner represents that it will apply to this Court to obtain that modest relief, and Respondent DPP agrees that such relief is appropriate. Although the Pennsylvania Supreme Court rejected Petitioner's request for that relief, we have been informed by the Pennsylvania Attorney General that the Secretary of the Commonwealth issued guidance today directing county boards of elections to segregate ballots received between 8:00 p.m. on November 3, 2020, and 5:00 p.m. on November 6, 2020. Nothing in the Court's order today precludes Petitioner from applying to this Court for relief if, for some reason, it is not satisfied with the Secretary's guidance.

Moore v. Circosta

141 S. Ct. 46 (2020)

[On October 28, the same day as the Court's ruling in the Pennsylvania case, the Court also denied a stay in this North Carolina case. Again, Justice Barrett did not participate. Again, the only justices who would have granted a stay were Thomas, Alito, and Gorsuch. The latter two issued the following statement, written by Justice Gorsuch:]

This summer, the General Assembly of North Carolina adopted new election laws expressly designed to address the challenges COVID posed to a fast-approaching election. Among other things, the General Assembly reduced the witness requirement for absentee ballots from two witnesses to one; freed up more individuals to staff polling centers; created a mechanism to allow voters to track their ballots; enabled voters to request absentee ballots online; and increased funding to ensure the State's in-person and absentee voting infrastructure could withstand the coronavirus pandemic. At the same time, the General Assembly judged it appropriate to retain certain other existing election rules, like the State's deadline for the receipt of absentee ballots. Accordingly, under state law, absentee ballots must be postmarked on or before election day, and they must be received "not later than three days after" election day.

Despite the General Assembly's considered judgment about the appropriate response to COVID, other state actors—including the State Board of Elections—recently chose to issue their own additional and supplemental set of amendments to state election laws. Relevant here, they purported to extend the absentee ballot receipt deadline by six days, up to November 12.

The parties before us all acknowledge that, under the Federal Constitution, only the state "Legislature" and "Congress" may prescribe "[t]he Times, Places and Manner of holding Elections." Art. I, § 4, cl. 1. Everyone agrees, too, that the North Carolina Constitution expressly vests all legislative power in the General Assembly, not the Board or anyone else. So we need not go rifling through state law to understand the Board's permissible role in (re)writing election laws. All we need to know about its authority to override state election laws is plain from the Federal and State Constitutions.

Besides, even assuming the North Carolina General Assembly could delegate its Elections Clause authority to other officials, its representatives contend before us that it has not authorized the deadline extension here, and understandably so. State law provides the Board with supervisory authority over elections. But that authority permits the Board to prescribe regulations only if "they do not conflict" with state statutory law. State law also furnishes the Board with power to fashion interim rules. But that power too is circumscribed, triggered when a state statute has been (or likely would be) invalidated by a court. That doesn't sound like a blank check to the Board allowing it to rewrite the election code in any and all consent decrees it may wish to enter. Finally, state law confers upon the Board certain emergency powers. But, relevant for our purposes, the Board may exercise those powers only when three conditions are met: (1) "the normal schedule for the election is disrupted" (2) by a "natural disaster" and (3) provided that the Board's actions do not "unnecessar[ily] conflict" with statutory law. There is no ground for thinking that the election "schedule" has been "disrupted": North Carolina stands fully equipped to conduct its election on November 3. Nor is COVID like the "natural disasters" the Board has pointed to in the past (*e.g.*, hurricanes or power outages) that can disrupt the mechanics of running an election, especially given that the General Assembly has long known about the pandemic's challenges and expressly prepared for them. Finally, the change the Board adopted was deemed "unnecessary" by the General Assembly when it *retained* the statutory ballot receipt deadline after considering COVID's impact on election processes. Any single one of these three problems is enough to sink the Board's action.

In the Fourth Circuit, Judges Wilkinson, Agee, and Niemeyer thoughtfully explained the Board's constitutional overreach and the broader problems with last-minute election-law-writing-by-lawsuit. As they observed, efforts like these not only offend the Elections Clause's textual commitment of responsibility for election lawmaking to state and federal legislators, they do damage to faith in the written Constitution as law, to the power of the people to oversee their own government, and to the authority of legislatures. Such last-minute changes by largely unaccountable bodies, too, invite confusion, risk altering election outcomes, and in the process threaten voter confidence in the results. Respectfully, for all these reasons I would grant the application to stay the Board's action.

Democratic National Committee v. Wisconsin State Legislature

141 S. Ct. 28 (2020)

[Meanwhile, on October 26—just two days before the U.S. Supreme Court released its orders in the Pennsylvania and North Carolina cases, which as we have just seen concerned purported deviations from state statutory law undertaken by parts of state government (judicial or administrative) — the Court addressed a deviation from state statutory law mandated by a lower federal court. This case came from Wisconsin, and it concerned essentially the same issue that the Court had considered back in April during the Wisconsin primary: whether to extend the deadline for submission of absentee ballots.]

The application to vacate stay presented to Justice Kavanhaugh and by him referred to the Court is denied.

Chief Justice Roberts, concurring in denial of application to vacate stay.

In this case, as in several this Court has recently addressed, a District Court intervened in the thick of election season to enjoin enforcement of a State's laws. Because I believe this intervention was improper, I agree with the decision of the Seventh Circuit to stay the injunction pending appeal. I write separately to note that this case presents different issues than the applications this Court recently denied in *Scarnati v. Boockvar* and *Republican Party of Pennsylvania v. Boockvar*. While the Pennsylvania applications implicated the authority of state courts to apply their own constitutions to election regulations, this case involves federal intrusion on state lawmaking processes. Different bodies of law and different precedents govern these two situations and require, in these particular circumstances, that we allow the modification of election rules in Pennsylvania but not Wisconsin.

Justice Kavanaugh, concurring in denial of application to vacate stay.

Approximately 30 States, including Wisconsin, require that absentee ballots be received by election day in order to be counted. Like most States, Wisconsin has retained that deadline for the November 2020 election, notwithstanding the COVID–19 pandemic. In advance of the November election, however, a Federal District Court in Wisconsin unilaterally changed the State's deadline for receipt of absentee ballots. Citing the pandemic, the court extended the deadline for receipt of absentee ballots by six days—from election day, November 3, to November 9, so long as the ballots are postmarked on or before election day, November 3.

The Seventh Circuit stayed the District Court's injunction, ruling that the District Court had violated this Court's precedents in two fundamental ways: first, by changing state election rules too close to an election; and second, by usurping the state legislature's authority to either keep or make changes to state election rules in light of the pandemic.

Applicants here ask that we vacate the Seventh Circuit's stay and reinstate the District Court's order extending the deadline for absentee ballots to be received in Wisconsin. The Court today denies the applications and maintains the Seventh Circuit's stay of the District Court's order. I agree with the Court's decision to deny the applications, and I write separately to explain why.

I

For three alternative and independent reasons, I conclude that the District Court's injunction was unwarranted.

First, the District Court changed Wisconsin's election rules too close to the election, in contravention of this Court's precedents. This Court has repeatedly emphasized that federal courts ordinarily should not alter state election laws in the period close to an election—a principle often referred to as the *Purcell* principle. See *Purcell v. Gonzalez* (2006) (*per curiam*);

The Court's precedents recognize a basic tenet of election law: When an election is close at hand, the rules of the road should be clear and settled. That is because running a statewide election is a complicated endeavor. Lawmakers initially must make a host of difficult decisions about how best to structure and conduct the election. Then, thousands of state and local officials and volunteers must participate in a massive coordinated effort to implement the lawmakers' policy choices on the ground before and during the election, and again in counting the votes afterwards. And at every step, state and local officials must communicate to voters how, when, and where they may cast their ballots through in-person voting on election day, absentee voting, or early voting.

Even seemingly innocuous late-in-the-day judicial alterations to state election laws can interfere with administration of an election and cause unanticipated consequences. If a court alters election laws near an election, election administrators must first understand the court's injunction, then devise plans to implement that late-breaking injunction, and then determine as necessary how best to inform voters, as well as state and local election officials and volunteers, about those last-minute changes. It is one thing for state legislatures to alter their own election rules in the late innings and to bear the responsibility for any unintended consequences. It is quite another thing for a federal district court to swoop in and alter carefully considered and democratically enacted state election rules when an election is imminent.

That important principle of judicial restraint not only prevents voter confusion but also prevents election administrator confusion—and thereby protects the State's interest in running an orderly, efficient election and in giving citizens (including the losing candidates and their supporters) confidence in the fairness of the election. See *Purcell*, 549 U.S., at 4-5, 127 S. Ct. 5; *Crawford v. Marion County Election Bd.* (2008) (plurality opinion). The principle also discourages last-minute litigation and instead encourages litigants to bring any substantial challenges to election rules ahead of time, in the ordinary litigation process. For those reasons, among others, this Court has regularly cautioned that a federal court's last-minute interference with state election laws is ordinarily inappropriate.

In this case, however, just six weeks before the November election and after absentee voting had already begun, the District Court ordered several changes to Wisconsin's election laws, including a change to Wisconsin's deadline for receipt of absentee ballots. Although the District Court's order was well intentioned and thorough, it nonetheless contravened this Court's longstanding precedents by usurping the proper role of the state legislature and rewriting state election laws in the period close to an election.

Applicants retort that the *Purcell* principle precludes an appellate court—such as the Seventh Circuit here—from overturning a district court's injunction of a state election rule in the period close to an election. That argument defies common sense and would turn *Purcell* on its head. Correcting an erroneous lower court injunction of a state election rule cannot itself constitute a *Purcell* problem. Otherwise, appellate courts could never correct a late-breaking lower court injunction of a state election rule. That obviously is not the law. To be sure, it would be preferable if federal district courts did not contravene the *Purcell* principle by rewriting state election laws close to an election. But when they do, appellate courts must step in.

Second, even apart from the late timing, the District Court misapprehended the limited role of the federal courts in COVID-19 cases. This Court has consistently stated that the Constitution principally entrusts politically accountable state legislatures, not unelected federal judges, with the responsibility to address the health and safety of the people during the COVID-19 pandemic.

The COVID-19 pandemic has caused the deaths of more than 200,000 Americans, and it remains a serious threat, including in Wisconsin. The virus poses a particular risk to the elderly and to those with certain pre-existing conditions. But federal judges do not possess special expertise or competence about how best to balance the costs and benefits of potential policy responses to the pandemic, including with respect to elections. For that reason, this Court's cases during the pandemic have adhered to a basic jurisprudential principle: When state and local officials "'undertake[] to act in areas fraught with medical and scientific uncertainties,' their latitude 'must be especially broad.'" *Andino*, ___ U.S., at ___, 141 S. Ct., at 10, *ante*, at 34-35 (Kavanaugh, J., concurring in grant of application for stay). It follows "that a State legislature's decision either to keep or to make changes to election rules to address COVID-19 ordinarily 'should not be subject to second-guessing by an unelected federal judiciary, which lacks the background, competence, and expertise to assess public health and is not accountable to the people.'" *Ibid.* (some internal quotation marks omitted). As the Seventh Circuit rightly explained, "the design of electoral procedures is a legislative task," including during the pandemic. *Democratic National Committee* v. *Bostelmann* (2020).

Over the last seven months, this Court has stayed numerous federal district court injunctions that second-guessed state legislative judgments about whether to keep or make changes to election rules during the pandemic.

To be sure, in light of the pandemic, some state legislatures have exercised their Article I, § 4, authority over elections and have changed their election rules for the November 2020 election. Of particular relevance here, a few States such as Mississippi no longer require that absentee ballots be received before election day. See, *e.g.*, Miss. Code Ann. § 23-15-637 (2020). Other States such as Vermont, by contrast, have decided not to make changes to their ordinary election-deadline rules, including to the election-day deadline for receipt of absentee ballots. See, *e.g.*, Vt. Stat. Ann., Tit. 17, § 2543 (2020). The variation in state responses reflects our constitutional system of federalism. Different state legislatures may make different choices. Assessing the complicated tradeoffs involved in changing or retaining election deadlines, or other election rules, in light of public health conditions in a particular State is primarily the responsibility of state legislatures and falls outside the competence of federal courts.

Applicants respond that this principle of deference to state legislatures applies only when a state legislature has affirmatively made some changes, but not others, to the election code in light of COVID-19. And they say that Wisconsin's legislature has not done so, unlike the South Carolina legislature in *Andino*, for example. But the Wisconsin State Legislature's decision *not* to modify its election rules in light of the pandemic is itself a policy judgment worthy of the same judicial deference that this Court afforded the South Carolina legislature in *Andino*. In short, state legislatures, not federal courts, primarily decide whether and how to adjust election rules in light of the pandemic.

Third, the District Court did not sufficiently appreciate the significance of election deadlines. This Court has long recognized that a State's reasonable deadlines for registering to vote, requesting absentee ballots, submitting absentee ballots, and voting in person generally raise no federal constitutional issues under the traditional *Anderson-Burdick* balancing test. See *Anderson v. Celebrezze* (1983); *Burdick v. Takushi* (1992).

To state the obvious, a State cannot conduct an election without deadlines. It follows that the right to vote is not substantially burdened by a requirement that voters "act in a timely fashion if they wish to express their views in the voting booth." *Burdick*, 504 U.S., at 438, 112 S. Ct. 2059. For the same reason, the right to vote is not substantially burdened by a requirement that voters act in a timely fashion if they wish to cast an *absentee ballot*. Either way, voters need to vote on time. A deadline is not unconstitutional merely because of voters' "own failure to take timely steps" to ensure their franchise. *Rosario v. Rockefeller* (1973). Voters who, for example, show up to vote at midnight after the polls close on election night do not have a right to demand that the State nonetheless count their votes. Voters who submit their absentee ballots after the State's deadline similarly do not have a right to demand that the State count their votes.

For important reasons, most States, including Wisconsin, require absentee ballots to be *received* by election day, not just *mailed* by election day. Those States want to avoid the chaos and suspicions of impropriety that can ensue if thousands of absentee ballots flow in after election day and potentially flip the results of an election. And those States also want to be able to definitively announce the results of the election on election night, or as soon as possible thereafter. Moreover, particularly in a Presidential election, counting all the votes quickly can help the State promptly resolve any disputes, address any need for recounts, and begin the process of canvassing and certifying the election results in an expeditious manner. See 3 U.S.C. § 5. The States are aware of the risks described by Professor Pildes: "[L]ate-arriving ballots open up one of the greatest risks of what might, in our era of hyperpolarized political parties and existential politics, destabilize the election result. If the apparent winner the morning after the election ends up losing due to late-arriving ballots, charges of a rigged election could explode." Pildes, How to Accommodate a Massive Surge in Absentee Voting, U. Chi. L. Rev. Online (June 26,

2020) (online source archived at www.supremecourt.gov). The "longer after Election Day any significant changes in vote totals take place, the greater the risk that the losing side will cry that the election has been stolen." *Ibid.*

One may disagree with a State's policy choice to require that absentee ballots be received by election day. Indeed, some States require only that absentee ballots be *mailed* by election day. See, *e.g.*, W. Va. Code Ann. § 3-3-5(g)(2) (Lexis 2020). But the States requiring that absentee ballots be received by election day do so for weighty reasons that warrant judicial respect. Federal courts have no business disregarding those state interests simply because the federal courts believe that later deadlines would be better.

That constitutional analysis of election deadlines still applies in the pandemic. After all, during the pandemic, a State still cannot conduct an election without deadlines. And the States that require absentee ballots to be received by election day still have strong interests in avoiding suspicions of impropriety and announcing final results on or close to election night.

To be sure, more people are voting absentee during the pandemic. But the State of Wisconsin has repeatedly instructed voters to request and mail their ballots well ahead of time, and the State has taken numerous steps to accommodate the increased number of absentee ballots. Moreover, the State now has some experience to draw upon when administering an election during the pandemic. Wisconsin conducted primary elections in April and August, and has incorporated the lessons from those experiences into its extensive planning for the November election. And that planning has paid off so far: For the November election, more than a million Wisconsin voters have *already* voted by absentee ballot.

In attempting to justify the District Court's injunction, Applicants also rely on this Court's decision in April regarding the Wisconsin primary election. They claim that the Court there approved the District Court's change of the deadline for receipt of absentee ballots in the primary election, so long as the ballots were postmarked by election day. That assertion is incorrect. In that case, this Court explicitly stated that the District Court's last-minute extension of the deadline for receipt of absentee ballots was "not challenged in this Court."

In sum, the District Court's injunction was unwarranted for three alternative and independent reasons: The District Court changed the state election laws too close to the election. It misapprehended the limited role of federal courts in COVID-19 cases. And it did not sufficiently appreciate the significance of election deadlines.[1]

1. [Important footnote by Justice Kavanaugh relating the debate within the Court over the so-called "independent state legislature" doctrine.—EDS.] A *federal court's* alteration of state election laws such as Wisconsin's differs in some respects from a *state court's* (or state agency's) alteration of state election laws. That said, under the U. S. Constitution, the state courts do not have a blank check to rewrite state election laws for federal elections. Article II expressly provides that the rules for Presidential elections are established by the States "in such Manner as the *Legislature* thereof may direct." § 1, cl. 2 (emphasis added). The text of Article II means that "the clearly expressed intent of the legislature must prevail" and that a state court may not depart from the state election code enacted by the legislature. *Bush v. Gore* (2000) (Rehnquist, C. J., concurring); see *Bush v. Palm Beach County Canvassing Bd.*

II

The dissent rejects all three of the above conclusions and applies the ordinary *Anderson-Burdick* balancing test for analyzing state election rules. In the dissent's view, the District Court permissibly concluded that the benefits of the State's deadline for receipt of absentee ballots are outweighed by the burdens of the deadline on voters. In light of the three alternative and independent conclusions outlined above, I do not think that we may conduct that kind of open-ended balancing test in this case. But even on its own terms, the dissent's balancing analysis is faulty, in my respectful view.

Start by considering the implications of the dissent's analysis. In reinstating the District Court's order extending Wisconsin's deadline for receipt of absentee ballots, the dissent's approach would necessarily invalidate (or at least call into question) the laws of approximately 30 States for the upcoming election and compel all of those States to accept absentee ballots received after election day. The dissent's *de facto* green light to federal courts to rewrite dozens of state election laws around the country over the next two weeks seems to be rooted in a belief that federal judges know better than state legislators about how to run elections during a pandemic. But over the last several months, this Court has consistently rejected that federal-judges-know-best vision of election administration.

The dissent does not fully come to grips with the destabilizing consequences of its analysis, saying that the facts may differ in other States. But the key facts underlying the District Court's injunction are similar in other States: the existence of the virus and its effects on election workers, voters, mail systems, and in-person voting. The dissent's claim that its reasoning would not necessarily invalidate the absentee-ballot deadlines of approximately 30 other States therefore rings hollow.

Turning to the dissent's balancing analysis, the dissent does not sufficiently appreciate the necessity of deadlines in elections, and does not sufficiently account for all the steps that Wisconsin has already taken to help voters meet those deadlines.

(2000) (*per curiam*); *McPherson v. Blacker* (1892). In a Presidential election, in other words, a state court's "significant departure from the legislative scheme for appointing Presidential electors presents a federal constitutional question." *Bush v. Gore,* 531 U.S. at 113, 121 S. Ct. 525 (Rehnquist, C. J., concurring). As Chief Justice Rehnquist explained in *Bush* v. *Gore,* the important federal judicial role in reviewing state-court decisions about state law in a federal Presidential election "does not imply a disrespect for state *courts* but rather a respect for the constitutionally prescribed role of state *legislatures.* To attach definitive weight to the pronouncement of a state court, when the very question at issue is whether the court has actually departed from the statutory meaning, would be to abdicate our responsibility to enforce the explicit requirements of Article II." *Id.,* at 115, 121 S. Ct. 525.

The dissent here questions why the federal courts would have a role in that kind of case. The answer to that question, as the unanimous Court stated in *Bush v. Palm Beach County Canvassing Bd.,* and as Chief Justice Rehnquist persuasively explained in *Bush* v. *Gore,* is that the text of the Constitution requires federal courts to ensure that state courts do not rewrite state election laws.

The dissent claims that the State's election-day deadline for receipt of absentee ballots will "disenfranchise" some Wisconsin voters. But that is not what a reasonable election deadline does. This Court has long explained that a State's election deadline does not disenfranchise voters who are capable of meeting the deadline but fail to do so. See *Rosario*, 410 U.S., at 757-758, 93 S. Ct. 1245. In other words, reasonable election deadlines do not "disenfranchise" anyone under any legitimate understanding of that term. And the dissent cannot plausibly argue that the absentee-ballot deadline imposed—and still in place as of today—in most of the States is not a reasonable one. Those voters who disregard the deadlines or who fail to take the state-prescribed steps for meeting the deadlines may have to vote in person. But no one is disenfranchised by Wisconsin's reasonable and commonplace deadline for receiving absentee ballots. Indeed, more than *one million* Wisconsin voters have already requested, received, *and returned* their absentee ballots.

To help voters meet the deadlines, Wisconsin makes it easy to vote absentee and has taken several extraordinary steps this year to inform voters that they should request and return absentee ballots well before election day.

For starters, Wisconsin has "lots of rules" that "make voting easier than do the rules of many other states." *Luft v. Evers* (2020). Wisconsin law allows voters to vote absentee without an excuse, no questions asked. Registered voters may request an absentee ballot by mail, e-mail, online, or fax.

Since August, moreover, the Wisconsin Elections Commission has been regularly reminding voters of the need to act early so as to avoid backlogs and potential mail delays. In August and September, for example, Wisconsin's chief elections official explicitly urged voters not to wait to request a ballot: "It takes time for Wisconsin clerks to process your request. Then it may take up to seven days for you to receive your ballot in the mail. It can then take another seven days for your ballot to be returned by mail."

Perhaps most importantly, in early September, Wisconsin decided to leave little to chance and mailed every registered voter in the State who had not already requested an absentee ballot (2.6 million of Wisconsin's registered voters) an absentee ballot application, as well as information about how to vote absentee.

Returning an absentee ballot in Wisconsin is also easy. To begin with, voters can return their completed absentee ballots by mail. But absentee voters who do not want to rely on the mail have several other options. Until election day, voters may, for example, hand-deliver their absentee ballots to the municipal clerk's office or other designated site, or they may place their absentee ballots in a secure absentee ballot drop box. Some absentee ballot drop boxes are located outdoors, either for drive-through or walk-up access, and some are indoors at a location like a municipal clerk's office.

Alternatively, absentee voters may vote "in-person absentee" beginning two weeks before election day. A Wisconsin voter who votes "in-person absentee" fills out an absentee ballot in person at a municipal clerk's office or other designated location before election day. Some municipalities have created drive-up absentee voting sites to allow voters to vote "in-person absentee" without leaving their cars.

Finally, on election day, a voter may drop off an absentee ballot at a polling place until 8:00 p.m. In sum, as the Governor of Wisconsin correctly said back in March as the COVID-19 crisis broke: "The good news is that absentee voting in Wisconsin is really easy."

The current statistics for the November election bear out the Governor's statement. In huge and unprecedented numbers, Wisconsin voters have already taken advantage of the State's generous absentee voting procedures for the November election. As of October 26, 2020, the Wisconsin Elections Commission has mailed 1,706,771 absentee ballots to Wisconsin voters. And it has already received back from voters 1,344,535 completed absentee ballots.

As those statistics suggest, the dissent's charge that Wisconsin has disenfranchised absentee voters is not tenable. As the Seventh Circuit explained, the "district court did not find that any person who wants to avoid voting in person on Election Day would be unable to cast a ballot in Wisconsin by planning ahead and taking advantage of the opportunities allowed by state law."

The dissent insists, however, that "tens of thousands" and perhaps even 100,000 votes will not be counted if we do not reinstate the District Court's extension of the deadline. The District Court arrived at the same prediction, but it was a prediction, not a finding of fact. For its part, the dissent makes the same prediction by looking at the number of absentee ballots that arrived after the primary election day in April. But in the April primary, the received-by deadline had been extended to allow receipt of absentee ballots after election day. The dissent's statistic tells us nothing about how many voters might miss the deadline when voters know that the ballots must be received by election day. To take an analogy: How many people would file their taxes after April 15 if the filing deadline were changed to April 21? Lots. That fact tells us nothing about how many people would file their taxes after April 15 if the deadline remained at April 15.

The dissent also seizes on the fact that Wisconsin law allows voters to request absentee ballots until October 29, five days before election day. But the dissent does not grapple with the good reason why the State allows such late requests. The State allows those late requests for ballots because it wants to accommodate late requesters who still want to obtain an absentee ballot so that they can drop it off in person and avoid lines at the polls on election day. No one thinks that voters who request absentee ballots as late as October 29 can both receive the ballots and *mail* them back in time to be received by election day. Rather, those late requesters would, after receiving the ballots, necessarily have to drop their absentee ballots off in person at one of the designated locations. In short, Wisconsin provides an option to request absentee ballots until October 29 for voters who decide relatively late in the game that they would prefer to avoid lines at the polls on election day.

The dissent's October 29-based argument falls short for another reason as well: The dissent's approach would actually penalize Wisconsin for being too generous with its absentee voting regime. Under the dissent's theory, if Wisconsin had just set a *more restrictive* deadline for voters to request absentee ballots—say, two weeks before election day—there presumably would not be a constitutional problem with the State's election-day deadline for receipt of absentee ballots. But it makes little sense to penalize Wisconsin for accommodating voters and making it easier for them to vote absentee and avoid lines on election day.

The dissent's rhetoric of "disenfranchisement" is misplaced for still another reason. As the dissent uses that term, the dissent's own position would itself "disenfranchise" voters. What about voters who request an absentee ballot after October 29? What about voters who mail their ballots after November 3? What about voters who mail their ballots by November 3 but whose ballots arrive after November 9? Even if we reinstated the District Court's order as the dissent would have us do, those votes would not count. The dissent's position would itself therefore "disenfranchise" some voters, at least as the dissent uses the term. All of which simply shows that the dissent's rhetoric of disenfranchisement is mistaken.

The dissent responds that I am just disagreeing with the facts found by the District Court. Not so. I do not disagree with any of the relevant historical facts that the District Court found and that the dissent highlights. The dissent, for example, calls attention to the District Court's finding that nearly two million Wisconsin voters in this election are likely to request mail ballots. I agree. Indeed, the Wisconsin Elections Commission has already sent nearly that number of absentee ballots to voters who have requested them. The dissent notes that the influx of ballots has imposed a serious burden on some local election offices. I agree. The dissent points out that the District Court found that ballots can sometimes take two weeks to be sent and returned in light of Postal Service delays. I agree. The dissent highlights that the pandemic has gotten worse, not better, in Wisconsin over the last few weeks. I agree. And the dissent notes that the in-person voting option can pose a health risk to elderly and ill voters. I agree; I am fully aware of and sensitive to that reality.

Contrary to the dissent's attempt to characterize our disagreement as factual, the facts in this case are largely undisputed. I have zero disagreement with the dissent on the question of whether COVID-19 is a serious problem. It is. Instead, I disagree with some of the District Court's and the dissent's speculative predictions about how the voting process might unfold with an election-day deadline for receipt of absentee ballots. And I disagree with the District Court's and the dissent's legal analysis of whether, given the agreed-upon facts, the State has done enough to protect the right to vote under the Constitution and this Court's precedents, given the necessity of having election deadlines.

In short, I agree with the dissent that COVID-19 is a serious problem. But you need deadlines to hold elections—there is just no wishing away or getting around that fundamental point. And Wisconsin's deadline is the same as that in 30 other States and is a reasonable deadline given all the circumstances.

To be clear, in every election a voter who requests an absentee ballot, particularly a voter who waits until the last moments to request an absentee ballot, might not receive a ballot in time to mail it back in, or in some cases may not receive a ballot until after election day. Or in some cases, a voter may mail a completed ballot, but it may get delayed and arrive too late to be counted. Indeed, in 2012 and 2016, the States rejected more than 70,000 ballots in each election because the ballots missed the deadlines. But moving a deadline would not prevent ballots from arriving after the newly minted deadline any more than moving first base would mean no more close plays. And more to the point, the fact that some ballots will be late in any system with deadlines does not make Wisconsin's widely used deadline facially unconstitutional. See *Crawford*, 553 U.S. at 202-203, 128 S. Ct. 1610.

Put another way, the relevant question is not whether any voter would ever miss the deadlines. After all, in every deadline case, the answer would always be yes, and no election deadline would ever be permissible. The proper question under the Constitution is whether the deadline is reasonable under the circumstances. See *Rosario*, 410 U.S. at 760, 93 S. Ct. 1245. Again, Wisconsin's deadline is the same as that in about 30 other States for the November election and is reasonable, for the reasons I have explained.

In any event, if a Wisconsin voter does not receive an absentee ballot in time to cast it, the voter still has the option of voting in person. And Wisconsin, like many other States, demonstrated in the April and August primary elections that it can run an in-person election in a way that is reasonably safe for Wisconsin voters, with socially distanced lines, mask requirements, and sanitizing protocols. The District Court acknowledged that in-person voting can be done "safely" again in November "if the majority of votes are cast in advance, sufficient poll workers, polling places, and PPE are available, and social distancing and masking protocols are followed." If a voter requests a ballot at the last minute—long after the State has told voters that they should request ballots—and if that voter does not receive a ballot by election day, the voter still has the option of voting in person. That said, the better option, as Wisconsin has repeatedly announced, is for voters who wish to vote absentee to request and submit their ballots well ahead of time. That is what tens of millions of voters across America—including more than one million voters in Wisconsin—have already done.

* * *

For those reasons, I concur in the denial of the applications to vacate the stay.

Justice GORSUCH, with whom Justice KAVANAUGH joins, concurring in denial of application to vacate stay.

Elections must end sometime, a single deadline supplies clear notice, and requiring ballots be in by election day puts all voters on the same footing.

Why did the district court seek to scuttle such a long-settled tradition in this area? COVID. Because of the current pandemic, the court suggested, it was free to substitute its own election deadline for the State's. Never mind that, in response to the pandemic, the Wisconsin Elections Commission decided to mail registered voters an absentee ballot application and return envelope over the summer, so no one had to ask for one. Never mind that voters have also been free to seek and return absentee ballots since September. Never mind that voters may return their ballots not only by mail but also by bringing them to a county clerk's office, or various "no touch" drop boxes staged locally, or certain polling places on election day. Never mind that those unable to vote on election day have still other options in Wisconsin, like voting in-person during a 2-week voting period before election day. And never mind that the court itself found the pandemic posed an insufficient threat to the health and safety of voters to justify revamping the State's in-person election procedures.

So it's indisputable that Wisconsin has made considerable efforts to accommodate early voting and respond to COVID. The district court's only possible complaint is that the State hasn't done *enough.* But how much is enough? If Wisconsin's statutory absentee voting deadline can be discarded on the strength of the State's status as a COVID "hotspot," what about the identical deadlines in 30 other States? How much of a "hotspot" must a State (or maybe some sliver of it) be before judges get to improvise? Then there's the question what these new ad hoc deadlines should be. The judge in this case tacked 6 days onto the State's election deadline, but what about 3 or 7 or 10, and what's to stop different judges choosing (as they surely would) different deadlines in different jurisdictions? A widely shared state policy seeking to make election day real would give way to a Babel of decrees. And what's to stop courts from tinkering with in-person voting rules too? This judge declined to go that far, but the plaintiffs thought he should have, and it's not hard to imagine other judges accepting invitations to unfurl the precinct maps and decide whether States should add polling places, revise their hours, rearrange the voting booths within them, or maybe even supplement existing social distancing, hand washing, and ventilation protocols.

The Constitution dictates a different approach to these how-much-is-enough questions. The Constitution provides that state legislatures—not federal judges, not state judges, not state governors, not other state officials—bear primary responsibility for setting election rules. Art. I, § 4, cl. 1. And the Constitution provides a second layer of protection too. If state rules need revision, Congress is free to alter them. Nothing in our founding document contemplates the kind of judicial intervention that took place here, nor is there precedent for it in 230 years of this Court's decisions.

Understandably so. Legislators can be held accountable by the people for the rules they write or fail to write; typically, judges cannot. Legislatures make policy and bring to bear the collective wisdom of the whole people when they do, while courts dispense the judgment of only a single person or a handful. Legislatures enjoy far greater resources for research and fact finding on questions of science and safety than usually can be mustered in litigation between discrete parties before a single judge. In reaching their decisions, legislators must compromise to achieve the broad social consensus necessary to enact new laws, something not easily replicated in courtrooms where typically one side must win and the other lose.

Of course, democratic processes can prove frustrating. Because they cannot easily act without a broad social consensus, legislatures are often slow to respond and tepid when they do. The clamor for judges to sweep in and address emergent problems, and the temptation for individual judges to fill the void of perceived inaction, can be great. But what sometimes seems like a fault in the constitutional design was a feature to the framers, a means of ensuring that any changes to the status quo will not be made hastily, without careful deliberation, extensive consultation, and social consensus.

Nor may we undo this arrangement just because we might be frustrated. Our oath to uphold the Constitution is tested by hard times, not easy ones. And succumbing to the temptation to sidestep the usual constitutional rules is never costless. It does damage to faith in the written Constitution as law, to the power of the people to oversee their own government, and to the authority of legislatures, for the more we assume their duties the less incentive they have to discharge them. Last-minute changes to longstanding election rules risk other problems too, inviting confusion and chaos and eroding public confidence in electoral outcomes. No one doubts that conducting a national election amid a pandemic poses serious challenges. But none of that means individual judges may improvise with their own election rules in place of those the people's representatives have adopted.

Justice KAGAN, with whom Justice BREYER and Justice SOTOMAYOR join, dissenting.

Wisconsin is one of the hottest of all COVID hotspots in the Nation. So rather than vote in person, many Wisconsinites will choose to vote by mail. State election officials report that 1.7 million people—about 50 percent of Wisconsin's voters—have already asked for mail ballots. And more are expected to do so, because state law gives voters until October 29, five days before Election Day, to make that request.

To ensure that these mail ballots are counted, the district court ordered in September the same relief afforded in April: a six-day extension of the receipt deadline for mail ballots postmarked by Election Day. The court supported that order with specific facts and figures about how COVID would affect the electoral process in Wisconsin. The court found that the surge in requests for mail ballots would overwhelm state officials in the weeks leading up to the October 29 ballot-application deadline. And it discovered unusual delays in the United States Postal Service's delivery of mail in the State. The combination of those factors meant, as a high-ranking elections official testified, that a typical ballot would take a full two weeks "to make its way through the mail from a clerk's office to a voter and back again"—even when the voter instantly turns the ballot around. Based on the April election experience, the court determined that many voters would not even *receive* mail ballots by Election Day, making it impossible to vote in that way. And as many as 100,000 citizens would not have their votes counted—even though timely requested and postmarked—without the six-day extension. (To put that number in perspective, a grand total of 284 Wisconsin mail ballots were not counted in the 2016 election.) In the court's view, the discarding of so many properly cast ballots would severely burden the constitutional right to vote. The fit remedy was to create a six-day grace period, to allow those ballots a little extra time to arrive in the face of unprecedented administrative and delivery delays.

But a court of appeals halted the district court's order, and today this Court leaves that stay in place. I respectfully dissent because the Court's decision will disenfranchise large numbers of responsible voters in the midst of hazardous pandemic conditions.

I

The court of appeals did not dispute any of the district court's careful findings about the effect of COVID on voting in Wisconsin. It did not deny that, because of those dangers, state election offices will be swamped until the end of October by timely mail-ballot applications. It did not contest that backlogs in those offices, combined with unusual delays in mail delivery, will prevent tens of thousands of Wisconsinites—through no fault of their own—from successfully casting a mail ballot. Nor did the appellate court express doubt that disenfranchisement of that kind, and on that scale, imposes a severe burden on the right to vote. In fact, the court never even addressed the constitutional issue.

How could that be? In the appellate court's view, this Court's decision in *Purcell v. Gonzalez* (2006) (*per curiam*), prohibited the district court from modifying Wisconsin's election rules so close to (*i.e.*, six weeks before) Election Day. But that is a misunderstanding of *Purcell*'s message. In fixating on timing alone, the court of appeals went astray.

The Court in *Purcell* considered an appellate decision reversing a district court's refusal to enjoin a voter identification law shortly before an election. We vacated the decision because the court of appeals—much like the one here—failed to "give deference to [a district court's] discretion" in assessing the propriety of injunctive relief. In doing so, we briefly addressed how to "weigh" whether an injunction of an election rule should issue. A court, we counseled, must balance the "harms attendant upon issuance or nonissuance of an injunction," together with "considerations specific to election cases" that may affect "the integrity of our electoral processes." Among those election-specific factors, we continued, was the potential for a court order, especially close to Election Day, to "result in voter confusion and consequent incentive to remain away from the polls.".

That statement, as the dissent below saw, "articulated not a rule but a caution." Last-minute changes to election processes may baffle and discourage voters; and when that is likely, a court has strong reason to stay its hand. But not every such change poses that danger. And a court must also take account of other matters—among them, the presence of extraordinary circumstances (like a pandemic), the clarity of a constitutional injury, and the extent of voter disenfranchisement threatened. At its core, *Purcell* tells courts to apply, not depart from, the usual rules of equity. And that means courts must consider all relevant factors, not just the calendar. Yes, there is a danger that an autumn injunction may confuse voters and suppress voting. But no, there is not a moratorium on the Constitution as the cold weather approaches. Remediable incursions on the right to vote can occur in September or October as well as in April or May.

It is hard to see how the extension of a ballot-receipt deadline could confuse citizens about how to vote: At worst, a voter not informed of the new deadline would (if she could) put her ballot in the mail a few days earlier than needed. Nor would that measure discourage Wisconsin citizens from exercising their right to the franchise. To the contrary, it would prevent the State from throwing away the votes of people actively participating in the democratic process. And what will undermine the "integrity" of that process is not the counting but instead the discarding of timely cast ballots that, because of pandemic conditions, arrive a bit after Election Day. *Purcell*, 549 U.S., at 4, 127 S. Ct. 5.[3] On the scales of both constitutional justice and electoral accuracy, protecting the right to vote in a health crisis outweighs conforming to a deadline created in safer days.

Indeed, I see no more apt time for the district court to have issued its injunction than when it did. The court of appeals insisted that the injunction would better have come in May, a half-year before Election Day; then, the court said, the order "could not be called untimely." But "untimely" can mean too early as well as

3. Justice Kavanaugh alleges that "suspicions of impropriety" will result if "absentee ballots flow in after election day and potentially flip the results of an election." *Ante*, at 33. But there are no results to "flip" until all valid votes are counted. And nothing could be more "suspicio[us]" or "improp[er]" than refusing to tally votes once the clock strikes 12 on election night. To suggest otherwise, especially in these fractious times, is to disserve the electoral process.

too late. And a May order could have been premature, perhaps even foolishly so. At that time, the district court could not have known the course COVID would take. Nor could the court have known about the current ability of Wisconsin election offices or the Postal Service to handle increased demand for mail ballots. (Doubts about the Postal Service's delivery performance, for example, did not arise until August.) In waiting until late September, the district court resolved to base its ruling on concrete evidence—not on unfounded speculation.

And without *Purcell*, not much is left in the appellate court's opinion to justify its stay. That court separately argued that "the design of electoral procedures" is a solely "legislative task." But that is not so when those procedures infringe the constitutionally enshrined right to vote. To be sure, deference is usually due to a legislature's decisions about how best to manage the COVID pandemic. But the Wisconsin legislature has not for a moment considered whether recent COVID conditions demand changes to the State's election rules; that body has not even met since April. And if there is one area where deference to legislators should not shade into acquiescence, it is election law. For in that field politicians' incentives often conflict with voters' interests—that is, whenever suppressing votes benefits the lawmakers who make the rules.

II

Justice Kavanaugh's concurring opinion goes further than the court of appeals. Rather than relying on *Purcell* and deference alone, he also concludes that Wisconsin's election rules, as applied during the COVID pandemic, do not violate the right to vote. That follows, in his view, because voting by mail is "easy" in Wisconsin and because in-person voting is "reasonably safe."

The first problem with that reasoning is that the district court found to the contrary. As this Court constantly states, a district court has the greatest familiarity with the facts in a case, because it oversees the development and presentation of evidence. That is why the court of appeals rightly did not question any of the lower court's findings. And why the concurrence is wrong to take a different tack.

Recall that the district court's findings include the following. The COVID pandemic has been getting worse and worse in Wisconsin. And as the State has "broken numerous new case records," in-person voting—according to credible expert testimony—creates a "significant [health] risk," especially for older and sicker citizens. For that reason, Wisconsinites have turned to the mails. According to the state elections commission, close to 2 million people are likely to request mail ballots. (That is about double the number of already-returned ballots that the concurrence chooses to emphasize.) State election offices have not received the resources they need to deal with that influx of applications, and severe administrative backlogs have therefore developed. Postal Service delays, detailed by both state and federal officials, compound the risk that voters will be unable to return timely requested mail ballots by Election Day. And if a voter discovers on Election Day that her mail ballot has not yet arrived, Wisconsin law prevents her from voting in person—even assuming she would undertake the risk. See Wis. Stat. § 6.86(6). All these facts would mean, as the chair of the Wisconsin Elections Commission testified, that many thousands of timely requested and postmarked votes—potentially into the six-figure range—would not be counted without a short extension of the ballot-receipt deadline.

The concurrence fails to give those findings the respect they are due. Of course, the concurrence *says* it is not committing that elementary error; according to Justice Kavanaugh, he disputes only the district court's "speculative predictions," not its statement of "historical facts." But the concurrence alternately rejects, ignores, or accepts only *pro forma* the district court's account of the facts. In responding to this dissent, the concurring opinion acknowledges that in-person voting in Wisconsin "can pose a health risk." Yet in condemning the injunction, it continues to insist—how else could it reach the decision it does?—that going to the polls is "reasonably safe" for Wisconsin's citizens, contrary to the expert testimony the district court relied on. Similarly, the concurrence nods glancingly to increased ballot applications, but it fails to recount (as the district court did in detail) how that influx has created heavy backlogs and prevented ballots from issuing in timely fashion. And it does not discuss the evidence of unusual, even unprecedented, delays in postal delivery service in Wisconsin. In short, the concurrence refuses to engage with the core of the analysis supporting the district court's injunction: that a veritable tsunami (in the form of a pandemic) has hit Wisconsin's election machinery, and disrupted all its usual mail ballot operations. And as to the supposedly "speculative prediction" that without the ballot-receipt extension as many as 100,000 timely cast mail votes would go uncounted? That estimate itself derived from the factual findings just listed, along with the credible testimony of the elections commission's chair—all matters indisputably entitled to deference from an appellate tribunal. Those findings, and not the concurrence's substitute facts purporting to show that voting in Wisconsin is safe and easy, should properly ground today's decision.[5]

A related flaw in the concurring opinion is how much it reasons from normal, pre-pandemic conditions. A "reasonable election deadline," the concurrence says, "does not disenfranchise voters." I have no argument with that statement, even though some voters may overlook the deadline. See *Rosario v. Rockefeller* (1973). But what is "reasonable" in one set of circumstances may become unreasonable in another. And when that switch occurs, a constitutional problem arises. So it matters not that Wisconsin could apply its ballot-receipt deadline when ballots moved rapidly through the mails and people could safely vote in person. At *this* time, neither condition holds—again, according to the district court's eminently believable findings. Today, mail ballots often travel at a snail's pace, and the elderly and ill put themselves in peril if they go to the polls. So citizens—thousands and thousands

5. Note as well that nothing rides on the exactness of the district court's estimate. Suppose that without the ballot-receipt extension, only (only?) half as many votes would be discarded as the district court thought. The court's decision would have remained the same, and so too everything I say here. But as for the concurrence? Who can know? Justice Kavanaugh does not reveal how many uncounted votes he thinks would violate the Constitution. Nor does he suggest how many votes short of that level will be discarded because of the Court's decision today.

of them—who have followed all the State's rules still cannot cast a successful vote. And because that is true, the ballot-receipt deadline that once survived constitutional review no longer does.[6]

That deadline, contrary to Justice Kavanaugh's view, now disenfranchises Wisconsin citizens—however much he objects to applying that term here. Far from using the word "rhetorically," I mean it precisely. During COVID, the State's ballot-receipt deadline and the Court's decision upholding it disenfranchise citizens by depriving them of their constitutionally guaranteed right to vote. Because the Court refuses to reinstate the district court's injunction, Wisconsin will throw out thousands of timely requested and timely cast mail ballots.[7]

NOTE: "LAST MINUTE" LITIGATION TO EXTEND POLLING HOURS

Even where there has been no "election eve" litigation, if long lines or other problems actually occur at polling places on Election Day, then there is also the possibility of lawsuits filed that day seeking to keep polls open later than their originally scheduled closing time. Many states have statutory provisions that require officials to permit voters who are standing in line at the time polls are scheduled to close to cast ballots that will be counted at the end of the day. But sometimes courts find this kind of provision inadequate: For example, if the problem that caused excessively long lines occurred early in the morning, when voters attempted to cast ballots before going to work, judges may wish to give these voters extra hours in the evening when they can show up to cast a ballot.

This kind of judicial extension of polling hours, however, can cause its own difficulties. If limited only to some precincts, does it give an extra advantage to voters in those precincts that is not available to voters in other precincts? Usually, a judicial order extending polling hours does not require that voters who take advantage of the extension show that they personally suffered the problem that triggered the extension. Thus, especially when they are limited to precincts where one political party has an advantage, this kind of extension can be abused: The favored party

6. The concurrence is wrong to view that conclusion as casting doubt on all similar deadlines in all other States. The district court rested its constitutional judgment, as I would too, on a confluence of factors: COVID conditions in Wisconsin, the scarce time between the State's ballot-application and ballot-receipt deadlines, evidence about in-state mail delivery and the administrative capacity of state election offices. In another State with all the same facts, the same result should obtain. But in another State with different facts—say, a less intense outbreak of COVID, an earlier ballot-application deadline, faster mail delivery, and better staffed and funded election offices—the constitutional analysis should come out a different way.

7. At the same time that Justice Kavanaugh defends this stance by decrying a "federal-judges-know-best vision of election administration," he calls for *more* federal court involvement in "reviewing state-court decisions about state [election] law." It is hard to know how to reconcile those two views about the federal judiciary's role in voting-rights cases. Contrary to Justice Kavanaugh's attempted explanation, neither the text of the Elections Clause nor our precedent interpreting it leads to his inconstant approach. See *Arizona State Legislature v. Arizona Independent Redistricting Comm'n* (2015); *Smiley v. Holm* (1932).

can target their Election Day campaigning to round up additional voters to cast ballots during the extended hours. Accordingly, HAVA requires any ballot cast pursuant to a judicial extension of polling hours to be a provisional ballot. Beyond that, state law can require the disqualification of these ballots if the extension was unwarranted.

For an example of a state-court decision that disapproved the extension of polling hours for those who were not already in line at the time the polls were scheduled to close, see *State ex rel. Bush-Cheney 2000, Inc. v. Baker*, 34 S.W.3d 410 (Mo. Ct. App. 2000). There the court rejected the problem of long lines as a justification for the extension of polling hours:

> Although the lines may be long and the number of working machines less than desirable, anyone in line at seven o'clock [the statutorily designated closing time] will eventually be permitted to vote no matter how late the hour and their vote will count. If any voters in line at seven o'clock are unwilling or unable to stay and vote, their inconvenience will not be lessened by extending the hours in which new voters can join the line. Extending the hours of voting simply permits voting by persons not entitled to vote due to their failure to come to the polls on time. [The trial court] has no authority to authorize voters who did not come to the polls during the hours established by the legislature to participate in the election.

D. *THE COUNTING OF BALLOTS*

1. *Ballot-Counting Disputes in the States*

There have been significant disputes over the counting of ballots since the 13 original states declared their independence from Britain. One major early dispute concerned New York's gubernatorial election of 1792. John Jay was willing to leave his position as the first Chief Justice of the United States to challenge the incumbent governor, George Clinton—a career move that shows the relative importance of the two offices at the time! America's first two-party system was beginning to emerge, with Jay representing the Federalists against the Jeffersonians (who were the forerunners of today's Democrats). The election was extremely close, as are all elections in which a dispute over the counting of specific ballots could make a difference in determining the winner. Jay would have won if ballots from Cooperstown, the future home of baseball's hall of fame, had been counted. But the town's ballots were disqualified by the state's canvassing committee, which split 7-4 along newly formed party lines. The reason the Jeffersonians gave for disqualifying the ballots was the fact that state law required the town's ballots to be delivered to the secretary of state by the local sheriff, but the Cooperstown sheriff's commission had expired and therefore he was no longer legally qualified to deliver the ballots (as he had done). The Federalists cried foul, believing that the election had been stolen from them based on a purely partisan pretext. They took to the streets, and for a while considered calling a new constitutional convention in the state to undo the result, but ultimately they acquiesced. The experience, however, left many of the Founders—above all Jay himself—believing that their own constitutional handiwork had been inadequate in a key moment in the life of a republic: when it is time to count ballots in a close election for a major office.*

Ballot-counting disputes that will determine the outcome of a major election continue to cause problems for state legal systems. Consider, for example, the dispute over the 2004 election for governor in the State of Washington. The dispute lasted seven months, until June 6, 2005, when the Republican candidate conceded after a state trial court rejected his challenge to the Democratic candidate's victory—a result that embittered many Republicans in the state.

A recount completed on December 30, 2004 showed the Democrat winning by just 127 votes, but the trial court found that 1,678 votes had been unlawfully cast and should not have been counted. (Most of these unlawful votes had been cast by felons, who were not entitled to participate in the election under Washington law. But several hundred were provisional ballots that should have been disqualified but were erroneously counted. There were also 19 ballots fraudulently cast on behalf of deceased voters, and six individuals who each illegally cast two ballots.)

The trial court, however, refused to order any remedy, neither voiding the election on the ground that the number of unlawful ballots far exceeded the Democrat's certified margin of victory, nor awarding the election to the Republican candidate based on a statistical calculation that most of the unlawful ballots had been cast in Democratic-leaning precincts. The trial court ruled, instead, that the Republican candidate was obligated to prove that enough unlawful ballots had actually been cast for the Democrat to erase the 127-vote margin. It did not matter that this burden of proof was a practical impossibility, as it would be extremely difficult for him to find and bring all of the unlawful voters to court and convince them to testify that they had voted illegally, and coercing them to testify would have violated the secrecy of the ballot by requiring them to testify under oath which candidate they supported. Absent this additional evidence, according to the trial court, the result of the election must stand even though the number of unlawful ballots was over ten times larger than the certified margin of victory.

Courts in other states would not necessarily agree with the Washington trial court's ruling. Reading precedents from around the country suggests that some state courts would be willing to void the election in this situation, whereas others might entertain the kind of statistical analysis that the Washington trial court refused to consider.

But one must be cautious when reading these other precedents because they did not involve a gubernatorial election, where the stakes are especially high. Even though the doctrine articulated in the precedents does not distinguish between gubernatorial and other types of elections, judges cannot help but be aware of the political context in which they adjudicate a particular ballot-counting dispute. When the consequence of voiding an election would leave a

* If you are interested in learning further details of this 1792 dispute (although doing so is not necessary for this introductory Election Law course), see Edward B. Foley, *The Founders' Bush v. Gore: The 1792 Election Dispute and Its Continuing Relevance*, 44 Ind. L. Rev. 23 (2010).

state without a newly elected governor, or would require the expense of holding another statewide vote, a state court may balk even if the state's most relevant judicial precedents would seem to require that result. Thus, as you read the following cases, ask yourself whether the opinions and outcomes would have been the same if the elections involved had been, like in Washington, for governor rather than a local office.

Gecy v. Bagwell

642 S.E.2d 569 (S.C. 2007)

Per Curiam [unanimous].

Appellant Tammy Bagwell, candidate for Simpsonville City Council, contested the results of the municipal election which resulted in respondent, Robert Gecy, being declared winner. The Simpsonville Election Commission ("Commission") invalidated the results and ordered a new election. The circuit court overturned the ruling of the Commission and reinstated Gecy as winner of the Simpsonville City Council seat. We reverse.

FACTS

On November 8, 2005, the city of Simpsonville held an election to fill three seats on its city council. The two candidates on the ballot for the Ward IV race were Bagwell and Gecy. The final vote tally was 430-427 in favor of Gecy, with one write-in vote for another individual.

On November 10, 2005, Bagwell filed a timely protest of the election. The Commission [after a hearing] decided that two illegal votes had been cast, and these votes rendered doubtful the result of the election. One of the illegal votes was cast by a voter who moved from her residence in one precinct to a residence in another precinct, and the other illegal vote came from a Simpsonville resident who voted in a precinct where his old business was located. The two illegal votes were subtracted from Gecy's total, leaving him with a total of 428 votes, preventing him from garnering a majority of the total votes cast [because Bagwell's 427 votes plus the one write-in equaled that number]. The Commission then ordered a new election.

Gecy appealed the Commission's ruling to the circuit court, [which] overturned the Commission. Bagwell appeals the order of the circuit court and seeks a new election for the contested seat.

ANALYSIS

Bagwell argues that the votes cast in the wrong precinct were illegal, and as a result, a new election should have been held. We agree.

In this case, two voters cast a ballot in a precinct where they previously were registered, but they no longer had a valid address in that precinct at the time of the election. Both parties agree that these two votes were not properly cast, and the question becomes whether these illegal votes should be thrown out, which would require a new election.

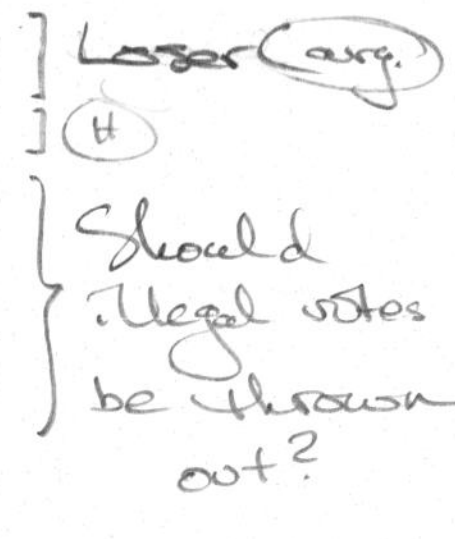

The election process is exclusively controlled by statute. S.C. Const. Art. II, § 10. We have recognized that perfect compliance with the election statutes is unlikely, and this Court will not nullify an election based on minor violations of technical requirements.

As a general rule, statutory provisions are mandatory when the statute expressly declares that a particular act is essential to the validity of an election. However, the Court may [also] deem such provisions to be mandatory, and thus non-compliance may nullify the results, when the provisions substantially affect the determination of the results, an essential element of the election, or the fundamental integrity of the election. Where there is a total disregard of the statute, the violation cannot be treated as an irregularity, but it must be held and adjudicated to be cause for declaring the election void and illegal. The Court will not sanction practices which circumvent the plain purposes of the law and open the door to fraud.

The use of precincts in our election process is a fundamental part of our statutory scheme. [The court cited various portions of the state's election code, including S.C. Code Ann. § 7-5-440 (Supp. 2005) (outlining specific procedures for voting by an elector who has moved to a new precinct but has not notified the county registration board).]

The disregard of the election statutes requiring electors to be residents of the precincts in which they vote, as well as failing to follow the procedure outlined in S.C. Code Ann. § 7-5-440 for those voters who have moved to a new precinct, constitutes more than a mere irregularity or illegality. The precinct system is an essential element of our voting process, and the failure of the two voters to adhere to the statutory requirements for registration and voting requires their votes to be rejected. Because the rejection of these two votes results in Gecy no longer carrying a majority of the total votes cast, a new election must be held.

Gecy also contends that S.C. Code Ann. § 7-13-810, which allows for post-election challenges based on after-discovered evidence, requires the protesting party to exercise due diligence in obtaining information that could have been acquired prior to the election. Gecy argues that because Bagwell could have determined before the election that the two illegal voters no longer lived in the precinct where they were registered, her protest fails because it was not based on after-discovered evidence. We disagree.

Although this Court has defined after-discovered evidence in other contexts, the applicable election statute clearly provides:

> A candidate may protest an election in which he is a candidate pursuant to 7-17-30 when the protest is based in whole or in part on evidence discovered after the election. This evidence may include, but is not limited to, after-discovered evidence of voters who have voted in a precinct or for a district office other than the one in which they are entitled by law to vote.

S.C. Code Ann. § 7-13-810. In this case, evidence of the two voters who cast their ballots in a precinct where they no longer resided qualifies as after-discovered evidence allowed by § 7-13-810. Even though Bagwell could have discovered the evidence on which she bases her challenge before the election, we decline to require a candidate to review all registration books and match each registered voter with his current address before the election.

CONCLUSION

We reverse the circuit court's decision to reinstate Gecy as the winner of the Simpsonville City Council seat. The two illegal votes cannot be counted, and a new election is required.

In re the Matter of the Protest of Election Returns and Absentee Ballots in the November 4, 1997 Election for the City of Miami, Florida

707 So.2d 1170 (Fla. Dist. Ct. App. 1998)

PER CURIAM.

This appeal involves an election contest [over Miami's 1997 election for mayor]. After considering the evidence, the lower tribunal issued a Final Judgment which found that the evidence demonstrated an extensive "pattern of fraudulent, intentional and criminal conduct that resulted in such an extensive abuse of the absentee ballot laws that it can fairly be said that the intent of these laws was totally frustrated." The lower court ordered that the appropriate remedy was to declare the entire Mayoral election void and order that a new election be held within sixty (60) days. While we find that substantial competent evidence existed to support the trial court's findings of massive fraud in the absentee ballots, we disagree as to the appropriateness of the trial court's remedy in ordering a new election.

On November 4, 1997, a general election was held for the position of Mayor, with Joe Carollo and Xavier Suarez as two of the contenders. Carollo received a majority of the precinct votes (51.41%) and Suarez received a majority of the absentee votes (61.48%), resulting in Carollo receiving 49.65% of the votes and Suarez receiving 46.80% of the votes when the absentee ballot votes were combined with the machine precinct votes.

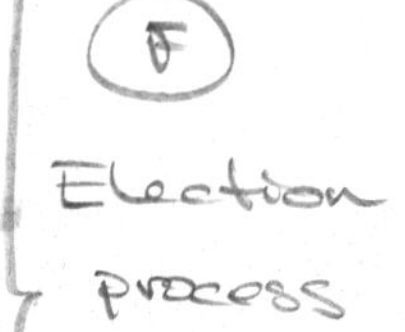

Since neither of the parties received a majority of the overall votes, a run-off election was held on November 13, 1997. In that election, Suarez defeated Carollo in both precinct votes and the absentee votes. On November 14, 1997, the results of the November 13, 1997, election were certified and Suarez assumed the position of Mayor. On the same day, Carollo filed a protest. The principal relief sought by Carollo was to be declared the victor of the Mayoral election, having received a majority of the "untainted" precinct votes or, in the alternative, for a new election.

A bench trial was held and, on March 3, 1998, the trial court declared the Mayoral election void. This judgment was based on the trial court's finding of massive absentee voter fraud which affected the electoral process.

The uncontradicted statistical evidence presented by Kevin Hill, Ph.D., a political scientist and expert in research methodology and statistical analysis, indicated that the amount of fraud involved in the absentee ballots was of such consequence so as to have affected the outcome of the election. Dr. Hill analyzed the absentee ballot voting, finding that the absentee ballots cast in Commission District 3 could not be explained by any normal statistical measurement. District 3 is the area which the trial court found "was the center of a massive, well conceived and well orchestrated absentee ballot voter fraud scheme." Dr. Hill referred to the results of the absentee ballots as an "outlier" and an "aberrant case" so unlikely that it was

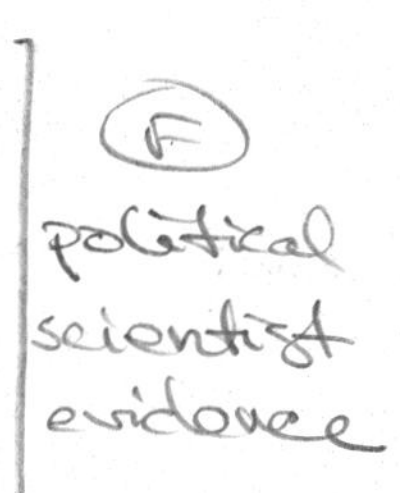

"literally off the charts" of probability tables. The odds of this occurring by chance were 5,000 to 1.

Dr. Hill finally concluded it was "reasonable" that the absentee ballot deviation in favor of Suarez resulted only from voting fraud, ruling "out almost every other conceivable possibility to a high degree of probability."[2]

An expert documents examiner, Linda Hart, concluded that 225 illegal absentee ballots were cast, in contravention of statutory requirements. An FBI agent with 26 years of experience, Hugh Cochran, identified 113 confirmed false voter addresses. There was evidence of 14 stolen ballots, and of 140 ballots that were falsely witnessed. In addition, evidence was presented that more than 480 ballots were procured or witnessed by the 29 so-called "ballot brokers" who invoked their privilege against self-incrimination instead of testifying at trial.

The trial court specifically found that the above described absentee ballot voter fraud scheme, "literally and figuratively, stole the ballot from the hands of every honest voter in the City of Miami." The trial court further found that, as a result thereof, "the integrity of the election was adversely affected." Based on our review of the record, there was certainly ample evidence of fraud to support the findings of the trial court's Final Judgment.

We are confronted with the question of whether the trial court erred in finding that the remedy for the instant absentee voting fraud was to order a new election. We hold that it did.

[In] *Bolden v. Potter* (Fla. 1984) [,] the Supreme Court of Florida expressly approve[d] the trial court's remedy, which was to invalidate all of the *absentee ballots* and, thereafter, to solely rely on the machine vote to determine the outcome of the election. Similarly, in *Boardman v. Esteva* (Fla. 1975), the Supreme Court of Florida held that "[T]he general rule is that where the number of invalid *absentee ballots* is more than enough to change the result of an election, then the election shall be determined solely upon the basis of machine vote." *Id.* (emphasis added).

We are mindful of the fact that the trial court found there was no evidence that Mr. Suarez knew of, or in any way participated in, the absentee voter fraud. However, as the Supreme Court stated in *Bolden v. Potter:*

> We also reject the district court's implication that the burden of proof, with regard to fraud or corruption, is dependent upon the status of the offender. It makes no difference whether the fraud is committed by candidates, election officials, or third parties. The evil to be avoided is the same, irrespective of the source. As long as the fraud, from whatever source, is such that the true result of the election cannot be ascertained with reasonable certainty, the ballots affected should be invalidated.

While we recognize that the above cases do not explicitly state that the exclusive remedy for massive absentee voter fraud is to determine the election solely based on machine vote, that form of remedy has historically been consistently approved since the 1930s. *See State ex rel. Whitley v. Rinehart* (Fla. 1939). In addition,

2. Dr. Hill estimated that the "aberrant" absentee ballots in Commission District 3 cost Mr. Carollo more than the 160 votes that he needed in order to secure outright victory in the November 4, 1997, election.

we note a complete absence of any Florida Appellate Court decision upholding the ordering of a new election in the face of such fraudulent conduct relating to absentee ballots. Mr. Suarez contends that to eliminate all of the absentee ballots would effectively disenfranchise those absentee voters who legally voted. We first note that unlike the right to vote, which is assured every citizen by the United States Constitution, the ability to vote by absentee ballot is a privilege. In fact, the Florida Legislature created this privilege by enacting statutory provisions separate from those applicable to voting at the polls. *See Bolden v. Potter* (expressly rejecting the contention that invalidating all absentee ballots, in the face of extensive absentee vote buying, was an unjustified disenfranchisement of those voters who cast legal ballots).

Consistent with the fact that there is no legal precedent in Florida to support the action of the trial court in ordering a new election as the proper remedy upon a finding of massive absentee voter fraud is the public policy of the State of Florida to not encourage such fraud. Rather, it must be remembered that the sanctity of free and honest elections is the cornerstone of a true democracy. As the Supervisor of Elections, David Leahy, noted during his trial testimony, were we to approve a new election as the proper remedy following extensive absentee voting fraud, we would be sending out the message that the worst that would happen in the face of voter fraud would be another election.

Further, we refuse to disenfranchise the more than 40,000 voters who, on November 4, 1997, exercised their constitutionally guaranteed right to vote in the polling places of Miami. In the absence of any findings of impropriety relating to the machine vote in this election, public policy dictates that we not void those constitutionally protected votes, the majority of which were cast for Mr. Carollo. In addition, a candidate who wins an election by virtue of obtaining a majority of the votes cast is entitled to take office as a result thereof, and not be forced into a second election, whether it is a statutorily mandated run-off election or a court ordered special election, when the said second election only comes about due to absentee ballot fraud, in the first election, that favored one of his or her opponents.

As a result, the voiding of the entire election and the ordering of a new election is hereby reversed, and this cause is remanded to the trial court with directions to enter a Final Judgment, forthwith, that voids and vacates the *absentee ballots only* and, furthermore, provides that the outcome of the November 4, 1997, City of Miami Mayoral election shall be determined solely upon the machine ballots cast at the polls, resulting in the election of Joe Carollo as Mayor of the City of Miami.

Huggins v. Superior Court

Supreme Court of Arizona 788 P.2d 81 (Ariz. 1990)

Noel FIDEL, Vice Chief Judge, Court of Appeals [sitting by designation, on behalf of unanimous court]:

In a contested primary election decided by an eight-vote margin, sixteen illegal votes were cast. The loser claims that the election must be set aside because one cannot know which of the candidates received the highest number of legal votes. We have taken jurisdiction to reexamine the law that governs elections when illegal votes exceed the margin of victory.

FACTS

In the 1988 primary election for Navajo County Attorney, petitioner Bret H. Huggins narrowly lost the Democratic Party nomination to Dale K. Patton. The Secretary of State reported that Patton had won by 3,593 votes to Huggins's 3,585. This eight-vote margin, however, was exceeded by sixteen votes illegally cast. Fifteen voters registered as independents or non–partisans had been improperly permitted to vote Democratic Party ballots. The sixteenth illegal voter was a convicted felon whose electoral rights were unrestored.

Huggins contested the election, but lost [in trial court] because he was unable to prove for whom the illegal votes were cast. Though he proved that illegal votes were cast in sufficient number to change the election result, he could not prove that they changed the result in fact.

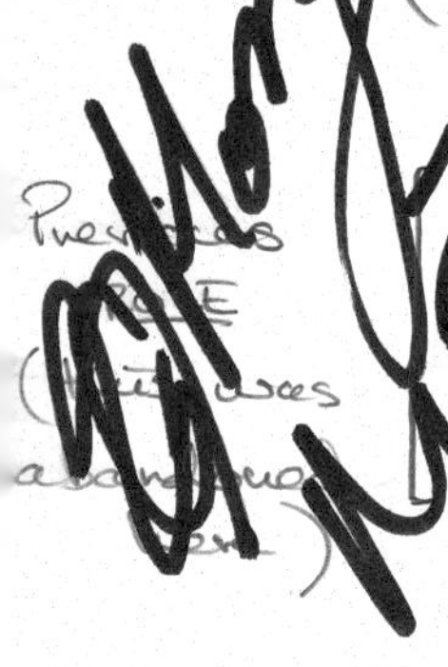

THE *MORGAN-MILLET* RULE

[Under prior Arizona precedent, known as *Morgan-Millet,* a candidate challenging the result of an election on the ground that the winner's margin of victory was smaller than the number of unlawful ballots cast, in addition to proving the illegality of disputed ballots, was required to prove for which candidate the disputed ballots were cast. In this respect, the *Morgan-Millet* rule was the same position as the one the trial court adopted in Washington's 2004 gubernatorial election, discussed above.]

In this case, the trial court criticized, but felt obliged to follow, the *Morgan-Millet* rule. Huggins now urges us to abandon that rule and to relieve election contestants of the burden of proving how illegal votes were cast. Huggins directs us to *Baggett v. State Election Board* (Okla. 1972), where, under circumstances similar to these, the Oklahoma Supreme Court nullified an election, stating:

> If election officials have not conducted an election according to law and knowingly permit non-registered Democrats to vote in a Democratic runoff primary election, the inexcusable conduct of the election officials should not inure to the benefit of any candidate either directly or indirectly.

The trial court described *Baggett* as having "the force of reason behind it," and Huggins urges us to make the Oklahoma approach our own.

We too see much reason in *Baggett.* Like the majority in that case, we recognize the inequity of burdening the challenger "to prove for which candidate the unlawful ballots were cast [in order] to be relieved from having the illegal ballots counted as legal ballots." *Id.* Moreover, the challenger's burden increases with the size of the unlawful vote. As Huggins argues persuasively, "it hardly seems fair that as the amount of illegal voting escalates, the likelihood of redressing the wrong diminishes."

There are additional difficulties with the *Morgan-Millet* rule, which stem from the need to prove how illegal votes were cast through the testimony of those who cast them. First, as Justice Jackson pointed out in concurrence in *Baggett,* voters who have cast unlawful ballots may choose to assert their fifth amendment privilege not to testify. Though an illegal voter might be motivated to maintain silence by a genuine fear of criminal sanctions, a supporter of the challenger's opponent might equally be motivated by the recognition that an invalid vote against the challenger would likely be cancelled only if the voter revealed how it was cast. Thus, the *Morgan-Millet* rule not only burdens a challenger onerously; it actually empowers partisans of the opposition to frustrate an election challenge and preserve illegal votes by exercising fifth amendment rights.

There is a second and related weakness to the *Morgan-Millet* rule. Voter disclosure testimony, even where offered, is highly suspect. Courts have long recognized this weakness when contemplating testimony by legal voters whose attempted votes were erroneously unrecorded. As the Utah Supreme Court stated:

> We know from common experience that those who do vote are usually unwilling that the character of their votes be made public, and that whenever there is an investigation as to the actual vote cast it is almost certain to bring about prevarication and uncertainty as to what the truth is. . . . The temptation to actual fraud and corruption on the part of the candidates and their political supporters is never so great as when it is known precisely how many votes it will take to change the result. . . .

Young v. Deming (Utah 1893); *see also Briscoe v. Between Consol. School Dist.* (Ga. 1931) ("[I]t would . . . be dangerous to receive and rely upon the subsequent statement of the voters as to their intentions, after it is ascertained precisely what effect their votes would have upon the result."). We concur in these comments and attribute comparable weakness to the testimony of illegal voters asked to disclose accomplished votes.

There is a third and especially troublesome problem associated with the *Morgan-Millet* rule: the prospect of judges compelling good faith voters who have cast invalid ballots to reveal what they supposed were private votes. The *McCavitt* opinion records the outrage of a voter so compelled: "I will not answer that question because, as far as I'm concerned, that is illegal. Nobody has the right to know who I voted for." *McCavitt v. Registrars of Voters* (Mass. 1982). Massachusetts rejects compelling voter testimony in these circumstances as "a kind of inquisitorial power unknown to the principles of our government and constitution." *Id.* This criticism strikes a responsive chord in Arizona, where our constitution explicitly assures secrecy in voting. We need not now determine whether, under any circumstances, our constitutional commitment to ballot secrecy might accommodate compelling good faith voters to disclose invalid votes. It is sufficient for present purposes to recognize the force of that commitment and to explore alternative solutions that permit us to avoid compulsion so offensive to democratic sensibilities and assumptions.

NULLIFICATION AND RESUBMISSION

The solution commended by Huggins is to nullify the contested election and to order a new election when, as here, a challenger has proven that the margin of victory is exceeded by the number of invalid votes. This solution, the one chosen in *Baggett* and *McCavitt*, permits the public a second effort to achieve a properly conducted election.

A second election, however, is not immune from illegal ballots and may prove no better than the first. Moreover, a second election is costly, and the costs are not limited to the heavy fiscal expense of running an election another time. Some votes will be lost in a second election that were properly recorded in the first; these include voters who have died, voters who have moved, and voters whose interest in the office or electoral issue is too attenuated to pull them to the polls a second time. Additionally,

> there may . . . be identifiable biases in second elections. Candidates with ready access to financing and with strong and continuing party organizations will be able to mobilize a second campaign in the short time available much more effectively than opponents who lack such advantages. Candidates with support concentrated among less active voters may be disadvantaged in a second election if such supporters do not turn out to cast ballots when only one office is at stake.

Note, *Developments in the Law: Elections*, 88 Harv. L. Rev. 1111, 1315 (1975).

These costs and biases make us hesitant to nullify first elections automatically upon proof that the winner's margin of victory was exceeded by the number of illegal votes.

THE *GROUNDS* RULE

[W]e find a better alternative in *Grounds v. Lawe* (Ariz. 1948). [There,] we considered whether the outcome would be altered by a proportionate, precinct-by-precinct extraction of the illegal votes. That is, for each district in which invalid votes were cast, we calculated a "pro rata deduction of the illegal votes according to the number of votes cast for the respective candidates in [that] election district." *Id.*[3] Because the illegal votes were insufficient, when extracted in this fashion, to change the election result, the victory of the declared winner was confirmed.

Grounds has also been cited with approval by the Supreme Court of Alaska, *Hammond v. Hickel* (Alaska 1978), and we reaffirm its application in this case.

We recognize an arbitrary element to proration. As we said in *Grounds:* "[T]he truth might be, if it could be shown, that all the illegal votes were on one side, while it is scarcely to be presumed that they would ever be divided between the candidates in exact proportion to their whole vote." [*Grounds*], quoting *McCrary on Elections,* 4th Ed., §§ 495-97. This element has led the Supreme Judicial Court of Massachusetts to reject proration in favor of nullification and resubmission to the voters "whenever the irregularity . . . of the election is such that the result . . . would be placed in doubt." *McCavitt.*

The Supreme Court of Alaska, however, has recognized that proration is a useful "analytical tool . . . for the limited purpose of determining whether . . . [there]

3. For example, consider a pair of hypothetical precincts with a mathematically convenient turnout of 100 voters in each. In the first precinct, Smith receives 60 votes, Jones receives 40, but 10 invalid votes are cast. Pro rata deduction would reduce Smith's tally by 6 votes (60% of the invalid votes) and Jones's tally by 4 (40%). In the second precinct, Jones wins 80 votes, Smith wins 20, but 5 invalid votes are cast. Here, pro rata deduction takes 4 of the invalid votes (80%) from Jones and 1 (20%) from Smith. Application of this method precinct-by-precinct is a neutral method to extract invalid ballots from the overall total.

were errors of sufficient magnitude to change the result. . . ." *Fischer v. Stout* (Alaska 1987). Alaska has not yet determined what it will do if a case arises where "the election result is put in doubt by application of the proportionate reduction rule." *Id.* Where, however, as in *Grounds,* proportionate reduction does not change the result, Alaska certifies the declared winner of the first election.

Huggins challenges the *Grounds* approach as constitutionally invalid. Article VII, § 7 of the Arizona Constitution, the source of Huggins's argument, provides: "in all elections held by the people in this state, the person, or persons, receiving the highest number of legal votes shall be declared elected." Huggins reasons from this provision that, because proration does not permit us to be certain who won the highest number of *legal* votes, it is constitutionally proscribed.

We disagree. The problem we confront is practical; the solution we choose is workable. The Arizona Constitution, in our view, permits us room to make this choice. While proration is imperfect, we lack the luxury of perfection, and proration strikes us as a sensible screening device in a multi-district case.[4] First, proration spares the body politic the offensive voter compulsion of the *Morgan-Millet* rule. Second, when limited as in *Fischer,* it permits us at least sometimes to avoid the cost and delay of a second election.

Moreover, though proration leaves some doubt that we have discovered the true winner, the other options fail to bring us nearer to that mark. The practical impact of the *Morgan-Millet* rule, with its virtually impossible burden on the challenger, is to let illegal votes count. The nullification remedy invalidates a multitude of first election legal votes, passes the choice to the inevitably different electorate that turns out for a second election, and accepts the second election biases and distortions earlier described. Proration, by comparison, has the virtue of neutrality; and in election contests, neutrality is a major constituent of fairness.

Like the Supreme Court of Alaska, we defer deciding what must be done when proration would change an election result. The law advances incrementally; we address the increment before us; the legislature may wish to consider the subject before we visit it again. For now, we reaffirm the *Grounds* approach as a limited screening device. When, as here, the margin of electoral victory is exceeded by the number of invalid votes and the invalid votes were cast in more than one precinct, the impact of those votes shall be tested by proportionate deduction. When, as here, proportionate reduction does not change the result, the declared victory may be confirmed.

CONCLUSION: PRORATION APPLIED

Proration in this case changes the tally in eight Navajo County precincts, taking six votes from Patton's overall tally and nine from that of Huggins. By this method Patton remains the winner with 3,587 votes to 3,576 for Huggins. Thus, we conclude that Huggins's election challenge was properly denied.

4. We observed in *Grounds* that proration can only work fairly where more than one district has undergone invalid ballots. Thus, we only announce a rule today for multi-district elections. We will deal with single district elections when the need arises.

NOTE ON THE VARIATION IN STATE LAW ON BALLOT-COUNTING DISPUTES

The above cases barely scratch the surface of the existing jurisprudence among state courts on how to resolve ballot-counting disputes.* One additional case worth a brief mention here is *Bauer v. Souto*, 896 A.2d 90 (Conn. 2006), in which the Supreme Court of Connecticut ordered a new citywide election even though the problem that triggered the dispute was confined to a specific polling location. One voting machine at that polling place had malfunctioned, failing to record votes cast on that machine for one of the candidates. Had the machine worked properly, it is likely (based on a statistical analysis) that the affected candidate would have won the city council election in which he was competing, but based on the votes actually recorded by the machine this candidate was not elected. The trial court ordered a revote in the electoral district served by the polling place where the machine had malfunctioned. The Connecticut Supreme Court, however, decided that it was necessary to hold an entirely new election among all voters eligible to vote for this city council seat, which happened to be the entire city since it was an "at-large" seat. The court reasoned that only a complete do-over of the original election was "consistent with the nature of elections [and] the democratic process."

Although the Connecticut Supreme Court based its decision on state rather than federal law, insofar as its reasoning was rooted in general philosophical principles about the nature of equal voting rights among members of the electorate in a democracy, this decision raises the question of whether it could have been based on the Equal Protection Clause of the Fourteenth Amendment to the U.S. Constitution, instead of on state law. In this respect, this case raises the more general question about what role federal law plays in resolving ballot-counting disputes. This federal law question can be asked with respect to any election, even for a state or local office (because the Fourteenth Amendment binds the states), but this issue is particularly germane to election for federal offices, especially the presidency—our next topic.

2. *The Federal Dimension to Disputed Elections: Historical Background*

The first presidential election involving a dispute over the counting of ballots occurred in 1876. (There had been a deadlocked presidential election in 1800, but that problem occurred because of the original design of the Electoral College, which caused Thomas Jefferson and his running mate Aaron Burr to receive the same number of Electoral Votes; it did not concern the counting of ballots cast by citizens to determine the presidential electors of a particular state.) The fight over the 1876 outcome primarily focused on ballots cast in three southern states: Florida, Louisiana, and South Carolina. Without any of these states, the Democratic

* For two systematic discussions in recent law review articles on this topic, see Steven F. Huefner, *Remedying Election Wrongs*, HARV. J. LEG. 265 (2007) and Joshua A. Douglas, *Procedural Fairness in Election Contests*, 88 IND. L.J. 1 (2013).

candidate, Samuel Tilden, was just one Electoral Vote shy of the majority necessary to win the presidency. Therefore, if Tilden could prevail in any of these three states, he would be President, whereas his Republican opponent, Rutherford Hayes, needed to prevail in all three to win.

The dispute ended up being decided by a specially created Electoral Commission of 15 members. The plan had been for the Commission to have seven Democrats, seven Republicans, and one independent. But the person intended to be the independent, Justice David Davis of the U.S. Supreme Court, declined to serve, and the congressional statute creating the Commission required that his replacement be another Supreme Court justice. There was, however, no other justice who was perceived as genuinely independent, and Justice Joseph Bradley was chosen as the most moderate Republican available on the Court.

When it came time for the Commission to decide the dispute over the ballots in each of the three states, the Commission split 8-7 each time on a straight party-line vote, with Bradley siding with his fellow Republicans to give all three states to Hayes. Although Bradley professed to base his decision on principle rather than partisanship, Democrats at the time saw it otherwise and began referring to President Hayes as "His Fraudulency." From our historical vantage point, it seems less important to determine whether Bradley reached the right decision, or even whether he acted in good faith—the legal issues involved were very complicated—than it is to observe that the design of the Electoral Commission was flawed given its purpose. Since the goal had been to create the Commission with a neutral tiebreaker, the plan failed once the Commission lost its genuinely independent member.

Whether because of this experience with the 1876 election or otherwise, the U.S. Supreme Court tended to stay out of ballot-counting disputes during the twentieth century, despite the efforts of candidates to invoke the Court's jurisdiction by claiming that a state's method of counting ballots violated the Fourteenth Amendment. In 1900, at the very beginning of the century, the Court ruled in *Taylor v. Beckham*, 178 U.S. 548 (1900), that a gubernatorial candidate could not claim a Fourteenth Amendment violation even when alleging systematic ballot-counting fraud in favor of his opponent. The case involved a particularly ugly dispute over Kentucky's election for governor, during which one of the candidates was assassinated. The consequence of the Court's refusal to intervene was that the state's own handling of the ballot-counting dispute would prevail no matter how fraudulent or antidemocratic it might be. The prophetic Justice John Marshall Harlan, who came from Kentucky and was the lone dissenter in *Plessy v. Ferguson*, 163 U.S. 537 (1896) (the railroad segregation case that accepted "separate but equal" as constitutional), also dissented alone in *Taylor v. Beckham*. "[T]he overturning of the public will, as expressed at the ballot box, . . . in order to accomplish partisan ends, is a crime against free government, and deserves the execration of all lovers of liberty," Justice Harlan decried. "I cannot believe the judiciary is helpless in the presence of such a crime," he added, making it clear he would have made an honest and accurate count of ballots one of the "rights protected by the 14th Amendment of the Constitution of the United States."

At mid-century, Justice Harlan's view was again rebuffed in the infamous primary election between Lyndon Johnson and Coke Stevenson to determine the Democratic Party's nominee for U.S. Senator from Texas in 1948. Certified returns showed Johnson ahead by a mere 87 votes, and there was damning evidence that 200 entirely fabricated votes for Johnson had been added to the tally sheet for one ballot box—the notorious Ballot Box 13—from one local county under the control of a political boss loyal to Johnson. Believing he could not receive a fair hearing in state court, Coke Stevenson went to federal court claiming that the stuffing of Ballot Box 13 violated the Fourteenth Amendment. The local federal judge was willing to hear the claim and was in the process of examining the evidence when Johnson secured an order from Justice Hugo Black to halt the proceedings on the ground that the federal judiciary had no business involving itself in a state's ballot-counting dispute. Johnson's 87-vote victory thus withstood Stevenson's judicial attack, thereby giving Johnson his nickname "Landslide Lyndon" and propelling him into national politics. The principle upon which Justice Black based his order was the same one that had prevailed a half-century earlier in *Taylor v. Beckham*: The Fourteenth Amendment does not provide a basis for the federal judiciary to supervise ballot-counting by a state, no matter how egregiously flawed and undemocratic the state's ballot-counting may be.

Thus was the prevailing jurisprudence on this point at mid-century, before the Reapportionment Revolution of *Baker v. Carr* and *Reynolds v. Sims*. Those new precedents from the 1960s, along with *Harper* and *Kramer*, laid the foundation for a new voting-rights jurisprudence that ultimately would have implications for ballot-counting cases.

These implications developed slowly and did not command the U.S. Supreme Court's attention until the 2000 presidential election. In 1978, for example, the U.S. Court of Appeals for the First Circuit ruled that Rhode Island had violated the Due Process Clause of the Fourteenth Amendment when its election officials, at the secretary of state's direction, encouraged voters to use absentee ballots but the state supreme court later refused to count them on the ground that the voters were not entitled to vote absentee. *Griffin v. Burns*, 570 F.2d 1065 (1st Cir. 1978). Then, in a case stemming from Alabama's 1994 election for Chief Justice of its supreme court, the U.S. Court of Appeals for the Eleventh Circuit found a Due Process violation when that same supreme court (other members having decided not to recuse themselves) ruled in favor of counting absentee ballots that previously would have been disqualified under Alabama law. *See Roe v. Alabama*, 43 F.3d 574 (announcing standard pretrial), 68 F.3d 404 (applying standard posttrial) (11th Cir. 1995).

Consequently, when the dispute over counting ballots in the 2000 presidential election reached the U.S. Supreme Court, there was an unresolved tension between two strands of jurisprudence. First was the longstanding principle of federal court nonintervention in these disputes, going back at least a century to *Taylor v. Beckham*. But second was the small but increasing corpus of case law among federal courts of appeals that the Fourteenth Amendment, as understood in the wake of the Warren Court's voting rights precedents from the 1960s, authorized limited federal-court intervention in state ballot-counting controversies to avoid deviations from "fundamental fairness" (in the words of both the *Burns* and *Roe* courts). The 2000 presidential election would cause the nine Justices of the U.S. Supreme Court to decide which of these two strands of jurisprudence each of them would embrace, and they would need to make this momentous decision working at what amounted to lightning speed under the glare of national spotlight as intense as it has ever been.

3. *The 2000 Presidential Election: Preliminary Proceedings*

The dispute over ballots in the 2000 presidential election ended with the U.S. Supreme Court's 5-4 ruling in *Bush v. Gore* on December 12 to halt any further recounting of ballots in Florida, and Al Gore's concession speech the next night. But to better understand the Court's ruling, as well as the four dissents from it, it helps to review the five weeks that occurred between the casting of ballots and the Court's decision, as well as the legal context from which the case arose. What follows is necessarily abbreviated. For those who want more, the most riveting account is Jeffery Toobin's *Too Close to Call* (2001), although it arguably tells the story from a pro-Gore perspective. Likewise, HBO's film *Recount* nicely dramatizes the events, but it too tilts in a pro-Gore direction. (A timeline summarizing key events in this chronology appears right before the opinions in *Bush v. Gore*, on page 729 below.)

As the nation watched the election returns on the night of Tuesday, November 7, it became clear that whichever candidate, George W. Bush or Al Gore, won Florida would win a majority of the Electoral College and thus the presidency. But despite the desire for a snap judgment on which candidate won Florida—the networks first called the state for Gore, then called it for Bush, and then in the early hours of the next morning left it "too close to call"—the candidates quickly realized that the outcome would depend on whether there were enough additional Gore ballots that had been cast but not yet counted to overcome Bush's miniscule lead (which stood at 327 on Friday, November 10, after ballots had been retabulated by vote-counting machines).

Figure 4-1

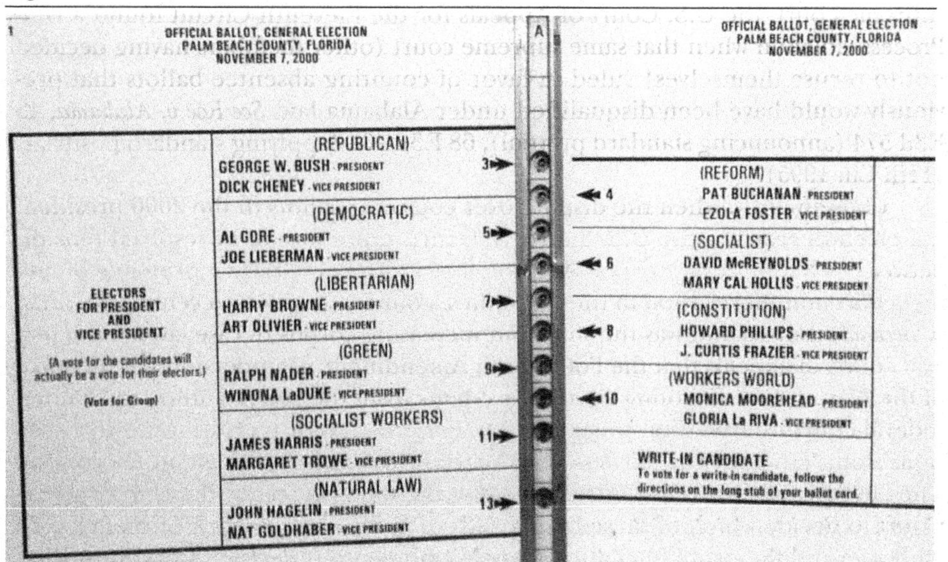

OFFICIAL BALLOT, GENERAL ELECTION
PALM BEACH COUNTY, FLORIDA
NOVEMBER 7, 2000

ELECTORS FOR PRESIDENT AND VICE PRESIDENT
(A vote for the candidates will actually be a vote for their electors.)
(Vote for Group)

(REPUBLICAN)
GEORGE W. BUSH - PRESIDENT
DICK CHENEY - VICE PRESIDENT 3

(DEMOCRATIC)
AL GORE - PRESIDENT
JOE LIEBERMAN - VICE PRESIDENT 5

(LIBERTARIAN)
HARRY BROWNE - PRESIDENT
ART OLIVIER - VICE PRESIDENT 7

(GREEN)
RALPH NADER - PRESIDENT
WINONA LaDUKE - VICE PRESIDENT 9

(SOCIALIST WORKERS)
JAMES HARRIS - PRESIDENT
MARGARET TROWE - VICE PRESIDENT 11

(NATURAL LAW)
JOHN HAGELIN - PRESIDENT
NAT GOLDHABER - VICE PRESIDENT 13

OFFICIAL BALLOT, GENERAL ELECTION
PALM BEACH COUNTY, FLORIDA
NOVEMBER 7, 2000

4 (REFORM)
PAT BUCHANAN - PRESIDENT
EZOLA FOSTER - VICE PRESIDENT

6 (SOCIALIST)
DAVID McREYNOLDS - PRESIDENT
MARY CAL HOLLIS - VICE PRESIDENT

8 (CONSTITUTION)
HOWARD PHILLIPS - PRESIDENT
J. CURTIS FRAZIER - VICE PRESIDENT

10 (WORKERS WORLD)
MONICA MOOREHEAD - PRESIDENT
GLORIA La RIVA - VICE PRESIDENT

WRITE-IN CANDIDATE
To vote for a write-in candidate, follow the directions on the long stub of your ballot card.

A variety of fascinating but ultimately tangential issues emerged during the five-week fight—including the controversy over the "butterfly ballot," which apparently caused thousands of elderly voters to mistakenly vote for Pat Buchanan rather than Al Gore (but for which there was no easy remedy available). See Figure 4-1 for an image of the butterfly ballot. But the dispute soon focused on the fact that the voting machines had not counted many thousands of punch-card ballots because the "chads" that the voters were supposed to punch out of the ballots to indicate their choices had not been completely dislodged and therefore the vote was not "readable" by the machine. Some of these chads had been left "hanging" (see Figure 4-2), whereas others were punctured (and thus would let light through the punch-card ballot), whereas still others were merely dimpled or "pregnant," to invoke one of the terms used at the time.

The legal question was whether any of these ballots, uncountable by machines, were still entitled to be counted in a recount conducted by hand and, if so, according to what standard. For example, should only "hanging chads" count according to a "two-corner" rule, which required a chad to be partially dislodged so that at least two corners were swinging free from the ballot itself? Or should any punctured chad count according to an examination that puts the ballot up to a light? Or should the standard even more generously permit the counting of any dimpled or "pregnant" chad, at least where the ballot contains no contrary indication that the voter did not wish to cast a vote for the candidate indicated by this indented chad?

Figure 4-2

Reprinted with permission from Professor Ted Herman at the University of Iowa.

When Gore's legal team initially confronted the issue of these uncounted punch-card ballots, there seemed to be two procedural avenues available in which to pursue a possible recount. The first, called a "protest" under Florida law at the time, was an administrative proceeding by which the candidate could ask each county in the state to conduct a manual recount before certification of the election's results. The second, called a "contest" under state law, was a judicial proceeding that challenged the administrative certification on the ground that it was erroneous. On Thursday, November 9, Gore decided to go the first route, in the hope of preventing Bush from achieving a certified victory, and Gore specifically asked for a manual administrative recount of uncounted ballots in four Florida counties that voted heavily in favor of Democratic candidates.

Two problems with this strategy emerged, however, at least from the perspective of those seeking the counting of additional votes. One was the fact that Florida's statutes specified a deadline of Tuesday, November 14—one week after Election Day—by which counties were required to submit their certified returns to the Secretary of State (to be accumulated into a single statewide certified result). That one-week deadline proved to be too tight for the urban counties that Gore most wanted to conduct a manual recount. Second, in an administrative "protest," Florida's statutes did not mandate that the counties conduct a manual recount but instead gave the counties the discretion to do so. As Gore would learn, Miami/Dade County would choose to exercise its discretion against completing a manual recount.

Gore nonetheless decided to fight the deadline. On the day of the deadline, he secured a ruling from respected state judge Terry Lewis that Secretary of State Katherine Harris must at least consider a county's reasons for conducting a manual recount past the statutory deadline. But on Friday, November 17 (the final date for receipt of military and overseas absentee ballots and thus the earliest date for an official statewide certification of the election results), Judge Lewis ruled that Secretary of State Harris need not accept a county's explanation for missing the statutory deadline. Later that same day, however, the Florida Supreme Court ordered that Secretary Harris must not certify a final result of the election absent further order of that court. Then on Tuesday, November 21 (two weeks after Election Day), the seven-member Florida Supreme Court released a unanimous opinion extending the deadline for final certification to Sunday, November 26, and requiring that the state include any manual recounts conducted by that deadline in the final certification.

Bush's legal team viewed the Florida Supreme Court's decision as a partisan distortion of the relevant statutory language, by judges who were Democrats and, thus, Gore supporters. Two statutory provisions, although in tension with each other, seemed contrary to the Florida Supreme Court's decision. One, Section 102.111, using the mandatory word "shall," required Secretary Harris to "ignore" late-filed returns: "If the county returns are not received by the Department of State by 5 p.m. of the seventh day following an election, all missing counties *shall be ignored*, and the results shown by the returns on file shall be certified." (Emphasis added.) The other, Section 102.112, permitted Secretary Harris to ignore late-filed returns: "If the returns are not received by the department by the time specified, such returns *may be ignored* and the results on file at that time may be certified by the department." (Emphasis added.) Neither statutory provision, however, *prohibited* Secretary Harris from ignoring late-filed returns after a manual recount, yet that result is precisely what the Florida Supreme Court's decision achieved.

The Florida Supreme Court justified its decision by observing that the state's statutory laws contemplated the possibility of a manual recount, which can be time consuming. But Bush's lawyers saw this justification as another distortion of the statutory scheme. In their view, a manual recount was unnecessary as long as the punch-card voting machines were functioning as designed, and the machines were working properly because they could not be expected to record votes when the chads had not been completely dislodged. Moreover, because a manual recount was discretionary under the statute, the Bush team believed that the counties were obligated to exercise their discretion in a way that satisfied the explicit statutory deadline.

The Bush team, however, faced a difficulty. While their side may have had the better argument in terms of interpreting the relevant state statutes, the Florida Supreme Court was the highest judicial authority on the meaning of Florida's statutory law, and that court had ruled against them. Bush could only go to the U.S. Supreme Court on a question of federal law. Bush's lawyers then developed a federal argument based on Article II of the U.S. Constitution, which provides: "Each State shall appoint, *in such Manner as the Legislature thereof may direct*, a Number of Electors, equal to the whole Number of Senators and Representatives to which the State may be entitled in the Congress." (Emphasis added.) Bush's argument was that because the state's *legislature* decides how to appoint the state's presidential electors, an interpretation of the legislative command by a state's supreme court that is so far off the mark as to undo the legislature's decision is a violation of Article II.

To the surprise of many observers, on Friday, November 24, the U.S. Supreme Court agreed to consider this argument. But after hearing the case on the next Friday, December 1, the nine Justices unanimously decided on the following Monday, December 4, to send the case back to the Florida Supreme Court for clarification. *Bush v. Palm Beach Canvassing Bd.*, 531 U.S. 70 (2000). The "per curiam" opinion for the Court hinted that the Justices, or at least a majority of them, were disturbed by the Florida Supreme Court's statutory interpretation: "There are expressions in the opinion of the Supreme Court of Florida that may be read to indicate that it construed the Florida Election Code without regard to the extent to which the Florida Constitution could, consistent with [Article II] circumscribe the legislative power." *Id.* at 77.

The Justices also wondered whether Florida wished to take advantage of the so-called "Safe Harbor Provision," 3 U.S.C. § 5, which purports to bind Congress to a state's resolution of a dispute over the counting of ballots cast by its citizens in a presidential election if the state's method of resolving the dispute meets certain conditions. Enacted by Congress as part of the Electoral Count Act of 1887 in the aftermath of the disputed Hayes-Tilden election, this Safe-Harbor Provision encourages states to resolve these disputes so that Congress can avoid the kind of unhappy ending that occurred with the Electoral Commission's partisan 8-7 decision. Specifically, if *before ballots are cast* a state's legislature establishes a procedure

Figure 4-3

to handle these disputes, and if by using that procedure the state resolves a dispute *six days before the meeting of the presidential Electors*, then that resolution "shall be conclusive" when Congress meets to count and announce the Electoral votes from each state.

In 2000, the meeting of the presidential Electors was scheduled for Monday, December 18, which made Tuesday, December 12 the Safe-Harbor Deadline. Seeing that Florida was running out of time when the U.S. Supreme Court remanded the controversy on December 1, and noting that taking advantage of the Safe-Harbor Provision required following the dictates of Florida's statutory law as it stood before the casting of ballots began, the nine Justices observed: "a legislative wish to take advantage of the 'safe harbor' would counsel against any construction of the Election Code that Congress might deem to be a change in the law."

Meanwhile, back in Florida, after the Florida Supreme Court's ruling on November 21, the manual recount continued in three of the four counties where Gore had requested them (the fourth had already finished). But the very next day, Miami-Dade County decided to stop its recount after the so-called "Brooks Brother riot," in which Republican activists protested what they perceived as the unfairness of the county's recount proceedings (including the fact that the recount was occurring behind closed doors, out of public view). When the Florida Supreme Court's November 26 deadline arrived, there was no Miami-Dade recount to include, and Palm Beach County had missed the deadline by two hours. Secretary of State Harris, excluding Palm Beach County's late return, certified Bush's slate of presidential Electors as victorious by 537 citizen-cast ballots.

Gore, having hoped to avoid a post-certification judicial "contest" by prevailing in the administrative "protest," now had no choice but to file a judicial contest, which he did on Monday, November 27. The state trial judge, Sander Sauls, held a trial of the contest over the weekend of December 2 and 3. On Monday, December 4 (the same day as the U.S. Supreme Court's remand of the protest case, which had become essentially moot since the post-certification contest was underway), Judge Sauls rejected Gore's claim that the certified result wrongfully excluded valid votes that had been lawfully cast. Judge Sauls accepted the Bush team's position that counties were not required to retrieve attempted votes that their voting machines were unable to read because the voters had not fully dislodged the chads. Gore immediately appealed, and on Friday, December 8, the Florida Supreme Court issued the following decision to require all counties (not just the four that Gore wanted) to conduct a manual recount of all ballots where the voting machine had failed to record a vote for president. This time, however, the Florida Supreme Court was not unanimous, but instead split 4-3. As you read this decision, and the dissents from it, imagine how the nine Justices of the U.S. Supreme Court perceived it when this decision came before them for their review in *Bush v. Gore.*

Gore v. Harris

772 So. 2d 1243 (Fla. 2000)

PER CURIAM.

Although we find that the appellants are entitled to reversal in part of the trial court's order and are entitled to a manual count of the Miami-Dade County undervote, we agree with the appellees that the ultimate relief would require a counting of the legal votes contained within the undervotes in all counties where the undervote has not been subjected to a manual tabulation.

I

[Omitted.]

II. APPLICABLE LAW

This case today is controlled by the language set forth by the Legislature in section 102.168, Florida Statutes (2000). Indeed, an important part of the statutory election scheme is the State's provision for a contest process, section 102.168, which laws were enacted by the Legislature prior to the 2000 election. Although courts are, and should be, reluctant to interject themselves in essentially political controversies, the Legislature has directed in section 102.168 that an election contest shall be resolved in a judicial forum.

In carefully construing the contest statute, no single statutory provision will be construed in such a way as to render meaningless or absurd any other statutory provision. In interpreting the various statutory components of the State's election process, then, a common-sense approach is required, so that the purpose of the statute is to give effect to the legislative directions ensuring that the right to vote will not be frustrated.

Section 102.168(3) outlines the grounds for contesting an election, and includes: "Receipt of a number of illegal votes or *rejection of a number of legal votes sufficient to change or place in doubt the result of the election.*" § 102.168(3)(c) (emphasis added). Although the right to contest an election is created by statute, it has been a long-standing right since 1845 when the first election contest statute was enacted. As is well established in this State by our contest statute, "[t]he right to a correct count of the ballots in an election is a substantial right which it is the privilege of every candidate for office to insist on, in every case where there has been a failure to make a *proper count,* call, tally, or return of the votes as required by law, and this fact has been duly established as the basis for granting such relief." *State ex rel. Millinor v. Smith* (Fla. 1932) (emphasis added). The Staff Analysis of the 1999 legislative amendment expressly endorses this important principle. Similarly, the Florida House of Representatives Committee on Election Reform 1997 Interim Project on Election Contests and Recounts expressly declared:

> Recounts are an integral part of the election process. For one's vote, when cast, to be translated into a true message, that vote must be accurately counted, and if necessary, recounted. The moment an individual's vote becomes subject to error in the vote tabulation process, the easier it is for that vote to be diluted.
>
> Furthermore, with voting statistics tracing a decline in voter turnout and in increase in public skepticism, every effort should be made to ensure the integrity of the electoral process.
>
> Integrity is particularly crucial at the tabulation stage because many elections occur in extremely competitive jurisdictions, where very close election results are always possible. In addition, voters and the media expect rapid and accurate tabulation of election returns, regardless of whether the election is close or one sided. Nonetheless, when large numbers of votes are to be counted, it can be expected that some error will occur in tabulation or in canvassing.

It is with the recognition of these legislative realities and abiding principles that we address whether the trial court made errors of law in rendering its decision.

III. ORDER ON REVIEW

Vice President Gore claims that the trial court erred in the following three ways: (1) The trial court held that an election contest proceeding was essentially an appellate proceeding where the County Canvassing Board's decision must be reviewed with an "abuse of discretion," rather than "de novo," standard of review; (2) The court held that in a contest proceeding in a statewide election a court must review all the ballots cast throughout the state, not just the contested ballots; (3) The court failed to apply the legal standard for relief expressly set forth in section 102.168(3)(c).

A. The Trial Court's Standard of Review

The Florida Election Code sets forth a two-pronged system for challenging vote returns and election procedures. The "protest" and "contest" provisions are distinct proceedings. A protest proceeding is filed with the County Canvassing Board and addresses the validity of the vote returns. The relief that may be granted includes a manual recount. A contest proceeding, on the other hand, is filed in circuit court and addresses the validity of the election itself. Relief that may be granted is varied and can be extensive. No appellate relationship exists between a "protest" and a "contest"; a protest is not a prerequisite for a contest. Moreover, the trial court in the contest action does not sit as an appellate court over the decisions of the Canvassing Board. Accordingly, while the Board's actions concerning the elections process may constitute evidence in a contest proceeding, the Board's decisions are not to be accorded the highly deferential "abuse of discretion" standard of review during a contest proceeding.

In applying the abuse of discretion standard of review to the Boards' actions, the trial court relinquished an improper degree of its own authority to the Boards. This was error.

B. Must All the Ballots be Counted Statewide?

Appellees contend that even if a count of the undervotes in Miami-Dade were appropriate, section 102.168, Florida Statutes (2000), requires a count of all votes in Miami-Dade County and the entire state [including overvotes, where a machine recorded more than one vote for a particular office on a ballot and thus voided those multiple votes] as opposed to a selected number of votes challenged. However, the plain language of section 102.168 refutes appellees' argument.

[S]ection 102.168(3)(c) explicitly contemplates contests based upon a "rejection of a number of legal votes sufficient to change the outcome of an election." Logic dictates that to bring a challenge based upon the rejection of a specific number of legal votes under section 102.168(3)(c), the contestant must establish the "number of legal votes" which the county canvassing board failed to count. This number, therefore, under the plain language of the statute, is limited to the votes identified and challenged under section 102.168(3)(c), rather than the entire county. Moreover, counting uncontested votes in a contest would be irrelevant to a determination of whether certain uncounted votes constitute legal votes that have been rejected.

We do agree, however, that it is absolutely essential in this proceeding and to any final decision, that a manual recount be conducted for all legal votes in this State, not only in Miami-Dade County, but in all Florida counties where there was an undervote and, hence, a concern that not every citizen's vote was counted. This election should be determined by a careful examination of the votes of Florida's citizens and not by strategies extraneous to the voting process. This essential principle, that the outcome of elections be determined by the will of the voters, forms the foundation of the election code enacted by the Florida Legislature and has been consistently applied by this Court in resolving elections disputes.

When an election contest is filed under section 102.168, Florida Statutes (2000), the contest statute charges the trial judge to:

> fashion such orders as he or she deems necessary to ensure that each allegation in the complaint is *investigated, examined, or checked,* to prevent or correct any alleged wrong, and to provide any relief appropriate under such circumstances.

Id. (emphasis added). Through this statute, the Legislature has granted trial courts broad authority to resolve election disputes and fashion appropriate relief. In turn, this Court, consistent with legislative policy, has pointed to the "will of the voters" as the primary guiding principle to be utilized by trial courts in resolving election contests. *Boardman v. Esteva* (Fla. 1975). For example, the Legislature has mandated that no vote shall be ignored "if there is a clear indication of the intent of the voter" on the ballot, unless it is "impossible to determine the elector's choice." § 101.5614(5)-(6) Fla. Stat. (2000). Section 102.166(7), Florida Statutes (2000), also provides that the focus of any manual examination of a ballot shall be to determine the voter's intent. The clear message from this legislative policy is that every citizen's vote be counted whenever possible, whether in an election for a local commissioner or an election for President of the United States.[11]

The demonstrated problem of not counting legal votes inures to any county utilizing a counting system which results in undervotes and "no registered vote" ballots. In a countywide election, one would not simply examine such categories of ballots from a single precinct to ensure the reliability and integrity of the countywide vote. Similarly, in this statewide election, review should not be limited to less than all counties whose tabulation has resulted in such categories of ballots. Relief would not be "appropriate under [the] circumstances" if it failed to address the "otherwise valid exercise of the right of a citizen to vote" of all those citizens of this State who, being similarly situated, have had their legal votes rejected. This is particularly important in a presidential election, which implicates both state and uniquely important national interests. The contestant here satisfied the threshold requirement by demonstrating that, upon consideration of the thousands of undervote or "no registered vote" ballots presented, the number of legal votes therein were sufficient to at least place in doubt the result of the election. However, a final decision as to the result of the statewide election should only be determined upon consideration of the legal votes contained within the undervote or "no registered vote" ballots of all Florida counties, as well as the legal votes already tabulated.

C. The Plaintiff's Burden of Proof

It is immediately apparent, in reviewing the trial court's ruling here, that the trial court failed to apply the statutory standard and instead applied an improper standard in determining the contestant's burden under the contest statute. The trial court began its analysis by stating:

> It is not enough to show a reasonable possibility that election results could have been altered by such irregularities, or inaccuracies, rather, a reasonable probability that the results of the election would have been changed must be shown.

11. The Legislature has not, beyond granting to Florida's voters the right to select presidential electors, indicated in any way that it intended that a different (and unstated) set of election rules should apply to the selection of presidential electors. Of course, because the selection and participation of Florida's electors in the presidential election process is subject to a stringent calendar controlled by federal law, the Florida election law scheme must yield in the event of a conflict. [Footnote relocated. —EDS.]

This analysis overlooks and fails to recognize the specific and material changes to the statute which the Legislature made in 1999 that control these proceedings. While the earlier version, like the current version, provided that a contestant shall file a complaint setting forth "the grounds on which the contestant intends to establish his or her right to such office or set aside the result of the election," the prior version did not specifically enumerate the "grounds for contesting an election under this section." Those grounds, as contained in the 1999 statute, now explicitly include, in subsection (c), the "[r]eceipt of a number of illegal votes or rejection of a number of legal votes sufficient to change *or place in doubt* the result of the election." (Emphasis supplied.) Assuming that reasonableness is an implied component of such a doubt standard, the determination of whether the plaintiff has met his or her burden of proof to establish that the result of an election is in doubt is a far different standard than the "reasonable probability" standard, which was applicable to contests under the old version of the statute, and erroneously applied and articulated as a "preponderance of a reasonable probability" standard by the trial court here. A person authorized to contest an election is required to demonstrate that there have been legal votes cast in the election that have not been counted (here characterized as "undervotes" or "no vote registered" ballots) and that available data shows that a number of legal votes would be recovered from the entire pool of the subject ballots which, if cast for the unsuccessful candidate, would change or place in doubt the result of the election. Here, there has been an undisputed showing of the existence of some 9000 "undervotes" in an election contest decided by a margin measured in the hundreds. Thus, a threshold contest showing that the result of an election has been placed in doubt, warranting a manual count of all undervotes or "no vote registered" ballots, has been made.

LEGAL VOTES

Having first identified the proper standard of review, we turn now to the allegations of the complaint filed in this election contest. To test the sufficiency of those allegations and the proof, it is essential to understand what, under Florida law, may constitute a "legal vote," and what constitutes rejection of such vote.

Section 101.5614(5), Florida Statutes (2000), provides that "[n]o vote shall be declared invalid or void if there is a clear indication of the intent of the voter as determined by the canvassing board." Section 101.5614(6) provides, conversely, that any vote in which the board cannot discern the intent of the voter must be discarded. Lastly, section 102.166(7)(b) provides that, "[i]f a counting team is unable to determine a voter's intent in casting a ballot, the ballot shall be presented to the county canvassing board for it to determine the voter's intent." This legislative emphasis on discerning the voter's intent is mirrored in the case law of this State, and in that of other states.

This Court has repeatedly held, in accordance with the statutory law of this State, that so long as the voter's intent may be discerned from the ballot, the vote constitutes a "legal vote" that should be counted. *See McAlpin v. State ex rel. Avriett* (Fla. 1944); *see also State ex rel. Peacock v. Latham* (Fla. 1936) (holding that the election contest statute "affords an efficient available remedy and legal procedure by which the circuit court can investigate and determine, not only the legality of the votes cast, but can correct any inaccuracies in the count of the ballots by having them brought into the court and examining the contents of the ballot boxes if properly preserved"). As the State has moved toward electronic voting, nothing in this evolution has diminished the longstanding case law and statutory law that the intent of the voter is of paramount concern and should always be given effect *if* the intent can be determined. *Cf. Boardman v. Esteva,* (Fla. 1975) (recognizing the over-arching principle that, where voters do all that statutes require them to do, they should not be disfranchised solely because of failure of election officials to follow directory statutes).

Not surprisingly, other states also have recognized this principle. *Cf. Delahunt v. Johnston,* (Mass. 1996) (holding that a vote should be counted as a legal vote if it properly indicates the voter's intent with reasonable certainty); *Duffy v. Mortenson* (S.D. 1993) (applying the rule that every marking found where a vote should be should be treated as an intended vote in the absence of clear evidence to the clear contrary); *Pullen v. Mulligan* (Ill. 1990) (holding that votes could be recounted by manual means to the extent that the voter's intent could be determined with reasonable certainty, despite the existence of a statute which provided that punch card ballots were to be recounted by automated tabulation equipment).

Accordingly, we conclude that a legal vote is one in which there is a "clear indication of the intent of the voter." We next address whether the term "rejection" used in section 102.168(3)(c) includes instances where the County Canvassing Board has not counted legal votes. Looking at the statutory scheme as a whole, it appears that the term "rejected" does encompass votes that may exist but have not been counted. As explained above, in 1999, the Legislature substantially revised the contest provision of the Election Code. One of the revisions to the contest provision included the codification of the grounds for contesting an election. The House Bill noted that one of the grounds for contesting an election at common law was the "Receipt of a number of illegal votes or rejection of a number of legal votes sufficient to change or place in doubt the result of the election." As noted above, the contest statute ultimately contained this ground for contesting the results of an election.

To further determine the meaning of the term "rejection", as used by the Legislature, we may also look to Florida case law. In *State ex rel. Clark v. Klingensmith* (Fla. 1935), an individual who lost an election brought an action for quo warranto challenging his opponent's right to hold office. The challenger challenged twenty-two ballots, which he divided into four groups. One of these groups included three ballots that the challenger claimed had not been counted. This Court concluded that "the *rejection* of votes from legal voters, not brought about by fraud, and not of such magnitude as to demonstrate that a free expression of the popular will has been suppressed," is insufficient to void an election, "at least unless it be shown that the votes rejected would have changed the result." Therefore, the Court appears to have equated a "rejection" of legal votes with the failure to count legal votes, while at the same time recognizing that a sufficient number of such votes must have been rejected to merit relief. This notion of "rejected" is also in accordance with the common understanding of rejection of votes as used in other election cases.

Here, then, it is apparent that there have been sufficient allegations made which, if analyzed pursuant to the proper standard, compel the conclusion that legal votes sufficient to place in doubt the election results have been rejected in this case.

THIS CASE

[Based on the foregoing, the Florida Supreme Court ruled that it was necessary to complete the as-yet-unfinished manual recount in Miami-Dade. The court, however, rejected Gore's contention that Palm Beach County was required to use the more lenient "dimpled" chad standard to count some 3,300 ballots that had been rejected using a more stringent standard. The court then held that those ballots that already had been manually recounted, either in Miami-Dade before the recount stopped there, or in Palm Beach's recount that was completed two hours late, needed to be added to the final certified total.]

CONCLUSION

Through no fault of appellants, a lawfully commenced manual recount in Dade County was never completed and recounts that were completed were not counted. Without examining or investigating the ballots that were not counted by the machines, the trial court concluded there was no reasonable probability of a different result. However, the proper standard required by section 102.168 was whether the results of the election were placed in doubt. On this record there can be no question that there are legal votes within the 9000 uncounted votes sufficient to place the results of this election in doubt. We know this *not* only by evidence of statistical analysis but also by the actual experience of recounts conducted. The votes for each candidate that have been counted are separated by no more than approximately 500 votes and may be separated by as little as approximately 100 votes. Thousands of uncounted votes could obviously make a difference.

Although in all elections the Legislature and the courts have recognized that the voter's intent is paramount, in close elections the necessity for counting all legal votes becomes critical. However, the need for accuracy must be weighed against the need for finality. The need for prompt resolution and finality is especially critical in presidential elections where there is an outside deadline established by federal law. Notwithstanding, consistent with the legislative mandate and our precedent, although the time constraints are limited, we must do everything required by law to ensure that legal votes that have not been counted are included in the final election results.

In addition to the relief requested by appellants to count the Miami-Dade undervote, claims have been made by the various appellees and intervenors that because this is a statewide election, statewide remedies would be called for. As we discussed in this opinion, we agree. While we recognize that time is desperately short, we cannot in good faith ignore the appellants' right to relief as to their claims concerning the uncounted votes in Miami-Dade County, nor can we ignore the correctness of the assertions that any analysis and ultimate remedy should be made on a statewide basis.[21]

21. The dissents would have us throw up our hands and say that because of looming deadlines and practical difficulties we should give up any attempt to have the election of the presidential electors rest upon the vote of Florida citizens as mandated by the Legislature. While we agree that practical difficulties may well end up controlling the outcome of the election we vigorously disagree that we should therefore abandon our responsibility to resolve this election dispute under the rule of law. We can only do the best we can to carry out our sworn responsibilities to the justice system and its role in this process. We, and our

We note that the contest statutes vest broad discretion in the circuit court to "provide any relief appropriate under the circumstances." § 102.168(5). Moreover, because venue of an election contest that covers more than one county lies in Leon County, *see* § 102.1685, Fla. Stat. (2000), the circuit court has jurisdiction, as part of the relief it orders, to order the Supervisor of Elections and the Canvassing Boards, as well as the necessary public officials, in all counties that have not conducted a manual recount or tabulation of the undervotes in this election to do so forthwith, said tabulation to take place in the individual counties where the ballots are located.[22]

Accordingly, we reverse the final judgment of the trial court dated December 4, 2000, and remand this cause for the circuit court to immediately tabulate by hand the approximate 9000 Miami-Dade ballots, which the counting machine registered as non-votes, but which have never been manually reviewed, and for other relief that may thereafter appear appropriate. The circuit court is directed to enter such orders as are necessary to add any legal votes to the total statewide certifications and to enter any orders necessary to ensure the inclusion of the additional legal votes for Gore in Palm Beach County and the 168 additional legal votes from Miami-Dade County.

Because time is of the essence, the circuit court shall commence the tabulation of the Miami-Dade ballots immediately. The circuit court is authorized, in accordance with the provisions of section 102.168(8), to be assisted by the Leon County Supervisor of Elections or his sworn designees. Moreover, since time is also of the essence in any statewide relief that the circuit court must consider, any further statewide relief should also be ordered forthwith and simultaneously with the manual tabulation of the Miami-Dade undervotes.

In tabulating the ballots and in making a determination of what is a "legal" vote, the standard to be employed is that established by the Legislature in our Election Code which is that the vote shall be counted as a "legal" vote if there is "clear indication of the intent of the voter." § 101.5614(5), Fla. Stat. (2000).

It is so ordered. ANSTEAD, PARIENTE, LEWIS and QUINCE, JJ., concur.

HARDING, J., [with whom SHAW, J., concurs,] dissenting.*

I would affirm Judge Sauls' order because I agree with his ultimate conclusion in this case, namely that the appellants failed to carry their requisite burden of proof and thus are not entitled to relief.

dissenting colleagues, have simply done the best we can, and remain confident that others charged with similar heavy responsibilities will also do the best they can to fulfill their duties as they see them.

22. We are mindful of the fact that due to the time constraints, the count of the undervotes places demands on the public servants throughout the State to work over this week-end. However, we are confident that with the cooperation of the officials in all the counties, the remaining undervotes in these counties can be accomplished within the required time frame. We note that public officials in many counties have worked diligently over the past thirty days in dealing with exigencies that have occurred because of this unique historical circumstance arising from the presidential election of 2000. We commend those dedicated public servants for attempting to make this election process truly reflect the vote of all Floridians.

* [The two dissenting opinions are printed here in the opposite order from which they appear in the official reported decision. It is evident that Chief Justice Wells wrote his impassioned separate dissent after reading Justice Harding's more muted dissent. —EDS.]

I agree with Judge Sauls that the appellants have not carried their burden of showing that the number of legal votes rejected by the canvassing boards is sufficient to change or place in doubt the result of this *statewide* election. That failure of proof controls the outcome here. Moreover, as explained below, I do not believe that an adequate remedy exists under the circumstances of this case.

The basis for appellants' claim for relief under section 102.168 is that there is a "no-vote" problem, i.e., ballots which, although counted by machines at least once, allegedly have not been counted in the presidential election. The evidence showed that this no-vote problem, to the extent it exists, is a statewide problem.[33] Appellants ask that only a subset of these no-votes be counted.

The action is to determine whether the Secretary of State certified the correct winner for the entire State of Florida. Appellants failed, however, to provide any meaningful statistical evidence that the outcome of the Florida election would be different if the "no-vote" in other counties had been counted; their proof that the outcome of the vote in two counties would likely change the results of the election was insufficient. It would be improper to permit appellants to carry their burden in a statewide election by merely demonstrating that there were a sufficient number of no-votes that could have changed the returns in isolated counties. Recounting a subset of counties selected by the appellants does not answer the ultimate question of whether a sufficient number of uncounted legal votes could be recovered from the statewide "no-votes" to change the result of the statewide election. At most, such a procedure only demonstrates that the losing candidate would have had greater success in the subset of counties most favorable to that candidate.

As such, I would find that the selective recounting requested by appellant is not available under the election contest provisions of section 102.168. Such an application does not provide for a more accurate reflection of the will of the voters but, rather, allows for an unfair distortion of the statewide vote. It is patently unlawful to permit the recount of "no-votes" in a single county to determine the outcome of the November 7, 2000, election for the next President of the United States. We are a nation of laws, and we have survived and prospered as a free nation because we have adhered to the rule of law. Fairness is achieved by following the rules.

Finally, even if I were to conclude that the appellants' allegations and evidence were sufficient to warrant relief, I do not believe that the rules permit an adequate remedy under the circumstances of this case. This Court, in its prior opinion, and all of the parties agree that election controversies and contests must be finally and conclusively determined by December 12, 2000. *See* 3 U.S.C.

33. No-votes (ballots for which the no vote for presidential electors was recorded) exist throughout the state, not just in the counties selected by appellants. Of the 177,655 no-votes in the November 7, 2000, election in Florida, 28,492 occurred in Miami-Dade County and 29,366 occurred in Palm Beach County.

§ 5. Clearly, the only remedy authorized by law would be a statewide recount of more than 170,000 "no-vote" ballots by December 12. Even if such a recount were possible, speed would come at the expense of accuracy, and it would be difficult to put any faith or credibility in a vote total achieved under such chaotic conditions. In order to undertake this unprecedented task, the majority has established standards for manual recounts—a step that this Court refused to take [in its decision during the administrative protest], presumably because there was no authority for such action and nothing in the record to guide the Court in setting such standards. The same circumstances exist in this case. All of the parties should be afforded an opportunity to be heard on this very important issue.

While this Court must be ever mindful of the Legislature's plenary power to appoint presidential electors, *see* U.S. CONST. art. II, § 1, cl. 2, I am more concerned that the majority is departing from the essential requirements of the law by providing a remedy which is impossible to achieve and which will ultimately lead to chaos. In giving Judge Sauls the direction to order a statewide recount, the majority permits a remedy which was not prayed for, which is based upon a premise for which there is no evidence, and which presents Judge Sauls with directions to order entities (i.e. local canvassing boards) to conduct recounts when they have not been served, have not been named as parties, but, most importantly, have not had the opportunity to be heard. In effect, the majority is allowing the results of the statewide election to be determined by the manual recount in Miami-Dade County because a statewide recount will be impossible to accomplish. Even if by some miracle a portion of the statewide recount is completed by December 12, a partial recount is not acceptable. The uncertainty of the outcome of this election will be greater under the remedy afforded by the majority than the uncertainty that now exists.

The circumstances of this election call to mind a quote from football coaching legend Vince Lombardi: "We didn't lose the game, we just ran out of time."

* * *

WELLS, C.J., dissenting.

I want to make it clear at the outset of my separate opinion that I do not question the good faith or honorable intentions of my colleagues in the majority. However, I could not more strongly disagree with their decision to reverse the trial court and prolong this judicial process. I also believe that the majority's decision cannot withstand the scrutiny which will certainly immediately follow under the United States Constitution.

My succinct conclusion is that the majority's decision to return this case to the circuit court for a count of the under-votes from either Miami-Dade County or all counties has no foundation in the law of Florida as it existed on November 7, 2000, or at any time until the issuance of this opinion. The majority returns the case to the circuit court for this partial recount of under-votes on the basis of unknown or, at best, ambiguous standards with authority to obtain help from others, the credentials, qualifications, and objectivity of whom are totally unknown. That is but a first glance at the imponderable problems the majority creates.[26]

Importantly to me, I have a deep and abiding concern that the prolonging of judicial process in this counting contest propels this country and this state into an unprecedented and unnecessary constitutional crisis. I have to conclude that there is a real and present likelihood that this constitutional crisis will do substantial damage to our country, our state, and to this Court as an institution.

On the basis of my analysis of Florida law as it existed on November 7, 2000, I conclude that the trial court's decision can and should be affirmed.

There are two fundamental and historical principles of Florida law that this Court has recognized which are relevant here. First, at common law, there was no right to contest an election; thus, any right to contest an election must be construed to grant only those rights that are explicitly set forth by the Legislature. *See McPherson v. Flynn* (Fla. 1981). Second, this Court gives deference to decisions made by executive officials charged with implementing Florida's election laws. *See Krivanek v. Take Back Tampa Political Committee* (Fla. 1993).

These two concepts are the foundation of my analysis of the present case.

At the outset, I note that, after an evidentiary hearing, the trial court expressly found no dishonesty, gross negligence, improper influence, coercion, or fraud in the balloting and counting processes based upon the evidence presented. I conclude this finding should curtail this Court's involvement in this election through this case and is a substantial basis for affirming the trial court. Historically, this Court has only been involved in elections when there have been substantial allegations of fraud and then only upon a high threshold because of the chill that a hovering judicial involvement can put on elections. Otherwise, we run a great risk that every election will result in judicial testing. Judicial restraint in respect to elections is absolutely necessary because the health of our democracy depends on elections being decided by voters — not by judges. We must have the self-discipline not to become embroiled in political contests whenever a judicial majority subjectively concludes to do so because the majority perceives it is "the right thing to do." Elections involve the other branches of government. A lack of self-discipline in being involved in elections, especially by a court of last resort, always has the potential of leading to a crisis with the other branches of government and raises serious separation-of-powers concerns.

26. Also problematic with the majority's analysis is that the majority only *requires* that the "under-votes" are to be counted. How about the "over-votes"? Section 101.5614(6) provides that a ballot should not be counted "[i]f an elector marks more names than there are persons to be elected to an office," meaning the voter voted for more than one person for president. The underlying premise of the majority's rationale is that in such a close race a manual review of ballots rejected by the machines is necessary to ensure that all legal votes cast are counted. The majority, however, ignores the over-votes. Could it be said, without reviewing the over-votes, that the machine did not err in not counting them? It seems patently erroneous to me to assume that the vote-counting machines can err when reading under-votes but not err when reading over-votes. Can the majority say, without having the over-votes looked at, that there are no legal votes among the over-votes? [Footnote relocated. — EDS.]

I find that the trial judge correctly concluded that plaintiffs were not entitled to a manual recount. I believe that the contest and protest statutes must logically be read together. It appears logical to me that a circuit judge in a section 102.168 contest should review a county canvassing board's determinations in a section 102.166 protest under an abuse-of-discretion standard.

The majority quotes section 101.5614(5) for the proposition of settling how a county canvassing board should count a vote. The majority states that "[n]o vote shall be declared invalid or void if there is a clear indication of the intent of the voter as determined by the canvassing board." § 101.5614(5), Fla. Stat. (2000). Section 101.5614(5), however, is a statute that authorizes the creation of a duplicate ballot where a "ballot card . . . is damaged or defective so that it cannot properly be counted by the automatic tabulating equipment." There is no basis in this record that suggests that the approximately 9000 ballots from Miami-Dade County were damaged or defective.

Laying aside this problem and assuming the majority is correct that section 101.5614(5) correctly annunciates the standard by which a county canvassing board should judge a questionable ballot, section 101.5614(5) utterly fails to provide any meaningful standard. There is no doubt that every vote should be counted where there is a "clear indication of the intent of the voter." The problem is how a county canvassing board translates that directive to these punch cards. Should a county canvassing board count or not count a "dimpled chad" where the voter is able to successfully dislodge the chad in every other contest on that ballot? Here, the county canvassing boards disagree. Apparently, some do and some do not. Continuation of this system of county-by-county decisions regarding how a dimpled chad is counted is fraught with equal protection concerns which will eventually cause the election results in Florida to be stricken by the federal courts or Congress.

Based upon this analysis, I conclude the circuit court properly looked at what the county canvassing boards had done and found that they did not abuse their discretion. Regarding Miami-Dade County, I find that the trial judge properly concluded that the Miami-Dade Canvassing Board did not abuse its discretion in deciding to discontinue the manual recount begun on November 19, 2000. I also agree with the trial judge that [Secretary of State Harris] did not abuse [her] discretion in refusing to accept either an amended return reflecting the results of a partial manual recount or a late amended return filed by the Palm Beach Board. [The majority's contrary decision] not only changes a rule after November 7, 2000, but it also changes a rule this Court made on November 26, 2000.

I conclude that this contest simply must end.

Directing the trial court to conduct a manual recount of the ballots violates article II, section 1, clause 2 of the United States Constitution, in that neither this Court nor the circuit court has the authority to create the standards by which it will count the under-voted ballots. The Legislature has given to the county canvassing boards—and only these boards—the authority to ascertain the intent of the voter. *See* § 102.166(7)(b), Fla. Stat. (2000). Clearly, in a presidential election, the Legislature has not authorized the courts of Florida to order partial recounts, either in a limited number of counties or statewide. This Court's order to do so appears to me to be in conflict with the United States Supreme Court decision [on December 4 in *Bush v. Palm Beach Canvassing Bd.*].

Laying aside the constitutional infirmities of this Court's action today, what the majority actually creates is an overflowing basket of practical problems. Assuming the majority recognizes a need to protect the votes of Florida's presidential electors, the entire contest must be completed "at least six days before" December 18, 2000, the date the presidential electors meet to vote. *See* 3 U.S.C. § 5 (1994). The safe harbor deadline day is December 12, 2000. Today is Friday, December 8, 2000. Thus, under the majority's time line, all manual recounts must be completed in five days, assuming the counting begins today.

In that time frame, all questionable ballots must be reviewed by the judicial officer appointed to discern the intent of the voter in a process open to the public. Fairness dictates that a provision be made for either party to object to how a particular ballot is counted. Additionally, this short time period must allow for judicial review. I respectfully submit this cannot be completed without taking Florida's presidential electors outside the safe harbor provision, creating the very real possibility of disenfranchising those nearly six million voters who were able to correctly cast their ballots on election day.

Another significant problem is that the majority returns this case to the circuit court for a recount with no standards. I do not, and neither will the trial judge, know whether to count or not count ballots on the criteria used by the canvassing boards, what those criteria are, or to do so on the basis of standards divined by Judge Sauls. A continuing problem with these manual recounts is their reliability. It only stands to reason that many times a reading of a ballot by a human will be subjective, and the intent gleaned from that ballot is only in the mind of the beholder. This subjective counting is only compounded where no standards exist or, as in this statewide contest, where there are no statewide standards for determining voter intent by the various canvassing boards, individual judges, or multiple unknown counters who will eventually count these ballots.

I must regrettably conclude that the majority ignores the magnitude of its decision. The Court fails to make provision for: (1) the qualifications of those who count; (2) what standards are used in the count—are they the same standards for all ballots statewide or a continuation of the county-by-county constitutionally suspect standards; (3) who is to observe the count; (4) how one objects to the count; (5) who is entitled to object to the count; (6) whether a person may object to a counter; (7) the possible lack of personnel to conduct the count; (8) the fatigue of the counters; and (9) the effect of the differing intra-county standards.

This Court's responsibility must be to balance the contest allegations against the rights of all Florida voters who are not involved in election contests to have their votes counted in the electoral college. To me, it is inescapable that there is no practical way for the contest to continue for the good of this country and state.

For a month, Floridians have been working on this problem. At this point, I am convinced of the following.

First, there have been an enormous number of citizens who have expended heroic efforts as members of canvassing boards, counters, and observers, and as legal counsel who have in almost all instances, in utmost good faith attempted to bring about a fair resolution of this election. I know that, regardless of the outcome, all of us are in their debt for their efforts on behalf of representative democracy.

Second, the local election officials, state election officials, and the courts have been attempting to resolve the issues of this election with an election code which any objective, frank analysis must conclude never contemplated this circumstance. Only to state a few of the incongruities, the time limits of sections 102.112, 102.166, and 102.168 and 3 U.S.C. §§ 1, 5, and 7 simply do not coordinate in any practical way with a presidential election in Florida in the year 2000. Therefore, section 102.168, Florida Statues, is inconsistent with the remedy being sought here because it is unclear in a presidential election as to: (1) whether the candidates or the presidential electors should be party to this election contest; (2) what the possible remedy would be; and (3) what standards to apply in counting the ballots statewide.

Third, under the United States Supreme Court's analysis in *Bush v. Palm Beach County Canvassing Board,* there is uncertainty as to whether the Florida Legislature has even given the courts of Florida any power to resolve contests or controversies in respect to presidential elections.

Fourth, there is no available remedy for the appellants on the basis of these allegations. Quite simply, courts cannot fairly continue to proceed without jeopardizing the votes and rights of other citizens through a further count of these votes.

This case has reached the point where finality must take precedence over continued judicial process. I agree with the view attributed to John Allen Paulos, a professor of mathematics at Temple University, who was quoted as saying, "The margin of error in this election is far greater than the margin of victory, no matter who wins." Further judicial process will not change this self-evident fact and will only result in confusion and disorder.

4. The Endgame of the 2000 Presidential Election

After the Florida Supreme Court issued the above 4-3 decision on Friday, December 8, two things happened immediately. First, the required statewide manual recount began under the supervision of Judge Terry Lewis, who took over the case after Judge Sauls recused himself. Second, the Bush team filed an emergency application in the U.S. Supreme Court, asking the Court to stop the recount on the ground that it violated either Article II or the Fourteenth Amendment. On Saturday, December 9, by a 5-4 vote, the Court granted the requested stay and scheduled oral argument on Monday, December 11, to consider the merits of Bush's constitutional claims. Although theoretically the Court could have lifted the stay if after oral argument it decided that these claims lacked merit, as a practical matter the Court's stay had the momentous effect of postponing any further recounting of ballots as the Safe Harbor Deadline of Tuesday, December 12, came ever closer.

Justice Stevens, joined by Justices Souter, Ginsburg, and Breyer, released a dissenting opinion to the stay order:

> To stop the counting of legal votes, the majority today departs from three venerable rules of judicial restraint that have guided the Court throughout its history. On questions of state law, we have consistently respected the opinions of the highest courts of the States. On questions whose resolution is committed at least in large measure to another branch of the

> Federal Government, we have construed our own jurisdiction narrowly and exercised it cautiously. On federal constitutional questions that were not fairly presented to the court whose judgment is being reviewed, we have prudently declined to express an opinion. The majority has acted unwisely.
>
> Time does not permit a full discussion of the merits. It is clear, however, that a stay should not be granted unless an applicant makes a substantial showing of a likelihood of irreparable harm. In this case, petitioners have failed to carry that heavy burden. Counting every legally cast vote cannot constitute irreparable harm. On the other hand, there is a danger that a stay may cause irreparable harm to respondents—and, more importantly, the public at large—because of the risk that the entry of the stay would be tantamount to a decision on the merits in favor of the applicants. Preventing the recount from being completed will inevitably cast a cloud on the legitimacy of the election.
>
> It is certainly not clear that the Florida decision violated federal law. The Florida Code provides elaborate procedures for ensuring that every eligible voter has a full and fair opportunity to cast a ballot and that every ballot so cast is counted. In fact, the statutory provision relating to damaged and defective ballots states that "[n]o vote shall be declared invalid or void if there is a clear indication of the intent of the voter as determined by the canvassing board." § 101.5614(5). In its opinion, the Florida Supreme Court gave weight to that legislative command. Its ruling was consistent with earlier Florida cases that have repeatedly described the interest in correctly ascertaining the will of the voters as paramount. Its ruling also appears to be consistent with the prevailing view in other States. As a more fundamental matter, the Florida court's ruling reflects the basic principle, inherent in our Constitution and our democracy, that every legal vote should be counted.

This dissent prompted Justice Scalia, writing solely for himself, to issue a concurrence to the Court's stay order:

> Though it is not customary for the Court to issue an opinion in connection with its grant of a stay, I believe a brief response is necessary to Justice Stevens' dissent. I will not address the merits of the case, since they will shortly be before us in the petition for certiorari that we have granted. It suffices to say that the issuance of the stay suggests that a majority of the Court, while not deciding the issues presented, believe that petitioners have a substantial probability of success.
>
> On the question of irreparable harm, however, a few words are appropriate. The issue is not, as the dissent puts it, whether "[c]ounting every legally cast vote ca[n] constitute irreparable harm." One of the principal issues in the appeal we have accepted is precisely whether the votes that have been ordered to be counted are, under a reasonable interpretation of Florida law, "legally cast vote[s]." The counting of votes that are of questionable legality does in my view threaten irreparable harm to petitioner Bush, and to the country, by casting a cloud upon what he claims

to be the legitimacy of his election. Count first, and rule upon legality afterwards, is not a recipe for producing election results that have the public acceptance democratic stability requires. Another issue in the case, moreover, is the propriety, indeed the constitutionality, of letting the standard for determination of voters' intent—dimpled chads, hanging chads, etc.—vary from county to county, as the Florida Supreme Court opinion permits. If petitioners are correct that counting in this fashion is unlawful, permitting the count to proceed on that erroneous basis will prevent an accurate recount from being conducted on a proper basis later, since it is generally agreed that each manual recount produces a degradation of the ballots, which renders a subsequent recount inaccurate.

For these reasons I have joined the Court's issuance of a stay, with a highly accelerated timetable for resolving this case on the merits.

The oral argument on the merits occurred as scheduled, and the next day—Tuesday, December 12, the day of the Safe-Harbor Deadline, the U.S. Supreme Court announced its decision in *Bush v. Gore.*

Bush v. Gore

531 U.S. 98 (2000)

PER CURIAM.

I

On December 8, 2000, the Supreme Court of Florida ordered that the Circuit Court of Leon County tabulate by hand 9,000 ballots in Miami-Dade County. It also ordered the inclusion in the certified vote totals of 215 votes identified in Palm Beach County and 168 votes identified in Miami-Dade County for Vice President Albert Gore, Jr., and Senator Joseph Lieberman, Democratic candidates for President and Vice President. The State Supreme Court noted that petitioner George W. Bush asserted that the net gain for Vice President Gore in Palm Beach County was 176 votes, and directed the Circuit Court to resolve that dispute on remand. The court further held that relief would require manual recounts in all Florida counties where so-called "undervotes" had not been subject to manual tabulation. The court ordered all manual recounts to begin at once. Governor Bush and Richard Cheney, Republican candidates for President and Vice President, filed an emergency application for a stay of this mandate. On December 9, we granted the application, treated the application as a petition for a writ of certiorari, and granted certiorari.

The proceedings leading to the present controversy are discussed in some detail in our opinion in *Bush v. Palm Beach County Canvassing Bd.* (2000). On November 8, 2000, the day following the Presidential election, the Florida Division of Elections reported that petitioner Bush had received 2,909,135 votes, and respondent Gore had received 2,907,351 votes, a margin of 1,784 for Governor Bush. Because Governor Bush's margin of victory was less than "one-half of a percent . . . of the votes cast," an automatic machine recount was conducted under § 102.141(4) of the election code, the results of which showed Governor Bush still winning the race but by a diminished margin. Vice President Gore then sought manual recounts in Volusia, Palm Beach, Broward, and Miami-Dade Counties, pursuant to Florida's election protest provisions. Fla. Stat. Ann. § 102.166 (Supp. 2001). A dispute arose concerning the deadline for local county canvassing boards to submit their returns to the Secretary of State (Secretary). The Secretary declined to waive the November 14 deadline imposed by statute. §§ 102.111, 102.112. The Florida Supreme Court, however, set the deadline at November 26. We granted certiorari and vacated the Florida Supreme Court's decision, finding considerable uncertainty as to the grounds on which it was based. On December 11, the Florida Supreme Court issued a decision on remand reinstating that date. *Palm Beach County Canvassing Bd. v. Harris* (2000).

On November 26, the Florida Elections Canvassing Commission certified the results of the election and declared Governor Bush the winner of Florida's 25 electoral votes. On November 27, Vice President Gore, pursuant to Florida's contest provisions, filed a complaint in Leon County Circuit Court contesting the certification. Fla. Stat. Ann. § 102.168 (Supp. 2001). He sought relief pursuant to § 102.168(3)(c), which provides that "[r]eceipt of a number of illegal votes or rejection of a number of legal votes sufficient to change or place in doubt the result of the election" shall be grounds for a contest. The Circuit Court denied relief, stating that Vice President Gore failed to meet his burden of proof. He appealed to the First District Court of Appeal, which certified the matter to the Florida Supreme Court.

Accepting jurisdiction, the Florida Supreme Court affirmed in part and reversed in part. *Gore v. Harris* (2000). The court held that the Circuit Court had been correct to reject Vice President Gore's challenge to the results certified in Nassau County and his challenge to the Palm Beach County Canvassing Board's determination that 3,300 ballots cast in that county were not, in the statutory phrase, "legal votes."

The Supreme Court held that Vice President Gore had satisfied his burden of proof under § 102.168(3)(c) with respect to his challenge to Miami-Dade County's failure to tabulate, by manual count, 9,000 ballots on which the machines had failed to detect a vote for President ("undervotes"). Noting the closeness of the election, the court explained that "[o]n this record, there can be no question that there are legal votes within the 9,000 uncounted votes sufficient to place the results of this election in doubt." A "legal vote," as determined by the Supreme Court, is "one in which there is a 'clear indication of the intent of the voter.' " The court therefore ordered a hand recount of the 9,000 ballots in Miami-Dade County. Observing that the contest provisions vest broad discretion in the circuit judge to "provide any relief appropriate under such circumstances," § 102.168(8), the Supreme Court further held that the Circuit Court could order "the Supervisor of Elections and the Canvassing Boards, as well as the necessary public officials, in all counties that have not conducted a manual recount or tabulation of the undervotes . . . to do so forthwith, said tabulation to take place in the individual counties where the ballots are located." *Id.*

The Supreme Court also determined that both Palm Beach County and Miami-Dade County, in their earlier manual recounts, had identified a net gain of 215 and 168 legal votes for Vice President Gore. Rejecting the Circuit Court's conclusion that Palm Beach County lacked the authority to include the 215 net votes submitted past the November 26 deadline, the Supreme Court explained that the deadline was not intended to exclude votes identified after that date through ongoing manual recounts. As to Miami-Dade County, the court concluded that although the 168 votes identified were the result of a partial recount, they were "legal votes [that] could change the outcome of the election." The Supreme Court therefore directed the Circuit Court to include those totals in the certified results, subject to resolution of the actual vote total from the Miami-Dade partial recount.

The petition presents the following questions: whether the Florida Supreme Court established new standards for resolving Presidential election contests, thereby violating Art. II, § 1, cl. 2, of the United States Constitution and failing to comply with 3 U.S.C. § 5, and whether the use of standardless manual recounts violates the Equal Protection and Due Process Clauses. With respect to the equal protection question, we find a violation of the Equal Protection Clause.

II

A

The closeness of this election, and the multitude of legal challenges which have followed in its wake, have brought into sharp focus a common, if heretofore unnoticed, phenomenon. Nationwide statistics reveal that an estimated 2% of ballots cast do not register a vote for President for whatever reason, including deliberately choosing no candidate at all or some voter error, such as voting for two candidates or insufficiently marking a ballot. *See* Ho, *More Than 2M Ballots Uncounted,* AP Online (Nov. 28, 2000); Kelley, *Balloting Problems Not Rare But Only in a Very Close Election Do Mistakes and Mismarking Make a Difference,* Omaha World-Herald (Nov. 15, 2000). In certifying election results, the votes eligible for inclusion in the certification are the votes meeting the properly established legal requirements.

This case has shown that punch card balloting machines can produce an unfortunate number of ballots which are not punched in a clean, complete way by the voter. After the current counting, it is likely legislative bodies nationwide will examine ways to improve the mechanisms and machinery for voting.

B

The individual citizen has no federal constitutional right to vote for electors for the President of the United States unless and until the state legislature chooses a statewide election as the means to implement its power to appoint members of the electoral college. U.S. Const., Art. II, § 1. This is the source for the statement in *McPherson v. Blacker* (1892) that the state legislature's power to select the manner for appointing electors is plenary; it may, if it so chooses, select the electors itself, which indeed was the manner used by state legislatures in several States for many years after the framing of our Constitution. History has now favored the voter, and in each of the several States the citizens themselves vote for Presidential electors. When the state legislature vests the right to vote for President in its people, the right to vote as the legislature has prescribed is fundamental; and one source of its fundamental nature lies in the equal weight accorded to each vote and the equal dignity owed to each voter. The State, of course, after granting the franchise in the special context of Article II, can take back the power to appoint electors.

The right to vote is protected in more than the initial allocation of the franchise. Equal protection applies as well to the manner of its exercise. Having once granted the right to vote on equal terms, the State may not, by later arbitrary and disparate treatment, value one person's vote over that of another. *See, e.g., Harper v. Virginia Bd. of Elections* [(1966)]. It must be remembered that "the right of suffrage can be denied by a debasement or dilution of the weight of a citizen's vote just as effectively as by wholly prohibiting the free exercise of the franchise." *Reynolds v. Sims* (1964).

There is no difference between the two sides of the present controversy on these basic propositions. Respondents say that the very purpose of vindicating the right to vote justifies the recount procedures now at issue. The question before us, however, is whether the recount procedures the Florida Supreme Court has adopted are consistent with its obligation to avoid arbitrary and disparate treatment of the members of its electorate.

Much of the controversy seems to revolve around ballot cards designed to be perforated by a stylus but which, either through error or deliberate omission, have not been perforated with sufficient precision for a machine to register the perforations. In some cases a piece of the card—a chad—is hanging, say, by two corners. In other cases there is no separation at all, just an indentation.

The Florida Supreme Court has ordered that the intent of the voter be discerned from such ballots. For purposes of resolving the equal protection challenge, it is not necessary to decide whether the Florida Supreme Court had the authority under the legislative scheme for resolving election disputes to define what a legal vote is and to mandate a manual recount implementing that definition. The recount mechanisms implemented in response to the decisions of the Florida Supreme Court do not satisfy the minimum requirement for nonarbitrary treatment of voters necessary to secure the fundamental right. Florida's basic command for the count of legally cast votes is to consider the "intent of the voter." This is unobjectionable as an abstract proposition and a starting principle. The problem inheres in the absence of specific standards to ensure its equal application. The formulation of uniform rules to determine intent based on these recurring circumstances is practicable and, we conclude, necessary.

The law does not refrain from searching for the intent of the actor in a multitude of circumstances; and in some cases the general command to ascertain intent is not susceptible to much further refinement. In this instance, however, the question is not whether to believe a witness but how to interpret the marks or holes or scratches on an inanimate object, a piece of cardboard or paper which, it is said, might not have registered as a vote during the machine count. The factfinder confronts a thing, not a person. The search for intent can be confined by specific rules designed to ensure uniform treatment.

The want of those rules here has led to unequal evaluation of ballots in various respects. *See* [Florida Supreme Court decision] (Wells, C.J., dissenting) ("Should a county canvassing board count or not count a 'dimpled chad' where the voter is able to successfully dislodge the chad in every other contest on that ballot? Here, the county canvassing boards disagree"). As seems to have been acknowledged at oral argument, the standards for accepting or rejecting contested ballots might vary not only from county to county but indeed within a single county from one recount team to another.

The record provides some examples. A monitor in Miami-Dade County testified at trial that he observed that three members of the county canvassing board applied different standards in defining a legal vote. And testimony at trial also revealed that at least one county changed its evaluative standards during the counting process. Palm Beach County, for example, began the process with a 1990 guideline which precluded counting completely attached chads, switched to a rule that considered a vote to be legal if any light could be seen through a chad, changed back to the 1990 rule, and then abandoned any pretense of a *per se* rule, only to have a court order that the county consider dimpled chads legal. This is not a process with sufficient guarantees of equal treatment.

An early case in our one-person, one-vote jurisprudence arose when a State accorded arbitrary and disparate treatment to voters in its different counties. *Gray v. Sanders* (1963). The Court found a constitutional violation. We relied on these principles in the context of the Presidential selection process in *Moore v. Ogilvie* (1969), where we invalidated a county-based procedure that diluted the influence of citizens in larger counties in the nominating process. There we observed that "[t]he idea that one group can be granted greater voting strength than another is hostile to the one man, one vote basis of our representative government." *Id.*

The State Supreme Court ratified this uneven treatment. It mandated that the recount totals from two counties, Miami-Dade and Palm Beach, be included in the certified total. The court also appeared to hold *sub silentio* that the recount totals from Broward County, which were not completed until after the original November 14 certification by the Secretary, were to be considered part of the new certified vote totals even though the county certification was not contested by Vice President Gore. Yet each of the counties used varying standards to determine what was a legal vote. Broward County used a more forgiving standard than Palm Beach County, and uncovered almost three times as many new votes, a result markedly disproportionate to the difference in population between the counties.

In addition, the recounts in these three counties were not limited to so-called undervotes but extended to all of the ballots. The distinction has real consequences. A manual recount of all ballots identifies not only those ballots which show no vote but also those which contain more than one, the so-called overvotes. Neither category will be counted by the machine. This is not a trivial concern. At oral argument, respondents estimated there are as many as 110,000 overvotes statewide. As a result, the citizen whose ballot was not read by a machine because he failed to vote for a candidate in a way readable by a machine may still have his vote counted in a manual recount; on the other hand, the citizen who marks two candidates in a way discernible by the machine will not have the same opportunity to have his vote count, even if a manual examination of the ballot would reveal the requisite indicia of intent. Furthermore, the citizen who marks two candidates, only one of which is discernible by the machine, will have his vote counted even though it should have been read as an invalid ballot. The State Supreme Court's inclusion of vote counts based on these variant standards exemplifies concerns with the remedial processes that were under way.

That brings the analysis to yet a further equal protection problem. The votes certified by the court included a partial total from one county, Miami-Dade. The Florida Supreme Court's decision thus gives no assurance that the recounts included in a final certification must be complete. Indeed, it is respondents' submission that it would be consistent with the rules of the recount procedures to include whatever partial counts are done by the time of final certification, and we interpret the Florida Supreme Court's decision to permit this. *See* [Florida Supreme Court decision] (noting "practical difficulties" may control outcome of election, but certifying partial Miami-Dade total nonetheless). This accommodation no doubt results from the truncated contest period established by the Florida Supreme Court in *Palm Beach County Canvassing Bd. v. Harris*, at respondents' own urging. The press of time does not diminish the constitutional concern. A desire for speed is not a general excuse for ignoring equal protection guarantees.

In addition to these difficulties the actual process by which the votes were to be counted under the Florida Supreme Court's decision raises further concerns. That order did not specify who would recount the ballots. The county canvassing boards were forced to pull together ad hoc teams of judges from various Circuits who had no previous training in handling and interpreting ballots. Furthermore, while others were permitted to observe, they were prohibited from objecting during the recount.

The recount process, in its features here described, is inconsistent with the minimum procedures necessary to protect the fundamental right of each voter in the special instance of a statewide recount under the authority of a single state judicial officer. Our consideration is limited to the present circumstances, for the problem of equal protection in election processes generally presents many complexities.*

The question before the Court is not whether local entities, in the exercise of their expertise, may develop different systems for implementing elections. Instead, we are presented with a situation where a state court with the power to assure uniformity has ordered a statewide recount with minimal procedural safeguards. When a court orders a statewide remedy, there must be at least some assurance that the rudimentary requirements of equal treatment and fundamental fairness are satisfied.

* [This sentence has been particularly controversial. Many have interpreted it as an explicit admission by the Court that its decision was unprincipled and lawless, refusing to set a precedent that would apply in future cases according to the rule of law. Others have seen the sentence as innocuous, consistent with the common law heritage of adjudicating cases one at a time and not creating judicial dicta broader than necessary to decide the specific case at hand. What do you think the Court meant by this sentence? Does it matter, or instead is it now more important how future courts treat *Bush v. Gore* as a precedent? To be sure, the Court itself has not relied upon it in a subsequent case. (Justice Thomas cited it in a dissent for a rather straightforward proposition.) But, as you already have seen and will continue to see elsewhere in this casebook, lower courts have started to use *Bush v. Gore* to generate significance new Equal Protection jurisprudence applicable to the casting and counting of ballots. Thus, will the fury that this sentence sparked in some quarters upon the immediate release of the opinion continue to subside, as more time passes since 2000?—Eds.]

Given the Court's assessment that the recount process underway was probably being conducted in an unconstitutional manner, the Court stayed the order directing the recount so it could hear this case and render an expedited decision. The contest provision, as it was mandated by the State Supreme Court, is not well calculated to sustain the confidence that all citizens must have in the outcome of elections. The State has not shown that its procedures include the necessary safeguards. The problem, for instance, of the estimated 110,000 overvotes has not been addressed, although Chief Justice Wells called attention to the concern in his dissenting opinion.

Upon due consideration of the difficulties identified to this point, it is obvious that the recount cannot be conducted in compliance with the requirements of equal protection and due process without substantial additional work. It would require not only the adoption (after opportunity for argument) of adequate statewide standards for determining what is a legal vote, and practicable procedures to implement them, but also orderly judicial review of any disputed matters that might arise. In addition, the Secretary has advised that the recount of only a portion of the ballots requires that the vote tabulation equipment be used to screen out undervotes, a function for which the machines were not designed. If a recount of overvotes were also required, perhaps even a second screening would be necessary. Use of the equipment for this purpose, and any new software developed for it, would have to be evaluated for accuracy by the Secretary, as required by Fla. Stat. Ann. § 101.015 (Supp. 2001).

The Supreme Court of Florida has said that the legislature intended the State's electors to "participat[e] fully in the federal electoral process," as provided in 3 U.S.C. § 5. That statute, in turn, requires that any controversy or contest that is designed to lead to a conclusive selection of electors be completed by December 12. That date is upon us, and there is no recount procedure in place under the State Supreme Court's order that comports with minimal constitutional standards. Because it is evident that any recount seeking to meet the December 12 date will be unconstitutional for the reasons we have discussed, we reverse the judgment of the Supreme Court of Florida ordering a recount to proceed.

Seven Justices of the Court agree that there are constitutional problems with the recount ordered by the Florida Supreme Court that demand a remedy. See *post*, (Souter, J., dissenting); *post*, (Breyer, J., dissenting). The only disagreement is as to the remedy. Because the Florida Supreme Court has said that the Florida Legislature intended to obtain the safe-harbor benefits of 3 U.S.C. § 5, Justice Breyer's proposed remedy—remanding to the Florida Supreme Court for its ordering of a constitutionally proper contest until December 18 contemplates action in violation of the Florida Election Code, and hence could not be part of an "appropriate" order authorized by Fla. Stat. Ann. § 102.168(8) (Supp. 2001).

* * *

None are more conscious of the vital limits on judicial authority than are the Members of this Court, and none stand more in admiration of the Constitution's design to leave the selection of the President to the people, through their legislatures, and to the political sphere. When contending parties invoke the process of the courts, however, it becomes our unsought responsibility to resolve the federal and constitutional issues the judicial system has been forced to confront.

The judgment of the Supreme Court of Florida is reversed, and the case is remanded for further proceedings not inconsistent with this opinion.

Pursuant to this Court's Rule 45.2, the Clerk is directed to issue the mandate in this case forthwith.

It is so ordered.

Chief Justice REHNQUIST, with whom Justice SCALIA and Justice THOMAS join, concurring.

We join the *per curiam* opinion. We write separately because we believe there are additional grounds that require us to reverse the Florida Supreme Court's decision.

I

In most cases, comity and respect for federalism compel us to defer to the decisions of state courts on issues of state law. That practice reflects our understanding that the decisions of state courts are definitive pronouncements of the will of the States as sovereigns. Of course, in ordinary cases, the distribution of powers among the branches of a State's government raises no questions of federal constitutional law, subject to the requirement that the government be republican in character. *See* U.S. CONST., Art. IV, § 4. But there are a few exceptional cases in which the Constitution imposes a duty or confers a power on a particular branch of a State's government. This is one of them. Article II, § 1, cl. 2, provides that "[e]ach State shall appoint, in such Manner as the *Legislature* thereof may direct," electors for President and Vice President. (Emphasis added.) Thus, the text of the election law itself, and not just its interpretation by the courts of the States, takes on independent significance.

Title 3 U.S.C. § 5 informs our application of Art. II, § 1, cl. 2, to the Florida statutory scheme, which, as the Florida Supreme Court acknowledged, took that statute into account. Section 5 provides that the State's selection of electors "shall be conclusive, and shall govern in the counting of the electoral votes" if the electors are chosen under laws enacted prior to election day, and if the selection process is completed six days prior to the meeting of the electoral college. As we noted in *Bush v. Palm Beach County Canvassing Bd.*:

> "Since § 5 contains a principle of federal law that would assure finality of the State's determination if made pursuant to a state law in effect before the election, a legislative wish to take advantage of the 'safe harbor' would counsel against any construction of the Election Code that Congress might deem to be a change in the law."

If we are to respect the legislature's Article II powers, therefore, we must ensure that postelection state-court actions do not frustrate the legislative desire to attain the "safe harbor" provided by § 5.

In Florida, the legislature has chosen to hold statewide elections to appoint the State's 25 electors. Importantly, the legislature has delegated the authority to run the elections and to oversee election disputes to the Secretary of State

(Secretary), Fla. Stat. Ann. § 97.012(1) (Supp. 2001), and to state circuit courts, §§ 102.168(1), 102.168(8). Isolated sections of the code may well admit of more than one interpretation, but the general coherence of the legislative scheme may not be altered by judicial interpretation so as to wholly change the statutorily provided apportionment of responsibility among these various bodies.

To attach definitive weight to the pronouncement of a state court, when the very question at issue is whether the court has actually departed from the statutory meaning, would be to abdicate our responsibility to enforce the explicit requirements of Article II.

II

Acting pursuant to its constitutional grant of authority, the Florida Legislature has created a detailed, if not perfectly crafted, statutory scheme that provides for appointment of Presidential electors by direct election. Fla. Stat. Ann. § 103.011 (1992). Under the statute, "[v]otes cast for the actual candidates for President and Vice President shall be counted as votes cast for the presidential electors supporting such candidates.". The legislature has designated the Secretary as the "chief election officer," with the responsibility to "[o]btain and maintain uniformity in the application, operation, and interpretation of the election laws." Fla. Stat. Ann. § 97.012 (Supp. 2001). The state legislature has delegated to county canvassing boards the duties of administering elections. § 102.141. Those boards are responsible for providing results to the state Elections Canvassing Commission, comprising the Governor, the Secretary of State, and the Director of the Division of Elections. § 102.111.

After the election has taken place, the canvassing boards receive returns from precincts, count the votes, and in the event that a candidate was defeated by 0.5% or less, conduct a mandatory recount. Fla. Stat. § 102.141(4) (2000). The county canvassing boards must file certified election returns with the Department of State by 5 p.m. on the seventh day following the election. § 102.112(1). The Elections Canvassing Commission must then certify the results of the election. § 102.111(1).

The state legislature has also provided mechanisms both for protesting election returns and for contesting certified election results. Section 102.166 governs protests. Any protest must be filed prior to the certification of election results by the county canvassing board. § 102.166(4)(b). Once a protest has been filed, "[t]he county canvassing board may authorize a manual recount." § 102.166(4)(c). If a sample recount conducted pursuant to § 102.166(5) "indicates an error in the vote tabulation which could affect the outcome of the election," the county canvassing board is instructed to: "(a) Correct the error and recount the remaining precincts with the vote tabulation system; (b) Request the Department of State to verify the tabulation software; or (c) Manually recount all ballots," § 102.166(5). In the event a canvassing board chooses to conduct a manual recount of all ballots, § 102.166(7) prescribes procedures for such a recount.

Contests to the certification of an election, on the other hand, are controlled by § 102.168. The grounds for contesting an election include "[r]eceipt of a number of illegal votes or rejection of a number of legal votes sufficient to change or place in doubt the result of the election." § 102.168(3)(c). Any contest must be filed in the appropriate Florida circuit court, § 102.168(1), and the canvassing board or election board is the proper party defendant, § 102.168(4). Section 102.168(8) provides that "[t]he circuit judge to whom the contest is presented may fashion such orders as he or she deems necessary to ensure that each allegation in the complaint is investigated, examined, or checked, to prevent or correct any alleged wrong, and to provide any relief appropriate under such circumstances." In Presidential elections, the contest period necessarily terminates on the date set by 3 U.S.C. § 5 for concluding the State's "final determination" of election controversies.

In its first decision, *Palm Beach Canvassing Bd. v. Harris* (2000) (*Harris I*), the Florida Supreme Court extended the 7-day statutory certification deadline established by the legislature.[2] This modification of the code, by lengthening the protest period, necessarily shortened the contest period for Presidential elections. Underlying the extension of the certification deadline and the shortchanging of the contest period was, presumably, the clear implication that certification was a matter of significance: The certified winner would enjoy presumptive validity, making a contest proceeding by the losing candidate an uphill battle. In its latest opinion, however, the court empties certification of virtually all legal consequence during the contest, and in doing so departs from the provisions enacted by the Florida Legislature.

The court determined that canvassing boards' decisions regarding whether to recount ballots past the certification deadline (even the certification deadline established by *Harris I*) are to be reviewed *de novo,* although the Election Code clearly vests discretion whether to recount in the boards, and sets strict deadlines subject to the Secretary's rejection of late tallies and monetary fines for tardiness. Moreover, the Florida court held that all late vote tallies arriving during the contest period should be automatically included in the certification regardless of the certification deadline (even the certification deadline established by *Harris I*), thus virtually eliminating both the deadline and the Secretary's discretion to disregard recounts that violate it.

Moreover, the court's interpretation of "legal vote," and hence its decision to order a contest-period recount, plainly departed from the legislative scheme. Florida statutory law cannot reasonably be thought to *require* the counting of improperly marked ballots. Each Florida precinct before election day provides instructions on how properly to cast a vote, Fla. Stat. Ann. § 101.46 (1992); each polling place on election day contains a working model of the voting machine it uses, Fla. Stat. Ann. § 101.5611 (Supp. 2001); and each voting booth contains a sample ballot, § 101.46. In precincts using punchcard ballots, voters are instructed to punch out the ballot cleanly:

> "AFTER VOTING, CHECK YOUR BALLOT CARD TO BE SURE YOUR VOTING SELECTIONS ARE CLEARLY AND CLEANLY PUNCHED AND THERE ARE NO CHIPS LEFT HANGING ON THE BACK OF THE CARD."
>
> Instructions to Voters, quoted in Brief for Respondent Harris et al. 13, n.5.

2. We vacated that decision and remanded that case; the Florida Supreme Court reissued the same judgment with a new opinion on December 11, 2000.

No reasonable person would call it "an error in the vote tabulation," Fla. Stat. Ann. § 102.166(5) (Supp. 2001), or a "rejection of . . . legal votes," § 102.168(3)(c),[4] when electronic or electromechanical equipment performs precisely in the manner designed, and fails to count those ballots that are not marked in the manner that these voting instructions explicitly and prominently specify. The scheme that the Florida Supreme Court's opinion attributes to the legislature is one in which machines are *required* to be "capable of correctly counting votes," § 101.5606(4), but which nonetheless regularly produces elections in which legal votes are predictably *not* tabulated, so that in close elections manual recounts are regularly required. This is of course absurd. The Secretary, who is authorized by law to issue binding interpretations of the Election Code, §§ 97.012, 106.23, rejected this peculiar reading of the statutes. See DE 00-13 (opinion of the Division of Elections). The Florida Supreme Court, although it must defer to the Secretary's interpretations, rejected her reasonable interpretation and embraced the peculiar one. *See Palm Beach County Canvassing Bd. v. Harris* (Fla. 2000) (*Harris III*).

But as we indicated in our remand of the earlier case, in a Presidential election the clearly expressed intent of the legislature must prevail. And there is no basis for reading the Florida statutes as requiring the counting of improperly marked ballots, as an examination of the Florida Supreme Court's textual analysis shows. We will not parse that analysis here, except to note that the principal provision of the Election Code on which it relied, § 101.5614(5), was, as Chief Justice Wells pointed out in his dissent in *Gore v. Harris* (Fla. 2000) (*Harris II*), entirely irrelevant. The State's Attorney General (who was supporting the Gore challenge) confirmed in oral argument here that never before the present election had a manual recount been conducted on the basis of the contention that "undervotes" should have been examined to determine voter intent. For the court to step away from this established practice, prescribed by the Secretary, the state official charged by the legislature with "responsibility to . . . [o]btain and maintain uniformity in the application, operation, and interpretation of the election laws," § 97.012(1), was to depart from the legislative scheme.

III

The scope and nature of the remedy ordered by the Florida Supreme Court jeopardizes the "legislative wish" to take advantage of the safe harbor provided by 3 U.S.C. § 5. December 12, 2000, is the last date for a final determination of the Florida electors that will satisfy § 5. Yet in the late afternoon of December 8th—four days before this deadline—the Supreme Court of Florida ordered recounts of tens of thousands of so-called "undervotes" spread through 64 of the State's 67 counties. This was done in a search for elusive—perhaps delusive—certainty as to the exact count of 6 million votes. But no one claims that these ballots have not previously been tabulated; they were initially read by voting machines at the time of the election, and thereafter reread by virtue of Florida's automatic recount provision.

4. It is inconceivable that what constitutes a vote that must be counted under the "error in the vote tabulation" language of the protest phase is different from what constitutes a vote that must be counted under the "legal votes" language of the contest phase.

No one claims there was any fraud in the election. The Supreme Court of Florida ordered this additional recount under the provision of the Election Code giving the circuit judge the authority to provide relief that is "appropriate under such circumstances." Fla. Stat. Ann. § 102.168(8) (Supp. 2001).

Surely when the Florida Legislature empowered the courts of the State to grant "appropriate" relief, it must have meant relief that would have become final by the cutoff date of 3 U.S.C. § 5. In light of the inevitable legal challenges and ensuing appeals to the Supreme Court of Florida and petitions for certiorari to this Court, the entire recounting process could not possibly be completed by that date. Whereas the majority in the Supreme Court of Florida stated its confidence that "the remaining undervotes in these counties can be [counted] within the required time frame," it made no assertion that the seemingly inevitable appeals could be disposed of in that time. [T]he federal deadlines for the Presidential election simply do not permit even a shortened process.

As the dissent noted:

> "In [the four days remaining], all questionable ballots must be reviewed by the judicial officer appointed to discern the intent of the voter in a process open to the public. Fairness dictates that a provision be made for either party to object to how a particular ballot is counted. Additionally, this short time period must allow for judicial review. I respectfully submit this cannot be completed without taking Florida's presidential electors outside the safe harbor provision, creating the very real possibility of disenfranchising those nearly six million voters who are able to correctly cast their ballots on election day." (opinion of Wells, C.J.).

Given all these factors, and in light of the legislative intent identified by the Florida Supreme Court to bring Florida within the "safe harbor" provision of 3 U.S.C. § 5, the remedy prescribed by the Supreme Court of Florida cannot be deemed an "appropriate" one as of December 8. It significantly departed from the statutory framework in place on November 7, and authorized open-ended further proceedings which could not be completed by December 12, thereby preventing a final determination by that date.

For these reasons, in addition to those given in the *per curiam* opinion, we would reverse.

Justice STEVENS, with whom Justice GINSBURG and Justice BREYER join, dissenting.*

[Article II Issue]

The federal questions that ultimately emerged in this case are not substantial. Article II provides that "[e]ach *State* shall appoint, in such Manner as the Legislature *thereof* may direct, a Number of Electors." (Emphasis added.) It does not

* [In the U.S. Reports, four dissenting opinions are printed in order of each author's seniority on the Court. For the sake of readability, we have ordered them in the sequence in which they appeared to have been drafted. — EDS.]

create state legislatures out of whole cloth, but rather takes them as they come—as creatures born of, and constrained by, their state constitutions. Lest there be any doubt, we stated over 100 years ago in *McPherson v. Blacker* (1892), that "[w]hat is forbidden or required to be done by a State" in the Article II context "is forbidden or required of the legislative power under state constitutions as they exist." The legislative power in Florida is subject to judicial review pursuant to Article V of the Florida Constitution, and nothing in Article II of the Federal Constitution frees the state legislature from the constraints in the State Constitution that created it. Moreover, the Florida Legislature's own decision to employ a unitary code for all elections indicates that it intended the Florida Supreme Court to play the same role in Presidential elections that it has historically played in resolving electoral disputes. The Florida Supreme Court's exercise of appellate jurisdiction therefore was wholly consistent with, and indeed contemplated by, the grant of authority in Article II.

It hardly needs stating that Congress, pursuant to 3 U.S.C. § 5, did not impose any affirmative duties upon the States that their governmental branches could "violate." Rather, § 5 provides a safe harbor for States to select electors in contested elections "by judicial or other methods" established by laws prior to the election day. Section 5, like Article II, assumes the involvement of the state judiciary in interpreting state election laws and resolving election disputes under those laws. Neither § 5 nor Article II grants federal judges any special authority to substitute their views for those of the state judiciary on matters of state law.

[Equal Protection Issue]

Nor are petitioners correct in asserting that the failure of the Florida Supreme Court to specify in detail the precise manner in which the "intent of the voter," Fla. Stat. Ann. § 101.5614(5) (Supp. 2001), is to be determined rises to the level of a constitutional violation.[2] We found such a violation when individual votes within the same State were weighted unequally, *see, e.g., Reynolds v. Sims,* (1964), but we have never before called into question the substantive standard by which a State determines that a vote has been legally cast. And there is no reason to think that the guidance provided to the factfinders, specifically the various canvassing boards, by the "intent of the voter" standard is any less sufficient—or will lead to results any less uniform—than, for example, the "beyond a reasonable doubt" standard employed every day by ordinary citizens in courtrooms across this country.

Admittedly, the use of differing substandards for determining voter intent in different counties employing similar voting systems may raise serious concerns. Those concerns are alleviated—if not eliminated—by the fact that a single impartial magistrate will ultimately adjudicate all objections arising from the recount process. Of course, as a general matter, "[t]he interpretation of constitutional principles must not be too literal. We must remember that the machinery of government would not work if it were not allowed a little play in its joints." *Bain Peanut Co.*

2. The Florida statutory standard is consistent with the practice of the majority of States, which apply either an "intent of the voter" standard or an "impossible to determine the elector's choice" standard in ballot recounts.

of Tex. v. Pinson (1931) (Holmes, J.). If it were otherwise, Florida's decision to leave to each county the determination of what balloting system to employ—despite enormous differences in accuracy[4]—might run afoul of equal protection. So, too, might the similar decisions of the vast majority of state legislatures to delegate to local authorities certain decisions with respect to voting systems and ballot design.

Even assuming that aspects of the remedial scheme might ultimately be found to violate the Equal Protection Clause, I could not subscribe to the majority's disposition of the case. As the majority explicitly holds, once a state legislature determines to select electors through a popular vote, the right to have one's vote counted is of constitutional stature. As the majority further acknowledges, Florida law holds that all ballots that reveal the intent of the voter constitute valid votes. Recognizing these principles, the majority nonetheless orders the termination of the contest proceeding before all such votes have been tabulated. Under their own reasoning, the appropriate course of action would be to remand to allow more specific procedures for implementing the legislature's uniform general standard to be established.

In the interest of finality, however, the majority effectively orders the disenfranchisement of an unknown number of voters whose ballots reveal their intent and are therefore legal votes under state law but were for some reason rejected by ballot-counting machines. It does so on the basis of the deadlines set forth in Title 3 of the United States Code. But, as I have already noted, those provisions merely provide rules of decision for Congress to follow when selecting among conflicting slates of electors. They do not prohibit a State from counting what the majority concedes to be legal votes until a bona fide winner is determined. Indeed, in 1960, Hawaii appointed two slates of electors and Congress chose to count the one appointed on January 4, 1961, well after the Title 3 deadlines. Thus, nothing prevents the majority, even if it properly found an equal protection violation, from ordering relief appropriate to remedy that violation without depriving Florida voters of their right to have their votes counted. As the majority notes, "[a] desire for speed is not a general excuse for ignoring equal protection guarantees."

[Article II Issue, Cont.]

Finally, neither in this case, nor in its earlier opinion in *Palm Beach County Canvassing Bd. v. Harris* (2000), did the Florida Supreme Court make any substantive change in Florida electoral law. Its decisions were rooted in long-established precedent and were consistent with the relevant statutory provisions, taken as a whole. It did what courts do—it decided the case before it in light of the legislature's intent to leave no legally cast vote uncounted. In so doing, it relied on the sufficiency of the general "intent of the voter" standard articulated by the state legislature, coupled with a procedure for ultimate review by an impartial judge, to resolve the concern

4. The percentage of nonvotes in this election in counties using a punchcard system was 3.92%; in contrast, the rate of error under the more modern optical-scan systems was only 1.43 Put in other terms, for every 10,000 votes cast, punchcard systems result in 250 more nonvotes than optical-scan systems. A total of 3,718,305 votes were cast under punchcard systems, and 2,353,811 votes were cast under optical-scan systems.

about disparate evaluations of contested ballots. If we assume—as I do—that the members of that court and the judges who would have carried out its mandate are impartial, its decision does not even raise a colorable federal question.

What must underlie petitioners' entire federal assault on the Florida election procedures is an unstated lack of confidence in the impartiality and capacity of the state judges who would make the critical decisions if the vote count were to proceed. Otherwise, their position is wholly without merit. The endorsement of that position by the majority of this Court can only lend credence to the most cynical appraisal of the work of judges throughout the land. It is confidence in the men and women who administer the judicial system that is the true backbone of the rule of law. Time will one day heal the wound to that confidence that will be inflicted by today's decision. One thing, however, is certain. Although we may never know with complete certainty the identity of the winner of this year's Presidential election, the identity of the loser is perfectly clear. It is the Nation's confidence in the judge as an impartial guardian of the rule of law.

I respectfully dissent.

Justice BREYER, with whom Justice STEVENS and Justice GINSBURG join except as to Part I-A-1, and with whom Justice SOUTER joins as to Part I, dissenting.

The Court was wrong to take this case. It was wrong to grant a stay. It should now vacate that stay and permit the Florida Supreme Court to decide whether the recount should resume.

I

The political implications of this case for the country are momentous. But the federal legal questions presented, with one exception, are insubstantial.

A

1

The majority raises three equal protection problems with the Florida Supreme Court's recount order: first, the failure to include overvotes in the manual recount; second, the fact that *all* ballots, rather than simply the undervotes, were recounted in some, but not all, counties; and third, the absence of a uniform, specific standard to guide the recounts. As far as the first issue is concerned, petitioners presented no evidence, to this Court or to any Florida court, that a manual recount of overvotes would identify additional legal votes. The same is true of the second, and, in addition, the majority's reasoning would seem to invalidate any state provision for a manual recount of individual counties in a statewide election.

The majority's third concern does implicate principles of fundamental fairness. The majority concludes that the Equal Protection Clause requires that a manual recount be governed not only by the uniform general standard of the "clear intent of the voter," but also by uniform subsidiary standards (for example, a uniform determination whether indented, but not perforated, "undervotes" should count). The opinion points out that the Florida Supreme Court ordered the inclusion of Broward County's undercounted "legal votes" even though those votes included ballots that were not perforated but simply "dimpled," while newly recounted ballots from other counties will likely include only votes determined to be "legal" on the basis of a stricter standard. In light of our previous remand, the Florida Supreme Court may have been reluctant to adopt a more specific standard than that provided for by the legislature for fear of exceeding its authority under Article II. However, since the use of different standards could favor one or the other of the candidates, since time was, and is, too short to permit the lower courts to iron out significant differences through ordinary judicial review, and since the relevant distinction was embodied in the order of the State's highest court, I agree that, in these very special circumstances, basic principles of fairness may well have counseled the adoption of a uniform standard to address the problem.

2

Nonetheless, there is no justification for the majority's remedy, which is simply to reverse the lower court and halt the recount entirely. An appropriate remedy would be, instead, to remand this case with instructions that, even at this late date, would permit the Florida Supreme Court to require recounting *all* undercounted votes in Florida, including those from Broward, Volusia, Palm Beach, and Miami-Dade Counties, whether or not previously recounted prior to the end of the protest period, and to do so in accordance with a single uniform standard.

The majority justifies stopping the recount entirely on the ground that there is no more time. In particular, the majority relies on the lack of time for the Secretary of State to review and approve equipment needed to separate undervotes. But the majority reaches this conclusion in the absence of *any* record evidence that the recount could not have been completed in the time allowed by the Florida Supreme Court. The majority finds facts outside of the record on matters that state courts are in a far better position to address. Of course, it is too late for any such recount to take place by December 12, the date by which election disputes must be decided if a State is to take advantage of the safe harbor provisions of 3 U.S.C. § 5. Whether there is time to conduct a recount prior to December 18, when the electors are scheduled to meet, is a matter for the state courts to determine. And whether, under Florida law, Florida could or could not take further action is obviously a matter for Florida courts, not this Court, to decide.

By halting the manual recount, and thus ensuring that the uncounted legal votes will not be counted under any standard, this Court crafts a remedy out of proportion to the asserted harm. And that remedy harms the very fairness interests the Court is attempting to protect. The manual recount would itself redress a problem of unequal treatment of ballots. [T]he ballots of voters in counties that use punchcard systems are more likely to be disqualified than those in counties using optical-scanning systems. According to recent news reports, variations in the undervote rate are even more pronounced. *See* Fessenden, *No-Vote Rates Higher in Punch Card Count,* N.Y. TIMES, Dec. 1, 2000, p. A29 (reporting that 0.3% of ballots cast in 30 Florida counties using optical-scanning systems registered no Presidential vote, in comparison to 1.53% in the 15 counties using Votomatic punchcard ballots). Thus, in a system that allows counties to use different types of voting systems, voters already arrive at the polls with an unequal chance that their votes will be counted. I do not see how the fact that this results from counties' selection of different voting machines rather than a court order makes the outcome any more fair. Nor do I understand why the Florida Supreme Court's recount order, which helps to redress this inequity, must be entirely prohibited based on a deficiency that could easily be remedied.

B

The remainder of petitioners' claims, which are the focus of The Chief Justice's concurrence, raise no significant federal questions. I cannot agree that The Chief Justice's unusual review of state law in this case is justified by reference either to Art. II, § 1, or to 3 U.S.C. § 5. Moreover, even were such review proper, the conclusion that the Florida Supreme Court's decision contravenes federal law is untenable.

The Chief Justice contends that our opinion in *Bush v. Palm Beach County Canvassing Bd.* (*per curiam*) (*Bush I*), in which we stated that "a legislative wish to take advantage of [§ 5] would counsel against" a construction of Florida law that Congress might deem to be a change in law now means that *this* Court "must ensure that post-election state-court actions do not frustrate the legislative desire to attain the 'safe harbor' provided by § 5." However, § 5 is part of the rules that govern Congress' recognition of slates of electors. Nowhere in *Bush I* did we establish that *this* Court had the authority to enforce § 5. Nor did we suggest that the permissive "counsel against" could be transformed into the mandatory "must ensure." And nowhere did we intimate, as the concurrence does here, that a state-court decision that threatens the safe harbor provision of § 5 does so in violation of Article II. The concurrence's logic turns the presumption that legislatures would wish to take advantage of § 5's "safe harbor" provision into a mandate that trumps other statutory provisions and overrides the intent that the legislature *did* express.

But, in any event, the concurrence, having conducted its review, now reaches the wrong conclusion. It says that "the Florida Supreme Court's interpretation of the Florida election laws impermissibly distorted them beyond what a fair reading required, in violation of Article II." But what precisely is the distortion? Apparently, it has three elements. First, the Florida court, in its earlier opinion, changed the election certification date from November 14 to November 26. Second, the Florida court ordered a manual recount of "undercounted" ballots that could not have been fully completed by the December 12 "safe harbor" deadline. Third, the Florida court, in the opinion now under review, failed to give adequate deference to the determinations of canvassing boards and the Secretary.

To characterize the first element as a "distortion," however, requires the concurrence to second-guess the way in which the state court resolved a plain conflict in the language of different statutes. *Compare* Fla. Stat. Ann. § 102.166 (Supp. 2001) (foreseeing manual recounts during the protest period) *with* § 102.111 (setting what is arguably too short a deadline for manual recounts to be conducted); *compare* § 102.112(1) (stating that the Secretary "may" ignore late returns) *with* § 102.111(1) (stating that the Secretary "shall" ignore late returns). In any event, that issue no longer has any practical importance and cannot justify the reversal of the different Florida court decision before us now.

To characterize the second element as a "distortion" requires the concurrence to overlook the fact that the inability of the Florida courts to conduct the recount on time is, in significant part, a problem of the Court's own making. The Florida

Supreme Court thought that the recount could be completed on time, and, within hours, the Florida Circuit Court was moving in an orderly fashion to meet the deadline. This Court improvidently entered a stay. As a result, we will never know whether the recount could have been completed.

Nor can one characterize the third element as "impermissibl[e] distort[ion]" once one understands that there are two sides to the opinion's argument that the Florida Supreme Court "virtually eliminat[ed] the Secretary's discretion." The Florida statute in question was amended in 1999 to provide that the "grounds for contesting an election" include the "rejection of a number of legal votes sufficient to . . . place in doubt the result of the election." Fla. Stat. Ann. §§ 102.168(3), (3)(c) (Supp. 2001). And the parties have argued about the proper meaning of the statute's term "legal vote." The Secretary has claimed that a "legal vote" is a vote "properly executed in accordance with the instructions provided to all registered voters." On that interpretation, punchcard ballots for which the machines cannot register a vote are not "legal" votes. The Florida Supreme Court did not accept her definition. But it had a reason. Its reason was that a different provision of Florida election laws (a provision that addresses damaged or defective ballots) says that no vote shall be disregarded "if there is a clear indication of the intent of the voter as determined by the canvassing board" (adding that ballots should not be counted "if it is impossible to determine the elector's choice"). Fla. Stat. Ann. § 101.5614(5) (Supp. 2001). Given this statutory language, certain roughly analogous judicial precedent, and somewhat similar determinations by courts throughout the Nation, the Florida Supreme Court concluded that the term "legal vote" means a vote recorded on a ballot that clearly reflects what the voter intended. That conclusion differs from the conclusion of the Secretary. But nothing in Florida law requires the Florida Supreme Court to accept as determinative the Secretary's view on such a matter. Nor can one say that the court's ultimate determination is so unreasonable as to amount to a constitutionally "impermissible distort[ion]" of Florida law.

The Florida Supreme Court, applying this definition, decided, on the basis of the record, that respondents had shown that the ballots undercounted by the voting machines contained enough "legal votes" to place "the result[s]" of the election "in doubt." Since only a few hundred votes separated the candidates, and since the "undercounted" ballots numbered tens of thousands, it is difficult to see how anyone could find this conclusion unreasonable—however strict the standard used to measure the voter's "clear intent." Nor did this conclusion "strip" canvassing boards of their discretion. The boards retain their traditional discretionary authority during the protest period. And during the contest period, as the court stated, "the Canvassing Board's actions [during the protest period] may constitute evidence that a ballot does or does not qualify as a legal vote." Whether a local county canvassing board's discretionary judgment during the protest period not to conduct a manual recount will be set aside during a contest period depends upon whether a candidate provides additional evidence that the rejected votes contain enough "legal votes" to place the outcome of the race in doubt. To limit the local canvassing board's discretion in this way is not to eliminate that discretion. At the least, one could reasonably so believe.

The statute goes on to provide the Florida circuit judge with authority to "fashion such orders as he or she deems necessary to ensure that each allegation . . . is *investigated, examined, or checked,* . . . and to provide any relief appropriate." Fla. Stat. Ann. § 102.168(8) (Supp. 2001) (emphasis added). The Florida Supreme Court did just that. One might reasonably disagree with the Florida Supreme Court's interpretation of these, or other, words in the statute. But I do not see how one could call its plain language interpretation of a 1999 statutory change so misguided as no longer to qualify as judicial interpretation or as a usurpation of the authority of the state legislature. Indeed, other state courts have interpreted roughly similar state statutes in similar ways.

I repeat, where is the "impermissible" distortion?

II

Despite the reminder that this case involves "an election for the President of the United States," no preeminent legal concern, or practical concern related to legal questions, required this Court to hear this case, let alone to issue a stay that stopped Florida's recount process in its tracks. Petitioners invoke fundamental fairness, namely, the need for procedural fairness, including finality. But with the one "equal protection" exception, they rely upon law that focuses, not upon that basic need, but upon the constitutional allocation of power. Respondents invoke a competing fundamental consideration—the need to determine the voter's true intent. But they look to state law, not to federal constitutional law, to protect that interest. Neither side claims electoral fraud, dishonesty, or the like. And the more fundamental equal protection claim might have been left to the state court to resolve if and when it was discovered to have mattered. It could still be resolved through a remand conditioned upon issuance of a uniform standard; it does not require reversing the Florida Supreme Court.

Of course, the selection of the President is of fundamental national importance. But that importance is political, not legal. And this Court should resist the temptation unnecessarily to resolve tangential legal disputes, where doing so threatens to determine the outcome of the election.

The Constitution and federal statutes themselves make clear that restraint is appropriate. They set forth a road-map of how to resolve disputes about electors, even after an election as close as this one. That road-map foresees resolution of electoral disputes by *state* courts. *See* 3 U.S.C. § 5 (providing that, where a "State shall have provided, by laws enacted prior to [election day], for its final determination of any controversy or contest concerning the appointment of . . . electors . . . by *judicial* or other methods," the subsequently chosen electors enter a safe harbor free from congressional challenge). But it nowhere provides for involvement by the United States Supreme Court.

To the contrary, the Twelfth Amendment commits to Congress the authority and responsibility to count electoral votes. A federal statute, the Electoral Count Act, enacted after the close 1876 Hayes-Tilden Presidential election, specifies that, after States have tried to resolve disputes (through "judicial" or other means), Congress is the body primarily authorized to resolve remaining disputes. *See* Electoral Count Act of 1887.

The legislative history of the Act makes clear its intent to commit the power to resolve such disputes to Congress, rather than the courts:

"The two Houses are, by the Constitution, authorized to make the count of electoral votes. They can only count legal votes, and in doing so must determine, from the best evidence to be had, what are legal votes. . . .

. . . .

"The power to determine rests with the two houses, and there is no other constitutional tribunal." H.R. Rep. No. 1638, 49th Cong., 1st Sess., 2 (1886).

The Act goes on to set out rules for the congressional determination of disputes about those votes. If, for example, a State submits a single slate of electors, Congress must count those votes unless both Houses agree that the votes "have not been . . . regularly given." 3 U.S.C. § 15. If, as occurred in 1876, a State submits two slates of electors, then Congress must determine whether a slate has entered the safe harbor of § 5, in which case its votes will have "conclusive" effect. If, as also occurred in 1876, there is controversy about "which of two or more of such State authorities . . . is the lawful tribunal" authorized to appoint electors, then each House shall determine separately which votes are "supported by the decision of such State so authorized by its law." If the two Houses of Congress agree, the votes they have approved will be counted. If they disagree, then "the votes of the electors whose appointment shall have been certified by the executive of the State, under the seal thereof, shall be counted."

Given this detailed, comprehensive scheme for counting electoral votes, there is no reason to believe that federal law either foresees or requires resolution of such a political issue by this Court. Nor, for that matter, is there any reason to think that the Constitution's Framers would have reached a different conclusion. Madison, at least, believed that allowing the judiciary to choose the Presidential electors "was out of the question."

The decision by both the Constitution's Framers and the 1886 Congress to minimize this Court's role in resolving close federal Presidential elections is as wise as it is clear. However awkward or difficult it may be for Congress to resolve difficult electoral disputes, Congress, being a political body, expresses the people's will far more accurately than does an unelected Court. And the people's will is what elections are about.

Moreover, Congress was fully aware of the danger that would arise should it ask judges, unarmed with appropriate legal standards, to resolve a hotly contested Presidential election contest. [Justice Breyer here recounts the history of the 1876 presidential election, which ended with the partisan 8-7 split of the Electoral Commission.]

For present purposes, the relevance of this history lies in the fact that the participation in the work of the electoral commission by five Justices, including Justice Bradley, did not lend that process legitimacy. Nor did it assure the public that the process had worked fairly, guided by the law. Rather, it simply embroiled Members of the Court in partisan conflict, thereby undermining respect for the judicial process. And the Congress that later enacted the Electoral Count Act knew it.

This history may help to explain why I think it not only legally wrong, but also most unfortunate, for the Court simply to have terminated the Florida recount. Those who caution judicial restraint in resolving political disputes have described the quintessential case for that restraint as a case marked, among other things, by the "strangeness of the issue," its "intractability to principled resolution," its "sheer momentousness, . . . which tends to unbalance judicial judgment," and "the inner vulnerability, the self-doubt of an institution which is electorally irresponsible and has no earth to draw strength from." [Alexander Bickel, The Least Dangerous Branch 184 (1962).] Those characteristics mark this case.

[A]bove all, in this highly politicized matter, the appearance of a split decision runs the risk of undermining the public's confidence in the Court itself. That confidence is a public treasure. It has been built slowly over many years, some of which were marked by a Civil War and the tragedy of segregation. It is a vitally necessary ingredient of any successful effort to protect basic liberty and, indeed, the rule of law itself. We run no risk of returning to the days when a President (responding to this Court's efforts to protect the Cherokee Indians) might have said, "John Marshall has made his decision; now let him enforce it!" But we do risk a self-inflicted wound—a wound that may harm not just the Court, but the Nation.

Justice Brandeis once said of the Court, "The most important thing we do is not doing." What it does today, the Court should have left undone. I would repair the damage done as best we now can, by permitting the Florida recount to continue under uniform standards.

I respectfully dissent.

Justice Ginsburg, with whom Justice Stevens joins, and with whom Justice Souter and Justice Breyer join as to Part I, dissenting.

I

The Chief Justice says that Article II, by providing that state legislatures shall direct the manner of appointing electors, authorizes federal superintendence over the relationship between state courts and state legislatures, and licenses a departure from the usual deference we give to state-court interpretations of state law. The Framers of our Constitution, however, understood that in a republican government, the judiciary would construe the legislature's enactments. Article II does not call for the scrutiny undertaken by this Court.

The extraordinary setting of this case has obscured the ordinary principle that dictates its proper resolution: Federal courts defer to a state high court's interpretations of the State's own law. This principle reflects the core of federalism, on which all agree. Were the other Members of this Court as mindful as they generally are of our system of dual sovereignty, they would affirm the judgment of the Florida Supreme Court.

II

I agree with Justice Stevens that petitioners have not presented a substantial equal protection claim. Ideally, perfection would be the appropriate standard for judging the recount. But we live in an imperfect world, one in which thousands of votes have not been counted. I cannot agree that the recount adopted by the Florida court, flawed as it may be, would yield a result any less fair or precise than the certification that preceded that recount.

Even if there were an equal protection violation, I would agree with Justice Stevens, Justice Souter, and Justice Breyer that the Court's concern about "the December 12 deadline" is misplaced. Time is short in part because of the Court's entry of a stay on December 9, several hours after an able circuit judge in Leon County had begun to superintend the recount process. More fundamentally, the Court's reluctance to let the recount go forward despite its suggestion that "[t]he search for intent can be confined by specific rules designed to ensure uniform treatment," ultimately turns on its own judgment about the practical realities of implementing a recount, not the judgment of those much closer to the process.

The Court assumes that time will not permit "orderly judicial review of any disputed matters that might arise." But no one has doubted the good faith and diligence with which Florida election officials, attorneys for all sides of this controversy, and the courts of law have performed their duties. Notably, the Florida Supreme Court has produced two substantial opinions within 29 hours of oral argument. In sum, the Court's conclusion that a constitutionally adequate recount is impractical is a prophecy the Court's own judgment will not allow to be tested. Such an untested prophecy should not decide the Presidency of the United States.

I dissent.

Justice SOUTER, with whom Justice BREYER joins, and with whom Justice STEVENS and Justice GINSBURG join as to all but Part III, dissenting.

The Court should not have reviewed either *Bush v. Palm Beach County Canvassing Bd.* (*per curiam*), or this case, and should not have stopped Florida's attempt to recount all undervote ballots by issuing a stay of the Florida Supreme Court's orders during the period of this review. If this Court had allowed the State to follow the course indicated by the opinions of its own Supreme Court, it is entirely possible that there would ultimately have been no issue requiring our review, and political tension could have worked itself out in the Congress following the procedure provided in 3 U.S.C. § 15. The case being before us, however, its resolution by the majority is another erroneous decision.

As will be clear, I am in substantial agreement with the dissenting opinions of Justice Stevens, Justice Ginsburg, and Justice Breyer. I write separately only to say how straightforward the issues before us really are.

There are three issues: whether the State Supreme Court's interpretation of the statute providing for a contest of the state election results somehow violates 3 U.S.C. § 5; whether that court's construction of the state statutory provisions governing contests impermissibly changes a state law from what the State's legislature has provided, in violation of Article II, § 1, cl. 2, of the National Constitution; and whether the manner of interpreting markings on disputed ballots failing to cause machines to register votes for President (the undervote ballots) violates the equal protection or due process guaranteed by the Fourteenth Amendment. None of these issues is difficult to describe or to resolve.

I

The 3 U.S.C. § 5 issue is not serious. That provision sets certain conditions for treating a State's certification of Presidential electors as conclusive in the event that a dispute over recognizing those electors must be resolved in the Congress under 3

U.S.C. § 15. Conclusiveness requires selection under a legal scheme in place before the election, with results determined at least six days before the date set for casting electoral votes. But no State is required to conform to § 5 if it cannot do that (for whatever reason); the sanction for failing to satisfy the conditions of § 5 is simply loss of what has been called its "safe harbor." And even that determination is to be made, if made anywhere, in the Congress.

II

The second matter here goes to the State Supreme Court's interpretation of certain terms in the state statute governing election "contests," Fla. Stat. Ann. § 102.168 (Supp. 2001); there is no question here about the state court's interpretation of the related provisions dealing with the antecedent process of "protesting" particular vote counts, § 102.166, which was involved in the previous case, *Bush v. Palm Beach County Canvassing Bd.* The issue is whether the judgment of the State Supreme Court has displaced the state legislature's provisions for election contests: is the law as declared by the court different from the provisions made by the legislature, to which the National Constitution commits responsibility for determining how each State's Presidential electors are chosen? Bush does not, of course, claim that any judicial act interpreting a statute of uncertain meaning is enough to displace the legislative provision and violate Article II; statutes require interpretation, which does not without more affect the legislative character of a statute within the meaning of the Constitution. What Bush does argue, as I understand the contention, is that the interpretation of § 102.168 was so unreasonable as to transcend the accepted bounds of statutory interpretation, to the point of being a nonjudicial act and producing new law untethered to the legislative Act in question.

The starting point for evaluating the claim that the Florida Supreme Court's interpretation effectively rewrote § 102.168 must be the language of the provision on which Gore relies to show his right to raise this contest: that the previously certified result in Bush's favor was produced by "rejection of a number of legal votes sufficient to change or place in doubt the result of the election." Fla. Stat. Ann. § 102.168(3)(c) (Supp. 2001). None of the state court's interpretations is unreasonable to the point of displacing the legislative enactment quoted. As I will note below, other interpretations were of course possible, and some might have been better than those adopted by the Florida court's majority; the two dissents from the majority opinion of that court and various briefs submitted to us set out alternatives. But the majority view is in each instance within the bounds of reasonable interpretation, and the law as declared is consistent with Article II.

1. The statute does not define a "legal vote," the rejection of which may affect the election. The State Supreme Court was therefore required to define it, and in doing that the court looked to another election statute, § 101.5614(5), dealing with damaged or defective ballots, which contains a provision that no vote shall be disregarded "if there is a clear indication of the intent of the voter as determined by the canvassing board." The court read that objective of looking to the voter's intent as indicating that the legislature probably meant "legal vote" to mean a vote recorded on a ballot indicating what the voter intended. It is perfectly true that the majority might have chosen a different reading. *See, e.g.*, Brief for Respondent Harris

(defining "legal votes" as "votes properly executed in accordance with the instructions provided to all registered voters in advance of the election and in the polling places"). But even so, there is no constitutional violation in following the majority view; Article II is unconcerned with mere disagreements about interpretive merits.

2. The Florida court next interpreted "rejection" to determine what act in the counting process may be attacked in a contest. Again, the statute does not define the term. The court majority read the word to mean simply a failure to count. That reading is certainly within the bounds of common sense, given the objective to give effect to a voter's intent if that can be determined. A different reading, of course, is possible. The majority might have concluded that "rejection" should refer to machine malfunction, or that a ballot should not be treated as "reject[ed]" in the absence of wrongdoing by election officials, lest contests be so easy to claim that every election will end up in one. There is, however, nothing nonjudicial in the Florida majority's more hospitable reading.

3. The same is true about the court majority's understanding of the phrase "votes sufficient to change or place in doubt" the result of the election in Florida. The court held that if the uncounted ballots were so numerous that it was reasonably possible that they contained enough "legal" votes to swing the election, this contest would be authorized by the statute. While the majority might have thought (as the trial judge did) that a probability, not a possibility, should be necessary to justify a contest, that reading is not required by the statute's text, which says nothing about probability. Whatever people of good will and good sense may argue about the merits of the Florida court's reading, there is no warrant for saying that it transcends the limits of reasonable statutory interpretation to the point of supplanting the statute enacted by the "legislature" within the meaning of Article II.

III

It is only on the third issue before us that there is a meritorious argument for relief, as this Court's *per curiam* opinion recognizes. It is an issue that might well have been dealt with adequately by the Florida courts if the state proceedings had not been interrupted, and if not disposed of at the state level it could have been considered by the Congress in any electoral vote dispute. But because the course of state proceedings has been interrupted, time is short, and the issue is before us, I think it sensible for the Court to address it.

Petitioners have raised an equal protection claim (or, alternatively, a due process claim) in the charge that unjustifiably disparate standards are applied in different electoral jurisdictions to otherwise identical facts. It is true that the Equal Protection Clause does not forbid the use of a variety of voting mechanisms within a jurisdiction, even though different mechanisms will have different levels of effectiveness in recording voters' intentions; local variety can be justified by concerns about cost, the potential value of innovation, and so on. But evidence in the record here suggests that a different order of disparity obtains under rules for determining a voter's intent that have been applied (and could continue to be applied) to identical types of ballots used in identical brands of machines and exhibiting identical physical characteristics (such as "hanging" or "dimpled" chads). I can conceive of no legitimate state interest served by these differing treatments of the expressions of voters' fundamental rights. The differences appear wholly arbitrary.

In deciding what to do about this, we should take account of the fact that electoral votes are due to be cast in six days. I would therefore remand the case to the courts of Florida with instructions to establish uniform standards for evaluating the several types of ballots that have prompted differing treatments, to be applied within and among counties when passing on such identical ballots in any further recounting (or successive recounting) that the courts might order.

Unlike the majority, I see no warrant for this Court to assume that Florida could not possibly comply with this requirement before the date set for the meeting of electors, December 18. Although one of the dissenting justices of the State Supreme Court estimated that disparate standards potentially affected 170,000 votes, the number at issue is significantly smaller. The 170,000 figure apparently represents all uncounted votes, both undervotes (those for which no Presidential choice was recorded by a machine) and overvotes (those rejected because of votes for more than one candidate). But as Justice Breyer has pointed out, no showing has been made of legal overvotes uncounted, and counsel for Gore made an uncontradicted representation to the Court that the statewide total of undervotes is about 60,000. To recount these manually would be a tall order, but before this Court stayed the effort to do that the courts of Florida were ready to do their best to get that job done. There is no justification for denying the State the opportunity to try to count all disputed ballots now.

I respectfully dissent.

NOTE ON *BUSH v. GORE*

One issue that the dissenters raised is whether the Court should have involved itself at all in the case. Because the Court's certiorari jurisdiction is discretionary, the Court could have stayed out of it. Although no one can ever know for sure what would have happened if the Court had refrained from taking the case, it is probable that Gore would have lost the recount ordered by the Florida Supreme Court. A media study of the ballots afterwards determined that Gore could have won only if the statewide manual recount included an examination of overvotes as well as undervotes, but overvotes were not part of the Florida Supreme Court's order.*

Delving into the realm of speculation, if Gore somehow would have won the recount, the situation could have become even messier. The Florida legislature, which at the time was controlled by Republicans, was prepared to enact new legislation, purporting to rely on its authority under Article II of the U.S. Constitution, to award Florida's Electoral Votes directly to Bush, thereby attempting to nullify any contrary result from the recount. One could then imagine two competing certificates arriving in Congress before January 6, 2001, the date for the congressional counting of Electoral Votes. One certificate, flowing from the recount, would declare Gore the winner of Florida's Electoral Votes. The other certificate, flowing from the contrary legislation, would name Bush the winner.

* *See* Keating & Balz, *Florida Recounts Would Have Favored Bush*, WASH. POST (Nov. 12, 2001), p. A01.

What would then happen in Congress? While Gore might try to claim that his victory under the recount was entitled to Safe Harbor status (assuming the recount had been completed by December 12, absent U.S. Supreme Court intervention), there is no guarantee that the Republicans who controlled the U.S. House of Representatives at the time would have agreed. If the House voted for Bush, and the Senate voted for Gore—perhaps based on a tie-breaking vote cast by Gore himself as the incumbent Vice President (and thus President of the Senate) at the time—then according to the Electoral Count Act of 1887, the victory belonged to whichever certificate from Florida was signed by the state's "executive," presumably meaning the state's governor, who was Jeb Bush, the Republican candidate's brother.

But what if the Florida Supreme Court ordered Governor Bush to sign the certificate consistent with the result of its mandated recount, and ordered him not to sign the contrary certificate mandated by the legislature? What if the state's Attorney General, who was a Democrat, signed as "acting Governor" to comply with the Florida Supreme Court's order? What if the Democrats in the U.S. Senate refused to accept any result other than Gore's victory, based on their belief (right or wrong) that he had won more votes in Florida?

Some, including Judge Richard Posner of the U.S. Court of Appeals for the Seventh Circuit, have argued that to avoid such possibilities it was better to have the Supreme Court intervene in *Bush v. Gore* even if the constitutional basis for its intervention was dubious.* That view would extend the Court's role beyond its function under *Marbury v. Madison* "to declare what the law is" to a more fuzzy power to act as it deems best in circumstances of overriding national interest. On this view, the criteria for evaluating whether the Court acted wisely in *Bush v. Gore* would be very different from assessing whether its decision was legally sound according to conventional methods of legal analysis.

5. *The Fight over Vote-Counting in 2020*

Twenty years after *Bush v. Gore*, another presidential election erupted in a monumental dispute starting on Election Night over the outcome—although the circumstances were almost entirely different from what they had been in 2000. Rather than been caught by surprise about the possibility of shifting vote tallies, as the campaigns in 2000 had been, it was widely known and reported by the media that the initial returns on Election Night were unlikely to be stable but instead would change significantly over the ensuing days because of a documented phenomenon called "the blue shift": valid ballots incapable of being counted on Election Night, but counted subsequently, tend to favor Democratic candidates. The blue shift had caused the 2018 U.S. Senate election in Arizona to flip from a Republican lead to a Democratic win, and it almost did the same to both the U.S. Senate and gubernatorial elections in Florida that same year. Thus, even before the Covid pandemic occurred, there was every reason to think that the blue shift could affect the 2020

* *See* Richard A. Posner, Breaking the Deadlock: The 2000 Election, the Constitution, and the Courts (2001).

presidential election. After the pandemic hit, and with the inevitable increased reliance on absentee ballots as a result—plus President Trump's sustained hostility to absentee voting throughout the 2020 campaign—it was obvious to all observers that Election Night tallies would tend to favor Republicans before the ensuing blue shift started to occur. In fact, some referred to the "red mirage" of Election Night tallies looking more favorable to Republicans than what the eventual count of all valid ballots would end up being.

Sure enough, what was predicted was exactly what happened. The initial Election Night returns were much more favorable to President Trump than the final count of ballots in battleground states, and by Saturday, November 7 the networks—including Fox—had seen enough to "call" the election unofficially a victory for Joe Biden and thus a defeat for incumbent President Trump. But Trump refused to accept defeat and began a sustained attack on the result in six battleground states that he lost: Arizona, Georgia, Michigan, Nevada, Pennsylvania, and Wisconsin.

The fact that Trump was challenging the outcome in six states, not one, was another clear difference between 2020 and *Bush v. Gore*. Trump would have had to overturn the result in three states to deprive Biden his Electoral College victory. Moreover, in none of the six states was the margin nearly as close as the 537-vote squeaker in favor of Bush in Florida twenty years earlier. Arizona and Georgia were the two closest states in 2020, but Biden still won by over 10,000 in each. The next closest was Wisconsin, where Biden won by over 20,000. He won Pennsylvania by more than 80,000, and Michigan by more than 150,000! Even so, President Trump wouldn't let go of his claim, which was either delusional or dishonest, that he rather than Biden was the actual winner of the election. One of Trump's more preposterous theories was that Georgia's machines to count votes was somehow hacked by Venezuela, but a manual recount of all ballots in Georgia readily disproved that bizarre conspiracy theory—although Trump and his supporters continued to peddle the demonstrably false claim afterwards, much like claiming the earth is flat even after astronauts have orbited the round globe with pictures to prove its roundness.

Trump and his allies went to court, including the U.S. Supreme Court, hoping that the judiciary would overturn Biden's victory. But his experience was nothing like Bush's judicial success in 2000. For one thing, Trump's lawyers were careful not to repeat his blatant lies about the election being stolen from him in court, for fear of being sanctioned for lying to judges. (One of Trump's attorneys, Sidney Powell, subsequently defended herself against a defamation claim by saying that her dishonest claims of election fraud should not have been taken seriously, and that no reasonable person would be misled by them!). Even paring down their claims to technical defects in the administration of the election, none of which challenged the eligibility of voters who cast ballots or the accuracy of the results from counting those ballots, Team Trump lost all but one of its claims (with the one exception being a minor matter not affecting many ballots in Pennsylvania). Essentially, Trump's argument boiled down to seeking the disqualification of ballots cast by eligible voters for procedural defects that Trump had the opportunity to raise before those ballots were cast but did not. No judge, not even ones appointed by Trump, were going to nullify the result of a presidential election based on that kind of argument.

Despite losing everywhere in court, Trump persisted in his spurious claim that the election had been wrongfully stolen from him. His persistence led to the insurrection at the Capitol on January 6, 2021, when Congress met in joint session pursuant to the Twelfth Amendment and the Electoral Count Act to receive and count the Electoral College votes sent from the states. Trump's supporters in the House of Representatives, as well as Senators Josh Hawley and Ted Cruz, mounted an effort to disqualify enough Electoral College votes for Biden to deprive him of his victory. It was an effort doomed to fail according to the procedures set forth in the Electoral Count Act, because as long as one of the two congressional chambers would vote to count the challenged votes, those votes would be counted. Moreover, weeks before January 6, enough Representatives and Senators had made clear that they were going to sustain Biden's victory despite whatever objections might be filed, and so the result was never in doubt. Still, Trump urged the crowd of his supporters to protest at the Capitol, and even after the rioting had resulted in death, Senator Hawley and numerous Representatives persisted with their objection to Biden's Electoral College votes. The objection was rejected in both houses of Congress, as expected, and Biden was duly inaugurated on January 20. Nonetheless, because ex-President Trump continues to claim that he was wrongly deprived of a second term, public opinion polls show that a large percentage of Republican voters—as high as 80 percent—continue to believe without any basis in evidence that Trump won more valid votes than Biden and that the election was stolen from Trump.

In preparation for the January 6 joint session of Congress, Representative Liz Cheney of Wyoming wrote this memo for her Republican colleagues to explain why it was wrong for them to object to Biden's victory:

2020 Presidential Election Challenges in Arizona, Georgia, Michigan, Nevada, Pennsylvania and Wisconsin, and Our Constitutional Process

Representative Liz Cheney

The following summary begins by addressing the Constitutional issues, then provides excerpts from and a description of the principal judicial decisions in each of the states. By objecting to electoral slates, members are unavoidably asserting that Congress has the authority to overturn elections and overrule state and federal courts. Such objections set an exceptionally dangerous precedent, threatening to steal states' explicit constitutional responsibility for choosing the President and bestowing it instead on Congress. This is directly at odds with the Constitution's clear text and our core beliefs as Republicans.

ARTICLE II AND THE 12TH AMENDMENT

Article II and the 12th Amendment to our Constitution govern how our Republic selects the President of the United States. Although the Framers considered whether to confer the power to select the President upon the Congress of the United States, that proposal was specifically rejected. Instead, the Framers conferred that specific power upon the States and the People. Article II creates the Electoral College, and provides that "[e]ach state shall appoint, in such manner as the Legislature thereof may direct, a number of electors, equal to the whole number of Senators and Representatives to which the State may be entitled in the Congress." "The person having the greatest Number of [Electoral College] votes for President, *shall be the President.*"

In accordance with Article II, every State Legislature has enacted a set of rules governing the manner in which the election of the President in that State will be conducted and how electors will be selected. Those laws not only instruct state election officials how to conduct elections (and explicitly delegate authority to those officials for that purpose), but also set forth a state law process for challenging an election when problems arise. The legal processes for challenging the election vary state to state, but generally provide a procedure for recounts and audits, and an opportunity to litigate disputed issues in state court. In certain circumstances, it may be possible to bring an appropriate claim in Federal Court as well (for example, if a State has violated the U.S. Constitution or federal law), but Federal Courts are bound to observe the Constitutional limits on their jurisdiction (under Article III).

Because Article II commits to the States the authority and responsibility to conduct the election for President, and because State Legislatures have (consistent with Article II) provided a specific manner for challenging a Presidential election, allegations of election irregularities, fraud or other illegality must be resolved in accordance with those state laws. This is our Constitutional process and the rule of law. To date, dozens of cases challenging the 2020 Presidential election have been litigated in the six states at issue. Many judges (including multiple federal judges appointed by President Trump himself), have already directly addressed the subject matter of objections members intend to make. For instance, multiple judges have ruled state election officials *were not* acting contrary to state election laws. And multiple judges have found that allegations about Dominion voting machines and other issues *are not* supported by evidence.

In addition to committing the power and responsibility for selecting the President to the People of the States, Article II and the 12th Amendment also explicitly identify the exceptionally limited role of Congress in this process. First, "the President of the Senate shall receive certified copies of the electoral votes from each state" and "in the presence of the Senate and House of Representatives, open all the certificates." The votes "shall then be counted." Nothing in Article II, the 12th Amendment or any other Constitutional text provides for any debate, objection or discretionary judgments by Congress in performing the ministerial task of counting the votes. Nothing in the Constitution remotely says that Congress is the court of last resort, with the authority to second-guess and invalidate state and federal court judicial rulings in election challenges. Indeed, the Constitutional text reads: "The person having the greatest Number of [Electoral College] votes for President, shall be the President." It does not say: "The person having the greatest Number of [Electoral College] votes for President, shall be the President, *unless Congress objects or Congress wants to investigate.*" The Constitution identifies specifically the *only* occasions when Congress can take any non-ministerial action – when no Presidential candidate has a majority of the electoral votes: "[I]f no person have such majority [of the electoral votes counted], then from the persons having the highest numbers not exceeding three on the list of those voted for as President, the

House of Representatives shall choose immediately, by ballot, the President. . . ." Thus, the Constitutional text tells us very clearly what Congress' role is and is not.

For most of our nation's history, the Framers' straight-forward instructions regarding selection of the President prevailed. In the aftermath of our nation's Civil War, officials in certain Reconstruction Era state governments submitted competing slates of electors. In 1887, Congress sought to resolve those issues by enacting the Electoral Count Act. A principal provision of that Act instructs that a certificate identifying the Electoral College electors and their votes received from the Governor of a state shall be regarded as "conclusive." 3. U.S.C. § 5. Although the Constitutionality of that Act has been the subject of substantial debate, here there is no dispute that each Governor of the six states at issue submitted an official certification of the election, and those electors' votes have been transmitted to this Congress. Thus, under the Electoral Count Act, those certificates are conclusive and must be counted. There is no discretion to do otherwise under that Act. Accordingly, both the clear text of the Constitution and the Electoral Count Act compel the same conclusion – there is no appropriate basis to object to the electors from any of the six states at issue.

DESCRIPTION AND EXCERPTS OF PRINCIPAL CASES IN ALL SIX STATES

I. Arizona

A. Litigation in Arizona State Court

Multiple challenges to the Arizona Presidential election were filed, litigated and resolved with no change to the election outcome. In the principal case (which ultimately reached the Arizona Supreme Court), the trial judge allowed the challengers to engage in inspection of mail-in and "duplicate" ballots, conduct multiple depositions, and present their evidence at a hearing. In response to allegations about allegedly forged signatures on mail-in ballots, the court found:

> "There is no evidence that the manner in which signatures were reviewed was designed to benefit one candidate or another, or that there was any misconduct, impropriety, or violation of Arizona law with respect to the review of mail-in ballots."

As the Court also explained, neither the plaintiffs nor the defense experts found evidence of "forgery or simulation" as to the examined mail-in ballots. Addressing the *process* for reviewing mail-in ballots under Arizona law, the trial court explained:

> "Under Arizona law, voters who vote by mail submit their ballot inside an envelope that is also an affidavit signed by the voter. Election officials review all mail-in envelope/affidavits to compare the signature on them with the signature in voter registration records. If the official is "satisfied that the signatures correspond," the unopened envelope is held until the time for counting votes. If not, officials attempt to contact the voter to validate the ballot. A.R.S. § 16-550(A). This legislatively-prescribed process is elaborated on in the Secretary of State's Election Procedures

Manual. . . . Maricopa County election officials followed this process faithfully in 2020."

The Court also allowed inspection of a sample of "duplicate ballots." Such duplicates must be made for overseas military voters and in cases when ballots cannot be properly read by a tabulation machine. As to that evidence, the Court found:

"The duplication process prescribed by the Legislature necessarily requires manual action and human judgment, which entail a risk of human error. Despite that, the duplication process for the presidential election was 99.45% accurate. And there is no evidence that the inaccuracies were intentional or part of a fraudulent scheme. They were mistakes. And given both the small number of duplicate ballots and the low error rate, the evidence does not show any impact on the outcome."

The trial court concluded that "Plaintiff has not proven that the Biden/Harris ticket did not receive the highest number of votes." The Arizona Supreme Court then unanimously affirmed that ruling, explaining as follows:

"The validity of an election is not voided by honest mistakes or omissions unless they affect the result, or at least render it uncertain. *Findley v. Sorenson*, 35Ariz. 265, 269 (1929). Where an election is contested on the ground of illegal voting, the contestant has the burden of showing that sufficient illegal votes were cast to change the result. *Morgan v. Board of Sup'rs* (1948). The legislature has expressly delegated to the Secretary the authority to promulgate rules and instructions for early voting. A.R.S. § 16-452(A). After consulting with county boards and election officials, the Secretary is directed to compile the rules "in an official instructions and procedures manual." The Election Procedures Manual or "EPM," has the force of law. The Court recently considered a challenge to an election process and granted relief where the county recorder adopted a practice contrary to the EPM. . . . *Here, however, there are no allegations of any violation of the EPM or any Arizona law.*"

"Because the challenge fails to present any evidence of "misconduct," "illegal votes" or that the Biden Electors "*did not* in fact receive the highest number of votes for office," let alone establish any degree of fraud or a sufficient error rate that would undermine the certainty of the election results, the Court need not decide if the challenge was in fact authorized under A.R.S. § 16-672 or if the federal "safe harbor" deadline applies to this contest. **IT IS ORDERED** affirming the trial court decision and confirming the election of the Biden Electors under A.R.S. § 16-676(B)."

B. Litigation in Federal Court in Arizona

Tyler Bowyer, et al., v. Doug Ducey, et al. Federal District Court, Arizona, CV-20-02321-PHX-DJH, 12/09/20. Judge Diana Humetewa.

In addition to litigating in the Arizona state judicial system, plaintiffs supporting President Trump also attempted to bring multiple claims in Federal District Court for the District of Arizona, with factual allegations addressing "destruction of absentee ballots," Dominion voting machines, voting fraud and manipulation, problems with the election observer process, and alleged "dilution of lawful votes." The Court explained why several of the allegations were insufficient to state a federal Constitutional claim, including because the plaintiffs lacked standing under Article III of the Constitution. The Court also addressed plaintiffs' allegations of fraud specifically. Below is a selection of excerpts from the Judge's opinion on those issues:

> "The allegations they put forth to support their claims of fraud fail in their particularity and plausibility. Plaintiffs append over three hundred pages of attachments, which are only impressive for their volume. The various affidavits and expert reports are largely based on anonymous witnesses, hearsay, and irrelevant analysis of unrelated elections."
>
> "The Complaint is equally void of plausible allegations that Dominion voting machines were actually hacked or compromised in Arizona during the 2020 General Election. Plaintiffs are clearly concerned about the vulnerabilities of voting machines used in some counties across Arizona and in other states. They cite sources that attest to knowledge of 'well-known' vulnerabilities, have included letters from concerned citizens, Arizona elected officials, and United States senators. Plaintiffs even attach an affidavit of an anonymous witness with connections to the late Venezuelan dictator Hugo Chavez claiming to be privy as to how officials in Venezuela rigged their elections with the help of a voting systems company whose software "DNA" is now used in voting machines in the United States. These concerns and stated vulnerabilities, however, do not sufficiently allege that any voting machine used in Arizona was in fact hacked or compromised in the 2020 General Election. Rather, what is present is a lengthy collection of phrases beginning with the words "could have, possibly, might," and "may have."
>
> "Plaintiffs next argue that they have expert witnesses who can attest to widespread voter fraud in Arizona. As an initial matter, none of Plaintiffs' witnesses identify Defendants as committing the alleged fraud, or state what their participation in the alleged fraudulent scheme was. Instead, they allege that absentee ballots "could have been filled out by anyone and then submitted in the name of another voter," "could be filled in by third parties to shift the election to Joe Biden," or that ballots were destroyed or replaced "with blank ballots filled out by election workers, Dominion or other third parties." These innuendoes fail to meet Rule 9(b) standards. But perhaps more concerning to the Court is that the 'expert reports' reach implausible conclusions, often because they are derived from wholly unreliable sources."
>
> "Not only have Plaintiffs failed to provide the Court with factual support for their extraordinary claims, but they have wholly failed to establish that they have standing for the Court to consider them. ***Allegations that find favor in the public sphere of gossip and innuendo cannot be a substitute for earnest pleadings and procedure in federal court.*** They most certainly cannot be the basis for upending Arizona's 2020 General Election. The Court is left with no alternative but to dismiss this matter in its entirety."

II. Georgia

A. Cases litigated in Georgia State Court

Multiple plaintiffs filed cases challenging the Georgia election in Georgia State Courts. The Georgia legislature has enacted a detailed series of laws governing elections. Those laws provide specific remedies to address election related concerns (including post-election audits). In certain of the cases filed, the litigants supporting President Trump made fundamental errors by, for example, failing to sue the appropriate Georgia officials as required by Georgia law, failing to serve the defendants in the case with process, and other routine filing errors delaying the cases. A summary of the issues appears in a brief filed in the U.S. Supreme Court by the Attorney General of the State of Georgia (a Republican appointee):

> "Since the November election, there have been at least six Georgia cases alleging that state election officials violated the law by acting in accordance with the State's settlement agreement or by adopting State Rule 183-1-14-0.9-.15. And none of that litigation has gone anywhere. The Eleventh Circuit, the Northern District of Georgia, and the Superior Courts of Fulton County and Cobb County, Georgia have rejected all the claims except for in one case, which was filed just this week and is thus still winding through Georgia's courts just as the Georgia Legislature envisioned."

The Georgia Attorney General also described how Georgia's legislature enacted measures for election recounts (and state court election challenges) in accordance with Article II of our Constitution, and how those measures were implemented in 2020:

> "Georgia's legislature enacted laws governing elections and election disputes, and the State and its officers have implemented and followed those laws. To ensure the accuracy of the results of that process, it has completed three total counts of the vote for its presidential electors, including a historic 100 percent manual recount—all in accordance with state law. It has, consistent with its authority under 3 U.S.C. § 5 [the Electoral Count Act], authorized its courts to resolve election disputes. . . . The Legislature has given the Election Board express authority to "promulgate rules and regulations" to ensure "uniformity" among election officials and a "fair, legal, and orderly" election. O.C.G.A. § 21-2-31. . . . First, in accordance with O.C.G.A. § 21-2-498, Georgia completed a risk-limiting audit. . . . The audit resulted in a manual count of nearly 5 million ballots cast—a process that lasted the better part of a week and required the State to deploy immense human and financial resources. Ultimately, the audit confirmed the initial election results, and Secretary Raffensperger certified the results on November 20, 2020. That was not all. Responding to the Trump Campaign's request, Georgia undertook a machine tabulation recount of the nearly 5 million ballots. Again, the recount confirmed the initial election results."

Georgia state courts have specifically addressed allegations of election irregularities. In *Boland v. Raffensperger*, for example, a Georgia State Court evaluated a range of allegations about misconduct by election officials and related matters. The Court described the plaintiffs' case as follows:

"Even if credited, the Complaint's factual allegations do not plausibly support his claims. The allegations in the Complaint rest on speculation rather than duly pled facts. They cannot, as a matter of law, sustain this contest. Count I, which alleges that 20,312 people may have voted illegally in Georgia, relies upon a YouTube video which purportedly is based upon United States Postal Service mail forwarding information. Count II alleges that the signature-matching process resulting from a Settlement Agreement entered into by the State nine months ago is inconsistent with Georgia's election code, and allegedly violates the federal Constitution. The Court finds that Plaintiff's allegations, as pled, do not support an allegation of impropriety or a conclusion that sufficient illegal votes were cast to change or place in doubt the result of the election. These arguments have been offered and rejected in other courts. Furthermore, the statutory changes put in place by the General Assembly permitting voters to cure signature issues on their ballot as a result of 2019 legislation, as well as regulatory changes adopted by the State Election Board contemporaneous with execution of the Settlement Agreement, would be expected to result in fewer signature rejections. This would not be because illegal votes are somehow evading review, but because subjecting signatures to more thorough verification and permitting voters to cure suspected errors should reduce the number of lawful ballots that are improperly thrown out."

Likewise, in the *Della Polla* case, a Georgia State Court Judge concluded as follows:

"[Georgia law] provides that a petition for an election contest must set forth the grounds for the election context. [Georgia law] further provides that it must set forth such facts as are necessary to 'provide a full particular and explicit statement of the cause of contest.' Georgia's Supreme Court has interpreted this to require a contestant to allege and prove a factual basis showing grounds for an election contest and to prohibit a contestant from basing a contest on a mere speculative belief that an error has occurred. *See Ellis v. Johnson* (1993). Plaintiffs' Complaint does not meet this requirement as it does not recite facts or evidence but relies on speculation as to this belief that an error in the election has occurred. Therefore, his complaint is dismissed for failure to state a claim."

In one remaining state court case, *Trump et al. v. Raffensperger et al.*, No. 2020-CV-343255, counsel for President Trump initially sought an emergency hearing to address his claims of fraud and illegality, but then withdrew that emergency motion on December 8, 2020, canceling the imminent hearing and delaying the case. This has slowed the ultimate resolution of that action.

B. Principal Cases litigated in Federal Court in Georgia

Lin Wood v. Raffensperger, Federal District Court for the Northern District of Georgia, Atlanta Division, Judge Stephen Grimburg (appointed by President Trump.)

The plaintiff in this Federal District Court case argued that Georgia officials took unauthorized actions and treated absentee ballots in a manner that favored candidate Biden. Plaintiff also asked the Court to order a "second recount" of Georgia ballots. The absentee ballot allegations related in part to a settlement in March 2020 by Georgia of a prior lawsuit. Plaintiff also argued that designated Republican monitors did not have proper access to an audit conducted by Georgia state officials in the days after the election.

Judge Grimberg, a Trump appointee, conducted a hearing with live witness testimony before issuing his ruling. His opinion begins by describing the foundational Constitutional problems with Plaintiff Wood's federal suit, including that Wood lacked standing and noting that Wood was relying upon a 1993 11th Circuit precedent that is "no longer good law." Judge Grimberg also explained why courts require the type of challenge Plaintiff brought to be made pre-election, before millions of voters cast their ballots. After addressing those issues, the Court turned to the substance of Wood's legal and factual arguments, explaining as follows:

> "Even assuming Wood possessed standing, and assuming Counts I and II are not barred by laches, the Court nonetheless finds Wood would not be entitled to the relief he seeks."

Allegations about Absentee Ballots: "Wood's argument is that the procedures in the Settlement Agreement regarding information and signature match so overwhelmed ballot clerks that the rate of rejection plummeted and, ergo, invalid ballots were passed over and counted. This argument is belied by the record; the percentage of absentee ballots rejected for missing or mismatched information and signature is the exact same for the 2018 election and the General Election (.15%). This is despite a substantial increase in the total number of absentee ballots submitted by voters during the General Election as compared to the 2018 election."

Elections and Electors Clauses: "In relevant part, the Constitution states: 'The Times, Places and Manner of holding Elections for Senators and Representatives, shall be prescribed in each State by the Legislature thereof." U.S. CONST. art. I, § 4, cl. 1. This provision—colloquially known as the Elections Clause—vests authority in the states to regulate the mechanics of federal elections. *Foster v. Love* (1997). The 'Electors Clause' of the Constitution similarly states that "[e]ach State shall appoint, in such Manner as the Legislature thereof may direct, a Number of [Presidential] Electors." U.S. CONST. art. II, § 1, cl. 2. Wood argues Defendants violated the Elections and Electors Clauses because the 'procedures set forth in the [Settlement Agreement] for the handling of defective absentee ballots is not consistent with the laws of the State of Georgia, and thus, Defendants' actions . . . exceed their authority.' Put another way, Wood argues Defendants usurped the role of the Georgia General Assembly—and thereby violated the United States Constitution—by enacting additional safeguards regarding absentee ballots not found in the Georgia Election Code. . . . State legislatures—such as the Georgia General Assembly—possess the authority to delegate their authority over elections to state officials in conformity with the Elections and Electors Clauses. [*Citing* U.S. Supreme Court precedent.] *Ariz. State Legislature*, 576 U.S. at 816 ("The Elections Clause [] is not reasonably read to disarm States from adopting modes of legislation that place the lead rein in the people's hands . . . it is characteristic of our federal system that States retain autonomy to establish their own governmental processes."). *See also Corman v. Torres* (M.D. Pa. 2018) ("The Elections Clause, therefore, affirmatively grants rights to state legislatures, and under Supreme Court precedent, to other entities to which a state may, consistent with the Constitution, delegate lawmaking authority.") . . . Recognizing that Secretary Raffensperger is "the state's chief election official," the General Assembly enacted legislation permitting him (in his official capacity) to "formulate, adopt, and promulgate such rules and regulations, consistent with law, as will be conducive to the fair, legal, and orderly conduct of primaries and elections." O.C.G.A. § 21-2-31(2). ***The Settlement Agreement is a manifestation of Secretary Raffensperger's statutorily granted authority. It does not override or rewrite state law.*** It simply adds an additional safeguard to ensure election security by having more than one individual review an absentee ballot's information and signature for accuracy before the ballot is rejected. Wood does not articulate how the Settlement Agreement is not "consistent with law" other than it not being a verbatim recitation of the statutory code. Taking Wood's argument at face value renders O.C.G.A. § 21-2-31(2) superfluous. A state official—such as Secretary Raffensperger—could never wield his or her authority to make rules for conducting elections that had not otherwise already been adopted by the Georgia General Assembly. The record in this case demonstrates that, if anything, Defendants' actions in entering into the Settlement Agreement sought to achieve consistency among the county election officials in Georgia, which furthers Wood's stated goals of conducting "[f]ree, fair, and transparent public elections."

Judge Grimberg's Conclusion: "Granting injunctive relief here would breed confusion, undermine the public's trust in the election, and potentially disenfranchise over one million Georgia voters. Viewed in comparison to the lack of any demonstrable harm to Wood, this Court finds no basis in fact or in law to grant him the relief he seeks."

On appeal, a three-judge panel of the Federal Circuit Court of Appeals for the 11th Circuit affirmed Judge Grimberg's ruling unanimously. The panel included Judge Lagoa (a Trump appointee who was considered by the President for the recent Supreme Court vacancy, and Judge William Pryor, a Bush appointee).

Finally, in the *Pearson* litigation filed by Sidney Powell in Federal District Court in Atlanta, Judge Batten (a Bush appointee) reviewed all the pleadings and held an argument on a motion for an injunction. Judge Batten concluded as follows:

> "Finally, in their complaint, the Plaintiffs essentially ask the Court for perhaps the most extraordinary relief ever sought in any Federal Court in connection with an election. They want this Court to substitute its judgment for that of two-and-a-half million Georgia voters who voted for Joe Biden, and this I am unwilling to do."

III. Michigan

A number of cases were launched in Federal and State Courts in Michigan challenging different elements of the Michigan election. Certain of the cases were summarily dismissed by the courts for a range of pleading or procedural errors – including suing the wrong state official. Certain other cases were voluntarily dismissed by those litigants who brought them after the election was certified under

Michigan law. Judge Stephens of the Court of Claims for Michigan described one set of evidentiary issues this way:

> "This 'supplemental evidence' is inadmissible as hearsay. The assertion that Connarn was informed by an unknown individual what "other hired poll workers at her table" had been told is inadmissible hearsay within hearsay, and plaintiffs have provided no hearsay exception for either level of hearsay that would warrant consideration of the evidence. Moreover, even overlooking the evidentiary issues, the Court notes that there are still no allegations implicating the Secretary of State's general supervisory control over the conduct of elections. . . . Not only can the relief requested not issue against the Secretary of State, who is the only named defendant in this action, but the factual record does not support the relief requested."

Another Federal District Court case brought by attorney Sidney Powell in the Eastern District of Michigan alleged many of the same irregularities publicized in the press, such as voting machines allegedly corrupted or hijacked in the same manner used in Venezuela by former President Hugo Chavez. Federal District Court Judge Parker systematically reviewed the evidence Powell submitted explained why the relief sought by Powell could not be granted. For example, Judge Parker wrote:

> "With nothing but speculation and conjecture that votes for President Trump were destroyed, discarded or switched to votes for Vice President Biden, Plaintiffs' equal protection claim fails."
>
> "Plaintiffs' equal protection claim is not supported by any allegation that Defendants' alleged schemes caused votes for President Trump to be changed to votes for Vice President Biden. For example, the closest Plaintiffs get to alleging that physical ballots were altered in such a way is the following statement in an election challenger's sworn affidavit: "I believe some of these workers were changing votes that had been cast for Donald Trump and other Republican candidates." But of course, "[a] belief is not evidence" and falls far short of what is required to obtain any relief, much less the extraordinary relief Plaintiffs request."
>
> "The closest Plaintiffs get to alleging that election machines and software changed votes for President Trump to Vice President Biden in Wayne County is an amalgamation of theories, conjecture, and speculation that such alterations were *possible*."
>
> "Plaintiffs' requested injunction would "upend the statutory process for election certification and the selection of Presidential Electors. Moreover, it w[ould] disenfranchise millions of Michigan voters in favor [of] the preferences of a handful of people who[are] disappointed with the official results." In short, none of the remaining factors weigh in favor of granting Plaintiffs' request for an injunction."

In the wake of Judge Parker's ruling, defense counsel has filed a motion seeking sanctions against Powell and others on her legal team: "Plaintiffs' egregious conduct and frivolous and fraudulent filings clearly warrant sanctions under 28 U.S.C. § 1927."

IV. Nevada

In Nevada, the Court [held] a full hearing vetting the factual basis for each legal claim. He ruled against the plaintiffs, and was affirmed unanimously by the Nevada Supreme Court.

Nevada District Judge Russell allowed each party to conduct 15 depositions, considered all the evidence from those depositions and all submitted affidavits in detail. His 34-page opinion is highly detailed and addresses all the principal allegations. He explained as follows:

Dominion Voting Machines: "Clark County, along with 15 other counties in Nevada uses Dominion Voting Systems to conduct in person voting. . . . These voting systems are subject to extensive testing and certification before each election and are audited after each election. For example, the electronic voting systems used by Clark County were certified by the federal government when they were first brought on the market, as well as any time a hardware or software component is upgraded. This certification is done by a voting system test laboratory. The electronic voting machines are also tested and certified by the Secretary. . . . These voting machines are also audited against a paper trail that is generated . . . when voters make their selections. A Clark County voting machine will not operate unless it is connected to a printer . . . which creates a paper record that voters can review. . . . After each election, Clark County, like Nevada's other counties, conducts a random audit of its voting machines. Specifically, it compares the paper trail created by the printer against the results recorded by the voting machine to ensure they match. . . . Clark County conducted this audit following the November election and there were no discrepancies between the paper audit trail created by the printer and the data from the voting machine."

"Contestants' evidence does not establish by clear and convincing proof, or under any standard of evidence, that 'there was a malfunction of any voting device or electronic tabulator, counting device or computer in a manner sufficient to raise reasonable doubt as to the outcome of the election."

Affidavits/Declarations from Non-Testifying Witnesses: "Much of Contestants' evidence consists of non-deposition evidence in the form of witness declarations. These declarations fall outside the scope of the contest statute, which provides that election contests 'shall be tried and submitted so far as may be possible upon depositions and written or oral argument as the court may order. . . . The reason for this is to allow for the cross-examination of the deponent under oath. . . . These declarations also constitute hearsay, as they are out-of-court statements offered in evidence to prove the truth of the matters asserted. Most of these declarations were self-serving statements of little or no evidentiary value. The Court nonetheless considers the totality of evidence provided by Contestants in reaching and ruling upon the merits of their claims."

Plaintiffs' Expert Evidence: The Court heard expert testimony from three individuals who sought to use telephone surveys and statistical information to infer that the vote tallies must be incorrect, and to opine upon the administration of mail-in voting. He found each proffered expert unreliable:

> "The Court questions Mr. Baselice's methodology because he was unable to identify the source of the data for his survey and conducted no quality control of the data he received."

> "The Court questions Mr. Kamzol's methodology because he had little to no information about or supervision over the origins of his data, the manner in which it had been matched and what the rate of false positives would be. Additionally, there was little to no verification of his numbers."
>
> "Mr. Gessler's report lacked citations to facts and evidence that he used to come to his conclusions and did not include a single exhibit to support any of his conclusions. The Court finds that Mr. Gessler's methodology is unsound because he based nearly all of his opinions on a handful of affidavits that he took no steps to corroborate through independent investigation."
>
> "As reflected herein, the Court finds that the expert testimony provided by Contestants was of little or no value. The Court did not exclude consideration of this evidence, which it could have, but gave it very little weight."

Illegal or Improper Votes: "Contestants allege that fraud occurred at multiple points in the voting process in Nevada that exceed the margin of victory in the presidential race. . . . The Court finds there is no evidence that voter fraud rates associated with mail-in voting are systematically higher than voter fraud rates associated with other forms of voting. . . . [T]he illegal vote rate totaled at most only 0.00054 percent."

Provisional Ballots, Mismatched Signatures, Illegal Votes from In-Person Voting Technology, Ineligible Voters and Double Voting, Deceased Voters, Voter Impersonation, Untimely Ballots: The court made detailed findings rebutting each of plaintiffs' claims about illegality on each of these topics.

Judge Russell concluded: "The Contestants failed to meet their burden to prove credible and relevant evidence to substantiate any of the grounds set forth in NRS 293.410 to contest the November 3, 2020 General Election." President Trump's legal team appealed each of the issues up through the Nevada Supreme Court. That Court unanimously affirmed the ruling of the trial court judge, explaining:

> "Despite our earlier order asking appellants to identify specific findings with which they take issue, appellants have not pointed to any unsupported factual findings, and we have identified none."

V. Pennsylvania

A. Cases Filed in State Court

In *Kelly v. Commonwealth of Pennsylvania*, a group of plaintiffs challenged the mail-in ballot measures enacted by the Pennsylvania legislature in Act 77. The case began in Pennsylvania state court, reached the Pennsylvania Supreme Court, and then was the subject of a petition for emergency injunctive relief to the U.S. Supreme Court.

The principal allegation in the case was that Pennsylvania's "mail-in ballot" law violated the Pennsylvania state Constitution's provision on absentee voting. The plaintiffs claimed that the state constitution's provision is a restriction on all forms of remote voting, *i.e.* other than in-person voting. But Pennsylvania does not interpret its own Constitution that way. Instead, the Pennsylvania legislature understood the absentee voting provision to require that the Legislature *provide an avenue for absentee voting* for anyone who will not vote in person because they will be out of town on business, are prevented from voting in person by illness, are physically disabled, are observing a religious holiday or are serving as poll workers that day. As Pennsylvania explains in its brief to the U.S. Supreme Court, the absentee voting provision ensures that people in those categories will be able to vote absentee, but does not prevent the legislature from going further and providing a broader provision for mail-in ballots:

> "Petitioners contend that by requiring the General Assembly to allow certain voters to cast absentee ballots, Article VII, § 14 somehow forbids the General Assembly from allowing others to vote by mail. But the inclusion of a particular legislative duty in the Pennsylvania Constitution does not prevent the General Assembly from crafting other legislation on that topic. In fact, the Pennsylvania Constitution originally said "may" and now says "shall" in Article VII, § 14—a change meant to further clarify that this provision provides a floor, not a ceiling, for absentee voting in Pennsylvania. Thus, the Pennsylvania Constitution provides that the General Assembly must allow voters in the enumerated four categories to cast absentee ballots, but may also go further—by exercising its broad power to "prescribe[]" the permissible "method[s]" of voting, PA. CONST. art. VII, § 4—and allow other categories of voters to vote by mail, including by allowing any voter to opt to cast a mail-in ballot."

When this issue reached the Pennsylvania Supreme Court, the court ruled against plaintiffs based on the state law doctrine of "laches" – explaining that the plaintiffs waited too long to bring their claims, and could have brought their claims before the November election. Pennsylvania also explained that multiple state elections have already been conducted under the "mail-in" ballot law. Pennsylvania's brief in the U.S. Supreme Court and characterized the argument this way:

> "Petitioners maintain that the doctrine of laches must yield because they "are not lawyers," and could not have "been reasonably expected to know[] that they had viable legal claims well-before the election occurred." This assertion of ignorance is implausible, given that several Petitioners are current legislators or candidates for legislative office. In any event, '[l]aches is not excused by simply saying, 'I did not know.' If by diligence a fact can be ascertained, the want of knowledge so caused is no excuse for a stale claim. The test is not what the plaintiff knows, 'but what he might have known by the use of the means of information within his reach with the vigilance the law requires of him.' "

As noted, after the Pennsylvania Supreme Court ruled, the plaintiffs in the case filed a request with the U.S. Supreme Court for an emergency injunction. The Supreme Court denied that request on December 8, 2020. No U.S. Supreme Court Justice dissented from that denial.

In addition to the *Kelly* case, several other state court cases have been unsuccessfully pursued. One such case, *Metcalf*, was brought 11 days after the state law deadline, and was dismissed on that basis. In another matter, 8,329 votes were challenged because the voters failed to properly print their names, addresses and the date in full on the ballot envelope. The Pennsylvania Supreme Court applied state law and ruled as follows:

> "Here we conclude that while failures to include a handwritten name, address or date in the voter declaration on the back of the outer envelope, while constituting technical violations of the Election Code, do not warrant the wholesale disenfranchisement of thousands of Pennsylvania voters."

B. Cases Filed in Federal Court

In *Donald J. Trump for President, Inc. v. Boockvar*, the Federal District Court for the Middle District of Pennsylvania addressed plaintiffs' concerns with what is known as a "notice and cure" policy. Under that policy Pennsylvania State election officials allowed Pennsylvania county officials to provide notice to voters who had not properly filled out mail-in or absentee ballots, so that the voters could correct them. Some of the counties in the state exercised this authority and others did not. Plaintiffs argued that the unequal application of this policy across the state required the Court to throw out the election result state-wide. The Court responded as follows:

> "One might expect that when seeking such a startling outcome, a plaintiff would come formidably armed with compelling legal arguments and factual proof of rampant corruption, such that this Court would have no option but to regrettably grant the proposed injunctive relief despite the impact it would have on such a large group of citizens. That has not happened. Instead, this Court has been presented with strained legal arguments without merit and speculative accusations, unpled in the operative complaint and unsupported by evidence. In the United States of America, this cannot justify the disenfranchisement of a single voter, let alone all the voters of its sixth most populated state."
>
> "Plaintiffs' claims fail because it is perfectly rational for a state to provide counties discretion to notify voters that they may cure procedurally defective mail-in ballots. Though states may not discriminatorily sanction procedures that are likely to burden some persons' right to vote more than others, they need not expand the right to vote in perfect uniformity. All Plaintiffs have alleged is that Secretary Boockvar allowed counties to choose whether or not they wished to use the notice-and-cure procedure. No county was forced to adopt notice-and-cure; each county made a choice to do so, or not. Because it is not irrational or arbitrary for a state to allow counties to expand the right to vote if they so choose, Individual Plaintiffs fail to state an equal-protection claim."
>
> "Crucially, Plaintiffs fail to understand the relationship between right and remedy. Though every injury must have its proper redress, a court may not prescribe a remedy unhinged from the underlying right being asserted. By seeking injunctive relief preventing certification of the Pennsylvania election results, Plaintiffs ask this Court to do exactly that. Even assuming that they can establish that their right to vote has been denied,

> which they cannot, Plaintiffs seek to remedy the denial of their votes by invalidating the votes of millions of others. Rather than requesting that their votes be counted, they seek to discredit scores of other votes, but only for one race. This is simply not how the Constitution works."

The Federal Court of Appeals for the Third Circuit affirmed the District Court ruling. Judge Bibas, *another nominee of President Trump,* wrote the extensive opinion:

> "Free, fair elections are the lifeblood of our democracy. Charges of unfairness are serious. But calling an election unfair does not make it so. Charges require specific allegations and then proof. We have neither here. The Trump Presidential Campaign asserts that Pennsylvania's 2020 election was unfair. But as lawyer Rudolph Giuliani stressed, the Campaign "doesn't plead fraud. . . . [T]his is not a fraud case." Instead, it objects that Pennsylvania's Secretary of State and some counties restricted poll watchers and let voters fix technical defects in their mail-in ballots. It offers nothing more."
>
> "So is the claim that, "[u]pon information and belief, a substantial portion of the approximately 1.5 million absentee and mail votes in Defendant Counties should not have been counted." 'Upon information and belief' is a lawyerly way of saying that the Campaign does not know that something is a fact but just suspects it or has heard it. 'While legal conclusions can provide the framework of a complaint, they must be supported by factual allegations.' *Iqbal,* 556 U.S. at 679. Yet the Campaign offers no specific facts to back up these claims."
>
> "The Campaign's claims have no merit. The number of ballots it specifically challenges is far smaller than the roughly 81,000-vote margin of victory. And it never claims fraud or that any votes were cast by illegal voters. Plus, tossing out millions of mail-in ballots would be drastic and unprecedented, disenfranchising a huge swath of the electorate *and upsetting all down-ballot races too.*"

Another case filed in Federal District Court addressed the State law deadline for *receipt of mailed ballots.* This case has now been the subject of multiple filings at the U.S. Supreme Court but addresses only a relatively small number of ballots – approximately 9400 votes, far short of the Biden margin of victory in Pennsylvania. The matter relates to a Pennsylvania State Court ruling extending the Pennsylvania statue's deadline for receipt of mailed ballots by a number of days because COVID-19 apparently threatened delays in mail delivery. On November 6, 2020, Justice Alito entered a brief order, requiring that:

> "All [Pennsylvania] county boards of election are hereby ordered, pending further order of the Court, to comply with the following guidance provided by the Secretary of the Commonwealth on October 28 and November 1, namely, (1) that all ballots received by mail after 8:00 p.m. on November 3 be segregated and kept "in a secure, safe and sealed container separate from other voted ballots," and (2) that all such ballots, if counted, be counted separately."

The procedural history in this matter is complicated, and multiple courts have ruled in various contexts. But the principal remaining issue pending before the

Supreme Court is this: "Do State courts and executive officials have authority to alter legislatively established election rules, despite the U.S. Constitution's vesting of authority to set the rules for federal elections in State legislatures?" Briefing on a petition for certiorari seeking Supreme Court review is complete now, and the Court could issue its decision on the petition at any time. But to be clear, *the parties involved in this case know that the matter being addressed will not impact the outcome of the Presidential Election in Pennsylvania or any other state.* Indeed, the Petitioner, who supports President Trump's position in this case has argued in a recent brief: "In reality, however, this case is an ideal vehicle [for Supreme Court review], in part precisely *because it will not affect the outcome of this election.*"

VI. Wisconsin

A. Cases litigated in Federal Court

Donald J. Trump v. Wisconsin Elections Commission, et al.

In Federal District Court for the Eastern District of Wisconsin, and then on appeal in the Seventh Circuit, *two Trump appointees,* Judges Ludwig and Scudder, ruled against the President. The case addressed a series of issues relating to Wisconsin Election Commission procedures for addressing absentee ballots during the pandemic. The President's counsel argued that those procedures were at odds with Wisconsin Legislative enactments and thus unconstitutional under the Electors Clause of Article II of our federal Constitution.

At the District Court, Judge Ludwig concluded that the President had standing and presented federal claims. He conducted an expedited hearing *on the merits of the President's claims* before ruling. Judge Ludwig summarized his conclusion as follows:

> "And, on the merits of plaintiff's claims, the Court now further concludes that plaintiff has not proved that defendants violated his rights under the Electors Clause. To the contrary, the record shows Wisconsin's Presidential Electors are being determined in the very manner directed by the Legislature, as required by Article II, Section 1 of the Constitution."

Judge Ludwig also explained how the Wisconsin Legislature specifically created the Wisconsin Election Commission (WEC) to carry out the election, and delegated to the Commission specific authority to create procedures for addressing election related issues (including absentee balloting) and created a right to seek relief in state court to remedy any "alleged irregularity, defect or mistake" related to the election:

> "The Wisconsin Legislature has also established laws detailing the particulars of election administration. For the last five years, responsibility for the administration of Wisconsin elections has rested with the WEC. The Wisconsin Legislature created the WEC in 2015 specifically to "have the responsibility for the administration of . . . laws relating to elections and election campaigns." 2015 Wis. Act 118 § 4; Wis. Stat. § 5.05. The Wisconsin Legislature has also assigned powers and duties under the state election laws to municipal and county clerks, municipal and county boards of canvassers, and in Milwaukee, the municipal and county boards

> of election commissioners. Wis. Stat. §§ 7.10, 7.15,7.21. The Wisconsin Legislature has directed that these officials, along with the WEC, administer elections in Wisconsin. To carry out these duties, the legislature has delegated significant authority to the WEC. . . . For the determination of Presidential Electors, the Wisconsin Legislature has directed the WEC to "prepare a certificate showing the determination of the results of the canvass and the names of the persons elected." Wis. Stat. § 7.70(5)(b). The legislature has further directed that "the governor shall sign [the certificate], affix the great seal of the state, and transmit the certificate by registered mail to the U.S. administrator of general services." *Id.* . . . In addition to logistically administering the election, the Wisconsin Legislature has directed the WEC to issue advisory opinions, Wis. Stat. § 5.05(6a), and "[p]romulgate rules . . . applicable to all jurisdictions for the purpose of interpreting or implementing the laws regulating the conduct of elections or election campaigns. Wis. Stat. § 5.05(1)(f). The WEC is to "conduct or prescribe requirements for educational programs to inform electors about voting procedures, voting rights, and voting technology." Wis. Stat. § 5.05(12). Finally, the Wisconsin Legislature has provided detailed recount procedures. Wis. Stat. § 9.01. After requesting a recount, "any candidate . . . may appeal to circuit court." Wis. Stat. § 9.01(6). The legislature has also directed that "[Wis. Stat. § 9.01] constitutes the exclusive judicial remedy for testing the right to hold an elective office as the result of an alleged irregularity, defect or mistake committed during the voting or canvassing process." Wis. Stat. § 9.01(11)."

Judge Ludwig then concluded that the WEC did not act inconsistently with the manner provided by the Wisconsin Legislature for conducting the election and selecting a slate for the Electoral College:

> "The approach, form, method, or mode the Wisconsin Legislature has set for appointing Presidential electors is by general ballot at the general election. There is no dispute that this is precisely how Wisconsin election officials, including all the defendants, determined the appointment of Wisconsin's Presidential Electors in the latest election. They used "general ballot[s] at the general election for choosing the president and vice president of the United States" and treated a "vote for the president and vice president nominations of any party is a vote for the electors of the nominees." Absent proof that defendants failed to follow this "Manner" of determining the state's Presidential Electors, plaintiff has not and cannot show a violation of the Electors Clause."

And Judge Ludwig also explained explicitly why the WEC actions regarding absentee ballots were consistent with the enactments of the Wisconsin Legislature:

> "These issues are ones the Wisconsin Legislature has expressly entrusted to the WEC. When the legislature created the WEC, it authorized the commission to issue guidance to help election officials statewide interpret the Wisconsin election statutes and new binding court decisions. Wis. Stat. § 5.05(5t). The WEC is also expressly authorized to issue advisory

> opinions, Wis. Stat. § 5.05(6a), and to "[p]romulgate rules . . . applicable to all jurisdictions for the purpose of interpreting or implementing the laws regulating the conduct of elections or election campaigns." Wis. Stat. § 5.05(1)(f). The Wisconsin Legislature also directed that the WEC would have "responsibility for the administration of . . . laws relating to elections and election campaigns." Wis. Stat. § 5.05(1). In sum, far from defying the will of the Wisconsin Legislature in issuing the challenged guidance, the WEC was in fact acting pursuant to the legislature's express directives. . . . Thus, the guidance that plaintiff claims constitutes an unconstitutional deviation from the Wisconsin Legislature's direction, is, to the contrary, the direct consequence of legislature's express *command.* And, defendants have acted consistent with the "Manner" of election administration prescribed by the legislature."
>
> "Because plaintiff has failed to show a clear departure from the Wisconsin Legislature's directives, his complaint must be dismissed. As Chief Justice Rehnquist stated, "in a Presidential election the clearly expressed intent of the legislature must prevail." Bush v. Gore (2000) (Rehnquist, C.J., concurring). That is what occurred here. There has been no violation of the Constitution."

As noted, the United States Court of Appeals for the Seventh Circuit affirmed Judge Ludwig's ruling, and addressed the issues in additional detail. Judge Scudder, *also a Trump appointee,* wrote for the unanimous three judge panel, explaining:

> "We agree that Wisconsin lawfully appointed its electors in the manner directed by its Legislature and add that the President's claim also fails because of the unreasonable delay that accompanied the challenges the President now wishes to advance against Wisconsin's election procedures."
>
> "On the merits, the district court was right to enter judgment for the defendants. We reach this conclusion in no small part because of the President's delay in bringing the challenges to Wisconsin law that provide the foundation for the alleged constitutional violation. Even apart from the delay, the claims fail under the Electors Clause."
>
> "In his concurring opinion in Bush v. Gore, Chief Justice Rehnquist suggested that the proper inquiry under the Electors Clause is to ask whether a state conducted the election in a manner substantially consistent with the "legislative scheme" for appointing electors. 531 U.S. 98, 113 (2000) (Rehnquist, C.J., concurring). . . . Whatever actions the Commission took here, it took under color of authority expressly granted to it by the Legislature."

B. Principal Case in State Court

After a recount conducted in Wisconsin increased candidate Biden's lead, President Trump's campaign filed suit in State Court in Wisconsin arguing that the absentee voting procedures in two specific heavily Democratic Wisconsin counties violated Wisconsin law. A Wisconsin state court trial judge conducted a hearing and then on December 11, 2020 entered findings against the President. The matter then reached the Wisconsin Supreme Court on appeal. That court again ruled against the President 4-3, which multiple concurrences and dissents.

The issues litigated related to absentee ballot procedures during the pandemic in the two specific heavily democratic counties selected by the President's counsel. The case did not address similar issues state-wide, or in other counties with vote totals predominantly favoring the President. One issue related to a county determination that, pursuant to the Governor's "Safer at Home" pandemic order, voters could qualify as "indefinitely confined" due to illness, and thus vote by mail or drop box without showing identification in person. The President's counsel sought to disqualify every absentee ballot in the two counties of an "indefinitely confined" person regardless of whether that "confinement" related to the pandemic or not. Another issue related to ballots collected by volunteers at various events in Madison, Wisconsin named "Democracy in the Park."

Judge Hagedorn, appointed by former Republican Governor Scott Walker, wrote the majority opinion. The majority first ruled against the Plaintiff as to the application of the definition of "indefinitely confined"—"The challenge to the indefinitely confined voter ballots is meritless on its face." As a concurrence explained:

> "Although the number of individuals claiming indefinitely confined status has increased throughout the state, the Campaign asks us to apply this blanket invalidation of indefinitely confined voters only to ballots cast in Dane and Milwaukee Counties. . . . The Campaign's request to strike indefinitely confined voters in Dane and Milwaukee Counties as a class without regard to whether any individual voter was in fact indefinitely confined has no basis in reason or law; it is wholly without merit."

Next, the Court declined to address the merits of other claims, explaining that the doctrine of "laches" applied:

> "Such doctrine is applied because the efficient use of public resources demands that a court not allow persons to gamble on the outcome of an election contest and then challenge it when dissatisfied with the results, especially when the same challenge could have been made before the public is put through the time and expense of the entire election process. Thus if a party seeking extraordinary relief in an election-related matter fails to exercise the requisite diligence, laches will bar the action. . . . Although it disagrees the elements were satisfied here, the Campaign does not dispute the proposition that laches may bar an untimely election challenge. This principle appears to be recognized and applied universally. . . . The relevant election officials, as well as Vice President Biden and Senator Harris, had no knowledge a claim to these broad categories of challenges would occur. The Campaign's delay in raising these issues was unreasonable in the extreme, and the resulting prejudice to the election officials, other candidates, voters of the affected counties, and to voters statewide, is obvious and immense."

Addressing the "Democracy in the Park" events specifically, the majority explained:

> "When the events were announced, an attorney for the Wisconsin Legislature sent a warning letter to the City of Madison suggesting the events were illegal. The City of Madison responded that the events were legally compliant, offering reasons why. Although these events and the legislature's concerns were widely publicized, the Campaign never challenged these events, nor did any other tribunal determine they were unlawful. The Campaign now asks us to determine that all 17,271 absentee ballots collected during the "Democracy in the Park"events were illegally cast. Once again, when the events were announced, the Campaign could have challenged its legality. It did not."

The Majority concluded:

> "Our laws allow the challenge flag to be thrown regarding various aspects of election administration. The challenges raised by the Campaign in this case, however, come long after the last play or even the last game; the Campaign is challenging the rulebook adopted before the season began. Election claims of this type must be brought expeditiously. The Campaign waited until after the election to raise selective challenges that could have been raised long before the election. We conclude the challenge to indefinitely confined voter ballots is without merit, and that laches bars relief on the remaining three categories of challenged ballots."

And the concurring justices added:

> "As acknowledged by the President's counsel at oral argument, the President would have the people of this country believe that fraud took place in Wisconsin during the November 3, 2020 election. Nothing could be further from the truth. The President failed to point to even one vote cast in this election by an ineligible voter; yet he asks this court to disenfranchise over 220,000 voters. The circuit court, whose decision we affirm, found no evidence of any fraud."

The three dissenting members of the Wisconsin Supreme Court each opposed application of the doctrine of laches, explaining that the people of Wisconsin deserved clarity on the law applicable for each of the circumstances identified:

> "Our constitutional responsibility is to analyze the law and determine if it was followed regardless of whether any remedy might be available. In this way future elections benefit from our analysis."
>
> "Petitioners assert troubling allegations of noncompliance with Wisconsin's election laws by public officials on whom the voters rely to ensure free and fair elections. It is our solemn judicial duty to say what the law is. The majority's failure to discharge its duty perpetuates violations of the law by those entrusted to administer it. I dissent."

Finally, one dissenter declined to reach a conclusion as to the "indefinite confinement" issue with absentee ballots, noting that the court lacked "sufficient information . . . to determine whether they lawfully asserted that they were indefinitely confined prior to receiving an absentee ballot." And multiple dissenters questioned the legality of the "Democracy in the Park" events. None of the dissenters explained whether or how a contrary ruling on the subject issues could change the outcome of the election.

NOTE ON TRUMP'S LITIGATION TO OVERTURN THE 2020 ELECTION

Two of the cases discussed in Liz Cheney's memo deserve more extensive treatment because they are opinions written by federal circuit courts of appeals, which tend to have more persuasive weight in our legal system that state court opinions, and because they raise the most significant procedural issues that in other contexts—where they might have made a difference to the outcome—would have raised at least colorable questions about the proper judicial remedy for administrative wrongdoing in the conduct of a presidential election. The first of these cases is from Pennsylvania, where the Republican claims of administrative malfeasance were most credible (although not nearly in a magnitude to affect the outcome of Biden's victory in the state) and Wisconsin, where technical deviations from existing state law (although sanctioned in advance by both parties) was arguably more widespread than elsewhere.

Donald J. Trump for President, Inc. v. Secretary of Pennsylvania

830 Fed.Appx. 377 (2020)

Before: SMITH, Chief Judge, and CHAGARES and BIBAS, Circuit Judges

BIBAS, Circuit Judge.

Free, fair elections are the lifeblood of our democracy. Charges of unfairness are serious. But calling an election unfair does not make it so. Charges require specific allegations and then proof. We have neither here.

The Trump Presidential Campaign asserts that Pennsylvania's 2020 election was unfair. But as lawyer Rudolph Giuliani stressed, the Campaign "doesn't plead fraud. . . . [T]his is not a fraud case." Mot. to Dismiss Hr'g Tr. 118:19–20, 137:18. Instead, it objects that Pennsylvania's Secretary of State and some counties restricted poll watchers and let voters fix technical defects in their mail-in ballots. It offers nothing more.

This case is not about whether those claims are true. Rather, the Campaign appeals on a very narrow ground: whether the District Court abused its discretion in not letting the Campaign amend its complaint a second time. It did not.

Most of the claims in the Second Amended Complaint boil down to issues of state law. But Pennsylvania law is willing to overlook many technical defects. It favors counting votes as long as there is no fraud. Indeed, the Campaign has already litigated and lost many of these issues in state courts.

The Campaign tries to repackage these state-law claims as unconstitutional discrimination. Yet its allegations are vague and conclusory. It never alleges that anyone treated the Trump campaign or Trump votes worse than it treated the Biden campaign or Biden votes. And federal law does not require poll watchers or specify how they may observe. It also says nothing about curing technical state-law errors in ballots. Each of these defects is fatal, and the proposed Second Amended Complaint does not fix them. So the District Court properly denied leave to amend again.

Nor does the Campaign deserve an injunction to undo Pennsylvania's certification of its votes. The Campaign's claims have no merit. The number of ballots it specifically challenges is far smaller than the roughly 81,000-vote margin of victory. And it never claims fraud or that any votes were cast by illegal voters. Plus, tossing out millions of mail-in ballots would be drastic and unprecedented, disenfranchising a huge swath of the electorate and upsetting all down-ballot races too. That remedy would be grossly disproportionate to the procedural challenges raised. So we deny the motion for an injunction pending appeal.

I. BACKGROUND

A. Pennsylvania Election Law

In Pennsylvania, each county runs its own elections. Counties choose and staff polling places. They buy their own ballot boxes and voting booths and machines. They even count the votes and post the results. In all this, counties must follow Pennsylvania's Election Code and regulations. But counties can, and do, adopt rules and guidance for election officers and electors. And they are charged with ensuring that elections are "honestly, efficiently, and uniformly conducted."

1. *Poll watchers and representatives.* Counties must admit qualified poll "watchers" to observe votes being tallied. Poll watchers must be registered to vote in the county where they will serve. Each candidate can pick two poll watchers per election district; each political party, three. The poll watchers remain at the polling place while election officials count in-person ballots. They can ask to check voting lists. And they get to be present when officials open and count all the mail-in ballots. Likewise, candidates' and political parties' "representatives" may be present when absentee and mail-in ballots are inspected, opened, or counted, or when provisional ballots are examined.

Still, counties have some control over these poll watchers and representatives. The Election Code does not tell counties how they must accommodate them. Counties need only allow them "in the polling place" or "in the room" where ballots are being inspected, opened, or counted. Counties are expected to set up "an enclosed space" for vote counters at the polling place, and poll watchers "shall remain outside the enclosed space." So the counties decide where the watchers stand and how close they get to the vote counters.

2. *Mail-in ballots.* For decades, Pennsylvania let only certain people, like members of the military and their families, vote by mail. But last year, as part of a bipartisan election reform, Pennsylvania expanded mail-in voting. Now, any Pennsylvania voter can vote by mail for any reason.

To vote by mail, a Pennsylvania voter must take several steps. First, he (or she) must ask the State (Commonwealth) or his county for a mail-in ballot. To do that, he must submit a signed application with his name, date of birth, address, and other information. He must also provide a driver's license number, the last four digits of his Social Security number, or the like. Once the application is correct and complete, the county will approve it.

Close to the election, the county will mail the voter a mail-in ballot package. The package has a ballot and two envelopes. The smaller envelope (also called the secrecy envelope) is stamped "Official Election Ballot." The larger envelope is stamped with the county board of election's name and address and bears a printed voter declaration.

Next, the voter fills out the ballot. He then folds the ballot; puts it into the first, smaller secrecy envelope; and seals it. After that, he puts the secrecy envelope inside the larger envelope and seals that too. He must also "fill out, date and sign the declaration printed" on the outside of the larger envelope. The declaration for the November 2020 election read thus:

> I hereby declare that I am qualified to vote from the below stated address at this election; that I have not already voted in this election; and I further declare that I marked my ballot in secret. I am qualified to vote the enclosed ballot. I understand I am no longer eligible to vote at my polling place after I return my voted ballot. However, if my ballot is not received by the county, I understand I may only vote by provisional ballot at my polling place, unless I surrender my balloting materials, to be voided, to the judge of elections at my polling place.
>
> [BAR CODE]
>
> Voter, sign or mark here/Votante firme o mar[q]ue aqui
>
> X______________
>
> ______________
>
> Date of signing (MM/DD/YYYY)/Fecha de firme (MM/DD/YYYY)
>
> ______________
>
> Voter, print name/Votante, nombre en letra de impreta

Once the voter assembles the ballot packet, he can mail it back or deliver it in person. 25 Pa. Stat. § 3150.16(a).

Not every voter can be expected to follow this process perfectly. Some forget one of the envelopes. Others forget to sign on the dotted line. Some major errors will invalidate a ballot. For instance, counties may not count mail-in ballots that lack secrecy envelopes. *Pa. Dem. Party v. Boockvar* (Pa. 2020). But the Election Code says nothing about what should happen if a county notices these errors before election day. Some counties stay silent and do not count the ballots; others contact the voters and give them a chance to correct their errors.

B. Facts and Procedural History

On appeal from the dismissal of a complaint, we take the factual allegations as true:

1. *Mail-in voting*. For months, Pennsylvanians went to the polls, so to speak. The first batch of mail-in ballots went out to voters in late September. As they trickled back in, election officials noticed that some voters had not followed the rules. Some ballots were not in secrecy envelopes, so those packages were lighter and

thinner than complete ballot packages. Others had declarations that voters had not completed. Some counties did not notify voters about these defective ballots. Others, including the counties named in this suit, decided to reach out to these voters to let them cure their mistakes by voting provisionally on Election Day or asking for a replacement ballot.

2. *Election Day.* Though more than two million Pennsylvanians voted by mail, even more voted in person. On Election Day, November 3, the Campaign set up poll watchers at polling places around the Commonwealth. Appellees' election officials kept poll watchers and representatives away from where ballots were opened, counted, and tallied. In Philadelphia, for instance, poll watchers were kept six to twenty-five feet back from officials. In comparison, other, "Republican[-]controlled" counties did give the Campaign's poll watchers and representatives full access.

In all, nearly seven million Pennsylvanians voted, more than a third of them by mail. *Unofficial Returns for the 2020 Presidential Election,* Pa. Dep't of State, https://www.electionreturns.pa.gov/ (last visited Nov. 27, 2020). As of today, former Vice President Biden leads President Trump in Pennsylvania by 81,660 votes.

Pennsylvania's counties certified their election results by the November 23 certification deadline. The next morning, the Secretary of State (technically, Secretary of the Commonwealth) certified the vote totals, and the Governor signed the Certificate of Ascertainment and sent it to the U.S. Archivist. *Department of State Certifies Presidential Election Results,* PA Media, https://www.media.pa.gov/Pages/State-details.aspx?newsid=435 (last visited Nov. 27, 2020). The certified margin of victory was 80,555 votes.

3. *This lawsuit.* Almost a week after the election, the Campaign (as well as two voters) sued seven Pennsylvania counties and Secretary of State Kathy Boockvar. It alleged that they had violated the Due Process, Equal Protection, and Electors and Elections Clauses of the U.S. Constitution by taking two basic actions: First, the counties (encouraged by Secretary Boockvar) identified defective mail-in ballots early and told voters how to fix them. Second, they kept poll watchers and representatives from watching officials count all ballots.

So far, the Campaign has filed or tried to file three complaints. The original Complaint, filed November 9, set out six counts (plus a duplicate). After Boockvar and the counties moved to dismiss, on November 15 the Campaign filed a First Amended Complaint as of right, dropping four of the six counts (plus the duplicate), including all the counts relating to poll watchers and representatives. The Campaign sought a preliminary injunction to block certifying the election results. Boockvar and the counties again moved to dismiss. On November 18, the Campaign sought to file a Second Amended Complaint, resurrecting four dropped claims from the original Complaint and adding three more about how Philadelphia had blocked poll watching.

The District Court ended these volleys, denying leave to file the Second Amended Complaint. Instead, it dismissed the First Amended Complaint with prejudice and denied the Campaign's motion for a preliminary injunction as moot. *Donald J. Trump for President, Inc. v. Boockvar* (M.D. Pa. Nov. 21, 2020). In doing so, it held that the individual voters lacked standing. We commend the District Court for its fast, fair, patient handling of this demanding litigation.

4. *This appeal.* The Campaign filed this appeal on Sunday, November 22, and we granted its motion to expedite. The Campaign filed its brief and another motion November 23; opposing briefs and filings arrived the next day. We are issuing this opinion nonprecedentially so we can rule by November 27.

The Campaign does not challenge the District Court's finding that the voters lacked standing, so we do not consider their claims. On appeal, it seeks only narrow relief: to overturn the District Court's decision not to let it amend its complaint again. We address that claim in Part II. Separately, the Campaign asks us for an injunction to prevent the certified vote totals from taking effect. We address that claim in Part III.

II. THE DISTRICT COURT PROPERLY DENIED LEAVE TO AMEND THE COMPLAINT AGAIN

After one amendment, the District Court denied the Campaign's motion to amend the complaint a second time. We review that denial for abuse of discretion. *Premier Comp. Sol., LLC v. UPMC* (3d Cir. 2020). But on any standard of review, the court got it right.

Courts should grant leave to amend "freely . . . when justice so requires." Fed. R. Civ. P. 15(a)(2). In civil-rights cases, that means granting leave unless "amendment would be futile or inequitable." *Vorchheimer v. Phila. Owners Ass'n* (3d Cir. 2018); *Cureton v. NCAA* (3d Cir. 2001) (giving undue delay as an example of inequity). Here, the Campaign's request fails as both inequitable and futile.

A. The Campaign's Delay Was Undue, Given Its Stress on Needing to Resolve the Case by November 23

When the Campaign was before the District Court, it focused its arguments on the need to resolve the case by Pennsylvania's deadline for counties to certify their votes: Monday, November 23. Indeed, all three iterations of the complaint focused their prayers for relief on blocking the certification of the vote tally. The Campaign said it could get no "meaningful remedy" after that date.

The Campaign filed its First Amended Complaint on November 15, eight days before the certification deadline. In response to several pending motions to dismiss, it dropped many of the challenged counts from the original Complaint. It did not then move to file a Second Amended Complaint until November 18, when its opposition to the new motions to dismiss was due. And it did not file a brief in support of that motion until Friday, November 20. Certification was three days away.

As the District Court rightly noted, amending that close to the deadline would have delayed resolving the issues. True, delay alone is not enough to bar amendment. *Cureton*, 252 F.3d at 273. But "at some point, the delay will become 'undue,' placing an unwarranted burden on the court." *Id.* (quoting *Adams v. Gould, Inc.* (3d Cir. 1984)). The Campaign's motion would have done just that. It would have mooted the existing motions to dismiss and required new briefing, possibly new oral argument, and a reasoned judicial opinion within seventy-two hours over a weekend. That is too much to ask—especially since the proposed Second Amended Complaint largely repleaded many claims abandoned by the first one. *Cf. Rolo v. City Investing Co. Liquidating Tr.* (3d Cir. 1998) (affirming denial of leave to amend because the movant sought largely to "replead facts and arguments that could have been pled much earlier").

Having repeatedly stressed the certification deadline, the Campaign cannot now pivot and object that the District Court abused its discretion by holding the Campaign to that very deadline. It did not.

B. Amending the Complaint Again Would Have Been Futile

The Campaign focuses on critiquing the District Court's discussion of undue delay. Though the court properly rested on that ground, we can affirm on any ground supported by the record. Another ground also supports its denial of leave to amend: it would have been futile.

1. *The Campaign had to plead plausible facts, not just conclusory allegations.* Plaintiffs must do more than allege conclusions. Rather, "a complaint must contain sufficient factual matter, accepted as true, to 'state a claim to relief that is plausible on its face.'" *Ashcroft v. Iqbal* (2009) (quoting *Bell Atl. Corp. v. Twombly* (2007)). "Threadbare recitals of the elements of a cause of action, supported by mere conclusory statements, do not suffice." *Id.* The Second Amended Complaint does not meet *Twombly* and *Iqbal's* baseline standard of specifics.

To start, note what it does not allege: fraud. Indeed, in oral argument before the District Court, Campaign lawyer Rudolph Giuliani conceded that the Campaign "doesn't plead fraud." Mot. to Dismiss Hr'g Tr. 118:19-20 (Nov. 17, 2020). He reiterated: "If we had alleged fraud, yes, but this is not a fraud case." *Id.* at 137:18.

Though it alleges many conclusions, the Second Amended Complaint is light on facts. Take the nearly identical paragraphs introducing Counts One, Two, Four, and Six: "Democrats who controlled the Defendant County Election Boards engaged in a deliberate scheme of intentional and purposeful discrimination . . . by excluding Republican and Trump Campaign observers from the canvassing of the mail ballots in order to conceal their decision not to enforce [certain ballot] requirements." Second Am. Compl. ¶¶ 167, 193, 222, 252. That is conclusory. So is the claim that, "[u]pon information and belief, a substantial portion of the approximately 1.5 million absentee and mail votes in Defendant Counties should not have been counted." *Id.* ¶¶ 168, 194, 223, 253. "Upon information and belief" is a lawyerly way of saying that the Campaign does not know that something is a fact but just suspects it or has heard it. "While legal conclusions can provide the framework of a complaint, they must be supported by factual allegations." *Iqbal*, 556 U.S. at 679, 129 S. Ct. 1937. Yet the Campaign offers no specific facts to back up these claims.

2. *The Campaign has already litigated and lost most of these issues.* Many of the Second Amended Complaint's claims have already had their day in court. The Campaign cannot use this lawsuit to collaterally attack those prior rulings. On Counts One, Two, Four, and Six, the Campaign has already litigated whether ballots that lack a handwritten name, address, or date on the outer envelope must be disqualified. *See In re: Canvass of Absentee and Mail-in Ballots*, ___ A.3d at ___, 2020 WL 6875017, at *1. The Pennsylvania Supreme Court ruled against the Campaign, holding: "[T]he Election Code does not require boards of elections to disqualify mail-in or absentee ballots submitted by qualified electors who signed the declaration on their ballot's outer envelope but did not handwrite their name, their

address, and/or date, where no fraud or irregularity has been alleged." *Id.* at ___, at *1. That holding undermines the Campaign's suggestions that defective ballots should not have been counted.

Counts One and Two also challenge the requirement that poll watchers be registered electors of the county they wish to observe and that observers be Pennsylvania lawyers. But a federal district court has already held "that the county-residency requirement for poll watching does not, as applied to the particular circumstances of this election, burden any of [the Campaign's] fundamental constitutional rights." *Donald J. Trump for President, Inc. v. Boockvar* (W.D. Pa. Oct. 10, 2020). The Campaign never appealed that decision, so it is bound by it.

Count Seven alleges that Philadelphia's Board of Elections violated due process by obstructing poll watchers and representatives. But nothing in the Due Process Clause requires having poll watchers or representatives, let alone watchers from outside a county or less than eighteen feet away from the nearest table. The Campaign cites no authority for those propositions, and we know of none. (Ditto for notice-and-cure procedures.) And the Campaign litigated and lost that claim under state law too. The Pennsylvania Supreme Court held that the Election Code requires only that poll watchers be in the room, not that they be within any specific distance of the ballots. *In re Canvassing Observation Appeal of: City of Phila. Bd. of Electors* (Pa. Nov. 17, 2020).

The Campaign does not even challenge the dismissal of Counts Three, Five, and Nine, the Electors and Elections Clause counts. It concedes that under our recent decision, it lacks standing to pursue alleged violations of those clauses. *Bognet v. Sec'y Commonwealth of Pa.* (3d Cir. Nov. 13, 2020). Given its concession, we need not consider the issue any more.

The Second Amended Complaint thus boils down to the equal-protection claims in Counts Two, Four, Six, and Eight. They require not violations of state law, but discrimination in applying it. Those claims fail too.

3. *The Campaign never pleads that any defendant treated the Trump and Biden campaigns or votes differently.* A violation of the Equal Protection Clause requires more than variation from county to county. It requires unequal treatment of similarly situated parties. But the Campaign never pleads or alleges that anyone treated it differently from the Biden campaign. Count One alleges that the counties refused to credential the Campaign's poll watchers or kept them behind metal barricades, away from the ballots. It never alleges that other campaigns' poll watchers or representatives were treated differently. Count Two alleges that an unnamed lawyer was able to watch all aspects of voting in York County, while poll watchers in Philadelphia were not. It also makes a claim about one Jared M. Mellott, who was able to poll watch in York County. Counts Four and Six allege that poll watcher George Gallenthin had no issues in Bucks County but was barred from watching in Philadelphia. And Count Eight alleges that Philadelphia officials kept Jeremy Mercer too far away to verify that ballots were properly filled out. None of these counts alleges facts showing improper vote counting. And none alleges facts showing that the Trump campaign was singled out for adverse treatment. The Campaign cites no authority suggesting that an actor discriminates by treating people equally while harboring a partisan motive, and we know of none.

These county-to-county variations do not show discrimination. "[C]ounties may, consistent with equal protection, employ entirely different election procedures and voting systems within a single state." *Donald J. Trump for President, Inc.*, ___ F. Supp. 3d at ___, 2020 WL 5997680, at *44 (collecting cases). Even when boards of elections "vary . . . considerably" in how they decide to reject ballots, those local differences in implementing statewide standards do not violate equal protection. *Ne. Ohio Coal. for the Homeless v. Husted* (6th Cir. 2016); *see also Wexler v. Anderson* (11th Cir. 2006) (recognizing that equal protection lets different counties use different voting systems).

Nor does *Bush v. Gore* help the Campaign. There, the Florida Supreme Court had ratified treating ballots unequally. That was because the principle it set forth, the "intent of the voter," lacked *any* "specific standards to ensure its equal application." The lack of any standards at all empowered officials to treat ballots arbitrarily, violating equal protection. Here, by contrast, Pennsylvania's Election Code gives counties specific guidelines. To be sure, counties vary in implementing that guidance, but that is normal. Reasonable county-to-county variation is not discrimination. *Bush v. Gore* does not federalize every jot and tittle of state election law.

4. *The relief sought — throwing out millions of votes — is unprecedented.* Finally, the Second Amended Complaint seeks breathtaking relief: barring the Commonwealth from certifying its results or else declaring the election results defective and ordering the Pennsylvania General Assembly, not the voters, to choose Pennsylvania's presidential electors. It cites no authority for this drastic remedy.

The closest the Campaign comes to justifying the relief it seeks is citing *Marks v. Stinson* (3d Cir. 1994). But those facts were a far cry from the ones here. In *Marks*, the district court found that the Stinson campaign had orchestrated "massive absentee ballot fraud, deception, intimidation, harassment and forgery." It had lied to voters, deceived election officials, and forged ballots. We remanded that case, instructing that "the district court should not direct the certification of a candidate unless it finds, on the basis of record evidence, that the designated candidate would have won the election but for wrongdoing." And that seemed likely: the Stinson campaign had gotten about 600 net absentee-ballot applications (roughly 1000 minus 400 that were later rejected), more than the 461-vote margin of victory.

Here, however, there is no clear evidence of massive absentee-ballot fraud or forgery. On the contrary, at oral argument in the District Court, the Campaign specifically disavowed any claim of fraud. And the margin of victory here is not nearly as close: not 461 votes, but roughly 81,000.

Though district courts should freely give leave to amend, they need not do so when amendment would be futile. Because the Second Amended Complaint would not survive a motion to dismiss, the District Court properly denied leave to file it.

III. NO STAY OR INJUNCTION IS WARRANTED

We could stop here. Once we affirm the denial of leave to amend, this case is over. Still, for completeness, we address the Campaign's emergency motion to stay the effect of certification. No stay or injunction is called for.

Though the Campaign styles its motion as seeking a stay or preliminary injunction, what it really wants is an injunction pending appeal. But it neither requested that from the District Court during the appeal nor showed that it could not make that request, as required by Federal Rule of Appellate Procedure 8(a)(2)(A). That failure bars the motion.

Even if we could grant relief, we would not. Injunctions pending appeal, like preliminary injunctions, are "extraordinary remed[ies] never awarded as of right." *Winter v. NRDC* (2008). For a stay or injunction pending appeal, the movant must show both (1) a "strong" likelihood of success on the merits and (2) irreparable injury absent a stay or injunction. *Hilton v. Braunskill* (1987). The[se] first two factors are "the most critical." *Nken v. Holder* (2009). After that, we also balance (3) whether a stay or injunction will injure other interested parties (also called the balance of equities) and (4) the public interest. *Hilton*, 481 U.S. at 776, 107 S. Ct. 2113; *In re Revel AC, Inc.* (3d Cir. 2015). None of the four factors favors taking this extraordinary step.

A. The Campaign Has No Strong Likelihood of Success on the Merits

As discussed, the Campaign cannot win this lawsuit. It conceded that it is not alleging election fraud. It has already raised and lost most of these state-law issues, and it cannot relitigate them here. It cites no federal authority regulating poll watchers or notice and cure. It alleges no specific discrimination. And it does not contest that it lacks standing under the Elections and Electors Clauses. These claims cannot succeed.

B. The Campaign Faces No Irreparable Harm

The Campaign has not shown that denying relief will injure it. "Upon information and belief," it suspects that many of the 1.5 million mail-in ballots in the challenged counties were improperly counted. Second Am. Compl. ¶¶ 168, 194, 223, 253. But it challenges no specific ballots. The Campaign alleges only that at most three specific voters cast ballots that were not counted. *Id.* ¶ 237 (one voter); First Am. Compl. ¶¶ 15-16, 112 (three). And it never alleges that anyone except a lawful voter cast a vote. Of the seven counties whose notice-and-cure procedures are challenged, four (including the three most populous) represented that they gave notice to only about 6,500 voters who sent in defective ballot packages. Allegheny Cty. Opp. Mot. TRO & PI 7-8, D. Ct. Dkt. No. 193 (Nov. 20, 2020). The Campaign never disputed these numbers or alleged its own. Even if 10,000 voters got notice and cured their defective ballots, and every single one then voted for Biden, that is less than an eighth of the margin of victory.

Without more facts, we will not extrapolate from these modest numbers to postulate that the number of affected ballots comes close to the certified margin of victory of 80,555 votes. Denying relief will not move the needle.

Plus, states are primarily responsible for running federal elections. U.S. Const. art. I, § 4, cl. 1; 3 U.S.C. § 5. Pennsylvania law has detailed mechanisms for disputing election results. 25 Pa. Stat. §§ 3261-3474. Because the Campaign can raise these issues and seek relief through state courts and then the U.S. Supreme Court, any harm may not be irreparable. *Touchston v. McDermott* (11th Cir. 2000) (per curiam) (en banc).

C. The Balance of Equities Opposes Disenfranchising Voters

Nor would granting relief be equitable. The Campaign has already litigated and lost most of these issues as garden-variety state-law claims. It now tries to turn them into federal constitutional claims but cannot. *See Bognet*, 980 F.3d at 354-56.

Even if it could, it has delayed bringing this suit. For instance, in proposed Count Four, it challenges giving voters notice and letting them cure ballot defects as violating equal protection. The Campaign could have disputed these practices while they were happening or during the canvassing period. Instead, it waited almost a week after Election Day to file its original complaint, almost another week to amend it, and then another three days to amend it again. Its delay is inequitable, and further delay would wreak further inequity.

And the Campaign's charges are selective. Though Pennsylvanians cast 2.6 million mail-in ballots, the Campaign challenges 1.5 million of them. It cherry-picks votes cast in "Democratic-heavy counties" but not "those in Republican-heavy counties." Second Am. Compl. ¶ 8. Without compelling evidence of massive fraud, not even alleged here, we can hardly grant such lopsided relief.

Granting relief would harm millions of Pennsylvania voters too. The Campaign would have us set aside 1.5 million ballots without even alleging fraud. As the deadline to certify votes has already passed, granting relief would disenfranchise those voters or sidestep the expressed will of the people. Tossing out those ballots could disrupt every down-ballot race as well. There is no allegation of fraud (let alone proof) to justify harming those millions of voters as well as other candidates.

D. The Public Interest Favors Counting All Lawful Voters' Votes

Lastly, relief would not serve the public interest. Democracy depends on counting all lawful votes promptly and finally, not setting them aside without weighty proof. The public must have confidence that our Government honors and respects their votes.

What is more, throwing out those votes would conflict with Pennsylvania election law. The Pennsylvania Supreme Court has long "liberally construed" its Election Code "to protect voters' right to vote," even when a ballot violates a technical requirement. *Shambach v. Bickhart* (2004). "Technicalities should not be used to make the right of the voter insecure." *Appeal of James* (1954) (internal quotation marks omitted). That court recently reiterated: "[T]he Election Code should be liberally construed so as not to deprive, *inter alia,* electors of their right to elect a candidate of their choice." *Pa. Dem. Party,* 238 A.3d at 356. Thus, unless there is evidence of fraud, Pennsylvania law overlooks small ballot glitches and respects the expressed intent of every lawful voter. *In re: Canvass of Absentee and Mail-in Ballots,* 2020 WL 6875017, at *1 (plurality opinion). In our federalist system, we must respect Pennsylvania's approach to running elections. We will not make more of ballot technicalities than Pennsylvania itself does.

***

Voters, not lawyers, choose the President. Ballots, not briefs, decide elections. The ballots here are governed by Pennsylvania election law. No federal law requires poll watchers or specifies where they must live or how close they may stand when votes are counted. Nor does federal law govern whether to count ballots with minor state-law defects or let voters cure those defects. Those are all issues of state law, not ones that we can hear. And earlier lawsuits have rejected those claims.

Seeking to turn those state-law claims into federal ones, the Campaign claims discrimination. But its alchemy cannot transmute lead into gold. The Campaign never alleges that any ballot was fraudulent or cast by an illegal voter. It never alleges that any defendant treated the Trump campaign or its votes worse than it treated the Biden campaign or its votes. Calling something discrimination does not make it so. The Second Amended Complaint still suffers from these core defects, so granting leave to amend would have been futile.

And there is no basis to grant the unprecedented injunction sought here. First, for the reasons already given, the Campaign is unlikely to succeed on the merits. Second, it shows no irreparable harm, offering specific challenges to many fewer ballots than the roughly 81,000-vote margin of victory. Third, the Campaign is responsible for its delay and repetitive litigation. Finally, the public interest strongly favors finality, counting every lawful voter's vote, and not disenfranchising millions of Pennsylvania voters who voted by mail. Plus, discarding those votes could disrupt every other election on the ballot.

We will thus affirm the District Court's denial of leave to amend, and we deny an injunction pending appeal. The Campaign asked for a very fast briefing schedule, and we have granted its request. Because the Campaign wants us to move as fast as possible, we also deny oral argument. We grant all motions to file overlength responses, to file amicus briefs, and to supplement appendices. We deny all other outstanding motions as moot. This Court's mandate shall issue at once.

Trump v. Wisconsin Elections Commission,

983 F.3d 919 (2020)

Before Flaum, Rovner, and Scudder, Circuit Judges.

Scudder, Circuit Judge.

Two days after Wisconsin certified the results of its 2020 election, President Donald J. Trump invoked the Electors Clause of the U.S. Constitution and sued the Wisconsin Elections Commission, Governor, Secretary of State, and several local officials in federal court. The district court concluded that the President's challenges lacked merit, as he objected only to the administration of the election, yet the Electors Clause, by its terms, addresses the authority of the State's Legislature to prescribe the manner of appointing its presidential electors. So, too, did the district court conclude that the President's claims would fail even under a broader, alternative reading of the Electors Clause that extended to a state's conduct of the presidential election. We agree that Wisconsin lawfully appointed its electors in the manner directed by its Legislature and add that the President's claim also fails because of the unreasonable delay that accompanied the challenges the President now wishes to advance against Wisconsin's election procedures.

I

A

On November 3, the United States held its 2020 presidential election. The final tally in Wisconsin showed that Joseph R. Biden, Jr. won the State by 20,682 votes. On November 30, the Wisconsin Elections Commission certified the results, the Governor signed an accompanying certification, and Wisconsin notified the National Archives that it had selected Biden's ten electors to represent the State in the Electoral College.

Two days later, the President brought this lawsuit challenging certain procedures Wisconsin had used in conducting the election. The President alleged that the procedures violated the Electors Clause of the U.S. Constitution:

> Each State shall appoint, in such Manner as the Legislature thereof may direct, a Number of Electors, equal to the whole Number of Senators and Representatives to which the State may be entitled in the Congress. . . .

U.S. CONST. art. II, § 1, cl. 2.

To implement the obligation imposed by the Electors Clause, Wisconsin's Legislature has directed that the State's electors be appointed "[b]y general ballot at the general election for choosing the president and vice president of the United States." Wis. Stat. § 8.25(1). It has further assigned "responsibility for the administration of . . . laws relating to elections and election campaigns" to the Commission. *Id.* § 5.05(1). Municipalities run the election, and each municipality's own clerk "has charge and supervision of elections and registration in the municipality." *Id.* § 7.15(1).

The President alleges that the Commission and municipal officials so misused the power granted to them by the Legislature that they had unconstitutionally altered the "Manner" by which Wisconsin appointed its electors. His allegations challenge three pieces of guidance issued by the Commission well in advance of the 2020 election. (Each guidance document is available on the Commission's website, https://elections.wi.gov.)

First, in March 2020, the Commission clarified the standards and procedures for voters to qualify as "indefinitely confined" and therefore be entitled to vote absentee without presenting a photo identification. See Wis. Stat. §§ 6.86(2)(a), 6.87(4)(b)2. The Commission explained that many voters would qualify based on their personal circumstances and the COVID-19 pandemic, adding that Wisconsin law established no method for a clerk to demand proof of a voter's individual situation. The Wisconsin Supreme Court endorsed the Commission's interpretation when it enjoined the Dane County Clerk from offering any contrary view of the law. See *Jefferson v. Dane County* (2020).

Second, the Commission issued guidance in August 2020 endorsing the use of drop boxes for the return of absentee ballots. The Commission explained that drop boxes could be "staffed or unstaffed, temporary or permanent," and offered advice on how to make them both secure and available to voters during the pandemic.

Third, four years ago, before the 2016 election, the Commission instructed municipal clerks on best practices for correcting a witness's address on an absentee ballot certificate. See Wis. Stat. § 6.87(2), (6d), (9). Clerks were able, the Commission explained, to contact the voter or witness or use another source of reliable information to correct or complete address information on an absentee ballot.

The President's complaint alleges that the Commission, in issuing this guidance, expanded the standards for "indefinitely confined" voters, invited voter fraud by authorizing the use of unstaffed drop boxes, and misled municipal clerks about their powers to complete or correct address information on absentee ballots, all contrary to Wisconsin statutory law. The President sought declaratory and injunctive relief on the view that these alleged misinterpretations of state law "infringed and invaded upon the Wisconsin Legislature's prerogative and directions under [the Electors Clause of] Article II of the U.S. Constitution."

B

After an evidentiary hearing, the district court rejected the President's claims on the merits and entered judgment for the Commission and other defendants. The Electors Clause, the court determined, addressed the "Manner"—the "approach, form, method, or mode"—by which Wisconsin appointed its electors. For Wisconsin, that meant only by "general ballot at the general election," Wis. Stat. § 8.25(1), with the court further observing that any mistakes in administering the election did not change that the electors were appointed by general election.

Even if the Electors Clause was read more broadly to address the "Manner" in which Wisconsin conducted the election, the district court determined that the Legislature had authorized the Commission to issue the guidance now challenged by the President. None of that guidance, the district court reasoned, reflected such a deviation from the Wisconsin Legislature's directives as to violate the Electors Clause.

The President promptly appealed, and we expedited the case for decision.

II

We begin, as we must, by assessing whether the President has presented a Case or Controversy over which we have jurisdiction. The inquiry turns on the doctrine of standing and, more specifically, whether the President has alleged an injury traceable to the actions of the defendants and capable of being redressed by a favorable judicial ruling. See *Lujan v. Defs. of Wildlife* (1992). The district court answered the question in the President's favor. We do too.

On the injury prong of standing, the President has alleged "concrete and particularized" harm stemming from the allegedly unlawful manner by which Wisconsin appointed its electors. *Id.* at 560, 112 S. Ct. 2130. As a candidate for elected office, the President's alleged injury is one that "affect[s] [him] in a personal and individual way." *Id.* at 560, 112 S. Ct. 2130 n.1; see also *Carson v. Simon* (8th Cir. 2020) ("An inaccurate vote tally is a concrete and particularized injury to candidates."). The alleged injury-in-fact is likewise "fairly traceable" to the challenged action of the defendants, see *Allen v. Wright* (1984), all of whom played some role in administering the election.

The final requirement for Article III standing—that the alleged injury "likely" would be redressed by a favorable decision—presents a closer question. *Lujan,* 504 U.S. at 561, 112 S. Ct. 2130. The difficulty is attributable to the gap between what the President ultimately desires (to be declared the victor of Wisconsin) on one hand, and what a court can award him on the other. But the President's complaint can be read as more modestly requesting a declaration that the defendants' actions violated the Electors Clause and that those violations tainted enough ballots to "void" the election. Were we to grant the President the relief he requests and declare the election results void, the alleged injury—the unlawful appointment of electors—would be redressed. True, our declaration would not result in a new slate of electors. But the fact that a judicial order cannot provide the full extent or exact type of relief a plaintiff might desire does not render the entire case nonjusticiable. See *Church of Scientology v. United States* (1992). A favorable ruling would provide the opportunity for the appointment of a new slate of electors. From there, it would be for the Wisconsin Legislature to decide the next steps in advance of Congress's count of the Electoral College's votes on January 6, 2021. See 3 U.S.C. § 15. All of this is enough to demonstrate Article III standing.

We also conclude that the President's complaint presents a federal question, despite its anchoring in alleged violations of state law. The Eleventh Amendment and principles of federalism bar federal courts from directing state officials to follow state law. See *Pennhurst State Sch. & Hosp. v. Halderman* (1984). But we can decide whether their interpretation of state law violated a provision of the federal Constitution, here the Electors Clause. This distinction alleviates any federalism concerns that might otherwise preclude our consideration of the President's claims.

III

On the merits, the district court was right to enter judgment for the defendants. We reach this conclusion in no small part because of the President's delay in bringing the challenges to Wisconsin law that provide the foundation for the alleged constitutional violation. Even apart from the delay, the claims fail under the Electors Clause.

A

The timing of election litigation matters. "[A]ny claim against a state electoral procedure must be expressed expeditiously." *Fulani v. Hogsett* (7th Cir. 1990) (citing *Williams v. Rhodes* (1968)). The Supreme Court underscored this precise point in this very election cycle, and with respect to this very State. See *Republican Nat'l Comm. v. Democratic Nat'l Comm.* (2020). The Court's direction was clear: federal courts should avoid announcing or requiring changes in election law and procedures close in time to voting. Doing so risks offending principles of federalism and reflects an improper exercise of the federal judicial power. Even more, belated election litigation risks giving voters "incentive to remain away from the polls." *Purcell v. Gonzalez* (2006); see also *Crookston v. Johnson* (6th Cir. 2016) ("Call it what you will—laches, the *Purcell* principle, or common sense—the idea is that courts will not disrupt imminent elections absent a powerful reason for doing so."). On this reasoning, we have rejected as late claims brought too close in time *before* an election occurs. See *Democratic Nat'l Comm. v. Bostelmann* (7th Cir. 2020); *Jones v. Markiewicz-Qualkinbush* (7th Cir. 2016); *Navarro v. Neal* (7th Cir. 2013).

The same imperative of timing and the exercise of judicial review applies with much more force on the back end of elections. Before a court can contemplate entering a judgment that would void election results, it "*must* consider whether the plaintiffs filed a timely pre-election request for relief." *Gjersten v. Bd. of Election Comm'rs* (7th Cir. 1986) (emphasis added) (footnote omitted).

These very considerations underpin the doctrine of laches. At its core, laches is about timing. "Laches cuts off the right to sue when the plaintiff has delayed 'too long' in suing. 'Too long' for this purpose means that the plaintiff delayed inexcusably and the defendant was harmed by the delay." *Teamsters & Emps. Welfare Tr. of Ill. v. Gorman Bros. Ready Mix* (7th Cir. 2002).

The President had a full opportunity before the election to press the very challenges to Wisconsin law underlying his present claims. Having foregone that opportunity, he cannot now—after the election results have been certified as final—seek to bring those challenges. All of this is especially so given that the Commission announced well in advance of the election the guidance he now challenges. Indeed, the witness-address guidance came four years ago, before the 2016 election. The Commission issued its guidance on indefinitely confined voters in March 2020 and endorsed the use of drop boxes in August.

Allowing the President to raise his arguments, at this late date, after Wisconsin has tallied the votes and certified the election outcome, would impose unquestionable harm on the defendants, and the State's voters, many of whom cast ballots in reliance on the guidance, procedures, and practices that the President challenges here. The President's delay alone is enough to warrant affirming the district court's judgment.

B

The President would fare no better even if we went further and reached the merits of his claims under the Electors Clause.

Defining the precise contours of the Electors Clause is a difficult endeavor. The text seems to point to at least two constructions, and the case law interpreting or applying the Clause is sparse. This case does not require us to answer the question, as the Commission's guidance did not amount to a violation under the two most likely interpretations.

Recall that the Electors Clause requires each State to "appoint, in such Manner as the Legislature thereof may direct," presidential electors. U.S. CONST. art. II, § 1, cl. 2. By its terms, the Clause could be read as addressing only the manner of appointing electors and thus nothing about the law that governs the administration of an election (polling place operations, voting procedures, vote tallying, and the like). The word "appoint" is capacious, "conveying the broadest power of determination," including but not limited to the "mode" of popular election. *McPherson v. Blacker* (1892). Historically, the states used a variety of manners for appointing electors, such as direct legislative appointment. See *id.* at 29-33, 13 S. Ct. 3. For its part, the Wisconsin Legislature has consistently chosen a general election to appoint its electors. See Wis. Stat. § 8.25(1) (2020); Wis. Stat. §§ 6.3, 7.3 (1849). The complaint does not allege that the Commission's guidance documents shifted Wisconsin from a general election to some other manner of appointing electors, like those used in other states in the past. On this reading of the Electors Clause, the President has failed to state a claim. See Fed. R. Civ. P. 12(b)(6).

But perhaps the better construction is to read the term "Manner" in the Electors Clause as also encompassing acts necessarily antecedent and subsidiary to the method for appointing electors—in short, Wisconsin's conduct of its general election. Even on this broader reading, the President's claims still would fall short. In his concurring opinion in *Bush v. Gore*, Chief Justice Rehnquist suggested that the proper inquiry under the Electors Clause is to ask whether a state conducted the election in a manner substantially consistent with the "legislative scheme" for appointing electors. 531 U.S. 98, 113, 121 S. Ct. 525, 148 L. Ed. 2d 388 (2000) (Rehnquist, C.J., concurring). We would not go further and ask, for example, whether Wisconsin's officials interpreted perfectly "[i]solated sections" of the elections code. *Id.* at 114, 121 S. Ct. 525.

The Wisconsin Legislature expressly assigned to the Commission "the responsibility for the administration of . . . laws relating to elections," Wis. Stat. § 5.05(1), just as Florida's Legislature had delegated a similar responsibility to its Secretary of State. See *Bush,* 531 U.S. at 116, 121 S. Ct. 525 (Rehnquist, C.J., concurring). Florida's legislative scheme included this "statutorily provided apportionment of responsibility," *id.* at 114, 121 S. Ct. 525, and three Justices found a departure from that scheme when the Florida Supreme Court rejected the Secretary's interpretation of state law. See *id.* at 119, 123, 121 S. Ct. 525. And it was the Minnesota Secretary of State's lack of a similar responsibility that prompted two judges of the Eighth Circuit to conclude that he likely violated the Electors Clause by adding a week to the deadline for receipt of absentee ballots. See *Carson,* 978 F.3d at 1060. By contrast, whatever actions the Commission took here, it took under color of authority expressly granted to it by the Legislature. And that authority is not diminished by allegations that the Commission erred in its exercise.

We confine our conclusions to applications of the Electors Clause. We are not the ultimate authority on Wisconsin law. That responsibility rests with the State's Supreme Court. Put another way, the errors that the President alleges occurred in the Commission's exercise of its authority are in the main matters of state law. They belong, then, in the state courts, where the President had an opportunity to raise his concerns. Indeed, the Wisconsin Supreme Court rejected his claims regarding the guidance on indefinitely confined voters, see *Trump v. Biden* (2020), and declined to reach the rest of his arguments on grounds of laches.

For our part, all we need to say is that, even on a broad reading of the Electors Clause, Wisconsin lawfully appointed its electors in the manner directed by its Legislature.

For these reasons, we AFFIRM.

FINAL NOTE ON THE AFTERMATH OF THE JANUARY 6 CAPITOL INSURRECTION

As the second edition of this casebook goes to press (in May of 2021), candor compels acknowledging that the future of American democracy looks disturbingly bleak. Liz Cheney has been ousted from her leadership role within the Republican Party because she denounces ex-President Trump's persistent—and baseless—effort to discredit the validity of President Biden's victory. Ever since the development of America's two-party system in the immediate aftermath of the Constitution's adoption, the ongoing success of the Republic has depended on robust but fair competition between the two parties vying to hold political power. But that fair two-party competition can occur only if both parties are willing to respect the results of the election, as revealed by honest and accurate counting of the votes cast by eligible voters. When one of the two major parties abandons its commitment to honest vote-counting, the system becomes unstable. Current conditions—including Republican leader Kevin McCarthy's decision to align himself with Trump over Cheney in their fight over the truth of the 2020 election, as well as efforts in various states to replace Republicans who were honest in their 2020 vote-counting (like Georgia's Secretary of State Brad Raffensperger) with Trump loyalists who vocally espouse the "Big Lie" that the 2020 election was stolen from Trump (like Georgia's Jody Hice, who is challenging Raffensperger in the 2022 GOP primary)—raise unsettling questions about America's capacity to count votes honestly in future elections.

Even as we focus on the current moment, it is important to recognize that the path leading to this bleak place includes problems plaguing both major political parties. Without engaging in false equivalence, it is necessary to note that Democrats in Congress objected to President Trump's Electoral College victory when there was no doubt that Trump had won the popular vote in enough states. It is also possible to imagine scenarios in 2024 that cause Democrats, rather than Republicans, to repudiate the official Electoral College result: Suppose the Democratic nominee wins the legally irrelevant "national popular vote" but the Republican nominee officially receives an Electoral College victory just because the Wisconsin Supreme Court, in a 4-3 decision, invalidates enough ballots to put the state in the GOP column.

As you reflect on the challenges facing American democracy, ask yourself the extent to which laws and legal institutions—in contrast to cultural conditions including respect for basic "fair play" norms that previously regulated social relations—are the problem and/or the potential solution? What would it take to guarantee that votes are counted honestly in America? A change in rules for counting votes? A change in the legal institutions responsible for counting votes? Or, instead, a change in attitudes about counting votes, including a recommitment to the basic "fair play" value against cheating and dishonesty? In other words, a willingness to count votes as cast and abiding by the result even if one's own side doesn't win? If the problem is ultimately cultural, and Americans collectively lack sufficient moral virtue to count votes fairly, is there anything that election law can do to remedy the deficiency? Or is the situation more complicated: The Founders recognized that there would be only a limited supply of virtue in politics, and that legal rules and institutions need to pursue the public interest by economizing on what little virtue exists; accordingly, is the task now to make necessary adjustments in the rules and institutions for counting votes in response to what appears to be a diminution in political virtue over the last several decades?

This last question brings us full circle with where we started this book. Although we end by focusing on the counting of votes, the question of how rules and institutions relate to political morality is essentially the same as it is for the topic of redistricting: gerrymandering, at bottom, is greed. It is the effort to manipulate district lines to maximize the advantage of one party, for the sake of retaining power, at the expense of what the voters themselves want. Although not the same as counting ballots dishonestly, the motivation is identical: politicians trying to keep power for themselves in defiance of the will of the voters, the exact opposite of what is supposed to happen in a system committed to the basic principle that "governments . . . deriv[e] their just powers from the consent of the governed" (in the immemorial words of the Declaration of Independence). Thus, we can ask the same question with respect to redistricting as we just did with respect to vote-counting: Is the solution to be found in new rules, new institutions, a resuscitated "fair play" morality, or some complicated combination thereof?

Finally, think about the interrelationship of all four parts of this book: districting, the nomination of candidates and the relationship of primary and general elections, campaign finance, and the voting process. All four domains are feeling the effect of the current hyper-polarization in American politics, as well as the willingness of some major American politicians (including ex-President Trump and his allies) to engage in disinformation in the pursuit of power. Will the effort to make electoral competition healthy in America again—so that the nation returns to robust but fair competition between the two major parties—require reforms in all four of these areas of election law?

E. A CONCLUDING OBSERVATION

As you reflect on your examination of election law, is there any overarching way to tie together all four units that we have studied? Scholars in the field have searched for the "holy grail" of a unified theory of all election law. But much like physicists who seek a Grand Unified Theory that would tie together all four forces in nature (gravity, electromagnetism, and the strong and weak nuclear interactions), election law scholars so far have been unsuccessful in this quest. Or, to be precise, some such "general theories of election law" have been offered, but none have commanded a prevailing consensus in the field.

To be sure, there are some overarching themes. The cases in all four Parts of this casebook raise questions about the meaning of the constitutional right to vote and the proper constitutional test for election regulations. The decisions force us to question whether the judiciary is competent to create fair, impartial, and manageable standards. Are judges a valid check on entrenchment, or the concern that incumbents will enact laws to favor their own reelection (or to keep their political party in power)? Should courts enter the "political thicket"? Is broad access to the ballot inconsistent with maintaining integrity of the electoral system, and if so, how do we reconcile these competing concerns? Thus, broad themes emerge, but we are still searching for a common overarching theory to harmonize the case law.

What is the best explanation for why there is no successful unified theory of election law? Is it perhaps the fault of the U.S. Supreme Court? After all, how can scholars be expected to make sense of the Court's jurisprudence in this area when the Justices themselves seem so confused and bewildered? Consider Justice Kennedy's ambivalence over the topic of political gerrymandering: If he cannot decide what to do, can scholars find the underlying truth lying behind his tentativeness? Or consider *Crawford*, where the Court was split 3-3-3, and the plurality's test was exceptionally vague and indeterminate: If the fundamental principle of constitutional law applicable to election cases—so-called *Anderson-Burdick-Crawford* balancing—is entirely "ad hoc" and fact-specific, what measure of predictability or insight could scholars be expected to bring to the field?

But maybe the Justices are not to blame. Maybe the difficulty lies inherently within the field itself. As you review the issues that the Justices have confronted—from partisan gerrymandering, to the regulation of party primaries, to the validity of various versions of voter identification laws—do you not appreciate that answers cannot be plucked easily from the air? Is it really possible for the Court to develop a more precise standard than *Anderson-Burdick-Crawford* balancing, which essentially condemns any electoral rule that imposes burdens that are excessive, or disproportionate, in relation to its justifiable benefits?

Moreover, even if we could come to understand three of the four areas of election law as governed by an overarching, and serviceable, "disproportionality" standard of the kind that *Anderson-Burdick-Crawford* balancing is striving for—these three areas being the Law of Districting, the Law of Nominating Candidates, and the Law of Voting—it is hard to see campaign finance (or the regulation of campaign practices more generally) as being governed by such a general "disproportionality" standard. Whether because it involves threats to Free Speech rights or otherwise, the specific area of campaign finance seems inevitably to remain governed by a different standard than other types of electoral regulation. In this respect, campaign finance seems to be analogous to gravity. Physicists have managed to unify three of the four basic forces of nature—but not gravity, which remains stubbornly immune to their efforts. Likewise, campaign finance presents theoretical problems for election law scholars that are distinct from other areas of election law. These theoretical obstacles, furthermore, seem deeper than simply the question whether the Court was right or wrong in *Citizens United* or any other particular case. Even proponents of robust campaign finance regulation, who oppose the current deregulatory trend in this area, acknowledge that the First Amendment imposes limits on how far legislatures can go: Traditional media enterprises, like the *New York Times*, are entitled to spend freely on their editorializing in favor of candidates. And once this proposition is accepted, it becomes difficult to fold the regulation of campaign finance into a single overarching principle of electoral regulation.

If the intrinsic nature of election law means that it is not susceptible to a single Grand Unified Theory, should that bother us? Who needs theoretical neatness if we can make our way pragmatically in the world? But does the "Big Lie" of 2020 and its aftermath indicate that whatever worked pragmatically in the past is no longer good enough to maintain a functional democracy in the future?

But if we remain uneasy about just muddling through in the area of election law (without a clear theoretical compass to guide us), is this unease because we have an intuitive sense that this field—above all others—should be comprehensible? Election law, after all, is about democracy, and our democracy belongs to all of us. We all should be able to understand it. Unlike theoretical physics, it should not remain inherently impenetrable. Therefore, if at its core democracy is intrinsically incomprehensible—we cannot make sense of what, even in principle, it should entail—something seems wrong with that conclusion. In other words, we want to think that at least in theory there should be right answers to the questions of how to do legislative districting, and the nomination of candidates, and the administration of the voting process, and so forth. Even if partisanship (or other frailties of the human spirit) sometimes impedes the implementation of these right answers in practice, we want a yardstick that can show us where and by how much we fall short.

But if there are no answers to these questions of how to conduct democracy even in principle, where does that leave us—and our desire to govern ourselves according to the fundamental ideal of popular sovereignty?

At the end of this book, we are going to leave you without a definitive answer to this most basic question. You must decide for yourself, based on your own study of this topic, whether the uncertainties and perplexities that currently exist in the field of election law are caused by the inadequacies of our existing system, including the Justices of the Supreme Court, or instead are intrinsic to the topic. You must decide for yourself, too, what you think the future of election law is capable of being.

But whatever you decide intellectually about the nature of election law and its potential trajectory, remember this: Ultimately, it is your democracy, whatever its limitations or capacities might be. Whether or not you will have a professional career that focuses on election law, you share in the responsibility for democracy as a citizen. Therefore, as the authors of this book, we hope that you will put it to use in making your own contributions to the future of democracy, as you think most appropriate. The need to do so has never been more pressing.

TABLE OF CASES

Principal cases are indicated by italics.

Q

R

S

Y

INDEX

E

F

P